Applet	Concept Illustrated	Descriptor	Applet Exercise Number and Page
Mean versus median	This applet illustrates the concept that the mean and the median of a data set respond differently to changes in the data. It can be used to investigate how skewedness and outliers affect measures of central tendency.	This applet is designed to allow the user to visualize the relationship between the mean and median of a data set. The user may easily add and delete data points. The applet automatically updates the mean and median for each change in the data.	**2.1**, p. 70; **2.2**, p. 70; **2.3**, p. 70
Standard deviation	This applet illustrates the concept that standard deviation measures the spread of a data set. It can be used to investigate how the shape and spread of a distribution affect the standard deviation.	This applet is designed to allow the user to visualize the relationship between the mean and standard deviation of a data set. The user may easily add and delete data points. The applet automatically updates the mean and standard deviation for each change in the data.	**2.4**, p. 78; **2.5**, p. 79; **2.6**, p. 79; **2.7**, p. 91
Confidence intervals for a proportion	This applet illustrates the concept that not all confidence intervals contain the population mean. It can be used to investigate the meaning of 95% and 99% confidence.	This applet generates confidence intervals for a population proportion. The user specifies the population proportion and the sample size. The applet simulates selecting 100 random samples from the population and finds the 95% and 99% confidence intervals for each sample. The confidence intervals are plotted and the number and proportion containing the true proportion are reported.	**5.5**, p. 318; **5.6**, p. 318
Confidence intervals for a mean (the impact of confidence level)	This applet illustrates the concept that not all confidence intervals contain the population proportion. It can be used to investigate the meaning of 95% and 99% confidence.	This applet generates confidence intervals for a population mean. The user specifies the sample size, the shape of the distribution, the population mean, and the population standard deviation. The applet simulates selecting 100 random samples from the population and finds the 95% and 99% confidence intervals for each sample. The confidence intervals are plotted and the number and proportion containing the true mean are reported.	**5.1**, p. 298; **5.2**, p. 298
Confidence intervals for a mean (the impact of not knowing the standard deviation)	This applet illustrates the concept that confidence intervals obtained using the sample standard deviation are different from those obtained using the population standard deviation. It can be used to investigate the effect of not knowing the population standard deviation.	This applet generates confidence intervals for a population mean. The user specifies the sample size, the shape of the distribution, the population mean, and the population standard deviation. The applet simulates selecting 100 random samples from the population and finds the 95% z-interval and 95% t-interval for each sample. The confidence intervals are plotted and the number and proportion containing the true mean are reported.	**5.3**, p. 309; **5.4**, p. 309
Hypothesis tests for a proportion	This applet illustrates the concept that not all tests of hypotheses lead correctly to either rejecting or failing to reject the null hypothesis. It can be used to investigate the relationship between the level of confidence and the probabilities of making Type I and Type II errors.	This applet performs hypotheses tests for a population proportion. The user specifies the population proportion, the sample size, and the null and alternative hypotheses. The applet simulates selecting 100 random samples from the population and calculates and plots the z statistic and p-value for each sample. The applet reports the number and proportion of times the null hypotheses is rejected at both the .05 level and the .01 level.	**6.5**, p. 377; **6.6**; p. 377
Hypothesis tests for a mean	This applet illustrates the concept that not all tests of hypotheses lead correctly to either rejecting or failing to reject the null hypothesis. It can be used to investigate the relationship between the level of confidence and the probabilities of making Type I and Type II errors.	This applet performs hypotheses tests for a population mean. The user specifies the shape of the population distribution, the population mean and standard deviation, the sample size, and the null and alternative hypotheses. The applet simulates selecting 100 random samples from the population and calculates and plots the t statistic and p-value for each sample. The applet reports the number and proportion of times the null hypotheses is rejected at both the .05 level and the .01 level.	**6.1**, p. 350; **6.2**; p. 357; **6.3**; p. 357; **6.4**; p. 357
Correlation by eye	This applet illustrates the concept that the correlation coefficient measures the strength of a linear relationship between two variables. It helps the user learn to assess the strength of a linear relationship from a scattergram.	This applet computes the correlation coefficient r for a set of bivariate data plotted on a scattergram. The user can easily add or delete points and guess the value of r. The applet then compares the guess to its calculated value.	**10.2**, p. 636
Regression by eye	This applet illustrates the concept that the least squares regression line has a smaller SSE than any other line that might approximate a set of bivariate data. It helps the user learn to approximate the location of a regression line on a scattergram.	This applet computes the least squares regression line for a set of bivariate data plotted on a scattergram. The user can easily add or delete points and guess the location of the regression line by manipulating a line provided on the scattergram. The applet will then plot the least squares line. It displays the equations and the SSEs for both lines.	**10.1**, p. 611

James T. McClave, P. George Benson, Terry Sincich, *Statistics for Business and Economics*, **10/e**
0-13-240956-9
© 2008 Pearson Education, Inc.
Pearson Prentice Hall
Pearson Education, Inc.
Upper Saddle River, NJ 07458
Pearson Prentice Hall™ is a trademark of Pearson Education, Inc.

YOU SHOULD CAREFULLY READ THE TERMS AND CONDITIONS BEFORE USING THE CD-ROM PACKAGE. USING THIS CD-ROM PACKAGE INDICATES YOUR ACCEPTANCE OF THESE TERMS AND CONDITIONS.

Pearson Education, Inc. provides this program and licenses its use. You assume responsibility for the selection of the program to achieve your intended results, and for the installation, use, and results obtained from the program. This license extends only to use of the program in the United States or countries in which the program is marketed by authorized distributors.

LICENSE GRANT
You hereby accept a nonexclusive, nontransferable, permanent license to install and use the program ON A SINGLE COMPUTER at any given time. You may copy the program solely for backup or archival purposes in support of your use of the program on the single computer. You may not modify, translate, disassemble, decompile, or reverse engineer the program, in whole or in part.

TERM
The License is effective until terminated. Pearson Education, Inc. reserves the right to terminate this License automatically if any provision of the License is violated. You may terminate the License at any time. To terminate this License, you must return the program, including documentation, along with a written warranty stating that all copies in your possession have been returned or destroyed.

LIMITED WARRANTY
THE PROGRAM IS PROVIDED "AS IS" WITHOUT WARRANTY OF ANY KIND, EITHER EXPRESSED OR IMPLIED, INCLUDING, BUT NOT LIMITED TO, THE IMPLIED WARRANTIES OF MERCHANTABILITY AND FITNESS FOR A PARTICULAR PURPOSE. THE ENTIRE RISK AS TO THE QUALITY AND PERFORMANCE OF THE PROGRAM IS WITH YOU. SHOULD THE PROGRAM PROVE DEFECTIVE, YOU (AND NOT PEARSON EDUCATION, INC. OR ANY AUTHORIZED DEALER) ASSUME THE ENTIRE COST OF ALL NECESSARY SERVICING, REPAIR, OR CORRECTION. NO ORAL OR WRITTEN INFORMATION OR ADVICE GIVEN BY PEARSON EDUCATION, INC., ITS DEALERS, DISTRIBUTORS, OR AGENTS SHALL CREATE A WARRANTY OR INCREASE THE SCOPE OF THIS WARRANTY.

SOME STATES DO NOT ALLOW THE EXCLUSION OF IMPLIED WARRANTIES, SO THE ABOVE EXCLUSION MAY NOT APPLY TO YOU. THIS WARRANTY GIVES YOU SPECIFIC LEGAL RIGHTS AND YOU MAY ALSO HAVE OTHER LEGAL RIGHTS THAT VARY FROM STATE TO STATE.

Pearson Education, Inc. does not warrant that the functions contained in the program will meet your requirements or that the operation of the program will be uninterrupted or error-free. However, Pearson Education, Inc. warrants the CD-ROM(s) on which the program is furnished to be free from defects in material and workmanship under normal use for a period of ninety (90) days from the date of delivery to you as evidenced by a copy of your receipt. The program should not be relied on as the sole basis to solve a problem whose incorrect solution could result in injury to person or property. If the program is employed in such a manner, it is at the user's own risk and Pearson Education, Inc. explicitly disclaims all liability for such misuse.

LIMITATION OF REMEDIES
Pearson Education, Inc.'s entire liability and your exclusive remedy shall be: 1. the replacement of any CD-ROM not meeting Pearson Education, Inc.'s "LIMITED WARRANTY" and that is returned to Pearson Education, or 2. if Pearson Education is unable to deliver a replacement CD-ROM that is free of defects in materials or workmanship, you may terminate this agreement by returning the program.

IN NO EVENT WILL PEARSON EDUCATION, INC. BE LIABLE TO YOU FOR ANY DAMAGES, INCLUDING ANY LOST PROFITS, LOST SAVINGS, OR OTHER INCIDENTAL OR CONSEQUENTIAL DAMAGES ARISING OUT OF THE USE OR INABILITY TO USE SUCH PROGRAM EVEN IF PEARSON EDUCATION, INC. OR AN AUTHORIZED DISTRIBUTOR HAS BEEN ADVISED OF THE POSSIBILITY OF SUCH DAMAGES, OR FOR ANY CLAIM BY ANY OTHER PARTY.

SOME STATES DO NOT ALLOW FOR THE LIMITATION OR EXCLUSION OF LIABILITY FOR INCIDENTAL OR CONSEQUENTIAL DAMAGES, SO THE ABOVE LIMITATION OR EXCLUSION MAY NOT APPLY TO YOU.

GENERAL
You may not sublicense, assign, or transfer the license of the program. Any attempt to sublicense, assign or transfer any of the rights, duties, or obligations hereunder is void.

This Agreement will be governed by the laws of the State of New York.

Should you have any questions concerning this Agreement, you may contact Pearson Education, Inc. by writing to:
ESM Media Development
Higher Education Division
Pearson Education, Inc.
1 Lake Street
Upper Saddle River, NJ 07458

Should you have any questions concerning technical support, you may write to:
New Media Production
Higher Education Division
Pearson Education, Inc.
1 Lake Street
Upper Saddle River, NJ 07458

YOU ACKNOWLEDGE THAT YOU HAVE READ THIS AGREEMENT, UNDERSTAND IT, AND AGREE TO BE BOUND BY ITS TERMS AND CONDITIONS. YOU FURTHER AGREE THAT IT IS THE COMPLETE AND EXCLUSIVE STATEMENT OF THE AGREEMENT BETWEEN US THAT SUPERSEDES ANY PROPOSAL OR PRIOR AGREEMENT, ORAL OR WRITTEN, AND ANY OTHER COMMUNICATIONS BETWEEN US RELATING TO THE SUBJECT MATTER OF THIS AGREEMENT.

System Requirements
-Windows
Pentium II 300 MHz processor
Windows NT, 2000, ME, or XP
64 MB RAM (128 MB RAM required for Windows XP)
4.3 MB available hard drive space (optional—for minimum QuickTime installation)
800 x 600 resolution
8x or faster CD-ROM drive
QuickTime 6.x
Sound card

-Macintosh
PowerPC G3 233 MHz or better
Mac OS 9.x or 10.x
64 MB RAM
10 MB available hard drive space for Mac OS 9, 19 MB on OS X (optional—if QuickTime installation is needed)
800 x 600 resolution
8x or faster CD-ROM drive
QuickTime 6.x

Support Information
If you are having problems with this software, call (800) 677-6337 between 8:00 a.m. and 8:00 p.m. EST, Monday through Friday, and 5:00 p.m. through Midnight EST on Sundays. You can also get support by filling out the web form located at: http://247.prenhall.com/mediaform

Our technical staff will need to know certain things about your system in order to help us solve your problems more quickly and efficiently. If possible, please be at your computer when you call for support. You should have the following information ready:
• Textbook ISBN
• CD-ROM ISBN
• corresponding product and title
• computer make and model
• Operating System (Windows or Macintosh) and Version
• RAM available
• hard disk space available
• Sound card? Yes or No
• printer make and model
• network connection
• detailed description of the problem, including the exact wording of any error messages.

NOTE: Pearson does not support and/or assist with the following:
• third-party software (i.e. Microsoft including Microsoft Office suite, Apple, Borland, etc.)
• homework assistance
• Textbooks and CD-ROMs purchased used are not supported and are non-replaceable. To purchase a new CD-ROM, contact Pearson Individual Order Copies at 1-800-282-0693.

Statistics
For Business and Economics

Statistics
For Business and Economics
TENTH EDITION

James T. McClave

Info Tech, Inc.
University of Florida

P. George Benson

College of Charleston

Terry Sincich

University of South Florida

PEARSON
Prentice Hall

Upper Saddle River, NJ 07458

Library of Congress Cataloging-in-Publication Data

McClave, James T.
   Statistics for business and economics / James T. McClave, P. George Benson, Terry
Sincich.—10th ed.
      p. cm.
   Includes bibliographical references and index.
   ISBN 0-13-240936-4
      1. Commercial statistics. 2. Economics—Statistical methods. 3. Statistics. I. Benson,
P. George. II. Sincich, Terry. III. Title.

HF1017.M36 2008
519.5—dc22
                                                                    2006053282

Executive Acquisitions Editor: *Petra Recter*
Vice President and Editorial Director, Mathematics: *Christine Hoag*
Project Manager: *Michael Bell*
Editorial Assistant/Print Supplements Editor: *Joanne Wendelken*
Production Management and Composition: *Elm Street Publishing Services, Inc.*
Senior Managing Editor: *Linda Mihatov Behrens*
Executive Managing Editor: *Kathleen Schiaparelli*
Media Project Manager, Developmental Math: *Audra J. Walsh*
Media Production Editor: *Robert Merenoff*
Manufacturing Buyer: *Maura Zaldivar*
Manufacturing Manager: *Alexis Heydt-Long*
Director of Marketing: *Patrice Jones*
Marketing Manager: *Wayne Parkins*
Marketing Assistant: *Jennifer DeLeeuwerk*
Art Director: *Maureen Eide*
Interior Designer: *Michael J. Fruhbeis*
Cover Designers: *Michael J. Fruhbeis/Maureen Eide*
Art Editor: *Thomas Benfatti*
Cover Photo: (tags) *Dorling Kindersley/Getty Images;* (shirts) *Iconica/Getty Images Inc.*
Manager, Cover Visual Research & Permissions: *Karen Sanatar*
Director, Image Resource Center: *Melinda Patelli*
Manager, Rights and Permissions: *Zina Arabia*
Manager, Visual Research: *Beth Brenzel*
Image Permission Coordinator: *Fran Toepfer*
Art Studio: *GEX*

© 2008 by Pearson Education, Inc.
Pearson Prentice Hall
Pearson Education, Inc.,
Upper Saddle River, New Jersey 07458

Photo Credits appear on pages P-1–P-2, which constitutes a continuation of the copyright page.

Printed in the United States of America
10 9 8 7 6 5 4 3

ISBN-13: 978-0-13-240935-3   ISBN-10: 0-13-240935-6

Pearson Education LTD., *London*
Pearson Education Australia PTY., Limited, *Sydney*
Pearson Education Singapore, Pte. Ltd.
Pearson Education North Asia Ltd., *Hong Kong*
Pearson Education Canada, Ltd., *Canada*
Pearson Educacíon de Mexico, S.A. de C.V.
Pearson Education—Japan, *Tokyo*
Pearson Education Malaysia, Pte. Ltd.

Contents

Preface   xiii

CHAPTER 6

Inferences Based on a Single Sample: Tests of Hypothesis   344

CHAPTER 7

Inferences Based on Two Samples: Confidence Intervals and Tests of Hypotheses   402

CHAPTER 11

Multiple Regression and Model Building   664

CHAPTER 12

Methods for Quality Improvement   788

CHAPTER

1

Statistics, Data, and Statistical Thinking

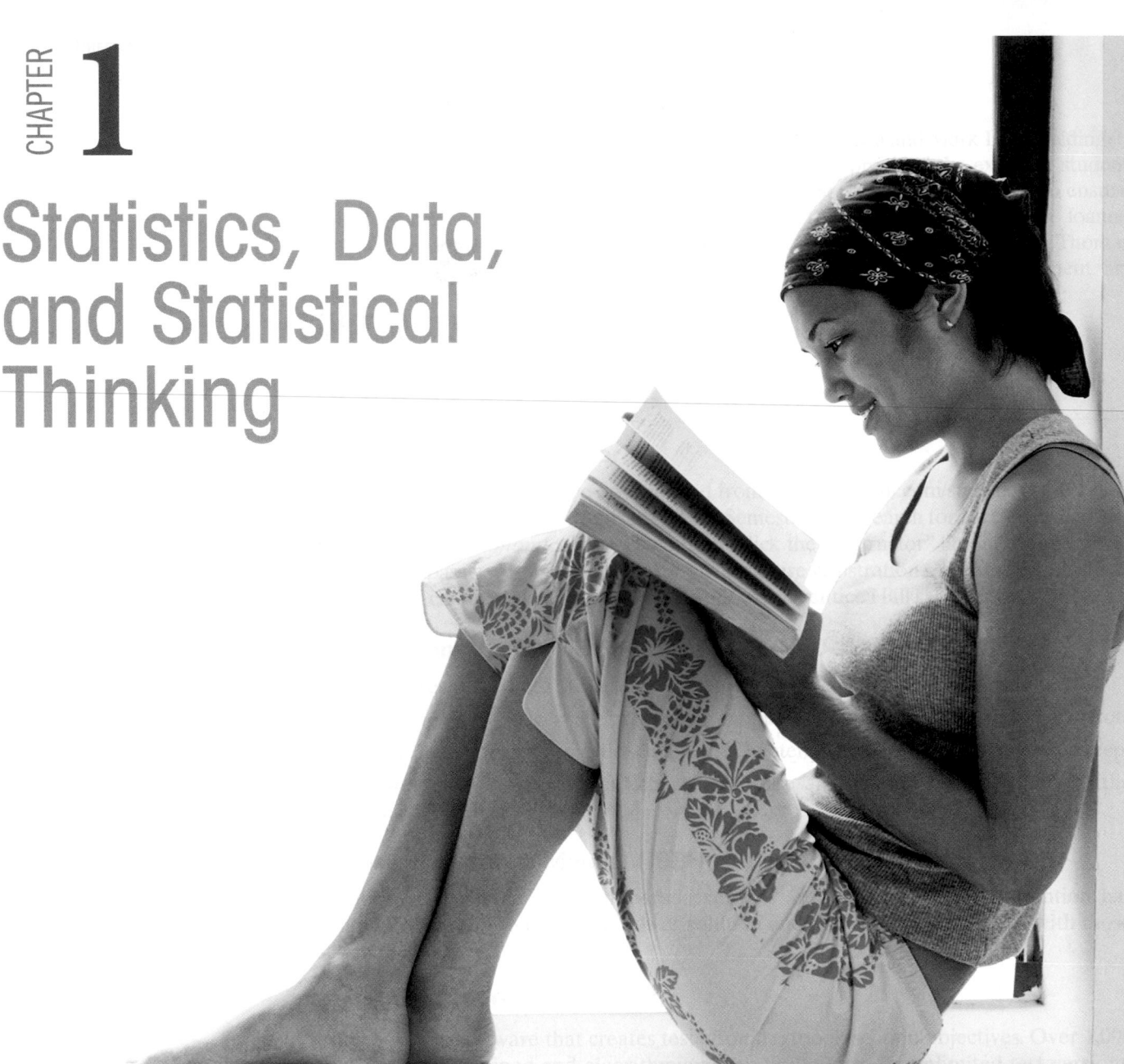

WHERE WE'RE GOING

■ Introduce the field of statistics.

■ Demonstrate how statistics applies to business.

■ Establish the link between statistics and data.

■ Identify the different types of data and data-collection methods.

■ Differentiate between population and sample data.

■ Differentiate between descriptive and inferential statistics.

STATISTICS IN ACTION

A 20/20 View of Surveys: Fact or Fiction?

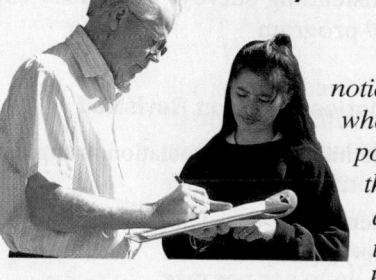

"Did you ever notice that, no matter where you stand on popular issues of the day, you can always find statistics or surveys to back up your point of view—whether to take vitamins, whether day-care harms kids, or what foods can hurt you or save you? There is an endless flow of information to help you make decisions, but is this information accurate, unbiased? John Stossel decided to check that out, and you may be surprised to learn if the picture you're getting doesn't seem quite right, maybe it isn't."

Barbara Walters gave this introduction to a March 31, 1995, segment of the popular prime-time ABC television program *20/20*. The story is titled "Facts or Fiction?—Exposés of So-Called Surveys." One of the surveys investigated by ABC correspondent John Stossel compared the discipline problems experienced by teachers in the 1940s and those experienced today. The results: In the 1940s, teachers worried most about students talking in class, chewing gum, and running in the halls. Today, they worry most about being assaulted! This information was highly publicized in the print media—in daily newspapers, weekly magazines, Ann Landers's column, the *Congressional Quarterly,*

and the *Wall Street Journal,* among others—and referenced in speeches by a variety of public figures, including former first lady Barbara Bush and former Education Secretary William Bennett.

"Hearing this made me yearn for the old days when life was so much simpler and gentler, but was life that simple then?" asks Stossel. "Wasn't there juvenile delinquency [in the 1940s]? Is the survey true?" With the help of a Yale School of Management professor, Stossel found the original source of the teacher survey—Texas oilman T. Colin Davis—and discovered it wasn't a survey at all! Davis had simply identified certain disciplinary problems encountered by teachers in a conservative newsletter—a list he admitted was not obtained from a statistical survey, but from Davis's personal knowledge of the problems in the 1940s. ("I was in school then") and his understanding of the problems today ("I read the papers").

Stossel's critical thinking about the teacher "survey" led to the discovery of research that is misleading at best and unethical at worst. Several more misleading (and possibly unethical) surveys, conducted by businesses or special interest groups with specific objectives in mind, were presented on the ABC program. These are listed below. A sixth study, published in the *New York Times,* is also discussed.

Reported Information (Source)	Actual Study Information
1. Eating oat bran is a cheap and easy way to achieve a slightly lower cholesterol. (Quaker Oats)	Diet must consist of nothing but oat bran to reduce your cholesterol count.
2. 150,000 women a year die from anorexia. (Feminist group)	Approximately 1,000 women a year die from problems that were likely caused by anorexia.
3. Domestic violence causes more birth defects than all medical issues combined. (March of Dimes)	No study—false report.
4. Only 29% of high school girls are happy with themselves, compared to 66% of elementary school girls. (American Association of University Women)	Of 3,000 high school girls, 29% responded "Always true" to the statement "I am happy the way I am." Most answered, "Sort of true" and "Sometimes true."
5. One in four American children under age 12 is hungry or at risk of hunger. (Food Research and Action Center)	Based on responses to questions: "Do you ever cut the size of meals?" "Do you ever eat less than you feel you should?" "Did you ever rely on limited numbers of foods to feed your children because you were running out of money to buy food for a meal?"
6. There is a strong correlation between a CEO's golf handicap and the company's stock performance: The lower the CEO's handicap (i.e., the better the golfer), the better the stock performs. (*New York Times,* May 31, 1998)	Survey sent to CEOs of 300 largest U.S. companies; only 74 revealed their golf handicaps. Data for several top-ranking CEOs were excluded from the analysis.

1.3 Fundamenta

3

Look Back A key to diagnosing a statistical problem is to identify the data set collected (in this example, the ages of the 500 ABC nightly news viewers) as a population or sample.

EXAMPLE 1.2

Key Elements of a Statistical Problem

Problem *Cola wars* is the popular term for the intense competition between Coca-Cola and Pepsi displayed in their marketing campaigns. Their campaigns have featured movie and television stars, rock videos, athletic endorsements, and claims of consumer preference based on taste tests. Suppose, as part of a Pepsi marketing campaign, 1,000 cola consumers are given a blind taste test (i.e., a taste test in which the two brand names are disguised). Each consumer is asked to state a preference for brand A or brand B.

a. Describe the population.

b. Describe the variable of interest.

c. Describe the sample.

d. Describe the inference.

Solution

a. Since we are interested in the responses of cola consumers in a taste test, a cola consumer is the experimental unit. Thus, the population of interest is the collection or set of all cola consumers.

b. The characteristic that Pepsi wants to measure is the consumer's cola preference as revealed under the conditions of a blind taste test, so cola preference is the variable of interest.

c. The sample is the 1,000 cola consumers selected from the population of all cola consumers.

d. The inference of interest is the *generalization* of the cola preferences of the 1,000 sampled consumers to the population of all cola consumers. In particular, the preferences of the consumers in the sample can be used to *estimate* the percentage of all cola consumers who prefer each brand.

Look Back In determining whether the inference is inferential or descriptive, we assess whether Pepsi is interested in the responses of only the 1,000 sampled customers (descriptive statistics) or in the responses for the entire population of consumers (inferential statistics).

Now Work Exercise 1.14b

The preceding definitions and examples identify four of the five elements of an inferential statistical problem: a population, one or more variables of interest in a sample, and an inference. But making the inference is only part of the story. We also need to know its **reliability**—that is, how good the inference is. The only way we can be certain that an inference about a population is correct is to include the entire population in our sample. However, because of *resource constraints* (i.e., insufficient time and/or money), we usually can't work with whole populations, so we base our inferences on just a portion of the population (a sample). Consequently, whenever possible, it is important to determine and report the reliability of each inference made. Reliability, then, is the fifth element of inferential statistical problems.

The measure of reliability that accompanies an inference separates the science of statistics from the art of fortune-telling. A palm reader, like a statistician, may examine a sample (your hand) and make inferences about the population (your life). However, unlike statistical inferences, the palm reader's inferences include no measure of reliability.

Suppose, like the TV executive in Example 1.1, we are interested in the *error of estimation* (i.e., the difference between the average age for the population of TV viewers and the average age of a sample of TV viewers). Using statistical methods, we can determine a *bound on the estimation error.* This bound is simply a number that our estimation error (the difference between the average age of the sample and the average age of the population) is not likely to exceed. We'll see in later chapters that this bound is a measure of the uncertainty of our inference. The reliability of statistical inferences is discussed throughout this text. For now, we simply want you to realize that an inference is incomplete without a measure of its reliability.

> **Definition 1.9**
>
> A **measure of reliability** is a statement (usually quantified) about the degree of uncertainty associated with a statistical inference.

Let's conclude this section with a summary of the elements of both descriptive and inferential statistical problems and an example to illustrate a measure of reliability.

Four Elements of Descriptive Statistical Problems

1. The population or sample of interest
2. One or more variables (characteristics of the population or sample units) that are to be investigated
3. Tables, graphs, or numerical summary tools
4. Identification of patterns in the data

Five Elements of Inferential Statistical Problems

1. The population of interest
2. One or more variables (characteristics of the population units) that are to be investigated
3. The sample of population units
4. The inference about the population based on information contained in the sample
5. A measure of reliability for the inference

EXAMPLE 1.3

Reliability of an Inference

Problem Refer to Example 1.2, in which the cola preferences of 1,000 consumers were indicated in a taste test. Describe how the reliability of an inference concerning the preferences of all cola consumers in the Pepsi bottler's marketing region could be measured.

Solution When the preferences of 1,000 consumers are used to estimate the preferences of all consumers in the region, the estimate will not exactly mirror the preferences of the population. For example, if the taste test shows that 56% of the 1,000 consumers chose Pepsi, it does not follow (nor is it likely) that exactly 56% of all cola drinkers in the region prefer Pepsi. Nevertheless, we can use sound statistical reasoning (which is presented later in the text) to ensure that our sampling procedure will generate estimates that are almost certainly within a specified limit of the true percentage of all consumers who prefer Pepsi. For example, such reasoning might assure us that the estimate of the preference for Pepsi from the sample is almost certainly within 5% of the actual population preference. The implication is that the actual preference for Pepsi is between 51% [i.e., $(56 - 5)\%$] and 61% [i.e., $(56 + 5)\%$]—that is, $(56 \pm 5)\%$. This interval represents a measure of reliability for the inference.

Look Back The interval 56 ± 5 is called a *confidence interval,* since we are "confident" that the true percentage of customers who prefer Pepsi in a taste test falls into the range (51, 61). In Chapter 5, we learn how to assess the degree of confidence (e.g., 90% or 95% confidence) in the interval.

EXAMPLE 1.4

Key Elements of
a Process

Problem A particular fast-food restaurant chain has 6,289 outlets with drive-through windows. To attract more customers to its drive-through services, the company is considering offering a 50% discount to customers who wait more than a specified number of minutes to receive their order. To help determine what the time limit should be, the company decided to estimate the average waiting time at a particular drive-through window in Dallas, Texas. For 7 consecutive days, the worker taking customers' orders recorded the time that every order was placed. The worker who handed the order to the customer recorded the time of delivery. In both cases, workers used synchronized digital clocks that reported the time to the nearest second. At the end of the 7-day period, 2,109 orders had been timed.

  a. Describe the process of interest at the Dallas restaurant.

  b. Describe the variable of interest.

  c. Describe the sample.

  d. Describe the inference of interest.

  e. Describe how the reliability of the inference could be measured.

Solution

  a. The process of interest is the drive-through window at a particular fast-food restaurant in Dallas, Texas. It is a process because it "produces," or "generates," meals over time—that is, it services customers over time.

  b. The variable the company monitored is customer waiting time, the length of time a customer waits to receive a meal after placing an order. Since the study is focusing only on the output of the process (the time to produce the output) and not the internal operations of the process (the tasks required to produce a meal for a customer), the process is being treated as a black box.

  c. The sampling plan was to monitor every order over a particular 7-day period. The sample is the 2,109 orders that were processed during the 7-day period.

  d. The company's immediate interest is in learning about the drive-through window in Dallas. They plan to do this by using the waiting times from the sample to make a statistical inference about the drive-through process. In particular, they might use the average waiting time for the sample to estimate the average waiting time at the Dallas facility.

  e. As for inferences about populations, measures of reliability can be developed for inferences about processes. The reliability of the estimate of the average waiting time for the Dallas restaurant could be measured by a bound on the error of estimation—that is, we might find that the average waiting time is 4.2 minutes, with a bound on the error of estimation of .5 minutes. The implication would be that we could be reasonably certain that the true average waiting time for the Dallas process is between 3.7 and 4.7 minutes.

Look Back Notice that there is also a population described in this example: the company's 6,289 existing outlets with drive-through facilities. In the final analysis, the company will use what it learns about the process in Dallas and, perhaps, similar studies at other locations to make an inference about the waiting times in its population of outlets.

Now Work Exercise 1.30

Note that output already generated by a process can be viewed as a population. Suppose a soft-drink canning process produced 2,000 twelve-packs yesterday, all of which were stored in a warehouse. If we were interested in learning something about those 2,000 twelve-packs—such as the percentage with defective cardboard packaging—we could treat the 2,000 twelve-packs as a population. We might draw a sample from the population in the warehouse, measure the variable of interest, and use the sample data to make a statistical inference about the 2,000 twelve-packs, as described in Sections 1.2 and 1.3.

In this optional section, we have presented a brief introduction to processes and the use of statistical methods to analyze and learn about processes. In Chapters 12 and 13 we present an in-depth treatment of these subjects.

1.5 Types of Data

You have learned that statistics is the science of data and that data are obtained by measuring the values of one or more variables on the units in the sample (or population). All data (and hence the variables we measure) can be classified as one of two general types: *quantitative* and *qualitative*.

Quantitative data are data that are measured on a naturally occurring numerical scale.* The following are examples of quantitative data:

1. The temperature (in degrees Celsius) at which each unit in a sample of 20 pieces of heat-resistant plastic begins to melt
2. The current unemployment rate (measured as a percentage) for each of the 50 states
3. The scores of a sample of 150 MBA applicants on the GMAT, a standardized business graduate school entrance exam administered nationwide
4. The number of female executives employed in each of a sample of 75 manufacturing companies

> **Definition 1.13**
>
> **Quantitative data** are measurements that are recorded on a naturally occurring numerical scale.

In contrast, qualitative data cannot be measured on a natural numerical scale; they can only be classified into categories.† Examples of qualitative data are as follows:

1. The political party affiliation (Democrat, Republican, or Independent) in a sample of 50 chief executive officers
2. The defective status (defective or not) of each of 100 computer chips manufactured by Intel
3. The size of a car (subcompact, compact, midsize, or full-size) rented by each of a sample of 30 business travelers
4. A taste tester's ranking (best, worst, etc.) of four brands of barbecue sauce for a panel of 10 testers

Often, we assign arbitrary numerical values to qualitative data for ease of computer entry and analysis. But these assigned numerical values are simply codes: They cannot be meaningfully added, subtracted, multiplied, or divided. For example, we might code Democrat = 1, Republican = 2, and Independent = 3. Similarly, a taste tester might rank the barbecue sauces from 1 (best) to 4 (worst). These are simply arbitrarily selected numerical codes for the categories and have no utility beyond that.

---

*Quantitative data can be subclassified as either *interval* or *ratio*. For ratio data, the origin (i.e., the value 0) is a meaningful number. But the origin has no meaning with interval data. Consequently, we can add and subtract interval data, but we can't multiply and divide them. Of the four quantitative data sets listed, (1) and (3) are interval data, while (2) and (4) are ratio data.

†Qualitative data can be subclassified as either *nominal* or *ordinal*. The categories of an ordinal data set can be ranked or meaningfully ordered, but the categories of a nominal data set can't be ordered. Of the four qualitative data sets listed above, (1) and (2) are nominal and (3) and (4) are ordinal.

> **Definition 1.14**
> **Qualitative data** are measurements that cannot be measured on a natural numerical scale; they can only be classified into one of a group of categories.

EXAMPLE 1.5
Types of Data

DDT

Problem Chemical and manufacturing plants sometimes discharge toxic-waste materials such as DDT into nearby rivers and streams. These toxins can adversely affect the plants and animals inhabiting the river and the riverbank. The U.S. Army Corps of Engineers conducted a study of fish in the Tennessee River (in Alabama) and its three tributary creeks: Flint Creek, Limestone Creek, and Spring Creek. A total of 144 fish were captured, and the following variables were measured for each:

1. River/creek where each fish was captured
2. Species (channel catfish, largemouth bass, or smallmouth buffalo fish)
3. Length (centimeters)
4. Weight (grams)
5. DDT concentration (parts per million)

These data are saved in the **DDT** file. Classify each of the five variables measured as quantitative or qualitative.

Solution The variables length, weight, and DDT are quantitative because each is measured on a numerical scale: length in centimeters, weight in grams, and DDT in parts per million. In contrast, river/creek and species cannot be measured quantitatively: They can only be classified into categories (e.g., channel catfish, largemouth bass, and smallmouth buffalo fish for species). Consequently, data on river/creek and species are qualitative.

Look Back It is essential that you understand whether data are quantitative or qualitative in nature, since the statistical method appropriate for describing, reporting, and analyzing the data depends on the data type (quantitative or qualitative).

Now Work Exercise 1.16

ACTIVITY 1.1: *Keep the Change:* Collecting Data

In 2006, Bank of America introduced a savings program called *Keep the Change.* Each time a customer enrolled in the program uses his or her debit card to make a purchase, the difference between the purchase total and the next higher dollar amount is transferred from the customer's checking account to a savings account. For example, if you were enrolled in the program and used your debit card to purchase a latte for $3.75, then $0.25 would be transferred from your checking to your savings account. For the first 90 days that a customer is enrolled in the program, Bank of America matches the amounts transferred up to $250. In this and subsequent activities, we will investigate the potential benefit to the customer and cost to the bank.

1. Simulate the program by keeping track of all purchases that you make during one week that could be made with a debit card even if you use a different form of payment. For each purchase, record both the purchase total and the amount that would be transferred from checking to savings with the *Keep the Change* program.

2. You now have two sets of data: *Purchase Totals* and *Amounts Transferred.* Both sets contain quantitative data. For each data set, identify the corresponding naturally occurring numerical scale. Explain why each set has an obvious lower bound but only one set has a definite upper bound.

3. Find the total of the amounts transferred for the one-week period. Since 90 days is approximately 13 weeks, multiply the total by 13 to estimate how much the bank would have to match during the first 90 days. Form a third data set, *Bank Matching,* by collecting the 90-day estimates of all the students in your class. Identify the naturally occurring scale, including bounds, for this set of data.

Keep the data sets from this activity for use in other activities. We suggest you save the data using statistical software (e.g., Minitab) or a graphing calculator.

We demonstrate many useful methods for analyzing quantitative and qualitative data in the remaining chapters of the text. But first, we discuss some important ideas on data collection.

1.6 Collecting Data

Once you decide on the type of data—quantitative or qualitative—appropriate for the problem at hand, you'll need to collect the data. Generally, you can obtain the data in four different ways:

1. Data from a *published source*
2. Data from a *designed experiment*
3. Data from a *survey*
4. Data collected *observationally*

Sometimes, the data set of interest has already been collected for you and is available in a **published source,** such as a book, journal, newspaper, or Web site. For example, you may want to examine and summarize the unemployment rates (i.e., percentages of eligible workers who are unemployed) in the 50 states of the United States. You can find this data set (as well as numerous other data sets) at your library in the *Statistical Abstract of the United States,* published annually by the U.S. government. Similarly, someone who is interested in monthly mortgage applications for new home construction would find this data set in the *Survey of Current Business,* another government publication. Other examples of published data sources include the *Wall Street Journal* (financial data) and the *The Sporting News* (sports information).*

A second method of collecting data involves conducting a **designed experiment,** in which the researcher exerts strict control over the units (people, objects, or events) in the study. For example, a recent medical study investigated the potential of aspirin in preventing heart attacks. Volunteer physicians were divided into two groups—the *treatment* group and the *control* group. In the treatment group, each physician took one aspirin tablet a day for 1 year, while each physician in the control group took an aspirin-free placebo (no drug) made to look like an aspirin tablet. The researchers, not the physicians under study, controlled who received the aspirin (the treatment) and who received the placebo. As you will learn in Chapter 10, a properly designed experiment allows you to extract more information from the data than is possible with an uncontrolled study.

Surveys are a third source of data. With a **survey,** the researcher samples a group of people, asks one or more questions, and records the responses. Probably the most familiar type of survey is the political polls conducted by any one of a number of organizations (e.g., Harris, Gallup, Roper, and CNN) and designed to predict the outcome of a political election. Another familiar survey is the Nielsen survey, which provides the major television networks with information on the most watched TV programs. Surveys can be conducted through the mail, with telephone interviews, or with in-person interviews. Although in-person interviews are more expensive than mail or telephone surveys, they may be necessary when complex information must be collected.

Finally, observational studies can be employed to collect data. In an **observational study,** the researcher observes the experimental units in their natural setting and records the variable(s) of interest. For example, a company psychologist might observe and record the level of "Type A" behavior of a sample of assembly line workers. Similarly, a finance researcher may observe and record the closing stock prices of companies that are acquired by other firms on the day prior to the buyout and compare them to the closing prices on the day the acquisition is announced. Unlike a designed experiment, an observational study is one in which the researcher makes no attempt to control any aspect of the experimental units.

Regardless of the data-collection method employed, it is likely that the data will be a sample from some population. And if we wish to apply inferential statistics, we must obtain a *representative sample.*

*With published data, we often make a distinction between the *primary source* and *secondary source*. If the publisher is the original collector of the data, the source is primary. Otherwise, the data are secondary source.

> **Definition 1.15**
>
> A **representative sample** exhibits characteristics typical of those possessed by the population of interest.

For example, consider a political poll conducted during a presidential election year. Assume the pollster wants to estimate the percentage of all 140,000,000 registered voters in the United States who favor the incumbent president. The pollster would be unwise to base the estimate on survey data collected for a sample of voters from the incumbent's own state. Such an estimate would almost certainly be *biased* high.

The most common way to satisfy the representative sample requirement is to select a random sample. A **random sample** ensures that every subset of fixed size in the population has the same chance of being included in the sample. If the pollster samples 1,500 of the 140,000,000 voters in the population so that every subset of 1,500 voters has an equal chance of being selected, he has devised a random sample. The procedure for selecting a random sample is discussed in Chapter 3. Here, however, let's look at two examples involving actual sampling studies.

> **Definition 1.16**
>
> A **random sample** of n experimental units is a sample selected from the population in such a way that every different sample of size n has an equal chance of selection.

EXAMPLE 1.6
Method of Data Collection

Problem How do consumers feel about using the Internet for online shopping? To find out, a customer-experience software company commissioned a nationwide survey of 1,859 U.S. adults who had conducted at least one online transaction at a banking, shopping, travel, or insurance Web site in the past year. The findings, reported on *BusinessWeek.com* (January 5, 2006), revealed that 1,655 respondents, or 89%, experienced technical problems with an online transaction. Also, more than one-third of the consumers go to a competitor's Web site when a glitch in the online transaction occurs.

  a. Identify the data-collection method.

  b. Identify the target population.

  c. Are the sample data representative of the population?

Solution

  a. The data-collection method is a survey: 1,859 adults completed the questionnaire.

  b. Presumably, the software company who commissioned the survey is interested in all consumers who have made at least one online transaction in the past year. Consequently, the target population is *all* consumers who use the Internet for online transactions.

  c. Because the 1,859 respondents clearly make up a subset of the target population, they do form a sample. Whether or not the sample is representative is unclear, since *BusinessWeek.com* provided no detailed information on how the 1,859 respondents were selected. If the respondents were obtained using, say, random-digit telephone dialing, then the sample is likely to be representative since it is a random sample. However, if the questionnaire was made available to anyone surfing the Internet, then the respondents are *self-selected* (i.e., each Internet user who saw the survey chose whether or not to respond to it). Such a survey often suffers from *nonresponse* bias. It is possible that many Internet users who chose not to respond (or who never saw the questionnaire) would have answered the questions differently, leading to a lower (or higher) sample percentage.

Look Back Any inferences based on survey samples that employ self-selection are suspect due to potential nonresponse bias.

EXAMPLE 1.7
Data-Collection Method; Representative Data

Problem Marketers use wording such as "was $100, now $80" to indicate a price promotion. The promotion is typically compared to the retailer's previous price or to a competitor's price. A study in the *Journal of Consumer Research* (September 1996) investigated whether between-store comparisons result in greater perceptions of value by consumers than within-store comparisons. Suppose 50 consumers were randomly selected from all consumers in a designated market area to participate in the study. The researchers randomly assigned 25 consumers to read a within-store price promotion advertisement ("was $100, now $80") and 25 consumers to read a between-store price promotion ("$100 there, $80 here"). The consumers then gave their opinion on the value of the discount offer on a 10-point scale (where 1 = lowest value and 10 = highest value). The value opinions of the two groups of consumers were compared.

a. Identify the data-collection method.
b. Are the sample data representative of the target population?

Solution

a. Here, the experimental units are the consumers. Since the researchers controlled which price promotion ad—"within-store" or "between-store"—the experimental units (consumers) were assigned to, a designed experiment was used to collect the data.

b. The sample of 50 consumers was randomly selected from all consumers in the designated market area. If the target population is all consumers in this market, it is likely that the sample is representative. However, the researchers warn that the sample data should not be used to make inferences about consumer behavior in other, dissimilar markets.

Look Back By using randomization in a designed experiment, the researcher is attempting to eliminate different types of bias, including self-selection bias.

Now Work Exercise 1.15

STATISTICS IN ACTION REVISITED

Identifying the Data-Collection Method and Data Type for the CEO Golf Handicap—Stock Performance Study

 GOLFCEO

Refer to the *New York Times* study on the link between a CEO's golf handicap and the company's stock performance. Recall that the newspaper gathered information on golf handicaps of corporate executives obtained from a *Golf Digest* survey that was sent to 300 corporate executives. Thus, the data-collection method is a survey. In addition to golf handicap (a numerical "index" that allows golfers to compare skills), the *Times* measured the CEO's company stock market performance over a 3-year period on a scale of 0 to 100. Since both variables, golf handicap and stock performance, are numerical in nature, they are quantitative data.

1.7 The Role of Statistics in Managerial Decision Making

According to H. G. Wells, author of such science-fiction classics as *The War of the Worlds* and *The Time Machine,* "*Statistical thinking* will one day be as necessary for efficient citizenship as the ability to read and write." Written more than a hundred years ago, Wells's prediction is proving true today.

Biography

H. G. WELLS
(1866–1946)

Writer and Novelist

English-born Herbert George Wells published his first novel, *The Time Machine,* in 1895 as a parody of the English class division and as a satirical warning that human progress is inevitable. Although most famous as a science-fiction novelist, Wells was a prolific writer as a journalist, sociologist, historian, and philosopher. Wells's prediction about statistical thinking (see above) is just one of a plethora of observations he made about life on this world. Here are a few more of H. G. Wells's more famous quotes:

"Advertising is legalized lying."

"Crude classification and false generalizations are the curse of organized life."

"The crisis of today is the joke of tomorrow."

"Fools make researchers and wise men exploit them."

"The only true measure of success is the ration between what we might have done and what we might have been on the one hand, and the thing we have made and the things we have made of ourselves on the other."

The growth in data collection associated with scientific phenomena, business operations, and government activities (quality control, statistical auditing, forecasting, etc.) has been remarkable in the past several decades. Every day the media present us with the published results of political, economic, and social surveys. In increasing government emphasis on drug and product testing, for example, we see vivid evidence of the need to be able to evaluate data sets intelligently. Consequently, each of us has to develop a discerning sense—an ability to use rational thought to interpret and understand the meaning of data. This ability can help you make intelligent decisions, inferences, and generalizations; that is, it helps you *think critically* using statistics.

> **Definition 1.17**
>
> **Statistical thinking** involves applying rational thought and the science of statistics to critically assess data and inferences. Fundamental to the thought process is that variation exists in populations and process data.

To gain some insight into the role statistics plays in critical thinking, let's look at a study evaluated by a group of 27 mathematics and statistics teachers attending an American Statistical Association course called "Chance." Consider the following excerpt from an article describing the problem:

> *There are few issues in the news that are not in some way statistical. Take one. Should motorcyclists be required by law to wear helmets? . . . In "The Case for No Helmets" (New York Times, June 17, 1995), Dick Teresi, editor of a magazine for Harley-Davidson bikers, argued that helmets may actually kill, since in collisions at speeds greater than 15 miles an hour the heavy helmet may protect the head but snap the spine. [Teresi] citing a "study," said "nine states without helmet laws had a lower fatality rate (3.05 deaths per 10,000 motorcycles) than those that mandated helmets (3.38)," and "in a survey of 2,500 [at a rally], 98% of the respondents opposed such laws."*

[The course instructors] asked: After reading this [New York Times] piece, do you think it is safer to ride a motorcycle without a helmet? Do you think 98% might be a valid estimate of bikers who oppose helmet laws? What further statistical information would you like? [From Cohn, V. "Chance in college curriculum," AmStat News, Aug.–Sept. 1995, No. 223, p. 2.]

You can use "statistical thinking" to help you critically evaluate the study. For example, before you can evaluate the validity of the 98% estimate, you would want to know how the data were collected for the study cited by the editor of the biker magazine. If a survey was conducted, it's possible that the 2,500 bikers in the sample were not selected at random from the target population of all bikers, but rather were "self-selected." (Remember, they were all attending a rally—a rally likely for bikers who oppose the law.) If the respondents were likely to have strong opinions regarding the helmet law (e.g., strongly oppose the law), the resulting estimate is probably biased high. Also, if the biased sample was intentional, with the sole purpose to mislead the public, the researchers would be guilty of **unethical statistical practice.**

You'd also want more information about the study comparing the motorcycle fatality rate of the nine states without a helmet law to those states that mandate helmets. Were the data obtained from a published source? Were all 50 states included in the study? That is, are you seeing sample data or population data? Furthermore, do the helmet laws vary among states? If so, can you really compare the fatality rates?

These questions led the Chance group to the discovery of two scientific and statistically sound studies on helmets. The first, a UCLA study of nonfatal injuries, disputed the charge that helmets shift injuries to the spine. The second study reported a dramatic *decline* in motorcycle crash deaths after California passed its helmet law.

As in the motorcycle helmet study, many statistical studies are based on survey data. Most of the problems with these surveys result from the use of *nonrandom* samples. These samples are subject to potential errors, such as *selection bias, nonresponse bias* (recall Example 1.6), and *measurement error*. Researchers who are aware of these problems and continue to use the sample data to make inferences are practicing unethical statistics.

Definition 1.18

Selection bias results when a subset of the experimental units in the population is excluded so that these units have no chance of being selected for the sample.

Definition 1.19

Nonresponse bias results when the researchers conducting a survey or study are unable to obtain data on all experimental units selected for the sample.

Definition 1.20

Measurement error refers to inaccuracies in the values of the data recorded. In surveys, the error may be due to ambiguous or leading questions and the interviewer's effect on the respondent.

Successful managers rely heavily on statistical thinking to help them make decisions. The role statistics can play in managerial decision making is displayed in the flow diagram in Figure 1.5. Every managerial decision-making problem begins with a real-world problem. This problem is then formulated in managerial terms and framed as a managerial question. The next sequence of steps (proceeding counterclockwise around

STATISTICS IN ACTION REVISITED

Critically Assessing the CEO Golf Handicap—Stock Performance Study   GOLFCEO

The *New York Times* reported a strong link between a corporate executive's golf handicap and his/her company's stock performance. Thus, the newspaper inferred that the better the CEO is at golf, the better the company's stock performance will be. To critically assess this study, consider the following facts:

1. *Golf Digest* sent surveys to the CEOs at the 300 largest U.S. firms. Only 74 executives agreed to reveal their golf handicaps. Of these 74 CEOs, the *Times* collected data on stock performance for only 51 of the companies. (The other 23 CEOs were not in the stock performance database used by the newspaper.)

2. The *New York Times* researcher who performed the analysis of the data stated that "for all the different factors I've tested as possible links to predicting which CEOs are going to perform well or poorly, [golf handicap] is certainly one of the . . . strongest."

3. According to the *Times*, the researcher "scientifically sifted out a handful of CEOs because of their statistical extremes," in effect "removing seven CEOs from the final analysis because [their data] destroyed the trend lines."

These observations lead a critical thinker to doubt the validity of the inference made by the *New York Times* researcher. Consider first that the sample of CEOs analyzed was not randomly selected from all CEOs in the United States. In fact, they were self-selected—only those CEOs who chose to report their golf handicap were included in the study. (Not even all these "self-reporters" were included; some were eliminated since the newspaper did not have information on their company's stock performance in the database.) Thus, the potential for selection and/or nonresponse bias is extremely high.

Second, based on fact #2, it is likely that the researcher tested a multitude of factors and found only one (golf handicap) that had a link to stock performance. We will learn in subsequent chapters that when a plethora of irrelevant variables are tested statistically, by chance one or more of the variables will be found "statistically significant."

Finally, the researcher removed the data for seven CEOs based on their "statistical extremes." In the next chapter, we learn about statistical "outliers"—how to detect them and how to treat them when discovered. However, it can be shown (using the methods outlined in the text) that these seven data points are not outliers. If the data points are included in the analysis, the link between golf handicap and stock performance is found to be weak, at best.

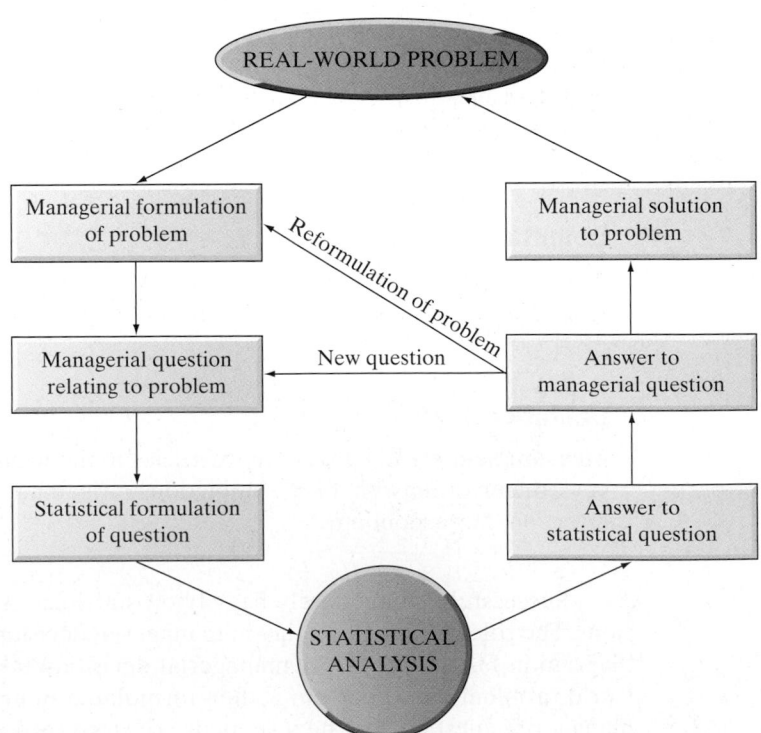

FIGURE 1.5

Flow diagram showing the role of statistics in managerial decision making
Source: Chervany, Benson, and Iyer (1980)

the flow diagram) identifies the role that statistics can play in this process. The managerial question is translated into a statistical question, the sample data are collected and analyzed, and the statistical question is answered. The next step in the process is using the answer to the statistical question to reach an answer to the managerial question. The answer to the managerial question may suggest a reformulation of the original managerial problem, suggest a new managerial question, or lead to the solution of the managerial problem.

One of the most difficult steps in the decision-making process—one that requires a cooperative effort among managers and statisticians—is the translation of the managerial question into statistical terms (for example, into a question about a population). This statistical question must be formulated so that, when answered, it will provide the key to the answer to the managerial question. Thus, as in the game of chess, you must formulate the statistical question with the end result, the solution to the managerial question, in mind.

In the remaining chapters of the text, you'll become familiar with the tools essential for building a firm foundation in statistics and statistical thinking.

ACTIVITY 1.2: Identifying Misleading Statistics

In the *Statistics in Action* feature at the beginning of this chapter, several examples of false or misleading statistics were discussed. Claims such as *One in four American children under age 12 is hungry or at risk of hunger* are often used to persuade the public or the government to donate or allocate more money to charitable groups that feed the poor. Researchers sometimes claim a relationship exists between two seemingly unrelated quantities such as a CEO's golf handicap and the company's stock performance; such relationships are often weak at best and of little practical importance. Read the *Statistics in Action* and *Statistics in Action Revisited* features in this chapter before completing this activity.

1. Look for an article in a newspaper or on the Internet in which a large proportion or percentage of a population is purported to be "at risk" of some calamity, as in the childhood hunger example. Does the article cite a source or provide any information to support the proportion or percentage reported? Is the goal of the article to persuade some individual or group to take some action? If so, what action is being requested? Do you believe that the writer of the article may have some motive for exaggerating the problem? If so, give some possible motives.

2. Look for another article in which a relationship between two seemingly unrelated quantities is purported to exist, as in the CEO golf handicap and stock performance study. Select an article that contains some information on how the data were collected. Identify the target population and the data collection method. Based on what is presented in the article, do you believe that the data are representative of the population? Explain. Is the purported relationship of any practical interest? Explain.

KEY TERMS

Note: Starred (*) terms are from the optional sections in this chapter.

*Black box   13
Census   8
Data   4
Descriptive statistics   5
Designed experiment   17
Experimental unit   7
Inference   5
Inferential statistics   5
Measurement   8

Measurement error   21
Measure of reliability   11
Nonresponse bias   21
Observational study   17
Population   7
*Process   12
Published source   17
Qualitative data   16
Quantitative data   15
Random sample   18
Reliability   10

Representative sample   18
Sample   8, 13
Selection bias   21
Statistical inference   8
Statistical thinking   20
Statistics   4
Survey   17
Unethical statistical practice   21
Variable   7

CHAPTER NOTES

Types of Statistical Applications

Descriptive

1. Identify **population** or **sample** (collection of **experimental units**)
2. Identify **variable(s)**
3. Collect **data**
4. **Describe** data

Inferential

1. Identify **population** (collection of *all* **experimental units**)
2. Identify **variable(s)**
3. Collect **sample** data (*subset* of population)
4. **Inference** about population based on sample
5. **Measure of reliability** for inference

Types of Data

1. **Quantitative** (numerical in nature)
2. **Qualitative** (categorical in nature)

Data-Collection Methods

1. **Observational**
2. **Published source**
3. **Survey**
4. **Designed experiment**

Problems with Nonrandom Samples

1. **Selection bias**
2. **Nonresponse bias**
3. **Measurement error**

EXERCISES 1.1–1.32

Note: Starred (*) exercises are from the optional section in this chapter.

Learning the Mechanics

1.1 What is statistics?

1.2 Explain the difference between descriptive and inferential statistics.

1.3 List and define the four elements of a descriptive statistics problem.

1.4 List and define the five elements of an inferential statistical analysis.

1.5 List the four major methods of collecting data and explain their differences.

1.6 Explain the difference between quantitative and qualitative data.

1.7 Explain how populations and variables differ.

1.8 Explain how populations and samples differ.

1.9 What is a representative sample? What is its value?

1.10 Why would a statistician consider an inference incomplete without an accompanying measure of its reliability?

*1.11 Explain the difference between a population and a process.

1.12 Define *statistical thinking*.

1.13 Suppose you're given a data set that classifies each sample unit into one of four categories: A, B, C, or D. You plan to create a computer database consisting of these data, and you decide to code the data as A = 1, B = 2, C = 3, and D = 4. Are the data consisting of the classifications A, B, C, and D qualitative or quantitative? After the data are input as 1, 2, 3, or 4, are they qualitative or quantitative? Explain your answers.

APPLET   Applet Exercise 1.1

The *Random Numbers* applet generates a list of *n* random numbers from 1 to *N*, where *n* is the size of the sample and *N* is the size of the population. The list generated often contains repetitions of one or more numbers.

a. Using the applet *Random Numbers*, enter 1 for the minimum value, 10 for the maximum value, and 10 for the sample size. Then click on *Sample*. Look at the results and list any numbers that are repeated and the number of times each of these numbers occurs.

b. Repeat part **a,** changing the maximum value to 20 and keeping the size of the sample fixed at 10. If you still have repetitions, repeat the process, increasing the maximum value by 10 each time but keeping the size of the sample fixed. What is the smallest maximum value for which you had no repetitions?

c. Describe the relationship between the population size (maximum value) and the number of repetitions in the list of random numbers as the population size increases and the sample size remains the same. What can you conclude about using a random number generator to choose a relatively small sample from a large population?

APPLET   Applet Exercise 1.2

The *Random Numbers* applet can be used to select a random sample from a population, but can it be used to simulate data? In parts **a** and **b,** you will use the applet to create data sets. Then you will explore whether those data sets are realistic.

a. In the activity *Keep the Change* on page 16, a data set called *Amounts Transferred* is described. Use the *Random Numbers* applet to simulate this data set by setting the minimum value equal to 0, the maximum value equal to 99, and the sample size equal to 30. Explain what the numbers in the list produced by the applet represent in the context of the activity. (You may need to read the activity.) Do the numbers produced by the applet seem reasonable? Explain.

b. Use the *Random Numbers* applet to simulate grades on a statistics test by setting the minimum value equal to 0, the maximum value equal to 100, and the sample size equal to 30. Explain what the numbers in the list produced by the applet represent in this context. Do the numbers produced by the applet seem reasonable? Explain.

c. Referring to parts **a** and **b**, why do the randomly generated data seem more reasonable in one situation than in the other? Comment on the usefulness of using a random number generator to produce data.

Applying the Concepts—Basic

1.14 Credit card market shares. Refer to the CardWeb.com, Inc., study of credit card purchases in the United States in Section 1.2 (Study 1, p. 5). Recall that the company tracked all credit card purchases during 2005 and measured two variables: (1) the type of credit card used (VISA, MasterCard, American Express, or Discover), and (2) the amount (in dollars) of each purchase.

a. Identify the type (quantitative or qualitative) of each variable measured.

NW **b.** Does the data set collected represent a population or a sample? Explain.

1.15 Opinion polls. Pollsters regularly conduct opinion polls to **NW** determine the popularity rating of the current president. Suppose a poll is to be conducted tomorrow in which 2,000 individuals will be asked whether the president is doing a good or bad job. The 2,000 individuals will be selected by random digit telephone dialing and asked the question over the phone.

a. What is the relevant population?

b. What is the variable of interest? Is it quantitative or qualitative?

c. What is the sample?

d. What is the inference of interest to the pollster?

e. What method of data collection is employed?

f. How likely is the sample to be representative?

1.16 College application data. Colleges and universities are re-**NW** quiring an increasing amount of information about applicants before making acceptance and financial aid decisions. Classify each of the following types of data required on a college application as quantitative or qualitative.

a. High school GPA

b. Honors, awards

c. Applicant's score on the SAT or ACT

d. Gender of applicant

e. Parents' income

f. Age of applicant

1.17 Microsoft survey of Windows. Windows is a computer software product made by Microsoft Corporation. In designing Windows XP, Microsoft telephoned thousands of users of an earlier version of Windows and asked them how the product could be improved. Assume customers were asked the following questions:

    I. Are you the most frequent user of Windows in your household?

    II. What is your age?

    III. Are the tutorial instructions that accompany Windows helpful?

    IV. When using a printer with Windows, do you most frequently use a laser printer or another type of printer?

    V. If the speed of Windows could be changed, which one of the following would you prefer: slower, unchanged, or faster?

    VI. How many people in your household have used Windows at least once?

Each of these questions defines a variable of interest to the company. Classify the data generated for each variable as quantitative or qualitative. Justify your classification.

1.18 E-Commerce in business. The Cutter Consortium surveyed 154 U.S. companies to determine the extent of their involvement in electronic commerce (called *e-commerce*). Four of the questions they asked follow. (*Internet Week*, September 6, 1999.)

    1. Do you have an overall e-commerce strategy?

    2. If you don't already have an e-commerce plan, when will you implement one?

    3. Are you delivering products over the Internet?

    4. What was your company's total revenue in the last fiscal year?

a. For each question, determine the variable of interest and classify it as quantitative or qualitative.

b. Do the data collected for the 154 companies represent a sample or a population? Explain.

CEOPAY05

1.19 The executive compensation scoreboard. Each year, *Forbes* publishes its Executive Compensation Scoreboard. (See Study #2, p. 6.) For the 2005 scoreboard, data were collected for chief executive officers at the 500 largest U.S. companies and the following variables were measured for each CEO: (1) the industry type of the CEO's company (e.g., banking, retailing, etc.), (2) the CEO's total compensation ($ millions) for the year, (3) the CEO's total compensation ($ millions) over the previous 5 years, (4) the number of company stock shares (millions) held, (5) the CEO's age (years), and (6) the CEO's efficiency rating.

a. Is the data for the 500 CEOs in the 2005 Executive Compensation Scoreboard a population or sample? Explain.

b. Identify the type (quantitative or qualitative) of each variable measured.

1.20 Annual survey of computer crimes. The Computer Security Institute (CSI) conducts an annual survey of computer crime at United States businesses. CSI sends survey questionnaires to computer security personnel at all U.S. corporations and government agencies. In 2006, 616 organizations responded to the CSI survey. Fifty-two percent of the respondents admitted unauthorized use of computer systems at their firms during the year. (*Computer Security Issues & Trends*, Spring 2006)

a. Identify the population of interest to CSI.

b. Identify the data-collection method used by CSI. Are there any potential biases in the method used?

c. Describe the variable measured in the CSI survey. Is it quantitative or qualitative?

d. What inference can be made from the study result?

Applying the Concepts—Intermediate

1.21 On-the-job mentoring of employees. To help employers better understand what employees value, Fort Lauderdale–based Interim Services, Inc., surveyed a random sample of 1,000 employees in the United States. One question they asked was, "If your employer provides you with mentoring opportunities are you likely to remain in your job for the next five years?" They found that 620 members of the sample said yes (*HRMagazine,* Sept. 1999).
   a. Identify the population of interest to Interim Services, Inc.
   b. Based on the question posed by Interim Services, Inc., what is the variable of interest?
   c. Is the variable quantitative or qualitative? Explain.
   d. Describe the sample.
   e. What inference can be made from the results of the survey?

1.22 New cancer screening method. According to the American Lung Association, lung cancer accounts for 28% of all cancer deaths in the United States. A new type of screening for lung cancer, computed tomography (CT), has been developed. Medical researchers believe CT scans are more sensitive than regular X-rays in pinpointing small tumors. The H. Lee Moffitt Cancer Center at the University of South Florida is currently conducting a clinical trial of 50,000 smokers nationwide to compare the effectiveness of CT scans with X-rays for detecting lung cancer (*Todays' Tomorrows,* Fall 2002). Each participating smoker is randomly assigned to one of two screening methods, CT or chest X-ray, and his or her progress is tracked over time. The age at which the scanning method first detects a tumor is the variable of interest.
   a. Identify the data-collection method used by the cancer researchers.
   b. Identify the experimental units of the study.
   c. Identify the type (quantitative or qualitative) of the variable measured.
   d. Identify the population and sample.
   e. What is the inference that will ultimately be drawn from the clinical trial?

1.23 Inspection of highway bridges. All highway bridges in the United States are inspected periodically for structural deficiency by the Federal Highway Administration (FHWA). Data from the FHWA inspections are compiled into the National Bridge Inventory (NBI). Several of the nearly 100 variables maintained by the NBI are listed below. Classify each variable as quantitative or qualitative.
   a. Length of maximum span (feet)
   b. Number of vehicle lanes
   c. Toll bridge (yes or no)
   d. Average daily traffic
   e. Condition of deck (good, fair, or poor)
   f. Bypass or detour length (miles)
   g. Route type (interstate, U.S., state, county, or city)

1.24 Structurally deficient highway bridges. Refer to Exercise 1.23. The most recent NBI data were analyzed and the results published in the *Journal of Infrastructure Systems* (June 1995). Using the FHWA inspection ratings, each of the 470,515 highway bridges in the United States was categorized as structurally deficient, functionally obsolete, or safe. About 26% of the bridges were found to be structurally deficient, while 19% were functionally obsolete.
   a. What is the variable of interest to the researchers?
   b. Is the variable of part a quantitative or qualitative?
   c. Is the data set analyzed a population or a sample? Explain.
   d. How did the researchers obtain the data for their study?

∗1.25 Monitoring product quality. The Wallace Company of Houston is a distributor of pipes, valves, and fittings to the refining, chemical, and petrochemical industries. The company was a recent winner of the Malcolm Baldrige National Quality Award. One of the steps the company takes to monitor the quality of its distribution process is to send out a survey twice a year to a subset of its current customers, asking the customers to rate the speed of deliveries, the accuracy of invoices, and the quality of the packaging of the products they have received from Wallace.
   a. Describe the process studied.
   b. Describe the variables of interest.
   c. Describe the sample.
   d. Describe the inferences of interest.
   e. What are some of the factors that are likely to affect the reliability of the inferences?

1.26 Audit sampling at accounting firms. To assess how extensively accounting firms in New York State use sampling methods in auditing their clients, the New York Society of CPAs mailed a questionnaire to 800 New York accounting firms employing two or more professionals. They received responses from 179 firms of which four responses were unusable and 12 reported they had no audit practice. The questionnaire asked firms whether they use audit sampling methods and, if so, whether or not they use random sampling (*CPA Journal,* July 1995).
   a. Identify the population, the variables, the sample, and the inferences of interest to the New York Society of CPAs.
   b. Speculate as to what could have made four of the responses unusable.
   c. In later chapters you will learn that the reliability of an inference is related to the size of the sample used. In addition to sample size, what factors might affect the reliability of the inferences drawn in the mail survey described above?

1.27 Job satisfaction and Machiavellian rating. The *Journal of Retailing* (Spring 1988) published a study of the relationship between job satisfaction and the degree of *Machiavellian orientation*. Briefly, the Machiavellian orientation is one in which the executive exerts very strong control, even to the point of deception and cruelty, over the employees he or she supervises. The authors administered a questionnaire to each in a sample of 218 department store executives and obtained both a job satisfaction score and a Machiavellian rating. They concluded that those with higher job satisfaction scores are likely to have a lower "Mach" rating.
   a. What is the population from which the sample was selected?
   b. What variables were measured by the authors?
   c. Identify the sample.
   d. Identify the data-collection method used.
   e. What inference was made by the authors?

1.28 Success/failure of software reuse. The PROMISE Software Engineering Repository, hosted by the University of Ottawa, is a collection of publicly available data sets to serve researchers in building prediction software models. A PROMISE data set on software reuse, saved in the **SWREUSE** file, provides information on the success or failure of reusing previously developed software for each in a sample of 24 new software development projects. (Data source: *IEEE Transactions on Software Engineering*, Vol. 28, 2002.) Of the 24 projects, 9 were judged failures and 15 were successfully implemented.
a. Identify the experimental units for this study.
b. Describe the population from which the sample is selected.
c. What is the variable of interest in the study? Is it quantitative or qualitative?
d. Use the sample information to make an inference about the population.

Applying the Concepts—Advanced

1.29 Bank corporate mergers. *Corporate merger* is a means through which one firm (the bidder) acquires control of the assets of another firm (the target). During the late 1990s, there was a frenzy of bank mergers in the United States, as the banking industry consolidated into more efficient and more competitive units.
a. Construct a brief questionnaire (two or three questions) that could be used to query a sample of bank presidents concerning their opinions of why the industry is consolidating and whether it will consolidate further.
b. Describe the population about which inferences could be made from the results of the survey.
c. Discuss the pros and cons of sending the questionnaire to all bank presidents versus a sample of 200.

*1.30 Monitoring the production of soft drink cans.** Coca-Cola and Schweppes Beverages Limited (CCSB), which was formed in 1987, is 49% owned by the Coca-Cola Company. According to *Industrial Management and Data Systems* (Vol. 92, 1992), CCSB's Wakefield plant can produce 4,000 cans of soft drink per minute. The automated process consists of measuring and dispensing the raw ingredients into storage vessels to create the syrup, and then injecting the syrup, along with carbon dioxide, into the beverage cans. In order to monitor the subprocess that adds carbon dioxide to the cans, five filled cans are pulled off the line every 15 minutes and the amount of carbon dioxide in each of these five cans is measured to determine whether the amounts are within prescribed limits.
a. Describe the process studied.
b. Describe the variable of interest.
c. Describe the sample.
d. Describe the inference of interest.
e. *Brix* is a unit for measuring sugar concentration. If a technician is assigned the task of estimating the average brix level of all 240,000 cans of beverage stored in a warehouse near Wakefield, will the technician be examining a process or a population? Explain.

1.31 Current population survey. The employment status (employed or unemployed) of each individual in the U.S. workforce is a set of data that is of interest to economists, businesspeople, and sociologists. To obtain information about the employment status of the workforce, the U.S. Bureau of the Census conducts what is known as the *Current Population Survey*. Each month interviewers visit about 59,000 of the 98 million households in the United States and question the occupants over 14 years of age about their employment status. Their responses enable the Bureau of the Census to *estimate* the percentage of people in the labor force who are unemployed (the *unemployment rate*).
a. Define the population of interest to the Census Bureau.
b. What variable is being measured? Is it quantitative or qualitative?
c. Is the problem of interest to the Census Bureau descriptive or inferential?
d. In order to monitor the rate of unemployment, it is essential to have a definition of *unemployed*. Different economists and even different countries define it in various ways. Develop your own definition of an "unemployed person." Your definition should answer such questions as: Are students on summer vacation unemployed? Are college professors who do not teach summer school unemployed? At what age are people considered to be eligible for the workforce? Are people who are out of work but not actively seeking a job unemployed?

Critical Thinking Challenge

1.32 20/20 survey expose. Refer to the "Statistics in Action" box of this chapter (p. 3). Recall that the popular prime-time ABC television program *20/20* presented several misleading (and possibly unethical) surveys in a segment titled "Facts or Fiction?—Exposés of So-Called Surveys." The information reported from four of these surveys are reproduced here (actual survey facts are provided in parentheses).
Quaker Oats study: Eating oat bran is a cheap and easy way to reduce your cholesterol count. (Fact: Diet must consist of nothing but oat bran to achieve a slightly lower cholesterol count.)
March of Dimes report: Domestic violence causes more birth defects than all medical issues combined. (Fact: No study—false report.)
American Association of University Women (AAUA) study: Only 29% of high school girls are happy with themselves, compared to 66% of elementary school girls. (Fact: Of 3,000 high school girls, 29% responded "Always true" to the statement "I am happy the way I am." Most answered, "Sort of true" and "Sometimes true.")
Food Research and Action Center study: One in four American children under age 12 is hungry or at risk of hunger. (Fact: Based on responses to questions "Do you ever cut the size of meals?" and "Do you ever eat less than you feel you should?" and "Did you ever rely on limited numbers of foods to feed your children because you were running out of money to buy food for a meal?")
a. Refer to the Quaker Oats study relating oat bran to cholesterol levels. Discuss why it is unethical to report the results as stated.
b. Consider the false March of Dimes report on domestic violence and birth defects. Discuss the type of data required to investigate the impact of domestic violence on

birth defects. What data-collection method would you recommend?

c. Refer to the AAUW study of self-esteem of high school girls. Explain why the results of the study are likely to be misleading. What data might be appropriate for assessing the self-esteem of high school girls?

d. Refer to the Food Research and Action Center study of hunger in America. Explain why the results of the study are likely to be misleading. What data would provide insight into the proportion of hungry American children?

REFERENCES

Brochures about Survey Research, Section on Survey Research Methods, American Statistical Association, 2004 (www.amstat.org).

Careers in Statistics, American Statistical Association, Biometric Society, Institute of Mathematical Statistics and Statistical Society of Canada, 2004 (www.amstat.org).

Cochran, W. G. *Sampling Techniques,* 3rd ed. New York: Wiley, 1977.

Deming, W. E. *Sample Design in Business Research.* New York: Wiley, 1963.

Ethical Guidelines for Statistical Practice, American Statistical Association, 1995.

Hansen, M. H., Hurwitz, W. N., and Madow, W. G. *Sample Survey Methods and Theory,* Vol. 1. New York: Wiley, 1953.

Kirk, R. E. ed. *Statistical Issues: A Reader for the Behavioral Sciences.* Monterey, Calif.: Brooks/Cole, 1972.

Kish, L. *Survey Sampling.* New York: Wiley, 1965.

Scheaffer, R., Mendenhall, W., and Ott, R. L. *Elementary Survey Sampling,* 2nd ed. Boston: Duxbury, 1979.

Tanur, J. M., Mosteller, F., Kruskal, W. H., Link, R. E., Pieters, R. S., and Rising, G. R. *Statistics: A Guide to the Unknown* (E. L. Lehmann, special editor). San Francisco: Holden-Day, 1989.

Yamane, T. *Elementary Sampling Theory,* 3rd ed. Englewood Cliffs, N.J.: Prentice Hall, 1967.

Using Technology

1.1 Accessing and Listing Data in SPSS

Upon entering into an SPSS session, you will see a screen similar to Figure 1.S.1. The main portion of the screen is an empty spreadsheet, with columns representing variables and rows representing observations (or cases). The very top of the screen is the SPSS main menu bar, with buttons for the different

Figure 1.S.1

Initial screen viewed by SPSS user

Figure 1.S.2
Data entered into the SPSS spreadsheet

Figure 1.S.3
SPSS options for reading data from an external file

functions and procedures available in SPSS. Once you have entered data into the spreadsheet, you can analyze the data by clicking the appropriate menu buttons.

Entering Data
You can create an SPSS data file by entering data directly into the spreadsheet. Figure 1.S.2 shows data entered on a variable called "Ratio." The variables (columns) can be named by selecting the "Variable View" button at the bottom of the screen and typing in the name of each variable.

Accessing Data from a File
If the data are saved in an external data file, you can access the data using the options available in SPSS. Click the "File" button on the menu bar, then click "Read Text Data," as shown in Figure 1.S.3. A dialog box similar to Figure 1.S.4 will appear.

Figure 1.S.4
Selecting the external data file in SPSS

Specify the disk drive and folder that contains the data file, click on the data file, then click "Open," as shown in Figure 1.S.4. This will invoke the SPSS Text Import Wizard. The Text Import Wizard presents a series of six screen menus, the first of which is shown in Figure 1.S.5. Make the appropriate selections on the screen, and click "Next" to go to the next screen. When finished, click "Finish." The SPSS spreadsheet will reappear with the data from the external data file, as shown in Figure 1.S.6.

Figure 1.S.5

The SPSS Text Import
Wizard, Screen 1

Figure 1.S.6

The SPSS spreadsheet with the imported data

Reminder: The variable (columns) can be named by selecting the "Variable View" button at the bottom of the spreadsheet screen and typing in the name of each variable.

To access a previously saved SPSS data file, click "File," then "open," then select the SPSS file name.

Listing Data

To obtain a listing (printout) of your data, click on the "Analyze" button on the SPSS main menu bar, then click on "Reports," then on "Report Summaries in Rows" (see Figure 1.S.7). The resulting menu, or dialog box, appears as in Figure 1.S.8. Enter the names of the variables you want to print in the "Data Columns" box (you can do this by simply clicking on the variables), check the "Display cases" box at the bottom left, then click "OK." The printout will show up on your screen.

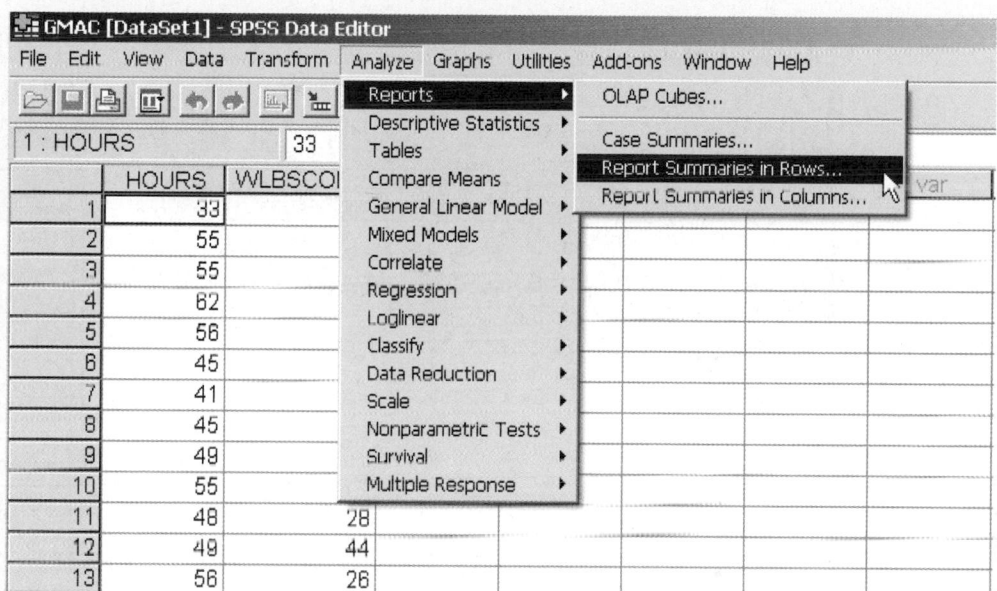

Figure 1.S.7
SPSS menu options for obtaining a data listing

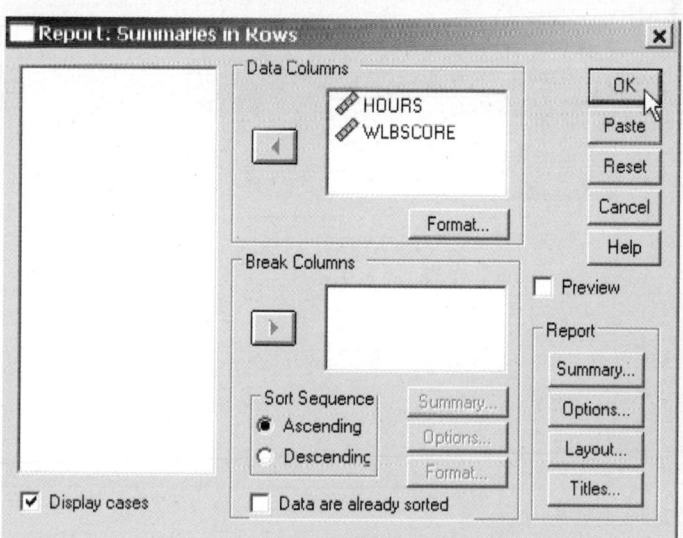

Figure 1.S.8
SPSS data report dialog box

1.2 Accessing and Listing Data in MINITAB

Upon entering into a MINITAB session, you will see a screen similar to Figure 1.M.1. The bottom portion of the screen is an empty spreadsheet—called a MINITAB worksheet—with columns representing variables and rows representing observations (or cases). The very top of the screen is the MINITAB main menu bar, with buttons for the different functions and procedures available in MINITAB. Once you have entered data into the spreadsheet, you can analyze the data by clicking the appropriate menu buttons. The results will appear in the Session window.

Entering Data

You can create a MINITAB data file by entering data directly into the worksheet. Figure 1.M.2 shows data entered for a variable called "Ratio." The variables (columns) can be named by typing in the name of each variable in the box below the column number.

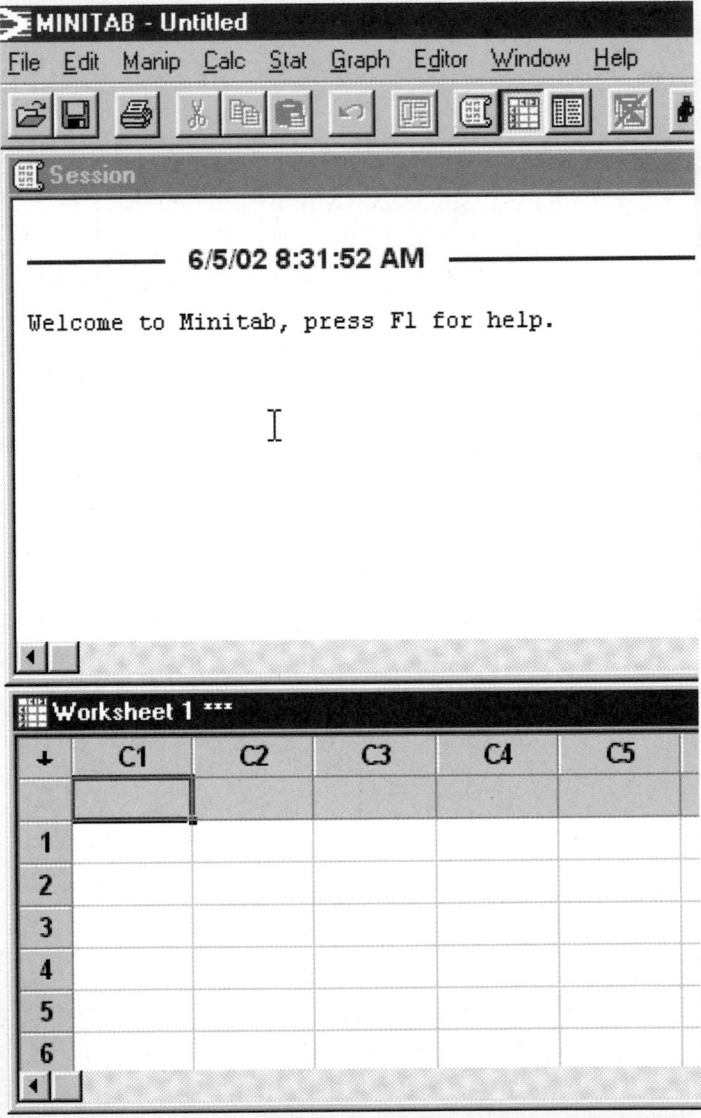

Figure 1.M.1
Initial screen viewed by MINITAB user

Figure 1.M.2
Data entered into the MINITAB worksheet

Accessing Data from a File

If the data are saved in an external data file, you can access the data using the options available in MINITAB. Click the "File" button on the menu bar, then click "Open Worksheet," as shown in Figure 1.M.3. A dialog box similar to Figure 1.M.4 will appear.

Specify the disk drive and folder that contains the external data file and the file type, then click on the file name, as shown in Figure 1.M.4. If the data set contains qualitative data or data with special characters, click on the "Options" button as shown in Figure 1.M.4. The Options dialog box, shown in Figure 1.M.5, will appear. Specify the appropriate options

Figure 1.M.4

Selecting the external data file in MINITAB

Figure 1.M.3

MINITAB options for reading data from
an external file

Figure 1.M.5

Selecting the MINITAB data
input options

for the data set, then click "OK" to return to the "Open Worksheet" dialog box (Figure 1.M.4). Click "Open" and the MINITAB worksheet will appear with the data from the external data file, as shown in Figure 1.M.6.

Reminder: The variables (columns) can be named by typing in the name of each variable in the box under the column number.

To access a previously saved MINITAB worksheet, click "File," then "Open Worksheet," then select the MINITAB file.

Listing Data

To obtain a listing (printout) of your data, click on the "Data" button on the MINITAB main menu bar, then click on "Display Data" (see Figure 1.M.7). The resulting menu, or dialog box, appears as in Figure 1.M.8. Enter the names of the variables you want to print in the "Columns, constants, and matrices to display" box (you can do this by simply clicking on the variables), then click "OK." The printout will show up on your MINITAB session screen.

	C1	C2	C3
	HOURS	WLB-SCORE	
1	33	42	
2	55	54	
3	55	40	
4	62	53	
5	56	40	
6	45	45	
7	41	52	
8	45	36	
9	49	49	
10	55	39	
11	48	28	
12	49	44	
13	56	26	
14	47	42	
15	60	50	

Figure 1.M.6
MINITAB worksheet with the imported data

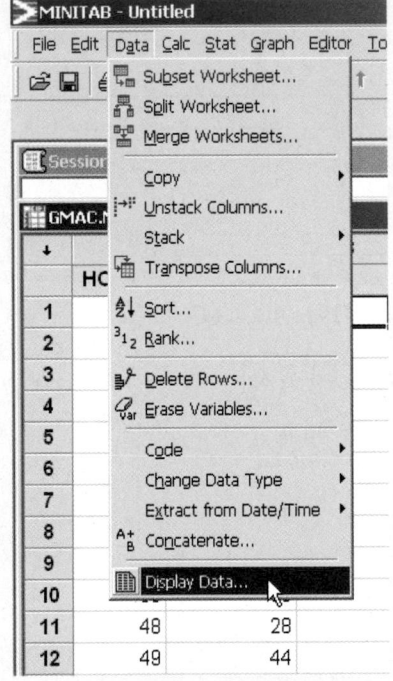

Figure 1.M.7
MINITAB menu options for obtaining a data listing

Figure 1.M.8
MINITAB Display Data dialog box

1.3 Accessing and Listing Data in Excel

Upon entering into an Excel session, you will see a screen similar to Figure 1.E.1. The majority of the screen window is comprised of a spreadsheet—called an Excel workbook—with columns (labeled A, B, C, etc.) representing variables and rows representing observations (or cases). The very top of the screen is the Excel main menu bar, with buttons for the different functions and procedures available in Excel. Once you have entered data into the spreadsheet, you can analyze the data by clicking the appropriate menu buttons. The results will appear in a new workbook.

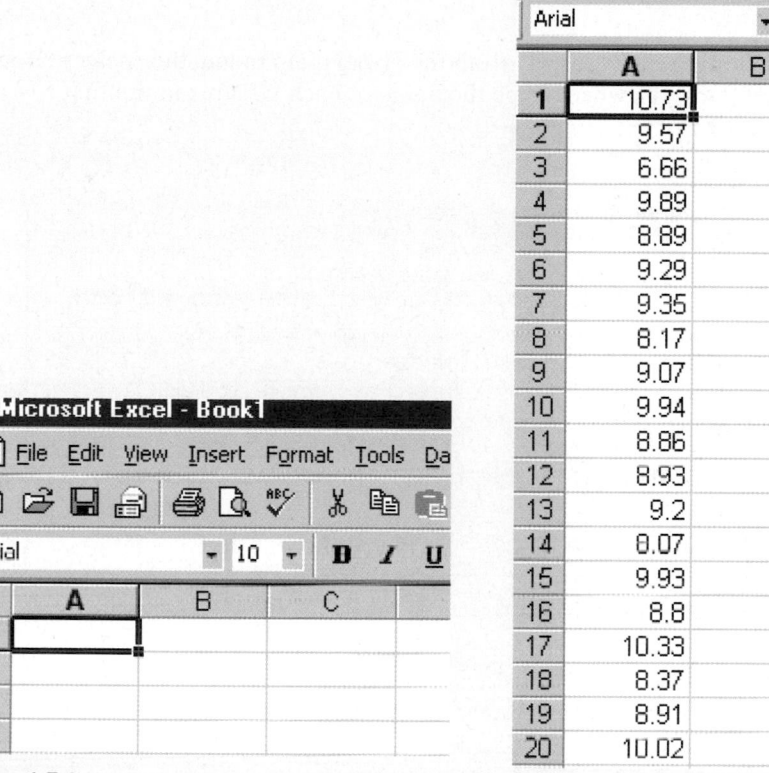

Figure 1.E.1
Initial screen viewed
by Excel user

Figure 1.E.2
Data entered into the
Excel workbook

Figure 1.E.3
Excel options for reading data from an
external file

Entering Data

You can create an Excel workbook by entering data directly into the appropriate row and column of the spreadsheet. Figure 1.E.2 shows data entered in the first (A) column. Optionally, you can add names for the variables (columns) in the first row of the workbook.

Accessing Data from a File

If the data are saved in an external data file, you can access it using the options available in EXCEL. Click the "File" button on the menu bar, then click "Open," as shown in Figure 1.E.3. A dialog box similar to Figure 1.E.4 will appear.

Figure 1.E.4
Selecting the external data file in Excel

Specify the disk drive and folder that contains the external data file and the file type, then click on the file name and click on "Open," as shown in Figure 1.E.4. This will invoke the Excel Text Import Wizard. The Text Import Wizard presents a series of three screen menus, the first of which is shown in Figure 1.E.5. Make the appropriate selections on the screen, and click "Next" to go to the next screen. When finished, click "Finish." The Excel workbook will reappear with the data from the external data file, as shown in Figure 1.E.6.

Note: The variables (columns) can be named as follows: Select "Insert" from the Excel main menu, then select "Rows." A blank (empty) row will be added in the first row of the spreadsheet. Type the name of each variable in the first row under the appropriate column.

Figure 1.E.5
Excel Text Import Wizard,
Screen 1

Figure 1.E.6
The Excel workbook with the
imported data

To access a previously created Excel workbook, click "File," then "Open," then select the Excel file.

Listing Data

To obtain a listing (printout) of the data in the Excel workbook, click on the "File" button on the Excel main menu bar, then click on "Print" (see Figure 1.E.7).

Figure 1.E.7

Excel menu options for obtaining a data listing

CHAPTER

2

Methods for Describing Sets of Data

WHERE WE'VE BEEN

- Examined the difference between inferential and descriptive statistics

- Described the key elements of a statistical problem

- Learned about the two types of data—quantitative and qualitative

- Discussed the role of statistical thinking in managerial decision making

WHERE WE'RE GOING

- Describe data using graphs

- Describe data using numerical measures

Factors That Influence a Doctor to Refuse Ethics Consultation

Ethical dilemmas commonly arise in the course of a physician's clinical practice. These dilemmas include (but are not limited to) end-of-life issues, treatment of patients without health insurance, providing nonbeneficial treatment at the patient's request, obtaining informed consent, maintaining patient autonomy, truth-telling and confidentiality, involvement of children in research, designing of clinical trials, and termination of subject participation in research protocols. Empirical studies have found that an ethical issue will arise in one of every five clinical encounters.

Over the past 10 years, ethics consultation has evolved as a means of assisting physicians who are confused about how to best approach an ethical dilemma. About 80% of general hospitals in the United States now provide ethics consultation services to staff physicians. When faced with a difficult ethical decision, the doctor may request advice from a panel of ethics experts, with assurances that all communications will be anonymous and confidential. However, not all physicians take advantage of this service; in fact, some doctors refuse to use ethics consultation.

Medical researchers at University Community Hospital (UCH) in Tampa, Florida, undertook a study to determine the factors that might influence a physician's decision request or to refuse ethics consultation.*

Survey questionnaires were distributed to all 746 physicians on staff at UCH; 118 of the questionnaires were returned, yielding a response rate of approximately 16%. The survey was designed to obtain data on the following variables for each physician:

1. *Level of previous ethics consultation use* **at UCH** ("used at least once" or "never used")
2. *Practitioner specialty* ("medical" or "surgical")
3. *Length of time in practice* (number of years)
4. *Amount of exposure to ethics in medical school* (number of hours)

5. *Would you ever consider using ethics consultation* **in the future** (yes or no)

The physicians were also asked to elicit opinions on the following statements about ethics consultants. (All responses were measured on a 5-point scale, where 1 = "strongly disagree," 2 = "somewhat disagree," 3 = "neither agree nor disagree," 4 = "somewhat disagree," or 5 = "strongly agree.")

6. *Ethics consultants have extensive training in ethics and ethics principles.*
7. *Ethics consultants participate in frequent ethics education.*
8. *Ethics consultants think they are "moral experts."*
9. *Ethics consultants cannot grasp the full picture from the "outside."*

 ETHICS

The UCH medical researchers wanted to use the survey results to develop insight into why certain physicians use ethics consultation and others do not. The researchers hypothesized that more experienced doctors and physicians who specialize in surgery would be less likely to use ethics consultation. The data for the study are stored in the file named **ETHICS** in SPSS, MINITAB, and Excel.

In the following *Statistics in Action Revisited* sections, we apply the graphical and numerical descriptive techniques of this chapter to the **ETHICS** data to answer some of the researchers' questions.

Statistics in Action Revisited

- Interpreting pie charts (p. 46)
- Interpreting histograms (p. 57)
- Interpreting numerical descriptive measures (p. 84)
- Detecting outliers (p. 98)
- Interpreting scatterplots (p. 103)

*Hein, S., Orlowski, J. P., Meinke, R., and Sincich, T. "Why Physicians Do or Do Not Use Ethics Consultation." Paper presented at the annual meeting of the American Society for Bioethics and Humanities, Nashville, TN, Oct. 2001.

S uppose you wish to evaluate the managerial capabilities of a class of 400 MBA students based on their Graduate Management Aptitude Test (GMAT) scores. How would you describe these 400 measurements? Characteristics of the data set include the typical or most frequent GMAT score, the variability in the scores, the highest and lowest scores, the "shape" of the data, and whether or not the data set contains any unusual scores. Extracting this information by "eye-balling" the data isn't easy. The 400 scores may provide too many bits of information for our minds to comprehend. Clearly we need some formal methods for summarizing and characterizing the information in such a data set. Methods for describing data sets are also essential for statistical inference. Most populations are large data sets. Consequently, we need methods for describing a sample data set that let us make descriptive statements (inferences) about the population from which the sample was drawn.

Two methods for describing data are presented in this chapter, one *graphical* and the other *numerical*. Both play an important role in statistics. Section 2.1 presents both graphical and numerical methods for describing qualitative data. Graphical methods for describing quantitative data are presented in Section 2.2 and optional Sections 2.8, 2.9, and 2.10; numerical descriptive methods for quantitative data are presented in Sections 2.3–2.7. We end this chapter with a section on the *misuse* of descriptive techniques.

2.1 Describing Qualitative Data

Recall the "Executive Compensation Scoreboard" tabulated annually by *Forbes* (see Study 2 in Section 1.2). In addition to salary information, *Forbes* collects and reports personal data on the CEOs, including level of education. Do most CEOs have advanced degrees, such as masters degrees or doctorates? To answer this question, Table 2.1 gives the highest college degree obtained (bachelors, MBA, masters, law, PhD, or none) for each of the 40 best-paid CEOs in 2006.

For this study, the variable of interest, highest college degree obtained, is qualitative in nature. Qualitative data are nonnumerical in nature; thus, the value of a qualitative variable can only be classified into categories called *classes*. The possible degree types— bachelors, MBA, masters, law, PhD, or none—represent the classes for this qualitative variable. We can summarize such data numerically in two ways: (1) by computing the *class frequency*—the number of observations in the data set that fall into each class; or (2) by computing the *class relative frequency*—the proportion of the total number of observations falling into each class.

Definition 2.1

A **class** is one of the categories into which qualitative data can be classified.

Definition 2.2

The **class frequency** is the number of observations in the data set falling into a particular class.

Definition 2.3

The **class relative frequency** is the class frequency divided by the total number of observations in the data set.

Examining Table 2.1, we observe that 2 of the 40 best-paid CEOs did not obtain a college degree, 8 obtained bachelors degrees, 20 MBAs, 4 masters degrees, 2 PhDs, and 4 law degrees. These numbers—2, 8, 20, 4, 2, and 4—represent the class frequencies for the six classes and are shown in the summary table, Figure 2.1, produced using SPSS.

Definition 2.4

The **class percentage** is the class relative frequency multiplied by 100.

FORBES40

TABLE 2.1 Data on 40 Best-Paid Executives

	CEO	Company	Salary ($ millions)	Age (years)	Degree
1	Richard D. Fairbank	Capital One Financial	249.42	55	MBA
2	Terry S. Semel	Yahoo.	230.55	63	MBA
3	Henry R. Silverman	Cendant	139.96	65	Law
4	Bruce Karatz	KB Home	135.53	60	Law
5	Richard S. Fuld Jr.	Lehman Bros	122.67	60	MBA
6	Ray R. Irani	Occidental Petroleum	80.73	71	PhD
7	Lawrence J. Ellison	Oracle	75.33	61	None
8	John W. Thompson	Symantec	71.84	57	Masters
9	Edwin M. Crawford	Caremark Rx	69.66	57	Bachelors
10	Angelo R. Mozilo	Countrywide Financial	68.96	67	Bachelors
11	John T. Chambers	Cisco Systems	62.99	56	MBA
12	R. Chad Dreier	Ryland Group	56.47	58	Bachelors
13	Lew Frankfort	Coach	55.99	60	MBA
14	Ara K. Hovnanian	Hovnanian Enterprises	47.83	48	MBA
15	John G. Drosdick	Sunoco	46.19	62	Masters
16	Robert I. Toll	Toll Brothers	41.31	65	Law
17	Robert J. Ulrich	Target	39.64	63	Bachelors
18	Kevin B. Rollins	Dell	39.32	53	MBA
19	Clarence P. Cazalot Jr.	Marathon Oil	37.48	55	Bachelors
20	David C. Novak	Yum Brands	37.42	53	Bachelors
21	Mark G. Papa	EOG Resources	36.54	59	MBA
22	Henri A. Termeer	Genzyme	36.38	60	MBA
23	Richard C. Adkerson	Freeport Copper	35.41	59	MBA
24	Kevin W. Sharer	Amgen	34.49	58	Masters
25	Jay Sugarman	IStar Financial	32.94	43	MBA
26	George David	United Technologies	32.73	64	MBA
27	Bob R. Simpson	XTO Energy	32.19	57	MBA
28	J. Terrence Lanni	MGM Mirage	31.54	63	MBA
29	Paul E. Jacobs	Qualcomm	31.44	64	PhD
30	Stephen F. Bollenbach	Hilton Hotels	31.43	63	MBA
31	James J. Mulva	ConocoPhillips	31.34	59	MBA
32	John J. Mack	Morgan Stanley	31.23	61	Bachelors
33	Ronald A. Williams	Aetna	30.87	57	Masters
34	David J. Lesar	Halliburton	29.36	53	MBA
35	H. Edward Hanway	Cigna	28.82	54	MBA
36	James E. Cayne	Bear Stearns Cos	28.40	72	None
37	Daniel P. Amos	Aflac	27.97	54	Bachelors
38	Kent J. Thiry	DaVita	27.89	50	MBA
39	John W. Rowe	Exelon	26.90	60	Law
40	James M. Cornelius	Guidant	25.18	62	MBA

Source: Forbes, May 8, 2006.

DEGREE

		Frequency	Percent	Valid Percent	Cumulative Percent
Valid	Bachelors	8	20.0	20.0	20.0
	Law	4	10.0	10.0	30.0
	Masters	4	10.0	10.0	40.0
	MBA	20	50.0	50.0	90.0
	None	2	5.0	5.0	95.0
	PhD	2	5.0	5.0	100.0
	Total	40	100.0	100.0	

FIGURE 2.1

SPSS summary table for degrees of 40 CEOs

Figure 2.1 also gives the relative frequency of each of the five degree classes. From Definition 2.3, we know that we calculate the relative frequency by dividing the class frequency by the total number of observations in the data set. Thus, the relative frequencies for the five degree types are

$$\text{Bachelors: } \frac{8}{40} = .20$$

$$\text{Law: } \frac{4}{40} = .10$$

$$\text{Masters: } \frac{4}{40} = .10$$

$$\text{MBA: } \frac{20}{40} = .50$$

$$\text{None: } \frac{2}{40} = .05$$

$$\text{PhD: } \frac{2}{40} = .05$$

These values, expressed as a percentage, are shown in the "Percent" column in the SPSS Summary table, Figure 2.1. If we sum the relative frequencies for MBA, masters, law, and PhD, we obtain .50 + .10 + .10 + .05 = .75. Therefore, 75% of the 40 best-paid CEOs obtained at least a masters degree (MBA, masters, law, or PhD).

Although the summary table of Figure 2.1 adequately describes the data of Table 2.1, we often want a graphical presentation as well. Figures 2.2 and 2.3 show two of the most widely used graphical methods for describing qualitative data—**bar graphs** and **pie charts.** Figures 2.2 is a bar graph for "highest degree obtained" produced with MINITAB. Note that the height of the rectangle, or "bar," over each class is equal to the class frequency. (Optionally, the bar heights can be proportional to class relative frequencies.) In contrast, Figure 2.3 (also created using MINITAB) shows the relative frequencies (expressed as a percentage) of the five degree types in a *pie chart*. Note that the pie is a circle (spanning 360°), and the size (angle) of the "pie slice" assigned to each class is proportional to the class relative frequency. For example, the slice assigned to the MBA degree is 50% of 360°, or (.50)(360°) = 180°.

Before leaving the data set in Table 2.1, consider the bar graph shown in Figure 2.4, produced using Excel with the PHStat2 add-in. Note that the bars for the CEO degree categories are arranged in descending order of height from left to right across the hori-

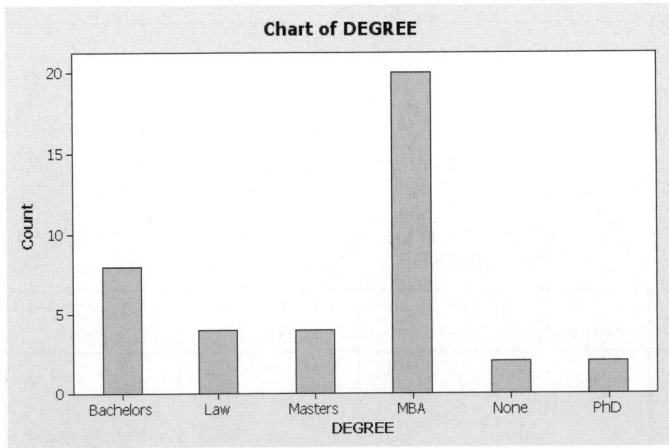

FIGURE 2.2
MINITAB bar graph for degrees of 40 CEOs

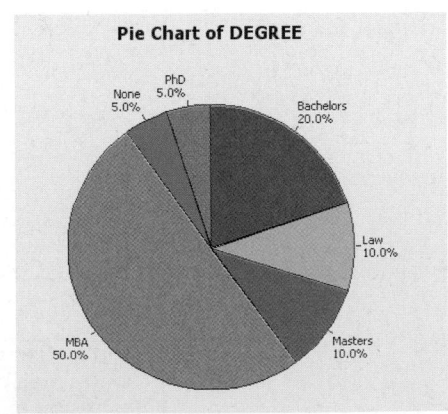

FIGURE 2.3
MINITAB pie chart for degrees of 40 CEOs

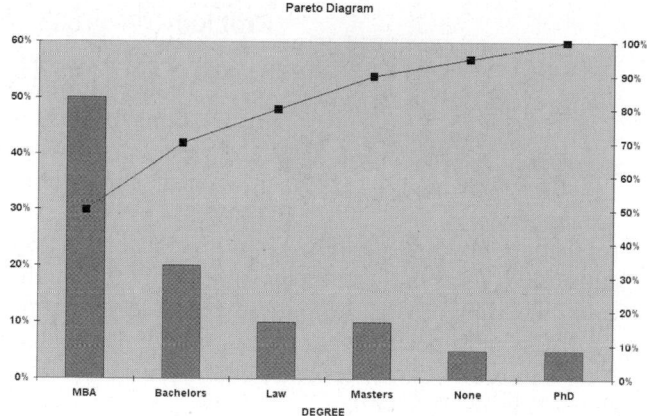

FIGURE 2.4

Excel/PHStat2 Pareto diagram for degrees of 40 CEOs

zontal axis—that is, the tallest bar (MBA) is positioned at the far left and the shortest bars (None and PhD) are at the far right. This rearrangement of the bars in a bar graph is called a Pareto diagram. One goal of a Pareto diagram (named for the Italian economist, Vilfredo Pareto) is to make it easy to locate the "most important" categories—those with the largest frequencies. For the 40 best-paid CEOs in 2006, an MBA degree was the highest degree obtained by the most CEOs (50%).

Note: In the Pareto diagram in Figure 2.4, the left vertical axis gives the scale for the relative frequencies (percentages) of the bars, and the right vertical axis gives the scale for the cumulative relative frequencies. The actual cumulative percentages are represented by the black squares connected with straight lines.

Biography

**VILFREDO PARETO
(1843–1923)**

The Pareto Principle

Born in Paris to an Italian aristocratic family, Vilfredo Pareto was educated at the University of Turin, where he studied engineering and mathematics. After the death of his parents, Pareto quit his job as an engineer and began writing and lecturing on the evils of the economic policies of the Italian government. While at the University of Lausanne in Switzerland in 1896, he published his first paper, "Cours d'economie politique." In the paper, Pareto derived a complicated mathematical formula to prove that the distribution of income and wealth in society is not random but that a consistent pattern appears throughout history in all societies. Essentially, Pareto showed that approximately 80% of the total wealth in a society lies with only 20% of the families. This famous law about the "vital few and the trivial many" is widely known as the Pareto principle in economics.

Summary of Graphical Descriptive Methods for Qualitative Data

Bar graph: The categories (classes) of the qualitative variable are represented by bars, where the height of each bar is either the class frequency, class relative frequency, or class percentage.

Pie chart: The categories (classes) of the qualitative variable are represented by slices of a pie (circle). The size of each slice is proportional to the class relative frequency.

Pareto diagram: A bar graph with the categories (classes) of the qualitative variable (i.e., the bars) arranged by height in descending order from left to right.

Now Work Exercise 2.4

Let's look at a practical example that requires interpretation of the graphical results.

EXAMPLE 2.1

Graphing and
Summarizing
Qualitative Data

BLOODLOSS

Problem A group of cardiac physicians in southwest Florida have been studying a new drug designed to reduce blood loss in coronary artery bypass operations. Blood loss data for 114 coronary artery bypass patients (some who received a dosage of the drug and others who did not) are saved in the **BLOODLOSS** file. Although the drug shows promise in reducing blood loss, the physicians are concerned about possible side effects and complications. So their data set includes not only the qualitative variable, DRUG, which indicates whether or not the patient received the drug, but also the qualitative variable, COMP, which specifies the type (if any) of complication experienced by the patient. The four values of COMP recorded by the physicians are (1) redo surgery, (2) post-op infection, (3) both, or (4) none.

a. Figure 2.5, generated using SPSS, shows summary tables for the two qualitative variables, DRUG and COMP. Interpret the results.

b. Interpret the MINITAB output shown in Figure 2.6 and the SPSS output shown in Figure 2.7.

DRUG

		Frequency	Percent	Valid Percent	Cumulative Percent
Valid	NO	57	50.0	50.0	50.0
	YES	57	50.0	50.0	100.0
	Total	114	100.0	100.0	

COMP

		Frequency	Percent	Valid Percent	Cumulative Percent
Valid	BOTH	6	5.3	5.3	5.3
	INFECT	15	13.2	13.2	18.4
	NONE	79	69.3	69.3	87.7
	REDO	14	12.3	12.3	100.0
	Total	114	100.0	100.0	

FIGURE 2.5

SPSS summary tables
for DRUG and COMP

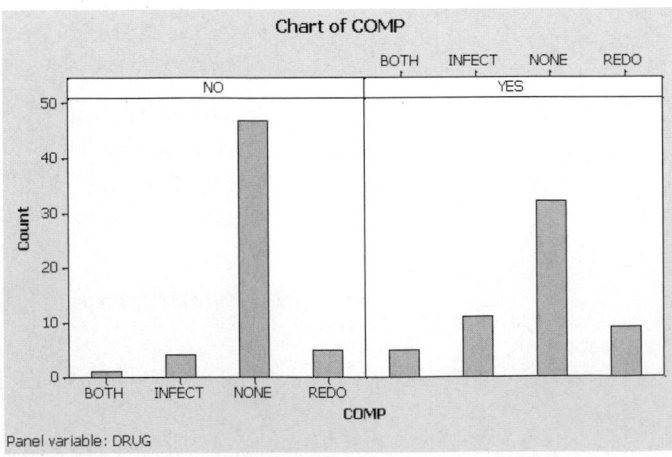

FIGURE 2.6

MINITAB side-by-side
bar graphs for COMP, by
value of DRUG

COMP

DRUG			Frequency	Percent	Valid Percent	Cumulative Percent
NO	Valid	BOTH	1	1.8	1.8	1.8
		INFECT	4	7.0	7.0	8.8
		NONE	47	82.5	82.5	91.2
		REDO	5	8.8	8.8	100.0
		Total	57	100.0	100.0	
YES	Valid	BOTH	5	8.8	8.8	8.8
		INFECT	11	19.3	19.3	28.1
		NONE	32	56.1	56.1	84.2
		REDO	9	15.8	15.8	100.0
		Total	57	100.0	100.0	

FIGURE 2.7

SPSS summary tables for COMP by value of DRUG

Solution

a. The top table in Figure 2.5 is a summary frequency table for DRUG. Note that exactly half (57) of the 114 coronary artery bypass patients received the drug and half did not. The bottom table in Figure 2.5 is a summary frequency table for COMP. We see that about 69% of the 114 patients had no complications, leaving about 31% who experienced either a redo surgery, a post-op infection, or both.

b. Figure 2.6 is a MINITAB side-by-side bar graph for the data. The four bars on the left represent the frequencies of COMP for the 57 patients who did not receive the drug; the four bars on the right represent the frequencies of COMP for the 57 patients who did receive a dosage of the drug. The graph clearly shows that patients who did not get the drug suffered fewer complications. The exact percentages are displayed in the SPSS summary tables of Figure 2.7. About 56% of the patients who got the drug had no complications, compared to about 83% for the patients who did not get the drug.

Look Back Although the drug may be effective in reducing blood loss, the results in Figures 2.6 and 2.7 also imply that patients on the drug may have a higher risk of complications. But before using this information to make a decision about the drug, the physicians will need to provide a measure of reliability for the inference—that is, the physicians will want to know whether the difference between the percentages of patients with complications observed in this sample of 114 patients is generalizable to the population of all coronary artery bypass patients.

Now Work Exercise 2.7

STATISTICS IN ACTION REVISITED

Interpreting Pie Charts

In the survey of University Community Hospital physicians, the medical researchers measured three qualitative variables: *Level of previous ethics consultation use* ("never used" or "used"), *Practitioner specialty* ("medical" or "surgical"), and *Future use of ethics consultation* ("yes" or "no"). Pie charts and bar graphs can be used to summarize and describe the physicians' responses to these survey questions. Recall that the data are saved in the **ETHICS** file. These variables are named PREVUSE, SPEC, and FUTUREUSE in the data file. We created pie charts for these variables using MINITAB.

Figure SIA2.1 is a pie chart for the PREVUSE variable. Clearly, a higher percentage of physicians (71.2%) has previously never used ethics consultation

Continued

at the hospital than have (28.8%). The researchers want to know if this "previous use" pattern differs for the two practitioner specialties. Figure SIA2.2 shows side-by-side pie charts of the PREVUSE variable for each level of the SPEC variable. The left-side chart describes the pattern of previous use by medical specialists, and the right-side chart describes the pattern of previous use by surgeons. Figure SIA2.2 shows that slightly fewer surgeons (27.9%) have used ethics consultation in the past than have medical practitioners (29.3%).

We produced a similar set of side-by-side pie charts to describe the qualitative variable FUTUREUSE in Figure SIA2.3. Apparently, the gap between surgeons and medical specialists has widened. These charts again show that fewer surgeons (76.7%) would consider using ethics consultation in the future than medical specialists (82.7%), but the difference in the percentages is greater than for previous use. The researchers' theory that surgical specialists at UCH are less likely to use ethics consultation than medical specialists is supported by the pie charts.

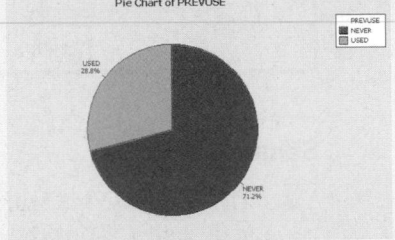

Figure SIA2.1

MINITAB pie chart for previous use of ethics consultation

Figure SIA2.2

MINITAB pie charts for previous use of ethics consultation — medical versus surgical specialty

Figure SIA2.3

MINITAB pie charts for future use of ethics consultation — medical versus surgical specialty

Exercises 2.1–2.15

Learning the Mechanics

2.1 Complete the following table.

Grade on Business Statistics Exam	Frequency	Relative Frequency
A: 90–100	—	.08
B: 80–89	36	—
C: 65–79	90	—
D: 50–64	30	—
F: Below 50	28	—
Total	200	1.00

2.2 A qualitative variable with three classes (X, Y, and Z) is measured for each of 20 units randomly sampled from a target population. The data (observed class for each unit) are listed below.

Y X X Z X Y Y Y X X Z X
Y Y X Z Y Y Y Y X

a. Compute the frequency for each of the three classes.
b. Compute the relative frequency for each of the three classes.
c. Display the results, part **a,** in a frequency bar graph.
d. Display the results, part **b,** in a pie chart.

Applying the Concepts—Basic

2.3 **Industrial robots.** The Robotics Industries Association reports that there were approximately 144,000 industrial robots operating in North America in 2004. The MINITAB graph below shows the percentages of industrial robot units assigned to each of six task categories: (1) spot welding, (2) arc welding, (3) material removal, (4) material handling, (5) assembly, and (6) dispensing/coating.
  a. What type of graph is used to describe the data?
  b. Identify the variable measured for each of the 144,000 industrial robots.
  c. Use the graph to identify the task that uses the highest percentage of industrial robots.
  d. How many of the 144,000 industrial robots are used for spot welding?
  e. What percentage of industrial robots are used for either spot welding or arc welding?

2.4 **Switching off air bags.** Driver-side and passenger-side air bags are installed in all new cars to prevent serious or fatal injury in an automobile crash. However, air bags have been found to cause deaths in children and small people or people with handicaps in low-speed crashes. Consequently, in 1998, the federal government began allowing vehicle owners to request installation of an on–off switch for air bags. The table describes the reasons for requesting the installation of passenger-side on–off switches given by car owners over a two-year period.

Reason	Number of Requests
Infant	1,852
Child	17,148
Medical	8,377
Infant & medical	44
Child & medical	903
Infant & child	1,878
Infant & child & medical	135
Total	30,337

Source: National Highway Transportation Safety Administration, September 2000.

  a. What type of variable, quantitative or qualitative, is summarized in the table? Give the values that the variable could assume.
  b. Calculate the relative frequencies for each reason.
  c. Display the information in the table in an appropriate graph.
  d. What proportion of the car owners who requested on–off air bag switches gave medical as one of the reasons?

2.5 **Defects in new automobiles.** Consider the following data from the automobile industry (adapted from Kane 1989). All cars produced on a particular day were inspected for defects. The 145 defects found were categorized by type as shown in the accompanying table.

Defect Type	Number
Accessories	50
Body	70
Electrical	10
Engine	5
Transmission	10

  a. Construct a Pareto diagram for the data. Use the graph to identify the most frequently observed type of defect.
  b. All 70 car body defects were further classified as to type. The frequencies are provided in the following table. Form a Pareto diagram for type of body defect. (Adding this graph to the original Pareto diagram of part **a** is called *exploding the Pareto diagram*.) Interpret the result. What type of body defect should be targeted for special attention?

Body Defect	Number
Chrome	2
Dents	25
Paint	30
Upholstery	10
Windshield	3

2.6 **Management system failures.** The U.S. Chemical Safety and Hazard Investigation Board (CSB) is responsible for determining the root cause of industrial accidents. Since its creation in 1998, the CSB has identified 83 incidents that were caused by management system failures (*Process Safety Progress*, Dec. 2004). The accompanying table gives a breakdown of the root causes of these 83 incidents.

Management System Cause Category	Number of Incidents
Engineering & Design	27
Procedures & Practices	24
Management & Oversight	22
Training & Communication	10
Total	83

Source: Blair, A. S. "Management System Failures Identified in Incidents Investigated by the U.S. Chemical Safety and Hazard Investigation Board." Process Safety Progress, Vol. 23, No. 4, Dec. 2004 (Table 1).

  a. Find the relative frequency of the number of incidents for each cause category.
  b. Construct a Pareto diagram for the data.
  c. From the Pareto diagram, identify the cause categories with the highest (and lowest) relative frequency of incidents.

2.7 **Store loyalty survey.** Customer satisfaction and loyalty are valued and monitored by all world-class organizations. But are satisfied customers necessarily loyal customers?

MINITAB graph for Exercise 2.3

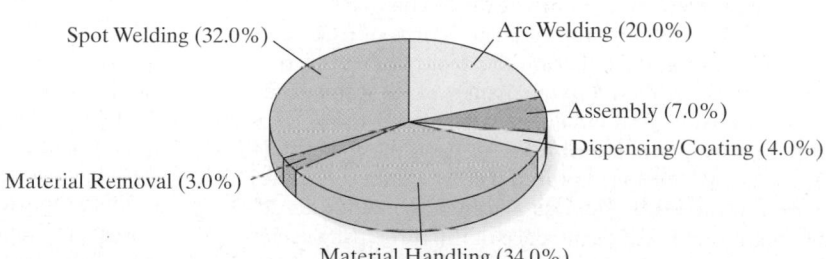

Harte-Hanks Market Research surveyed customers of department stores and banks and published the following results in *American Demographics* (Aug. 1999).

	Banks	Department Stores
Totally satisfied and very loyal	27%	4%
Totally satisfied and not very loyal	18%	25%
Not totally satisfied and very loyal	13%	2%
Not totally satisfied and not very loyal	42%	69%
	100%	100%

Source: American Demographics, Aug. 1999.

a. Construct side-by-side relative frequency bar charts for banks and department stores.

b. Could these data have been described using pie charts? Explain.

c. Do the data indicate that customers who are totally satisfied are very loyal? Explain.

Applying the Concepts—Intermediate

2.8 **Products "Made in the USA."** "Made in the USA" is a claim stated in many product advertisements or on product labels. Advertisers want consumers to believe that the product is manufactured with 100% U.S. labor and materials—which is often not the case. What does "Made in the USA" mean to the typical consumer? To answer this question, a group of marketing professors conducted an experiment at a shopping mall in Muncie, Indiana (*Journal of Global Business*, Spring 2002). They asked every fourth adult entrant to the mall to participate in the study. A total of 106 shoppers agreed to answer the question, "'Made in the USA' means what percentage of U.S. labor and materials?" The responses of the 106 shoppers are summarized in the following table.

Response to "Made in the USA"	Number of Shoppers
100%	64
75 to 99%	20
50 to 74%	18
Less than 50%	4

Source: "'Made in the USA': Consumer Perceptions, Deception and Policy Alternatives." *Journal of Global Business,* Vol. 13, No. 24, Spring 2002 (Table 3).

a. What type of data-collection method was used?

b. What type of variable, quantitative or qualitative, is measured?

c. Present the data in the table in graphical form. Use the graph to make a statement about the percentage of consumers who believe "Made in the USA" means 100% U.S. labor and materials.

DDT

2.9 **Fish contaminated by a plant's toxic discharge.** Refer to Example 1.5 (p. 16) and the U.S. Army Corps of Engineers data on fish contaminated from the toxic discharges of a chemical plant located on the banks of the Tennessee River in Alabama. The engineers determined the species (channel catfish, largemouth bass, or smallmouth buffalo fish) for each of the 144 captured fish. The data on species are saved in the **DDT** file. Use a graphical method to describe the frequency of occurrence of the three fish species in the 144 captured fish.

CEOPAY05

2.10 **The Executive Compensation Scoreboard.** Refer to the *Forbes* "Executive Compensation Scoreboard" for 2005, described in Chapter 1 (p. 6) and in Exercise 1.19 (p. 25). Recall that the industry type of the CEO's company (e.g., banking, retailing, etc.) was recorded for each of the 500 CEOs in the survey. (See Table 1.1, p. 6, for a list of the industries.) Access the **CEOPAY05** file and use a graphical method to describe the frequency of occurrence of the industry types.

DIAMONDS

2.11 **Color and clarity of diamonds.** Diamonds are categorized according to the "four C's": carats, clarity, color, and cut. Each diamond stone that is sold on the open market is provided a certificate by an independent diamond assessor that lists these characteristics. Data for 308 diamonds were extracted from Singapore's *Business Times* and are saved in the **DIAMONDS** file (*Journal of Statistics Education*, Vol. 9, No. 1, 2001). Color is classified as D, E, F, G, H, or I, while clarity is classified as IF, VVS1, VVS2, VS1, or VS2. Use a graphical technique to summarize the color and clarity of the 308 diamond stones. What is the color and clarity that occurs most often? Least often?

2.12 **Survey of computer crime.** Refer to the Computer Security Institute (CSI) annual survey of computer crime at United States businesses, Exercise 1.20 (p. 25). One question asked, "Did your business suffer unauthorized use of computer systems within the past year?" The responses are summarized in the next table for two survey years, 1999 and 2006. Compare the responses for the 2 years using side-by-side bar charts. What inference can be made from the charts?

Unauthorized Use of Computer Systems	Percentage in 1999	Percentage in 2006
Yes	62	52
No	17	38
Don't know	21	10
Totals	100	100

Source: "2006 CSI/FBI Computer Crime and Security Survey." *Computer Security Issues & Trends,* Spring 2006.

Applying the Concepts—Advanced

2.13 **Advertising with reader-response cards.** "Reader-response cards" are used by marketers to advertise their product and obtain sales leads. These cards are placed in magazines and trade publications. Readers detach and mail in the cards to indicate their interest in the product, expecting literature or a phone call in return. How effective are these cards (called "bingo cards" in the industry) as a marketing tool? Performark, a Minneapolis business that helps companies close on sales leads, attempted to answer this question by responding to 17,000 card-advertisements placed by industrial marketers in a wide variety of trade publications over a 6-year period. Performark kept track of how long it took for each advertiser to respond. A summary of the response times, reported in *Inc.* magazine (July 1995), is given in the following table.

a. Describe the variable measured by Performark.

b. *Inc.* displayed the results in the form of a pie chart. Reconstruct the pie chart from the information given in the table.

c. How many of the 17,000 advertisers never responded to the sales lead?

d. Advertisers typically spend at least a million dollars on a reader-response card marketing campaign. Many industrial marketers feel these "bingo cards" are not worth their expense. Does the information in the pie chart, part **b,** support this contention? Explain why or why not. If not, what information can be gleaned from the pie chart to help potential "bingo card" campaigns?

Advertiser's Response Time	Percentage
Never responded	21
13–59 days	33
60–120 days	34
More than 120 days	12
Total	100

2.14 Stewardship at MBA programs. *Business Ethics* (Fall 2005) reported on a survey designed to rank master in business administration (MBA) programs worldwide on how well they prepare students for social and environmental stewardship. Each business school was ranked according to four criteria: *student exposure* (class time dedicated to social and environmental issues), *student opportunity* (courses with social and environmental content), *course content* (courses emphasize business as a force for positive social and environmental change), and *faculty research* (published articles that examine business in a social/environmental context). Each area was rated from 1 star (lowest rating) to 5 stars (highest rating). Overall, Stanford University received the top ranking, followed by ESADE (Spain), York University (Canada), Monterrey Technical Institute (Mexico), and the University of Notre Dame. A summary of the rankings (star ratings) for the top 30 MBA programs is shown in the table.

a. Illustrate the differences and similarities of the star ranking distributions for the four different criteria.

b. Give a plausible reason why there were no 1-star ratings for the 30 MBA programs.

Criteria	5 Stars	4 Stars	3 Stars	2 Stars	1 Star	Total
Student Exposure	2	9	14	5	0	30
Student Opportunity	3	10	14	3	0	30
Course Content	3	9	17	1	0	30
Faculty Research	3	10	11	4	0	28

Source: Biello, D. "MBA Programs for Social and Environmental Stewardship." *Business Ethics*, Fall 2005, p. 25.

2.15 Foreign investments in China. Since opening its doors to Western investors 25 years ago, the People's Republic of China has been steadily moving toward a market economy. However, because of the considerable political and economic uncertainties in China, Western investors remain uneasy about the investments in China. An agency of the Chinese government surveyed 402 foreign investors to ascertain their concerns with the investment environment. Each was asked to indicate their most serious concern. The results appear below.

a. Construct a Pareto diagram for the 10 categories.

b. According to your Pareto diagram, which environmental factors most concern investors?

c. In this case, are 80% of the investors concerned with 20% of the environmental factors as the Pareto principle would suggest? Justify your answer.

⊙ CHINA

Investor's Concern	Frequency
Communication infrastructure	8
Environmental protection	13
Financial services	14
Government efficiency	30
Inflation rate	233
Labor supply	11
Personal safety	2
Real estate prices	82
Security of personal property	4
Water supply	5

Source: Adapted from China Marketing News, No. 26, November 1995.

2.2 Graphical Methods for Describing Quantitative Data

Recall from Section 1.5 that quantitative data sets consist of data that are recorded on a meaningful numerical scale. For describing, summarizing, and detecting patterns in such data, we can use three graphical methods: **dot plots, stem-and-leaf displays,** and **histograms.** Since almost all statistical software packages can produce these graphs, we'll focus here on their interpretations rather than their construction.

For example, suppose a financial analyst is interested in the amount of resources spent by computer hardware and software companies on research and development (R&D). She samples 50 of these high-technology firms and calculates the amount each spent last year on R&D as a percentage of their total revenue. The results are given in Table 2.2. As numerical measurements made on the sample of 50 units (the firms), these percentages represent quantitative data. The analyst's initial objective is to summarize and describe these data in order to extract relevant information.

A visual inspection of the data indicates some obvious facts. For example, the smallest R&D percentage is 5.2% (company 45) and the largest is 13.5% (companies 1 and 16). But it is difficult to provide much additional information on the 50 R&D percentages without resorting to some method of summarizing the data. One such method is a dot plot.

R&D

TABLE 2.2 Percentage of Revenues Spent on Research and Development

Company	Percentage	Company	Percentage	Company	Percentage	Company	Percentage
1	13.5	14	9.5	27	8.2	39	6.5
2	8.4	15	8.1	28	6.9	40	7.5
3	10.5	16	13.5	29	7.2	41	7.1
4	9.0	17	9.9	30	8.2	42	13.2
5	9.2	18	6.9	31	9.6	43	7.7
6	9.7	19	7.5	32	7.2	44	5.9
7	6.6	20	11.1	33	8.8	45	5.2
8	10.6	21	8.2	34	11.3	46	5.6
9	10.1	22	8.0	35	8.5	47	11.7
10	7.1	23	7.7	36	9.4	48	6.0
11	8.0	24	7.4	37	10.5	49	7.8
12	7.9	25	6.5	38	6.9	50	6.5
13	6.8	26	9.5				

Dot Plots

A **dot plot** for the 50 R&D percentages, produced using MINITAB software, shown in Figure 2.8. The horizontal axis of Figure 2.8 is a scale for the quantitative variable, percent. The numerical value of each measurement in the data set is located on the horizontal scale by a dot. When data values repeat, the dots are placed above one another, forming a pile at that particular numerical location. As you can see, this dot plot shows that almost all of the R&D percentages are between 6% and 12%, with most falling between 7% and 9%.

Stem-and-Leaf Display

We used Excel and PHStat2 to generate another graphical representation of these same data, a **stem-and-leaf display,** in Figure 2.9. In this display the *stem* is the portion of the measurement (percentage) to the left of the decimal point, while the remaining portion to the right of the decimal point is the *leaf.*

The stems for the data set are listed in a column from the smallest (5) to the largest (13). Then the leaf for each observation is recorded in the row of the display corresponding to the observation's stem. For example, the leaf 5 of the first observation (13.5) in Table 2.2 is placed in the row corresponding to the stem 13. Similarly, the leaf 4 for the second observation (8.4) in Table 2.2 is recorded in the row corresponding to the stem 8, while the leaf 5 for the third observation (10.5) is recorded in the row corresponding to the stem 10. (The leaves for these first three observations are shaded in Figure 2.9.) Typically, the leaves in each row are ordered as shown in Figure 2.9.

The stem-and-leaf display presents another compact picture of the data set. You can see at a glance that most of the sampled computer companies (37 of 50) spent between 6.0% and 9.9% of their revenues on R&D, and 11 of them spent between 7.0% and 7.9%. Relative to the rest of the sampled companies, three spent a high percentage of revenues on R&D—in excess of 13%.

D	E	F
Stem-and-Leaf Display		
for RDPct		
Stem unit: 1		
5	2 6 9	
6	0 5 5 5 6 8 9 9 9	
7	1 1 2 2 4 5 5 7 7 8 9	
8	0 0 1 2 2 2 4 5 8	
9	0 2 4 5 5 6 7 9	
10	1 5 5 6	
11	1 3 7	
12		
13	2 5 5	

FIGURE 2.9

Excel/PHStat2 stem-and-leaf display for 50 R&D percentages

FIGURE 2.8

MINITAB dot plot for 50 R&D percentages

The definitions of the stem and leaf can be modified to alter the graphical description. For example, suppose we had defined the stem as the tens digit for the R&D percentage data, rather than the ones and tens digits. With this definition, the stems and leaves corresponding to the measurements 13.5 and 8.4 would be as follows:

Stem	Leaf		Stem	Leaf
1	3		0	8

Note that the decimal portion of the numbers has been dropped. Generally, only one digit is displayed in the leaf.

If you look at the data, you'll see why we didn't define the stem this way, All the R&D measurements fall below 13.5, so all the leaves would fall into just two stem rows—1 and 0—in this display. The resulting picture would not be nearly as informative as Figure 2.9.

Now Work Exercise 2.22

Biography

**JOHN TUKEY
(1915–2000)**

The Picasso of Statistics

Like the legendary artist Pablo Picasso, who mastered and revolutionized a variety of art forms during his lifetime, John Tukey is recognized for his contributions to many subfields of statistics. Born in Massachusetts, Tukey was home-schooled, graduated with his bachelor's and master's degrees in chemistry from Brown University, and received his PhD in mathematics from Princeton University. While at Bell Telephone Laboratories in the 1960s and early 1970s, Tukey developed "exploratory data analysis," a set of graphical descriptive methods for summarizing and presenting huge amounts of data. Many of these tools, including the stem-and-leaf display and the box plot, are now standard features of modern statistical software packages. (In fact, it was Tukey himself who coined the term *software* for computer programs.)

Histograms

A **MINITAB histogram** for these 50 R&D measurements is displayed in Figure 2.10. The horizontal axis for Figure 2.10, which gives the percentage amounts spent on R&D for each company, is divided into **class intervals** commencing with the interval (4.5−5.5) and proceeding in intervals of equal size to (13.5−14.5). (*Note:* MINITAB shows the midpoint of every other class interval on the histogram.) The vertical axis gives the number (or *frequency*) of the 50 measurements that fall in each class interval. You can see that the class intervals (6.5−7.5) and (7.5−8.5, i.e., the classes with the two highest bars) contain the largest frequencies—both intervals contain 13 R&D percentage measurements; the remaining class intervals tend to contain a smaller number of measurements as R&D percentage gets smaller or larger.

Histograms can be used to display either the frequency or relative frequency of the measurements falling into the class intervals. The class intervals, frequencies, and relative frequencies for the 50 R&D measurements are shown in Table 2.3.* By summing the relative frequencies in the intervals (6.5−7.5), (7.5−8.5), (8.5−9.5), (9.5−10.5), and (10.5−11.5), we find that .26 + .26 + .10 + .12 + .10 = .84, or 84%, of the R&D measurements are between 6.5 and 11.5. Similarly, summing the relative frequencies in the last two intervals, (12.5−13.5) and (13.5−14.5), we find that or 6%, of the companies spent over 12.5% of their revenues on R&D. Many other summary statements can be made by further study of the histogram.

When interpreting a histogram (say, the histogram in Figure 2.10), consider two important facts. First, the proportion of the total area under the histogram that falls above a particular interval of the horizontal axis is equal to the relative frequency of

---

*MINITAB, like many statistical software packages, will classify an observation that falls on the borderline of a class interval into the next highest class interval. For example, the R&D measurement of 13.5, which falls on the border between the intervals (12.5−13.5) and (13.5−14.5), is classified into the (13.5−14.5) interval. The frequencies in Table 2.3 reflect this convention.

FIGURE 2.10

MINITAB histogram for
50 R&D percentages

**TABLE 2.3 Class Intervals, Frequencies, and Relative Frequencies
for the 50 R&D Measurements**

Class	Class Interval	Class Frequency	Class Relative Frequency
1	4.5–5.5	1	1/50 = .02
2	5.5–6.5	3	3/50 = .06
3	6.5–7.5	13	13/50 = .26
4	7.5–8.5	13	13/50 = .26
5	8.5–9.5	5	5/50 = .10
6	9.5–10.5	6	6/50 = .12
7	10.5–11.5	5	5/50 = .10
8	11.5–12.5	1	1/50 = .02
9	12.5–13.5	1	1/50 = .02
10	13.5–14.5	2	2/50 = .04
Totals		50	1.00

measurements falling in the interval. For example, the relative frequency for the class interval 7.5–8.5 is .26. Consequently, the rectangle above the interval contains .26 of the total area under the histogram.

Second, you can imagine the appearance of the relative frequency histogram for a very large set of data (say, a population). As the number of measurements in a data set is increased, you can obtain a better description of the data by decreasing the width of the class intervals. When the class intervals become small enough, a relative frequency histogram will (for all practical purposes) appear as a smooth curve (see Figure 2.11). Some recommendations for selecting the number of intervals in a histogram for smaller data sets are given in the box.

While histograms provide good visual descriptions of data sets—particularly very large ones—they do not let us identify individual measurements. In contrast, each of the original measurements is visible to some extent in a dot plot and clearly visible in a stem-and-leaf display. The stem-and-leaf display arranges the data in ascending order, so it's easy to locate the individual measurements. For example, in Figure 2.9, we can easily

FIGURE 2.11

Effect of the size of a data set
on the outline of a histogram

a. Small data set

b. Larger data set

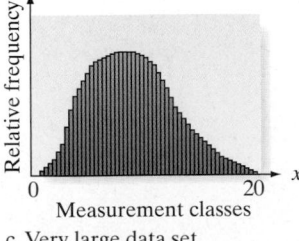

c. Very large data set

see that three of the R&D measurements are equal to 8.2, but we can't see that fact by inspecting the histogram in Figure 2.10. However, stem-and-leaf displays can become unwieldy for very large data sets. A very large number of stems and leaves causes the vertical and horizontal dimensions of the display to become cumbersome, diminishing the usefulness of the visual display.

Determining the Number of Classes in a Histogram

Number of Observations in Data Set	Number of Classes
Less than 25	5–6
25–50	7–14
More than 50	15–20

EXAMPLE 2.2

Graphs for a Quantitative Variable

Problem A manufacturer of industrial wheels suspects that profitable orders are being lost because of the long time the firm takes to develop price quotes for potential customers. To investigate this possibility, 50 requests for price quotes were randomly selected from the set of all quotes made last year, and the processing time was determined for each quote. The processing times are displayed in Table 2.4, and each quote was classified according to whether the order was "lost" or not (i.e., whether or not the customer placed an order after receiving a price quote).

a. Use a statistical software package to create a frequency histogram for these data. Then shade the area under the histogram that corresponds to lost orders. Interpret the result.

b. Use a statistical software package to create a stem-and-leaf display for these data. Then shade each leaf of the display that corresponds to a lost order. Interpret the result.

PRICEQUOTES

TABLE 2.4 Price Quote Processing Time (Days)

Request Number	Processing Time	Lost?	Request Number	Processing Time	Lost?
1	2.36	No	26	3.34	No
2	5.73	No	27	6.00	No
3	6.60	No	28	5.92	No
4	10.05	Yes	29	7.28	Yes
5	5.13	No	30	1.25	No
6	1.88	No	31	4.01	No
7	2.52	No	32	7.59	No
8	2.00	No	33	13.42	Yes
9	4.69	No	34	3.24	No
10	1.91	No	35	3.37	No
11	6.75	Yes	36	14.06	Yes
12	3.92	No	37	5.10	No
13	3.46	No	38	6.44	No
14	2.64	No	39	7.76	No
15	3.63	No	40	4.40	No
16	3.44	No	41	5.48	No
17	9.49	Yes	42	7.51	No
18	4.90	No	43	6.18	No
19	7.45	No	44	8.22	Yes
20	20.23	Yes	45	4.37	No
21	3.91	No	46	2.93	No
22	1.70	No	47	9.95	Yes
23	16.29	Yes	48	4.46	No
24	5.52	No	49	14.32	Yes
25	1.44	No	50	9.01	No

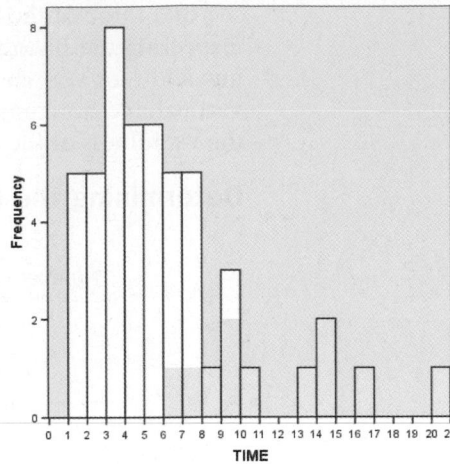

FIGURE 2.12
SPSS frequency histogram
for price quote data
(lost orders shaded)

Solution

a. We used SPSS to generate the frequency histogram in Figure 2.12. Note that 20 classes were formed by the SPSS program. The class intervals are (1.0–2.0), (2.0–3.0), . . ., (20.0–21.0). This histogram clearly shows the clustering of the measurements in the lower end of the distribution (between approximately 1 and 8 days), and the relatively few measurements in the upper end of the distribution (greater than 12 days). The shading of the area of the frequency histogram corresponding to lost orders clearly indicates that they lie in the upper tail of the distribution.

b. We used MINITAB to generate the stem-and-leaf display in Figure 2.13. Note that the stem (the second column of the printout) consists of the number of whole days (digits to the left of the decimal). The leaf (the third column of the printout) is the tenths digit (first digit after the decimal) of each measurement.* Thus, the leaf 2 in the stem 20 (the last row of the printout) represents the time of 20.23 days. Like the histogram, the stem-and-leaf display shows the shaded "lost" orders in the upper-tail of the distribution.

```
Stem-and-leaf of TIME   N  = 50
Leaf Unit = 0.10


  5    1    24789
 10    2    03569
 18    3    23344699
 24    4    034469
(6)    5    114579
 20    6    01467
 15    7    24557
 10    8    2
  9    9    049
  6   10    0
  5   11
  5   12
  5   13    4
  4   14    03
  2   15
  2   16    2
  1   17
  1   18
  1   19
  1   20    2
```

FIGURE 2.13
MINITAB stem-and-leaf
display for price quote data

Look Back As is usually the case for data sets that are not too large (say, fewer than 100 measurements), the stem-and-leaf display provides more detail than the histogram without being unwieldy. For instance, the stem-and-leaf display in Figure 2.13 clearly indicates that the lost orders are associated with high processing times (as does the histogram in Figure 2.12), and exactly which of the times correspond to lost orders. Histograms are most useful for displaying very large data sets, when the overall shape of the distribution of measurements is more important than the identification of individual measurements. Nevertheless, the message of both graphical displays is clear: Establishing processing time limits may well result in fewer lost orders.

Now Work Exercise 2.20

---

*The first column of the MINITAB stem-and-leaf display represents the cumulative number of measurements from the class interval to the nearest extreme class interval.

Most statistical software packages can be used to generate histograms, stem-and-leaf displays, and dot plots. All three are useful tools for graphically describing data sets. We recommend that you generate and compare the displays whenever you can. You'll find that histograms are generally more useful for very large data sets, while stem-and-leaf displays and dot plots provide useful detail for smaller data sets.

Summary of Graphical Descriptive Methods for Quantitative Data

Dot plot: The numerical value of each quantitative measurement in the data set is represented by a dot on a horizontal scale. When data values repeat, the dots are placed above one another vertically.

Stem-and-leaf display: The numerical value of the quantitative variable is partitioned into a "stem" and a "leaf." The possible stems are listed in order in a column. The leaf for each quantitative measurement in the data set is placed in the corresponding stem row. Leaves for observations with the same stem value are listed in increasing order horizontally.

Histogram: The possible numerical values of the quantitative variable are partitioned into class intervals, where each interval has the same width. These intervals form the scale of the horizontal axis. The frequency or relative frequency of observations in each class interval is determined. A vertical bar is placed over each class interval with height equal to either the class frequency or class relative frequency.

Histograms

Using the TI-83/TI-84 Graphing Calculator

I. Making a Histogram from Raw Data

Step 1 *Enter the data*

> Press **STAT** and select **1:Edit**
> Note: If the list already contains data, clear the old data. Use the up arrow to highlight "**L1**". Press **CLEAR ENTER.**
> Use the arrow and **ENTER** keys to enter the data set into **L1**.

Step 2 *Set up the histogram plot*

> Press **2nd** and press **Y** – for **STAT PLOT**
> Press **1** for **Plot 1**
> Set the cursor so that **ON** is flashing.
> For **Type,** use the arrow and Enter keys to highlight and select the histogram.
> For **Xlist,** choose the column containing the data (in most cases, L1).
> Note: Press **2nd 1** for **L1**
> **Freq** should be set to 1.

Step 3 *Select your window settings*

> Press **WINDOW** and adjust the settings as follows:

$$\text{X min} = \text{lowest class boundary}$$
$$\text{X max} = \text{highest class boundary}$$
$$\text{X scl} = \text{class width}$$
$$\text{Y min} = 0$$
$$\text{Y max} \geq \text{greatest class frequency}$$
$$\text{Y scl} = 1$$
$$\text{X res} = 1$$

Step 4 *View the graph*

> Press **GRAPH**

Continued

Optional   *Read class frequencies and class boundaries*
     Step   You can press **TRACE** to read the class frequencies and class boundaries. Use the arrow keys to move between bars.

Example   The following figures show TI-83 window settings and histogram for the following sample data:

86, 70, 62, 98, 73, 56, 53, 92, 86, 37, 62, 83, 78, 49, 78, 37, 67, 79, 57

II. Making a Histogram from a Frequency Table

Step 1   *Enter the data*

Press **STAT** and select **1:Edit**
Note: If a list already contains data, clear the old data. Use the up arrow to highlight the list name, "**L1**" or "**L2**".
Press **CLEAR ENTER.**
Enter the midpoint of each class into **L1**
Enter the class frequencies or relative frequencies into **L2**

Step 2   *Set up the histogram plot*

Press **2nd** and **Y =** for **STAT PLOT**
Press **1** for **Plot 1**
Set the cursor so that **ON** is flashing.
For **Type,** use the arrow and Enter keys to highlight and select the histogram.
For **Xlist,** choose the column containing the midpoints.
For **Freq,** choose the column containing the frequencies or relative frequencies.

Steps 3–4   *Follow steps 3–4 given above.*

Note: To set up the Window for relative frequencies, be sure to set **Ymax** to a value that is greater than or equal to the largest relative frequency.

STATISTICS IN ACTION REVISITED

Interpreting Histograms

One of the quantitative variables measured in the ethics consultation survey of physicians was *Length of time in practice* (i.e., years of experience). Recall that the medical researchers hypothesize that older, more experienced physicians will be less likely to use ethics consultation in the future. To check the believability of this claim, we accessed the **ETHICS** data file in MINITAB and created two frequency histograms for years of experience—one for physicians who indicated they would use ethics consultation in the future, and one for physicians who would not use ethics consultation. These side-by-side histograms are displayed in Figure SIA2.4.

From the histograms, you can see there is some support for the researchers' assertion. The histogram for the physicians who indicated they would use ethics consultation (the histogram on the right in Figure SIA2.4) shows that most of these physicians have been in practice between 10 and 20 years, while the histogram for nonusers (the histogram on the left in Figure SIA2.4) shows a tendency for these physicians to have more experience (over 20 years). However, the lack of data (only 21 observations) for the sample of physicians who would not use ethics consultation makes it difficult to reliably extend this inference to the population of physicians. In later chapters, we'll learn how to attach a measure of reliability to such an inference, even for small samples.

Figure SIA2.4

MINITAB histograms for years of practice—ethics consultation users versus nonusers

Exercises 2.16–2.32

Learning the Mechanics

2.16 Graph the relative frequency histogram for the 500 measurements summarized in the accompanying relative frequency table.

Measurement Class	Relative Frequency
.5–2.5	.10
2.5–4.5	.15
4.5–6.5	.25
6.5–8.5	.20
8.5–10.5	.05
10.5–12.5	.10
12.5–14.5	.10
14.5–16.5	.05

2.17 Refer to Exercise 2.16. Calculate the number of the 500 measurements falling into each of the measurement classes. Then graph a frequency histogram for these data.

2.18 Consider the stem-and-leaf display shown here.

Stem	Leaf
5	1
4	457
3	00036
2	1134599
1	2248
0	012

a. How many observations were in the original data set?
b. In the bottom row of the stem-and-leaf display, identify the stem, the leaves, and the numbers in the original data set represented by this stem and its leaves.
c. Re-create all the numbers in the data set and construct a dot plot.

2.19. MINITAB was used to generate the following histogram:

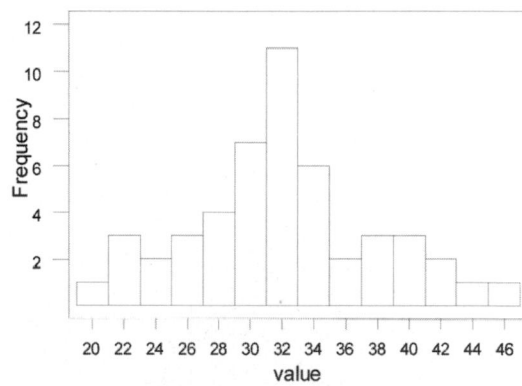

a. Is this a frequency histogram or a relative frequency histogram? Explain.
b. How many measurement classes were used in the construction of this histogram?
c. How many measurements are in the data set described by this histogram?

Applying the Concepts—Basic

2.20 Computer security survey. Refer to the 2006 CSI/FBI
NW Computer Crime and Security Survey, Exercise 2.12 (p. 48)
One of the survey questions asked respondents to indicate
the percentage of computer security functions that their
company outsources. Consequently, the quantitative variable of interest is measured as a percentage for each of 609
respondents in the 2006 survey. The following histogram
summarizes the data.

   a. Which measurement class contains the highest proportion
of respondents?

   b. What proportion of the 609 respondents indicate that
they outsource between 20% and 40% of computer security functions?

   c. What proportion of the 609 respondents outsource at
least 40% of computer security functions?

   d. How many of the 609 respondents outsource less than
20% of computer security functions?

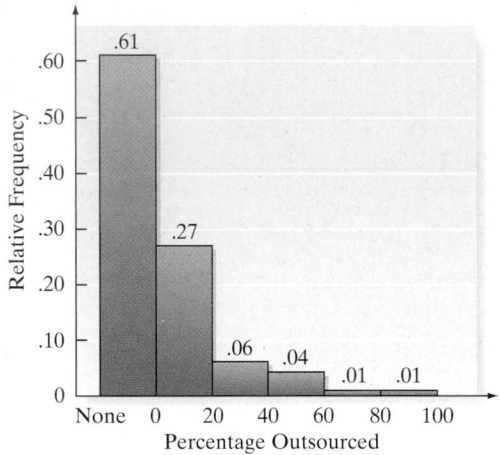

2.21 USGA golfing handicaps. The United States Golf
Association (USGA) Handicap System is designed to allow
golfers of differing abilities to enjoy fair competition. The
handicap index is a measure of a player's potential scoring
ability on an 18-hole golf course of standard difficulty. For
example, on a par-72 course, a golfer with a handicap of 7
will typically have a score of 79 (seven strokes over par).
Over 4.5 million golfers have an official USGA handicap
index. The handicap indexes for both male and female
golfers were obtained from the USGA and are summarized
in the following two histograms.

USGA Male Golfers

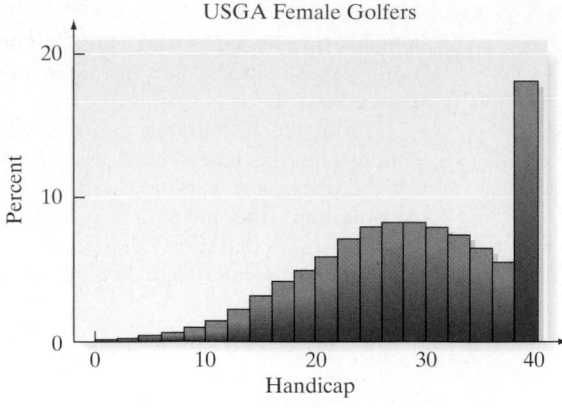

   a. What percentage of male USGA golfers have a handicap
greater than 20?

   b. What percentage of female USGA golfers have a
handicap greater than 20?

2.22 Sanitation inspection of cruise ships. To minimize the poten-
NW tial for gastrointestinal disease outbreaks, all passenger
cruise ships arriving at U.S. ports are subject to unan-
nounced sanitation inspections. Ships are rated on a
100-point scale by the Centers for Disease Control and
Prevention. A score of 86 or higher indicates that the ship is
providing an accepted standard of sanitation. The latest (as
of May 2006) sanitation scores for 169 cruise ships are saved
in the **SHIPSANIT** file. The first five and last five observations in the data set are listed in the accompanying table.

🔹 **SHIPSANIT (selected observations)**

Ship Name	Sanitation Score
Adventure of the Seas	95
Albatross	96
Amsterdam	98
Arabella	94
Arcadia	98
.	.
.	.
Wind Surf	95
Yorktown Clipper	91
Zaandam	98
Zenith	94
Zuiderdam	94

Source: National Center for Environmental Health, Centers for
Disease Control and Prevention, May 24, 2006.

   a. Generate a stem-and-leaf display of the data. Identify
the stems and leaves of the graph.

   b. Use the stem-and-leaf display to estimate the proportion
of ships that have an accepted sanitation standard.

   c. Locate the inspection score of 84 (*Sea Bird*) on the
stem-and-leaf display.

2.23 Investigating a link between home runs and runs scored.
Mark McGwire of the St. Louis Cardinals hit 70 home runs
during the 1998 Major League Baseball season, breaking a
record held by Roger Maris (61 home runs) since 1961. (In
2001, Barry Bonds broke the record again with 73 home
runs.) J. S. Simonoff of New York University collected data on
the number of runs scored by the Cardinals in games in which
McGwire hit home runs (*Journal of Statistics Education*,
Vol. 6, 1998). The data are reproduced in the table.

⊙ **STLRUNS**

6	6	3	11	13
8	1	10	6	7
5	8	9	6*	3
8	2	3	6*	6
15*	2	8*	5	6
8	6	2	3	5
5	8	4	10*	
8	9	4	4	
3	5	3	11*	
5	7	6	1	
2	3	8	4	
6	2	7*	6*	
3	7	14*	4*	

a. Construct a stem-and-leaf display for the number of runs scored by St. Louis during games when McGwire hit a home run.

b. The asterisks in the table represent games in which McGwire hit multiple home runs. On the stem-and-leaf display, circle the run values for these games. Do you detect any patterns?

Applying the Concepts—Intermediate

⊙ **DDT**

2.24 Fish contaminated by a plant's toxic discharge. Refer to Exercise 2.9 (p. 48) and the U.S. Army Corps of Engineers data on contaminated fish saved in the **DDT** file. In addition to species (channel catfish, largemouth bass, or smallmouth buffalo fish), the length (in centimeters), weight (in grams), and DDT level (in parts per million) was measured for each of the 144 captured fish.

a. Use a graphical method to describe the distribution of the 144 fish lengths.

b. Use a graphical method to describe the distribution of the 144 fish weights.

c. Use a graphical method to describe the distribution of the 144 DDT measurements.

⊙ **DIAMONDS**

2.25 Color and clarity of diamonds. Refer to the *Journal of Statistics Education* study of diamonds, Exercise 2.11 (p. 48). In addition to color and clarity, the independent certification group (GIA, HRD, or IGI) and the number of carats were recorded for each of 308 diamonds for sale on the open market. Recall that the data are saved in the **DIAMONDS** file.

a. Use a graphical method to describe the carat distribution of all 308 diamonds.

b. Use a graphical method to describe the carat distribution of diamonds certified by the GIA group.

c. Repeat part **b** for the HRD and IGI certification groups.

d. Compare the three carat distributions, parts **b** and **c**. Is there one particular certification group that appears to be assessing diamonds with higher carats than the others?

2.26 Items arriving and departing a work center. In a manufacturing plant, a *work center* is a specific production facility that consists of one or more people and/or machines and is treated as one unit for the purposes of capacity requirements planning and job scheduling. If jobs arrive at a particular work center at a faster rate than they depart, the work center impedes the overall production process and is referred to as a *bottleneck* (Fogarty, Blackstone, and Hoffmann, *Production and Inventory Management*, 1991). The data in the table at the bottom of this page were collected by an operations manager for use in investigating a potential bottleneck work center. Construct dot plots for the two sets of data. Do the dot plots suggest that the work center may be a bottleneck? Explain.

2.27 Environmental failures of Arkansas companies. Any corporation doing business in the United States must be aware of and obey both federal and state environmental regulations. Failure to do so may result in irreparable damage to the environment and costly financial penalties to guilty corporations. Of the 55 civil actions filed against corporations within the state of Arkansas by the U.S. Department of Justice on behalf of the Environmental Protection Agency, 38 resulted in financial penalties. These penalties along with the laws that were violated are listed in the table on the top of page 60. (*Note:* Some companies were involved in more than one civil action.)

a. Construct a stem-and-leaf display for all 38 penalties.

b. Circle the individual leaves that are associated with penalties imposed for violations of the Clean Air Act (CAA).

c. What does the pattern of circles in part **b** suggest about the severity of the penalties imposed for Clean Air Act violations relative to the other types of violations reported in the table? Explain.

2.28 Comparing task completion times. In order to estimate how long it will take to produce a particular product, a manufacturer will study the relationship between production time per unit and the number of units that have been produced. The line or curve characterizing this relationship is called a *learning curve* (Adler and Clark, *Management Science*, Mar. 1991). Twenty-five employees, all of whom were performing the same production task for the 10th time, were observed. Each person's task completion time (in minutes) was recorded. The same 25 employees were observed again the 30th time they performed the same task and the 50th time they performed the task. The resulting completion times are shown in the table at the bottom left column of page 60.

⊙ **WORKCTR**

Number of Items Arriving at Work Center per Hour											
155	115	156	150	159	163	172	143	159	166	148	175
151	161	138	148	129	135	140	152	139			

Number of Items Departing Work Center per Hour											
156	109	127	148	135	119	140	127	115	122	99	106
171	123	135	125	107	152	111	137	161			

CLEANAIR

Company Identification Number	Penalty	Law*	Company Identification Number	Penalty	Law*
01	$ 930,000	CERCLA	17	20,000	CWA
02	10,000	CWA	18	40,000	CWA
03	90,600	CAA	19	20,000	CWA
04	123,549	CWA	20	40,000	CWA
05	37,500	CWA	21	850,000	CWA
06	137,500	CWA	22	35,000	CWA
07	2,500	SDWA	23	4,000	CAA
08	1,000,000	CWA	24	25,000	CWA
09	25,000	CAA	25	40,000	CWA
09	25,000	CAA	26	30,000	CAA
10	25,000	CWA	27	15,000	CWA
10	25,000	RCRA	28	15,000	CAA
11	19,100	CAA	29	105,000	CAA
12	100,000	CWA	30	20,000	CWA
12	30,000	CWA	31	400,000	CWA
13	35,000	CAA	32	85,000	CWA
13	43,000	CWA	33	300,000	CWA/ RCRA/ CERCLA
14	190,000	CWA			
15	15,000	CWA			
16	90,000	RCRA	34	30,000	CWA

*CAA: Clean Air Act: CERCLA: Comprehensive Environmental Response, Compensation, and Liability Act: RCRA: Resource Conservation and Recovery Act: SDWA: Safe Drinking Water Act.

Source: Tabor, R. H., and Stanwick, S. D. "Arkansas: An Environmental Perspective." *Arkansas Business and Economic Review,* Vol. 28. Summer 1995, pp. 22–32 (Table 4).

a. Use a statistical software package to construct a frequency histogram for each of the three data sets.

b. In most production processes, the time required to complete a particular task will be shorter each time the task is undertaken. Do the histograms, part **a,** follow this trend? Explain.

COMPTIME

	PERFORMANCE		
Employee	10th	30th	50th
1	15	16	10
2	21	10	5
3	30	12	7
4	17	9	9
5	18	7	8
6	22	11	11
7	33	8	12
8	41	9	9
9	10	5	7
10	14	15	6
11	18	10	8
12	25	11	14
13	23	9	9
14	19	11	8
15	20	10	10
16	22	13	8
17	20	12	7
18	19	8	8
19	18	20	6
20	17	7	5
21	16	6	6
22	20	9	4
23	22	10	15
24	19	10	7
25	24	11	20

Applying the Concepts—Advanced

2.29 State SAT scores. Educators are constantly evaluating the efficacy of public schools in the education and training of American students. One quantitative assessment of change over time is the difference in scores on the SAT, which has been used for decades by colleges and universities as one criterion for admission. The file **SATSCORES** contains the average SAT scores for each of the 50 states and District of Columbia for the years 1990 and 2005. The first five observations and last two observations in the data set are shown in the table.

a. Use graphs to display the two SAT score distributions. How have the distributions of state scores changed over time?

b. As another method of comparing the 1990 and 2005 SAT scores, compute the *paired difference* by subtracting the 1990 score from the 2005 score for each state. Summarize these differences with a graph.

c. Interpret the graph, part **b.** How do your conclusions compare to those of part **a?**

d. Based on the graph, part **b,** what is the largest improvement in SAT score between 1990 and 2005? Identify the state associated with this improvement.

SATSCORES

State	1990	2005
Alabama	1079	1126
Alaska	1015	1042
Arizona	1041	1056
Arkansas	1077	1115
California	1002	1026
.	.	.
Wisconsin	1111	1191
Wyoming	1072	1087

Source: College Entrance Examination Board, 2006.

2.30 Time in bankruptcy. Financially distressed firms can gain protection from their creditors while they restructure by filing for protection under U.S. Bankruptcy Codes. In a *prepackaged bankruptcy,* a firm negotiates a reorganization plan with its creditors prior to filing for bankruptcy. This can result in a much quicker exit from bankruptcy than traditional bankruptcy filings. Brian Betker conducted a study of 49 prepackaged bankruptcies that were filed between 1986 and 1993 and reported the results in *Financial Management* (Spring 1995). The table on the right lists the time (in months) in bankruptcy for these 49 companies. The table also lists the results of a vote by each company's board of directors concerning their preferred reorganization plan. (*Note:* "Joint" = joint exchange offer with prepackaged bankruptcy solicitation; "Prepack" = prepackaged bankruptcy solicitation only; "None" = no prefiling vote held.)

a. Construct a stem-and-leaf display for the length of time in bankruptcy for all 49 companies.

b. Summarize the information reflected in the stem-and-leaf display, part **a.** Make a general statement about the length of time in bankruptcy for firms using "prepacks."

c. Select a graphical technique that will permit a comparison of the time-in-bankruptcy distributions for the three types of "prepack" firms: those who held no prefiling vote; those who voted their preference for a joint solution; and those who voted their preference for a prepack.

d. The companies that were reorganized through a leveraged buyout are identified by an asterisk in the table. Identify these firms on the stem-and-leaf display, part **a,** by circling their bankruptcy times. Do you observe any pattern in the graph? Explain.

2.31 Malfunctioning hearing aids. It's not uncommon for hearing aids to malfunction and cancel the desired signal. *IEEE Transactions on Speech and Audio Processing* (May 1995) reported on a new audio processing system designed to limit the amount of signal cancellation that may occur. The system utilizes a mathematical equation that involves a variable, V, called a *sufficient norm constraint.* A histogram for realizations of V, produced using simulation, is shown below

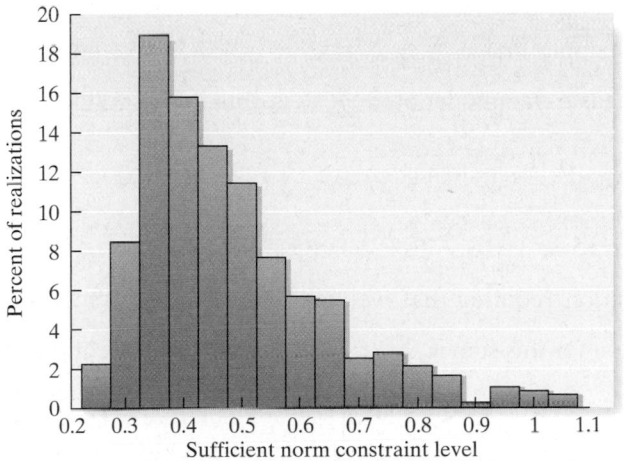

Source: Hoffman, M. W., and Buckley, K. M. "Robust Time-Domain Processing of Broadband Microphone Array Data." *IEEE Transactions on Speech and Audio Processing,* Vol. 3, No. 3, May 1995, p. 199 (Figure 4). © 1995 IEEE.

a. Estimate the percentage of realizations of V with values ranging from .425 to .675.

b. Cancellation of the desired signal is limited by selecting a norm constraint V. Find the value of V for a company that

⊙ **BANKRUPT**

Company	Prefiling Votes	Time in Bankruptcy (months)
AM International	None	3.9
Anglo Energy	Prepack	1.5
Arizona Biltmore*	Prepack	1.0
Astrex	None	10.1
Barry's Jewelers	None	4.1
Calton	Prepack	1.9
Cencor	Joint	1.4
Charter Medical*	Prepack	1.3
Cherokee*	Joint	1.2
Circle Express	Prepack	4.1
Cook Inlet Comm.	Prepack	1.1
Crystal Oil	None	3.0
Divi Hotels	None	3.2
Edgell Comm.*	Prepack	1.0
Endevco	Prepack	3.8
Gaylord Container	Joint	1.2
Great Amer. Comm.*	Prepack	1.0
Hadson	Prepack	1.5
In-Store Advertising	Prepack	1.0
JPS Textiles*	Prepack	1.4
Kendall*	Prepack	1.2
Kinder-Care	None	4.2
Kroy*	Prepack	3.0
Ladish*	Joint	1.5
LaSalle Energy*	Prepack	1.6
LIVE Entertainment	Joint	1.4
Mayflower Group*	Prepack	1.4
Memorex Telex*	Prepack	1.1
Munsingwear	None	2.9
Nat'l Environmental	Joint	5.2
Petrolane Gas	Prepack	1.2
Price Communications	None	2.4
Republic Health*	Joint	4.5
Resorts Int'l*	None	7.8
Restaurant Enterprises*	Prepack	1.5
Rymer Foods	Joint	2.1
SCI TV*	Prepack	2.1
Southland*	Joint	3.9
Specialty Equipment*	None	2.6
SPI Holdings*	Joint	1.4
Sprouse-Reitz	Prepack	1.4
Sunshine Metals	Joint	5.4
TIE/Communications	None	2.4
Trump Plaza	Prepack	1.7
Trump Taj Mahal	Prepack	1.4
Trump's Castle	Prepack	2.7
USG	Prepack	1.2
Vyquest	Prepack	4.1
West Point Acq.*	Prepack	2.9

*Leveraged buyout.

Source: Betker, B. L. "An Empirical Examination of Prepackaged Bankruptcy." *Financial Management,* Vol. 24, No. 1, Spring 1995, p. 6 (Table 2).

wants to market the new hearing aid so that only 10% of the realizations have values below the selected level.

2.32 Made-to-order delivery times. Production processes may be classified as *make-to-stock processes* or *make-to-order processes.* Make-to-stock processes are designed to produce a standardized product that can be sold to customers from the firm's inventory. Make-to-order processes are designed to produce products according to customer specifications (Schroeder, *Operations Management,* 1993). In general, performance of make-to-order processes is measured by delivery time—the time from receipt of an order until the product is delivered to the customer. The following data set is a sample of delivery times (in days) for a particular make-to-order firm last year. The delivery times marked by an asterisk are associated with customers who subsequently placed additional orders with the firm.

Concerned that they are losing potential repeat customers because of long delivery times, the management would like to establish a guideline for the maximum tolerable delivery time. Use a graphical method to help suggest a guideline. Explain your reasoning.

DELTIMES

50*	64*	56*	43*	64*	82*	65*	49*	32*	63*	44*	71
54*	51*	102	49*	73*	50*	39*	86	33*	95	59*	51*
68											

2.3 Summation Notation

Now that we've examined some graphical techniques for summarizing and describing quantitative data sets, we turn to numerical methods for accomplishing this objective. Before giving the formulas for calculating numerical descriptive measures, let's look at some shorthand notation that will simplify our calculation instructions. Remember that such notation is used for one reason only—to avoid repeating the same verbal descriptions over and over. If you mentally substitute the verbal definition of a symbol each time you read it, you'll soon get used to it.

We denote the measurements of a quantitative data set as follows: $x_1, x_2, x_3, \ldots, x_n$ where x_1 is the first measurement in the data set, x_2 is the second measurement in the data set, x_3 is the third measurement in the data set, $\ldots$, and x_n is the nth (and last) measurement in the data set. Thus, if we have five measurements in a set of data, we will write x_1, x_2, x_3, x_4, x_5 to represent the measurements. If the actual numbers are 5, 3, 8, 5, and 4, we have $x_1 = 5$, $x_2 = 3$, $x_3 = 8$, $x_4 = 5$, and $x_5 = 4$.

Most of the formulas we use require a summation of numbers. For example, one sum we'll need to obtain is the sum of all the measurements in the data set, or $x_1 + x_2 + x_3 + \cdots + x_n$. To shorten the notation, we use the symbol Σ for the summation—that is, $x_1 + x_2 + x_3 + \cdots + x_n = \sum_{i=1}^{n} x_i$. Verbally translate $\sum_{i=1}^{n} x_i$ as follows: "The sum of the measurements, whose typical member is x_i, beginning with the member x_1, and ending with the member x_n."

Suppose, as in our earlier example, that $x_1 = 5$, $x_2 = 3$, $x_3 = 8$, $x_4 = 5$, and $x_5 = 4$. Then the sum of the five measurements, denoted $\sum_{i=1}^{n} x_i$, is obtained as follows:

$$\sum_{i=1}^{5} x_i = x_1 + x_2 + x_3 + x_4 + x_5$$

$$= 5 + 3 + 8 + 5 + 4 = 25$$

Another important calculation requires that we square each measurement and then sum the squares. The notation for this sum is $\sum_{i=1}^{n} x_i^2$. For the preceding five measurements, we have

$$\sum_{i=1}^{5} x_i^2 = x_1^2 + x_2^2 + x_3^2 + x_4^2 + x_5^2$$

$$= 5^2 + 3^2 + 8^2 + 5^2 + 4^2$$

$$= 25 + 9 + 64 + 25 + 16 = 139$$

In general, the symbol following the summation sign represents the variable (or function of the variable) that is to be summed.

The Meaning of Summation Notation $\displaystyle\sum_{i=1}^{n} x_i$

Sum the measurements on the variable that appears to the right of the summation symbol, beginning with the 1st measurement and ending with the nth measurement.

Exercises 2.33–2.36

Learning the Mechanics

Note: In all exercises, Σ represents $\displaystyle\sum_{i=1}^{n}$.

2.33 A data set contains the observations 5, 1, 3, 2, 1. Find
  a. Σx **b.** Σx^2 **c.** $\Sigma(x-1)$
  d. $\Sigma(x-1)^2$ **e.** $(\Sigma x)^2$

2.34 Suppose a data set contains the observations 3, 8, 4, 5, 3, 4, 6. Find
  a. Σx **b.** Σx^2 **c.** $\Sigma(x-5)^2$
  d. $\Sigma(x-2)^2$ **e.** $(\Sigma x)^2$

2.35 Refer to Exercise 2.33. Find
  a. $\Sigma x^2 - \dfrac{(\Sigma x)^2}{5}$ **b.** $\Sigma(x-2)^2$ **c.** $\Sigma x^2 - 10$

2.36 A data set contains the observations 6, 0, −2, −1, 3. Find
  a. Σx **b.** Σx^2 **c.** $\Sigma x^2 - \dfrac{(\Sigma x)^2}{5}$

2.4 Numerical Measures of Central Tendency

When we speak of a data set, we refer to either a sample or a population. If statistical inference is our goal, we'll wish ultimately to use sample **numerical descriptive measures** to make inferences about the corresponding measures for the population.

As you'll see, a large number of numerical methods are available to describe quantitative data sets. Most of these methods measure one of two data characteristics:

1. The **central tendency** of the set of measurements—that is, the tendency of the data to cluster, or center, about certain numerical values (see Figure 2.14a).

2. The **variability** of the set of measurements—that is, the spread of the data (see Figure 2.14b).

In this section we concentrate on measures of central tendency. In the next section, we discuss measures of variability.

The most popular and best-understood measure of central tendency for quantitative data set is the arithmetic mean (or simply the mean) of a data set.

Definition 2.4

The **mean** of a set of quantitative data is the sum of the measurements divided by the number of measurements contained in the data set.

In everyday terms, the mean is the average value of the data set and is often used to represent a "typical" value. We denote the **mean of a sample** of measurements by $\bar{x}$ (read "x-bar"), and represent the formula for its calculation as shown in the box.

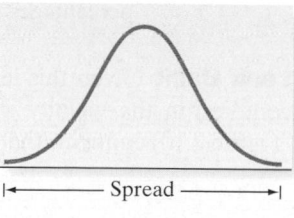

FIGURE 2.14
Numerical descriptive measures

Center
a.

|— Spread —|
b.

Formula for a Sample Mean

$$\bar{x} = \frac{\sum_{i=1}^{n} x_i}{n}$$

EXAMPLE 2.3

Calculating the
Sample Mean

Problem Calculate the mean of the following five sample measurements: 5, 3, 8, 5, 6.

Solution Using the definition of sample mean and the summation notation, we find

$$\bar{x} = \frac{\sum_{i=1}^{5} x_i}{5} = \frac{5 + 3 + 8 + 5 + 6}{5} = \frac{27}{5} = 5.4$$

Thus, the mean of this sample is 5.4.

Look Back There is no specific rule for rounding when calculating $\bar{x}$ because $\bar{x}$ is specifically defined to be the sum of all measurements divided by n—that is, it is a specific fraction. When $\bar{x}$ is used for descriptive purposes, it is often convenient to round the calculated value of $\bar{x}$ to the number of significant figures used for the original measurements. When $\bar{x}$ is to be used in other calculations, however, it may be necessary to retain more significant figures.

Now Work Exercise 2.38

EXAMPLE 2.4

The Sample Mean
on a Printout

Problem Calculate the sample mean for the R&D expenditure percentages of the 50 companies given in Table 2.2.

Solution The mean R&D percentage for the 50 companies is denoted

$$\bar{x} = \frac{\sum_{i=1}^{50} x_i}{50}$$

Rather than compute $\bar{x}$ by hand (or calculator), we employed Excel to compute the mean. The Excel printout is shown in Figure 2.15. The sample mean, highlighted on the printout, is $\bar{x} = 8.492$.

	A	B
1	RDPct	
2		
3	Mean	8.492
4	Standard Error	0.2801
5	Median	8.05
6	Mode	6.9
7	Standard Deviation	1.980604
8	Sample Variance	3.922792
9	Kurtosis	0.419288
10	Skewness	0.854601
11	Range	8.3
12	Minimum	5.2
13	Maximum	13.5
14	Sum	424.6
15	Count	50
16		

FIGURE 2.15

Excel numerical descriptive
measures for 50 R&D
percentages

Look Back Given this information, you can visualize a distribution of R&D percentages centered in the vicinity $\bar{x} = 8.492$. An examination of the relative frequency histogram (Figure 2.10) confirms that $\bar{x}$ does in fact fall near the center of the distribution.

The sample mean $\bar{x}$ will play an important role in accomplishing our objective of making inferences about populations based on sample information. For this reason, we need to use a different symbol for the *mean of a population*—the mean of the set of measurements on every unit in the population. We use the Greek letter μ(mu) for the population mean.

Symbols for the Sample and Population Mean

In this text, we adopt a general policy of using Greek letters to represent population numerical descriptive measures and Roman letters to represent corresponding descriptive measures for the sample. The symbols for the mean are

$$\bar{x} = \text{Sample mean}$$
$$\mu = \text{Population mean}$$

We'll often use the sample mean, $\bar{x}$ to estimate (make an inference about) the population mean, μ. For example, the percentages of revenues spent on R&D by the population consisting of *all* U.S. companies has a mean equal to some value, μ. Our sample of 50 companies yielded percentages with a mean of $\bar{x} = 8.492$. If, as is usually the case, we don't have access to the measurements for the entire population, we could use $\bar{x}$ as an estimator or approximator for μ. Then we'd need to know something about the reliability of our inference—that is, we'd need to know how accurately we might expect $\bar{x}$ to estimate μ. In Chapter 5, we'll find that this accuracy depends on two factors:

1. The *size of the sample*. The larger the sample, the more accurate the estimate will tend to be.

2. The *variability*, or *spread, of the data*. All other factors remaining constant, the more variable the data, the less accurate the estimate.

Another important measure of central tendency is the *median*.

Definition 2.5

The **median** of a quantitative data set is the middle number when the measurements are arranged in ascending (or descending) order.

The median is of most value in describing large data sets. If the data set is characterized by a relative frequency histogram (Figure 2.16), the median is the point on the x-axis such that half the area under the histogram lies above the median and half lies below. [*Note:* In Section 2.2 we observed that the relative frequency associated with a particular interval on the horizontal axis is proportional to the amount of area under the histogram that lies above the interval.] We denote the *median of a sample* by m.

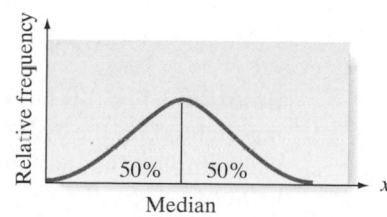

FIGURE 2.16
Location of the median

> **Calculating a Sample Median, m**
>
> Arrange the n measurements from smallest to largest.
>
> 1. If n is odd, m is the middle number.
> 2. If n is even, m is the mean of the middle two numbers.

EXAMPLE 2.5

Finding the Median

Problem Consider the following sample of $n = 7$ measurements: 5, 7, 4, 5, 20, 6, 2.

a. Calculate the median m of this sample.

b. Eliminate the last measurement (the 2) and calculate the median of the remaining $n = 6$ measurements.

Solution

a. The seven measurements in the sample are ranked in ascending order: 2, 4, 5, 5, 6, 7, 20. Because the number of measurements is odd, the median is the middle measurement. Thus, the median of this sample is $m = 5$ (the second 5 listed in the sequence).

b. After removing the 2 from the set of measurements, we rank the sample measurements in ascending order as follows: 4, 5, 5, 6, 7, 20.

Now the number of measurements is even, so we average the middle two measurements. The median is $m = (5 + 6)/2 = 5.5$.

Look Back When the sample size n is even and the two middle numbers are different (as in part **b**), exactly half of the measurements will fall below the calculated median m. However, when n is odd (as in part **a**), the percentage of measurements that fall below m is approximately 50%. This approximation improves as n increases.

Now Work Exercise 2.37

In certain situations, the median may be a better measure of central tendency than the mean. In particular, the median is less sensitive than the mean to extremely large or small measurements. Note, for instance, that all but one of the measurements in part **a** of Example 2.5 center about $x = 5$. The single relatively large measurement, $x = 20$, does not affect the value of the median, 5, but it causes the mean, $\bar{x} = 7$, to lie to the right of most of the measurements.

As another example of data for which the central tendency is better described by the median than the mean, consider the salaries of professional athletes (e.g., National Basketball Association players). The presence of just a few athletes (e.g., Labron James) with extremely high salaries will affect the mean more than the median. Thus, the median will provide a more accurate picture of the typical salary for the professional league. The mean could exceed the vast majority of the sample measurements (salaries), making it a misleading measure of central tendency.

EXAMPLE 2.6

The Median
on a Printout

Problem Calculate the median for the 50 R&D percentages given in Table 2.2. Compare the median to the mean found in Example 2.4.

Solution For this large data set, we again resort to a computer analysis. The median is highlighted on the Excel printout, Figure 2.15. You can see that the median is 8.05. This value implies that half of the 50 R&D percentages in the data set fall below 8.05 and half lie above 8.05.

Note that the mean (8.492) for these data is larger than the median. This fact indicates that the data are **skewed** to the right—that is, there are more extreme measurements in the right tail of the distribution than in the left tail (recall the histogram in Figure 2.10).

Look Back In general, extreme values (large or small) affect the mean more than the median since these values are used explicitly in the calculation of the mean. On the other hand, the median is not affected directly by extreme measurements since only the middle measurement (or two middle measurements) is explicitly used to calculate the median. Consequently, if measurements are pulled toward one end of the distribution (as with the R&D percentages), the mean will shift toward that tail more than the median.

Definition 2.6

A data set is said to be **skewed** if one tail of the distribution has more extreme observations than the other tail.

A comparison of the mean and median gives us a general method for detecting skewness in data sets, as shown in the next box.

Detecting Skewness by Comparing the Mean and the Median

If the data set is skewed to the right, then the median is less than the mean.

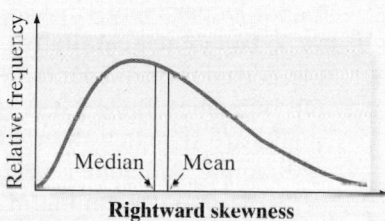

Rightward skewness

If the data set is symmetric, the mean equals the median.

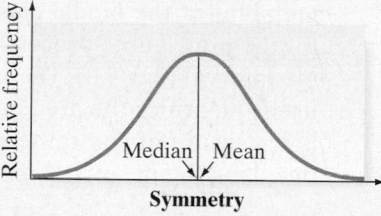

Symmetry

If the data set is skewed to the left, the mean is less than (to the left of) the median.

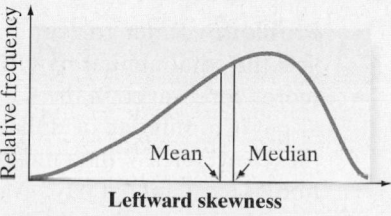

Leftward skewness

Now Work Exercise 2.43

A third measure of central tendency is the *mode* of a set of measurements.

> **Definition 2.7**
> The **mode** is the measurement that occurs most frequently in the data set.

EXAMPLE 2.7

Finding the Mode

Problem Each of 10 taste testers rated a new brand of barbecue sauce on a 10-point scale, where 1 = awful and 10 = excellent. Find the mode for the 10 = ratings shown below.

$$8 \quad 7 \quad 9 \quad 6 \quad 8 \quad 10 \quad 9 \quad 9 \quad 5 \quad 7$$

Solution Since 9 occurs most often, the mode of the 10 taste ratings is 9.

Look Back Note that the data are actually qualitative in nature (e.g., "awful," "excellent"). The mode is particularly useful for describing qualitative data. The modal category is simply the category (or class) that occurs most often.

Now Work Exercise 2.41

Because it emphasizes data concentration, the mode is used with quantitative data sets to locate the region in which much of the data is concentrated. A retailer of men's clothing would be interested in the modal neck size and sleeve length of potential customers. The modal income class of the laborers in the United States is of interest to the Labor Department.

For some quantitative data sets, the mode may not be very meaningful. For example, consider the percentages of revenues spent on research and development (R&D) by 50 companies, Table 2.2. A reexamination of the data reveals that three of the measurements are repeated three times: 6.5%, 6.9%, and 8.2%. Thus, there are three modes in the sample, and none is particularly useful as a measure of central tendency.

A more meaningful measure can be obtained from a relative frequency histogram for quantitative data. The class interval containing the largest relative frequency is called the **modal class.** Several definitions exist for locating the position of the mode within a modal class, but the simplest is to define the mode as the midpoint of the modal class. For example, examine the relative frequency histogram for the price quote processing times in Figure 2.12. You can see that the modal class is the interval (3.0–4.0). The mode (the midpoint) is 3.5. This modal class (and the mode itself) identifies the area in which the data are most concentrated, and in that sense it is a measure of central tendency. However, for most applications involving quantitative data, the mean and median provide more descriptive information than the mode.

EXAMPLE 2.8

Comparing the Mean, Median, and Mode of CEO Salaries

 CEOPAY05

Problem Refer to *Forbes* magazine's "Executive Compensation Scoreboard," which lists the total annual pay for CEOs at the 500 largest U.S. firms. The data for the 2005 scoreboard, saved in the **CEOPAY05** file, includes the quantitative variables total annual pay (in millions of dollars) and age. Find the mean, median, and mode for both of these variables. Which measure of central tendency is better for describing the distribution of total annual pay? Age?

Solution Measures of central tendency for the two variables were obtained using SPSS. The means, medians, and modes are displayed at the top of the SPSS printout, Figure 2.17.

Statistics

		PAY2005	AGE
N	Valid	497	500
	Missing	3	0
Mean		10.93027	55.63
Median		5.54000	56.00
Mode		1.000ᵃ	57ᵃ

a. Multiple modes exist. The smallest value is shown

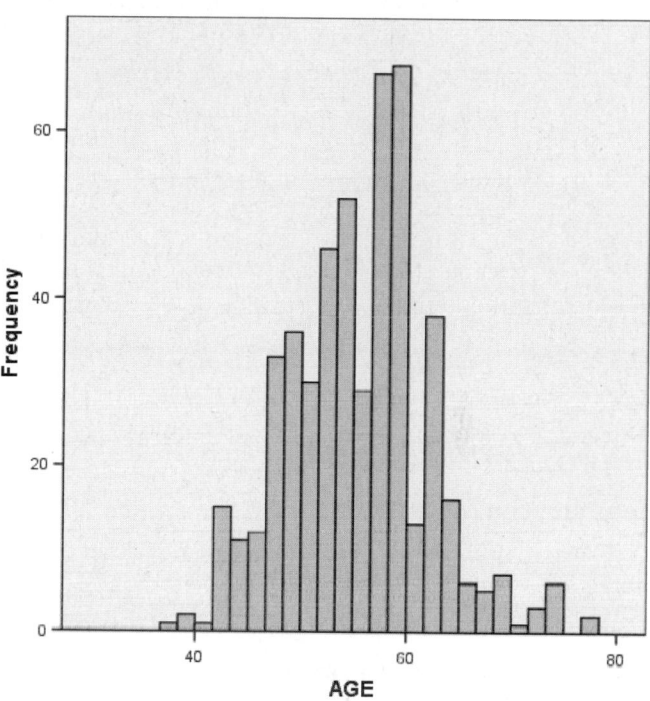

FIGURE 2.17

SPSS Analysis of total 2005 pay and age for CEOs in Executive Compensation Scoreboard

For total annual pay, the mean, median, and mode are $10.93 million, $5.54 million, and $1 million, respectively. Note that the mean is much greater than the median, indicating that the data is highly skewed right. This rightward skewness (graphically shown on the histogram for total pay in Figure 2.17) is due to several exceptionally high CEO salaries in 2005. Consequently, we would probably want to use the median, $5.54 million, as the "typical" value for annual pay for CEOs at the 500 largest firms. The mode of $1 million is the total pay value that occurs most often in the data set, but it is not very descriptive of the "center" of the total annual pay distribution.

For age, the mean, median, and mode are 55.63, 56, and 57 years, respectively. All three values are nearly the same, which is typical of symmetric distributions. From the age histogram to the right in Figure 2.17, you can see that the age distribution is nearly symmetric. Consequently, any of the three measures of central tendency could be used to describe the "middle" of the age distribution.

Look Back The choice of which measure of central tendency to use will depend on the properties of the data set analyzed and on the application. Consequently, it is vital that you understand how the mean, median, and mode are computed.

Now Work Exercise 2.46a,b

ACTIVITY 2.1: *Real Estate Sales:* **Measures of Central Tendency**

In recent years, the price of real estate in America's major metropolitan areas has skyrocketed. Newspapers usually report recent real estate sales data in their Saturday editions, both hard copies and online. This data usually includes the actual prices paid for homes by geographical location during a certain time period, usually a one-week period six to eight weeks earlier, and some summary statistics, which might include comparisons to real estate sales data in other geographical locations or during other time periods.

1. Locate the real estate sales data in a newspaper for a major metropolitan area. From the information given, identify the time period during which the homes listed were sold. Then describe the way the sales prices are organized. Are they categorized by type of home (single family or condominium), by neighborhood or address, by sales price, etc.?

2. What summary statistics and comparisons are provided with the sales data? Describe several groups of people who might be interested in this data and how each of the summary statistics and comparisons would be helpful to them. Why are the measures of central tendency listed more useful in the real estate market than other measures of central tendency?

3. Based on the lowest and highest sales prices represented in the data, create ten intervals of equal size and use these intervals to create a relative frequency histogram for the sales data. Describe the shape of the histogram and explain how the summary statistics provided with the data are illustrated in the histogram. Based on the histogram, describe the "typical" home price.

Exercises 2.37–2.54

Learning the Mechanics

2.37 Calculate the mean and median of the following grade
NW point averages:

$$3.2 \quad 2.5 \quad 2.1 \quad 3.7 \quad 2.8 \quad 2.0$$

2.38 Calculate the mean for samples where
NW   **a.** $n = 10, \Sigma x = 85$
  b. $n = 16, \Sigma x = 400$
  c. $n = 45, \Sigma x = 35$
  d. $n = 18, \Sigma x = 242$

2.39 Explain how the relationship between the mean and median provides information about the symmetry or skewness of the data's distribution.

2.40 Explain the difference between the calculation of the median for an odd and an even number of measurements. Construct one data set consisting of five measurements and another consisting of six measurements for which the medians are equal.

2.41 Calculate the mode, mean, and median of the following
NW data:

$$18 \quad 10 \quad 15 \quad 13 \quad 17 \quad 15 \quad 12 \quad 15 \quad 18 \quad 16 \quad 11$$

2.42 Calculate the mean, median, and mode for each of the following samples:
  a. $7, -2, 3, 3, 0, 4$
  b. $2, 3, 5, 3, 2, 3, 4, 3, 5, 1, 2, 3, 4$
  c. $51, 50, 47, 50, 48, 41, 59, 68, 45, 37$

APPLET **Applet Exercise 2.1**

Use the applet entitled *Mean versus Median* to find the mean and median of each of the three data sets in Exercise 2.42. For each data set, set the lower limit to a number less than all of the

data, set the upper limit to a number greater than all of the data, and then click on *Update*. Click on the approximate location of each data item on the number line. You can get rid of a point by dragging it to the trash can. To clear the graph between data sets, simply click on the trash can.
  a. Compare the means and medians generated by the applet to those you calculated by hand in Exercise 2.42. If there are differences, explain why the applet might give values slightly different from the hand calculations.
  b. Despite providing only approximate values of the mean and median of a data set, describe some advantages of using the applet to find these values.

2.43 Describe how the mean compares to the median for a dis-
NW tribution as follows:
  a. Skewed to the left
  b. Skewed to the right
  c. Symmetric

APPLET **Applet Exercise 2.2**

Use the applet *Mean versus Median* to illustrate your descriptions in Exercise 2.43. For each part **a, b,** and **c,** create a data set with ten items that has the given property. Using the applet, verify that the mean and median have the relationship you described in Exercise 2.43.

APPLET **Applet Exercise 2.3**

Use the applet *Mean versus Median* to study the effect that an extreme value has on the difference between the mean and median. Begin by setting appropriate limits and plotting the given data on the number line provided in the applet.

$$0 \quad 6 \quad 7 \quad 7 \quad 8 \quad 8 \quad 8 \quad 9 \quad 9 \quad 10$$

  a. Describe the shape of the distribution and record the value of the mean and median. Based on the shape of the distrib-

One-Variable Descriptive Statistics

Using the TI-83/TI-84 Graphing Calculator

Step 1 *Enter the data*

Press STAT and select 1:Edit
Note: If the list already contains data, clear the old data. Use the up arrow to highlight "L1". Press CLEAR ENTER.
Use the arrow and ENTER keys to enter the data set into L1.

Step 2 *Calculate descriptive statistics*

Press STAT
Press the right arrow key to highlight CALC

Press ENTER for 1-Var Stats
Enter the name of the list containing your data.
Press 2nd 1 for L1 (or 2nd 2 for L2, etc.)
Press ENTER

You should see the statistics on your screen. Some of the statistics are off the bottom of the screen. Use the down arrow to scroll through to see the remaining statistics. Use the up arrow to scroll back up.

Example The descriptive statistics for the sample data set

86, 70, 62, 98, 73, 56, 53, 92, 86, 37, 62, 83, 78, 49, 78, 37, 67, 79, 57

The output screens for this example are shown below.

Sorting Data

The descriptive statistics do not include the mode. To find the mode, sort your data as follows:

Press STAT
Press 2 for SORTA(
Enter the name of the list your data is in. If your data is in L1, press 2nd 1

Press ENTER
The screen will say: DONE
To see the sorted data, press STAT and select 1:Edit
Scroll down through the list and locate the data value that occurs most frequently.

---

ution, do the mean and median have the relationship that you would expect?

b. Replace the extreme value of 0 with 2, then 4, and then 6. Record the mean and median each time. Describe what is happening to the mean as 0 is replaced by higher numbers. What is happening to the median? How is the difference between the mean and the median changing?

c. Now replace 0 with 8. What values does the applet give you for the mean and the median? Explain why the mean and the median should be the same.

Applying the Concepts—Basic

2.44 Top Florida law firms. Data on the top-ranked law firms in Florida, obtained from *Florida Trend* magazine (April 2002), are provided in the table on page 72.

a. Find the mean, median, and mode for the number of lawyers at the top-ranked Florida law firms. Interpret these values.

b. Find the mean, median, and mode for the number of offices open by top-ranked Florida law firms. Interpret these values.

FLALAW

Rank	Firm	Headquarters	Number of Lawyers	Number of Offices
1	Holland & Knight	Tallahassee	529	11
2	Akerman Senterfit	Orlando	355	9
3	Greenberg Traurig	Miami	301	6
4	Carlton Fields	Tampa	207	6
5	Gruden McClosky Smit	Ft. Lauder	175	9
6	Fowler White Boggs	Tampa	175	7
7	Foley & Lardner	Orlando	159	5
8	GrayHarris	Orlando	158	6
9	Broad and Cassel	Orlando	150	7
10	Shutts & Bowen	Miami	144	5
11	Steel Hector & Davis	Miami	141	5
12	Gunster Yoakley	WPalmBeach	140	6
13	Adorno & Zeder	Miami	105	4
14	Becker & Poliakoff	Ft. Lauder	100	12
15	Lowndes Drosdick	Orlando	100	1
16	Conroy Simberg Ganon	Hollywood	91	6
17	Stearns Weaver	Miami	85	3
18	Wicker Smith O'Hara	Miami	85	6
19	Rogers Towers Bailey	Jacksonville	80	2
20	Butler Burnette	Tampa	77	3
21	Bilzin Sumberg Dunn	Miami	70	1
22	Morgan Colling	Orlando	70	4
23	White & Case	Miami	70	1
24	Fowler White Burnett	Miami	64	4
25	Rissman Weisberg	Orlando	63	3
26	Rumberger Kirk	Orlando	63	4

Source: Florida Trend magazine, April 2002, p. 105.

2.45 Most powerful women in America. *Fortune* (Nov. 14, 2005) published a list of the 50 most powerful women in America. The data on age (in years) and title of each of these 50 women are stored in the **WPOWER50** file. The first five and last two observations of the data are listed in the table below.

a. Find the mean, median, and modal age of these 50 women.

b. What do the mean and median indicate about the skewness of the age distribution?

c. Construct a relative frequency histogram for the age data. What is the modal age class?

WPOWER50

Rank	Name	Age	Company	Title
1	Meg Whitman	49	eBay	CEO/chairman
2	Anne Mulcahy	52	Xerox	CEO/chairman
3	Brenda Barnes	51	Sara Lee	CEO/president
4	Oprah Winfrey	51	Harpo	Chairman
5	Andrea Jung	47	Avon	CEO/chairman
.	.	.		
.	.	.		
49	Safra Catz	43	Oracle	President
50	Kathy Cassidy	51	General Electric	Treasurer

Source: Fortune, Nov. 14, 2005.

2.46 Surface roughness of oil field pipe. Oil field pipes are internally coated in order to prevent corrosion. Researchers at the University of Louisiana, Lafayette, investigated the influence that coating may have on the surface roughness of oil field pipes (*Anti-corrosion Methods and Materials,* Vol. 50, 2003). A scanning probe instrument was used to measure the surface roughness of each in a sample of 20 sections of coated interior pipe. The data (in micrometers) is provided in the table.

ROUGHPIPE

1.72	2.50	2.16	2.13	1.06	2.24	2.31	2.03	1.09	1.40
2.57	2.64	1.26	2.05	1.19	2.13	1.27	1.51	2.41	1.95

Source: Farshad, F., and Pesacreta, T. "Coated Pipe Interior Surface Roughness as Measured by Three Scanning Probe Instruments." *Anti-corrosion Methods and Materials,* Vol. 50, No. 1, 2003 (Table III).

NW a. Find and interpret the mean of the sample.

NW b. Find and interpret the median of the sample.

c. Which measure of central tendency—the mean or the median—best describes the surface roughness of the sampled pipe sections? Explain.

DIAMONDS

2.47 Size of diamonds sold at retail. Refer to Exercise 2.25 (p. 59) and the *Journal of Statistics Education* data on diamonds saved in the **DIAMONDS** file. Consider the quantitative variable, number of carats, recorded for each of the 308 diamonds for sale on the open market.

a. Find and interpret the mean of the data set.

b. Find and interpret the median of the data set.

c. Find and interpret the mode of the data set.

d. Which measure of central tendency best describes the 308 carat values? Explain.

Applying the Concepts—Intermediate

2.48 Efficacy of Chinese herbal drugs. Platelet-activating factor (PAF) is a potent chemical that occurs in patients suffering from shock, inflammation, hypotension, and allergic responses as well as respiratory and cardiovascular disorders. Consequently, drugs that effectively inhibit PAF, keeping it from binding to human cells, may be successful in treating these disorders. A bioassay was undertaken to investigate the potential of 17 traditional Chinese herbal drugs in PAF inhibition (H. Guiqui, *Progress in Natural Science,* June 1995). The prevention of the PAF binding process, measured as a percentage, for each drug is provided in the accompanying table.

DRUGPAF

Drug	PAF Inhibition (%)
Hai-feng-teng (Fuji)	77
Hai-feng-teng (Japan)	33
Shan-ju	75
Zhang-yiz-hu-jiao	62
Shi-nan-teng	70
Huang-hua-hu-jiao	12
Hua-nan-hu-jiao	0
Xiao-yie-pa-ai-xiang	0
Mao-ju	0
Jia-ju	15
Xie-yie-ju	25
Da-yie-ju	0
Bian-yie-hu-jiao	9
Bi-bo	24
Duo-mai-hu-jiao	40
Yan-sen	0
Jiao-guo-hu-jiao	31

Source: Guiqui, H. "PAF Receptor Antagonistic Principles from Chinese Traditional Drugs." *Progress in Natural Science,* Vol. 5, No. 3, June 1995, p. 301 (Table 1).

a. Construct a stem-and-leaf display for the data.

b. Compute the median inhibition percentage for the 17 herbal drugs. Interpret the result.

c. Compute the mean inhibition percentage for the 17 herbal drugs. Interpret the result.

d. Compute the mode of the 17 inhibition percentages. Interpret the result.

e. Locate the median, mean, and mode on the stem-and-leaf display, part **a.** Do these measures of central tendency appear to locate the center of the data?

2.49 Semester hours taken by CPA candidates. In order to become a certified public accountant (CPA), you must pass the Uniform CPA Exam. Many states require a minimum of 150 semester hours of college education before a candidate can sit for the CPA exam. However, traditionally, colleges only require 128 semester hours for an undergraduate degree. A study of whether the "extra" 22 hours of college credit is warranted for CPA candidates was published in the *Journal of Accounting and Public Policy* (Spring 2002). For one aspect of the study, researchers sampled over 100,000 first-time candidates for the CPA exam and recorded the total semester hours of college credit for each candidate. The mean and median for the data set were 141.31 and 140 hours, respectively. Interpret these values. Make a statement about the type of skewness, if any, that exists in the distribution of total semester hours.

DDT

2.50 Fish contaminated by a plant's toxic discharge. Refer to Exercise 2.24 (p. 59) and the U.S. Army Corps of Engineers data on contaminated fish saved in the **DDT** file. Consider the quantitative variables length (in centimeters), weight (in grams), and DDT level (in parts per million).

a. Find three numerical measures of central tendency for the 144 fish lengths. Interpret these values.

b. Find three numerical measures of central tendency for the 144 fish weights. Interpret these values

c. Find three numerical measures of central tendency for the 144 DDT measurements. Interpret these values.

d. Use the results, part **a,** and the graph of the data from Exercise 2.24a to make a statement about the type of skewness in the fish length distribution.

e. Use the results, part **b,** and the graph of the data from Exercise 2.22b to make a statement about the type of skewness in the fish weight distribution.

f. Use the results, part **c,** and the graph of the data from Exercise 2.22c to make a statement about the type of skewness in the fish DDT distribution.

2.51 Symmetric or skewed? Would you expect the data sets described below to possess relative frequency distributions that are symmetric, skewed to the right, or skewed to the left? Explain.

a. The salaries of all persons employed by a large university

b. The grades on an easy test

c. The grades on a difficult test

d. The amounts of time students in your class studied last week

e. The ages of automobiles on a used-car lot

f. The amounts of time spent by students on a difficult examination (maximum time is 50 minutes)

2.52 Professional athletes' salaries. The salaries of superstar professional athletes receive much attention in the media. The multimillion-dollar long-term contract is now commonplace among this elite group. Nevertheless, rarely does a season pass without negotiations between one or more of the players' associations and team owners for additional salary and fringe benefits for *all* players in their particular sports.

a. If a players' association wanted to support its argument for higher "average" salaries, which measure of central tendency do you think it should use? Why?

b. To refute the argument, which measure of central tendency should the owners apply to the players' salaries? Why?

Applying the Concepts—Advanced

2.53 Time in bankruptcy. Refer to the *Financial Management* (Spring 1995) study of prepackaged bankruptcy filings, Exercise 2.30 (p. 61). Recall that each of 49 firms that negotiated a reorganization plan with its creditors prior to filing for bankruptcy was classified in one of three categories: joint exchange offer with prepack, prepack solicitation only, and no prefiling vote held. Consider the quantitative variable length of time in bankruptcy (months). Is it reasonable to use a single number (e.g., mean or median) to describe the center of the time-in-bankruptcy distributions? Or should three "centers" be calculated, one for each of the three categories of prepack firms? Explain.

2.54 Active nuclear power plants. The U.S. Energy Information Administration monitors all nuclear power plants operating in the United States. The table on the next page lists the number of active nuclear power plants operating in each of a sample of 20 states.

a. Find the mean, median, and mode of this data set.

b. Eliminate the largest value from the data set and repeat part **a.** What effect does dropping this measurement have on the measures of central tendency found in part **a**?

c. Arrange the 20 values in the table from lowest to highest. Next, eliminate the lowest two values and the highest two values from the data set and find the mean of the remaining data values. The result is called a *10% trimmed mean*, since it is calculated after removing the highest 10% and the lowest 10% of the data values. What advantages does a trimmed mean have over the regular arithmetic mean?

NUCLEAR

State	Number of Power Plants	State	Number of Power Plants
Alabama	5	New Hampshire	1
Arizona	3	New York	6
California	4	North Carolina	5
Florida	5	Ohio	2
Georgia	4	Pennsylvania	9
Illinois	13	South Carolina	7
Kansas	1	Tennessee	3
Louisiana	2	Texas	4
Massachusetts	1	Vermont	1
Mississippi	1	Wisconsin	3

Source: Statistical Abstract of the United States, 2000 (Table 966). U.S. Energy Information Administration, Electric Power Annual.

2.5 Numerical Measures of Variability

Measures of central tendency provide only a partial description of a quantitative data set. The description is incomplete without a **measure of the variability,** or **spread,** of the data set. Knowledge of the data's variability along with its center can help us visualize the shape of a data set as well as its extreme values.

For example, suppose we are comparing the profit margin per construction job (as a percentage of the total bid price) for 100 construction jobs for each of two cost estimators working for a large construction company. The histograms for the two sets of 100 profit margin measurements are shown in Figure 2.18. If you examine the two histograms, you will notice that both data sets are symmetric with equal modes, medians, and means. However, cost estimator A (Figure 2.18a) has profit margins spread with almost equal relative frequency over the measurement classes, while cost estimator B (Figure 2.18b) has profit margins clustered about the center of the distribution. Thus, estimator B's profit margins are *less variable* than estimator A's. Consequently, you can see that we need a measure of variability as well as a measure of central tendency to describe a data set.

Perhaps the simplest measure of the variability of a quantitative data set is its *range*.

Definition 2.8
The **range** of a quantitative data set is equal to the largest measurement minus the smallest measurement.

a. Cost estimator A

b. Cost estimator B

FIGURE 2.18
Profit margin histograms for two cost estimators

TABLE 2.5 Two Hypothetical Data Sets

	Sample 1	Sample 2
Measurements	1, 2, 3, 4, 5	2, 3, 3, 3, 4
Mean	$\bar{x} = \dfrac{1 + 2 + 3 + 4 + 5}{5} = \dfrac{15}{5} = 3$	$\bar{x} = \dfrac{2 + 3 + 3 + 3 + 4}{5} = \dfrac{15}{5} = 3$
Deviations of measurement values from $\bar{x}$	$(1 - 3), (2 - 3), (3 - 3), (4 - 3),$ $(5 - 3)$, or $-2, -1, 0, 1, 2$	$(2 - 3), (3 - 3), (3 - 3), (3 - 3), (3 - 3),$ $(4 - 3)$, or $-1, 0, 0, 1$

The range is easy to compute and easy to understand, but it is a rather insensitive measure of data variation when the data sets are large. This is because two data sets can have the same range and be vastly different with respect to data variation. This phenomenon is demonstrated in Figure 2.18. Although the ranges are equal and all central tendency measures are the same for these two symmetric data sets, there is an obvious difference between the two sets of measurements. The difference is that estimator B's profit margins tend to be more stable—that is, to pile up or to cluster about the center of the data set. In contrast estimator A's profit margins are more spread out over the range, indicating a higher incidence of some high profit margins, but also a greater risk of losses. Thus, even though the ranges are equal, the profit margin record of estimator A is more variable than that of estimator B, indicating a distinct difference in their cost-estimating characteristics.

Let's see if we can find a measure of data variation that is more sensitive than the range. Consider the two samples in Table 2.5: Each has five measurements. (We have ordered the numbers for convenience.)

Note that both samples have a mean of 3 and that we have also calculated the distance and direction, or *deviation*, between each measurement and the mean. What information do these deviations contain? If they tend to be large in magnitude, as in sample 1, the data are spread out, or highly variable. If the deviations are mostly small, as in sample 2, the data are clustered around the mean, $\bar{x}$, and therefore do not exhibit much variability. You can see that these deviations, displayed graphically in Figure 2.19, provide information about the variability of the sample measurements.

The next step is to condense the information in these deviations into a single numerical measure of variability. Averaging the deviations from $\bar{x}$ won't help because the negative and positive deviations cancel; that is, the sum of the deviations (and thus the average deviation) is always equal to zero.

Two methods come to mind for dealing with the fact that positive and negative deviations from the mean cancel. The first is to treat all the deviations as though they were positive, ignoring the sign of the negative deviations. We won't pursue this line of thought because the resulting measure of variability (the mean of the absolute values of the deviations) presents analytical difficulties beyond the scope of this text. A second method of eliminating the minus signs associated with the deviations is to square them. The quantity we can calculate from the squared deviations will provide a meaningful description of the variability of a data set and presents fewer analytical difficulties in inference making.

To use the squared deviations calculated from a data set, we first calculate the *sample variance*.

FIGURE 2.19
Dots plots for two data sets

Definition 2.9

The **sample variance** for a sample of n measurements is equal to the sum of the squared deviations from the mean divided by $(n-1)$. In symbols, using s^2 to represent the sample variance,

$$s^2 = \frac{\sum_{i=1}^{n}(x_i - \bar{x})^2}{n-1}$$

Note: A shortcut formula for calculating s^2 is

$$s^2 = \frac{\sum_{i=1}^{n} x_i^2 - \frac{\left(\sum_{i=1}^{n} x_i\right)^2}{n}}{n-1}$$

Referring to the two samples in Table 2.5, you can calculate the variance for sample 1 as follows:

$$s^2 = \frac{(1-3)^2 + (2-3)^2 + (3-3)^2 + (4-3)^2 + (5-3)^2}{5-1}$$

$$= \frac{4+1+0+1+4}{4} = 2.5$$

The second step in finding a meaningful measure of data variability is to calculate the *standard deviation* of the data set.

Definition 2.10

The **sample standard deviation,** s, is defined as the positive square root of the sample variance, s^2. Thus, $s = \sqrt{s^2}$.

The population variance, denoted by the symbol σ^2 (sigma squared), is the average of the squared distances of the measurements on *all* units in the population from the mean, μ, and σ (sigma) is the square root of this quantity. Since we never really compute σ^2 or σ from the population (the object of sampling is to the avoid this costly procedure), we simply denote these two quantities by their respective symbols.

Symbols for Variance and Standard Deviation

s^2 = Sample variance

s = Sample standard deviation

σ^2 = Population variance

σ = Population standard deviation

Notice that, unlike the variance, the standard deviation is expressed in the original units of measurement. For example, if the original measurements are in dollars, the variance is expressed in the peculiar units "dollar squared," but the standard deviation is expressed in dollars.

You may wonder why we use the divisor $(n-1)$ instead of n when calculating the sample variance. Wouldn't using n be more logical so that the sample variance would be the average squared deviation from the mean? The trouble is using n tends to produce an underestimate of the population variance, σ^2, so we use $(n-1)$ in the denominator to provide the appropriate correction for this tendency.* Since sample statistics such as s^2 are primarily used to estimate population parameters such as σ^2, $(n-1)$ is preferred to n when defining the sample variance.

EXAMPLE 2.9
Computing Measures of Variation

Problem Calculate the variance and standard deviation of the following sample: 2, 3, 3, 3, 4.

Solution If you calculate the values of s and s^2 by hand, it is advantageous to use the shortcut formula provided in Definition 2.8. To do this, we need two summations: Σx and Σx^2. These can easily be obtained from the following type of tabulation:

x	x^2
2	4
3	9
3	9
3	9
4	16
$\Sigma x = 15$	$\Sigma x^2 = 47$

Then we use†

$$s^2 = \frac{\sum_{i=1}^{n} x_i^2 - \frac{\left(\sum_{i=1}^{n} x_i\right)^2}{n}}{n-1} = \frac{47 - \frac{(15)^2}{5}}{5-1} = \frac{2}{4} = .5$$

$$s = \sqrt{.5} = .71$$

Look Back As the sample size n increases, these calculations can become very tedious. As the next example shows, we can use the computer to find s^2 and s.

Now Work Exercise 2.57

	A	B
1	RDPct	
2		
3	Mean	8.492
4	Standard Error	0.2801
5	Median	8.05
6	Mode	6.9
7	Standard Deviation	1.980604
8	Sample Variance	3.922792
9	Kurtosis	0.419288
10	Skewness	0.854601
11	Range	8.3
12	Minimum	5.2
13	Maximum	13.5
14	Sum	424.6
15	Count	50
16		

FIGURE 2.20

Reproduction of Excel numerical descriptive measures for 50 R&D percentages

EXAMPLE 2.10
Measures of Variation on the Computer

Problem Use the computer to find the sample variance s^2 and the sample standard deviation s for the 50 companies' percentages of revenues spent on R&D.

Solution The Excel printout describing the R&D percentage data is reproduced in Figure 2.20. The variance and standard deviation, highlighted on the printout, are $s^2 = 3.922792$ and $s = 1.980604$.

You now know that the standard deviation measures the variability of a set of data. The larger the standard deviation, the more variable the data. The smaller the standard deviation, the less variable the data. But how can we practically interpret the standard deviation and use it to make inferences? This is the topic of Section 2.6.

---

*Appropriate here means that s^2 with the divisor $(n-1)$ is an *unbiased estimator* of σ^2. We define and discuss *unbiasedness* of estimators in Chapter 4.
†When calculating s^2 how many decimal places should you carry? Although there are no rules for the rounding procedure, it's reasonable to retain twice as many decimal places in s^2 as you ultimately wish to have in s. If you wish to calculate s^2 to the nearest hundredth (two decimal places), for example, you should calculate s^2 to the nearest ten-thousandth (four decimal places).

ACTIVITY 2.2: *Keep the Change:* Measures of Central Tendency and Variability

In this activity, we continue our study of the Bank of America *Keep the Change* savings program by looking at the measures of central tendency and variability for the three data sets collected in Activity 1.1 (p. 16).

1. Before performing any calculations, explain why you would expect greater variability in the data set *Purchase Totals* than in *Amounts Transferred.* Then find the mean and median of each of these two data sets. Are the mean and median essentially the same for either of these sets? If so, which one? Can you offer an explanation for these results?

2. Make a histogram for each of the data sets *Amounts Transferred* and *Bank Matching.* Describe any properties of the data that are evident in the histograms. Explain why it is more likely that *Bank Matching* is skewed to the right than *Amounts Transferred.* Based on your data and histogram,

how concerned does Bank of America need to be about matching the maximum amount of $250 for its customers who are college students?

3. Form a fourth data set *Mean Amounts Transferred* by collecting the mean of the data set *Amounts Transferred* for each student in your class. Before performing any calculations, inspect the new data and describe any trends that you notice. Then find the mean and standard deviation of *Mean Amounts Transferred.* How close is the mean to $0.50? Without performing further calculations, determine whether the standard deviation of *Amounts Transferred* is less than or greater than the standard deviation of *Mean Amounts Transferred.* Explain.

Keep your results from this activity for use in other activities.

Exercises 2.55–2.68

Learning the Mechanics

2.55 Answer the following questions about variability of data sets:
   a. What is the primary disadvantage of using the range to compare the variability of data sets?
   b. Describe the sample variance using words rather than a formula. Do the same with the population variance.
   c. Can the variance of a data set ever be negative? Explain. Can the variance ever be smaller than the standard deviation? Explain.

2.56 Calculate the variance and standard deviation for samples where
   a. $n = 10$, $\Sigma x^2 = 84$, $\Sigma x = 20$
   b. $n = 40$, $\Sigma x^2 = 380$, $\Sigma x = 100$
   c. $n = 20$, $\Sigma x^2 = 18$, $\Sigma x = 17$

2.57 Calculate the range, variance, and standard deviation for
NW the following samples:
   a. $4, 2, 1, 0, 1$
   b. $1, 6, 2, 2, 3, 0, 3$
   c. $8, -2, 1, 3, 5, 4, 4, 1, 3, 3$
   d. $0.2, 0, 0, -1, 1, -2, 1, 0, -1, 1, -1, 0, -3, -2, -1, 0, 1$

APPLET Applet Exercise 2.4

Use the applet entitled *Standard Deviation* to find the standard deviation of each of the four data sets in Exercise 2.57. For each data set, set the lower limit to a number less than all of the data, set the upper limit to a number greater than all of the data, and then click on *Update.* Click on the approximate location of each data item on the number line. You can get rid of a point by dragging it to the trash can. To clear the graph between data sets, simply click on the trash can.
   a. Compare the standard deviations generated by the applet to those you calculated by hand in Exercise 2.57. If there are differences, explain why the applet might give values slightly different from the hand calculations.

   b. Despite providing a slightly different value of the standard deviation of a data set, describe some advantages of using the applet.

2.58 Calculate the range, variance, and standard deviation for the following samples:
   a. $39, 42, 40, 37, 41$
   b. $100, 4, 7, 96, 80, 3, 1, 10, 2$
   c. $100, 4, 7, 30, 80, 30, 42, 2$

2.59 Compute $\bar{x}$, s^2, and s for each of the following data sets. If appropriate, specify the units in which your answer is expressed.
   a. $3, 1, 10, 10, 4$
   b. 8 feet, 10 feet, 32 feet, 5 feet
   c. $-1, -4, -3, 1, -4, -4$
   d. $\frac{1}{5}$ ounce, $\frac{1}{5}$ ounce, $\frac{1}{5}$ ounce, $\frac{2}{5}$ ounce, $\frac{1}{5}$ ounce, $\frac{4}{5}$ ounce,

2.60 Using only integers between 0 and 10, construct two data sets with at least 10 observations each so that the two sets have the same mean but different variances. Construct dot plots for each of your data sets and mark the mean of each data set on its dot diagram.

2.61 Using only integers between 0 and 10, construct two data sets with at least 10 observations each that have the same range but different means. Construct a dot plot for each of your data sets, and mark the mean of each data set on its dot diagram.

2.62 Consider the following sample of five measurements: 2, 1, 1, 0, 3.
   a. Calculate the range, s^2 and s.
   b. Add 3 to each measurement and repeat part **a.**
   c. Subtract 4 from each measurement and repeat part **a.**
   d. Considering your answers to parts **a, b,** and **c,** what seems to be the effect on the variability of a data set by adding the same number to or subtracting the same number from each measurement?

Applet Exercise 2.5

Use the applet *Standard Deviation* to study the effect that multiplying or dividing each number in a data set by the same number has on the standard deviation. Begin by setting appropriate limits and plotting the given data on the number line provided in the applet.

$$0 \quad 1 \quad 1 \quad 1 \quad 2 \quad 2 \quad 3 \quad 4$$

a. Record the standard deviation. Then multiply each data item by 2, plot the new data items, and record the standard deviation. Repeat the process first multiplying each of the original data items by 3 and then by 4. Describe what is happening to the standard deviation as the data items are multiplied by higher numbers. Divide each standard deviation by the standard deviation of the original data set. Do you see a pattern? Explain.

b. Divide each of the original data items by 2, plot the new data, and record the standard deviation. Repeat the process first dividing each of the original data items by 3 and then by 4. Describe what is happening to the standard deviation as the data items are divided by higher numbers. Divide each standard deviation by the standard deviation of the original data set. Do you see a pattern? Explain.

c. Using your results from parts a and b, describe what happens to the standard deviation of a data set when each of the data items in the set is multiplied or divided by a fixed number n. Experiment by repeating parts a and b for other data sets if you need to.

Applet Exercise 2.6

Use the applet *Standard Deviation* to study the effect that an extreme value has on the standard deviation. Begin by setting appropriate limits and plotting the given data on the number line provided in the applet.

$$0 \quad 6 \quad 7 \quad 7 \quad 8 \quad 8 \quad 8 \quad 9 \quad 9 \quad 10$$

a. Record the standard deviation. Replace the extreme value of 0 with 2, then 4, and then 6. Record the standard deviation each time. Describe what is happening to the standard deviation as 0 is replaced by higher numbers.

b. How would the standard deviation of the data set compare to the original standard deviation if the 0 were replaced by 16? Explain.

Applying the Concepts—Basic

FLALAW

2.63 **Top Florida law firms.** Refer to the data on the top-ranked law firms in Florida, Exercise 2.44 (p. 71), collected by *Florida Trend* magazine (April 2002). The data are saved in the **FLALAW** file.
  a. Find the range of the number of lawyers at the top-ranked law firms with headquarters in Orlando.
  b. Find the range of the number of lawyers at the top-ranked law firms with headquarters in Miami.
  c. Using only the ranges in parts a and b, is it possible to determine which city, Orlando or Miami, has the largest law firms?

WPOWER50

2.64 **Most powerful women in America.** Refer to Exercise 2.45 (p. 72) and *Fortune*'s (Nov. 14, 2006) list of the 50 most powerful women in America. The data are stored in the **WPOWER50** file.
  a. Find the range of the ages for these 50 women.
  b. Find the variance of the ages for these 50 women.
  c. Find the standard deviation of the ages for these 50 women.
  d. Suppose the standard deviation of the ages of the most powerful women in Europe is 10 years. For which location, the United States or Europe, is the age data more variable?

DDT

2.65 **Fish contaminated by a plant's toxic discharge.** Refer to Exercise 2.24 (p. 59) and the U.S. Army Corps of Engineers data on contaminated fish saved in the **DDT** file. Consider the quantitative variables length (in centimeters), weight (in grams), and DDT level (in parts per million).
  a. Find three different measures of variation for the 144 fish lengths. Give the units of measurement for each.
  b. Find three different measures of variation for the 144 fish weights. Give the units of measurement for each.
  c. Find three different measures of variation for the 144 DDT values. Give the units of measurement for each.

Applying the Concepts—Intermediate

DIAMONDS

2.66 **Size of diamonds sold at retail.** Refer to Exercise 2.25 (p. 59) and the *Journal of Statistics Education* data on diamonds saved in the **DIAMONDS** file. Consider the data on the number of carats for each of the 308 diamonds.
  a. Find the range of the data set.
  b. Find the variance of the data set.
  c. Find the standard deviation of the data set.
  d. Which measure of variation best describes the spread of the 308 carat values? Explain.

NUCLEAR

2.67 **Active nuclear power plants.** Refer to Exercise 2.54 (p. 73) and the U.S. Energy Information Administration's data on the number of nuclear power plants operating in each of 20 states. The data are saved in the **NUCLEAR** file.
  a. Find the range, variance, and standard deviation of this data set.
  b. Eliminate the largest value from the data set and repeat part a. What effect does dropping this measurement have on the measures of variation found in part a?
  c. Eliminate the smallest and largest value from the data set and repeat part a. What effect does dropping both of these measurement have on the measures of variation found in part a?

Applying the Concepts—Advanced

2.68 **Estimating production time.** A widely used technique for estimating the length of time it takes workers to produce a product is the **time study.** In a time study, the task to be studied is divided into measurable parts, and each is timed with a stop-watch or filmed for later analysis. For each worker, this process is repeated many times for each subtask. Then the average and standard deviation of the time required to complete each subtask are computed for each worker. A worker's overall time to complete the task under study is then determined by adding his or her subtask-time averages (Gaither, *Production and Operations Management*, 1996). The data (in minutes) given in the table are the result of a time study of a production operation involving two subtasks.

a. Find the overall time it took each worker to complete the manufacturing operation under study.

b. For each worker, find the standard deviation of the seven times for subtask 1.

c. In the context of this problem, what are the standard deviations you computed in part **b** measuring?

d. Repeat part **b** for subtask 2.

e. If you could choose workers similar to A or workers similar to B to perform subtasks 1 and 2, which type would you assign to each subtask? Explain your decisions on the basis of your answers to parts **a–d**.

TIMESTUDY

	WORKER A		WORKER B	
Repetition	Subtask 1	Subtask 2	Subtask 1	Subtask 2
1	30	2	31	7
2	28	4	30	2
3	31	3	32	6
4	38	3	30	5
5	25	2	29	4
6	29	4	30	1
7	30	3	31	4

2.6 Interpreting the Standard Deviation

We've seen that if we are comparing the variability of two samples selected from a population, the sample with the larger standard deviation is the more variable of the two. Thus, we know how to interpret the standard deviation on a relative or comparative basis, but we haven't explained how it provides a measure of variability for a single sample.

To understand how the standard deviation provides a measure of variability of a data set, consider a specific data set and answer the following questions: How many measurements are within 1 standard deviation of the mean? How many measurements are within 2 standard deviations? For a specific data set, we can answer these questions by counting the number of measurements in each of the intervals. However, if we are interested in obtaining a general answer to these questions, the problem is more difficult.

Tables 2.6 and 2.7 give two sets of answers to the questions of how many measurements fall within 1, 2, and 3 standard deviations of the mean. The first, which applies to *any* set of data, is derived from a theorem proved by the Russian mathematician P. L. Chebyshev. The second, which applies to **mound-shaped,** symmetric distributions of data (where the mean, median, and mode are all about the same), is based upon empirical evidence that has accumulated over the years. However, the percentages given for the intervals in Table 2.7 provide remarkably good approximations even when the distribution of the data is slightly skewed or asymmetric. Note that both rules apply to either population data sets or sample data sets.

TABLE 2.6   Interpreting the Standard Deviation: Chebyshev's Rule

Chebyshev's Rule applies to any data set, regardless of the shape of the frequency distribution of the data.

a. No useful information is provided on the fraction of measurements that fall within 1 standard deviation of the mean [i.e., within the interval $(\bar{x} - s, \bar{x} + s)$ for samples and $(\mu - \sigma, \mu + \sigma)$ for populations].

b. At least $\frac{3}{4}$ will fall within 2 standard deviations of the mean [i.e., within the interval $(\bar{x} - 2s, \bar{x} + 2s)$ for samples and $(\mu - 2\sigma, \mu + 2\sigma)$ for populations].

c. At least $\frac{8}{9}$ of the measurements will fall within 3 standard deviations of the mean [i.e., within the interval $(\bar{x} - 3s, \bar{x} + 3s)$ for samples and $(\mu - 3\sigma, \mu + 3\sigma)$ for populations].

d. Generally, for any number k greater than 1, at least $(1 - 1/k^2)$ of the measurements will fall within k standard deviations of the mean [i.e., within the interval $(\bar{x} - ks, \bar{x} + ks)$ for samples and $(\mu - 3\sigma, \mu + 3\sigma)$ for populations].

TABLE 2.7   Interpreting the Standard Deviation: The Empirical Rule

The **Empirical Rule** is a rule of thumb that applies to data sets with frequency distributions that are mound-shaped and symmetric, as shown below.

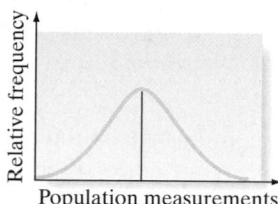

a. Approximately 68% of the measurements will fall within 1 standard deviation of the mean [i.e., within the interval $(\bar{x} - s, \bar{x} + s)$ for samples and $(\mu - \sigma, \mu + \sigma)$ for populations].
b. Approximately 95% of the measurements will fall within 2 standard deviations of the mean [i.e., within the interval $(\bar{x} - 2s, \bar{x} + 2s)$ for samples and $(\mu - 2\sigma, \mu + 2\sigma)$ for populations].
c. Approximately 99.7% (essentially all) of the measurements will fall within 3 standard deviations of the mean [i.e., within the interval $(\bar{x} - 3s, \bar{x} + 3s)$ for samples and $(\mu - 3\sigma, \mu + 3\sigma)$ for populations].

Biography

PAFNUTY L. CHEBYSHEV
(1821–1894)

The Splendid Russian Mathematician

P. L. Chebyshev was educated in mathematical science at Moscow University, eventually earning his master's degree. Following his graduation, Chebyshev joined St. Petersburg (Russia) University as a professor, becoming part of the well-known "Petersburg mathematical school." It was here that Chebyshev proved his famous the-

orem about the probability of a measurement being within k standard deviations of the mean (Table 2.6). His fluency in French allowed him to gain international recognition in probability theory. In fact, Chebyshev once objected to being described as a "splendid Russian mathematician," saying he surely was a "worldwide mathematician." One student remembered Chebyshev as "a wonderful lecturer" who "was always prompt for class," and "as soon as the bell sounded, he immediately dropped the chalk, and, limping, left the auditorium."

EXAMPLE 2.11

Interpreting the Standard Deviation

PROBLEM   The 50 companies' percentages of revenues spent on R&D are repeated in Table 2.8. We have previously shown (see Figure 2.20, p. 77) that the mean and standard deviation of these data (rounded) are 8.49 and 1.98, respectively. Calculate the fraction of these measurements that lie within the intervals $\bar{x} \pm s$, $\bar{x} \pm 2s$, and $\bar{x} \pm 3s$, and compare the results with those predicted in Tables 2.6 and 2.7.

Solution   We first form the interval

$$(\bar{x} - s, \bar{x} + s) = (8.49 - 1.98, 8.49 + 1.98) = (6.51, 10.47)$$

A check of the measurements reveals that 34 of the 50 measurements, or 68%, are within 1 standard deviation of the mean.

 R&D

TABLE 2.8   R&D Percentages for 50 Companies

13.5	9.5	8.2	6.5	8.4	8.1	6.9	7.5	10.5	13.5
7.2	7.1	9.0	9.9	8.2	13.2	9.2	6.9	9.6	7.7
9.7	7.5	7.2	5.9	6.6	11.1	8.8	5.2	10.6	8.2
11.3	5.6	10.1	8.0	8.5	11.7	7.1	7.7	9.4	6.0
8.0	7.4	10.5	7.8	7.9	6.5	6.9	6.5	6.8	9.5

The next interval of interest,

$$(\bar{x} - 2s, \bar{x} + 2s) = (8.49 - 3.96, 8.49 + 3.96) = (4.53, 12.45),$$

contains 47 of the 50 measurements, or 94%.

Finally, the 3-standard-deviation interval around $\bar{x}$,

$$(\bar{x} - 3s, \bar{x} + 3s) = (8.49 - 5.94, 8.49 + 5.94) = (2.55, 14.43),$$

contains all, or 100%, of the measurements.

In spite of the fact that the distribution of these data is skewed to the right (see Figure 2.10), the percentages within 1, 2, and 3 standard deviations (68%, 94%, and 100%) agree very well with the approximations of 68%, 95%, and 99.7% given by the Empirical Rule (Table 2.7).

Look Back You will find that unless the distribution is extremely skewed, the mound-shaped approximations will be reasonably accurate. Of course, no matter what the shape of the distribution, Chebyshev's Rule (Table 2.6) assures that at least 75% and at least 89% of the measurements will lie within 2 and 3 standard deviations of the mean, respectively.

Now Work Exercise 2.72

EXAMPLE 2.12

Check on the Calculation of s

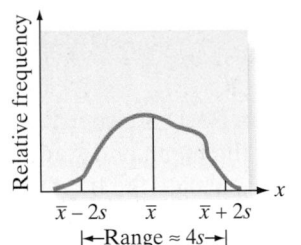

FIGURE 2.21
The relation between the range and the standard deviation

Problem Chebyshev's Rule and the Empirical Rule are useful as a check on the calculation of the standard deviation. For example, suppose we calculated the standard deviation for the R&D percentages (Table 2.8) to be 3.92. Are there any "clues" in the data that enable us to judge whether this number is reasonable?

Solution The range of the R&D percentages in Table 2.8 is $13.5 - 5.2 = 8.3$. From Chebyshev's Rule and the Empirical Rule we know that most of the measurements (approximately 95% if the distribution is mound-shaped) will be within 2 standard deviations of the mean. And, regardless of the shape of the distribution and the number of measurements, almost all of them will fall within 3 standard deviations of the mean. Consequently, we would expect the range of the measurements to be between 4 (i.e., $\pm 2s$) and 6 (i.e., $\pm 3s$) standard deviations in length (see Figure 2.21).

For the R&D data, this means that s should fall between

$$\frac{\text{Range}}{6} = \frac{8.3}{6} = 1.38 \quad \text{and} \quad \frac{\text{Range}}{4} = \frac{8.3}{4} = 2.08$$

In particular, the standard deviation should not be much larger than $\frac{1}{4}$ of the range, particularly for the data set with 50 measurements. Thus, we have reason to believe that the calculation of 3.92 is too large. A check of our work reveals that 3.92 is the variance s^2, not the standard deviation s (see Example 2.10). We "forgot" to take the square root (a common error); the correct value is $s = 1.98$. Note that this value is between $\frac{1}{6}$ and $\frac{1}{4}$ of the range.

Look Back In examples and exercises we'll sometimes use $s \approx \text{range}/4$ to obtain a crude, and usually conservatively large, approximation for s. However, we stress that this is no substitute for calculating the exact value of s when possible.

Now Work Exercise 2.73

In the next example, we use the concepts in Chebyshev's Rule and the Empirical Rule to build the foundation for statistical inference making.

EXAMPLE 2.13
Making a Statistical Inference

Problem   A manufacturer of automobile batteries claims that the average length of life for its grade A battery is 60 months. However, the guarantee on this brand is for just 36 months. Suppose the standard deviation of the life length is known to be 10 months, and the frequency distribution of the life-length data is known to be mound-shaped.

a. Approximately what percentage of the manufacturer's grade A batteries will last more than 50 months, assuming the manufacturer's claim is true?

b. Approximately what percentage of the manufacturer's batteries will last less than 40 months, assuming the manufacturer's claim is true?

c. Suppose your battery lasts 37 months. What could you infer about the manufacturer's claim?

Solution   If the distribution of life length is assumed to be mound-shaped with a mean of 60 months and a standard deviation of 10 months, it would appear as shown in Figure 2.22. Note that we can take advantage of the fact that mound-shaped distributions are (approximately) symmetric about the mean, so that the percentages given by the Empirical Rule can be split equally between the halves of the distribution on each side of the mean.

For example, since approximately 68% of the measurements will fall within 1 standard deviation of the mean, the distribution's symmetry implies that approximately $\frac{1}{2}(68\%) = 34\%$ of the measurements will fall between the mean and 1 standard deviation on each side. This concept is illustrated in Figure 2.22. The figure also shows that 2.5% of the measurements lie beyond 2 standard deviations in each direction from the mean. This result follows from the fact that if approximately 95% of the measurements fall within 2 standard deviations of the mean, then about 5% fall outside 2 standard deviations; if the distribution is approximately symmetric, then about 2.5% of the measurements fall beyond 2 standard deviations on each side of the mean.

a. It is easy to see in Figure 2.22 that the percentage of batteries lasting more than 50 months is approximately 34% (between 50 and 60 months) plus 50% (greater than 60 months). Thus, approximately 84% of the batteries should have life length exceeding 50 months.

b. The percentage of batteries that last less than 40 months can also be easily determined from Figure 2.22. Approximately 2.5% of the batteries should fail prior to 40 months, assuming the manufacturer's claim is true.

c. If you are so unfortunate that your grade A battery fails at 37 months, you can make one of two inferences: either your battery was one of the approximately 2.5% that fail prior to 40 months, or something about the manufacturer's claim is not true. Because the chances are so small that a battery fails before 40 months, you would have good reason to have serious doubts about the manufacturer's claim. A mean smaller than 60 months and/or a standard deviation longer than 10 months would both increase the likelihood of failure prior to 40 months.*

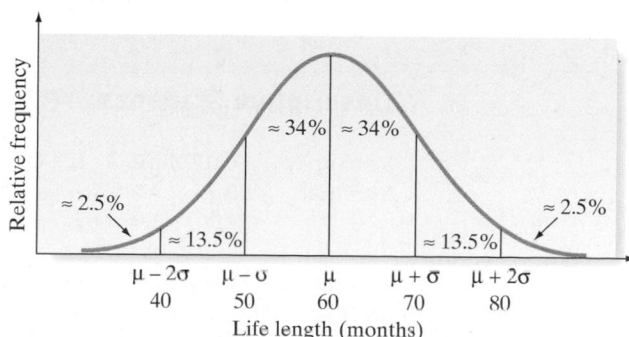

FIGURE 2.22
Battery life-length distribution: Manufacturer's claim assumed true

*The assumption that the distribution is mound-shaped and symmetric may also be incorrect. However, if the distribution were skewed to the right, as life-length distributions often tend to be, the percentage of measurements more than 2 standard deviations *below* the mean would be even less than 2.5%.

Look Back The approximations given in Figure 2.22 are more dependent on the assumption of a mound-shaped distribution than those given by the Empirical Rule (Table 2.7), because the approximations in Figure 2.22 depend on the (approximate) symmetry of the mound-shaped distribution. We saw in Example 2.11 that the Empirical Rule can yield good approximations even for skewed distributions. This will *not* be true of the approximations in Figure 2.22; the distribution *must* be mound-shaped and approximately symmetric.

Example 2.13 is our initial demonstration of the statistical inference-making process. At this point you should realize that we'll use sample information (in Example 2.13, your battery's failure at 37 months) to make inferences about the population (in Example 2.13, the manufacturer's claim about the life length for the population of all batteries). We'll build on this foundation as we proceed.

STATISTICS IN ACTION REVISITED

Interpreting Numerical Descriptive Measures

We return to the analysis of length of time in practice for two groups of University Community Hospital physicians—those who indicate they are willing to use ethics consultation and those who would not use ethics consultation. Recall that the researchers propose that nonusers of ethics consultation will be more experienced than users. The MINITAB descriptive statistics printout for the **ETHICS** data is displayed in Figure SIA2.5, with the means and standard deviations highlighted.

The sample mean for ethics consultation (EC) nonusers is 16.43 and the mean for EC users is 14.18. Our interpretation is that nonusers have slightly more experience (16.43 years, on average) than users (14.18 years, on average).

To interpret the standard deviation, we substitute into the formula, mean ± 2(standard deviation), to obtain the intervals:

EC Nonusers:

$16.43 \pm 2(10.05) = 16.43 \pm 20.10 = (-3.67, 36.53)$

EC Users:

$14.18 \pm 2(8.95) = 14.18 \pm 17.90 = (-3.72, 32.08)$

Since years of experience cannot take on a negative value, essentially the standard deviation intervals for EC nonusers and EC users are $(0, 36.53)$ $(0, 32.08)$, respectively.

From the Chebyshev's Rule (Table 2.6), we know that at least 75% of the physicians who would not use ethics consultation will have anywhere between 0 and 36.5 years of experience. Similarly, we know that at least 75% of the EC users will have anywhere from 0 to 32.08 years of experience. Note that these ranges indicate that there is very little difference in the experience distributions of the two groups of physicians. However, if a physician on staff has 35 years of experience, it is very unlikely that the doctor would use ethics consultation since 35 years is above the mean ± 2(standard deviation) interval for EC users. Rather, the experience value of 35 is more likely to come from the distribution of years of experience for nonusers of ethics consultation.

Descriptive Statistics: YRSPRAC

Variable	FUTUREUSE	N	N*	Mean	SE Mean	StDev	Variance	Minimum	Q1
YRSPRAC	NO	21	2	16.43	2.19	10.05	100.96	1.00	7.50
	YES	91	4	14.176	0.938	8.950	80.102	1.000	7.000

Variable	FUTUREUSE	Median	Q3	Maximum
YRSPRAC	NO	18.00	25.00	35.00
	YES	14.000	20.000	40.000

Figure SIA2.5
MINITAB analysis of physicians' experience

Exercises 2.69–2.85

Learning the Mechanics

2.69 The output from a statistical software package indicates that the mean and standard deviation of a data set consisting of 200 measurements are \$1,500 and \$300, respectively.

a. What are the units of measurement of the variable of interest? Based on the units, what type of data is this: quantitative or qualitative?

b. What can be said about the number of measurements between \$900 and \$2,100? Between \$600 and \$2,400? Between \$1,200 and \$1,800? Between \$1,500 and \$2,100?

2.70 For any set of data, what can be said about the percentage of the measurements contained in each of the following intervals?

a. $\bar{x} - s$ to $\bar{x} + s$
b. $\bar{x} - 2s$ to $\bar{x} + 2s$
c. $\bar{x} - 3s$ to $\bar{x} + 3s$

2.71 For a set of data with a mound-shaped relative frequency distribution, what can be said about the percentage of the measurements contained in each of the intervals specified in Exercise 2.70?

2.72 The following is a sample of 25 measurements:

⊙ **LM2_72**

7	6	6	11	8	9	11	9	10	8	7	7
5	9	10	7	7	7	7	9	12	10	10	8	6

NW **a.** Compute $\bar{x}$, s^2, and s for this sample.

b. Count the number of measurements in the intervals $\bar{x} \pm s$, $\bar{x} \pm 2s$, $\bar{x} \pm 3s$. Express each count as a percentage of the total number of measurements.

c. Compare the percentages found in part **b** to the percentages given by the Empirical Rule and Chebyshev's Rule.

d. Calculate the range and use it to obtain a rough approximation for s. Does the result compare favorably with the actual value for s found in part **a**?

2.73 Given a data set with a largest value of 760 and a smallest
NW value of 135, what would you estimate the standard deviation to be? Explain the logic behind the procedure you used to estimate the standard deviation. Suppose the standard deviation is reported to be 25. Is this feasible? Explain.

Applying the Concepts—Basic

⊙ **DIAMONDS**

2.74 Size of diamonds sold at retail. Refer to the *Journal of Statistics Education* data on diamonds saved in the **DIAMONDS** file. In Exercise 2.47 (p. 72) you found the mean number of carats for the 308 diamonds in the data set, and in Exercise 2.66 (p. 79) you found the standard deviation. Use the mean and standard deviation to form an interval that will contain at least 75% of the carat values in the data set.

2.75 Semester hours taken by CPA candidates. Refer to the *Journal of Accounting and Public Policy* (Spring 2002) study of 100,000 first-time candidates for the CPA exam, Exercise 2.49 (p. 73). Recall that the mean number of se-

mester hours of college credit taken by the candidates was 141.31 hours. The standard deviation was reported to be 17.77 hours.

a. Compute the 2-standard deviation interval around the mean.

b. Make a statement about the proportion of first-time candidates for the CPA exam that have total college credit hours within the interval, part **a.**

c. For the statement, part **b,** to be true, what must be known about the shape of the distribution of total semester hours?

2.76 Vehicle use of an intersection. For each day of last year, the number of vehicles passing through a certain intersection was recorded by a city engineer. One objective of this study was to determine the percentage of days that more than 425 vehicles used the intersection. Suppose the mean for the data was 375 vehicles per day and the standard deviation was 25 vehicles.

a. What can you say about the percentage of days that more than 425 vehicles used the intersection? Assume you know nothing about the shape of the relative frequency distribution for the data.

b. What is your answer to part **a** if you know that the relative frequency distribution for the data is mound-shaped?

⊙ **SHIPSANIT**

2.77 Sanitation inspection of cruise ships. Refer to the Centers for Disease Control and Prevention listing of the May 2006 sanitation scores for 169 cruise ships, Exercise 2.22 (p. 58). The data are saved in the **SHIPSANIT** File.

a. Find the mean and standard deviation of the sanitation scores.

b. Calculate the intervals $\bar{x} \pm s$, $\bar{x} \pm 2s$, $\bar{x} \pm 3s$.

c. Find the percentage of measurements in the data set that fall within each of the intervals, part **b.** Do these percentages agree with Chebyshev's Rule? The Empirical Rule?

Applying the Concepts—Intermediate

2.78 How long do you expect to work at one company? The New Jersey State Chamber of Commerce and Rutgers Business School—with sponsorship by Arthur Anderson—conducted a survey to investigate Generation Xers' expectations of the future workplace and their careers. Telephone interviews were conducted with 662 randomly selected New Jerseyans between the ages of 21 and 28. One question asked, "What is the maximum number of years you expect to spend with any one employer over the course of your career?" The 590 useable responses to this question are summarized below:

$$n = 590$$
$$\bar{x} = 18.2 \text{ years}$$
$$\text{median} = 15 \text{ years}$$
$$s = 10.64$$
$$\min = 2.0$$
$$\max = 50$$

Sources: N.J. State Chamber of Commerce, press release, June 18, 1998, and personal communication from P. George Benson.

a. What evidence exists to suggest that the distribution of years is not mound-shaped?

b. Suppose you did not know the sample standard deviation, s. Use the range of the data set to estimate s. Compare your estimate to the actual sample standard deviation.

c. In the last decade, workers moved between companies much more frequently than in the 1980s. Consequently, the researchers were surprised by the expectations of longevity expressed by the Generation Xers. What can you say about the percentage of Generation Xers in the sample whose response was 40 years or more? 8 years or more?

2.79 Bearing strength of concrete FRP strips. Fiber reinforced polymer (FRP) composite materials are the standard for strengthening, retrofitting, and repairing concrete structures. Typically, FRP strips are fastened to the concrete with epoxy adhesive. Engineers at the University of Wisconsin-Madison have developed a new method of fastening the FRP strips using mechanical anchors (*Composites Fabrication Magazine*, Sep. 2004). To evaluate the new fastening method, 10 specimens of pultruded FRP strips mechanically fastened to highway bridges were tested for bearing strength. The strength measurements (recorded in mega pascal units, Mpa) are shown in the table. Use the sample data to find an interval that is likely to contain the bearing strength of a pultruded FRP strip.

⚙ **FRP**

240.9	248.8	215.7	233.6	231.4	230.9	225.3	247.3	235.5	238.0

Source: Data are simulated from summary information provided in *Composites Fabrication Magazine*, Sep. 2004, p. 32 (Table 1).

⚙ **BANKRUPT**

2.80 Time in bankruptcy. Refer to the *Financial Management* (Spring 1995) study of 49 firms filing for prepackaged bankruptcy, Exercise 2.30 (p. 61). Data on the variable of interest, length of time (months) in bankruptcy for each firm, are saved in the **BANKRUPT** file.

a. Construct a histogram for the 49 bankruptcy times. Comment on whether the Empirical Rule is applicable for describing the bankruptcy time distribution for firms filing for prepackaged bankruptcy.

b. Find numerical descriptive statistics for the data set. Use this information to construct an interval that captures at least 75% of the bankruptcy times.

c. Count the number of the 49 bankruptcy times that fall within the interval, part **b**, and convert the result to a percentage. Does the result agree with Chebyshev's Rule? The Empirical Rule?

d. A firm is considering filing a prepackaged bankruptcy plan. Estimate the length of time the firm will be in bankruptcy.

2.81 Velocity of Winchester bullets. The *American Rifleman* (June 1993) reported on the velocity of ammunition fired from the FEG P9R pistol, a 9 mm gun manufactured in Hungary. Field tests revealed that Winchester bullets fired from the pistol had a mean velocity (at 15 feet) of 936 feet per second and a standard deviation of 10 feet per second.

Tests were also conducted with Uzi and Black Hills ammunition.

a. Describe the velocity distribution of Winchester bullets fired from the FEG P9R pistol.

b. A bullet, brand unknown, is fired from the FEG P9R pistol. Suppose the velocity (at 15 feet) of the bullet is 1,000 feet per second. Is the bullet likely to be manufactured by Winchester? Explain.

2.82 Amount of zinc phosphide in commercial rat poison. A chemical company produces a substance composed of 98% cracked corn particles and 2% zinc phosphide for use in controlling rat populations in sugarcane fields. Production must be carefully controlled to maintain the 2% zinc phosphide because too much zinc phosphide will cause damage to the sugarcane and too little will be ineffective in controlling the rat population. Records from past production indicate that the distribution of the actual percentage of zinc phosphide present in the substance is approximately mound-shaped, with a mean of 2.0% and a standard deviation of .08%.

a. If the production line is operating correctly, approximately what proportion of batches from a day's production will contain less than 1.84% of zinc phosphide?

b. Suppose one batch chosen randomly actually contains 1.80% zinc phosphide. Does this indicate that there is too little zinc phosphide in today's production? Explain your reasoning.

Applying the Concepts—Advanced

2.83 Land purchase decision. A buyer for a lumber company must decide whether to buy a piece of land containing 5,000 pine trees. If 1,000 of the trees are at least 40 feet tall, the buyer will purchase the land; otherwise, he won't. The owner of the land reports that the height of the trees has a mean of 30 feet and a standard deviation of 3 feet. Based on this information, what is the buyer's decision?

2.84 Improving SAT Scores. The National Education Longitudinal Survey (NELS) tracks a nationally representative sample of U.S. students from eighth grade through high school and college. Research published in *Chance* (Winter 2001) examined the Standardized Admission Test (SAT) scores of 265 NELS students who paid a private tutor to help them improve their scores. The table summarizes the changes in both the SAT–Mathematics and SAT–Verbal scores for these students.

	SAT–Math	SAT–Verbal
Mean change in score	19	7
Standard deviation of score changes	65	49

a. Suppose one of the 265 students who paid a private tutor is selected at random. Give an interval that is likely to contain this student's change in the SAT–Math score.

b. Repeat part **a** for the SAT–Verbal score.

c. Suppose the selected student increased their score on one of the SAT tests by 140 points. Which test, the

SAT–Math or SAT–Verbal, is the one most likely to have the 140-point increase? Explain.

2.85 Monitoring weights of flour bags. When it is working properly, a machine that fills 25-pound bags of flour dispenses an average of 25 pounds per fill; the standard deviation of the amount of fill is .1 pound. To monitor the performance of the machine, an inspector weighs the contents of a bag coming off the machine's conveyor belt every half hour during the day. If the contents of two consecutive bags fall more than 2 standard deviations from the mean (using the mean and standard deviation given above), the filling process is said to be out of control and the machine is shut down briefly for adjustments. The data given in the following table are the weights measured by the inspector yesterday. Assume the machine is never shut down for more than 15 minutes at a time. At what times yesterday was the process shut down for adjustment? Justify your answer.

FLOUR

Time	Weight (pounds)
8:00 A.M.	25.10
8:30	25.15
9:00	24.81
9:30	24.75
10:00	25.00
10:30	25.05
11:00	25.23
11:30	25.25
12:00	25.01
12:30 P.M.	25.06
1:00	24.95
1:30	24.80
2:00	24.95
2:30	25.21
3:00	24.90
3:30	24.71
4:00	25.31
4:30	25.15
5:00	25.20

2.7 Numerical Measures of Relative Standing

We've seen that numerical measures of central tendency and variability describe the general nature of a quantitative data set (either a sample or a population). In addition, we may be interested in describing the *relative* quantitative location of a particular measurement within a data set. Descriptive measures of the relationship of a measurement to the rest of the data are called **measures of relative standing.**

One measure of the relative standing of a measurement is its **percentile ranking,** or **percentile score.** For example, if oil company A reports that its yearly sales are in the 90th percentile of all companies in the industry, the implication is that 90% of all oil companies have yearly sales less than company A's, and only 10% have yearly sales exceeding company A's. This is demonstrated in Figure 2.23. Similarly, if the oil company's yearly sales are in the 50th percentile (the median of the data set), 50% of all oil companies would have lower yearly sales and 50% would have higher yearly sales.

FIGURE 2.23

Location of 90th percentile for yearly sales of oil companies

Percentile rankings are of practical value only for large data sets. Finding them involves a process similar to the one used in finding a median. The measurements are ranked in order, and a rule is selected to define the location of each percentile. Since we are primarily interested in interpreting the percentile rankings of measurements (rather than finding particular percentiles for a data set), we define the *pth percentile* of a data set as shown in Definition 2.11.

Definition 2.11

For any set of *n* measurements (arranged in ascending or descending order), the *pth* **percentile** is a number such that $p\%$ of the measurements fall below the *pth* percentile and $(100 - p)\%$ fall above it.

EXAMPLE 2.14
Finding and
Interpreting
Percentiles

Problem   Refer to the percentages spent on research and development by the 50 high-technology firms listed in Table 2.8 (p. 81). A portion of the SPSS descriptive statistics printout is shown in Figure 2.24. Locate the 25th percentile and 95th percentile on the printout and interpret these values.

Solution   Both the 25th percentile and 95th percentile are highlighted on the SPSS printout, Figure 2.24. These values are 7.05 and 13.335, respectively. Our interpretations are as follows: 25% of the 50 R&D percentages fall below 7.05 and 95% of the R&D percentages fall below 13.335.

Look Back   The method for computing percentiles varies according to the software used. Some packages, like SPSS, gives two different methods of computing percentiles. As the data set increases in size, these percentile values will converge to a single number.

Statistics

RDPCT

N	Valid	50
	Missing	0
Percentiles	5	5.765
	10	6.500
	25	7.050
	50	8.050
	75	9.625
	90	11.280
	95	13.335

FIGURE 2.24
SPSS percentiles for
50 R&D percentages

Now Work Exercise 2.87

Another measure of relative standing in popular use is the *z-score*. As you can see in Definition 2.12, the *z*-score makes use of the mean and standard deviation of the data set in order to specify the relative location of a measurement. Note that the *z*-score is calculated by subtracting $\bar{x}$ (or μ) from the measurement x and then dividing the result by s (or σ). The final result, the *z*-score, represents the distance between a given measurement x and the mean, expressed in standard deviations.

Definition 2.12

The **sample z-score** for a measurement x is

$$z = \frac{x - \bar{x}}{s}$$

The **population z-score** for a measurement x is

$$z = \frac{x - \mu}{\sigma}$$

EXAMPLE 2.15
Finding A z-Score

Problem   Suppose 200 steelworkers are selected, and the annual income of each is determined. The mean and standard deviation are $\bar{x} = \$34{,}000$ and $s = \$2{,}000$. Suppose Joe Smith's annual income is $32,000. What is his sample *z*-score?

Solution   Joe Smith's annual income lies below the mean income of the 200 steelworker (see Figure 2.25). We compute

$$z = \frac{x - \bar{x}}{s} = \frac{\$32{,}000 - \$34{,}000}{2{,}000} = -1.0$$

$$z = -1.0$$

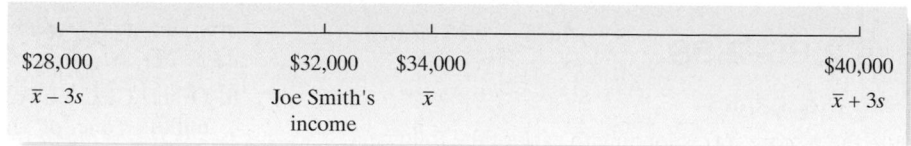

FIGURE 2.25
Annual income of steel workers

which tells us that Joe Smith's annual income is 1.0 standard deviation *below* the sample mean, or, in short, his sample z-score is -1.0.

Look Back The numerical value of the z-score reflects the relative standing of the measurement. A large positive z-score implies that the measurement is larger than almost all other measurements, whereas a large (in magnitude) negative z-score indicates that the measurement is smaller than almost every other measurement. If a z-score is 0 or near 0, the measurement is located at or near the mean of the sample or population.

Now Work Exercise 2.86

If we know that the frequency distribution of the measurements is mound-shaped, the following interpretation of the z-score can be given.

Interpretation of z-Scores for Mound-Shaped Distributions of Data

1. Approximately 68% of the measurements will have a z-score between -1 and 1.
2. Approximately 95% of the measurements will have a z-score between -2 and 2.
3. Approximately 99.7% (almost all) of the measurements will have a z-score between -3 and 3.

Note that this interpretation of z-scores is identical to that given by the Empirical Rule for mound-shaped distributions (Table 2.7). The statement that a measurement falls in the interval $(\mu - \sigma)$ to $(\mu + \sigma)$ is equivalent to the statement that a measurement has a population z-score between -1 and 1, since all measurements between $(\mu - \sigma)$ and $(\mu + \sigma)$ are within 1 standard deviation of μ. These z-scores are displayed in Figure 2.26.

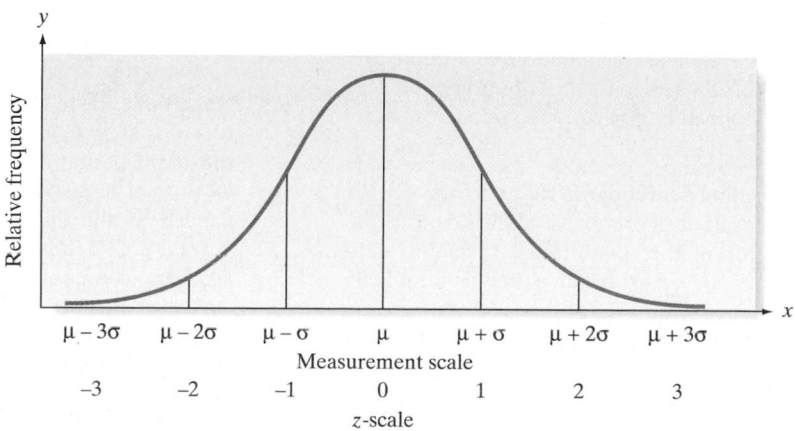

FIGURE 2.26
Population z-scores for a mound-shaped distribution

Exercises 2.86–2.98

Learning the Mechanics

2.86 Compute the z-score corresponding to each of the following
NW values of x:
  a. $x = 40, s = 5, \bar{x} = 30$
  b. $x = 90, \mu = 89, \sigma = 2$
  c. $\mu = 50, \sigma = 5, x = 50$
  d. $s = 4, x = 20, \bar{x} = 30$
  e. In parts **a–d,** state whether the z-score locates x within a sample or a population.
  f. In parts **a–d,** state whether each value of x lies above or below the mean and by how many standard deviations.

2.87 Give the percentage of measurements in a data set that are
NW above and below each of the following percentiles:
  a. 75th percentile
  b. 50th percentile
  c. 20th percentile
  d. 84th percentile

2.88 What is the 50th percentile of a quantitative data set called?

2.89 Compare the z-scores to decide which of the following x values lie the greatest distance above the mean and the greatest distance below the mean.
  a. $x = 100, \mu = 50, \sigma = 25$
  b. $x = 1, \mu = 4, \sigma = 1$
  c. $x = 0, \mu = 200, \sigma = 100$
  d. $x = 10, \mu = 5, \sigma = 3$

2.90 Suppose that 40 and 90 are two elements of a population data set and that their z-scores are -2 and 3, respectively. Using only this information, is it possible to determine the population's mean and standard deviation? If so, find them. If not, explain why it's not possible.

Applying the Concepts—Basic

2.91 **Mathematics assessment test scores.** According to the National Center for Education Statistics (2005), scores on a mathematics assessment test for United States eighth-graders have a mean of 279, a 10th percentile of 231, a 25th percentile of 255, a 75th percentile of 304, and a 90th percentile of 324. Interpret each of these numerical descriptive measures.

2.92 **Drivers stopped by police.** According to the Bureau of Justice Statistics (March 2002), 73.5% of all licensed drivers stopped by police are 25 years or older. Give a percentile ranking for the age of 25 years in the distribution of all ages of licensed drivers stopped by police.

CEOPAY05

2.93 **Executive compensation scoreboard.** Refer to the *Forbes* "Executive Compensation Scoreboard" data saved in the **CEOPAY05** file. One of the quantitative variables measured for each of the 500 CEOs in the survey is total 2005 pay (in $ millions).
  a. Find the mean and standard deviation of the total 2005 pay values.

  b. Oracle CEO Lawrence Ellison had a total pay of $75.33 million (one of the highest in the survey). Find the z-score for this value.
  c. Microsoft CEO S. A. Ballmer had a total pay of $1.1 million. Find the z-score for this value.
  d. Use the z-scores, parts **b** and **c,** to make a statement about the two CEOs' total 2005 pay relative to the total pay values for all CEOs in the survey.

SHIPSANIT

2.94 **Sanitation inspection of cruise ships.** Refer to the May 2006 sanitation levels of cruise ships, Exercise 2.77 (p. 85). The data are saved in the **SHIPSANIT** file.
  a. Give a measure of relative standing for the Nautilus Explorer score of 78. Interpret the result.
  b. Give a measure of relative standing for the Rotterdam's score of 98. Interpret the result.

Applying the Concepts—Intermediate

2.95 **Lead in drinking water.** The U.S. Environmental Protection Agency (EPA) sets a limit on the amount of lead permitted in drinking water. The EPA *Action Level* for lead is .015 milligrams per liter (mg/L) of water. Under EPA guidelines, if 90% of a water system's study samples have a lead concentration less than .015 mg/L, the water is considered safe for drinking. I (coauthor Sincich) received a recent report on a study of lead levels in the drinking water of homes in my subdivision. The 90th percentile of the study sample had a lead concentration of .00372 mg/L. Are water customers in my subdivision at risk of drinking water with unhealthy lead levels? Explain.

2.96 **Using z-scores for grades.** At one university, the students are given z-scores at the end of each semester rather than the traditional GPAs. The mean and standard deviation of all students' cumulative GPAs, on which the z-scores are based, are 2.7 and .5, respectively.
  a. Translate each of the following z-scores to corresponding GPA: $z = 2.0, z = -1.0, z = .5, z = -2.5$.
  b. Students with z-scores below -1.6 are put on probation. What is the corresponding probationary GPA?
  c. The president of the university wishes to graduate the top 16% of the students with *cum laude* honors and the top 2.5% with *summa cum laude* honors. Where (approximately) should the limits be set in terms of z-scores? In terms of GPAs? What assumption, if any, did you make about the distribution of the GPAs at the university?

2.97 **Hazardous waste cleanup in Arkansas.** The Superfund Act was passed by Congress to encourage state participation in the implementation of a law relating to the release and cleanup of hazardous substances. Hazardous waste sites financed by the Superfund Act are called *Superfund sites.* A total of 393 Superfund sites are operated by waste management companies in Arkansas (Tabor and Stanwick, *Arkansas Business and Economic Review,* Summer 1995). The number of these Superfund sites in each of Arkansas's 75 counties is shown in the next table.

⊙ **ARKFUND**

3	3	2	1	2	0	5	3	5	2	1	8	2
12	3	5	3	1	3	0	8	0	9	6	8	6
2	16	0	6	0	5	5	0	1	25	0	0	0
6	2	10	12	3	10	3	17	2	4	2	1	21
4	2	1	11	5	2	2	7	2	3	1	8	2
0	0	0	2	3	10	2	3	48	21			

Source: Tabor. R. H., and Stanwick, S. D. *"Arkansas: An Environmental Perspective." Arkansas Business and Economic Review*, Vol. 28, No. 2, Summer 1995, pp. 22–32 (Table 1).

a. Find the 10th percentile of the data set. Interpret the result.

b. Find the 95th percentile of the data set. Interpret the result.

c. Find the mean and standard deviation of the data; then use these values to calculate the *z*-score for an Arkansas county with 48 Superfund sites.

d. Based on your answer to part **c**, would you classify 48 as an extreme number of Superfund sites?

Applying the Concepts—Advanced

2.98 Blue versus red-colored exam study. In a study of how external clues influence performance, professors at the University of Alberta and Pennsylvania State University gave two different forms of a midterm examination to a large group of introductory students. The questions on the exam were identical and in the same order, but one exam was printed on blue paper and the other on red paper (*Teaching Psychology*, May 1998). Grading only the difficult questions on the exam, the researchers found that scores on the blue exam had a distribution with a mean of 53% and a standard deviation of 15%, while scores on the red exam had a distribution with a mean of 39% and a standard deviation of 12%. (Assume that both distributions are approximately mound-shaped and symmetric.)

a. Give an interpretation of the standard deviation for the students who took the blue exam.

b. Give an interpretation of the standard deviation for the students who took the red exam.

c. Suppose a student is selected at random from the group of students who participated in the study and the student's score on the difficult questions is 20%. Which exam form is the student more likely to have taken, the blue or the red exam? Explain.

APPLET **Applet Exercise 2.7**

Use the applet *Standard Deviation* to determine whether an item in a data set may be an outlier. Begin by setting appropriate limits and plotting the data below on the number line provided in the applet.

10 80 80 85 85 85 85 90 90 90 90 90 95 95 95 95 100 100

a. The green arrow shows the approximate location of the mean. Multiply the standard deviation given by the applet by 3. Is the data item 10 more than three standard deviations away from the green arrow (the mean)? Can you conclude that the 10 is an outlier?

b. Using the mean and standard deviation from part **a**, move the point at 10 on your plot to a point that appears to be about three standard deviations from the mean. Repeat the process in part **a** for the new plot and the new suspected outlier.

c. When you replaced the extreme value in part **a** with a number that appeared to be within three standard deviations of the mean, the standard deviation got smaller and the mean moved to the right, yielding a new data set where the extreme value was not within three standard deviations of the mean. Continue to replace the extreme value with higher numbers until the new value is within three standard deviations of the mean in the new data set. Use trial and error to estimate the smallest number that can replace the 10 in the original data set so that the replacement is not considered to be an outlier.

2.8 Methods for Detecting Outliers (Optional)

Sometimes it is important to identify inconsistent or unusual measurements in a data set. An observation that is unusually large or small relative to the data values we want to describe is called an *outlier*.

Outliers are often attributable to one of several causes. First, the measurement associated with the outlier may be invalid. For example, the experimental procedure used to generate the measurement may have malfunctioned, the experimenter may have misrecorded the measurement, or the data might have been coded incorrectly in the computer. Second, the outlier may be the result of a misclassified measurement—that is, the measurement belongs to a population different from that from which the rest of the sample was drawn. Finally, the measurement associated with the outlier may be recorded correctly and from the same population as the rest of the sample, but represents a rare (chance) event. Such outliers occur most often when the relative frequency distribution of the sample data is extremely skewed, because such a distribution has a tendency to include extremely large or small observations relative to the others in the data set.

Definition 2.13

An observation (or measurement) that is unusually large or small relative to the other values in a data set is called an **outlier.** Outliers typically are attributable to one of the following causes:

1. The measurement is observed, recorded, or entered into the computer incorrectly.
2. The measurement comes from a different population.
3. The measurement is correct but represents a rare (chance) event.

Two useful methods for detecting outliers, one graphical and one numerical, are **box plots** and z-scores. The box plot is based on the *quartiles* of a data set. **Quartiles** are values that partition the data set into four groups, each containing 25% of the measurements. The *lower quartile* Q_L is the 25th percentile, the *middle quartile* is the median m (the 50th percentile), and the *upper quartile* Q_U is the 75th percentile (see Figure 2.27).

FIGURE 2.27

The quartiles for a data set

Definition 2.14

The **lower quartile** Q_L is the 25th percentile of a data set. The **middle quartile** m is the median. The **upper quartile** Q_U is the 75th percentile.

A box plot is based on the *interquartile range* (IQR), the distance between the lower and upper quartiles:

$$IQR = Q_U - Q_L$$

Definition 2.15

The **interquartile range (IQR)** is the distance between the lower and upper quartiles:

$$IQR = Q_U - Q_L$$

An annotated MINITAB box plot for the 50 companies' percentages of revenues spent on R&D (Table 2.2) is shown in Figure 2.28.* Note that a rectangle (the box) is drawn, with the top and bottom sides of the rectangle (the **hinges**) drawn at the quartiles Q_L and Q_U respectively. By definition, then, the "middle" 50% of the observations— those between Q_L and Q_U—fall inside the box. For the R&D data, these quartiles are at 7.05 and 9.625 (see Figure 2.24, p. 88). Thus,

$$IQR = 9.625 - 7.05 = 2.575$$

The median is shown at 8.05 by a horizontal line within the box.

To guide the construction of the "tails" of the box plot, two sets of limits, called **inner fences** and **outer fences,** are used. Neither set of fences actually appears on the box plot. Inner fences are located at a distance of 1.5(IQR) from the hinges. Emanating from the hinges of the box are vertical lines called the **whiskers.** The two whiskers extend to the most extreme observation inside the inner fences. For example, the inner fence on the lower side (bottom) of the R&D percentage box plot is

---

*Although box plots can be generated by hand, the amount of detail required makes them particularly well suited for computer generation. We use computer software to generate the box plots in this section.

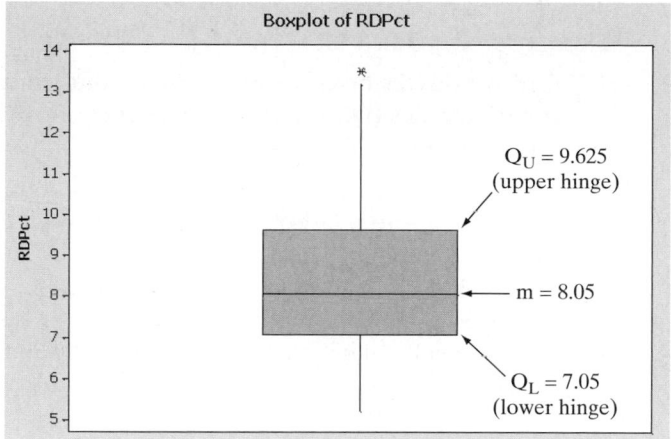

FIGURE 2.28

Annotated MINITAB box plot for 50 R&D percentages

$$\text{Lower inner fence} = \text{Lower hinge} - 1.5(\text{IQR})$$
$$= 7.05 - 1.5(2.575)$$
$$= 7.05 - 3.863 = 3.187$$

The smallest measurement in the data set is 5.2, which is well inside this inner fence. Thus, the lower whisker extends to 5.2. Similarly, the upper whisker extends to the most extreme observation inside the upper inner fence, where

$$\text{Upper inner fence} = \text{Upper hinge} + 1.5(\text{IQR})$$
$$= 9.625 + 1.5(2.575)$$
$$= 9.625 + 3.863 = 13.488$$

The largest measurement inside this fence is the third largest measurement, 13.2. Note that the longer upper whisker reveals the rightward skewness of the R&D distribution.

Values that are beyond the inner fences are deemed *potential outliers* because they are extreme values that represent relatively rare occurrences. In fact, for mound-shaped distributions, fewer than 1% of the observations are expected to fall outside the inner fences. Two of the 50 R&D measurements, both at 13.5, fall outside the upper inner fence. Each of these potential outliers is represented by the asterisk (*) at 13.5.

The other two imaginary fences, the outer fences, are defined at a distance 3(IQR) from each end of the box. Measurements that fall beyond the outer fence are represented by 0s (zeros) and are very extreme measurements that require special analysis. Since less than one-hundredth of 1% (.01% or .0001) of the measurements from mound-shaped distributions are expected to fall beyond the outer fence, these measurements are considered to be *outliers*. No measurement in the R&D percentage box plot (Figure 2.28) is represented by a 0; thus there are no outliers.

Recall that outliers are extreme measurements that stand out from the rest of the sample and may be faulty: They may be incorrectly recorded observations, members of a population different from the rest of the sample, or, at the least, very unusual measurements from the same population. For example, the two R&D measurements at 13.5 (identified by an asterisk) may be considered outliers. When we analyze these measurements, we find that they are correctly recorded. However, it turns out that both represent R&D expenditures of relatively young and fast-growing companies. Thus, the outlier analysis may have revealed important factors that relate to the R&D expenditures of high-tech companies: their age and rate of growth. Outlier analysis often reveals useful information of this kind and therefore plays an important role in the statistical inference-making process.

In addition to detecting outliers, box plots provide useful information on the variation in a data set. The elements (and nomenclature) of box plots are summarized in the next box. Some aids to the interpretation of box plots are also given.

Elements of a Box Plot

1. A rectangle (the **box**) is drawn with the ends (the **hinges**) drawn at the lower and upper quartiles (Q_L and Q_U). The median of the data is shown in the box, usually by a line or a symbol (such as "+").

2. The points at distances 1.5(IQR) from each hinge define the **inner fences** of the data set. Lines (the **whiskers**) are drawn from each hinge to the most extreme measurement inside the inner fence.

3. A second pair of fences, the **outer fences,** are defined at a distance of 3 interquartile ranges, 3(IQR), from the hinges. One symbol (usually "*") is used to represent measurements falling between the inner and outer fences, and another (usually "0") is used to represent measurements beyond the outer fences.

4. The symbols used to represent the median and the extreme data points (those beyond the fences) will vary depending on the software you use to construct the box plot. (You may use your own symbols if you are constructing a box plot by hand.) You should consult the program's documentation to determine exactly which symbols are used.

Aids to the Interpretation of Box Plots

1. Examine the length of the box. The IQR is a measure of the sample's variability and is especially useful for the comparison of two samples (see Example 2.17).

2. Visually compare the lengths of the whiskers. If one is clearly longer, the distribution of the data is probably skewed in the direction of the longer whisker.

3. Analyze any measurements that lie beyond the fences. Fewer than 5% should fall beyond the inner fences, even for very skewed distributions. Measurements beyond the outer fences are probably outliers, with one of the following explanations:

   a. The measurement is incorrect. It may have been observed, recorded, or entered into the computer incorrectly.

   b. The measurement belongs to a population different from the population that the rest of the sample was drawn from (see Example 2.17).

   c. The measurement is correct *and* from the same population as the rest. Generally, we accept this explanation only after carefully ruling out all others.

EXAMPLE 2.16
Box Plots Using the Computer

Problem In Example 2.2 (p. 53) we analyzed 50 processing times (listed in Table 2.4) for the development of price quotes by the manufacturer of industrial wheels. The intent was to determine whether the success or failure in obtaining the order was related to the amount of time to process the price quotes. Each quote that corresponds to "lost" business was so classified. Use a statistical software package to draw a box plot for all 50 processing times. What does the box plot reveal about the data?

Solution The MINITAB box plot printout for these data is shown in Figure 2.29. Note that the upper whisker is much longer than the lower whisker, indicating rightward skewness of the data. However, the most important feature of the data is made very obvious by the box plot: There are four measurements (indicated by asterisks) that are beyond the upper inner fence. Thus, the distribution is extremely skewed to the right, and several measurements—or outliers—need special attention in our analysis.

Look Back Before removing outliers from the data set, a good analyst will make a concerted effort to find the cause of the outliers. We offer an explanation for these processing time outliers in the next example.

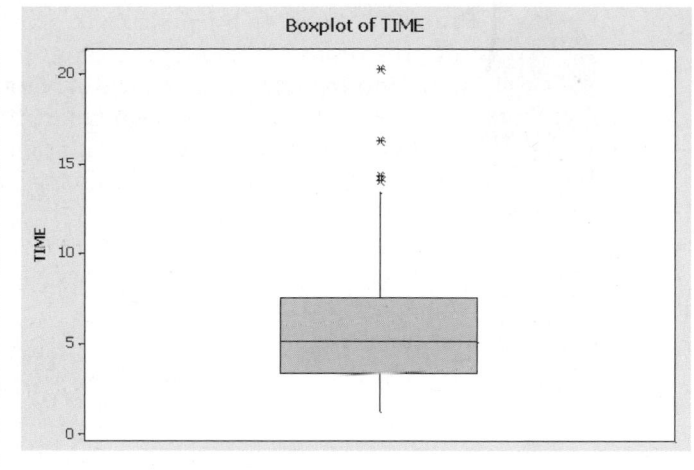

FIGURE 2.29

MINITAB box plot for processing time data

Now Work Exercise 2.102

EXAMPLE 2.17

Comparing Box Plots

Problem The box plot for the 50 processing times (Figure 2.29) does not explicitly reveal the differences, if any, between the set of times corresponding to the success and the set of times corresponding to the failure to obtain the business. Box plots corresponding to the 39 "won" and 11 "lost" bids were generated using SPSS and are shown in Figure 2.30. Interpret them.

Solution The division of the data set into two parts, corresponding to won and lost bids eliminates any observations that are beyond the inner fences. Furthermore, the skewness in the distributions has been reduced, as evidenced by the fact that the upper whiskers are only slightly longer than the lower. The box plots also reveal that the processing times corresponding to the lost bids tend to exceed those of the won bids. A plausible explanation for the outliers in the combined box plot (Figure 2.29) is that they are from a different population than the bulk of the times. In other words, there are two populations represented by the sample of processing times—one corresponding to lost bids and the other to won bids.

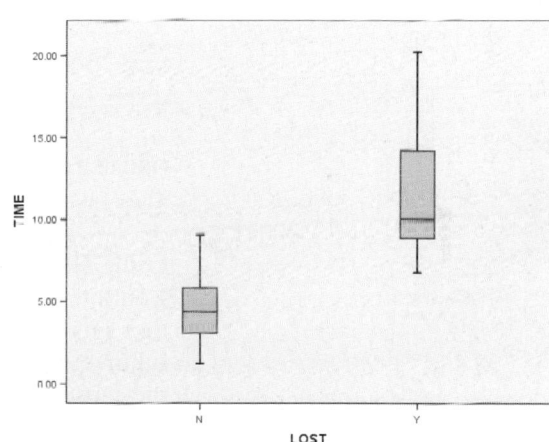

FIGURE 2.30

SPSS box plots of processing times for won and lost bids

Look Back The box plots lend support to the conclusion that the price quote processing time and the success of acquiring the business are related. However, whether the visual differences between the box plots generalize to inferences about the populations corresponding to these two samples is a matter for inferential statistics, not graphical descriptions. We'll discuss how to use samples to compare two populations using inferential statistics in Chapter 7.

The following example illustrates how z-scores can be used to detect outliers and make inferences.

EXAMPLE 2.18

Inference Using z-Scores

Problem Suppose a female bank employee believes that her salary is low as a result of sex discrimination. To substantiate her belief, she collects information on the salaries of her male counterparts in the banking business. She finds that their salaries have a mean of $54,000 and a standard deviation of $2,000. Her salary is $47,000. Does this information support her claim of sex discrimination?

Solution The analysis might proceed as follows: First, we calculate the z-score for the woman's salary with respect to those of her male counterparts. Thus,

$$z = \frac{\$47,000 - \$54,000}{\$2,000} = -3.5$$

The implication is that the woman's salary is 3.5 standard deviations *below* the mean of the male salary distribution. Furthermore, if a check of the male salary data shows that the frequency distribution is mound-shaped, we can infer that very few salaries in this distribution should have a z-score less than −3, as shown in Figure 2.31. Clearly, a z-score of −3.5 represents an outlier. Either this female's salary is from a distribution different from the male salary distribution, or it is a very unusual (highly improbable) measurement from a distribution that is no different than the male salary distribution.

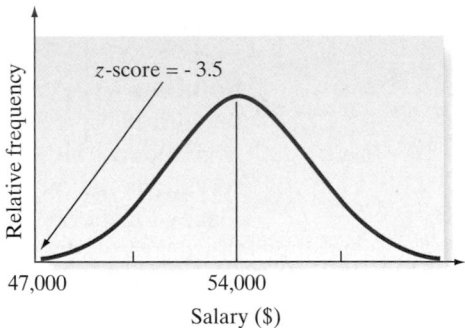

FIGURE 2.31
Male salary distribution

Look Back Which of the two situations do you think prevails? Statistical thinking would lead us to conclude that her salary does not come from the male salary distribution, lending support to the female bank employee's claim of sex discrimination. A careful investigator should require more information before inferring sex discrimination as the cause. We would want to know more about the data-collection technique the woman used and more about her competence at her job. Also perhaps other factors such as length of employment should be considered in the analysis.

Now Work Exercise 2.99

Examples 2.17 and 2.18 exemplify an approach to statistical inference that might be called the **rare-event approach.** An experimenter hypothesizes a specific frequency distribution to describe a population of measurements. Then a sample of measurements is drawn from the population. If the experimenter finds it unlikely that the sample came from the hypothesized distribution, the hypothesis is concluded to be false. Thus, in Example 2.18 the woman believes her salary reflects discrimination. She hypothesizes that her salary should be just another measurement in the distribution of her male counterparts' salaries if no discrimination exists. However, it is so unlikely that the sample (in this case, her salary) came from the male frequency distribution that she rejects that hypothesis, concluding that the distribution from which her salary was drawn is different from the distribution for the men.

This rare-event approach to inference-making is discussed further in later chapters. Proper application of the approach requires a knowledge of probability, the subject of our next chapter.

We conclude this section with some rules of thumb for detecting outliers.

> **Rules of Thumb for Detecting Outliers**[*]
>
> **Box Plots:** Observations falling between the inner and outer fences are deemed *suspect outliers*. Observations falling beyond the outer fence are deemed *highly suspect outliers*.
>
> **z-scores:** Observations with z-scores greater than 3 in absolute value are considered outliers. (For some highly skewed data sets, observations with z-scores greater than 2 in absolute value may be outliers).

Exercises 2.99–2.110

Learning the Mechanics

2.99 A sample data set has a mean of 57 and a standard deviation of 11. Determine whether each of the following sample measurements are outliers.
  a. 65
  b. 21
  c. 72
  d. 98

2.100 Define the 25th, 50th, and 75th percentiles of a data set. Explain how they provide a description of the data.

2.101 Suppose a data set consisting of exam scores has a lower quartile $Q_L = 60$, a median $m = 75$, and an upper quartile $Q_U = 85$. The scores on the exam range from 18 to 100. Without having the actual scores available to you, construct as much of the box plot as possible.

2.102 Consider the horizontal box plot shown below.
  a. What is the median of the data set (approximately)?
  b. What are the upper and lower quartiles of the data set (approximately)?
  c. What is the interquartile range of the data set (approximately)?
  d. Is the data set skewed to the left, skewed to the right, or symmetric?
  e. What percentage of the measurements in the data set lie to the right of the median? To the left of the upper quartile?
  f. Identify any outliers in the data.

Applying the Concepts—Basic

2.103 Semester hours taken by CPA candidates. Refer to the *Journal of Accounting and Public Policy* (Spring 2002) study of 100,000 first-time candidates for the CPA exam,

Exercise 2.49 (p. 73). The number of semester hours of college credit earned by the candidates had a mean of 141.31 hours and a standard deviation of 17.77 hours.
  a. Find the z-score for a first-time candidate for the CPA exam who earned 160 semester hours of college credit. Is this observation considered an outlier?
  b. Give a value of number of semester hours that would, in fact, be considered an outlier in this data set.

2.104 Salary offers to MBAs. The following table contains the top salary offer (in thousands of dollars) received by each member of a sample of 50 MBA students who recently graduated from the Graduate School of Management at Rutgers, the state university of New Jersey.

 MBASAL

61.1	48.5	47.0	49.1	43.5
50.8	62.3	50.0	65.4	58.0
53.2	39.9	49.1	75.0	51.2
41.7	40.0	53.0	39.6	49.6
55.2	54.9	62.5	35.0	50.3
41.5	56.0	55.5	70.0	59.2
39.2	47.0	58.2	59.0	60.8
72.3	55.0	41.4	51.5	63.0
48.4	61.7	45.3	63.2	41.3
47.0	43.2	44.6	47.7	58.6

Source: Career Services Office, Graduate School of Management, Rutgers University.

  a. The mean and standard deviation are 52.33 and 9.22, respectively. Find and interpret the z-score associated with the highest salary offer, the lowest salary offer, and the mean salary offer. Would you consider the highest offer to be unusually high? Why or why not?
  b. Construct a box plot for this data set. Which salary offers (if any) are potentially faulty observations? Explain.

 BANKRUPT

2.105 Time in bankruptcy. Refer to the *Financial Management* (Spring 1995) study of 49 firms filing for prepackaged

STATISTICS IN ACTION REVISITED

Detecting Outliers

In the ethics survey of University Community Hospital physicians, the medical researchers measured two qualitative variables: *Length of time in practice* (number of years) and *Amount of exposure to ethics in medical school* (number of hours). Are there any unusual values of these variables in the **ETHICS** data set? We will employ both the box plot and z-score methods to aid in identifying outliers in the data.

Descriptive statistics for these two variables, produced using MINITAB, are shown in Figure SIA2.6. To employ the z-score method, we need the means and standard deviations. These values are highlighted on Figure SIA2.6. Then the 3-standard-deviation intervals are

$$\text{YRSPRAC:} \quad 14.6 \pm 3(9.2) = 14.6 \pm 27.6$$
$$= (-13.0, 42.2)$$

$$\text{EDHRS:} \quad 23.9 \pm 3(109.6) = 23.9 \pm 328.8$$
$$= (-304.9, 352.7)$$

[*Note:* Since neither of the variables can be negative, for practical purposes the intervals all begin at 0.]

In this application, we will focus on only the three largest values of the variables in the data set. For length of time in practice, these values are 35, 40, and 40 years. Note that all three values fall within the 3-standard-deviation interval—that is, they all have z-scores less than 3 in absolute value. Consequently, no outliers exist for the data on length of time in practice.

For ethics exposure, the three largest values are 75, 80, and 1,000 hours. Note that only one of these values, 1,000, falls beyond the 3-standard-deviation interval. Thus, the data for the physician who was exposed to 1,000 hours of ethics in medical school is considered an outlier using the z-score approach. However, notice that the standard deviation for the variable (109.6) is much larger than the mean (23.9). Typically, when S exceeds $\bar{x}$ (for a non-negative variable), a high degree of skewness exists. This skewness is due, in large part, to the extreme value of 1,000 hours. When such an extreme outlier occurs in the data, the standard deviation is inflated and the z-score method is less likely to detect unusual observations. (See the footnote on p. 97.) When this occurs, the box plot method for detecting outliers is preferred.

Rather than produce a box plot for the ethics exposure variable, we'll use the descriptive statistics in Figure SIA2.6 to find the inner and outer fences. From the MINITAB printout, we see that $Q_L = 1$, $Q_U = 20$, and IQR = 19. Then the upper inner and outer fence boundaries of the box plot are

Upper inner fence:
$$Q_U + (1.5)\text{IQR} = 20 + (1.5)(19) = 48.5$$

Upper outer fence:
$$Q_U + (3)\text{IQR} = 20 + (3)(19) = 77.0$$

Now we see that the ethics exposure value of 80 hours is, indeed, a highly suspect outlier, since it falls beyond the upper outer fence. Also, the exposure value of 75 hours is a suspect outlier, since it falls beyond the upper inner fence. Thus, the box plot method detected an additional two outliers.

Before any type of inference is made concerning the population of ethics exposure values, we should consider whether these three outliers are legitimate observations (in which case they will remain in the data set) or are associated with physicians that are not members of the population of interest (in which case they will be removed from the data set).

Descriptive Statistics: YRSPRAC, EDHRS

Variable	N	N*	Mean	StDev	Q1	Median	Q3	IQR
YRSPRAC	112	6	14.598	9.161	7.000	14.000	20.000	13.000
EDHRS	83	35	23.9	109.6	1.0	5.0	20.0	19.0

Figure SIA2.6

MINITAB descriptive statistics for practice experience and ethics exposure

bankruptcies, Exercise 2.30 (p. 61). Recall that three types of "prepack" firms exist: (1) those who hold no prefiling vote, (2) those who vote their preference for a joint solution; and (3) those who vote their preference for a prepack.

a. Construct a box plot for the time in bankruptcy (months) for each type of firm.

b. Find the median bankruptcy times for the three types

c. How do the variabilities of the bankruptcy times compare for the three types?

d. The standard deviations of the bankruptcy times are 2.47 for "none," 1.72 for "joint," and 0.96 for "prepack." Do the standard deviations agree with the interquartile ranges with regard to the comparison of the variabilities of the bankruptcy times?

e. Is there evidence of outliers in any of the three distributions?

Box Plots

Using the TI-83/TI-84 Graphing Calculator

Making a Box Plot

Step 1 *Enter the data*

Press STAT and select 1:Edit
Note: If the list already contains data, clear the old data. Use the up arrow to highlight "L1". Press CLEAR ENTER.
Use the arrow and ENTER keys to enter the data set into L1.

Step 2 *Set up the box plot*

Press **2nd Y** = for **STAT PLOT**
Press **1** for **Plot 1**

Set the cursor so that "ON" is flashing.
For TYPE, use the right arrow to scroll through the plot icons and select the box plot in the middle of the second row.
For XLIST, choose L1.
Set FREQ to 1.

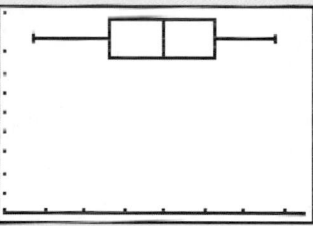

Step 3 *View the graph*

Press ZOOM and select 9:ZoomStat

Optional *Read the five number summary*

Step Press TRACE
Use the left and right arrow keys to move between minX, Q1, Med, Q3, and maxX.

Example Make a box plot for the given data,

86, 70, 62, 98, 73, 56, 53, 92, 86, 37, 62, 83, 78, 49, 78, 37, 67, 79, 57

The output screen for this example is shown below.

Applying the Concepts—Intermediate

⊘ **WPOWER50**

2.106 Most powerful women in America. Refer to the *Fortune* (Nov. 14, 2006) ranking of the 50 most powerful women in America, Exercise 2.45 (p. 72). The data are saved in the **WPOWER50** file. Use side-by-side box plots to compare the ages of the women in three groups based on their position within the firm: Group 1 (CEO/Chairman, CEO/president, or CFO/ president); Group 2 (CEO, CFO, CFO/EVP, CIO/EVP, chairman, COO, CRO, or president); Group 3 (EVP, executive, founder, SVP, treasurer, or vice chair). Do you detect any outliers?

⊘ **SHIPSANIT**

2.107 Sanitation inspection of cruise ships. Refer to Exercise 2.77 (p. 85) and the data on the sanitation levels of passenger cruise ships. The data are saved in the **SHIPSANIT** file.
   a. Use the box plot method to detect any outliers in the data set.
   b. Use the z-score method to detect any outliers in the data set.
   c. Do the two methods agree? If not, explain why.

⊘ **ARKFUND**

2.108 Hazardous waste cleanup in Arkansas. Refer to Exercise 2.97 (p. 90) and the data on the number of Superfund sites in each of 75 Arkansas counties. The data are saved in the **ARKFUND** file.

a. There is at least one outlier in the data. Use the methods of this chapter to detect the outliers.

b. Delete the outlier(s) found in part **a** from the data set and recalculate measures of central tendency and variation. Which measures are most affected by the removal of the outlier(s)?

2.109 Network server downtime. A manufacturer of network computer server systems is interested in improving its customer support services. As a first step, its marketing department has been charged with the responsibility of summarizing the extent of customer problems in terms of system downtime. The 40 most recent customers were surveyed to determine the amount of downtime (in hours) they had experienced during the previous month. These data are listed in the table.

⊙ DOWNTIME

Customer Number	Down Time	Customer Number	Down Time
230	12	250	4
231	16	251	10
232	5	252	15
233	16	253	7
234	21	254	20
235	29	255	9
236	38	256	22
237	14	257	18
238	47	258	28
239	0	259	19
240	24	260	34
241	15	261	26
242	13	262	17
243	8	263	11
244	2	264	64
245	11	265	19
246	22	266	18
247	17	267	24
248	31	268	49
249	10	269	50

a. Construct a box plot for these data. Use the information reflected in the box plot to describe the frequency distribution of the data set. Your description should address central tendency, variation, and skewness.

b. Use your box plot to determine which customers are having unusually lengthy downtimes.

c. Find and interpret the z-scores associated with the customers you identified in part **b**.

Applying the Concepts—Advanced

2.110 Sensor motion of a robot. Researchers at Carnegie Mellon University developed an algorithm for estimating the sensor motion of a robotic arm by mounting a camera with inertia sensors on the arm (*International Journal of Robotics Research*, Dec. 2004). One variable of interest is the error of estimating arm translation (measured in centimeters). Data for 10 experiments are listed in the following table. In each experiment, the perturbation of camera intrinsics and projections were varied. Suppose a trial resulted in a translation error of 4.5 cm. Is this value an outlier for trials with perturbed intrinsics but no perturbed projections? For trials with perturbed projections but no perturbed intrinsics? What type of camera perturbation most likely occurred for this trial?

⊙ SENSOR

Trial	Perturbed Intrinsics	Perturbed Projections	Translation Error (cm)
1	Yes	No	1.0
2	Yes	No	1.3
3	Yes	No	3.0
4	Yes	No	1.5
5	Yes	No	1.3
6	No	Yes	22.9
7	No	Yes	21.0
8	No	Yes	34.4
9	No	Yes	29.8
10	No	Yes	17.7

Source: Strelow, D. and Singh, S. "Motion Estimation Form Image and Inertial Measurements." *International Journal of Robotics Research*, Vol. 23, No. 12, Dec. 2004 (Table 4).

2.9 Graphing Bivariate Relationships (Optional)

The claim is often made that the crime rate and the unemployment rate are "highly correlated." Another popular belief is that the gross domestic product (GDP) and the rate of inflation are "related." Some people even believe that the Dow Jones Industrial Average and the lengths of fashionable skirts are "associated." The words *correlated*, *related*, and *associated* imply a relationship between two variables—in the examples above, two *quantitative* variables.

One way to describe the relationship between two quantitative variables—called a **bivariate relationship**—is to plot the data in a **scattergram** (or **scatterplot**). A scattergram is a two-dimensional plot, with one variable's values plotted along the vertical axis and the other along the horizontal axis. For example, Figure 2.32 is a scattergram relating (1) the cost of mechanical work (heating, ventilating, and plumbing) to (2) the floor area of the building for a sample of 26 factory and warehouse buildings. Note that the scattergram suggests a general tendency for mechanical cost to increase as building floor area increases.

When an increase in one variable is generally associated with an increase in the second variable, we say that the two variables are "positively related" or "positively cor-

FIGURE 2.32

Scattergram of cost
vs. floor area

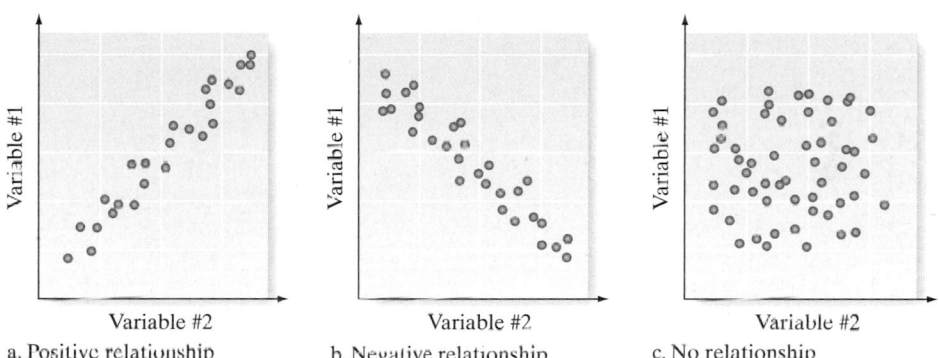

FIGURE 2.33

Hypothetical bivariate
relationship

a. Positive relationship

b. Negative relationship

c. No relationship

related."* Figure 2.32 implies that mechanical cost and floor area are positively correlated. Alternatively, if one variable has a tendency to decrease as the other increases, we say the variables are "negatively correlated." Figure 2.33 shows several hypothetical scattergrams that portray a positive bivariate relationship (Figure 2.33a), a negative bivariate relationship (Figure 2.33b), and a situation where the two variables are unrelated (Figure 2.33c).

EXAMPLE 2.19

Graphing Bivariate
Data from a Hospital

Problem   A medical item used to administer to a hospital patient is called a *factor*. For example, factors can be intravenous (IV) tubing, IV fluid, needles, shave kits, bedpans, diapers, dressings, medications, and even code carts. The coronary care unit at Bayonet Point Hospital (St. Petersburg, Florida) recently investigated the relationship between the number of factors administered per patient and the patient's length of stay (in days). Data on these two variables for a sample of 50 coronary care patients are given in Table 2.9. Use a scattergram to describe the relationship between the two variables of interest, number of factors, and length of stay.

Solution   Rather than construct the plot by hand, we resort to a statistical software package. The Excel plot of the data in Table 2.9, with length of stay (LOS) on the vertical axis and number of factors (FACTORS) on the horizontal axis, is shown in Figure 2.34.

Although the plotted points exhibit a fair amount of variation, the scattergram clearly shows an increasing trend. It appears that a patient's length of stay is positively correlated with the number of factors administered to the patient.

---

*A formal definition of correlation is given in Chapter 10. We will learn that correlation measures the strength of the linear (or straight-line) relationship between two variables.

MEDFACTORS

TABLE 2.9 Data on Patient's Factors and Length of Stay

Number of Factors	Length of Stay (days)	Number of Factors	Length of Stay (days)
231	9	354	11
323	7	142	7
113	8	286	9
208	5	341	10
162	4	201	5
117	4	158	11
159	6	243	6
169	9	156	6
55	6	184	7
77	3	115	4
103	4	202	6
147	6	206	5
230	6	360	6
78	3	84	3
525	9	331	9
121	7	302	7
248	5	60	2
233	8	110	2
260	4	131	5
224	7	364	4
472	12	180	7
220	8	134	6
383	6	401	15
301	9	155	4
262	7	338	8

Source: Bayonet Point Hospital, Coronary Care Unit.

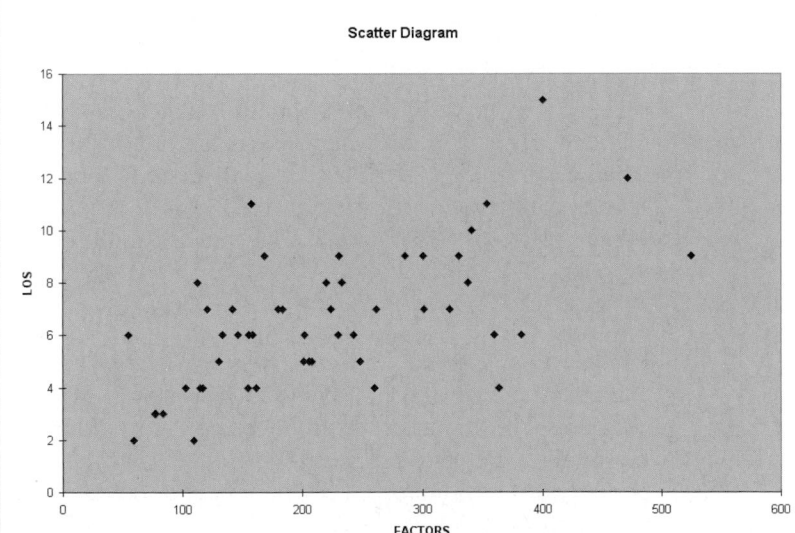

FIGURE 2.34

Excel/PHStat2 scatterplot of data in Table 2.9

Look Back If hospital administrators can be confident that the sample trend shown in Figure 2.34 accurately describes the trend in the population, then they may use this information to improve their forecasts of lengths of stay for future patients.

The scattergram is a simple but powerful tool for describing a bivariate relationship. However, keep in mind that it is only a graph. No measure of reliability can be attached to inferences made about bivariate populations based on scattergrams of sample data. The statistical tools that enable us to make inferences about bivariate relationships are presented in Chapter 10.

STATISTICS IN ACTION REVISITED

Interpreting Scatterplots

Consider the two qualitative variables, *Length of time in practice* (number of years) and *Amount of exposure to ethics in medical school* (number of hours), measured on a sample of University Community Hospital physicians. To investigate a possible relationship between these two variables, we created a scatterplot for the data in Figure SIA2.7 using MINITAB.

At first glance, the graph appears to show almost no relationship between the variables. However, note the outlying data point to the far right of the scatter-

plot. This point corresponds to a physician who reported 1,000 hours of exposure to ethics in medical school. Recall that we classified this data point as a highly suspect outlier in the previous SIA Revisited section (p. 98). If we remove this observation from the data set and rerun the scatterplot option of MINITAB, the graph shown in Figure SIA2.8 is produced. Now the trend in the relationship is more apparent. For physicians with 20 or fewer hours of ethics exposure, there is little or no trend. However, for physicians with more than 20 hours of exposure to ethics, there appears to be a decreasing trend; that is, for physicians with high exposure to ethics, practice experience and exposure time are apparently negatively related.

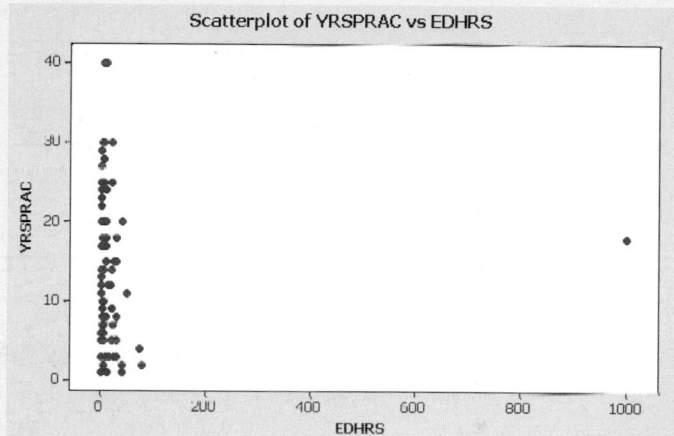

Figure SIA2.7

MINITAB scatterplot of practice experience versus ethics exposure

Figure SIA2.8

MINITAB scatterplot of practice experience versus ethics exposure—outlier deleted

Scatterplots

Using the TI-83/T1-84 Graphing Calculator

Making Scatterplots

Step 1   *Enter the data*

Press STAT and select 1:Edit
Note: If a list already contains data, clear the old data. Use the up arrow to highlight the list name, "L1" or "L2".
Press CLEAR ENTER.
Enter your x-data in L1 and your y-data in L2.

Step 2   *Set up the scatterplot*

Press 2nd Y = for STAT PLOT
Press 1 for Plot1
Set the cursor so that ON is flashing.
For Type, use the arrow and Enter keys to highlight and select the scatterplot (first icon in the first row).
For Xlist, choose the column containing the x-data.
For Ylist, choose the column containing the y-data.

Step 3   *View the scatterplot*

Press ZOOM 9 for ZoomStat

Example   The figures below show a table of data entered on the T1-83 and the scatterplot of the data obtained using the steps given above.

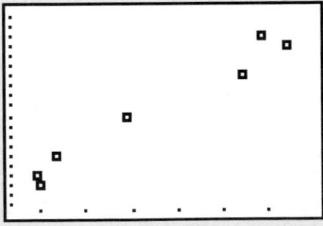

Exercises 2.111–2.118

Learning the Mechanics

2.111 Construct a scattergram for the data in the following table.

Variable 1	5	1	1.5	2	2.5	3	3.5	4	4.5	5
Variable 2	2	1	3	4	6	10	9	12	17	17

2.112 Construct a scattergram for the data in the following table.

Variable 1	5	3	−1	2	7	6	4	0	8
Variable 2	14	3	10	1	8	5	3	2	12

Applying the Concepts—Basic

SATSCORES

2.113 State SAT scores. Refer to Exercise 2.29 (p. 61) and the data on state SAT scores saved in the **SATSCORES** file. Construct a scatterplot for the data, with 1990 SAT score on the horizontal axis and 2005 SAT score on the vertical axis. What type of trend do you detect?

FLALAW

2.114 Top Florida law firms. Refer to Exercise 2.44 (p. 71) and the data on law firms with headquarters in the state of Florida. For each firm, the number of lawyers and number of law offices are saved in the **FLALAW** file. Construct a scatterplot for the data, with number of law offices on the horizontal axis and number of lawyers on the vertical axis. What type of trend do you detect?

DIAMONDS

2.115 Characteristics of diamonds sold at retail. Refer to the *Journal of Statistics Education* data on diamonds saved in the **DIAMONDS** file. In addition to the number of carats, the asking price for the each of the 308 diamonds for sale on the open market was recorded. Construct a scatterplot for the data, with number of carats on the horizontal axis and price on the vertical axis. What type of trend do you detect?

Applying the Concepts—Intermediate

COMPTIME

2.116 Comparing task completion times. Refer to Exercise 2.28 (p. 60) and the *Management Science* experiment on task completion times. Recall that each of 25 employees performed a production task a multiple number of times. The time to complete the task (in minutes) after the 10th, 30th, and 50th time it was performed was recorded for each employee; these data are saved in the **COMPTIME** file.
a. Use a graph to investigate a possible relationship between completion times after the 10th and 30th time the task was performed.
b. Use a graph to investigate a possible relationship between completion times after the 10th and 50th time the task was performed.
c. Use a graph to investigate a possible relationship between completion times after the 30th and 50th time the task was performed.

DDT

2.117 Fish contaminated by a plant's toxic discharge. Refer to the U.S. Army Corps of Engineers data on contaminated fish saved in the **DDT** file. Three quantitative variables are measured for each of the 144 captured fish: length (in centimeters), weight (in grams), and DDT level (in parts per million). Form a scatterplot for each pair of these variables. What trends, if any, do you detect?

2.118 Spreading rate of spilled liquid. A contract engineer at DuPont Corp. studied the rate at which a spilled volatile liquid will spread across a surface (*Chemical Engineering Progress*, Jan. 2005). Assume 50 gallons of methanol spills onto a level surface outdoors. The engineer used derived empirical formulas (assuming a state of turbulent-free convection) to calculate the mass (in pounds) of the spill after a period of time ranging from 0 to 60 minutes. The calculated mass values are given in the accompanying table. Is there evidence to indicate that the mass of the spill tends to diminish as time increases? Support your answer with a scatterplot.

LIQUIDSPILL

Time (minutes)	Mass (pounds)
0	6.64
1	6.34
2	6.04
4	5.47
6	4.94
8	4.44
10	3.98
12	3.55
14	3.15
16	2.79
18	2.45
20	2.14
22	1.86
24	1.60
26	1.37
28	1.17
30	0.98
35	0.60
40	0.34
45	0.17
50	0.06
55	0.02
60	0.00

Source: Barry, J. "Estimating Rates of Spreading and Evaporation of Volatile Liquids." *Chemical Engineering Progress*, Vol. 101, No. 1, Jan. 2005.

2.10 The Time Series Plot (Optional)

Each of the previous sections has been concerned with describing the information contained in a sample or population of data. Often these data are viewed as having been produced at essentially the same point in time. Thus, time has not been a factor in any of the graphical methods described so far.

Data of interest to managers are often produced and monitored over time. Examples include the daily closing price of their company's common stock, the company's weekly sales volume and quarterly profits, and characteristics—such as weight and length—of products produced by the company.

Definition 2.16

Data that are produced and monitored over time are called **time series data.**

Recall from Section 1.4 that a process is a series of actions or operations that generates output over time. Accordingly, measurements taken of a sequence of units produced by a process—such as a production process—are time series data. In general, any sequence of numbers produced over time can be thought of as being generated by a process.

When measurements are made over time, it is important to record both the numerical value and the time or the time period associated with each measurement. With this information, a **time series plot**—sometimes called a **run chart**—can be constructed to describe the time series data and to learn about the process that generated the data. A time series plot is simply a scatterplot with the measurements on the vertical axis and time or the order in which the measurements were made on the horizontal axis. The plotted points are usually connected by straight lines to make it easier to see the changes and movement in the measurements over time. For example, Figure 2.35 is a time series plot of a particular company's monthly sales (number of units sold per month). And Figure 2.36 is a time series plot of the weights of 30 one-gallon paint cans that were consecutively filled by the same filling head. Notice that the weights are plotted against the order in which the cans were filled rather than some unit of time. When monitoring production processes, it is often more convenient to record the order rather than the exact time at which each measurement was made.

Time series plots reveal the movement (trend) and changes (variation) in the variable being monitored. Notice how sales trend upward in the summer and how the variation in the weights of the paint cans increases over time. This kind of information would not be revealed by stem-and-leaf displays or histograms, as the following example illustrates.

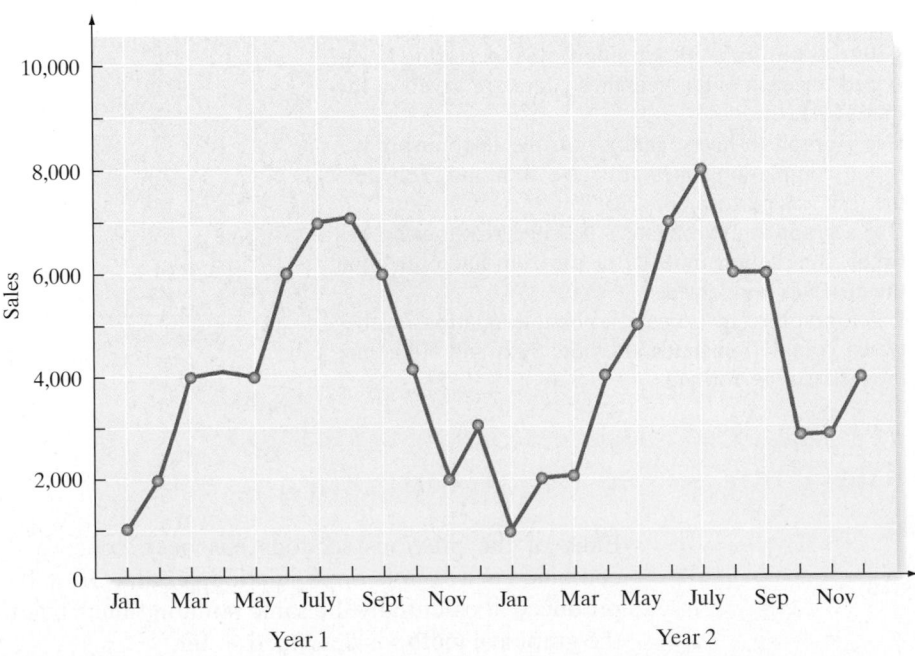

FIGURE 2.35

Time series plot
of company sales

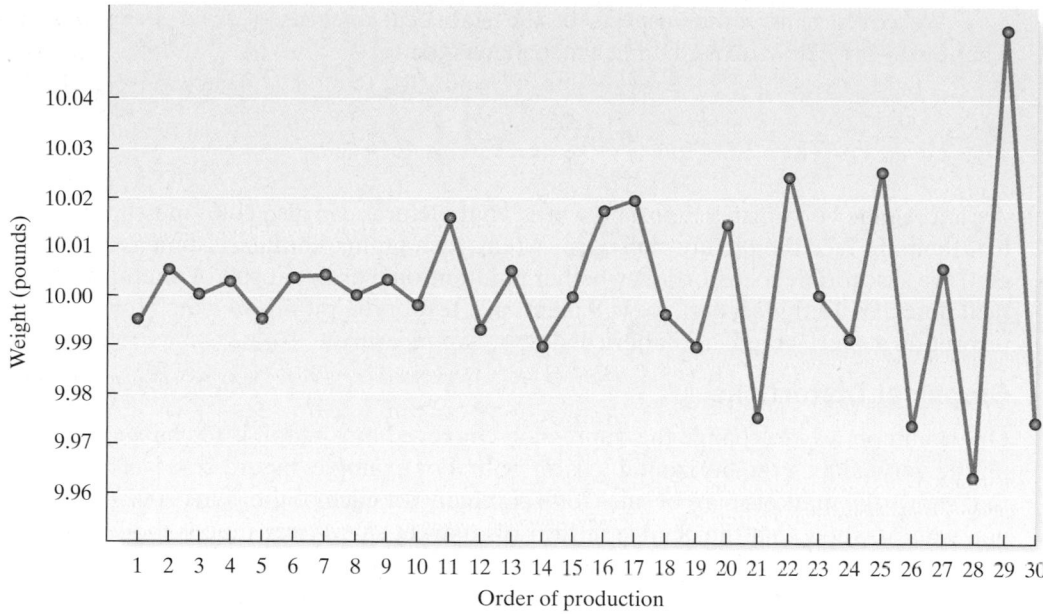

FIGURE 2.36

Time series plot of paint can weights

EXAMPLE **2.20**

Time Series Plot
versus a Histogram

Problem   W. Edwards Deming was one of America's most famous statisticians. He was best known for the role he played after World War II in teaching the Japanese how to improve the quality of their products by monitoring and continually improving their production processes. In his book *Out of the Crisis* (1986), Deming warned against the knee-jerk (i.e., automatic) use of histograms to display and extract information from data. As evidence, he offered the following example.

Fifty camera springs were tested in the order in which they were produced. The elongation of each spring was measured under the pull of 20 grams. Both a time series plot and a histogram were constructed from the measurements. They are shown in Figure 2.37, which has been reproduced from Deming's book. If you had to predict the elongation measurement of the next spring to be produced (i.e., spring 51) and could use only one of the two plots to guide your prediction, which would you use? Why?

Solution   Only the time series plot describes the behavior *over time* of the process that produces the springs. The fact that the elongation measurements are decreasing over time can only be gleaned from the time series plot. Because the histogram does not reflect the order in which the springs were produced, it in effect represents all observations as having been produced simultaneously. Using the histogram to predict the elongation of the 51st spring would very likely lead to an overestimate.

Look Back   The lesson from Deming's example is this: For displaying and analyzing data that have been generated over time by a process, the primary graphical tool is the time series plot, not the histogram.

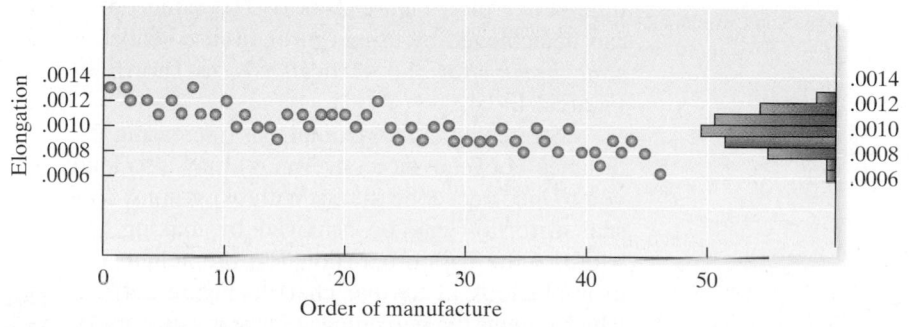

FIGURE 2.37

Deming's time series plot
and histogram

We cover many other aspects of the statistical analysis of time series data in Chapter 13 (available on a CD that accompanies the text).

2.11 Distorting the Truth with Descriptive Techniques

A picture may be "worth a thousand words," but pictures can also color messages or distort them. In fact, the pictures in statistics (e.g., histograms, bar charts, time series plots, etc.) are susceptible to distortion, whether unintentional or as a result of unethical statistical practices. In this section, we will mention a few of the pitfalls to watch for when interpreting a chart, graph, or numerical descriptive measure.

Graphical Distortions

One common way to change the impression conveyed by a graph is to change the scale on the vertical axis, the horizontal axis, or both. For example, Figure 2.38 is a bar graph that shows the market share of sales for a company for each of the years 2002 to 2007. If you want to show that the change in firm A's market share over time is moderate, you should pack in a large number of units per inch on the vertical axis—that is, make the distance between successive units on the vertical scale small, as shown in Figure 2.38. You can see that a change in the firm's market share over time is barely apparent.

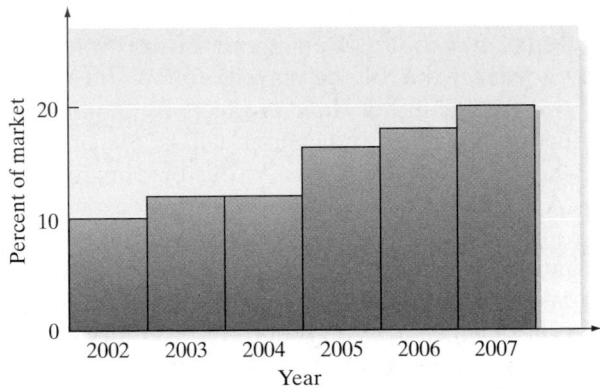

FIGURE 2.38
Firm A's market share from 2002 to 2007—packed vertical axis

If you want to use the same data to make the changes in firm A's market share appear large, you should increase the distance between successive units on the vertical axis—that is, stretch the vertical axis by graphing only a few units per inch as in Figure 2.39. A telltale sign of stretching is a long vertical axis, but this is often hidden by starting the vertical axis at some point above 0, as shown in the time series plot, Figure 2.40(a). The same effect can be achieved by using a broken line—called a *scale break*—for the vertical axis, as shown in Figure 2.40(b).

Stretching the horizontal axis (increasing the distance between successive units) may also lead you to incorrect conclusions. With bar graphs, a visual distortion can be achieved by making the width of the bars proportional to the height. For example, look at the bar chart in Figure 2.41(a), which depicts the percentage of a year's total automobile sales attributable to each of the four major

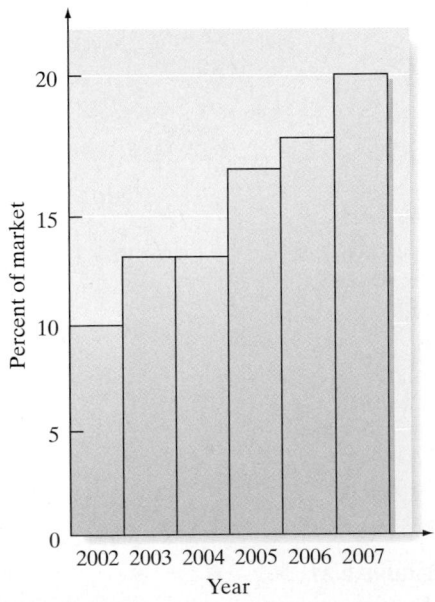

FIGURE 2.39
Firm A's market share from 2002 to 2007—stretched vertical axis

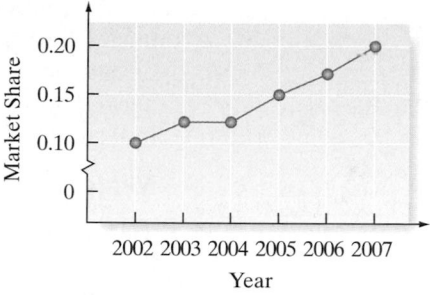

FIGURE 2.40

Firm A's market share from 2002 to 2007

a. Vertical axis started at a point greater than 0

b. Gap in vertical axis

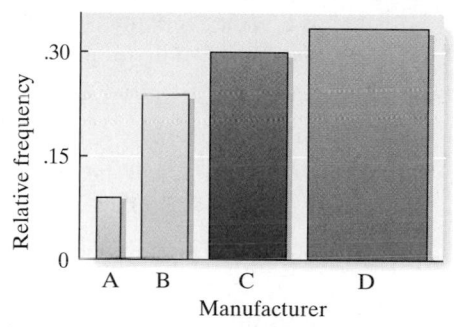

FIGURE 2.41

Relative share of the automobile market for each of four major manufacturers

a. Bar chart

b. Width of bars grows with height

manufacturers. Now suppose we make both the width and the height grow as the market share grows. This change is shown in Figure 2.41(b). The reader may tend to equate the *area* of the bars with the relative market share of each manufacturer. But the fact is the true relative market share is proportional only to the *height* of the bars.

Sometimes we do not need to manipulate the graph to distort the impression it creates. Modifying the verbal description that accompanies the graph can change the interpretation that will be made by the viewer. Figure 2.42 provides good illustration of this ploy.

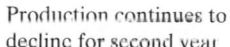

Production continues to decline for second year

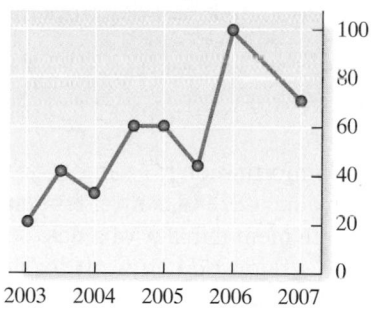

For our production, we need not even change the chart, so we can't be accused of fudging the data. Here we'll simply change the title so that for the Senate subcommittee, we'll indicate that we're not doing as well as in the past...

2007: 2nd best year for production

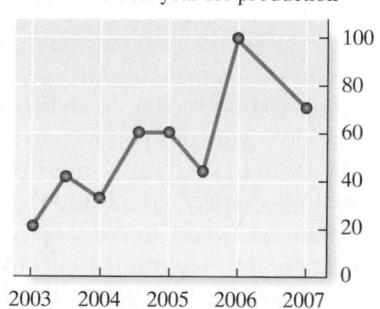

whereas for the general public, we'll tell them that we're still in the prime years.

FIGURE 2.42

Changing the verbal description to change a viewer's interpretation
Source: Adapted from Selazny, G. "Grappling with Graphics," *Management Review,* Oct. 1975, p. 7.

Although we've discussed only a few of the ways that graphs can be used to convey misleading pictures of phenomena, the lesson is clear. Look at all graphical descriptions of data with a critical eye. Particularly, check the axes and the size of the units on each axis. Ignore the visual changes and concentrate on the actual numerical changes indicated by the graph or chart.

Misleading Numerical Descriptive Statistics

The information in a data set can also be distorted by using numerical descriptive measures, as Example 2.20 indicates.

EXAMPLE 2.20

Misleading Descriptive Statistics

Problem   Suppose you're considering working for a small law firm—one that currently has a senior member and three junior members. You inquire about the salary you could expect to earn if you join the firm. Unfortunately, you receive two answers:

> *Answer A:* The senior member tells you that an "average employee" earns $87,500.

> *Answer B:* One of the junior members later tells you that an "average employee" earns $75,000

Which answer can you believe?

Solution   The confusion exists because the phrase "average employee" has not been clearly defined. Suppose the four salaries paid are $75,000 for each of the three junior members and $125,000 for the senior member. Thus,

$$\text{Mean} = \frac{3(\$75,000) + \$125,000}{4} = \frac{\$350,000}{4} = \$87,500$$

$$\text{Median} = \$75,000$$

You can now see how the two answers were obtained. The senior member reported the mean of the four salaries, and the junior member reported the median. The information you received was distorted because neither person stated which measure of central tendency was being used.

Look Back   Based on our earlier discussion of the mean and median, we would probably prefer the median as the measure that best describes the salary of the "average" employee.

Another distortion of information in a sample occurs when *only* a measure of central tendency is reported. Both a measure of central tendency and a measure of variability are needed to obtain an accurate mental image of a data set.

Suppose you want to buy a new car and are trying to decide which of two models to purchase. Since energy and economy are both important issues, you decide to purchase model A because its EPA mileage rating is 32 miles per gallon in the city, whereas the mileage rating for model B is only 30 miles per gallon in the city.

However, you may have acted too quickly. How much variability is associated with the ratings? As an extreme example, suppose that further investigation reveals that the standard deviation for model A mileages is 5 miles per gallon, whereas that for model B is only 1 mile per gallon. If the mileages form a mound-shaped distribution, they might appear as shown in Figure 2.43. Note that the larger amount of variability associated with model A implies that more risk is involved in purchasing

FIGURE 2.43

Mileage distributions for two car models

model A—that is, the particular car you purchase is more likely to have a mileage rating that will greatly differ from the EPA rating of 32 miles per gallon if you purchase model A, while a model B car is not likely to vary from the 30-miles-per-gallon rating by more than 2 miles per gallon.

We conclude this section with another example on distorting the truth with numerical descriptive measures.

EXAMPLE 2.22

More Misleading Descriptive Statistics

Problem   *Children out of School in America* is a report on delinquency of school-age children prepared by the Children's Defense Fund (CDF), a government-sponsored organization. Consider the following three reported results of the CDF survey.

- Reported result 1: 25 percent of the 16- and 17-year-olds in the Portland, Maine, Bayside East Housing Project were out of school. Fact: *Only eight children were surveyed; two were found to be out of school.*

- Reported result 2: Of all the secondary-school students who had been suspended more than once in census tract 22 in Columbia, South Carolina, 33% had been suspended two times and 67% had been suspended three or more times. Fact: *CDF found only three children in that entire census tract who had been suspended; one child was suspended twice and the other two children, three or more times.*

- Reported result 3: In the Portland Bayside East Housing Project, 50% of all the secondary-school children who had been suspended more than once had been suspended three or more times. Fact: *The survey found two secondary-school children had been suspended in that area; one of them had been suspended three or more times.*

Identify the potential distortions in the results reported by the CDF.

Solution   In each of these examples, the reporting of percentages (i.e., relative frequencies) instead of the numbers themselves is misleading. No inference we might draw from the cited examples would be reliable. (We'll see how to measure the reliability of estimated percentages in Chapter 5.) In short, either the report should state the numbers alone instead of percentages, or, better yet, it should state that the numbers were too small to report by region.

Look Back   If several regions were combined, the numbers (and percentages) would be more meaningful.

KEY TERMS

Note: Starred (*) items are from the optional sections in this chapter.

Bar graph   43
*Bivariate relationship   100
*Box plots   92
Central tendency   63
Chebyshev's Rule   80
Class   40
Class frequency   40
Class interval   51
Class percentage   40
Class relative frequency   40
Dot plot   50
Empirical Rule   81
*Hinges   92
Histogram   51
*Inner fences   92
*Interquartile range   92

*Lower quartile   92
Mean   63
Measures of central tendency   63
Measures of relative standing   87
Measures of variation or spread   63
Median   65
*Middle quartile   92
Modal class   68
Mode   68
Mound-shaped distribution   80
Numerical descriptive measures   63
*Outer fences   92
*Outliers   92
Pareto diagram   43
Percentile   87
Pie chart   43
*Quartiles   92
Range   74

*Rare-event approach   96
Relative frequency histogram   51
*Run chart   106
*Scattergram   100
*Scatterplot   100
Skewness   67
Spread   74
Standard deviation   76
Stem-and-leaf display   50
Symmetric distribution   67
*Time series data   106
*Time series plot   106
*Upper quartile   92
Variability   63
Variance   76
*Whiskers   92
z-score   88

GUIDE TO SELECTING THE DATA DESCRIPTION METHOD

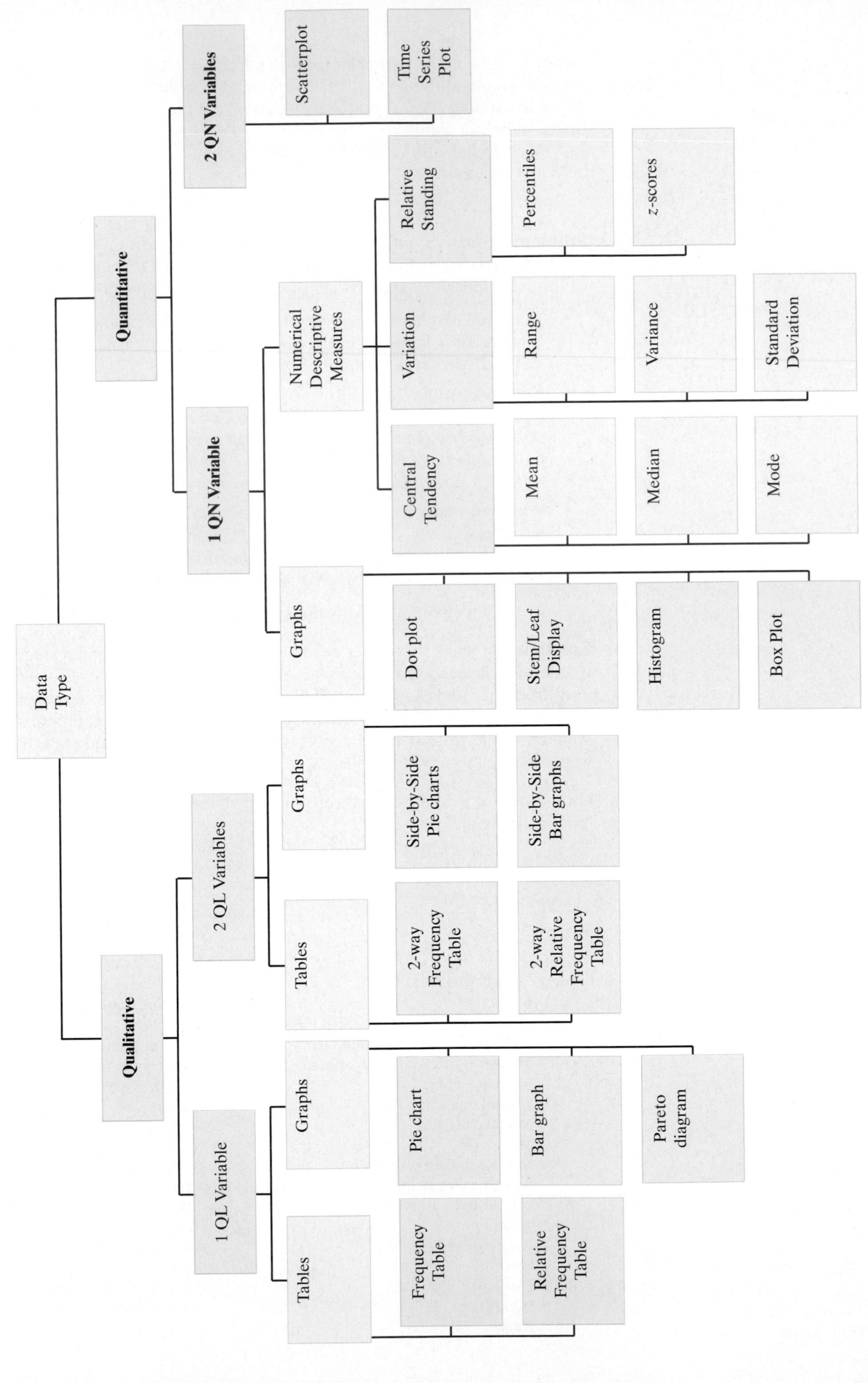

CHAPTER NOTES

Describing QUALITATIVE Data

1. Identify **category classes**
2. Determine **class frequencies**
3. **Class relative frequency** = (class frequency)/n
4. **Graph** relative frequencies

   Pie Chart:

   Bar Graph:

   Pareto Diagram:

Graphing QUANTITATIVE Data

1 Variable

1. Identify class intervals
2. Determine **class interval frequencies**
3. **Class interval relative frequency** = (class interval frequency)/n
4. **Graph** class interval relative frequencies

   Dot Plot:

   Stem-and-Leaf Display:

   ```
   1 | 3
   2 | 2489
   3 | 126678
   4 | 37
   5 | 2
   ```

   Histogram:

   Box plot:

2 Variables

   Scatterplot:

KEY SYMBOLS

	Sample	Population
Mean:	$\overline{x}$	μ
Variance:	s^2	σ^2
Std. Dev.	s	σ
Median:	m	
Lower Quartile:	Q_L	
Upper Quartile:	Q_U	
Interquartile Range:	IQR	

Numerical Description of QUANTITATIVE Data

Central Tendency

Mean: $\bar{x} = (\Sigma x_i)/n$

Median: Middle value when data ranked in order

Mode: Value that occurs most often

Variation

Range: Difference between largest and smallest value

Variance:

$$s^2 = \frac{\Sigma(x_i - \bar{x})^2}{n-1} = \frac{\Sigma x_i^2 - \frac{(\Sigma x_i)^2}{n}}{n-1}$$

Std Dev.: $s = \sqrt{s^2}$

Interquartile Range:

$$IQR = Q_U - Q_L$$

Relative Standing

Percentile Score: Percentage of values that fall below *x*-score

z-score:

$$z = (x - \bar{x})/s$$

Rules for Detecting Quantitative Outliers

Interval	Chebyshev's Rule	Empirical Rule
$\bar{x} \pm s$	At least 0%	$\approx 68\%$
$\bar{x} \pm 2s$	At least 75%	$\approx 95\%$
$\bar{x} \pm 3s$	At least 89%	$\approx$ All

Rules for Detecting Quantitative Outliers

Method	Suspect	Highly Suspect
Box plot:	Values between inner & outer fences	Values beyond outer fences
z-score:	$2 < |z| < 3$	$|z| > 3$

SUPPLEMENTARY EXERCISES 2.119–2.149

Starred (*) exercises are from the optional sections in this chapter.

Learning the Mechanics

2.119 Construct a relative frequency histogram for the data summarized in the accompanying table.

Measurement Class	Relative Frequency
.00–.75	.02
.75–1.50	.01
1.50–2.25	.03
2.25–3.00	.05
3.00–3.75	.10
3.75–4.50	.14
4.50–5.25	.19
5.25–6.00	.15
6.00–6.75	.12
6.75–7.50	.09
7.50–8.25	.05
8.25–9.00	.04
9.00–9.75	.01

2.120 Discuss the conditions under which the median is preferred to the mean as a measure of central tendency.

2.121 Consider the following three measurements: 50, 70, 80. Find the z-score for each measurement if they are from a population with a mean and standard deviation equal to
a. $\mu = 60, \sigma = 10$ b. $\mu = 50, \sigma = 5$
c. $\mu = 40, \sigma = 10$ d. $\mu = 40, \sigma = 100$

*2.122 Refer to Exercise 2.121. For parts **a–d**, determine whether the values 50, 70, and 80 are outliers.

2.123 For each of the following data sets, compute $\bar{x}$, s^2, and s:
a. 13, 1, 10, 3, 3
b. 13, 6, 6, 0
c. 1, 0, 1, 10, 11, 11, 15
d. 3, 3, 3, 3

2.124 For each of the following data sets, compute $\bar{x}$, s^2, and s. If appropriate, specify the units in which your answers are expressed.
a. 4, 6, 6, 5, 6, 7
b. −$1, $4, −$3, $0, −$3, −$6
c. $\frac{3}{5}\%, \frac{4}{5}\%, \frac{2}{5}\%, \frac{1}{5}\%, \frac{1}{16}\%$
d. Calculate the range of each data set in parts **a–c**.

2.125 Explain why we generally prefer the standard deviation to the range as a measure of variability for quantitative data.

2.126 If the range of a set of data is 20, find a rough approximation to the standard deviation of the data set.

2.127 Construct a scattergram for the data in the following table.

Variable 1	174	268	345	119	400	520	190	448	307	252
Variable 2	8	10	15	7	22	31	15	20	11	9

Applying the Concepts—Basic

SWDEFECTS

2.128 Software defects. The Promise Software Engineering Repository is a collection of data sets available to serve businesses in building predictive software models. One such data set, saved in the **SWDEFECTS** files, contains information on 498 modules of software code. Each module was analyzed for defects and classified as "true" if it contained defective code and "false" if not. Access the data file and produce a bar graph or a pie chart for the defect variable. Use the graph to make a statement about the likelihood of defective software code.

CRASH

2.129 Crash tests on new cars. The National Highway Traffic Safety Administration (NHTSA) crash-tests new car models to determine how well they protect the driver and front-seat passenger in a head-on collision. The NHTSA has developed a "star" scoring system for the frontal crash test, with results ranging from one star (*) to five stars (*****). The more stars in the rating, the better the level of crash protection in a head-on collision. The NHTSA crash test results for 98 cars (in a recent model year) are stored in the data file named **CRASH**. The driver-side star ratings for the 98 cars are summarized in the MINITAB printout shown below. Use the information in the printout to form a pie chart. Interpret the graph.

Tally for Discrete Variables: DRIVSTAR

DRIVSTAR	Count	Percent
2	4	4.08
3	17	17.35
4	59	60.20
5	18	18.37
N=	98	

2.130 Crash tests on new cars (cont'd). Refer to Exercise 2.129. One quantitative variable recorded by the NHTSA is driver's severity of head injury (measured on a scale from 0 to 1,500). The mean and standard deviation for the 98 driver head-injury ratings in the **CRASH** file are displayed in the MINITAB printout below. Use these values to find the z-score for a driver head-injury rating of 408. Interpret the result.

MINITAB Output for Exercise 2.130

Descriptive Statistics: DRIVHEAD

Variable	N	Mean	StDev	Minimum	Q1	Median	Q3	Maximum
DRIVHEAD	98	603.7	185.4	216.0	475.0	605.0	724.3	1240.0

2.131 Orlando theme park prices. The entrance fees for adults to 14 theme parks and attractions in Orlando, Florida, are listed in the following table. Find and interpret the mean, median, and mode of the entrance fees. Which measure of central tendency best describes the entrance-fee distribution of the data?

PARKFEES

Theme Park/Attraction	Entrance Fee ($)
Blue Water Hot Air Balloons	185.00
Disney Animal Kingdom	56.70
Disney EPCOT Center	56.70
Disney Magic Kingdom	56.70
Disney MGM Studios	56.70
Disney Pleasure Island	20.95
Disney Wide World of Sports Complex	9.00
DisneyQuest	35.00
Gatorland	21.95
Holy Land Experience	29.99
SeaWorld Adventure Park	61.95
Universal CityWalk	11.95
Universal Islands of Adventure	63.00
Universal Studios	63.00

Source: American Automobile Association, 2006.

2.132 Library acquisitions study. Many librarians rely on book reviews to determine which new books to purchase for their library. A random sample of 375 book reviews in American history, geography, and area studies was selected and the "overall opinion" of the book stated in each review was ascertained (*Library Acquisitions: Practice and Theory*, Vol. 19, 1995). Overall opinion was coded as follows: 1 = would not recommend, 2 = cautious or very little recommendation, 3 = little or no preference, 4 = favorable/contribution, 5 = outstanding/significant contribution. A summary of the data is provided in the bar graph.

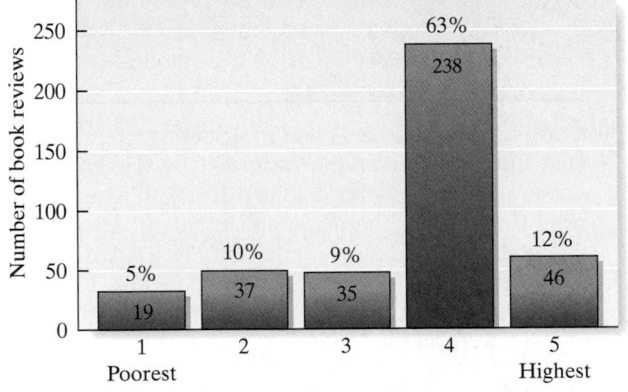

Source: Reprinted from *Library Acquisitions: Practice and Theory*, Vol. 19, No. 2, P. W. Carlo and A. Natowitx, "Choice Book Reviews in American History, Geography, and Area Studies: An analysis for 1988–1993," p. 159. Copyright 1995, with permission from Elsevier Science Ltd, The Boulevard, Langford Lane, Kidlington OX5 1 GB, UK.

a. Is the variable measured quantitative or qualitative? Explain.

b. Interpret the bar graph.

c. Comment on the following statement extracted from the study: "A majority (more than 75%) of books reviewed are evaluated favorably and recommended for purchase."

2.133 Testing a new method for imprinting napkins. In experimenting with a new technique for imprinting paper napkins with designs, names, etc., a paper-products company discovered that four different results were possible:
(A) Imprint successful
(B) Imprint smeared
(C) Imprint off-center to the left
(D) Imprint off-center to the right
To test the reliability of the technique, the company imprinted 1,000 napkins and obtained the results shown in the graph below.

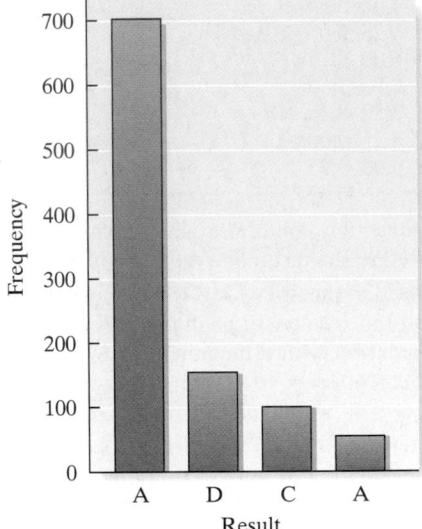

a. What type of graphical tool is the figure?

b. What information does the graph convey to you?

c. From the information provided by the graph, how might you numerically describe the reliability of the imprinting technique?

2.134 Collecting Beanie Babies. Beanie Babies are toy stuffed animals that have become valuable collector's items. *Beanie World Magazine* provided the age, retired status, and value of 50 Beanie Babies. The data are saved in the **BEANIE** file, with several of the observations shown in the table (p. 117).

a. Summarize the retired/current status of the 50 Beanie Babies with an appropriate graph. Interpret the graph.

b. Summarize the values of the 50 Beanie Babies with an appropriate graph. Interpret the graph.

c. Use a graph to portray the relationship between a Beanie Baby's value and its age. Do you detect a trend?

d. According to Chebyshev's Rule, what percentage of the age measurements would you expect to find in the intervals $\bar{x} \pm .75s$, $\bar{x} \pm 2.5s$, $\bar{x} \pm 4s$?

e. What percentage of the age measurements actually fall in the intervals of part **e**? Compare your results with those of part

f. Repeat parts **d** and **e** for value.

BEANIE (Selective observations)

Name	Age (Months)	Retired (R) Current (C)	Value ($)
1. Ally the Alligator	52	R	55.00
2. Batty the Bat	12	C	12.00
3. Bongo the Brown Monkey	28	R	40.00
4. Blackie the Bear	52	C	10.00
5. Bucky the Beaver	40	R	45.00
⋮	⋮	⋮	⋮
46. Stripes the Tiger (Gold/Black)	40	R	400.00
47. Teddy the 1997 Holiday Bear	12	R	50.00
48. Tuffy the Terrier	17	C	10.00
49. Tracker the Basset Hound	5	C	15.00
50. Zip the Black Cat	28	R	40.00

Source: Beanie World Magazine, Sept. 1998.

Applying the Concepts—Intermediate

OILSPILL

2.135 Hull failures of oil tankers. Owing to several major ocean oil spills by tank vessels, Congress passed the 1990 Oil Pollution Act, which requires all tankers to be designed with thicker hulls. Further improvements in the structural design of a tank vessel have been proposed since then, each with the objective of reducing the likelihood of an oil spill and decreasing the amount of outflow in the event of a hull puncture. To aid in this development, *Marine Technology* (Jan. 1995) reported on the spillage amount (in thousands of metric tons) and cause of puncture for 42 recent major oil spills from tankers and carriers. [*Note:* Cause of puncture is classified as either collision (C), fire/explosion (FE), hull failure (HF), or grounding (G).] The data are saved in the **OILSPILL** file.
a. Use a graphical method to describe the cause of oil spillage for the 42 tankers. Does the graph suggest that any one cause is more likely to occur than any other? How is this information of value to the design engineers?
b. Find and interpret descriptive statistics for the 42 spillage amounts. Use this information to form an interval that can be used to predict the spillage amount of the next major oil spill.

2.136 Evaluating toothpaste brands. *Consumer Reports*, published by Consumers Union, is a magazine that contains ratings and reports for consumers on goods, services, health, and personal finances. Consumers Union reported on the testing of 46 brands of toothpaste (*Consumer Reports*, Sept. 1992). Each was rated on package design, flavor, cleaning ability, fluoride content, and cost per month (a cost estimate based on brushing with half-inch of toothpaste twice daily). The data in the next table are costs per month for the 46 brands. Costs marked by an asterisk represent those brands that carry the American Dental Association (ADA) seal verifying effective decay prevention.
a. Construct a stem-and-leaf display for the data.
b. Circle the individual leaves that represent those brands that carry the ADA seal.

c. What does the pattern of circles suggest about the costs of those brands approved by the ADA?

TOOTHPASTE

.58	.66	1.02	1.11	1.77	1.40	.73*	53*	.57*	1.34
1.29	.89*	.49	.53*	.52	3.90	4.73	1.26	.71*	.55*
.59*	.97	.44*	.74*	.51*	.68*	.67	1.22	.39	.55
.62	.66*	1.07	.64	1.32*	1.77*	.80*	.79	.89*	.64
.81*	.79*	.44*	1.09	1.04	1.12				

2.137 Time to develop price quotes. A manufacturer of industrial wheels is losing many profitable orders because of the long time it takes the firm's marketing, engineering, and accounting departments to develop price quotes for potential customers. To remedy this problem, the firm's management would like to set guidelines for the length of time each department should spend developing price quotes. To help develop these guidelines, 50 requests for price quotes were randomly selected from the set of price quotes made last year: the processing time (in days) was determined for each price quote for each department. These times are saved in the **LOSTQUOTES** file. Several observations are displayed in the table below. The price quotes are also classified by whether they were "lost" (i.e., whether or not the customer placed an order after receiving the price quote).
a. Construct a stem-and-leaf display for the total processing time for each department. Shade the leaves that correspond to "lost" orders in each of the displays, and interpret each of the displays.
b. Using your results from part **a**, develop "maximum processing time" guidelines for each department that, if followed, will help the firm reduce the number of lost orders.

LOSTQUOTES

Request Number	Marketing	Engineering	Accounting	Lost?
1	7.0	6.2	.1	No
2	4	5.2	.1	No
3	2.4	4.6	.6	No
4	6.2	13.0	.8	Yes
5	4.7	.9	.5	No
⋮	⋮	⋮	⋮	⋮
46	6.4	1.3	6.2	No
47	4.0	2.4	13.5	Yes
48	10.0	5.3	.1	No
49	8.0	14.4	1.9	Yes
50	7.0	10.0	2.0	No

2.138 Time to develop price quotes (cont'd). Refer to Exercise 2.137.
a. Generate summary statistics for the processing times. Interpret the results.
b. Calculate the z-score corresponding to the maximum processing time guideline you developed in Exercise 2.137 for each department, and for the total processing time.
c. Calculate the maximum processing time corresponding to a z-score of 3 for each of the departments. What percentage of the orders exceed these guidelines? How does this agree with Chebyshev's Rule and the Empirical Rule?
d. Repeat part **c** using a z-score of 2.
e. Compare the percentage of "lost" quotes with corresponding times that exceed at least one of the guidelines in part **c** to the same percentage using the guidelines in

part **d.** Which set of guidelines would you recommend be adopted? Why?

*2.139 **Misleading advertisement.** A time series plot similar to the one shown next appeared in a recent advertisement for a well-known golf magazine. One person might interpret the plot's message as the longer you subscribe to the magazine, the better golfer you should become. Another person might interpret it as indicating that if you subscribe for 3 years, your game should improve dramatically.

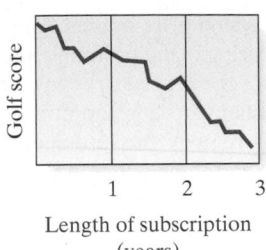

Length of subscription
(years)

a. Explain why the plot can be interpreted in more than one way.
b. How could the plot be altered to rectify the current distortion?

2.140 **Safety record of a company.** A company has roughly the same number of people in each of five departments: Production, Sales, R&D, Maintenance, and Administration. The following table lists the number and type of major injuries that occurred in each department last year.

INJURY

Type of Injury	Department	Number of Injuries
Burn	Production	3
	Maintenance	6
Back strain	Production	2
	Sales	1
	R&D	1
	Maintenance	5
	Administration	2
Eye damage	Production	1
	Maintenance	2
	Administration	1
Deafness	Production	1
Cuts	Production	4
	Sales	1
	R&D	1
	Maintenance	10
Broken arm	Production	2
	Maintenance	2
Broken leg	Sales	1
	Maintenance	1
Broken finger	Administration	1
Concussion	Maintenance	3
	Administration	1
Hearing loss	Maintenance	2

a. Construct a Pareto diagram to identify which department or departments have the worst safety record.
b. Explode the Pareto diagram of part **a** to identify the most prevalent type of injury in the department with the worst safety record.

2.141 **Radiation levels in homes.** In some locations, radiation levels in homes are measured at well above normal background levels in the environment. As a result, many architects and builders are making design changes to ensure

adequate air exchange so that radiation will not be "trapped" in homes. In one such location, 50 homes levels were measured, and the mean level was 10 parts per billion (ppb), the median was 8 ppb, and the standard deviation was 3 ppb. Background levels in this location are at about 4 ppb.

a. Based on these results, is the distribution of the 50 homes' radiation levels symmetric, skewed to the left, or skewed to the right? Why?
b. Use both Chebyshev's Rule and the Empirical Rule to describe the distribution of radiation levels. Which do you think is most appropriate in this case? Why?
c. Use the results from part **b** to approximate the number of homes in this sample that have radiation levels above the background level.
d. Suppose another home is measured at a location 10 miles from the one sampled and has a level of 20 ppb. What is the z-score for this measurement relative to the 50 homes sampled in the other location? Is it likely that this new measurement comes from the same distribution of radiation levels as the other 50? Why? How would you go about confirming your conclusion?

2.142 **Improving gasoline mileage of a car.** As a result of government and consumer pressure, automobile manufacturers in the United States are deeply involved in research to improve their products' gasoline mileage. One manufacturer, hoping to achieve 40 miles per gallon on one of its compact models, measured the mileage obtained by 36 test versions of the model with the following results (rounded to the nearest mile for convenience):

MPG36

43	35	41	42	42	38	40	41	41	40	40	41
42	36	43	40	38	40	38	45	39	41	42	37
40	40	44	39	40	37	39	41	39	41	37	40

a. Find the mean and standard deviation of these data and give the units in which they are expressed.
b. If the manufacturer would be satisfied with a (population) mean of 40 miles per gallon, how would it react to the above test data?
c. Use the information in Tables 2.6–2.7 to check to reasonableness of the calculated standard deviation $s = 2.2$.
d. Construct a relative frequency histogram of the data set. Is the data set mound-shaped?
e. What percentage of the measurements would you expect to find within the intervals $\bar{x} \pm s$, $\bar{x} \pm 2s$, $\bar{x} \pm 3s$?
f. Count the number of measurements that actually fall within the intervals of part **e.** Express each interval count as a percentage of the total number of measurements. Compare these results with your answers to part **e.**

2.143 **Monetary values of NFL Teams.** *Forbes* magazine (Sep. 1, 2005) reported the financial standings of each team in the National Football League (NFL). The next table lists current team value (without deduction for debt, except stadium debt) and operating income for each team in 2004.

a. Use a statistical software package to construct a stem-and-leaf plot for an NFL team's current value.
b. Does the distribution of current values appear to be skewed? Explain.
c. Use the stem-and-leaf plot of part **a** to find the median of the current values.
d. Calculate the z-scores for the Pittsburgh Steelers' current value and operating income.

e. Interpret the two z-scores of part **d.**

f. Which other NFL teams have positive current value z-scores and negative operating income z-scores?

*g. Identify any outliers in the current value data set.

*h. Construct a graph to investigate a possible trend between an NFL team's current value and its operating income. What do you observe?

NFLVALUE

Team	Current Value ($ millions)	Operating Income ($ millions)
Dallas Cowboys	1,063	54.3
Washington Redskins	1,264	53.8
New England Patriots	1,040	50.5
Denver Broncos	907	49.4
Cincinnati Bengals	716	45.6
Tampa Bay Buccaneers	877	45.4
San Francisco 49ers	699	43.6
New Orleans Saints	718	42.6
Houston Texans	946	41.3
Cleveland Browns	892	41.1
Chicago Bears	871	40.1
St. Louis Rams	757	39.8
Pittsburgh Steelers	820	36.5
Buffalo Bills	708	36.1
Green Bay Packers	849	35.4
Tennessee Titans	839	35.1
Jacksonville Jaguars	691	34.6
San Diego Chargers	678	32.8
Baltimore Ravens	864	32.7
Kansas City Chiefs	762	31
Atlanta Falcons	690	26.8
New York Giants	806	26.7
Philadelphia Eagles	952	24.5
Carolina Panthers	878	24.3
Indianapolis Colts	715	16.4
Arizona Cardinals	673	16.2
Miami Dolphins	856	15.8
Minnesota Vikings	658	15.6
Detroit Lions	780	15.4
Seattle Seahawks	823	14.4
New York Jets	739	12
Oakland Raiders	676	7.8

Source: Forbes, Sep. 1, 2005.

2.144 U.S. peanut production. If not examined carefully, the graphical description of U.S. peanut production shown below can be misleading.

a. Explain why the graph may mislead some readers.

b. Construct an undistorted graph of U.S. peanut production for the given years.

2.145 Length of time for an oil change. A national chain of automobile oil-change franchises claims that "your hood will be open for less than 12 minutes when we service your car." To check their claim, an undercover consumer reporter from a local television station monitored the "hood time" of 25 consecutive customers at one of the chain's franchises. The resulting data are shown below. Construct a time series plot for these data and describe in words what it reveals.

HOODTIME

Customer Number	Hood Open (Minutes)	Customer Number	Hood Open (Minutes)
1	11.50	14	12.50
2	13.50	15	13.75
3	12.25	16	12.00
4	15.00	17	11.50
5	14.50	18	14.25
6	13.75	19	15.50
7	14.00	20	13.00
8	11.00	21	18.25
9	12.75	22	11.75
10	11.50	23	12.50
11	11.00	24	11.25
12	13.00	25	14.75
13	16.25		

Applying the Concepts—Advanced

2.146 Investigating the claims of weight-loss clinics. The U.S. Federal Trade Commission assesses fines and other penalties against weight-loss clinics that make unsupported or misleading claims about the effectiveness of their programs. Brochures from two weight-loss clinics both advertise "statistical evidence" about the effectiveness of their programs. Clinic A claims that the *mean* weight loss during the first month is 15 pounds; Clinic B claims a *median* weight loss of 10 pounds.

a. Assuming the statistics are accurately calculated, which clinic would you recommend if you had no other information? Why?

b. Upon further research, the median and standard deviation for Clinic A are found to be 10 pounds and 20 pounds, respectively, while the mean and standard

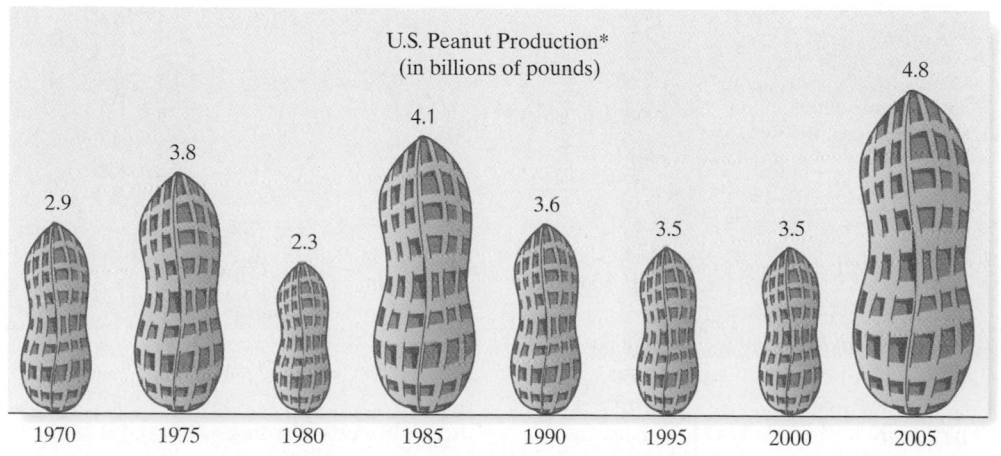

U.S. Peanut Production*
(in billions of pounds)

1970	1975	1980	1985	1990	1995	2000	2005
2.9	3.8	2.3	4.1	3.6	3.5	3.5	4.8

deviation for Clinic B are found to be 10 and 5 pounds, respectively. Both are based on samples of more than 100 clients. Describe the two clinics' weight-loss distributions as completely as possible given this additional information. What would you recommend to a prospective client now? Why?

c. Note that nothing has been said about how the sample of clients upon which the statistics are based was selected. What additional information would be important regarding the sampling techniques employed by the clinics?

2.147 Age discrimination study. The Age Discrimination in Employment Act mandates that workers 40 years of age or older be treated without regard to age in all phases of employment (hiring, promotions, firing, etc.). Age discrimination cases are of two types: *disparate treatment* and *disparate impact*. In the former, the issue is whether workers have been intentionally discriminated against. In the latter, the issue is whether employment practices adversely affect the protected class (i.e., workers 40 and over) even though no such effect was intended by the employer (Zabell 1989). A small computer manufacturer laid off 10 of its 20 software engineers. The ages of all engineers at the time of the layoff are below. Analyze the data to determine whether the company may be vulnerable to a disparate impact claim.

LAYOFF

Not laid off:	34	55	42	38	42	32	40	40	46	29
Laid off:	52	35	40	41	40	39	40	64	47	44

Critical Thinking Challenges

2.148 No Child Left Behind Act. According to the government, federal spending on K-12 education has increased dramatically over the past 20 years, but student performance has essentially stayed the same. Hence, in 2002, President George Bush signed into law the No Child Left Behind Act, a bill that promised improved student achievement for all U.S. children. *Chance* (Fall 2003) reported on a graphic obtained from the U.S. Department of Education Web site (www.ed.gov) that was designed to support the new legislation. The graphic is reproduced below. The bars in the graph represent annual federal spending on education, in billions of dollars (left-side vertical axis). The horizontal line represents the annual average fourth-grade children's reading ability score (right-side vertical axis). Critically assess the information portrayed in the graph. Does it, in fact, support the government's position that our children are not making classroom improvements despite federal spending on educations? Use the following facts (divulged in the *Chance* article) to help you frame your answer: (1) The U.S. student population has also increased dramatically over the past 20 years, (2) fourth-grade reading test scores are designed to have an average of 250 with a standard deviation of 50, and (3) the reading test scores of seventh and twelfth grades and the mathematics scores of fourth graders did improve substantially over the past 20 years.

2.149 Steel rod quality. In his essay "Making Things Right," W. Edwards Deming considered the role of statistics in the quality control of industrial products.* In one example, Deming examined the quality-control process for a manufacturer of steel rods. Rods produced with diameters smaller than I centimeter fit too loosely in their bearings and ultimately must be rejected (thrown out). To determine whether the diameter setting of the machine that produces the rods is correct, 500 rods are selected from the day's production and their diameters are recorded. The distribution of the 500 diameters for one day's production is shown in the figure below. Note that the symbol LSL in the figure represents the 1-centimeter lower specification limit of the steel rod diameters. There has been speculation that some of the inspectors are unaware of the trouble that an undersized rod diameter would cause later in the manufacturing process. Consequently, these inspectors may be passing rods with diameters that were barely below the lower specification limit and recording them in the interval centered at 1.000 centimeter. According to the figure, is there any evidence to support this claim? Explain.

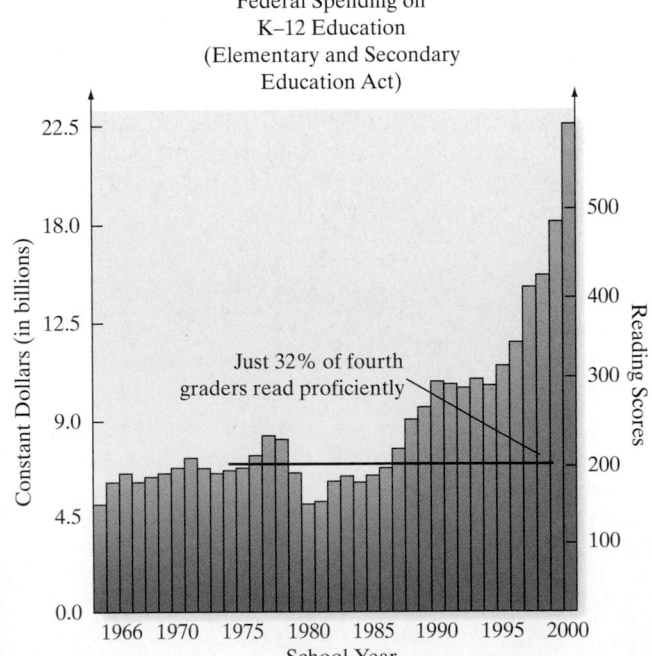

Federal Spending on
K–12 Education
(Elementary and Secondary
Education Act)

Just 32% of fourth graders read proficiently

Source: U.S. Department of Education.

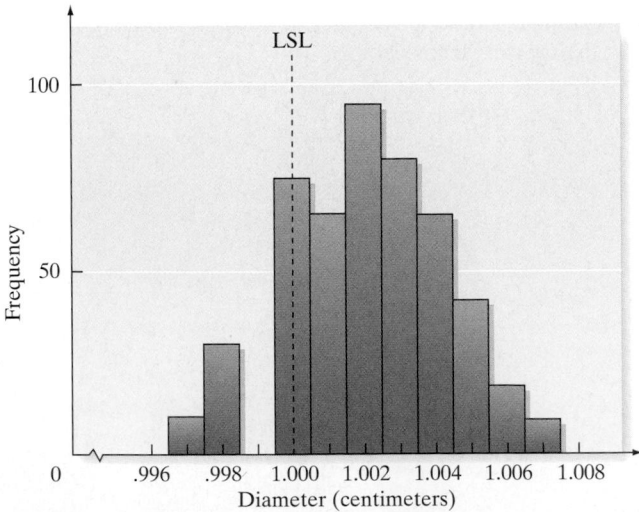

*From Tanur; J., et al., eds. *Statistics: A Guide to the Unknown*. San Francisco: Holden-Day, 1978, pp. 279–81.

REFERENCES

Deming, W. E. *Out of the Crisis*. Cambridge, Mass.: M.I.T. Center for Advanced Engineering Study, 1986.

Gitlow, H., Oppenheim, A., and Oppenheim, R. *Quality Management: Methods for Improvement*, 2nd ed. Burr Ridge, Ill.: Irwin, 1995.

Huff, D. *How to Lie with Statistics*. New York: Norton, 1954.

Ishikawa, K. *Guide to Quality Control*, 2nd ed. White Plains, N.Y.: Kraus International Publications, 1982.

Juran, J. M. *Juran on Planning for Quality*. New York: The Free Press, 1988.

Mendenhall, W., Beaver, R. J., and Beaver, B. M. *Introduction to Probability and Statistics*, 12th ed. North Scituate, Mass.: Duxbury, 2006.

Zabel, S. L. "Statistical Proof of Employment Discrimination." *Statistics: A Guide to the Unknown*, 3rd ed. Pacific Grove, Calif.: Wadsworth, 1989.

Tufte, E. R. *Envisioning Information*. Cheshire, Conn.: Graphics Press, 1990.

Tufte, E. R. *Visual Display of Quantiative Information*. Cheshire, Conn.: Graphics Press, 1983.

Tufte, E. R. *Visual Explanations*. Cheshire, Conn.: Graphics Press, 1997.

Tukey, J. *Exploratory Data Analysis*. Reading, Mass.: Addison-Wesley, 1977.

Using Technology

2.1 Describing Data Using SPSS

Graphing Data

To obtain graphical descriptions of data that appear in the SPSS spreadsheet, click on the "Graphs" button on the SPSS menu bar. The resulting menu list appears as shown in Figure 2.S.1. Several of the options covered in this text are "Bar (graph)", "Pie (chart)", "Pareto (diagram)", "Boxplot", "Scatter (plot)", and "Histogram". Click on the graph of your choice to view the appropriate dialog

Figure 2.S.1

SPSS menu options for graphing data

box. For example, the dialog box for a histogram is shown in Figure 2.S.2. Make the appropriate variable selections and click "OK" to view the graph.

Stem-and-leaf plots can be obtained by selecting "Analyze" from the main SPSS menu, then "Descriptive Statistics", then "Explore", as shown in Figure 2.S.3. In the "Explore" dialog box, select the variable to be analyzed in the "Dependent List" box, as shown in Figure 2.S.4. Click on either "Both" or "Plots" in the "Display" options, then click "OK" to display the stem-and-leaf graph.

Numerical Descriptive Statistics

To obtain numerical descriptive measures for a quantitative variable, click on the "Analyze" button on the main menu bar, then click on "Descriptive Statistics", as shown in Figure 2.S.3. To obtain standard descriptive statistics (e.g.,

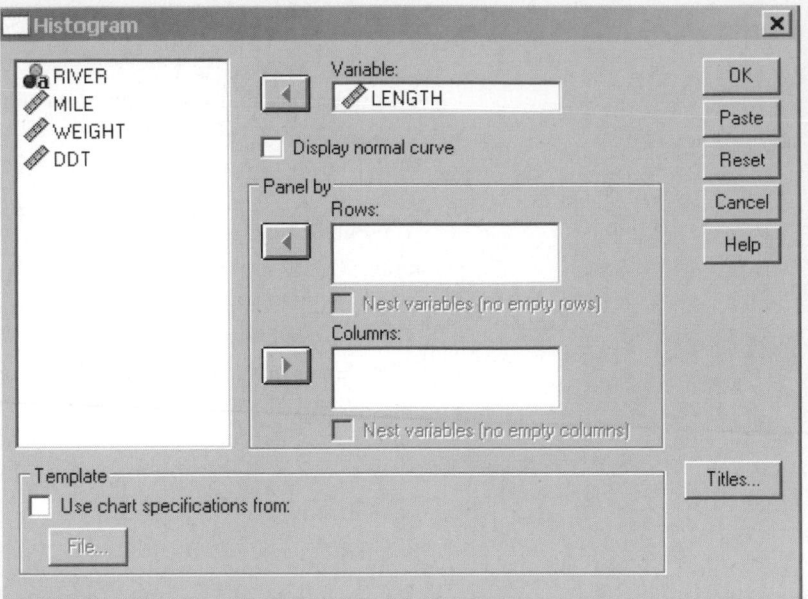

Figure 2.S.2
SPSS Histogram dialog box

Figure 2.S.3
SPSS menu options for descriptive statistics

Figure 2.S.4
SPSS Explore dialog box

Figure 2.S.5
SPSS Descriptive statistics
dialog box

mean, variance, standard deviation), select "Descriptives" from the menu; the dialog box shown in Figure 2.S.5 will appear. Select the quantitative variables you want to analyze and place them in the "Variable(s)" box. You can control which particular descriptive statistics appear by clicking the "Options" button on the dialog box and making your selections. Click on "OK" to view the descriptive statistics printout.

If you want these standard statistics as well as percentiles, select "Explore" from the main SPSS menu, as shown in Figure 2.S.3. In the resulting dialog box (see Figure 2.S.4), select the "Statistics" button and check the "Percentiles" box on the resulting menu. Return to the "Explore Dialog Box" and click "OK" to generate the descriptive statistics.

2.2 Describing Data Using MINITAB

Graphing Data

To obtain graphical descriptions of your data, click on the "Graph" button on the MINITAB menu bar. The resulting menu list appears as shown in Figure 2.M.1. Several of the options covered in this text are "Bar Chart," "Pie Chart," "Scatterplot", "Histogram", "Dotplot", and "Stem-and-Leaf (display)". Click on the graph of your choice to view the appropriate dialog box. For example, the dialog box for a histogram is shown in Figure 2.M.2. Make the appropriate variable selections and click "OK" to view the graph.

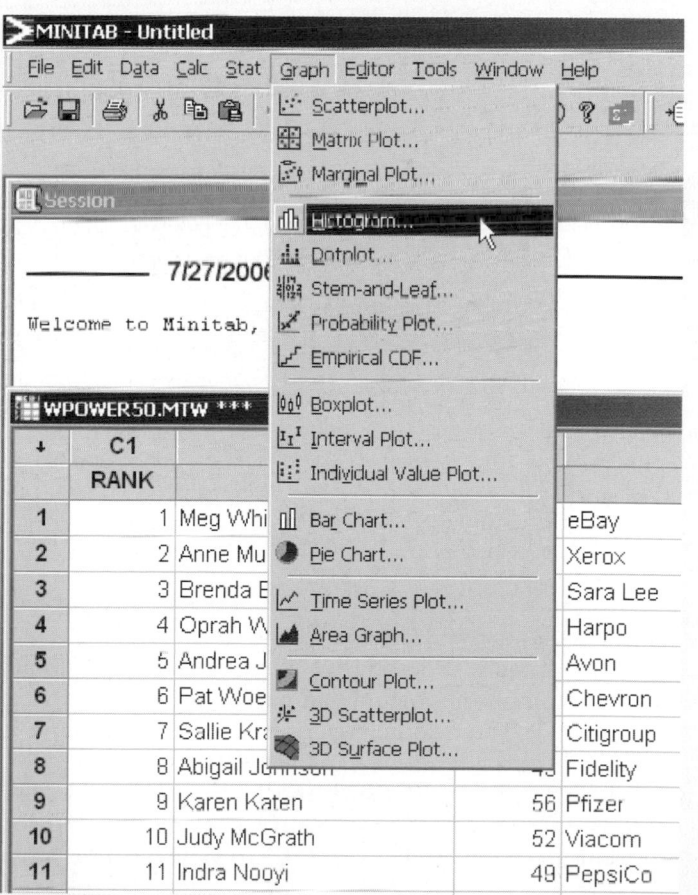

Figure 2.M.1
MINITAB menu options for graphing data

Figure 2.M.2
MINITAB Histogram
dialog box

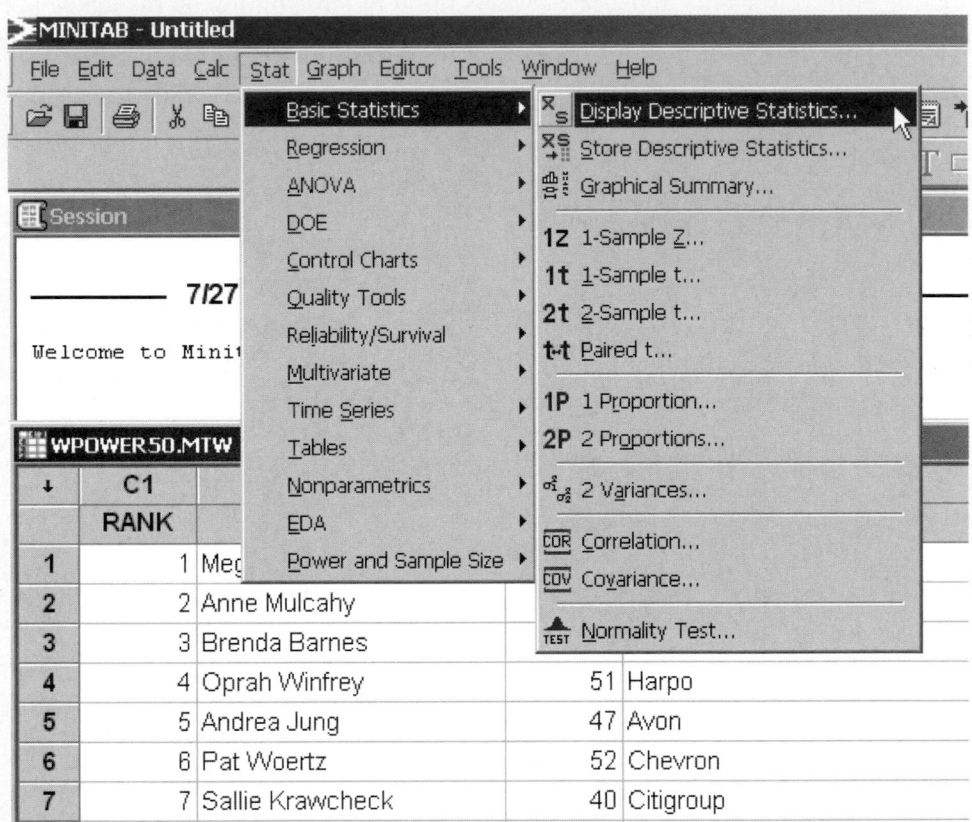

Figure 2.M.3
MINITAB options for
descriptive statistics

Numerical Descriptive Statistics

To obtain numerical descriptive measures for a quantitative variable (e.g., mean, standard deviation, etc.), click on the "Stat" button on the main menu bar, then click on "Basic Statistics", then click on "Display Descriptive Statistics" (see Figure 2.M.3). The resulting dialog box appears in Figure 2.M.4.

Select the quantitative variables you want to analyze and place them in the "Variables" box. You can control which particular descriptive statistics appear by clicking the "Statistics" button on the dialog box and making your selections. (As an option, you can create histograms and dot plots for the data by clicking the "Graphs" button and making the appropriate selections.) Click on "OK" to view the descriptive statistics printout.

Figure 2.M.4
MINITAB Descriptive
Statistics dialog box

2.3 Describing Data Using Excel/PHStat2

Graphing Data

To graph the data for a single variable in your Excel spreadsheet, click on the "PHStat" button on the Excel main menu bar, then on "Descriptive Statistics." The resulting menu will appear as shown in Figure 2.E.1. To obtain a pie chart, bar graph, or Pareto diagram for a qualitative variable, click on "One-Way Tables & Charts" (see Figure 2.E.1). The resulting dialog box appears as shown in Figure 2.E.2. Select the type of data, input the cell range of the variable, and select the type of graph (bar graph, pie chart, or Pareto diagram). Then click "OK" to view the graph.

Figure 2.E.1

Excel and PHStat2 menu
options for graphing your data

To obtain a graph for a single quantitative variable, select the appropriate option—"Boxplot", "Dot (scale diagram) plot", "Histograms", or "Stem-and-Leaf (display)"—from the available options shown in Figure 2.E.1. Make the appropriate menu choices in the resulting dialog box. For example, the dialog box for a histogram is shown in Figure 2.E.3. [*Note*: For a histogram, you will have to create two new variables with data on your Excel spreadsheet—"Bins" (which represent the right endpoints of the class intervals) and the "Midpoints" of each bin (or class interval).]

After making the menu selections, click "OK" to view the graph.

To obtain a scatterplot for two quantitative variables, click on the Chart Wizard on the Excel main menu selection. A series of four menus will appear. Step 1 of the Chart Wizard is shown in Figure 2.E.4. Make the appropriate menu choices, then click "Finish" to view the scatterplot. [*Note*: The two variables you want to graph must be in adjacent columns on the Excel spreadsheet.]

Figure 2.E.2
One-way charts dialog box

Figure 2.E.3
Histogram dialog box

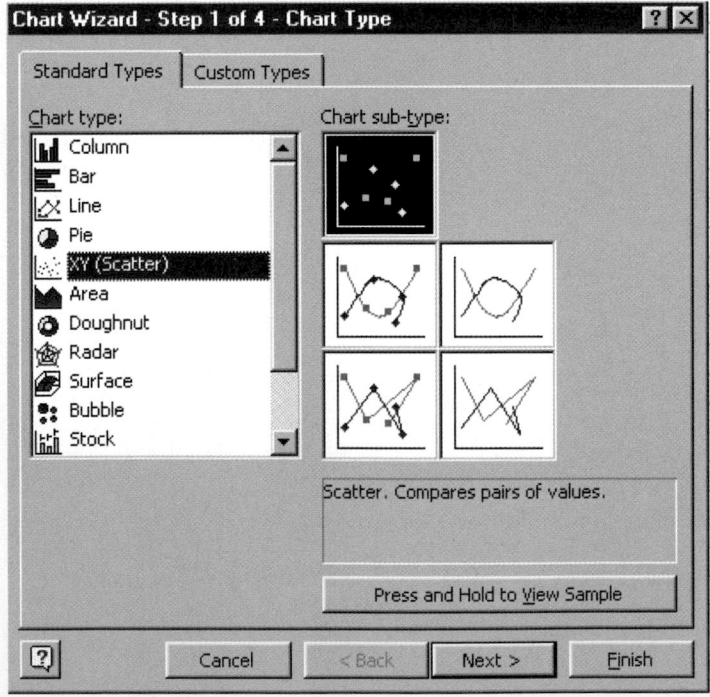

Figure 2.E.4
Step 1 of Chart Wizard for a scatterplot

Numerical Descriptive Statistics

To obtain numerical descriptive measures for a quantitative variable (e.g., mean, standard deviation, etc.), click on the "Tools" button on the main menu bar, then click on "Data Analysis", as shown in Figure 2.E.5. Select "Descriptive Statistics" from the resulting menu (see Figure 2.E.6). The resulting dialog box appears in Figure 2.E.7. Input the cell range of the variable to be analyzed and select "Summary Statistics". Then click on "OK" to view the descriptive statistics printout.

Figure 2.E.5

Main menu options for descriptive statistics

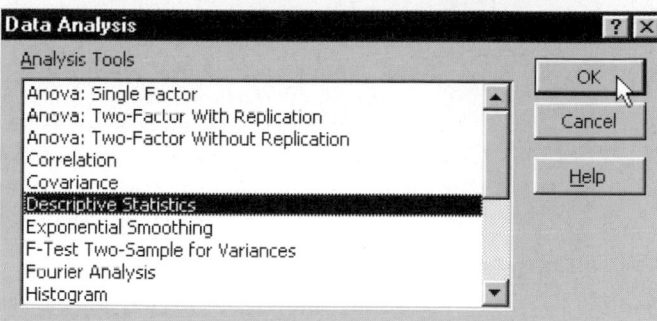

Figure 2.E.6

Data analysis menu

Figure 2.E.7

Descriptive statistics dialog box

Real-World Case

The Kentucky Milk Case—Part 1

(A Case Covering Chapters 1 and 2)

Many products and services are purchased by governments, cities, states, and businesses on the basis of scaled bids, and contracts are awarded to the lowest bidders. This process works extremely well in competitive markets, but it has the potential to increase the cost of purchasing if the markets are noncompetitive or if collusive practices are present. An investigation that began with a statistical analysis of bids in the Florida school milk market in 1986 led to the recovery of more than $33,000,000 from dairies that had conspired to rig the bids there in the 1980s. The investigation spread quickly to other states, and to date, settlements and fines from dairies exceed $100.000,000 for school milk bid-rigging in 20 other states. This case concerns a school milk bidrigging investigation in Kentucky.

Each year, the Commonwealth of Kentucky invites bids from dairies to supply half-pint containers of fluid milk products for its school districts. The products include whole white milk, low-fat white milk, and low-fat chocolate milk. In 13 school districts in northern Kentucky, the suppliers (dairies) were accused of "price-fixing" what is, conspiring to allocate the districts so that the "winner" was predetermined. Since these districts are located in

Boone, Campbell, and Kenton counties, the geographic market they represent is designated as the "tri-county" market. Between 1983 and 1991, two dairies—Meyer Dairy and Trauth Dairy—were the only bidders on the milk contracts in the school districts in the tri-county market. Consequently, these two companies were awarded all the milk contracts in the market. (In contrast, a large number of different dairies won the milk contracts for the school districts in the remainder of the northern Kentucky market—called the "surrounding" market.) The Commonwealth of Kentucky alleged that Meyer and Trauth conspired to allocate the districts in the tri-county market. To date, one of the dairies (Meyer) has admitted guilt, while the other (Trauth) steadfastly maintains its innocence.

The Commonwealth of Kentucky maintains a database on all bids received from the dairies competing for the milk contracts. Some of these data have been made available to you to analyze to determine whether there is empirical evidence of bid collusion in the tri-county market. The data, saved in the **MILK** file, are described in detail below. Some background information on the data and important economic theory regarding bid collusion is also provided. Use this information to guide your analysis. Prepare a professional document that presents the results of your analysis and gives your opinion regarding collusion.

 MILK (Number of observation: 392)

Variable	Type	Description
YEAR	QN	Year in which milk contract awarded
MARKET	QL	Northern Kentucky Market(TRI-COUNTY or SURROUND)
WINNER	QL	Name of winning dairy
WWBID	QN	Winning bid price of whole white milk(dollars per half-pint)
WWQTY	QN	Quantity of whole white milk purchased (number of half-pints)
LFWBID	QN	Winning bid price of low-far white milk (dollars per half-pints)
LFWQTY	QN	Quantity of low-fat white milk purchased (number of half-pint)
LFCBID	QN	Winning bid price of low-fat chocolate milk(dollars per half-pint)
LFCQTY	QN	Quantity of low-fat chocolate milk purchased (number of half-pints)
DISTRICT	QL	School district number
KYFMO	QN	FMO minimum raw cost of milk (dollars per half-pint)
MILESM	QN	Distance (miles) from Meyer processing plant to school district
MILEST	QN	Distance (miles) from Trauth processing plant to school district
LETDATE	QL	Date on which bidding on milk contract began (month/day/year)

Background Information

Collusive Market Environment

Certain economic features of a market create an environment in which collusion may be found. These basic features include the following:

1. *Few sellers and high concentration.* Only a few dairies control all or nearly all of the milk business in the market.

2. *Homogeneous products.* The products sold are essentially the same from the standpoint of the buyer (i.e., the school district).

3. *Inelastic demand.* Demand is relatively insensitive to price. (*Note:* The quantity of milk required by a school district is primarily determined by school enrollment, not price.)

4. *Similar costs.* The dairies bidding for the milk contracts face similar cost conditions. (*Note:* Approximately 60% of a dairy's production cost is raw milk, which is federally regulated. Meyer and Trauth are dairies of similar size and both bought their raw milk from the same supplier.)

Although these market structure characteristics create an environment that makes collusive behavior easier, they do not necessarily indicate the existence of collusion. An analysis of the actual bid prices may provide additional information about the degree of competition in the market.

Collusive Bidding Patterns

The analyses of patterns in sealed bids reveal much about the level of competition, or lack thereof, among the vendors serving the market. Consider the following bid analyses:

1. *Market shares.* A market share for a dairy is the number of milk half-pints supplied by the dairy over a given school year, divided by the total number of half-pints supplied to the entire market. One sign of potential collusive behavior is stable, nearly equal market shares over time for the dairies under investigation.

2. *Incumbency rates.* Market allocation is a common form of collusive behavior in bidrigging conspiracies. Typically, the same dairy controls the same school districts year after year. The incumbency rate for a market in a given school year is defined as the percentage of school districts that are won by the same vendor who won the previous year. An incumbency rate that exceeds 70% has been considered a sign of collusive behavior.

3. *Bid levels and dispersion.* In competitive sealed bid markets, vendors do not share information about their bids. Consequently, more dispersion or variability among the bids is observed than in collusive markets, where vendors communicate about their bids and have a tendency to submit bids in close proximity to one an-

other in an attempt to make the bidding appear competitive. Furthermore, in competitive markets the bid dispersion tends to be directly proportional to the level of the bid: When bids are submitted at relatively high levels, there is more variability among the bids than when they are submitted at or near marginal cost. Which will be approximately the same among dairies in the same geographic market.

4. *Price versus cost/distance.* In competitive markets, bid prices are expected to track costs over time. Thus, if the market is competitive, the bid price of milk should be highly correlated with the raw milk cost. Lack of such a relationship is another sign of collusion. Similarly, bid price should be correlated to the distance the product must travel from the processing plant to the school (due to delivery costs) in a competitive market.

5. *Bid sequence.* School milk bids are submitted over the spring and summer months, generally at the end of one school year and before the beginning of the next. When the bids are examined in sequence in competitive markets, the level of bidding is expected to fall as the bidding season progresses. (This phenomenon is attributable to the learning process that occurs during the season, with bids adjusted accordingly. Dairies may submit relatively high bids early in the season to "test the market," confident that volume can be picked up later if the early high bids lose. But, dairies who do not win much business early in the season are likely to become more aggressive in their bidding as the season progresses, driving price levels down.) Constant or slightly increasing price patterns of sequential bids in a market where a single dairy wins year after year is considered another indication of collusive behavior.

6. *Comparison of average winning bid prices.* Consider two similar markets, one in which bids are possibly rigged and the other in which bids are competitively determined. In theory, the mean winning price in the "rigged" market will be significantly higher than the mean price in the competitive market for each year in which collusion occurs.

CHAPTER

3

Probability

CONTENTS

STATISTICS IN ACTION
Lotto Buster!

USING TECHNOLOGY

WHERE WE'VE BEEN
- Identified the objective of inferential statistics: to make inferences about a population based on information in a sample

- Introduced graphical and numerical descriptive measures for both quantitative and qualitative data

WHERE WE'RE GOING
- Develop probability as a measure of uncertainty.

- Introduce basic rules for finding probabilities.

- Use probability as a measure of reliability for an inference.

Lotto Buster!

"Welcome to the Wonderful World of Lottery Bus$ters." So began the premier issue of Lottery Buster, *a monthly publication for players of the state lottery games.* Lottery Buster *provides interesting facts and figures on the 42 state lotteries and 2 multi-state lotteries currently operating in the United States and, more important, tips on how to increase a player's odds of winning the lottery.*

New Hampshire, in 1963, was the first state in modern times to authorize a state lottery as an alternative to increasing taxes. (Prior to this time, beginning in 1895, lotteries were banned in America because of corruption.) Since then, lotteries have become immensely popular for two reasons. First, they lure you with the opportunity to win millions of dollars with a $1 investment, and second, when you lose, at least you believe your money is going to a good cause. Many state lotteries, like Florida, designate a high percentage of lottery revenues to fund state education.

The popularity of the state lottery has brought with it an avalanche of "experts" and "mathematical wizards" (such as the editors of *Lottery Buster*) who provide advice on how to win the lottery—for a fee, of course! Many offer guaranteed "systems" of winning through computer software products with catchy names such as lotto Wizard, Lottorobics, Win4d, and Loto-luck.

For example, most knowledgeable lottery players would agree that the "golden rule" or "first rule" in winning lotteries is *game selection.* State lotteries generally offer three types of games: Instant (scratch-off tickets or online) game, Daily Numbers (Pick-3 or Pick-4), and weekly Pick-6 lotto' game.

One version of the Instant game involves scratching off the thin opaque covering on a ticket with the edge of a coin to determine whether you have won or lost. The cost of a ticket ranges from 50¢ to $5, and the amount won ranges from $1 to $100,000 in most states, and to as much as $1 million in others. *Lottery Buster* advises against playing the Instant game because it is "a pure chance play, and you can win only by dumb luck. No skill can be applied to this game."

The Daily Numbers game permits you to choose either a three-digit (Pick-3) or four-digit (Pick-4) number at a cost of $1 per ticket. Each night, the winning number is drawn. If your number matches the winning number, you win a large sum of money, usually $100,000. You do have some control over the Daily Numbers game (since you pick the numbers that you play), and, consequently, there are strategies available to increase your chances of winning. However, the Daily Numbers game, like the Instant game, is not available for out-of-state play.

To play Pick-6 Lotto, you select six numbers of your choice from a field of numbers ranging from 1 to *N*, where *N* depends on which state's game you are playing. For example, Florida's current Lotto game involves picking six numbers ranging from 1 to 53. (See Figure SIA3.1.) The cost of a ticket is $1 and the payoff, if your six numbers match the winning numbers drawn, is $7 million or more, depending on the number of

Figure SIA3.1

Reproduction of Florida's 6/53 Lotto ticket

tickets purchased. (To date, Florida has had the largest individual state weekly payoff of over $200 million.) In addition to the grand prize, you can win second-, third-, and fourth-prize payoffs by matching five, four, and three of the six numbers drawn, respectively. And you don't have to be a resident of the state to play the state's Lotto game.

In this chapter, several Statistics in Action Revisited examples demonstrate how to use the basic concepts of probability to compute the odds of winning a state lottery game and to assess the validity of the strategies suggested by lottery "experts."

Statistics in Action Revisited

- Computing and Understanding the Probability of Winning Lotto (p. 142)
- The Probability of Winning Lotto with a Wheel System (p. 151)
- The Probability of Winning Cash 3 or Play 4 (p. 165)

Recall that one branch of statistics is concerned with decisions about a population based on sample information. You can see how this is accomplished more easily if you understand the relationship between population and sample—a relationship that becomes clearer if we reverse the statistical procedure of making inferences from sample to population. In this chapter, then, we assume that the population is known and calculate the chances of obtaining various samples from the population. Thus, we show that probability is the reverse of statistics: In probability, we use the population information to infer the probable nature of the sample.

Probability plays an important role in inference-making. Suppose, for example, you have an opportunity to invest in an oil exploration company. Past records show that out of 10 previous oil drillings (a sample of the company's experiences), all 10 came up dry. What do you conclude? Do you think the chances are better than 50:50 that the company will hit a gusher? Should you invest in this company? Chances are, your answer to these questions will be an emphatic "no." If the company's exploratory prowess is sufficient to hit a producing well 50% of the time, a record of 10 dry wells out of 10 drilled is an event that is just too improbable.

Or suppose you're playing poker with what your opponents assure you is a well-shuffled deck of cards. In three consecutive five-card hands, the person on your right is dealt four aces. Based on this sample of three deals, do you think the cards are being adequately shuffled? Again, your answer is likely to be "no" because dealing three hands of four aces is just too improbable if the cards were properly shuffled.

Note that the decisions concerning the potential success of the oil drilling company and the adequacy of card shuffling both involve knowing the chance—or probability—of a certain sample result. Both situations were contrived so that you could easily conclude that the probabilities of the sample results were small. Unfortunately, the probabilities of many observed sample results aren't so easy to evaluate intuitively. For these cases we will need the assistance of a theory of probability.

3.1 Events, Sample Spaces, and Probability

Let's begin our treatment of probability with simple examples that are easily described. With the aid of simple examples, we can introduce important definitions that will help us develop the notion of probability more easily.

Suppose a coin is tossed once and the up face is recorded. The result we see and record is called an *observation*, or *measurement*, and the process of making an observation is called an *experiment*. Notice that our definition of *experiment* is broader than the one used in the physical sciences, where you would picture test tubes, microscopes, and other laboratory equipment. Among other things, statistical experiments may include recording an Internet user's preference for a Web browser, recording a change in the Dow Jones Industrial Average from one day to the next, recording the weekly sales of a business firm, and counting the number of errors on a page of an accountant's ledger. The point is that a statistical experiment can be almost any act of observation as long as the outcome is uncertain.

> **Definition 3.1**
>
> An **experiment** is an act or process of observation that leads to a single outcome that cannot be predicted with certainty.

Consider another simple experiment consisting of tossing a die and observing the number on the up face. The six basic possible outcomes to this experiment are as follows:

1. Observe a 1
2. Observe a 2
3. Observe a 3
4. Observe a 4
5. Observe a 5
6. Observe a 6

Note that if this experiment is conducted once, *you can observe one and only one of these six basic outcomes, and the outcome cannot be predicted with certainty.* Also, these possibilities cannot be decomposed into more basic outcomes. Because observing the outcome of an experiment is similar to selecting a sample from a population, the basic possible outcomes to an experiment are called *sample points.**

> **Definition 3.2**
>
> A **sample point** is the most basic outcome of an experiment.

EXAMPLE 3.1

Listing the Sample Points for a Coin-Tossing Experiment

Problem Two coins are tossed, and their up faces are recorded. List all the sample points for this experiment.

Solution Even for a seemingly trivial experiment, we must be careful when listing the sample points. At first glance, we might expect three basic outcomes: Observe two heads, Observe two tails, or Observe one head and one tail. However, further reflection reveals that the last of these, Observe one head and one tail, can be decomposed into two outcomes: Head on coin 1, Tail on coin 2; and Tail on coin 1, Head on coin 2. Thus, we have four sample points:

1. Observe *HH*
2. Observe *HT*
3. Observe *TH*
4. Observe *TT*

where *H* in the first position means "Head on coin 1," *H* in the second position means "Head on coin 2," and so on.

Look Back Even if the coins are identical in appearance, there are, in fact, two distinct coins. Thus, the sample points must account for this distinction.

Now Work Exercise 3.7a

We often wish to refer to the collection of all the sample points of an experiment. This collection is called the *sample space* of the experiment. For example, there are six sample points in the sample space associated with the die-toss experiment. The sample spaces for the experiments discussed thus far are shown in Table 3.1.

*Alternatively, the term *simple event* can be used.

TABLE 3.1   Experiments and Their Sample Spaces

Experiment: Observe the up face on a coin.
Sample space: 1. Observe a head
                    2. Observe a tail
This sample space can be represented in set notation as a set containing two sample points:

$$S: \{H, T\}$$

where H represents the sample point Observe a head and T represents the sample point Observe a tail.

Experiment: Observe the up face on a die.
Sample space: 1. Observe a 1
                    2. Observe a 2
                    3. Observe a 3
                    4. Observe a 4
                    5. Observe a 5
                    6. Observe a 6
This sample space can be represented in set notation as a set of six sample points:

$$S: \{1, 2, 3, 4, 5, 6\}$$

Experiment: Observe the up faces on two coins.
Sample space: 1. Observe HH
                    2. Observe HT
                    3. Observe TH
                    4. Observe TT
This sample space can be represented in set notation as a set of four sample points:

$$S: \{HH, HT, TH, TT\}$$

Definition 3.3

The **sample space** of an experiment is the collection of all its sample points.

Just as graphs are useful in describing sets of data, a pictorial method for presenting the sample space will often be useful. Figure 3.1 shows such a representation for each of the experiments in Table 3.1. In each case, the sample space is shown as a closed figure, labeled S, containing all possible sample points. Each sample point is represented by a solid dot (i.e., a "point") and labeled accordingly. Such graphical representations are called **Venn diagrams**.

Now that we know that an experiment will result in *only one* basic outcome—called a *sample point*—and that the sample space is the collection of all possible sample points, we're ready to discuss the probabilities of the sample points. You've undoubtedly used the term *probability* and have some intuitive idea about its meaning. Probability is generally used synonymously with "chance," "odds," and similar concepts. For example, if a fair coin is tossed, we might reason that both the sample points, Observe a head and Observe a tail, have the same *chance* of occurring. Thus, we might state that "the probability of observing a head is 50%" or "the *odds* of seeing a head are 50:50." Both of these statements are based on an informal knowledge of probability. We'll begin our treatment of probability by using such informal concepts and then solidify what we mean later.

The probability of a sample point is a number between 0 and 1 inclusive that measures the likelihood that the outcome will occur when the experiment is performed. This number is usually taken to be the relative frequency of the occurrence of a sample point in a very long series of repetitions of an experiment.* For example, if we are assigning probabilities to the two sample points (Observe a head and Observe a tail) in the coin-

a. Experiment: Observe the up face on a coin

b. Experiment: Observe the up face on a die

c. Experiment: Observe the up faces on two coins

FIGURE 3.1

Venn diagrams for the three experiments from Table 3.1

*The result derives from an axiom in probability theory called the **Law of Large Numbers**. Phrased informally, this law states that the relative frequency of the number of times that an outcome occurs when an experiment is replicated over and over again (i.e., a large number of times) approaches the theoretical probability of the outcome.

toss experiment, we might reason that if we toss a balanced coin a very large number of times, the sample points Observe a head and Observe a tail will occur with the same relative frequency of .5.

Biography

**JOHN VENN
(1834–1923)**

The English Logician

Born in Hull, England, John Venn is probably best know for his pictorial representation of unions and intersections (the Venn diagram). While lecturing in Moral Science at Cambridge University, Venn wrote *The Logic of Chance* and two other treatises on logic. In these works, Venn probably had his greatest contribution to the field of probability and statistics—the notion that the probability of an event is simply the long-run proportion of times the event occurs. Besides being a well-known mathematician, Venn was also a historian, philosopher, priest, and skilled machine builder. (His machine for bowling cricket balls once beat a top star on the Australian cricket team.)

Our reasoning is supported by Figure 3.2. The figure plots the relative frequency of the number of times that a head occurs when simulating (by computer) the toss of a coin N times, where N ranges from as few as 25 tosses to as many as 1,500 tosses of the coin. You can see that when N is large (i.e., $N = 1,500$), the relative frequency is converging to .5. Thus, the probability of each sample point in the coin-tossing experiment is .5.

For some experiments, we may have little or no information on the relative frequency of occurrence of the sample points; consequently, we must assign probabilities to the sample points based on general information about the experiment. For example, if the experiment is to invest in a business venture and to observe whether it succeeds or fails, the sample space would appear as in Figure 3.3. We are unlikely to be able to assign probabilities to the sample points of this experiment based on a long series of repetitions since unique factors govern each performance of this kind of experiment. Instead, we may consider factors such as the personnel managing the venture, the general state of the economy at the time, the rate of success of similar ventures, and any other pertinent information. If we finally decide that the venture has an 80% chance of succeeding, we assign a probability of .8 to the sample point Success. This probability can be interpreted as a measure of our degree of belief in the outcome of the business venture; that is, it is a subjective probability. Notice, however, that such probabilities should be based

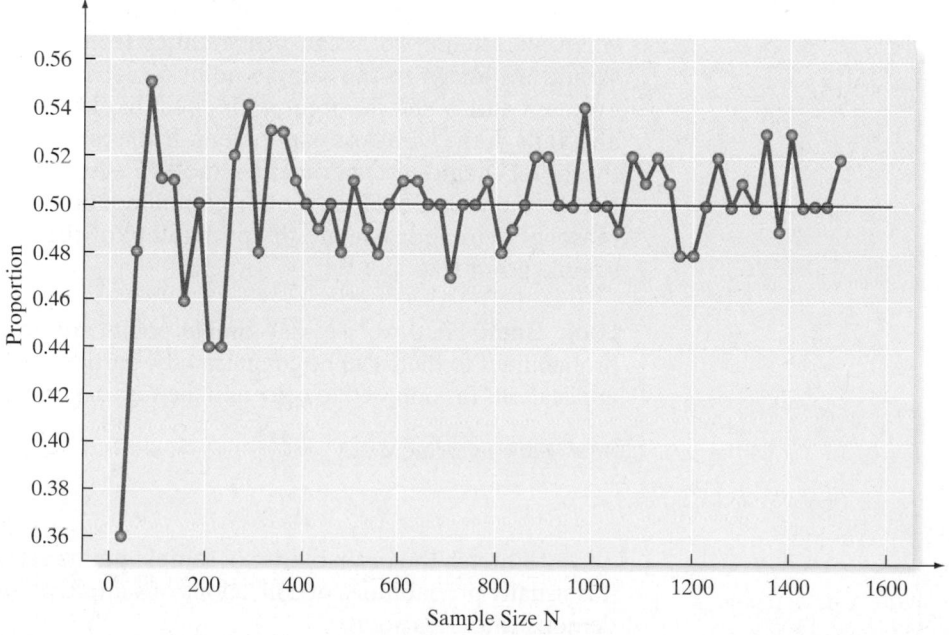

FIGURE 3.2

Proportion of heads
in N coin tosses

FIGURE 3.3
Experiment: Invest in a
business venture and observe
whether it succeeds (*S*) or
fails (*F*)

on expert information that is carefully assessed. If not, we may be misled on any decisions based on these probabilities or based on any calculations in which they appear. [*Note*: For a text that deals in detail with the subjective evaluation of probabilities, see Winkler (1972) or Lindley (1985).]

No matter how you assign the probabilities to sample points, the probabilities assigned must obey two rules:

Probability Rules for Sample Points

Let p_i represent the probability of sample point *i*.

1. All sample point probabilities *must* lie between 0 and 1 (i.e., $0 \leq p_i \leq 1$).
2. The probabilities of all the sample points within a sample space *must* sum to 1 (i.e., $\Sigma p_i = 1$).

Assigning probabilities to sample points is easy for some experiments. For example, if the experiment is to toss a fair coin and observe the face, we would probably all agree to assign a probability of $\frac{1}{2}$ to the two sample points, Observe a head and Observe a tail. However, many experiments have sample points whose probabilities are more difficult to assign.

EXAMPLE 3.2

Assigning
Probabilities to the
Sample Points for a
Hotel Guest Room
Survey

Problem Many American hotels offer complimentary shampoo in their guest rooms. Suppose you randomly select one hotel from a registry of all hotels in the United States and check whether or not the hotel offers complimentary shampoo. Show how this problem might be formulated in the framework of an experiment with sample points and a sample space. Indicate how probabilities might be assigned to the sample points.

Solution The experiment can be defined as the selection of an American hotel and the observation of whether or not complimentary shampoo is offered in the hotel's guest rooms. There are two sample points in the sample space corresponding to this experiment:

S: {The hotel offers complimentary shampoo}

N: {No complimentary shampoo is offered by the hotel}

The difference between this and the coin-toss experiment becomes apparent when we attempt to assign probabilities to the two sample points. What probability should we assign to the sample point *S*? If you answer .5, you are assuming that the events *S* and *N* should occur with equal likelihood, just like the sample points Heads and Tails in the coin-toss experiment. But assignment of sample point probabilities for the hotel-shampoo experiment is not so easy. In fact, a recent survey of American hotels found that 80% now offer complimentary shampoo to guests. Then it might be reasonable to approximate the probability of the sample point *S* as .8 and that of the sample point *N* as .2.

Look Back Here we see that sample points are not always equally likely, so assigning probabilities to them can be complicated—particularly for experiments that represent real applications (as opposed to coin- and die-toss experiments).

Now Work Exercise 3.12

Although the probabilities of sample points are often of interest in their own right, it is usually probabilities of collections of sample points that are important. Example 3.3 demonstrates this point.

EXAMPLE 3.3

Finding the Probability of a Collection of Sample Points from a Die-Tossing Experiment

Problem A fair die is tossed, and the up face is observed. If the face is even, you win $1. Otherwise, you lose $1. What is the probability that you win?

Solution Recall that the sample space for this experiment contains six sample points:

$$S: \{1, 2, 3, 4, 5, 6\}$$

Since the die is balanced, we assign a probability of $\frac{1}{6}$ to each of the sample points in this sample space. An even number will occur if one of the sample points, Observe a 2, Observe a 4, or Observe a 6, occurs. A collection of sample points such as this is called an *event*, which we denote by the letter A. Since the event A contains three sample points—each with probability $\frac{1}{6}$—and since no sample points can occur simultaneously, we reason that the probability of A is the sum of the probabilities of the sample points in A. Thus, the probability of A (i.e., the probability that you will win) is $\frac{1}{6} + \frac{1}{6} + \frac{1}{6} = \frac{1}{2}$.

Look Back Based on our notion of probability, $P(A) = \frac{1}{2}$ implies that, *in the long run*, you will win $1 half the time and lose $1 half the time.

Now Work Exercise 3.6

FIGURE 3.4
Die-toss experiment with event A: Observe an even number

Figure 3.4 is a Venn diagram depicting the sample space associated with a die-toss experiment and the event A, Observe an even number. The event A is represented by the closed figure inside the sample space S. This closed figure A contains all the sample points that comprise it.

To decide which sample points belong to the set associated with an event A, test each sample point in the sample space S. If event A occurs, then that sample point is in the event A. For example, the event A, Observe an even number, in the die-toss experiment will occur if the sample point Observe a 2 occurs. By the same reasoning, the sample points Observe a 4 and Observe a 6 are also in event A.

To summarize, we have demonstrated that an event can be defined in words or it can be defined as a specific set of sample points. This leads us to the following general definition of an event:

Definition 3.4

An **event** is a specific collection of sample points.

EXAMPLE 3.4

The Probability of an Event in a Coin-Tossing Experiment

Problem Consider the experiment of tossing two *unbalanced* coins. Because the coins are *not* balanced, their outcomes (H or T) are not equiprobable. Suppose the correct probabilities associated with the sample points are given in the table. [*Note:* The necessary properties for assigning probabilities to sample points are satisfied.]
Consider the events

$$A: \{\text{Observe exactly one head}\}$$
$$B: \{\text{Observe at least one head}\}$$

Calculate the probability of A and the probability of B.

Sample Point	Probability
HH	$\frac{4}{9}$
HT	$\frac{2}{9}$
TH	$\frac{2}{9}$
TT	$\frac{1}{9}$

Solution   Event A contains the sample points HT and TH. Since two or more sample points cannot occur at the same time, we can easily calculate the probability of event A by summing the probabilities of the two sample points. Thus, the probability of observing exactly one head (event A), denoted by the symbol $P(A)$, is

$$P(A) = P(\text{Observe } HT) + P (\text{Observe } TH) = \frac{2}{9} + \frac{2}{9} = \frac{4}{9}$$

Similarly, since B contains the sample points HH, HT, and TH,

$$P(B) = \frac{4}{9} + \frac{2}{9} + \frac{2}{9} = \frac{8}{9}$$

Look Back   Again, these probabilities should be interpreted *in the long run*. For example, $P(B) = 8/9 \approx .89$ implies that if we were to toss two coins an infinite number of times, we would observe at least 2 heads on about 89% of the tosses.

Now Work Exercise 3.3

The preceding example leads us to a general procedure for finding the probability of an event A:

Probability of an Event

The probability of an event A is calculated by summing the probabilities of the sample points in the sample space for A.

Thus, we can summarize the steps for calculating the probability of any event, as indicated in the next box.

Steps for Calculating Probabilities of Events

Step 1   Define the experiment; that is, describe the process used to make an observation and the type of observation that will be recorded.

Step 2   List the sample points.

Step 3   Assign probabilities to the sample points.

Step 4   Determine the collection of sample points contained in the event of interest.

Step 5   Sum the sample point probabilities to get the event probability.

EXAMPLE 3.5

Applying the Five Steps to Find a Probability in Diversity Training

Problem   Diversity training of employees is the latest trend in U.S. business. *USA Today* reported on the primary reasons businesses give for making diversity training part of their strategic planning process. The reasons are summarized in Table 3.2. Assume that one business is selected at random from all U.S. businesses that use diversity training, and the primary reason is determined.

TABLE 3.2   Primary Reasons for Diversity Training

Reason	Percentage
Comply with personnel policies (CPP)	7
Increase productivity (IP)	47
Stay competitive (SC)	38
Social responsibility (SR)	4
Other (O)	4
Total	100%

FIGURE 3.5
Venn diagram for diversity
training survey

**TABLE 3.3 Sample Point
Probabilities for Diversity
Training Survey**

Sample Point	Probability
CPP	.07
IP	.47
SC	.38
SR	.04
O	.04

a. Define the experiment that generated the data in Table 3.2, and list the sample points.

b. Assign probabilities to the sample points.

c. What is the probability that the primary reason for diversity training is business related; that is, related to competition or productivity?

d. What is the probability that social responsibility is not a primary reason for diversity training?

Solution

a. The experiment is the act of determining the primary reason for diversity training of employees at a U.S. business. The sample points, the simplest outcomes of the experiment, are the five response categories listed in Table 3.2. These sample points are shown in the Venn diagram in Figure 3.5.

b. If, as in Example 3.1, we were to assign equal probabilities in this case, each of the response categories would have a probability of one-fifth ($\frac{1}{5}$), or .20. But, by examining Table 3.2 you can see that equal probabilities are not reasonable here because the response percentages were not even approximately the same in the five classifications. It is more reasonable to assign a probability equal to the response percentage in each class, as shown in Table 3.3.*

c. Let the symbol B represent the event that the primary reason for diversity training is business related. B is not a sample point because it consists of more than one of the response classifications (the sample points). In fact, as shown in Figure 3.5, B consists of two sample points, IP and SC. The probability of B is defined to be the sum of the probabilities of the sample points in B.

$$P(B) = P(IP) + P(SC) = .47 + .38 = .85$$

d. Let NSR represent the event that social responsibility is not a primary reason for diversity training. Then NSR consists of all sample points except SR, and the probability is the sum of the corresponding sample point probabilities:

$$P(NSR) = P(CPP) + P(IP) + P(SC) + P(O)$$
$$= .07 + .47 + .38 + .04 = .96$$

Look Back The key to solving this problem is to follow the steps outlined in the box. We defined the experiment (Step 1) and listed the sample points (Step 2) in part a. The assignment of probabilities to the sample points (Step 3) was done in part b. For each probability in parts c and d, we identified the collection of points in the event (Step 4) and summed their probabilities (Step 5).

Now Work Exercise 3.13

EXAMPLE 3.6

The Probability of
Investing in a
Successful Venture

Problem You have the capital to invest in two of four ventures, each of which requires approximately the same amount of investment capital. Unknown to you, two of the investments will eventually fail and two will be successful. You research the four ventures because you think that your research will increase your probability of a successful choice over a purely random selection, and you eventually decide on two. If you used none of the information generated by your research, and selected two ventures at random, what is the probability that you would select at least one successful venture?

*The response percentages were based on a sample of U.S. businesses: consequently, these assigned probabilities are estimates of the true population-response percentages. You'll learn how to measure the reliability of probability estimates in Chapter 5.

Solution

Step 1: Denote the two successful enterprises as S_1 and S_2 and the two failing enterprises as F_1 and F_2. The experiment involves a random selection of two out of the four ventures, and each possible pair of ventures represents a sample point.

Step 2: The six sample points that make up the sample space are

1. (S_1, S_2)
2. (S_1, F_1)
3. (S_1, F_2)
4. (S_2, F_1)
5. (S_2, F_2)
6. (F_1, F_2)

Step 3: Next, we assign probabilities to the sample points. If we assume that the choice of any one pair is as likely as any other, then the probability of each sample point is $1/6$.

Step 4: The event of selecting at least one of the two successful ventures includes all the sample points except (F_1, F_2).

Step 5: Now, we find

$$P(\text{Select at least one success}) = P(S_1, S_2) + P(S_1, F_1) + P(S_1, F_2) + P(S_2, F_1) \\ + P(S_2, F_2)$$
$$= \tfrac{1}{6} + \tfrac{1}{6} + \tfrac{1}{6} + \tfrac{1}{6} + \tfrac{1}{6} = \tfrac{5}{6}$$

Therefore, with a random selection, the probability of selecting at least one successful venture out of two is $5/6$.

The preceding examples have one thing in common: The number of sample points in each of the sample spaces was small; hence, the sample points were easy to identify and list. How can we manage this when the sample points run into the thousands or millions? For example, suppose you wish to select five business ventures from a group of 1,000. Then each different group of five ventures would represent a sample point. How can you determine the number of sample points associated with this experiment?

One method of determining the number of sample points for a complex experiment is to develop a counting system. Start by examining a simple version of the experiment. For example, see if you can develop a system for counting the number of ways to select two ventures from a total of four (this is exactly what was done in Example 3.6). If the ventures are represented by the symbols V_1, V_2, V_3, and V_4, the sample points could be listed in the following pattern:

$$(V_1, V_2) \qquad (V_2, V_3) \qquad (V_3, V_4)$$
$$(V_1, V_3) \qquad (V_2, V_4)$$
$$(V_1, V_4)$$

Note the pattern and now try a more complex situation—say, sampling three ventures out of five. List the sample points and observe the pattern. Finally, see if you can deduce the pattern for the general case. Perhaps you can program a computer to produce the matching and counting for the number of samples of 5 selected from a total of 1,000.

A second method of determining the number of sample points for an experiment is to use **combinatorial mathematics.** This branch of mathematics is concerned with developing counting rules for given situations. For example, there is a simple rule for finding the number of different samples of five ventures selected from 1,000. This rule, called the **Combinations Rule,** is given in the box.

Combinations Rule

A sample of n elements is to be drawn from a set of N elements. Then, the number of different samples possible is denoted by $\binom{N}{n}$ and is equal to

$$\binom{N}{n} = \frac{N!}{n!(N-n)!}$$

where the factorial symbol (!) means that

$$n! = n(n-1)(n-2)\cdots(3)(2)(1)$$

For example, $5! = 5 \cdot 4 \cdot 3 \cdot 2 \cdot 1$. [*Note:* The quantity $0!$ is defined to be equal to 1.]

EXAMPLE 3.7

Using the Combinations Rule to Determine the Number of Possible Investments: Selecting 2 from 4

Problem Refer to Example 3.6, where we selected two ventures from four in which to invest. Use the combinations counting rule to determine how many different selections can be made.

Solution For this example, $N = 4$, $n = 2$, and

$$\binom{4}{2} = \frac{4!}{2!2!} = \frac{4 \cdot 3 \cdot 2 \cdot 1}{(2 \cdot 1)(2 \cdot 1)} = 6$$

Look Back You can see that this agrees with the number of sample points obtained in Example 3.6.

Now Work Exercise 3.4

EXAMPLE 3.8

Using the Combinations Rule to Determine the Number of Possible Investments: Selecting 5 from 20

Problem Suppose you plan to invest equal amounts of money in each of five business ventures. If you have 20 ventures from which to make the selection, how many different samples of five ventures can be selected from the 20?

Solution For this example, $N = 20$ and $n = 5$. Then the number of different samples of 5 that can be selected from the 20 ventures is

$$\binom{20}{5} = \frac{20!}{5!(20-5)!} = \frac{20!}{5!15!}$$

$$= \frac{20 \cdot 19 \cdot 18 \cdots 3 \cdot 2 \cdot 1}{(5 \cdot 4 \cdot 3 \cdot 2 \cdot 1)(15 \cdot 14 \cdot 13 \cdot \cdots \cdot 3 \cdot 2 \cdot 1)} = \frac{20 \cdot 19 \cdot 18 \cdot 17 \cdot 16}{5 \cdot 4 \cdot 3 \cdot 2 \cdot 1} = 15{,}504$$

Look Back You can see that attempting to list all the sample points for this experiment would be an extremely tedious and time consuming, if not practically impossible, task.

The Combinations Rule is just one of a large number of counting rules that have been developed by combinatorial mathematicians. This counting rule applies to situations in which the experiment calls for selecting n elements from a total of N elements, without replacing each element before the next is selected. If you are interested in learning other methods for counting sample points for various types of experiments, you will find a few of the basic counting rules in Appendix A. Others can be found in the chapter references.

STATISTICS IN ACTION REVISITED

Computing and Understanding the Probability of Winning Lotto

In Florida's state lottery game, called Pick-6 Lotto, you select six numbers of your choice from a set of numbers ranging from 1 to 53. We can apply the Combinations Rule to determine the total number of combinations of 6 numbers selected from 53 (i.e., the total number of sample points [or possible winning tickets]). Here, $N = 53$ and $n = 6$; therefore, we have

$$\binom{N}{n} = \frac{N!}{n!(N-n)!} = \frac{53!}{6!47!}$$
$$= \frac{(53)(52)(51)(50)(49)(48)(47!)}{(6)(5)(4)(3)(2)(1)(47!)}$$
$$= 22{,}957{,}480$$

Now, since the Lotto balls are selected at random, each of these 22,957,480 combinations is equally likely to occur. Therefore, the probability of winning Lotto is

$$P(\text{Win 6/53 Lotto}) = 1/(22{,}957{,}480) = .00000004356$$

This probability is often stated as follows: The odds of winning the game with a single ticket are 1 in 22,957,480, or, 1 in approximately 23 million. For all practical purposes, this probability is 0, implying that you have almost no chance of winning the lottery with a single ticket. Yet each week there is almost always a winner in the Florida Lotto. This apparent contradiction can be explained with the following analogy.

Suppose there is a line of minivans, front-to-back, from New York City to Los Angeles, California. Based on the distance between the two cities and the length of a standard minivan, there would be approximately 23 million minivans in line. Lottery officials will select, at random, one of the minivans and put a check for $10 million dollars in the glove compartment. For a cost of $1, you may roam the country and select one (and only one) minivan and check the glove compartment. Do you think you will find $10 million in the minivan you choose? You can be almost certain that you won't. But now permit anyone to enter the lottery for $1 and suppose that 50 million people do so. With such a large number of participants, it is very likely that someone will find the minivan with the $10 million—but it almost certainly won't be you! (This example illustrates an axiom in statistics called the Law of Large Numbers. See the footnote at the bottom of p. 134.)

Exercises 3.1–3.21

Learning the Mechanics

3.1 An experiment results in one of the following sample points: $E_1, E_2, E_3, E_4,$ or E_5.
    a. Find $P(E_3)$ if $P(E_1) = .1, P(E_2) = .2, P(E_4) = .1,$ and $P(E_5) = .1$.
    b. Find $P(E_3)$ if $P(E_1) = P(E_3), P(E_2) = .1, P(E_4) = .2,$ and $P(E_5) = .1$.
    c. Find $P(E_3)$ if $P(E_1) = P(E_2) = P(E_4) = P(E_5) = .1$.

3.2 The accompanying diagram describes the sample space of a particular experiment and events A and B.
    a. What is this type of diagram called?
    b. Suppose the sample points are equally likely. Find $P(A)$ and $P(B)$.
    c. Suppose $P(1) = P(2) = P(3) = P(4) = P(5) = \frac{1}{20}$ and $P(6) = P(7) = P(8) = P(9) = P(10) = \frac{3}{20}$. Find $P(A)$ and $P(B)$.

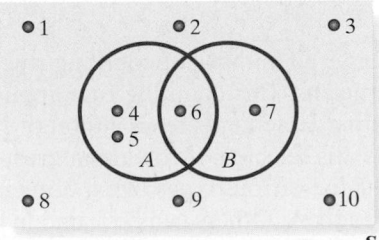

3.3 The sample space for an experiment contains five sample points with probabilities as shown in the table. Find the probability of each of the following events:

Sample Points	Probabilities
1	.05
2	.20
3	.30
4	.30
5	.15

A: {Either 1, 2, or 3 occurs}
B: {Either 1, 3, or 5 occurs}
C: {4 does not occur}

3.4 Compute each of the following:
    a. $\binom{9}{4}$ **b.** $\binom{7}{2}$ **c.** $\binom{4}{4}$
    d. $\binom{5}{0}$ **e.** $\binom{6}{5}$

3.5 Compute the number of ways you can select n elements from N elements for each of the following:
    a. $n = 2, N = 5$
    b. $n = 3, N = 6$
    c. $n = 5, N = 20$

3.6 Two fair dice are tossed, and the face on each die is
NW observed.
- **a.** List the 36 sample points contained in the sample space.
- **b.** Assign probabilities to the sample points in part a.
- **c.** Find the probability of each of the following events:

$$A = \{3 \text{ showing on each die}\}$$
$$B = \{\text{sum of two numbers showing is 7}\}$$
$$C = \{\text{sum of two numbers showing is even}\}$$

3.7 Two marbles are drawn at random and without replacement from a box containing two blue marbles and three red marbles.
NW **a.** List the sample points for this experiment.
- **b.** Assign probabilities to the sample points.
- **c.** Determine the probability of observing each of the following events:

$$A: \{\text{Two blue marbles are drawn}\}$$
$$B: \{\text{A red and a blue marble are drawn}\}$$
$$C: \{\text{Two red marbles are drawn}\}$$

3.8 Simulate the experiment described in Exercise 3.7 using any five identically shaped objects, two of which are one color and three, another. Mix the objects, draw two, record the results, and then replace the objects. Repeat the experiment a large number of times (at least 100). Calculate the proportion of time events A, B, and C occur. How do these proportions compare with the probabilities you calculated in Exercise 3.7? Should these proportions equal the probabilities? Explain.

APPLET **Applet Exercise 3.1**

Use the applet entitled *Simulating the Probability of Rolling a 6* to explore the relationship between the proportion of 6s rolled on several rolls of a die and the theoretical probability of rolling a 6 on a fair die.
- **a.** To simulate rolling a die one time, click on the *Roll* button on the screen while $n = 1$. The outcome of the roll appears in the list at the right, and the cumulative proportion of 6s for one roll is shown above the graph and as a point on the graph corresponding to 1. Click *Reset* and repeat the process with $n = 1$ several times. What are the possible values of the cumulative proportion of 6s for one roll of a die? Can the cumulative proportion of 6s for one roll of a die equal the theoretical probability of rolling a 6 on a fair die? Explain.
- **b.** Set $n = 10$ and click the *Roll* button. Repeat this several times, resetting after each time. Record the cumulative proportion of 6s for each roll. Compare the cumulative proportions for $n = 10$ to those for $n = 1$ in part **a.** Which tend to be closer to the theoretical probability of rolling a 6 on a fair die?
- **c.** Repeat part **b** for $n = 1000$, comparing the cumulative proportions for $n = 1000$ to those for $n = 1$ in part **a** and for $n = 10$ in part **b.**
- **d.** Based on your results for parts **a, b,** and **c,** do you believe that we could justifiably conclude that a die is unfair because we rolled it 10 times and didn't roll any 6s? Explain.

APPLET **Applet Exercise 3.2**

Use the applet entitled *Simulating the Probability of a Head with a Fair Coin* to explore the relationship between the proportion of heads on several flips of a coin and the theoretical probability of getting heads on one flip of a fair coin.
- **a.** Repeat parts **a–c** of Applet Exercise 3.1 for the experiment of flipping a coin and the event of getting heads.
- **b.** Based on your results for part **a,** do you believe that we could justifiably conclude that a coin is unfair because we flipped it 10 times and didn't roll any heads? Explain.

Applying the Concepts—Basic

3.9 **Annual compensation and benefits report.** Each year, Hudson Institute surveys 10,000 U.S. workers about their total compensation packages. One question in Hudson's *2006 Compensation and Benefits Report* focused on employees who received raises in the past year. Of these employees, 35% reported that their raise was based on job performance, 50% reported that it was based on a standard cost of living, and the remainder (15%) were unsure how their raises were determined. Suppose we select (at random) one of the U.S. workers surveyed who received a raise last year and inquire about how that worker's raise was determined.
- **a.** List the sample points for this experiment.
- **b.** Assign reasonable probabilities to the sample points.
- **c.** Find the probability that the raise was based either on job performance or a standard cost of living.

3.10 **Assaults against postal workers.** *The Wall Street Journal* (Sept. 1, 2000) reported on an independent study of postal workers and violence at post offices. In a sample of 12,000 postal workers, 600 of them were physically assaulted on the job in the past year. Use this information to estimate the probability that a randomly selected postal worker will be physically assaulted on the job during the year.

3.11 **USDA chicken inspection.** The United States Department of Agriculture (USDA) reports that, under its standard inspection system, one in every 100 slaughtered chickens pass inspection with fecal contamination. (*Tampa Tribune*, Mar. 31, 2000.)
- **a.** If a slaughtered chicken is selected at random, what is the probability that it passes inspection with fecal contamination?
- **b.** The probability of part **a** was based on a USDA study that found that 306 of 32,075 chicken carcasses passed inspection with fecal contamination. Do you agree with the USDA's statement about the likelihood of a slaughtered chicken passing inspection with fecal contamination?

3.12 **Identifying urban counties.** *Urban* and *rural* describe geo-
NW graphic areas upon which land zoning regulations, school district policy, and public service policy are often set. However, the characteristics of urban/rural areas are not clearly defined. Researchers at the University of Nevada (Reno) asked a sample of county commissioners to give their perception of the single most important factor in identifying urban counties (*Professional Geographer*, Feb. 2000). In all, five factors were mentioned by the commissioners: total population, agricultural change, presence of industry, growth, and population concentration. The survey

order): Infiniti M35, Toyota Prius, and Chevrolet Corvette. (*Consumer Reports*, Apr. 2006).

a. List all possible sets of rankings for these top three cars.

b. Assuming that each set of rankings in part **a** is equally likely, what is the probability that readers ranked Toyota Prius first? That readers ranked Infiniti M35 third? That readers ranked Toyota Prius first and Chevrolet Corvette second (which is, in fact, what they did)?

Applying the Concepts—Advanced

3.19 Odds of winning a race. Handicappers for greyhound races express their belief about the probabilities that each greyhound will win a race in terms of **odds.** If the probability of event E is $P(E)$, then the *odds in favor of E* are $P(E)$ to $1 - P(E)$. Thus, if a handicapper assesses a probability of .25 that Oxford Shoes will win its next race, the odds in favor of Oxford Shoes are $^{25}/_{100}$ to $^{75}/_{100}$, or 1 to 3. It follows that the *odds against E* are $1 - P(E)$ to $P(E)$, or 3 to 1 against a win by Oxford Shoes. In general, if the odds in favor of event E are a to b, then $P(E) = a/(a + b)$.

a. A second handicapper assesses the probability of a win by Oxford Shoes to be $^1/_3$. According to the second handicapper, what are the odds in favor of Oxford Shoes winning?

b. A third handicapper assesses the odds in favor of Oxford Shoes to be 1 to 1. According to the third handicapper, what is the probability of Oxford Shoes winning?

c. A fourth handicapper assesses the odds against Oxford Shoes winning to be 3 to 2. Find this handicapper's assessment of the probability that Oxford Shoes will win.

3.20 Lead bullets as forensic evidence. *Chance* (Summer 2004) published an article on the use of lead bullets as forensic evidence in a federal criminal case. Typically, the Federal Bureau of Investigation (FBI) will use a laboratory method to match the lead in a bullet found at the crime scene with unexpended lead cartridges found in possession of the suspect. The value of this evidence depends on the chance of a *false positive* (i.e., the probability that the FBI finds a match given that the lead at the crime scene and the lead in possession of the suspect are actually from two different "melts," or sources). To estimate the false-positive rate, the FBI collected 1,837 bullets that they were confident all came from different melts. The FBI then examined every possible pair of bullets and counted the number of matches using its established criteria. According to *Chance*, the FBI found 693 matches. Use this information to compute the chance of a false positive. Is this probability small enough for you to have confidence in the FBI's forensic evidence?

3.21 Profile of a sustainable farmer. *Sustainable development or sustainable farming* means "finding ways to live and work the Earth without jeopardizing the future" (*Minneapolis Star Tribune*, June 20, 1992). Studies were conducted in five Midwestern states to develop a profile of a sustainable farmer. The results revealed that farmers can be classified along a sustainability scale, depending on whether they are likely (L) or unlikely (U) to engage in the following practices: (1) Raise a broad mix of crops; (2) raise livestock; (3) use chemicals sparingly; and (4) use techniques for regenerating the soil, such as crop rotation.

a. List the different sets of classifications that are possible for the four practices (e.g., LUUL).

b. Suppose you are planning to interview farmers across the country to determine the frequency with which they fall into the classification sets you listed for part a. Since no information is yet available, assume initially that there is an equal chance of a farmer falling into any single classification set. Using that assumption, what is the probability that a farmer will be classified as unlikely on all four criteria (i.e., classified as a nonsustainable farmer)?

c. Using the same assumption as in part b, what is the probability that a farmer will be classified as likely on at least three of the criteria (i.e., classified as a near-sustainable farmer)?

3.2 Unions and Intersections

An event can often be viewed as a composition of two or more other events. Such events, which are called **compound events,** can be formed (composed) in two ways, as defined and illustrated here.

Definition 3.5

The **union** of two events A and B is the event that occurs if either A or B or both occur on a single performance of the experiment. We denote the union of events A and B by the symbol $A \cup B$. $A \cup B$ consists of all the sample points that belong to A or B or both. (See Figure 3.6a.)

Definition 3.6

The **intersection** of two events A and B is the event that occurs if both A and B occur on a single performance of the experiment. We write $A \cap B$ for the intersection of A and B. $A \cap B$ consists of all the sample points belonging to *both A and B*. (See Figure 3.6b.)

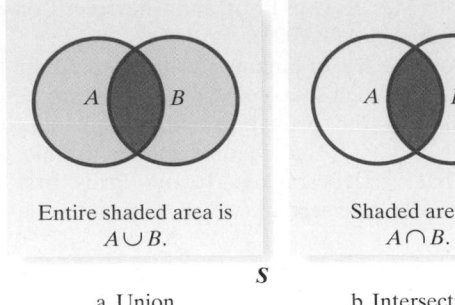

Entire shaded area is $A \cup B$.	Shaded area is $A \cap B$.
a. Union	b. Intersection

FIGURE 3.6
Venn diagrams for union and intersection

EXAMPLE 3.9

Probabilities of Unions and Intersections in a Die-Toss Experiment

Problem   Consider the die-toss experiment. Define the following events:

A: {Toss an even number}
B: {Toss a number less than or equal to 3}

a. Describe $A \cup B$ for this experiment.
b. Describe $A \cap B$ for this experiment.
c. Calculate $P(A \cup B)$ and $P(A \cap B)$ assuming the die is fair.

Solution   Draw the Venn diagram as shown in Figure 3.7.

a. The union of A and B is the event that occurs if we observe either an even number, a number less than or equal to 3, or both on a single throw of the die. Consequently, the sample points in the event $A \cup B$ are those for which A occurs, B occurs, or both A and B occur. Checking the sample points in the entire sample space, we find that the collection of sample points in the union of A and B is

$$A \cup B = \{1, 2, 3, 4, 6\}$$

b. The intersection of A and B is the event that occurs if we observe *both* an even number and a number less than or equal to 3 on a single throw of the die. Checking the sample points to see which imply the occurrence of *both* events A and B, we see that the intersection contains only one sample point:

$$A \cap B = \{2\}$$

In other words, the intersection of A and B is the sample point Observe a 2.

c. Recalling that the probability of an event is the sum of the probabilities of the sample points of which the event is composed, we have

$$P(A \cup B) = P(1) + P(2) + P(3) + P(4) + P(6)$$
$$= \tfrac{1}{6} + \tfrac{1}{6} + \tfrac{1}{6} + \tfrac{1}{6} + \tfrac{1}{6} = \tfrac{5}{6}$$

and

$$P(A \cap B) = P(2) = \tfrac{1}{6}$$

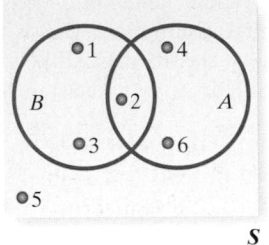

FIGURE 3.7
Venn diagram for die toss

Now Work Exercise 3.25 a–d

EXAMPLE 3.10

Finding Probabilities in a Two-Way Table for a Mass Mailing: Income Versus Age

Problem   Many firms undertake direct marketing campaigns to promote their products. The campaigns typically involve mailing information to millions of households. The response rates are carefully monitored to determine the demographic characteristics of respondents. By studying tendencies to respond, the firms can better target future mailings to those segments of the population most likely to purchase their products.

TABLE 3.4 Two-Way Table with Percentage of Respondents in Age-Income Classes

AGE	INCOME		
	< $25,000	$25,000–$50,000	> $50,000
< 30 yrs	5%	12%	10%
30–50 yrs	14%	22%	16%
> 50 yrs	8%	10%	3%

Suppose a distributor of mail-order tools is analyzing the results of a recent mailing. The probability of response is believed to be related to income and age. The percentages of the total number of respondents to the mailing are given by income and age classification in Table 3.4. This table is called a **two-way table** since responses are classified according to two variables, income (columns) and age (rows).

Define the following events:

> A: {A respondent's income is more than $50,000}
>
> B: {A respondent's age is 30 or more}

a. Find $P(A)$ and $P(B)$.

b. Find $P(A \cup B)$.

c. Find $P(A \cap B)$.

Solution Following the steps for calculating probabilities of events, we first note that the objective is to characterize the income and age distribution of respondents to the mailing. To accomplish this, we define the experiment to consist of selecting a respondent from the collection of all respondents and observing which income and age class he or she occupies. The sample points are the nine different age-income classifications:

E_1: {< 30 yrs, < $25,000} E_4: {< 30 yrs, $25,000–$50,000} E_7: {< 30 yrs, > $50,000}

E_2: {30–50 yrs, < $25,000} E_5: {30–50 yrs, $25,000–$50,000} E_8: {30–50 yrs, > $50,000}

E_3: {> 50 yrs, < $25,000} E_6: {> 50 yrs, $25,000–$50,000} E_9: {> 50 yrs, > $50,000}

Next, we assign probabilities to the sample points. If we blindly select one of the respondents, the probability that he or she will occupy a particular age-income classification is just the proportion, or relative frequency, of respondents in the classification. These proportions are given (as percentages) in Table 3.4. Thus,

$$P(E_1) = \text{Relative frequency of respondents in age-income class}$$
$$\{< 30 \text{ yrs}, < \$25,000\} = .05$$
$$P(E_2) = .14$$
$$P(E_3) = .08$$
$$P(E_4) = .12$$
$$P(E_5) = .22$$
$$P(E_6) = .10$$
$$P(E_7) = .10$$
$$P(E_8) = .16$$
$$P(E_9) = .03$$

You may verify that the sample points probabilities add to 1.

a. To find $P(A)$, we first determine the collection of sample points contained in event A. Since A is defined as {>$50,000}, we see from Table 3.4 that A contains the three sample points represented by the last column of the table. In other words, the event A consists of the income classification $\{>\$50,000\}$ in all three age classifications. The probability of A is the sum of the probabilities of the sample points in A:

$$P(A) = P(E_7) + P(E_8) + P(E_9) = .10 + .16 + .03 = .29$$

Similarly, $B = \{\geq 30 \text{ yrs}\}$ consists of the six sample points in the second and third rows of Table 3.4:

$$P(B) = P(E_2) + P(E_3) + P(E_5) + P(E_6) + P(E_8) + P(E_9)$$
$$= .14 + .08 + .22 + .10 + .16 + .03 = .73$$

b. The union of events A and B, $A \cup B$, consists of all the sample points in *either A or B or both*—that is, the union of A and B consists of all respondents whose income exceeds \$50,000 *or* whose age is 30 or more. In Table 3.4 this is any sample point found in the third column *or* the last two rows. Thus,

$$P(A \cup B) = .10 + .14 + .22 + .16 + .08 + .10 + .03 = .83$$

c. The intersection of events A and B, $A \cap B$, consists of all sample points in *both A and B*—that is, the intersection of A and B consists of all respondents whose income exceeds \$50,000 *and* whose age is 30 or more. In Table 3.4 this is any sample point found in the third column *and* the last two rows. Thus,

$$P(A \cap B) = .16 + .03 = .19$$

Look Back As with previous problems, the key to finding the probabilities of parts **b** and **c** is to identify the sample points that comprise the event of interest. In a two-way table like Table 3.4, the number of sample points will be equal to the number of rows times the number of columns.

Now Work Exercise 3.27f–g

3.3 Complementary Events

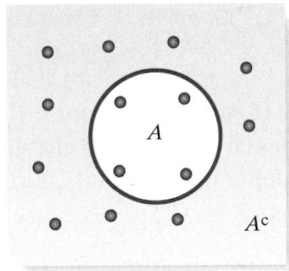

FIGURE 3.8

Venn diagram of complementary events

A very useful concept in the calculation of event probabilities is the notion of *complementary events:*

> **Definition 3.7**
>
> The **complement** of an event A is the event that A does *not* occur—that is, the event consisting of all sample points that are not in event A. We denote the complement of A by A^c.

An event A is a collection of sample points, and the sample points included in A^c are those not in A. Figure 3.8 demonstrates this idea. Note from the figure that all sample points in S are included in *either A or A^c* and that *no* sample point is in both A and A^c. This leads us to conclude that the probabilities of an event and its complement *must sum to 1:*

> **Rule of Complements**
>
> The sum of the probabilities of complementary events equals 1; that is,
> $P(A) + P(A^c) = 1$.

In many probability problems, calculating the probability of the complement of the event of interest is easier than calculating the event itself. Then, because

$$P(A) + P(A^c) = 1$$

we can calculate $P(A)$ by using the relationship

$$P(A) = 1 - P(A^c)$$

EXAMPLE 3.11

Probabilities of Complementary Events in a Coin-Tossing Experiment

Problem Consider the experiment of tossing two fair coins. Use the complementary relationship to calculate the probability of event A: {Observing at least one head}.

Solution We know that the event A: {Observing at least one head} consists of the sample points

$$A: \{HH, HT, TH\}$$

The complement of A is defined as the event that occurs when A does not occur. Therefore,

$$A^c: \{\text{Observe no heads}\} = \{TT\}$$

This complementary relationship is shown in Figure 3.9. Assuming the coins are balanced,

$$P(A^c) = P(TT) = {}^1\!/_4$$

and

$$P(A) = 1 - P(A^c) = 1 - {}^1\!/_4 = {}^3\!/_4$$

Look Back Note that we could have found $P(A)$ by summing the probabilities of the sample points HH, HT, and TH in A. Many times it is easier to find the probability of A^c and use the rule of complements.

Now Work Exercise 3.25e–f

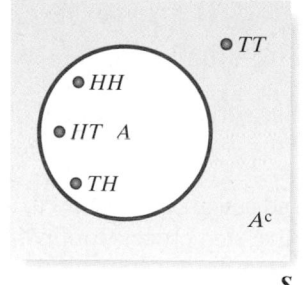

FIGURE 3.9
Complementary events in the toss of two coins

3.4 The Additive Rule and Mutually Exclusive Events

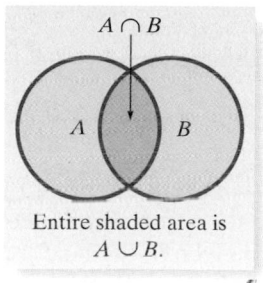

Entire shaded area is $A \cup B$.

FIGURE 3.10
Venn diagram of union

In Section 3.2 we saw how to determine which sample points are contained in a union and how to calculate the probability of the union by adding the probabilities of the sample points in the union. It is also possible to obtain the probability of the union of two events by using the **additive rule of probability.**

The union of two events will often contain many sample points, since the union occurs if either one or both of the events occur. By studying the Venn diagram in Figure 3.10, you can see that the probability of the union of two events, A and B, can be obtained by summing $P(A)$ and $P(B)$ and subtracting the probability corresponding to $A \cap B$. Therefore, the formula for calculating the probability of the union of two events is given in the next box.

Additive Rule of Probability

The probability of the union of events A and B is the sum of the probabilities of events A and B minus the probability of the intersection of events A and B—that is,

$$P(A \cup B) = P(A) + P(B) - P(A \cap B)$$

EXAMPLE 3.12

Applying the Additive Rule to a Hospital Admission Study

Problem Hospital records show that 12% of all patients are admitted for surgical treatment, 16% are admitted for obstetrics, and 2% receive both obstetrics and surgical treatment. If a new patient is admitted to the hospital, what is the probability that the patient will be admitted either for surgery, obstetrics, or both? Use the additive rule of probability to arrive at the answer.

Solution Consider the following events:

A: {A patient admitted to the hospital receives surgical treatment}

B: {A patient admitted to the hospital receives obstetrics treatment}

Then, from the given information,

$$P(A) = .12$$
$$P(B) = .16$$

and the probability of the event that a patient receives both obstetrics and surgical treatment is

$$P(A \cap B) = .02$$

The event that a patient admitted to the hospital receives either surgical treatment, obstetrics treatment, or both is the union $A \cup B$. The probability of $A \cup B$ is given by the additive rule of probability:

$$P(A \cup B) = P(A) + P(B) - P(A \cap B) = .12 + .16 - .02 = .26$$

Thus, 26% of all patients admitted to the hospital receive either surgical treatment, obstetrics treatment, or both.

Look Back From the information given, it is not possible to list and assign probabilities to all the sample points. Consequently, we cannot proceed through the five-step process for finding the probability of an event and must use the Additive Rule.

Now Work Exercise 3.22

A very special relationship exists between events A and B when $A \cap B$ contains no sample points. In this case we call the events A and B *mutually exclusive events*.

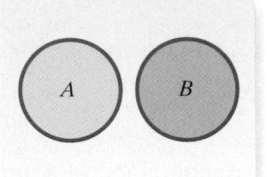

FIGURE 3.11
Venn diagram of mutually exclusive events

> **Definition 3.8**
> Events A and B are **mutually exclusive** if $A \cap B$ contains no sample points—that is, if A and B have no sample points in common.

Figure 3.11 shows a Venn diagram of two mutually exclusive events. The events A and B have no sample points in common—that is, A and B cannot occur simultaneously, and $P(A \cap B) = 0$. Thus, we have the important relationship given in the box.

> **Probability of Union of Two Mutually Exclusive Events**
>
> If two events A and B are *mutually exclusive*, the probability of the union of A and B equals the sum of the probabilities of A and B; that is, $P(A \cup B) = P(A) + P(B)$.

Caution
The formula just shown is *false* if the events are *not* mutually exclusive. In this case (i.e., two nonmutually exclusive events), you must apply the general additive rule of probability.

EXAMPLE 3.13
The Union of Two Mutually Exclusive Events in a Coin-Tossing Experiment

Problem   Consider the experiment of tossing two balanced coins. Find the probability of observing at *least* one head.

Solution   Define the events

A: {Observe at least one head}
B: {Observe exactly one head}
C: {Observe exactly two heads}

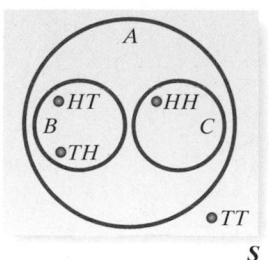

FIGURE 3.12

Venn diagram for coin-toss experiment

Note that

$$A = B \cup C$$

and that $B \cap C$ contains no sample points (see Figure 3.12). Thus, B and C are mutually exclusive, so that

$$P(A) = P(B \cup C) = P(B) + P(C) = \tfrac{1}{2} + \tfrac{1}{4} = \tfrac{3}{4}$$

Look Back Although this example is very simple, it shows us that writing events with verbal descriptions that include the phrases "at least" or "at most" as unions of mutually exclusive events is very useful. This practice enables us to find the probability of the event by adding the probabilities of the mutually exclusive events.

STATISTICS IN ACTION REVISITED

The Probability of Winning Lotto with a Wheel System

Refer to Florida's Pick-6 Lotto game in which you select six numbers of your choice from a field of numbers ranging from 1 to 53. In Section 3.1, we learned that the probability of winning Lotto on a single ticket is only 1 in approximately 23 million. The "experts" at Lotto Buster recommend many strategies for increasing the odds of winning the lottery. One strategy is to employ a wheeling system. In a complete wheeling system, you select more than six numbers, say, seven, and play every combination of six of those seven numbers.

Suppose you choose to "wheel" the following seven numbers: 2, 7, 18, 23, 30, 32, and 51. Every combination of six of these seven numbers is listed in Table SIA3.1. You can see that there are seven different possibilities. (Use the Combinations Rule with $N = 7$ and $n = 6$ to verify this.) Thus, we would purchase seven tickets (at a cost of $7) corresponding to these different combinations in a complete wheeling system.

To determine if this strategy does, in fact, increase our odds of winning, we need to find the probability that one of these seven combinations occurs during the 6/53 Lotto draw—that is, we need to find the probability that either Ticket 1 or Ticket 2 or Ticket 3 or Ticket 4 or Ticket 5 or Ticket 6 or Ticket 7 is the winning combination. Note that this probability is stated using the word *or*, implying a union of seven events. Letting T1 represent the event that Ticket 1 wins, and defining T2, T3, . . ., T7 in a similar fashion, we want to find

$$P(\text{T1 or T2 or T3 or T4 or T5 or T6 of T7})$$

Recall (Section 3.1) that the 22,957,480 possible combinations in Pick-6 Lotto are mutually exclusive and equally likely to occur. Consequently, the probability of the union of the seven events is simply the sum of the probabilities of the individual events, where each event has probability of 1/(22,957,480):

$$P(\text{win Lotto with 7 wheeled numbers})$$
$$= P(\text{T1 or T2 or T3 or T4 or T5 or T6 or T7})$$
$$= 7/(22,957,480) = .0000003$$

In terms of odds, we now have 3 chances in 10 million of winning the Lotto with the complete wheeling system. The "experts" are correct—our odds of winning Lotto have increased (from 1 in 23 million). However, the probability of winning is so close to 0 we question whether the $7 spent on lottery tickets is worth the negligible increase in odds. In fact, it can be shown that to increase your chance of winning the 6/53 Lotto to 1 chance in 100 (i.e., .01) using a complete wheeling system, you would have to wheel 26 of your favorite numbers—a total of 230,230 combinations at a cost of $230,230!

TABLE SIA3.1 Wheeling the Six Numbers 2, 7, 18, 23, 30, 32, and 51

Ticket 1	2	7	18	23	30	32
Ticket 2	2	7	18	23	30	51
Ticket 3	2	7	18	23	32	51
Ticket 4	2	7	18	30	32	51
Ticket 5	2	7	23	30	32	51
Ticket 6	2	18	23	30	32	51
Ticket 7	7	18	23	30	32	51

Exercises 3.22–3.40

Learning the Mechanics

3.22 Suppose $P(A) = .4$, $P(B) = .7$, and $P(A \cap B) = .3$. Find
NW the following probabilities:
   a. $P(B^c)$ **b.** $P(A^c)$ **c.** $P(A \cup B)$

3.23 A fair coin is tossed three times and the events A and B are
defined as follows:

   A: {At least one head is observed}
   B: {The number of heads observed is odd}

   a. Identify the sample points in the events A, B, $A \cup B$, A^c
   and $A \cap B$.
   b. Find $P(A)$, $P(B)$, $P(A \cup B)$, $P(A^c)$, and $P(A \cap B)$ by
   summing the probabilities of the appropriate sample
   points.
   c. Find $P(A \cup B)$ using the additive rule. Compare your
   answer to the one you obtained in part **b**.
   d. Are the events A and B mutually exclusive? Why?

3.24 A pair of fair dice is tossed. Define the following events:

   A: {You will roll a 7} (i.e., the sum of the dots
       on the up faces of the two dice is equal to 7)

   B: {At least one of the two dice shows a 4}

   a. Identify the sample points in the events A, B, $A \cap B$,
   $A \cup B$, and A^c.
   b. Find $P(A)$, $P(B)$, $P(A \cap B)$, $P(A \cup B)$, and $P(A^c)$ by
   summing the probabilities of the appropriate sample
   points.
   c. Find $P(A \cup B)$ using the additive rule. Compare your
   answer to that for the same event in part **b**.
   d. Are A and B mutually exclusive? Why?

3.25 Consider the accompanying Venn diagram, where
NW
$$P(E_1) = P(E_2) = P(E_3) = \tfrac{1}{5}, P(E_4) = P(E_5) = \tfrac{1}{20},$$
$$P(E_6) = \tfrac{1}{10}, \text{ and } P(E_7) = \tfrac{1}{5}.$$

Find each of the following probabilities:
   a. $P(A)$ **b.** $P(B)$
   c. $P(A \cup B)$ **d.** $P(A \cap B)$
   e. $P(A^c)$ **f.** $P(B^c)$
   g. $P(A \cup A^c)$ **h.** $P(A^c \cap B)$

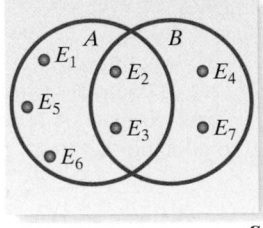

3.26 Consider the next Venn diagram, where

$$P(E_1) = .10, P(E_2) = .05, P(E_3) = P(E_4) = .2,$$
$$P(E_5) = .06, P(E_6) = .3, P(E_7) = .06, \text{ and}$$
$$P(E_8) = .03.$$

Find the following probabilities:
   a. $P(A^c)$ **b.** $P(B^c)$ **c.** $P(A^c \cap B)$
   d. $P(A \cup B))$ **e.** $P(A \cap B)$ **f.** $P(A^c \cup B^c)$
   g. Are events A and B mutually exclusive? Why?

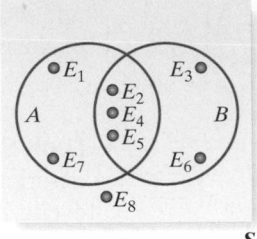

3.27 The outcomes of two variables are (Low, Medium, High) and
(On, Off), respectively. An experiment is conducted in which
the outcomes of each of the two variables are observed. The
probabilities associated with each of the six possible outcome pairs are given in the accompanying two-way table.

	Low	Medium	High
On	.50	.10	.05
Off	.25	.07	.03

Consider the following events:

   A: {On}
   B: {Medium or On}
   C: {Off and Low}
   D: {High}

   a. Find $P(A)$.
   b. Find $P(B)$.
   c. Find $P(C)$.
   d. Find $P(D)$.
   e. Find $P(A^c)$.
NW **f.** Find $P(A \cup B)$.
NW **g.** Find $P(A \cap C)$.
   h. Consider each pair of events (A and B, A and C, A and D,
   B and C, B and D, C and D). List the pairs of events that
   are mutually exclusive. Justify your choices.

3.28 Refer to Exercise 3.27. Use the same event definitions to do
the following exercises.
   a. Write the event that the outcome is "On" and "High" as
   an intersection of two events.
   b. Write the event that the outcome is "Low" or "Medium"
   as the complement of an event.

APPLET Applet Exercise 3.3

Use the applets entitled *Simulating the Probability of Rolling a 6*
and *Simulating the Probability of Rolling a 3 or 4* to explore the
additive rule for probability.
   a. Explain why the applet *Simulating the Probability of
   Rolling a 6* can also be used to simulate the probability of
   rolling a 3. Then use the applet with $n = 1000$ to simulate
   the probability of rolling a 3. Record the cumulative proportion. Repeat the process to simulate the probability of
   rolling a 4.
   b. Use the applet *Simulating the Probability of Rolling a 3 or 4*
   with $n = 1000$ to simulate the probability of rolling a 3 or 4.
   Record the cumulative proportion.
   c. Add the two cumulative proportions from part **a**. How does
   this sum compare to the cumulative proportion in part **b**?
   How does this illustrate the additive rule for probability?

APPLET **Applet Exercise 3.4**

Use the applets entitled *Simulating the Probability of Rolling a 6* and *Simulating the Probability of Rolling a 3 or 4* to simulate the probability of the complement of an event.

a. Explain how the applet *Simulating the Probability of Rolling a 6* can also be used to simulate the probability of the event *rolling a 1, 2, 3, 4, or 5*. Then use the applet with $n = 1000$ to simulate this probability.

b. Explain how the applet *Simulating the Probability of Rolling a 3 or 4* can also be used to simulate the probability of the event *rolling a 1, 2, 5, or 6*. Then use the applet with $n = 1000$ to simulate this probability.

c. Which applet could be used to simulate the probability of the event *rolling a 1, 2, 3, or 4*? Explain.

Applying the Concepts—Basic

3.29 Ownership of small businesses. According to the *Journal of Business Venturing* (Vol. 17, 2002), 27% of all small businesses owned by non-Hispanic whites nationwide are women-owned firms. If we select, at random, a small business owned by a non-Hispanic white, what is the probability that it is a male-owned firm?

3.30 Problems at major companies. The *Organization Development Journal* (Summer 2006) reported on the results of a survey of human resource officers (HROs) at major employers located in a southeastern city. The focus of the study was employee behavior, namely absenteeism, promptness to work, and turnover. The study found that 55% of the HROs had problems with employee absenteeism; also, 41% had problems with turnover. Suppose that 22% of the HROs had problems with both absenteeism and turnover. Use this information to find the probability that a human resource officer selected from the group surveyed had problems with either employee absenteeism or employee turnover.

3.31 Use of cellular phone features. Harris Interactive conducted a survey of cellular phone owners to estimate the likelihood of using extra phone features, such as the calendar, address book, instant messaging, e-mail, and so on. The results were reported online at *BusinessWeek.com* (Aug. 17, 2005). The following table shows the percentage of 18- to 34-year-olds who use the extra cell phone features. (Note that the percentages in the table do not sum to 100% since a cell phone owner may use more than one feature.)

Cell Phone Feature	Percentage of 18- to 34-Year-Olds
Calendar and address book	56%
Download and/or play games	54%
Download ringtones	47%
Instant messaging	43%
Take pictures	35%
Send and receive e-mail	28%
Access the Internet	34%
None of the above	16%

Source: BusinessWeek.com, Aug. 17, 2005.

a. Estimate the probability that an 18- to 34-year-old cell phone owner uses instant messaging.

b. Estimate the probability that an 18- to 34-year-old cell phone owner uses at least one of the features listed in the table.

3.32 The game of roulette. *Roulette* is a very popular game in many American casinos. In roulette, a ball spins on a circular wheel that is divided into 38 arcs of equal length, bearing the numbers 00, 0, 1, 2, . . . , 35, 36. The number of the arc on which the ball stops is the outcome of one play of the game. The numbers are also colored in the following manner:

Red: 1, 3, 5, 7, 9, 12, 14, 16, 18, 19, 21, 23, 25, 27, 30, 32, 34, 36
Black: 2, 4, 6, 8, 10, 11, 13, 15, 17, 20, 22, 24, 26, 28, 29, 31, 33, 35
Green: 00, 0

Players may place bets on the table in a variety of ways, including bets on odd, even, red, black, high, low, etc. Define the following events:

> *A:* {Outcome is an odd number (00 and 0 are considered neither odd nor even)}
> *B:* {Outcome is a black number}
> *C:* {Outcome is a low number (1–18)}

a. Define the event $A \cap B$ as a specific set of sample points.

b. Define the event $A \cup B$ as a specific set of sample points.

c. Find $P(A)$, $P(B)$, $P(A \cap B)$, $P(A \cup B)$, and $P(C)$ by summing the probabilities of the appropriate sample points.

d. Define the event $A \cap B \cap C$ as a specific set of sample points.

e. Find $P(A \cup B)$ using the additive rule. Are events A and B mutually exclusive? Why?

f. Find $P(A \cap B \cap C)$ by summing the probabilities of the sample points given in part d.

g. Define the event $A \cup B \cup C$ as a specific set of sample points.

h. Find $P(A \cup B \cup C)$ by summing the probabilities of the sample points given in part g.

3.33 Inactive oil and gas structures. U.S. federal regulations require that operating companies clear all inactive offshore oil and gas structures within 1 year after production ceases. Researchers at the Louisiana State University Center for Energy Studies gathered data on both active and inactive oil and gas structures in the Gulf of Mexico (*Oil & Gas Journal,* Jan. 3, 2005). They discovered that the gulf had 2,175 active and 1,225 idle (inactive) structures at the end of 2003. The following table breaks down these structures by type (caisson, well protector, or fixed platform). Consider the structure type and active status of one of these oil/gas structures.

	STRUCTURE TYPE			
	Caisson	Well Protector	Fixed Platform	Totals
Active	503	225	1,447	2,175
Inactive	598	177	450	1,225

Source: Kaiser, M., and Mesyanzhinov, D. "Study Tabulates Idle Gulf of Mexico Structures." *Oil & Gas Journal,* Vol 103, No. 1, Jan. 3, 2005 (Table 2).

a. List the simple events for this experiment.

b. Assign reasonable probabilities to the simple events.

c. Find the probability that the structure is active.

d. Find the probability that the structure is a well protector.

e. Find the probability that the structure is an inactive caisson.

f. Find the probability that the structure is either inactive or a fixed platform.

g. Find the probability that the structure is not a caisson.

3.34 Characteristics of a new product. The long-run success of a business depends on its ability to market products with superior characteristics that maximize consumer satisfaction and that give the firm a competitive advantage (Kotler, *Marketing Management*, 1994). Ten new products have been developed by a food-products firm. Market research has indicated that the 10 products have the characteristics described by the following Venn diagram:

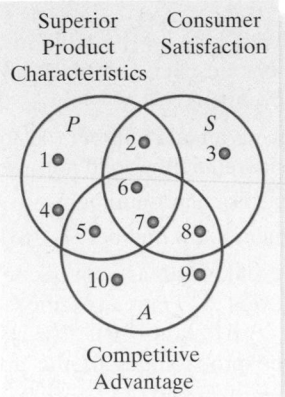

Superior Product Characteristics   Consumer Satisfaction

Competitive Advantage

a. Write the event that a product possesses all the desired characteristics as an intersection of the events defined in the Venn diagram. Which products are contained in this intersection?

b. If one of the 10 products were selected at random to be marketed, what is the probability that it would possess all the desired characteristics?

c. Write the event that the randomly selected product would give the firm a competitive advantage or would satisfy consumers as a union of the events defined in the Venn diagram. Find the probability of this union.

d. Write the event that the randomly selected product would possess superior product characteristics and satisfy consumers. Find the probability of this intersection.

Applying the Concepts—Intermediate

3.35 Appeals of federal civil trials. The *Journal of the American Law and Economics Association* (Vol. 3, 2001) published the results of a study of appeals of federal civil trials. The following table, extracted from the article, gives a breakdown of 2,143 civil cases that were appealed by either the plaintiff or the defendant. The outcome of the appeal, as well as the type of trial (judge or jury), was determined for each civil case. Suppose one of the 2,143 cases is selected at random and both the outcome of the appeal and type of trial are observed.

	Jury	Judge	Totals
Plaintiff trial win—reversed	194	71	265
Plaintiff trial win—affirmed/dismissed	429	240	669
Defendant trial win—reversed	111	68	179
Defendant trial win—affirmed/dismissed	731	299	1,030
Totals	1,465	678	2,143

a. Find $P(A)$, where $A = $ {jury trial}.

b. Find $P(B)$, where $B = $ {plaintiff trial win is reversed}.

c. Are A and B mutually exclusive events?

d. Find $P(A^c)$.

e. Find $P(A \cup B)$.

f. Find $P(A \cap B)$.

3.36 Part-time workers in Japan. Corporate downsizing in Japan has caused a significant increase in the demand for temporary and part-time workers. The distribution (in percent) of nonregular workers in Japan (by age) is provided in the next table (adapted from *Monthly Labor Review*, Oct. 1995). Column headings are defined below the table. Suppose a nonregular worker is to be chosen at random from this population. Define the following events:

A: {The worker is 40 or over}
B: {The worker is a teenager and part time}
C: {The worker is under 40 and either arubaito or dispatched}
D: {The worker is part time}

a. Find the probability of each of the above events.

b. Find $P(A \cap D)$ and $P(A \cup D)$.

c. Describe in words the following events: A^c, B^c, and D^c.

d. Find the probability of each of the events you described in part **c**.

Age	Part Time	Arubaito	Temporary and Day	Dispatched	Totals
15–19	.3	3.7	2.3	.2	6.5
20–29	3.4	7.8	6.1	4.7	22.0
30–39	8.4	1.6	4.5	2.7	17.2
40–49	15.6	1.6	7.3	1.4	25.9
50–59	9.4	1.1	5.8	.6	16.9
60 and over	4.3	1.8	4.8	.6	11.5
Totals	41.4	17.6	30.8	10.2	100.0

Part time: Work fewer hours per day or days per week than regular workers; arubaito: someone with a "side" job who is in school or has regular employment elsewhere; temporary: employed on a contract lasting more than 1 month but less than 1 year; day: employed on a contract of less than 1 month's duration; dispatched: hired from a temporary-help agency.

Source: Houseman, S., and Osawa, M. "Part-Time and Temporary Employment in Japan." *Monthly Labor Review*, October 1995, pp. 12–13 (Tables 1 and 2).

3.37 Online securities trading. E*Trade Group Inc. was the first to provide online securities trading for its clients, offering an alternative to traditional investment firms. According to *Business Week*, online securities trading accounts for a significant share of the brokerage business. The table at the top of p. 155 reports the number of online and traditional accounts for five leading brokerages.

Suppose a customer account is to be drawn at random from the population of accounts described in the table. Consider the following events:

A: {The account is with Merrill Lynch}
B: {The account is an online account}
C: {The account is with E*Trade and is an online account}
D: {The account is either with TD Waterhouse or E*Trade, and is an online account}
E: {The account is with E*Trade}

a. Find the probability of each of the afore-mentioned events.

b. Find $P(A \cap B)$.

Table for Exercise 3.37

Brokerage Firms	Online Accounts	Traditional Accounts	Total Accounts
Fidelity Investments	2.8 million	8.0 million	10.8 million
Merrill Lynch & Co.	0	8.0 million	8.0 million
Charles Schwab & Co.	2.8 million	3.5 million	6.3 million
TD Waterhouse Group Inc.	1.0 million	1.1 million	2.1 million
E*Trade Group Inc.	1.24 million	0	1.24 million
Totals	7.84 million	20.6 million	28.44 million

Source: Business Week, October 18, 1999, pp. 185–186.

c. Find $P(A \cup B)$.
d. Find $P(B^c \cap E)$.
e. Find $P(A \cup E)$.
f. Which pairs of events are mutually exclusive?

3.38 Home modifications for wheelchair users. The *American Journal of Public Health* (Jan. 2002) reported on a study of elderly wheelchair users who live at home. A sample of 306 wheelchair users, age 65 or older, were surveyed about whether they had an injurious fall during the year and whether their home features any one of five structural modifications: bathroom modifications, widened doorways/hallways, kitchen modifications, installed railings, and easy-open doors. The responses are summarized in the accompanying table. Suppose we select, at random, one of the 306 surveyed wheelchair users.

Home Features	Injurious Fall(s)	No Falls	Totals
All 5	2	7	9
At least 1, but not all	26	162	188
None	20	89	109
Totals	48	258	306

Source: Berg, K., Hines, M., and Allen, S. "Wheelchair Users at Home: Few Home Modifications and Many Injurious Falls." American Journal of Public Health, Vol. 92, No. 1, Jan. 2002 (Table 1).

a. Find the probability that the wheelchair user had an injurious fall
b. Find the probability that the wheelchair user had all five features installed in the home.
c. Find the probability that the wheelchair user had no falls and none of the features installed in the home.

3.39 Reliability of gas station air pumps. Tire and automobile manufacturers and consumer safety experts all recommend that drivers maintain proper tire pressure in their cars. Consequently, many gas stations now provide air pumps and air gauges for their customers. In a *Research Note* (Nov. 2001), the National Highway Traffic Safety Administration studied the reliability of gas station air pumps. The following

table gives the percentage of gas stations that provide air gauges that overreport the pressure level in the tire.

Station Gauge Pressure	Overreport by 4 psi or more (%)	Overreport by 6 psi or more (%)	Overreport by 8 psi or more (%)
25 psi	16	2	0
35 psi	19	9	0
45 psi	19	14	5
55 psi	20	15	9

a. If the gas station air pressure gauge reads 35 psi, what is the probability that the pressure is overreported by 6 psi or more?
b. If the gas station air pressure gauge reads 55 psi, what is the probability that the pressure is overreported by 8 psi or more?
c. If the gas station air pressure gauge reads 25 psi, what is the probability that the pressure is not overreported by 4 psi or more?
d. Are the events A = {overreport by 4 psi or more} and B = {overreport by 6 psi or more} mutually exclusive? Explain.
e. Based on your answer to part d, why do the probabilities in the table not sum to 1?

Applying the Concepts—Advanced

3.40 Galileo's Passedix game. Passedix is a game of chance played with three fair dice. Players bet whether the sum of the faces shown on the dice will be above or below 10. During the late sixteenth century, the astronomer and mathematician Galileo Galilei was asked by the Grand Duke of Tuscany to explain why "the chance of throwing a total of 9 with three fair dice was less than that of throwing a total of 10" (*Interstat*, Jan. 2004). The grand duke believed that the chance should be the same since "there are an equal number of partitions of the numbers 9 and 10." Find the flaw in the grand duke's reasoning and answer the question posed to Galileo.

3.5 Conditional Probability

The event probabilities we've been discussing give the relative frequencies of the occurrences of the events when the experiment is repeated a very large number of times. Such probabilities are often called **unconditional probabilities** because no special conditions are assumed, other than those that define the experiment.

Often, however, we have additional knowledge that might affect the likelihood of the outcome of an experiment, so we need to alter the probability of an event of interest. A probability that reflects such additional knowledge is called the **conditional probability** of the event. For example, we've seen that the probability of observing an even number (event A) on a toss of a fair die is $\frac{1}{2}$. But suppose we're given the information that on a particular throw of the die, the result was a number less than or equal to 3 (event B). Would the probability of observing an even number on that throw of the die still be equal to $\frac{1}{2}$? It can't be, because making the assumption that B has occurred reduces the sample space from six sample points to three sample points (namely, those contained in event B). This reduced sample space is as shown in Figure 3.13.

Because the sample points for the die-toss experiment are equally likely, each of the three sample points in the reduced sample space is assigned an equal *conditional probability* of $\frac{1}{3}$. Since the only even number of the three in the reduced sample space B is the number 2 and the die is fair, we conclude that the probability that A occurs *given that B occurs* is $\frac{1}{3}$. We use the symbol $P(A|B)$ to represent the probability of event A given that event B occurs. For the die-toss example, $P(A|B) = \frac{1}{3}$.

To get the probability of event A given that event B occurs, we proceed as follows: We divide the probability of the part of A that falls within the reduced sample space B, namely $P(A \cap B)$, by the total probability of the reduced sample space, namely $P(B)$. Thus, for the die-toss example with event A: {Observe an even number} and event B: {Observe a number less than or equal to 3}, we find

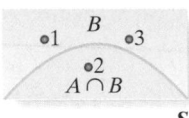

FIGURE 3.13

Reduced sample space for the die-toss experiment given that event B has occurred

$$P(A|B) = \frac{P(A \cap B)}{P(B)} = \frac{P(2)}{P(1) + P(2) + P(3)} = \frac{\frac{1}{6}}{\frac{3}{6}} = \frac{1}{3}$$

The formula for $P(A|B)$ is true in general:

Conditional Probability Formula

To find the *conditional probability that event A occurs given that event B occurs*, divide the probability that *both* A and B occur by the probability that B occurs—that is,

$$P(A|B) = \frac{P(A \cap B)}{P(B)} \quad \text{[We assume that } P(B) \neq 0.]$$

This formula adjusts the probability of $A \cap B$ from its original value in the complete sample space S to a conditional probability in the reduced sample space B. If the sample points in the complete sample space are equally likely, then the formula will assign equal probabilities to the sample points in the reduced sample space, as in the die-toss experiment. If, on the other hand, the sample points have unequal probabilities, the formula will assign conditional probabilities proportional to the probabilities in the complete sample space. This is illustrated by the following examples.

EXAMPLE 3.14

The Conditional Probability Formula Applied to Executives Who Cheat at Golf

Problem   To develop programs for business travelers staying at convention hotels, Hyatt Hotels Corp. commissioned a study of executives who play golf. The study revealed that 55% of the executives admitted they had cheated at golf. Also, 20% of the executives admitted they had cheated at golf and had lied in business. Given an executive had cheated at golf, what is the probability that the executive also had lied in business?

Solution   Let's define events A and B as follows:

$$A = \{\text{Executive who had cheated at golf}\}$$
$$B = \{\text{Executive who had lied in business}\}$$

From the study, we know that 55% of executives had cheated at golf, so $P(A) = .55$. Now, executives who both cheat at golf (event A) *and* lie in business (event B) represent the compound event $A \cap B$. From the study, $P(A \cap B) = .20$. We want to know the probability that an executive lied in business (event B), given he or she cheated at golf (event A)—that is, we want to know the conditional probability $P(A|B)$. Applying the preceding conditional probability formula, we have

$$P(B|A) = \frac{P(A \cap B)}{P(A)} = \frac{.20}{.55} = .364$$

Thus, given an executive had cheated at golf, the probability that the executive also had lied in business is .364.

Look Back One of the keys to correctly applying the formula is to write the information in the study in the form of probability statements involving the events of interest. The word *and* in the statement "cheat at golf *and* lie in business" implies an intersection of the two events, A and B. The word *given* in the phrase "*given* an executive cheats at golf" implies that event A is the given event.

Now Work Exercise 3.50

EXAMPLE 3.15

Applying the Conditional Probability Formula to a Two-Way Table on Customer Desire to Buy

Problem Suppose you are interested in the probability of the sale of a large piece of earthmoving equipment. A single prospect is contacted. Let F be the event that the buyer has sufficient money (or credit) to buy the product and let F^c denote the complement of F (the event that the prospect does not have the financial capability to buy the product). Similarly, let B be the event that the buyer wishes to buy the product and let B^c be the complement of that event. Then the four sample points associated with the experiment are shown in Figure 3.14, and their probabilities are given in Table 3.5. Use the sample point probabilities to find the probability that a single prospect will buy, given that the prospect is able to finance the purchase.

FIGURE 3.14

Sample space for contacting a sales prospect

TABLE 3.5 Probabilities of Customer Desire to Buy and Ability to Finance

		DESIRE	
		To Buy, B	Not to Buy, B^c
Able to Finance	Yes, F	.2	.1
	No, F^c	.4	.3

Solution Suppose you consider the large collection of prospects for the sale of your product and randomly select one person from this collection. What is the probability that the person selected will buy the product? In order to buy the product, the customer must be financially able *and* have the desire to buy, so this probability would correspond to the entry in Table 3.5 {To buy, B} and next to {Yes, F}, or $P(B \cap F) = .2$. This is the unconditional probability of the event $B \cap F$.

In contrast, suppose you know that the prospect selected has the financial capability for purchasing the product. Now you are seeking the probability that the customer will buy given (the condition) that the customer has the financial ability to pay. This probability, the conditional probability of B given that F has occurred and denoted by the symbol $P(B|F)$, would be determined by considering only the sample points in the reduced sample space containing the sample points $B \cap F$ and $B^c \cap F$—that is, sample points that imply the prospect is financially able to buy. (This subspace is shaded in Figure 3.15.) From our definition of conditional probability,

$$P(B|F) = \frac{P(B \cap F)}{P(F)}$$

FIGURE 3.15
Subspace (shaded) containing
sample points implying a
financially able prospect

where $P(F)$ is the sum of the probabilities of the two sample points corresponding to $B \cap F$ and $B^c \cap F$ (given in Table 3.5). Then

$$P(F) = P(B \cap F) + P(B^c \cap F) = .2 + .1 = .3$$

and the conditional probability that a prospect buys, given that the prospect is financially able, is

$$P(B|F) = \frac{P(B \cap F)}{P(F)} = \frac{.2}{.3} = .667$$

As we would expect, the probability that the prospect will buy, given that he or she is financially able, is higher than the unconditional probability of selecting a prospect who will buy.

Look Back Note that the conditional probability formula assigns a probability to the event $(B \cap F)$ in the reduced sample space that is proportional to the probability of the event in the complete sample space. To see this, note that the two sample points in the reduced sample space, $(B \cap F)$ and $(B^c \cap F)$, have probabilities of .2 and .1, respectively, in the complete sample space S. The formula assigns conditional probabilities $\frac{2}{3}$ and $\frac{1}{3}$ (use the formula to check the second one) to these sample points in the reduced sample space F, so that the conditional probabilities retain the 2-to-1 proportionality of the original sample point probabilities.

Now Work Exercise 3.41a–b

EXAMPLE 3.16

Applying the
Conditional
Probability Formula
to a Two-Way Table
on Customer
Complaints

Problem   The investigation of consumer product complaints by the Federal Trade Commission (FTC) has generated much interest by manufacturers in the quality of their products. A manufacturer of an electromechanical kitchen utensil conducted an analysis of a large number of consumer complaints and found that they fell into the six categories shown in Table 3.6. If a consumer complaint is received, what is the probability that the cause of the complaint was product appearance given that the complaint originated during the guarantee period?

TABLE 3.6   Distribution of Product Complaints

	REASON FOR COMPLAINT			
Complaint Origin	Electrical	Mechanical	Appearance	Totals
During Guarantee Period	18%	13%	32%	63%
After Guarantee Period	12%	22%	3%	37%
Totals	30%	35%	35%	100%

Solution   Let A represent the event that the cause of a particular complaint is product appearance, and let B represent the event that the complaint occurred during the guarantee period. Checking Table 3.6, you can see that $(18 + 13 + 32)\% = 63\%$ of the complaints occur during the guarantee period. Hence, $P(B) = .63$. The percentage of complaints that were caused by the appearance and occurred during the guarantee period (the event $A \cap B$) is 32%. Therefore, $P(A \cap B) = .32$.

Using these probability values, we can calculate the conditional probability $P(A|B)$ that the cause of a complaint is appearance, given that the complaint occurred during the guarantee time:

$$P(A|B) = \frac{P(A \cap B)}{P(B)} = \frac{.32}{.63} = .51$$

Consequently, we can see that slightly more than half the complaints that occurred during the guarantee period were due to scratches, dents, or other imperfections in the surface of the kitchen devices.

Look Back Note that the answer, $\frac{.32}{.63}$, is the proportion for the event of interest A (.32) divided by the row total proportion for the given event B (.63)—that is, it is the proportion of the time A occurs within the given event B.

Now Work Exercise 3.52

3.6 The Multiplicative Rule and Independent Events

The probability of an intersection of two events can be calculated using the multiplicative rule, which employs the conditional probabilities we defined in the previous section. Actually, we have already developed the formula in another context (Section 3.5). You will recall that the formula for calculating the conditional probability of A given B is

$$P(A|B) = \frac{P(A \cap B)}{P(B)}$$

Multiplying both sides of this equation by $P(B)$, we obtain a formula for the probability of the intersection of events A and B. This is often called the **Multiplicative Rule of Probability.**

> **Multiplicative Rule of Probability**
> $$P(A \cap B) = P(A)P(B|A) \text{ or, equivalently, } P(A \cap B) = P(B)P(A|B)$$

EXAMPLE 3.17

Applying the Multiplicative Rule to Find a Probability Associated with Wheat Futures

Problem   An investor in wheat futures is concerned with the following events:

B:{U.S. production of wheat will be profitable next year}

A:{A serious drought will occur next year}

Based on available information, the investor believes that the probability is .01 that production of wheat will be profitable *assuming* a serious drought will occur in the same year and that the probability is .05 that a serious drought will occur—that is,

$$P(B|A) = .01 \text{ and } P(A) = .05$$

Based on the information provided, what is the probability that a serious drought will occur and that a profit will be made? That is, find $P(A \cap B)$, the probability of the intersection of events A and B.

Solution   We want to calculate $P(A \cap B)$. Using the formula for the multiplicative rule, we obtain

$$P(A \cap B) = P(A)P(B|A) = (.05)(.01) = .0005$$

The probability that a serious drought occurs and the production of wheat is profitable is only .0005. As we might expect, this intersection is a very rare event.

Now Work Exercise 3.54

Intersections often contain only a few sample points. In this case, the probability of an intersection is easy to calculate by summing the appropriate sample point probabilities. However, the formula for calculating intersection probabilities is invaluable when the intersection contains numerous sample points, as the next example illustrates.

ACTIVITY 3.1: *Exit Polls:* **Conditional Probability**

Exit polls are conducted in selected locations as voters leave their polling places after voting. In addition to being used to predict the outcome of elections before the votes are counted, these polls are used to gauge tendencies among voters. The results are usually stated in terms of conditional probabilities.

The following table shows the results of exit polling that suggest men were more likely to vote for George W. Bush while women were more likely to vote for John F. Kerry in the 2004 Presidential Election. In addition, the table also suggests that more women than men voted in the election. The six percentages in the last three columns represent conditional probabilities where the given event is gender.

2004 Presidential Election, Vote by Gender

	Bush	Kerry	Other
Male (46%)	55%	44%	1%
Female (54%)	48%	51%	1%

Source: CNN.com

1. Find similar exit poll results where the voters are categorized by race, income, education, or some other criterion for a recent national, state, or local election. Choose two different examples and interpret the percentages given as probabilities, or conditional probabilities where appropriate.

2. Use the multiplicative rule of probability to find the probabilities related to the percentages given. [For example, in the accompanying table find P (Bush and Male) using the multiplicative rule.] Then interpret each of these probabilities and use them to determine the total percentage of the electorate who voted for each candidate.

3. Describe a situation where a business might use a form of exit polling to gauge customer reaction to a new product or service. Identify the type of business, the product or service, the criterion used to categorize customers, and how the customers' reactions will be determined. Then describe how the results will be summarized as conditional probabilities. How might the results of the poll benefit the business?

EXAMPLE 3.18

Applying The Multiplicative Rule to a Study of Welfare Workers

Problem   A county welfare agency employs 10 welfare workers who interview prospective food stamp recipients. Periodically the supervisor selects, at random, the forms completed by two workers to audit for illegal deductions. Unknown to the supervisor, three of the workers have regularly been giving illegal deductions to applicants. What is the probability that both of the two workers chosen have been giving illegal deductions?

Solution   Define the following two events:

A: {First worker selected gives illegal deductions}

B: {Second worker selected gives illegal deductions}

We want to find the probability of the event that both selected workers have been giving illegal deductions. This event can be restated as: {First worker gives illegal deductions *and* second worker gives illegal deductions}. Thus, we want to find the probability of the intersection, $A \cap B$. Applying the multiplicative rule, we have

$$P(A \cap B) = P(A)P(B|A)$$

To find $P(A)$, it is helpful to consider the experiment as selecting one worker from the 10. Then the sample space for the experiment contains 10 sample points (representing the 10 welfare workers), where the three workers giving illegal deductions are denoted by the symbol I (I_1, I_2, I_3), and the seven workers not giving illegal deductions are denoted by the symbol N ($N_1, \ldots, N_7$). The resulting Venn diagram is illustrated in Figure 3.16.

Since the first worker is selected at random from the 10, it is reasonable to assign equal probabilities to the 10 sample points. Thus, each sample point has a probability of $1/10$. The sample points in event A are $\{I_1, I_2, I_3\}$—the three workers who are giving illegal deductions. Thus,

$$P(A) = P(I_1) + P(I_2) + P(I_3) = 1/10 + 1/10 + 1/10 = 3/10$$

FIGURE 3.16
Venn diagram for finding $P(A)$

FIGURE 3.17

Venn diagram for finding $P(B|A)$

To find the conditional probability, $P(B|A)$, we need to alter the sample space S. Since we know A has occurred [the first worker selected is giving illegal deductions (say I_3), only two of the nine remaining workers in the sample space are giving illegal deductions]. The Venn diagram for this new sample space (S') is shown in Figure 3.17. Each of these nine sample points are equally likely, so each is assigned a probability of $\frac{1}{9}$. Since the event $(B|A)$ contains the sample points $\{I_1, I_2\}$, we have

$$P(B|A) = P(I_1) + P(I_2) = \frac{1}{9} + \frac{1}{9} = \frac{2}{9}$$

Substituting $P(A) = \frac{3}{10}$ and $P(B|A) = \frac{2}{9}$ into the formula for the multiplicative rule, we find

$$P(A \cap B) = P(A)P(B|A) = (\tfrac{3}{10})(\tfrac{2}{9}) = \tfrac{6}{90} = \tfrac{1}{15}$$

Thus, there is a 1 in 15 chance that both workers chosen by the supervisor have been giving illegal deductions to food stamp recipients.

Look Back The key words *both* and *and* in the statement "both A and B occur" imply an intersection of two events, which in turn implies that we should *multiply* probabilities to obtain the probability of interest.

Now Work Exercise 3.45c

The sample space approach is only one way to solve the problem posed in Example 3.18. An alternative method employs the concept of a **tree diagram.** Tree diagrams are helpful for calculating the probability of an intersection.

To illustrate, a tree diagram for Example 3.18 is displayed in Figure 3.18. The tree begins at the far left with two branches. These branches represent the two possible outcomes N (no illegal deductions) and I (illegal deductions) for the first worker selected. The unconditional probability of each outcome is given (in parentheses) on the appropriate branch—that is, for the first worker selected, $P(N) = \frac{7}{10}$ and $P(I) = \frac{3}{10}$. (These can be obtained by summing sample point probabilities as in Example 3.18.)

The next level of the tree diagram (moving to the right) represents the outcomes for the second worker selected. The probabilities shown here are conditional probabilities since the outcome for the first worker is assumed to be known. For example, if the

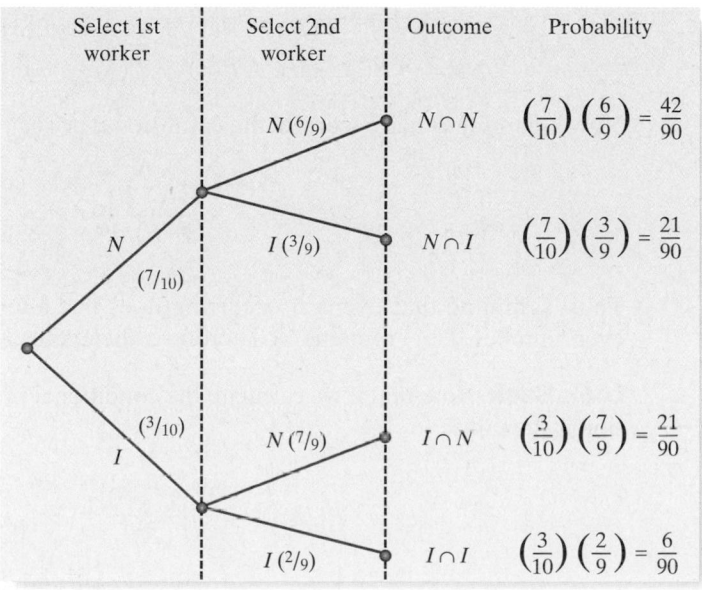

FIGURE 3.18

Tree diagram for Example 3.18

first worker is giving illegal deductions (*I*), the probability that the second worker is also giving illegal deductions (*I*) is $^2/_9$ since of the nine workers left to be selected, only two remain who are giving illegal deductions. This conditional probability, $^2/_9$, is shown in parentheses on the bottom branch of Figure 3.18.

Finally, the four possible outcomes of the experiment are shown at the end of each of the four tree branches. These events are intersections of two events (outcome of first worker and outcome of second worker). Consequently, the multiplicative rule is applied to calculate each probability, as shown in Figure 3.18. You can see that the intersection$\{I \cap I\}$ (i.e., the event that both workers selected are giving illegal deductions) has probability $^6/_{90} = ^1/_{15}$—the same value obtained in Example 3.18.

In Section 3.5 we showed that the probability of an event *A* may be substantially altered by the knowledge that an event *B* has occurred. However, this will not always be the case. In some instances, the assumption that event *B* has occurred will *not* alter the probability of event *A* at all. When this is true, we say that the two events *A* and *B* are *independent events*.

Definition 3.9

Events *A* and *B* are **independent events** if the occurrence of *B* does not alter the probability that *A* has occurred; that is, events *A* and *B* are independent if

$$P(A|B) = P(A)$$

When events *A* and *B* are independent, it is also true that

$$P(B|A) = P(B)$$

Events that are not independent are said to be **dependent.**

EXAMPLE 3.19

Checking for Independence in a Die-Tossing Experiment

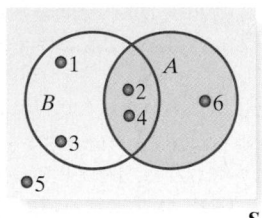

FIGURE 3.19
Venn diagram for die-toss experiment

Problem Consider the experiment of tossing a fair die and let

$$A: \{\text{Observe an even number}\}$$
$$B: \{\text{Observe a number less than or equal to 4}\}$$

Are events *A* and *B* independent?

Solution The Venn diagram for this experiment is shown in Figure 3.19. We first calculate

$$P(A) = P(2) + P(4) + P(6) = ^1/_2$$
$$P(B) = P(1) + P(2) + P(3) + P(4) = ^2/_3$$
$$P(A \cap B) = P(2) + P(4) = ^1/_3$$

Now assuming *B* has occurred, the conditional probability of *A* given *B* is

$$P(A|B) = \frac{P(A \cap B)}{P(B)} = \frac{\frac{1}{3}}{\frac{2}{3}} = \frac{1}{2} = P(A)$$

Thus, assuming that event *B* occurring does not alter the probability of observing an even number, $P(A)$ remains $^1/_2$. Therefore, the events *A* and *B* are independent.

Look Back Note that if we calculate the conditional probability of *B* given *A*, our conclusion is the same:

$$P(B|A) = \frac{P(A \cap B)}{P(A)} = \frac{\frac{1}{3}}{\frac{1}{2}} = \frac{2}{3} = P(B)$$

Biography

**BLAISE PASCAL
(1623–1662)**

Solver of Chevalier's Dilemma

As a precocious child growing up in France, Blaise Pascal showed an early inclination toward mathematics. Although his father would not permit Pascal to study mathematics before the age of 15 (removing all math texts from his house), at age 12 Blaise discovered on his own that the sum of the angles of a triangle are two right triangles.

Pascal went on to become a distinguished mathematician, as well as a physicist, theolo-

gian, and the inventor of the first digital calculator. Most historians attribute the beginning of the study of probability to the correspondence between Pascal and Pierre de Fermat in 1654. The two solved the Chevalier's dilemma–a gambling problem related to Pascal by his friend and Paris gambler the Chevalier de Mere. The problem involved determining the expected number of times one could roll two dice without throwing a double 6. (Pascal proved that the break-even point was 25 rolls.)

EXAMPLE 3.20

Checking for Independence in the Consumer Product Complaint Study

Problem   Refer to the consumer product complaint study in Example 3.16. The percentages of complaints of various types during and after the guarantee period are shown in Table 3.6. Define the following events:

A: {Cause of complaint is product appearance}

B: {Complaint occurred during the guarantee term}

Are A and B independent events?

Solution   Events A and B are independent if $P(A|B) = P(A)$. We calculated $P(A|B)$ in Example 3.15 to be .51, and from Table 3.6 we see that

$$P(A) = .32 + .03 = .35$$

Therefore, $P(A|B)$ is not equal to $P(A)$, and A and B are dependent events.

Now Work Exercise 3.41c

To gain an intuitive understanding of independence, think of situations in which the occurrence of one event does not alter the probability that a second event will occur. For example, suppose two small companies are being monitored by a financier for possible investment. If the businesses are in different industries and they are otherwise unrelated, then the success–or failure of one company may be *independent* of the success or failure of the other—that is, the event that company A fails may not alter the probability that company B will fail.

As a second example, consider an election poll in which 1,000 registered voters are asked their preference between two candidates. Pollsters try to use procedures for selecting a sample of voters so that the responses are independent—that is, the objective of the pollster is to select the sample so the event that one polled voter prefers candidate A does not alter the probability that a second polled voter prefers candidate A.

We will make three final points about independence. The first is that the property of independence, unlike the mutually exclusive property, cannot be shown on or gleaned from a Venn diagram. This means *you can't trust your intuition*. In general, the only way to check for independence is by performing the calculations of the probabilities in the definition.

The second point concerns the relationship between the mutually exclusive and independence properties. Suppose that events A and B are mutually exclusive, as shown in Figure 3.20, and both events have nonzero probabilities. Are these events independent or dependent? That is, does the assumption that B occurs alter the probability of the occurrence of A? It certainly does, because if we assume that B has occurred, it is impossible for A to have occurred simultaneously—that is, $P(A|B) = 0$. Thus, *mutually exclusive events are dependent events* since $P(A) \neq P(A|B)$.

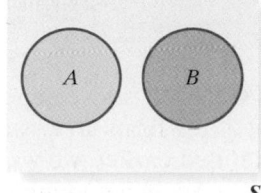

FIGURE 3.20

Mutually exclusive events are dependent events

The third point is that the probability of the intersection of independent events is very easy to calculate. Referring to the formula for calculating the probability of an intersection, we find

$$P(A \cap B) = P(A)P(B|A)$$

Thus, since $P(B|A) = P(B)$ when A and B are independent, we have the following useful rule:

Probability of Intersection of Two Independent Events

If events A and B are independent, the probability of the intersection of A and B equals the product of the probabilities of A and B; that is,

$$P(A \cap B) = P(A)P(B)$$

The converse is also true: If $P(A \cap B) = P(A)P(B)$, then events A and B are independent.

In the die-toss experiment, we showed in Example 3.19 that the events A: {Observe an even number} and B: {Observe a number less than or equal to 4} are independent if the die is fair. Thus,

$$P(A \cap B) = P(A)P(B) = (\tfrac{1}{2})(\tfrac{2}{3}) = \tfrac{1}{3}$$

This agrees with the result that we obtained in the example:

$$P(A \cap B) = P(2) + P(4) = \tfrac{2}{6} = \tfrac{1}{3}$$

EXAMPLE 3.21

Probability of Independent Events Occurring Simultaneously in the Diversity Training Study

Problem   Refer to Example 3.5 (p. 138). Recall that *USA Today* found that of all U.S. firms that use diversity training, 38% state that their primary reason for using it is to stay competitive.

a.   What is the probability that in a sample of two firms that use diversity training, both primarily use it to stay competitive?

b.   What is the probability that in a sample of 10 firms that use diversity training, all 10 primarily use it to stay competitive?

Solution

a.   Let C_1 represent the event that firm 1 gives "stay competitive" as the primary reason for using diversity training. Define C_2 similarly for firm 2. The event that *both* firms give "stay competitive" as their primary reason is the intersection of the two events, $C_1 \cap C_2$. Based on the survey that found that 38% of U.S. firms use diversity training to stay competitive, we could reasonably conclude that $P(C_1) = .38$ and $P(C_2) = .38$ However, in order to compute the probability of $C_1 \cap C_2$ from the Multiplicative Rule, we must make the assumption that the two events are independent. Since the classification of any firm using diversity training is not likely to affect the classification of another firm, this assumption is reasonable. Assuming independence, we have

$$P(C_1 \cap C_2) = P(C_1)P(C_2) = (.38)(.38) = .1444$$

b.   To see how to compute the probability that 10 of 10 firms will give "stay competitive" as their primary reason, first consider the event that 3 of 3 firms give "stay competitive" as the primary reason. Using the notation defined earlier, we want to compute the probability of the intersection $C_1 \cap C_2 \cap C_3$. Again assuming independence of the classifications, we have

$$P(C_1 \cap C_2 \cap C_3) = P(C_1)P(C_2)P(C_3) = (.38)(.38)(.38) = .054872$$

Similar reasoning leads us to the conclusion that the intersection of 10 such events can be calculated as follows:

$$P(C_1 \cap C_2 \cap C_3 \cap \ldots \cap C_{10}) = P(C_1)P(C_2)\ldots P(C_{10}) = (.38)^{10} = .0000628$$

Thus, the probability that 10 of 10 firms all give "stay competitive" as their primary reason for using diversity training is about 63 in 1 million, assuming the events (stated reasons for using diversity training) are independent.

Look Back The very small probability in part b makes it extremely unlikely that 10 of 10 firms would give "stay competitive" as their primary reason for diversity training. If this event should actually occur, we would need to reassess our estimate of the probability of .38 used in the calculation. If all 10 firms' reason is staying competitive, then the probability that any one firm gives staying competitive as their reason is much higher than .38. (This conclusion is another application of the rare event approach to statistical inference.)

Now Work Exercise 3.62a

STATISTICS IN ACTION REVISITED

The Probability of Winning Cash 3 or Play 4

In addition to biweekly Lotto 6/53, the Florida Lottery runs several other games. Two popular daily games are "Cash 3" and "Play 4." In Cash 3, players pay $1 to select three numbers in sequential order, where each number ranges from 0 to 9. If the three numbers selected (e.g., 2-8-4) match exactly the order of the three numbers drawn, the player wins $500. Play 4 is similar to Cash 3, but players must match four numbers (each number ranging from 0 to 9). For a $1 Play 4 ticket (e.g., 3-8-3-0), the player will win $5,000 if the numbers match the order of the four numbers drawn.

During the official drawing for Cash 3, 10 Ping-Pong balls numbered 0, 1, 2, 3, 4, 5, 6, 7, 8, and 9 are placed into each of three chambers. The balls in the first chamber are colored pink, the balls in the second chamber are blue, and the balls in the third chamber are yellow. One ball of each color is randomly drawn, with the official order as pink-blue-yellow. In Play 4, a fourth chamber with orange balls is added and the official order is pink-blue-yellow-orange. Since the draws of the colored balls are

random and independent, we can apply an extension of the Probability Rule for the Intersection of Two Independent Events to find the odds of winning Cash 3 and Play 4. The probability of matching a numbered ball being drawn from a chamber is 1/10; therefore,

P(Win Cash 3) = P(match pink AND match blue)
= P(match pink) × P(match blue) ×
= (1/10)(1/10)(1/10) = 1/1000 = .001

P(Win Play 4) = P(match pink AND match blue)
= P(match pink) × P(match blue) ×
P(match yellow) × P(match orange)
= (1/10)(1/10)(1/10)(1/10)
= 1/10,000 = .0001

Although the odds of winning one of these daily games is much better than the odds of winning Lotto 6/53, there is still only a 1 in 1,000 chance (for Cash 3) or 1 in 10,000 chance (for Play 4) of winning the daily game. And the payoffs ($500 or $5,000) are much smaller. In fact, it can be shown that you will lose an average of 50¢ every time you play either Cash 3 or Play 4!

Exercises 3.41–3.67

Learning the Mechanics

3.41 For two events, A and B, $P(A) = .4$, $P(B) = .2$, and NW $P(A \cap B) = .1$.
 a. Find $P(A|B)$. b. Find $P(B|A)$.
 c. Are A and B independent events?

3.42 For two events, A and B, $P(A) = .4$, $P(B) = .2$, and $P(A|B) = .6$.
 a. Find $P(A \cap B)$.
 b. Find $P(B|A)$.

3.43 For two independent events, A and B, $P(A) = .4$ and $P(B) = .2$.
 a. Find $P(A \cap B)$.
 b. Find $P(A|B)$.
 c. Find $P(A \cup B)$.

3.44 An experiment results in one of three mutually exclusive events, A, B, or C. It is known that $P(A) = .30$, $P(B) = .55$, and $P(C) - .15$. Find each of the following probabilities:

a. $P(A \cup B)$

b. $P(A \cap C)$

c. $P(A|B))$

d. $P(B \cup C)$

e. Are B and C independent events? Explain.

3.45 Consider the experiment depicted by the Venn diagram, with the sample space S containing five sample points. The sample points are assigned the following probabilities: $P(E_1) = .20$, $P(E_2) = .30$, $P(E_3) = .30$, $P(E_4) = .10$, $P(E_5) = .10$.

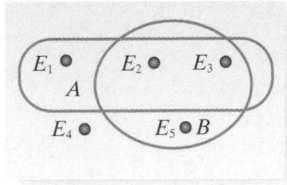

S

a. Calculate $P(A)$, $P(B)$, and $P(A \cap B)$.

b. Suppose we know that event A has occurred, so that the reduced sample space consists of the three sample points in A—namely, E_1, E_2, and E_3. Use the formula for conditional probability to adjust the probabilities of these three sample points for the knowledge that A has occurred [i.e., $P(E_i|A)$]. Verify that the conditional probabilities are in the same proportion to one another as the original sample point probabilities.

NW c. Calculate the conditional probability $P(B|A)$ in two ways: (1) Add the adjusted (conditional) probabilities of the sample points in the intersection $A \cap B$ since these represent the event that B occurs given that A has occurred; (2) use the formula for conditional probability:

$$P(B|A) = \frac{P(A \cap B)}{P(A)}$$

Verify that the two methods yield the same result.

d. Are events A and B independent? Why or why not?

3.46 Two fair coins are tossed, and the following events are defined:

A: {Observe at least one head}

B: {Observe exactly one head}

a. Draw a Venn diagram for the experiment, showing events A and B. Assign probabilities to the sample points.

b. Find $P(A)$, $P(B)$, and $P(A \cap B)$.

c. Use the formula for conditional probability to find $P(A|B)$ and $P(B|A)$. Verify your answer by inspecting the Venn diagram and using the concept of reduced sample spaces.

3.47 An experiment results in one of five sample points with the following probabilities: $P(E_1) = .22$, $P(E_2) = .31$, $P(E_3) = .15$, $P(E_4) = .22$, and $P(E_5) = .1$. The following events have been defined:

A: $\{E_1, E_3\}$

B: $\{E_2, E_3, E_4\}$

C: $\{E_1, E_5\}$

Find each of the following probabilities:

a. $P(A)$

b. $P(B)$

c. $P(A \cap B))$

d. $P(A|B)$

e. $P(B \cap C)$

f. $P(C|B)$

g. Consider each pair of events: A and B, A and C, and B and C. Are any of the pairs of events independent? Why?

3.48 Two fair dice are tossed, and the following events are defined:

A: {Sum of the numbers showing is odd}

B: {Sum of the numbers showing is 9, 11, or 12}

Are events A and B independent? Why?

3.49 A sample space contains six sample points and events A, B, and C as shown in the Venn diagram. The probabilities of the sample points are

$P(1) = .20$, $P(2) = .05$, $P(3) = .30$, $P(4) = .10$,

$P(5) = .10$, $P(6) = .25$.

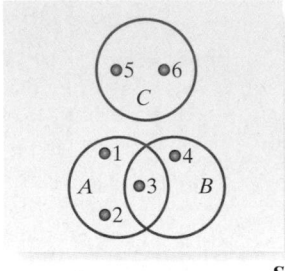

S

a. Which pairs of events, if any, are mutually exclusive? Why?

b. Which pairs of events, if any, are independent? Why?

c. Find $P(A \cup B)$ by adding the probabilities of the sample points and then by using the additive rule. Verify that the answers agree. Repeat for $P(A \cup C)$.

APPLET Applet Exercise 3.5

Use the applet entitled *Simulating the Probability of Rolling a 6* to simulate conditional probabilities. Begin by running the applet twice with $n = 10$ without resetting between runs. The data on your screen represent 20 rolls of a die. The diagram above the *Roll* button shows the frequency of each of the six possible outcomes. Use this information to find each of the probabilities.

a. The probability of 6 given the outcome is 5 or 6

b. The probability of 6 given the outcome is even

c. The probability of 4 or 6 given the outcome is even

d. The probability of 4 or 6 given the outcome is odd

Applying the Concepts—Basic

3.50 Speeding linked to fatal car crashes. According to the
NW National Highway Traffic and Safety Administration's National Center for Statistics and Analysis (NCSA), "speeding is one of the most prevalent factors contributing to fatal traffic crashes" (*NHTSA Technical Report*, Aug. 2005). The probability that speeding is a cause of a fatal

crash is .3. Furthermore, the probability that speeding and missing a curve are causes of a fatal crash is .12. Given speeding is a cause of a fatal crash, what is the probability that the crash occurred on a curve?

3.51 Largest nondomestic public companies. *Forbes* (July 26, 1999) conducted a survey of the 20 largest nondomestic public companies in the world. Of these 20 companies, 6 were trading companies based in Japan. A total of 11 Japanese companies were on the top 20 list. Suppose we select one of these 20 companies at random. Given the company is based in Japan, what is the probability that it is a trading company?

3.52 World Series winners. The New York Yankees, a member of
NW the Eastern Division of the American League in Major League Baseball (MLB), won three consecutive World Series between 1998 and 2000. The following table summarizes the 15 MLB World Series winners from 1990 to 2005 by division and league. (There was no World Series in 1994 due to a players' strike.) One of these 15 World Series winners is to be chosen at random.

a. Given that the winner is a member of the American League, what is the probability that the winner plays in the Eastern Division?

b. If the winner plays in the Central Division, what is the probability that the winner is a member of the National League?

c. If the winner is a member of the National League, what is the probability that the winner plays in either the Central or Western Division?

		LEAGUE	
		National	American
Division	Eastern	3	7
	Central	1	2
	Western	1	1

Source: Major League Baseball.

3.53 Internet user study. In a study of Internet users, researchers discovered that 80% of the users own at least one computer and that 25% of the users log on to the Internet for more than 30 hours per week. (*Internet Research*, Vol. 11, 2001.) Suppose that 15% of the users own at least one computer and log on to the Internet for more than 30 hours per week.

a. Given an Internet user owns at least one computer, what is the probability that he or she logs on to the Internet for more than 30 hours per week?

b. Given an Internet user logs on to the Internet for more than 30 hours per week, what is the probability that he or she owns at least one computer?

3.54 Monitoring quality of power equipment. *Mechanical*
NW *Engineering* (Feb. 2005) reported on the need for wireless networks to monitor the quality of industrial equipment. For example, consider Eaton Corp., a company that develops distribution products. Eaton estimates that 90% of the electrical switching devices it sells can monitor the quality of the power running through the device. Eaton further estimates that of the buyers of electrical switching devices capable of monitoring quality, 90% do not wire the equipment up for that purpose. Use this information to estimate the probability that an Eaton electrical switching device is capable of monitoring power quality and is wired up for that purpose.

Applying the Concepts—Intermediate

3.55 Reversible errors in capital punishment cases. New York's Columbia University Law School released a report in February 2002 on all capital punishment (death-penalty) cases that occurred over the past 25 years in the United States. Two of the findings are stated as follows: 68% of all capital punishment cases had a serious, reversible error. Of the cases that were overturned due to reversible error, 7% resulted in acquittal for the defendant upon retrial.

a. Write each of these findings in the form of a probability.

b. Use the findings to find the probability that a capital case had a serious, reversible error and an innocent defendant.

3.56 Degrees of best-paid CEOs. Refer to the results of the *Forbes* (May 8, 2006) survey of the top 40 best-paid chief executive officers shown in Table 2.1 (p. 41). The data on highest degree obtained are summarized in the following SPSS printout. Suppose you randomly select five of the CEOs (without replacement) and record the highest degree obtained by each.

a. What is the probability that the highest degree obtained by the first CEO you select is a bachelor's degree?

b. Suppose the highest degree obtained by each of the first four CEOs you select is a bachelor's degree. What is the probability that the highest degree obtained by the fifth CEO you select is a bachelor's degree?

3.57 Home modifications for wheelchair users. Refer to the *American Journal of Public Health* (Jan. 2002) study of elderly wheelchair users who live at home, Exercise 3.38 (p. 155). The table classifying a sample of 306 wheelchair users according to type of features installed in the home

SPSS Output for Exercise 3.56

DEGREE

		Frequency	Percent	Valid Percent	Cumulative Percent
Valid	Bachelors	8	20.0	20.0	20.0
	Law	4	10.0	10.0	30.0
	Masters	4	10.0	10.0	40.0
	MBA	20	50.0	50.0	90.0
	None	2	5.0	5.0	95.0
	PhD	2	5.0	5.0	100.0
	Total	40	100.0	100.0	

and whether or not they had an injurious fall follows. Suppose we select, at random, one of the 306 surveyed wheelchair users.

Home Features	Injurious Fall(s)	No Falls	Totals
All 5	2	7	9
At least 1	26	162	188
None	20	89	109
Totals	48	258	306

Source: Berg, K., Hines, M., and Allen, S. "Wheelchair Users at Home: Few Home Modifications and Many Injurious Falls." *American Journal of Public Health,* Vol. 92, No. 1, Jan. 2002 (Table 1).

a. Given the wheelchair user had all five features installed, what is the probability that the user had an injurious fall?

b. Given the wheelchair user had none of the features installed, what is the probability that the user had an injurious fall?

3.58 Working mothers with children. The U.S. Census Bureau reports a decline in the percentage of mothers with infant children in the workforce. The following table gives a breakdown of the marital status and working status of the 3.9 million mothers with infant children in the year 2000. (The numbers in the table are reported in millions.) Consider the following events: $A = \{$Mom with infant works$\}$, $B = \{$Mom with infant is married and living with husband$\}$. Are A and B independent events?

	Working	Not Working
Married/living with husband	1,385	1,175
All other arrangements	786	588

Source: U.S. Census Bureau; *American Demographics,* Feb. 2002.

3.59 Intrusion detection systems. A computer intrusion detection system (IDS) is designed to provide an alarm whenever an intrusion (e.g., unauthorized access) is being attempted into a computer system. A probabilistic evaluation of a system with two independently operating intrusion detection systems (a double IDS) was published in the *Journal of Research of the National Institute of Standards and Technology* (November/December 2003). Consider a double IDS with system A and system B. If there is an intruder, system A sounds an alarm with probability .9, and system B sounds an alarm with probability .95. If there is no intruder, the probability that system A sounds an alarm (i.e., a false alarm) is .2 and the probability that system B sounds an alarm is .1.

a. Using symbols, express the four probabilities given in the example.

b. If there is an intruder, what is the probability that both systems sound an alarm?

c. If there is no intruder, what is the probability that both systems sound an alarm?

d. Given an intruder, what is the probability that at least one of the systems sounds an alarm?

3.60 Detecting traces of TNT. University of Florida researchers in the Department of Materials Science and Engineering have invented a technique to rapidly detect traces of TNT. (*Today,* Spring 2005.) The method, which involves shining a laser light on a potentially contaminated object, provides instantaneous results and gives no false positives. In this application, a false positive would occur if the laser light detects traces of TNT when, in fact, no TNT is actually present on the object. Let A be the event that the laser light detects traces of TNT. Let B be the event that the object contains no traces of TNT. The probability of a false positive is 0. Write this probability in terms of A and B using symbols such as $\cup$, $\cap$, and $|$.

SWDEFECTS

3.61 Software defects in NASA spacecraft instrument code. Portions of computer software code that may contain undetected defects are called *blind spots.* The issue of blind spots in software code evaluation was addressed at the *8th IEEE International Symposium on High Assurance Software Engineering* (March 2004). The researchers developed guidelines for assessing methods of predicting software defects using data on 498 modules of software code written in "C" language for a NASA spacecraft instrument. One simple prediction algorithm is to count the lines of code in the module; any module with more than 50 lines of code is predicted to have a defect. The **SWDEFECTS** file contains the predicted and actual defect status of all 498 modules. A standard approach to evaluating a software defect prediction algorithm is to form a two-way summary table similar to the one shown here. In the table, *a, b, c,* and *d* represent the number of modules in each cell. Software engineers use these table entries to compute several probability measures, called *accuracy, detection rate, false alarm rate,* and *precision.*

		MODULE HAS DEFECTS	
		False	True
Algorithm	No	*a*	*b*
Predicts			
Defects	Yes	*c*	*d*

a. *Accuracy* is defined as the probability that the prediction algorithm is correct. Write a formula for *accuracy* as a function of the table values *a, b, c,* and *d.*

b. The *detection rate* is defined as the probability that the algorithm predicts a defect, given that the module actually is a defect. Write a formula for *detection rate* as a function of the table values *a, b, c,* and *d.*

c. The *false alarm rate* is defined as the probability that the algorithm predicts a defect, given that the module actually has no defect. Write a formula for *false alarm rate* as a function of the table values *a, b, c,* and *d.*

d. *Precision* is defined as the probability that the module has a defect, given that the algorithm predicts a defect. Write a formula for *precision* as a function of the table values *a, b, c,* and *d.*

e. Access the **SWDEFECTS** file and compute the values of accuracy, detection rate, false alarm rate, and precision. Interpret the results.

3.62 Lie detector test. A new type of lie detector—called the Computerized Voice Stress Analyzer (CVSA)—has been developed. The manufacturer claims that the CVSA is 98% accurate, and, unlike a polygraph machine, will not be thrown off by drugs and medical factors. However, laboratory studies by the U.S. Defense Department found that the CVSA had an accuracy rate of 49.8%—slightly less than pure chance (*Tampa Tribune,* Jan. 10, 1999). Suppose the CVSA is used to test the veracity of four suspects. Assume the suspects' responses are independent.

NW **a.** If the manufacturer's claim is true, what is the probability that the CVSA will correctly determine the veracity of all four suspects?

b. If the manufacturer's claim is true, what is the probability that the CVSA will yield an incorrect result for at least one of the four suspects?

c. Suppose that in a laboratory experiment conducted by the U.S. Defense Department on four suspects, the CVSA yielded incorrect results for two of the suspects. Use this result to make an inference about the true accuracy rate of the new lie detector.

3.63 Success of firms using TQM. One definition of *Total Quality Management* (TQM) is a "management philosophy and a system of management techniques to improve product and service quality and worker productivity" (Benson, *Minnesota Management Review*, Fall 1992). One hundred U.S. companies were surveyed, and it was found that 30 had implemented TQM. Among the 100 companies surveyed, 60 reported an increase in sales last year. Of those 60, 20 had implemented TQM. Suppose one of the 100 surveyed companies is to be selected at random for additional analysis.

a. What is the probability that a firm that implemented TQM is selected? That a firm whose sales increased is selected?

b. Are the two events {TQM implemented} and {Sales increased} independent or dependent? Explain.

c. Suppose that instead of 20 TQM implementers among the 60 firms reporting sales increases, there were 18. Now are the events {TQM implemented} and {Sales increased} independent or dependent? Explain.

Applying the Concepts—Advanced

3.64 Risk of a natural gas pipeline accident. *Process Safety Progress* (Dec. 2004) published a risk analysis for a natural gas pipeline between Bolivia and Brazil. The most likely scenario for an accident would be natural gas leakage from a hole in the pipeline. The probability that the leak ignites immediately (causing a jet fire) is .01. If the leak does not immediately ignite, it may result in a delayed ignition of a gas cloud. Given no immediate ignition, the probability of delayed ignition (causing a flash fire) is .01. If there is no delayed ignition, the gas cloud will harmlessly disperse. Suppose a leak occurs in the natural gas pipeline. Find the probability that either a jet fire or a flash fire will occur. Illustrate with a tree diagram.

3.65 Patient medical instruction sheets. Physicians and pharmacists sometimes fail to inform patients adequately about the proper application of prescription drugs and about the precautions to take in order to avoid potential side effects. One method of increasing patients' awareness of the problem is for physicians to provide Patient Medication Instruction (PMI) sheets. The American Medical Association, however, has found that only 20% of the doctors who prescribe drugs frequently distribute PMI sheets to their patients. Assume that 20% of all patients receive the PMI sheet with their prescriptions and that 12% receive the PMI sheet and are hospitalized because of a drug-related problem. What is the probability that a person will be hospitalized for a drug-related problem given that the person has received the PMI sheet?

3.66 Strategy in the game "Go." "Go" is one of the oldest and most popular strategic board games in the world, especially in Japan and Korea. This two-player game is played on a flat surface marked with 19 vertical and 19 horizontal lines. The objective is to control territory by placing pieces called *stones* on vacant points on the board. Players alternate placing their stones. The player using black stones goes first, followed by the player using white stones.

[*Note:* The University of Virginia requires MBA students to learn Go to understand how the Japanese conduct business.] *Chance* (Summer 1995) published an article that investigated the advantage of playing first (i.e., using the black stones) in Go. The results of 577 games recently played by professional Go players were analyzed.

a. In the 577 games, the player with the black stones won 319 times and the player with the white stones won 258 times. Use this information to assess the probability of winning when you play first in Go.

b. Professional Go players are classified by level. Group C includes the top-level players followed by Group B (middle-level) and Group A (low-level) players. The following table describes the number of games won by the player with the black stones, categorized by level of the black player and level of the opponent. Assess the probability of winning when you play first in Go for each combination of player and opponent level.

c. If the player with the black stones is ranked higher than the player with the white stones, what is the probability that black wins?

d. Given the players are of the same level, what is the probability that the player with the black stones wins?

🔵 **GO**

Black Player Level	Opponent Level	Number of Wins	Number of Games
C	A	34	34
C	B	69	79
C	C	66	118
B	A	40	54
B	B	52	95
B	C	27	79
A	A	15	28
A	B	11	51
A	C	5	39
	Totals	319	577

Source: Kim, J. and Kim, H. J. "The Advantage of Playing First in Go." *Chance,* Vol. 8, No. 3, Summer 1995, p. 26 (Table 3).

3.67 Most likely coin-tossing sequence. In *Parade Magazine*'s (Nov. 26, 2000) column "Ask Marilyn," the following question was posed: "I have just tossed a [balanced] coin 10 times, and I ask you to guess which of the following three sequences was the result. One (and only one) of the sequences is genuine."

(1) H H H H H H H H H H
(2) H H T T H T T H H H
(3) T T T T T T T T T T

a. Demonstrate that prior to actually tossing the coins, the three sequences are equally likely to occur.

b. Find the probability that the 10 coin tosses result in all heads or all tails.

ACTIVITY 3.2: *Keep the Change:* **Independent Events**

Once again we return to the Bank of America *Keep the Change* savings program, Activity 1.1 (p. 16). This time we look at whether certain events involving purchase totals and amounts transferred to savings are independent. Throughout this activity, the experiment consists of randomly selecting one purchase from a large group of purchases.

1. Define events *A* and *B* as follows:

A: {Purchase total ends in $0.25}
B: {Amount transferred is less than $0.50}

Explain why events *A* and *B* are not independent. Are events *A* and *B* mutually exclusive? Use this example to explain the difference between independent events and mutually exclusive events.

2. Now define events *A* and *B* in this manner:

A: {Purchase total is greater than $10}
B: {Amount transferred is less than $0.50}

Do you believe that these events are independent? Explain your reasoning.

3. To investigate numerically whether the events in Question 2 are independent, we will use the data collected in the activity on page 16. Pool your data with the data from other students or the entire class so that the combined data set represents at least 100 purchases. Complete the table by counting the number of purchases in each category.

Distribution of Purchases

Transfer Amount	Purchase ≤$10	Total >$10	Totals
$0.00–$0.49 $0.99–$0.99			
Totals			

Compute appropriate probabilities based on your completed table to test whether the events of Question 2 are independent. If you conclude that the events are not independent, can you explain your conclusion in terms of the original data?

c. Find the probability that the 10 coin tosses result in a mix of heads and tails.

d. Marilyn's answer to the question posed was "Though the chances of the three specific sequences occurring randomly are equal ... it's reasonable for us to choose sequence (2) as the most likely genuine result." If you know that only one of the three sequences actually occurred, explain why Marilyn's answer is correct. [*Hint:* Compare the probabilities in parts **b** and **c**.]

3.7 Random Sampling

How a sample is selected from a population is of vital importance in statistical inference because the probability of an observed sample will be used to infer the characteristics of the sampled population. To illustrate, suppose you deal yourself four cards from a deck of 52 cards and all four cards are aces. Do you conclude that your deck is an ordinary bridge deck, containing only four aces, or do you conclude that the deck is stacked with more than four aces? It depends on how the cards were drawn. If the four aces were always placed at the top of a standard bridge deck, drawing four aces is not unusual—it is certain. On the other hand, if the cards are thoroughly mixed, drawing four aces in a sample of four cards is highly improbable. The point, of course, is that in order to use the observed sample of four cards to draw inferences about the population (the deck of 52 cards), you need to know how the sample was selected from the deck.

One of the simplest and most frequently employed sampling procedures is implied in many of the previous examples and exercises. It produces what is known as a *random sample*. We learned in Section 1.5 (p. 16) that a random sample is likely to be *representative* of the population that it is selected from.

> **Definition 3.10**
>
> If *n* elements are selected from a population in such a way that every set of *n* elements in the population has an equal probability of being selected, the *n* elements are said to be a **random sample.** *

---

*Strictly speaking, this is a **simple random sample.** There are many different types of random samples. The simple random sample is the most common.

If a population is not too large and the elements can be numbered on slips of paper, poker chips, and so on, you can physically mix the slips of paper or chips and remove n elements from the total. The numbers that appear on the chips selected would indicate the population elements to be included in the sample. Since it is often difficult to achieve a thorough mix, such a procedure only provides an approximation to random sampling. Most researchers rely on **random number generators** to automatically generate the random sample. Random number generators are available in table form, and they are built into most statistical software packages.

EXAMPLE 3.22
Selecting a Random Sample of Households

Problem   Suppose you wish to randomly sample five households from a population of 100,000 households to participate in a study.

a. How many different samples can be selected?
b. Use a random number generator to select a random sample.

Solution

a. To determine the number of samples, we'll apply the combinatorial rule of Section 3.1. In this case, $N = 100,000$ and $n = 5$. Then

$$\binom{N}{n} = \binom{100,000}{5} = \frac{100,000!}{5!\,99,995!}$$

$$= \frac{100,000 \cdot 99,999 \cdot 99,998 \cdot 99,997 \cdot 99,996}{5 \cdot 4 \cdot 3 \cdot 2 \cdot 1}$$

$$= 8.33 \times 10^{22}$$

Thus, there are 83.3 billion trillion different samples of five households that can be selected from 100,000.

b. To ensure that each of the possible samples has an equal chance of being selected, as required for random sampling, we can employ a **random number table,** as provided in Table I of Appendix B. Random number tables are constructed in such a way that every number occurs with (approximately) equal probability. Furthermore, the occurrence of any one number in a position is independent of any of the other numbers that appear in the table. To use a table of random numbers, number the N elements in the population from 1 to N. Then turn to Table I and select a starting number in the table. Proceeding from this number either across the row or down the column, remove and record n numbers from the table.

To illustrate, first we number the households in the population from 1 to 100,000. Then, we turn to a page of Table I, say the first page. (A partial reproduction of the first page of Table I is shown in Table 3.7.) Now we arbitrarily select a starting number, say the random number appearing in the third row, second column. This number is 48,360. Then we proceed down the second column to obtain the remaining four random numbers. In this case we have selected five random numbers, which are shaded in Table 3.7. Using the first five digits to represent households from 1 to 99,999 and the number 00000 to represent household 100,000, we can see that the households numbered

48,360
93,093
39,975
6,907
72,905

should be included in our sample.

FIGURE 3.21

MINITAB worksheet
with random sample of
50 households

TABLE 3.7 Partial Reproduction of Table I in Appendix B

ROW	Column 1	2	3	4	5	6
1	10480	15011	01536	02011	81647	91646
2	22368	46573	25595	85393	30995	89198
3	24130	48360	22527	97265	76393	64809
4	42167	93093	06243	61680	07856	16376
5	37570	39975	81837	16656	06121	91782
6	77921	06907	11008	42751	27756	53498
7	99562	72905	56420	69994	98872	31016
8	96301	91977	05463	07972	18876	20922
9	89579	14342	63661	10281	17453	18103
10	85475	36857	53342	53988	53060	59533
11	28918	69578	88231	33276	70997	79936
12	63553	40961	48235	03427	49626	69445
13	09429	93969	52636	92737	88974	33488

Note: Use only the necessary number of digits in each random number to identify the element to be included in the sample. If, in the course of recording the n numbers from the table, you select a number that has already been selected, simply discard the duplicate and select a replacement at the end of the sequence. Thus, you may have to record more than n numbers from the table to obtain a sample of n unique numbers.

Look Back Can we be perfectly sure that all 83.3 billion trillion samples have an equal chance of being selected? The fact is, we can't; but to the extent that the random number table contains truly random sequences of digits, the sample should be very close to random.

Now Work Exercise 3.68

Table I in Appendix B is just one example of a random number generator. For most scientific studies that require a large random sample, computers are used to generate the random sample. The EXCEL, MINITAB, and SPSS statistical software packages all have easy-to-use random number generators.

For example, suppose we required a random sample of $n = 50$ households from the population of 100,000 households in Example 3.21. Here, we might employ the MINITAB random number generator. Figure 3.21 shows a MINITAB printout listing 50 random numbers (from a population of 100,000). The households with these identification numbers would be included in the random sample.

Exercises 3.68–3.75

Learning the Mechanics

3.68 Suppose you wish to sample $n = 2$ elements from a total of
NW $N = 10$ elements.
  a. Count the number of different samples that can be drawn, first by listing them, and then by using combinatorial mathematics. (See Section 3.1.)
  b. If random sampling is to be employed, what is the probability that any particular sample will be selected?
  c. Show how to use the random number table, Table I in Appendix B, to select a random sample of 2 elements

from a population of 10 elements. Perform the sampling procedure 20 times. Do any two of the samples contain the same 2 elements? Given your answer to part **b**, did you expect repeated samples?

3.69 Suppose you wish to sample $n = 3$ elements from a total of $N = 600$ elements.
  a. Count the number of different samples by using combinatorial mathematics (see Section 3.1).
  b. If random sampling is to be employed, what is the probability that any particular sample will be selected?

c. Show how to use the random number table, Table I in Appendix B, to select a random sample of 3 elements from a population of 600 elements. Perform the sampling procedure 20 times. Do any two of the samples contain the same three elements? Given your answer to part **b**, did you expect repeated samples?

d. Use a computer to generate a random sample of 3 from the population of 600 elements.

3.70 Suppose that a population contains $N = 200,000$ elements. Use a computer or Table I of Appendix B to select a random sample of $n = 10$ elements from the population. Explain how you selected your sample.

Applying the Concepts—Basic

3.71 Random-digit dialing. To ascertain the effectiveness of their advertising campaigns, firms frequently conduct telephone interviews with consumers using *random-digit dialing*. With this approach, a random number generator mechanically creates the sample of phone numbers to be called.

a. Explain how the random number table (Table I of Appendix B) or a computer could be used to generate a sample of seven-digit telephone numbers.

b. Use the procedure you described in part **a** to generate a sample of 10 seven-digit telephone numbers.

c. Use the procedure you described in part **a** to generate five seven-digit telephone numbers whose first three digits are 373.

3.72 Census sampling. In addition to its decennial enumeration of the population, the U.S. Bureau of the Census regularly samples the population to estimate level of and changes in a number of other attributes, such as income, family size, employment, and marital status. Suppose the bureau plans to sample 1,000 households in a city that has a total of 534,322 households. Show how the bureau could use the random number table in Appendix B or a computer to generate the sample. Select the first 10 households to be included in the sample.

Applying the Concepts—Intermediate

3.73 Auditing an accounting system. In auditing a firm's financial statements, an auditor will (1) assess the capability of the firm's accounting system to accumulate, measure, and synthesize transactional data properly, and (2) assess the operational effectiveness of the accounting system. In performing the second assessment, the auditor frequently relies on a random sample of actual transactions (Stickney and Weil, *Financial Accounting: An Introduction to Concepts, Methods, and Uses*, 2002). A particular firm has 5,382 customer accounts that are numbered from 0001 to 5382.

a. One account is to be selected at random for audit. What is the probability that account number 3,241 is selected?

b. Draw a random sample of 10 accounts and explain in detail the procedure you used.

c. Refer to part **b**. The following are two possible random samples of size 10. Is one more likely to be selected than the other? Explain.

Sample Number 1				
5011	0082	0963	0772	3415
2663	1126	0008	0026	4189

Sample Number 2				
0001	0003	0005	0007	0009
0002	0004	0006	0008	0010

3.74 Sampling stocks on the NYSE. The results of the previous business day's transactions for stocks traded on the New York Stock Exchange (NYSE) and five regional exchanges—the Chicago, Pacific, Philadelphia, Boston, and Cincinnati stock exchanges—are summarized each business day in the NYSE–Composite Transactions table in the *Wall Street Journal.*

a. Examine the NYSE–Composite Transactions table in a recent issue of the *Wall Street Journal* and explain how to draw a random sample of stocks from the table.

b. Use the procedure you described in part **a** to draw a random sample of 20 stocks from a recent NYSE–Composite Transactions table. For each stock in the sample, list its name (i.e., the abbreviation given in the table), its sales volume, and its closing price.

Applying the Concepts—Advanced

3.75 Sampling TV markets for a court case. A recent court case involved a claim of satellite television subscribers obtaining illegal access to local TV stations. The defendant (the satellite TV company) wanted to sample TV markets nationwide and determine the percentage of its subscribers in each sampled market who have illegal access to local TV stations. To do this, defendant's expert witness drew a rectangular grid over the continental United States, with horizontal and vertical grid lines every .02 degrees of latitude and longitude, respectively. This created a total of 500 rows and 1,000 columns, or $(500)(1,000) = 500,000$ intersections. The plan was to randomly sample 900 intersection points and include the TV market at each intersection in the sample. Explain how you could use a random number generator to obtain a random sample of 900 intersections. Develop at least two plans: one that numbers the intersections from 1 to 500,000 prior to selection and another that selects the row and column of each sampled intersection (from the total of 500 rows and 1,000 columns).

3.8 Bayes's Rule (Optional)

An early attempt to employ probability in making inferences is the basis for a branch of statistical methodology known as **Bayesian statistical methods.** The logic employed by the English philosopher Thomas Bayes in the mid-1700s, involves converting an unknown conditional probability, say $P(B|A)$, to one involving a known conditional probability, say $P(A|B)$. The method is illustrated in the next example.

EXAMPLE 3.23
Applying Bayes's
Logic to an Intruder
Detection System

Problem An unmanned monitoring system uses high-tech video equipment and micro-processors to detect intruders. A prototype system has been developed and is in use out-doors at a weapons munitions plant. The system is designed to detect intruders with a probability of .90. However, the design engineers expect this probability to vary with weather conditions. The system automatically records the weather condition each time an intruder is detected. Based on a series of controlled tests, in which an intruder was released at the plant under various weather conditions, the following information is available: Given the intruder was, in fact, detected by the system, the weather was clear 75% of the time, cloudy 20% of the time, and raining 5% of the time. When the system failed to detect the intruder, 60% of the days were clear, 30% cloudy, and 10% rainy. Use this information to find the probability of detecting an intruder, given rainy weather conditions. (Assume that an intruder has been released at the plant.)

Solution Define D to be the event that the intruder is detected by the system. Then D^c is the event that the system failed to detect the intruder. Our goal is to calculate the conditional probability, $P(D|\text{Rainy})$. From the statement of the problem, the following information is available:

$$P(D) = .90 \qquad P(D^c) = .10$$
$$P(\text{Clear}|D) = .75 \qquad P(\text{Clear}|D^c) = .60$$
$$P(\text{Cloudy}|D) = .20 \qquad P(\text{Cloudy}|D^c) = .30$$
$$P(\text{Rainy}|D) = .05 \qquad P(\text{Rainy}|D^c) = .10$$

Note that $P(D|\text{Rainy})$ is not one of the conditional probabilities that is known. However, we can find

$$P(\text{Rainy} \cap D) = P(D)P(\text{Rainy}|D) = (.90)(.05) = .045$$

and

$$P(\text{Rainy} \cap D^c) = P(D^c)P(\text{Rainy}|D^c) = (.10)(.10) = .01$$

using the Multiplicative Probability Rule. These two probabilities are highlighted on the tree diagram for the problem in Figure 3.22.

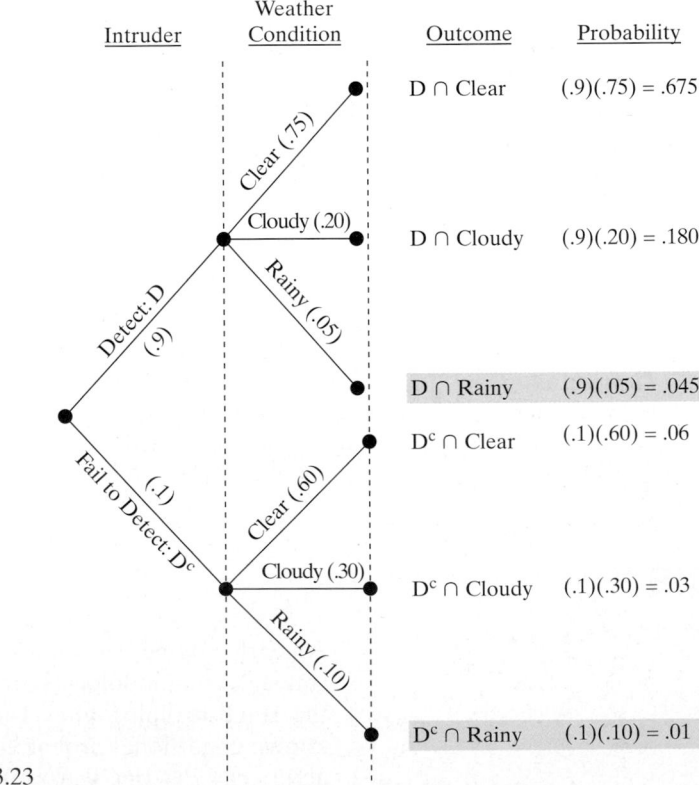

FIGURE 3.22

Tree Diagram for Example 3.23

Now the event Rainy is the union of two mutually exclusive events, (Rainy $\cap D$) and (Rainy $\cap D^c$). Thus, applying the Additive Probability Rule, we have

$$P(\text{Rainy}) = P(\text{Rainy} \cap D) + P(\text{Rainy} \cap D^c) = .045 + .01 = .055$$

We now apply the formula for conditional probability to obtain

$$P(D|\text{Rainy}) = \frac{P(\text{Rainy} \cap D)}{P(\text{Rainy})} = \frac{P(\text{Rainy} \cap D)}{P(\text{Rainy} \cap D) + P(\text{Rainy} \cap D^c)}$$
$$= .045/.055 = .818$$

Therefore, under rainy weather conditions, the prototype system can detect the intruder with a probability of .818—a value lower than the designed probability of .90.

Now Work Exercise 3.76

The technique utilized in Example 3.23, called **Bayes's Rule,** can be applied when an observed event A occurs with any one of several mutually exclusive and exhaustive events, $B_1, B_2, \ldots, B_k$. The formula for finding the appropriate conditional probabilities is given in the box.

Bayes's Rule

Given k mutually exclusive and exhaustive events, $B_1, B_2, \ldots, B_k$, such that $P(B_1) + P(B_2) + \cdots + P(B_k) = 1$, and an observed event A, then

$$P(B_i|A) = P(B_i \cap A)/P(A)$$
$$= \frac{P(B_i)P(A|B_i)}{P(B_1)P(A|B_1) + P(B_2)P(A|B_2) + \cdots + P(B_k)P(A|B_k)}$$

In applying Bayes's Rule to Example 3.23, the observed event $A = \{\text{Rainy}\}$ and the $k = 2$ mutually exclusive and exhaustive events are the complementary events $D = \{\text{intruder detected}\}$ and $D^c = \{\text{intruder not detected}\}$. Hence, the formula

$$P(D|\text{Rainy}) = \frac{P(D)P(\text{Rainy}|D)}{P(D) \, P(\text{Rainy}|D) + P(D^c) \, P(\text{Rainy}|D^c)}$$
$$= \frac{(.90)(.05)}{(.90)(.05) + (.10)(.10)} = .818$$

Biography

THOMAS BAYES (1702–1761)

The Inverse Probabilist

The Reverend Thomas Bayes was an ordained English Presbyterian minister who became a Fellow of the Royal Statistical Society without benefit of any formal training in mathematics or any published papers in science during his lifetime. His manipulation of the formula for conditional probability in 1761 is now known as Bayes's Theorem. At the time and for 200 years afterward, use of Bayes's Theorem (or inverse probability, as it was called) was controversial and, to some, considered an inappropriate practice. It was not until the 1960s that the power of the Bayesian approach to decision making began to be tapped.

Exercises 3.76–3.85

Learning the Mechanics

3.76 Suppose the events B_1 and B_2 are mutually exclusive and
NW complementary events, such that $P(B_1) = .75$ and
$P(B_2) = .25$. Consider another event A such that
$P(A|B_1) = .3$ and $P(A|B_2) = .5$.
  a. Find $P(B_1 \cap A)$.
  b. Find $P(B_2 \cap A)$.
  c. Find $P(A)$ using the results in parts a and b.
  d. Find $P(B_1|A)$.
  e. Find $P(B_2|A)$.

3.77 Suppose the events B_1, B_2, and B_3 are mutually exclusive and
complementary events, such that $P(B_1) = .2$, $P(B_2) = .15$,
and $P(B_3) = .65$. Consider another event A such that
$P(A|B_1) = .4$, $P(A|B_2) = .25$, and $P(A|B_3) = .6$. Use
Bayes's Rule to find
  a. $P(B_1|A)$ b. $P(B_2|A)$ c. $P(B_3|A)$

3.78 Suppose the events B_1, B_2, and B_3 are mutually exclusive and
complementary events, such that $P(B_1) = .2$, $P(B_2) = .15$,
and $P(B_3) = .65$. Consider another event A such that
$P(A) = .4$. If A is independent of B_1, B_2, and B_3, use Bayes's
Rule to show that $P(B_1|A) = P(B_1) = .2$.

Applying the Concepts—Basic

DDT

3.79 Fish contaminated by a plant's toxic discharge. Refer to
the U.S. Army Corps of Engineers' study on the DDT contamination of fish in the Tennessee River (Alabama),
Example 1.5 (p. 16). Part of the investigation focused on
how far upstream the contaminated fish have migrated. (A
fish is considered to be contaminated if its measured DDT
concentration is greater than 5.0 parts per million.)
  a. Considering only the contaminated fish captured from
     the Tennessee River, the data reveal that 52% of the fish
     are found between 275 and 300 miles upstream, 39% are
     found 305 to 325 miles upstream, and 9% are found 330
     to 350 miles upstream. Use these percentages to deter-
     mine the probabilities, $P(275–300)$, $P(305–325)$, and
     $P(330–350)$.
  b. Given that a contaminated fish is found a certain dis-
     tance upstream, the probability that it is a channel catfish
     (CC) is determined from the data as $P(CC|275–300) =$
     $.775$, $P(CC|305–325) = .77$, and $P(CC|330–350) = .86$. If
     a contaminated channel catfish is captured from the
     Tennessee River, what is the probability that it was cap-
     tured 275–300 miles upstream?

3.80 Errors in estimating job costs. A construction company employs three sales engineers. Engineers 1, 2, and 3 estimate
the costs of 30%, 20%, and 50%, respectively, of all jobs bid
by the company. For $i = 1, 2, 3$, define E_i to be the event
that a job is estimated by engineer i. The following probabilities describe the rates at which the engineers make serious errors in estimating costs:

$P(\text{error}|E_1) = .01$, $P(\text{error}|E_2) = .03$, and
$P(\text{error}|E_3) = .02$

  a. If a particular bid results in a serious error in estimating
     job cost, what is the probability that the error was made
     by engineer 1?

  b. If a particular bid results in a serious error in estimating
     job cost, what is the probability that the error was made
     by engineer 2?
  c. If a particular bid results in a serious error in estimating
     job cost, what is the probability that the error was made
     by engineer 3?
  d. Based on the probabilities, parts **a–c**, which engineer is
     most likely responsible for making the serious error?

3.81 Drug testing in athletes. Due to inaccuracies in drug-testing
procedures (e.g., false positives and false negatives) in the
medical field, the results of a drug test represent only one
factor in a physician's diagnosis. Yet, when Olympic athletes
are tested for illegal drug use (i.e., doping), the results of a
single test are used to ban the athlete from competition. In
Chance (Spring 2004), University of Texas biostatisticians
D. A. Berry and L. Chastain demonstrated the application
of Bayes's Rule for making inferences about testosterone
abuse among Olympic athletes. They used the following example: In a population of 1,000 athletes, suppose 100 are il-
legally using testosterone. Of the users, suppose 50 would
test positive for testosterone. Of the nonusers, suppose 9
would test positive.
  a. Given that the athlete is a user, find the probability that
     a drug test for testosterone will yield a positive result.
     (This probability represents the *sensitivity* of the drug
     test.)
  b. Given the athlete is a nonuser, find the probability that a
     drug test for testosterone will yield a negative result. (This
     probability represents the *specificity* of the drug test.)
  c. If an athlete tests positive for testosterone, use Bayes's
     Rule to find the probability that the athlete is really dop-
     ing. (This probability represents the *positive predictive
     value* of the drug test.)

Applying the Concepts—Intermediate

3.82 Nondestructive evaluation. Nondestructive evaluation
(NDE) describes methods that quantitatively characterize
materials, tissues, and structures by noninvasive means such
as X-ray computed tomography, ultrasonics, and acoustic
emission. Recently, NDE was used to detect defects in steel
castings (*JOM*, May 2005). Assume that the probability that
NDE detects a "hit" (i.e., predicts a defect in a steel casting)
when, in fact, a defect exists is .97. (This is often called the
probability of detection.) Also assume that the probability
that NDE detects a hit when, in fact, no defect exists is .005.
(This is called the *probability of a false call.*) Past experience has shown a defect occurs once in every 100 steel castings. If NDE detects a hit for a particular steel casting, what
is the probability that an actual defect exists?

3.83 Malfunctioning production lines. A manufacturing operation utilizes two production lines to assemble electronic
fuses. Both lines produce fuses at the same rate and generally produce 2.5% defective fuses. However, production line 1
recently suffered mechanical difficulty and produced 6.0%
defectives during a 3-week period. This situation was not
known until several lots of electronic fuses produced in this
period were shipped to customers. If one of the two fuses
tested by a customer was found to be defective, what is the
probability that the lot from which it came was produced on

malfunctioning line 1? (Assume all the fuses in the lot were produced on the same line.)

3.84 Intrusion detection systems. Refer to the *Journal of Research of the National Institute of Standards and Technology* (Nov.–Dec. 2003) study of a double intrusion detection system with independent systems, Exercise 3.59 (p. 168). Recall that if there is an intruder, system A sounds an alarm with probability .9 and system B sounds an alarm with probability .95. If there is no intruder, system A sounds an alarm with probability .2 and system B sounds an alarm with probability .1. Now assume that the probability of an intruder is .4. If both systems sound an alarm, what is the probability that an intruder is detected?

3.85 Purchasing microchips. An important component of your desktop or laptop personal computer (PC) is a microchip. The table gives the proportions of microchips that a certain PC manufacturer purchases from seven suppliers.

Supplier	Proportion
S_1	.15
S_2	.05
S_3	.10
S_4	.20
S_5	.12
S_6	.20
S_7	.18

a. It is known that the proportions of defective microchips produced by the seven suppliers are .001, .0003, .0007, .006, .0002, .0002, and .001, respectively. If a single PC microchip failure is observed, which supplier is most likely responsible?

b. Suppose the seven suppliers produce defective microchips at the same rate, .0005. If a single PC microchip failure is observed, which supplier is most likely responsible?

KEY TERMS

[Note: Items marked with an asterisk (*) are from the optional section in this chapter.]

GUIDE TO SELECTING PROBABILITY RULES

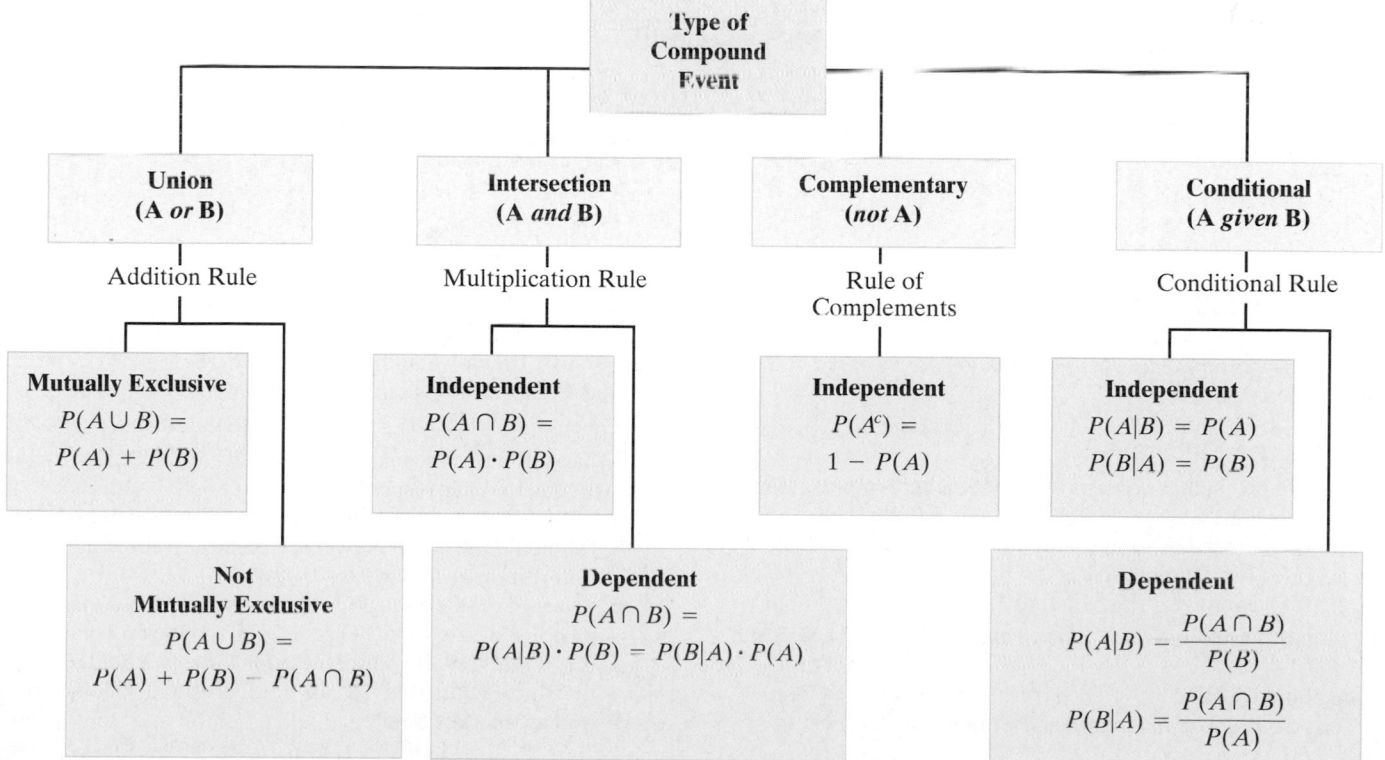

CHAPTER NOTES

Probability Rules for *k* Sample Points, $S_1, S_2, S_3, \ldots S_k$

1. $0 \le P(S_i) \le 1$
2. $\Sigma P(S_i) = 1$

Random Sample

All possible such samples have equal probability of being selected

Combinations Rule

Counting number of samples of *n* elements selected from *N* elements

$$\binom{N}{n} = \frac{N!}{n!(N-n)!}$$
$$= \frac{N(N-1)(N-2)\ldots(N-n+1)}{n(n-1)(n-2)\ldots(2)(1)}$$

KEY SYMBOLS

S	**Sample space** (collection of all sample points)
A: {1,2}	Set of **sample points in event A**
$P(A)$	**Probability** of event A
$A \cup B$	**union** of events A and B (either A or B can occur)
$A \cap B$	**intersection** of events A and B (both A and B occur)
A^c	**complement** of A (event A does not occur)
$A\|B$	event A occurs, **given** event B occurs
$\binom{N}{n}$	Number of **combinations** of N elements taken n at a time
$N!$	**N factorial** $= N(N-1)(N-2)\ldots(2)(1)$

Bayes's Rule

For sample points $S_1, S_2, S_3, \ldots, S_k$,

$$P(S_i|A) = \frac{P(S_i)P(A|S_i)}{P(S_1)P(A|S_1) + P(S_2)P(A|S_2) + \cdots + P(S_k)P(A|S_k)}$$

SUPPLEMENTARY EXERCISES 3.86–3.123

[Note: Exercises marked with an asterisk (*) are from the optional section.]

Learning the Mechanics

3.86 A sample space consists of four sample points, where $P(S_1) = .2$, $P(S_2) = .1$, $P(S_3) = .3$, and $P(S_4) = .4$.
  a. Show that the sample points obey the two probability rules for a sample space.
  b. If an event $A = \{S_1, S_4\}$, find $P(A)$.

3.87 A and B are mutually exclusive events, with $P(A) = .2$ and $P(B) = .3$.
  a. Find $P(A|B)$.
  b. Are A and B independent events?

3.88 For two events A and B, suppose $P(A) = .7$, $P(B) = .5$, and $P(A \cap B) = .4$. Find $P(A \cup B)$.

3.89 Given that $P(A \cap B) = .4$ and $P(A|B) = .8$, find $P(B)$.

3.90 Which of the following pairs of events are mutually exclusive? Justify your response.
  a. {The Dow Jones Industrial Average increases on Monday}, {A large New York bank decreases its prime interest rate on Monday}
  b. {The next sale by a PC retailer is a laptop computer}, {The next sale by a PC retailer is a desktop computer}
  c. {You reinvest all your dividend income in a limited partnership}, {You reinvest all your dividend income in a money market fund}

3.91 The accompanying Venn diagram illustrates a sample space containing six sample points and three events, *A*, *B*, and *C*. The probabilities of the sample points are $P(1) = .3$, $P(2) = .2, P(3) = .1, P(4) = .1, P(5) = .1,$ and $P(6) = .2.$

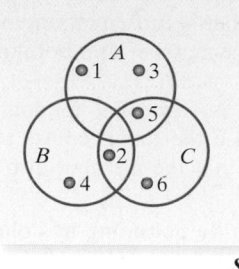

S

a. Find $P(A \cap B)$, $P(B \cap C)$, $P(A \cup C)$, $P(A \cup B \cup C)$, $P(B^c)$, $P(A^c \cap B)$, $P(B|C)$, and $P(B|A)$.
b. Are *A* and *B* independent? Mutually exclusive? Why?
c. Are *B* and *C* independent? Mutually exclusive? Why?

3.92 Two events, *A* and *B*, are independent, with $P(A) = .3$ and $P(B) = .1$.
a. Are *A* and *B* mutually exclusive? Why?
b. Find $P(A|B)$ and $P(B|A)$.
c. Find $P(A \cup B)$.

3.93 Find the numerical value of
a. 6! **b.** $\binom{10}{9}$ **c.** $\binom{10}{1}$ **d.** $\binom{6}{3}$ **e.** 0!

3.94 A random sample of five graduate students is to be selected from 50 MBA majors for participation in a case competition.
a. In how many different ways can the sample be drawn?
b. Show how the random number table, Table I of Appendix B, can be used to select the sample of students.

APPLET Applet Exercise 3.6

Use the applet entitled *Random Numbers* to generate a list of 50 numbers between 1 and 100, inclusive. Use this list to find each of the probabilities.
a. The probability that a number chosen from the list is less than or equal to 50
b. The probability that a number chosen from the list is even
c. The probability that a number chosen from the list is less than or equal to 50 and even
d. The probability that a number chosen from the list is less than or equal to 50 given that the number is even
e. Do your results from parts **a–d** support the conclusion that the events *less than or equal to 50* and *even* are independent? Explain.

Applying the Concepts—Basic

3.95 According to *USA Today* (Sep. 19, 2000), there are 650 members of the International Nanny Association (INA). Of these, only three are men. Find the probability that a randomly selected member of the INA is a man.

3.96 Condition of public school facilities. The National Center for Education Statistics (NCES) conducted a survey on the condition of America's public school facilities. The survey revealed the following information. The probability that a public school building has inadequate plumbing

is .25. Of the buildings with inadequate plumbing, the probability that the school has plans for repairing the building is .38. Find the probability that a public school building has inadequate plumbing and will be repaired.

3.97 New car crash tests. Refer to the National Highway Traffic Safety Administration (NHTSA) crash tests of new car models, Exercise 2.129 (p. 115). Recall that the NHTSA has developed a "star" scoring system, with results ranging from one star (*) to five stars (*****). The more stars in the rating, the better the level of crash protection in a head-on collision. A summary of the driver-side star ratings for 98 cars is reproduced in the accompanying MINITAB printout. Assume that one of the 98 cars is selected at random. State whether each of the following is true or false.
a. The probability that the car has a rating of two stars is 4.
b. The probability that the car has a rating of four or five stars is .7857.
c. The probability that the car has a rating of one star is 0.
d. The car has a better chance of having a two-star rating than of having a five-star rating.

Tally for Discrete Variables: DRIVSTAR

DRIVSTAR	Count	Percent
2	4	4.08
3	17	17.35
4	59	60.20
5	18	18.37
N=	98	

3.98 ISO 9000 registered companies. The ISO 9000 is a series of standards for setting up and documenting quality systems, processes, and procedures. To gauge how managers view the standards or how the standards were achieved, a sample of 40 ISO 9000–registered companies in Colorado was selected and the manager most responsible for ISO 9000 implementation was interviewed (*Quality Progress*, 1995). The following are some of the data obtained by the study:

Level of Top Management Involvement in the ISO 9000 Registration Process	Frequency
Very involved	9
Moderate involvement	16
Minimal involvement	12
Not involved	3

Length of Time to Achieve ISO 9000 Registration	Frequency
Less than 1 year	5
1–1.5 years	21
1.6–2 years	9
2.1–2.5 years	2
More than 2.5 years	3

Source: Weston, F. C. "What Do Managers Really Think of the ISO 9000 Registration Process?" *Quality Progress*, October 1995, p. 68–69 (Tables 3 and 4).

Suppose one of the 40 managers who were interviewed is to be randomly selected for additional questioning. Consider the events defined as follows:

A: {The manager was involved in the ISO 9000 registration}

B: {The length of time to achieve ISO 9000 registration was more than 2 years}

a. Find $P(A)$.
b. Find $P(B)$.
c. Explain why the preceding data are not sufficient to determine whether events A and B are independent.

3.99   Survey on energy conservation. A state energy agency mailed questionnaires on energy conservation to 1,000 homeowners in the state capital. Five hundred questionnaires were returned. Suppose an experiment consists of randomly selecting and reviewing one of the returned questionnaires. Consider the events:

A: {The home is constructed of brick}

B: {The home is more than 30 years old}

C: {The home is heated with oil}

Describe each of the following events in terms of unions, intersections, and complements (i.e., $A \cup B$, $A \cap B$, A^c, etc.):

a. The home is more than 30 years old and is heated with oil.
b. The home is not constructed of brick.
c. The home is heated with oil or is more than 30 years old.
d. The home is constructed of brick and is not heated with oil.

3.100   Management's commitment to TQM. *Total Quality Management* (TQM) involves responsive customer service through continuously improved and redesigned work processes (*Quality Progress*, July 1995). In evaluating perceptions of TQM, a University of North Carolina in Charlotte study asked 159 employees to indicate how strongly they agreed or disagreed with a series of statements, including "I believe that management is committed to TQM." The following responses were received:

Strongly Agree	Agree	Neither Agree nor Disagree	Disagree	Strongly Disagree
30	64	41	18	6

Source: Buch, K., and Shelnut, J. W. "UNC Charlotte Measures the Effects of Its Quality Initiative." *Quality Progress,* July 1995, p. 75 (Table 2).

a. Define the experiment and list the sample points.
b. Assign probabilities to the sample points.
c. What is the probability that an employee agrees or strongly agrees with the above statement?
d. What is the probability that an employee does not strongly agree with the above statement?

3.101   Use of country club facilities. A local country club has a membership of 600 and operates facilities that include an 18-hole championship golf course and 12 tennis courts. Before deciding whether to accept new members, the club president would like to know how many members regularly use each facility. A survey of the membership indicates that 70% regularly use the golf course, 50% regularly use the tennis courts, and 5% use neither of these facilities regularly.

a. Construct a Venn diagram to describe the results of the survey.
b. If one club member is chosen at random, what is the probability that the member uses either the golf course or the tennis courts or both?
c. If one member is chosen at random, what is the probability that the member uses both the golf and the tennis facilities?
d. A member is chosen at random from among those known to use the tennis courts regularly. What is the probability that the member also uses the golf course regularly?

3.102   Carbon monoxide poisoning in Colorado. *The American Journal of Public Health* (July 1995) published a study on unintentional carbon monoxide (CO) poisoning of Colorado residents. A total of 981 cases of CO poisoning were reported during a 6 year period. Each case was classified as fatal or nonfatal and by source of exposure. The number of cases occurring in each of the categories is shown in the next table. Assume that one of the 981 cases of unintentional CO poisoning is randomly selected.

Source of Exposure	Fatal	Nonfatal	Total
Fire	63	53	116
Auto exhaust	60	178	238
Furnace	18	345	363
Kerosene or space heater	9	18	27
Appliance	9	63	72
Other gas-powered motor	3	73	76
Fireplace	0	16	16
Other	3	19	22
Unknown	9	42	51
Total	174	807	981

Source: Cook, M. C., Simon, P. A., and Hoffman, R. E. "Unintentional Carbon Monoxide Poisoning in Colorado, 1986 through 1991." *American Journal of Public Health,* Vol. 85, No. 7, July 1995, p. 989 (Table 1). American Public Health Association.

a. List all sample points for this experiment.
b. What is the set of all sample points called?
c. Let A be the event that the CO poisoning is caused by fire. Find $P(A)$.
d. Let B be the event that the CO poisoning is fatal. Find $P(B)$.
e. Let C be the event that the CO poisoning is caused by auto exhaust. Find $P(C)$.
f. Let D be the event that the CO poisoning is caused by auto exhaust and is fatal. Find $P(D)$.
g. Let E be the event that the CO poisoning is caused by fire but is nonfatal. Find $P(E)$.
h. Given that the source of the poisoning is fire, what is the probability that the case is fatal?
i. Given that the case is nonfatal, what is the probability that it is caused by auto exhaust?
j. If the case is fatal, what is the probability that the source is unknown?
k. If the case is nonfatal, what is the probability that the source is not fire or a fireplace?

Applying the Concepts—Intermediate

3.103   Effect of stock market on consumer spending and saving. According to *Economic Inquiry* (Jan. 2002), 50% of all U.S. households own stock. A sample of these stockholders was asked what effect recent trends in the stock market have had on their saving and spending the last few years. The responses are summarized in the table. A U.S. household is selected at random.

Stock Market Effect on Spending/Saving	Percent of Stockholders
No effect	85.0
Spend more/save less	3.4
Spend less/save more	11.6
Total	100.0

Source: Starr-McCluer, M. "Stock Market Wealth and Consumer Spending." *Economic Inquiry,* Vol. 40, No. 1, January 2002 (Table 3).

a. What is the probability that the household does not own stock?

b. Given the household owns stock, what is the probability that the household spends more and saves less due to recent trends in the stock market?

c. What is the probability that the household owns stock but spends less and saves more due to recent trends in the stock market?

3.104 Assembling a panel of energy experts. The state legislature has appropriated $1 million to be distributed in the form of grants to individuals and organizations engaged in the research and development of alternative energy sources. You have been hired by the state's energy agency to assemble a panel of five energy experts whose task it will be to determine which individuals and organizations should receive the grant money. You have identified 11 equally qualified individuals who are willing to serve on the panel. How many different panels of five experts could be formed from these 11 individuals?

3.105 Testing a watch manufacturer's claim. A manufacturer of electronic digital watches claims that the probability of its watch running more than 1 minute slow or 1 minute fast after 1 year of use is .05. A consumer protection agency has purchased four of the manufacturer's watches with the intention of testing the claim.

a. Assuming that the manufacturer's claim is correct, what is the probability that none of the watches are as accurate as claimed?

b. Assuming that the manufacturer's claim is correct, what is the probability that exactly two of the four watches are as accurate as claimed?

c. Suppose that only one of the four tested watches is as accurate as claimed. What inference can be made about the manufacturer's claim? Explain.

d. Suppose that none of the watches tested are as accurate as claimed. Is it necessarily true that the manufacturer's claim is false? Explain.

3.106 Ranking razor blades. The corporations in the highly competitive razor blade industry do a tremendous amount of advertising each year. Corporation G gave a supply of three top-name brands, G, S, and W, to a consumer and asked her to use them and rank them in order of preference. The corporation was, of course, hoping the consumer would prefer its brand and rank it first, thereby giving them some material for a consumer interview advertising campaign. If the consumer did not prefer one blade over any other, but was still required to rank the blades, what is the probability that

a. The consumer ranked brand G first?

b. The consumer ranked brand G last?

c. The consumer ranked brand G last and brand W second?

d. The consumer ranked brand W first, brand G second, and brand S third?

3.107 Predicting the success of a new product. Acupoll is a consumer preference poll used to predict whether newly developed products will succeed if they are brought to market. The reliability of the Acupoll has been described as follows: The probability that Acupoll predicts the success of a particular product, given that later the product actually is successful, is .89 (*Minneapolis Star Tribune,* Dec. 16, 1992). A company is considering the introduction of a new product and assesses the product's probability of success to be .90. If this company were to have its product evaluated through Acupoll, what is the probability that Acupoll predicts success for the product and the product actually turns out to be successful?

3.108 Which events are independent? Use your intuitive understanding of independence to form an opinion about whether each of the following scenarios represent independent events.

a. The results of consecutive tosses of a coin

b. The opinions of randomly selected individuals in a pre-election poll

c. A major league baseball player's results in two consecutive at-bats

d. The amount of gain or loss associated with investments in different stocks if these stocks are bought on the same day and sold on the same day one month later

e. The amount of gain or loss associated with investments in different stocks that are bought and sold in different time periods, 5 years apart

f. The prices bid by two different development firms in response to a building construction proposal

3.109 Link between cigar smoking and cancer. The *Journal of the National Cancer Institute* (Feb. 16, 2000) published the results of a study that investigated the association between cigar smoking and death from tobacco-related cancers. Data were obtained for a national sample of 137,243 American men. The results are summarized in the accompanying table. Each male in the study was classified according to his cigar-smoking status and whether or not he died from a tobacco-related cancer.

a. Find the probability that a man who never smoked cigars died from cancer.

b. Find the probability that a former cigar smoker died from cancer.

c. Find the probability that a current cigar smoker died from cancer.

	Died from Cancer	Did Not Die from Cancer	Totals
Never Smoked Cigars	782	120,747	121,529
Former Cigar Smoker	91	7,757	7,848
Current Cigar Smoker	141	7,725	7,866
Totals	1,014	136,229	137,243

Source: Shapiro, J. A., Jacobs, E. J., and Thun, M. J. "Cigar Smoking in Men and Risk of Death from Tobacco-related Cancers." *Journal of the National Cancer Institute,* Vol. 92, No. 4, February 16, 2000 (Table 2).

3.110 Reliability of an automatic sprinkler system. A particular automatic sprinkler system for high-rise apartment buildings, office buildings, and hotels has two different types of activation devices for each sprinkler head. One type has a reliability of .91 (i.e., the probability that it will activate the sprinkler when it should is .91). The other type, which operates independently of the first type, has a reliability of .87. Suppose a serious fire starts near a particular sprinkler head.

  a. What is the probability that the sprinkler head will be activated?

  b. What is the probability that the sprinkler head will not be activated?

  c. What is the probability that both activation devices will work properly?

  d. What is the probability that only the device with reliability .91 will work properly?

3.111 Employees' choices of health care plans. Most companies offer their employees a variety of health care plans to choose from—e.g., preferred provider organizations (PPOs) and health maintenance organizations (HMOs) (*Monthly Labor Review*, Oct. 1995). A survey of 100 large, 100 medium, and 100 small companies that offer their employees HMOs, PPOs, and fee-for-service plans was conducted; each firm provided information on the plans chosen by their employees. These companies had a total employment of 833,303 people. A breakdown of the number of employees in each category by firm size and plan is provided in the table.

Company Size	Fee-for-Service	PPO	HMO	Totals
Small	1,808	1,757	1,456	5,021
Medium	8,953	6,491	6,938	22,382
Large	330,419	241,770	233,711	805,900
Totals	341,180	250,018	242,105	833,303

Source: Adapted from Bucci, M., and Grant, R. "Employer-Sponsored Health Insurance: What's Offered: What's Chosen?" *Monthly Labor Review,* October 1995, pp. 38–43.

One employee from the 833,303 total employees is to be chosen at random for further analysis. Define the events A and B as follows:

  A: {Observe an employee that chose fee-for-service}
  B: {Observe an employee from a small company}

  a. Find $P(B)$.
  b. Find $P(A \cap B)$.
  c. Find $P(A \cup B)$.
  d. Find $P(A|B)$.
  e. Are A and B independent? Justify your answer.

*3.112 Repairing a computer network. The local area network (LAN) for the College of Business computing system at a large university is temporarily shut down for repairs. Previous shutdowns have been due to hardware failure, software failure, or power failure. Maintenance engineers have determined that the probabilities of hardware, software, and power problems are .01, .05, and .02, respectively. They have also determined that if the system experiences hardware problems, it shuts down 73% of the time. Similarly, if software problems occur, the system shuts down 12% of the time; and, if power failure occurs, the system shuts down 88% of the time. What is the probability that the current shutdown of the LAN is due to hardware failure? Software failure? Power failure?

3.113 Chance of an Avon sale. The probability that an Avon salesperson sells beauty products to a prospective customer on the first visit to the customer is .4. If the salesperson fails to make the sale on the first visit, the probability that the sale will be made on the second visit is .65. The salesperson never visits a prospective customer more than twice. What is the probability that the salesperson will make a sale to a particular customer?

3.114 Evaluating the performance of quality inspectors. The performance of quality inspectors affects both the quality of outgoing products and the cost of the products. A product that passes inspection is assumed to meet quality standards; a product that fails inspection may be reworked, scrapped, or reinspected. Quality engineers at Westinghouse Electric Corporation evaluated performances of inspectors in judging the quality of solder joints by comparing each inspector's classifications of a set of 153 joints with the consensus evaluation of a panel of experts. The results for a particular inspector are shown in the next table.

	Inspector's Judgment	
Committee's Judgment	Joint Acceptable	Joint Rejectable
Joint acceptable	101	10
Joint rejectable	23	19

Source: American Society for Quality Control.

One of the 153 solder joints is to be selected at random.

  a. What is the probability that the inspector judges the joint to be acceptable? That the committee judges the joint to be acceptable?

  b. What is the probability that both the inspector and the committee judge the joint to be acceptable? That neither judge the joint to be acceptable?

  c. What is the probability that the inspector and the committee disagree? Agree?

3.115 System components operating in series. The figure shown at the top of page 183 is a schematic representation of a system comprised of three components. The system operates properly only if all three components operate properly. The three components are said to operate *in series*. The components could be mechanical or electrical; they could be work stations in an assembly process; or they could represent the functions of three different departments in an organization. The probability of failure for each component is listed in the table. Assume the components operate independently of each other.

Component	Probability of Failure
1	.12
2	.09
3	.11

  a. Find the probability that the system operates properly.

  b. What is the probability that at least one of the components will fail and therefore that the system will fail?

Figure for Exercise 3.115

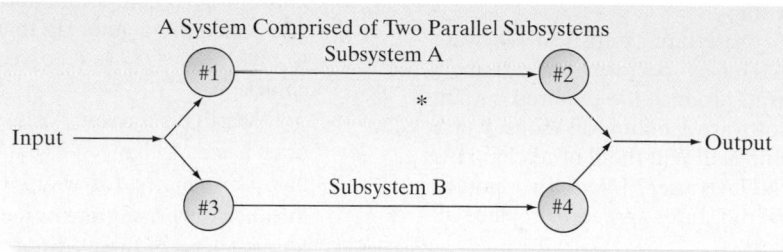

Figure for Exercise 3.116

3.116 Subsystems operating in parallel. The figure directly above is a representation of two subsystems that are said to operate *in parallel*. Each subsystem has two components that operate in series (refer to Exercise 3.115). The system will operate properly as long as at least one of the subsystems functions properly. The probability of failure for each component in the system is .1. Assume the components operate independently of each other.

a. Find the probability that the system operates properly.

b. Find the probability that exactly one subsystem fails.

c. Find the probability that the system fails to operate properly.

d. How many parallel subsystems like the two shown here would be required to guarantee that the system would operate properly at least 99% of the time?

Applying the Concepts—Advanced

3.117 Value line stock survey. The Value Line Survey, a service for common stock investors, provides its subscribers with up-to-date evaluations of the prospects and risks associated with the purchase of a large number of common stocks. Each stock is ranked 1 (highest) to 5 (lowest) according to Value Line's estimate of the stock's potential for price appreciation during the next 12 months. Suppose you plan to purchase stock in three electrical utility companies from among seven that possess rankings of 2 for price appreciation. Unknown to you, two of the companies will experience serious difficulties with their nuclear facilities during the coming year. If you randomly select the three companies from among the seven, what is the probability that you select:

a. None of the companies with prospective nuclear difficulties?

b. One of the companies with prospective nuclear difficulties?

c. Both of the companies with prospective nuclear difficulties?

*3.118 Rejected bottles of a brewery. A small brewery has two bottling machines. Machine A produces 75% of the bottles and machine B produces 25%. One out of every 20 bottles filled by A is rejected for some reason, while one out of every 30 bottles from B is rejected. What proportion of bottles is rejected? What is the probability that a randomly selected bottle comes from machine A, given that it is accepted?

*3.119 Scrap rate of machine parts. A press produces parts used in the manufacture of large-screen plasma televisions. If the press is correctly adjusted, it produces parts with a scrap rate of 5%. If it is not adjusted correctly, it produces scrap at a 50% rate. From past company records, the machine is known to be correctly adjusted 90% of the time. A quality control inspector randomly selects one part from those recently produced by the press and discovers it is defective. What is the probability that the machine is incorrectly adjusted?

3.120 Chance of winning at "craps." A version of the dice game "craps" is played in the following manner. A player starts by rolling two balanced dice. If the roll (the sum of the two numbers showing on the dice) results in a 7 or 11, the player wins. If the roll results in a 2 or a 3 (called *craps*), the player loses. For any other roll outcome, the player continues to throw the dice until the original roll outcome recurs (in which case the player wins) or until a 7 occurs (in which case the player loses).

a. What is the probability that a player wins the game on the first roll of the dice?

b. What is the probability that a player loses the game on the first roll of the dice?

c. If the player throws a total of 4 on the first roll, what is the probability that the game ends (win or lose) on the next roll?

3.121 Chance of winning blackjack. Blackjack, a favorite game of gamblers, is played by a dealer and at least one opponent (called a *player*). In one version of the game, 2 cards of a standard 52-card bridge deck are dealt to the player and 2 cards to the dealer. For this exercise, assume that drawing an ace and a face card is called *blackjack*. If the dealer does not draw a blackjack and the player does, the player wins. If both the dealer and player draw blackjack, a "push" (i.e., a tie) occurs.

a. What is the probability that the dealer will draw a blackjack?

b. What is the probability that the player wins with a blackjack?

Critical Thinking Challenges

3.122 Flawed Pentium computer chip. In October 1994, a flaw was discovered in the Pentium microchip installed in personal computers. The chip produced an incorrect result when dividing two numbers. Intel, the manufacturer of the Pentium chip, initially announced that such an error would occur once in 9 billion divides, or "once in every 27,000 years" for a typical user; consequently, it did not immediately offer to replace the chip.

Depending on the procedure, statistical software packages (e.g., MINITAB) may perform an extremely large number of divisions to produce the required output. For heavy users of the software 1 billion divisions over a short time frame is not unusual. Will the flawed chip be a problem for a heavy MINITAB user? [*Note:* Two months after the flaw was discovered, Intel agreed to replace all Pentium chips free of charge.]

3.123 "Let's Make a Deal." Marilyn vos Savant, who is listed in *Guinness Book of World Records Hall of Fame* for

"Highest IQ," writes a weekly column in the Sunday newspaper supplement, *Parade Magazine*. Her column, "Ask Marilyn," is devoted to games of skill, puzzles, and mind-bending riddles. In one issue (*Parade Magazine*, Feb. 24, 1991), vos Savant posed the following question:

Suppose you're on a game show, and you're given a choice of three doors. Behind one door is a car; behind the others, goats. You pick a door—say, #1—and the host, who knows what's behind the doors, opens another door—say #3—which has a goat. He then says to you, "Do you want to pick door #2?" Is it to your advantage to switch your choice?

Marilyn's answer: "Yes, you should switch. The first door has a $\frac{1}{3}$ chance of winning [the car], but the second has a $\frac{2}{3}$ chance [of winning the car]." Predictably, vos Savant's surprising answer elicited thousands of critical letters, many of them from PhD mathematicians, who disagreed with her. Who is correct, the PhDs or Marilyn?

REFERENCES

Bennett, D. J. *Randomness*. Cambridge, Mass.: Harvard University Press, 1998.

Epstein, R. A. *The Theory of Gambling and Statistical Logic*, rev. ed. New York: Academic Press, 1977.

Feller, W. *An Introduction to Probability Theory and Its Applications*, 3rd ed., Vol. 1. New York: Wiley, 1968.

Lindley, D. V. *Making Decisions*, 2nd ed. London: Wiley, 1985.

Parzen, E. *Modern Probability Theory and Its Applications*. New York: Wiley, 1960.

Wackerly, D., Mendenhall, W., and Scheaffer, R. L. *Mathematical Statistics with Applications*, 6th ed. Boston: Duxbury, 2002.

Williams, B. *A Sampler on Sampling*. New York: Wiley, 1978.

Winkler, R. L. *An Introduction to Bayesian Inference and Decision*. New York: Holt, Rinehart and Winston, 1972.

Wright, G., and Ayton, P., eds. *Subjective Probability*. New York: Wiley, 1994.

Using Technology

3.1 Generating a Random Sample Using SPSS

To obtain a random sample of observations (cases) from a data set stored in the SPSS spreadsheet, click on the "Data" button on the SPSS menu bar, then click on "Select Cases," as shown in Figure 3.S.1. The resulting menu list appears as shown in Figure 3.S.2. Select "Random sample of cases" from the list, then click on the "Sample" button. The dialog box shown in Figure 3.S.3 will appear. You will specify the sample size either as a percentage of cases or a raw number. After you specify the sample size, click "Continue" to return to the "Select Cases" dialog box (Figure 3.S.2) and click "OK." The SPSS spreadsheet will reappear with the selected (sampled) cases.

Figure 3.S.1
SPSS Menu Options for
Sampling from a Data Set

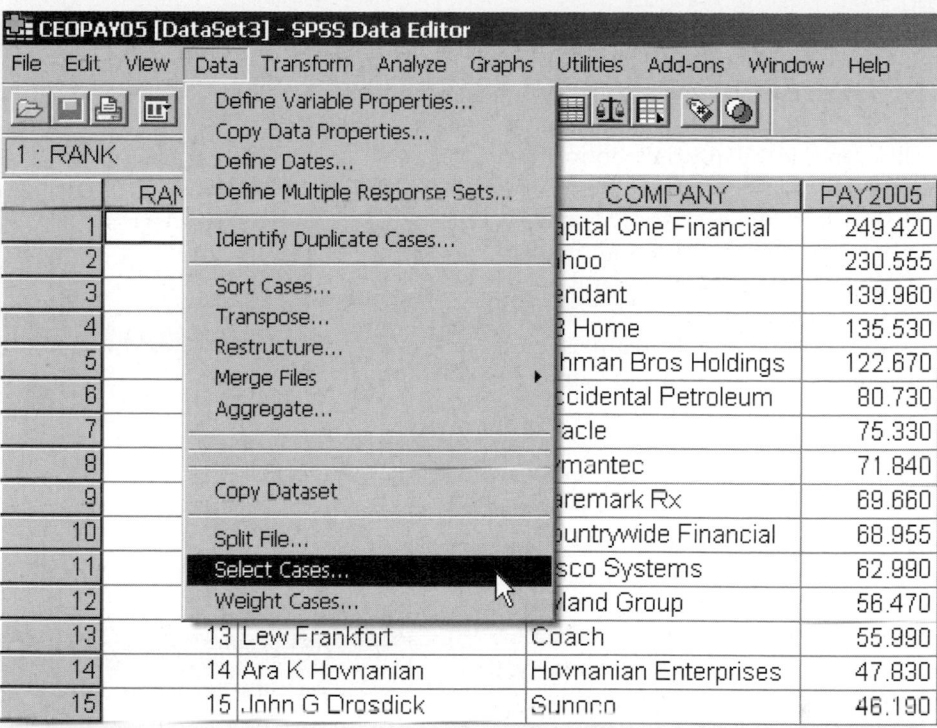

Figure 3.S.3
SPSS Random Sample Dialog Box

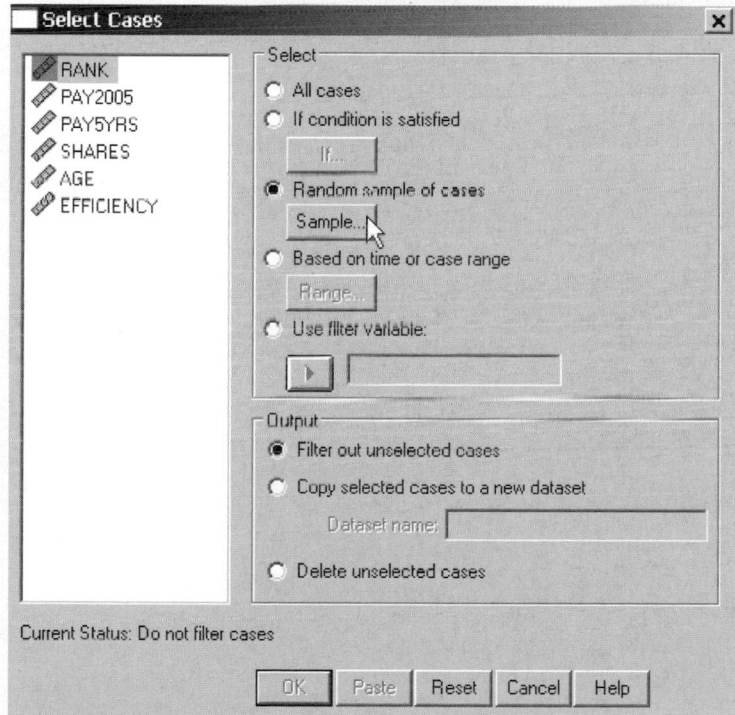

Figure 3.S.2
SPSS Options for Selecting a Random Sample

3.2 Generating a Random Sample Using MINITAB

To obtain a random sample of observations (cases) from a data set stored in the MINITAB worksheet, click on the "Calc" button on the MINITAB menu bar, then click on "Random Data," and finally, click on "Sample from Columns," as shown in Figure 3.M.1. The resulting dialog box appears as shown in Figure 3.M.2. Specify the sample size (i.e., number of rows), the variable(s) to be sampled, and the column(s) where you want to save the sample. Click "OK" and the MINITAB worksheet will reappear with the values of the variable for the selected (sampled) cases in the column specified.

In MINITAB, you can also generate a sample of case numbers. From the MINITAB menu, click on the "Calc" button, then click on "Random Data," and finally, click on the "Uniform" option (see Figure 3.M.1). The resulting dialog box appears as shown in Figure 3.M.3. Specify the number of cases (rows, i.e., the sample size), and the column where the case numbers selected will be stored. Click "OK" and the MINITAB worksheet will reappear with the case numbers for the selected (sampled) cases in the column specified.

[*Note:* If you want the option of generating the same (identical) sample multiple times from the data set, then first click on the "Set Base" option shown in Figure 3.M.1. Specify an integer in the resulting dialog box. If you always select the same integer, MINITAB will select the same sample when you choose the random sampling options.]

Figure 3.M.1

MINITAB Menu Options for Sampling from a Data Set

Figure 3.M.2

MINITAB Options for Selecting a Random Sample from Worksheet Columns

Figure 3.M.3

MINITAB Options for Selecting a Random Sample of Cases

3.3 Generating a Random Sample Using Excel/PHStat2

To obtain a random sample of observations (cases) from a data set stored in the EXCEL spreadsheet, enter into a PHStat2 session. From the PHStat2 main menu, click on the "PHStat" button, then click on "Sampling," and finally, click on "Random Sample Generator," as shown in Figure 3.E.1. The resulting dialog box appears as shown in Figure 3.E.2. Specify the sample size (i.e., number of cases), then decide whether you want a list of case numbers or a list of values of the variable of interest. For a list of case numbers, select "Generate list of random numbers" and specify the population size (see Figure 3.E.2). For a list of the values of the variable, select "Values from range" and specify the cell range (see Figure 3.E.3). After making your selections, click "OK" and a new EXCEL worksheet with the random numbers will appear on the screen.

Figure 3.E.1
EXCEL/PHStat Menu Options for Sampling from a Data Set

Figure 3.E.2
EXCEL/PHStat Random Sample Generator Dialog Box with Options for Selecting Case Numbers

Figure 3.E.3
EXCEL/PHStat Random Sample Generator Dialog Box with Options for Selecting Values of a Variable

CHAPTER

4

Random Variables and Probability Distributions

CONTENTS

STATISTICS IN ACTION

Super Weapons Development—Optimizing the Hit Ratio

USING TECHNOLOGY

Binomial Probabilities, Normal Probabilities, and Simulated Sampling Distributions Using SPSS, MINITAB, and Excel/PHStat2

WHERE WE'VE BEEN

- Used probability to make an inference about a population from data in an observed sample

- Used probability to measure the reliability of the inference

WHERE WE'RE GOING

- Develop the notion of a random variable.

- Learn that numerical data are observed values of either discrete or continuous random variables.

- Study two important types of random variables and their probability models: the binomial and normal model.

- Define a sampling distribution as the probability distribution of a sample statistic.

- Learn that the sampling distribution of $\bar{x}$ follows a normal model.

STATISTICS IN ACTION

Super Weapons Development—Optimizing the Hit Ratio

The U.S. Army is working with a major defense contractor to develop a "super" weapon. The weapon is designed to fire a large number of sharp tungsten bullets— called flechettes—*with a single shot that will destroy a large number of enemy soldiers. Flechettes are about the size of an average nail, with small fins at one end to stabilize them in flight. Since World War I, when France dropped them in large quantities from aircraft on masses of ground troops, munitions experts have experimented with using flechettes in a variety of guns. The problem with using flechettes as ammunition is accuracy—current weapons that fire large quantities of flechettes have unsatisfactory hit ratios when fired at long distances.*

The defense contractor (not named here for both confidentiality and security reasons) has developed a prototype gun that fires 1,100 flechettes with a single round. In range tests, three 2-feet-wide targets were set up a distance of 500 meters (approximately 1,500 feet) from the weapon. Using a number line as a reference, the centers of the three targets were at 0, 5, and 10 feet, respectively, as shown in Figure SIA4.1. The prototype gun was aimed at the middle target (center at 5 feet) and fired once. The point where each of the 1,100 flechettes landed at the 500-meter distance was measured using a horizontal and vertical grid. For the purposes of this application, only the horizontal measurements are considered. These 1,100 measurements are saved in the **MOAGUN** file. (The data are simulated for confidentiality reasons.) For example, a flechette with a value of $x = 5.5$ hit the middle target, but a flechette with a value of

Figure SIA4.1
Target placement on gun range

$x = 2.0$ did not hit any of the three targets (see Figure SIA4.1).

The defense contractor is interested in the likelihood of any one of the targets being hit by a flechette and, in particular, wants to set the gun specifications to maximize the number of target hits. The weapon is designed to have a mean horizontal value equal to the aim point (e.g., $\mu = 5$ feet when aimed at the center target). By changing specifications, the contractor can vary the standard deviation, σ. The **MOAGUN** file contains flechette measurements for three different range tests—one with a standard deviation of $\sigma = 1$ foot, one with $\sigma = 2$ feet, and one with $\sigma = 4$ feet.

In this chapter, three Statistics in Action Revisited examples demonstrate how we can use one of the probability models discussed in this chapter—the normal probability distribution—to aid the defense contractor in developing its "super" weapon.

 MOAGUN

Statistics in Action Revisited

- Using the Normal Model to Maximize the Probability of a Hit with the Super Weapon (p. 239)
- Assessing whether the Normal Distribution Is Appropriate for Modeling the Super Weapon Hit Data (p. 246)
- Making an Inference about the Mean Accuracy of the Super Weapon (p. 269)

Y ou may have noticed that many of the examples of experiments in Chapter 3 generated quantitative (numerical) observations. The Consumer Price Index, the unemployment rate, the number of sales made in a week, and the yearly profit of a company are all examples of numerical measurements of some phenomenon. Thus, most experiments have sample points that correspond to values of some numerical variable.

To illustrate, consider the coin-tossing experiment of Chapter 3. Figure 4.1 is a Venn diagram showing the sample points when two coins are tossed and the up faces (heads or tails) of the coins are observed. One possible numerical outcome is the total

HH
●
(2)

HT
●
(1)

TT
●
(0)

TH
●
(1)

S

FIGURE 4.1
Venn diagram for coin-tossing
experiment

number of heads observed. These values (0, 1, or 2) are shown in parentheses on the Venn diagram, one numerical value associated with each sample point. In the jargon of probability, the variable "total number of heads observed when two coins are tossed" is called a *random variable*.

> **Definition 4.1**
>
> A **random variable** is a variable that assumes numerical values associated with the random outcomes of an experiment, where one (and only one) numerical value is assigned to each sample point.

The term *random variable* is more meaningful than the term *variable* because the adjective *random* indicates that the coin-tossing experiment may result in one of the several possible values of the variable—0, 1, and 2—according to the *random* outcome of the experiment, *HH, HT, TH,* and *TT*. Similarly, if the experiment is to count the number of customers who use the drive-up window of a bank each day, the random variable (the number of customers) will vary from day to day, partly because of the random phenomena that influence whether customers use the drive-up window. Thus, the possible values of this random variable range from 0 to the maximum number of customers the window could possibly serve in a day.

We define two different types of random variables, *discrete* and *continuous*, in Section 4.1. Then we spend the remainder of this chapter discussing specific types of both discrete and continuous random variables and the aspects that make them important in business applications.

4.1 Two Types of Random Variables

Recall that the sample point probabilities corresponding to an experiment must sum to 1. Dividing one unit of probability among the sample points in a sample space and consequently assigning probabilities to the values of a random variable is not always as easy as the examples in Chapter 3 might lead you to believe. If the number of sample points can be completely listed, the job is straightforward. But if the experiment results in an infinite number of numerical sample points that are impossible to list, the task of assigning probabilities to the sample points is impossible without the aid of a probability model. The next three examples demonstrate the need for different probability models depending on the number of values that a random variable can assume.

EXAMPLE 4.1

Values of a Discrete
Random Variable—
Wine Ratings

Problem A panel of 10 experts for the *Wine Spectator* (a national publication) is asked to taste a new white wine and assign a rating of 0, 1, 2, or 3. A score is then obtained by adding together the ratings of the 10 experts. How many values can this random variable assume?

Solution A sample point is a sequence of 10 numbers associated with the rating of each expert. For example, one sample point is

$$\{1, 0, 0, 1, 2, 0, 0, 3, 1, 0\}$$

The random variable assigns a score to each one of these sample points by adding the 10 numbers together. Thus, the smallest score is 0 (if all 10 ratings are 0), and the largest score is 30 (if all 10 ratings are 3). Since every integer between 0 and 30 is a possible score, the random variable denoted by the symbol x can assume 31 values. Note that the value of the random variable for the sample point above is $x = 8$.*

*The standard mathematical convention is to use a capital letter (e.g., X) to denote the theoretical random variable. The possible values (or realizations) of the random variable are typically denoted with a lowercase letter (e.g., x). Thus, in Example 4.1, the random variable X can take on the values $x = 0, 1, 2, \ldots, 30$. Since this notation can be confusing for introductory statistics students, we simplify the notation by using the lowercase x to represent the random variable throughout.

Look Back This is an example of a *discrete random variable*, since there is a finite number of distinct possible values. Whenever all the possible values a random variable can assume can be listed (or counted), the random variable is discrete.

EXAMPLE 4.2
Values of a Discrete Random Variable— EPA Application

Problem   Suppose the Environmental Protection Agency (EPA) takes readings once a month on the amount of pesticide in the discharge water of a chemical company. If the amount of pesticide exceeds the maximum level set by the EPA, the company is forced to take corrective action and may be subject to penalty. Consider the random variable, x, number of months before the company's discharge exceeds the EPA's maximum level. What values can x assume?

Solution   The company's discharge of pesticide may exceed the maximum allowable level on the first month of testing, the second month of testing, and so on. It is possible that the company's discharge will *never* exceed the maximum level. Thus, the set of possible values for the number of months until the level is first exceeded is the set of all positive integers

$$1, 2, 3, 4, \ldots$$

Look Back   If we can list the values of a random variable x, even though the list is never ending, we call the list **countable** and the corresponding random variable *discrete*. Thus, the number of months until the company's discharge first exceeds the limit is a *discrete random variable*.

Now Work Exercise 4.4

EXAMPLE 4.3
Values of a Continuous Random Variable—Another EPA Application

Problem   Refer to Example 4.2. A second random variable of interest is the amount x of pesticide (in milligrams per liter) found in the monthly sample of discharge waters from the chemical company. What values can this random variable assume?

Solution   Unlike the *number* of months before the company's discharge exceeds the EPA's maximum level, the set of all possible values for the *amount* of discharge *cannot be listed*—that is, is not countable. The possible values for the amounts of pesticide would correspond to the points on the interval between 0 and the largest possible value the amount of the discharge could attain, the maximum number of milligrams that could occupy 1 liter of volume. (Practically, the interval would be much smaller, say, between 0 and 500 milligrams per liter.)

Look Back   When the values of a random variable are not countable but instead correspond to the points on some interval, we call it a *continuous random variable*. Thus, the *amount* of pesticide in the chemical plant's discharge waters is a *continuous random variable*.

Now Work Exercise 4.5

Definition 4.2

Random variables that can assume a *countable* number of values are called **discrete.**

Definition 4.3

Random variables that can assume values corresponding to any of the points contained in one or more intervals (i.e., values that are *uncountable*) are called **continuous.**

Several more examples of discrete random variables follow:

1. The number of sales made by a salesperson in a given week: $x = 0, 1, 2, \ldots$
2. The number of consumers in a sample of 500 who favor a particular product over all competitors: $x = 0, 1, 2, \ldots, 500$
3. The number of bids received in a bond offering: $x = 0, 1, 2, \ldots$
4. The number of errors on a page of an accountant's ledger: $x = 0, 1, 2, \ldots$
5. The number of customers waiting to be served in a restaurant at a particular time: $x = 0, 1, 2, \ldots$

Note that each of the examples of discrete random variables begins with the words "The number of . . . " This wording is very common, since the discrete random variables most frequently observed are counts.

We conclude this section with some more examples of continuous random variables:

1. The length of time between arrivals at a hospital clinic: $0 \leq x < \infty$ (infinity)
2. For a new apartment complex, the length of time from completion until a specified number of apartments are rented: $0 \leq x < \infty$
3. The amount of carbonated beverage loaded into a 12-ounce can in a can-filling operation: $0 \leq x \leq 12$
4. The depth at which a successful oil-drilling venture first strikes oil: $0 \leq x \leq c$, where c is the maximum depth obtainable
5. The weight of a food item bought in a supermarket: $0 \leq x \leq 500$ [*Note*: Theoretically, there is no upper limit on x, but it is unlikely that it would exceed 500 pounds.]

Discrete random variables and their probability distributions are discussed in Sections 4.2–4.4. Continuous random variables and their probability distributions are the topic of Sections 4.5–4.7.

Exercises 4.1–4.10

Applying the Concepts—Basic

4.1 Types of random variables. Which of the following describe continuous random variables, and which describe discrete random variables?
a. The number of newspapers sold by the *New York Times* each month
b. The amount of ink used in printing a Sunday edition of the *New York Times*
c. The actual number of ounces in a one-gallon bottle of laundry detergent
d. The number of defective parts in a shipment of nuts and bolts
e. The number of people collecting unemployment insurance each month

4.2 Types of finance random variables. Security analysts are professionals who devote full-time efforts to evaluating the investment worth of a narrow list of stocks. The following variables are of interest to security analysts (Radcliffe, *Investments: Concepts, Analysis and Strategy,* 1997). Which are discrete and which are continuous random variables?
a. The closing price of a particular stock on the New York Stock Exchange
b. The number of shares of a particular stock that are traded each business day

c. The quarterly earnings of a particular firm
d. The percentage change in yearly earnings between 2005 and 2006 for a particular firm
e. The number of new products introduced per year by a firm
f. The time until a pharmaceutical company gains approval from the U.S. Food and Drug Administration to market a new drug

CRASH

4.3 NHTSA crash tests. Refer to the National Highway Traffic Safety Administration crash tests of new car models, Exercise 2.129 (p. 115). Recall that the NHTSA developed a driver-side "star" scoring system, with results ranging from one star (*) to five stars (*****). The more stars in the rating, the better the level of crash protection in a head-on collision. Suppose that a car is selected and its driver-side star rating is determined. Let x equal the number of stars in the rating. Is x a discrete or continuous random variable?

4.4 Customers in line at a Subway shop. The number of customers, x, waiting in line to order sandwiches at a Subway shop at noon is of interest to the store manager. What values can x assume? Is x a discrete or continuous random variable?

4.5 **Executive Compensation Scoreboard.** Refer to *Forbes'*
NW 2005 "Executive Compensation Scoreboard." One variable
saved in the file is the CEO's compensation (in $ millions)
in 2005. Is *x* a discrete or continuous random variable?

Applying the Concepts—Intermediate

⍥ **4.6** **Banking.** Give an example of a discrete random variable
that would be of interest to a banker.

4.7 **Economics.** Give an example of a continuous random
variable that would be of interest to an economist.

4.8 **Hotel management.** Give an example of a discrete
random variable that would be of interest to the manager
of a hotel.

4.9 **Retailing.** Give two examples of discrete random variables
that would be of interest to the manager of a clothing
store.

⍥ **4.10** **Stock market.** Give an example of a continuous random
variable that would be of interest to a stockbroker.

4.2 Probability Distributions for Discrete Random Variables

A complete description of a discrete random variable requires that we *specify the possible values the random variable can assume and the probability associated with each value.* To illustrate, consider Example 4.4.

EXAMPLE 4.4

Finding a Probability Distribution for a Coin-Tossing Experiment

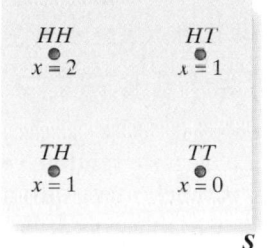

S

FIGURE 4.2

Venn diagram for the two-coin-toss experiment

Problem Recall the experiment of tossing two coins (Section 4.1), and let *x* be the number of heads observed. Find the probability associated with each value of the random variable *x*, assuming the two coins are fair. Display these values in a table or graph.

Solution The sample space and sample points for this experiment are reproduced in Figure 4.2. Note that the random variable *x* can assume values 0, 1, 2. Recall (from Chapter 3) that the probability associated with each of the four sample points is $\frac{1}{4}$. Then, identifying the probabilities of the sample points associated with each of these values of *x*, we have

$$P(x = 0) = P(TT) = \tfrac{1}{4}$$
$$P(x = 1) = P(TH) + P(HT) = \tfrac{1}{4} + \tfrac{1}{4} = \tfrac{1}{2}$$
$$P(x = 2) = P(HH) = \tfrac{1}{4}$$

Thus, we now know the values the random variable can assume (0, 1, 2) and how the probability is *distributed over* these values ($\frac{1}{4}, \frac{1}{2}, \frac{1}{4}$). This completely describes the random variable and is referred to as the *probability distribution*, denoted by the symbol *p(x)*.* The probability distribution for the coin-toss example is shown in tabular form in Table 4.1 and in graphical form in Figure 4.3. Since the probability distribution for a discrete random variable is concentrated at specific points (values of *x*), the graph in Figure 4.3(a) represents the probabilities as the heights of vertical lines over the corresponding values of *x*. Although the representation of the probability distribution as a histogram, as in Figure 4.3(b), is less precise (since the probability is spread over a unit interval), the histogram representation will prove useful when we approximate probabilities of certain discrete random variables in Section 4.4.

Look Back We could also present the probability distribution for *x* as a formula, but this would unnecessarily complicate a very simple example. We give the formulas for the probability distributions of some common discrete random variables later in this chapter.

Now Work Exercise 4.15

TABLE 4.1 Probability Distribution for Coin-Toss Experiment: Tabular Form

x	p(x)
0	$\frac{1}{4}$
1	$\frac{1}{2}$
2	$\frac{1}{4}$

*In standard mathematical notation, the probability that a random variable *X* takes on a value *x* is denoted $P(X = x) = p(x)$. Thus, $P(X = 0) = p(0)$, $P(X = 1) = p(1)$, etc. In this introductory text, we adopt the simpler *p(x)* notation.

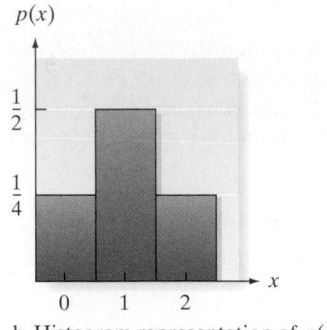

a. Point representation of $p(x)$ b. Histogram representation of $p(x)$

FIGURE 4.3
Probability distribution
for coin-toss experiment:
graphical form

Definition 4.4

The **probability distribution** of a **discrete random variable** is a graph, table, or formula that specifies the probability associated with each possible value the random variable can assume.

Two requirements must be satisfied by all probability distributions for discrete random variables.

Requirements for the Probability Distribution of a Discrete Random Variable, x

1. $p(x) \geq 0$ for all values of x
2. $\Sigma p(x) = 1$

where the summation of $p(x)$ is over all possible values of x.*

Now Work Exercise 4.12

Example 4.4 illustrates how the probability distribution for a discrete random variable can be derived, but for many practical situations, the task is much more difficult. Fortunately, many experiments and associated discrete random variables observed in business possess identical characteristics. Thus, you might observe a random variable in a marketing experiment that would possess the same characteristics as a random variable observed in accounting, economics, or management. We classify random variables according to type of experiment, derive the probability distribution for each of the different types, and then use the appropriate probability distribution when a particular type of random variable is observed in a practical situation. The probability distributions for most commonly occurring discrete random variables have already been derived. This fact simplifies the problem of finding the appropriate probability distributions for the business analyst, as the next example illustrates.

EXAMPLE 4.5

Probability
Distribution for
Texas Droughts
Using a Formula

Problem   A drought is a period of abnormal dry weather that causes serious problems in the farming industry of the region. University of Arizona researchers used historical annual data to study the severity of droughts in Texas (*Journal of Hydrologic Engineering*, Sept./Oct. 2003). The researchers showed that the distribution of x, the number of consecutive years that must be sampled until a dry (drought) year is observed, can be modeled using the formula

$$p(x) = (.3)(.7)^{x-1}, \; x = 1, 2, 3, \ldots$$

Find the probability that exactly 3 years must be sampled before a drought year occurs.

---

*Unless otherwise indicated, summations will always be over all possible values of x.

Solution We want to find the probability that $x = 3$. Using the formula, we have

$$p(3) = (.3)(.7)^{3-1} = (.3)(.7)^2 = (.3)(.49) = .147$$

Thus, there is about a 15% chance that exactly 3 years must be sampled before a drought year occurs in Texas.

Look Back The probability of interest can also be derived using the principles of probability developed in Chapter 3. The event of interest is $N_1 N_2 D_3$, where N_1 represents no drought occurs in the first sampled year, N_2 represents no drought occurs in the second sampled year, and D_3 represents a drought occurs in the third sampled year. The researchers discovered that the probability of a drought occurring in any sampled year is .3 (and consequently, the probability of no drought occurring in any sampled year is .7). Using the Multiplicative Law of Probability for independent events, the probability of interest is $(.7)(.7)(.3) = .147$.

Since probability distributions are analogous to the relative frequency distributions of Chapter 2, it should be no surprise that the mean and standard deviation are useful descriptive measures.

If a discrete random variable x were observed a very large number of times and the data generated were arranged in a relative frequency distribution, the relative frequency distribution would be indistinguishable from the probability distribution for the random variable. Thus, the probability distribution for a random variable is a theoretical model for the relative frequency distribution of a population. To the extent that the two distributions are equivalent (and we will assume they are), the probability distribution for x possesses a mean μ and a variance σ^2 that are identical to the corresponding descriptive measures for the population. How can you find the mean value for a random variable? We illustrate the procedure with an example.

Examine the probability distribution for x (the number of heads observed in the toss of two fair coins) in Figure 4.4. Try to locate the mean of the distribution intuitively. We may reason that the mean μ of this distribution is equal to 1 as follows: In a large number of experiments, $\frac{1}{4}$ should result in $x = 0$, $\frac{1}{2}$ in $x = 1$, and $\frac{1}{4}$ in $x = 2$ heads. Therefore, the average number of heads is

$$\mu = 0\left(\tfrac{1}{4}\right) + 1\left(\tfrac{1}{2}\right) + 2\left(\tfrac{1}{4}\right) = 0 + \tfrac{1}{2} + \tfrac{1}{2} = 1$$

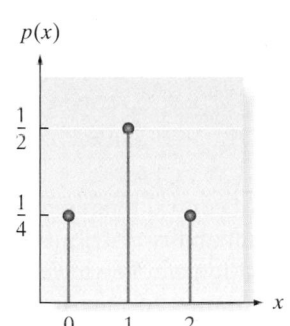

FIGURE 4.4
Probability distribution for a two-coin toss

Note that to get the population mean of the random variable x, we multiply each possible value of x by its probability $p(x)$, and then sum this product over all possible values of x. The *mean of x* is also referred to as the *expected value of x*, denoted $E(x)$.

Definition 4.5

The **mean,** or **expected value,** of a discrete random variable x is

$$\mu = E(x) = \sum x p(x)$$

Expected is a mathematical term and should not be interpreted as it is typically used. Specifically, a random variable might never be equal to its "expected value." Rather, the expected value is the mean of the probability distribution or a measure of its central tendency. You can think of μ as the mean value of x in a *very large* (actually, *infinite*) number of repetitions of the experiment, where the values of x occur in proportions equivalent to the probabilities of x.

EXAMPLE 4.6
Finding an Expected Value—An Insurance Application

Problem Suppose you work for an insurance company, and you sell a $10,000 one-year term insurance policy at an annual premium of $290. Actuarial tables show that the probability of death during the next year for a person of your customer's age, sex, health, etc., is .001. What is the expected gain (amount of money made by the company) for a policy of this type?

Solution   The experiment is to observe whether the customer survives the upcoming year. The probabilities associated with the two sample points, Live and Die, are .999 and .001, respectively. The random variable you are interested in is the gain x, which can assume the values shown in the following table.

Gain, x	Sample Point	Probability
$290	Customer lives	.999
−$9,710	Customer dies	.001

If the customer lives, the company gains the $290 premium as profit. If the customer dies, the gain is negative because the company must pay $10,000, for a net "gain" of $(290 − 10,000) = −$9,710$. The expected gain is therefore

$$\mu = E(x) = \sum_{\text{all } x} xp(x)$$

$$= (290)(.999) + (-9,710)(.001) = \$280$$

In other words, if the company were to sell a very large number of one-year $10,000 policies to customers possessing the characteristics previously described it would (on the average) net $280 per sale in the next year.

Look Back   Note that $E(x)$ need not equal a possible value of x—that is, the expected value is $280, but x will equal either $290 or −$9,710 each time the experiment is performed (a policy is sold and a year elapses). The expected value is a measure of central tendency—and in this case represents the average over a very large number of one-year policies—but is not a possible value of x.

Now Work Exercise 4.28a

We learned in Chapter 2 that the mean and other measures of central tendency tell only part of the story about a set of data. The same is true about probability distributions. We need to measure variability as well. Since a probability distribution can be viewed as a representation of a population, we will use the population variance to measure its variability.

The *population variance* σ^2 is defined as the average of the squared distance of x from the population mean μ. Since x is a random variable, the squared distance, $(x − \mu)^2$, is also a random variable. Using the same logic used to find the mean value of x, we find the mean value of $(x − \mu)^2$ by multiplying all possible values of $(x − \mu)^2$ by $p(x)$ and then summing over all possible x values.* This quantity,

$$E[(x − \mu)^2] = \sum_{\text{all } x} (x − \mu)^2 p(x)$$

is also called the *expected value of the squared distance from the mean;* that is, $\sigma^2 = E[(x − \mu)^2]$. The standard deviation of x is defined as the square root of the variance σ^2.

Definition 4.6

The **variance** of a **discrete random variable** x is

$$\sigma^2 = E[(x − \mu)^2] = \sum (x − \mu)^2 p(x)$$

Definition 4.7

The **standard deviation** of a **discrete random variable** is equal to the square root of the variance, i.e., $\sigma = \sqrt{\sigma^2}$.

*It can be shown that $E[(x − \mu)^2] = E(x)^2 − \mu^2$, where $E(x^2) = \sum x^2 p(x)$. Note the similarity between this expression and the shortcut formula $\sum(x − \bar{x})^2 = \sum x^2 − (\sum x)^2/n$ given in Chapter 2.

Knowing the mean μ and standard deviation σ of the probability distribution of x, in conjunction with Chebyshev's Rule (Table 2.6) and the Empirical Rule (Table 2.7), we can make statements about the likelihood that values of x will fall within the intervals $\mu \pm \sigma, \mu \pm 2\sigma$, and $\mu \pm 3\sigma$. These probabilities are given in the box.

Probability Rules for a Discrete Random Variable

Let x be a discrete random variable with probability distribution $p(x)$, mean μ, and standard deviation σ. Then, depending on the shape of $p(x)$, the following probability statements can be made:

	Chebyshev's Rule	Empirical Rule
	Applies to any probability distribution (see Figure 4.5a)	Applies to probability that distributions are mound-shaped and symmetric (see Figure 4.5b)
$P(\mu - \sigma < x < \mu + \sigma)$	≥ 0	$\approx.68$
$P(\mu - 2\sigma < x < \mu + 2\sigma)$	$\geq {}^3\!/_4$	$\approx.95$
$P(\mu - 3\sigma < x < \mu + 3\sigma)$	$\geq {}^8\!/_9$	≈1.00

FIGURE 4.5

Shapes of two probability distributions for a discrete random variable x

a. Skewed distribution

b. Mound-shaped, symmetric

EXAMPLE 4.7

Finding μ and σ for an Internet Business Venture

Problem   Suppose you invest a fixed sum of money in each of five Internet business ventures. Assume you know that 70% of such ventures are successful, the outcomes of the ventures are independent of one another, and the probability distribution for the number, x, of successful ventures out of five is

x	0	1	2	3	4	5
$p(x)$	.002	.029	.132	.309	.360	.168

a. Find $\mu = E(x)$. Interpret the result.

b. Find $\sigma = \sqrt{E[(x - \mu)^2]}$. Interpret the result.

c. Graph $p(x)$. Locate μ and the interval $\mu \pm 2\sigma$ on the graph. Use either Chebyshev's Rule or the Empirical Rule to approximate the probability that x falls in this interval. Compare this result with the actual probability.

d. Would you expect to observe fewer than two successful ventures out of five?

Solution

a. Applying the formula,

$$\mu = E(x) = \sum xp(x) = 0(.002) + 1(.029) + 2(.132) + 3(.309)$$
$$+ 4(.360) + 5(.168) = 3.50$$

On average, the number of successful ventures out of five will equal 3.5. Remember that this expected value only has meaning when the experiment—investing in five Internet business ventures—is repeated a large number of times.

b. Now we calculate the variance of x:

$$\sigma^2 = E[(x - \mu)^2] = \sum (x - \mu)^2 p(x)$$

$$= (0 - 3.5)^2(.002) + (1 - 3.5)^2(.029) + (2 - 3.5)^2(.132)$$
$$+ (3 - 3.5)^2 (.309) + (4 - 3.5)^2 (.360) + (5 - 3.5)^2(.168)$$
$$= 1.05$$

Thus, the standard deviation is

$$\sigma = \sqrt{\sigma^2} = \sqrt{1.05} = 1.02$$

This value measures the spread of the probability distribution of x, the number of successful ventures out of five. A more useful interpretation is obtained by answering parts **c** and **d**.

c. The graph of $p(x)$ in histogram form is shown in Figure 4.6 with the mean μ and the interval $\mu \pm 2\sigma = 3.50 \pm 2(1.02) = 3.50 \pm 2.04 = (1.46, 5.54)$ shown on the graph. Note particularly that $\mu = 3.5$ locates the center of the probability distribution. Since this distribution is a theoretical relative frequency distribution that is moderately mound-shaped (see Figure 4.6), we expect (from Chebyshev's Rule) at least 75% and, more likely (from the Empirical Rule), approximately 95% of observed x values to fall in the interval $\mu \pm 2\sigma$—that is, between 1.46 and 5.54. You can see from Figure 4.6 that the actual probability that x falls in the interval $\mu \pm 2\sigma$ includes the sum of $p(x)$ for the values $x = 2$, $x = 3$, $x = 4$, and $x = 5$. This probability is $p(2) + p(3) + p(4) + p(5) = .132 + .309 + .360 + .168 = .969..$ Therefore, 96.9% of the probability distribution lies within 2 standard deviations of the mean. This percentage is consistent with both Chebyshev's Rule and the Empirical Rule.

d. Fewer than two successful ventures out of five implies that $x = 0$ or $x = 1$. Since both these values of x lie outside the interval $\mu \pm 2\sigma$, we know from the Empirical

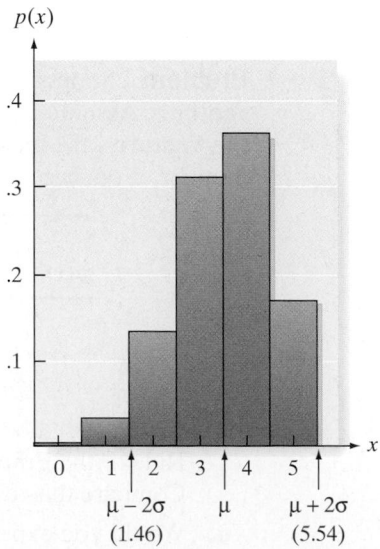

FIGURE 4.6

Graph of $p(x)$ for
Example 4.6

Rule that such a result is unlikely (approximate probability of .05). The exact probability, $P(x \leq 1)$, is $p(0) + p(1) = .002 + .029 = .031$. Consequently, in a single experiment where we invest in five Internet business ventures, we would not expect to observe fewer than two successful ones.

Now Work Exercise 4.17

Discrete Random Variables
Using the TI-83/TI-84 Graphing Calculator

Calculating the Mean and Standard Deviation of a Discrete Random Variable

Step 1   *Enter the data.*

Press **STAT** and select **1:Edit**.
Note: If the lists already contain data, clear the old data. Use the up **ARROW** to highlight '**L1**'.
Press **CLEAR ENTER**.
Use the up **ARROW** to highlight '**L2**'.
Press **CLEAR ENTER**.
Use the **ARROW** and **ENTER** keys to enter the *x*-values of the variable into **L1**.
Use the **ARROW** and **ENTER** keys to enter the probabilities, $P(x)$, into **L2**.

Step 2   *Access the Calc Menu*

Press **STAT**.
Arrow right to **CALC**.
Select **1-Var Stats**.
Press **ENTER**.

```
EDIT CALC TESTS
1█1-Var Stats
2:2-Var Stats
3:Med-Med
4:LinReg(ax+b)
5:QuadReg
6:CubicReg
7↓QuartReg
```

Press **2nd 1** for **L1**.
Press **COMMA**.
Press **2nd 2** for **L2**.
Press **ENTER**.

The mean and standard deviation will be displayed on the screen, as well as the quartiles, min, and max.

Continued

Example   Find the mean and the standard deviation of the following discrete probability distribution.

x	0	1	2	3
$p(x)$	.05	.10	.25	.60

First enter the data into **L1** and **L2**.

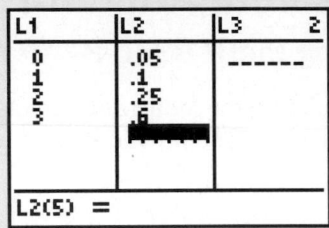

The output screens for this example are shown below.

```
1-Var Stats
 x̄=2.4
 Σx=2.4
 Σx²=6.5
 Sx=
 σx=.8602325267
↓n=1
■
```

```
1-Var Stats
↑n=1
 minX=0
 Q₁=2
 Med=3
 Q₃=3
 maxX=3
■
```

The mean of this discrete variable is 2.4 and the standard deviation is .86.

Exercises 4.11–4.34

Learning the Mechanics

4.11 A die is tossed. Let x be the number of spots observed on the upturned face of the die.
  a. Find the probability distribution of x and display it in tabular form.
  b. Display the probability distribution of x in graphical form.

4.12 The random variable x has the following discrete probabili-
NW ty distribution:

x	1	3	5	7	9
$p(x)$	.1	.2	.4	.2	.1

  a. List the values x may assume.
  b. What value of x is most probable?
  c. Display the probability distribution as a graph.
  d. Find $P(x = 7)$.
  e. Find $P(x \geq 5)$.
  f. Find $P(x > 2)$.

4.13 A discrete random variable x can assume five possible values: 2, 3, 5, 8, and 10. Its probability distribution is shown here:

x	2	3	5	8	10
$p(x)$	.15	.10	–	.25	.25

a. What is $p(5)$?
b. What is the probability that x equals 2 or 10?
c. What is $P(x \le 8)$?

4.14 Explain why each of the following is or is not a valid probability distribution for a discrete random variable x:

a.

x	0	1	2	3
$p(x)$	.1	.3	.3	.2

b.

x	−2	−1	0
$p(x)$	.25	.50	.25

c.

x	4	9	20
$p(x)$	−.3	.4	.3

d.

x	2	3	5	6
$p(x)$	.15	.15	.45	.35

4.15 Toss three fair coins and let x equal the number of heads
NW observed.
a. Identify the sample points associated with this experiment and assign a value of x to each sample point.
b. Calculate $p(x)$ for each value of x.
c. Construct a graph for $p(x)$.
d. What is $P(x = 2 \text{ or } x = 3)$?

APPLET Applet Exercise 4.1

Use the applet entitled *Random Numbers* to generate a list of 25 numbers between 1 and 3, inclusive. Let x represent a number chosen from this list.
a. What are the possible values of x?
b. Write down a probability distribution for x in table form.
c. Use the probability distribution in part **b** to find the expected value of x.
d. Let y be a number randomly chosen from the set {1, 2, 3}. Write down a probability distribution for y in table form and use it to find the expected value of y.
e. Compare the expected values of x and y in parts **c** and **d**. Why should these two numbers be approximately the same?

APPLET Applet Exercise 4.2

Run the applet entitled *Simulating the Probability of a Head with a Fair Coin* ten times with $n = 2$, resetting between runs, to simulate flipping two coins ten times. Count and record the number of heads each time. Let x represent the number of heads on a single flip of the two coins.
a. What are the possible values of x?
b. Use the results of the simulation to write down a probability distribution for x in table form and then use it to find the expected value of x.
c. Explain why the expected value in part **b** should be close to 1.

4.16 Consider the probability distribution for the random variable x shown here.

x	10	20	30	40	50	60
$p(x)$	.05	.20	.30	.25	.10	.10

a. Find μ, σ^2, and σ.
b. Graph $p(x)$.
c. Locate μ and the interval $\mu \pm 2\sigma$ on your graph. What is the probability that x will fall within the interval $\mu \pm 2\sigma$?

4.17 Consider the probability distribution shown here.

x	−4	−3	−2	−1	0	1	2	3	4
$p(x)$	.02	.07	.10	.15	.30	.18	.10	.06	.02

NW a. Calculate μ, σ^2, and σ.
b. Graph $p(x)$. Locate $\mu, \mu - 2\sigma$, and $\mu + 2\sigma$ on the graph.
c. What is the probability that x is in the interval $\mu \pm 2\sigma$?

4.18 Consider the probability distributions shown here.

x	0	1	2
$p(x)$	.3	.4	.3

y	0	1	2
$p(y)$	.1	.8	.1

a. Use your intuition to find the mean for each distribution. How did you arrive at your choice?
b. Which distribution appears to be more variable? Why?
c. Calculate μ and σ^2 for each distribution. Compare these answers to your answers in parts **a** and **b**.

Applying the Concepts—Basic

CRASH

4.19 NHTSA crash tests. Refer to the National Highway Traffic Safety Administration (NHTSA) crash tests of new car models, Exercise 4.3 (p. 192). A summary of the driver-side star ratings for the 98 cars in the **CRASH** file is reproduced in the accompanying MINITAB printout. Assume that one of the 98 cars is selected at random and let x equal the number of stars in the car's driver-side star rating.

Tally for Discrete Variables: DRIVSTAR

DRIVSTAR	Count	Percent
2	4	4.08
3	17	17.35
4	59	60.20
5	18	18.37
N=	98	

a. Use the information in the printout to find the probability distribution for x.
b. Find $P(x = 5)$.
c. Find $P(x \le 2)$.
d. Find $\mu = E(x)$ and practically interpret the result.

4.20 Ages of "dot-com" employees. The age distribution for the employees of a highly successful "dot-com" company headquartered in Atlanta is shown at the top of page 202. An employee is to be randomly selected from this population.
a. Can the relative frequency distribution in the table be interpreted as a probability distribution? Explain.
b. Graph the probability distribution.
c. What is the probability that the randomly selected employee is over 30 years of age? Over 40 years of age? Under 30 years of age?
d. What is the probability that the randomly selected employee will be 25 or 26 years old?

Table for Exercise 4.20

Age	20	21	22	23	24	25	26	27	28	29	30	31	32	33
Proportion	.02	.04	.05	.07	.04	.02	.07	.02	.11	.07	.09	.13	.15	.12

Source: Personal communication from P. George Benson.

4.21 Customer arrivals at Wendy's. The probability distribution for the number of customer arrivals per 15-minute period at a Wendy's in New Jersey is shown below.

    a. Does this distribution meet the two requirements for the probability distribution of a discrete random variable? Justify your answer.

    b. What is the probability that exactly 16 customers enter the restaurant in the next 15 minutes?

    c. Find $p(x \le 10)$.

    d. Find $p(5 \le x \le 15)$.

x	5	6	7	8	9	10	11	12	13	14	15
$p(x)$	.01	.02	.03	.05	.08	.09	.11	.13	.12	.10	.08

x	16	17	18	19	20	21
$p(x)$	.06	.05	.03	.02	.01	.01

Source: Ford, R., Roberts, D., and Saxton. P. *Queuing Models.* Graduate School of Management, Rutgers University, 1992.

4.22 Choosing portable grill displays. Refer to the *Journal of Consumer Research* (Mar. 2003) marketing study of influencing consumer choices by offering undesirable alternatives, Exercise 3.17 (p. 145). Recall that each of 124 college students selected showroom displays for portable grills. Five different displays (representing five different-sized grills) were available, but the students were instructed to select only three displays in order to maximize purchases of Grill #2 (a smaller-sized grill). The table shows the grill display combinations and the number of each selected by the 124 students. Suppose one of the 124 students is selected at random. Let x represent the sum of the grill numbers selected by this student. (This value is an indicator of the size of the grills selected.)

    a. Find the probability distribution for x.

    b. What is the probability that x exceeds 10?

Grill Display Combination	Number of Students
1-2-3	35
1-2-4	8
1-2-5	42
2-3-4	4
2-3-5	1
2-4-5	34

Source: Hamilton, R. W. "Why Do People Suggest What They Do Not Want? Using Context Effects to Influence Others' Choices," *Journal of Consumer Research,* Vol. 29, Mar. 2003 (Table 1).

Applying the Concepts—Intermediate

4.23 Mailrooms contaminated with anthrax. During autumn 2001, there was a highly publicized outbreak of anthrax cases among U.S. Postal Service workers. In *Chance* (Spring 2002), research statisticians discussed the problem of sampling mailrooms for the presence of anthrax spores. Let x equal the number of mailrooms contaminated with anthrax spores in a random sample of n mailrooms selected from a population of N mailrooms. The researchers showed that the probability distribution for x is given by the formula

$$p(x) = \frac{\binom{k}{x}\binom{N-k}{n-x}}{\binom{N}{n}}$$

where k is the number of contaminated mailrooms in the population. (This probability distribution is known as the *hypergeometric distribution.*) Suppose $N = 100, n = 3$, and $k = 20$.

    a. Find $p(0)$.

    b. Find $p(1)$.

    c. Find $p(2)$.

    d. Find $p(3)$.

4.24 USDA chicken inspection. In Exercise 3.11 (p. 144) you learned that one in every 100 slaughtered chickens passes USDA inspection with fecal contamination. Consider a random sample of three slaughtered chickens that all pass USDA inspection. Let x equal the number of chickens in the sample that have fecal contamination.

    a. Find $p(x)$ for $x = 0, 1, 2, 3$.

    b. Graph $p(x)$.

    c. Find $P(x \le 1)$.

4.25 Contaminated gun cartridges. A weapons manufacturer uses a liquid propellant to produce gun cartridges. During the manufacturing process, the propellant can get mixed with another liquid to produce a contaminated cartridge. A University of South Florida statistician, hired by the company to investigate the level of contamination in the stored cartridges, found that 23% of the cartridges in a particular lot were contaminated. Suppose you randomly sample (without replacement) gun cartridges from this lot until you find a contaminated one. Let x be the number of cartridges sampled until a contaminated one is found. It is known that the probability distribution for x is given by the formula

$$p(x) = (.23)(.77)^{x-1}, \quad x = 1, 2, 3, \ldots$$

    a. Find $p(1)$. Interpret this result.

    b. Find $p(5)$. Interpret this result.

    c. Find $P(x \ge 2)$. Interpret this result.

4.26 Appeals of Federal civil trials. Refer to the *Journal of the American Law and Economics Association* (Vol. 3, 2001) study of appeals of Federal civil trials, Exercise 3.35 (p. 155). A breakdown of the 678 civil cases that were originally tried in front of a judge (rather than a jury) and appealed by either the plaintiff or defendant is reproduced in the following table. Suppose each civil case is awarded points (positive or negative) based on the outcome of the appeal for the purpose of evaluating Federal judges. If the appeal is affirmed or dismissed, +5 points are awarded. If the appeal of a plaintiff trial win is reversed, -1 point is awarded. If the appeal of a defendant trial win is reversed, -3 points are awarded. Suppose one of the 678 cases is selected at random and the number, x, of points awarded is determined. Find and graph the probability distribution for x.

Outcome of Appeal	Number of Cases
Plaintiff trial win—reversed	71
Plaintiff trial win— affirmed/dismissed	240
Defendant trial win—reversed	68
Defendant trial win— affirmed/dismissed	299
Total	678

4.27 Reliability of a bridge network. A team of Chinese university professors investigated the reliability of several capacitated-flow networks in the journal *Networks* (May 1995). One network examined in the article, illustrated below, is a bridge network with arcs a_1, a_2, a_3, a_4, a_5, and a_6. The probability distribution of the capacity x for each of the six arcs is provided in the following table.

Arc	Capacity (x)	$p(x)$	Arc	Capacity (x)	$p(x)$
a_1	3	.60	a_4	1	.90
	2	.25		0	.10
	1	.10			
	0	.05			
a_2	2	.60	a_5	1	.90
	1	.30		0	.10
	0	.10			
a_3	1	.90	a_6	2	.70
	0	.10		1	.25
				0	.05

Source: Lin, J., et al. "On Reliability Evaluation of Capacitated-Flow Network in Terms of Minimal Pathsets." *Networks*, Vol. 25, No. 3, May 1995, p. 135 (Table 1), 1995, John Wiley and Sons.

a. Verify that the properties of discrete probability distributions are satisfied for each arc capacity distribution.
b. Find the probability that the capacity for arc a_1 will exceed 1.
c. Repeat part **b** for each of the remaining five arcs.
d. Compute the mean capacity for each arc and interpret its value.
e. Compute σ for each arc and interpret the results.

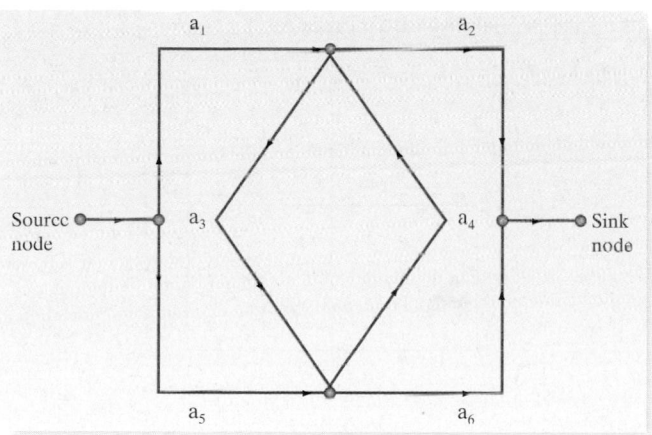

4.28 Investment risk analysis. The risk of a portfolio of financial assets is sometimes called *investment risk* (Radcliffe, 1997). In general, investment risk is typically measured by computing the variance or standard deviation of the probability distribution that describes the decision maker's potential outcomes (gains or losses). The greater the variation in potential outcomes, the greater the uncertainty faced by the decision maker; the smaller the variation in potential outcomes, the more predictable the decision maker's gains or losses. The two discrete probability distributions given in the next table were developed from historical data. They describe the potential total physical damage losses next year to the fleets of delivery trucks of two different firms.

FIRM A		FIRM B	
Loss Next Year	Probability	Loss Next Year	Probability
$ 0	.01	$ 0	.00
500	.01	200	.01
1,000	.01	700	.02
1,500	.02	1,200	.02
2,000	.35	1,700	.15
2,500	.30	2,200	.30
3,000	.25	2,700	.30
3,500	.02	3,200	.15
4,000	.01	3,700	.02
4,500	.01	4,200	.02
5,000	.01	4,700	.01

NW a. Verify that both firms have the same expected total physical damage loss.
b. Compute the standard deviation of each probability distribution, and determine which firm faces the greater risk of physical damage to its fleet next year.

4.29 Expected loss due to flood damage. The National Weather Service issues precipitation forecasts that indicate the likelihood of measurable precipitation ($\geq.01$ inch) at a specific point (the official rain gauge) during a given time period (Doswell and Brooks, *Probabilistic Forecasting: A Primer*, 1996). Suppose that if a measurable amount of rain falls during the next 24 hours, a river will reach flood stage and a business will incur damages of $300,000. The National Weather Service has indicated that there is a 30% chance of a measurable amount of rain during the next 24 hours.
a. Construct the probability distribution that describes the potential flood damages.
b. Find the firm's expected loss due to flood damage.

4.30 Checkout lanes at a supermarket. A team of consultants working for a large national supermarket chain based in the New York metropolitan area developed a statistical model for predicting the annual sales of potential new store locations. Part of their analysis involved identifying variables that influence store sales, such as the size of the store (in square feet), the size of the surrounding population, and the number of checkout lanes. They surveyed 52 supermarkets in a particular region of the country and constructed the relative frequency distribution shown below to describe the number of checkout lanes per store, x.
a. Why do the relative frequencies in the table represent the approximate probabilities of a randomly selected supermarket having x number of checkout lanes?
b. Find $E(x)$ and interpret its value in the context of the problem.
c. Find the standard deviation of x.
d. According to Chebyshev's Rule (Chapter 2), what percentage of supermarkets would be expected to fall within $\mu \pm \sigma$? Within $\mu \pm 2\sigma$?
e. What is the actual number of supermarkets that fall within $\mu \pm \sigma$? $\mu \pm 2\sigma$? Compare your answers to those of part **d**. Are the answers consistent?

x	1	2	3	4	5	6	7	8	9	10
Relative Frequency	.01	.04	.04	.08	.10	.15	.25	.20	.08	.05

Source: Adapted from Chow, W. et. al. "A Model for Predicting a Supermarket's Annual Sales per Square Foot." Graduate School of Management, Rutgers University, 1994.

4.31 The showcase showdown. On the popular television game show *The Price Is Right*, contestants can play "The Showcase Showdown." The game involves a large wheel with 20 nickel values, 5, 10, 15, 20, . . . , 95, 100, marked on it. Contestants spin the wheel once or twice, with the objective of obtaining the highest total score *without going over a dollar* (*100*). [According to the *American Statistician* (Aug. 1995), the optimal strategy for the first spinner in a three-player game is to spin a second time only if the value of the initial spin is 65 or less.] Let *x* represent the total score for a single contestant playing "The Showcase Showdown." Assume a "fair" wheel (i.e., a wheel with equally likely outcomes). If the total of the player's spins exceeds 100, the total score is set to 0.

a. If the player is permitted only one spin of the wheel, find the probability distribution for *x*.

b. Refer to part **a.** Find $E(x)$ and interpret this value.

c. Refer to part **a.** Give a range of values within which *x* is likely to fall.

d. Suppose the player will spin the wheel twice, no matter what the outcome of the first spin. Find the probability distribution for *x*.

e. What assumption did you make to obtain the probability distribution, part **d**? Is it a reasonable assumption?

f. Find μ and σ for the probability distribution, part **d**, and interpret the results.

g. Refer to part **d.** What is the probability that in two spins the player's total score exceeds a dollar (i.e., is set to 0)?

h. Suppose the player obtains a 20 on the first spin and decides to spin again. Find the probability distribution for *x*.

i. Refer to part **h.** What is the probability that the player's total score exceeds a dollar?

j. Given the player obtains a 65 on the first spin and decides to spin again, find the probability that the player's total score exceeds a dollar.

k. Repeat part **j** for different first-spin outcomes. Use this information to suggest a strategy for the one-player game.

4.32 Expected lotto winnings. Most states offer weekly lotteries to generate revenue for the state. Despite the long odds of winning, residents continue to gamble on the lottery each week. In SIA, Chapter 3 (p. 143), you learned that the chance of winning Florida's Pick-6 Lotto game is 1 in approximately 23 million. Suppose you buy a $1 Lotto ticket in anticipation of winning the $7 million grand prize. Calculate your expected net winnings. Interpret the result.

Applying the Concepts—Advanced

4.33 Parlay card betting. Odds makers try to predict which professional and college football teams will win and by how much (the *spread*). If the odds makers do this accurately, adding the spread to the underdog's score should make the final score a tie. Suppose a bookie will give you $6 for every $1 you risk if you pick the winners in three ball-games (adjusted by the spread) on a "parlay" card. Thus, for every $1 bet you will either lose $1 or gain $5. What is the bookie's expected earnings per dollar wagered?

4.34 Robot-sensor system configuration. Engineers at Broadcom Corp. and Simon Fraser University collaborated on research involving a robot-sensor system in an unknown environment (*International Journal of Robotics Research*, Dec. 2004). As an example, the engineers presented the three-point, single-link robotic system shown in the accompanying figure. Each point (A, B, or C) in the physical space of the system has either an "obstacle" status or a "free" status. There are two single links in the system: A $\leftrightarrow$ B and B $\leftrightarrow$ C. A link has a "free" status if and only if both points in the link are "free." Otherwise, the link has an "obstacle" status. Of interest is the random variable Y, the total number of links in the system that are "free."

a. List the possible values of Y for the system.

b. The researchers stated that the probability of any point in the system having a "free" status is .5. Assuming the three points in the system operate independently, find the probability distribution for Y.

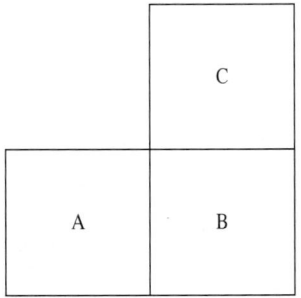

4.3 The Binomial Distribution

Many experiments result in *dichotomous* responses—that is, responses for which there exist two possible alternatives, such as Yes-No, Pass-Fail, Defective-Nondefective, or Male-Female. A simple example of such an experiment is the coin-toss experiment. A coin is tossed a number of times, say 10. Each toss results in one of two outcomes, Head or Tail. Ultimately, we are interested in the probability distribution of *x*, the number of heads observed. Many other experiments are equivalent to tossing a coin (either balanced or unbalanced) a fixed number *n* of times and observing the number *x* of times that one of the two possible outcomes occurs. Random variables that possess these characteristics are called **binomial random variables.**

Public opinion and consumer preference polls (e.g., the CNN, Gallup, and Harris polls) frequently yield observations on binomial random variables. For example, suppose a sample of 100 current customers is selected from a firm's database and each person is asked whether he or she prefers the firm's product (a Head) or prefers a competitor's product (a Tail). Suppose we are interested in *x*, the number of customers in the sample who prefer the firm's product. Sampling 100 customers is analogous to tossing the coin 100 times. Thus, you can see that consumer preference polls like the one described here are real-life equivalents of coin-toss experiments. We have been describing a **binomial experiment;** it is identified by the following characteristics.

Characteristics of a Binomial Random Variable

1. The experiment consists of n identical trials.

2. There are only two possible outcomes on each trial. We will denote one outcome by S (for Success) and the other by F (for Failure).

3. The probability of S remains the same from trial to trial. This probability is denoted by p, and the probability of F is denoted by q. Note that $q = 1 - p$.

4. The trials are independent.

5. The binomial random variable x is the number of S's in n trials.

Biography

JACOB BERNOULLI (1654–1705)

The Bernoulli Distribution

Son of a magistrate and spice maker in Basel, Switzerland, Jacob Bernoulli completed a degree in theology at the University of Basel. While at the university, however, he studied mathematics secretly and against the will of his father. Jacob taught mathematics to his younger brother Johan, and they both went on to become distinguished European math-

ematicians. At first the brothers collaborated on the problems of the time (e.g., calculus); unfortunately, they later became bitter mathematical rivals. Jacob applied his philosophical training and mathematical intuition to probability and the theory of games of chance, where he developed the law of large numbers. In his book *Ars Conjectandi*, published in 1713 (eight years after his death), the binomial distribution was first proposed. Jacob showed that the binomial distribution was a sum of independent 0–1 variables, now known as "Bernoulli" random variables.

EXAMPLE 4.8
Assessing Whether x Is Binomial

Problem   For the following examples, decide whether x is a binomial random variable.

a. You randomly select 3 bonds out of a possible 10 for an investment portfolio. Unknown to you, 8 of the 10 will maintain their present value, and the other 2 will lose value due to a change in their ratings. Let x be the number of the 3 bonds you select that lose value.

b. Before marketing a new product on a large scale, many companies will conduct a consumer preference survey to determine whether the product is likely to be successful. Suppose a company develops a new diet soda and then conducts a taste preference survey in which 100 randomly chosen consumers state their preferences among the new soda and the two leading sellers. Let x be the number of the 100 who choose the new brand over the two others.

c. Some surveys are conducted by using a method of sampling other than simple random sampling (defined in Chapter 3). For example, suppose a television cable company plans to conduct a survey to determine the fraction of households in the city that would use the cable television service. The sampling method is to choose a city block at random and then survey every household on that block. This sampling technique is called *cluster sampling*. Suppose 10 blocks are so sampled, producing a total of 124 household responses. Let x be the number of the 124 households that would use the television cable service.

Solution

a. In checking the binomial characteristics in the box, a problem arises with both characteristic 3 (probabilities remaining the same from trial to trial) and characteristic 4

ACTIVITY 4.1: *Warehouse Club Memberships:* **Exploring a Binomial Random Variable**

Warehouse clubs are retailers that offer lower prices than traditional retailers but they only sell to customers who have purchased memberships and often merchandise must be purchased in large quantities. A warehouse club may offer more than one type of membership, such as a regular membership R for a low annual fee and an upgraded membership U for a higher annual fee. The upgraded membership has additional benefits which might include extended shopping hours, additional discounts on certain products, or cash back on purchases.

A local warehouse club has determined that 20% of its customer base has the upgraded membership.

1. What is the probability $P(U)$ that a randomly chosen customer entering the store has an upgraded membership? What is the probability $P(R)$ that a randomly chosen customer entering the store has a regular (not upgraded) membership?

   In an effort to sell more upgraded memberships, sales associates are placed at the entrance to the store to explain the benefits of the upgraded membership to customers as they enter. Suppose that in a given time period five customers enter the store.

2. Given that 20% of the store's customers have an upgraded membership, how many of the five customers would you expect to have an upgraded membership?

3. Since there are five customers and each customer either has an upgraded membership (U) or does not (R), there are $2^5 = 32$ different possible combinations of membership types among the five customers. List these 32 possibilities.

4. Find the probability of each of the 32 outcomes. Assume that each of the five customers' membership type is independent of each of the other customers' membership type and use your probabilities $P(U)$ and $P(R)$ with the multiplicative rule. For example, $P(RRUUR) = P(R)P(R)P(U)P(U)P(R)$.

5. Notice that $P(URRRR) = P(RURRR) = P(RRURR) = P(RRRUR) = P(RRRRU) = P(U)^1 P(R)^4$ so that $P(\text{exactly one } U) = P(URRRR) + P(RURRR) + P(RRURR) + P(RRRUR) + P(RRRRU) = 5P(U)^1 P(R)^4$ where 5 is the number of ways that exactly one U can occur. Find $P(\text{exactly one } U)$. Use similar reasoning to establish that $P(\text{no } Us) = 1P(U)^0 P(R)^5$, $P(\text{exactly two } Us) = 10P(U)^2 P(R)^3$, $P(\text{exactly three } Us) = 10P(U)^3 P(R)^2$, $P(\text{exactly four } Us) = 5P(U)^4 P(R)^1$, and $P(\text{five } Us) = 1P(U)^5 P(R)^0$.

6. Let x be the number of upgraded memberships U in a sample of five customers. Use the results of Part 5 to write a probability distribution for the random variable x in table form. Find the mean and standard deviation of the distribution using the formulas in Section 4.2.

7. Calculate np and $\sqrt{npq}$ where $n = 5$, $p = P(U)$, and $q = P(R)$. How do these numbers compare to the mean and standard deviation of the random variable x in Part 6 and to the expected number of customers with upgraded memberships in Part 1?

8. Explain how the characteristics of a binomial random variable are illustrated in this activity.

(independence). The probability that the first bond you pick loses value is clearly $\frac{2}{10}$. Now suppose the first bond you picked was one of the two that will lose value. This reduces the chance that the second bond you pick will lose value to $\frac{1}{9}$, since now only one of the nine remaining bonds are in that category. Thus, the choices you make are dependent, and therefore x, the number of three bonds you select that lose value, is *not* a binomial random variable.

b. Surveys that produce dichotomous responses and use random sampling techniques are classic examples of binomial experiments. In our example, each randomly selected consumer either states a preference for the new diet soda or does not. The sample of 100 consumers is a very small proportion of the totality of potential consumers, so the response of one would be, for all practical purposes, independent of another.* Thus, x is a binomial random variable.

c. This example is a survey with dichotomous responses (Yes or No to the cable service), but the sampling method is not simple random sampling. Again, the binomial characteristic of independent trials would probably not be satisfied. The responses of households within a particular block would be dependent, since the

---

*In most real-life applications of the binomial distribution, the population of interest has a finite number of elements (trials), denoted N. When N is large and the sample size n is small relative to N, say $n/N \leq .05$, the sampling procedure, for all practical purposes, satisfies the conditions of a binomial experiment.

households within a block tend to be similar with respect to income, level of education, and general interests. Thus, the binomial model would not be satisfactory for x if the cluster sampling technique were employed.

Look Back Nonbinomial random variables with two outcomes on every trial typically occur because they do not satisfy characteristics 3 or 4 of a binomial distribution.

Now Work Exercise 4.42a

EXAMPLE 4.9

Deriving the
Binomial Probability
Distribution in a PC
Purchase Application

Problem A computer retailer sells both desktop and laptop personal computers (PCs) online. Assume that 80% of the PCs that the retailer sells online are desktops and 20% are laptops.

a. Use the steps given in Chapter 3 (box on page 139) to find the probability that all of the next four online PC purchases are laptops.

b. Find the probability that three of the next four online PC purchases are laptops.

c. Let x represent the number of the next four online PC purchases that are laptops. Explain why x is a binomial random variable.

d. Use the answers to parts a and b to derive a formula for $p(x)$, the probability distribution of the binomial random variable x.

Solution

a. 1. The first step is to define the experiment. Here we are interested in observing the type of PC purchased online by each of the next four (buying) customers: desktop (D) or laptop (L).

2. Next, we list the sample points associated with the experiment. Each sample point consists of the purchase decisions made by the four online customers. For example, $DDDD$ represents the sample point that all four purchase desktop PCs, while $LDDD$ represents the sample point that customer 1 purchases a laptop, while customers 2, 3, and 4 purchase desktops. The 16 sample points are listed in Table 4.2.

3. We now assign probabilities to the sample points. Note that each sample point can be viewed as the intersection of four customers' decisions and, assuming the decisions are made independently, the probability of each sample point can be obtained using the multiplicative rule, as follows:

$$P(DDDD) = P[(\text{customer 1 chooses desktop}) \cap (\text{customer 2 chooses desktop})$$
$$\cap (\text{customer 3 chooses desktop}) \cap (\text{customer 4 chooses desktop})]$$

$$= P(\text{customer 1 chooses desktop}) \times P(\text{customer 2 chooses desktop}) \times P(\text{customer 3 chooses desktop})$$
$$\times P(\text{customer 4 chooses desktop})$$

$$= (.8)(.8)(.8)(.8) = (.8)^4 = .4096$$

TABLE 4.2 Sample Points for PC Experiment of Example 4.9

$DDDD$	$LDDD$	$LLDD$	$DLLL$	LLLL
	$DLDD$	$LDLD$	$LDLL$	
	$DDLD$	$LDDL$	$LLDL$	
	$DDDL$	$DLLD$	$LLLD$	
		$DLDL$		
		$DDLL$		

All other sample point probabilities are calculated using similar reasoning. For example,

$$P(LDDD) = (.2)(.8)(.8)(.8) = (.2)(.8)^3 = .1024$$

You can check that this reasoning results in sample point probabilities that add to 1 over the 16 points in the sample space.

4. Finally, we add the appropriate sample point probabilities to obtain the desired event probability. The event of interest is that all four online customers purchase laptops. In Table 4.2 we find only one sample point, LLLL, contained in this event. All other sample points imply that at least one desktop is purchased. Thus,

$$P(\text{All four purchase laptops}) = P(LLLL) = (.2)^4 = .0016$$

That is, the probability is only 16 in 10,000 that all four customers purchase laptop PCs.

b. The event that three of the next four online buyers purchase laptops consists of the four sample points in the fourth column of Table 4.2: $DLLL$, $LDLL$, $LLDL$, and $LLLD$. To obtain the event probability we add the sample point probabilities:

P(3 of next 4 customers purchase laptops)

$$= P(DLLL) + P(LDLL) + P(LLDL) + P(LLLD)$$
$$= (.2)^3(.8) + (.2)^3(.8) + (.2)^3(.8) + (.2)^3(.8)$$
$$= 4(.2)^3(.8) = .0256$$

Note that each of the four sample point probabilities is the same, because each sample point consists of three L's and one D; the order does not affect the probability because the customers' decisions are (assumed) independent.

c. We can characterize the experiment as consisting of four identical trials—the four customers' purchase decisions. There are two possible outcomes to each trial, D or L, and the probability of L, $p = .2$, is the same for each trial. Finally, we are assuming that each customer's purchase decision is independent of all others, so that the four trials are independent. Then it follows that x, the number of the next four purchases that are laptops, is a binomial random variable.

d. The event probabilities in parts **a** and **b** provide insight into the formula for the probability distribution $p(x)$. First, consider the event that three purchases are laptops (part b). We found that

$$P(x = 3) = (\text{Number of sample points for which } x = 3) \times$$
$$(.2)^{\text{Number of laptops purchased}} \times (.8)^{\text{Number of desktops purchased}}$$
$$= 4(.2)^3(.8)^1$$

In general, we can use combinatorial mathematics to count the number of sample points. For example,

Number of sample points for which $x = 3$

= Number of different ways of selecting 3 of the 4 trials for L purchases

$$= \binom{4}{3} = \frac{4!}{3!(4-3)!} = \frac{4 \cdot 3 \cdot 2 \cdot 1}{(3 \cdot 2 \cdot 1) \cdot 1} = 4$$

The formula that works for any value of x can be deduced as follows. Since

$$P(x = 3) = \binom{4}{3}(.2)^3(.8)^1,$$

then $p(x) = \binom{4}{x}(.2)^x(.8)^{4-x}$

The component $\begin{pmatrix} 4 \\ x \end{pmatrix}$ counts the number of sample points with x laptops and the component $(.2)^x(.8)^{4-x}$ is the probability associated with each sample point having x laptops. For the general binomial experiment, with n trials and probability of Success p on each trial, the probability of x Successes is

$$p(x) = \binom{n}{x} \cdot p^x(1 - p)^{n-x}$$

Number of sample points with x S's

Probability of x S's and $(n - x)$ F's in any sample point

Look Back In theory, you could always resort to the principles developed in this example to calculate binomial probabilities; list the sample points and sum their probabilities. However, as the number of trials (n) increases, the number of sample points grows very rapidly (the number of sample points is 2^n). Thus, we prefer the formula for calculating binomial probabilities, since its use avoids listing sample points.

The binomial distribution* is summarized in the box.

The Binomial Probability Distribution

$$p(x) = \binom{n}{x} p^x q^{n-x} \quad (x = 0, 1, 2, \dots, n)$$

where

p = Probability of a success on a single trial

$q = 1 - p$

n = Number of trials

x = Number of successes in n trials

$\binom{n}{x} = \dfrac{n!}{x!(n - x)!}$

As noted in Chapter 3, the symbol 5! means $5 \cdot 4 \cdot 3 \cdot 2 \cdot 1 = 120$. Similarly, $n! = n(n - 1)(n - 2) \cdots 3 \cdot 2 \cdot 1$; remember, $0! = 1$.

EXAMPLE 4.10

Applying the Binomial Distribution to the Manufacture of Automobiles

Problem A machine that produces stampings for automobile engines is malfunctioning and producing 10% defectives. The defective and nondefective stampings proceed from the machine in a random manner. If the next five stampings are tested, find the probability that three of them are defective.

Solution Let x equal the number of defectives in $n = 5$ trials. Then x is a binomial random variable with p, the probability that a single stamping will be defective, equal to .1, and $q = 1 - p = 1 - .1 = .9$. The probability distribution for x is given by the expression

$$p(x) = \binom{n}{x} p^x q^{n-x} = \binom{5}{x} (.1)^x(.9)^{5-x}$$

$$= \frac{5!}{x!(5 - x)!} (.1)^x(.9)^{5-x} \quad (x = 0, 1, 2, 3, 4, 5)$$

---

*The binomial distribution is so named because the probabilities, $p(x)$, $x = 0, 1, \dots, n$, are terms of the binomial expansion $(q + p)^n$.

To find the probability of observing $x = 3$ defectives in a sample of $n = 5$, substitute $x = 3$ into the formula for $p(x)$ to obtain

$$p(3) = \frac{5!}{3!(5-3)!} (.1)^3 (.9)^{5-3} = \frac{5!}{3!2!} (.1)^3(.9)^2$$

$$= \frac{5 \cdot 4 \cdot 3 \cdot 2 \cdot 1}{(3 \cdot 2 \cdot 1)(2 \cdot 1)} (.1)^3(.9)^2 = 10(.1)^3(.9)^2$$

$$= .0081$$

Look Back Note that the binomial formula tells us that there are 10 sample points having 3 defectives (check this by listing them), each with probability $(.1)^3(.9)^2$.

Now Work Exercise 4.37

The mean, variance, and standard deviation for the binomial random variable x are shown in the box.

Mean Variance, and Standard Deviation for a Binomial Random Variable

Mean: $\mu = np$

Variance: $\sigma^2 = npq$

Standard deviation: $\sigma = \sqrt{npq}$

As we demonstrated in Chapter 2, the mean and standard deviation provide measures of the central tendency and variability, respectively, of a distribution. Thus, we can use μ and σ to obtain a rough visualization of the probability distribution for x when the calculation of the probabilities is too tedious. The next example illustrates this idea.

EXAMPLE 4.11

Finding μ and σ in the Automobile Manufacturing Application

Problem Refer to Example 4.10 and find the values of $p(0)$, $p(1)$, $p(2)$, $p(4)$, and $p(5)$. Graph $p(x)$. Calculate the mean μ and standard deviation σ. Locate μ and the interval $\mu - 2\sigma$ to $\mu + 2\sigma$ on the graph. If the experiment were to be repeated many times, what proportion of the x observations would fall within the interval $\mu - 2\sigma$ to $\mu + 2\sigma$?

Solution Again, $n = 5$, $p = .1$, and $q = .9$. Then, substituting into the formula for $p(x)$:

$$p(0) = \frac{5!}{0!(5-0)!} (.1)^0 (.9)^{5-0} = \frac{5 \cdot 4 \cdot 3 \cdot 2 \cdot 1}{(1)(5 \cdot 4 \cdot 3 \cdot 2 \cdot 1)} (1)(.9)^5 = .59049$$

$$p(1) = \frac{5!}{1!(5-1)!} (.1)^1 (.9)^{5-1} = 5(.1) (.9)^4 = .32805$$

$$p(2) = \frac{5!}{2!(5-2)!} (.1)^2(.9)^{5-2} = (10) (.1)^2 (.9)^3 = .07290$$

$$p(4) = \frac{5!}{4!(5-4)!} (.1)^4(.9)^{5-4} = 5(.1)^4 (.9) = .00045$$

$$p(5) = \frac{5!}{5!(5-5)!} (.1)^5 (.9)^{5-5} = 5(.1)^5 = .00001$$

The graph of $p(x)$ is shown as a probability histogram in Figure 4.7 [$p(3)$ is taken from Example 4.10 to be .0081].

To calculate the values of μ and σ, substitute $n = 5$ and $p = .1$ into the following formulas:

$$\mu = np = (5)(.1) = .5$$
$$\sigma = \sqrt{npq} = \sqrt{(5)(.1)(.9)} = \sqrt{.45} = .67$$

To find the interval $\mu - 2\sigma$ to $\mu + 2\sigma$, we calculate

$$\mu - 2\sigma = .5 - 2(.67) = -.84$$
$$\mu + 2\sigma = .5 + 2(.67) = 1.84$$

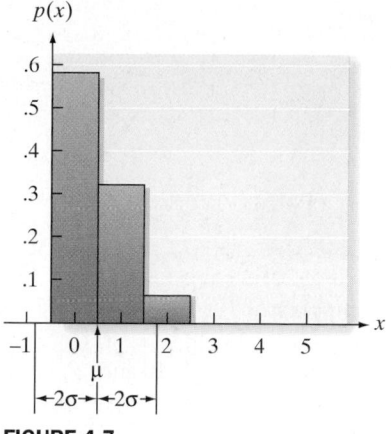

If the experiment was repeated a large number of times, what proportion of the x observations would fall within the interval $\mu - 2\sigma$ to $\mu + 2\sigma$? You can see from Figure 4.7 that all observations equal to 0 or 1 will fall within the interval. The probabilities corresponding to these values are .5905 and .3280, respectively. Consequently, you would expect $.5905 + .3280 = .9185$, or approximately 91.9%, of the observations to fall within the interval $\mu - 2\sigma$ to $\mu + 2\sigma$.

FIGURE 4.7
The binomial distribution: $n = 5, p = .1$

Look Back This result again emphasizes that for most probability distributions, observations rarely fall more than 2 standard deviations from μ.

Using Binomial Tables

Calculating binomial probabilities becomes tedious when n is large. For some values of n and p, the binomial probabilities have been tabulated in Table II of Appendix B. Part of Table II is shown in Table 4.3; a graph of the binomial probability distribution for $n = 10$ and $p = .10$ is shown in Figure 4.8. Table II actually contains a total of nine tables, labeled (a) through (i), each one corresponding to $n = 5, 6, 7, 8, 9, 10, 15, 20,$ and 25. In each of these tables, the columns correspond to values of p, and the rows correspond to values (k) of the random variable x. The entries in the table represent **cumulative binomial probabilities**, $p(x \leq k)$. Thus, for example, the entry in the column corresponding to $p = .10$ and the row corresponding to $k = 2$ is .930 (shaded), and its interpretation is

$$P(x \leq 2) = P(x = 0) + P(x = 1) + P(x = 2) = .930$$

TABLE 4.3 Reproduction of Part of Table II of Appendix B: Binomial Probabilities for $n = 10$

k	.01	.05	.10	.20	.30	.40	.50	.60	.70	.80	.90	.95	.99
0	.904	.599	.349	.107	.028	.006	.001	.000	.000	.000	.000	.000	.000
1	.996	.914	.736	.376	.149	.046	.011	.002	.000	.000	.000	.000	.000
2	1.000	.988	.930	.678	.383	.167	.055	.012	.002	.000	.000	.000	.000
3	1.000	.999	.987	.879	.650	.382	.172	.055	.011	.001	.000	.000	.000
4	1.000	1.000	.998	.967	.850	.633	.377	.166	.047	.006	.000	.000	.000
5	1.000	1.000	1.000	.994	.953	.834	.623	.367	.150	.033	.002	.000	.000
6	1.000	1.000	1.000	.999	.989	.945	.828	.618	.350	.121	.013	.001	.000
7	1.000	1.000	1.000	1.000	.998	.988	.945	.833	.617	.322	.070	.012	.000
8	1.000	1.000	1.000	1.000	1.000	.998	.989	.954	.851	.624	.264	.086	.004
9	1.000	1.000	1.000	1.000	1.000	1.000	.999	.994	.972	.893	.651	.401	.096

FIGURE 4.8
Binomial probability
distribution for $n = 10$ and
$p = .10$; $P(x \le 2)$ shaded

This probability is also shaded in the graphical representation of the binomial distribution with $n = 10$ and $p = .10$ in Figure 4.8.

You can also use Table II to find the probability that x equals a specific value. For example, suppose you want to find the probability that $x = 2$ in the binomial distribution with $n = 10$ and $p = .10$. This is found by subtraction as follows:

$$P(x = 2) = [P(x = 0) + P(x = 1) + P(x = 2)] - [P(x = 0) + P(x = 1)]$$
$$= P(x \le 2) - P(x \le 1) = .930 - .736 = .194$$

The probability that a binomial random variable exceeds a specified value can be found using Table II and the notion of complementary events. For example, to find the probability that x exceeds 2 when $n = 10$ and $p = .10$, we use

$$P(x > 2) = 1 - P(x \le 2) = .930 = .070$$

Note that this probability is represented by the unshaded portion of the graph in Figure 4.8.

All probabilities in Table II are rounded to three decimal places. Thus, although none of the binomial probabilities in the table is exactly zero, some are small enough (less than .0005) to round to .000. For example, using the formula to find $P(x = 0)$ when $n = 10$ and $p = .6$, we obtain

$$P(x = 0) = \binom{10}{0}(.6)^0(.4)^{10-0} = .4^{10} = .00010486$$

but this is rounded to .000 in Table II of Appendix B (see Table 4.3).

Similarly, none of the table entries is exactly 1.0, but when the cumulative probabilities exceed .9995, they are rounded to 1.000. The row corresponding to the largest possible value for x, $x = n$, is omitted, because all the cumulative probabilities in that row are equal to 1.0 (exactly). For example, in Table 4.3, with $n = 10$, $P(x \le 10) = 1.0$, no matter what the value of p.

The following example further illustrates the use of Table II.

EXAMPLE 4.12

Using the Binomial
Table to Find
Probabilities
Associated with
Worker Unionization

Problem Suppose a poll of 20 employees is taken in a large company. The purpose is to determine x, the number who favor unionization. Suppose that 60% of all the company's employees favor unionization.

a. Find the mean and standard deviation of x.

b. Use Table II of Appendix B to find the probability that $x \le 10$.

c. Use Table II to find the probability that $x > 12$.

d. Use Table II to find the probability that $x = 11$.

e. Graph the probability distribution of x and locate the interval $\mu \pm 2\sigma$ on the graph.

Solution

a. The number of employees polled is presumably small compared with the total number of employees in this company. Thus, we may treat x, the number of the 20 who favor unionization, as a binomial random variable. The value of p is the fraction of the total employees who favor unionization; that is, $p = .6$. Therefore, we calculate the mean and variance:

$$\mu = np = 20(.6) = 12$$
$$\sigma^2 = npq = 20(.6)(.4) = 4.8$$
$$\sigma = \sqrt{4.8} = 2.19$$

b. Looking in the $k = 10$ row and the $p = .6$ column of Table II (Appendix B) for $n = 20$, we find the value of .245. Thus,

$$P(x \leq 10) = .245$$

c. To find the probability

$$P(x > 12) = \sum_{x=13}^{20} p(x)$$

we use the fact that for all probability distributions, $\sum_{\text{All } x} p(x) = 1$. Therefore,

$$P(x > 12) = 1 - P(x \leq 12) = 1 - \sum_{x=0}^{12} p(x)$$

Consulting Table II, we find the entry in row $k = 12$, column $p = .6$ to be .584. Thus,

$$P(x > 12) = 1 - .584 = .416$$

d. To find the probability that exactly 11 employees favor unionization, recall that the entries in Table II are cumulative probabilities and use the relationship

$$P(x = 11) = [p(0) + p(1) + \cdots + p(11)] - [p(0) + p(1) + \cdots + p(10)]$$
$$= P(x \leq 11) - P(x \leq 10)$$

Then

$$P(x = 11) = .404 - .245 = .159$$

e. The probability distribution for x in this example is shown in Figure 4.9. Note that

$$\mu - 2\sigma = 12 - 2(2.2) = 7.6 \quad \mu + 2\sigma = 12 + 2(2.2) = 16.4$$

The interval (7.6, 16.4) is also shown in Figure 4.9. The probability that x falls in this interval is $P(x = 8, 9, 10, \ldots, 16) = P(x \leq 16) - P(x \leq 7) = .984 - .021 = .963$. This probability is very close to the .95 given by the Empirical Rule. Thus, we expect the number of employees in the sample of 20 who favor unionization to be between 8 and 16.

FIGURE 4.9

The binomial probability distribution for x in Example 4.12: $n = 20, p = .6$

Binomial Probabilities
Using the TI-83/TI-84 Graphing Calculator
Calculating Binomial Probabilities

I. $P(x = k)$

To compute the probability of k successes in n trials, where p is the probability of success for each trial, use the **binompdf(** command. *Binompdf* stands for "binomial probability density function." This command is under the **DISTR**ibution menu and has the format **binompdf(n, p, k).**

Example Compute the probability of 5 successes in 8 trials where the probability of success for a single trial is 40%. In this example, $n = 8$, $p = .4$, and $k = 5$.

Step 1 *Enter the binomial parameters*

Press **2nd VARS** for **DISTR**
Press the down **ARROW** key until **binompdf** is highlighted
Press **ENTER**
After **binompdf(**, type **8, .4, 5)** (Note: be sure to use the **COMMA** key between each parameter)
Press **ENTER**
You should see

```
binompdf(8,.4,5)
          .12386304
```

Thus, $P(x = 5)$ is about 12.4%.

II. $P(x \leq k)$

To compute the probability of k or fewer successes in n trials, where p is the probability of success for each trial, use the **binomcdf(** command. *Binomcdf* stands for "binomial *cumulative* probability density function." This command is under the **DISTR**ibution menu and has the format **binomcdf(n, p, k)**.

Example Compute the probability of 5 or less successes in 8 trials where the probability of success for a single trial is 40%. In this example, $n = 8$, $p = .4$, and $k = 5$.

Step 2 *Enter the binomial parameters*

Press **2nd VARS** for **DISTR**
Press down the **ARROW** key until **binomcdf** is highlighted
Press **ENTER**
After **binomcdf(**, type **8, .4, 5)**
Press **ENTER**
You should see

```
binomcdf(8,.4,5)
          .95019264
```

Thus, $P(x \leq k)$ is about 95%.

III. $P(x < k)$, $P(x > k)$, $P(x \geq k)$

To find the probability of less than k successes $P(x < k)$, more than k successes $P(x > k)$, or at least k successes $P(x \geq k)$, variations of the **binomcdf(** command must be used as shown below.

$P(x < k)$ use **binomcdf(n, p, k − 1)**
$P(x > k)$ use **1 − binomcdf(n, p, k)**
$P(x \geq k)$ use **1 − binomcdf(n, p, k − 1)**

Exercises 4.35–4.54

Learning the Mechanics

4.35 Compute the following:

a. $\dfrac{6!}{2!(6 - 2)!}$ b. $\dbinom{5}{2}$ c. $\dbinom{7}{0}$ d. $\dbinom{6}{6}$ e. $\dbinom{4}{3}$

4.36 Consider the following probability distribution:

$$p(x) = \binom{5}{x}(.7)^x (.3)^{5-x} \quad (x = 0, 1, 2, \ldots, 5)$$

a. Is x a discrete or a continuous random variable?
b. What is the name of this probability distribution?
c. Graph the probability distribution.
d. Find the mean and standard deviation of x.
e. Show the mean and the 2-standard-deviation interval on each side of the mean on the graph you drew in part **c**.

4.37 If x is a binomial random variable, compute $p(x)$ for each of
NW the following cases:
a. $n = 5, x = 1, p = .2$
b. $n = 4, x = 2, q = .4$
c. $n = 3, x = 0, p = .7$
d. $n = 5, x = 3, p = .1$
e. $n = 4, x = 2, q = .6$
f. $n = 3, x = 1, p = .9$

4.38 Suppose x is a binomial random variable with $n = 3$ and $p = .3$.
a. Calculate the value of $p(x)$, $x = 0, 1, 2, 3$, using the formula for a binomial probability distribution.
b. Using your answers to part **a**, give the probability distribution for x in tabular form.

4.39 If x is a binomial random variable, calculate μ, σ^2, and σ for each of the following:
a. $n = 25, p = .5$
b. $n = 80, p = .2$
c. $n = 100, p = .6$
d. $n = 70, p = .9$
e. $n = 60, p = .8$
f. $n = 1,000, p = .04$

4.40 If x is a binomial random variable, use Table II in Appendix B to find the following probabilities:
a. $P(x = 2)$ for $n = 10, p = .4$
b. $P(x \leq 5)$ for $n = 15, p = .6$
c. $P(x > 1)$ for $n = 5, p = .1$
d. $P(x < 10)$ for $n = 25, p = .7$
e. $P(x \geq 10)$ for $n = 15, p = .9$
f. $P(x = 2)$ for $n = 20, p = .2$

4.41 The binomial probability distribution is a family of probability distributions with each single distribution depending on the values of n and p. Assume that x is a binomial random variable with $n = 4$.

a. Determine a value of p such that the probability distribution of x is symmetric.
b. Determine a value of p such that the probability distribution of x is skewed to the right.
c. Determine a value of p such that the probability distribution of x is skewed to the left.
d. Graph each of the binomial distributions you obtained in parts **a, b**, and **c**. Locate the mean for each distribution on its graph.
e. In general, for what values of p will a binomial distribution be symmetric? Skewed to the right? Skewed to the left?

APPLET **Applet Exercise 4.3**

Use the applets entitled *Simulating the Probability of a Head with an Unfair Coin (P(H) = .2)*, and *Simulating the Probability of a Head with an Unfair Coin (P(H) = .8)* to study the mean μ of a binomial distribution.

a. Run each applet mentioned above once with $n = 1000$ and record the cumulative proportions. How does the cumulative proportion for each applet compare to the value of $P(H)$ given for the applet?
b. Using the cumulative proportion from each applet as p, compute $\mu = np$ for each applet where $n = 1000$. What does the value of μ represent in terms of the results from running each applet in part **a**?
c. In your own words, describe what the mean μ of a binomial distribution represents.

APPLET **Applet Exercise 4.4**

Open the applet entitled *Sample from a Population*. On the pull-down menu to the right of the top graph, select *Binary*. Set $n = 10$ as the sample size and repeatedly choose samples from the population. For each sample, record the number of 1s in the sample. Let x be the number of 1s in a sample of size 10. Explain why x is a binomial random variable.

APPLET **Applet Exercise 4.5**

Use the applet entitled *Simulating the Stock Market* to estimate the probability that the stock market will go up each of the next two days. Repeatedly run the applet for $n = 2$, recording the number of up's each time. Use the proportion of 2s among your results as the estimate of the probability. Compare to the binomial probability where $x = 2, n = 2$, and $p = 0.5$.

Applying the Concepts—Basic

4.42 Mobile phones with Internet access. According to a Jupiter/NPD Consumer Survey of young adults (18–24 years of age) who shop online, 20% own a mobile phone with Internet access (*American Demographics*, May 2002). In a random sample of 200 young adults who shop online, let x be the number who own a mobile phone with Internet access.

NW **a.** Explain why x is a binomial random variable (to a reasonable degree of approximation).

b. What is the value of p? Interpret this value.

c. What is the expected value of x? Interpret this value.

4.43 **Women-owned businesses.** According to the *Journal of Business Venturing* (Vol. 17, 2002), 27% of all small businesses owned by non-Hispanic whites nationwide are women-owned firms.

a. In a sample of 200 small businesses owned by non-Hispanic whites, how many would you expect to be female owned?

b. If eight small businesses owned by non-Hispanic whites were randomly selected, what is the probability that none are female owned? That half are female owned?

4.44 **Analysis of bottled water.** Is the bottled water you're drinking really purified water? A four-year study of bottled water brands conducted by the Natural Resources Defense Council found that 25% of bottled water is just tap water packaged in a bottle (*Scientific American*, July 2003). Consider a sample of five bottled water brands, and let x equal the number of these brands that use tap water.

a. Explain why x is (approximately) a binomial random variable.

b. Give the probability distribution for x as a formula.

c. Find $P(x = 2)$.

d. Find $P(x \leq 1)$.

4.45 **Tracking missiles with satellite imagery.** The U.S. government has devoted considerable funding to missile defense research over the past 20 years. The latest development is the Space-Based Infrared System (SBIRS), which uses satellite imagery to detect and track missiles (*Chance*, Summer 2005). The probability that an intruding object (e.g., a missile) will be detected on a flight track by SBIRS is .8. Consider a sample of 20 simulated tracks, each with an intruding object. Let x equal the number of these tracks where SBIRS detects the object.

a. Demonstrate that x is (approximately) a binomial random variable.

b. Give the values of p and n for the binomial distribution.

c. Find $P(x = 15)$, the probability that SBIRS will detect the object on exactly 15 tracks.

d. Find $P(x \geq 15)$, the probability that SBIRS will detect the object on at least 15 tracks.

e. Find $E(x)$ and interpret the result.

4.46 **Back injuries at work.** A poll by the Gallup Organization sponsored by Philadelphia-based CIGNA Integrated Care found that about 40% of employees have missed work due to a musculoskeletal (back) injury of some kind (*National Underwriter*, Apr. 5, 1999). Let x be the number of sampled workers who have missed work due to a back injury.

a. Explain why x is approximately a binomial random variable.

b. Use the Gallup poll data to estimate p for the binomial random variable of part **a**.

c. A random sample of 10 workers is to be drawn from a particular manufacturing plant. Use the p from part **b** to find the mean and standard deviation of x, the number of workers who missed work due to back injuries.

d. For the sample in part **c**, find the probability that exactly one worker missed work due to a back injury. That more than one worker missed work due to a back injury.

Applying the Concepts—Intermediate

4.47 **Bridge inspection ratings.** According to the National Bridge Inspection Standard (NBIS), public bridges over 20 feet in length must be inspected and rated every 2 years. The NBIS rating scale ranges from 0 (poorest rating) to 9 (highest rating). University of Colorado engineers used a probabilistic model to forecast the inspection ratings of all major bridges in Denver (*Journal of Performance of Constructed Facilities*, Feb. 2005). For the year 2020, the engineers forecast that 9% of all major Denver bridges will have ratings of 4 or below.

a. Use the forecast to find the probability that in a random sample of 10 major Denver bridges, at least 3 will have an inspection rating of 4 or below in 2020.

b. Suppose that you actually observe 3 or more of the sample of 10 bridges with inspection ratings of 4 or below in 2020. What inference can you make? Why?

4.48 **Detecting a computer virus attack.** *Chance* (Winter 2004) presented basic methods for detecting virus attacks (e.g., Trojan programs or worms) on a network computer that are sent from a remote host. These viruses reach the network through requests for communication (e.g., e-mail, Web chat, or remote log-in) that are identified as "packets." For example, the "SYN flood" virus ties up the network computer by "flooding" the network with multiple packets. Cybersecurity experts can detect this type of virus attack if at least one packet is observed by a network sensor. Assume that the probability of observing a single packet sent from a new virus is only .001. If the virus actually sends 150 packets to a network computer, what is the probability that the virus is detected by the sensor?

4.49 **Tax returns audited by the IRS.** According to the Internal Revenue Service (IRS), the chances of your tax return being audited are about 15 in 1,000 if your income is less than $100,000 and 30 in 1,000 if your income is $100,000 or more (*Statistical Abstract of the United States*).

a. What is the probability that a taxpayer with income less than $100,000 will be audited by the IRS? With income $100,000 or more?

b. If five taxpayers with incomes under $100,000 are randomly selected, what is the probability that exactly one will be audited? That more than one will be audited?

c. Repeat part **b** assuming that five taxpayers with incomes of $100,000 or more are randomly selected.

d. If two taxpayers with incomes under $100,000 are randomly selected and two with incomes more than $100,000 are randomly selected, what is the probability that none of these taxpayers will be audited by the IRS?

e. What assumptions did you have to make in order to answer these questions using the methodology presented in this section?

4.50 Switching banks after a merger. Banks that merge with others to form "mega-banks" sometimes leave customers dissatisfied with the impersonal service. A poll by the Gallup Organization found 20% of retail customers switched banks after their banks merged with another (*Bank Marketing*, Feb. 1999). One year after the acquisition of First Fidelity by First Union, a random sample of 25 retail customers who had banked with First Fidelity were questioned. Let x be the number of those customers who switched their business from First Union to a different bank.

a. What assumptions must hold in order for x to be a binomial random variable? In the remainder of this exercise, use the data from the Gallop Poll to estimate p.

b. What is the probability that $x \leq 10$?

c. Find $E(x)$ and the standard deviation of x.

d. Calculate the interval $\mu \pm 2\sigma$.

e. If samples of size 25 were drawn repeatedly a large number of times and x determined for each sample, what proportion of the x values would fall within the interval you calculated in part **d**?

4.51 FDA report on pesticides in food. Every quarter, the Food and Drug Administration (FDA) produces a report called the *Total Diet Study*. The FDA's report covers a variety of food items, each of which is analyzed for potentially harmful chemical compounds. A recent *Total Diet Study* reported that no pesticides at all were found in 60% of the domestically produced food samples (*FDA Pesticide Program: Residue Monitoring*, 2001). Consider a random sample of 800 food items analyzed for the presence of pesticides.

a. Compute μ and σ for the random variable x, the number of food items found that showed no trace of pesticide.

b. Based on a sample of 800 food items, is it likely you would observe less than half without any traces of pesticide? Explain.

Applying the Concepts—Advanced

4.52 Purchasing decision. Suppose you are a purchasing officer for a large company. You have purchased 5 million electrical switches, and your supplier has guaranteed that the shipment will contain no more than .1% defectives. To check the shipment, you randomly sample 500 switches, test them, and find that four are defective. Based on this evidence, do you think the supplier has complied with the guarantee? Explain.

4.53 USGA golf ball specifications. According to the U.S. Golf Association (USGA), "The weight of the [golf] ball shall not be greater than 1.620 ounces avoirdupois (45.93 grams).... The diameter of the ball shall not be less than 1.680 inches. ... The velocity of the ball shall not be greater than 250 feet per second" (USGA 2002). The USGA periodically checks the specifications of golf balls sold in the United States by randomly sampling balls from pro shops around the country. Two dozen of each kind are sampled, and if more than three do not meet size and/or velocity requirements, that kind of ball is removed from the USGA's approved-ball list.

a. What assumptions must be made and what information must be known in order to use the binomial probability distribution to calculate the probability that the USGA will remove a particular kind of golf ball from its approved-ball list?

b. Suppose 10% of all balls produced by a particular manufacturer are less than 1.680 inches in diameter, and assume that the number of such balls, x, in a sample of two dozen balls can be adequately characterized by a binomial probability distribution. Find the mean and standard deviation of the binomial distribution.

c. Refer to part **b**. If x has a binomial distribution, then so does the number, y, of balls in the sample that meet the USGA's minimum diameter. [*Note:* $x + y = 24$.] Describe the distribution of y. In particular, what are p, q, and n? Also, find $E(y)$ and the standard deviation of y.

4.54 Reliability of a "one-shot" device. A "one-shot" device can only be used once; after use, the device (e.g., a nuclear weapon, space shuttle, automobile air bag) is either destroyed or must be rebuilt. The destructive nature of a one-shot device makes repeated testing either impractical or too costly. Hence, the reliability of such a device must be determined with minimal testing. Consider a one-shot device that has some probability, p, of failure. Of course, the true value of p is unknown, so designers will specify a value of p that is the largest defective rate they are willing to accept. Designers will conduct n tests of the device and determine the success or failure of each test. If the number of observed failures, x, is less than or equal to some specified value, K, then the device is considered to have the desired failure rate. Consequently, the designers want to know the minimum sample size n needed so that observing K or fewer defectives in the sample will demonstrate that the true probability of failure for the one-shot device is no greater than p.

a. Suppose the desired failure rate for a one-shot device is $p = .10$. Also, suppose designers will conduct $n = 20$ tests of the device and conclude that the device is performing to specifications if $K = 1$ (i.e., if 1 or no failures are observed in the sample). Find $P(x \leq 1)$.

b. In reliability analysis, $1 - P(x \leq K)$ is often called the *level of confidence* for concluding that the true failure rate is less than or equal to p. Find the level of confidence for the one-shot device described in part **a**. In your opinion, is this an acceptable level? Explain.

c. Demonstrate that the confidence level can be increased by either (1) increasing the sample size n or (2) decreasing the number K of failures allowed in the sample.

d. Typically, designers want a confidence level of .90, .95, or .99. Find the values of n and K to use so that the designers can conclude (with at least 95% confidence) that the failure rate for the one-shot device of part **a** is no greater than $p = .10$.

[*Note:* The U.S. Department of Defense Reliability Analysis Center (DoD RAC) provides designers with free access to tables and toolboxes that give the minimum sample size n required to obtain a desired confidence level for a specified number of observed failures in the sample.]

4.4 The Poisson Distribution (Optional)

A type of probability distribution that is often useful in describing the number of events that will occur in a specific period of time or in a specific area or volume is the **Poisson distribution** (named after the 18th-century physicist and mathematician, Siméon Poisson). Typical examples of random variables for which the Poisson probability distribution provides a good model are as follows:

1. The number of industrial accidents per month at a manufacturing plant
2. The number of noticeable surface defects (scratches, dents, etc.) found by quality inspectors on a new automobile
3. The parts per million of some toxin found in the water or air emission from a manufacturing plant
4. The number of customer arrivals per unit of time at a supermarket checkout counter
5. The number of death claims received per day by an insurance company
6. The number of errors per 100 invoices in the accounting records of a company

---

Characteristics of a Poisson Random Variable

1. The experiment consists of counting the number of times a certain event occurs during a given unit of time or in a given area or volume (or weight, distance, or any other unit of measurement).
2. The probability that an event occurs in a given unit of time, area, or volume is the same for all the units.
3. The number of events that occur in one unit of time, area, or volume is independent of the number that occur in any other mutually exclusive unit.
4. The mean (or expected) number of events in each unit is denoted by the Greek letter lambda, λ.

The characteristics of the Poisson random variable are usually difficult to verify for practical examples. The examples given satisfy them well enough that the Poisson distribution provides a good model in many instances. As with all probability models, the real test of the adequacy of the Poisson model is in whether it provides a reasonable approximation to reality—that is, whether empirical data support it.

The probability distribution, mean, and variance for a Poisson random variable are shown in the next box.

Probability Distribution, Mean, and Variance for a Poisson Random Variable*

$$p(x) = \frac{\lambda^x e^{-\lambda}}{x!} \quad (x = 0, 1, 2, \ldots)$$

$$\mu = \lambda$$

$$\sigma^2 = \lambda$$

where

λ = Mean number of events during given unit of time, area, volume, etc.

$e = 2.71828\ldots$

The calculation of Poisson probabilities is made easier by the use of Table III in Appendix B, which gives the cumulative probabilities $P(x \leq k)$ for various values of λ. The use of Table III is illustrated in Example 4.13.

---

*The Poisson probability distribution also provides a good approximation to a binomial distribution with mean $\lambda = np$ when n is large and p is small (say, $np \leq 7$).

Biography

EXAMPLE 4.13

Finding Poisson Probabilities Associated with Worker Absenteeism

Problem Suppose the number, x, of a company's employees who are absent on Mondays has (approximately) a Poisson probability distribution. Furthermore, assume that the average number of Monday absentees is 2.6.

a. Find the mean and standard deviation of x, the number of employees absent on Monday.

b. Use Table III to find the probability that fewer than two employees are absent on a given Monday.

c. Use Table III to find the probability that more than five employees are absent on a given Monday.

d. Use Table III to find the probability that exactly five employees are absent on a given Monday.

Solution

a. The mean and variance of a Poisson random variable are both equal to λ. Thus, for this example,

$$\mu = \lambda = 2.6$$
$$\sigma^2 = \lambda = 2.6$$

Then the standard deviation of x is

$$\sigma = \sqrt{2.6} = 1.61$$

Remember that the mean measures the central tendency of the distribution and does not necessarily equal a possible value of x. In this example, the mean is 2.6 absences, and although there cannot be 2.6 absences on a given Monday, the average number of Monday absences is 2.6. Similarly, the standard deviation of 1.61 measures the variability of the number of absences per week. Perhaps a more helpful measure is the interval $\mu \pm 2\sigma$, which in this case stretches from $-.62$ to 5.82. We expect the number of absences to fall in this interval most of the time—with at least 75% relative frequency (according to Chebyshev's Rule) and probably with approximately 95% relative frequency (the Empirical Rule). The mean and the 2-standard-deviation interval around it are shown in Figure 4.10.

b. A partial reproduction of Table III is shown in Table 4.4. The rows of the table correspond to different values of λ, and the columns correspond to different values (k) of the Poisson random variable x. The entries in the table (like the binomial probabilities in Table II) give the cumulative probability $P(x \le k)$. To find the probability that fewer than two employees are absent on Monday, we first note that

$$P(x < 2) = P(x \le 1)$$

FIGURE 4.10
Probability distribution for
number of Monday absences

TABLE 4.4 Reproduction of Part of Table III in Appendix B

λ\k	0	1	2	3	4	5	6	7	8	9
2.2	.111	.355	.623	.819	.928	.975	.993	.998	1.000	1.000
2.4	.091	.308	.570	.779	.904	.964	.988	.997	.999	1.000
2.6	.074	.267	.518	.736	.877	.951	.983	.995	.999	1.000
2.8	.061	.231	.469	.692	.848	.935	.976	.992	.998	.999
3.0	.050	.199	.423	.647	.815	.916	.966	.988	.996	.999
3.2	.041	.171	.380	.603	.781	.895	.955	.983	.994	.998
3.4	.033	.147	.340	.558	.744	.871	.942	.977	.992	.997
3.6	.027	.126	.303	.515	.706	.844	.927	.969	.988	.996
3.8	.022	.107	.269	.473	.668	.816	.909	.960	.984	.994
4.0	.018	.092	.238	.433	.629	.785	.889	.949	.979	.992
4.2	.015	.078	.210	.395	.590	.753	.867	.936	.972	.989
4.4	.012	.066	.185	.359	.551	.720	.844	.921	.964	.985
4.6	.010	.056	.163	.326	.513	.686	.818	.905	.955	.980
4.8	.008	.048	.143	.294	.476	.651	.791	.887	.944	.975
5.0	.007	.040	.125	.265	.440	.616	.762	.867	.932	.968
5.2	.006	.034	.109	.238	.406	.581	.732	.845	.918	.960
5.4	.005	.029	.095	.213	.373	.546	.702	.822	.903	.951
5.6	.004	.024	.082	.191	.342	.512	.670	.797	.886	.941
5.8	.003	.021	.072	.170	.313	.478	.638	.771	.867	.929
6.0	.002	.017	.062	.151	.285	.446	.606	.744	.847	.916

This probability is cumulative and therefore is the entry in Table III in the row corresponding to $\lambda = 2.6$ and the column corresponding to $k = 1$. The entry is .267, shown shaded in Table 4.4. This probability corresponds to the shaded area in Figure 4.10 and may be interpreted as meaning that there is a 26.7% chance that fewer than two employees will be absent on a given Monday.

c. To find the probability that more than five employees are absent on a given Monday, we consider the complementary event

$$P(x > 5) = 1 - P(x \le 5) = 1 - .951 = .049$$

where .951 is the entry in Table III corresponding to $\lambda = 2.6$ and $k = 5$ (see Table 4.4). Note from Figure 4.10 that this is the area in the interval $\mu \pm 2\sigma$, or $-.62$ to 5.82. Then the number of absences should exceed 5—or, equivalently, should be more than 2 standard deviations from the mean—during only about 4.9% of all Mondays. Note that this percentage agrees remarkably well with that given by the Empirical Rule for mound-shaped distributions, which tells us to expect approximately 5% of the measurements (values of the random variable) to lie farther than 2 standard deviations from the mean.

d. To use Table III to find the probability that *exactly* five employees are absent on a Monday, we must write the probability as the difference between two cumulative probabilities:

$$P(x = 5) = P(x \le 5) - P(x \le 4) = .951 - .877 = .074$$

Now Work Exercise 4.56

Note that the probabilities in Table III are all rounded to three decimal places. Thus, although in theory a Poisson random variable can assume infinitely large values, the values of k in Table III are extended only until the cumulative probability is 1.000. This does not mean that x *cannot* assume larger values, but only that the likelihood is less than .001 (in fact, less than .0005) that it will do so.

Finally, you may need to calculate Poisson probabilities for values of λ not found in Table III. You may be able to obtain an adequate approximation by interpolation, but if not, consult more extensive tables for the Poisson distribution.

Exercises 4.55–4.68

Learning the Mechanics

4.55 Consider the probability distribution shown here:

$$p(x) = \frac{3^x e^{-3}}{x!} \ (x = 0, 1, 2, \dots)$$

a. Is x a discrete or continuous random variable? Explain.

b. What is the name of this probability distribution?
c. Graph the probability distribution.
d. Find the mean and standard deviation of x.

4.56 Assume that x is a random variable having a Poisson prob-
NW ability distribution with a mean of 1.5. Use Table III to find the following probabilities:
a. $P(x \le 3)$
b. $P(x \ge 3)$
c. $P(x = 3)$
d. $P(x = 0)$
e. $P(x > 0)$
f. $P(x > 6)$

4.57 Given that x is a random variable for which a Poisson probability distribution provides a good approximation, use Table III to compute the following:
a. $P(x < 2)$ when $\lambda = 1$
b. $P(x \le 2)$ when $\lambda = 2$
c. $P(x \le 2)$ when $\lambda = 3$
d. What happens to the probability of the event $\{x \le 2\}$ as λ increases from 1 to 3? Is this intuitively reasonable?

4.58 Suppose x is a random variable for which a Poisson probability distribution with $\lambda = 5$ provides a good characterization.
a. Graph $p(x)$ for $x = 0, 1, 2, \dots, 15$.
b. Find μ and σ for x, and locate μ and the interval $\mu \pm 2\sigma$ on the graph.
c. What is the probability that x will fall within the interval $\mu \pm 2\sigma$?

Applying the Concepts—Basic

4.59 LAN video conferencing. A network administrator is installing a video conferencing module to a local area network (LAN) computer system. Of interest is the capacity of the LAN to handle users who attempt to call in for video conferencing during peak hours. Calls are blocked if the user finds all LAN lines are "busy." The capacity is directly related to the rate at which calls are blocked ("Traffic Engineering Model for LAN Video Conferencing," Intel, 2005). Let x equal the number of calls blocked during the peak hour (busy) video conferencing call time. The network administrator believes that x has a Poisson distribution with mean $\lambda = 5$.

a. Find the probability that fewer than 3 calls are blocked during the peak hour.
b. Find $E(x)$ and interpret its value.

4.60 FDIC bank failures. The Federal Deposit Insurance Corporation (FDIC) insures deposits of up to $100,000 in banks that are members of the Federal Reserve System against losses due to bank failure or theft. Over the last 5 years, the average number of bank failures per year among insured banks was 5.8 (*FDIC Stats at a Glance*, Mar. 2003). Assume that x, the number of bank failures per year among insured banks, can be adequately characterized by a Poisson probability distribution with mean 6.
a. Find the expected value and standard deviation of x.

b. In 1997, only one insured bank failed. How far (in standard deviations) does $x = 1$ lie below the mean of the Poisson distribution? That is, find the z-score for $x = 1$.
c. In 2002, 10 insured banks failed. Find $P(x \le 10)$.

4.61 Airline fatalities. U.S. airlines average about 1.2 fatalities per month (*Statistical Abstract of the United States: 2006*). Assume the probability distribution for x, the number of fatalities per month, can be approximated by a Poisson probability distribution.
a. What is the probability that no fatalities will occur during any given month?
b. What is the probability that one fatality will occur during a month?
c. Find $E(x)$ and the standard deviation of x.

4.62 Deep-draft vessel casualties. University of New Mexico economists Gawande and Wheeler modeled the number of casualties experienced by a deep-draft marine vessel over a 3-year period as a Poisson random variable, x. They estimated $E(x)$ to be .03 (*Management Science*, January 1999).
a. Find the variance x.
b. Discuss the conditions that would make the researchers' Poisson assumption plausible.
c. What is the probability that a deep-draft U.S. flag vessel will have exactly one casualty in a 3-year time period? No casualties in a 3-year period?

Applying the Concepts—Intermediate

4.63 Vinyl chloride emissions. The Environmental Protection Agency (EPA) limits the amount of vinyl chloride in plant air emissions to no more than 10 parts per million. Suppose the mean emission of vinyl chloride for a particular plant is 4 parts per million. Assume that the number of parts per million of vinyl chloride in air samples, x, follows a Poisson probability distribution.

Poisson Probabilities

Using the TI-83/TI-84 Graphing Calculator

Calculating Poisson Probabilities

I. $P(x = k)$

To compute $P(x = k)$, the probability of exactly k successes in a specified interval where λ is the mean number of successes in the interval, use the **poissonpdf(** command. *Poissonpdf* stands for "Poisson probability density function." This command is under the **DISTR**ibution menu and has the format **poissonpdf( )**.

Example   Suppose that the number, x, of reported sightings per week of blue whales is recorded. Assume that x has approximately a Poisson probability distribution and that the average number of weekly sightings is 2.6.
Compute the probability that exactly five sightings are made during a given week. In this example, $\lambda = 2.6$ and $k = 5$.

Step 1   *Enter the poisson parameters*
Press **2nd VARS** for **DISTR**
Press the down **ARROW** key until **poissonpdf** is highlighted
Press **ENTER**
After **poissonpdf(**, type **2.6, 5** (Note: be sure to use the **COMMA** key between each parameter)
Press **ENTER**

You should see

```
poissonpdf(2.6,5
)
            .0735393591
```

Thus, the $P(x = 5)$ is about 7.4%.

II. $P(x \le k)$

To compute the probability of k or fewer successes in a specified interval, where λ is the mean number of successes in the interval, use the **poissoncdf(** command. *Poissoncdf* stands for "Poisson *cumulative* probability density function." This command is under the **DISTR**ibution menu and has the format **poissoncdf(**

Example   In the preceding example compute the probability that five or fewer sightings are made during a given week. In this example, $\lambda = 2.6$ and $k = 5$.

Step 1   *Enter the poisson parameters*
Press **2nd VARS** for **DISTR**
Press the down **ARROW** key until **poissoncdf** is highlighted
Press **ENTER**
After **poissoncdf(**, type **2.6, 5**
Press **ENTER**

You should see:

```
poissoncdf(2.6,5
)
            .9509628481
```

Thus, the $P(x = 5)$ is about 95.1%.

III. $P(x < k)$, $P(x > k)$, $P(x \ge k)$

To find the probability of less than k successes, more than k successes, or at least k successes, variations of **poissoncdf(** command must be used as shown below.
$P(x < k)$ use **poissoncdf($\lambda, k - 1$)**
$P(x > k)$ use **1 − poissoncdf(λ, k)**
$P(x \ge k)$ use **1 − poissoncdf($\lambda, k - 1$)**

a. What is the standard deviation of x for the plant?

b. Is it likely that a sample of air from the plant would yield a value of x that would exceed the EPA limit? Explain.

c. Discuss conditions that would make the Poisson assumption plausible.

4.64 Customer arrivals at a bakery. As part of a project targeted at improving the services of a local bakery, a management consultant (L. Lei of Rutgers University) monitored customer arrivals for several Saturdays and Sundays. Using the arrival data, she estimated the average number of customer arrivals per 10-minute period on Saturdays to be 6.2. She assumed that arrivals per 10-minute interval followed the Poisson distribution (some of whose values are missing) shown in the table below.

a. Compute the missing probabilities.

b. Plot the distribution.

c. Find μ and σ and plot the intervals $\mu \pm \sigma$, $\mu \pm 2\sigma$, and $\mu \pm 3\sigma$ on your plot of part **b**.

d. The owner of the bakery claims that more than 75 customers per hour enter the store on Saturdays. Based on the consultant's data, is this likely? Explain.

4.65 Mainframe computer life cycle. In studying the product life cycle in the commercial mainframe computer market Greenstein (Northwestern University) and Wade (University of Illinois) found that the number of new product introductions per year per firm, x, could be approximated by a Poisson random variable with mean equal to .37 (*Rand Journal of Economics*, Winter 1998).

a. Find the standard deviation of x.

b. Plot $p(x)$, the probability distribution for x.

c. Is it likely that the mainframe manufacturer would introduce more than two new products per year? Less than one new product per year? Justify your answers.

4.66 Flaws in wooden doors. As a check on the quality of the wooden doors produced by a company, its owner requested that each door undergo inspection for defects before leaving the plant. The plant's quality control inspector found that one square foot of door surface contains, on the average, .5 minor flaws. Subsequently, one square foot of each door's surface was examined for flaws. The owner decided to have all doors reworked that were found to have two or more minor flaws in the square foot of surface that was inspected. What is the probability that a door will fail inspection and be sent back for reworking? What is the probability that a door will pass inspection?

4.67 Reliability of incandescent lightbulbs. A large manufacturing plant has 3,200 incandescent lightbulbs illuminating the manufacturing floor. The rate at which the bulbs fail follows a Poisson distribution with a mean of three bulbs per hour. What is the probability that no bulbs fail in an 8-hour shift?

Applying the Concepts—Advanced

4.68 Waiting for a car wash. An automatic car wash takes exactly 5 minutes to wash a car. On average, 10 cars per hour arrive at the car wash. Suppose that 30 minutes before closing time, 5 cars are in line. If the car wash is in continuous use until closing time, is it likely anyone will be in line at closing time?

Probability Distribution for Exercise 4.64

x	0	1	2	3	4	5	6	7	8	9	10	11	12	13
$p(x)$	.002	.013	—	.081	.125	.155	—	.142	.110	.076	—	.026	.014	.007

Source: Lei, L. *Dorsi's Bakery: Modeling Service Operations.* Graduate School of Management. Rutgers University, 1993.

4.5 Probability Distributions for Continuous Random Variables

The graphical form of the probability distribution for a **continuous random variable** x is a smooth curve that might appear as shown in Figure 4.11. This curve, a function of x, is denoted by the symbol $f(x)$ and is variously called a **probability density function (pdf),** a **frequency function,** or a **probability distribution.**

The areas under a probability distribution correspond to probabilities for x. For example, the area A beneath the curve between the two points a and b, as shown in Figure 4.11, is the probability that x assumes a value between a and b ($a < x < b$). Because there is no area over a point, say $x = a$, it follows that (according to our model) the probability associated with a particular value of x is equal to 0; that is, $P(x = a) = 0$ and hence $P(a < x < b) = P(a \leq x \leq b)$. In other words, the probability is the same whether or not you include the endpoints of the interval. Also, because areas over intervals represent probabilities, it follows that the total area under a probability distribution, the probability assigned to all values of x, should equal 1. Note that probability distributions for continuous random variables possess different shapes depending on the relative frequency distributions of real data that the probability distributions are supposed to model.

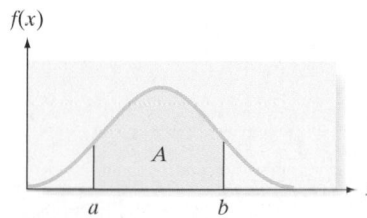

FIGURE 4.11

A probability distribution $f(x)$ for a continuous random variable x

The areas under most probability distributions are obtained by using calculus or numerical methods.* Because these methods often involve difficult procedures, we will give the areas for some of the most common probability distributions in tabular form in Appendix B. Then, to find the area between two values of x, say $x = a$ and $x = b$, you simply have to consult the appropriate table.

For each of the continuous random variables presented in this chapter, we will give the formula for the probability distribution along with its mean μ and standard deviation σ. These two numbers will enable you to make some approximate probability statements about a random variable even when you do not have access to a table of areas under the probability distribution.

4.6 The Uniform Distribution (Optional)

All the probability problems discussed in Chapter 3 had sample spaces that contained a finite number of sample points. In many of these problems, the sample points were assigned equal probabilities—for example, the die toss or the coin toss. For continuous random variables, there is an infinite number of values in the sample space, but in some cases the values may appear to be equally likely. For example, if a short exists in a 5-meter stretch of electrical wire, it may have an equal probability of being in any particular 1-centimeter segment along the line. Or if a safety inspector plans to choose a time at random during the four afternoon work hours to pay a surprise visit to a certain area of a plant, then each 1-minute time interval in this 4-work-hour period will have an equally likely chance of being selected for the visit.

Continuous random variables that appear to have equally likely outcomes over their range of possible values possess a **uniform probability distribution,** perhaps the simplest of all continuous probability distributions. Suppose the random variable x can assume values only in an interval $c \le x \le d$. Then the uniform frequency function has a rectangular shape, as shown in Figure 4.12. Note that the possible values of x consist of all points in the interval between point c and point d. The height of $f(x)$ is constant in that interval and equals $1/(d - c)$. Therefore, the total area under $f(x)$ is given by

$$\text{Total area of rectangle} = (\text{Base})(\text{Height}) = (d - c)\left(\frac{1}{d - c}\right) = 1$$

The uniform probability distribution provides a model for continuous random variables that are *evenly distributed* over a certain interval—that is, a uniform random variable is one that is just as likely to assume a value in one interval as it is to assume a value in any other interval of equal size. There is no clustering of values around any value; instead, there is an even spread over the entire region of possible values.

The uniform distribution is sometimes referred to as the **randomness distribution,** since one way of generating a uniform random variable is to perform an experiment in which a point is *randomly selected* on the horizontal axis between the points c and d. If we were to repeat this experiment infinitely often, we would create a uniform probability distribution like that shown in Figure 4.12. The random selection of points in an interval can also be used to generate random numbers such as those in Table I of Appendix B. Recall that random numbers are selected in such a way that every number would have an

FIGURE 4.12
The uniform probability distribution

---

*Students with knowledge of calculus should note that the probability that x assumes a value in the interval $a < x < b$ is $P(a < x < b) = \int_a^b f(x)\, dx$, assuming the integral exists. Similar to the requirement for a discrete probability distribution, we require $f(x) \ge 0$ and $\int_{-\infty}^{\infty} f(x)\, dx = 1$.

equal probability of selection. Therefore, random numbers are realizations of a uniform random variable. (Random numbers were used to draw random samples in Section 3.7.) The formulas for the uniform probability distribution, its mean, and standard deviation are shown in the box.

Probability Distribution for a Uniform Random Variable x

Probability density function: $f(x) = \dfrac{1}{d - c} \quad c \leq x \leq d$

$$\text{Mean: } \mu = \frac{c + d}{2} \qquad \text{Standard deviation: } \sigma = \frac{d - c}{\sqrt{12}}$$

$$P(a < x < b) = (b - a)/(d - c), \, c \leq a < b \leq d$$

Suppose the interval $a < x < b$ lies within the domain of x; that is, it falls within the larger interval $c \leq x \leq d$. Then the probability that x assumes a value within the interval $a < x < b$ is equal to the area of the rectangle over the interval, namely, $(b - a)/(d - c)$.* (See the shaded area in Figure 4.12.)

EXAMPLE 4.14

Applying the Uniform Distribution to Steel Manufacturing

Problem   Suppose the research department of a steel manufacturer believes that one of the company's rolling machines is producing sheets of steel of varying thickness. The thickness is a uniform random variable with values between 150 and 200 millimeters. Any sheets less than 160 millimeters must be scrapped because they are unacceptable to buyers.

a. Calculate and interpret the mean and standard deviation of x, the thickness of the sheets produced by this machine.

b. Graph the probability distribution of x, and show the mean on the horizontal axis. Also show 1- and 2-standard-deviation intervals around the mean.

c. Calculate the fraction of steel sheets produced by this machine that have to be scrapped.

Solution

a. To calculate the mean and standard deviation for x, we substitute 150 and 200 millimeters for c and d, respectively, in the formulas for uniform random variables. Thus,

$$\mu = \frac{c + d}{2} = \frac{150 + 200}{2} = 175 \text{ millimeters}$$

and

$$\sigma = \frac{d - c}{\sqrt{12}} = \frac{200 - 150}{\sqrt{12}} = \frac{50}{3.464} = 14.43 \text{ millimeters}$$

Our interpretations follow:

The average thickness of all manufactured steel sheets is $\mu = 175$ millimeters. From Chebyshev's Theorem (Table 2.6, p. 80), we know that at least 75% of the thickness values, x, in the distribution will fall in the interval

$$\mu \pm 2\sigma = 175 \pm 2(14.43)$$
$$= 175 \pm 28.86$$

---

*The student with knowledge of calculus should note that
$$P(a < x < b) = \int_a^b f(x)\, d(x) = \int_a^b 1/(d - c)\, dx = (b - a)/(d - c)$$

FIGURE 4.13
Distribution for x
in Example 4.14

FIGURE 4.14
Probability that sheet
thickness, x, is between
150 and 160 millimeters

or, between 146.14 and 203.86 millimeters. (This demonstrates, once again, the conservativeness of Chebyshev's Theorem since we know that all values of x fall between 150 and 200 millimeters.)

b. The uniform probability distribution is

$$f(x) = \frac{1}{d-c} = \frac{1}{200-150} = \frac{1}{50} \; (150 \le x \le 200)$$

The graph of this function is shown in Figure 4.13. The mean and 1- and 2-standard-deviation intervals around the mean are shown on the horizontal axis.

c. To find the fraction of steel sheets produced by the machine that have to be scrapped, we must find the probability that x, the thickness, is less than 160 millimeters. As indicated in Figure 4.14, we need to calculate the area under the frequency function $f(x)$ between the points $x = 150$ and $x = 160$. Therefore, in this case, $a = 150$ and $b = 160$. Applying the formula in the box, we have

$$P(x < 160) = P(150 < x < 160)$$

$$= \frac{b-a}{d-c} = \frac{160-150}{200-150} = \frac{10}{50} = \frac{1}{5}$$

That is, 20% of all the sheets made by this machine must be scrapped.

Look Back The calculated probability in part **c** is the area of a rectangle with base $160 - 150 = 10$ and height $\frac{1}{50}$. Alternatively, we can find the fraction that has to be scrapped as

$$P(x < 160) = (\text{Base})(\text{Height}) = (10)\left(\frac{1}{50}\right) = \frac{1}{5}$$

> **Now Work Exercise 4.76**

Exercises 4.69–4.83

Learning the Mechanics

4.69 Suppose x is a random variable best described by a uniform probability distribution with $c = 20$ and $d = 45$.

    a. Find $f(x)$.

    b. Find the mean and standard deviation of x.

    c. Graph $f(x)$ and locate μ and the interval $\mu \pm 2\sigma$ on the graph. Note that the probability that x assumes a value within the interval $\mu \pm 2\sigma$ is equal to 1.

4.70 Refer to Exercise 4.69. Find the following probabilities:

    a. $P(20 \le x \le 30)$ **b.** $P(20 < x \le 30)$

c. $P(x \geq 30)$

d. $P(x \geq 45)$

e. $P(x \leq 40)$

f. $P(x < 40)$

g. $P(15 \leq x \leq 35)$

h. $P(21.5 \leq x \leq 31.5)$

4.71 Suppose x is a random variable best described by a uniform probability distribution with $c = 3$ and $d = 7$.

a. Find $f(x)$.

b. Find the mean and standard deviation of x.

c. Find $P(\mu - \sigma \leq x \leq \mu + \sigma)$.

4.72 Refer to Exercise 4.71. Find the value of a that makes each of the following probability statements true.

a. $P(x \geq a) = .6$

b. $P(x \leq a) = .25$

c. $P(x \leq a) = 1$

d. $P(4 \leq x \leq a) = .5$

4.73 The random variable x is best described by a uniform probability distribution with $c = 100$ and $d = 200$. Find the probability that x assumes a value

a. More than 2 standard deviations from μ.

b. Less than 3 standard deviations from μ.

c. Within 2 standard deviations of μ.

4.74 The random variable x is best described by a uniform probability distribution with mean 10 and standard deviation 1. Find c, d, and $f(x)$. Graph the probability distribution.

APPLET Applet Exercise 4.6

Open the applet entitled *Sample from a Population*. On the pull-down menu to the right of the top graph, select *Uniform*. The box to the left of the top graph displays the population mean, median, and standard deviation.

a. Run the applet for each available value of n on the pull-down menu for the sample size. Go from the smallest to the largest value of n. For each value of n, observe the shape of the graph of the sample data and record the mean, median, and standard deviation of the sample.

b. Describe what happens to the shape of the graph and the mean, median, and standard deviation of the sample as the sample size increases.

APPLET Applet Exercise 4.7

Suppose we set the *Random Numbers* applet to generate one number between 1 and 100, inclusive. We let the value of the random variable x be the number generated when the *Sample* button is clicked. Explain why the distribution of x is approximately uniform even though x is a discrete rather than continuous random variable.

Applying the Concepts—Basic

4.75 Maintaining pipe wall temperature. Maintaining a constant pipe wall temperature in some hot-process applications is critical. A new technique that utilizes bolt-on trace elements to maintain temperature was presented in the *Journal of Heat Transfer* (Nov. 2000). Without bolt-on trace elements, the pipe wall temperature of a switch condenser used to produce plastic has a uniform distribution ranging from 260° to 290°F. When several bolt-on trace elements are attached to the piping, the wall temperature is uniform from 278° to 285°F.

a. Ideally, the pipe wall temperature should range between 280° and 284°F. What is the probability that the temperature will fall in this ideal range when no bolt-on trace elements are used? When bolt-on trace elements are attached to the pipe?

b. When the temperature is 268°F or lower, the hot liquid plastic hardens (or plates), causing a buildup in the piping. What is the probability of plastic plating when no bolt-on trace elements are used? When bolt-on trace elements are attached to the pipe?

4.76 Trajectory of an electrical circuit. Researchers at the **NW** University of California—Berkeley have designed, built, and tested a switched-capacitor circuit for generating random signals (*International Journal of Circuit Theory and Applications*, May–June 1990). The circuit's trajectory was shown to be uniformly distributed on the interval $(0, 1)$.

a. Give the mean and variance of the circuit's trajectory.

b. Compute the probability that the trajectory falls between .2 and .4.

c. Would you expect to observe a trajectory that exceeds .995? Explain.

4.77 Random numbers. The data set listed in the table was created using the MINITAB random number generator. Construct a relative frequency histogram for the data. Except for the expected variation in relative frequencies among the class intervals, does your histogram suggest that the data are observations on a uniform random variable with $c = 0$ and $d = 100$? Explain.

RANUNI

38.8759	98.0716	64.5788	60.8422	.8413
88.3734	31.8792	32.9847	.7434	93.3017
12.4337	11.7828	87.4506	94.1727	23.0892
47.0121	43.3629	50.7119	88.2612	69.2875
62.6626	55.6267	78.3936	28.6777	71.6829
44.0466	57.8870	71.8318	28.9622	23.0278
35.6438	38.6584	46.7404	11.2159	96.1009
95.3660	21.5478	87.7819	12.0605	75.1015

Applying the Concepts—Intermediate

4.78 Marine losses for an oil company. The frequency distribution shown in the table depicts the property and marine losses incurred by a large oil company over the last two years. This distribution can be used by the company to predict future losses and to help determine an appropriate level of insurance coverage. In analyzing the losses within an interval of the distribution, for simplification, analysts may treat the interval as a uniform probability distribution (*Research Review*, Summer 1998). In the insurance business, intervals like these are often called *layers*.

Layer	Property and Marine Losses (millions of $)	Frequency
1	0.00–0.01	668
2	0.01–0.05	38
3	0.05 0.10	7
4	0.10–0.25	4
5	0.25–0.50	2
6	0.50–1.00	1
7	1.00–2.50	0

Source: Cozzolino, John M., and Mikolaj, Peter J. "Applications of the Piecewise Constant Pareto Distribution." *Research Review*, Summer 1998.

a. Use a uniform distribution to model the loss amount in layer 2. Graph the distribution. Calculate and interpret its mean and variance.

b. Repeat part a for layer 6.

c. If a loss occurs in layer 2, what is the probability that it exceeds $10,000? That it is under $25,000?

d. If a layer-6 loss occurs, what is the probability that it is between $750,000 and $1,000,000? That it exceeds $900,000? That it is exactly $900,000?

4.79 Soft-drink dispenser. The manager of a local soft-drink bottling company believes that when a new beverage-dispensing machine is set to dispense 7 ounces, it in fact dispenses an amount x at random anywhere between 6.5 and 7.5 ounces inclusive. Suppose x has a uniform probability distribution.

a. Is the amount dispensed by the beverage machine a discrete or a continuous random variable? Explain.

b. Graph the frequency function for x, the amount of beverage the manager believes is dispensed by the new machine when it is set to dispense 7 ounces.

c. Find the mean and standard deviation for the distribution graphed in part **b**, and locate the mean and the interval $\mu \pm 2\sigma$ on the graph.

d. Find $P(x \geq 7)$.

e. Find $P(x < 6)$.

f. Find $P(6.5 \leq x \leq 7.25)$.

g. What is the probability that each of the next six bottles filled by the new machine will contain more than 7.25 ounces of beverage? Assume that the amount of beverage dispensed in one bottle is independent of the amount dispensed in another bottle.

4.80 Cycle availability of a system. In the jargon of system maintenance, *cycle availability* is defined as the probability that the system is functioning at any point in time. The United States Department of Defense developed a series of performance measures for assessing system cycle availability (*START*, Vol. 11, 2004). Under certain assumptions about the failure time and maintenance time of a system, cycle availability is shown to be uniformly distributed between 0 and 1. Find the following parameters for cycle availability: mean, standard deviation, 10th percentile, lower quartile, and upper quartile. Interpret the results.

4.81 Time delays at a bus stop. A bus is scheduled to stop at a certain bus stop every half hour on the hour and the half hour. At the end of the day, buses still stop after every 30 minutes, but because delays often occur earlier in the day, the bus is never early and likely to be late. The director of the bus line claims

that the length of time a bus is late is uniformly distributed, and the maximum time that a bus is late is 20 minutes.

a. If the director's claim is true, what is the expected number of minutes a bus will be late?

b. If the director's claim is true, what is the probability that the last bus on a given day will be more than 19 minutes late?

c. If you arrive at the bus stop at the end of a day at exactly half past the hour and must wait more than 19 minutes for the bus, what would you conclude about the director's claim? Why?

Applying the Concepts—Advanced

4.82 Reliability of a robotic device. The *reliability* of a piece of equipment is frequently defined to be the probability, p, that the equipment performs its intended function successfully for a given period of time under specific conditions (Render and Heizer, *Principles of Operations Management*, 1995). Because p varies from one point in time to another, some reliability analysts treat p as if it were a random variable. Suppose an analyst characterizes the uncertainty about the reliability of a particular robotic device used in an automobile assembly line using the following distribution:

$$f(p) = \begin{cases} 1 & 0 \leq p \leq 1 \\ 0 & \text{otherwise} \end{cases}$$

a. Graph the analyst's probability distribution for p.

b. Find the mean and variance of p.

c. According to the analyst's probability distribution for p, what is the probability that p is greater than .95? Less than .95?

d. Suppose the analyst receives the additional information that p is definitely between .90 and .95, but that there is complete uncertainty about where it lies between these values. Describe the probability distribution the analyst should now use to describe p.

4.83 Gouges on a spindle. A tool-and-die machine shop produces extremely high-tolerance spindles. The spindles are 18-inch slender rods used in a variety of military equipment. A piece of equipment used in the manufacture of the spindles malfunctions on occasion and places a single gouge somewhere on the spindle. However, if the spindle can be cut so that it has 14 consecutive inches without a gouge, then the spindle can be salvaged for other purposes. Assuming that the location of the gouge along the spindle is random, what is the probability that a defective spindle can be salvaged?

4.7 The Normal Distribution

One of the most commonly observed continuous random variables has a **bell-shaped** probability distribution (or **bell curve**) as shown in Figure 4.15. It is known as a **normal random variable,** and its probability distribution is called a **normal distribution.**

The normal distribution plays a very important role in the science of statistical inference. Moreover, many business phenomena generate random variables with probability distributions that are very well approximated by a normal distribution. For example, the monthly rate of return for a particular stock is approximately a normal random variable, and the probability distribution for the weekly sales of a corporation might be approximated by a normal probability distribution. The normal distribution

$f(x)$

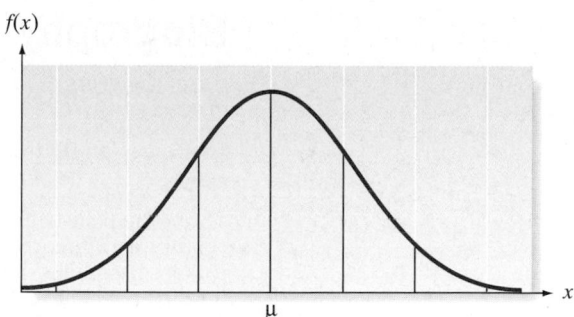

FIGURE 4.15

A normal probability
distribution

might also provide an accurate model for the distribution of scores on an employment
aptitude test. You can determine the adequacy of the normal approximation to an existing population by comparing the relative frequency distribution of a large sample of the
data to the normal probability distribution. Methods to detect disagreement between a
set of data and the assumption of normality are presented in Section 4.8.

The normal distribution is perfectly symmetric about its mean μ, as can be seen in the
examples in Figure 4.16. Its spread is determined by the value of its standard deviation σ.

The formula for the normal probability distribution is shown in the box. When
plotted, this formula yields a curve like that shown in Figure 4.15.

Probability Distribution for a Normal Random Variable x

Probability density function: $f(x) = \dfrac{1}{\sigma\sqrt{2\pi}}\, e^{-(1/2)[(x-\mu)/\sigma]^2}$

where

μ = Mean of the normal random variable x

σ = Standard deviation

π = 3.1416 . . .

e = 2.71828 . . .

$P(x < a)$ is obtained from a table of normal probabilities

Note that the mean μ and standard deviation σ appear in this formula, so no separate formulas for μ and σ are necessary. To graph the normal curve, we have to know the
numerical values of μ and $\sigma\sigma$.

Computing the area over intervals under the normal probability distribution is a
difficult task.* Consequently, we will use the computed areas listed in Table IV of

$f(x)$

FIGURE 4.16

Several normal distributions
with different means and
standard deviations

---

*The student with knowledge of calculus should note that there is not a closed-form expression for

$P(a < x < b) = \displaystyle\int_a^b f(x)\,dx$ for the normal probability distribution. The value of this definite integral
can be obtained to any desired degree of accuracy by numerical approximation procedures. For this
reason, it is tabulated for the user.

Biography

**CARL F. GAUSS
(1777–1855)**

The Gaussian Distribution

The normal distribution began in the 18th century as a theoretical distribution for errors in disciplines where fluctuations in nature were believed to behave randomly. Although he may not have been the first to discover the formula, the normal distribution was named the Gaussian distribution after Carl Friedrich Gauss. A well-known and respected German mathematician, physicist, and astronomer, Gauss applied the normal distribution while studying the motion of planets and stars. Gauss's prowess as a mathematician was exemplified by one of his most important discoveries. At the young age of 22, Gauss constructed a regular 17-gon by ruler and compasses—a feat that was the most major advance in mathematics since the time of the ancient Greeks. In addition to publishing close to 200 scientific papers, Gauss invented the heliograph as well as a primitive telegraph device.

Appendix B. Although there are an infinitely large number of normal curves—one for each pair of values for μ and σ—we have formed a single table that will apply to any normal curve.

Table IV is based on a normal distribution with mean $\mu = 0$ and standard deviation $\sigma = 1$, called a *standard normal distribution*. A random variable with a standard normal distribution is typically denoted by the symbol z. The formula for the probability distribution of z is given by

$$f(z) = \frac{1}{\sqrt{2\pi}}\, e^{-(1/2)z^2}$$

Figure 4.17 shows the graph of a standard normal distribution.

Definition 4.8

The **standard normal distribution** is a normal distribution with $\mu = 0$ and $\sigma = 1$. A random variable with a standard normal distribution, denoted by the symbol z, is called a *standard normal random variable*.

Since we will ultimately convert all normal random variables to standard normal in order to use Table IV to find probabilities, it is important that you learn to use Table IV well. A partial reproduction of Table IV is shown in Table 4.5. Note that the values of the standard normal random variable z are listed in the left-hand column. The entries in the body of the table give the area (probability) between 0 and z. Examples 4.15–4.18 illustrate the use of the table.

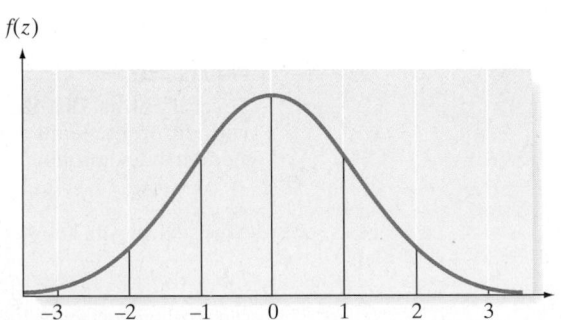

FIGURE 4.17

Standard normal
distribution: $\mu = 0, \sigma = 1$

TABLE 4.5 Reproduction of Part of Table IV in Appendix B

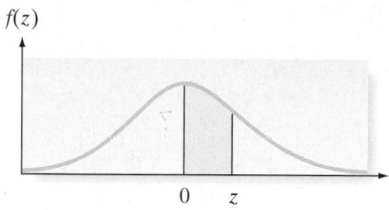

$f(z)$

z	.00	.01	.02	.03	.04	.05	.06	.07	.08	.09
.0	.0000	.0040	.0080	.0120	.0160	.0199	.0239	.0279	.0319	.0359
.1	.0398	.0438	.0478	.0517	.0557	.0596	.0636	.0675	.0714	.0753
.2	.0793	.0832	.0871	.0910	.0948	.0987	.1026	.1064	.1103	.1141
.3	.1179	.1217	.1255	.1293	.1331	.1368	.1406	.1443	.1480	.1517
.4	.1554	.1591	.1628	.1664	.1700	.1736	.1772	.1808	.1844	.1879
.5	.1915	.1950	.1985	.2019	.2054	.2088	.2123	.2157	.2190	.2224
.6	.2257	.2291	.2324	.2357	.2389	.2422	.2454	.2486	.2517	.2549
.7	.2580	.2611	.2642	.2673	.2704	.2734	.2764	.2794	.2823	.2852
.8	.2881	.2910	.2939	.2967	.2995	.3023	.3051	.3078	.3106	.3133
.9	.3159	.3186	.3212	.3238	.3264	.3289	.3315	.3340	.3365	.3389
1.0	.3413	.3438	.3461	.3485	.3508	.3531	.3554	.3577	.3599	.3621
1.1	.3643	.3665	.3686	.3708	.3729	.3749	.3770	.3790	.3810	.3830
1.2	.3849	.3869	.3888	.3907	.3925	.3944	.3962	.3980	.3997	.4015
1.3	.4032	.4049	.4066	.4082	.4099	.4115	.4131	.4147	.4162	.4177
1.4	.4192	.4207	.4222	.4236	.4251	.4265	.4279	.4292	.4306	.4319
1.5	.4332	.4345	.4357	.4370	.4382	.4394	.4406	.4418	.4429	.4441

EXAMPLE 4.15

Using the Standard Normal Table to Find $P(-z_0 < z < z_0)$

Problem Find the probability that the standard normal random variable z falls between -1.33 and 1.33.

Solution The standard normal distribution is shown again in Figure 4.18. Since all probabilities associated with standard normal random variables can be depicted as areas under the standard normal curve, you should always draw the curve and then equate the desired probability to an area.

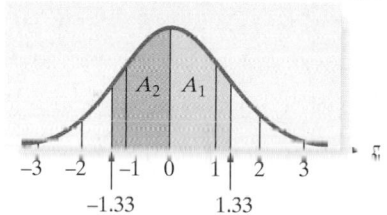

FIGURE 4.18

Areas under the standard normal curve for Example 4.15

In this example we want to find the probability that z falls between -1.33 and 1.33, which is equivalent to the area between -1.33 and 1.33, shown shaded in Figure 4.18. Table IV provides the area between $z = 0$ and any value of z, so that if we look up $z = 1.33$, we find that the area between $z = 0$ and $z = 1.33$ is .4082. (The value of 1.33 and the area of .4082 are both highlighted in Table 4.5.) This is the area labeled A_1 in Figure 4.18. To find the area A_2 located between $z = 0$ and $z = -1.33$, we note that the symmetry of the normal distribution implies that the area between $z = 0$ and any point to the left is equal to the area between $z = 0$ and the point equidistant to the right. Thus, in this example the area between $z = 0$ and $z = -1.33$ is equal to the area between $z = 0$ and $z = 1.33$. That is,

$$A_1 = A_2 = .4082$$

The probability that z falls between -1.33 and 1.33 is the sum of the areas of A_1 and A_2. We summarize in probabilistic notation:

$$P(-1.33 < z < 1.33) = P(-1.33 < z < 0) + P(0 < z < 1.33)$$
$$= A_1 + A_2 = .4082 + .4082 = .8164$$

Look Back Remember that "<" and "≤" are equivalent in events involving z, because the inclusion (or exclusion) of a single point does not alter the probability of an event involving a continuous random variable.

Now Work Exercise 4.87

EXAMPLE 4.16

Using the Standard
Normal Table to Find
$P(z > z_0)$

Problem Find the probability that a standard normal random variable exceeds 1.64; that is, find $P(z > 1.64)$.

Solution The area under the standard normal distribution to the right of 1.64 is the shaded area labeled A_1 in Figure 4.19. This area represents the desired probability that z exceeds 1.64. However, when we look up $z = 1.64$ in Table IV, we must remember that the probability given in the table corresponds to the area between $z = 0$ and $z = 1.64$ (the area labeled A_2 in Figure 4.19). From Table IV we find that $A_2 = .4495$. To find the area A_1 to the right of 1.64, we make use of two facts:

FIGURE 4.19
Areas under the standard normal curve for Example 4.16

1. The standard normal distribution is symmetric about its mean, $z = 0$.
2. The total area under the standard normal probability distribution equals 1.

Taken together, these two facts imply that the areas on either side of the mean $z = 0$ equal .5; thus, the area to the right of $z = 0$ in Figure 4.19 is $A_1 + A_2 = .5$. Then

$$P(z > 1.64) = A_1 = .5 - A_2 = .5 - .4495 = .0505$$

Look Back To attach some practical significance to this probability, note that the implication is that the chance of a standard normal random variable exceeding 1.64 is approximately .05.

Now Work Exercise 4.85a

EXAMPLE 4.17

Using the Standard
Normal Table to Find
$P(z < z_0)$

Problem Find the probability that a standard normal random variable lies to the left of .67.

Solution The event is shown as the highlighted area in Figure 4.20. We want to find $P(z < .67)$. We divide the highlighted area into two parts: the area A_1 between $z = 0$ and $z = .67$, and the area A_2 to the left of $z = 0$. We must always make such a division when the desired area lies on both sides of the mean ($z = 0$) because Table IV contains areas between $z = 0$ and the point you look up. We look up $z = .67$ in Table IV to find that $A_1 = .2486$. The symmetry of the standard normal distribution also implies that half the distribution lies on each side of the mean, so the area A_2 to the left of $z = 0$ is .5. Then

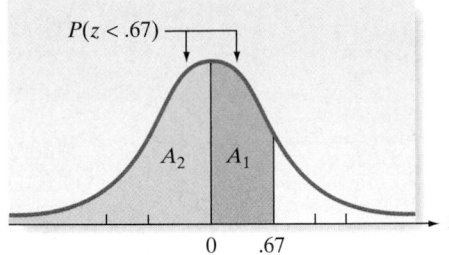

FIGURE 4.20
Areas under the standard normal curve for Example 4.17

$$P(z < .67) = A_1 + A_2 = .2486 + .5 = .7486$$

Look Back Note that this probability is approximately .75. Thus, about 75% of the time the standard normal random variable z will fall below .67. This implies that $z = .67$ represents the approximate 75th percentile for the distribution.

Now Work Exercise 4.86f

EXAMPLE 4.18

Using the Standard Normal Table to Find $P(|z| > z_0)$

Problem   Find the probability that a standard normal random variable exceeds 1.96 in absolute value.

Solution   We want to find

$$P(|z| > 1.96) = P(z < -1.96 \text{ or } z > 1.96)$$

FIGURE 4.21
Areas under the standard normal curve for Example 4.18

This probability is the shaded area in Figure 4.21. Note that the total shaded area is the sum of two areas, A_1 and A_2—areas that are equal because of the symmetry of the normal distribution.

We look up $z = 1.96$ and find the area between $z = 0$ and $z = 1.96$ to be .4750. Then the area to the right of $1.96, A_2$, is $.5 - .4750 = .0250$, so that

$$P(|z| > 1.96) = A_1 + A_2 = .0250 + .0250 = .05$$

Look Back   We emphasize, again, the importance of drawing the standard normal curve when finding normal probabilities.

To apply Table IV to a normal random variable x with any mean μ and any standard deviation σ, we must first convert the value of x to a z-score. The population z-score for a measurement was defined (in Section 2.7) as the *distance* between the measurement and the population mean, divided by the population standard deviation. Thus, the z-score gives the distance between a measurement and the mean in units equal to the standard deviation. In symbolic form, the z-score for the measurement x is

$$z = \frac{x - \mu}{\sigma}$$

Note that when $x = \mu$, we obtain $z = 0$.

An important property of the normal distribution is that if x is normally distributed with any mean and any standard deviation, z is always normally distributed with mean 0 and standard deviation 1. That is, z is a standard normal random variable.

Property of Normal Distributions

If x is a normal random variable with mean μ and standard deviation σ, then the random variable z, defined by the formula

$$z = \frac{x - \mu}{\sigma}$$

has a standard normal distribution. The value z describes the number of standard deviations between x and μ.

Recall from Example 4.18 that $P(|z| > 1.96) = .05$. This probability coupled with our interpretation of z implies that any normal random variable lies more than 1.96 standard deviations from its mean only 5% of the time. Compare this to the Empirical Rule (Chapter 2), which tells us that about 5% of the measurements in mound-shaped distributions will lie beyond 2 standard deviations from the mean. The normal distribution actually provides the model on which the Empirical Rule is based, along with much "empirical" experience with real data that often approximately obey the rule, whether drawn from a normal distribution or not.

EXAMPLE 4.19

Finding the Probability of a Normal Random Variable—Cell Phone Application

Problem Assume that the length of time, x, between charges of a cellular phone is normally distributed with a mean of 10 hours and a standard deviation of 1.5 hours. Find the probability that the cell phone will last between 8 and 12 hours between charges.

Solution The normal distribution with mean $\mu = 10$ and $\sigma = 1.5$ is shown in Figure 4.22. The desired probability that the charge lasts between 8 and 12 hours is shaded. In order to find the probability, we must first convert the distribution to standard normal, which we do by calculating the z-score:

$$z = \frac{x - \mu}{\sigma}$$

The z-scores corresponding to the important values of x are shown beneath the x values on the horizontal axis in Figure 4.22. Note that $z = 0$ corresponds to the mean of $\mu = 10$ hours, whereas the x values 8 and 12 yield z-scores of -1.33 and 1.33, respectively. Thus, the event that the cell phone charge lasts between 8 and 12 hours is equivalent to the event that a standard normal random variable lies between -1.33 and 1.33. We found this probability in Example 4.15 (see Figure 4.18) by doubling the area corresponding to $z = 1.33$ in Table IV. That is,

$$P(8 \le x \le 12) = P(-1.33 \le z \le 1.33) = 2(.4082) = .8164$$

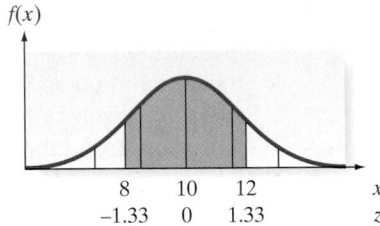

FIGURE 4.22
Areas under the normal curve for Example 4.19

Now Work Exercise 4.98a,b,c

The steps to follow when calculating a probability corresponding to a normal random variable are shown in the box.

Steps for Finding a Probability Corresponding to a Normal Random Variable

1. Sketch the normal distribution and indicate the mean of the random variable x. Then shade the area corresponding to the probability you want to find.

2. Convert the boundaries of the shaded area from x values to standard normal random variable z values using the formula

$$z = \frac{x - \mu}{\sigma}$$

Show the z values under the corresponding x values on your sketch.

3. Use Table IV in Appendix B to find the areas corresponding to the z values. If necessary, use the symmetry of the normal distribution to find areas corresponding to negative z values and the fact that the total area on each side of the mean equals .5 to convert the areas from Table IV to the probabilities of the event you have shaded.

Standard Normal Probabilities

Using the TI-83/TI-84 Graphing Calculator

Graphing the Area under the Standard Normal Curve

Step 1   *Turn off all plots.*

Press **2nd PRGM** and select **1:ClrDraw**
Press **ENTER** and "Done" will appear on the screen.
Press **2nd Y=** and select **4:PlotsOff**
Press **ENTER** and "Done" will appear on the screen.

Step 2   *Set the viewing window. (Recall that almost all of the area under the standard normal curve falls between −5 and 5. A height of 0.5 is a good choice for Ymax.)*

Note: When entering a negative number, be sure to use the negative sign (−), and not the minus sign.

Set **Xmin** = −5
Xmax = 5
Xscl = 1
Ymin = 0
Ymax = .5
Yscl = 0
Xres = 1

Step 3   *View graph.*

Press **2nd VARS**
Arrow right to **DRAW**
Press **ENTER** to select **1:ShadeNorm(**
Enter your lower limit
Press **COMMA**
Enter your upper limit
Press **)** Press **ENTER**
The graph will be displayed along with the area, lower limit, and upper limit.

Example   Using the standard normal curve, what is the probability that *z* is less than 1.5? In this example, set the window as shown in **Step 2.** For the limits in **Step 3,** use −5 for the lower limit and 1.5 for the upper limit.

The screens for this example are shown here.

Thus, $P(z < 1.5) = .9332$.

EXAMPLE 4.20

Using Normal Probabilities to Make an Inference about Advertised Gas Mileage

Problem   Suppose an automobile manufacturer introduces a new model that has an advertised mean in-city mileage of 27 miles per gallon. Although such advertisements seldom report any measure of variability, suppose you write the manufacturer for the details of the tests, and you find that the standard deviation is 3 miles per gallon. This information leads you to formulate a probability model for the random variable *x*, the in-city mileage for this car model. You believe that the probability distribution of *x* can be approximated by a normal distribution with a mean of 27 and a standard deviation of 3.

a. If you were to buy this model of automobile, what is the probability that you would purchase one that averages less than 20 miles per gallon for in-city driving? In other words, find $P(x < 20)$.

b. Suppose you purchase one of these new models and it does get less than 20 miles per gallon for in-city driving. Should you conclude that your probability model is incorrect?

FIGURE 4.23

Areas under the normal curve for Example 4.20

Solution

a. The probability model proposed for x, the in-city mileage, is shown in Figure 4.23.

We are interested in finding the area A to the left of 20 since this area corresponds to the probability that a measurement chosen from this distribution falls below 20. In other words, if this model is correct, the area A represents the fraction of cars that can be expected to get less than 20 miles per gallon for in-city driving. To find A, we first calculate the z value corresponding to $x = 20$. That is,

$$z = \frac{x - \mu}{\sigma} = \frac{20 - 27}{3} = -\frac{7}{3} = -2.33$$

Then

$$P(x < 20) = P(z < -2.33)$$

as indicated by the shaded area in Figure 4.23. Since Table IV gives only areas to the right of the mean (and because the normal distribution is symmetric about its mean), we look up 2.33 in Table IV and find that the corresponding area is .4901. This is equal to the area between $z = 0$ and $z = -2.33$, so we find

$$P(x < 20) = A = .5 - .4901 = .0099 \approx .01$$

According to this probability model, you should have only about a 1% chance of purchasing a car of this make with an in-city mileage under 20 miles per gallon.

b. Now you are asked to make an inference based on a sample—the car you purchased. You are getting less than 20 miles per gallon for in-city driving. What do you infer? We think you will agree that one of two possibilities is true:

1. The probability model is correct. You simply were unfortunate to have purchased one of the cars in the 1% that get less than 20 miles per gallon in the city.
2. The probability model is incorrect. Perhaps the assumption of a normal distribution is unwarranted or the mean of 27 is an overestimate, or the standard deviation of 3 is an underestimate, or some combination of these errors was made. At any rate, the form of the actual probability model certainly merits further investigation.

You have no way of knowing with certainty which possibility is correct, but the evidence points to the second one. We are again relying on the rare-event approach to statistical inference that we introduced earlier. The sample (one measurement in this case) was so unlikely to have been drawn from the proposed probability model that it casts serious doubt on the model. We would be inclined to believe that the model is somehow in error.

Look Back When applying the rare event approach, the calculated probability must be small (say, less than or equal to .05) in order to infer that the observed event is, indeed, unlikely.

Now Work Exercise 4.98d

Occasionally you will be given a probability and will want to find the values of the normal random variable that correspond to the probability. For example, suppose the scores on a college entrance examination are known to be normally distributed, and a certain prestigious university will consider for admission only those applicants whose scores exceed the 90th percentile of the test score distribution. To determine the minimum score for admission consideration, you will need to be able to use Table IV in reverse, as demonstrated in the following example.

EXAMPLE 4.21

Using the Normal Table in Reverse

Problem Find the value of z, call it z_0, in the standard normal distribution that will be exceeded only 10% of the time—that is, find z_0 such that $P(z \ge z_0) = .10$.

.2090

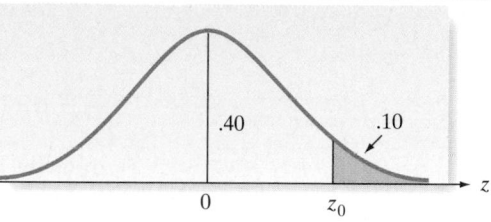

FIGURE 4.24
Area under the standard normal curve for Example 4.21

Solution In this case we are given a probability, or an area, and asked to find the value of the standard normal random variable that corresponds to the area. Specifically, we want to find the value z_0 such that only 10% of the standard normal distribution exceeds z_0 (see Figure 4.24).

We know that the total area to the right of the mean $z = 0$ is .5, which implies that z_0 must lie to the right of (above) 0. To pinpoint the value, we use the fact that the area to the right of z_0 is .10, which implies that the area between $z = 0$ and z_0 is $.5 - .1 = .4$. But areas between $z = 0$ and some other z value are exactly the types given in Table IV. Therefore, we look up the area .4000 in the body of Table IV and find that the corresponding z value is (to the closest approximation) $z_0 = 1.28$. The implication is that the point 1.28 standard deviations above the mean is the 90th percentile of a normal distribution.

Look Back As with earlier problems, it is critical to draw correctly the normal probability of interest on the normal curve. Placement of z_0 to the left or right of 0 is the key. Be sure to shade the probability (area) involving z_0. If it does not agree with the probability of interest (i.e., the shaded area is greater than .5 and the probability of interest is smaller than .5), then you need to place z_0 on the opposite side of 0.

Now Work Exercise 4.89

EXAMPLE 4.22

Using the Normal Table in Reverse

Problem Find the value of z_0 such that 95% of the standard normal z values lie between $-z_0$ and z_0; that is, $P(-z_0 < z \le z_0) = .95$.

Solution Here we wish to move an equal distance z_0 in the positive and negative directions from the mean $z = 0$ until 95% of the standard normal distribution is enclosed. This means that the area on each side of the mean will be equal to $\frac{1}{2}(.95) = .475$, as shown in Figure 4.25. Since the area between $z = 0$ and z_0 is .475, we look up .475 in the body of Table IV to find the value $z_0 = 1.96$. Thus, as we found in the reverse order in Example 4.18, 95% of a normal distribution lies between -1.96 and 1.96 standard deviations of the mean.

FIGURE 4.25
Areas under the standard normal curve for Example 4.22

Now Work Exercise 4.94

Now that you have learned to use Table IV to find a standard normal z value that corresponds to a specified probability, we demonstrate a practical application in Example 4.23.

EXAMPLE 4.23

Using the Normal
Table in Reverse—
Paint Manufacturing
Application

Problem Suppose a paint manufacturer has a daily production, x, that is normally distributed with a mean of 100,000 gallons and a standard deviation of 10,000 gallons. Management wants to create an incentive bonus for the production crew when the daily production exceeds the 90th percentile of the distribution, in hopes that the crew will, in turn, become more productive. At what level of production should management pay the incentive bonus?

Solution In this example, we want to find a production level, x_0, such that 90% of the daily levels (x values) in the distribution fall below x_0 and only 10% fall above x_0—that is,

$$P(x \leq x_0) = .90$$

Converting x to a standard normal random variable, where $\mu = 100{,}000$ and $\sigma = 10{,}000$, we have

$$P(x \leq x_0) = P\left(z \leq \frac{x_0 - \mu}{\sigma}\right)$$

$$= P\left(z \leq \frac{x_0 - 100{,}000}{10{,}000}\right) = .90$$

In Example 4.21 (see Figure 4.24) we found the 90th percentile of the standard normal distribution to be $z_0 = 1.28$—that is, we found $P(z \leq 1.28) = .90$. Consequently, we know the production level x_0 at which the incentive bonus is paid corresponds to a z-score of 1.28; that is,

$$\frac{x_0 - 100{,}000}{10{,}000} = 1.28$$

If we solve this equation for x_0, we find

$$x_0 = 100{,}000 + 1.28(10{,}000) = 100{,}000 + 12{,}800 = 112{,}800$$

This x value is shown in Figure 4.26. Thus, the 90th percentile of the production distribution is 112,800 gallons. Management should pay an incentive bonus when a day's production exceeds this level if its objective is to pay only when production is in the top 10% of the current daily production distribution.

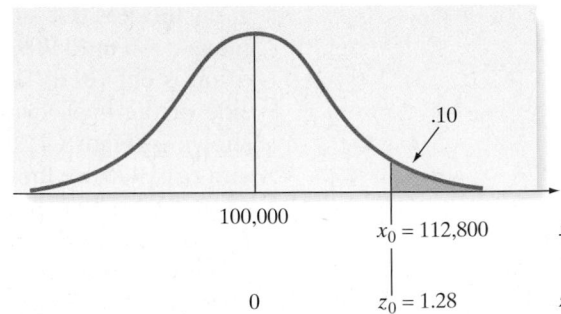

FIGURE 4.26
Area under the normal curve
for Example 4.23

Look Back As this example shows, in practical applications of the normal table in reverse, first find the value of z_0, then convert the value to the units of x using the z-score formula in reverse.

STATISTICS IN ACTION REVISITED

I WANT YOU
FOR U.S. ARMY
NEAREST RECRUITING STATION

Using the Normal Model to Maximize the Probability of a Hit with the Super Weapon

Recall that a defense contractor has developed a prototype gun for the U.S. Army that fires 1,100 flechettes with a single round. The specifications of the weapon are set so that when the gun is aimed at a target 500 meters away, the mean horizontal grid value of the flechettes is equal to the aim point. In the range test, the weapon was aimed at the center target in Figure SIA4.1 (p. 189); thus, $\mu = 5$ feet. For three different tests, the standard deviation was set at $\sigma = 1$ feet, $\sigma = 2$ feet, and $\sigma = 4$ feet. From past experience, the defense contractor has found that the distribution of the horizontal hit point measurements is closely approximated by a normal distribution. Therefore, we can use the normal distribution to find the probability that a single flechette shot from the weapon will hit any one of the three targets. Recall from Figure SIA4.1 (p. 189) that the three targets range from -1 to 1, 4 to 6, and 9 to 11 feet on the horizontal grid.

Consider, first, the middle target. Letting x represent the horizontal measurement for a flechette shot from the gun, the flechette will hit the target if $4 \le x \le 6$. The probability that this flechette will hit the target when $\mu = 5$ and $\sigma = 1$ is, using the normal probability table (Table IV, Appendix B),

Middle:
$\sigma = 1$
$$P(4 \le x \le 6) = P\left(\frac{4-5}{1} < z < \frac{6-5}{1}\right)$$
$$= P(-1 < z < 1)$$
$$= 2(.3413) = .6826$$

Similarly, we find the probability that the flechette hits the left and right targets shown in Figure SIA4.1.

Left:
$\sigma = 1$
$$P(-1 \le x \le 1) = P\left(\frac{-1-5}{1} < z < \frac{1-5}{1}\right)$$
$$= P(-6 < z < -4) \approx 0$$

Right:
$\sigma = 1$
$$P(9 \le x \le 11) = P\left(\frac{9-5}{1} < z < \frac{11-5}{1}\right)$$
$$= P(4 < z < 6) \approx 0$$

You can see that there is about a 68% chance that a flechette will hit the middle target but virtually no chance that one will hit the left and right targets when the standard deviation is set at 1 foot.

To find these three probabilities for $\sigma = 2$ and $\sigma = 4$, we use the normal probability function in MINITAB. Figure SIA4.2 is a MINITAB worksheet giving the cumulative probabilities of a normal random variable (with $\mu = 5, \sigma = 1$) falling below the x-values in the first column. The cumulative probabilities for $\sigma = 2$ and $\sigma = 4$ are given in the columns named "sigma2" and "sigma4," respectively.

Using the cumulative probabilities in the figure to find the three probabilities when $\sigma = 2$, we have

Middle:
$\sigma = 2$
$$P(4 \le x \le 6) = P(x \le 6) - P(x \le 4)$$
$$= .6915 - .3085 = .3830$$

Left:
$\sigma = 2$
$$P(-1 \le x \le 1) = P(x \le 1) - P(x \le -1)$$
$$= .0227 - .0013 = .0214$$

Right:
$\sigma = 2$
$$P(9 \le x \le 11) = P(x \le 11) - P(x \le 9)$$
$$= .9987 - .9773 = .0214$$

Thus, when $\sigma = 2$, there is about a 38% chance that a flechette will hit the middle target, a 2% chance that one will hit the left target, and a 2% chance that one will hit the right target. The probability that a flechette will hit either the middle or left or right target is simply the sum of these three probabilities (an application of the Additive Rule of probability). This sum is $.3830 + .0214 + .0214 = .4258$; consequently, there is about a 42% chance of hitting any one of the three targets when specifications are set so that $\sigma = 2$.

Figure SIA4.2

MINITAB worksheet with cumulative normal probabilities

↓	C1	C2	C3	C4	C5
	x	sigma1	sigma2	sigma4	
1	-1	0.00000	0.001350	0.066807	
2	1	0.00003	0.022750	0.158655	
3	4	0.15866	0.308538	0.401294	
4	6	0.84134	0.691462	0.598706	
5	9	0.99997	0.977250	0.841345	
6	11	1.00000	0.998650	0.933193	
7					

Continued

Now, we use the cumulative probabilities in Figure SIA4.2 to find the three hit probabilities when $\sigma = 4$:

Middle:
$\sigma = 4$
$P(4 \leq x \leq 6) = P(x \leq 6) - P(x \leq 4)$
$= .5987 - .4013 = .1974$

Left:
$\sigma = 4$
$P(-1 \leq x \leq 1) = P(x \leq 1) - P(x \leq -1)$
$= .1587 - .0668 = .0919$

Right:
$\sigma = 9$
$P(9 \leq x \leq 11) = P(x \leq 11) - P(x \leq 9)$
$= .9332 - .8413 = .0919$

Thus, when $\sigma = 4$, there is about a 20% chance that a flechette will hit the middle target, a 9% chance that one will hit the left target, and a 9% chance that one

will hit the right target. The probability that a flechette will hit any one of the three targets is $.1974 + .0919 + .0919 = .3812$.

These probability calculations reveal a few patterns. First, the probability of hitting the middle target (the target where the gun is aimed) is reduced as the standard deviation is increased. Obviously, if the U.S. Army wants to maximize the chance of hitting the target that the prototype gun is aimed at, it will want specifications set with a small value of σ. But if the Army wants to hit multiple targets with a single shot of the weapon, σ should be increased. With a larger σ, not as many of the flechettes will hit the target aimed at, but more will hit peripheral targets. Whether σ should be set at 4 or 6 (or some other value) depends on how high of a hit rate is required for the peripheral targets.

Exercises 4.84–4.110

Learning the Mechanics

4.84 Find the area under the standard normal probability distribution between the following pairs of z-scores:
  a. $z = 0$ and $z = 2.00$ **b.** $z = 0$ and $z = 3$
  c. $z = 0$ and $z = 1.5$ **d.** $z = 0$ and $z = .80$

4.85 Find the following probabilities for the standard normal random variable z:
NW   **a.** $P(z > 1.46)$ **b.** $P(z < -1.56)$
  c. $P(.67 \leq z \leq 2.41)$ **d.** $P(-1.96 \leq z < -.33)$
  e. $P(z \geq 0)$ **f.** $P(-2.33 < z < 1.50)$

4.86 Find the following probabilities for the standard normal random variable z:
  a. $P(-1 \leq z \leq 1)$ **b.** $P(-2 \leq z \leq 2)$
  c. $P(-2.16 \leq z \leq .55)$ **d.** $P(-.42 < z < 1.96)$
  e. $P(z \geq -2.33)$ **NW f.** $P(z < 2.33)$

4.87 Find each of the following probabilities for the standard
NW   normal random variable z:
  a. $P(-1 \leq z \leq 1)$ **b.** $P(-1.96 \leq z \leq 1.96)$
  c. $P(-1.645 \leq z \leq 1.645)$ **d.** $P(-2 \leq z \leq 2)$

4.88 Find each of the following probabilities for a standard normal random variable z:
  a. $P(z = 1)$ **b.** $P(z \leq 1)$
  c. $P(z < 1)$ **d.** $P(z > 1)$

4.89 Find a value of the standard normal random variable z,
NW   call it z_0, such that
  a. $P(z \leq z_0) = .2090$
  b. $P(z \leq z_0) = .7090$
  c. $P(-z_0 \leq z < z_0) = .8472$
  d. $P(-z_0 \leq z \leq z_0) = .1664$
  e. $P(z_0 \leq z \leq 0) = .4798$
  f. $P(-1 < z < z_0) = .5328$

4.90 Find a value of the standard normal random variable z, call it z_0, such that
  a. $P(z \geq z_0) = .05$
  b. $P(z \geq z_0) = .025$
  c. $P(z \leq z_0) = .025$

  d. $P(z \geq z_0) = .10$
  e. $P(z > z_0) = .10$

4.91 Suppose the random variable x is best described by a normal distribution with $\mu = 30$ and $\sigma = 4$. Find the z-score that corresponds to each of the following x values:
  a. $x = 20$ **b.** $x = 30$
  c. $x = 27.5$ **d.** $x = 15$
  e. $x = 35$ **f.** $x = 25$

4.92 Give the z-score for a measurement from a normal distribution for the following:
  a. 1 standard deviation above the mean
  b. 1 standard deviation below the mean
  c. Equal to the mean
  d. 2.5 standard deviations below the mean
  e. 3 standard deviations above the mean

4.93 Suppose x is a normally distributed random variable with $\mu = 11$ and $\sigma = 2$. Find each of the following:
  a. $P(10 \leq x \leq 12)$ **b.** $P(6 \leq x \leq 10)$
  c. $P(13 \leq x \leq 16)$ **d.** $P(7.8 \leq x \leq 12.6)$
  e. $P(x \geq 13.24)$ **f.** $P(x \geq 7.62)$

4.94 The random variable x has a normal distribution with
NW $\mu = 1{,}000$ and $\sigma = 10$.
  a. Find the probability that x assumes a value more than 2 standard deviations from its mean. More than 3 standard deviations from μ.
  b. Find the probability that x assumes a value within 1 standard deviation of its mean. Within 2 standard deviations of μ.
  c. Find the value of x that represents the 80th percentile of this distribution. The 10th percentile.

4.95 Suppose x is a normally distributed random variable with mean 120 and variance 36. Draw a rough graph of the distribution of x. Locate μ and the interval $\mu \pm 2\sigma$ on the graph. Find the following probabilities:
  a. $P(\mu - 2\sigma \leq x \leq \mu + 2\sigma)$ **b.** $P(x \geq 128)$
  c. $P(x \leq 108)$ **d.** $P(112 \leq x \leq 130)$

e. $P(114 \le x \le 116)$ **f.** $P(115 \le x \le 128)$

4.96 Suppose x is a normally distributed random variable with $\mu = 50$ and $\sigma = 3$. Find a value of the random variable, call it x_0, such that

a. $P(x \le x_0) = .8413$

b. $P(x > x_0) = .025$

c. $P(x > x_0) = .95$

d. $P(41 \le x < x_0) = .8630$

e. 10% of the values of x are less than x_0.

f. 1% of the values of x are greater than x_0.

APPLET   Applet Exercise 4.8

Open the applet entitled *Sample from a Population*. On the pull-down menu to the right of the top graph, select *Bell shaped*. The box to the left of the top graph displays the population mean, median, and standard deviation.

a. Run the applet for each available value of n on the pull-down menu for the sample size. Go from the smallest to the largest value of n. For each value of n, observe the shape of the graph of the sample data and record the mean, median, and standard deviation of the sample.

b. Describe what happens to the shape of the graph and the mean, median, and standard deviation of the sample as the sample size increases.

Applying the Concepts—Basic

WPOWER50

4.97 Most powerful women in America. Refer to the *Fortune* (Nov. 14, 2005) list of the 50 most powerful women in America, Exercise 2.45 (p.72). Recall that the data on age (in years) of each woman is stored in the **WPOWER50** file. The ages in the data set can be shown to be approximately normally distributed with a mean of 50 years and a standard deviation of 5.3 years. A powerful woman is randomly selected from the data and her age is observed.

a. Find the probability that her age will fall between 55 and 60 years.

b. Find the probability that her age will fall between 48 and 52 years.

c. Find the probability that her age will be less than 35 years.

d. Find the probability that her age will exceed 40 years.

4.98 The business of casino gaming. Casino gaming yields over $35 billion in revenue each year in the United States. In *Chance* (Spring 2005), University of Denver statistician R. C. Hannum discussed the business of casino gaming and its reliance on the laws of probability. Casino games of pure chance (e.g., craps, roulette, baccarat, and keno) always yield a "house advantage." For example, in the game of double-zero roulette, the expected casino win percentage is 5.26% on bets made on whether the outcome will be either black or red. (This implies that for every $5 bet on black or red, the casino will earn a net of about 25 cents.) It can be shown that in 100 roulette plays on black/red, the average casino win percentage is normally distributed with mean 5.26% and standard deviation 10%. Let x represent the average casino win percentage after 100 bets on black/red in double-zero roulette.

a. Find $P(x > 0)$. (This is the probability that the casino wins money.)

b. Find $P(5 < x < 15)$.

c. Find $P(x < 1)$.

d. If you observed an average casino win percentage of -25% after 100 roulette bets on black/red, what would you conclude?

DDT

4.99 Fish contaminated by a plant's discharge. Refer to the U.S. Army Corps of Engineers data on contaminated fish in the Tennessee River, saved in the **DDT** file. Recall that one of the variables measured for each captured fish is weight (in grams). The weights in the data set can be shown to be approximately normally distributed with a mean of 1,050 grams and a standard deviation of 375 grams. An observation is randomly selected from the data and the fish weight is observed.

a. Find the probability that the weight will fall between 1,000 and 1,400 grams.

b. Find the probability that the weight will fall between 800 and 1,000 grams.

c. Find the probability that the weight will be less than 1,750 grams.

d. Find the probability that the weight will exceed 500 grams.

CRASH

4.100 NHTSA crash safety tests. Refer to Exercise 4.19 (p. 201) and the National Highway Traffic Safety Administration (NHTSA) crash test data for new cars. One of the variables saved in the **CRASH** file is the severity of a driver's head injury when the car is in a head-on collision with a fixed barrier while traveling at 35 miles per hour. The more points assigned to the head injury rating, the more severe the injury. The head injury ratings can be shown to be approximately normally distributed with a mean of 605 points and a standard deviation of 185 points. One of the crash-tested cars is randomly selected from the data and the driver's head injury rating is observed.

a. Find the probability that the rating will fall between 500 and 700 points.

b. Find the probability that the rating will fall between 400 and 500 points.

c. Find the probability that the rating will be less than 850 points.

d. Find the probability that the rating will exceed 1,000 points.

4.101 Transmission delays in wireless technology. Resource reservation protocol (RSVP) was originally designed to establish signaling links for stationary networks. In *Mobile Networks and Applications* (Dec. 2003), RSVP was applied to mobile wireless technology (e.g., a PC notebook with wireless LAN card for Internet access). A simulation study revealed that the transmission delay (measured in milliseconds) of an RSVP linked wireless device has an approximate normal distribution with mean $\mu = 48.5$ milliseconds and $\sigma = 8.5$ milliseconds.

a. What is the probability that the transmission delay is less than 57 milliseconds?

b. What is the probability that the transmission delay is between 40 and 60 milliseconds?

Applying the Concepts—Intermediate

4.102 Cotton crop yield study. The crop yield for a particular farm in a particular year is typically measured as the amount of the crop produced per acre. For example, cotton is measured in pounds per acre. It has been demonstrated that the normal distribution can be used to characterize crop yields over time (*American Journal of Agricultural Economics*, May 1999). Historical data indicate that next summer's cotton yield for a particular Georgia farmer can be characterized by a normal distribution with mean 1,500 pounds per acre and standard deviation 250. The farm in question will be profitable if it produces at least 1,600 pounds per acre.

a. What is the probability that the farm will lose money next summer?

b. Assume the same normal distribution is appropriate for describing cotton yield in each of the next two summers. Also assume that the two yields are statistically independent. What is the probability that the farm will lose money for two straight years?

c. What is the probability that the cotton yield falls within 2 standard deviations of 1,500 pounds per acre next summer?

4.103 **Airline flight assignment problem.** The problem of matching aircraft to passenger demand on each flight leg is called the *flight assignment problem* in the airline industry. *Spill* is defined as the number of passengers not carried because the aircraft's capacity is insufficient. A solution to the flight assignment problem at Delta Airlines was published in *Interfaces* (Jan.–Feb. 1994). The authors—four Delta Airlines researchers and a Georgia Tech professor (Roy Marsten)—demonstrated their approach with an example in which passenger demand for a particular flight leg is normally distributed with a mean of 125 passengers and a standard deviation of 45. Consider a Boeing 727 with a capacity of 148 passengers and a Boeing 757 with a capacity of 182.

a. What is the probability that passenger demand will exceed the capacity of the Boeing 727? The Boeing 757?

b. If the 727 is assigned to the flight leg, what is the probability that the flight will depart with one or more empty seats? Answer the same question for the Boeing 757.

c. If the 727 is assigned to the flight, what is the probability that the spill will be more than 100 passengers?

4.104 **Manufacturing hourly pay rate.** Government data indicate that the mean hourly wage for manufacturing workers in the United States is $16 (*Statistical Abstract of the United States: 2006*). Suppose the distribution of manufacturing wage rates nationwide can be approximated by a normal distribution with standard deviation $1.25 per hour. The first manufacturing firm contacted by a particular worker seeking a new job pays $17.30 per hour.

a. If the worker were to undertake a nationwide job search, approximately what proportion of the wage rates would be greater than $17.30 per hour?

b. If the worker were to randomly select a U.S. manufacturing firm, what is the probability the firm would pay more than $17.30 per hour?

c. The population median, call it η, of a continuous random variable x is the value such that $P(x \geq \eta) = P(x \leq \eta) = .5$—that is, the median is the value η such that half the area under the probability distribution lies above η and half lies below it. Find the median of the random variable corresponding to the wage rate and compare it to the mean wage rate.

4.105 **Personnel dexterity tests.** Personnel tests are designed to test a job applicant's cognitive and/or physical abilities. An IQ test is an example of the former; a speed test involving the arrangement of pegs on a peg board is an example of the latter (Cowling and James, *The Essence of Personnel Management and Industrial Relations*, 1994). A particular dexterity test is administered nationwide by a private testing service. It is known that for all tests administered last year, the distribution of scores was approximately normal with mean 75 and standard deviation 7.5.

a. A particular employer requires job candidates to score at least 80 on the dexterity test. Approximately what percentage of the test scores during the past year exceeded 80?

b. The testing service reported to a particular employer that one of its job candidate's scores fell at the 98th percentile of the distribution (i.e., approximately 98% of the scores were lower than the candidate's, and only 2% were higher). What was the candidate's score?

4.106 **Model for long-term construction cost.** Before negotiating a long-term construction contract, building contractors must carefully estimate the total cost of completing the project. Benzion Barlev of New York University proposed a model for total cost of a long-term contract based on the normal distribution (*Journal of Business Finance and Accounting*, July 1995). For one particular construction contract, Barlev assumed total cost, x, to be normally distributed with mean $850,000 and standard deviation $170,000. The revenue, R, promised to the contractor is $1,000,000.

a. The contract will be profitable if revenue exceeds total cost. What is the probability that the contract will be profitable for the contractor?

b. What is the probability that the project will result in a loss for the contractor?

c. Suppose the contractor has the opportunity to renegotiate the contract. What value of R should the contractor strive for in order to have a .99 probability of making a profit?

4.107 **Evaluating a stock's performance.** The *monthly rate of return* of a stock is a measure investors frequently use for evaluating the behavior of a stock over time. A stock's monthly rate of return generally reflects the amount of money an investor makes (or loses if the return is negative) for every dollar invested in the stock in a given month. In his classic text, *Foundations of Finance* (1976), Eugene Fama demonstrated that the probability distribution for the monthly rate of return of a stock can be approximated by a normal probability distribution. Suppose the monthly rates of return to stock ABC are normally distributed with mean .05 and standard deviation .03, and the monthly rates of return to stock XYZ are normally distributed with mean .07 and standard deviation .05. Assume that you have $100 invested in each stock.

a. Over the long run, which stock will yield the higher average monthly rate of return? Why?

b. Suppose you plan to hold each stock for only one month. What is the expected value of each investment at the end of one month?

c. Which stock offers greater protection against incurring a loss on your investment next month? Why?

Applying the Concepts—Advanced

4.108 Industrial filling process. The characteristics of an industrial filling process in which an expensive liquid is injected into a container was investigated in *Journal of Quality Technology* (July 1999). The quantity injected per container is approximately normally distributed with mean 10 units and standard deviation .2 units. Each unit of fill costs $20 per unit. If a container contains less than 10 units (i.e., is underfilled), it must be reprocessed at a cost of $10. A properly filled container sells for $230.

  a. Find the probability that a container is underfilled. Not underfilled.

  b. A container is initially underfilled and must be reprocessed. Upon refilling, it contains 10.60 units. How much profit will the company make on this container?

  c. The operations manager adjusts the mean of the filling process upward to 10.10 units in order to make the probability of underfilling approximately zero. Under these conditions, what is the expected profit per container?

4.109 Dye discharged in paint. A machine used to regulate the amount of dye dispensed for mixing shades of paint can be set so that it discharges an average of μ milliliters (mL) of dye per can of paint. The amount of dye discharged is known to have a normal distribution with a standard deviation of .4 mL. If more than 6 mL of dye are discharged when making a certain shade of blue paint, the shade is unacceptable. Determine the setting for μ so that only 1% of the cans of paint will be unacceptable.

4.110 Box plots and the standard normal distribution. What relationship exists between the standard normal distribution and the box-plot methodology (optional Section 2.8) for describing distributions of data using quartiles? The answer depends on the true underlying probability distribution of the data. Assume for the remainder of this exercise that the distribution is normal.

  a. Calculate the values of the standard normal random variable z, call them z_L and z_U, that correspond to the hinges of the box plot—that is, the lower and upper quartiles, Q_L and Q_U—of the probability distribution.

  b. Calculate the z values that correspond to the inner fences of the box plot for a normal probability distribution.

  c. Calculate the z values that correspond to the outer fences of the box plot for a normal probability distribution.

  d. What is the probability that an observation lies beyond the inner fences of a normal probability distribution? The outer fences?

  e. Can you better understand why the inner and outer fences of a box plot are used to detect outliers in a distribution? Explain.

4.8 Descriptive Methods for Assessing Normality

In the chapters that follow, we learn how to make inferences about the population based on information in the sample. Several of these techniques are based on the assumption that the population is approximately normally distributed. Consequently, it will be important to determine whether the sample data come from a normal population before we can properly apply these techniques.

Several descriptive methods can be used to check for normality. In this section, we consider the four methods summarized in the box.

Determining Whether the Data Are from an Approximately Normal Distribution

1. Construct either a histogram or stem-and-leaf display for the data and note the shape of the graph. If the data are approximately normal, the shape of the histogram or stem-and-leaf display will be similar to the normal curve, Figure 4.15 (i.e., mound-shaped and symmetric about the mean).

2. Compute the intervals $\bar{x} \pm s$, $\bar{x} \pm 2s$, and $\bar{x} \pm 3s$, and determine the percentage of measurements falling in each. If the data are approximately normal, the percentages will be approximately equal to 68%, 95%, and 100%, respectively.

3. Find the interquartile range, IQR, and standard deviation, s, for the sample, then calculate the ratio IQR/s. If the data are approximately normal, then IQR/$s \approx 1.3$.

4. Construct a *normal probability plot* for the data. If the data are approximately normal, the points will fall (approximately) on a straight line.

The first two methods come directly from the properties of a normal distribution established in Section 4.7. Method 3 is based on the fact that for normal distributions, the z values corresponding to the 25th and 75th percentiles are $-.67$ and $.67$, respectively (see Example 4.17). Since $\sigma = 1$ for a standard normal distribution,

$$\frac{\text{IQR}}{\sigma} = \frac{Q_U - Q_L}{\sigma} = \frac{.67 - (-.67)}{1} = 1.34$$

The final descriptive method for checking normality is based on a *normal probability plot*. In such a plot, the observations in a data set are ordered from smallest to largest and then plotted against the expected z-scores of observations calculated under the assumption that the data come from a normal distribution. When the data are, in fact, normally distributed, a linear (straight-line) trend will result. A nonlinear trend in the plot suggests that the data are nonnormal.

Definition 4.9

A **normal probability plot** for a data set is a scatterplot with the ranked data values on one axis and their corresponding expected z-scores from a standard normal distribution on the other axis. [*Note:* Computation of the expected standard normal z-scores are beyond the scope of this text. Therefore, we will rely on available statistical software packages to generate a normal probability plot.]

EXAMPLE 4.24

Checking for Normal Data—EPA Estimated Gas Mileages

Problem   The Environmental Protection Agency (EPA) performs extensive tests on all new car models to determine their mileage ratings. The results of 100 EPA tests on a certain new car model are displayed in Table 4.6. Numerical and graphical descriptive measures for the data are shown on the MINITAB and SPSS printouts, Figures 4.27(a)–(c). Determine whether the EPA mileage ratings are from an approximate normal distribution.

 EPAGAS

TABLE 4.6   EPA Gas Mileage Ratings for 100 Cars (miles per gallon)

36.3	41.0	36.9	37.1	44.9	36.8	30.0	37.2	42.1	36.7
32.7	37.3	41.2	36.6	32.9	36.5	33.2	37.4	37.5	33.6
40.5	36.5	37.6	33.9	40.2	36.4	37.7	37.7	40.0	34.2
36.2	37.9	36.0	37.9	35.9	38.2	38.3	35.7	35.6	35.1
38.5	39.0	35.5	34.8	38.6	39.4	35.3	34.4	38.8	39.7
36.3	36.8	32.5	36.4	40.5	36.6	36.1	38.2	38.4	39.3
41.0	31.8	37.3	33.1	37.0	37.6	37.0	38.7	39.0	35.8
37.0	37.2	40.7	37.4	37.1	37.8	35.9	35.6	36.7	34.5
37.1	40.3	36.7	37.0	33.9	40.1	38.0	35.2	34.8	39.5
39.9	36.9	32.9	33.8	39.8	34.0	36.8	35.0	38.1	36.9

FIGURE 4.27a
MINITAB histogram for gas mileage data

Descriptive Statistics: MPG

Variable	N	Mean	StDev	Minimum	Q1	Median	Q3	Maximum
MPG	100	36.994	2.418	30.000	35.625	37.000	38.375	44.900

FIGURE 4.27b
MINITAB descriptive statistics for gas mileage data

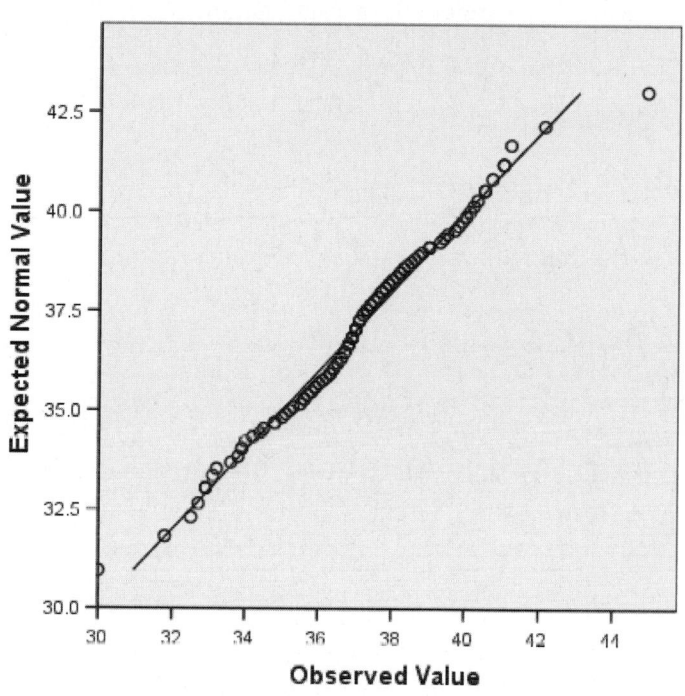

Normal Q-Q Plot of MPG

FIGURE 4.27c

SPSS normal probability plot for gas mileage data

Solution   As a first check, we examine the MINITAB histogram of the data shown in Figure 4.27(a). Clearly, the mileages fall in an approximately mound-shaped, symmetric distribution centered around the mean of approximately 37 mpg. Note that a normal curve is superimposed on the figure. Therefore, using check #1 in the box, the data appear to be approximately normal.

To apply check #2, we obtain $\bar{x} - 37$ and $s = 2.4$ from the MINITAB printout, Figure 4.27(b). The intervals $\bar{x} \pm s, \bar{x} \pm 2s$, and $\bar{x} \pm 3s$, are shown in Table 4.7, as well as the percentage of mileage ratings that fall in each interval. These percentages agree almost exactly with those from a normal distribution.

Check #3 in the box requires that we find the ratio IQR/s. From Figure 4.27(b), the 25th percentile (called Q_1 by MINITAB) is $Q_L = 35.625$ and the 75th percentile (labeled Q_3 by MINITAB) is $Q_U = 38.375$. Then, IQR $= Q_U - Q_L = 2.75$ and the ratio is

$$\frac{IQR}{s} = \frac{2.75}{2.4} = 1.15$$

Since this value is approximately equal to 1.3, we have further confirmation that the data are approximately normal.

TABLE 4.7   Describing the 100 EPA Mileage Ratings

Interval	Percentage in Interval
$\bar{x} \pm s = (34.6, 39.4)$	68
$\bar{x} \pm 2s = (32.2, 41.8)$	96
$\bar{x} \pm 3s = (29.8, 44.2)$	99

A fourth descriptive method is to interpret a normal probability plot. An SPSS normal probability plot for the mileage data is shown in Figure 4.27(c). Notice that the ordered mileage values (shown on the horizontal axis) fall reasonably close to a straight line when plotted against the expected z-scores from a normal distribution. Thus, check #4 also suggests that the EPA mileage data are likely to be approximately normally distributed.

Look Back The checks for normality given in the box are simple, yet powerful, techniques to apply, but they are only descriptive in nature. It is possible (although unlikely) that the data are nonnormal even when the checks are reasonably satisfied. Thus, we should be careful not to claim that the 100 EPA mileage ratings of Example 4.24 are, in fact, normally distributed. We can only state that it is reasonable to believe that the data are from a normal distribution.*

Now Work Exercise 4.114

As we will learn in the next chapter, several inferential methods of analysis require the data to be approximately normal. If the data are clearly nonnormal, inferences derived from the method may be invalid. Therefore, it is advisable to check the normality of the data prior to conducting the analysis.

STATISTICS IN ACTION REVISITED

Assessing Whether the Normal Distribution Is Appropriate for Modeling the Super Weapon Hit Data

In Statistics in Action Revisited, Section 4.7, we used the normal distribution to find the probability that a single flechette from a super weapon that shoots 1,100 flechettes at once hits one of three targets at 500 meters. Recall that for three range tests, the weapon was always aimed at the center target (i.e., the specification mean was set at $\mu = 5$ feet), but the specification standard deviation was varied at $\sigma = 1$ foot, $\sigma = 2$ feet, and $\sigma = 4$ feet. Table SIA4.1 shows the calculated normal probabilities of hitting the three targets for the different values of σ, as well as the actual results of the three range tests. (Recall that the actual data are saved in the **MOAGUN** file.) You can see that the proportion of the 1,100 flechettes that actually hit each target—called the *hit ratio*—agrees very well with the estimated probability of a hit using the normal distribution.

Consequently, it appears that our assumption that the horizontal hit measurements are approximately normally distributed is reasonably satisfied. Further evidence of this is provided by the MINITAB histograms of the horizontal hit measurements shown in Figures SIA4.3(a)–(c). The normal curves superimposed on the histograms fit the data very well.

 MOAGUN

TABLE SIA4.1 **Summary of Normal Probability Calculations and Actual Range Test Results**

TARGET	Specification	Normal Probability	Actual Number of Hits	Hit Ratio (Hits/1100)
LEFT (−1 to 1)	$\sigma = 1$	.0000	0	.000
	$\sigma = 2$	.0214	30	.027
	$\sigma = 4$	.0919	73	.066
MIDDLE (4 to 6)	$\sigma = 1$	.6826	764	.695
	$\sigma = 2$	.3820	409	.372
	$\sigma = 4$	.1974	242	.220
RIGHT (9 to 11)	$\sigma = 1$	.0000	0	.000
	$\sigma = 2$	.0214	23	.021
	$\sigma = 4$	.0919	93	.085

*Statistical tests of normality that provide a measure of reliability for the inference are available. However, these tests tend to be very sensitive to slight departures from normality (i.e., they tend to reject the hypothesis of normality for any distribution that is not perfectly symmetrical and mound shaped). Consult the references (see Ramsey & Ramsey, 1990) if you want to learn more about these tests.

Figure SIA4.3a

MINITAB histogram for the horizontal hit measurements when $\sigma = 1$

Figure SIA4.3b

MINITAB histogram for the horizontal hit measurements when $\sigma = 2$

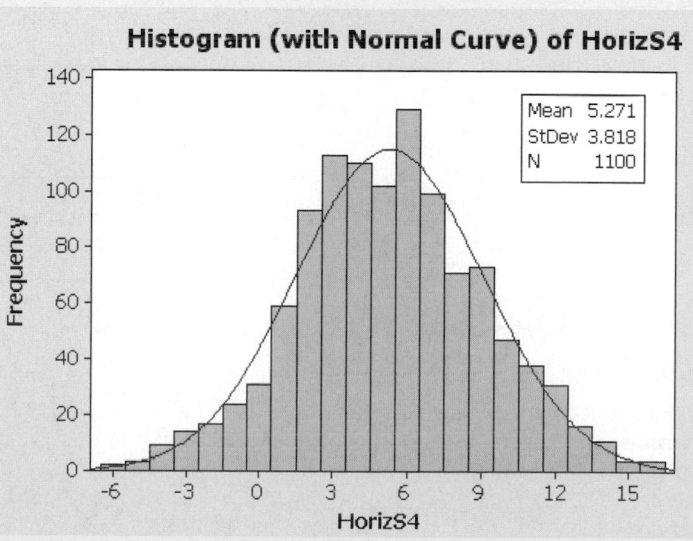

Figure SIA4.3c

MINITAB histogram for the horizontal hit measurements when $\sigma = 4$

Normal Probability Plot

Using the TI-83/TI-84 Graphing Calculator

Graphing a Normal Probability Plot

Step 1   *Enter the data*

Press **STAT** and select **1:Edit**
Note: If the list already contains data, clear the old data. Use the up
arrow to highlight **L1**. Press **CLEAR ENTER**.
Use the **ARROW** and **ENTER** keys to enter the data set into **L1**.

Step 2   *Set up the normal probability plot*

Press **Y=** and **CLEAR** all functions from the Y registers
Press **2nd** and press **Y=** for **STAT PLOT**
Press **1** for **Plot 1**
Set the cursor so that **ON** is flashing.
For **Type**, use the **ARROW** and **ENTER** keys to highlight and select the last graph
in the bottom row.
For **Data List**, choose the column containing the data (in most cases, L1). (Note:
Press **2nd** 1 for **L1**)
For **Data Axis**, choose **X** and press **ENTER**.

Step 3   *View plot*

Press **ZOOM 9**
Your data will be displayed against the expected *z*-scores from a normal distribution.
If you see a "generally" linear relationship, your data set is approximately normal.

Example   Using a normal probability plot, test whether or not the data are normally distributed.

9.7	93.1	33.0	21.2	81.4	51.1
43.5	10.6	12.8	7.8	18.1	12.7

The following screen shows the normal probability plot. There is a noticeable curve to the plot,
indicating that the data set is not normally distributed.

Exercises 4.111–4.122

Learning the Mechanics

4.111 If a population data set is normally distributed, what is the
proportion of measurements you would expect to fall
within the following intervals?
  a. $\mu \pm \sigma$
  b. $\mu \pm 2\sigma$
  c. $\mu \pm 3\sigma$

4.112 Consider a sample data set with the following summary
statistics: $s = 95, Q_L = 72, Q_U = 195$.
  a. Calculate IQR.
  b. Calculate IQR/s.
  c. Is the value of IQR/s approximately equal to 1.3? What
does this imply?

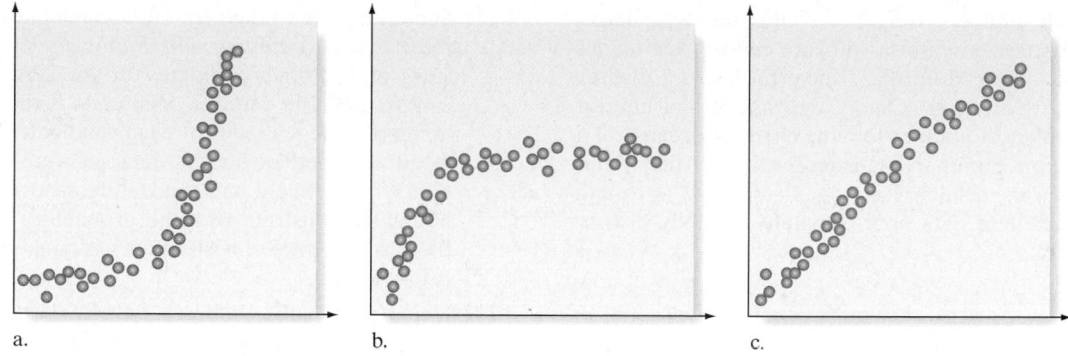

a.   b.   c.

Normal Probability Plots for Exercise 4.113

4.113 Normal probability plots for three data sets are shown above. Which plot indicates that the data are approximately normally distributed?

4.114 Examine the sample data below.

⚙ **LM4_114**

5.9	5.3	1.6	7.4	8.6	1.2	2.1
4.0	7.3	8.4	8.9	6.7	4.5	6.3
7.6	9.7	3.5	1.1	4.3	3.3	8.4
1.6	8.2	6.5	1.1	5.0	9.4	6.4

NW **a.** Construct a stem-and-leaf plot to assess whether the data are from an approximately normal distribution.

b. Compute s for the sample data.

c. Find the values of Q_L and Q_U and the value of s from part **b** to assess whether the data come from an approximately normal distribution.

d. Generate a normal probability plot for the data and use it to assess whether the data are approximately normal.

Applying the Concepts—Basic

⚙ **WPOWER50**

4.115 Most powerful women in America. Refer to the *Fortune* (Nov. 14, 2005) list of the 50 most powerful women in America. In Exercise 4.97 (p. 241), you assumed that the ages (in years) of these women are approximately normally distributed. A MINITAB printout with summary statistics for the age distribution is reproduced below.

a. Use the relevant statistics on the printout to find the interquartile range, IQR.

b. Locate the value of the standard deviation, s, on the printout.

c. Use the results, parts **a** and **b**, to demonstrate that the age distribution is approximately normal.

d. In Exercise 2.45c (p. 72) you constructed a relative frequency histogram for the age data. Use this graph to support your assumption of normality.

⚙ **STLRUNS**

4.116 Runs scored by the St. Louis Cardinals. Refer to the *Journal of Statistics Education* study of Mark McGwire's record-breaking 1998 Major League Baseball season, Exercise 2.23 (p. 59). The data on number of runs scored by McGwire's team, the St. Louis Cardinals, in games in which McGwire hit a home run are saved in the **STLRUNS** file. An SPSS normal probability plot for the data is shown below. Use the graph to assess whether the data are approximately normal.

Normal Q-Q Plot of runs

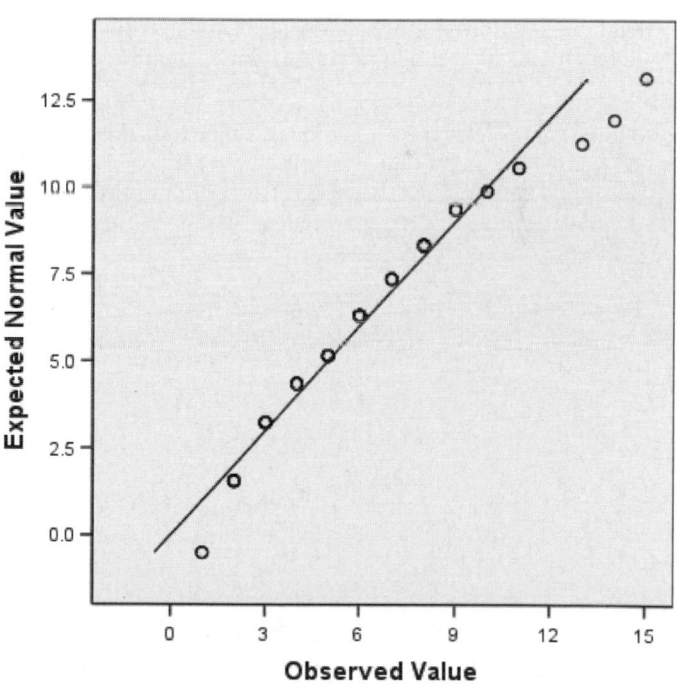

MINITAB Output for Exercise 4.115

Descriptive Statistics: AGE

Variable	N	Mean	StDev	Minimum	Q1	Median	Q3	Maximum
AGE	50	49.880	5.275	39.000	47.000	49.500	53.000	64.000

4.117 Software file updates. Software configuration management was used to monitor a software engineering team's performance at Motorola, Inc. (*Software Quality Professional*, Nov. 2004). One of the variables of interest was the number of updates to a file changed because of a problem report. Summary statistics for $n = 421$ files yielded the following results: $\bar{x} = 4.71$, $s = 6.09$, $Q_L = 1$, and $Q_U = 6$. Are these data approximately normally distributed? Explain.

Applying the Concepts—Intermediate

DDT

4.118 Fish contaminated by a plant's discharge. Refer to the U.S. Army Corps of Engineers data on contaminated fish in the Tennessee River.
  a. In Exercise 4.99 (p. 241), you assumed that the weight (in grams) of a captured fish is approximately normally distributed. Apply the methods of this chapter to the data saved in the **DDT** file to support this assumption.
  b. Another variable saved in the **DDT** file is the amount of DDT (in parts per million) detected in each fish captured. Determine whether DDT level is approximately normal.

CRASH

4.119 NHTSA crash tests. Refer to the National Highway Traffic Safety Administration (NHTSA) crash test data for new cars. In Exercise 4.100 (p. 241), you assumed that the driver's head-injury rating is approximately normally distributed. Apply the methods of this chapter to the data saved in the **CRASH** file to support this assumption.

SHIPSANIT

4.120 Sanitation inspection of cruise ships. Refer to the data on the May, 2006, sanitation scores for 151 cruise ships, first presented in Exercise 2.22 (p. 58). The data are saved in the **SHIPSANIT** file. Assess whether the sanitation scores are approximately normally distributed.

4.121 Semester hours taken by CPA candidates. Refer to the *Journal of Accounting and Public Policy* (Spring 2002) study of first-time candidates for the CPA exam, Exercise 2.49 (p. 73). The variable of interest is the total semester hours of college credit for each candidate. Recall that the mean and median for the data set were 141.31 and 140 hours, respectively, and the standard deviation was 17.77 hours. Demonstrate why the probability distribution for the variable, total semester hours, is unlikely to be normally distributed.

4.122 Department of Defense START sheets. The U.S. Department of Defense (DoD) Reliability Analysis Center publishes *Selected Topics in Assurance Related Technologies (START)* sheets for government and industry. These *START* sheets are designed to improve the reliability, maintainability, supportability, and quality of manufactured components and systems. In *START* (Volume 11, 2004), the DoD analyzed the following data set on tensile strength measurements taken at two different temperatures. In the *START* sheet, the DoD demonstrated that the data for the 11 tensile strength measurements were sampled from an approximately normal distribution. Do you agree?

TENSILE

Temperature	Strength
75	328.2
75	334.7
75	347.8
75	346.3
75	338.7
75	340.8
−67	343.6
−67	334.2
−67	348.7
−67	356.3
−67	344.1

4.9 Approximating a Binomial Distribution with a Normal Distribution (Optional)

When the discrete binomial random variable (Section 4.3) can assume a large number of values, the calculation of its probabilities may become very tedious. To contend with this problem, we provide tables in Appendix B to give the probabilities for some values of n and p, but these tables are by necessity incomplete. Recall that the binomial probability table (Table II) can be used only for $n = 5, 6, 7, 8, 9, 10, 15, 20,$ or 25. To deal with this limitation, we seek approximation procedures for calculating the probabilities associated with a binomial probability distribution.

When n is large, a normal probability distribution may be used to provide a good approximation to the probability distribution of a binomial random variable. To show how this approximation works, we refer to Example 4.12, in which we used the binomial distribution to model the number x of 20 employees who favor unionization. We assumed that 60% of all the company's employees favored unionization. The mean and standard deviation of x were found to be $\mu = 12$ and $\sigma = 2.2$. The binomial distribution for $n = 20$ and $p = .6$ is shown in Figure 4.28 and the approximating normal distribution with mean $\mu = 12$ and standard deviation $\sigma = 2.2$ is superimposed.

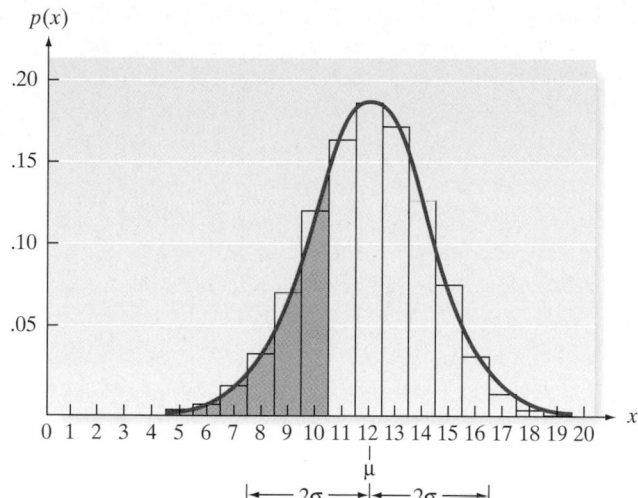

FIGURE 4.28

Binomial distribution for
$n = 20, p = .6$ and normal
distribution with $\mu = 12, \sigma = 2.2$

As part of Example 4.12, we used Table II to find the probability that $x \le 10$. This probability, which is equal to the sum of the areas contained in the rectangles (shown in Figure 4.28) that correspond to $p(0), p(1), p(2), \ldots, p(10)$, was found to equal .245. The portion of the approximating normal curve that would be used to approximate the area $p(0) + p(1) + p(2) + \cdots + p(10)$ is shaded in Figure 4.28. Note that this shaded area lies to the left of 10.5 (not 10), so we may include all of the probability in the rectangle corresponding to $p(10)$. Because we are approximating a discrete distribution (the binomial) with a continuous distribution (the normal), we call the use of 10.5 (instead of 10 or 11) a **correction for continuity,** that is, we are correcting the discrete distribution so that it can be approximated by the continuous one. The use of the correction for continuity leads to the calculation of the following standard normal z value:

$$z = \frac{x - \mu}{\sigma} = \frac{10.5 - 12}{2.2} = -.68$$

Using Table IV, we find the area between $z = 0$ and $z = .68$ to be .2517. Then the probability that x is less than or equal to 10 is approximated by the area under the normal distribution to the left of 10.5, shown shaded in Figure 4.28 — that is,

$$P(x \le 10) \approx P(z \le -.68) = .5 - P(-.68 < z \le 0) = .5 - .2517 = .2483$$

The approximation differs only slightly from the exact binomial probability, .245. Of course, when tables of exact binomial probabilities are available, we will use the exact value rather than a normal approximation.

Use of the normal distribution will not always provide a good approximation for binomial probabilities. The following is a useful rule of thumb to determine when n is large enough for the approximation to be effective: *The interval $\mu \pm 3\sigma$ should lie within the range of the binomial random variable x (i.e., 0 to n) in order for the normal approximation to be adequate.* The rule works well because almost all of the normal distribution falls within 3 standard deviations of the mean, so if this interval is contained within the range of x values, there is "room" for the normal approximation to work.

As shown in Figure 4.29(a) for the preceding example with $n = 20$ and $p = .6$, the interval $\mu \pm 3\sigma = 12 \pm 3(2.2) = (5.4, 18.6)$ lies within the range 0 to 20. However, if we were to try to use the normal approximation with $n = 10$ and $p = .1$, the interval $\mu \pm 3\sigma$ is $1 \pm 3(.95)$, or $(-1.85, 3.85)$. As shown in Figure 4.29(b), this interval is not contained within the range of x since $x = 0$ is the lower bound for a binomial random variable. Note in Figure 4.29(b) that the normal distribution will not "fit" in the range of x, and therefore it will not provide a good approximation to the binomial probabilities.

a. $n = 20$, $p = .6$: Normal approximation is good

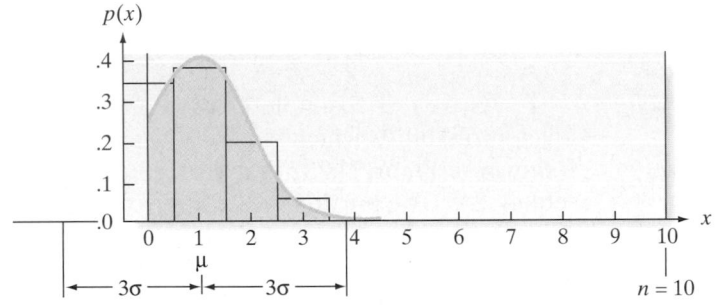

FIGURE 4.29

Rule of thumb for normal approximation to binomial probabilities

b. $n = 10$, $p = .1$: Normal approximation is poor

Biography

ABRAHAM DE MOIVRE (1667–1754)

Advisor to Gamblers

French-born mathematician Abraham de Moivre moved to London when he was 21 years old to escape religious persecution. In England, he earned a living first as a traveling teacher of mathematics and then as an advisor to gamblers, underwriters, and annuity brokers. De Moivre's major contribu- tions to probability theory are contained in two of his books. *The Doctrine of Chances* (1718) and *Miscellanea Analytica* (1730). In these works he defines statistical indepen- dence, develops the formula for the normal probability distribution, and derives the nor- mal curve as an approximation to the bino- mial distribution. Despite his eminence as a mathematician, de Moivre died in poverty. He is famous for predicting the day of his own death using an arithmetic progression.

EXAMPLE 4.25

Applying the Normal Approximation to a Binomial Probability—Lot Acceptance Sampling

Problem One problem with any product (e.g., a graphing calculator) that is mass pro- duced is quality control. The process must somehow be monitored or audited to be sure the output of the process conforms to requirements. One method of dealing with this problem is *lot acceptance sampling*, in which items being produced are sampled at vari- ous stages of the production process and are carefully inspected. The lot of items from which the sample is drawn is then accepted or rejected, based on the number of defec- tives in the sample. Lots that are accepted may be sent forward for further processing or may be shipped to customers; lots that are rejected may be reworked or scrapped. For example, suppose a manufacturer of calculators chooses 200 stamped circuits from the day's production and determines x, the number of defective circuits in the sample. Suppose that up to a 6% rate of defectives is considered acceptable for the process.

a. Find the mean and standard deviation of x, assuming the defective rate is 6%.

b. Use the normal approximation to determine the probability that 20 or more defec- tives are observed in the sample of 200 circuits (i.e., find the approximate probabil- ity that $x \geq 20$).

FIGURE 4.30
Normal approximation to
the binomial distribution
with $n = 200, p = .06$

Solution

a. The random variable x is binomial with $n - 200$ and the fraction defective $p - .06$. Thus,

$$\mu = np = 200(.06) = 12$$
$$\sigma = \sqrt{npq} = \sqrt{200(.06)(.94)} = \sqrt{11.28} = 3.36$$

We first note that

$$\mu \pm 3\sigma = 12 \pm 3(3.36) = 12 \pm 10.08 = (1.92, 22.08)$$

lies completely within the range from 0 to 200. Therefore, a normal probability distribution should provide an adequate approximation to this binomial distribution.

b. Using the rule of complements, $P(x \geq 20) = 1 - P(x \leq 19)$. To find the approximating area corresponding to $x \leq 19$, refer to Figure 4.30. Note that we want to include all the binomial probability histogram from 0 to 19, inclusive. Since the event is of the form $x < a$, the proper correction for continuity is $a + .5 = 19 + .5 = 19.5$. Thus, the z value of interest is

$$z = \frac{(a + .5) - \mu}{\sigma} = \frac{19.5 - 12}{3.36} = \frac{7.5}{3.36} = 2.23$$

Referring to Table IV in Appendix B, we find that the area to the right of the mean 0 corresponding to $z = 2.23$ (see Figure 4.31) is .4871. So the area $A = P(z \leq 2.23)$ is

$$A = .5 + .4871 = .9871$$

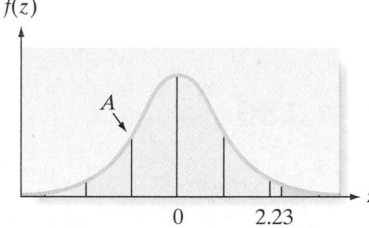

FIGURE 4.31
Standard normal distribution

Thus, the normal approximation to the binomial probability we seek is

$$P(x \geq 20) = 1 - P(x \leq 19) \approx 1 - .9871 = .0129$$

In other words, the probability is extremely small that 20 or more defectives will be observed in a sample of 200 circuits—*if in fact the true fraction of defectives is .06.*

Look Back If the manufacturer observes $x \geq 20$, the likely reason is that the process is producing more than the acceptable 6% defectives. The lot acceptance sampling procedure is another example of using the rare-event approach to make inferences.

Now Work Exercise 4.124

The steps for approximating a binomial probability by a normal probability are given in the accompanying box.

Using a Normal Distribution to Approximate Binomial Probabilities

1. After you have determined n and p for the binomial distribution, calculate the interval

$$\mu \pm 3\sigma = np \pm 3\sqrt{npq}$$

If the interval lies in the range 0 to n, the normal distribution will provide a reasonable approximation to the probabilities of most binomial events.

2. Express the binomial probability to be approximated in the form $P(x \leq a)$ or $P(x \leq b) - P(x \leq a)$. For example,

$$P(x < 3) = P(x \leq 2)$$
$$P(x \geq 5) = 1 - P(x \leq 4)$$
$$P(7 \leq x \leq 10) = P(x \leq 10) - P(x \leq 6)$$

3. For each value of interest a, the correction for continuity is $(a + .5)$, and the corresponding standard normal z value is

$$z = \frac{(a + .5) - \mu}{\sigma} \quad \text{(See Figure 4.32)}$$

4. Sketch the approximating normal distribution and shade the area corresponding to the probability of the event of interest, as in Figure 4.32. Verify that the rectangles you have included in the shaded area correspond to the event probability you wish to approximate. Using Table IV and the z value(s) you calculated in step 3, find the shaded area. This is the approximate probability of the binomial event.

FIGURE 4.32

Approximating binomial probabilities by normal probabilities

Exercises 4.123–4.136

Learning the Mechanics

4.123 Assume that x is a binomial random variable with n and p as specified in parts **a–f**. For which cases would it be appropriate to use a normal distribution to approximate the binomial distribution?
  a. $n = 100, p = .01$
  b. $n = 20, p = .6$
  c. $n = 10, p = .4$
  d. $n = 1,000, p = .05$
  e. $n = 100, p = .8$
  f. $n = 35, p = .7$

4.124 Suppose x is a binomial random variable with $p = .4$ and
NW $n = 25$.
  a. Would it be appropriate to approximate the probability distribution of x with a normal distribution? Explain.

  b. Assuming that a normal distribution provides an adequate approximation to the distribution of x, what are the mean and variance of the approximating normal distribution?
  c. Use Table II of Appendix B to find the exact value of $P(x \geq 9)$.
  d. Use the normal approximation to find $P(x \geq 9)$

4.125 Assume that x is a binomial random variable with $n = 100$ and $p = .40$. Use a normal approximation to find the following:
  a. $P(x \leq 35)$
  b. $P(40 \leq x \leq 50)$
  c. $P(x \geq 38)$

4.126 Assume that x is a binomial random variable with $n = 1,000$ and $p = .50$. Use a normal approximation to find each of the following probabilities:

a. $P(x > 500)$
b. $P(490 \leq x < 500)$
c. $P(x > 550)$

Applying the Concepts—Basic

4.127 Mobile phones with Internet access. In Exercise 4.42 (p. 215), you learned that 20% of young adults who shop online own a mobile phone with Internet access (*American Demographics*, May 2002.) In a random sample of 200 young adults who shop online, let x be the number who own a mobile phone with Internet access.

a. Find the mean of x. (This value should agree with your answer to Exercise 4.42c.)
b. Find the standard deviation of x.
c. Find the z-score for the value $x = 50.5$.
d. Find the approximate probability that the number of young adults who own a mobile phone with Internet access in a sample of 200 is less than or equal to 50.

4.128 Women-owned businesses. In Exercise 4.43 (p. 216), you learned that 27% of all small businesses owned by non-Hispanic whites nationwide are women-owned firms (*Journal of Business Venturing*, Vol. 17, 2002). In a random sample of 350 small businesses owned by non-Hispanic whites, let x be the number that are owned by a woman.

a. Find the mean of x.
b. Find the standard deviation of x.
c. Find the z-score for the value $x = 99.5$.
d. Find the approximate probability that the number of small businesses in the sample of 350 that are owned by a woman is 100 or more.

4.129 LASIK surgery complications. According to recent studies 1% of all patients who undergo laser surgery (i.e., LASIK) to correct their vision have serious postlaser vision problems (*All About Vision*, 2006). In a sample of 100,000 patients, what is the approximate probability that fewer than 950 will experience serious postlaser vision problems?

4.130 Stress in white-collar workers. An article in *The International Journal of Sports Psychology* (July–Sept. 1990) evaluated the relationship between physical fitness and stress. The research revealed that white-collar workers in good physical condition have only a 10% probability of developing a stress-related health problem. What is the probability that more than 60 in a random sample of 400 white-collar employees in good physical condition will develop stress-related illnesses?

Applying the Concepts—Intermediate

4.131 Analysis of bottled water. Refer to the *Scientific American* (July 2003) report on whether bottled water is really purified water, Exercise 4.44 (p. 216). Recall that the Natural Resources Defense Council found that 25% of bottled water brands fill their bottles with just tap water. In a random sample of 65 bottled water brands, is it likely that 20 or more brands will contain tap water? Explain.

4.132 Defects in semiconductor wafers. The computer chips in today's notebook and laptop computers are produced from semiconductor wafers. Certain semiconductor wafers are exposed to an environment that generates up to 100 possible defects per wafer. The number of defects per wafer, x, was found to follow a binomial distribution if the manufacturing process is stable and generates defects that are randomly distributed on the wafers (*IEEE Transactions on Semiconductor*

Manufacturing, May 1995). Let p represent the probability that a defect occurs at any one of the 100 points of the wafer. For each of the following cases, determine whether the normal approximation can be used to characterize x.

a. $p = .01$
b. $p = .50$
c. $p = .90$

4.133 Testing a manufacturer's claim. A manufacturer of CD-ROMs claims that 99.4% of its CDs are defect-free. A large software company that buys and uses a large number of the CDs wants to verify this claim, so it selects 1,600 CDs to be tested. The tests reveal 12 CDs to be defective. Assuming that the manufacturer's claim is correct, what is the probability of finding 12 or more defective CDs in a sample of 1,600? Does your answer cast doubt on the manufacturer's claim? Explain.

4.134 Credit card market shares. The following table reports the U.S. credit card industry's market share data for 2005. A random sample of 100 credit card users is to be questioned regarding their satisfaction with their credit card company. For simplification, assume that each credit card user carries just one credit card and that the market share percentages are the percentages of all credit card customers that carry each brand.

Credit Card	Market Share %
Visa	53.9
MasterCard	28.9
American Express	13.2
Discover	4.0

Source: CardWeb.com, Inc., Nov. 2005.

a. Propose a procedure for randomly selecting the 100 credit card users.
b. For random samples of 100 credit card users, what is the expected number of customers who carry Visa? Discover?
c. What is the probability that half or more of the sample of credit card users carry Visa? American Express?
d. Justify the use of the normal approximation to the binomial in answering the question in part **c**.

4.135 Financial aid for college students. The *Chronicle of Higher Education Almanac* reports that the percentage of undergraduates in the United States receiving federal financial aid is 45% at public four-year institutions and 52% at private four-year institutions. The U.S. Department of Education is interested in questioning a random sample of 100 U.S. undergraduate students to assess their satisfaction with federal financial aid procedures and policies.

a. Explain the difficulties of obtaining the desired random sample.
b. Assume the appropriate percentage above applies to your institution. If a random sample of 100 students from your institution were contacted, what is the approximate probability that 50 or more receive financial aid? Less than 25?
c. What assumptions must be made in order to answer part **b** using the normal approximation to the binomial?

Applying the Concepts—Advanced

4.136 Luggage inspection at Newark airport. According to *New Jersey Business* (Feb. 1996), Newark International

Airport's new terminal handles an average of 3,000 international passengers an hour but is capable of handling twice that number. Also, 80% of arriving international passengers pass through without their luggage being inspected and the remainder are detained for inspection. The inspection facility can handle 600 passengers an hour without unreasonable delays for the travelers.

a. When international passengers arrive at the rate of 1,500 per hour, what is the expected number of passengers who will be detained for luggage inspection?

b. In the future, it is expected that as many as 4,000 international passengers will arrive per hour. When that occurs, what is the expected number of passengers who will be detained for luggage inspection?

c. Refer to part **b.** Find the approximate probability that more than 600 international passengers will be detained for luggage inspection. (This is also the probability that travelers will experience unreasonable luggage inspection delays.)

4.10 Sampling Distributions

In the previous sections we assumed that we knew the probability distribution of a random variable, and using this knowledge we were able to compute the mean, variance, and probabilities associated with the random variable. However, in most practical applications, this information is not available. In reality, the true mean and standard deviation are unknown quantities that would have to be estimated. Numerical quantities that describe probability distributions are called *parameters*. Thus, p, the probability of a success in a binomial experiment, and μ and σ, the mean and standard deviation of a normal distribution, are examples of parameters.

> **Definition 4.10**
>
> A **parameter** is a numerical descriptive measure of a population. Because it is based on the observations in the population, its value is almost always unknown.

We have also discussed the sample mean $\bar{x}$, sample variance s^2, sample standard deviation s, etc., which are numerical descriptive measures calculated from the sample. We will often use the information contained in these *sample statistics* to make inferences about the parameters of a population.

> **Definition 4.11**
>
> A **sample statistic** is a numerical descriptive measure of a sample. It is calculated from the observations in the sample.

TABLE 4.8   List of Population Parameters and Corresponding Sample Statistics

	Population Parameter	Sample Statistic
Mean:	μ	$\bar{x}$
Variance:	σ^2	s^2
Standard deviation:	σ	s
Binomial proportion:	p	$\hat{p}$

Note that the term *statistic* refers to a *sample* quantity and the term *parameter* refers to a *population* quantity.

Before we can show you how to use sample statistics to make inferences about population parameters, we need to be able to evaluate their properties. Does one sample statistic contain more information than another about a population parameter? On what basis should we choose the "best" statistic for making inferences about a parameter? For example, if we want to estimate a parameter of a population—say, the population mean μ—we could use a number of sample statistics for our estimate. Two possibilities are the sample mean $\bar{x}$ and the sample median m. Which of these do you think will provide a better estimate of μ?

Before answering this question, consider the following example: Toss a fair die, and let x equal the number of dots showing on the up face. Suppose the die is tossed three

FIGURE 4.33

Comparing the sample mean ($\bar{x}$) and sample median (m) as estimators of the population mean (μ)

a. Sample 1: $\bar{x}$ is closer than m to μ

b. Sample 2: m is closer than $\bar{x}$ to μ

times, producing the sample measurements 2, 2, 6. The sample mean is $\bar{x} = 3.33$ and the sample median is $m = 2$. Since the population mean of x is $\mu = 3.5$, you can see that for this sample of three measurements, the sample mean $\bar{x}$ provides an estimate that falls closer to μ than does the sample median (see Figure 4.33a). Now suppose we toss the die three more times and obtain the sample measurements 3, 4, 6. The mean and median of this sample are $\bar{x} = 4.33$ and $m = 4$, respectively. This time m is closer to μ (see Figure 4.33b).

This simple example illustrates an important point: Neither the sample mean nor the sample median will *always* fall closer to the population mean. Consequently, we cannot compare these two sample statistics, or, in general, any two sample statistics, on the basis of their performance for a single sample. Instead, we need to recognize that sample statistics are themselves random variables, because different samples can lead to different values for the sample statistics. As random variables, sample statistics must be judged and compared on the basis of their probability distributions (i.e., the *collection* of values and associated probabilities of each statistic that would be obtained if the sampling experiment was repeated a *very large number of times*). We will illustrate this concept with another example.

Suppose it is known that the connector module manufactured for a certain brand of pacemaker has a mean length of $\mu = .3$ inch and a standard deviation of .005 inch. Consider an experiment consisting of randomly selecting 25 recently manufactured connector modules, measuring the length of each, and calculating the sample mean length $\bar{x}$. If this experiment was repeated a very large number of times, the value of $\bar{x}$ would vary from sample to sample. For example, the first sample of 25 length measurements might have a mean $\bar{x} = .301$, the second sample a mean $\bar{x} = .298$, the third sample a mean $\bar{x} = .303$, etc. If the sampling experiment was repeated a very large number of times, the resulting histogram of sample means would be approximately the probability distribution of $\bar{x}$. If $\bar{x}$ is a good estimator of μ, we would expect the values of $\bar{x}$ to cluster around μ, as shown in Figure 4.34. This probability distribution is called a *sampling distribution* because it is generated by repeating a sampling experiment a very large number of times.

Definition 4.12

The **sampling distribution** of a sample statistic calculated from a sample of n measurements is the probability distribution of the statistic.

In actual practice, the sampling distribution of a statistic is obtained mathematically or (at least approximately) by simulating the sample on a computer using a procedure similar to that just described.

If $\bar{x}$ has been calculated from a sample of $n = 25$ measurements selected from a population with mean $\mu = .3$ and standard deviation $\sigma = .005$, the sampling distribution (Figure 4.34) provides information about the behavior of $\bar{x}$ in repeated sampling. For - example, the probability that you will draw a sample of 25 length measurements and

FIGURE 4.34

Sampling distribution for $\bar{x}$ based on a sample of $n = 25$ length measurements

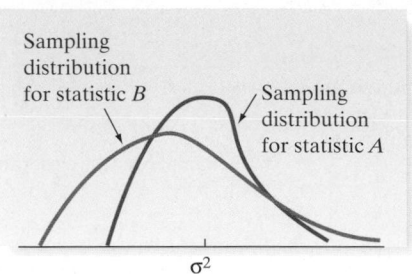

FIGURE 4.35

Two sampling distributions for estimating the population variance, σ^2

obtain a value of $\bar{x}$ in the interval $.299 \le \bar{x} \le .3$ will be the area under the sampling distr that interval.

Since the properties of a statistic are typified by its sampling distribution, it follows that to compare two sample statistics you compare their sampling distributions. For example, if you have two statistics, A and B, for estimating the same parameter (for purposes of illustration, suppose the parameter is the population variance σ^2) and if their sampling distributions are as shown in Figure 4.35, you would choose statistic A in preference to statistic B. You would make this choice because the sampling distribution for statistic A centers over σ^2 and has less spread (variation) than the sampling distribution for statistic B. When you draw a single sample in a practical sampling situation, the probability is higher that statistic A will fall nearer σ^2.

Remember that in practice we will not know the numerical value of the unknown parameter σ^2, so we will not know whether statistic A or statistic B is closer to σ^2 for a sample. We have to rely on our knowledge of the theoretical sampling distributions to choose the best sample statistic and then use it sample after sample. The procedure for finding the sampling distribution for a statistic is demonstrated in Example 4.26

EXAMPLE 4.26

Finding a Sampling Distribution

Problem   Consider a game played with a standard 52-card bridge deck in which you can score 0, 3, or 12 points per hand. Suppose the population of points per hand is described by the probability distribution shown here. A random sample of $n = 3$ hands is selected from the population.

Points, x	0	3	12
$p(x)$	$^1/_2$	$^1/_4$	$^1/_4$

a.   Find the sampling distribution of the sample mean number of points, $\bar{x}$.

b.   Find the sampling distribution of the sample median number of points, m.

Solution   Points for every possible sample of $n = 3$ hands is listed in Table 4.9 (p. 259) along with the sample mean and median. The probability of each sample is obtained using the Multiplicative Rule. For example, the probability of the sample $(0, 0, 3)$ is $p(0) \cdot p(0) \cdot p(3) = \left(^1/_2\right) \left(^1/_2\right) \left(^1/_4\right) = {}^1/_{16}$. The probability for each sample is also listed in Table 4.9. Note that the sum of these probabilities is equal to 1.

a.   From Table 4.9 you can see that $\bar{x}$ can assume the values $0, 1, 2, 3, 4, 5, 6, 8, 9,$ and 12. Because $\bar{x} = 0$ occurs in only the first listed sample, $P(\bar{x} = 0) = 8/64$. Similarly, $\bar{x} = 1$ occurs in three samples: $(0, 0, 3), (0, 3, 0),$ and $(3, 0, 0)$. Therefore, $P(\bar{x} = 1)$ is the sum of the probabilities for these three samples, i.e., $P(\bar{x} = 1) = 4/64 + 4/64 + 4/64 = 12/64$. Calculating the probabilities of the remaining values of $\bar{x}$ and arranging them in a table, we obtain the probability distribution shown below.

$\bar{x}$	0	1	2	3	4	5	6	8	9	12
$p(\bar{x})$	$^8/_{64}$	$^{12}/_{64}$	$^6/_{64}$	$^1/_{64}$	$^{12}/_{64}$	$^{12}/_{64}$	$^3/_{64}$	$^6/_{64}$	$^3/_{64}$	$^1/_{64}$

TABLE 4.9   All Possible Samples of $n = 3$ Hands of a Card Game, Example 4.26

Possible Samples	$\bar{x}$	m	Probability
0, 0, 0	0	0	$(\frac{1}{2})(\frac{1}{2})(\frac{1}{2}) = \frac{1}{8} = \frac{8}{64}$
0, 0, 3	1	0	$(\frac{1}{2})(\frac{1}{2})(\frac{1}{4}) = \frac{1}{16} = \frac{4}{64}$
0, 0, 12	4	0	$(\frac{1}{2})(\frac{1}{2})(\frac{1}{4}) = \frac{1}{16} = \frac{4}{64}$
0, 3, 0	1	0	$(\frac{1}{2})(\frac{1}{4})(\frac{1}{2}) = \frac{1}{16} = \frac{4}{64}$
0, 3, 3	2	3	$(\frac{1}{2})(\frac{1}{4})(\frac{1}{4}) = \frac{1}{32} = \frac{2}{64}$
0, 3, 12	5	3	$(\frac{1}{2})(\frac{1}{4})(\frac{1}{4}) = \frac{1}{32} = \frac{2}{64}$
0, 12, 0	4	0	$(\frac{1}{2})(\frac{1}{4})(\frac{1}{2}) = \frac{1}{16} = \frac{4}{64}$
0, 12, 3	5	3	$(\frac{1}{2})(\frac{1}{4})(\frac{1}{4}) = \frac{1}{32} = \frac{2}{64}$
0, 12, 12	8	12	$(\frac{1}{2})(\frac{1}{4})(\frac{1}{4}) = \frac{1}{32} = \frac{2}{64}$
3, 0, 0	1	0	$(\frac{1}{4})(\frac{1}{2})(\frac{1}{2}) = \frac{1}{16} = \frac{4}{64}$
3, 0, 3	2	3	$(\frac{1}{4})(\frac{1}{2})(\frac{1}{4}) = \frac{1}{32} = \frac{2}{64}$
3, 0, 12	5	3	$(\frac{1}{4})(\frac{1}{2})(\frac{1}{4}) = \frac{1}{32} = \frac{2}{64}$
3, 3, 0	2	3	$(\frac{1}{4})(\frac{1}{4})(\frac{1}{2}) = \frac{1}{32} = \frac{2}{64}$
3, 3, 3	3	3	$(\frac{1}{4})(\frac{1}{4})(\frac{1}{4}) = \frac{1}{64}$
3, 3, 12	6	3	$(\frac{1}{4})(\frac{1}{4})(\frac{1}{4}) = \frac{1}{64}$
3, 12, 0	5	3	$(\frac{1}{4})(\frac{1}{4})(\frac{1}{2}) = \frac{1}{32} = \frac{2}{64}$
3, 12, 3	6	3	$(\frac{1}{4})(\frac{1}{4})(\frac{1}{4}) = \frac{1}{64}$
3, 12, 12	9	12	$(\frac{1}{4})(\frac{1}{4})(\frac{1}{4}) = \frac{1}{64}$
12, 0, 0	4	0	$(\frac{1}{4})(\frac{1}{2})(\frac{1}{2}) = \frac{1}{16} = \frac{4}{64}$
12, 0, 3	5	3	$(\frac{1}{4})(\frac{1}{2})(\frac{1}{4}) = \frac{1}{32} = \frac{2}{64}$
12, 0, 12	8	12	$(\frac{1}{4})(\frac{1}{2})(\frac{1}{4}) = \frac{1}{32} = \frac{2}{64}$
12, 3, 0	5	3	$(\frac{1}{4})(\frac{1}{4})(\frac{1}{2}) = \frac{1}{32} = \frac{2}{64}$
12, 3, 3	6	3	$(\frac{1}{4})(\frac{1}{4})(\frac{1}{4}) = \frac{1}{64}$
12, 3, 12	9	12	$(\frac{1}{4})(\frac{1}{4})(\frac{1}{4}) = \frac{1}{64}$
12, 12, 0	8	12	$(\frac{1}{4})(\frac{1}{4})(\frac{1}{2}) = \frac{1}{32} = \frac{2}{64}$
12, 12, 3	9	12	$(\frac{1}{4})(\frac{1}{4})(\frac{1}{4}) = \frac{1}{64}$
12, 12, 12	12	12	$(\frac{1}{4})(\frac{1}{4})(\frac{1}{4}) = \frac{1}{64}$

$$\text{Sum} = \frac{64}{64} = 1$$

This is the sampling distribution for $\bar{x}$ because it specifies the probability associated with each possible value of $\bar{x}$.

b. In Table 4.9 you can see that the median m can assume one of the three values $0, 3$, or 12. The value $m = 0$ occurs in seven different samples. Therefore, $P(m = 0)$ is the sum of the probabilities of these seven samples, i.e., $P(m = 0) = \frac{8}{64} + \frac{4}{64} + \frac{4}{64} + \frac{4}{64} + \frac{4}{64} + \frac{4}{64} = \frac{32}{64}$. Similarly, $m = 3$ occurs in 13 samples and $m = 12$ occurs in seven samples, and these probabilities are obtained by summing the probabilities of their respective sample points. Therefore, the probability distribution (i.e., the sampling distribution) for the median m is as shown below.

m	0	3	12
$p(m)$	$\frac{32}{64}$	$\frac{22}{64}$	$\frac{10}{64}$

Look Back   The sampling distributions of parts **a** and **b** are found by first listing all possible distinct values of the statistic, and then calculating the probability of each value. Note that if the values of x were equally likely, then the 27 sample points in Table 4.9 would all have the same probability of occurring, namely $\frac{1}{27}$.

Now Work Exercise 4.137

Example 4.26 demonstrates the procedure for finding the exact sampling distribution of a statistic when the number of different samples that could be selected from the population is relatively small. In the real world, populations often consist of a large number of different values, making samples difficult (or impossible) to enumerate. When this situation occurs, we may choose to obtain the approximate sampling distribution for a statistic by simulating the sampling over and over again and recording the proportion of times different values of the statistic occur. Example 4.27 illustrates this procedure.

EXAMPLE 4.27

Simulating a
Sampling
Distribution

Problem   Refer to Example 4.14 (p. 225). Recall that the thickness of a steel sheet follows a uniform distribution with values between 150 and 200 millimeters. Suppose we perform the following experiment over and over again: Randomly sample 11 steel sheets from the production line and record the thickness, x, of each. Calculate the two sample statistics

$$\bar{x} = \text{Sample mean} = \frac{\Sigma x}{11}$$

$$m = \text{Median} = \text{Sixth sample measurement when the 11 thicknesses}$$
$$\text{are arranged in ascending order}$$

Obtain approximations to the sampling distributions of $\bar{x}$ and m.

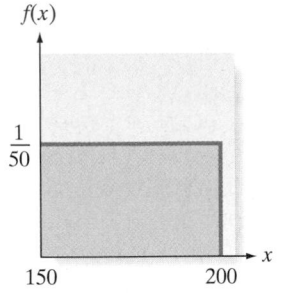

FIGURE 4.36
Uniform distribution for
thickness of steel sheets

Solution   Recall from Section 4.6 that the population of thicknesses follows the uniform distribution shown in Figure 4.36. We used MINITAB to generate 1,000 samples from this population, each with $n = 11$ observations. Then we compute $\bar{x}$ and m for each sample. Our goal is to obtain approximations to the sampling distributions of $\bar{x}$ and m to find out which sample statistic ($\bar{x}$ or m) contains more information about μ. [*Note:* In this particular example, we *know* the population mean is $\mu = 175$ mm. (See optional Section 4.6.)] The first 10 of the 1,000 samples generated are presented in Table 4.10. For instance, the first computer-generated sample from the uniform distribution (arranged in ascending order) contained the following thickness measurements: 151, 157, 162, 169, 171, 173, 181, 182, 187, 188, and 193 millimeters. The sample mean $\bar{x}$ and median m computed for this sample are

$$\bar{x} = \frac{151 + 157 + \cdots + 193}{11} = 174.0$$

$$m = \text{Sixth ordered measurement} = 173$$

The MINITAB relative frequency histograms for $\bar{x}$ and m for the 1,000 samples of size $n = 11$ are shown in Figure 4.37. These histograms represent approximations to the true sampling distributions of $\bar{x}$ and m.

 SIMUNI

TABLE 4.10   First 10 Samples of *n* = 11 Thickness Measurements from Uniform Distribution

Sample	Thickness Measurements											Mean	Median
1	173	171	187	151	188	181	182	157	162	169	193	174.00	173
2	181	190	182	171	187	177	162	172	188	200	193	182.09	182
3	192	195	187	187	172	164	164	189	179	182	173	180.36	182
4	173	157	150	154	168	174	171	182	200	181	187	172.45	173
5	169	160	167	170	197	159	174	174	161	173	160	169.46	169
6	179	170	167	174	173	178	173	170	173	198	187	176.55	173
7	166	177	162	171	154	177	154	179	175	185	193	172.09	175
8	164	199	152	153	163	156	184	151	198	167	180	169.73	164
9	181	193	151	166	180	199	180	184	182	181	175	179.27	181
10	155	199	199	171	172	157	173	187	190	185	150	176.18	173

FIGURE 4.37

MINITAB histograms for sample mean and sample median, Example 4.27

Look Back You can see that the values of $\bar{x}$ tend to cluster around μ to a greater extent than do the values of m. Thus, on the basis of the observed sampling distributions, we conclude that $\bar{x}$ contains more information about μ than m does—at least for samples of $n = 11$ measurements from the uniform distribution.

Now Work Exercise 4.142

As noted earlier, many sampling distributions can be derived mathematically, but the theory necessary to do this is beyond the scope of this text. Consequently, when we need to know the properties of a statistic, we will present its sampling distribution and simply describe its properties. The important properties of the sampling distribution of the sample mean are discussed in the next section.

Exercises 4.137–4.143

Learning the Mechanics

4.137 The probability distribution shown here describes a population of measurements that can assume values of 0, 2, 4, and 6, each of which occurs with the same relative frequency:

x	0	2	4	6
$p(x)$	$\frac{1}{4}$	$\frac{1}{4}$	$\frac{1}{4}$	$\frac{1}{4}$

a. List all the different samples of $n = 2$ measurements that can be selected from this population.
b. Calculate the mean of each different sample listed in part **a.**
c. If a sample of $n = 2$ measurements is randomly selected from the population, what is the probability that a specific sample will be selected?
d. Assume that a random sample of $n = 2$ measurements is selected from the population. List the different values of $\bar{x}$ found in part **b,** and find the probability of each. Then give the sampling distribution of the sample mean $\bar{x}$ in tabular form.

e. Construct a probability histogram for the sampling distribution of $\bar{x}$.

4.138 Simulate sampling from the population described in Exercise 4.137 by marking the values of x, one on each of four identical coins (or poker chips, etc.). Place the coins (marked 0, 2, 4, and 6) into a bag, randomly select one, and observe its value. Replace this coin, draw a second coin, and observe its value. Finally, calculate the mean $\bar{x}$ for this sample of $n = 2$ observations randomly selected from the population (Exercise 4.137, part **b**). Replace the coins, mix, and using the same procedure, select a sample of $n = 2$ observations from the population. Record the numbers and calculate $\bar{x}$ for this sample. Repeat this sampling process until you acquire 100 values of $\bar{x}$. Construct a relative frequency distribution for these 100 sample means. Compare this distribution to the exact sampling distribution of $\bar{x}$ found in part **e** of Exercise 4.137. [*Note:* The distribution obtained in this exercise is an approximation to the exact sampling distribution. But, if you were to repeat the sampling procedure, drawing two coins not 100 times but 10,000 times, the relative frequency distribution for the 10,000 sample means would be almost identical to the sampling distribution of $\bar{x}$ found in Exercise 4.137, part **e.**]

4.139 Consider the population described by the probability distribution shown below.

x	1	2	3	4	5
$p(x)$	.2	.3	.2	.2	.1

The random variable x is observed twice. If these observations are independent, verify that the different samples of size 2 and their probabilities are as shown below.

Sample	Probability	Sample	Probability
1, 1	.04	3, 4	.04
1, 2	.06	3, 5	.02
1, 3	.04	4, 1	.04
1, 4	.04	4, 2	.06
1, 5	.02	4, 3	.04
2, 1	.06	4, 4	.04
2, 2	.09	4, 5	.02
2, 3	.06	5, 1	.02
2, 4	.06	5, 2	.03
2, 5	.03	5, 3	.02
3, 1	.04	5, 4	.02
3, 2	.06	5, 5	.01
3, 3	.04		

a. Find the sampling distribution of the sample mean $\bar{x}$.
b. Construct a probability histogram for the sampling distribution of $\bar{x}$.
c. What is the probability that $\bar{x}$ is 4.5 or larger?
d. Would you expect to observe a value of $\bar{x}$ equal to 4.5 or larger? Explain.

4.140 Refer to Exercise 4.139 and find $E(x) = \mu$. Then use the sampling distribution of $\bar{x}$ found in Exercise 4.139 to find the expected value of $\bar{x}$. Note that $E(\bar{x}) = \mu$.

4.141 Refer to Exercise 4.139. Assume that a random sample of $n = 2$ measurements is randomly selected from the population.
a. List the different values that the sample median m may assume and find the probability of each. Then give the sampling distribution of the sample median.
b. Construct a probability histogram for the sampling distribution of the sample median and compare it with the probability histogram for the sample mean (Exercise 4.139, part **b**).

4.142 In Example 4.27 we used the computer to generate 1,000
NW samples, each containing $n = 11$ observations, from a uniform distribution over the interval from 150 to 200. For this exercise, use the computer to generate 500 samples, each containing $n = 15$ observations, from this population.
a. Calculate the sample mean for each sample. To approximate the sampling distribution of $\bar{x}$, construct a relative frequency histogram for the 500 values of $\bar{x}$.
b. Repeat part **a** for the sample median. Compare this approximate sampling distribution with the approximate sampling distribution of $\bar{x}$ found in part **a**.

4.143 Consider a population that contains values of x equal to 00, 01, 02, 03, . . . , 96, 97, 98, 99. Assume that these values of x occur with equal probability. Use the computer to generate 500 samples, each containing $n = 25$ measurements, from this population. Calculate the sample mean $\bar{x}$ and sample variance s^2 for each of the 500 samples.
a. To approximate the sampling distribution of $\bar{x}$, construct a relative frequency histogram for the 500 values of $\bar{x}$.
b. Repeat part **a** for the 500 values of s^2.

4.11 The Sampling Distribution of $\bar{x}$ and the Central Limit Theorem

Estimating the mean useful life of automobiles, the mean monthly sales for all computer dealers in a large city, and the mean breaking strength of new plastic are practical problems with something in common. In each case we are interested in making an inference about the mean μ of some population. As we mentioned in Chapter 2, the sample mean $\bar{x}$ is, in general, a good estimator of μ. We now develop pertinent information about the sampling distribution for this useful statistic.

EXAMPLE 4.28
Describing the Sampling Distribution of $\bar{x}$

Problem Suppose a population has the uniform probability distribution given in Figure 4.38. The mean and standard deviation of this probability distribution are $\mu = 175$ and $\sigma = 14.43$. (See optional Section 4.6 for the formulas for μ and σ.) Now suppose a sample of 11 measurements is selected from this population. Describe the sampling distribution of the sample mean $\bar{x}$ based on the 1,000 sampling experiments discussed in Example 4.27.

FIGURE 4.38
Sampled uniform population

Solution You will recall that in Example 4.27 we generated 1,000 samples of $n = 11$ measurements each. The MINITAB histogram for the 1,000

FIGURE 4.39

MINITAB histogram for sample mean in 1,000 samples

sample means is shown in Figure 4.39 with a normal probability distribution superimposed. You can see that this normal probability distribution approximates the computer-generated sampling distribution very well.

To fully describe a normal probability distribution, it is necessary to know its mean and standard deviation. MINITAB gives these statistics for the 1,000 $\bar{x}$'s in the upper right corner of the histogram, Figure 4.39. You can see that the mean is 175.2 and the standard deviation is 4.383.

To summarize our findings based on 1,000 samples, each consisting of 11 measurements from a uniform population, the sampling distribution of $\bar{x}$ appears to be approximately normal with a mean of about 175 and a standard deviation of about 4.38.

Look Back Note that the simulated value $\mu_{\bar{x}} = 175.2$ is very close to $\mu = 175$ for the uniform distribution—that is, the simulated sampling distribution of $\bar{x}$ appears to provide an accurate estimate of μ.

The true sampling distribution of $\bar{x}$ has the properties given in the next box, assuming only that a random sample of n observations has been selected from *any* population.

Properties of the Sampling Distribution of $\bar{x}$

1. Mean of sampling distribution equals mean of sampled population*, that is, $\mu_{\bar{x}} = E(\bar{x}) = \mu$.

2. Standard deviation of sampling distribution equals

$$\frac{\text{Standard deviation of sampled population}}{\text{Square root of sample size}}$$

That is, $\sigma_{\bar{x}} = \sigma/\sqrt{n}.$†

The standard deviation $\sigma_{\bar{x}}$ is often referred to as the **standard error of the mean.**

*When this property holds, we say that $\bar{x}$ is an *unbiased* estimate of μ.
†If the sample size, n, is large relative to the number, N, of elements in the population (e.g., 5% or more), $\sigma/\sqrt{n}$ must be multiplied by a finite population correction factor, $\sqrt{(N - n)/(N - 1)}$. For most sampling situations, this correction factor will be close to 1 and can be ignored.

You can see that our approximation to $\mu_{\bar{x}}$ in Example 4.28 was precise, since property 1 assures us that the mean is the same as that of the sampled population: 175 mm. Property 2 tells us how to calculate the standard deviation of the sampling distribution of $\bar{x}$. Substituting $\sigma = 14.43$, the standard deviation of the sampled uniform distribution, and the sample size $n = 11$ into the formula for $\sigma_{\bar{x}}$, we find

$$\sigma_{\bar{x}} = \frac{\sigma}{\sqrt{n}} = \frac{14.43}{\sqrt{11}} = 4.35$$

Thus, the approximation we obtained in Example 4.28, $\sigma_{\bar{x}} = 4.38$, is very close to the exact value, $\sigma_{\bar{x}} = 4.35$.*

What can be said about the shape of the sampling distribution of $\bar{x}$? Two important theorems provide this information.

Theorem 4.1

If a random sample of n observations is selected from a population with a normal distribution, the sampling distribution of $\bar{x}$ will be a normal distribution.

Theorem 4.2 (Central Limit Theorem)

Consider a random sample of n observations selected from a population (*any* probability distribution) with mean μ and standard deviation σ. Then, when n is sufficiently large, the sampling distribution of $\bar{x}$ will be approximately a normal distribution with mean $\mu_{\bar{x}} = \mu$ and standard deviation $\sigma_{\bar{x}} = \sigma/\sqrt{n}$. The larger the sample size, the better will be the normal approximation to the sampling distribution of $\bar{x}$.†

Biography

PIERRE-SIMON LAPLACE (1749–1827)

The CLT Originator

As a boy growing up in Normandy, France, Pierre-Simon Laplace attended a Benedictine priory school. Upon graduation, he entered Caen University to study theology. During his 2 years there he discovered his mathematical talents and began his career as an eminent mathematician. In fact, he considered himself the best mathematician in France. Laplace's contributions to mathematics ranged from introducing new methods of solving differential equations to complex analyses of motions of astronomical bodies. While studying the angles of inclination of comet orbits in 1778, Laplace showed that the sum of the angles were normally distributed. Consequently, he is considered to be the originator of the Central Limit Theorem. (A rigorous proof of the theorem, however, was not provided until the early 1930s by another French mathematician, Paul Levy.) Laplace also discovered Bayes's theorem and established Bayesian statistical analysis as a valid approach to many practical problems of his time.

Thus, for sufficiently large samples the sampling distribution of $\bar{x}$ is approximately normal. How large must the sample size n be so that the normal distribution provides a good approximation for the sampling distribution of $\bar{x}$? The answer depends on the shape of the distribution of the sampled population, as shown by Figure 4.40. Generally speaking, the greater the skewness of the sampled population distribution, the larger

*It can be shown (proof omitted) that the value of $\sigma_{\bar{x}}^2$ is the smallest variance among all unbiased estimators of μ—thus, $\bar{x}$ is the MVUE (minimum variance unbiased estimator) for μ.
†Moreover, because of the Central Limit Theorem, the sum of a random sample of n observations, Σx, will possess a sampling distribution that is approximately normal for large samples. This distribution will have a mean equal to $n\mu$ and a variance equal to $n\sigma^2$. Proof of the Central Limit Theorem is beyond the scope of this book, but it can be found in many mathematical statistics texts.

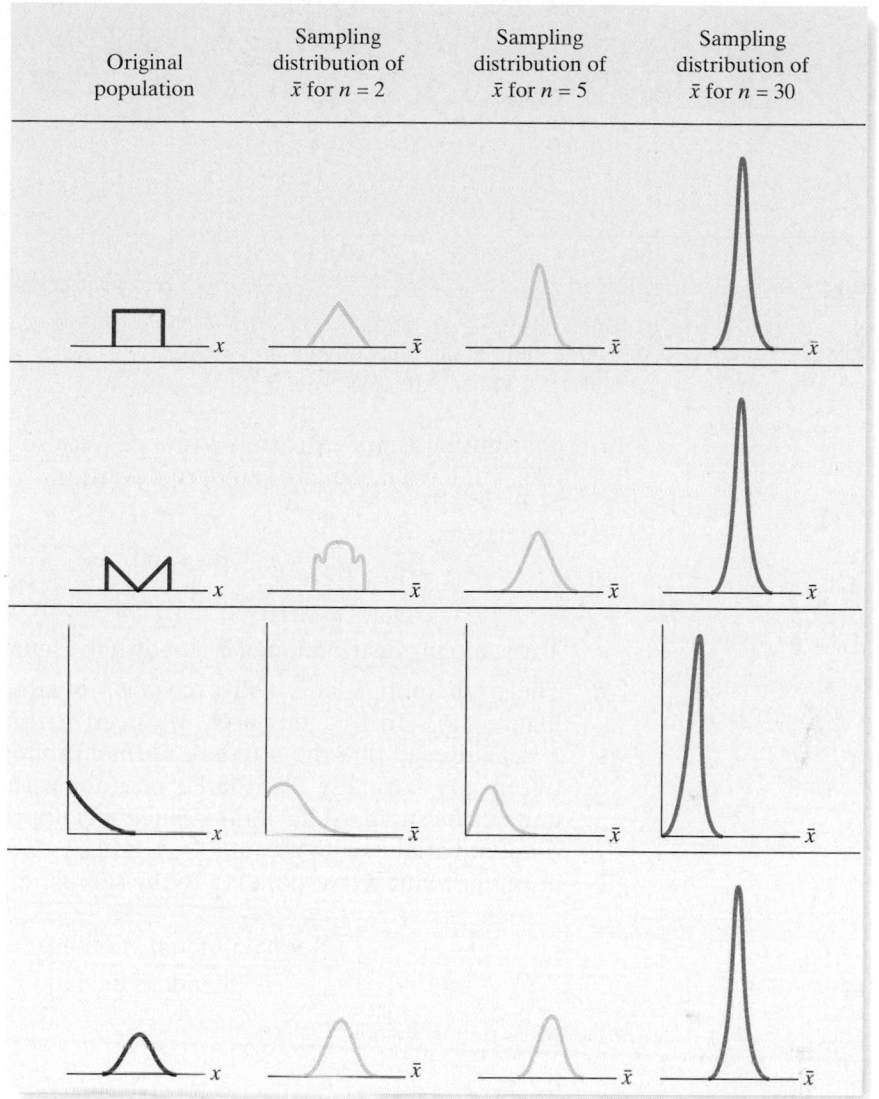

FIGURE 4.40

Sampling distributions of x̄ for different populations and different sample sizes

the sample size must be before the normal distribution is an adequate approximation for the sampling distribution of $\bar{x}$. For most sampled populations, sample sizes of $n \geq 30$ will suffice for the normal approximation to be reasonable. We will use the normal approximation for the sampling distribution of $\bar{x}$ when the sample size is at least 30.

EXAMPLE 4.29

Using the Central Limit Theorem to Find a Probability

Problem   Suppose we have selected a random sample of $n = 36$ observations from a population with mean equal to 80 and standard deviation equal to 6. It is known that the population is not extremely skewed.

a.   Sketch the relative frequency distributions for the population and for the sampling distribution of the sample mean, $\bar{x}$.

b.   Find the probability that $\bar{x}$ will be larger than 82.

Solution

a.   We do not know the exact shape of the population relative frequency distribution, but we do know that it should be centered about $\mu = 80$, its spread should be measured by $\sigma = 6$, and it is not highly skewed. One possibility is shown in Figure 4.41(a). From the Central Limit Theorem, we know that the sampling distribution of $\bar{x}$ will be approximately normal since the sampled population

a. Population relative frequency distribution

b. Sampling distribution of $\bar{x}$

FIGURE 4.41

A population relative frequency distribution and the sampling distribution for $\bar{x}$

distribution is not extremely skewed. We also know that the sampling distribution will have mean and standard deviation

$$\mu_{\bar{x}} = \mu = 80 \quad \text{and} \quad \sigma_{\bar{x}} = \frac{\sigma}{\sqrt{n}} = \frac{6}{\sqrt{36}} = 1$$

The sampling distribution of $\bar{x}$ is shown in Figure 4.41(b).

b. The probability that $\bar{x}$ will exceed 82 is equal to the darker shaded area in Figure 4.42. To find this area, we need to find the z value corresponding to $\bar{x} = 82$. Recall that the standard normal random variable z is the difference between any normally distributed random variable and its mean, expressed in units of its standard deviation. Since $\bar{x}$ is approximately a normally distributed random variable with mean $\mu_{\bar{x}} = \mu$ and $\sigma_{\bar{x}} = \sigma/\sqrt{n}$, it follows that the standard normal z value corresponding to the sample mean, $\bar{x}$, is

$$z = \frac{(\text{Normal random variable}) - (\text{Mean})}{\text{Standard deviation}} = \frac{\bar{x} - \mu_{\bar{x}}}{\sigma_{\bar{x}}}$$

FIGURE 4.42

The sampling distribution
of $\bar{x}$

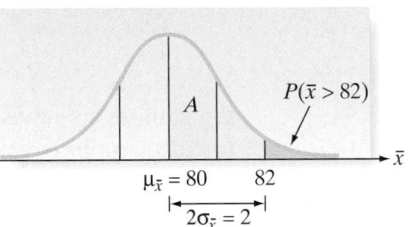

Therefore, for $\bar{x} = 82$, we have

$$z = \frac{\bar{x} - \mu_{\bar{x}}}{\sigma_{\bar{x}}} = \frac{82 - 80}{1} = 2$$

The area A in Figure 4.42 corresponding to $z = 2$ is given in the table of areas under the normal curve (see Table IV of Appendix B) as .4772. Therefore, the tail area corresponding to the probability that $\bar{x}$ exceeds 82 is

$$P(\bar{x} > 82) = P(z > 2) = .5 - .4772 = .0228$$

Look Back The key to finding the probability, part **b,** is to recognize that the distribution of $\bar{x}$ is normal with mean $\mu_{\bar{x}} = \mu$ and $\sigma_{\bar{x}} = \sigma/\sqrt{n}$.

Now Work Exercises 4.148–4.149

EXAMPLE 4.30

A Practical Application of the Central Limit Theorem to Test a Manufacturer's Claim

Problem A manufacturer of automobile batteries claims that the distribution of the lengths of life of its best battery has a mean of 54 months and a standard deviation of 6 months. Recently, the manufacturer has received a rash of complaints from unsatisfied customers whose batteries have died earlier than expected. Suppose a consumer group decides to check the manufacturer's claim by purchasing a sample of 50 of these batteries and subjecting them to tests that determine battery life.

a. Assuming that the manufacturer's claim is true, describe the sampling distribution of the mean lifetime of a sample of 50 batteries.

b. Assuming that the manufacturer's claim is true, what is the probability that the consumer group's sample has a mean life of 52 or fewer months?

Solution

a. Even though we have no information about the shape of the probability distribution of the lives of the batteries, we can use the Central Limit Theorem to deduce that the sampling distribution for a sample mean lifetime of 50 batteries is approximately normally distributed. Furthermore, the mean of this sampling distribution is the same as the mean of the sampled population, which is $\mu = 54$ months according to the manufacturer's claim. Finally, the standard deviation of the sampling distribution is given by

$$\sigma_{\bar{x}} = \frac{\sigma}{\sqrt{n}} = \frac{6}{\sqrt{50}} = .85 \text{ month}$$

FIGURE 4.43

Sampling distribution of $\bar{x}$ in Example 4.30 for $n = 50$

Note that we used the claimed standard deviation of the sampled population, $\sigma = 6$ months. Thus, if we assume that the claim is true, the sampling distribution for the mean life of the 50 batteries sampled is as shown in Figure 4.43.

b. If the manufacturer's claim is true, the probability that the consumer group observes a mean battery life of 52 or fewer months for their sample of 50 batteries, $P(\bar{x} \le 52)$, is equivalent to the darker shaded area in Figure 4.43. Since the sampling distribution is approximately normal, we can find this area by computing the standard normal z value:

$$z = \frac{\bar{x} - \mu_{\bar{x}}}{\sigma_{\bar{x}}} = \frac{52 - 54}{.85} = -2.35$$

where $\mu_{\bar{x}}$, the mean of the sampling distribution of $\bar{x}$, is equal to μ, the mean of the lives of the sampled population, and σ_x is the standard deviation of the sampling distribution of $\bar{x}$. Note that z is the familiar standardized distance (z-score) of Section 2.7 and, since $\bar{x}$ is approximately normally distributed, it will possess (approximately) the standard normal distribution of Section 4.7.

The area A shown in Figure 4.43 between $\bar{x} = 52$ and $\bar{x} = 54$ (corresponding to $z = -2.35$) is found in Table IV of Appendix B to be .4906. Therefore, the area to the left of $\bar{x} = 52$ is

$$P(\bar{x} \le 52) = .5 - A = .5 - .4906 = .0094$$

Thus, the probability that the consumer group will observe a sample mean of 52 or less is only .0094 if the manufacturer's claim is true.

Look Back If the 50 tested batteries do exhibit a mean of 52 or fewer months, the consumer group will have strong evidence that the manufacturer's claim is untrue, because such an event is very unlikely to occur if the claim is true. (This is still another application of the *rare-event approach to statistical inference.*)

Now Work Exercise 4.154

We conclude this section with two final comments on the sampling distribution of $\bar{x}$. First, from the formula $\sigma_{\bar{x}} = \sigma/\sqrt{n}$, we see that the standard deviation of the sampling distribution of $\bar{x}$ gets smaller as the sample size n gets larger. For example, we computed $\sigma_{\bar{x}} = .85$ when $n = 50$ in Example 4.30. However, for $n = 100$, we obtain $\sigma_{\bar{x}} = \sigma/\sqrt{n} = 6/\sqrt{100} = .60$. This relationship will hold true for most of the sample statistics encountered in this text—that is, *the standard deviation of the sampling distribution decreases as the sample size increases.* Consequently, the larger the sample size, the more accurate the sample statistic (e.g., $\bar{x}$) is in estimating a population parameter (e.g., μ). We will use this result in Chapter 5 to help us determine the sample size needed to obtain a specified accuracy of estimation.

Our second comment concerns the Central Limit Theorem. In addition to providing a very useful approximation for the sampling distribution of a sample mean, the Central Limit Theorem offers an explanation for the fact that many relative frequency distributions of data possess mound-shaped distributions. Many of the measurements we take in business are really means or sums of a large number of small phenomena. For example, a company's sales for 1 year are the total of the many individual sales the company made during the year. Similarly, we can view the length of time a construction company takes to build a house as the total of the times taken to complete a multitude of distinct jobs, and we can regard the monthly demand for blood at a hospital as the total of the many individual patients' needs. Whether or not the observations entering into these sums satisfy the assumptions basic to the Central Limit Theorem is open to question. However, it is a fact that many distributions of data in nature are mound-shaped and possess the appearance of normal distributions.

ACTIVITY 4.2: *Keep the Change:* Simulating a Sampling Distribution

In this activity, we will once again be working with the data set *Amounts Transferred* from Activity 1.1 on page 16. This activity is designed for small groups or the entire class.

1. Pool your *Amounts Transferred* data with other class members or the entire class so that the pooled data set has at least 100 data items. Have someone in the group calculate the mean and the standard deviation of the pooled data set.

2. Devise a convenient way to choose random samples from the pooled data set. You can assign each data item a number beginning with 1 and use a random number generator to select a sample or

you can write each data item on a small card and then draw cards without looking.

3. Choose a random sample of size $n = 30$ from the pooled data and find the mean of the sample, called a *sample mean*. Group members should repeat the process of choosing a sample of size $n = 30$ from the pooled data and finding the sample mean until the group has accumulated at least 25 sample means. Call this new data set *Sample Means*.

4. Find the mean and standard deviation of the data set *Sample Means*. Explain how the Central Limit Theorem is illustrated in this activity.

Keep the data set from this activity for use in other activities.

Exercises 4.144–4.163

Learning the Mechanics

4.144 Will the sampling distribution of $\bar{x}$ always be approximately normally distributed? Explain.

4.145 Suppose a random sample of n measurements is selected from a population with mean $\mu = 100$ and variance $\sigma^2 = 100$.

For each of the following values of n, give the mean and standard deviation of the sampling distribution of the sample mean $\bar{x}$.

a. $n = 4$ 100, 5

b. $n = 25$ 100, 2

STATISTICS IN ACTION REVISITED

Making an Inference about the Mean Accuracy of the Super Weapon

Consider, again, the prototype gun developed for the U.S. Army that fires over 1,000 flechettes with a single round. Suppose the specifications of the weapon are set so that when the gun is aimed at the center target (see Figure SIA4.1) from 500 meters away, the mean horizontal grid value is $\mu = 5$ feet (i.e., the aim point) and the standard deviation is $\sigma = 1$ foot. After firing one round of the super weapon, the U.S. Army randomly samples 100 of the discharged flechettes and records x, the horizontal measurement, for each. The sample mean was determined to be $\bar{x} = 5.3$. Is this result consistent with the gun specifications or is the true mean μ set higher than 5?

To answer this question, we need to examine the likelihood of obtaining the sample result, given that the gun specifications are met — that is, how likely is it to observe a sample mean of $\bar{x} = 5.3$ or higher for a sample of $n = 100$ flechettes when the mean and standard deviation of the population of horizontal grid measurements are set at $\mu = 5$ and $\sigma = 1$? Thus, the probability of interest is $P(\bar{x} > 5.3)$.

To find this probability, we invoke the Central Limit Theorem (CLT). According to the theorem, the sampling distribution of $\bar{x}$ is approximately normally distributed with the following mean and standard deviation:

$$\mu_{\bar{x}} = \mu = 5 \qquad \sigma_{\bar{x}} = \sigma/\sqrt{n} = 1/\sqrt{100} = .1$$

[Note that since we've already established (see SIA on p. 246) that the population of horizontal grid measurements are normally distributed, Theorem 4.1 also guarantees that the distribution of $\bar{x}$ will be normally distributed.] Therefore, we find the desired probability (using the standard normal table) as follows:

$$P(\bar{x} > 5.3) = P\left(z > \frac{5.3 - \mu_{\bar{x}}}{\sigma_{\bar{x}}}\right)$$

$$= P\left(z > \frac{5.3 - 5}{.1}\right) = P(z > 3) = .0013$$

In other words, the probability that we observe a sample mean at least as large as $\bar{x} = 5.3$ feet *if the mean and standard deviation of the horizontal grid measurements are $\mu = 5$ and $\sigma = 1$ (i.e., if the desired specifications are met) is almost 0.*

This small probability leads us to make one of two conclusions: Either the gun specifications are met and the U.S. Army has observed an extremely rare event (one with almost no chance of happening), or one or both of the gun specifications ($\mu = 5$ and $\sigma = 1$) are not being met. The *rare event approach* to making statistical inferences, of course, would favor the second conclusion. Possibly the gun specifications were set so that the true mean μ is higher than 5 feet, or the standard deviation was set at some number other than $\sigma = 1$. [In fact, you can show that if the specifications are set at $\sigma = 4$, $P(\bar{x} > 5.3) = .2266$. Thus, the observed sample mean has a reasonable chance of occurring if the standard deviation is inadvertently set at $\sigma = 4$.]

---

c. $n = 100$
d. $n = 50$
e. $n = 500$
f. $n = 1,000$

4.146 Suppose a random sample of $n = 25$ measurements is selected from a population with mean μ and standard deviation σ. For each of the following values of μ and σ, give the values of $\mu_{\bar{x}}$ and $\sigma_{\bar{x}}$.
a. $\mu = 10, \sigma = 3$ **b.** $\mu = 100, \sigma = 25$
c. $\mu = 20, \sigma = 40$ **d.** $\mu = 10, \sigma = 100$

4.147 Consider the probability distribution shown here.

x	1	2	3	8
$p(x)$	.1	.4	.4	.1

a. Find μ, σ^2, and σ.
b. Find the sampling distribution of $\bar{x}$ for random samples of $n = 2$ measurements from this distribution by listing all possible values of $\bar{x}$, and find the probability associated with each.
c. Use the results of part **b** to calculate $\mu_{\bar{x}}$ and $\sigma_{\bar{x}}$. Confirm that $\mu_{\bar{x}} = \mu$ and $\sigma_{\bar{x}} = \sigma/\sqrt{n} = \sigma/\sqrt{2}$.

4.148 A random sample of $n = 64$ observations is drawn from a population with a mean equal to 20 and standard deviation equal to 16.
a. Give the mean and standard deviation of the (repeated) sampling distribution of $\bar{x}$.
b. Describe the shape of the sampling distribution of $\bar{x}$. Does your answer depend on the sample size?
c. Calculate the standard normal z-score corresponding to a value of $\bar{x} = 15.5$.
d. Calculate the standard normal z-score corresponding to $\bar{x} = 23$.

4.149 Refer to Exercise 4.148. Find the probability that
a. $\bar{x}$ is less than 16
b. $\bar{x}$ is greater than 23
c. $\bar{x}$ is greater than 25
d. $\bar{x}$ falls between 16 and 22
e. $\bar{x}$ is less than 14

4.150 A random sample of $n = 900$ observations is selected from a population with $\mu = 100$ and $\sigma = 10$.
a. What are the largest and smallest values of $\bar{x}$ that you would expect to see?

b. How far, at the most, would you expect $\bar{x}$ to deviate from μ?

c. Did you have to know μ to answer part **b**? Explain.

4.151 A random sample of $n = 100$ observations is selected from a population with $\mu = 30$ and $\sigma = 16$. Approximate the following probabilities:

a. $P(\bar{x} \geq 28)$
b. $P(22.1 \leq \bar{x} \leq 26.8)$
c. $P(\bar{x} \leq 28.2)$
d. $P(\bar{x} \geq 27.0)$

4.152 Consider a population that contains values of x equal to $0, 1, 2, \ldots, 97, 98, 99$. Assume that the values of x are equally likely. For each of the following values of n, use a computer to generate 500 random samples and calculate $\bar{x}$ for each sample. For each sample size, construct a relative frequency histogram of the 500 values of $\bar{x}$. What changes occur in the histograms as the value of n increases? What similarities exist? Use $n = 2, n = 5, n = 10, n = 30$, and $n = 50$.

APPLET **Applet Exercise 4.9**

Open the applet entitled *Sampling Distributions*. On the pull-down menu to the right of the top graph, select *Binary*.

a. Run the applet for the sample size $n = 10$ and the number of samples $N = 1000$. Observe the shape of the graph of the sample proportions and record the mean, median, and standard deviation of the sample proportions.

b. How does the mean of the sample proportions compare to the mean $\mu = 0.5$ of the original distribution?

c. Compute the standard deviation of the original distribution using the formula $\sigma = \sqrt{np(1 - p)}$ where $n = 1$ and $p = 0.5$. Divide the result by $\sqrt{10}$, the square root of the sample size used in the sampling distribution. How does this result compare to the standard deviation of the sample proportions?

d. Explain how the graph of the distribution of sample proportions suggests that the distribution may be approximately normal.

e. Explain how the results of parts **b–d** illustrate the Central Limit Theorem.

APPLET **Applet Exercise 4.10**

Open the applet entitled *Sampling Distributions*. On the pull-down menu to the right of the top graph, select *Uniform*. The box to the left of the top graph displays the population mean, median, and standard deviation of the original distribution.

a. Run the applet for the sample size $n = 30$ and the number of samples $N = 1000$. Observe the shape of the graph of the sample means and record the mean, median, and standard deviation of the sample means.

b. How does the mean of the sample means compare to the mean of the original distribution?

c. Divide the standard deviation of the original distribution by $\sqrt{30}$, the square root of the sample size used in the sampling distribution. How does this result compare to the standard deviation of the sample proportions?

d. Explain how the graph of the distribution of sample means suggests that the distribution may be approximately normal.

e. Explain how the results of parts **b–d** illustrate the Central Limit Theorem.

Applying the Concepts—Basic

4.153 **Semester hours taken by CPA candidates.** Refer to the *Journal of Accounting and Public Policy* (Spring 2002) study of first-time candidates for the CPA exam, Exercise 2.49 (p. 73). The number of semester hours of college credit taken by candidates has a distribution with a mean of 141 hours and a standard deviation of 18 hours. Consider a random sample of 100 first-time candidates for the CPA exam and let $\bar{x}$ represent the mean number of hours of college credit taken for the sample.

a. What is $\mu_{\bar{x}}$?
b. What is $\sigma_{\bar{x}}$?
c. Describe the shape of the sampling distribution of $\bar{x}$.
d. Find the z-score for the value $\bar{x} = 142$ hours .
e. Find $P(\bar{x} > 142)$

4.154 **Salary of a travel management professional.** According
NW to *Business Travel News* (July 17, 2006), the average salary of a travel management professional is $98,500. Assume that the standard deviation of such salaries is $30,000. Consider a random sample of 50 travel management professionals and let $\bar{x}$ represent the mean salary for the sample.

a. What is $\mu_{\bar{x}}$?
b. What is $\sigma_{\bar{x}}$?
c. Describe the shape of the sampling distribution of $\bar{x}$.
d. Find the z-score for the value $\bar{x} = 89,500$.
e. Find $P(\bar{x} > 89,500)$.

4.155 **Improving SAT scores.** Refer to the *Chance* (Winter 2001) examination of Standardized Admission Test (SAT) scores of students who pay a private tutor to help them improve their results, Exercise 2.84 (p. 86). On the SAT–Mathematics test, these students had a mean score change of +19 points, with a standard deviation of 65 points. In a random sample of 100 students who pay a private tutor to help them improve their results, what is the likelihood that the sample mean score change is less than 10 points?

4.156 **Ocean quahog harvesting.** The ocean quahog is a type of clam found in the coastal waters of New England and the mid-Atlantic states. A federal survey of offshore ocean quahog harvesting in New Jersey, conducted from 1980 to 1992, revealed an average catch per unit effort (CPUE) of 89.34 clams. The CPUE standard deviation was 7.74 (*Journal of Shellfish Research*, June 1995). Let $\bar{x}$ represent the mean CPUE for a sample of 35 attempts to catch ocean quahogs off the New Jersey shore.

a. Compute $\mu_{\bar{x}}$ and $\sigma_{\bar{x}}$. Interpret their values.
b. Sketch the sampling distribution of $\bar{x}$.
c. Find $P(\bar{x} > 88)$.
d. Find $P(\bar{x} < 87)$.

Applying the Concepts—Intermediate

4.157 **Levelness of concrete slabs.** Geotechnical engineers use water-level "manometer" surveys to assess the levelness of newly constructed concrete slabs. Elevations are typically measured at eight points on the slab; of interest is the maximum differential between elevations. The *Journal of Performance of Constructed Facilities* (Feb. 2005) published an article on the levelness of slabs in California residential developments. Elevation data collected for over 1,300 concrete slabs *before tensioning* revealed that maximum differential, x, has a mean of $\mu = .53$ inch and a standard deviation of $\sigma = .193$ inch. Consider a sample of $n = 50$ slabs selected from those surveyed and let $\bar{x}$ represent the mean of the sample.

a. Fully describe the sampling distribution of $\bar{x}$.

b. Find $P(\bar{x} > .58)$.

c. The study also revealed that the mean maximum differential of concrete slabs measured *after tensioning and loading* is $\mu = .58$ inch. Suppose the sample data yields $\bar{x} = .59$ inch . Comment on whether the sample measurements were obtained before tensioning or after tensioning and loading.

4.158 **Surface roughness of pipe.** Refer to the *Anti-Corrosion Methods and Materials* (Vol. 50, 2003) study of the surface roughness of oil field pipes, Exercise 2.46 (p. 72). Recall that a scanning probe instrument was used to measure the surface roughness x (in micrometers) of 20 sampled sections of coated interior pipe. Consider the sample mean, $\bar{x}$.

a. Assume that the surface roughness distribution has a mean of $\mu = 1.8$ micrometers and a standard deviation of $\sigma = .5$ micrometer. Use this information to find the probability that $\bar{x}$ exceeds 1.85 micrometers.

b. The sample data is reproduced in the following table. Compute $\bar{x}$.

c. Based on the result, part **b,** comment on the validity of the assumptions made in part **a.**

ⓢ ROUGHPIPE

1.72	2.50	2.16	2.13	1.06	2.24	2.31	2.03	1.09	1.40
2.57	2.64	1.26	2.05	1.19	2.13	1.27	1.51	2.41	1.95

Source: Farshad, F., and Pesacreta, T. "Coated Pipe Interior Surface Roughness as Measured by Three Scanning Probe Instruments." *Anti-Corrosion Methods and Materials*, Vol. 50, No. 1, 2003 (Table III).

4.159 **Length of time working for an employer.** Workers are much less likely to remain with one employer for many years than their parents were a generation before. (*Georgia Trend*, December 1999). Do today's college students understand that the workplace they are about to enter is vastly different than the one their parents entered? To help answer this question, researchers at the Terry College of Business at the University of Georgia sampled 344 business students and asked them this question. Over the course of your lifetime, what is the maximum number of years you expect to work for any one employer? The resulting sample had $\bar{x} = 19.1$ years and $s = 6$ years. Assume the sample of students was randomly selected from the 5,800 undergraduate students in the Terry College.

a. Describe the sampling distribution of $\bar{x}$.

b. If the population mean was 18.5 years, what is $P(\bar{x} \geq 19.1 \text{ years})$?

c. If the population mean was 19.5 years, what is $P(\bar{x} \geq 19.1 \text{ years})$?

d. If $P(\bar{x} \geq 19.1) = .5$, what is the population mean?

e. If $P(\bar{x} \geq 19.1) = .2$, is the population mean greater or less than 19.1 years? Justify your answer.

4.160 **Rental car fleet evaluation.** National Car Rental Systems. Inc., commissioned the United States Automobile Club (USAC) to conduct a survey of the general condition of the cars rented to the public by Hertz, Avis, National, and Budget Rent-a-Car.* USAC officials evaluate each

---

*Information by personal communication with Rajiv Tandon, corporate vice president and general manager of the Car Rental Division, National Car Rental Systems, Inc., Minneapolis, Minnesota.

company's cars using a demerit point system. Each car starts with a perfect score of 0 points and incurs demerit points for each discrepancy noted by the inspectors. One measure of the overall condition of a company's cars is the mean of all scores received by the company (i.e., the company's *fleet mean score*). To estimate the fleet mean score of each rental car company, 10 major airports were randomly selected, and 10 cars from each company were randomly rented for inspection from each airport by USAC officials (i.e., a sample of size $n = 100$ cars from each company's fleet was drawn and inspected).

a. Describe the sampling distribution of $\bar{x}$, the mean score of a sample of $n = 100$ rental cars.

b. Interpret the mean of $\bar{x}$ in the context of this problem.

c. Assume $\mu = 30$ and $\sigma = 60$ for one rental car company. For this company, find $P(\bar{x} \geq 45)$.

d. Refer to part **c.** The company claims that their true fleet mean score "couldn't possibly be as high as 30." The sample mean score tabulated by USAC for this company was $\bar{x} = 45$. Does this result tend to support or refute the claim? Explain.

4.161 **Analysis of supplier lead time.** In determining when to place orders to replenish depleted product inventories, a retailer should take into consideration the lead times for the products. *Lead time* is the time between placing the order and having the product available to satisfy customer demand. It includes time for placing the order, receiving the shipment from the supplier, inspecting the units received, and placing them in inventory (Clauss, *Applied Management Science and Spreadsheet Modeling*, 1996). Interested in average lead time, μ, for a particular supplier of men's apparel, the purchasing department of a national department store chain randomly sampled 50 of the supplier's lead times and found $\bar{x} = 44$ days.

a. Describe the shape of the sampling distribution of $\bar{x}$.

b. If μ and σ are really 40 and 12, respectively, what is the probability that a second random sample of size 50 would yield $\bar{x}$ greater than or equal to 44?

c. Using the values for μ and σ in part **b,** what is the probability that a sample of size 50 would yield a sample mean within the interval $\mu \pm 2\sigma/\sqrt{n}$?

Applying the Concepts—Advanced

4.162 **Plastic fill process.** University of Louisville researchers J. Usher, S. Alexander, and D. Duggins examined the process of filling plastic pouches of dry blended biscuit mix (*Quality Engineering*, Vol. 91, 1996). The current fill mean of the process is set at $\mu = 406$ grams, and the process fill standard deviation is $\sigma = 10.1$ grams. (According to the researchers, "The high level of variation is due to the fact that the product has poor flow properties and is, therefore, difficult to fill consistently from pouch to pouch.") Operators monitor the process by randomly sampling 36 pouches each day and measuring the amount of biscuit mix in each. Consider $\bar{x}$, the mean fill amount of the sample of 36 products. Suppose that on one particular day, the operators observe $\bar{x} = 400.8$. One of the operators believes that this indicates that the true process fill mean μ for that day is less than 406 grams. Another operator argues that $\mu = 406$, and the small value of $\bar{x}$ observed is due to random variation in the fill process. Which operator do you agree with? Why?

4.163 Handwashing versus handrubbing. The *British Medical Journal* (Aug. 17, 2002) published the results of a study to compare the effectiveness of handwashing with soap and handrubbing with alcohol. Health care workers who used handrubbing had a mean bacterial count of 35 per hand with a standard deviation of 59. Health care workers who used handwashing had a mean bacterial count of 69 per hand with a standard deviation of 106. In a random sample of 50 health care workers, all using the same method of cleaning their hands, the mean bacterial count per hand, $\bar{x}$, is less than 30. Give your opinion on whether this sample of workers used handrubbing with alcohol or handwashing with soap.

KEY TERMS

Note: Starred (*) terms are from the optional sections in this chapter.

Bell curve   228
Bell-shaped distribution   228
Binomial distribution   209
Binomial experiment   205
Binomial random variable   205
Central Limit Theorem   264
Continuous probability distribution   223
Continuous random variable   191
*Correction for continuity   251
Countable   191
Cumulative binomial probabilities   211

Discrete probability distribution   194
Discrete random variable   191
Expected value   195
Frequency function   223
Mean of a discrete random
   variable   195
Normal distribution   228
Normal probability plot   244
Normal random variable   229
Parameter   256
*Poisson distribution   218
*Poisson random variable   218
Probability density function   223

Random variable   190
*Randomness distribution   224
Sample statistic   256
Sampling distribution   257
Standard deviation of a discrete random
   variable   196
Standard error of the mean   263
Standard normal distribution   230
Standard normal random variable   230
Variance of a discrete random
   variable   196
*Uniform distribution   224
*Uniform random variable   225

GUIDE TO SELECTING A PROBABILITY DISTRIBUTION

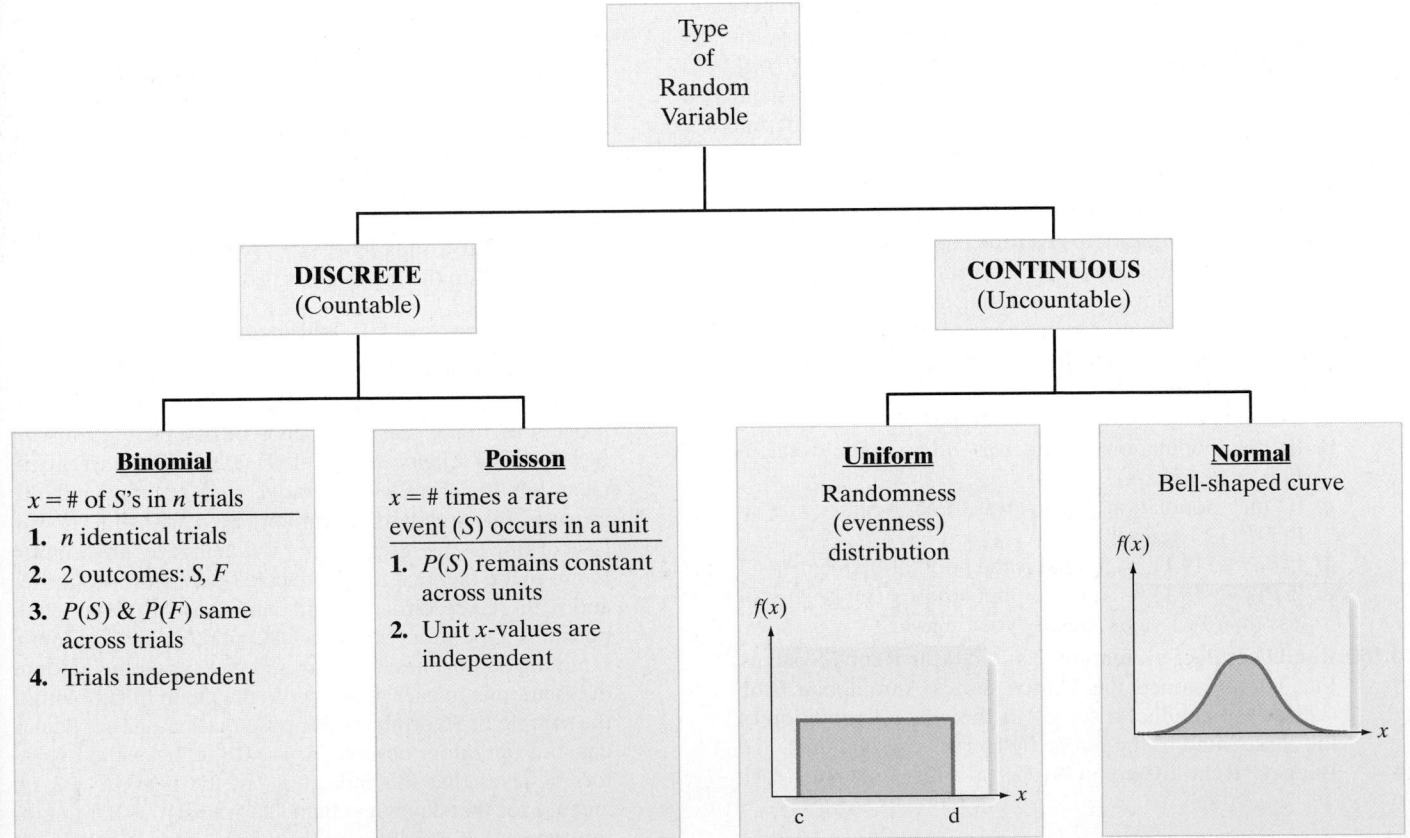

CHAPTER NOTES

Properties of Probability Distributions

Discrete Distributions:

(1) $p(x) \geq 0$

(2) $\displaystyle\sum_{\text{all } x} p(x) = 1$

Continuous Distributions:

(1) $P(x = a) = 0$

(2) $P(a < x < b)$ is area under curve between a and b

KEY SYMBOLS

$p(x)$	Probability distribution for discrete random variable, x
$f(x)$	Probability distribution for continuous random variable, x
S	Outcome of binomial trial denoted "success"
F	Outcome of binomial trial denoted "failure"
p	$P(S)$ in binomial trial
q	$P(F)$ in binomial trial $= 1 - p$
e	Constant used in normal & Poisson probability distributions, $e = 2.71828\ldots$
π	Constant used in normal probability distributions, $\pi = 3.1416\ldots$
$\mu_{\bar{x}}$	Mean of the population sampling distribution of $\bar{x}$
$\sigma_{\bar{x}}$	Standard deviation of the population sampling distribution of $\bar{x}$

KEY FORMULAS

Random Variable	Prob. Dist'n	Mean	Variance
General Discrete:	Table, formula, or graph for $p(x)$	$\displaystyle\sum_{\text{all } x} x \cdot p(x)$	$\displaystyle\sum_{\text{all } x} (x - \mu)^2 \cdot p(x)$
Binomial:	$p(x) = \dbinom{n}{x} p^x q^{n-x}$ $x = 0, 1, 2, \ldots, n$	np	npq
Poisson:	$p(x) = \dfrac{\lambda^x e^{-\lambda}}{x!}$ $x = 0, 1, 2, \ldots$	λ	λ
Uniform:	$f(x) = 1/(d - c)$ $(c \leq x \leq d)$	$(c + d)/2$	$(d - c)^2/12$
Normal:	$f(x) = \dfrac{1}{\sigma\sqrt{2\pi}} e^{-\frac{1}{2}[(x-\mu)/\sigma]^2}$	σ	σ^2
Standard Normal:	$f(z) = \dfrac{1}{\sqrt{2\pi}} e^{-\frac{1}{2}(z)^2}$ $z = (x - \mu)/\sigma$	$\mu = 0$	$\sigma^2 = 1$
Sample Mean: (large n)	$f(\bar{x}) = \dfrac{1}{\sigma_{\bar{x}}\sqrt{2\pi}} e^{-\frac{1}{2}[(x-\mu)/\sigma_{\bar{x}}]^2}$	$\mu_x = \mu$	$\sigma_{\bar{x}}^2 = \sigma^2/n$

CHAPTER NOTES (Cont'd)

<table>
<tr><td colspan="2">

Methods for Assessing Normality

</td><td>

Normal Approximation to Binomial

</td></tr>
</table>

(1) *Histogram*

(2) *Stem-and-leaf display*

1	7
2	3389
3	245677
4	19
5	2

(3) $(IQR)/\approx 1.3$

(4) *Normal probability plot*

x

z-scores

x is binomial (n, p)

$$P(x \le a) \approx P\{z < (a + .5) - \mu\}$$

Generating the Sampling Distribution of $\bar{x}$

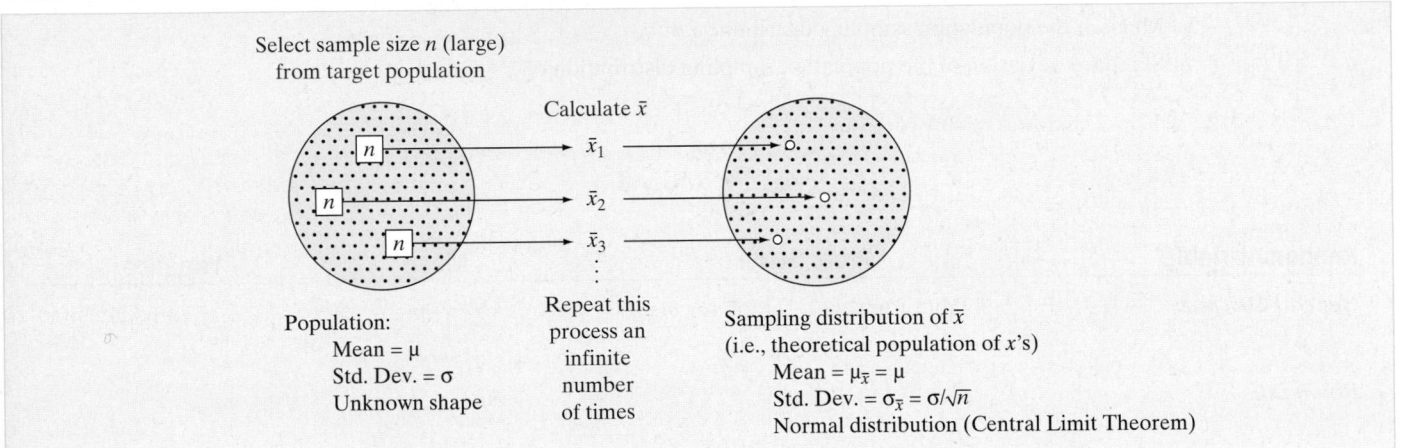

Select sample size n (large) from target population

Calculate $\bar{x}$

$\bar{x}_1$

$\bar{x}_2$

$\bar{x}_3$

Population:
Mean = μ
Std. Dev. = σ
Unknown shape

Repeat this process an infinite number of times

Sampling distribution of $\bar{x}$
(i.e., theoretical population of x's)
Mean = $\mu_{\bar{x}} = \mu$
Std. Dev. = $\sigma_{\bar{x}} = \sigma/\sqrt{n}$
Normal distribution (Central Limit Theorem)

SUPPLEMENTARY EXERCISES 4.164–4.201

Note: Starred (*) exercises refer to the optional sections in this chapter.

Learning the Mechanics

4.164 For each of the following examples, decide whether x is a binomial random variable and explain your decision:

    a. A manufacturer of computer chips randomly selects 100 chips from each hour's production in order to estimate the proportion defective. Let x represent the number of defectives in the 100 sampled chips.

    b. Of five applicants for a job, two will be selected. Although all applicants appear to be equally qualified, only three have the ability to fulfill the expectations of the company. Suppose that the two selections are made at random from the five applicants, and let x be the number of qualified applicants selected.

    c. A software developer establishes a support hotline for customers to call in with questions regarding use of the software. Let x represent the number of calls received on the support hotline during a specified workday.

    d. Florida is one of a minority of states with no state income tax. A poll of 1,000 registered voters is conducted to determine how many would favor a state income tax in light of the state's current fiscal condition. Let x be the number in the sample who would favor the tax.

4.165 Given that x is a binomial random variable, compute $p(x)$ for each of the following cases:

a. $n = 7, x = 3, p = .5$
b. $n = 4, x = 3, p = .8$
c. $n = 15, x = 1 \ p = .1$

4.166 Consider the discrete probability distribution shown here.

x	10	12	18	20
$p(x)$	.2	.3	.1	.4

a. Calculate μ, σ^2, and σ.
b. What is $P(x < 15)$?
c. Calculate $\mu \pm 2\sigma$.
d. What is the probability that x is in the interval $\mu \pm 2\sigma$?

4.167 Suppose x is a binomial random variable with $n = 20$ and $p = .7$.
a. Find $P(x = 14)$.
b. Find $P(x \le 12)$.
c. Find $P(x > 12)$.
d. Find $P(9 \le x \le 18)$.
e. Find $P(8 < x < 18)$.
f. Find μ, σ^2, and σ.
g. What is the probability that x is in the interval $\mu \pm 2\sigma$?

*4.168 Suppose x is a Poisson random variable. Compute $p(x)$ for each of the following cases:
a. $\lambda = 2, x = 3$
b. $\lambda = 1, x = 4$
c. $\lambda = .5, x = 2$

4.169 Which of the following describe discrete random variables, and which describe continuous random variables?
a. The number of damaged inventory items
b. The average monthly sales revenue generated by a salesperson over the past year
c. Square feet of warehouse space a company rents
d. The length of time a firm must wait before its copying machine is fixed

*4.170 Assume that x is a random variable best described by a uniform distribution with $c = 10$ and $d = 90$.
a. Find $f(x)$.
b. Find the mean and standard deviation of x.
c. Graph the probability distribution for x and locate its mean and the interval $\mu \pm 2\sigma$ on the graph.
d. Find $P(x \le 60)$.
e. Find $P(x \ge 90)$.
f. Find $P(x \le 80)$.
g. Find $P(\mu - \sigma \le x \le \mu + \sigma)$.
h. Find $P(x > 75)$.

4.171 Find the following probabilities for the standard normal random variable z:
a. $P(z \le 2.1)$
b. $P(z \ge 2.1)$
c. $P(z \ge -1.65)$
d. $P(-2.13 \le z \le -.41)$
e. $P(-1.45 \le z \le 2.15)$
f. $P(z \le -1.43)$

4.172 Find a z-score, call it z_0, such that
a. $P(z \le z_0) = .5080$
b. $P(z \ge z_0) = .5517$
c. $P(z \ge z_0) = .1492$
d. $P(z_0 \le z \le .59) = .4773$

4.173 The random variable x has a normal distribution with $\mu = 75$ and $\sigma = 10$. Find the following probabilities:
a. $P(x \le 80)$
b. $P(x \ge 85)$
c. $P(70 \le x \le 75)$
d. $P(x > 80)$
e. $P(x = 78)$
f. $P(x \le 110)$

*4.174 Assume that x is a binomial random variable with $n = 100$ and $p = .5$. Use the normal probability distribution to approximate the following probabilities:
a. $P(x \le 48)$
b. $P(50 \le x \le 65)$
c. $P(x \ge 70)$
d. $P(55 \le x \le 58)$
e. $P(x = 62)$
f. $P(x \le 49$ or $x > 72)$

4.175 The random variable x has a normal distribution with $\mu = 40$ and $\sigma^2 = 36$. Find a value of x, call it x_0, such that
a. $P(x \ge x_0) = .10$
b. $P(\mu \le x < x_0) = .40$
c. $P(x < x_0) = .05$
d. $P(x \ge x_0) = .40$
e. $P(x_0 \le x < \mu) = .45$

4.176 A random sample of 40 observations is to be drawn from a large population of measurements. It is known that 30% of the measurements in the population are 1s, 20% are 2s, 20% are 3s, and 30% are 4s.
a. Give the mean and standard deviation of the (repeated) sampling distribution of $\bar{x}$, the sample mean of the 40 observations.
b. Describe the shape of the sampling distribution of $\bar{x}$. Does your answer depend on the sample size?

4.177 A random sample of $n = 68$ observations is selected from a population with $\mu = 19.6$ and $\sigma = 3.2$. Approximate each of the following probabilities.
a. $P(\bar{x} \le 19.6)$
b. $P(\bar{x} \le 19)$
c. $P(\bar{x} \ge 20.1)$
d. $P(19.2 \le \bar{x} \le 20.6)$

4.178 Use a statistical software package to generate 100 random samples of size $n = 2$ from a population characterized by a uniform probability distribution (optional Section 4.6) with $c = 0$ and $d = 10$. Compute $\bar{x}$ for each sample, and plot a frequency distribution for the 100 $\bar{x}$ values. Repeat this process for $n = 5, 10, 30$, and 50. Explain how your plots illustrate the Central Limit Theorem.

4.179 A random sample of size n is to be drawn from a large population with mean 100 and standard deviation 10, and the sample mean $\bar{x}$ is to be calculated. To see the effect of different sample sizes on the standard deviation of the sampling distribution of $\bar{x}$, plot $\sigma/\sqrt{n}$ against n for $n = 1, 5, 10, 20, 30, 40$, and 50.

Applying the Concepts—Basic

4.180 **Accuracy of electronic checkout scanners.** A Federal Trade Commission (FTC) study of the pricing accuracy of electronic checkout scanners at stores found that one of every 30 items is priced incorrectly (*Price Check II: A Follow-up Report on the Accuracy of Checkout Scanner*

Prices, Dec. 16, 1998). Suppose the FTC randomly selects five items at a retail store and checks the accuracy of the scanner price of each. Let x represent the number of the five items that is priced incorrectly.

a. Show that x is (approximately) a binomial random variable.

b. Use the information in the FTC study to estimate p for the binomial experiment.

c. What is the probability that exactly one of the five items is priced incorrectly by the scanner?

d. What is the probability that at least one of the five items is priced incorrectly by the scanner?

*e. Suppose 10,000 supermarket items are scanned. What is the approximate probability that you observe at least 100 items with incorrect prices?

*f. Suppose 100 items are scanned and you are interested in the probability that fewer than five are incorrectly priced. Explain why the approximate method of part **a** may not yield an accurate estimate of the probability.

4.181 Dentists' use of laughing gas. According to the American Dental Association, 60% of all dentists use nitrous oxide in their practice (*New York Times*, June 20, 1995). If x equals the number of dentists in a random sample of five dentists who use laughing gas in practice, then the probability distribution of x is

x	0	1	2	3	4	5
$p(x)$	.0102	.0768	.2304	.3456	.2592	.0778

a. Verify that the probabilities for x sum to 1.

b. Find $P(x = 4)$.

c. Find $P(x < 2)$.

d. Find $P(x \geq 3)$.

e. Find $\mu = E(x)$ and practically interpret this value.

4.182 Analysis of "no-hitters" in baseball. In baseball, a *no-hitter* is a regulation nine-inning game in which the pitcher yields no hits to the opposing batters. *Chance* (Summer 1994) reported on a study of no-hitters in Major League Baseball (MLB). The initial analysis focused on the total number of hits yielded per game per team for nine-inning MLB games. The distribution of hits/nine-innings is approximately normal with mean 8.72 and standard deviation 1.10.

a. What percentage of nine-inning MLB games result in fewer than six hits?

b. Demonstrate, statistically, why a no-hitter is considered an extremely rare occurrence in MLB.

*4.183 Reimbursements to employees. A company found that monthly reimbursements to their employees, x, could be adequately modeled by a uniform distribution over the interval $\$10,000 \leq x \leq \$15,000$.

a. Find $E(x)$ and interpret it in the context of the exercise.

b. What is the probability of employee reimbursements exceeding $12,000 next month?

c. For budgeting purposes, the company needs to estimate next month's employee reimbursement expenses. How much should the company budget for employee reimbursements if they want the probability of exceeding the budgeted amount to be only .20?

*4.184 Arrivals at a cashier's counter. The number x of people who arrive at a cashier's counter in a bank during a specified period of time exhibits a Poisson probability distribution with mean arrival rate λ. Suppose you estimate that the mean number of arrivals per minute for cashier service at a bank is one person per minute (i.e., $\lambda = 1$).

a. What is the probability that in a given minute the number of arrivals will equal three?

b. What is the probability that the number of arrivals will exceed two per minute?

4.185 Evaluating elevator performance. One measure of elevator performance is cycle time—the time between successive elevator starts. *Simulation* (Oct. 1993) published a study on the use of a microcomputer based simulator for estimating elevator cycle times. The simulator produced an average cycle time μ of 26 seconds when traffic intensity was set at 50 persons every 5 minutes. Consider a sample of 200 simulated elevator runs and let $\bar{x}$ represent the mean cycle time of this sample.

a. What do you know about the distribution of x, the time between successive elevator starts? (Give the value of the mean and standard deviation of x and the shape of the distribution, if possible.)

b. What do you know about the distribution of $\bar{x}$? (Give the value of the mean and standard deviation of $\bar{x}$ and the shape of the distribution, if possible.)

c. Assume σ, the standard deviation of cycle time x, is 20 seconds. Use this information to calculate $P(\bar{x} > 26.8)$.

d. Repeat part **c** but assume $\sigma = 10$

Applying the Concepts—Intermediate

4.186 Substance abuse in the workplace. A study conducted in New Jersey by the Governor's Council for a Drug-Free Workplace concluded that 70% of New Jersey's businesses have employees whose performance is affected by drugs and/or alcohol. In those businesses, it was estimated that 8.5% of their workforces have alcohol problems and 5.2% have drug problems (*Report: The Governor's Council for a Drug-Free Workplace*, Spring/Summer 1995).

a. In a New Jersey company that acknowledges it has performance problems caused by substance abuse, out of every 1,000 employees, approximately how many have drug problems?

b. In the company referred to in part **a**, if 10 employees are randomly selected to form a committee to address alcohol abuse problems, what is the probability that at least one member of the committee is an alcohol abuser? That exactly two are alcohol abusers?

c. What assumptions did you have to make in order to answer part **b** using the methodology of this section?

4.187 GenXers' expectation of the future. Refer to the New Jersey Chamber of Commerce/Rutgers Business School/Arthur Anderson study of Generation Xers' expectations of their future careers, Exercise 2.78 (p. 85). Recall that a total of 590 GenXers responded to the question "What is the maximum number of years you expect to spend with any one employer?" The mean response was 18.2 years with a standard deviation of 10.64 years. Demonstrate why the distribution of years for all GenXers who respond is unlikely to be normally distributed.

4.188 Estimating demand for white bread. A bakery has determined that the number of loaves of its white bread demanded daily has a normal distribution with mean 7,200 loaves and standard deviation 300 loaves. Based on cost considerations, the company has decided that its best strategy is to produce a sufficient number of loaves so that it will fully supply demand on 94% of all days.

a. How many loaves of bread should the company produce?

b. Based on the production in part **a**, on what percentage of days will the company be left with more than 500 loaves of unsold bread?

*4.189 Millions of suburban commuters are finding railroads to be a convenient, time-saving, less stressful alternative to the automobile. While generally perceived as a safe mode of transportation, the average number of deaths per week due to railroad accidents is a surprisingly high 20 (U.S. National Center for Health Statistics, *Vital Statistics of the United States, 2001*).

a. Construct arguments both for and against the use of the Poisson distribution to characterize the number of deaths per week due to railroad accidents.

b. For the remainder of this exercise, assume the Poisson distribution is an adequate approximation for x, the number of deaths per week due to railroad accidents. Find $E(x)$ and the standard deviation of x.

c. Based strictly on your answers to part **b**, is it likely that only four or fewer deaths occur next week? Explain.

d. Find $P(x \le 4)$. Is this probability consistent with your answer to part **c**? Explain.

CLEANAIR

4.190 Environmental failures of Arkansas Companies. Refer to the study of 38 Arkansas corporations that were penalized for violating one or more environmental laws, Exercise 2.27 (p. 60). The financial penalties assessed to the companies are saved in the **CLEANAIR** file. Determine whether the financial penalties are approximately normally distributed.

BANKRUPT

4.191 Time in bankruptcy. Refer to the *Financial Management* (Spring 1995) study of 49 companies that filed for a prepackaged bankruptcy, Exercise 2.30 (p. 61). The time in bankruptcy (measured in months) for each company is saved in the **BANKRUPT** file. Determine whether the bankruptcy times are approximately normally distributed.

4.192 Comparing traditional and nontraditional college students. The *College Student Journal* (Dec. 1992) investigated differences in traditional and nontraditional students, where nontraditional students are generally defined as those 25 years or older and who are working full or part-time. Based on the study results, we can assume that the population mean and standard deviation for the GPA of all nontraditional students is $\mu = 3.5$ and $\sigma = .5$. Suppose that a random sample of $n = 100$ nontraditional students is selected from the population of all nontraditional students, and the GPA of each student is determined. Then $\bar{x}$, the sample mean, will be approximately normally distributed (because of the Central Limit Theorem).

a. Calculate $\mu_{\bar{x}}$ and $\sigma_{\bar{x}}$

b. What is the approximate probability that the nontraditional student sample has a mean GPA between 3.40 and 3.60?

c. What is the approximate probability that the sample of 100 nontraditional students has a mean GPA that exceeds 3.62?

d. How would the sampling distribution of $\bar{x}$ change if the sample size n were doubled from 100 to 200? How do your answers to parts **b** and **c** change when the sample size is doubled?

4.193 Errors in measuring truck weights. To help highway planners anticipate the need for road repairs and design future construction projects, data are collected on the estimated volume and weight of truck traffic on specific roadways (*Transportation Planning Handbook*, 1992) using specialized "weigh-in-motion" equipment. In an experiment performed by the Minnesota Department of Transportation involving repeated weighing of a 27,907-pound truck, it was found that the weights recorded by the weigh-in-motion equipment were approximately normally distributed with mean 27,315 and a standard deviation of 628 pounds (Minnesota Department of Transportation). It follows that the difference between the actual weight and recorded weight, the error of measurement, is normally distributed with mean 592 pounds and standard deviation 628 pounds.

a. What is the probability that the weigh-in-motion equipment understates the actual weight of the truck?

b. If a 27,907-pound truck was driven over the weigh-in-motion equipment 100 times, approximately how many times would the equipment overstate the truck's weight?

c. What is the probability that the error in the weight recorded by the weigh-in-motion equipment for a 27,907-pound truck exceeds 400 pounds?

d. It is possible to adjust (or *calibrate*) the weigh-in-motion equipment to control the mean error of measurement. At what level should the mean error be set so the equipment will understate the weight of a 27,907-pound truck 50% of the time? Only 40% of the time?

4.194 Errors in filling prescriptions A large number of preventable errors (e.g., overdoses, botched operations, misdiagnoses) are being made by doctors and nurses in U.S. hospitals (*New York Times*, July 18, 1995). A study of a major metropolitan hospital revealed that of every 100 medications prescribed or dispensed, one was in error; but, only 1 in 500 resulted in an error that caused significant problems for the patient. It is known that the hospital prescribes and dispenses 60,000 medications per year.

a. What is the expected number of errors per year at this hospital? The expected number of significant errors per year?

b. Within what limits would you expect the number of significant errors per year to fall?

c. What assumptions did you need to make in order to answer these questions?

4.195 Whistle-blowing among federal employees. The *Journal of Applied Psychology* (Vol. 71, 1986) reported the results of an extensive survey conducted to determine the extent of whistle-blowing among federal employees. *Whistle-blowing* refers to an employee's reporting of wrongdoing by coworkers. The survey found that about 5% of employees contacted had reported wrongdoing during the past 12 months. Assume that a sample of 25 employees in one agency are contacted, and let x be the number who have observed and reported wrongdoing in the last 12 months. Assume that the probability of whistle-blowing is .05 for any federal employee over the past 12 months.

a. Find the mean and standard deviation of x. Can x be equal to its expected value? Explain.

b. Write the event that at least five of the employees are whistle-blowers in terms of x. Find the probability of the event.

c. If 5 of the 25 contacted have been whistle-blowers over the past 12 months, what would you conclude about the applicability of the 5% assumption to this agency? Use your answer to part **b** to justify your conclusion.

4.196 A manufacturer produces safety jackets for competitive fencers. These jackets are rated by the minimum force, in newtons, that will allow a weapon to pierce the jacket. When this process is operating correctly, it produces jackets that have ratings with an average of 840 newtons and a standard deviation of 15 newtons. FIE, the international governing body for fencing, requires jackets to be rated at a minimum of 800 newtons. To check whether the process is operating correctly, a manager takes a sample of 50 jackets from the process, rates them, and calculates $\bar{x}$, the mean rating for jackets in the sample. She assumes that the standard deviation of the process is fixed but is worried that the mean rating of the process may have changed.

a. What is the sampling distribution of $\bar{x}$ if the process is still operating correctly?

b. Suppose the manager's sample has a mean rating of 830 newtons. What is the probability of getting an $\bar{x}$ of 830 newtons or lower if the process is operating correctly?

c. Given the manager's assumption that the standard deviation of the process is fixed, what does your answer to part **b** suggest about the current state of the process (i.e., does it appear that the mean jacket rating is still 840 newtons)?

d. Now suppose that the mean of the process has not changed, but the standard deviation of the process has increased from 15 newtons to 45 newtons. What is the sampling distribution of $\bar{x}$ in this case? What is the probability of getting an $\bar{x}$ of 830 newtons or lower when $\bar{x}$ has this distribution?

4.197 **How many questionnaires to mail?** The probability that a consumer responds to a marketing department's mailed questionnaire is .4. How many questionnaires should be mailed if you want to be reasonably certain that at least 100 will be returned?

Applying the Concepts—Advanced

4.198 **Establishing tolerance limits.** The *tolerance limits* for a particular quality characteristic (e.g., length, weight, or strength) of a product are the minimum and/or maximum values at which the product will operate properly. Tolerance limits are set by the engineering design function of the manufacturing operation (Moss, *Applying TQM to*

Product Design and Development, 1996). The tensile strength of a particular metal part can be characterized as being normally distributed with a mean of 25 pounds and a standard deviation of 2 pounds. The upper and lower tolerance limits for the part are 30 pounds and 21 pounds, respectively. A part that falls within the tolerance limits results in a profit of $10. A part that falls below the lower tolerance limit costs the company $2; a part that falls above the upper tolerance limit costs the company $1. Find the company's expected profit per metal part produced.

∗**4.199** **Purchasing decision.** A building contractor has decided to purchase a load of factory-reject aluminum siding as long as the average number of flaws per piece of siding in a sample of size 35 from the factory's reject pile is 2.1 or less. If it is known that the number of flaws per piece of siding in the factory's reject pile has a Poisson probability distribution with a mean of 2.5, find the approximate probability that the contractor will not purchase a load of siding.

Critical Thinking Challenges

4.200 **Reverse cocaine sting.** *The American Statistician* (May 1991) described an interesting application of a probability distribution in a case involving illegal drugs. During a drug bust, police seized 496 foil packets of a white, powdery substance that appeared to be cocaine. The police laboratory randomly selected four packets and found that all four tested positive for cocaine. This finding led to the conviction of the drug traffickers. Following the conviction, the police used two of the remaining 492 foil packets (i.e., those not tested) in a reverse sting operation. The two randomly selected packets were sold by undercover officers to a buyer who disposed of the evidence before being arrested. Is there beyond a reasonable doubt that the two packets contained cocaine? To solve the dilemma, assume that of the 496 original packets confiscated, 331 contained genuine cocaine and 165 contained an inert (legal) powder. (A statistician, hired as an expert witness on the case, showed that the chance of the defendant being found not guilty is maximized when 331 packets contain cocaine and 165 do not.) [Hint: First, find the probability that four packets randomly selected from the original 496 will test positive for cocaine. Next find the probability that the two packets sold in the reverse sting did not contain cocaine. Finally, find the probability that both events occur (i.e., that the first four packets selected test positive for cocaine but that the next two pack selected do not). In each of these probability calculations, apply the binomial probability distribution to approximate the probabilities.]

4.201 **The insomnia pill.** A research report published in the *Proceedings of the National Academy of Sciences* (Mar. 1994) brought encouraging news to insomniacs and international business travelers who suffer from jet lag. Neuroscientists at the Massachusetts Institute of Technology (MIT) have been experimenting with melatonin—a hormone secreted by the pineal gland in the brain—as a sleep-inducing hormone. Since the hormone is naturally produced, it is nonaddictive. The researchers believe melatonin may be effective in treating jet lag. In the MIT study, young male volunteers were given various doses of melatonin or a placebo (a dummy medication containing no melatonin). Then they were placed in a dark room at midday and told to close their eyes for 30 minutes. The variable of interest was the time (in minutes) elapsed before each volunteer fell asleep.

Now, consider a random sample of 40 young males, each of whom is given a dosage of the sleep-inducing hormone, melatonin. The times (in minutes) to fall asleep for these 40 males are listed in the table and saved in the **INSOMNIA** file. The researchers know that with the placebo (i.e., no hormone), the mean time to fall asleep is

$\mu = 15$ minutes and the standard deviation is $\sigma = 10$ minutes. They want to use the data to make an inference about the true value of μ for those taking the melatonin. Is melatonin an effective drug against insomnia?

INSOMNIA

7.6	2.1	1.4	1.5	3.6	17.0	14.9	4.4	4.7	20.1
7.7	2.4	8.1	1.5	10.3	1.3	3.7	2.5	3.4	10.7
2.9	1.5	15.9	3.0	1.9	8.5	6.1	4.5	2.2	2.6
7.0	6.4	2.8	2.8	22.8	1.5	4.6	2.0	6.3	3.2

[Note: These data are simulated sleep times based on summary information provided in the MIT study.]

REFERENCES

Deming, W. E. *Out of the Crisis*. Cambridge, Mass.: MIT Center for Advanced Engineering Study, 1986.

Hogg, R. V., and Craig, A. T. *Introduction to Mathematical Statistics*, 5th ed. Upper Saddle River, N.J.: Prentice Hall, 1995.

Larsen, R. J., and Marx, M. I. *An Introduction to Mathematical Statistics and Its Applications*, 3rd ed. Upper Saddle River, N.J.: Prentice Hall, 2001.

Lindgren, B. W. *Statistical Theory*, 3rd ed. New York: Macmillan, 1976.

Ramsey, P. P., and Ramsey, P. H. "Simple Tests of Normality in Small Samples." *Journal of Quality Technology*, Vol. 22, 1990.

Wackerly, D., Mendenhall, W., and Scheaffer, R, *Mathematical Statistics with Applications*, 6th ed. North Scituate, Mass.: Duxbury, 2002.

Using Technology

Binomial Probabilities, Normal Probabilities, and Simulated Sampling Distributions Using SPSS

Binomial Probabilities

To obtain binomial probabilities using SPSS, click on the "Transform" button on the SPSS menu bar, then click on "Compute", as shown in Figure 4.S.1. The resulting dialog box appears as shown in Figure 4.S.2. Specify a name for the "Target Variable" (e.g., the name of the probability you want to find), then select the appropriate probability function in the "Numeric Expression" box. SPSS allows you to compute cumulative probabilities or probabilities of exact values. For cumulative probabilities of the binomial, use the function CDF.BINOM. For exact binomial probabilities, use the PDF.BINOM function. You will need to enter the parameters of each distribution you select.

Figure 4.S.1

SPSS menu options for obtaining probabilities

Figure 4.S.2
SPSS Compute Variable dialog box

For example, Figure 4.S.2 shows the cumulative binomial function with parameters of $x = 3$ (the first number in the function), $n = 10$ (the second number), and $p = .2$ (the third number). When you click "OK", SPSS will compute the requested probability (in this example, the cumulative binomial probability that x is less than or equal to 3) and display it on the SPSS spreadsheet.

Normal Probabilities
To obtain cumulative probabilities for the normal random variable using SPSS, click on the "Transform" button on the SPSS menu bar, then click on "Compute". The resulting dialog box appears as shown in Figure 4.S.3. Specify a name for the "Target Variable" (e.g., the name of the probability you want to find), then select the appropriate probability function in the "Numeric Expression" box. For cumulative probabilities of the normal distributions, use the CDF.NORMAL function. You will need to enter the parameters of each distribution you select.

For example, Figure 4.S.3 shows the cumulative normal function with parameters of $x = 3.7$ (the first number in the function), $\mu = 5$ (the second number), and $\sigma = 2$ (the third number). When you click "OK", SPSS will compute the requested probability (in this example, the cumulative normal probability that x is less than 3.7) and display it on the SPSS spreadsheet.

Figure 4.S.3
SPSS Compute Variable
dialog box

Normal Probability Plot

To obtain a normal probability plot using SPSS, click on the "Graphs" button on the SPSS menu bar, then click on "Q-Q", as shown in Figure 4.S.4. The resulting dialog box appears as shown in Figure 4.S.5. Specify the variable of interest in the "Variables" box, select "Normal" in the "Test Distribution" box, then click "OK" to generate the normal probability plot.

Figure 4.S.4
SPSS options for a normal probability plot

Figure 4.S.5
SPSS Normal Probability Plot
dialog box

Sampling Distributions

Generating sampling distributions with SPSS is not a simple process. Consult the SPSS user's guide for help with this feature.

Binomial Probabilities, Normal Probabilities, and Simulated Sampling Distributions Using MINITAB

Binomial Probabilities

To obtain binomial probabilities using MINITAB, first enter the values of x for which you desire probabilities in a column (e.g., C1) on the MINITAB worksheet. Now click on the "Calc" button on the MINITAB menu bar, click on "Probability Distributions", then finally click on the distribution of your choice (e.g., "Binomial"), as shown in Figure 4.M.1. The resulting

Figure 4.M.1
MINITAB menu options for
obtaining probabilities

Figure 4.M.2
MINITAB Binomial
Distribution dialog box

dialog box appears as shown in Figure 4.M.2. Select either "Probabilities" or "Cumulative probabilities", specify the parameters of the distribution (e.g., sample size n and probability of success p), and enter "C1" in the "Input column". When you click "OK", the binomial probabilities for the values of x (saved in C1) will appear on the MINITAB worksheet.

Normal Probabilities

To obtain cumulative probabilities for the normal random variable using MINITAB, click on the "Calc" button on the MINITAB menu bar, click on "Probability Distributions", then click on the distribution of your choice (e.g., "Normal"), as shown in Figure 4.M.1. The resulting dialog box appears as shown in Figure 4.M.3. Select "Cumulative probability", specify the parameters of the distribution (e.g., the mean μ and standard deviation σ), and enter the value of x in the "Input constant" box. When you click "OK", the cumulative normal probability for the value of x will appear on the MINITAB session window.

Figure 4.M.3
MINITAB Normal
Distribution dialog box

Normal Probability Plot

To obtain a normal probability plot using MINITAB, click on the "Graph" button on the MINITAB menu bar, then click on "Probability Plot", as shown in Figure 4.M.4. Select "Single" (for one variable) on the next box, and the dialog box will appear as shown in Figure 4.M.5. Specify the variable of interest in the "Graph variables" box, then click the "Distribution" button and select the "Normal" option. Click "OK" to return to the Probability Plot dialog box, then click "OK" to generate the normal probability plot.

Figure 4.M.4
MINITAB options for a
normal probability plot

Figure 4.M.5
MINITAB Probability Plot
dialog box

Sampling Distributions

To generate a sampling distribution for a sample statistic using MINITAB, click on the "Calc" button on the MINITAB menu bar, click on "Random Data", then click on the distribution of your choice (e.g., "Uniform"). A dialog box similar to the one (the Uniform Distribution) shown in Figure 4.M.6 will appear. Specify the number of samples (e.g., 1000) to generate in the "Generate . . . rows of data" box and the columns where the data will be stored in the "Store in columns" box. (The number of columns will be equal to the sample size, e.g., 40.) Finally, specify the parameters of the distribution (e.g., the lower and upper range of the uniform distribution). When you click "OK", the simulated data will appear on the MINITAB worksheet.

Next, calculate the value of the sample statistic of interest for each sample. To do this, click on the "Calc" button on the MINITAB menu bar, then click on "Row Statistics", as shown in Figure 4.M.7. The resulting dialog box appears in Figure 4.M.8. Check the sample statistic (e.g., the mean) you want to calculate, specify the "Input variables" (or columns), and the column where you want the value of the sample statistic to be saved. Click "OK" and the value of the statistic for each sample will appear on the MINITAB worksheet.

Figure 4.M.6
MINITAB dialog box for simulating the uniform distribution

Figure 4.M.7
MINITAB selections for generating sample statistics for the simulated data

Figure 4.M.8
MINITAB Row Statistics
dialog box

[*Note:* Use the MINITAB menu choices provided in the "Chapter 2 Technology Tutorial" to generate a histogram of the sampling distribution of the statistic or to find the mean and variance of the sampling distribution.]

Binomial Probabilities, Normal Probabilities, and Simulated Sampling Distributions Using Excel/PHStat2

Binomial Probabilities

To obtain binomial probabilities using Excel, first enter into a PHStat2 session. Now click on the "PHStat2" button on the main menu bar, click on "Probability Distributions", then finally click on the distribution of your choice (e.g., "Binomial"), as shown in Figure 4.E.1. The resulting dialog box appears as shown in Figure 4.E.2. Specify the parameters of the distribution (e.g., sample size n and probability of success p), and give the values of x you want to compute probabilities for in the "Outcomes from" box. When you click "OK", the binomial probabilities for the values of x specified will appear on a new Excel workbook.

Figure 4.E.1
Excel/PHStat2 menu options for obtaining probabilities

Figure 4.E.2

Excel/PHStat2 Binomial dialog box

Figure 4.E.3

Excel/PHStat2 Normal dialog box

Normal Probabilities

To obtain cumulative probabilities for the normal random variable using Excel, first enter into a PHStat2 session. Now click on the "PHStat2" button on the main menu bar, then click on "Probability Distributions", as shown in Figure 4.E.1. Then, click on the distribution of your choice (e.g., "Normal"). The resulting dialog box appears as shown in Figure 4.E.3. Specify the parameters of the distribution (e.g., the mean μ and standard deviation σ), click the cumulative probability you desire ($X <=$ or $X >$), and specify the value of x of interest in the box. When you click "OK", the cumulative normal probability for the value of x specified will appear on a new Excel workbook.

Normal Probability Plot

To obtain a normal probability plot, click on the "PHStat" button on the Excel menu bar, select "Probability & Prob. Distributions", then click on "Normal Probability Plot", as shown in Figure 4.E.4. The dialog box will appear as shown in Figure 4.E.5. Specify the cell range for the variable of interest, then click "OK" to generate the normal probability plot.

Figure 4.E.4

Excel/PHStat2 options for a normal probability plot

Figure 4.E.5
PHStat2 Normal Probability
Plot dialog box

Sampling Distributions

To generate a sampling distribution for the sample mean using Excel, click on the "PHStat" button on the main menu bar, click on "Sampling", then click on "Sampling Distributions Simulation", as shown in Figure 4.E.6. The dialog box shown in Figure 4.E.7 will appear. Specify the number of samples (e.g., 250) to generate and the sample size of each (e.g., 30). Finally, specify the distribution (either Uniform or Standardized Normal) that the samples will be selected from. When you click "OK", the simulated data will appear on a new Excel spreadsheet, as well as the means for each sample and a histogram of the sample means.

Figure 4.E.6
Excel options for simulating a sampling distribution

Figure 4.E.7
Excel/PHStat2 dialog box for
simulating the sampling distribution of the mean

Real-World Case
The Furniture Fire Case

(A Case Covering Chapters 3–4)

A wholesale furniture retailer stores in-stock items at a large warehouse located in Tampa, Florida. In early 1992, a fire destroyed the warehouse and all the furniture in it. After determining the fire was an accident, the retailer sought to recover costs by submitting a claim to its insurance company.

As is typical in a fire insurance policy of this type, the furniture retailer must provide the insurance company with an estimate of "lost" profit for the destroyed items. Retailers calculate profit margin in percentage form using the Gross Profit Factor (GPF). By definition, the GPF for a single sold item is the ratio of the profit to the item's selling price measured as a percentage, that is,

Item GPF = (Profit/Sales price) × 100%

Of interest to both the retailer and the insurance company is the average GPF for all of the items in the warehouse. Since these furniture pieces were all destroyed, their eventual selling prices and profit values are obviously unknown. Consequently, the average GPF for all the warehouse items is unknown.

One way to estimate the mean GPF of the destroyed items is to use the mean GPF of similar, recently sold items. The retailer sold 3,005 furniture items in 1991 (the year prior to the fire) and kept paper invoices on all sales. Rather than calculate the mean GPF for all 3,005 items (the data were not computerized), the retailer sampled a total of 253 of the invoices and computed the mean GPF for these items. The 253 items were obtained by first selecting a sample of 134 items and then augmenting this sample with a second sample of 119 items. The mean GPFs for the two subsamples were calculated to be 50.6% and 51.0%, respectively, yielding an overall average GPF of 50.8%. This average GPF can be applied to the costs of the furniture items destroyed in the fire to obtain an estimate of the "lost" profit.

According to experienced claims adjusters at the insurance company, the GPF for sale items of the type destroyed in the fire rarely exceeds 48% Consequently, the estimate of 50.8% appeared to be unusually high. (A 1% increase in GPF for items of this type equates to, approximately, an additional $16,000 in profit.) When the insurance company questioned the retailer on this issue, the retailer responded "Our estimate was based on selecting two independent, random samples from the population of 3,005 invoices in 1991. Since the samples were selected randomly and the total sample size is large, the mean GPF estimate of 50.8% is valid."

A dispute arose between the furniture retailer and the insurance company, and a lawsuit was filed. In one portion of the suit, the insurance company accused the retailer of fraudulently representing their sampling methodology. Rather than selecting the samples randomly, the retailer was accused of selecting an unusual number of "high-profit" items from the population in order to increase the average GPF of the overall sample.

To support their claim of fraud, the insurance company hired a CPA firm to independently assess the retailer's 1991 Gross Profit Factor. Through the discovery process, the CPA firm legally obtained the paper invoices for the entire population of 3,005 items sold and input the information into a computer. The selling price, profit, profit margin, and month sold for these 3,005 furniture items are stored in the **FIRE** file, described below.

Your objective in this case is to use these data to determine the likelihood of fraud. Is it likely that a random sample of 253 items selected from the population of 3,005 items would yield a mean GPF of at least 50.8%? Or, is it likely that two independent, random samples of size 134 and 119 will yield mean GPFs of at least 50.6% and 51.0%, respectively? (These were the questions posed to a statistician retained by the CPA firm.) Use the ideas of probability and sampling distributions to guide your analysis.

Prepare a professional document that presents the results of your analysis and gives your opinion regarding fraud. Be sure to describe the assumptions and methodology used to arrive at your findings.

FIRE

Variable	Type	Description
MONTH	QL	Month in which item was sold in 1991
INVOICE	QN	Invoice number
SALES	QN	Sales price of item in dollars
PROFIT	QN	Profit amount of item in dollars
MARGIN	QN	Profit margin of item = (Profit/Sales) × 100%

CHAPTER **5**

Inferences Based on a Single Sample

Estimation with Confidence Intervals

CONTENTS

STATISTICS IN ACTION
Scallops, Sampling, and the Law

USING TECHNOLOGY

WHERE WE'VE BEEN

■ Learned that populations are characterized by numerical descriptive measures called *parameters*

■ Found that decisions about population parameters are based on *statistics* computed from the sample

■ Discovered that *inferences* about parameters are subject to uncertainty and that this uncertainty is reflected in the *sampling distribution* of a statistic

WHERE WE'RE GOING

■ Estimate a population parameter (means or proportion) based on a large sample selected from the population.

■ Use the sampling distribution of a statistic to form a confidence interval for the population parameter.

■ Show how to select the proper sample size for estimating a population parameter.

STATISTICS IN ACTION

Scallops, Sampling, and the Law

Arnold Bennett, a Sloan School of Management professor at the Massachusetts Institute of Technology (MIT), described a legal case in Interfaces *(Mar.–Apr. 1995) in which he served as a statistical "expert." The case involved a ship that fishes for scallops off the coast of New England. In order to protect baby scallops from being harvested, the U.S. Fisheries and Wildlife Service requires that the average meat per scallop weigh at least 1/36 of a pound. The ship was accused of violating this weight standard. Bennett lays out the scenario:*

The vessel arrived at a Massachusetts port with 11,000 bags of scallops, from which the harbormaster randomly selected 18 bags for weighing. From each such bag, his agents took a large scoop full of scallops; then, to estimate the bag's average meat per scallop, they divided the total weight of meat in the scoop by the number of scallops it contained. Based on the 18 [numbers] thus generated, the harbormaster estimated that each of the ship's scallops possessed an average of 1/39 of a pound of meat (that is, they were about seven percent lighter than the minimum requirement). Viewing this outcome as conclusive evidence that the weight standard had been violated, federal authorities at once confiscated 95 percent of the catch (which they then sold at auction). The fishing voyage was thus transformed into a financial catastrophe for its participants.

Bennett provided the estimated scallop weight measurements (in pounds) for each of the 18 sampled bags in the article. These data are available in the file called **SCALLOPS.** [*Note:* 1/36 of a pound, the minimum permissible average weight per scallop, is equivalent to .0278 pound. Consequently, weights below .0278 indicate individual bags that do not meet the standard.] The ship's owner filed a lawsuit against the federal government, declaring that his vessel had fully complied with the weight standard. A Boston law firm was hired to represent the owner in legal proceedings, and Bennett was retained by the firm to provide statistical litigation support and, if necessary, expert witness testimony.

In this chapter, several Statistics in Action Revisited examples demonstrate how confidence intervals can be used to support the ship's owner in the lawsuit.

 SCALLOPS

Statistics in Action Revisited

- Estimating the Mean Weight per Scallop (p. 307)
- Estimating the Proportion of Underweight Scallop Bags (p. 317)
- Determining the Number of Bags of Scallops to Sample (p. 325)

5.1 Identifying the Target Parameter

In this chapter, our goal is to estimate the value of an unknown population parameter, such as a population mean or a proportion from a binomial population. For example, we might want to know the mean gas mileage for a new car model, or the average expected life of a flat-screen computer monitor, or the proportion of dot-com companies that fail within a year of start-up.

You'll see that different techniques are used for estimating a mean or proportion, depending on whether a sample contains a large or small number of measurements. Nevertheless, our objectives remain the same. We want to use the sample information to estimate the population parameter of interest (called the **target parameter**) and to assess the reliability of the estimate.

> **Definition 5.1**
>
> The unknown population parameter (e.g., mean or proportion) that we are interested in estimating is called the **target parameter.**

Often, there are one or more key words in the statement of the problem that indicate the appropriate target parameter. Some key words associated with the two parameters covered in this section are listed in the accompanying table.

Determining the Target Parameter

Parameter	Key Words or Phrases	Type of Data
μ	Mean; average	Quantitative
p	Proportion; percentage; fraction; rate	Qualitative

For the examples given above, the words *mean* in *mean gas mileage*, and *average* in *average life expectancy* imply that the target parameter is the population mean, μ. The word *proportion* in *proportion of dot-com companies that fail within one year of start-up* indicates that the target parameter is the binomial proportion, p.

In addition to key words and phrases, the type of data (quantitative or qualitative) collected is indicative of the target parameter. With quantitative data, you are likely to be estimating the mean of the data. With qualitative data with two outcomes (success or failure), the binomial proportion of successes is likely to be the parameter of interest.

We consider a method of estimating a population mean using a large sample in Section 5.2 and a small sample in Section 5.3. Estimation of a population proportion is presented in Section 5.4. In Section 5.5, we show how to determine the sample sizes necessary for reliable estimates of the target parameters based on simple random sampling. Finally, in optional Sections 5.6 and 5.7 we introduce more complex sample survey designs and their application to business.

5.2 Large-Sample Confidence Interval for a Population Mean

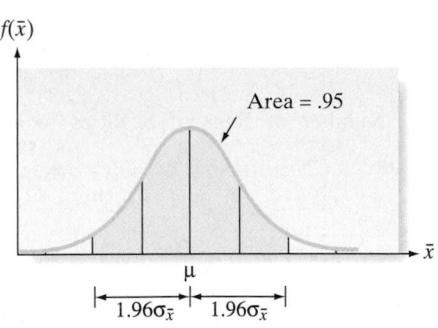

$f(\bar{x})$

Area = .95

μ

$1.96\sigma_{\bar{x}}$ $1.96\sigma_{\bar{x}}$

$\bar{x}$

FIGURE 5.1
Sampling distribution of $\bar{x}$

Suppose a large bank wants to estimate the average amount of money owed by its delinquent debtors (i.e., debtors who are more than 2 months behind in payment). To accomplish this objective, the bank plans to randomly sample 100 of its delinquent accounts and to use the sample mean, $\bar{x}$, of the amounts overdue to estimate μ, the mean for *all* delinquent accounts. The sample mean $\bar{x}$ represents a single number estimator—called a *point estimator*—of the population mean μ. How can we assess the accuracy of this point estimator?

> **Definition 5.2**
>
> A **point estimator** of a population parameter is a rule or formula that tells us how to use the sample data to calculate a *single* number that can be used as an *estimate* of the population parameter.

According to the Central Limit Theorem, the sampling distribution of the sample mean is approximately normal for large samples, as shown in Figure 5.1. Let us calculate the interval

$$\bar{x} \pm 1.96\sigma_{\bar{x}} = \bar{x} \pm \frac{1.96\sigma}{\sqrt{n}}$$

OVERDUE

TABLE 5.1   Overdue Amounts (in Dollars) for 100 Delinquent Accounts

195	243	132	133	209	400	142	312	221	289
221	162	134	275	355	293	242	458	378	148
278	222	236	178	202	222	334	208	194	135
363	221	449	265	146	215	113	229	221	243
512	193	134	138	209	207	206	310	293	310
237	135	252	365	371	238	232	271	121	134
203	178	180	148	162	160	86	234	244	266
119	259	108	289	328	331	330	227	162	354
304	141	158	240	82	17	357	187	364	268
368	274	278	190	344	157	219	77	171	280

That is, we form an interval from 1.96 standard deviations below the sample mean to 1.96 standard deviations above the mean. *Prior to drawing the sample*, what are the chances that this interval will enclose μ, the population mean?

To answer this question, refer to Figure 5.1. If the 100 measurements yield a value of $\bar{x}$ that falls between the two lines on either side of μ (i.e., within 1.96 standard deviations of μ), then the interval $\bar{x} \pm 1.96\sigma_{\bar{x}}$ will contain μ; if $\bar{x}$ falls outside these boundaries, the interval $\bar{x} \pm 1.96\sigma_{\bar{x}}$ will not contain μ. From Section 4.7, we know that the area under the normal curve (the sampling distribution of $\bar{x}$) between these boundaries is exactly .95. Thus, the probability that a randomly selected interval, $\bar{x} \pm 1.96\sigma_{\bar{x}}$, will contain μ is equal to .95.

For instance, consider the overdue amounts for 100 delinquent accounts shown in Table 5.1. An Excel printout of summary statistics for the sample of 100 overdue amounts is shown in Figure 5.2a. From the shaded portion of the printout, we find $\bar{x} = \$233.28$ and $s = \$90.34$. To achieve our objective, we must construct the interval

$$\bar{x} \pm 1.96\sigma_{\bar{x}} = 233.28 \pm 1.96\frac{\sigma}{\sqrt{100}}$$

	A	B
1		AMOUNT
2		
3	Mean	233.28
4	Standard Error	9.033988347
5	Median	222
6	Mode	221
7	Standard Deviation	90.33988347
8	Sample Variance	8161.294545
9	Kurtosis	0.254810234
10	Skewness	0.476799829
11	Range	495
12	Minimum	17
13	Maximum	512
14	Sum	23328
15	Count	100

FIGURE 5.2a

Excel summary statistics for overdue amounts

But now we face a problem. You can see that without knowing the standard deviation σ of the original population—that is, the standard deviation of the overdue amounts of *all* delinquent accounts—we cannot calculate this interval. However, since we have a large sample ($n = 100$ measurements), we can approximate the interval by using the sample standard deviation s to approximate σ. Thus,

$$\bar{x} \pm 1.96\frac{\sigma}{\sqrt{100}} \approx \bar{x} \pm 1.96\frac{s}{\sqrt{100}} = 233.28 \pm 1.96\left(\frac{90.34}{10}\right) = 233.28 \pm 17.71$$

	A	B
1	Confidence Interval Estimate for the Mean	
2		
3	Data	
4	Sample Standard Deviation	90.33988347
5	Sample Mean	233.28
6	Sample Size	100
7	Confidence Level	95%
8		
9	Intermediate Calculations	
10	Standard Error of the Mean	9.033988347
11	Degrees of Freedom	99
12	t Value	1.984217306
13	Interval Half Width	17.92539602
14		
15	Confidence Interval	
16	Interval Lower Limit	215.35
17	Interval Upper Limit	251.21

FIGURE 5.2b

Excel/PHStat2 output showing 95% confidence interval for mean

That is, we estimate the mean amount of delinquency for all accounts to fall within the interval $215.57 to $250.99. (This interval is highlighted at the bottom of the Excel/PHStat2 printout, Figure 5.2b. Differences are due to rounding.)

Can we be sure that μ, the true mean, is in the interval (215.57, 250.99)? We cannot be certain, but we can be reasonably confident that it is. This confidence is derived from the knowledge that if we were to draw repeated random samples of 100 measurements from this population and form the interval $\bar{x} \pm 1.96\sigma_{\bar{x}}$ each time, 95% of the intervals would contain μ. We have no way of knowing (without looking at all the delinquent accounts) whether our sample interval is one of the 95% that contains μ or one of the 5% that does not, but the odds certainly favor its containing μ. Consequently, the interval $215.57 to $250.99 provides a reliable estimate of the mean delinquency per account.

The formula that tells us how to calculate an interval estimate based on sample data is called an *interval estimator*, or *confidence interval*. The probability, .95, that measures the confidence we can place in the interval estimate is called a *confidence coefficient*. The percentage, 95%, is called the *confidence level* for the interval estimate. It is not usually possible to assess precisely the reliability of point estimators because they are single points rather than intervals. So, because we prefer to use estimators for which a measure of reliability can be calculated, we will generally use interval estimators.

Definition 5.3

An **interval estimator** (or **confidence interval**) is a formula that tells us how to use sample data to calculate an interval that estimates a population parameter.

Definition 5.4

The **confidence coefficient** is the probability that a randomly selected confidence interval encloses the population parameter—that is, the relative frequency with which similarly constructed intervals enclose the population parameter when the estimator is used repeatedly a very large number of times. The **confidence level** is the confidence coefficient expressed as a percentage.

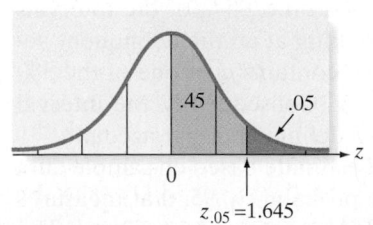

FIGURE 5.3

Confidence intervals for μ: 10 samples

Now we have seen how an interval can be used to estimate a population mean. When we use an interval estimator, we can usually calculate the probability that the estimation *process* will result in an interval that contains the true value of the population mean—that is, the probability that the interval contains the parameter in repeated usage is usually known. Figure 5.3 shows what happens when 10 different samples are drawn from a population, and a confidence interval for μ is calculated from each. The location of μ is indicated by the vertical line in the figure. Ten confidence intervals, each based on one of 10 samples, are shown as horizontal line segments. Note that the confidence intervals move from sample to sample—sometimes containing μ and other times missing μ. *If our confidence level is 95%, then in the long run, 95% of our confidence intervals will contain μ and 5% will not.*

Suppose you wish to choose a confidence coefficient other than .95. Notice in Figure 5.1 that the confidence coefficient .95 is equal to the total area under the sampling distribution, less .05 of the area, which is divided equally between the two tails. Using this idea, we can construct a confidence interval with any desired confidence coefficient by increasing or decreasing the area (call it α) assigned to the tails of the sampling distribution (see Figure 5.4). For example, if we place area $\alpha/2$ in each tail and if $z_{\alpha/2}$ is the z value such that the area $\alpha/2$ lies to its right, then the confidence interval with confidence coefficient $(1 - \alpha)$ is

$$\bar{x} \pm z_{\alpha/2}\sigma_{\bar{x}}$$

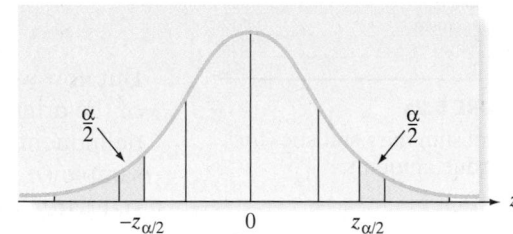

FIGURE 5.4

Locating $z_{\alpha/2}$ on the standard normal curve

Conditions Required for a Valid Large-Sample Confidence Interval for μ

1. A random sample is selected from the target population.
2. The sample size n is large (i.e., $n \geq 30$, due to the Central Limit Theorem, this condition guarantees that the sampling distribution of $\bar{x}$ is approximately normal. Also, for large n, s will be a good estimator of σ).

FIGURE 5.5

The z value ($z_{.05}$) corresponding to an area equal to .05 in the upper tail of the z-distribution

To illustrate, for a confidence coefficient of .90, we have $(1 - \alpha) = .90$, $\alpha = .10$, and $\alpha/2 = .05$; $z_{.05}$ is the z value that locates area .05 in the upper tail of the sampling distribution. Recall that Table IV in Appendix B gives the areas between the mean and a specified z value. Since the total area to the right of the mean is .5, we find that $z_{.05}$ will be the z value corresponding to an area of $.5 - .05 = .45$ to the right of the mean (see Figure 5.5). This z value is $z_{.05} = 1.645$.

Confidence coefficients used in practice usually range from .90 to .99. The most commonly used confidence coefficients with corresponding values of α and $z_{\alpha/2}$ are shown in Table 5.2.

Biography

TABLE 5.2 Commonly Used Values of $z_{\alpha/2}$

CONFIDENCE LEVEL			
$100(1 - \alpha)$	α	$\alpha/2$	$z_{\alpha/2}$
90%	.10	.05	1.645
→ 95%	.05	.025	1.96
99%	.01	.005	2.575

Now Work Exercise 5.1

Large-Sample $(1 - \alpha)\%$ Confidence Interval for μ

$$\overline{x} \pm z_{\alpha/2}\sigma_{\overline{x}} = \overline{x} \pm z_{\alpha/2}\frac{\sigma}{\sqrt{n}}$$

where $z_{\alpha/2}$ is the z value with an area $\alpha/2$ to its right (see Figure 5.4) and $\sigma_{\overline{x}} = \sigma/\sqrt{n}$. The parameter σ is the standard deviation of the sampled population and n is the sample size.

Note: When σ is unknown (as is almost always the case) and n is large (say, $n \geq 30$), the confidence interval is approximately equal to

$$\overline{x} \pm z_{\alpha/2}\left(\frac{s}{\sqrt{n}}\right)$$

where s is the sample standard deviation.

EXAMPLE 5.1

Finding a Large-Sample Confidence Interval for the Mean Number of Unoccupied Seats per Flight, μ

Problem Unoccupied seats on flights cause airlines to lose revenue. Suppose a large airline wants to estimate its average number of unoccupied seats per flight over the past year. To accomplish this, the records of 225 flights are randomly selected, and the number of unoccupied seats is noted for each of the sampled flights. (The data are saved in the **AIRNOSHOWS** file.) Descriptive statistics for the data are displayed in the MINITAB printout, Figure 5.6.

Estimate μ, the mean number of unoccupied seats per flight during the past year, using a 90% confidence interval.

AIRNOSHOWS

Solution The general form of the 90% confidence interval for a population mean is

$$\bar{x} \pm z_{\alpha/2}\sigma_{\bar{x}} = \bar{x} \pm z_{.05}\sigma_{\bar{x}} = \bar{x} \pm 1.645\left(\frac{\sigma}{\sqrt{n}}\right)$$

From Figure 5.6, we find (after rounding) $\bar{x} = 11.6$. Since we do not know the value of σ (the standard deviation of the number of unoccupied seats per flight for all flights of the year), we use our best approximation—the sample standard deviation s. Then the 90% confidence interval is, approximately,

$$11.6 \pm 1.645\left(\frac{4.1}{\sqrt{225}}\right) = 11.6 \pm .45$$

or from 11.15 to 12.05—that is, at the 90% confidence level, we estimate the mean number of unoccupied seats per flight to be between 11.15 and 12.05 during the sampled year. This result is verified (except for rounding) on the right side of the MINITAB printout in Figure 5.6.

FIGURE 5.6

MINITAB confidence interval for mean, Example 5.1

Variable	N	Mean	StDev	SE Mean	90% CI
NOSHOWS	225	11.5956	4.1026	0.2735	(11.1438, 12.0473)

Look Back We stress that the confidence level for this example, 90%, refers to the procedure used. If we were to apply this procedure repeatedly to different samples, approximately 90% of the intervals would contain μ. Although we do not know whether this particular interval (11.15, 12.05) is one of the 90% that contain μ or one of the 10% that do not, our knowledge of probability gives us "confidence" that the interval contains μ.

Now Work Exercise 5.10

The interpretation of confidence intervals for a population mean is summarized in the next box.

> **Interpretation of a Confidence Interval for a Population Mean**
>
> When we form a $100(1 - \alpha)\%$ confidence interval for m, we usually express our confidence in the interval with a statement such as, "We can be $100(1 - \alpha)\%$ confident that μ lies between the lower and upper bounds of the confidence interval," where for a particular application, we substitute the appropriate numerical values for the confidence and for the lower and upper bounds. *The statement reflects our confidence in the estimation process rather than in the particular interval that is calculated from the sample data.* We know that repeated application of the same procedure will result in different lower and upper bounds on the interval. Furthermore, we know that $100(1 - \alpha)\%$ of the resulting intervals will contain μ. There is (usually) no way to determine whether any particular interval is one of those that contain μ, or one that does not. However, unlike point estimators, confidence intervals have some measure of reliability, the confidence coefficient, associated with them. For that reason they are generally preferred to point estimators.

Sometimes, the estimation procedure yields a confidence interval that is too wide for our purposes. In this case, we will want to reduce the width of the interval to obtain a more precise estimate of μ. One way to accomplish this is to decrease the confidence coefficient, $1 - \alpha$. For example, reconsider the problem of estimating the mean amount owed, μ, for all delinquent accounts. Recall that for a sample of 100 accounts, $\bar{x} = \$233.28$ and $s = \$90.34$. A 90% confidence interval for μ is

$$\bar{x} \pm 1.645\sigma/\sqrt{n} \approx 233.28 \pm (1.645)(90.34/\sqrt{100}) = 233.28 \pm 14.86$$

or ($218.42, $248.14). You can see that this interval is narrower than the previously calculated 95% confidence interval ($215.57, $250.99). Unfortunately, we also have "less confidence" in the 90% confidence interval. An alternative method used to decrease the width of an interval without sacrificing "confidence" is to increase the sample size n. We demonstrate this method in Section 5.5.

Confidence Interval for a Population Mean (known σ or $n \geq 30$)

Using the TI-83/TI-84 Graphing Calculator
Creating a Confidence Interval for a Population Mean

Step 1 *Enter the data (Skip to Step 2 if you have summary statistics, not raw data)*

Press **STAT** and select **1:Edit**
Note: If the list already contains data, clear the old data. Use the up **ARROW** to highlight '**L1**'.
Press **CLEAR ENTER**.
Use the **ARROW** and **ENTER** keys to enter the data set into **L1**.

Step 2 *Access the Statistical Tests Menu*

Press **STAT**
Arrow right to **TESTS**
Arrow down to **ZInterval**
Press **ENTER**

```
EDIT CALC TESTS
1:Z-Test…
2:T-Test…
3:2-SampZTest…
4:2-SampTTest…
5:1-PropZTest…
6:2-PropZTest…
7↓ZInterval…
```

Step 3 *Choose "**Data**" or "**Stats.**" ("Data" is selected when you have entered the raw data into a List. "Stats" is selected when you are given only the mean, standard deviation, and sample size.)*

Press **ENTER**
If you selected "Data" enter a value for σ (the best approximation is s, the sample standard deviation)
Set **List** to **L1**
Set **Freq** to **1**
Set **C-Level** to the confidence level
Arrow down to "**Calculate**"
Press **ENTER**

```
ZInterval
 Inpt:Data Stats
 σ:8
 List:L1
 Freq:1
 C-Level:.95
 Calculate
```

If you selected "Stats" enter a value for σ (the best approximation is s, the sample standard deviation)
Enter the sample mean and sample size
Set **C-Level** to the confidence level
Arrow down to "**Calculate**"
Press **ENTER**
(The screen at right is set up for an example with a standard deviation of 20, a mean of 200 and a sample size of 40.)

```
ZInterval
 Inpt:Data Stats
 σ:20
 x̄:200
 n:40
 C-Level:.95
 Calculate
```

Continued

The confidence interval will be displayed along with the sample mean and the sample size.

Example Compute a 90% confidence interval for the mean number of unoccupied seats per flight using the the following information.

$$\bar{x} = 11.6 \text{ seats}, \quad s = 4.1 \text{ seats}, \quad n = 225 \text{ flights}$$

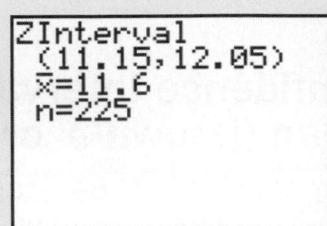

```
ZInterval
 (11.15,12.05)
 x̄=11.6
 n=225
```

As you can see from the screen, our 90% confidence interval is (11.5, 12.05). You will also notice the output displays the sample mean and sample size.

Exercises 5.1–5.20

Learning the Mechanics

5.1 Find $z_{\alpha/2}$ for each of the following:
NW **a.** $\alpha = .10$ **b.** $\alpha = .01$
      c. $\alpha = .05$ **d.** $\alpha = .20$

5.2 What is the confidence level of each of the following confidence intervals for μ?

a. $\bar{x} \pm 1.96 \left(\dfrac{\sigma}{\sqrt{n}} \right)$ **b.** $\bar{x} \pm 1.645 \left(\dfrac{\sigma}{\sqrt{n}} \right)$

c. $\bar{x} \pm 2.575 \left(\dfrac{\sigma}{\sqrt{n}} \right)$ **d.** $\bar{x} \pm 1.282 \left(\dfrac{\sigma}{\sqrt{n}} \right)$

e. $\bar{x} \pm .99 \left(\dfrac{\sigma}{\sqrt{n}} \right)$

5.3 A random sample of n measurements was selected from a population with unknown mean μ and standard deviation σ. Calculate a 95% confidence interval for μ for each of the following situations:
a. $n = 75, \bar{x} = 28, s^2 = 12$
b. $n = 200, \bar{x} = 102, s^2 = 22$
c. $n = 100, \bar{x} = 15, s = .3$
d. $n = 100, \bar{x} = 4.05, s = .83$
e. Is the assumption that the underlying population of measurements is normally distributed necessary to ensure the validity of the confidence intervals in parts **a–d**? Explain.

5.4 A random sample of 90 observations produced a mean $\bar{x} = 25.9$ and a standard deviation $s = 2.7$.
a. Find a 95% confidence interval for the population mean μ.
b. Find a 90% confidence interval for μ.
c. Find a 99% confidence interval for μ.

5.5 A random sample of 70 observations from a normally distributed population possesses a mean equal to 26.2 and a standard deviation equal to 4.1.
a. Find a 95% confidence interval for μ. $26.2 \pm .96$
b. What do you mean when you say that a confidence coefficient is .95? 95% of all intervals will include μ

c. Find a 99% confidence interval for μ. $\pm 1.2l.$ 26.2
d. What happens to the width of a confidence interval as the value of the confidence coefficient is increased while the sample size is held fixed?
e. Would your confidence intervals of parts **a** and **c** be valid if the distribution of the original population was not normal? Explain.

APPLET **Applet Exercise 5.1**

Use the applet entitled *Confidence Intervals for a Mean (the impact of confidence level)* to investigate the situation in Exercise 5.5 further. For this exercise, assume that $\mu = 2.62$ is the population mean and $\sigma = 4.1$ is the population standard deviation.
a. Using $n = 70$ and the normal distribution with the mean and standard deviation above, run the applet one time. How many of the 95% confidence intervals contain the mean? How many would you expect to contain the mean? How many of the 99% confidence intervals contain the mean? How many would you expect to contain the mean?
b. Which confidence level has a greater frequency of intervals that contain the mean? Is this result what you would expect? Explain.
c. Without clearing, run the applet several more times. What happens to the proportion of 95% confidence intervals that contain the mean as you run the applet more and more? What happens to the proportion of 99% confidence intervals that contain the mean as you run the applet more and more? Interpret these results in terms of the meanings of the 95% confidence interval and the 99% confidence interval.
d. Change the distribution to *right skewed*, clear, and run the applet several more times. Do you get the same results as in part **c**? Would you change your answer to part **e** of Exercise 5.5? Explain.

APPLET **Applet Exercise 5.2**

Use the applet entitled *Confidence Intervals for a Mean (the impact of confidence level)* to investigate the effect of the sample size on the proportion of confidence intervals that contain the mean when the underlying distribution is skewed. Set the distribution to *right skewed*, the mean to 10, and the standard deviation to 1.

a. Using $n = 30$, run the applet several times without clearing. What happens to the proportion of 95% confidence intervals that contain the mean as you run the applet more and more? What happens to the proportion of 99% confidence intervals that contain the mean as you run the applet more and more? Do the proportions seem to be approaching the values that you would expect?

b. Clear and run the applet several times using $n = 100$. What happens to the proportions of 95% confidence intervals and 99% confidence intervals that contain the mean this time? How do these results compare to your results in part **a**?

c. Clear and run the applet several times using $n = 1000$. How do the results compare to your results in parts **a** and **b**?

d. Describe the effect of sample size on the likelihood that a confidence interval contains the mean for a skewed distribution.

5.6 Explain what is meant by the statement, "We are 95% confident that an interval estimate contains μ."

5.7 Explain the difference between an interval estimator and a point estimator for μ.

5.8 The mean and standard deviation of a random sample of n measurements are equal to 33.9 and 3.3, respectively.

a. Find a 95% confidence interval for μ if $n = 100$.

b. Find a 95% confidence interval for μ if $n = 400$.

c. Find the widths of the confidence intervals found in parts **a** and **b**. What is the effect on the width of a confidence interval of quadrupling the sample size while holding the confidence coefficient fixed?

5.9 Will a large-sample confidence interval be valid if the population from which the sample is taken is not normally distributed? Explain.

Applying the Concepts—Basic

5.10 **Latex allergy in health care workers.** Health care workers who use latex gloves with glove powder on a daily basis are particularly susceptible to developing a latex allergy. Symptoms of a latex allergy include conjunctivitis, hand eczema, nasal congestion, skin rash, and shortness of breath. Each in a sample of 46 hospital employees who were diagnosed with latex allergy based on a skin-prick test reported on their exposure to latex gloves (*Current Allergy & Clinical Immunology*, Mar. 2004). Summary statistics for the number of latex gloves used per week are: $\bar{x} = 19.3, s = 11.9$.

a. Give a point estimate for the average number of latex gloves used per week by all health care workers with a latex allergy.

b. Form a 95% confidence interval for the average number of latex gloves used per week by all health care workers with a latex allergy.

c. Give a practical interpretation of the interval, part **b**.

d. Give the conditions required for the interval, part **b**, to be valid.

CEOPAY05

5.11 **Executive Compensation Scoreboard.** Refer to *Forbes'* 2006 "Executive Compensation Scoreboard." Recall that the **CEOPAY05** file contains the 2005 salaries (in $ millions) of the 500 chief executive officers that participated in the *Forbes'* survey. Suppose you are interested in estimating the mean 2005 salary for these 500 CEOs.

a. What is the target parameter?

b. Obtain a random sample of 50 salaries from the data set.

c. Find the mean and standard deviation of the 50 salaries, part **b**.

d. Use the information, part **c**, to form a 99% confidence interval for the true mean 2005 salary of the 500 CEOs in the *Forbes'* survey.

e. Give a practical interpretation of the interval, part **d**.

f. Find the true mean salary of the 500 CEOs and check to see if this value falls within the 99% confidence interval, part **d**.

5.12 **Tax-exempt charities.** Donations to tax-exempt organizations such as the Red Cross, the Salvation Army, the YMCA, and the American Cancer Society not only go to the stated charitable purpose, but are also used to cover fund-raising expenses and overhead. For a sample of 30 charities, the next table lists their *charitable commitment*, the percentage of their expenses that go toward the stated charitable purpose. A MINITAB analysis of the data is shown on p. 300.

a. Give a point estimate for the mean charitable commitment of tax-exempt organizations.

b. Locate a 95% confidence interval for the true mean charitable commitment of tax-exempt organizations on the printout. Interpret the result.

c. Why is the confidence interval of part **b** a better estimator of the mean charitable commitment than the point estimator of part **a**? Explain.

CHARITY

Organization	Charitable Commitment
American Cancer Society	62%
American National Red Cross	91
Big Brothers Big Sisters of America	77
Boy Scouts of America National Council	81
Boys & Girls Clubs of America	81
CARE	91
Covenant House	15
Disabled American Veterans	65
Ducks Unlimited	78
Feed the Children	90
Girl Scouts of the USA	83
Goodwill Industries International	89
Habitat for Humanity International	81
Mayo Foundation	26
Mothers Against Drunk Drivers	71
Multiple Sclerosis Association of America	56
Museum of Modern Art	79
Nature Conservancy	77
Paralyzed Veterans of America	50
Planned Parenthood Federation	81
Salvation Army	84
Shriners Hospital for Children	95
Smithsonian Institution	87
Special Olympics	72
Trust for Public Land	88
United Jewish Appeal/Federation-NY	75
United States Olympic Committee	78
United Way of New York City	85
WGBH Educational Foundation	81
YMCA of the USA	80

Source: "Look Before You Give." *Forbes*, Dec. 27, 1999, pp. 206–216.

5.13 **Semester hours taken by CPA candidates.** Refer to the *Journal of Accounting and Public Policy* (Spring 2002)

MINITAB output for Exercise 5.12

```
Variable    N    Mean    StDev  SE Mean       95% CI
COMMIT     30  74.9667  18.0220  3.2903  (68.2371, 81.6962)
```

study of 100,000 first-time candidates for the CPA exam, Exercise 2.49 (p. 73). Recall that the mean number of semester hours of college credit taken by the candidates was 141.31 hours. The standard deviation was reported to be 17.77 hours.

a. Compute a 99% confidence interval for the mean number of semester hours taken by all first-time candidates for the CPA exam.

b. Give a practical interpretation of the interval, part **a**.

c. For the interpretation, part **b**, to be valid, what conditions must hold?

5.14 Performance appraisal process. The relationship between an employee's participation in the performance appraisal process and subsequent subordinate reactions toward the appraisal was investigated in the *Journal of Applied Psychology* (Aug. 1998). In Chapter 10 we will discuss a quantitative measure of the relationship between two variables, called the *coefficient* of *correlation r*. The researchers obtained *r* for a sample of 34 studies that examined the relationship between appraisal participation and a subordinate's satisfaction with the appraisal. These correlations are listed in the table. (Values of *r* near +1 reflect a strong positive relationship between the variables.) Find a 95% confidence interval for the mean of the data and interpret it in the words of the problem.

CORR34

.50	.58	.71	.46	.63	.66	.31	.35	.51	.06	.35	.19
.40	.63	.43	.16	−.08	.51	.59	.43	.30	.69	.25	.20
.39	.20	.51	.68	.74	.65	.34	.45	.31	.27		

Source: Cawley, B. D., Keeping, L. M., and Levy, P. E. "Participation in the Performance Appraisal Process and Employee Reactions: A Meta-Analytic Review of Field Investigations." *Journal of Applied Psychology*, Vol. 83, No. 4, Aug. 1998, pp. 632–633 (Appendix).

Applying the Concepts—Intermediate

5.15 Improving SAT scores. Refer to the *Chance* (Winter 2001) and National Education Longitudinal Survey (NELS) study of 265 students who paid a private tutor to help them improve their SAT scores, Exercise 2.84 (p. 86). The changes in both the SAT–Mathematics and SAT–Verbal scores for these students are reproduced in the table.

	SAT–Math	SAT–Verbal
Mean change in score	19	7
Standard deviation of score changes	65	49

a. Construct and interpret a 90% confidence interval for the population mean change in SAT–Mathematics score for students who pay a private tutor.

b. Repeat part **a** for the population mean change in SAT–Verbal score.

c. Suppose the true population mean change in score on one of the SAT tests for all students who paid a private tutor is 15. Which of the two tests, SAT–Mathematics or SAT–Verbal, is most likely to have this mean change? Explain.

5.16 401(k) Participation rates. Named for the section of the 1978 Internal Revenue Code that authorized them, 401(k) plans permit employees to shift part of their before-tax salaries into investments such as mutual funds. Employers typically match 50% of the employee's contribution up to about 6% of salary (*Fortune*, Dec. 28, 1992). One company, concerned with what it believed was a low employee participation rate in its 401(k) plan, sampled 30 other companies with similar plans and asked for their 401(k) participation rates. The following rates (in percentages) were obtained:

RATE401K

80	76	81	77	82	80	85	60	80	79	82	70
88	85	80	79	83	75	87	78	80	84	72	75
90	84	82	77	75	86						

a. Construct a 90% confidence interval for the mean participation rate for all companies that have 401(k) plans.

b. Interpret the interval in the context of this problem.

c. What assumption is necessary to ensure the validity of this confidence interval?

d. If the company that conducted the sample has a 71% participation rate, can it safely conclude that its rate is below the population mean rate for all companies with 401(k) plans? Explain.

e. If in the data set the 60% had been 80%, how would the center and width of the confidence interval you constructed in part **a** be affected?

5.17 IQ comparison of older vs. younger workers. The 1967 Age Discrimination in Employment Act (ADEA) made it illegal to discriminate against workers 40 years of age and older. Opponents of the law argue that there are sound economic reasons why employers would not want to hire and train workers who are very close to retirement. They also argue that people's abilities tend to deteriorate with age. In fact, *Forbes* (Dec. 13, 1999) reported that 25-year-olds did significantly better than 60-year-olds on the Wechsler Adult Intelligence Scale, the most popular IQ test. The data in the next table are raw test scores (i.e., not the familiar normalized IQ scores) for a sample of 36 25-year-olds and 36 60-year-olds:

a. Estimate the mean raw test score for all 25-year-olds using a 99% confidence interval. Give a practical interpretation of the confidence interval.

b. What assumption(s) must hold for the method of estimation used in part **a** to be appropriate?

c. Find a 95% confidence interval for the mean raw score of all 60-year-olds and interpret your result.

IQ25

25-Year-Olds					
54	61	80	92	41	63
59	68	66	76	82	80
82	47	81	77	88	94
49	86	55	82	45	51
70	72	63	50	52	67
75	60	58	49	63	68

IQ60

60-Year-Olds					
42	54	38	22	58	37
60	49	51	60	45	42
73	28	65	65	60	34
34	33	40	28	36	60
45	61	47	30	45	45
45	37	27	40	37	58

Source: Adapted from "The Case for Age Discrimination." *Forbes,* Dec. 13, 1999, p. 13.

DIAMONDS

5.18 Size of diamonds sold at retail. Refer to Exercise 2.47 (p. 72) and the *Journal of Statistics Education* data on diamonds saved in the **DIAMONDS** file. Consider the quantitative variable, number of carats, recorded for each of the 308 diamonds for sale on the open market.

a. Select a random sample of 30 diamonds from the 308 diamonds.

b. Find the mean and standard deviation of the number of carats per diamond for the sample.

c. Use the sample information, part **b,** to construct a 95% confidence interval for the mean number of carats in the population of 308 diamonds.

d. Interpret the phrase "95% confidence" when applied to the interval, part **c.**

e. Refer to the mean of all 308 diamonds you calculated in Exercise 2.47. Does the "population" mean fall within the confidence interval of part **c**?

Applying the Concepts—Advanced

5.19 Job satisfaction of workers. Research reported in the *Journal of Psychology and Aging* (May 1992) studied the role that the age of workers has in determining their level of job satisfaction. The researcher hypothesized that both younger and older workers would have a higher job satisfaction rating than middle-age workers. Each of a sample of 1,686 adults was given a job satisfaction score based on answers to a series of questions. Higher job satisfaction scores indicate higher levels of job satisfaction. The data, arranged by age group, are summarized below.

	AGE GROUP		
	Younger 18–24	Middle Age 25–44	Older 45–64
$\bar{x}$	4.17	4.04	4.31
s	.75	.81	.82
n	241	768	677

a. Construct 95% confidence intervals for the mean job satisfaction scores of each age group. Carefully interpret each interval.

b. In the construction of three 95% confidence intervals, is it more or less likely that at least one of them will *not* contain the population mean it is intended to estimate than it is for a single confidence interval to miss the population mean? [*Hint:* Assume the three intervals are independent, and calculate the probability that at least one of them will not contain the population mean it estimates. Compare this probability to the probability that a single interval fails to enclose the mean.]

c. Based on these intervals, does it appear that the researcher's hypothesis is supported? [*Caution:* We'll learn how to use sample information to compare population means in Chapter 7, and we'll return to this exercise at that time. Here, simply base your opinion on the individual confidence intervals you constructed in part **a.**]

5.20 The "Raid" test kitchen. According to scientists, the cockroach has had 300 million years to develop a resistance to destruction. In a study conducted by researchers for S.C. Johnson & Son, Inc. (manufacturers of Raid and Off), 5,000 roaches (the expected number in a roach-infested house) were released in the Raid test kitchen. One week later, the kitchen was fumigated and 16,298 dead roaches were counted, a gain of 11,298 roaches for the 1-week period. Assume that none of the original roaches died during the 1-week period and that the standard deviation of x, the number of roaches produced per roach in a 1-week period, is 1.5. Use the number of roaches produced by the sample of 5,000 roaches to find a 95% confidence interval for the mean number of roaches produced per week for each roach in a typical roach-infested house.

5.3 Small-Sample Confidence Interval for a Population Mean

Federal legislation requires pharmaceutical companies to perform extensive tests on new drugs before they can be marketed. Initially, a new drug is tested on animals. If the drug is deemed safe after this first phase of testing, the pharmaceutical company is then permitted to begin human testing on a limited basis. During this second phase, inferences must be made about the safety of the drug based on information in very small samples.

Suppose a pharmaceutical company must estimate the average increase in blood pressure of patients who take a certain new drug. Assume that only six patients (randomly selected from the population of all patients) can be used in the initial phase of human testing. The use of a *small sample* in making an inference about μ presents two immediate problems when we attempt to use the standard normal z as a test statistic.

Problem 1   The shape of the sampling distribution of the sample mean $\bar{x}$ (and the z statistic) now depends on the shape of the population that is sampled. We can no longer assume that the sampling distribution of $\bar{x}$ is approximately normal, because the Central Limit Theorem ensures normality only for samples that are sufficiently large.

Solution to Problem 1   According to Theorem 4.1, the sampling distribution of $\bar{x}$ (and z) is exactly normal even for small samples if the sampled population is normal. It is approximately normal if the sampled population is approximately normal.

Problem 2   The population standard deviation σ is almost always unknown. Although it is still true that $\sigma_{\bar{x}} = \sigma/\sqrt{n}$, the sample standard deviation s may provide a poor approximation for σ when the sample size is small.

Solution to Problem 2   Instead of using the standard normal statistic

$$z = \frac{\bar{x} - \mu}{\sigma_{\bar{x}}} = \frac{\bar{x} - \mu}{\sigma/\sqrt{n}}$$

which requires knowledge of or a good approximation to σ, we define and use the statistic

$$t = \frac{\bar{x} - \mu}{s/\sqrt{n}}$$

in which the sample standard deviation, s, replaces the population standard deviation, σ.

If we are sampling from a normal distribution, the ***t*-statistic** has a sampling distribution very much like that of the z statistic: mound-shaped, symmetric, with mean 0. The primary difference between the sampling distributions of t and z is that the t-statistic is more variable than the z, which follows intuitively when you realize that t contains two random quantities ($\bar{x}$ and s), whereas z contains only one ($\bar{x}$).

The actual amount of variability in the sampling distribution of t depends on the sample size n. A convenient way of expressing this dependence is to say that the t-statistic has $(n - 1)$ **degrees of freedom (df).** Recall that the quantity $(n - 1)$ is the divisor that appears in the formula for s^2. This number plays a key role in the sampling distribution of s^2 and appears in discussions of other statistics in later chapters. In particular, the smaller the number of degrees of freedom associated with the t-statistic, the more variable will be its sampling distribution.

Biography

WILLIAM S. GOSSET (1876–1937)

Student's *t*-Distribution

At the age of 23, William Gosset earned a degree in chemistry and mathematics at prestigious Oxford University. He was immediately hired by the Guinness Brewing Company in Dublin, Ireland for his expertise in chemistry. However, Gosset's mathematical skills allowed him to solve numerous practical problems associated with brewing beer. For example, Gosset applied the Poisson distribution to model the number of yeast cells per unit volume in the fermentation process. His most important discovery was that of the t-distribution in 1908. Since most applied researchers worked with small samples, Gosset was interested in the behavior of the mean in the small sample case. He tediously took numerous small sets of numbers, calculated the mean and standard deviation, obtained their t-ratio, and plotted the results on graph paper. The shape of the distribution was always the same—the t-distribution. Under company policy, employees were forbidden to publish their research results, so Gosset used the pen name *Student* to publish a paper on the subject. Hence, the distribution has been called Student's t-distribution.

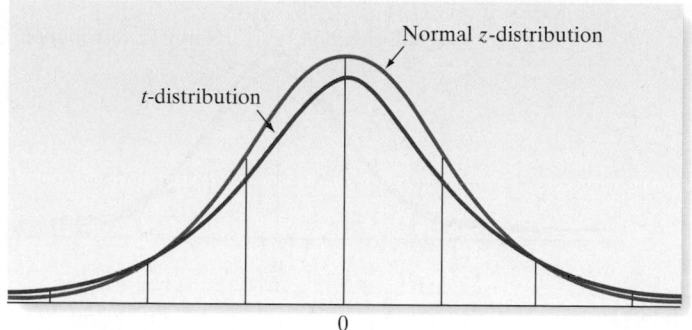

FIGURE 5.7

Standard normal (z)
distribution and t-distribution
with 4 df

In Figure 5.7 we show both the sampling distribution of z and the sampling distribution of a t-statistic with 4 df. You can see that the increased variability of the t-statistic means that the t-value, t_α, that locates an area α in the upper tail of the t-distribution is larger than the corresponding value z_α. For any given value of α, the t-value t_α increases as the number of degrees of freedom (df) decreases. Values of t that will be used in forming small-sample confidence intervals of μ are given in Table V of Appendix B. A partial reproduction of this table is shown in Table 5.3.

Note that t_α values are listed for various degrees of freedom, where α refers to the tail area under the t-distribution to the right of t_α. For example, if we want the t-value with an area of .025 to its right and 4 df, we look in the table under the column $t_{.025}$ for the entry in the row corresponding to 4 df. This entry is $t_{.025} = 2.776$, as shown in Figure 5.8. The corresponding standard normal z-score is $z_{.025} - 1.96$.

Note that the last row of Table V, where df $= \infty$ (infinity), contains the standard normal z values. This follows from the fact that as the sample size n grows very large, s becomes closer to σ and thus t becomes closer in distribution to z. In fact, when df = 29, , there is little difference between corresponding tabulated values of z and t. Thus, researchers often choose the arbitrary cutoff of $n = 30$ (df = 29) to distinguish between the large-sample and small-sample inferential techniques.

Returning to the example of testing a new drug, suppose that the six test patients have blood pressure increases of 1.7, 3.0, .8, 3.4, 2.7, and 2.1 points. (These data are saved

TABLE 5.3 Reproduction of Part of Table V in Appendix B

Degrees of Freedom	$t_{.100}$	$t_{.050}$	$t_{.025}$	$t_{.010}$	$t_{.005}$	$t_{.001}$	$t_{.0005}$
1	3.078	6.314	12.706	31.821	63.657	318.13	636.62
2	1.886	2.920	4.303	6.965	9.925	22.326	21.598
3	1.638	2.353	3.182	4.541	5.841	10.213	12.924
4	1.533	2.132	2.776	3.747	4.604	7.173	8.610
5	1.476	2.015	2.571	3.365	4.032	5.893	6.869
6	1.440	1.943	2.447	3.132	3.707	5.208	5.959
7	1.415	1.895	2.365	2.998	3.499	4.785	5.408
8	1.397	1.860	2.306	2.896	3.355	4.501	5.041
9	1.383	1.833	2.262	2.821	3.250	4.297	4.781
10	1.372	1.812	2.228	2.764	3.169	4.144	4.587
11	1.363	1.796	2.201	2.718	3.106	4.025	4.437
12	1.356	1.782	2.179	2.681	3.055	3.930	4.318
13	1.350	1.771	2.160	2.650	3.012	3.852	4.221
14	1.345	1.761	2.145	2.624	2.977	3.787	4.140
15	1.341	1.753	2.131	2.602	2.947	3.733	4.073
⋮	⋮	⋮	⋮	⋮	⋮	⋮	⋮
∞	1.282	1.645	1.960	2.326	2.576	3.090	3.291

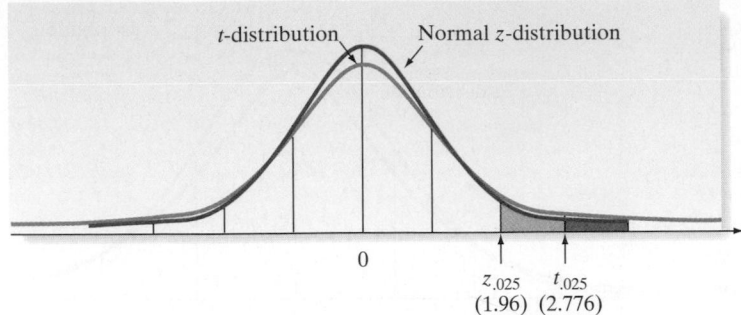

FIGURE 5.8

The $t_{.025}$ value in a t-distribution with 4 df and the corresponding $z_{.025}$ value

BPINCR

in the **BPINCR** file.) How can we use this information to construct a 95% confidence interval for μ the mean increase in blood pressure associated with the new drug for all patients in the population?

First, we know that we are dealing with a sample too small to assume that the sample mean $\bar{x}$ is approximately normally distributed by the Central Limit Theorem—that is, we do not get the normal distribution of $\bar{x}$ "automatically" from the Central Limit Theorem when the sample size is small. Instead, the measured variable, in this case the increase in blood pressure, must be normally distributed in order for the distribution of $\bar{x}$ to be normal.

Second, unless we are fortunate enough to know the population standard deviation σ, which in this case represents the standard deviation of *all* the patients' increases in blood pressure when they take the new drug, we cannot use the standard normal z statistic to form our confidence interval for μ. Instead, we must use the t-distribution, with $(n - 1)$ degrees of freedom.

In this case, $n - 1 = 5$ df, and the t-value is found in Table 5.3 to be $t_{.025} = 2.571$ with 5 df. Recall that the large-sample confidence interval would have been of the form

$$\bar{x} \pm z_{\alpha/2}\sigma_{\bar{x}} = \bar{x} \pm z_{\alpha/2}\frac{\sigma}{\sqrt{n}} = \bar{x} \pm z_{.025}\frac{\sigma}{\sqrt{n}}$$

where 95% is the desired confidence level. To form the interval for a small sample from *a normal distribution, we simply substitute t for z and s for σ in the preceding formula:*

$$\bar{x} \pm t_{\alpha/2}\frac{s}{\sqrt{n}}$$

An SPSS printout showing descriptive statistics for the six blood pressure increases is displayed in Figure 5.9. Note that $\bar{x} = 2.283$ and $s = .950$. Substituting these numerical values into the confidence interval formula, we get

$$2.283 \pm (2.571)\left(\frac{.950}{\sqrt{6}}\right) = 2.283 \pm .997$$

or 1.286 to 3.280 points. Note that this interval agrees (except for rounding) with the confidence interval generated by SPSS in Figure 5.9.

We interpret the interval as follows: We can be 95% confident that the mean increase in blood pressure associated with taking this new drug is between 1.286 and 3.28 points. As with our large-sample interval estimates, our confidence is in the process, not in this particular interval. We know that if we were to repeatedly use this estimation procedure, 95% of the confidence intervals produced would contain the true mean μ, *assuming that the probability distribution of changes in blood pressure from which our sample was selected is normal.* The latter assumption is necessary for the small-sample interval to be valid.

What price did we pay for having to utilize a small sample to make the inference? First, we had to assume the underlying population is normally distributed, and if

Descriptives

			Statistic	Std. Error
BPINCR	Mean		2.283	.3877
	95% Confidence Interval for Mean	Lower Bound	1.287	
		Upper Bound	3.280	
	5% Trimmed Mean		2.304	
	Median		2.400	
	Variance		.902	
	Std. Deviation		.9496	
	Minimum		.8	
	Maximum		3.4	
	Range		2.6	
	Interquartile Range		1.625	
	Skewness		-.573	.845
	Kurtosis		-.389	1.741

FIGURE 5.9
SPSS confidence interval for mean blood pressure increase

the assumption is invalid, our interval might also be invalid.* Second, we had to form the interval using a t-value of 2.571 rather than a z value of 1.96, resulting in a wider interval to achieve the same 95% level of confidence. If the interval from 1.286 to 3.28 is too wide to be of use, then we know how to remedy the situation: increase the number of patients sampled to decrease the interval width (on average).

Now Work Exercise 5.22

The procedure for forming a small-sample confidence interval is summarized in the accompanying boxes.

Small-Sample Confidence Interval† for μ

$$\bar{x} \pm t_{\alpha/2} \left(\frac{s}{\sqrt{n}} \right)$$

where $t_{\alpha/2}$ is based on $(n - 1)$ degrees of freedom

---

Conditions Required for a Valid Small-Sample Confidence Internal for μ

1. A random sample is selected from the target population.
2. The population has a relative frequency distribution that is approximately normal.

EXAMPLE 5.2

Finding a Small-Sample Confidence Interval for μ in Destructive Sampling

Problem Some quality-control experiments require *destructive sampling* (i.e., the test to determine whether the item is defective destroys the item) in order to measure some particular characteristic of the product. The cost of destructive sampling often dictates small samples. For example, suppose a manufacturer of printers for personal computers wishes to estimate the mean number of characters printed before the printhead fails. Suppose the printer manufacturer tests $n = 15$ randomly selected printheads and

---

*By *invalid*, we mean that the probability that the procedure will yield an interval that contains μ is not equal to $(1 - \alpha)$. Generally, if the underlying population is approximately normal, then the confidence coefficient will approximate the probability that a randomly selected interval contains μ.
†The procedure given in the box assumes that the population standard deviation σ is unknown, which is almost always the case. If σ is known, we can form the small-sample confidence interval just as we would a large-sample confidence interval using a standard normal z value instead of t. However, we must still assume that the underlying population is approximately normal.

PRINTHEAD

TABLE 5.4 Number of Characters (in Millions) for $n = 15$ Printhead Tests

1.13	1.55	1.43	.92	1.25
1.36	1.32	.85	1.07	1.48
1.20	1.33	1.18	1.22	1.29

records the number of characters printed until failure for each. These 15 measurements (in millions of characters) are listed in Table 5.4, followed by an Excel/PHStat2 summary statistics printout in Figure 5.10.

a. Form a 99% confidence interval for the mean number of characters printed before the printhead fails. Interpret the result.

b. What assumption is required for the interval, part **a**, to be valid? Is it reasonably satisfied?

Solution

a. For this small sample ($n = 15$), we use the t-statistic to form the confidence interval. We use a confidence coefficient of .99 and $n - 1 = 14$ degrees of freedom to find $t_{\alpha/2}$ in Table V:

$$t_{\alpha/2} = t_{.005} = 2.977$$

[*Note*: The small sample forces us to extend the interval almost 3 standard deviations (of $\bar{x}$) on each side of the sample mean in order to form the 99% confidence interval.] From the Excel/PHStat2 printout, Figure 5.10, we find $\bar{x} = 1.239$ and $s = .193$. Substituting these values into the confidence interval formula, we obtain

$$\bar{x} \pm t_{.005}\left(\frac{s}{\sqrt{n}}\right) = 1.239 \pm 2.977\left(\frac{.193}{\sqrt{15}}\right)$$

$$= 1.239 \pm .148 \text{ or } (1.091, 1.387)$$

This interval is shown at the bottom of the printout, Figure 5.10.

Our interpretation is as follows: The manufacturer can be 99% confident that the printhead has a mean life of between 1.091 and 1.387 million characters. If the manufacturer were to advertise that the mean life of its printheads is (at least) 1 million characters, the interval would support such a claim. Our confidence is derived from the fact that 99% of the intervals formed in repeated applications of this procedure would contain μ.

b. Since n is small, we must assume that the number of characters printed before printhead failure is a random variable from a normal distribution—that is, we

Confidence Interval Estimate for the Mean

Data	
Sample Standard Deviation	0.19316413
Sample Mean	1.238666667
Sample Size	15
Confidence Level	99%

Intermediate Calculations	
Standard Error of the Mean	0.049874764
Degrees of Freedom	14
t Value	2.976848918
Interval Half Width	0.148469637

Confidence Interval	
Interval Lower Limit	1.09
Interval Upper Limit	1.39

FIGURE 5.10

Excel/PHStat2 summary statistics and confidence interval for data in Table 5.4

Stem-and-Leaf Display: NUMBER

```
Stem-and-leaf of NUMBER   N  = 15
Leaf Unit = 0.010


    1    8    5
    2    9    2
    3   10    7
    5   11    38
   (4)  12    0259
    6   13    236
    3   14    38
    1   15    5
```

FIGURE 5.11

MINITAB stem-and-leaf
display of data in Table 5.4

assume that the population from which the sample of 15 measurements is selected is distributed normally. One way to check this assumption is to graph the distribution of data in Table 5.4. If the sample data are approximately normal, then the population from which the sample is selected is very likely to be normal. A MINITAB stem-and-leaf plot for the sample data is displayed in Figure 5.11. The distribution is mound-shaped and nearly symmetric. Therefore, the assumption of normality appears to be reasonably satisfied.

Look Back Other checks for normality, such as a normal probability plot and the ratio IQR/S, may also be used to verify the normality condition.

Now Work Exercise 5.33

We have emphasized throughout this section that an assumption that the population is approximately normally distributed is necessary for making small-sample inferences about μ when using the t-statistic. Although many phenomena do have approximately normal distributions, it is also true that many random phenomena have distributions that are not normal or even mound-shaped. Empirical evidence acquired over the years has shown that the t-distribution is rather insensitive to moderate departures from normality—that is, use of the t-statistic when sampling from slightly or moderately skewed mound-shaped populations generally produces credible results; however, for cases in which the distribution is distinctly nonnormal, we must either take a large sample or use a *nonparametric method* (the topic of Chapter 14).

What Do You Do When the Population Relative Frequency Distribution Departs Greatly from Normality?

Answer: Use the nonparametric statistical methods of Chapter 14.

STATISTICS IN ACTION REVISITED

Estimating the Mean Weight per Scallop

Refer to the scallop lawsuit described on p 291. Recall that a ship, returning from a fishing expedition with 11,000 bags of scallops, was accused of vi-olating the U.S. Fisheries and Wildlife Service weight standard for baby scallops. The law requires that the average meat per scallop weigh at least 1/36 of a pound. The harbormaster randomly selected 18 bags for weighing and estimated that the ship caught scallops that averaged only

Continued

SCALLOPS

TABLE SIA5.1 Scallop Weight Measurements (in Pounds) for 18 Bags Sampled

.0258	.0244	.0236	.0253	.0253	.0233	.0250	.0272	.0244
.0247	.0272	.0242	.0253	.0256	.0275	.0317	.0294	.0258

Adapted from Bennett, A. "Misapplications Review: Jail Terms." *Interfaces*, Vol. 25, No. 2, March–April 1995, p. 20.

1/39 of a pound of meat. Consequently, federal authorities confiscated the catch. Was the ship really in violation of the scallop weight standard?

One way to answer this question is to form a confidence interval for the true mean weight per scallop for all 11,000 bags caught by the fishing vessel. The data for the 18 sampled bags in the **SCALLOPS** file are shown in Table SIA5.1. (Each measurement in the table is the estimated average weight per scallop of the bag. A measurement less than 1/36 = .0278 pound indicates an individual bag that does not meet the standard.)

MINITAB software was used to find a 95% confidence interval for the population mean weight per scallop. The MINITAB printout is displayed in Figure SIA5.1. The interval shown on the printout is

(.024830, .026915). Note that the upper endpoint of the interval falls below .0278 (or 1/36 of a pound). Consequently, we are 95% confident that the true mean weight per scallop for the 11,000 bags caught by the fishing vessel falls below the 1/36 pound minimum set by the U.S. Fisheries and Wildlife Service. It appears that the ship was in violation of the government minimum weight requirement for baby scallops.

[*Note:* Because the ship violated the baby scallop weight rule, federal authorities confiscated 95% of the ship's catch. The ship's owner complained that this was not fair, since not all (or even 95%) of the bags of scallops had an average weight per scallop under 1/36 of a pound. We address this issue in the next Statistics in the Action Revisited (p. 317).]

One-Sample T: Weight

```
Variable    N      Mean     StDev    SE Mean        95% CI
Weight     18   0.025872  0.002096  0.000494   (0.024830, 0.026915)
```

Figure SIA5.1
MINITAB confidence interval for scallop weight data

Confidence Interval for a Population Mean ($n < 30$)

Using the TI-83/TI-84 Graphing Calculator
Creating a Confidence Interval for a Population Mean

Step 1 *Enter the data (skip to Step 2 if you have summary statistics, not raw data)*

Press **STAT** and select **1:Edit**
Note: If the list already contains data, clear the old data. Use the up ARROW to highlight "L1".
Press **CLEAR ENTER**.
Use the **ARROW** and **ENTER** keys to enter the data set into **L1**.

Step 2 *Access the Statistical Tests Menu*

Press **STAT**
Arrow right to **TESTS**
Arrow down to **TInterval**
Press **ENTER**

```
EDIT CALC TESTS
2↑T-Test…
3:2-SampZTest…
4:2-SampTTest…
5:1-PropZTest…
6:2-PropZTest…
7:ZInterval…
8↓TInterval…
```

Step 3 *Choose "**Data**" or "**Stats**". ("Data" is selected when you have entered the raw data into a List. "Stats" is selected when you are given only the mean, standard deviation, and sample size.)*

Press **ENTER**
If you selected "Data", set **List** to **L1**
Set **Freq** to **1**
Set **C-Level** to the confidence level
Arrow down to "**Calculate**"
Press **ENTER**

If you selected "Stats", enter the mean, standard deviation, and sample size.
Set **C-Level** to the confidence level
Arrow down to "**Calculate**"
Press **ENTER**
(The screen below is set up for an example with a mean of 100 and a standard deviation of 10.)

The confidence interval will be displayed with the mean, standard deviation, and sample size.

Example Compute a 99% confidence interval for the mean using the 15 pieces of data given in Example 5.2.

1.13	1.55	1.43	0.92	1.25
1.36	1.32	0.85	1.07	1.48
1.20	1.33	1.18	1.22	1.29

As you can see from the screen, our 99% confidence interval is **(1.0902, 1.3871)**.

You will also notice the output displays the mean, standard deviation, and sample size.

Exercises 5.21–5.35

Learning the Mechanics

5.21 Suppose you have selected a random sample of $n = 5$ measurements from a normal distribution. Compare the standard normal z values with the corresponding t-values if you were forming the following confidence intervals.
  a. 80% confidence interval
  b. 90% confidence interval
  c. 95% confidence interval
  d. 98% confidence interval
  e. 99% confidence interval
  f. Use the table values you obtained in parts **a–e** to sketch the z- and t-distributions. What are the similarities and differences?

APPLET **Applet Exercise 5.3**

Use the applet entitled *Confidence Intervals for a Mean (the impact of not knowing the standard deviation)* to compare proportions of z-intervals and t-intervals that contain the mean for a population that is normally distributed.
  a. Using $n = 5$ and the normal distribution with mean 50 and standard deviation 10, run the applet several times. How do the proportions of z-intervals and t-intervals that contain the mean compare?
  b. Repeat part **a** first for $n = 10$ and then for $n = 20$. Compare your results to part **a**.
  c. Describe any patterns you observe between the proportion of z-intervals that contain the mean and the proportion of t-intervals that contain the mean as the sample size increases.

APPLET **Applet Exercise 5.4**

Use the applet entitled *Confidence Intervals for a Mean (the impact of not knowing the standard deviation)* to compare proportions of z-intervals and t-intervals that contain the mean for a population with a skewed distribution.
  a. Using $n = 5$ and the right skewed distribution with mean 50 and standard deviation 10, run the applet several times. How do the proportions of z-intervals and t-intervals that contain the mean compare?
  b. Repeat part **a** first for $n = 10$ and then for $n = 20$. Compare your results to part **a**.
  c. Describe any patterns you observe between the proportion of z-intervals that contain the mean and the proportion of t-intervals that contain the mean as the sample size increases.
  d. How does skewedness of the underlying distribution affect the proportions of z-intervals and t-intervals that contain the mean?

5.22 Explain the differences in the sampling distributions of $\bar{x}$ for
NW large and small samples under the following assumptions.
  a. The variable of interest, x, is normally distributed.
  b. Nothing is known about the distribution of the variable x.

5.23 Let t_0 be a particular value of t. Use Table V of Appendix B to find t_0 values such that the following statements are true.
  a. $P(-t_0 < t < t_0) = .95$ where df $= 10$
  b. $P(t \le -t_0 \text{ or } t \ge t_0) = .05$ where df $= 10$
  c. $P(t \le t_0) = .05$ where df $= 10$ -1.812

d. $P(t \le -t_0 \text{ or } t \ge t_0) = .10$ where df $= 20$

e. $P(t \le -t_0 \text{ or } t \ge t_0) = .01$ where df $= 5$

5.24 Let t_0 be a specific value of t. Use Table V in Appendix B to find t_0 values such that the following statements are true.

a. $P(t \ge t_0) = .025$ where df $= 11$

b. $P(t \ge t_0) = .01$ where df $= 9$

c. $P(t \le t_0) = .005$ where df $= 6$

d. $P(t \le t_0) = .05$ where df $= 18$

5.25 The following random sample was selected from a normal distribution: 4, 6, 3, 5, 9, 3.

a. Construct a 90% confidence interval for the population mean μ.

b. Construct a 95% confidence interval for the population mean μ.

c. Construct a 99% confidence interval for the population mean μ.

d. Assume that the sample mean $\bar{x}$ and sample standard deviation s remain exactly the same as those you just calculated but that are based on a sample of $n = 25$ observations rather than $n = 6$ observations. Repeat parts **a–c.** What is the effect of increasing the sample size on the width of the confidence intervals?

5.26 The following sample of 16 measurements was selected from a population that is approximately normally distributed:

LM5_26

91	80	99	110	95	106	78	121	106	100	97	82
100	83	115	104								

a. Construct an 80% confidence interval for the population mean.

b. Construct a 95% confidence interval for the population mean and compare the width of this interval with that of part **a.**

c. Carefully interpret each of the confidence intervals and explain why the 80% confidence interval is narrower.

Applying the Concepts—Basic

5.27 **Assessing the bending strength of a wooden roof.** The white wood material used for the roof of an ancient Japanese temple is imported from Northern Europe. The wooden roof must withstand as much as 100 centimeters of snow in the winter. Architects at Tohoku University (Japan) conducted a study to estimate the mean bending strength of the white wood roof (*Journal of the International Association for Shell and Spatial Structures*, Aug. 2004). A sample of 25 pieces of the imported wood were tested and yielded the following statistics on breaking strength (MPa): $\bar{x} = 75.4$, $s = 10.9$. Estimate the true mean breaking strength of the white wood with a 90% confidence interval. Interpret the result.

5.28 **Contamination of New Jersey wells.** Methyl t-butyl ether (MTBE) is an organic water contaminant that often results from gasoline spills. The level of MTBE (in parts per billion) was measured for a sample of 12 well sites located near a gasoline service station in New Jersey (*Environmental Science & Technology*, Jan. 2005). The data are listed in the accompanying table.

NJGAS

150	367	38	12	11	134
12	251	63	8	13	107

Source: Kuder, T., et al. "Enrichment of Stable Carbon and Hydrogen Isotopes during Anaerobic Biodegradation of MTBE: Microcosm and Field Evidence." *Environmental Science & Technology*, Vol. 39, No. 1, Jan. 2005 (Table 1).

a. Give a point estimate for μ, the true mean MTBE level for all well sites located near the New Jersey gasoline service station.

b. Calculate and interpret a 99% confidence interval for μ.

c. What assumptions are required for the interval, part **b,** to be valid? Are these assumptions reasonably satisfied?

5.29 **Lead and copper in drinking water.** Periodically, the Hillsborough County (Florida) Water Department tests the drinking water of homeowners for contaminants such as lead and copper. The lead and copper levels in water specimens collected for a sample of 10 residents of the Crystal Lakes Manors subdivision are shown below.

LEADCOPP

Lead (μg/L)	Copper (mg/L)
1.32	.508
0	.279
13.1	.320
.919	.904
.657	.221
3.0	.283
1.32	.475
4.09	.130
4.45	.220
0	.743

Source: Hillsborough County Water Department Environmental Laboratory, Tampa, Florida.

a. Construct a 99% confidence interval for the mean lead level in water specimens from Crystal Lakes Manors.

b. Construct a 99% confidence interval for the mean copper level in water specimens from Crystal Lakes Manors.

c. Interpret the intervals, parts **a** and **b,** in the words of the problem.

d. Discuss the meaning of the phrase, "99% confident."

5.30 **Hospital length of stay.** Health insurers and the federal government are both putting pressure on hospitals to shorten the average length of stay (LOS) of their patients. The average LOS for men in the United States is 5.3 days and the average for women is 4.6 days (*Statistical Abstract of the United States: 2005*). A random sample of 20 hospitals in one state had a mean LOS for women of 3.8 days and a standard deviation of 1.2 days.

a. Use a 90% confidence interval to estimate the population mean LOS for women for the state's hospitals.

b. Interpret the interval in terms of this application.

c. What is meant by the phrase "90% confidence interval"?

5.31 **Technology Fast 500.** Deloitte & Touche rank the 500 fastest-growing technology companies in the United States based on percentage growth over a 5-year period. Their rankings are called the *Technology Fast 500*. A random sample of 12 companies from the 2005 *Technology Fast 500*

MINITAB output for Exercise 5.31

One-Sample T: GrwthRate

```
Variable   N     Mean    StDev   SE Mean       95% CI
GrwthRate  12  4935.42  11289.53 3259.01  (-2237.61, 12108.44)
```

Stem-and-Leaf Display: GrwthRate

```
Stem-and-leaf of GrwthRate  N  = 12
Leaf Unit = 1000


(10)  0  0000000012
  2   0
  2   1  2
  1   1
  1   2
  1   2
  1   3
  1   3  9
```

and their growth rates are shown in the table; a MINITAB analysis of the data appears above.

FAST500

Rank	Company	5-year Revenue Growth Rate
4	Case Stack	39,071%
22	Go2Call.com	12,514
88	Active Motiv	2,789
160	Netspoke	1,185
193	Conduant Corp.	860
268	ARGON ST.	576
274	Immtech Int'l.	555
323	Open Solutions	430
359	eCopy	384
397	:Basis	331
444	Espial Group	281
485	Pacific Biometrics	249

Source: Technology Fast 500, Deloitte & Touche 2005, (www.fast500.com)

a. Find a 95% confidence interval for the true mean 5-year revenue growth rate for the 2005 *Technology Fast 500*. Interpret the result.

b. In order to estimate the mean described in part **a** with a small-sample confidence interval, what characteristic must the population possess?

c. Explain why the required population characteristics may not hold in this case.

5.32 Surface roughness of pipe. Refer to the *Anti-corrosion Methods and Materials* (Vol. 50, 2003) study of the surface roughness of coated interior pipe used in oil fields, Exercise 2.46 (p. 72). The data (in micrometers) for 20 sampled pipe sections are reproduced in the next table; a MINITAB analysis of the data appears below.

a. Locate a 95% confidence interval for the mean surface roughness of coated interior pipe on the accompanying MINITAB printout.

b. Would you expect the average surface roughness to be as high as 2.5 micrometers? Explain.

ROUGHPIPE

1.72	2.50	2.16	2.13	1.06	2.24	2.31	2.03	1.09	1.40
2.57	2.64	1.26	2.05	1.19	2.13	1.27	1.51	2.41	1.95

Source: Farshad, F., and Pesacreta, T. "Coated Pipe Interior Surface Roughness as Measured by Three Scanning Probe Instruments." *Anti-corrosion Methods and Materials*, Vol. 50, No. 1, 2003 (Table III).

5.33 Minimizing tractor skidding distance. When planning for a new forest road to be used for tree harvesting, planners must select the location to minimize tractor skidding distance. In the *Journal of Forest Engineering* (July 1999), researchers wanted to estimate the true mean skidding distance along a new road in a European forest. The skidding distances (in meters) were measured at 20 randomly selected road sites. These values are given in the accompanying table.

a. Estimate the true mean skidding distance for the road with a 95% confidence interval.

b. Give a practical interpretation of the interval, part **a.**

c. What conditions are required for the inference, part **b,** to be valid? Are these conditions reasonably satisfied?

d. A logger working on the road claims the mean skidding distance is at least 425 meters. Do you agree?

SKIDDING

488	350	457	199	285	409	435	574	439	546
385	295	184	261	273	400	311	312	141	425

Source: Tujek, J., and Pacola, E. "Algorithms for Skidding Distance Modeling on a Raster Digital Terrain Model." *Journal of Forest Engineering*, Vol. 10, No. 1, July 1999 (Table 1).

MINITAB output for Exercise 5.32

One-Sample T: ROUGH

```
Variable   N    Mean    StDev   SE Mean       95% CI
ROUGH      20  1.88100  0.52391 0.11715  (1.63580, 2.12620)
```

TRAFFIC

Station	Type of Route	30th Highest Hour	100th Highest Hour
0117	small city	1,890	1,736
0087	recreational	2,217	2,069
0166	small city	1,444	1,345
0013	rural	2,105	2,049
0161	urban	4,905	4,815
0096	urban	2,022	1,958
0145	rural	594	548
0149	rural	252	229
0038	urban	2,162	2,048
0118	rural	1,938	1,748
0047	rural	879	811
0066	urban	1,913	1,772
0094	rural	3,494	3,403
0105	small city	1,424	1,309
0113	small city	4,571	4,425
0151	urban	3,494	3,359
0159	rural	2,222	2,137
0160	small city	1,076	989
0164	recreational	2,167	2,039
0165	recreational	3,350	3,123

Source: Ewing, R. "Roadway Levels of Service in an Era of Growth Management." *Journal of STAR Research,* Vol. 3, July 1994, p. 103 (Table 2).

5.34 DOT traffic counts. It is customary practice in the United States to base roadway design on the 30th highest hourly volume in a year. Thus, all roadway facilities are expected to operate at acceptable levels of service for all but 29 hours of the year. The Florida Department of Transportation (DOT), however, has shifted from the 30th highest hour to the 100th highest hour as the basis for level-of-service determinators. Florida Atlantic University researcher Reid Ewing investigated whether this shift was warranted in the *Journal of STAR Research* (July 1994). The table above gives the traffic counts at the 30th highest hour and the 100th highest hour of a recent year for 20 randomly selected DOT permanent count stations.

a. Describe the population from which the sample data is selected.

b. Does the sample appear to be representative of the population? Explain.

c. Compute and interpret a 95% confidence interval for the mean traffic count at the 30th highest hour.

d. What assumption is necessary for the confidence interval to be valid? Does it appear to be satisfied? Explain.

e. Repeat parts **c** and **d** for the 100th highest hour.

f. If $\mu = 2,700$, is it likely to be the mean traffic count for the 30th highest hour or the 100th highest hour? Explain.

5.35 Largest private companies. IPOs—initial public offerings of stock—create billions of dollars of new wealth for owners, managers, and employees of companies that were previously privately owned. Nevertheless, hundreds of large and thousands of small companies remain privately owned. The revenues of a random sample of 15 firms from *Forbes* 339 Largest Private Companies list is given in the next table.

PRIVCOMP

Company	Revenue (in billions)
Enterprise Rent-A-Car	$8.23
Flying J	5.91
Tenaska Energy	6.67
Wawa	3.08
Ergon	2.68
Brookshire Grocery	1.96
BrightStar	1.74
Bose	1.80
Mary Kay	2.00
LL Bean	1.41
Rooms to Go	1.40
SAS Institute	1.53
Anderson News	1.30
Printpack	1.10
US Oil	1.05

Source: "Largest Private Companies," *Forbes,* Nov. 28, 2005.

a. Describe the population from which the random sample was drawn.

b. Use a 98% confidence interval to estimate the mean revenue of the population of companies in question.

c. Interpret your confidence interval in the context of the problem.

d. What characteristic must the population possess to ensure the appropriateness of the estimation procedure used in part **b**?

e. *Forbes* reports that the true mean revenue of the 339 companies on the list is $3.04 billion. Is *Forbes*' claim believable?

5.4 Large-Sample Confidence Interval for a Population Proportion

The number of public opinion polls has grown at an astounding rate in recent years. Almost daily, the news media report the results of some poll. Pollsters regularly determine the percentage of people who approve of the president's on-the-job performance, the fraction of voters in favor of a certain candidate, the fraction of customers who prefer a particular product, and the proportion of households that watch a particular TV program. In each case, we are interested in estimating the percentage (or proportion) of some group with a certain characteristic. In this section we consider methods for making inferences about population proportions when the sample is large.

EXAMPLE 5.3

Estimating a
Population
Proportion—
Preference for
Breakfast Cereal

Problem   A food-products company conducted a market study by randomly sampling and interviewing 1,000 consumers to determine which brand of breakfast cereal they prefer. Suppose 313 consumers were found to prefer the company's brand. How would you estimate the true fraction of *all* consumers who prefer the company's cereal brand?

Solution   In this study, consumers are asked which brand of breakfast cereal they prefer. Note that "brand" is a qualitative variable and what we are asking is how you would estimate the probability p of success in a binomial experiment, where p is the probability that a chosen consumer prefers the company's brand. One logical method of estimating p for the population is to use the proportion of successes in the sample—that is, we can estimate p by calculating

$$\hat{p} = \frac{\text{Number of consumers sampled who prefer the company's brand}}{\text{Number of consumers sampled}}$$

where $\hat{p}$ is read "p hat." Thus, in this case,

$$\hat{p} = \frac{313}{1,000} = .313$$

Look Back   To determine the reliability of the estimator $\hat{p}$, we need to know its sampling distribution—that is, if we were to draw samples of 1,000 consumers over and over again, each time calculating a new estimate $\hat{p}$, what would be the frequency distribution of all the $\hat{p}$ values? The answer lies in viewing $\hat{p}$ as the average, or mean, number of successes per trial over the n trials. If each success is assigned a value equal to 1 and a failure is assigned a value of 0, then the sum of all n sample observations is x, the total number of successes, and $\hat{p} = x/n$ is the average, or mean, number of successes per trial in the n trials. The Central Limit Theorem tells us that the relative frequency distribution of the sample mean for any population is approximately normal for sufficiently large samples.

Now Work Exercise 5.43a

The repeated sampling distribution of $\hat{p}$ has the characteristics listed in the next box and shown in Figure 5.12.

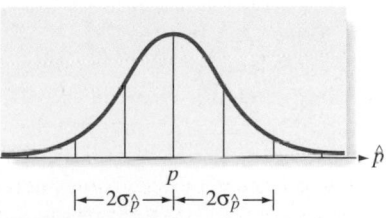

FIGURE 5.12
Sampling distribution of $\hat{p}$

Sampling Distribution of $\hat{p}$

1. The mean of the sampling distribution of $\hat{p}$ is p; that is, $\hat{p}$ is an unbiased estimator of p.
2. The standard deviation of the sampling distribution of $\hat{p}$ is $\sqrt{pq/n}$; that is, $\sigma_{\hat{p}} = \sqrt{pq/n}$, where $q = 1 - p$.
3. For large samples, the sampling distribution of $\hat{p}$ is approximately normal. A sample size is considered large if both $n\hat{p} \geq 15$ and $n\hat{q} \geq 15$.

The fact that $\hat{p}$ is a "sample mean number of successes per trial" allows us to form confidence intervals about p in a manner that is completely analogous to that used for large-sample estimation of μ.

Large-Sample Confidence Interval for p

$$\hat{p} \pm z_{\alpha/2}\sigma_{\hat{p}} = \hat{p} \pm z_{\alpha/2}\sqrt{\frac{pq}{n}} \approx \hat{p} \pm z_{\alpha/2}\sqrt{\frac{\hat{p}\hat{q}}{n}}$$

where $\hat{p} = \dfrac{x}{n}$ and $\hat{q} = 1 - \hat{p}$

Note: When n is large, $\hat{p}$ can approximate the value of p in the formula for $\sigma_{\hat{p}}$.

Conditions Required for a Valid Large-Sample Confidence Interval for p

1. A random sample is selected from the target population.
2. The sample size n is large. (This condition will be satisfied if both $n\hat{p} \geq 15$ and $n\hat{q} \geq 15$. Note that $n\hat{p}$ and $n\hat{q}$ are simply the number of successes and number of failures, respectively, in the sample.)

Thus, if 313 of 1,000 consumers prefer the company's cereal brand, a 95% confidence interval for the proportion of *all* consumers who prefer the company's brand is

$$\hat{p} \pm z_{\alpha/2}\sigma_{\hat{p}} = .313 \pm 1.96\sqrt{\frac{pq}{1,000}}$$

TABLE 5.6 Values of pq for Several Different Values of p

p	pq	$\sqrt{pq}$
.5	.25	.50
.6 or .4	.24	.49
.7 or .3	.21	.46
.8 or .2	.16	.40
.9 or .1	.09	.30

where $q = 1 - p$. Just as we needed an approximation for σ in calculating a large-sample confidence interval for μ, we now need an approximation for p. As Table 5.6 shows, the approximation for p does not have to be especially accurate, because the value of $\sqrt{pq}$ needed for the confidence interval is relatively insensitive to changes in p. Therefore, we can use $\hat{p}$ to approximate p. Keeping in mind that $\hat{q} = 1 - \hat{p}$, we substitute these values into the formula for the confidence interval:

$$\hat{p} \pm 1.96\sqrt{\frac{pq}{1,000}} \approx \hat{p} \pm 1.96\sqrt{\frac{\hat{p}\hat{q}}{1,000}}$$

$$= .313 \pm 1.96\sqrt{\frac{(.313)(.687)}{1,000}}$$

$$= .313 \pm .029$$

$$= (.284, .342)$$

The company can be 95% confident that the interval from 28.4% to 34.2% contains the true percentage of *all* consumers who prefer its brand—that is, in repeated construction of confidence intervals, approximately 95% of all samples would produce confidence intervals that enclose p. Note that the guidelines for interpreting a confidence interval about μ also apply to interpreting a confidence interval for p because p is the "population fraction of successes" in a binomial experiment.

EXAMPLE 5.4

Finding a Large-Sample Confidence Interval for p, the Proportion Optimistic about the Economy

Problem Many public polling agencies conduct surveys to determine the current consumer sentiment concerning the state of the economy. For example, the Bureau of Economic and Business Research (BEBR) at the University of Florida conducts quarterly surveys to gauge consumer sentiment in the Sunshine State. Suppose that BEBR randomly samples 484 consumers and finds that 257 are optimistic about the state of the economy. Use a 90% confidence interval to estimate the proportion of all consumers in Florida who are optimistic about the state of the economy. Based on the confidence interval, can BEBR infer that the majority of Florida consumers are optimistic about the economy?

Solution The number, x, of the 484 sampled consumers who are optimistic about the Florida economy is a binomial random variable if we can assume that the sample was randomly selected from the population of Florida consumers and that the poll was conducted identically for each sampled consumer.

The point estimate of the proportion of Florida consumers who are optimistic about the economy is

$$\hat{p} = \frac{x}{n} - \frac{257}{484} = .531$$

We first check to be sure that the sample size is sufficiently large that the normal distribution provides a reasonable approximation for the sampling distribution of $\hat{p}$. We require both $n\hat{p}$ and $n\hat{q}$ to be at least 15. Now

$$n\hat{p} = 484(.531) = 257$$

and

$$n\hat{q} = 484(1 - .531) = 227$$

Since both of these values are at least 15, we may conclude that the normal approximation is reasonable.

We now proceed to form the 90% confidence interval for p, the true proportion of Florida consumers who are optimistic about the state of the economy:

$$\hat{p} \pm z_{\alpha/2}\sigma_{\hat{p}} = \hat{p} \pm z_{\alpha/2}\sqrt{\frac{pq}{n}} \approx \hat{p} \pm z_{\alpha/2}\sqrt{\frac{\hat{p}\hat{q}}{n}}$$

$$= .531 \pm 1.645\sqrt{\frac{(.531)(.469)}{484}} = .531 \pm .037 = (.494, .568)$$

(This interval is also shown on the MINITAB printout, Figure 5.13.) Thus, we can be 90% confident that the proportion of all Florida consumers who are confident about the economy is between .494 and .568. As always, our confidence stems from the fact that 90% of all similarly formed intervals will contain the true proportion p and not from any knowledge about whether this particular interval does.

Can we conclude that the majority of Florida consumers are optimistic about the economy based on this interval? If we wished to use this interval to infer that a majority

FIGURE 5.13
Portion of MINITAB printout with 90% confidence interval for p

```
Sample    X    N   Sample p        90% CI
1        257  484  0.530992  (0.493681, 0.568303)
```

is optimistic, the interval would have to support the inference that p exceeds .5—that is, that more than 50% of the Florida consumers are optimistic about the economy. Note that the interval contains some values below .5 (as low as .494) as well as some above .5 (as high as .568). Therefore, we cannot conclude that the true value of p exceeds .5 based on this 90% confidence interval.

Look Back If the entire confidence interval fell above .5 (e.g., an interval from .52 to .54), then we could conclude (with 90% confidence) that the true proportion of consumers who are optimistic exceeds .5.

Now Work Exercise 5.43b,c

Caution

Unless n is extremely large, the large-sample procedure presented in this section performs poorly when p is near 0 or 1. For example, suppose you want to estimate the proportion of executives who die from a work-related injury. This proportion is likely to be near 0 (say, $p \approx .001$). Confidence intervals for p based on a sample of size $n = 100$ will probably be misleading. (Note that $np \approx 100(.001) = .1 < 15$.)

To overcome this potential problem, an extremely large sample size is required. Since the value of n required to satisfy "extremely large" is difficult to determine, statisticians (see Agresti & Coull, 1998) have proposed an alternative method, based on the Wilson (1927) point estimator of p. The procedure is outlined in the box. Researchers have shown that this confidence interval works well for any p, even when the sample size n is very small.

Adjusted $(1 - \alpha)100\%$ Confidence Interval for a Population Proportion, p

$$\tilde{p} \pm z_{\alpha/2}\sqrt{\frac{\tilde{p}(1 - \tilde{p})}{n + 4}}$$

where $\tilde{p} = \frac{x + 2}{n + 4}$ is the adjusted sample proportion of observations with the characteristic of interest, x is the number of successes in the sample, and n is the sample size.

EXAMPLE 5.5

Applying the Adjusted Confidence Interval Procedure for p, Proportion Who Are Victims of a Violent Crime

Problem According to *True Odds: How Risk Affects Your Everyday Life* (Walsh, 1997), the probability of being the victim of a violent crime is less than .01. Suppose that in a random sample of 200 Americans, 3 were victims of a violent crime. Estimate the true proportion of Americans who were victims of a violent crime using a 95% confidence interval.

Solution Let p represent the true proportion of Americans who were victims of a violent crime. Since p is near 0, an "extremely large" sample is required to estimate its value using the usual large-sample method. Note that the number of "successes," 3, is less than 15. Thus, we doubt whether the sample size of 200 is large enough to apply the large-sample method. Alternatively, we will apply the adjustment outlined in the box.

Since the number of "successes" (i.e., number of violent crime victims) in the sample is $x = 3$, the adjusted sample proportion is

$$\tilde{p} = \frac{x + 2}{n + 4} = \frac{3 + 2}{200 + 4} = \frac{5}{204} = .025$$

Note that this adjusted sample proportion is obtained by adding a total of four observations—two "successes" and two "failures"—to the sample data. Substituting $\tilde{p} = .025$ into the equation for a 95% confidence interval, we obtain

$$\tilde{p} \pm 1.96\sqrt{\frac{\tilde{p}(1-\tilde{p})}{n+4}} = .025 \pm 1.96\sqrt{\frac{(.025)(.975)}{204}}$$

$$= .025 \pm .021$$

or (.004, .046). Consequently, we are 95% confident that the true proportion of Americans who are victims of a violent crime falls between .004 and .046.

STATISTICS IN ACTION REVISITED

Estimating the Proportion of Underweight Scallop Bags

In the previous Statistics in Action Revisited (p. 307), we discovered that a ship returning from a fishing expedition with 11,000 bags of scallops was in violation of the U.S. Fisheries and Wildlife Service weight standard for baby scallops. (The law requires that the average meat per scallop weigh at least 1/36 of a pound.) Consequently, federal authorities confiscated 95% of the ship's catch. Is this fair? Did 95% of the ship's 11,000 bags contain underweight scallops?

To answer this question, we want to estimate p, the true fraction of the 11,000 bags of scallops that have an average weight per scallop less than $1/36 = .0278$ pound. If you examine the data for the 18 sampled bags (saved in the **SCALLOPS** file and listed in Table SIA5.1, p. 307), you will find that 16 of the 18 bags had an average weight per scallop less than .0278. Thus, our estimate of p is

$$\hat{p} = 16/18 = .889$$

A 95% confidence interval for p can be obtained using the confidence interval formula or with statistical software. A MINITAB printout of the analysis is displayed in Figure SIA5.2. The 95% confidence interval, highlighted on the printout, is (0.7437, 1.0000). Thus, we are 95% confident that the true percentage of the 11,000 bags of scallops that are under the 1/36 pound weight minimum is between 74.4% and 100%. This implies that the percentage of underweight bags could be as low as 74.4%. By confiscating 95% of the 11,000 bags of scallops, federal agents may have overestimated the fraction of bags that were in violation of the weight minimum.

Note: The MINITAB confidence interval in Figure SIA5.2 is based on a normal approximation that requires a "large" sample. A sample size of $n = 18$ bags is very small; thus, the interval may be inaccurate (as stated at the bottom of the MINITAB printout). To arrive at a more reliable estimate of the true proportion of underweight bags, federal agents should have selected a larger number of bags to weigh. In the next Statistics in Action Revisited (p. 325), we show how large of a sample needs to be selected.

Test and CI for One Proportion: Limit

```
Test of p = 0.5 vs p not = 0.5

Event = Below

Variable    X    N   Sample p       95% CI          Z-Value   P-Value
Limit      16   18   0.888889  (0.743706, 1.000000)   3.30     0.001


* NOTE * The normal approximation may be inaccurate for small samples.
```

Figure SIA 5.2
MINITAB confidence interval for proportion I of underweight bags

Confidence Interval for a Population Proportion (Large Sample Case)

Using the TI-83/TI-84 Graphing Calculator
Creating a Confidence Interval for a Population Proportion

Step 1 *Access the Statistical Tests Menu*

> Press **STAT**
> Arrow right to **TESTS**
> Arrow down to **1-PropZInt**
> Press **ENTER**

Step 2 *Enter the values for **x, n,** and **C-Level***

> where **x** = number of successes
> **n** = sample size
> **C-Level** = level of confidence
> Arrow down to "**Calculate**"
> Press **ENTER**

Example Suppose that 1,100 U.S. citizens are randomly chosen and 532 answer that they favor a flat income tax rate. Use a 95% confidence interval to estimate the true proportion of citizens who favor a flat income tax rate. In this example, $x = 532$, $n = 1,100$, and C-Level = .95.

The screens for this example are shown below.

Thus, a 95% confidence interval for the true percentage of all U.S. citizens who favor a flat income tax rate is 45.4% to 51.3%.

Exercises 5.36–5.51

Learning the Mechanics

5.36 Describe the sampling distribution of $\hat{p}$ based on large samples of size n—that is, give the mean, the standard deviation, and the (approximate) shape of the distribution of $\hat{p}$ when large samples of size n are (repeatedly) selected from the binomial distribution with probability of success p.

APPLET **Applet Exercise 5.5**

Use the applet entitled *Confidence Intervals for a Proportion* to investigate the effect of the value of p on the number of confidence intervals that contain the population proportion p for a fixed sample size. For this exercise, use sample size $n = 10$.
  a. Run the applet several times without clearing for $p = .1$. What proportion of the 95% confidence intervals

contain p? What proportion of the 99% confidence intervals contain p? Do the results surprise you? Explain.
  b. Repeat part **a** for each value of p: $p = .2, p = .3, p = .4, p = .5, p = .6, p = .7, p = .8$, and $p = .9$.
  c. Which value of p yields the greatest proportion of each type of interval that contain p?
  d. Based on your results, what values of p will yield more reliable confidence intervals for a fixed sample size n? Explain.

APPLET **Applet Exercise 5.6**

Use the applet entitled *Confidence Intervals for a Proportion* to investigate the effect of the sample size on the number of confidence intervals that contain the population proportion p for a value of p close to 0 or 1.

a. Run the applet several times without clearing for $p = .5$ and $n = 50$. Record the proportion of the 99% confidence intervals containing p.

b. Now set $p = .1$ and run the applet several times without clearing for $n = 50$. How does the proportion of the 99% confidence intervals containing p compare to that in part **a**?

c. Repeat part **b** keeping $p = .1$ and increasing the sample size by 50 until you find a sample size that yields a similar proportion of the 99% confidence intervals containing p as that in part **a**.

d. Based on your results, describe how the value of p effects the sample size needed to guarantee a certain level of confidence.

5.37 For the binomial sample information summarized in each part, indicate whether the sample size is large enough to use the methods of this chapter to construct a confidence interval for p.
   a. $n = 400$, $\hat{p} = .10$
   b. $n = 50$, $\hat{p} = .10$
   c. $n = 20$, $\hat{p} = .5$
   d. $n = 20$, $\hat{p} = .3$

5.38 A random sample of size $n = 121$ yielded $\hat{p} = .88$.
   a. Is the sample size large enough to use the methods of this section to construct a confidence interval for p? Explain.
   b. Construct a 90% confidence interval for p.
   c. What assumption is necessary to ensure the validity of this confidence interval?

5.39 A random sample of size $n = 225$ yielded $\hat{p} = .46$.
   a. Is the sample size large enough to use the methods of this section to construct a confidence interval for p? Explain.
   b. Construct a 95% confidence interval for p.
   c. Interpret the 95% confidence interval.
   d. Explain what is meant by the phrase "95% confidence interval."

5.40 A random sample of 50 consumers taste-tested a new snack food. Their responses were coded (0: do not like; 1: like; 2: indifferent) and recorded as follows:

⊙ **SNACK**

1	0	0	1	2	0	1	1	0	0
0	1	0	2	0	2	2	0	0	1
1	0	0	0	0	1	0	2	0	0
0	1	0	0	1	0	0	1	0	1
0	2	0	0	1	1	0	0	0	1

   a. Use an 80% confidence interval to estimate the proportion of consumers who like the snack food.
   b. Provide a statistical interpretation for the confidence interval you constructed in part **a**.

Applying the Concepts—Basic

5.41 Contractors with a company Web site. Each year, construction contractors and equipment distributors from across the United States participate in a survey called the CIT Construction Industry Forecast. Recently, 900 contractors were interviewed for the survey. Of these, 414 indicated that they either already have a company Web site or plan to have a company Web site by the end of the year (*Contractor Magazine*, Jan. 2005).
   a. Use the survey information to find a point estimate for the true proportion of contractors in the United States who have a company Web site or who will have one by the end of the year.
   b. Find an interval estimate for the proportion, part **a**. Use a 90% confidence interval.
   c. Give a practical interpretation of the interval, part **b**. Your answer should begin with "We are 90% confident . . ."
   d. Explain the meaning of the phrase, "90% confident."

5.42 Material safety data sheets. For over 20 years, the Occupational Safety & Health Administration has required companies that handle hazardous chemicals to complete material safety data sheets (MSDS). These MSDS have been criticized for being too hard to understand and complete by workers. Although improvements were implemented in 1990, a recent study of 150 MSDS revealed that only 11% were satisfactorily completed (*Chemical & Engineering News*, Feb. 7, 2005).
   a. Give a point estimate of p, the true proportion of MSDS that are satisfactorily completed.
   b. Find a 95% confidence interval for p.
   c. Give a practical interpretation of the interval, part **b**.

5.43 Cell phone use by drivers. In a July 2001 research note, the U.S. Department of Transportation reported the results of the *National Occupant Protection Use Survey*. One focus of the survey was to determine the level of cell phone use by drivers while they are in the act of driving a motor passenger vehicle. Data collected by observers at randomly selected intersections across the country revealed that in a sample of 1,165 drivers, 35 were using their cell phone.
   a. Give a point estimate of p, the true driver cell phone use rate (i.e., the true proportion of drivers who are using a cell phone while driving).
   b. Compute a 95% confidence interval for p.
   c. Give a practical interpretation of the interval, part **b**.

⊙ **DIAMONDS**

5.44 Diamonds sold on the open market. Refer to the sample of 308 diamond stones that were listed for sale on the open market in Singapore's *Business Times*. The data are saved in the **DIAMONDS** file. Recall that the color of each diamond is classified as D, E, F, G, H, or I, while the clarity of each is classified as VVS1, VVS2, VS1, or VS2.
   a. Find a 99% confidence interval for the proportion of all diamonds for sale on the open market that are classified as "D" color. Interpret the result.
   b. Find a 99% confidence interval for the proportion of all diamonds for sale on the open market that are classified as "VS1" clarity. Interpret the result.

5.45 Products made in the USA. Refer to Exercise 2.8 (p. 48) and the *Journal of Global Business* (Spring 2002) survey to determine what "Made in the USA" means to consumers. Recall that 106 shoppers at a shopping mall in Muncie, Indiana, responded to the question, " 'Made in the USA' means what percentage of US labor and materials?" Sixty-four shoppers answered "100%."
   a. Define the population of interest in the survey.
   b. What is the characteristic of interest in the population?
   c. Estimate the true proportion of consumers who believe "Made in the USA" means 100% US labor and materials using a 90% confidence interval.
   d. Give a practical interpretation of the interval, part **c**.
   e. Explain what the phrase "90% confidence" means for this interval.

Applying the Concepts—Intermediate

5.46 Interviewing candidates for a job. The costs associated with conducting interviews for a job opening have skyrocketed over the years. According to a Harris Interactive survey, 211 of 502 senior human resources executives at U.S. companies believe that their hiring managers are interviewing too many people to find qualified candidates for the job (*Business Wire*, June 8, 2006).

a. Describe the population of interest in this study.

b. Identify the population parameter of interest, p.

c. Is the sample size large enough to provide a reliable estimate of p?

d. Find and interpret an interval estimate for the true proportion of senior human resources executives who believe that their hiring managers interview too many candidates during a job search. Use a confidence level of 98%.

e. If you had constructed a 90% confidence interval, would it be wider or narrower?

5.47 Security of information submitted over the Internet. As Internet usage proliferates, so do questions of security and confidentiality of personal information, including such things as social security and credit card numbers. NCR Corporation surveyed 1,000 U.S. adults and asked them under what circumstances they would give personal information to a company. Twenty-nine percent said they would never give personal data to a company, while 51% said they would if the company had strict privacy guidelines in place (*Precision Marketing*, Oct. 4, 1999).

a. Verify that the sample size is large enough to construct a valid confidence interval for p, the proportion of all U.S. adults who would never give personal information to a company.

b. Construct a 95% confidence interval for p and interpret your result in the context of the problem.

c. Other than the size of the sample, what assumption must be made about the sample in order for the estimation procedure of part **b** to be valid?

5.48 Air bags pose danger for children. By law, all new cars must be equipped with both driver-side and passenger-side safety air bags. There is concern, however, over whether air bags pose a danger for children sitting on the passenger side. In a National Highway Traffic Safety Administration (NHTSA) study of 55 people killed by the explosive force of air bags, 35 were children seated on the front-passenger side (*Wall Street Journal*, Jan. 22, 1997). This study led some car owners with children to disconnect the passenger-side air bag. Consider all fatal automobile accidents in which it is determined that air bags were the cause of death. Let p represent the true proportion of these accidents involving children seated on the front-passenger side.

a. Use the data from the NHTSA study to estimate p.

b. Construct a 99% confidence interval for p.

c. Interpret the interval, part **b**, in the words of the problem.

d. NHTSA investigators determined that 24 of 35 children killed by the air bags were not wearing seat belts or were improperly restrained. How does this information impact your assessment of the risk of an air bag fatality?

5.49 Accuracy of price scanners at Wal-Mart. The National Institute for Standards and Technology (NIST) mandates that for every 100 items scanned through the electronic checkout scanner at a retail store, no more than 2 should have an inaccurate price. A recent study of the accuracy of checkout scanners at Wal-Mart stores in California was conducted (*Tampa Tribune*, Nov. 22, 2005). At each of 60 randomly selected Wal-Mart stores, 100 random items were scanned. The researchers found that 52 of the 60 stores had more than 2 items that were inaccurately priced.

a. Give an estimate of p, the proportion of Wal-Mart stores in California that have more than 2 inaccurately priced items per 100 items scanned.

b. Construct a 95% confidence interval for p.

c. Give a practical interpretation of the interval, part **b**.

d. Suppose a Wal-Mart spokesperson claims that 99% of California Wal-Mart stores are in compliance with the NIST mandate on accuracy of price scanners. Comment on the believability of this claim.

5.50 Latex allergy in health care workers. Refer to the *Current Allergy & Clinical Immunology* (Mar. 2004) study of health care workers who use latex gloves, Exercise 5.10 (p. 299). In addition to the 46 hospital employees who were diagnosed with a latex allergy based on a skin-prick test, another 37 health care workers were diagnosed with the allergy using a latex-specific serum test. Of these 83 workers with confirmed latex allergy, only 36 suspected that they had the allergy when asked on a questionnaire. Make a statement about the likelihood that a health care worker with latex allergy suspects he or she actually has the allergy. Attach a measure of reliability to your inference.

Applying the Concepts—Advanced

5.51 U.S. Postal services performance. The accounting firm of Price Waterhouse annually monitors the U.S. Postal Service's performance. One parameter of interest is the percentage of mail delivered on time. In a sample of 332,000 items mailed between Dec. 10 and Mar. 3—the most difficult delivery season due to bad weather and holidays—Price Waterhouse determined that 282,200 items were delivered on time (*Tampa Tribune*, Mar. 26, 1995). Use this information to make a statement about the likelihood of an item being delivered on time by the U.S. Postal Service.

5.5 Determining the Sample Size

Recall (Section 1.6) that one way to collect the relevant data for a study used to make inferences about the population is to implement a designed (planned) experiment. Perhaps the most important design decision faced by the analyst is to determine the size of the sample. We show in this section that the appropriate sample size for making an inference about a population mean or proportion depends on the desired reliability.

Estimating a Population Mean

Consider the example from Section 5.2 in which we estimated the mean overdue amount for all delinquent accounts in a large credit corporation. A sample of 100 delinquent accounts produced the 95% confidence interval $\bar{x} \pm 1.96\sigma_{\bar{x}} \approx 233.28 \pm 17.71$. Consequently, our estimate $\bar{x}$ was within \$17.71 of the true mean amount due, μ, for all the delinquent accounts at the 95% confidence level—that is, the 95% confidence interval for μ was $2(17.71) = \$35.42$ wide when 100 accounts were sampled. This is illustrated in Figure 5.14(a).

Now suppose we want to estimate μ to within \$5 with 95% confidence—that is, we want to narrow the width of the confidence interval from \$35.42 to \$10, as shown in Figure 5.14(b). How much will the sample size have to be increased to accomplish this? If we want the estimator $\bar{x}$ to be within \$5 of μ, we must have

$$2\sigma_{\bar{x}} = 5 \quad \text{or, equivalently,} \quad 2\left(\frac{\sigma}{\sqrt{n}}\right) = 5$$

The necessary sample size is obtained by solving this equation for n. To do this, we need an approximation for σ. We have an approximation from the initial sample of 100 accounts—namely, the sample standard deviation, $s = 90.34$. Thus,

$$2\left(\frac{\sigma}{\sqrt{n}}\right) \approx 2\left(\frac{s}{\sqrt{n}}\right) = 2\left(\frac{90.34}{\sqrt{n}}\right) = 5$$

$$\sqrt{n} = \frac{2(90.34)}{5} = 36.136$$

$$n = (36.136)^2 = 1,305.81 \approx 1,306$$

Approximately 1,306 accounts will have to be randomly sampled to estimate the mean overdue amount μ to within \$5 with (approximately) 95% confidence. The confidence interval resulting from a sample of this size will be approximately \$10 wide (see Figure 5.14b).

a. $n = 100$

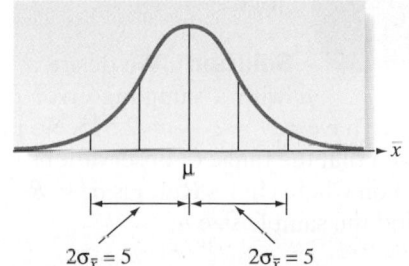

b. $n = 1,306$

FIGURE 5.14

Relationship between sample size and width of confidence interval: delinquent debtors example

FIGURE 5.15
Specifying the sampling error
SE as the half-width of a
confidence interval

In general, we express the reliability associated with a confidence interval for the population mean μ by specifying the **sampling error**, within which we want to estimate μ with $100(1 - \alpha)\%$ confidence. The sampling error (denoted SE), then, is equal to the half-width of the confidence interval, as shown in Figure 5.15.

Sample Size Determination for $100(1 - \alpha)\%$ Confidence Interval for μ

In order to estimate μ with a sampling error SE and with $100(1 - \alpha)\%$ confidence, the required sample size is found as follows:

$$z_{\alpha/2}\left(\frac{\sigma}{\sqrt{n}}\right) = SE$$

The solution for n is given by the equation

$$n = \frac{(z_{\alpha/2})^2\sigma^2}{(SE)^2}$$

Note: The value of σ is usually unknown. It can be estimated by the standard deviation, s, from a prior sample. Alternatively, we may approximate the range R of observations in the population, and (conservatively) estimate $\sigma \approx R/4$. In any case, you should round the value of n obtained *upward* to ensure that the sample size will be sufficient to achieve the specified reliability.

EXAMPLE 5.6

Finding the Sample
Size for Estimating
μ, the Mean Inflation
Pressure of Footballs

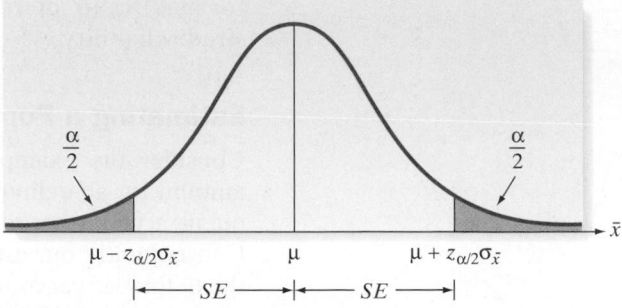

Problem   The manufacturer of official NFL footballs uses a machine to inflate its new balls to a pressure of 13.5 pounds. When the machine is properly calibrated, the mean inflation pressure is 13.5 pounds, but uncontrollable factors cause the pressures of individual footballs to vary randomly from about 13.3 to 13.7 pounds. For quality-control purposes, the manufacturer wishes to estimate the mean inflation pressure to within .025 pound of its true value with a 99% confidence interval. What sample size should be used?

Solution   We desire a 99% confidence interval that estimates μ with a sampling error of SE = .025 pound. For a 99% confidence interval, we have $z_{\alpha/2} = z_{.005} = 2.575$. No previous estimate of σ is available; however, we are given that the range of observations is $R = 13.7 - 13.3 = .4$. A conservative estimate (based on Chebychev's Rule) is $\sigma \approx R/4 = .1$. Now we use the formula derived in the box to find the sample size n:

$$n = \frac{(z_{\alpha/2})^2\sigma^2}{(SE)^2} \approx \frac{(2.575)^2(.1)^2}{(.025)^2} = 106.09$$

We round this up to $n = 107$. Realizing that σ was approximated by $R/4$, we might even advise that the sample size be specified as $n = 110$ to be more certain of attaining the objective of a 99% confidence interval with a sampling error of .025 pound or less.

Look Back To determine the value of the sampling error SE, look for the value that follows the key words "estimate μ to within. . . ."

Now Work Exercise 5.62

Sometimes the formula will yield a small sample size (say, $n < 30$). Unfortunately, this solution is invalid because the procedures and assumptions for small samples differ from those for large samples, as we discovered in Section 5.3. Therefore, if the formulas yield a small sample size, one simple strategy is to select a sample size $n = 30$.

Estimating a Population Proportion

The method outlined above is easily applied to a population proportion p. For example, in Section 5.4 a company used a sample of 1,000 consumers to calculate a 95% confidence interval for the proportion of consumers who preferred its cereal brand, obtaining the interval $.313 \pm .029$. Suppose the company wishes to estimate its market share more precisely, say to within .015 with a 95% confidence interval.

The company wants a confidence interval with a sampling error for the estimate of p of SE = .015. The sample size required to generate such an interval is found by solving the following equation for n (see Figure 5.16):

$$z_{\alpha/2}\sigma_{\hat{p}} = SE \qquad \text{or} \qquad z_{\alpha/2}\sqrt{\frac{pq}{n}} = .015$$

Since a 95% confidence interval is desired, the appropriate z value is $z_{\alpha/2} = z_{.025} = 1.96 \approx 2$. We must approximate the value of the product pq before we can solve the equation for n. As shown in Table 5.6, the closer the values of p and q to .5, the larger the product pq. Thus, to find a conservatively large sample size that will generate a confidence interval with the specified reliability, we generally choose an approximation of p close to .5. In the case of the food-products company, however, we have an initial sample estimate of $\hat{p} = .313$. A conservatively large estimate of pq can therefore be obtained by using, say, $p = .35$. We now substitute into the equation and solve for n:

$$2\sqrt{\frac{(.35)(.65)}{n}} = .015$$

$$n = \frac{(2)^2(.35)(.65)}{(.015)^2}$$

$$= 4,044.44 \approx 4,045$$

The company must sample about 4,045 consumers to estimate the percentage who prefer its brand to within .015 with a 95% confidence interval.

The procedure for finding the sample size necessary to estimate a population proportion p with a specified sampling error SE is given in the box.

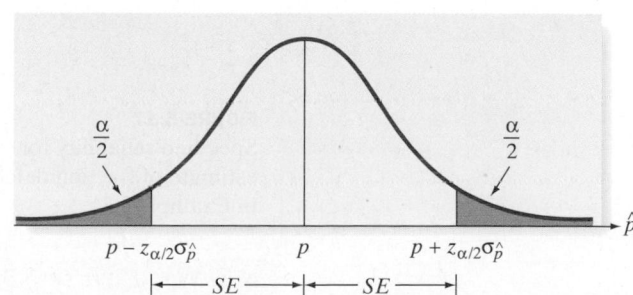

FIGURE 5.16
Specifying the sampling error SE of a confidence interval for a population proportion p

---

Sample Size Determination for $100(1 - \alpha)\%$ Confidence Interval for p

In order to estimate a binomial probability p with sampling error SE and with $100(1 - \alpha)$ % confidence, the required sample size is found by solving the following equation for n:

$$z_{\alpha/2}\sqrt{\frac{pq}{n}} = \text{SE}$$

The solution for n can be written as follows:

$$n = \frac{(z_{\alpha/2})^2(pq)}{(\text{SE})^2}$$

Note: Since the value of the product pq is unknown, it can be estimated by using the sample fraction of successes, $\hat{p}$, from a prior sample. Remember (Table 5.6) that the value of pq is at its maximum when p equals .5, so you can obtain conservatively large values of n by approximating p by .5 or values close to .5. In any case, you should round the value of n obtained *upward* to ensure that the sample size will be sufficient to achieve the specified reliability.

EXAMPLE 5.7

Finding the Sample Size for Estimating *p*, the Fraction of Defective Cell Phones

Problem   A cellular telephone manufacturer that entered the postregulation market too quickly has an initial problem with excessive customer complaints and consequent returns of the cell phones for repair or replacement. The manufacturer wants to determine the magnitude of the problem in order to estimate its warranty liability. How many cellular telephones should the company randomly sample from its warehouse and check in order to estimate the fraction defective, p, to within .01 with 90% confidence?

Solution   In order to estimate p to within .01 of its true value, we set the half-width of the confidence interval equal to SE = .01, as shown in Figure 5.17.
   The equation for the sample size n requires an estimate of the product pq. We could most conservatively estimate $pq = .25$ (i.e., use $p = .5$), but this may be overly conservative when estimating a fraction defective. A value of .1, corresponding to 10% defective, will probably be conservatively large for this application. The solution is therefore

$$n = \frac{(z_{\alpha/2})^2(pq)}{(\text{SE})^2} = \frac{(1.645)^2(.1)(.9)}{(.01)^2} = 2,435.4 \approx 2,436$$

Thus, the manufacturer should sample 2,436 cellular telephones in order to estimate the fraction defective, p, to within .01 with 90% confidence.

Look Back   Remember that this answer depends on our approximation for pq, where we used .09. If the fraction defective is closer to .05 than to .10, we can use a sample of 1,286 cell phones (check this) to estimate p to within .01 with 90% confidence.

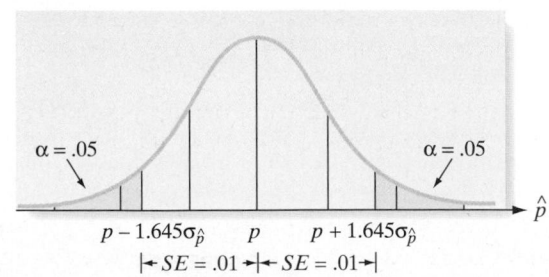

FIGURE 5.17
Specified reliability for estimate of fraction defective in Example 5.7

Now Work Exercise 5.61

STATISTICS IN ACTION REVISITED

Determining the Number of Bags of Scallops to Sample

In the previous Statistics in Action applications in this chapter, we used confidence intervals to (1) estimate μ, the population mean weight per scallop (p. 307), and (2) estimate p, the population proportion of scallop bags with average weight less than 1/36 pound (p. 317). The confidence interval for p was fairly wide due to the small number of bags sampled ($n = 18$) from the over 11,000 bags in the ship's catch. Also, with such a small sample, the use of the normal (z) statistic to form the confidence interval may be invalid. In order to find a valid, narrower confidence interval for the true proportion, the harbormaster would need to take a larger sample of scallop bags.

How many bags should be sampled from the ship's catch to estimate p to within .03 with 95% confidence? Here, we have the sampling error, $SE = .03$ and $z_{.025} = 1.96$ (since, for a 95% confidence interval, $\alpha = .05$ and $\alpha/2 = .025$). From our analysis on page 317, the estimated proportion is $\hat{p} = .89$. Substituting these values into the following equation, we obtain

$$n = \frac{(z_{.025})^2(\hat{p})(1 - \hat{p})}{(SE)^2} = \frac{(1.96)^2(.89)(.11)}{(.03)^2} = 417.88$$

Consequently, the harbormaster would have to sample 418 of the ship's 11,000 bags of scallops in order to find a valid 95% confidence interval for p.

The cost of sampling will also play an important role in the final determination of the sample size to be selected to estimate either μ or p. Although more complex formulas can be derived to balance the reliability and cost considerations, we will solve for the necessary sample size and note that the sampling budget may be a limiting factor. Consult the references for a more complete treatment of this problem.

Exercises 5.52–5.68

Learning the Mechanics

5.52 If you wish to estimate a population mean with a sampling error $SE = .3$ using a 95% confidence interval and you know from prior sampling that σ^2 is approximately equal to 7.2, how many observations would have to be included in your sample?

5.53 Suppose you wish to estimate a population mean correct to within .20 with probability equal to .90. You do not know σ^2, but you know that the observations will range in value between 30 and 34.
   a. Find the approximate sample size that will produce the desired accuracy of the estimate. You wish to be conservative to ensure that the sample size will be ample to achieve the desired accuracy of the estimate. [*Hint:* Using your knowledge of data variation from Section 2.6, assume that the range of the observations will equal 4σ.]
   b. Calculate the approximate sample size, making the less conservative assumption that the range of the observations is equal to 6σ.

5.54 In each case, find the approximate sample size required to construct a 95% confidence interval for p that has sampling error $SE = .08$.
   a. Assume p is near .2.
   b. Assume you have no prior knowledge about p, but you wish to be certain that your sample is large enough to achieve the specified accuracy for the estimate.

5.55 The following is a 90% confidence interval for p: (.26, .54). How large was the sample used to construct this interval?

5.56 It costs you $10 to draw a sample of size $n = 1$ and measure the attribute of interest. You have a budget of $1,500.
   a. Do you have sufficient funds to estimate the population mean for the attribute of interest with a 95% confidence interval 5 units in width? Assume $\sigma = 14$.
   b. If you used a 90% confidence level, would your answer to part **a** change? Explain.

5.57 Suppose you wish to estimate the mean of a normal population using a 95% confidence interval, and you know from prior information that $\sigma^2 \approx 1$.
   a. To see the effect of the sample size on the width of the confidence interval, calculate the width of the confidence interval for $n = 16, 25, 49, 100,$ and 400.
   b. Plot the width as a function of sample size n on graph paper. Connect the points by a smooth curve and note how the width decreases as n increases.

5.58 If nothing is known about p, .5 can be substituted for p in the sample-size formula for a population proportion. But when this is done, the resulting sample size may be larger than needed. Under what circumstances will using $p = .5$ in the sample-size formula yield a sample size larger than needed to construct a confidence interval for p with a specified bound and a specified confidence level?

Applying the Concepts—Basic

5.59 **Assessing the bending strength of a wooden roof.** Refer to the *Journal of the International Association for Shell and Spatial Structures* (Aug. 2004) study to estimate the mean bending strength of imported white wood used on the roof of an ancient Japanese temple, Exercise 5.27 (p. 310). Suppose you want to estimate the true mean breaking strength of the white wood to within 4 MPa using a 90% confidence interval. How many pieces of the imported wood need to be tested? Recall that the sample standard deviation of the breaking strengths from the study was 10.9 MPa.

5.60 **"Made in the USA" survey.** Refer to Exercise 5.45 (p. 319) and the *Journal of Global Business* (Spring 2002) survey to determine what "Made in the USA" means to consumers. Recall that 64 of 106 shoppers at a shopping mall in Muncie, Indiana, believe that "Made in the USA" implies all labor and materials are produced in the United States. Suppose the researchers want to increase the sample size in order to estimate the true proportion, p, to within .05 of its true value using a 90% confidence interval.

    a. What is the confidence level desired by the researchers?

    b. What is the sampling error desired by the researchers?

    c. Compute the sample size necessary to obtain the desired estimate.

5.61 **Aluminum cans contaminated by fire.** A gigantic warehouse located in Tampa, Florida, stores approximately 60 million empty aluminum beer and soda cans. Recently, a fire occurred at the warehouse. The smoke from the fire contaminated many of the cans with blackspot, rendering them unusable. A University of South Florida statistician was hired by the insurance company to estimate p, the true proportion of cans in the warehouse that were contaminated by the fire. How many aluminum cans should be randomly sampled to estimate p to within .02 with 90% confidence?

5.62 **Water pollution testing.** The EPA wants to test a randomly selected sample of n water specimens and estimate the mean daily rate of pollution produced by a mining operation. If the EPA wants a 95% confidence interval estimate with a sampling error of 1 milligram per liter (mg/L), how many water specimens are required in the sample? Assume prior knowledge indicates that pollution readings in water samples taken during a day are approximately normally distributed with a standard deviation equal to 5 mg/L.

Applying the Concepts—Intermediate

5.63 **Bacteria in bottled water.** Is the bottled water you drink safe? According to an article in *U.S. News & World Report* (April 12, 1999), the Natural Resources Defense Council warns that the bottled water you are drinking may contain more bacteria and other potentially carcinogenic chemicals than allowed by state and federal regulations. Of the more than 1,000 bottles studied, nearly one-third exceeded government levels. Suppose that the Natural Resources Defense Council wants an updated estimate of the population proportion of bottled water that violates at least one government standard. Determine the sample size (number of bottles) needed to estimate this proportion to within ±0.01 with 99% confidence.

5.64 **IRS answers to gift tax questions.** According to estimates made by the General Accounting Office, the Internal Revenue Service (IRS) answered 18.3 million telephone inquiries during a recent tax season, and 17% of the IRS offices provided answers that were wrong. These esti-

mates were based on data collected from sample calls to numerous IRS offices. How many IRS offices should be randomly selected and contacted in order to estimate the proportion of IRS offices that fail to correctly answer questions about gift taxes with a 90% confidence interval of width .06?

5.65 **Monitoring phone calls to a toll-free number.** A large food-products company receives about 100,000 phone calls a year from consumers on its toll-free number. A computer monitors and records how many rings it takes for an operator to answer, how much time each caller spends "on hold," and other data. However, the reliability of the monitoring system has been called into question by the operators and their labor union. As a check on the computer system, approximately how many calls should be manually monitored during the next year to estimate the true mean time that callers spend on hold to within 3 seconds with 95% confidence? Answer this question for the following values of the standard deviation of waiting times (in seconds): 10, 20, and 30.

5.66 **USGA golf ball tests.** The United States Golf Association (USGA) tests all new brands of golf balls to ensure that they meet USGA specifications. One test conducted is intended to measure the average distance traveled when the ball is hit by a machine called "Iron Byron," a name inspired by the swing of the famous golfer Byron Nelson. Suppose the USGA wishes to estimate the mean distance for a new brand to within 1 yard with 90% confidence. Assume that past tests have indicated that the standard deviation of the distances Iron Byron hits golf balls is approximately 10 yards. How many golf balls should be hit by Iron Byron to achieve the desired accuracy in estimating the mean?

Applying the Concepts—Advanced

5.67 **Is caffeine addictive?** Does the caffeine in coffee, tea, and cola induce an addiction similar to that induced by alcohol, tobacco, heroine, and cocaine? In an attempt to answer this question, researchers at Johns Hopkins University examined 27 caffeine drinkers and found 25 who displayed some type of withdrawal symptoms when abstaining from caffeine. [*Note*: The 27 caffeine drinkers volunteered for the study.] Furthermore, of 11 caffeine drinkers who were diagnosed as caffeine dependent, 8 displayed dramatic withdrawal symptoms (including impairment in normal functioning) when they consumed a caffeine-free diet in a controlled setting. The National Coffee Association claimed, however, that the study group was too small to draw conclusions (*Los Angeles Times*, Oct. 5, 1994). Is the sample large enough to estimate the true proportion of caffeine drinkers who are caffeine dependent to within .05 of the true value with 99% confidence? Explain.

5.68 **Preventing production of defective items.** It costs more to produce defective items—since they must be scrapped or reworked—than it does to produce nondefective items. This simple fact suggests that manufacturers should ensure the quality of their products by perfecting their production processes rather than through inspection of finished products (Deming, 1986). In order to better understand a particular metal-stamping process, a manufacturer wishes to estimate the mean length of items produced by the process during the past 24 hours.

a. How many parts should be sampled in order to estimate the population mean to within .1 millimeter (mm) with 90% confidence? Previous studies of this machine have indicated that the standard deviation of lengths produced by the stamping operation is about 2 mm.

b. Time permits the use of a sample size no larger than 100. If a 90% confidence interval for μ is constructed using $n = 100$, will it be wider or narrower than would have been obtained using the sample size determined in part **a**? Explain.

c. If management requires that μ be estimated to within .1 mm and that a sample size of no more than 100 be used, what is (approximately) the maximum confidence level that could be attained for a confidence interval that meets management's specifications?

5.6 Finite Population Correction for Simple Random Sampling (Optional)

The large-sample confidence intervals for a population mean μ and a population proportion p presented in the previous sections are based on a simple random sample selected from the target population. Although we did not state it, the procedure also assumes that the number N of measurements (i.e., sampling units) in the population is large relative to the sample size n.

In some sampling situations, the sample size n may represent 5% or perhaps 10% of the total number N of sampling units in the population. When the sample size is large relative to the number of measurements in the population (see the next box), the standard errors of the estimators of μ and p given in Sections 5.2 and 5.4, respectively, should be multiplied by a **finite population correction factor.**

The form of the finite population correction factor depends on how the population variance σ^2 is defined. In order to simplify the formulas of the standard errors, it is common to define σ^2 as division of the sum of squares of deviations by $N - 1$ rather than by N (analogous to the way we defined the sample variance). If we adopt this convention, the finite population correction factor becomes $\sqrt{(N - n)/N}$. Then the estimated standard errors of $\bar{x}$ (the estimator of μ) and $\hat{p}$ (the estimator of p) are as shown in the box.*

Rule of Thumb for Finite Population Correction Factor

Use the finite population correction factor (shown in the next box) when $n/N > .05$.

Simple Random Sampling with Finite Population of Size N
Estimation of the Population Mean

Estimated standard error:

$$\hat{\sigma}_{\bar{x}} = \frac{s}{\sqrt{n}}\sqrt{\frac{N - n}{N}}$$

Approximate 95% confidence interval: $\bar{x} \pm 2\hat{\sigma}_{\bar{x}}$

Estimation of the Population Proportion

Estimated standard error:

$$\hat{\sigma}_{\hat{p}} = \sqrt{\frac{\hat{p}(1 - \hat{p})}{n}}\sqrt{\frac{N - n}{N}}.$$

Approximate 95% confidence interval: $\hat{p} \pm 2\hat{\sigma}_{\hat{p}}$

Note: The confidence intervals are "approximate" since we are using 2 to approximate the value $z_{.025} = 1.96$.

---

*For most surveys and opinion polls, the finite population correction factor is approximately equal to 1 and, if desired, can be safely ignored. However, if $n/N > .05$, the finite population correction factor should be included in the calculation of the standard error.

EXAMPLE 5.8

Applying the Finite Population Correction Factor in the Manufacture of Sheet Aluminum Foil

Problem A specialty manufacturer wants to purchase remnants of sheet aluminum foil. The foil, all of which is the same thickness, is stored on 1,462 rolls, each containing a varying amount of foil. To obtain an estimate of the total number of square feet of foil on all the rolls, the manufacturer randomly sampled 100 rolls and measured the number of square feet on each roll. The sample mean was 47.4, and the sample standard deviation was 12.4.

a. Find an approximate 95% confidence interval for the mean amount of foil on the 1,462 rolls.

b. Estimate the total number of square feet of foil on all the rolls by multiplying the confidence interval, part **a**, by 1,462. Interpret the result.

Solution

a. Each roll of foil is a sampling unit, and there are $N = 1,462$ units in the population, and the sample size is $n = 100$. Since $n/N = 100/1,462 = .068$ exceeds .05, we need to apply the finite population correction. We have $n = 100$, $\bar{x} = 47.4$, and $s = 12.4$. Substituting these quantities, we obtain the approximate 95% confidence interval

$$\bar{x} \pm 2\frac{s}{\sqrt{n}}\sqrt{\frac{(N-n)}{N}} = (47.4) \pm 2\frac{12.4}{\sqrt{100}}\sqrt{\frac{(1,462-100)}{1,462}}$$

$$= 47.4 \pm 2.39$$

or (45.01, 49.79).

b. For finite populations of size N, the sum of all measurements in the population— called a *population total*—is

$$\sum_{i=1}^{N} x_i = N\mu$$

Since the confidence interval, part **a**, estimates μ, an estimate of the population total is obtained by multiplying the endpoints of the interval by N. For we have

Lower Limit $= N(45.01) = 1,462(45.01) = 65,804.6$

Upper Limit $= N(49.79) = 1,462(49.79) = 72,793.0$

Consequently, the manufacturer estimates the total amount of foil to be in the interval 65,805 square feet to 72,793 square feet with 95% confidence.

Look Back If the manufacturer wants to adopt a conservative approach, the bid for the foil will be based on the lower confidence limit, 65,805 square feet of foil.

Now Work Exercise 5.76a

Exercises 5.69–5.81

Learning the Mechanics

5.69 Calculate the percentage of the population sampled and the finite population correction factor for each of the following situations.
  a. $n = 1,000, N = 2,500$
  b. $n = 1,000, N = 5,000$
  c. $n = 1,000, N = 10,000$
  d. $n = 1,000, N = 100,000$

5.70 Suppose the standard deviation of the population is known to be $\sigma = 200$. Calculate the standard error of $\bar{x}$ for each of the situations described in Exercise 5.69.

5.71 Suppose $N = 10,000, n = 2,000$, and $s = 50$.

  a. Compute the standard error of $\bar{x}$ using the finite population correction factor.
  b. Repeat part **a** assuming $n = 4,000$.
  c. Repeat part **a** assuming $n = 10,000$
  d. Compare parts **a, b,** and **c,** and describe what happens to the standard error of $\bar{x}$ as n increased.
  e. The answer to part **c** is 0. This indicates that there is no sampling error in this case. Explain.

5.72 Suppose $N = 5,000, n = 64$, and $s = 24$.
  a. Compare the size of the standard error of $\bar{x}$ computed with and without the finite population correction factor.
  b. Repeat part **a,** but this time assume $n = 400$.

c. Theoretically, when sampling from a finite population, the finite population correction factor should always be used in computing the standard error of $\bar{x}$. However, when n is small relative to N, the finite population correction factor is close to 1 and can safely be ignored. Explain how parts **a** and **b** illustrate this point.

5.73 Suppose you want to estimate a population proportion, p, and $\hat{p} = .42$, $N = 6,000$, and $n = 1,600$. Find an approximate 95% confidence interval for p.

5.74 Suppose you want to estimate a population mean, μ, and $\bar{x} = 422$, $s = 14$, $N = 375$, and $n = 40$. Find an approximate 95% confidence interval for μ.

5.75 A random sample of size $n = 30$ was drawn from a population of size $N = 300$. The following measurements were obtained:

⊙ **LM5_75**

21	33	19	29	22	38	58	29	52	36	37	30
53	37	29	18	35	42	36	41	35	36	33	38
29	38	39	54	42	42						

a. Estimate μ with an approximate 95% confidence interval.

b. Estimate p, the proportion of measurements in the population that are greater than 30, with an approximate 95% confidence interval.

Applying the Concepts—Basic

5.76 **Magazine subscriber salaries.** The trade magazine *Quality Progress* (Dec. 2002) published a study of subscribers' salaries. The 223 vice presidents sampled had a mean salary of $116,754 and a standard deviation of $39,185. Suppose the goal of the study is to estimate the true mean salary of all vice presidents who subscribe to *Quality Progress*.

NW **a.** If 2,193 vice presidents subscribe to *Quality Progress*, estimate the mean with an approximate 95% confidence interval.

b. Interpret the result.

5.77 **Employees with substance abuse problems.** According to the New Jersey *Governor's Council for a Drug-Free Workplace Report* (Spring/Summer 1995), 50 of the 72 sampled businesses that are members of the council admitted that they had employees with substance abuse problems. At the time of the survey, 251 New Jersey businesses were members of the Governor's Council. Based on this information, find a 95% confidence interval for the proportion of all New Jersey Governor's Council business members that have employees with substance abuse problems. Interpret the resulting interval.

Applying the Concepts—Intermediate

5.78 **Furniture brand familiarity.** A brand name that consumers recognize is a highly valued commodity in any industry. To assess brand familiarity in the furniture industry, NPD (a market research firm) surveyed 1,333 women who head U.S. households that have incomes of $25,000 or more. The sample was drawn from a database of 25,000 households that match the criteria listed above. Of the 10 furniture brands evaluated, La-Z-Boy was the most recognized brand; 70.8% of the

respondents indicated they were "very familiar" with La-Z-Boy (*HFN*, Oct. 11, 1999).

a. Describe the population being investigated by NPD.

b. In constructing a confidence interval to estimate the proportion of households that are very familiar with the La-Z-Boy brand, is it necessary to use the finite population correction factor? Explain

c. What estimate of the standard error of $\hat{p}$ should be used in constructing the confidence interval of part **b**?

d. Construct a 90% confidence interval for the true proportion and interpret it in the context of the problem.

5.79 **Auditing sampling methods.** Since the early 1950s, auditors have relied to a great extent on sampling techniques, rather than 100% audits, to help them test and evaluate the financial records of a client firm. When sampling is used to obtain an estimate of the total dollar value of an account—the account balance—the examination is known as *a substantive test* (Arkin, *Sampling Methods for the Auditor*, 1982). In order to evaluate the reasonableness of a firm's stated total value of its parts inventory, an auditor randomly samples 100 of the total of 500 parts in stock, prices each part, and reports the results shown in the table.

⊙ **AUDPARTS**

Part Number	Part Price	Sample Size
002	$ 108	3
101	55	2
832	500	1
077	73	10
688	300	1
910	54	4
839	92	6
121	833	5
271	50	9
399	125	12
761	1,000	2
093	62	8
505	205	7
597	88	11
830	100	19

a. Give a point estimate of the mean value of the parts inventory.

b. Find the estimated standard error of the point estimate of part **a.**

c. Construct an approximate 95% confidence interval for the mean value of the parts inventory.

d. The firm reported a mean parts inventory value of $300. What does your confidence interval of part **c** suggest about the reasonableness of the firm's reported figure? Explain.

5.80 **Invoice errors in a billing system.** In a study of invoice errors in a company's new billing system, an auditor randomly sampled 35 invoices produced by the new system and recorded actual amount (A), invoice amount (I), and the difference (or error), $x = (A - I)$. The results were $\bar{x} = \$1$ and $s = \$124$. At the time that the sample was drawn, the new system had produced 1,500 invoices. Use this information to find an approximate 95% confidence interval for the true mean error per invoice of the new system. Interpret the result.

Applying the Concepts—Advanced

5.81 Pesticide residue in corn products. The U.S. Environmental Protection Agency (EPA) bans use of the cancer-causing pesticide ethylene dibromide (EDB) as a fumigant for grain- and flour-milling equipment. EDB was once used to protect against infestation by microscopic roundworms called *nematodes*. The EPA sets maximum safe levels for EDB presence in raw grain, flour, cake mixes, cereals, bread, and other grain products on supermarket shelves and in warehouses. Of the 3,000 corn-related products sold in one state, tests indicated that 15 of a random sample of 175 had EDB residues above the safe level. Will more than 7% of the corn-related products in this state have to be removed from shelves and warehouses? Explain.

5.7 Sample Survey Designs (Optional)

The confidence interval methodology developed in Sections 5.2–5.5 is based on simple random sampling (Chapter 3). A (simple) random sample is just one of several different sampling designs used in *sample surveys*.

The term **sample survey** is used in conjunction with the sampling of populations (i.e., collections of people, households, businesses, etc.). A consumer preference poll is an example of a sample survey. Samplings conducted to estimate the general level of business inventories or to estimate the proportion of households that watched a particular television program are also examples of sample surveys.

Sample surveys cost time and money, and sometimes they are almost impossible to conduct. For example, suppose we want to obtain an estimate of the proportion of households in the United States that plan to purchase new television sets next year, and we plan to base our estimate on the intentions of a random sample of 3,000 households. What are the problems associated with collecting these data? In order to use a random number generator (Chapter 3) to select the sample, we would need a list of all the households in the United States. Obtaining such a list would be a monumental obstacle. After we obtain a list of households, we need to contact each of the 3,000 selected for the sample. Will all be at home when the surveyor reaches the household? And will all answer the surveyor's question? You can see that collecting a random sample is easier said than done.

The large body of knowledge underlying **survey sampling** or **sample survey design** was developed to help solve some of the problems we have noted. It includes sample survey designs that help reduce the cost and time involved in conducting a sample survey, and it includes the confidence interval procedures associated with those designs. Since survey sampling is a course in itself, we will present only a few of the most widely used sample survey designs and address only a few of the problems you might encounter in this optional section. Further information on this important subject can be found in the references at the end of the text.

One of the most common sampling designs (besides random sampling) is called *stratified random sampling*. **Stratified random sampling** is used when the sampling units (i.e., the units that are sampled) associated with the population can be physically separated into two or more groups of sampling units (called **strata**) where the within-stratum response variation is less than the variation within the entire population. For example, suppose we want to estimate the average amount of rent paid for a two-bedroom apartment in New York City. Since the variation in rent paid within New York City is likely to be large, we may want to divide the city into regions (strata) where the rents within each stratum are relatively homogeneous. Then we would estimate the population mean by selecting random samples from within each stratum and combining the stratum estimates.

Stratified random sampling often produces estimators with smaller standard errors than those achieved using simple random sampling. Furthermore, by sampling from each stratum, we are more likely to obtain a sample representative of the entire population. In addition, the administrative and labor costs of selecting the stratum samples are often less than those for simple random sampling.

Sometimes it is difficult or too costly to select random samples. For example, it would be easier to obtain a sample of student opinions at a large university by systematically selecting every hundredth name from the student directory. This type of sample design is called a **systematic sample.** Although systematic samples are usually easier to select than other types of samples, one difficulty is the possibility of a systematic sampling bias. For example, if every fifth item in an assembly line is selected for quality-control inspection, and if five different machines are sequentially producing the items, all the items sampled may have been manufactured by the same machine. If we use systematic sampling, we must be certain that no cycles (like every fifth item manufactured by the same machine) exist in the list of the sampling units.

A third alternative to the simple random sampling design is *randomized response sampling.* **Randomized response sampling** is particularly useful when the questions of the pollsters are likely to elicit false answers. For example, suppose each person in a sample of wage earners is asked whether he or she cheated on an income tax return. A person who has not cheated most likely would give an honest answer to this question. A cheater might lie, thus biasing an estimate of what proportion of persons cheats on their income tax return.

One method of coping with the false responses produced by sensitive questions is randomized response sampling. Each person is presented *two* questions; one question is the object of the survey and the other is an innocuous question to which the interviewee will give an honest answer. For example, each person might be asked these two questions:

1. Did you cheat on your income tax return?
2. Did you drink coffee this morning?

Then a procedure is used to select randomly which of the two questions the person is to answer. For example, the interviewee might be asked to flip a coin. If the coin shows a head, the interviewee answers the sensitive question, 1. If the coin shows a tail, the interviewee answers the innocuous question, 2. Since the interviewer never has the opportunity to see the coin, the interviewee can answer the question and feel assured that his or her guilt (if guilty) will not be exposed. Consequently, the random response procedure can elicit an honest response to a sensitive question. Sophisticated methodology is then used to derive an estimate of the percentage of "yes" responses to the sensitive question.

As mentioned earlier, in any sample survey design, cost (either in time, labor, or money) may be an issue. Two methods for reducing the cost of random sampling are to use a telephone survey or a mailed survey. Although this type of sampling eliminates transportation costs and reduces labor costs, it introduces a serious difficulty—the problem of **nonresponse.** By this, we mean that sampling units contained in a sample do not produce sample observations. For example, an individual may not be at home when telephoned or may refuse to complete and mail back a questionnaire.

Nonresponse is a serious problem because it may lead to very biased results. There may be a high correlation between the type of response and whether or not a person responds. For example, most citizens in a community might have an opinion on a school bond issue, but the respondents in a mail survey might very well be those with vested interests in the outcome of the survey—say, parents with children of school age, or school teachers, or those whose taxes might be substantially affected. Others with no vested interests might have opinions on the issue but might not take the time to respond. For this example, the absence of the nonrespondents' data could lead to a larger estimate of the percentage in favor of the issue than was actually the case. In other words, the absence of the nonrespondents' data could lead to a biased estimate.

Nonresponse is a very important sampling problem. If your sampling plan calls for a specific collection of sampling units, failure to acquire the responses from those units may violate your sampling plan and lead to biased estimates. If you intend to select a random sample and you cannot obtain the responses from some of the sampling units, then your sampling procedure is *no longer random*, and the methodology based on it (e.g., confidence intervals) and the product of the methodology (e.g., inferences) are suspect.

There are ways for coping with nonresponse. Most involve tracking down and questioning all or part of the nonrespondents and using the additional information to adjust for the missing nonrespondent data. For mailed surveys, however, it has been found that the inclusion of a monetary incentive with the questionnaire—even as little as 25¢—will substantially increase the response rate of the survey.

There are many sampling designs available to a sample surveyor; some are variations on simple random sampling and stratified random sampling, and others are completely different. In addition, different types of estimators can be used with these designs. In this brief introduction to survey sampling, our intent was to present only a few of the most important sample survey designs and some of their inherent problems. Thorough presentations of the different sample survey designs are given in textbooks devoted to this topic (see the references at the end of this text).

KEY TERMS

Note: Starred (*) items are from the optional sections in this chapter.

Confidence coefficient   294
Confidence interval   294
Confidence level   294
Degrees of freedom   302

*Finite population correction factor   327
Interval estimator   294
*Nonresponse   331
*Randomized response sampling   331
*Sample survey design   330
Sampling error   322

*Strata   330
*Stratified random sampling   330
*Survey sampling   330
*Systematic sampling   331
t-statistic   302
Wilson adjustment for estimating p 316

GUIDE TO FORMING A CONFIDENCE INTERVAL

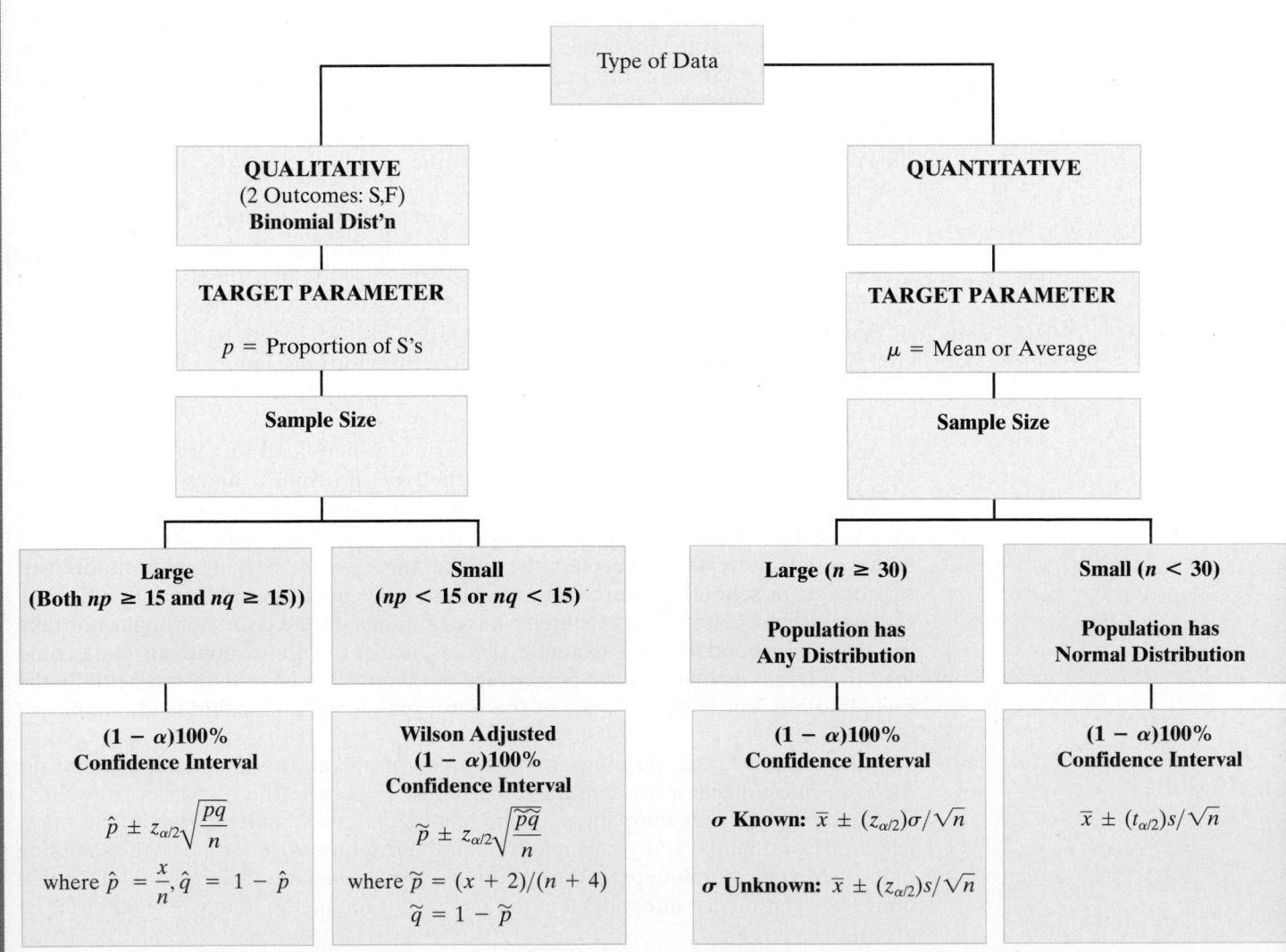

CHAPTER NOTES

Population Parameters, Estimators, & Standard Errors

Parameter (θ)	Estimator($\hat{\theta}$)	Standard Error of Estimator ($\hat{\sigma}_{\hat{\theta}}$)	Estimated Std. Error ($\hat{\sigma}_{\hat{\theta}}$)
Mean, μ	$\bar{x}$	$\sigma/\sqrt{n}$	$s/\sqrt{n}$
Proportion, p	$\hat{p}$	$\sqrt{pq/n}$	$\sqrt{\hat{p}\hat{q}/n}$

KEY SYMBOLS

θ	General population parameter (theta)
μ	Population mean
σ	Population standard deviation
p	Population proportion; P(Success) in binomial trial
q	$1 - p$
$\bar{x}$	Sample mean (estimator of μ)
$\hat{p}$	Sample proportion (estimator of p)
$\mu_{\bar{x}}$	Mean of the population sampling distribution of $\bar{x}$
$\sigma_{\bar{x}}$	Standard deviation of the sampling distribution of x
$\sigma_{\hat{p}}$	Standard deviation of the sampling distribution of $\hat{p}$
SE	Sampling error in estimation
α	$(1 - \alpha)$ represents the confidence coefficient
$z_{\alpha/2}$	z-value used in a $100(1 - \alpha)$% large-sample confidence interval
$t_{\alpha/2}$	Student's t-value used in a $100(1 - \alpha)$% small-sample confidence interval
N	Number of observations in the target population

Confidence Interval: An interval that encloses an unknown population parameter with a certain level of confidence $(1 - \alpha)$

Confidence Coefficient: The probability $(1 - \alpha)$ that a randomly selected confidence interval encloses the true value of the population parameter.

Key Words for Identifying the Target Parameter:

μ Mean, Average

p—Proportion, Fraction, Percentage, Rate, Probability

Sample Survey Designs:

1. *Simple random sampling*
2. *Stratified random sampling*
3. *Systematic sampling*
4. *Random response sampling*

Commonly Used z-values for a Large-Sample Confidence Interval:

90% CI:	$(1 - \alpha) = .10$	$z_{.05} = 1.645$
95% CI:	$(1 - \alpha) = .05$	$z_{.025} = 1.96$
99% CI:	$(1 - \alpha) = .01$	$z_{.005} = 2.575$

Determining the Sample Size n:

Estimating μ: $n = (z_{\alpha/2})^2(\sigma^2)/(\text{SE})^2$

Estimating p: $n = (z_{\alpha/2})^2(pq)/(\text{SE})^2$

Finite Population Correction Factor:

Required when $n/N > .05$

Illustrating the Notion of "95% Confidence"

SUPPLEMENTARY EXERCISES 5.82–5.110

Note: List the assumptions necessary for the valid implementation of the statistical procedures you use in solving all these exercises. Starred (*) exercises refer to the optional sections in this chapter.

Learning the Mechanics

5.82 In each of the following instances, determine whether you would use a z- or t-statistic (or neither) to form a 95% confidence interval, and then look up the appropriate z- or t-value.
   a. Random sample of size $n = 23$ from a normal distribution with unknown mean μ and standard deviation σ
   b. Random sample of size $n = 135$ from a normal distribution with unknown mean μ and standard deviation σ
   c. Random sample of size $n = 10$ from a normal distribution with unknown mean μ and standard deviation $\sigma = 5$
   d. Random sample of size $n = 73$ from a distribution about which nothing is known
   e. Random sample of size $n = 12$ from a distribution about which nothing is known

5.83 Let t_0 represent a particular value of t from Table V of Appendix B. Find the table values such that the following statements are true.
   a. $P(t \leq t_0) = .05$ where df $= 20$
   b. $P(t \geq t_0) = .005$ where df $= 9$
   c. $P(t \leq -t_0 \text{ or } t \geq t_0) = .10$ where df $= 8$
   d. $P(t \leq -t_0 \text{ or } t \geq t_0) = .01$ where df $= 17$

5.84 In a random sample of 400 measurements, 227 of the measurements possess the characteristic of interest, A.
   a. Use a 95% confidence interval to estimate the true proportion p of measurements in the population with characteristic A.
   b. How large a sample would be needed to estimate p to within .02 with 95% confidence?

5.85 A random sample of 225 measurements is selected from a population, and the sample mean and standard deviation are $\bar{x} = 32.5$ and $s = 30.0$, respectively.
   a. Use a 99% confidence interval to estimate the mean of the population, μ.
   b. How large a sample would be needed to estimate μ to within .5 with 99% confidence?
   c. What is meant by the phrase "99% confidence" as it is used in this exercise?

*5.86 Calculate the finite population correction factor for each of the following situations:
   a. $n = 50, N = 2,000$
   b. $n = 20, N = 100$
   c. $n = 300, N = 1,500$

Applying the Concepts—Basic

5.87 General health survey. The Centers for Disease Control and Prevention (CDCP) in Atlanta, Georgia, conducts an annual survey of the general health of the U.S. population as part of its Behavioral Risk Factor Surveillance System (*New York Times*, Mar. 29, 1995). Using random-digit dialing, the CDCP telephones U.S. citizens over 18 years of age and asks them the following four questions:
   1. Is your health generally excellent, very good, good, fair, or poor?
   2. How many days during the previous 30 days was your physical health not good because of injury or illness?
   3. How many days during the previous 30 days was your mental health not good because of stress, depression, or emotional problems?
   4. How many days during the previous 30 days did your physical or mental health prevent you from performing your usual activities?

Identify the parameter of interest for each question.

MINITAB Output for Exercise 5.88

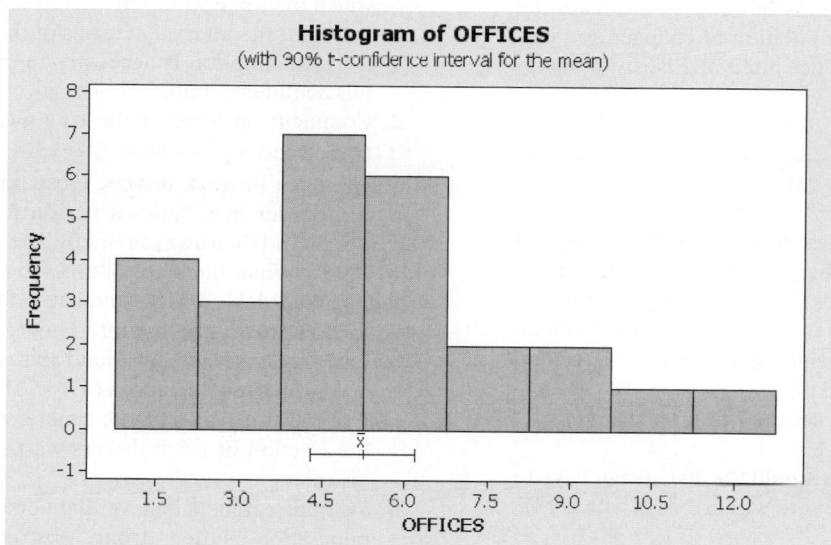

One-Sample T: OFFICES

```
Variable   N    Mean    StDev  SE Mean      90% CI
OFFICES    26  5.23077 2.84686 0.55832  (4.27709, 6.18445)
```

Histogram of OFFICES
(with 90% t-confidence interval for the mean)

◉ FLALAW

5.88 Top Florida law firms. Refer to Exercise 2.44 (p. 71) and the data on number of offices at the top law firms in Florida, as ranked by *Florida Trend Magazine* (April 2002). The data, saved in the **FLALAW** file, were analyzed using MINITAB. The MINITAB printout is shown above.

  a. Find a 90% confidence interval for the mean number of offices operated by all Florida law firms. Interpret the resulting interval.

  b. Does the condition of a normally distributed population appear to be satisfied for this application of the small-sample confidence interval method?

  c. Give a reason why the interval, part **a,** may be invalid.

◉ OILSPILL

5.89 Oil spills caused by hull failure. Refer to the *Marine Technology* (Jan. 1995) study of the causes of 50 recent major oil spills from tankers and carriers, Exercise 2.135 (p. 117). Recall that 12 of the spills were caused by hull failure.

  a. Give a point estimate for the proportion of major oil spills that are caused by hull failure.

  b. Form a 95% confidence interval for the estimate, part **a.** Interpret the result.

5.90 Homicide on the job. In a study of homicide on the job, University of North Carolina researchers collected data on workplaces where an employee was murdered (*American Journal of Epidemiology*, Vol. 154, 2001). In a sample of 105 cases, 67 of the homicides occurred during night hours (between 9:00 P.M. and 6:00 A.M.).

  a. Give a point estimate of p, the true proportion of on-the-job homicide cases that occurred at night.

  b. Compute a 95% confidence interval for p.

  c. Give a practical interpretation of the interval, part **b.**

5.91 Magazine subscriber salaries. The *Quality Progress* 2002 salary survey of quality professionals described in Exercise

5.76 (p. 329) generated responses from 2,413 quality managers. The lowest salary reported by a manager was $20,000; the highest was $205,000.

  a. Plans are being made to repeat the survey next year. Use the above information to determine how large a sample would need to be drawn to estimate the mean income of managers to within $5,000 with 95% confidence.

  b. In the survey, the standard deviation of managers' salaries was $19,830. Use this information and recalculate the sample size asked for in part **a.**

  c. Compare your answers to parts **a** and **b.** Which sample size would you use to estimate next year's mean salary? Justify your answer.

5.92 New Jersey residential property values. As part of a study of residential property values in Cedar Grove, New Jersey, the county tax assessor sampled 20 single-family homes that recently sold and recorded their sales prices (in thousands of dollars). The data are given below.

◉ NJVALUES

189.9	235.0	159.0	190.9	239.0	559.0	875.0	635.0
265.0	330.0	669.0	935.0	210.0	179.9	334.9	219.0
1,190.0	739.0	424.7	229.0				

Source: Multiple Listing Service of Suburban Essex County, New Jersey.

  a. Construct a 95% confidence interval for the mean sale price of all single-family homes in Cedar Grove, New Jersey.

  b. Give a practical interpretation of the interval, part **a.**

  c. What is meant by the phrase "95% confidence" as it is used in this exercise?

  d. Comment on the validity of any assumptions required to properly apply the estimation procedure.

5.93 College endowment funds. Private and public colleges and universities rely on money contributed by individuals, corporations, and foundations for both salaries and operating expenses. Much of this money is put into a fund called an *endowment*, and the college spends only the interest earned by the fund. A random sample of eight college endowments drawn from the list of endowments in the *Chronicle of Higher Education Almanac* yielded the following endowments (in millions of dollars). Estimate the mean endowment for this population of colleges and universities using a 95% confidence interval. List any assumptions you make.

⊙ **ENDOW**

148.6	66.1	340.8	500.2	212.8	55.4	72.6	83.4

5.94 Sick leave taken by employees. A company is interested in estimating μ, the mean number of days of sick leave taken by all its employees. The firm's statistician selects at random 100 personnel files and notes the number of sick days taken by each employee. The following sample statistics are computed: $\bar{x} = 12.2$ days, $s = 10$ days.
  a. Estimate μ using a 90% confidence interval. Interpret the result.
  b. How many personnel files would the statistician have to select in order to estimate μ to within 2 days with a 99% confidence interval?

⊙ **DDT**

5.95 Fish contaminated by a plant's discharge. Refer to the U.S. Army Corps of Engineers data on a sample of 144 contaminated fish collected from the river adjacent to a chemical plant. The data are saved in the **DDT** file. Estimate the proportion of contaminated fish that are of the channel catfish species. Use a 90% confidence interval and interpret the result.

Applying the Concepts—Intermediate

5.96 Improving the productivity of chickens. Farmers have discovered that the more domestic chickens peck at objects placed in their environment, the healthier and more productive the chickens seem to be. White string has been found to be a particularly attractive pecking stimulus. In one experiment, 72 chickens were exposed to a string stimulus. Instead of white string, blue-colored string was used. The number of pecks each chicken took at the blue string over a specified time interval was recorded. Summary statistics for the 72 chickens were: $\bar{x} = 1.13$ pecks, $s = 2.21$ pecks (*Applied Animal Behaviour Science*, Oct. 2000).
  a. Estimate the population mean number of pecks made by chickens pecking at blue string using a 99% confidence interval. Interpret the result.
  b. Previous research has shown that $\mu = 7.5$ pecks if chickens are exposed to white string. Based on the results, part **a**, is there evidence that chickens are more apt to peck at white string than blue string? Explain.

5.97 Petroleum waste contamination. Accidental spillage and misguided disposal of petroleum wastes have resulted in extensive contamination of soils across the country. A common hazardous compound found in the contaminated soil is benzo(a)pyrene [B(a)p]. An experiment was conducted to determine the effectiveness of a method designed to remove B(a)p from soil (*Journal of Hazardous Materials*, June 1995). Three soil specimens contaminated with a known amount of B(a)p were treated with a toxin that inhibits microbial growth. After 95 days of incubation, the

percentage of B(a)p removed from each soil specimen was measured. The experiment produced the following summary statistics: $\bar{x} = 49.3$ and $s = 1.5$.
  a. Use a 99% confidence interval to estimate the mean percentage of B(a)p removed from a soil specimen in which the toxin was used.
  b. Interpret the interval in terms of this application.
  c. What assumption is necessary to ensure the validity of this confidence interval?
  d. Comment on whether the true mean percent removed could be as high as 50%.

5.98 Sleep apnea in truck drivers. Obstructive sleep apnea is a sleep disorder that causes a person to stop breathing momentarily and then awaken briefly. These sleep interruptions, which may occur hundreds of times in a night, can drastically reduce the quality of rest and cause fatigue during waking hours. Researchers at Stanford University studied 159 commercial truck drivers and found that 124 of them suffered from obstructive sleep apnea (*Chest*, May 1995).
  a. Use the study results to estimate, with 90% confidence, the fraction of truck drivers who suffer from the sleep disorder.
  b. Sleep researchers believe that about 25% of the general population suffer from obstructive sleep apnea. Comment on whether or not this value represents the true percentage of truck drivers who suffer from the sleep disorder.

5.99 Distance traveled to work by men and women. Research reported in the *Professional Geographer* (May 1992) investigates the hypothesis that the disproportionate housework responsibility of women in two-income households is a major factor in determining the proximity of a woman's place of employment. The researcher studied the distance (in miles) to work for both men and women in two-income households. Random samples of men and women yielded the following results:

	CENTRAL CITY RESIDENCE		SUBURBAN RESIDENCE	
	Men	Women	Men	Women
Sample Size	159	119	138	93
Mean	7.4	4.5	9.3	6.6
Std. Deviation	6.3	4.2	7.1	5.6

  a. For central city residences, calculate a 95% confidence interval for the average distance to work for men and women in two-income households. Interpret the intervals. Is there a difference between men and women?
  b. Repeat part **a** for suburban residences. [*Note:* We will show how to use statistical techniques to compare two population means in Chapter 7.]

5.100 Using debit cards on the Internet. The Gallup Organization surveyed 1,252 debit cardholders in the United States and found that 180 had used the debit card to purchase a product or service on the Internet (*Card Fax*, November 12, 1999).
  a. Describe the population of interest to the Gallup Organization.
  b. If you personally were charged with drawing a random sample from this population, what difficulties would you encounter? Assume in the remainder of the exercise that the 1,252 debit cardholders were randomly selected.

c. Is the sample size large enough to construct a valid confidence interval for the proportion of debit cardholders who have used their card in making purchases over the Internet? Justify your answer.

d. Estimate the proportion referred to in part c using a 98% confidence interval. Interpret your result in the context of the problem.

e. If you had constructed a 90% confidence interval instead, would it be wider or narrower?

5.101 Vacation times at major companies. The primary determinant of the amount of vacation time U.S. employees receive is their length of service. According to data released by Hewitt Associates (*Management Review*, Nov. 1995), more than 8 of 10 employers provide 2 weeks of vacation after the first year. After 5 years, 75% of employers provide 3 weeks and after 15 years most provide 4-week vacations. To more accurately estimate p, the proportion of U.S. employers who provide only 2 weeks of vacation to new hires, a random sample of 24 major U.S. companies was contacted. The following vacation times were reported (in days):

🔵 **VACTIMES**

10	12	10	10	10	10
15	10	10	10	10	10
10	10	10	10	10	15
10	10	15	10	10	10

a. Construct a 95% confidence interval for p.

b. Is the sample size large enough to ensure that the normal distribution provides a reasonable approximation to the sampling distribution of $\hat{p}$? Justify your answer.

c. How large a sample would be required to estimate p to within .02 with 95% confidence?

5.102 Laying off cancer patients. According to the U.S. Bureau of Labor Statistics, 1 of every 80 American workers (i.e., 1.3%) is fired or laid off. Are employees with cancer fired or laid off at the same rate? To answer this question, *Working Women* magazine and Amgen—a company that makes drugs to lessen chemotherapy side effects—conducted a telephone survey of 100 cancer survivors who worked while undergoing treatment (*Tampa Tribune*, Sept. 25, 1996). Of these 100 cancer patients, 7 were fired or laid off due to their illness.

a. Construct a 90% confidence interval for the true percentage of all cancer patients who are fired or laid off due to their illness.

b. Give a practical interpretation of the interval, part **a**.

c. Are employees with cancer fired or laid off at the same rate as all U.S. workers? Explain.

*5.103 Interpreting "sampling error." When a poll reports, for example, that 61% of the public supports a program of national health insurance, it usually also reports the sampling error. For example, a poll might report that the estimate is accurate to within plus or minus 3%. An essay in *Time* magazine ("How not to read polls," Apr. 28, 1980) points out the following:

> *Readers consistently misinterpret the meaning of this "warning label."... [The sampling error warning] says nothing about errors that might be caused by a sloppily worded question or a biased one or a single question that evokes complex feelings. Example: "Are you*

> *satisfied with your job?" Most important of all, warning labels about sampling error say nothing about whether or not the public is conflict-ridden or has given a subject much thought. This is the most serious source of opinion poll misinterpretation.*

Carefully explain the difference between sampling error and nonsampling error, both in general and in the context of the above quote.

*5.104 Survey of magazine subscribers. Publishers of a weekly nationwide business magazine believe that a large proportion of their Florida subscribers invest in the stock market. They would like to be able to use this information to persuade brokerage firms in Florida to advertise in their magazine. The publishers send each of the 500,000 subscribers in Florida a questionnaire about stock investments. A total of 10,000 of the questionnaires are returned, and of these, 9,296 subscribers respond that they do currently have stock market investments.

a. Use this information to estimate the proportion of Florida subscribers who invest in the stock market with an approximate 95% confidence interval.

b. Should a brokerage firm in Florida consider the estimate in part a to be reliable? Explain.

5.105 Air bags pose danger for children. Refer to the National Highway Traffic Safety Administration (NHTSA) study of fatal auto accidents caused by air bags, Exercise 5.48 (p. 320). Recall that the NHTSA wants to estimate the proportion of such accidents in which children seated on the front passenger side were killed. How many fatal accidents should the NHTSA sample in order to estimate the proportion to within .1 of its true value using a 99% confidence interval?

5.106 Salmonella poisoning from eating an ice cream bar. Recently, a case of salmonella (bacterial) poisoning was traced to a particular brand of ice cream bar, and the manufacturer removed the bars from the market. Despite this response, many consumers refused to purchase *any* brand of ice cream bars for some period of time after the event (McClave, personal consulting). One manufacturer conducted a survey of consumers 6 months after the outbreak. A sample of 244 ice cream bar consumers was contacted, and 23 respondents indicated that they would not purchase ice cream bars because of the potential for food poisoning.

a. What is the point estimate of the true fraction of the entire market who refuse to purchase bars 6 months after the outbreak?

b. Is the sample size large enough to use the normal approximation for the sampling distribution of the estimator of the binomial probability? Justify your response.

c. Construct a 95% confidence interval for the true proportion of the market who still refuse to purchase ice cream bars 6 months after the event.

d. Interpret both the point estimate and confidence interval in terms of this application.

5.107 Salmonella poisoning from eating an ice cream bar (cont'd). Refer to Exercise 5.106. Suppose it is now 1 year after the outbreak of food poisoning was traced to ice cream bars. The manufacturer wishes to estimate the proportion who still will not purchase bars to within .02 using a 95% confidence interval. How many consumers should be sampled?

Applying the Concepts—Advanced

5.108 Accountants salary survey. Each year, *Management Accounting* reports the results of a salary survey of the members of the Institute of Management Accountants (IMA). One year, the 2,112 members responding had a salary distribution with a 20th percentile of $35,100; a median of $50,000; and an 80th percentile of $73,000.

a. Use this information to determine the minimum sample size that could be used in next year's survey to estimate the mean salary of IMA members to within $2,000 with 98% confidence. [Hint: To estimate s, first apply Chebyshev's Theorem to find k such that at least 60% of the data fall within k standard deviations of μ. Then find $s \approx$ (80th percentile–20th percentile)/k.]

b. Explain how you estimated the standard deviation required for the sample size calculation.

c. List any assumptions you make.

5.109 Internal auditing of invoices. A firm's president, vice presidents, department managers, and others use financial data generated by the firm's accounting system to help them make decisions regarding such things as pricing, budgeting, and plant expansion. To provide reasonable certainty that the system provides reliable data, internal auditors periodically perform various checks of the system (Horngren, Foster, and Datar, *Cost Accounting: A Managerial Emphasis*, 2005). Suppose an internal auditor is interested in determining the proportion of sales invoices in a population of 5,000 sales invoices for which the "total sales" figure is in error. She plans to estimate the true proportion of invoices in error based on a random sample of size 100.

a. Assume that the population of invoices is numbered from 1 to 5,000 and that every invoice ending with a 0 is in error (i.e., 10% are in error). Use a random number generator to draw a random sample of 100 invoices from the population of 5,000 invoices. For example, random number 456 stands for invoice number 456. List the invoice numbers in your sample and indicate which of your sampled invoices are in error (i.e., those ending in a 0).

b. Use the results of your sample of part **a** to construct a 90% confidence interval for the true proportion of invoices in error.

c. Recall that the true population proportion of invoices in error is equal to .1. Compare the true proportion with the estimate of the true proportion you developed in part **b**. Does your confidence interval include the true proportion?

Critical Thinking Challenge

5.110 "Out of control" production process. When companies employ control charts to monitor the quality of their products, a series of small samples is typically used to determine if the process is "in control" during the period of time in which each sample is selected. (We cover quality-control charts in Chapter 12.) Suppose a concrete-block manufacturer samples nine blocks per hour and tests the breaking strength of each. During 1 hour's test, the mean and standard deviation are 985.6 pounds per square inch (psi) and 22.9 psi, respectively. The process is to be considered "out of control" if the true mean strength differs from 1,000 psi. The manufacturer wants to be reasonably certain that the process is really out of control before shutting down the process and trying to determine the problem. What is your recommendation?

REFERENCES

Agresti, A., and Coull, B. A. "Approximate Is Better Than 'Exact' for Interval Estimation of Binomial Proportions." *The American Statistician*, Vol. 52, No. 2, May 1998, pp. 119–126.

Arkin, H. *Sampling Methods for the Auditor.* New York: McGraw-Hill, 1982.

Cochran, W. G. *Sampling Techniques*, 3rd ed. New York: Wiley, 1977.

Freedman, D., Pisani, R., and Purves, R. *Statistics.* New York: Norton, 1978.

Kish, L. *Survey Sampling.* New York: Wiley, 1965.

Mendenhall, W., Beaver, R. J., and Beaver, B. *Introduction to Probability and Statistics*, 11th ed. North Scituate, Mass.: Duxbury, 2002.

Wilson, E. G. "Probable Inference, the Law of Succession, and Statistical Inference." *Journal of the American Statistical Association*, Vol. 22, 1927, pp. 209–212.

Using Technology

5.1 Confidence Intervals Using SPSS

SPSS can be used to obtain one-sample confidence intervals for a population mean but cannot currently produce confidence intervals for a population proportion. To generate a confidence interval for the mean, first access the SPSS spreadsheet file that contains the sample data. Next, click on the "Analyze" button on the SPSS menu bar, then click on "Descriptive Statistics" and "Explore", as shown in Figure 5.S.1. The resulting dialog box appears as shown in Figure 5.S.2. Specify the quantitative variable of interest in the "Dependent List", then click on the "Statistics" button at the bottom of the box. Specify the confidence level in the resulting dialog box as shown in Figure 5.S.3. Click "Continue" to return to the "Explore" dialog box, then click "OK" to produce the confidence interval.

Figure 5.S.1
SPSS menu options—confidence interval for the mean

Figure 5.S.2
SPSS Explore dialog box

Figure 5.S.3
SPSS Explore Statistics options

5.2 Confidence Intervals Using MINITAB

MINITAB can be used to obtain one-sample confidence intervals for both a population mean and a population proportion. To generate a confidence interval for the mean using a previously created sample data set, first access the MINITAB data worksheet. Next, click on the "Stat" button on the MINITAB menu bar, then click on "Basic Statistics" and "1-sample t", as shown in Figure 5.M.1. The resulting dialog box appears as shown in Figure 5.M.2. Click on "Samples in Columns", then

Figure 5.M.1
MINITAB menu options—
confidence interval for the
mean

Figure 5.M.2
MINITAB 1-Sample
t dialog box

specify the quantitative variable of interest in the open box. Now, click on the "Options" button at the bottom of the dialog box and specify the confidence level in the resulting dialog box as shown in Figure 5.M.3. Click "OK" to return to the "1-Sample t" dialog box, then click "OK" again to produce the confidence interval.

If you want to produce a confidence interval for the mean from summary information (e.g., the sample mean, sample standard deviation, and sample size), then click on "Summarized data" in the "1-Sample t" dialog box as shown in Figure 5.M.4. Enter the values of the summary statistics, then click "OK".

Important Note: The MINITAB 1-sample t procedure uses the *t*-statistic to generate the confidence interval. When the sample size *n* is small, this is the appropriate method. When the sample size *n* is large, the *t*-value will be approximately equal to the large-sample *z*-value and the resulting interval will still be valid. If you have a large sample and you know the value of the population standard deviation σ (which is rarely the case), then select "1-sample Z" from the "Basic Statistics" menu options (see Figure 5.M.1) and make the appropriate selections.

Figure 5.M.3
MINITAB 1-Sample t Options dialog box

Figure 5.M.4
MINITAB 1-Sample t dialog box with summary statistics

To generate a confidence interval for a population proportion mean using a previously created sample data set, first access the MINITAB data worksheet. Next, click on the "Stat" button on the MINITAB menu bar, then click on "Basic Statistics" and "1 Proportion" (see Figure 5.M.1). The resulting dialog box appears as shown in Figure 5.M.5. Click on "Samples in Columns", then specify the qualitative variable of interest in the open box. Now, click on the

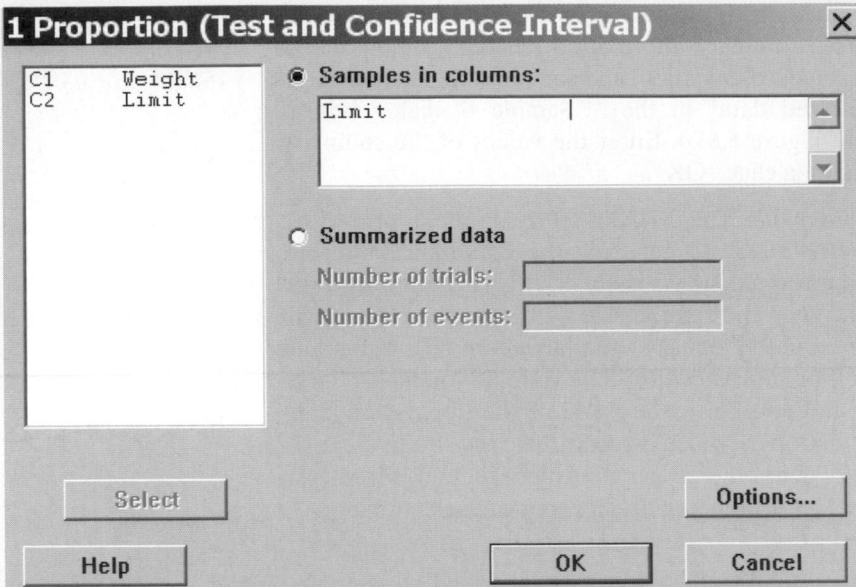

Figure 5.M.5
MINITAB 1-Proportion
dialog box

"Options" button at the bottom of the dialog box and specify the confidence level in the resulting dialog box, as shown in Figure 5.M.6. Also, check the "Use test and interval based on normal distribution" box at the bottom. Click "OK" to return to the "1-Proportion" dialog box, then click "OK" again to produce the confidence interval.

If you want to produce a confidence interval for a proportion from summary information (e.g., the number of successes and the sample size), then click on "Summarized data" in the "1-Proportion" dialog box (see Figure 5.M.5). Enter the value for the number of trials (i.e., the sample size) and the number of events (i.e., the number of successes), then click "OK".

Figure 5.M.6
MINITAB 1-Proportion dialog box

5.3 Confidence Intervals Using Excel/PHStat2

Excel with the PHStat2 add-in can be used to obtain one-sample confidence intervals for both a population mean and a population proportion. To generate a confidence interval for the mean using a previously created sample data set, first access the Excel worksheet. Next, click on the "PHStat" button on the Excel menu bar, then click on "Confidence Intervals" and "Estimate for the Mean, sigma unknown", as shown in Figure 5.E.1. The resulting dialog box appears as shown in Figure 5.E.2. Specify the confidence level, then click on "Sample Statistics Unknown" and specify cell range for the quantitative variable of interest (see Figure 5.E.2). Click "OK" to produce the confidence interval. If you want to produce a confidence interval for the mean from summary information (e.g., the sample mean, sample standard deviation, and sample size), then click on "Sample Statistics Known" on the dialog box as shown in Figure 5.E.2. Enter the values of the summary statistics, then click "OK".

Important Note: The Excel/PHStat2 one-sample procedure outlined above uses the t-statistic to generate the confidence interval when σ is unknown. When the sample size n is small, this is the appropriate method. When the sample size n is

Figure 5.E.1

Excel/PHStat2 menu options for a confidence interval for μ

Figure 5.E.2

Excel confidence interval for mean dialog box

large, the t-value will be approximately equal to the large-sample z-value and the resulting interval will still be valid. If you have a large sample and you know the value of the population standard deviation σ (which is rarely the case), then select "Estimate for the Mean, sigma known" from the "Confidence Intervals" menu options (see Figure 5.E.1) and make the appropriate selections.

To generate a confidence interval for a population proportion using Excel, you must first determine the sample size and the number of successes in the sample of interest. Next, click on the "PHStat" button on the Excel menu bar, then click on "Confidence Intervals" and "Estimate for the Proportion" (see Figure 5.E.1). The resulting dialog box appears as shown in Figure 5.E.3. Specify the sample size, number of successes, and confidence level in the appropriate boxes, then click "OK" to produce the confidence interval.

Figure 5.E.3

Excel confidence interval for Proportion dialog box

CHAPTER 6

Inferences Based on a Single Sample

Tests of Hypothesis

CONTENTS

WHERE WE'VE BEEN

- Used sample information to provide a *point estimate* of a population parameter

- Used the sampling distribution of a statistic to assess the reliability of an estimate through a *confidence interval*

WHERE WE'RE GOING

- Test a specific value of a population parameter (mean or proportion), called a *test of hypothesis*.

- Provide a measure of reliability for the hypothesis test, called the *significance level* of the test.

Diary of a Kleenex® User

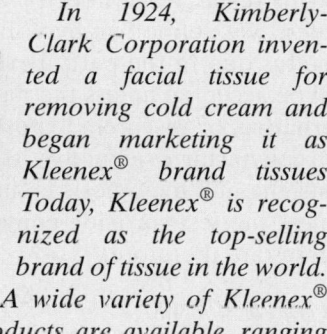

In 1924, Kimberly-Clark Corporation invented a facial tissue for removing cold cream and began marketing it as Kleenex® brand tissues Today, Kleenex® is recognized as the top-selling brand of tissue in the world. A wide variety of Kleenex® products are available, ranging from extra-large tissues to tissues with lotion. Over the past 80 years, Kimberly-Clark Corporation has packaged the tissues in boxes of different sizes and shapes and varied the number of tissues packaged in each box. For example, currently a family-size box contains 144 two-ply tissues, a cold-care box contains 70 tissues (coated with lotion), and a convenience pocket pack contains 15 miniature tissues.

How does Kimberly-Clark Corp. decide how many tissues to put in each box? According to the Wall Street Journal, marketing experts at the company use the results of a survey of Kleenex® customers to help determine how many tissues are packed in a box. In the mid-1980s, when Kimberly-Clark Corp. developed the cold-care box designed especially for people who have a cold, the company conducted their initial survey of customers for this purpose. Hundreds of customers were asked to keep count of their Kleenex® use in diaries. According to the Wall Street Journal report, the survey results left "little doubt that the company should put 60 tissues in each box." The number 60 was "the average number of times people blow their nose during a cold." (Note: In 2000, the company increased the number of tissues packaged in a cold-care box to 70.)

From summary information provided in the Wall Street Journal (Sept. 21, 1984) article, we constructed a data set that represents the results of a survey similar to the one described above. In the data file named **TISSUES**, we recorded the number of tissues used by each of 250 consumers during a period when they had a cold. We apply the hypothesis testing methodology presented in this chapter to this data set in several Statistics in Action Revisited examples.

 TISSUES

Statistics in Action Revisited

- Identifying the Key Elements of a Hypothesis Test Relevant to the Kleenex® Survey (p. 351)
- Testing a Population Mean in the Kleenex® Survey (p. 363)
- Testing a Population Proportion in the Kleenex® Survey (p. 376)

Suppose you wanted to determine whether the mean waiting time in the drive-through line of a fast-food restaurant is less than 5 minutes, or whether the majority of consumers are optimistic about the economy. In both cases you are interested in making an inference about how the value of a parameter relates to a specific numerical value. Is it less than, equal to, or greater than the specified number? This type of inference, called a **test of hypothesis,** is the subject of this chapter.

We introduce the elements of a test of hypothesis in Section 6.1. We then show how to conduct a large-sample test of hypothesis about a population mean in Sections 6.2 and 6.3. In Section 6.4 we utilize small samples to conduct tests about means. Large-sample tests about binomial probabilities are the subject of Section 6.5, and some advanced methods for determining the reliability of a test are covered in optional Section 6.6. Finally, we show how to conduct a test about a population variance in optional Section 6.7.

6.1 The Elements of a Test of Hypothesis

Suppose building specifications in a certain city require that the average breaking strength of residential sewer pipe be more than 2,400 pounds per foot of length (i.e., per linear foot). Each manufacturer who wants to sell pipe in this city must demonstrate that its product meets the specification. Note that we are again interested in making an inference about the mean μ of a population. However, in this example we are less interested in estimating the value of μ than we are in testing a *hypothesis* about its value—that is, *we want to decide whether the mean breaking strength of the pipe exceeds 2,400 pounds per linear foot.*

The method used to reach a decision is based on the rare-event concept explained in earlier chapters. We define two hypotheses: (1) The **null hypothesis** is that which represents the status quo to the party performing the sampling experiment— the hypothesis that will be accepted unless the data provide convincing evidence that it is false. (2) The **alternative,** or **research, hypothesis** is that which will be accepted only if the data provide convincing evidence of its truth. From the point of view of the city conducting the tests, the null hypothesis is that the manufacturer's pipe does *not* meet specifications unless the tests provide convincing evidence otherwise. The null and alternative hypotheses are therefore

Null hypothesis (H_0): $\mu \leq 2{,}400$

(i.e., the manufacturer's pipe does not meet specifications)

Alternative (research) hypothesis (H_a): $\mu > 2{,}400$

(i.e., the manufacturer's pipe meets specifications)

> **Now Work Exercise 6.10**

How can the city decide when enough evidence exists to conclude that the manufacturer's pipe meets specifications? Since the hypotheses concern the value of the population mean μ, it is reasonable to use the sample mean $\bar{x}$ to make the inference, just as we did when forming confidence intervals for μ in Sections 5.2 and 5.3. The city will conclude that the pipe meets specifications only when the sample mean $\bar{x}$ convincingly indicates that the population mean exceeds 2,400 pounds per linear foot.

"Convincing" evidence in favor of the alternative hypothesis will exist when the value of $\bar{x}$ exceeds 2,400 by an amount that cannot be readily attributed to sampling variability. To decide, we compute a **test statistic,** which is the z value that measures the distance between the value of $\bar{x}$ and the value of μ specified in the null hypothesis. When the null hypothesis contains more than one value of μ, as in this case (H_0: $\mu \leq 2{,}400$), we use the value of μ closest to the values specified in the alternative hypothesis. The idea is that if the hypothesis that μ *equals* 2,400 can be rejected in favor of $\mu > 2{,}400$, then μ *less than or equal to* 2,400 can certainly be rejected. Thus, the test statistic is

$$z = \frac{\bar{x} - 2{,}400}{\sigma_{\bar{x}}} = \frac{\bar{x} - 2{,}400}{\sigma / \sqrt{n}}$$

Note that a value of $z = 1$ means that $\bar{x}$ is 1 standard deviation above $\mu = 2{,}400$; a value of $z = 1.5$ means that $\bar{x}$ is 1.5 standard deviations above $\mu = 2{,}400$, etc. How large must z be before the city can be convinced that the null hypothesis can be rejected in favor of the alternative and conclude that the pipe meets specifications?

If you examine Figure 6.1, you will note that the chance of observing $\bar{x}$ more than 1.645 standard deviations above 2,400 is only .05—*if in fact the true mean μ is 2,400.* Thus, if the sample mean is more than 1.645 standard deviations above 2,400, either H_0 is true and a relatively rare event has occurred (.05 probability) or H_a is true and the population mean exceeds 2,400. Since we would most likely reject the notion that a rare event has occurred, we would reject the null hypothesis ($\mu \leq 2{,}400$) and conclude that the alternative hypothesis ($\mu > 2{,}400$) is true. What is the probability that this procedure will lead us to an incorrect decision?

Such an incorrect decision—deciding that the null hypothesis is false when in fact it is true—is called a **Type I error.** As indicated in Figure 6.1, the risk of making a Type I error is denoted by the symbol α—that is,

$\alpha = P(\text{Type I error})$

$= P(\text{Rejecting the null hypothesis when in fact the null hypothesis is true})$

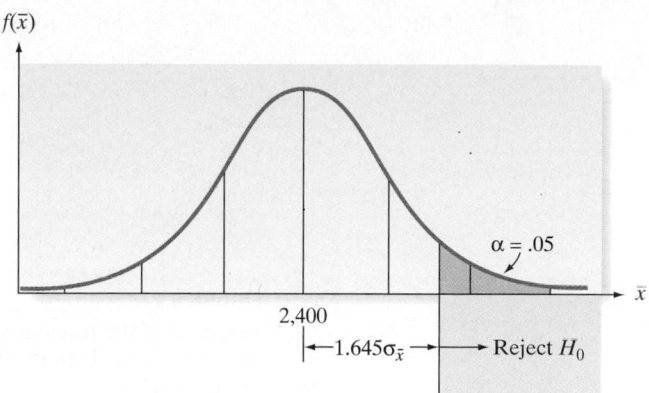

FIGURE 6.1

The sampling distribution of $\bar{x}$, assuming $\mu = 2{,}400$

In our example,

$$\alpha = P(z > 1.645 \text{ when in fact } \mu = 2{,}400) = .05$$

We now summarize the elements of the test:

> H_0: $\mu \leq 2{,}400$ (Pipe does not meet specifications)
>
> H_a: $\mu > 2{,}400$ (Pipe meets specifications)
>
> Test statistic: $z = \dfrac{\bar{x} - 2{,}400}{\sigma_{\bar{x}}}$
>
> Rejection region: $z > 1.645$, which corresponds to $\alpha = .05$

Note that the **rejection region** refers to the values of the test statistic for which we will *reject the null hypothesis.*

To illustrate the use of the test, suppose we test 50 sections of sewer pipe and find the mean and standard deviation for these 50 measurements to be

$$\bar{x} = 2{,}460 \text{ pounds per linear foot}$$
$$s = 200 \text{ pounds per linear foot}$$

As in the case of estimation, we can use s to approximate σ when s is calculated from a large set of sample measurements.

The test statistic is

$$z = \frac{\bar{x} - 2{,}400}{\sigma_{\bar{x}}} = \frac{\bar{x} - 2{,}400}{\sigma/\sqrt{n}} \approx \frac{\bar{x} - 2{,}400}{s/\sqrt{n}}$$

Substituting $\bar{x} = 2{,}460$, $n = 50$, and $s = 200$, we have

$$z \approx \frac{2{,}460 - 2{,}400}{200/\sqrt{50}} = \frac{60}{28.28} = 2.12$$

Therefore, the sample mean lies $2.12\sigma_{\bar{x}}$ above the hypothesized value of μ, 2,400, as shown in Figure 6.2. Since this value of z exceeds 1.645, it falls in the rejection region. That is, we reject the null hypothesis that $\mu = 2{,}400$ and conclude that $\mu > 2{,}400$. Thus, it appears that the company's pipe has a mean strength that exceeds 2,400 pounds per linear foot.

How much faith can be placed in this conclusion? What is the probability that our statistical test could lead us to reject the null hypothesis (and conclude that the company's pipe meets the city's specifications) when in fact the null hypothesis is true? The answer is $\alpha = .05$ —that is, we selected the level of risk, α, of making a Type I error when we constructed the test. Thus, the chance is only 1 in 20 that our test would lead us to conclude the

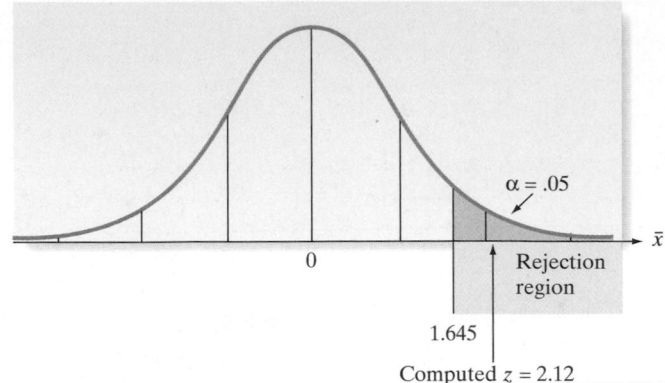

FIGURE 6.2

Location of the test statistic
for a test of the hypothesis
$H_0: \mu = 2{,}400$

manufacturer's pipe satisfies the city's specifications when in fact the pipe does *not* meet
specifications.

Now, suppose the sample mean breaking strength for the 50 sections of sewer pipe
turned out to be $\bar{x} = 2{,}430$ pounds per linear foot. Assuming that the sample standard
deviation is still $s = 200$, the test statistic is

$$z = \frac{2{,}430 - 2{,}400}{200/\sqrt{50}} = \frac{30}{28.28} = 1.06$$

Therefore, the sample mean $\bar{x} = 2{,}430$ is only 1.06 standard deviations above the null
hypothesized value of $\mu = 2{,}400$. As shown in Figure 6.3, this value does not fall into the
rejection region ($z > 1.645$). Therefore, we know that we cannot reject H_0 using
$\alpha = .05$. Even though the sample mean exceeds the city's specification of 2,400 by 30
pounds per linear foot, it does not exceed the specification by enough to provide
convincing evidence that the *population mean* exceeds 2,400.

Biography

EGON S. PEARSON
(1895–1980)

The Neyman-Pearson Lemma

Egon Pearson was the only son of note-
worthy British statistician Karl Pearson (see
Biography, p. 556). As you might expect,
Egon developed an interest in the statistical
methods developed by his father and, upon
completing graduate school, accepted a position to work for Karl in the Department of
Applied Statistics at University College,
London. Egon is best known for his collabo-

ration with Jerzey Neyman (see Biography,
p. 295) on the development of the theory of
hypothesis testing. One of the basic concepts
in the Neyman-Pearson approach was that of
the "null" and "alternative" hypotheses.
Their famous Neyman-Pearson lemma was
published in *Biometrika* in 1928. Egon
Pearson had numerous other contributions
to statistics and was known as an excellent
teacher and lecturer. In his last major work,
Egon fulfilled a promise made to his father
by publishing an annotated version of Karl
Pearson's lectures on the early history of
statistics.

Should we accept the null hypothesis $H_0: \mu \le 2{,}400$ and conclude that the manufacturer's pipe does not meet specifications? To do so would be to risk a **Type II error**—
that of concluding that the null hypothesis is true (the pipe does not meet specifications)
when in fact it is false (the pipe does meet specifications). We denote the probability of
committing a Type II error by β, and we show in optional Section 6.6 that β is often difficult to determine precisely. Rather than make a decision (accept H_0) for which the
probability of error (β) is unknown, we avoid the potential Type II error by avoiding the
conclusion that the null hypothesis is true. Instead, we will simply state that *the sample
evidence is insufficient to reject H_0 at $\alpha = .05$*. Since the null hypothesis is the "status-
quo" hypothesis, the effect of not rejecting H_0 is to maintain the status quo. In our pipe-
testing example, the effect of having insufficient evidence to reject the null hypothesis
that the pipe does not meet specifications is probably to prohibit the utilization of the

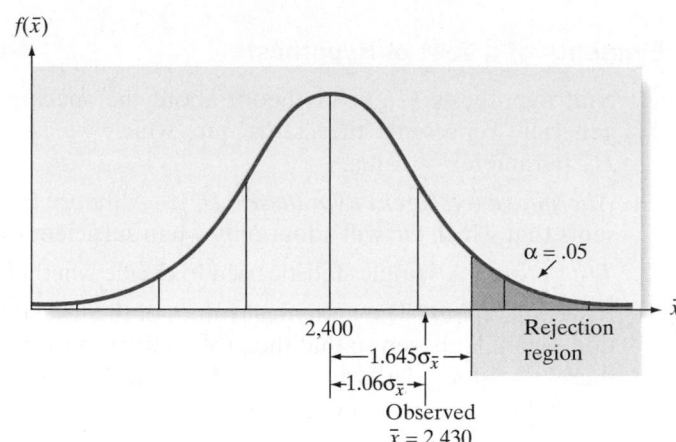

FIGURE 6.3
Location of test statistic
when $\bar{x} = 2{,}430$

manufacturer's pipe unless and until there is sufficient evidence that the pipe does meet specifications—that is, until the data indicate convincingly that the null hypothesis is false, we usually maintain the status quo implied by its truth.

Table 6.1 summarizes the four possible outcomes of a test of hypothesis. The "true state of nature" columns in Table 6.1 refer to the fact that either the null hypothesis H_0 is true or the alternative hypothesis H_a is true. Note that the true state of nature is unknown to the researcher conducting the test. The "decision" rows in Table 6.1 refer to the action of the researcher, assuming that he or she will either conclude that H_0 is true or that H_a is true, based on the results of the sampling experiment. Note that a Type I error can be made *only* when the null hypothesis is rejected in favor of the alternative hypothesis, and a Type II error can be made *only* when the null hypothesis is accepted. Our policy will be to make a decision only when we know the probability of making the error that corresponds to that decision. Since α is usually specified by the analyst, we will generally be able to reject H_0 (accept H_a) when the sample evidence supports that decision. However, since β is usually not specified, *we will generally avoid the decision to accept H_0, preferring instead to state that the sample evidence is insufficient to reject H_0 when the test statistic is not in the rejection region.*

Caution

Be careful not to "accept H_0" when conducting a test of hypothesis since the measure of reliability, $\beta = P(\text{Type II error})$, is almost always unknown. If the test statistic does not fall into the rejection region, it is better to state the conclusion as "insufficient evidence to reject H_0."*

The elements of a test of hypothesis are summarized in the following box. Note that the first four elements are all specified *before* the sampling experiment is performed. In no case will the results of the sample be used to determine the hypotheses—the data are collected to test the predetermined hypotheses, not to formulate them.

Now Work Exercise 6.13b

TABLE 6.1 Conclusions and Consequences for a Test of Hypothesis

	TRUE STATE OF NATURE	
Conclusion	H_0 True	H_a True
Accept H_0 (Assume H_0 True)	Correct decision	Type II error (probability β)
Reject H_0 (Assume H_a True)	Type I error (probability α)	Correct decision

*In many practical business applications of hypothesis testing, nonrejection leads management to behave as if the null hypothesis were accepted. Accordingly, the distinction between acceptance and nonrejection is frequently blurred in practice. We discuss the issues connected with the acceptance of the null hypothesis and the calculation of β in more detail in (optional) Section 6.6.

Elements of a Test of Hypothesis

1. *Null hypothesis* (H_0): A theory about the specific values of one or more population parameters. The theory generally represents the status quo, which we adopt until it is proven false. The theory is always stated as H_0: parameter = value.

2. *Alternative (research) hypothesis* (H_a): A theory that contradicts the null hypothesis. The theory generally represents that which we will adopt only when sufficient evidence exists to establish its truth.

3. *Test statistic:* A sample statistic used to decide whether to reject the null hypothesis.

4. *Rejection region:* The numerical values of the test statistic for which the null hypothesis will be rejected. The rejection region is chosen so that the probability is α that it will contain the test statistic when the null hypothesis is true, thereby leading to a Type I error. The value of α is usually chosen to be small (e.g., .01, .05, or .10) and is referred to as the **level of significance** of the test.

5. *Assumptions:* Clear statement(s) of any assumptions made about the population(s) being sampled.

6. *Experiment and calculation of test statistic:* Performance of the sampling experiment and determination of the numerical value of the test statistic.

7. *Conclusion:*
   a. If the numerical value of the test statistic falls in the rejection region, we reject the null hypothesis and conclude that the alternative hypothesis is true. We know that the hypothesis-testing process will lead to this conclusion incorrectly (Type I error) only $100\alpha\%$ of the time when H_0 is true.
   b. If the test statistic does not fall in the rejection region, we do not reject H_0. Thus, we reserve judgment about which hypothesis is true. We do not conclude that the null hypothesis is true because we do not (in general) know the probability β that our test procedure will lead to an incorrect acceptance of H_0 (Type II error).

As with confidence intervals, the methodology for testing hypotheses varies depending on the target population parameter. In this chapter, we develop methods for testing a population mean, a population proportion, and a population variance. Some key words and the type of data associated with these target parameters are listed in the accompanying box.

Determining the Target Parameter

Parameter	Key Words or Phrases	Type of Data
μ	Mean; average	Quantitative
p	Proportion; percentage; fraction; rate	Qualitative
σ^2	Variance; variability; spread	Quantitative

Exercises 6.1–6.16

Learning the Mechanics

6.1 Which hypothesis, the null or the alternative, is the status-quo hypothesis? Which is the research hypothesis?

6.2 Which element of a test of hypothesis is used to decide whether to reject the null hypothesis in favor of the alternative hypothesis?

6.3 What is the level of significance of a test of hypothesis?

6.4 What is the difference between Type I and Type II errors in hypothesis testing? How do α and β relate to Type I and Type II errors?

6.5 List the four possible results of the combinations of decisions and true states of nature for a test of hypothesis.

6.6 We (generally) reject the null hypothesis when the test statistic falls in the rejection region, but we do not accept the null hypothesis when the test statistic does not fall in the rejection region. Why?

6.7 If you test a hypothesis and reject the null hypothesis in favor of the alternative hypothesis, does your test prove that the alternative hypothesis is correct? Explain.

APPLET **Applet Exercise 6.1**

Use the applet entitled *Hypotheses Test for a Mean* to investigate the frequency of Type I and Type II errors. For this exercise, use $n = 100$ and the normal distribution with mean 50 and standard deviation 10.

a. Set the null mean equal to 50 and the alternative to *not equal.* Run the applet one time. How many times was the null hypothesis rejected at level .05? In this case, the null hypothesis is true. Which type of error occurred each time the true null hypothesis was rejected? What is the probability of rejecting a true null hypothesis at level .05? How does the proportion of times the null hypothesis was rejected compare to this probability?

b. Clear the applet, then set the null mean equal to 47, and keep the alternative at *not equal.* Run the applet one time. How

STATISTICS IN ACTION REVISITED

Identifying the Key Elements of a Hypothesis Test Relevant to the Kleenex® Survey

In Kimberly-Clark Corporation's survey of people with colds, each of 250 customers was asked to keep count of his or her use of Kleenex® tissues in diaries. One goal of the company was to determine how many tissues to package in a cold-care box of Kleenex®; consequently, the total number of tissues used was recorded for each person surveyed. Since number of tissues is a quantitative variable, the parameter of interest is μ, the mean number of tissues used by all customers with colds.

Now, according to a *Wall Street Journal* report, there was "little doubt that the company should put 60 tissues" in a cold-care box of Kleenex® tissues. This statement was based on a claim made by marketing experts that 60 is the average number of times a person will blow his or her nose during a cold. Consequently, the marketers are claiming that $\mu = 60$. Suppose we disbelieve the claim that $\mu = 60$, believing instead that the population mean is smaller than 60 tissues. In order to test the claim against our belief, we set up the following null and alternative hypothesis:

$$H_0: \mu = 60 \qquad H_a: \mu < 60$$

We'll conduct this test in the next Statistics in Action Revisited on p. 363.

ACTIVITY 6.1: *Challenging a Company's Claim:* Tests of Hypotheses

Use the Internet or a newspaper or magazine to find an example of a claim made by a company about the reliability or efficiency of one of its products. In this activity, you represent a consumer group that believes the claim may be false.

1. In your example, what kinds of evidence might exist that would cause one to suspect that the claim might be false and therefore worthy of a statistical study? Be specific. If the claim were false, how would consumers be hurt?

2. Explain the steps necessary to reject the company's claim at level α. State the null and alternative hypotheses. If you reject the claim, does it mean that the claim is false?

3. If you reject the claim when the claim is actually true, what type of error has occurred? What is the probability of this error occurring?

4. If you were to file a lawsuit against the company based on your rejection of its claim, how might the company use your results to defend itself?

---

many times was the null hypothesis *not* rejected at level .05? In this case, the null hypothesis is false. Which type of error occurred each time the null hypothesis was *not* rejected? Run the applet several more times without clearing. Based on your results, what can you conclude about the probability of failing to reject the null hypothesis for the given conditions?

Applying the Concepts—Basic

6.8 Work travel policy. American Express Consulting reported in *USA Today* (June 15, 2001) that 80% of U.S. companies have formal, written travel and entertainment policies for their employees. Give the null hypothesis for testing the claim made by American Express Consulting.

6.9 Student loan default rate. The national student loan default rate has dropped steadily over the last decade. The Department of Education reported the default rate (i.e., the proportion of college students who default on their loans) at .045 in fiscal year 2003. Set up the null and alternative hypotheses if you want to determine if the student loan default rate in 2006 is less than .045.

6.10 Libor interest rate. The interest rate at which London
NW banks lend money to one another is called the *London interbank offered rate,* or *Libor.* The British Bankers

Association regularly surveys international banks for the Libor rate. One recent report (Bankrate.com, Aug. 23, 2006) had the average Libor rate at 5.40% for 3-month loans—a value considered high by many Western banks. Set up the null and alternative hypothesis for testing the reported value.

6.11 Calories in school lunches. A University of Florida economist conducted a study of Virginia elementary school lunch menus. During the state-mandated testing period, school lunches averaged 863 calories (National Bureau of Economic Research, Nov. 2002). The economist claims that after the testing period ends, the average caloric content of Virginia school lunches drops significantly. Set up the null and alternative hypothesis to test the economist's claim.

6.12 A camera that detects liars. According to *NewScientist* (Jan. 2, 2002), a new thermal imaging camera that detects small temperature changes is now being used as a polygraph device. The United States Department of Defense Polygraph Institute (DDPI) claims the camera can correctly detect liars 75% of the time by monitoring the temperatures of their faces. Give the null hypothesis for testing the claim made by the DDPI.

Applying the Concepts—Intermediate

6.13 FDA certification of new drugs. According to *Chemical Marketing Reporter,* pharmaceutical companies spend $15 billion per year on research and development of new drugs. The pharmaceutical company must subject each new drug to lengthy and involved testing before receiving the necessary permission from the Food and Drug Administration (FDA) to market the drug. The FDA's policy is that the pharmaceutical company must provide substantial evidence that a new drug is safe prior to receiving FDA approval, so that the FDA can confidently certify the safety of the drug to potential consumers.

   a. If the new drug testing were to be placed in a test of hypothesis framework, would the null hypothesis be that the drug is safe or unsafe? The alternative hypothesis?

NW   **b.** Given the choice of null and alternative hypotheses in part **a**, describe Type I and Type II errors in terms of this application. Define α and β in terms of this application.

   c. If the FDA wants to be very confident that the drug is safe before permitting it to be marketed, is it more important that α or β be small? Explain.

6.14 Authorizing computer users. One of the most pressing problems in high-technology industries is computer security. Computer security is typically achieved by use of a *password*—a collection of symbols (usually letters and numbers) that must be supplied by the user before the computer permits access to the account. The problem is that persistent hackers can create programs that enter millions of combinations of symbols into a target system until the correct password is found. The newest systems solve this problem by requiring authorized users to identify themselves by unique body characteristics. For example, a system developed by Palmguard, Inc. tests the hypothesis

H_0: The proposed user is authorized

versus H_a: The proposed user is unauthorized

by checking characteristics of the proposed user's palm against those stored in the authorized users' data bank (*Omni*, 1984).

   a. Define a Type I error and Type II error for this test. Which is the more serious error? Why?

   b. Palmguard reports that the Type I error rate for its system is less than 1%, whereas the Type II error rate is .00025%. Interpret these error rates.

   c. Another successful security system, the EyeDentifyer, "spots authorized computer users by reading the one-of-a-kind patterns formed by the network of minute blood vessels across the retina at the back of the eye." The EyeDentifyer reports Type I and II error rates of .01% (1 in 10,000) and .005% (5 in 100,000), respectively. Interpret these rates.

Applying the Concepts—Advanced

6.15 Jury trial outcomes. Sometimes, the outcome of a jury trial defies the "common sense" expectations of the general public (e.g., the O. J. Simpson verdict in the "Trial of the Century"). Such a verdict is more acceptable if we understand that the jury trial of an accused murderer is analogous to the statistical hypothesis-testing process. The null hypothesis in a jury trial is that the accused is innocent. (The status-quo hypothesis in the U.S. system of justice is innocence, which is assumed to be true until proven *beyond a reasonable doubt.*) The alternative hypothesis is guilt, which is accepted only when sufficient evidence exists to establish its truth. If the vote of the jury is unanimous in favor of guilt, the null hypothesis of innocence is rejected and the court concludes that the accused murderer is guilty. Any vote other than a unanimous one for guilt results in a "not guilty" verdict. The court never accepts the null hypothesis; that is, the court never declares the accused "innocent." A "not guilty" verdict (as in the O. J. Simpson case) implies that the court could not find the defendant guilty *beyond a reasonable doubt.*

   a. Define Type I and Type II errors in a murder trial.

   b. Which of the two errors is the more serious? Explain.

   c. The court does not, in general, know the values of α and β; but ideally, both should be small. One of these probabilities is assumed to be smaller than the other in a jury trial. Which one, and why?

   d. The court system relies on the belief that the value of α is made very small by requiring a unanimous vote before guilt is concluded. Explain why this is so.

   e. For a jury prejudiced against a guilty verdict as the trial begins, will the value of α increase or decrease? Explain.

   f. For a jury prejudiced against a guilty verdict as the trial begins, will the value of β increase or decrease? Explain.

6.16 Intrusion detection systems. Refer to the *Journal of Research of the National Institute of Standards and Technology* (Nov.–Dec. 2003) study of a computer intrusion detection system (IDS), Exercise 3.84 (p. 177). Recall that an IDS is designed to provide an alarm whenever unauthorized access (e.g., an intrusion) to a computer system occurs. The probability of the system giving a false alarm (i.e., providing a warning when no intrusion occurs) is defined by the symbol α, while the probability of a missed detection (i.e., no warning given when an intrusion occurs) is defined by the symbol β. These symbols are used to represent Type I and Type II error rates, respectively, in a hypothesis testing scenario.

   a. What is the null hypothesis, H_0?

   b. What is the alternative hypothesis, H_a?

   c. According to actual data on the EMERALD system collected by the Massachusetts Institute of Technology Lincoln Laboratory, only 1 in 1,000 computer sessions with no intrusions resulted in a false alarm. For the same system, the laboratory found that only 500 of 1,000 intrusions were actually detected. Use this information to estimate the values of α and β.

6.2 Large-Sample Test of Hypothesis about a Population Mean

In Section 6.1 we learned that the null and alternative hypotheses form the basis for a test of hypothesis inference. The null and alternative hypotheses may take one of several forms. In the sewer pipe example, we tested the null hypothesis that the population mean strength of the pipe is less than or equal to 2,400 pounds per linear foot against the alternative hypothesis that the mean strength exceeds 2,400 — that is, we tested

$$H_0: \mu \leq 2,400 \quad \text{(Pipe does not meet specifications)}$$
$$H_a: \mu > 2,400 \quad \text{(Pipe meets specifications)}$$

This is a **one-tailed** (or **one-sided**) **statistical test** because the alternative hypothesis specifies that the population parameter (the population mean μ, in this example) is strictly greater than a specified value (2,400, in this example). If the null hypothesis had been $H_0: \mu \geq 2,400$ and the alternative hypothesis had been $H_a: \mu < 2,400$, the test would still be one sided, because the parameter is still specified to be on "one side" of the null hypothesis value. Some statistical investigations seek to show that the population parameter is *either larger or smaller* than some specified value. Such an alternative hypothesis is called a **two-tailed** (or **two-sided**) **hypothesis.**

While alternative hypotheses are always specified as strict inequalities, such as $\mu < 2,400$, $\mu > 2,400$, or $\mu \neq 2,400$, null hypotheses are usually specified as equalities, such as $\mu = 2,400$. Even when the null hypothesis is an inequality, such as $\mu \leq 2,400$, we specify $H_0: \mu = 2,400$, reasoning that if sufficient evidence exists to show that $H_a: \mu > 2,400$ is true when tested against $H_0: \mu = 2,400$, then surely sufficient evidence exists to reject $\mu < 2,400$ as well. Therefore, the null hypothesis is specified as the value of μ closest to a one-sided alternative hypothesis and as the only value *not* specified in a two-tailed alternative hypothesis. The steps for selecting the null and alternative hypotheses are summarized in the accompanying box.

Steps for Selecting the Null and Alternative Hypotheses

1. Select the *alternative hypothesis* as that which the sampling experiment is intended to establish. The alternative hypothesis will assume one of three forms:
   a. One-tailed, upper-tailed   (e.g., $H_a: \mu > 2,400$)
   b. One-tailed, lower-tailed   (e.g., $H_a: \mu < 2,400$)
   c. Two-tailed   (e.g., $H_a: \mu \neq 2,400$)

2. Select the *null hypothesis* as the status quo, that which will be presumed true unless the sampling experiment conclusively establishes the alternative hypothesis. The null hypothesis will be specified as that parameter value closest to the alternative in one-tailed tests and as the complementary (or only unspecified) value in two-tailed tests.

$$\text{(e.g., } H_0: \mu = 2,400\text{)}$$

The rejection region for a two-tailed test differs from that for a one-tailed test. When we are trying to detect departure from the null hypothesis in *either* direction, we must establish a rejection region in both tails of the sampling distribution of the test statistic. Figures 6.4(a) and 6.4(b) show the one-tailed rejection regions for lower- and upper-tailed tests, respectively. The two-tailed rejection region is illustrated in Figure 6.4(c). Note that a rejection region is established in each tail of the sampling distribution for a two-tailed test.

The rejection regions corresponding to typical values selected for α are shown in Table 6.2 for one- and two-tailed tests. Note that the smaller α you select, the more evidence (the larger z) you will need before you can reject H_0.

FIGURE 6.4

Rejection regions corresponding to one- and two-tailed tests

a. Form of $H_a: <$

b. Form of $H_a: >$

c. Form of $H_a: \neq$

TABLE 6.2 Rejection Regions for Common Values of α

	ALTERNATIVE HYPOTHESES		
	Lower-Tailed	Upper-Tailed	Two-Tailed
$\alpha = .10$	$z < -1.28$	$z > 1.28$	$z < -1.645$ or $z > 1.645$
$\alpha = .05$	$z < -1.645$	$z > 1.645$	$z < -1.96$ or $z > 1.96$
$\alpha = .01$	$z < -2.33$	$z > 2.33$	$z < -2.575$ or $z > 2.575$

EXAMPLE 6.1

Setting Up a Hypothesis Test for μ, the Mean Amount of Cereal in a Box

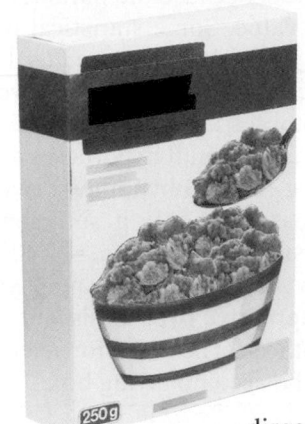

Problem A manufacturer of cereal wants to test the performance of one of its filling machines. The machine is designed to discharge a mean amount of 12 ounces per box, and the manufacturer wants to detect any departure from this setting. This quality study calls for randomly sampling 100 boxes from today's production run and determining whether the mean fill for the run is 12 ounces per box. Set up a test of hypothesis for this study, using $\alpha = .01$.

Solution The key word *mean* in the statement of the problem implies that the target parameter is μ, the mean amount of cereal discharged into the box. Since the manufacturer wishes to detect a departure from the setting of $\mu = 12$ in either direction, $\mu < 12$ or $\mu > 12$, we conduct a two-tailed statistical test.

Following the procedure for selecting the null and alternative hypotheses, we specify as the alternative hypothesis that the mean differs from 12 ounces, since detecting the machine's departure from specifications is the purpose of the quality control study. The null hypothesis is the presumption that the fill machine is operating properly unless the sample data indicate otherwise. Thus,

$H_0: \mu = 12$ (Population mean fill amount is 12 ounces)

$H_a: \mu \neq 12$ (i.e., $\mu < 12$ or $\mu > 12$; machine is under- or overfilling the box)

The test statistic measures the number of standard deviations between the observed value of $\overline{x}$ and the null hypothesized value $\mu = 12$:

$$Test\ statistic: \frac{\overline{x} - 12}{\sigma_{\overline{x}}}$$

The rejection region must be designated to detect a departure from $\mu = 12$ in *either* direction, so we will reject H_0 for values of z that are either too small (negative) or too large (positive). To determine the precise values of z that comprise the rejection region, we first select α, the probability that the test will lead to incorrect rejection of the null hypothesis. Then we divide α equally between the lower and upper tail of the distribution of z, as shown in Figure 6.5. In this example, $\alpha = .01$, so $\alpha/2 = .005$ is placed in each tail. The areas in the tails correspond to $z = -2.575$ and $z = 2.575$, respectively (from Table 6.2):

FIGURE 6.5
Two-tailed rejection region: $\alpha = .01$

Rejection region: $z < -2.575$ or $z > 2.575$, (see Figure 6.5)

Assumptions: Since the sample size of the experiment is large enough ($n > 30$), the Central Limit Theorem will apply, and no assumptions need be made about the population of fill measurements. The sampling distribution of the sample mean fill of

100 boxes will be approximately normal regardless of the distribution of the individual boxes' fills.

Look Back Note that the test is set up *before* the sampling experiment is conducted. The data are not used to develop the test. Evidently, the manufacturer does not want to disrupt the filling process to adjust the machine unless the sample data provide very convincing evidence that it is not meeting specifications, because the value of α has been set quite low at .01. If the sample evidence results in the rejection of H_0, the manufacturer will confidently conclude that the machine needs adjustment, since there is only a .01 probability of a Type I error.

Now Work Exercise 6.17

Once the test is set up, the manufacturer is ready to perform the sampling experiment and conduct the test. The test is performed in Example 6.2.

EXAMPLE 6.2

Carrying Out a
Hypothesis Test for
μ, the Mean Amount
of Cereal in a Box

Problem   Refer to the quality control test set up in Example 6.1. The sample of 100 boxes yielded the results (in ounces) shown in Table 6.3. Use these data to conduct the test of hypothesis.

 CEREAL

TABLE 6.3 Fill Amounts from Quality Control Tests, Example 6.2

12.3	12.2	12.9	11.8	12.1	11.7	11.8	11.3	12.0	11.7
11.0	12.7	11.2	11.8	11.4	11.3	11.5	12.1	12.5	11.7
12.3	11.7	11.6	11.6	11.1	12.1	12.4	11.4	11.6	11.4
10.9	11.0	11.5	11.6	11.6	11.4	11.9	11.1	11.7	12.1
12.2	11.7	11.6	11.4	12.4	11.0	11.8	12.9	13.2	11.5
11.5	12.0	11.9	11.8	12.5	11.8	12.4	12.0	12.2	12.4
11.8	12.6	11.8	11.8	11.5	12.0	12.7	11.5	11.0	11.8
11.2	12.6	12.0	12.6	12.0	12.0	12.5	12.0	12.8	11.8
12.6	12.4	10.9	12.0	11.9	11.6	11.3	12.1	11.8	12.2
12.2	11.5	12.7	11.5	11.0	11.7	12.5	11.6	11.3	11.1

Solution   To carry out the test, we need to find the values of $\bar{x}$ and s. These values, $\bar{x} = 11.851$ and $s = .512$, are shown (highlighted) on the MINITAB printout, Figure 6.6. Now, we substitute these sample statistics into the test statistic and obtain:

$$z = \frac{\bar{x} - 12}{\sigma_{\bar{x}}} = \frac{\bar{x} - 12}{\sigma/\sqrt{n}} = \frac{11.851 - 12}{\sigma/\sqrt{100}}$$

$$\approx \frac{11.851 - 12}{s/10} = \frac{-.149}{.512/10} = -2.91$$

The implication is that the sample mean, 11.851, is (approximately) 3 standard deviations below the null hypothesized value of 12.0 in the sampling distribution of $\bar{x}$. You can see in Figure 6.5 that this value of z is in the lower-tail rejection region, which consists of all values of $z < -2.575$. These sample data provide sufficient evidence to reject H_0 and conclude, at the $\alpha = .01$ level of significance, that the mean fill differs from the specification of $\mu = 12$ ounces. It appears that the machine is, on average, underfilling the boxes.

Descriptive Statistics: FILL

```
Variable     N    Mean   StDev  Minimum      Q1  Median      Q3  Maximum
FILL       100  11.851   0.512   10.900  11.500  11.800  12.200   13.200
```

FIGURE 6.6
MINITAB Descriptive Statistics for Fill Amounts, Example 6.2

Look Back Three points about the test of hypothesis in this example apply to all statistical tests:

1. Since z is less than -2.575, it is tempting to state our conclusion at a significance level lower than $\alpha = .01$. We resist the temptation because the level of α is determined before the sampling experiment is performed. If we decide that we are willing to tolerate a 1% Type I error rate, the result of the sampling experiment should have no effect on that decision. In general, *the same data should not be used both to set up and to conduct the test.*

2. When we state our conclusion at the .01 level of significance, we are referring to the failure rate of the procedure, not the result of this particular test. We know that the test procedure will lead to the rejection of the null hypothesis only 1% of the time when in fact $\mu = 12$. Therefore, *when the test statistic falls in the rejection region, we infer that the alternative $\mu \neq 12$ is true and express our confidence in the procedure by quoting the α level of significance, or the $100(1 - \alpha)\%$ confidence level.*

3. Although a test may lead to a "statistically significant" result (i.e., rejecting H_0 at significance level α, as in the test above), it may not be "practically significant." For example, suppose the quality control study tested $n = 100.000$ cereal boxes, resulting in $\bar{x} = 11.995$ and $s = .5$. Now, a two-tailed hypothesis test of $H_0: \mu = 12$ results in a test statistic of $z = \dfrac{(11.995 - 12)}{.5/\sqrt{100,000}} = -3.16$.

This result at $\alpha = .05$ leads us to "reject H_0" and conclude that the mean, μ, is "statistically different" from 12. However, for all practical purposes, the sample mean, $\bar{x} = 11.995$ and hypothesized mean, $\mu = 12$, are the same. Because the result is not "practically significant," the company is not likely to spend money fixing a machine, that, for all practical purposes, is dispensing an average of 12 ounces of cereal into the boxes. Consequently, *not all "statistically significant" results are "practically significant."*

Now Work Exercise 6.21

The setup of a large-sample test of hypothesis about a population mean is summarized in the following boxes. Both the one- and two-tailed tests are shown.

Large-Sample Test of Hypothesis about μ

One-Tailed Test	Two-Tailed Test
$H_0: \mu = \mu_0$	$H_0: \mu = \mu_0$
$H_a: \mu < \mu_0$	$H_a: \mu \neq \mu_0$
(or $H_a: \mu > \mu_0$)	
Test statistic: $z = \dfrac{\bar{x} - \mu_0}{\sigma_{\bar{x}}}$	Test statistic: $z = \dfrac{\bar{x} - \mu_0}{\sigma_{\bar{x}}}$
Rejection region: $z < -z_\alpha$	Rejection region: $|z| > z_{\alpha/2}$
(or $z > z_\alpha$ when $H_a: \mu > \mu_0$)	
where z_α is chosen so that	where $z_{\alpha/2}$ is chosen so that
$P(z > z_\alpha) = \alpha$	$P(|z| > z_{\alpha/2}) = \alpha/2$

Note: μ_0 is the symbol for the numerical value assigned to μ under the null hypothesis.

Conditions Required for a Valid Large-Sample Hypothesis Test for μ

1. A random sample is selected from the target population.
2. The sample size n is large (i.e., $n \geq 30$). (Due to the Central Limit Theorem, this condition guarantees that the test statistic will be approximately normal regardless of the shape of the underlying probability distribution of the population.)

Once the test has been set up, the sampling experiment is performed and the test statistic calculated. The next box contains possible conclusions for a test of hypothesis, depending on the result of the sampling experiment.

> **Possible Conclusions for a Test of Hypothesis**
>
> 1. If the calculated test statistic falls in the rejection region, reject H_0 and conclude that the alternative hypothesis H_a is true. State that you are rejecting H_0 at the α level of significance. Remember that the confidence is in the testing *process*, not the particular result of a single test.
>
> 2. If the test statistic does not fall in the rejection region, conclude that the sampling experiment does not provide sufficient evidence to reject H_0 at the α level of significance. [Generally, we will not "accept" the null hypothesis unless the probability β of a Type II error has been calculated (see optional Section 6.6).]

Exercises 6.17–6.31

Learning the Mechanics

6.17 For each of the following rejection regions, sketch the sampling distribution for z and indicate the location of the rejection region.
a. $z > 1.96$
b. $z > 1.645$
c. $z > 2.575$
d. $z < -1.28$
e. $z < -1.645$ or $z > 1.645$
f. $z < -2.575$ or $z > 2.575$
g. For each of the rejection regions specified in parts **a–f**, what is the probability that a Type I error will be made?

6.18 Suppose you are interested in conducting the statistical test of $H_0: \mu = 255$ against $H_a: \mu > 255$, and you have decided to use the following decision rule: Reject H_0 if the sample mean of a random sample of 81 items is more than 270. Assume that the standard deviation of the population is 63.
a. Express the decision rule in terms of z.
b. Find α, the probability of making a Type I error, by using this decision rule.

6.19 A random sample of 100 observations from a population with standard deviation 60 yielded a sample mean of 110.
a. Test the null hypothesis that $\mu = 100$ against the alternative hypothesis that $\mu > 100$ using $\alpha = .05$. Interpret the results of the test.
b. Test the null hypothesis that $\mu = 100$ against the alternative hypothesis that $\mu \neq 100$ using $\alpha = .05$. Interpret the results of the test.
c. Compare the results of the two tests you conducted. Explain why the results differ.

6.20 A random sample of 64 observations produced the following summary statistics: $\bar{x} = .323$ and $s^2 = .034$.
a. Test the null hypothesis that $\mu = .36$ against the alternative hypothesis that $\mu < .36$ using $\alpha = .10$.
b. Test the null hypothesis that $\mu = .36$ against the alternative hypothesis that $\mu \neq .36$ using $\alpha = .10$. Interpret the result.

APPLET Applet Exercise 6.2

Use the applet entitled *Hypotheses Test for a Mean* to investigate the effect of the underlying distribution on the proportion of

Type I errors. For this exercise use $n = 100$, mean $= 50$, standard deviation $= 10$, null mean $= 50$, and alternative $<$.
a. Select the normal distribution and run the applet several times without clearing. What happens to the proportion of times the null hypothesis is rejected at the .05 level as the applet is run more and more times?
b. Clear the applet and then repeat part **a** using the right skewed distribution. Do you get similar results? Explain.
c. Describe the effect that the underlying distribution has on the probability of making a Type I error.

APPLET Applet Exercise 6.3

Use the applet entitled *Hypotheses Test for a Mean* to investigate the effect of the underlying distribution on the proportion of Type II errors. For this exercise use $n = 100$, mean $= 50$, standard deviation $= 10$, null mean $= 52$, and alternative $<$.
a. Select the normal distribution and run the applet several times without clearing. What happens to the proportion of times the null hypothesis is rejected at the .01 level as the applet is run more and more times? Is this what you would expect? Explain.
b. Clear the applet and then repeat part **a** using the right skewed distribution. Do you get similar results? Explain.
c. Describe the effect that the underlying distribution has on the probability of making a Type II error.

APPLET Applet Exercise 6.4

Use the applet entitled *Hypotheses Test for a Mean* to investigate the effect of the null mean on the probability of making a Type II error. For this exercise use $n = 100$, mean $= 50$, standard deviation $= 10$, and alternative $<$ with the normal distribution. Set the null mean to 55 and run the applet several times without clearing. Record the proportion of Type II errors that occurred at the .01 level. Clear the applet and repeat for null means of 54, 53, 52, and 51. What can you conclude about the probability of a Type II error as the null mean gets closer to the actual mean? Can you offer a reasonable explanation for this?

Applying the Concepts—Basic

6.21 Latex allergy in health care workers. Refer to the *Current Allergy & Clinical Immunology* (Mar. 2004) study of $n = 46$

hospital employees who were diagnosed with a latex allergy from exposure to the powder on latex gloves, Exercise 5.10 (p. 299). The number of latex gloves used per week by the sampled workers is summarized as follows: $\bar{x} = 19.3$ and $s = 11.9$. Let μ represent the mean number of latex gloves used per week by all hospital employees. Consider testing $H_0: \mu = 20$ against $H_a: \mu < 20$.

a. Give the rejection region for the test at a significance level of $\alpha = .01$.

b. Calculate the value of the test statistic.

c. Use the results, parts a and b, to make the appropriate conclusion.

HYBRIDCARS

6.22 Prices of hybrid cars. *BusinessWeek.com* provides consumers with retail prices of new cars at dealers from across the country. The July 2006 prices for the hybrid Toyota Prius were obtained from a sample of 160 dealers. These 160 prices are saved in the **HYBRIDCARS** file.

a. Give the null and alternative hypotheses for testing whether the mean July 2006 dealer price of the Toyota Prius, μ, differs from $25,000.

b. Access the **HYBRIDCARS** file and find the sample mean and sample standard deviation.

c. Use the information in part b to find the test statistic for the hypothesis test.

d. Give the rejection region for the hypothesis test, using $\alpha = .05$.

e. State the appropriate conclusion for the hypothesis test.

6.23 Semester hours taken by CPA candidates. Refer to the *Journal of Accounting and Public Policy* (Spring 2002) study of $n = 100,000$ first-time candidates for the CPA exam, Exercise 5.13 (p. 300). The number of semester hours of college credit taken by the sampled candidates is summarized as follows: $\bar{x} = 141.31$ hours and $s = 17.77$ hours. Let μ represent the mean number of semester hours taken by all first-time candidates for the CPA exam. Consider testing $H_0: \mu = 140$ against $H_a: \mu > 140$.

a. Give the rejection region for the test at a significance level of $\alpha = .01$.

b. Calculate the value of the test statistic.

c. Use the results, parts a and b, to make the appropriate conclusion.

DIAMONDS

6.24 Size of diamonds sold at retail. Refer to the *Journal of Statistics Education* data on diamonds saved in the DIAMONDS file. In Exercise 5.18 (p. 301) you selected a random sample of 30 diamonds from the 308 diamonds and found the mean and standard deviation of the number of carats per diamond for the sample. Let μ represent the

mean number of carats in the population of 308 diamonds. Suppose you want to test $H_0: \mu = .6$ against $H_a: \mu \neq .6$.

a. In the words of the problem, define a Type I error and a Type II error.

b. Use the sample information to conduct the test at a significance level of $\alpha = .05$.

c. Conduct the test, part b, using $\alpha = .10$.

d. What do the results suggest about the choice of α in a test of hypothesis?

6.25 Producer's and consumer's risk. In quality control applications of hypothesis testing, the null and alternative hypotheses are frequently specified as

H_0: The production process is performing satisfactorily

H_a: The process is performing in an unsatisfactory manner

Accordingly, α is sometimes referred to as the *producer's risk*, while β is called the *consumer's risk* (Stevenson, *Production/Operations Management*, 2000). An injection molder produces plastic golf tees. The process is designed to produce tees with a mean weight of .250 ounce. To investigate whether the injection molder is operating satisfactorily, 40 tees were randomly sampled from the last hour's production. Their weights (in ounces) are listed in the following table.

TEES

.247	.251	.254	.253	.253	.248	.253	.255	.256	.252
.253	.252	.253	.256	.254	.256	.252	.251	.253	.251
.253	.253	.248	.251	.253	.256	.254	.250	.254	.255
.249	.250	.254	.251	.251	.255	.251	.253	.252	.253

a. Write H_0 and H_a in terms of the true mean weight of the golf tees, μ.

b. Do the data provide sufficient evidence to conclude that the process is not operating satisfactorily? Test using $\alpha = .01$.

c. In the context of this problem, explain why it makes sense to call α the producer's risk and β the consumer's risk.

Applying the Concepts—Intermediate

6.26 Cooling method for gas turbines. During periods of high electricity demand, especially during the hot summer months, the power output from a gas turbine engine can drop dramatically. One way to counter this drop in power is by cooling the inlet air to the gas turbine. An increasingly popular cooling method uses high pressure inlet fogging. The performance of a sample of 67 gas turbines augmented with high-pressure inlet fogging was investigated in the *Journal of Engineering for Gas Turbines and Power* (Jan. 2005). One measure of performance is heat rate (kilojoules per kilowatt per hour). Heat rates for the 67 gas turbines, saved in the **GASTURBINE** file, are list-

GASTURBINE

14622	13196	11948	11289	11964	10526	10387	10592	10460	10086
14628	13396	11726	11252	12449	11030	10787	10603	10144	11674
11510	10946	10508	10604	10270	10529	10360	14796	12913	12270
11842	10656	11360	11136	10814	13523	11289	11183	10951	9722
10481	9812	9669	9643	9115	9115	11588	10888	9738	9295
9421	9105	10233	10186	9918	9209	9532	9933	9152	9295
16243	14628	12766	8714	9469	11948	12414			

ed in the table. Suppose that a standard gas turbine has, on average, a heat rate of 10,000 kJ/kWh. Conduct a test to determine if the mean heat rate of gas turbines augmented with high-pressure inlet fogging exceeds 10,000 kJ/kWh. Use $\alpha = .05$.

6.27 Point spreads of NFL games. During the National Football League (NFL) season, Las Vegas oddsmakers establish a point spread on each game for betting purposes. For example, the Seattle Seahawks were established as 4.5-point favorites over the champion Pittsburgh Steelers in the 2006 Super Bowl. The final scores of NFL games were compared against the final point spreads established by the oddsmakers in *Chance* (Fall 1998). The difference between the game outcome and point spread (called a *point-spread error*) was calculated for 240 NFL games. The mean and standard deviation of the point-spread errors are $\bar{x} = -1.6$ and $s = 13.3$. Use this information to test the hypothesis that the true mean point-spread error for all NFL games differs from 0. Conduct the test at $\alpha = .01$ and interpret the result.

6.28 Revenue for a full-service funeral. According to the National Funeral Directors Association (NFDA), the nation's 22,000 funeral homes collected an average of $6,500 per full-service funeral in 2005 (*NFDA Fact Sheet*, 2006). A random sample of 36 funeral homes reported revenue data for 2006. Among other measures, each reported its average fee for a full-service funeral. These data (in thousands of dollars) are shown in the following table, rounded to the nearest hundred.

FUNERAL

7.4	9.4	5.3	8.4	7.5	6.5	6.2	8.3	6.7
11.6	6.3	5.9	6.7	5.8	5.2	6.4	6.0	7.4
7.2	6.6	6.3	5.3	6.6	5.6	8.4	7.2	7.4
5.8	6.3	6.1	7.0	7.2	6.1	5.4	7.4	6.6

a. What are the appropriate null and alternative hypotheses to test whether the average full-service fee of U. S. funeral homes in 2006 exceeds $6,500?

b. Conduct the test at $\alpha = .05$. Do the sample data provide sufficient evidence to conclude that the average fee in 2006 was higher than in 2005?

c. In conducting the test, was it necessary to assume that the population of average full-service fees was normally distributed? Justify your answer.

6.29 Salaries of postgraduates. The *Economics of Education Review* (Vol. 21, 2002) published a paper on the relationship between education level and earnings. The data for the research were obtained from the National Adult Literacy Survey of over 25,000 respondents. The survey revealed that males with a postgraduate degree had a mean salary of $61,340 (with standard error $s_{\bar{x}} = \$2,185$), while females with a postgraduate degree had a mean of $32,227 (with standard error $s_{\bar{x}} = \$932$).

a. The article reports that a 95% confidence interval for μ_M, the population mean salary of all males with postgraduate degrees, is ($57,050, $65,631). Based on this interval, is there evidence to say that μ_M differs from $60,000? Explain.

b. Use the summary information to test the hypothesis that the true mean salary of males with postgraduate degrees differs from $60,000. Use $\alpha = .05$. (*Note:* $s_{\bar{x}} = s/\sqrt{n}$.)

c. Explain why the inferences in parts **a** and **b** agree.

d. The article reports that a 95% confidence interval for μ_F, the population mean salary of all females with postgraduate degrees, is ($30,396, $34,058). Based on this interval, is there evidence to say that μ_F differs from $33,000? Explain.

e. Use the summary information to test the hypothesis that the true mean salary of females with postgraduate degrees differs from $33,000. Use $\alpha = .05$. (*Note:* $s_{\bar{x}} = s/\sqrt{n}$.)

f. Explain why the inferences in parts **d** and **e** agree.

6.30 Solder-joint inspections. Current technology uses X-rays and lasers for inspection of solder-joint defects on printed circuit boards (PCBs) (*Quality Congress Transactions*, 1986). A particular manufacturer of laser-based inspection equipment claims that its product can inspect on average at least 10 solder joints per second when the joints are spaced .1 inch apart. The equipment was tested by a potential buyer on 48 different PCBs. In each case, the equipment was operated for exactly 1 second. The number of solder joints inspected on each run follows:

PCB

10	9	10	10	11	9	12	8	8	9	6	10
7	10	11	9	9	13	9	10	11	10	12	8
9	9	9	7	12	6	9	10	10	8	7	9
11	12	10	0	10	11	12	9	7	9	9	10

a. The potential buyer wants to know whether the sample data refute the manufacturer's claim. Specify the null and alternative hypotheses that the buyer should test.

b. In the context of this exercise, what is a Type I error? A Type II error?

c. Conduct the hypothesis test you described in part **a**, and interpret the test's results in the context of this exercise. Use $\alpha = .05$.

Applying the Concepts—Advanced

6.31 Why do small firms export? What motivates small firms to export their products? To answer this question, California State University professor Ralph Pope conducted a survey of 137 exporting firms listed in the *California International Trade Register* (*Journal of Small Business Management*, Vol. 40, 2002.) Firm CEOs were asked to respond to the statement "Management believes that the firm can achieve economies of scale by exporting" on a scale of 1 (strongly disagree) to 5 (strongly agree). Summary statistics for the $n = 137$ scale scores were reported as: $\bar{x} = 3.85$ and $s = 1.5$. In the journal article, the researcher hypothesized that if the true mean scale score exceeds 3.5, then CEOs at all California small firms generally agree with the statement.

a. Conduct the appropriate test using $\alpha = .05$. State your conclusion in the words of the problem.

b. Explain why the results of the study, although "statistically significant," may not be practically significant.

c. The scale scores for the sample of 137 small firms are unlikely to be normally distributed. Does this invalidate the inference you made in part **a**? Explain.

6.3 Observed Significance Levels: *p*-Values

According to the statistical test procedure described in Section 6.2, the rejection region and, correspondingly, the value of α are selected prior to conducting the test, and the conclusions are stated in terms of rejecting or not rejecting the null hypothesis. A second method of presenting the results of a statistical test is one that reports the extent to which the test statistic disagrees with the null hypothesis and leaves to the reader the task of deciding whether to reject the null hypothesis. This measure of disagreement is called the *observed significance level* (or *p-value*) for the test.

> **Definition 6.1**
>
> The **observed significance level,** or *p*-value, for a specific statistical test is the probability (assuming H_0 is true) of observing a value of the test statistic that is at least as contradictory to the null hypothesis, and supportive of the alternative hypothesis, as the actual one computed from the sample data.

For example, the value of the test statistic computed for the sample of $n = 50$ sections of sewer pipe was $z = 2.12$. Since the test is one-tailed—that is, the alternative (research) hypothesis of interest is $H_a\colon \mu > 2{,}400$—values of the test statistic even more contradictory to H_0 than the one observed would be values larger than $z = 2.12$. Therefore, the observed significance level (*p*-value) for this test is

$$p\text{-value} = P(z > 2.12)$$

or, equivalently, the area under the standard normal curve to the right of $z = 2.12$ (see Figure 6.7).

The area A in Figure 6.7 is given in Table IV in Appendix B as .4830. Therefore, the upper-tail area corresponding to $z = 2.12$ is

$$p\text{-value} = .5 - .4830 = .0170$$

FIGURE 6.7

Finding the *p*-value for an upper-tailed test when $z = 2.12$

Consequently, we say that these test results are "very significant" (i.e., they disagree rather strongly with the null hypothesis, $H_0\colon \mu = 2{,}400$, and favor $H_a\colon \mu > 2{,}400$. The probability of observing a *z* value as large as 2.12 is only .0170, if in fact the true value of μ is 2,400.

If you are inclined to select $\alpha = .05$ for this test, then you would reject the null hypothesis because the *p*-value for the test, .0170, is less than .05. In contrast, if you choose $\alpha = .01$, you would not reject the null hypothesis because the *p*-value for the test is larger than .01. Thus, the use of the observed significance level is identical to the test procedure described in the preceding sections except that the choice of α is left to you.

The steps for calculating the *p*-value corresponding to a test statistic for a population mean are given in the next box.

> **Steps for Calculating the *p*-value for a Test of Hypothesis**
>
> 1. Determine the value of the test statistic *z* corresponding to the result of the sampling experiment.
> 2. a. If the test is one-tailed, the *p*-value is equal to the tail area beyond *z* in the same direction as the alternative hypothesis. Thus, if the alternative hypothesis is of the form >, the *p*-value is the area to the right of, or above, the observed *z* value. Conversely, if the alternative is of the form <, the *p*-value is the area to the left of, or below, the observed *z* value. (See Figure 6.8.)

b. If the test is two-tailed, the *p*-value is equal to twice the tail area beyond the observed *z* value in the direction of the sign of *z*—that is, if *z* is positive, the *p*-value is twice the area to the right of, or above, the observed *z* value. Conversely, if *z* is negative, the *p*-value is twice the area to the left of, or below, the observed *z* value. (See Figure 6.9.)

FIGURE 6.8
Finding the *p*-value for a one-tailed test

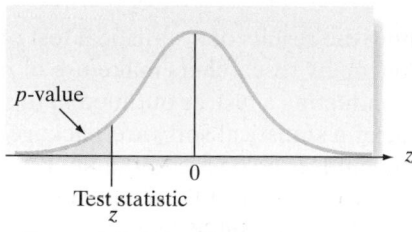

a. Lower-tailed test, $H_a: \mu < \mu_0$

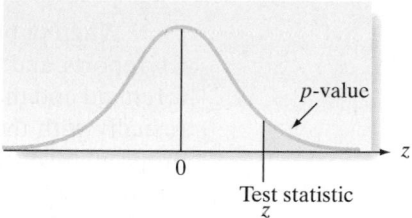

b. Upper-tailed test, $H_a: \mu > \mu_0$

FIGURE 6.9
Finding the *p*-value for a two-tailed test: *p*-value = 2(*p*/2)

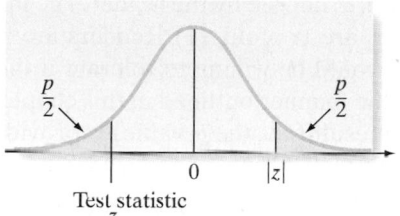

a. Test statistic *z* negative

b. Test statistic *z* positive

EXAMPLE 6.3

Computing a *p*-Value for the Test of Mean Filling Weight

Problem Find the observed significance level for the test of the mean filling weight in Examples 6.1 and 6.2.

Solution Example 6.1 presented a two-tailed test of the hypothesis

$$H_0: \mu = 12 \text{ ounces}$$

against the alternative hypothesis

$$H_a: \mu \neq 12 \text{ ounces}$$

The observed value of the test statistic in Example 6.2 was $z = -2.91$, and any value of z less than -2.91 or greater than 2.91 (because this is a two-tailed test) would be even more contradictory to H_0. Therefore, the observed significance level for the test is

$$p\text{-value} = P(z < -2.91 \text{ or } z > 2.91) = P(|z| > 2.91)$$

Thus, we calculate the area below the observed z value, $z = -2.91$, and double it. Consulting Table IV in Appendix B, we find that $P(z < -2.91) = .5 - .4982 = .0018$. Therefore, the *p*-value for this two-tailed test is

$$2P(z < -2.91) = 2(.0018) = .0036$$

This *p*-value can also be obtained using statistical software. The rounded *p*-value is shown (highlighted) on the MINITAB Printout, Figure 6.10.

Test of mu = 12 vs not = 12

Variable	N	Mean	StDev	SE Mean	95% CI	T	P
FILL	100	11.8510	0.5118	0.0512	(11.7495, 11.9525)	-2.91	0.004

FIGURE 6.10
MINITAB Test of Mean Fill Amount, Example 6.3

Look Back We can interpret this p-value as a strong indication that the machine is not filling the boxes according to specifications, since we would observe a test statistic this extreme or more extreme only 36 in 10,000 times if the machine were meeting specifications ($\mu = 12$). The extent to which the mean differs from 12 could be better determined by calculating a confidence interval for μ.

Now Work Exercise 6.37

When publishing the results of a statistical test of hypothesis in journals, case studies, reports, and so on, many researchers make use of p-values. Instead of selecting α beforehand and then conducting a test, as outlined in this chapter, the researcher computes (usually with the aid of a statistical software package) and reports the value of the appropriate test statistic and its associated p-value. It is left to the reader of the report to judge the significance of the result (i.e., the reader must determine whether to reject the null hypothesis in favor of the alternative hypothesis, based on the reported p-value). Usually, the null hypothesis is rejected if the observed significance level is *less than* the fixed significance level, α, chosen by the reader. The inherent advantage of reporting test results in this manner are twofold: (1) Readers are permitted to select the maximum value of α that they would be willing to tolerate if they actually carried out a standard test of hypothesis in the manner outlined in this chapter, and (2) a measure of the degree of significance of the result (i.e., the p-value) is provided.

Reporting Test Results as p-values: How to Decide Whether to Reject H_0

1. Choose the maximum value of α that you are willing to tolerate.
2. If the observed significance level (p-value) of the test is less than the chosen value of α, reject the null hypothesis. Otherwise, do not reject the null hypothesis.

EXAMPLE 6.4
Using p-Values to Test Mean Hospital Length of Stay

Problem   Knowledge of the amount of time a patient occupies a hospital bed—called *length of stay* (LOS)—is important for allocating resources. At one hospital, the mean length of stay was determined to be 5 days. A hospital administrator believes that the mean LOS may now be less than 5 days due to a newly adopted managed care system. To check this, the LOSs (in days) for 100 randomly selected hospital patients were recorded; these are listed in Table 6.4. Test the hypothesis that the true mean LOS at the hospital is less than 5 days; that is,

$$H_0: \mu = 5 \quad \text{(Mean LOS is 5 days)}$$
$$H_a: \mu < 5 \quad \text{(Mean LOS is less than 5 days)}$$

Use the data in the table to conduct the test at $\alpha = .05$.

Solution   The data were entered into a computer, and Excel/PHStat2 was used to conduct the analysis. The Excel printout for the lower-tailed test is displayed in

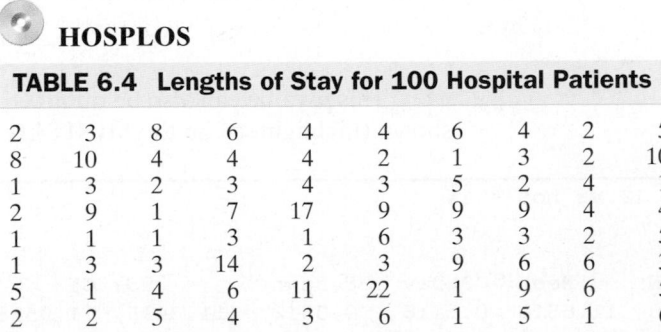

🔘 **HOSPLOS**

TABLE 6.4   Lengths of Stay for 100 Hospital Patients

2	3	8	6	4	4	6	4	2	5
8	10	4	4	4	2	1	3	2	10
1	3	2	3	4	3	5	2	4	1
2	9	1	7	17	9	9	9	4	4
1	1	1	3	1	6	3	3	2	5
1	3	3	14	2	3	9	6	6	3
5	1	4	6	11	22	1	9	6	5
2	2	5	4	3	6	1	5	1	6
17	1	2	4	5	4	4	3	2	3
3	5	2	3	3	2	10	2	4	2

t Test for Hypothesis of the Mean	
Data	
Null Hypothesis μ=	5
Level of Significance	0.05
Sample Size	100
Sample Mean	4.53
Sample Standard Deviation	3.677545844
Intermediate Calculations	
Standard Error of the Mean	0.367754584
Degrees of Freedom	99
t Test Statistic	-1.278026216
Lower-Tail Test	
Lower Critical Value	-1.660391717
***p*-Value**	0.102114325
Do not reject the null hypothesis	

FIGURE 6.11

Excel and PHStat2 printout for the hypothesis test of Example 6.4

Figure 6.11. Both the test statistic, $z = -1.278$, and *p*-value of the test, $p = .102$, are shown at the bottom of the printout. Since the *p*-value exceeds our selected α value, $\alpha = .05$, we cannot reject the null hypothesis. Hence, there is insufficient evidence (at $\alpha = .05$) to conclude that the true mean LOS at the hospital is less than 5 days.

Now Work Exercise 6.40

STATISTICS IN ACTION REVISITED

Testing a Population Mean in the Kleenex® Survey

Refer to Kimberly-Clark Corporation's survey of 250 people who kept a count of their use of Kleenex® tissues in diaries (p. 351). We want to test the claim made by marketing experts that $\mu = 60$ is the average number of tissues used by people with colds against our belief that the population mean is smaller than 60 tissues—that is, we want to test

$$H_0: \mu = 60 \quad H_a: \mu < 60$$

We will select $\alpha = .05$ as the level of significance for the test.

The survey results for the 250 sampled Kleenex® users are stored in the **TISSUES** data file. A MINITAB analysis of the data yielded the printout displayed in Figure SIA6.1.

The observed significance level of the test, highlighted on the printout, is *p*-value = .018. Since this *p*-value is less than $\alpha = .05$, we have sufficient evidence to reject H_0; therefore, we conclude that the mean number of tissues used by a person with a cold is less than 60 tissues.

[*Note:* If we conduct the same test using $\alpha = .01$ as the level of significance, we would have insufficient evidence to reject H_0 since the *p*-value = .018 is greater than $\alpha = .01$. Thus, at $\alpha = .01$, there is not sufficient evidence to support our alternative that the population mean is less than 60.]

```
Test of mu = 60 vs < 60

                                          95%
                                        Upper
Variable    N    Mean    StDev  SE Mean  Bound      T      P
NUMUSED   250  56.6760  25.0343  1.5833  59.2900  -2.10  0.018
```

Figure SIA6.1

MINITAB test of $\mu = 60$ for Kleenex® survey

Note: Some statistical software packages (e.g., SPSS) will conduct only two-tailed tests of hypothesis. For these packages, you obtain the *p*-value for a one-tailed test as shown in the box:

Converting a Two-Tailed *p*-value from a Printout to a One-Tailed *p*-value

$$p = \frac{\text{Reported } p\text{-value}}{2} \qquad \text{if} \begin{cases} H_a \text{ is of form } > \text{ and } z \text{ is positive} \\ H_a \text{ is of form } < \text{ and } z \text{ is negative} \end{cases}$$

$$p = 1 - \left(\frac{\text{Reported } p\text{-value}}{2} \right) \qquad \text{if} \begin{cases} H_a \text{ is of form } > \text{ and } z \text{ is negative} \\ H_a \text{ is of form } < \text{ and } z \text{ is positive} \end{cases}$$

Hypothesis Test for a Population Mean (Large Sample Case)

Using The TI-83/TI-84 Graphing Calculator

Step 1 *Enter the Data (Skip to Step 2 if you have summary statistics, not raw data)*

Press **STAT** and select **1:Edit**
Note: If the list already contains data, clear the old data. Use the up **ARROW** to highlight "**L1**".
Press **CLEAR ENTER**.
Use the **ARROW** and **ENTER** keys to enter the data set into **L1**.

Step 2 *Access the Statistical Tests Menu*

Press **STAT**
Arrow right to **TESTS**
Press **ENTER** to select **Z-Test**

Step 3 *Choose "**Data**" or "**Stats**". ("Data" is selected when you have entered the raw data into a List. "Stats" is selected when you are given only the mean, standard deviation, and sample size.)*

Press **ENTER**
If you selected "Data", enter the values for the hypothesis test where μ_0 = the value for μ in the null hypothesis, σ = assumed value of the population standard deviation.
Set **List** to **L1**
Set **Freq** to **1**
Use the **ARROW** to highlight the appropriate alternative hypothesis.
Press **ENTER**
Arrow down to "**Calculate**"
Press **ENTER**

If you selected "Stats", enter the values for the hypothesis test where μ_0 = the value for μ in the null hypothesis, σ = assumed value of the population standard deviation.
Enter the sample mean and sample size.
Use the **ARROW** to highlight the appropriate alternative hypothesis.
Press **ENTER**
Arrow down to "**Calculate**"
Press **ENTER**

The chosen test will be displayed as well as the *z*-test statistic, the *p*-value, the sample mean, and the sample size.

Example A manufacturer claims the average life expectancy of this particular model light-bulb is at least 10,000 hours with $\sigma = 1,000$ hours. A simple random sample of 40 lightbulbs shows a sample mean of 9,755 hours. Using $\sigma = .05$, test the manufacturer's claim.

For this problem, the hypotheses will be:

$$H_0: \mu \geq 10{,}000$$
$$H_a: \mu < 10{,}000$$

The screens are shown at right:

As you can see, the *p*-value is 0.061. Since $p > .05$, ***do not*** reject H_0.

Exercises 6.32–6.46

Learning the Mechanics

6.32 If a hypothesis test were conducted using $\alpha = .05$, for which of the following *p*-values would the null hypothesis be rejected?
a. .06   **b.** .10   **c.** .01
d. .001   **e.** .251   **f.** .042

6.33 For each α and observed significance level (*p*-value) pair, indicate whether the null hypothesis would be rejected.
a. $\alpha = .05$, *p*-value $= .10$
b. $\alpha = .10$, *p*-value $= .05$
c. $\alpha = .01$, *p*-value $= .001$
d. $\alpha = .025$, *p*-value $= .05$
e. $\alpha = .10$, *p*-value $= .45$

6.34 In a test of the hypothesis $H_0: \mu = 50$ versus $H_a: \mu > 50$, a sample of $n = 100$ observations possessed mean $\bar{x} = 49.4$ and standard deviation $s = 4.1$. Find and interpret the *p*-value for this test.

6.35 In a test of $H_0: \mu = 100$ against $H_a: \mu > 100$, the sample data yielded the test statistic $z = 2.17$. Find and interpret the *p*-value for the test.

6.36 In a test of the hypothesis $H_0: \mu = 10$ versus $H_a: \mu \neq 10$, a sample of $n = 50$ observations possessed mean $\bar{x} = 10.7$ and standard deviation $s = 3.1$. Find and interpret the *p*-value for this test.

6.37 In a test of $H_0: \mu = 100$ against $H_a: \mu \neq 100$, the sample
NW data yielded the test statistic $z = 2.17$. Find the *p*-value for the test.

6.38 In a test of $H_0: \mu = 75$ performed using the computer, SPSS reports a two-tailed *p*-value of .1032. Make the appropriate conclusion for each of the following situations:
a. $H_a: \mu < 75$, $z = -1.63$, $\alpha = .05$
b. $H_a: \mu < 75$, $z = 1.63$, $\alpha = .10$

c. $H_a: \mu > 75$, $z = 1.63$, $\alpha = .10$
d. $H_a: \mu \neq 75$, $z = -1.63$, $\alpha = .01$

6.39 An analyst tested the null hypothesis $\mu \geq 20$ against the alternative hypothesis that $\mu < 20$. The analyst reported a *p*-value of .06. What is the smallest value of α for which the null hypothesis would be rejected?

Applying the Concepts—Basic

HYBRIDCARS

6.40 **Prices of hybrid cars.** Refer to the *BusinessWeek.com* list-
NW ing of the July 2006 dealers prices for the hybrid Toyota Prius, Exercise 6.22 (p. 358). Recall that the data are saved in the **HYBRIDCARS** file. The results of the test of $H_0: \mu = 25{,}000$ versus $H_a: \mu \neq 25{,}000$ is shown in the accompanying MINITAB printout below. Find and interpret the *p*-value of the test.

DIAMONDS

6.41 **Size of diamonds sold at retail.** Refer to the carat data for 308 diamonds saved in the **DIAMONDS** file. In Exercise 6.24 (p. 358) you tested $H_0: \mu = .6$ against $H_a: \mu \neq .6$ based on a random sample of 30 diamonds.
a. Use a statistical software package to find the *p*-value of the test.
b. Compare the *p*-value to $\alpha = .05$ and make the appropriate conclusion.

TEES

6.42 **Testing mean weight of golf tees.** In Exercise 6.25 (p. 358) you tested $H_0: \mu = .250$ versus $H_a: \mu \neq .250$, where μ is the population mean weight of plastic golf tees. An SPSS printout for the hypothesis test is at the top of p. 366. Locate the *p*-value on the printout and interpret its value.

MINITAB Output for Exercise 6.40

```
Test of mu = 25000 vs not = 25000


Variable    N     Mean    StDev   SE Mean        95% CI           T       P
PRICE      160  25476.7  2429.8    192.1   (25097.3, 25856.1)   2.48    0.014
```

SPSS Output for Exercise 6.42

One-Sample Test

					95% Confidence Interval of the Difference	
				Test Value = .250		
	t	df	Sig. (2-tailed)	Mean Difference	Lower	Upper
WEIGHT	7.019	39	.000	.002475	.00176	.00319

FUNERAL

6.43 Revenue for a full-service funeral. Refer to the National Funeral Directors Association study of the average fee charged for a full-service funeral, Exercise 6.28 (p. 359). Recall that a test was conducted to determine if the true mean fee charged exceeds $6,500. The data (recorded in thousands of dollars) for the sample of 36 funeral homes were analyzed using Excel/PHStat2. The resulting printout of the test of hypothesis is shown below.

	A	B
1	t Test for Hypothesis of the Mean	
2		
3	Data	
4	Null Hypothesis μ=	6.5
5	Level of Significance	0.05
6	Sample Size	36
7	Sample Mean	6.819444444
8	Sample Standard Deviation	1.26487028
9		
10	Intermediate Calculations	
11	Standard Error of the Mean	0.210811713
12	Degrees of Freedom	35
13	t Test Statistic	1.515306903
14		
15	Upper-Tail Test	
16	Upper Critical Value	1.689572855
17	p-Value	0.069337376
18	Do not reject the null hypothesis	

a. Locate the p-value for this upper-tailed test of hypothesis.

b. Use the p-value to make a decision regarding the null hypothesis tested. Does the decision agree with your decision in Exercise 6.28?

Applying the Concepts—Intermediate

6.44 Ages of cable TV shoppers. In a paper presented at the 2000 Conference of the International Association for Time Use Research, professor Margaret Sanik of Ohio State University reported the results of her study on American cable TV viewers who purchase items from one of the home shopping channels. She found that the average age of these cable TV shoppers was 51 years. Suppose you want to test the null hypothesis, $H_0: \mu = 51$, using a sample of $n = 50$ cable TV shoppers.

a. Find the p-value of a two-tailed test if $\bar{x} = 52.3$ and $s = 7.1$.

b. Find the p-value of an upper-tailed test if $\bar{x} = 52.3$ and $s = 7.1$.

c. Find the p-value of a two-tailed test if $\bar{x} = 52.3$ and $s = 10.4$.

d. For each of the tests, parts **a–c**, give a value of α that will lead to a rejection of the null hypothesis.

e. If $\bar{x} = 52.3$, give a value of s that will yield a two-tailed p-value of .01 or less.

6.45 Cigarette smoking in China. An article published in the *Journal of the American Medical Association* (Oct. 16, 1995) calls smoking in China "a public health emergency." The researchers found that smokers in China smoke an average of 16.5 cigarettes a day. The high smoking rate is one reason why the tobacco industry is the central government's largest source of tax revenue. Has the average number of cigarettes smoked per day by Chinese smokers increased over the past 2 years? Consider that in a random sample of 200 Chinese smokers in 2007, the number of cigarettes smoked per day had a mean of 17.05 and a standard deviation of 5.21.

a. Set up the null and alternative hypotheses for testing whether Chinese smokers smoke, on average, more cigarettes a day in 2007 than in 1995. (Assume that the population mean for 1995 is $\mu = 16.5$.)

b. Compute and interpret the observed significance level of the test.

c. Why is a two-tailed test inappropriate for this problem?

6.46 Feminized faces in TV commercials. Television commercials most often employ females, or "feminized" males, to pitch a company's product. Research published in *Nature* (Aug. 27, 1998) revealed that people are, in fact, more attracted to "feminized" faces, regardless of gender. In one experiment, 50 human subjects viewed both a Japanese female and a Caucasian male face on a computer. Using special computer graphics, each subject could morph the faces (by making them more feminine or more masculine) until they attained the "most attractive" face. The level of feminization x (measured as a percentage) was measured.

a. For the Japanese female face, $\bar{x} = 10.2\%$ and $s = 31.3\%$. The researchers used this sample information to test the null hypothesis of a mean level of feminization equal to 0%. Verify that the test statistic is equal to 2.3.

b. Refer to part **a**. The researchers reported the p-value of the test as $p = .021$. Verify and interpret this result.

c. For the Caucasian male face, $\bar{x} = 15.0\%$ and $s = 25.1\%$. The researchers reported the test statistic (for the test of the null hypothesis stated in part **a**) as 4.23 with an associated p-value of approximately 0. Verify and interpret these results.

6.4 Small-Sample Test of Hypothesis about a Population Mean

A manufacturing operation consists of a single-machine-tool system that produces an average of 15.5 transformer parts every hour. After undergoing a complete overhaul, the system was monitored by observing the number of parts produced in each of 17 randomly selected 1-hour periods. The mean and standard deviation for the 17 production runs are

$$\bar{x} = 15.42 \qquad s = .16$$

Does this sample provide sufficient evidence to conclude that the true mean number of parts produced every hour by the overhauled system differs from 15.5?

This inference can be placed in a test of hypothesis framework. We establish the preoverhaul mean as the null hypothesized value and utilize a two-tailed alternative that the true mean of the overhauled system differs from the preoverhaul mean:

H_0: $\mu = 15.5$ (Mean of overhauled system equals 15.5 parts per hour)

H_a: $\mu \neq 15.5$ (Mean of overhauled system differs from 15.5 parts per hour)

Recall from Section 5.3 that when we are faced with making inferences about a population mean using the information in a small sample, two problems emerge:

1. The normality of the sampling distribution for $\bar{x}$ does not follow from the Central Limit Theorem when the sample size is small. We must assume that the distribution of measurements from which the sample was selected is approximately normally distributed in order to ensure the approximate normality of the sampling distribution of $\bar{x}$.

2. If the population standard deviation σ is unknown, as is usually the case, then we cannot assume that s will provide a good approximation for σ when the sample size is small. Instead, we must use the t-distribution rather than the standard normal z-distribution to make inferences about the population mean μ.

Therefore, as the test statistic of a small-sample test of a population mean, we use the t-statistic:

$$\text{Test statistic: } t = \frac{\bar{x} - \mu_0}{s/\sqrt{n}} = \frac{\bar{x} - 15.5}{s/\sqrt{n}}$$

where μ_0 is the null hypothesized value of the population mean, μ. In our example, $\mu_0 = 15.5$.

To find the rejection region, we must specify the value of α, the probability that the test will lead to rejection of the null hypothesis when it is true, and then consult the t-table (Table V of Appendix B). Using $\alpha = .05$, the two-tailed rejection region is

$$\text{Rejection region: } t_{\alpha/2} = t_{.025} = 2.120 \text{ with } n - 1 = 16 \text{ degrees of freedom}$$

Reject H_0 if $t < -2.120$ or $t > 2.120$

The rejection region is shown in Figure 6.12.

We are now prepared to calculate the test statistic and reach a conclusion:

$$t = \frac{\bar{x} - \mu_0}{s/\sqrt{n}} = \frac{15.42 - 15.50}{.16/\sqrt{17}} = \frac{-.08}{.0388} = -2.06$$

Since the calculated value of t does not fall in the rejection region (Figure 6.12), we cannot reject H_0 at the $\alpha = .05$ level of significance. Based on the sample evidence, we should not conclude that the mean number of parts produced per hour by the overhauled system differs from 15.5.

It is interesting to note that the calculated t value, -2.06, is *less than* the .05 level z value, -1.96. The implication is that if we had *incorrectly* used a z-statistic for this test, we would have rejected the null hypothesis at the .05 level, concluding that the mean production per hour of the overhauled system differs from 15.5 parts. The important point is that the statistical procedure to be used must always be closely scrutinized and all the assumptions understood. Many statistical distortions are the result of misapplications of otherwise valid procedures.

FIGURE 6.12

Two-tailed rejection region for small-sample t-test

The technique for conducting a small-sample test of hypothesis about a population mean is summarized in the following box.

Small-Sample Test of Hypothesis about μ

One-Tailed Test	Two-Tailed Test
H_0: $\mu = \mu_0$	H_0: $\mu = \mu_0$
H_a: $\mu < \mu_0$ (or H_a: $\mu > \mu_0$)	H_a: $\mu \neq \mu_0$
Test statistic: $t = \dfrac{\bar{x} - \mu_0}{s/\sqrt{n}}$	Test statistic: $t = \dfrac{\bar{x} - \mu_0}{s/\sqrt{n}}$
Rejection region: $t < -t_\alpha$	Rejection region: $|t| > t_{\alpha/2}$
(or $t > t_\alpha$ when H_a: $\mu > \mu_0$)	

where t_α and $t_{\alpha/2}$ are based on $(n-1)$ degrees of freedom

---

Conditions Required for a Valid Small-Sample Hypothesis Test for μ

1. A random sample is selected from the target population.
2. The population from which the sample is selected has a distribution that is approximately normal.

EXAMPLE 6.5

Conducting a Small-Sample Test for μ— Does a New Engine Meet Air Pollution Standards?

Problem   A major car manufacturer wants to test a new engine to determine whether it meets new air pollution standards. The mean emission μ of all engines of this type must be less than 20 parts per million of carbon. Ten engines are manufactured for testing purposes, and the emission level of each is determined. The data (in parts per million) are listed in Table 6.5.

Do the data supply sufficient evidence to allow the manufacturer to conclude that this type of engine meets the pollution standard? Assume that the production process is stable and the manufacturer is willing to risk a Type I error with probability $\alpha = .01$.

 EMISSIONS

TABLE 6.5   Emission Levels for Ten Engines

15.6	16.2	22.5	20.5	16.4	19.4	16.6	17.9	12.7	13.9

Solution   The manufacturer wants to support the research hypothesis that the mean emission level μ for all engines of this type is less than 20 parts per million. The elements of this small-sample one-tailed test are

$$H_0: \mu = 20 \quad \text{(Mean emission level equals 20 ppm)}$$
$$H_a: \mu < 20 \quad \text{(Mean emission level is less than 20 ppm—}$$
$$\text{i.e., engine meets pollution standard)}$$

$$\text{Test statistic: } t = \frac{\bar{x} - 20}{s/\sqrt{n}}$$

Assumption: The relative frequency distribution of the population of emission levels for all engines of this type is approximately normal.

Rejection region: For $\alpha = .01$ and df $= n - 1 = 9$, the one-tailed rejection region (see Figure 6.13) is $t < -t_{.01} = -2.821$.

To calculate the test statistic, we entered the data into a computer and analyzed it using MINITAB. The MINITAB printout is shown in Figure 6.14. From the printout, we obtain $\bar{x} = 17.17$, $s = 2.98$. Substituting these values into the test statistic formula, we get

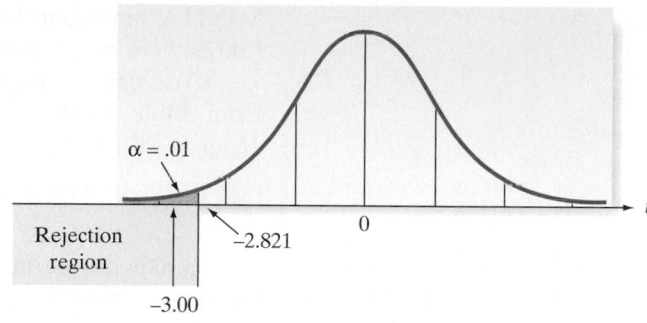

FIGURE 6.13

A t-distribution with 9 df
and the rejection region for
Example 6.5

FIGURE 6.14

MINITAB printout for test
of mean emissions

```
Test of mu = 20 vs < 20


                                            95%
                                          Upper
Variable    N      Mean    StDev  SE Mean   Bound      T      P
EMIT       10   17.1700   2.9814   0.9428  18.8983  -3.00  0.007
```

$$t = \frac{\bar{x} - 20}{s/\sqrt{n}} = \frac{17.17 - 20}{2.98/\sqrt{10}} = -3.00$$

Since the calculated t falls in the rejection region (see Figure 6.13), the manufacturer concludes that $\mu < 20$ parts per million and the new engine type meets the pollution standard.

Look Back Are you satisfied with the reliability associated with this inference? The probability is only $\alpha = .01$ that the test would support the research hypothesis if in fact it were false.

Now Work Exercise 6.50a,b

EXAMPLE 6.6

The p-Value for a
Small-Sample Test of μ

Problem Find the observed significance level for the test described in Example 6.5. Interpret the result.

Solution The test of Example 6.5 was a lower-tailed test: $H_0: \mu = 20$ versus $H_a: \mu < 20$. Since the value of t computed from the sample data was $t = -3.00$, the observed significance level (or p-value) for the test is equal to the probability that t would assume a value less than or equal to -3.00 if in fact H_0 were true. This is equal to the area in the lower tail of the t-distribution (shaded in Figure 6.15).

One way to find this area (i.e., the p-value for the test) is to consult the t-table (Table V in Appendix B). Unlike the table of areas under the normal curve, Table V gives only the t values corresponding to the areas .100, .050, .025, .010, .005, .001, and .0005. Therefore, we can only approximate the p-value for the test. Since the observed t-value was based on 9 degrees of freedom, we use the df = 9 row in Table V and move across the row until we reach the t values that are closest to the observed $t = -3.00$. [*Note:* We ignore the minus sign.] The t-values corresponding to p-values of .010 and .005 are 2.821 and 3.250, respectively. Since the observed t value falls between $t_{.010}$ and $t_{.005}$, the p-value for the test lies between .005 and .010. In other words, $.005 < p$-value $< .01$. Thus, we would reject the null hypothesis, $H_0: \mu = 20$ parts per million, for any value of α larger than .01 (the upper bound of the p-value).

A second, more accurate, way to obtain the p-value is to use a statistical software package to conduct the test of hypothesis. The

FIGURE 6.15

The observed significance level for the test of Example 6.5

MINITAB printout shown in Figure 6.14 gives both the test statistic (-3.00) and p-value $(.007)$.

You can see that the actual p-value of the test falls within the bounds obtained from Table V. Thus, the two methods agree; we will reject $H_0: \mu = 20$ in favor of $H_a: \mu < 20$ for any α level larger than .01.

> **Now Work Exercise 6.50c**

Small-sample inferences typically require more assumptions and provide less information about the population parameter than do large-sample inferences. Nevertheless, the t-test is a method of testing a hypothesis about a population mean of a normal distribution when only a small number of observations are available. What can be done if you know that the population relative frequency distribution is decidedly nonnormal, say highly skewed?

> **What Can Be Done If the Population Relative Frequency Distribution Departs Greatly from Normal?**
>
> *Answer:* Use one of the nonparametric statistical methods of Chapter 14.

ACTIVITY 6.2: *Keep the Change:* Tests of Hypotheses

In this activity, we will test claims that the mean amount transferred for any single purchase is $0.50 and that the mean amount that Bank of America matches for a customer during the first 90 days of enrollment is at least $25. We will be working with data sets from Activity 1.1, p. 16 and Activity 4.2, p. 268.

1. Based on the assumption that all transfer amounts between $0.00 and $0.99 seem to be equally likely to occur, one may conclude that the mean of the amounts transferred is about $0.50. Explain how someone who doesn't believe this conclusion would use a test of hypothesis to argue that the conclusion is false.

2. Suppose that your original data set *Amounts Transferred* from Activity 1.1 represents a random sample of amounts transferred for all Bank of America customers' purchases. Does your sample meet the requirements for performing either a large-sample or a small-sample test of hypothesis about the population mean? Explain. If your data meet the criteria for one of the tests, perform that test at $\alpha = .05$.

3. Use the pooled data set of *Amounts Transferred* from Activity 4.2 to represent a random sample of amounts transferred for all Bank of America customers' purchases. Explain how the conditions for the large-sample test of hypothesis about a population mean are met. Then perform the test at $\alpha = .05$. Do your results suggest that the mean may be something other than $0.50? Explain.

4. A friend suggests to you that the mean amount the bank matches for a customer during the first 90 days is at least $25. Explain how you could use a test of hypothesis to argue that your friend is wrong.

5. Suppose that your data set *Bank Matching* from Activity 1.1 represents a random sample of all Bank of America customers' bank matching. Perform an appropriate test of hypotheses at $\alpha = .05$ against your friend's claim. Assume that the underlying distribution is normal, if necessary. Does the test provide evidence that your friend's claim is false?

Keep the results from this activity for use in other activities.

Exercises 6.47–6.60

Learning the Mechanics

6.47 a. Consider testing $H_0: \mu = 80$. Under what conditions should you use the t-distribution to conduct the test?

b. In what ways are the distributions of the z-statistic and t-test statistic alike? How do they differ?

6.48 For each of the following rejection regions, sketch the sampling distribution of t, and indicate the location of the rejection region on your sketch:

a. $t > 1.440$ where df $= 6$
b. $t < -1.782$ where df $= 12$
c. $t < -2.060$ or $t > 2.060$ where df $= 25$
d. For each of parts **a–c**, what is the probability that a Type I error will be made?

6.49 A random sample of n observations is selected from a normal population to test the null hypothesis that $\mu = 10$. Specify the rejection region for each of the following combinations of H_a, α, and n:

a. $H_a: \mu \neq 10; \alpha = .05; n = 14$
b. $H_a: \mu > 10; \alpha = .01; n = 24$
c. $H_a: \mu > 10; \alpha = .10; n = 9$
d. $H_a: \mu < 10; \alpha = .01; n = 12$
e. $H_a: \mu \neq 10; \alpha = .10; n = 20$
f. $H_a: \mu < 10; \alpha = .05; n = 4$

6.50 A sample of five measurements, randomly selected from a
NW normally distributed population, resulted in the following
summary statistics: $\bar{x} = 4.8$, $s = 1.3$.
   a. Test the null hypothesis that the mean of the population is 6 against the alternative hypothesis, $\mu < 6$. Use $\alpha = .05$.
   b. Test the null hypothesis that the mean of the population is 6 against the alternative hypothesis, $\mu \neq 6$. Use $\alpha = .05$.
   c. Find the observed significance level for each test.

6.51 Suppose you conduct a t-test for the null hypothesis $H_0: \mu = 1,000$ versus the alternative hypothesis $H_a: \mu > 1,000$ based on a sample of 17 observations. The test results are: $t = 1.89$ and p-value $= .038$.
   a. What assumptions are necessary for the validity of this procedure?
   b. Interpret the results of the test.
   c. Suppose the alternative hypothesis had been the two-tailed $H_a: \mu \neq 1,000$. If the t-statistic were unchanged, then what would the p-value be for this test? Interpret the p-value for the two-tailed test.

Applying the Concepts—Basic

6.52 A new dental bonding agent. When bonding teeth, orthodontists must maintain a dry field. A new bonding adhesive (called *Smartbond*) has been developed to eliminate the necessity of a dry field. However, there is concern that the new bonding adhesive is not as strong as the current standard, a composite adhesive (*Trends in Biomaterials & Artificial Organs*, Jan. 2003). Tests on a sample of 10 extracted teeth bonded with the new adhesive resulted in a mean breaking strength (after 24 hours) of $\bar{x} = 5.07$ Mpa and a standard deviation of $s = .46$ Mpa. Orthodontists want to know if the true mean breaking strength of the new bonding adhesive is less than 5.70 Mpa, the mean breaking strength of the composite adhesive.
   a. Set up the null and alternative hypothesis for the test.
   b. Find the rejection region for the test using $\alpha = .01$.
   c. Compute the test statistic.
   d. Give the appropriate conclusion for the test.
   e. What conditions are required for the test results to be valid?

6.53 Surface roughness of pipe. Refer to the *Anti-corrosion Methods and Materials* (Vol. 50, 2003) study of the surface

roughness of coated interior pipe used in oil fields, Exercise 5.32 (p. 311). The data (in micrometers) for 20 sampled pipe sections are reproduced in the table.
   a. Give the null and alternative hypotheses for testing whether the mean surface roughness of coated interior pipe, μ, differs from 2 micrometers.
   b. Find the test statistic for the hypothesis test.
   c. Give the rejection region for the hypothesis test, using $\alpha = .05$.
   d. State the appropriate conclusion for the hypothesis test.
   e. A MINITAB printout giving the test results is shown below. Find and interpret the p-value of the test.
   f. In Exercise 5.32 you found a 95% confidence interval for μ. Explain why the confidence interval and test lead to the same conclusion about μ.

⊙ **ROUGHPIPE**

| 1.72 | 2.50 | 2.16 | 2.13 | 1.06 | 2.24 | 2.31 | 2.03 | 1.09 | 1.40 |
| 2.57 | 2.64 | 1.26 | 2.05 | 1.19 | 2.13 | 1.27 | 1.51 | 2.41 | 1.95 |

Source: Farshad, F., and Pesacreta, T. "Coated Pipe Interior Surface Roughness as Measured by Three Scanning Probe Instruments." *Anti-corrosion Methods and Materials*, Vol. 50, No. 1, 2003 (Table III).

6.54 Product usage index. Information Resources, Inc., a Chicago-based research organization, tracks supermarket sales in 28 metropolitan markets in the United States. They convert their data for specific products to an index that measures product usage relative to the national average usage. For example, Green Bay, Wisconsin's, ketchup index is 143, the highest in the nation. This means that Green Bay residents consume 43% more ketchup, on average, than the mean national consumption rate. The table lists the salad dressings index for each in a sample of seven Southeastern cities.

⊙ **SALAD**

Salad Dressings Index (U.S. mean = 100)

Charlotte, N.C.	124	Memphis, Tenn.	90
Birmingham, Al.	99	Atlanta, Ga.	111
Raleigh, N.C.	124	Nashville, Tenn.	89
Knoxville, Tenn.	99		

Source: Wall Street Journal Interactive Edition, Jan. 5, 2000.

   a. Specify the appropriate null and alternative hypotheses for testing whether the true mean consumption rate of salad dressings in the Southeastern United States is different than the mean national consumption rate of 100.
   b. What assumptions about the sample and population must hold in order for it to be appropriate to use a t-statistic in conducting the hypothesis test?

MINITAB Output for Exercise 6.53

One-Sample T: ROUGH

```
Test of mu = 2 vs not = 2


Variable    N    Mean     StDev   SE Mean        95% CI           T      P
ROUGH      20  1.88100  0.52391  0.11715  (1.63580, 2.12620)  -1.02  0.322
```

SPSS Output for Exercise 6.55

One-Sample Test

| | Test Value = 2550 | | | | 95% Confidence Interval of the Difference | |
	t	df	Sig. (2-tailed)	Mean Difference	Lower	Upper
POURTEMP	1.210	9	.257	8.70	-7.57	24.97

c. Conduct the hypothesis test using $\alpha = .05$.

d. Is the observed significance level of the test greater or less than .05? Justify your answer.

6.55 Pouring temperature of an iron automotive casting. The Cleveland Casting Plant produces iron automotive castings for Ford Motor Company (*Quality Engineering*, Vol. 7, 1995). The pouring temperatures (in degrees Fahrenheit) for a sample of 10 crankshafts produced at the plant are listed below. When the process is stable, the target pouring temperature of the molton iron is 2,550 degrees. Conduct a test to determine whether the true mean pouring temperature differs from the target setting. Test using $\alpha = .01$. Use the SPSS printout above to carry out the test.

IRONTEMP

2,543	2,541	2,544	2,620	2,560	2,559	2,562
2,553	2,552	2,553				

Source: Price, B., and Barth, B. "A Structural Model Relating Process Inputs and Final Product Characteristics." *Quality Engineering*, Vol. 7, No. 4, 1995, p. 696 (Table 2).

Applying the Concepts—Intermediate

6.56 Testing the effectiveness of a new mosquito repellent. A study was conducted to evaluate the effectiveness of a new mosquito repellent designed by the U.S. Army to be applied as camouflage face paint (*Journal of the Mosquito Control Association,* June 1995). The repellent was applied to the forearms of five volunteers, and then the arms were exposed to 15 active mosquitoes for a 10-hour period. The percentage of the forearm surface area protected from bites (called *percent repellency*) was calculated for each of the five volunteers. For one color of paint (loam), the following summary statistics were obtained:

$$\bar{x} = 83\% \qquad s = 15\%$$

a. The new repellent is considered effective if it provides a percent repellency of at least 95. Conduct a test to determine whether the mean repellency percentage of the new mosquito repellent is less than 95. Test using $\alpha = .10$

b. What assumptions are required for the hypothesis test in part **a** to be valid?

6.57 Minimizing tractor skidding distance. Refer to the *Journal of Forest Engineering* (July 1999) study of minimizing tractor skidding distances along a new road in a European forest, Exercise 5.33 (p. 311). The skidding distances (in meters) were measured at 20 randomly selected road sites. The data are repeated below. Recall that a logger working on the road claims the mean skidding distance is at least 425 meters. Is there sufficient evidence to refute this claim? Use $\alpha = .10$.

SKIDDING

488	350	457	199	285	409	435	574	439	546
385	295	184	261	273	400	311	312	141	425

Source: Tujek, J., and Pacola, E. "Algorithms for Skidding Distance Modeling on a Raster Digital Terrain Model." *Journal of Forest Engineering,* Vol. 10, No. 1, July 1999 (Table 1).

6.58 Active nuclear power plants. Refer to the U.S. Energy Information Administration's list of active nuclear power plants operating in each of a sample of 20 states, Exercise 2.54 (p. 73). The data, saved in the **NUCLEAR** file, are reproduced in the next table.

a. Is there sufficient evidence to claim that the mean number of active nuclear power plants operating in all states exceeds 3? Test using $\alpha = .10$.

b. Are the conditions required for a valid small-sample test reasonably satisfied? Explain.

c. Eliminate the lowest two values and the highest two values from the data set, then conduct the test of part **a** on the smaller data set. What impact does this have on the test results?

d. Why is it dangerous to eliminate data points in order to satisfy an assumption for a test of hypothesis?

NUCLEAR

State	Number of Power Plants	State	Number of Power Plants
Alabama	5	New Hampshire	1
Arizona	3	New York	6
California	4	North Carolina	5
Florida	5	Ohio	2
Georgia	4	Pennsylvania	9
Illinois	13	South Carolina	7
Kansas	1	Tennessee	3
Louisiana	2	Texas	4
Massachusetts	1	Vermont	1
Mississippi	1	Wisconsin	3

Source: Statistical Abstract of the United States, 2000 (Table 966). U.S. Energy Information Administration, Electric Power Annual.

6.59 Crack intensity of paved highways. The Mississippi Department of Transportation collected data on the number of cracks (called *crack intensity*) in an undivided two-lane highway using van-mounted state-of-the-art video technology (*Journal of Infrastructure Systems,* Mar. 1995). The mean number of cracks found in a sample of eight 50-meter sections of the highway was $\bar{x} = .210$, with a variance of $s^2 = .011$. Suppose the American Association of State Highway and Transportation Officials (AASHTO) recommends a maximum mean crack intensity of .100 for safety purposes. Is there evidence to say that the true mean crack intensity of the

Mississippi highway exceeds the AASHTO recommended maximum? Use $\alpha = .01$ in the test.

Applying the Concepts—Advanced

6.60 Arsenic in smelters. The Occupational Safety and Health Act (OSHA) allows issuance of engineering standards to ensure safe workplaces for all Americans. The maximum allowable mean level of arsenic in smelters, herbicide production facilities, and other places where arsenic is used is .004 milligrams per cubic meter of air. Suppose smelters at two plants are being investigated to determine whether they are meeting OSHA standards. Two analyses of the air are made

at each plant, and the results (in milligrams per cubic meter of air) are shown in the table. A claim is made that the OSHA standard is violated at Plant 2 but not at Plant 1. Do you agree?

ARSENIC

PLANT 1		PLANT 2	
Observation	Arsenic Level	Observation	Arsenic Level
1	.01	1	.05
2	.005	2	.09

6.5 Large-Sample Test of Hypothesis about a Population Proportion

Inferences about population proportions (or percentages) are often made in the context of the probability, p, of "success" for a binomial distribution. We saw how to use large samples from binomial distributions to form confidence intervals for p in Section 5.4. We now consider tests of hypotheses about p.

For example, consider the problem of *insider trading* in the stock market. Insider trading is the buying and selling of stock by an individual privy to inside information in a company, usually a high level executive in the firm. The Securities and Exchange Commission (SEC) imposes strict guidelines about insider trading so that all investors can have equal access to information that may affect the stock's price. An investor wishing to test the effectiveness of the SEC guidelines monitors the market for a period of a year and records the number of times a stock price increases the day following a significant purchase of stock by an insider. For a total of 576 such transactions, the stock increased the following day 327 times. Does this sample provide evidence that the stock price may be affected by insider trading?

We first view this as a binomial experiment, with the 576 transactions as the trials, and success representing an increase in the stock's price the following day. Let p represent the probability that the stock price will increase following a large insider purchase. If the insider purchase has no effect on the stock price (that is, if the information available to the insider is identical to that available to the general market), then the investor expects the probability of a stock increase to be the same as that of a decrease, or $p = .5$. On the other hand, if insider trading affects the stock price (indicating that the market has not fully accounted for the information known to the insiders), then the investor expects the stock either to decrease or to increase more than half the time following significant insider transactions; that is, $p \neq .5$.

We can now place the problem in the context of a test of hypothesis:

$$H_0: p = .5 \text{ (Probability of stock increase equals .5 —}$$
$$\text{i.e., insider purchase has no effect on stock price)}$$

$$H_a: p \neq .5 \text{ (Probability of stock increase differs from .5 —}$$
$$\text{i.e., insider trading effects stock price)}$$

Recall that the sample proportion, $\hat{p}$, is really just the sample mean of the outcomes of the individual binomial trials and, as such, is approximately normally distributed (for large samples) according to the Central Limit Theorem. Thus, for large samples we can use the standard normal z as the test statistic:

$$\text{Test statistic: } z = \frac{\text{Sample proportion} - \text{Null hypothesized proportion}}{\text{Standard deviation of sample proportion}}$$

$$= \frac{\hat{p} - p_0}{\sigma_{\hat{p}}}$$

where we use the symbol p_0 to represent the null hypothesized value of p.

FIGURE 6.16

Rejection region for insider trading example

Rejection region: We use the standard normal distribution to find the appropriate rejection region for the specified value of α. Using $\alpha = .05$, the two-tailed rejection region is

$$z < -z_{\alpha/2} = -z_{.025} = -1.96 \quad \text{or} \quad z > z_{\alpha/2} = z_{.025} = 1.96$$

See Figure 6.16.

We are now prepared to calculate the value of the test statistic. Before doing so, we want to be sure that the sample size is large enough to ensure that the normal approximation for the sampling distribution of $\hat{p}$ is reasonable. Recall from Section 5.4 that we require both np and nq to be at least 15. Since the null hypothesized value, p_0, is assumed to be the true value of p until our test procedure indicates otherwise, then we check to see if $np_0 \geq 15$ and $nq_0 \geq 15$ (where $q_0 = 1 - p_0$). Now, $np_0 = (576)(.5) = 288$ and $nq_0 = (576)(.5) = 288$; therefore, the normal distribution will provide a reasonable approximation for the sampling distribution of $\hat{p}$.

Returning to the hypothesis test at hand, the proportion of the sampled transactions that resulted in a stock increase is

$$\hat{p} = \frac{327}{576} = .568$$

Finally, we calculate the number of standard deviations (the z value) between the sampled and hypothesized value of the binomial proportion:

$$z = \frac{\hat{p} - p_0}{\sigma_{\hat{p}}} = \frac{\hat{p} - p_0}{\sqrt{p_0 q_0 / n}} = \frac{.568 - .5}{.021} = \frac{.068}{.021} = 3.24$$

The implication is that the observed sample proportion is (approximately) 3.24 standard deviations above the null hypothesized proportion .5 (Figure 6.16). Therefore, we reject the null hypothesis, concluding at the .05 level of significance that the true probability of an increase or decrease in a stock's price differs from .5 the day following insider purchase of the stock. It appears that an insider purchase significantly increases the probability that the stock price will increase the following day. (To estimate the magnitude of the probability of an increase, a confidence interval can be constructed.)

The test of hypothesis about a population proportion p is summarized in the next box. Note that the procedure is entirely analogous to that used for conducting large-sample tests about a population mean.

Large-Sample Test of Hypothesis about *p*

One-Tailed Test	Two-Tailed Test
H_0: $p = p_0$ (p_0 = hypothesized value of p)	H_0: $p = p_0$
H_a: $p < p_0$ (or H_a: $p > p_0$)	H_a: $p \neq p_0$
Test statistic: $z = \dfrac{\hat{p} - p_0}{\sigma_{\hat{p}}}$	Test statistic: $z = \dfrac{\hat{p} - p_0}{\sigma_{\hat{p}}}$

where, according to H_0, $\sigma_{\hat{p}} = \sqrt{p_0 q_0 / n}$ and $q_0 = 1 - p_0$

Rejection region: | *Rejection region:* $|z| > z_{\alpha/2}$
$z < -z_{\alpha}$ (or $z > z_{\alpha}$ when H_a: $p > p_0$) |

Conditions Required for a Valid Large-Sample Hypothesis Test for *p*

1. A random sample is selected from a binomial population.

2. The sample size n is large. (This condition will be satisfied if both $np_0 \geq 15$ and $nq_0 \geq 15$.)

EXAMPLE 6.7

Conducting a
Hypothesis Test for p,
the Proportion
of Defective Batteries.

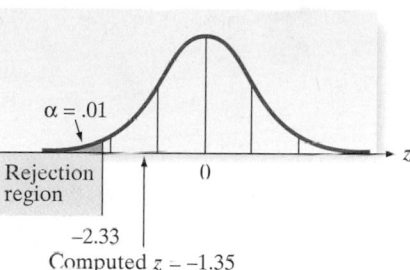

Problem The reputations (and hence sales) of many businesses can be severely damaged by shipments of manufactured items that contain a large percentage of defectives. For example, a manufacturer of alkaline batteries may want to be reasonably certain that fewer than 5% of its batteries are defective. Suppose 300 batteries are randomly selected from a very large shipment; each is tested and 10 defective batteries are found. Does this provide sufficient evidence for the manufacturer to conclude that the fraction defective in the entire shipment is less than .05? Use $\alpha = .01$.

Solution The objective of the sampling is to determine whether there is sufficient evidence to indicate that the fraction defective, p, is less than .05. Consequently, we will test the null hypothesis that $p = .05$ against the alternative hypothesis that $p < .05$. The elements of the test are

H_0: $p = .05$ (Fraction of defective batteries equals .05)

H_a: $p < .05$ (Fraction of defective batteries is less than .05)

Test statistic: $z = \dfrac{\hat{p} - p_0}{\sigma_{\hat{p}}}$

Rejection region: $z < -z_{.01} = -2.33$
(see Figure 6.17)

Before conducting the test, we check to determine whether the sample size is large enough to use the normal approximation to the sampling distribution of $\hat{p}$. Since $np_0 = (300)(.05) = 15$ and $nq_0 = (300)(.95) = 285$ are both at least 15, the normal approximation will be adequate.

We now calculate the test statistic:

$$z = \frac{\hat{p} - .05}{\sigma_{\hat{p}}} = \frac{(10/300) - .05}{\sqrt{p_0 q_0/n}} = \frac{.033 - .05}{\sqrt{p_0 q_0/300}}$$

FIGURE 6.17
Rejection region for Example 6.7

Notice that we use p_0 to calculate $\sigma_{\hat{p}}$ because, in contrast to calculating $\sigma_{\hat{p}}$ for a confidence interval, the test statistic is computed on the assumption that the null hypothesis is true—that is, $p = p_0$. Therefore, substituting the values for $\hat{p}$ and p_0 into the z-statistic, we obtain

$$z \approx \frac{-.017}{\sqrt{(.05)(.95)/300}} = \frac{-.017}{.0126} = -1.35$$

As shown in Figure 6.17, the calculated z value does not fall in the rejection region. Therefore, there is insufficient evidence at the .01 level of significance to indicate that the shipment contains fewer than 5% defective batteries.

Now Work Exercise 6.62a,b

EXAMPLE 6.8

The p-Value for
a Test about p

Problem In Example 6.7 we found that we did not have sufficient evidence, at the $\alpha = .01$ level of significance, to indicate that the fraction defective p of alkaline batteries was less than $p = .05$. How strong was the weight of evidence favoring the alternative hypothesis (H_a: $p < .05$)? Find the observed significance level for the test.

Solution The computed value of the test statistic z was $z = -1.35$. Therefore, for this lower-tailed test, the observed significance level is

FIGURE 6.18

The observed significance level for Example 6.8

$$\text{Observed significance level} = P(z \le -1.35)$$

This lower-tail area is shown in Figure 6.18. The area between $z = 0$ and $z = 1.35$ is given in Table IV in Appendix B as .4115. Therefore, the observed significance level is $.5 - .4115 = .0885$.

Look Back Note that this probability is quite small. Although we did not reject H_0: $p = .05$ at $\alpha = .01$, the probability of observing a z value as small as or smaller than -1.35 is only .0885 if in fact H_0 is true. Therefore, we would reject H_0 if we choose $\alpha = .10$ (since the observed significance level is less than .10), and we would not reject H_0 (the conclusion of Example 6.7) if we choose $\alpha = .05$ or $\alpha = .01$

Now Work Exercise 6.62c

Small-sample test procedures are also available for p, although most surveys use samples that are large enough to employ the large-sample tests presented in this section. A test of proportions that can be applied to small samples is discussed in Chapter 9.

STATISTICS IN ACTION REVISITED

Testing a Population Proportion in the Kleenex® Survey

In the previous "Statistics in Action Revisited" (p. 363), we investigated Kimberly-Clark Corporation's assertion that the company should put 60 tissues in a cold-care box of Kleenex® tissues. We did this by testing the claim that the mean number of tissues used by a person with a cold is $\mu = 60$ using data collected from a survey of 250 Kleenex® users. Another approach to the problem is to consider the proportion of Kleenex® users who use fewer than 60 tissues when they have a cold. Now the population parameter of interest is p, the proportion of all Kleenex® users who use fewer than 60 tissues when they have a cold.

Kimberly-Clark Corporation's belief that the company should put 60 tissues in a cold-care box will be supported if the *median* number of tissues used is 60. Now, if the true median is, in fact, 60, then half of the Kleenex® users will use less than 60 tissues and half will use more than 60 tissues (i.e., $p = .5$). Is there evidence to indicate that the population proportion differs from .5? To answer

this question, we set up the following null and alternative hypothesis:

$$H_0: p = .5 \qquad H_a: p \ne .5$$

Recall that the survey results for the 250 sampled Kleenex® users are stored in the **TISSUES** data file. In addition to the number of tissues used by each person, the file contains a qualitative variable—called USED60—representing whether the person used fewer or more than 60 tissues. (The values of USED60 in the data set are "BELOW" or "ABOVE".) A MINITAB analysis of this variable yielded the printout displayed in Figure SIA6.2.

On the MINITAB printout, X represents the number of the 250 people with colds who used less than 60 tissues. Note that $X = 143$. This value is used to compute the test statistic, $z = 2.28$, highlighted on the printout. The p-value of the test, also highlighted on the printout, is p-value $= .023$. Since this value is less than $\alpha = .05$, there is sufficient evidence (at $\alpha = .05$) to reject H_0; we conclude that the proportion of all Kleenex® users who use fewer than 60 tissues when they have a cold differs from .5. However, if we test at $\alpha = .01$, there is insufficient evidence to reject H_0. Consequently, our choice of α (as in the previous "Statistics in the Action Revisited") is critical to our decision.

```
Test of p = 0.5 vs p not = 0.5

Event = BELOW


Variable    X    N   Sample p        95% CI        Z-Value   P-Value
USED60     143  250  0.572000  (0.510666, 0.633334)   2.28     0.023
```

Figure SIA6.2

MINITAB test of $p = .5$ for Kleenex® survey

Exercises 6.61–6.75

Learning the Mechanics

6.61 For the binomial sample sizes and null hypothesized values of p in each part, determine whether the sample size is large enough to use the normal approximation methodology presented in this section to conduct a test of the null hypothesis $H_0: p = p_0$.
  a. $n = 900, p_0 = .975$
  b. $n = 125, p_0 = .01$
  c. $n = 40, p_0 = .75$
  d. $n = 15, p_0 = .75$
  e. $n = 12, p_0 = .62$

6.62 Suppose a random sample of 100 observations from a binomial population gives a value of $\hat{p} = .63$ and you wish to test the null hypothesis that the population parameter p is equal to .70 against the alternative hypothesis that p is less than .70.
  a. Noting that $\hat{p} = .63$, what does your intuition tell you? Does the value of $\hat{p}$ appear to contradict the null hypothesis?
  b. Use the large-sample z-test to test $H_0: p = .70$ against the alternative hypothesis, $H_a: p < .70$. Use $\alpha = .05$. How do the test results compare with your intuitive decision from part **a**?
  c. Find and interpret the observed significance level of the test you conducted in part **b**.

6.63 Suppose the sample in Exercise 6.62 has produced $\hat{p} = .83$ and we wish to test $H_0: p = .9$ against the alternative $H_a: p < .9$.
  a. Calculate the value of the z statistic for this test.
  b. Note that the numerator of the z statistic ($\hat{p} - p_0 = .83 - .90 = -.07$) is the same as for Exercise 6.62. Considering this, why is the absolute value of z for this exercise larger than that calculated in Exercise 6.62?
  c. Complete the test using $\alpha = .05$ and interpret the result.
  d. Find the observed significance level for the test and interpret its value.

6.64 A statistics student used a computer program to test the null hypothesis $H_0: p = .5$ against the one-tailed alternative, $H_a: p > .5$. A sample of 500 observations are input into SPSS, which returns the following results: $z = .44$, two-tailed p-value = .33
  a. The student concludes, based on the p-value, that there is a 33% chance that the alternative hypothesis is true. Do you agree? If not, correct the interpretation.
  b. How would the p-value change if the alternative hypothesis was two-tailed, $H_a: p \neq .5$? Interpret this p-value.

6.65 Refer to Exercise 5.40 (p. 319), in which 50 consumers taste-tested a new snack food. Their responses (where $0 = $ do not like; $1 = $ like; $2 = $ indifferent) are reproduced below.

SNACK

1	0	0	1	2	0	1	1	0	0	0	1
0	2	0	2	2	0	0	1	1	0	0	0
0	1	0	2	0	0	0	1	0	0	1	0
0	1	0	1	0	2	0	0	1	1	0	0
0	1										

  a. Test $H_0: p = .5$ against $H_a: p > .5$, where p is the proportion of customers who do not like the snack food. Use $\alpha = .10$.
  b. Find the observed significance level of your test.

APPLET Applet Exercise 6.5

Use the applet entitled *Hypotheses Test for a Proportion* to investigate the relationships between the probabilities of Type I and Type II errors occurring at level .05 and .01. For this exercise, use $n = 100$, true $p = 0.5$, and alternative *not equal*.
  a. Set null $p = .5$. What happens to the proportion of times the null hypothesis is rejected at the .05 level and at the .01 level as the applet is run more and more times? What type of error has occurred when the null hypothesis is rejected in this situation? Based on your results, is this type of error more likely to occur at level .05 or at level .01? Explain.
  b. Set null $p = .6$. What happens to the proportion of times the null hypothesis is *not* rejected at the .05 level and at the .01 level as the applet is run more and more times? What type of error has occurred when the null hypothesis is *not* rejected in this situation? Based on your results, is this type of error more likely to occur at level .05 or at level .01? Explain.
  c. Use your results from parts **a** and **b** to make a general statement about the probabilities of Type I and Type II errors at levels .05 and .01.

APPLET Applet Exercise 6.6

Use the applet entitled *Hypotheses Test for a Proportion* to investigate the effect of the true population proportion p on the probability of a Type I error occurring. For this exercise, use $n = 100$, and alternative *not equal*.
  a. Set true $p = .5$ and null $p = .5$. Run the applet several times and record the proportion of times the null hypothesis is rejected at the .01 level.
  b. Clear the applet and repeat part **a** for true $p = .1$ and null $p = .1$. Then repeat one more time for true $p = .01$ and null $p = .01$.
  c. Based on your results from parts **a** and **b**, what can you conclude about the probability of a Type I error occurring as the true population proportion gets closer to 0?

Applying the Concepts—Basic

6.66 **"Made in the USA" survey.** Refer to the *Journal of Global Business* (Spring 2002) study of what "Made in the USA" means to consumers, Exercise 2.8 (p. 48). Recall that 64 of 106 randomly selected shoppers believed "Made in the USA" means 100% of labor and materials are from the United States. Let p represent the true proportion of consumers who believe "Made in the USA" means 100% of labor and materials are from the United States.
  a. Calculate a point estimate for p.
  b. A claim is made that $p = .70$. Set up the null and alternative hypothesis to test this claim.
  c. Calculate the test statistic for the test, part **b**.
  d. Find the rejection region for the test if $\alpha = .01$.
  e. Use the results, parts **c** and **d**, to make the appropriate conclusion.

6.67 Unauthorized computer use. Refer to the Computer Security Institute (CSI) survey of computer crime, Exercise 2.12 (p. 48). Recall that in 1999, 62% of businesses suffered unauthorized use of computer systems. In a survey taken 7 years later, 320 of a sample of 616 businesses reported unauthorized use of computer systems. (*Computer Security Issues & Trends,* Spring 2006). Let p represent the true proportion of businesses that reported unauthorized use of computer systems in 2006.
a. Calculate a point estimate for p.
b. Set up the null and alternative hypothesis to test whether the value of p has changed since 1999.

c. Calculate the test statistic for the test, part **b**.
d. Find the rejection region for the test if $\alpha = .05$.

e. Use the results, parts **c** and **d**, to make the appropriate conclusion.
f. Find the p-value of the test and confirm that the conclusion based on the p-value agrees with the conclusion in part **e**.

6.68 Accuracy of price scanners at Wal-Mart. Refer to Exercise 5.49 (p. 320) and the study of the accuracy of checkout scanners at Wal-Mart stores in California. Recall that the National Institute for Standards and Technology (NIST) mandates that for every 100 items scanned through the electronic checkout scanner at a retail store, no more than two should have an inaccurate price. A study of random items purchased at California Wal-Mart stores found that 8.3% had the wrong price (*Tampa Tribune,* Nov. 22, 2005). Assume that the study included 1,000 randomly selected items.
a. Identify the population parameter of interest in the study.
b. Set up H_0 and H_a for a test to determine if the true proportion of items scanned at California Wal-Mart stores exceeds the 2% NIST standard.
c. Find the test statistic and rejection region (at $\alpha = .05$) for the test.
d. Give a practical interpretation of the test.
e. What conditions are required for the inference, part **d**, to be valid? Are these conditions met?

6.69 Toothpaste brands with the ADA seal. *Consumer Reports* evaluated and rated 46 brands of toothpaste. One attribute examined in the study was whether or not a toothpaste brand carries an American Dental Association (ADA) seal verifying effective decay prevention. The data for the 46 brands (coded 1 = ADA seal, 0 = no ADA seal) are listed here.

ADA

0	0	0	0	0	0	1	1	1	0	0	1
0	1	0	0	0	0	1	1	1	0	1	1
1	1	0	0	0	0	0	1	0	0	1	1
1	0	1	0	1	1	1	0	0	0		

a. Give the null and alternative hypotheses for testing whether the true proportion of toothpaste brands with the ADA seal verifying effective decay prevention is less than .5.
b. Locate the p-value on the MINITAB printout at the top of the page.
c. Make the appropriate conclusion using $\alpha = .10$.

MINITAB Output for Exercise 6.69

```
Test of p = 0.5 vs p < 0.5

Event = 1

                                         95%
                                       Upper      Exact
Variable    X    N   Sample p         Bound      P-Value
ADASEAL    20   46   0.434783       0.566289      0.231
```

6.70 Minority vacation-home owners. The *National Association of Realtors* (NAR) reported the results of a May 2006 survey of vacation-home owners. In a sample of 416 households that owned one or more vacation homes, 46 were minorities. Prior to 2003, 6% of vacation-home owners were minorities.
a. Do the survey results allow the NAR to conclude (at $\alpha = .01$) that the percentage of vacation-home owners in 2006 who are minorities is larger than 6%?
b. The NAR sent the survey questionnaire to a nationwide sample of 45,000 households that owned vacation homes. Only 416 of the households responded to the survey. How might this bias the survey results?

Applying the Concepts—Intermediate

6.71 Effectiveness of skin cream. Pond's Age-Defying Complex, a cream with alpha hydroxy acid, advertises that it can reduce wrinkles and improve the skin. In a study published in *Archives of Dermatology* (June 1996), 33 middle-aged women used a cream with alpha hydroxy acid for 22 weeks. At the end of the study period, a dermatologist judged whether each woman exhibited skin improvement. The results for the 33 women (where I = improved skin and N = no improvement) are listed in the accompanying table.
a. Do the data provide sufficient evidence to conclude that the cream will improve the skin of more than 60% of middle-aged women? Test using $\alpha = .05$.
b. Find and interpret the p-value of the test.

SKINCREAM

I	I	N	I	N	N	I	I	I	I	I	I
N	I	I	I	N	I	I	N	I	N	N	I
I	I	I	I	I	N	I	I	N			

6.72 Reporting company changes to the SEC. The Securities Exchange Commission (SEC) requires a company to file Form 8-K to report material changes in its financial condition or operation. Common material events are changes in directors, auditors, and assets disposition. Up until 2004, companies had 15 business days to submit Form 8-K. Currently, the SEC requires the form be submitted within 4 business days of the material event (*Sarbanes-Oxley Act,* Section 409). Previous research has indicated that as high as 10% of firms were in violation of the old, 15-day rule. Old Dominion University accounting professor Rob Pinsker conducted a study to determine if firms with material changes were able to comply with the new "4-day" rule (Information Systems Mid-Year Meeting, 2004). In a sample of 462 firms with material events, only 23 were in violation of the new 4-day requirement for filing. Are you able to conclude that the true percentage of firms in violation of the new 4-day rule for reporting material changes is less than 10%? Make your inference at a significance level of $\alpha = .01$.

6.73 Choosing portable grill displays. Refer to the *Journal of Consumer Research* (Mar. 2003) experiment on influencing the choices of others by offering undesirable alternatives, Exercise 3.17 (p. 144). Recall that each of 124 college students selected three portable grills from five to display on the showroom floor. The students were instructed to include Grill #2 (a smaller-sized grill) and select the remaining two grills in the display to maximize purchases of Grill #2. If the six possible grill display combinations (1-2-3, 1-2-4, 1-2-5, 2-3-4, 2-3-5, and 2-4-5) are selected at random, then the proportion of students selecting any display will be $1/6 = .167$. One theory tested by the researcher is that the students will tend to choose the three-grill display so that Grill #2 is a compromise between a more desirable and a less desirable grill. Of the 124 students, 85 selected a three-grill display that was consistent with this theory. Use this information to test the theory proposed by the researcher at $\alpha = .05$.

Applying the Concepts—Advanced

6.74 Testing the placebo effect. *Is the placebo effective?* Describes the phenomenon of improvement in the condition of a pa

tient taking a placebo—a pill that looks and tastes real but contains no medically active chemicals. Physicians at a clinic in La Jolla, California, gave what they thought were drugs to 7,000 asthma, ulcer, and herpes patients. Although the doctors later learned that the drugs were really placebos, 70% of the patients reported an improved condition (*Forbes*, May 22, 1995). Use this information to test (at $\alpha = .05$) the placebo effect at the clinic. Assume that if the placebo is ineffective, the probability of a patient's condition improving is .5.

6.75 The Pepsi Challenge. "Take the Pepsi Challenge" was a marketing campaign used by the Pepsi-Cola Company. Coca-Cola drinkers participated in a blind taste test where they were asked to taste unmarked cups of Pepsi and Coke and were asked to select their favorite. In one Pepsi television commercial, an announcer states that "in recent blind taste tests, more than half the Diet Coke drinkers surveyed said they preferred the taste of Diet Pepsi" (*Consumer's Research*, May 1993). Suppose 100 Diet Coke drinkers took the Pepsi Challenge and 56 preferred the taste of Diet Pepsi. Determine if more than half of all Diet Coke drinkers will select Diet Pepsi in the blind taste test. Select α to minimize the probability of a Type I error. What are the consequences of the test results from Coca-Cola's perspective?

6.6 Calculating Type II Error Probabilities: More about β (Optional)

In our introduction to hypothesis testing in Section 6.1, we showed that the probability of committing a Type I error, α, can be controlled by the selection of the rejection region for the test. Thus, when the test statistic falls in the rejection region and we make the decision to reject the null hypothesis, we do so knowing the error rate for incorrect rejections of H_0. The situation corresponding to accepting the null hypothesis, and thereby risking a Type II error, is not generally as controllable. For that reason, we adopted a policy of nonrejection of H_0 when the test statistic does not fall in the rejection region, rather than risking an error of unknown magnitude.

To see how β, the probability of a Type II error, can be calculated for a test of hypothesis, recall the example in Section 6.1 in which a city tests a manufacturer's pipe to see whether it meets the requirement that the mean strength exceeds 2,400 pounds per linear foot. The setup for the test is as follows:

$$H_0: \mu = 2,400$$
$$H_a: \mu > 2,400$$

Test statistic: $z = \dfrac{\bar{x} - 2,400}{\sigma/\sqrt{n}}$

Rejection region: $z > 1.645$ for $\alpha = .05$

Figure 6.19(a) shows the rejection region for the **null distribution**—that is, the distribution of the test statistic assuming the null hypothesis is true. The area in the rejection region is .05, and this area represents α, the probability that the test statistic leads to rejection of H_0 when in fact H_0 is true.

The Type II error probability β is calculated assuming that the null hypothesis is false, because it is defined as the *probability of accepting H_0 when it is false*. Since H_0 is false for any value of μ exceeding 2,400, one value of β exists for each possible value of μ greater than 2,400 (an infinite number of possibilities). Figures 6.19(b)–(d) show three of the possibilities, corresponding to alternative hypothesis values of μ equal to 2,425, 2,450, and 2,475, respectively. Note that β is the area in the *nonrejection* (or *acceptance*) *region* in each of these distributions and that β decreases as the true value of μ moves

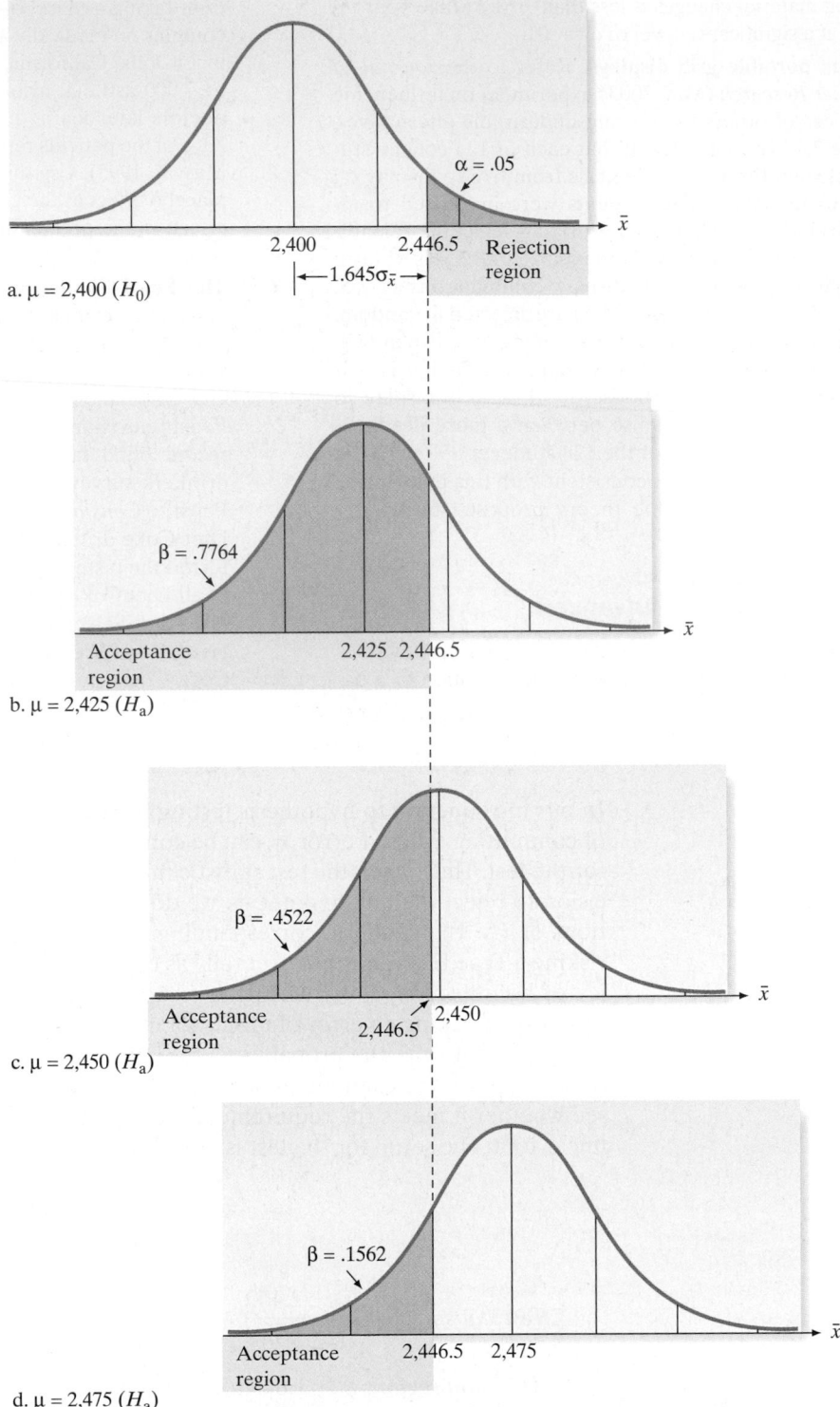

FIGURE 6.19

Values of α and β for various values of μ

a. $\mu = 2,400$ (H_0)

b. $\mu = 2,425$ (H_a)

c. $\mu = 2,450$ (H_a)

d. $\mu = 2,475$ (H_a)

farther from the null hypothesized value of $\mu = 2,400$. This is sensible because the probability of incorrectly accepting the null hypothesis should decrease as the distance between the null and alternative values of μ increases.

In order to calculate the value of β for a specific value of μ in H_a, we proceed as follows:

1. Calculate the value of $\bar{x}$ that corresponds to the border between the acceptance and rejection regions. For the sewer pipe example, this is the value of $\bar{x}$ that lies 1.645 standard deviations above $\mu = 2,400$ in the sampling distribution of $\bar{x}$.

Denoting this value by $\bar{x}_0$, corresponding to the largest value of $\bar{x}$ that supports the null hypothesis, we find (recalling that $s = 200$ and $n = 50$)

$$\bar{x}_0 = \mu_0 + 1.645\sigma_{\bar{x}} = 2{,}400 + 1.645\left(\frac{\sigma}{\sqrt{n}}\right)$$

$$\approx 2{,}400 + 1.645\left(\frac{s}{\sqrt{n}}\right) = 2{,}400 + 1.645\left(\frac{200}{\sqrt{50}}\right)$$

$$= 2{,}400 + 1.645(28.28) = 2{,}446.5$$

2. For a particular alternative distribution corresponding to a value of μ, denoted by μ_a, we calculate the z value corresponding to $\bar{x}_0$, the border between the rejection and acceptance regions. We then use this z value and Table IV of Appendix B to determine the area in the *acceptance region* under the alternative distribution. This area is the value of β corresponding to the particular alternative μ_a. For example, for the alternative $\mu_a = 2{,}425$, we calculate

$$z = \frac{\bar{x}_0 - 2{,}425}{\sigma_{\bar{x}}} = \frac{\bar{x}_0 - 2{,}425}{\sigma/\sqrt{n}}$$

$$\approx \frac{\bar{x}_0 - 2{,}425}{s/\sqrt{n}} = \frac{2{,}446.5 - 2{,}425}{28.28} = .76$$

Note in Figure 6.19(b) that the area in the acceptance region is the area to the left of $z = .76$. This area is

$$\beta = .5 + .2764 = .7764$$

Thus, the probability that the test procedure will lead to an incorrect acceptance of the null hypothesis $\mu = 2{,}400$ when in fact $\mu = 2{,}425$ is about .78. As the average strength of the pipe increases to 2,450, the value of β decreases to .4522 (Figure 6.19c). If the mean strength is further increased to 2,475, the value of β is further decreased to .1562 (Figure 6.19d). Thus, even if the true mean strength of the pipe exceeds the minimum specification by 75 pounds per linear foot, the test procedure will lead to an incorrect acceptance of the null hypothesis (rejection of the pipe) approximately 16% of the time. The upshot is that the pipe must be manufactured so that the mean strength well exceeds the minimum requirement if the manufacturer wants the probability of its acceptance by the city to be large (i.e., β to be small).

The steps for calculating β for a large-sample test about a population mean are summarized in the next box.

Steps for Calculating β for a Large-Sample Test about μ

1. Calculate the value(s) of $\bar{x}$ corresponding to the border(s) of the rejection region. There will be one border value for a one-tailed test and two for a two-tailed test. The formula is one of the following, corresponding to a test with level of significance α::

$$\text{Upper-tailed test: } \bar{x}_0 = \mu_0 + z_\alpha\sigma_{\bar{x}} \approx \mu_0 + z_\alpha\left(\frac{s}{\sqrt{n}}\right)$$

$$\text{Lower-tailed test: } \bar{x}_0 = \mu_0 - z_\alpha\sigma_{\bar{x}} \approx \mu_0 - z_\alpha\left(\frac{s}{\sqrt{n}}\right)$$

$$\text{Two-tailed test: } \bar{x}_{0.L} = \mu_0 - z_{\alpha/2}\sigma_{\bar{x}} \approx \mu_0 - z_{\alpha/2}\left(\frac{s}{\sqrt{n}}\right)$$

$$\bar{x}_{0.U} = \mu_0 + z_{\alpha/2}\sigma_{\bar{x}} \approx \mu_0 + z_{\alpha/2}\left(\frac{s}{\sqrt{n}}\right)$$

Continued

2. Specify the value of μ_a in the alternative hypothesis for which the value of β is to be calculated. Then convert the border value(s) of $\bar{x}_0$ to z value(s) using the alternative distribution with mean μ_a. The general formula for the z value is

$$z = \frac{\bar{x}_0 - \mu_a}{\sigma_{\bar{x}}}$$

Sketch the alternative distribution (centered at μ_a), and shade the area in the acceptance (nonrejection) region. Use the z statistic(s) and Table IV of Appendix B to find the shaded area, which is β.

Following the calculation of β for a particular value of μ_a, you should interpret the value in the context of the hypothesis testing application. It is often useful to interpret the value of $1 - \beta$, which is known as the *power of the test* corresponding to a particular alternative, μ_a. Since β is the probability of accepting the null hypothesis when the alternative hypothesis is true with $\mu = \mu_a$, $1 - \beta$ is the probability of the complementary event, or the probability of rejecting the null hypothesis when the alternative $H_a: \mu = \mu_a$ is true—that is, the power $1 - \beta$ measures the likelihood that the test procedure will lead to the correct decision (reject H_0) for a particular value of the mean in the alternative hypothesis.

> **Definition 6.2**
>
> The **power of a test** is the probability that the test will correctly lead to the rejection of the null hypothesis for a particular value of μ in the alternative hypothesis. The power is equal to $1 - \beta$ for the particular alternative considered.

For example, in the sewer pipe example we found that $\beta = .7764$ when $\mu = 2,425$. This is the probability that the test leads to the (incorrect) acceptance of the null hypothesis when $\mu = 2,425$. Or, equivalently, the power of the test is $1 - .7764 = .2236$, which means that the test will lead to the (correct) rejection of the null hypothesis only 22% of the time when the pipe exceeds specifications by 25 pounds per linear foot. When the manufacturer's pipe has a mean strength of 2,475 (that is, 75 pounds per linear foot in excess of specifications), the power of the test increases to $1 - .1562 = .8438$—that is, the test will lead to the acceptance of the manufacturer's pipe 84% of the time if $\mu = 2,475$.

EXAMPLE 6.9

Finding the Power of the Test

Problem Recall the quality control study in Examples 6.1 and 6.2, in which we tested to determine whether a cereal box filling machine was deviating from the specified mean fill of $\mu = 12$ ounces. The test setup is repeated here:

$$H_0: \mu = 12$$
$$H_a: \mu \neq 12 \ (\text{i.e., } \mu < 12 \text{ or } \mu > 12)$$

Test statistic: $z = \dfrac{\bar{x} - 12}{\sigma_{\bar{x}}}$

Rejection region: $z < -1.96 \quad \text{or} \quad z > 1.96 \qquad$ for $\alpha = .05$
$$z < -2.575 \quad \text{or} \quad z > 2.575 \qquad \text{for } \alpha = .01$$

Note that two rejection regions have been specified corresponding to values of $\alpha = .05$ and $\alpha = .01$, respectively. Assume that $n = 100$ and $s = .5$.

a. Suppose the machine is underfilling the boxes by an average of .1 ounce (i.e., $\mu = 11.9$). Calculate the values of β corresponding to the two rejection regions. Discuss the relationship between the values of α and β.

b. Calculate the power of the test for each of the rejection regions when $\mu = 11.9$.

Solution

a. We first consider the rejection region corresponding to $\alpha = .05$. The first step is to calculate the border values of $\bar{x}$ corresponding to the two-tailed rejection region, $z < -1.96$ or $z > 1.96$:

$$\bar{x}_{0.L} = \mu_0 - 1.96\sigma_{\bar{x}} \approx \mu_0 - 1.96\left(\frac{s}{\sqrt{n}}\right) = 12 - 1.96\left(\frac{.5}{10}\right) = 11.902$$

$$\bar{x}_{0.U} = \mu_0 + 1.96\sigma_{\bar{x}} \approx \mu_0 + 1.96\left(\frac{s}{\sqrt{n}}\right) = 12 + 1.96\left(\frac{.5}{10}\right) = 12.098$$

These border values are shown in Figure 6.20.

Next, we convert these values to z values in the alternative distribution with $\mu_a = 11.9$:

$$z_L = \frac{\bar{x}_{0.L} - \mu_a}{\sigma_{\bar{x}}} \approx \frac{11.902 - 11.9}{.05} = .04$$

$$z_U = \frac{\bar{x}_{0.U} - \mu_a}{\sigma_{\bar{x}}} \approx \frac{12.098 - 11.9}{.05} = 3.96$$

These z values are shown in Figure 6.20(b). You can see that the acceptance (or nonrejection) region is the area between them. Using Table IV of Appendix B, we

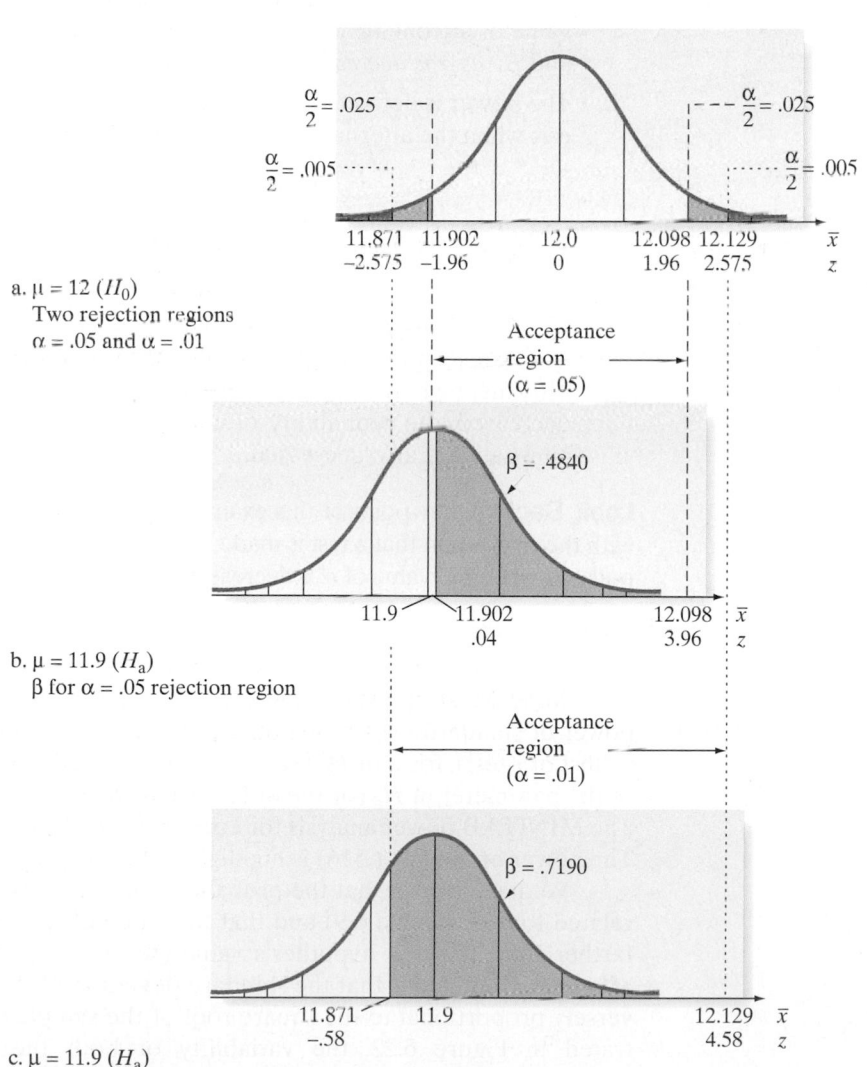

a. $\mu = 12$ (H_0)
   Two rejection regions
   $\alpha = .05$ and $\alpha = .01$

b. $\mu = 11.9$ (H_a)
   β for $\alpha = .05$ rejection region

c. $\mu = 11.9$ (H_a)
   β for $\alpha = .01$ rejection region

FIGURE 6.20

Calculation of β for filling machine example

find that the area between $z = 0$ and $z = .04$ is $.0160$, and the area between $z = 0$ and $z = 3.96$ is (approximately) $.5$ (since $z = 3.96$ is off the scale of Table IV). Then the area between $z = .04$ and $z = 3.96$ is, approximately,

$$\beta = .5 - .0160 = .4840$$

Thus, the test with $\alpha = .05$ will lead to a Type II error about 48% of the time when the machine is underfilling, on average, by .1 ounce.

For the rejection region corresponding to $\alpha = .01$, $z < -2.575$, or $z > 2.575$, we find

$$\bar{x}_{0,L} = 12 - 2.575\left(\frac{.5}{10}\right) = 11.871$$

$$\bar{x}_{0,U} = 12 + 2.575\left(\frac{.5}{10}\right) = 12.129$$

These border values of the rejection region are shown in Figure 6.20(c).

Converting these to z values in the alternative distribution with $\mu_a = 11.9$, we find $z_L = -.58$ and $z_U = 4.58$. The area between these values is, approximately,

$$\beta = .2190 + .5 = .7190$$

Thus, the chance that the test procedure with $\alpha = .01$ will lead to an incorrect acceptance of H_0 is about 72%.

Note that the value of β increases from $.4840$ to $.7190$ when we decrease the value of α from $.05$ to $.01$. This is a general property of the relationship between α and β: *as α is decreased (increased), β is increased (decreased).*

b. The power is defined to be the probability of (correctly) rejecting the null hypothesis when the alternative is true. When $\mu = 11.9$ and $\alpha = .05$, we find

$$\text{Power} = 1 - \beta = 1 - .4840 = .5160$$

When $\mu = 11.9$ and $\alpha = .01$, we find

$$\text{Power} = 1 - \beta = 1 - .7190 = .2810$$

You can see that the power of the test is decreased as the level of α is decreased. This means that as the probability of incorrectly rejecting the null hypothesis is decreased, the probability of correctly accepting the null hypothesis for a given alternative is also decreased.

Look Back A key point of this example is that the value of α must be selected carefully, with the realization that a test is made less capable of detecting departures from the null hypothesis when the value of α is decreased.

Note: Most statistical software packages now have options for computing the power of standard tests of hypothesis. Usually you will need to specify the type of test (z-test or t-test), form of H_a ($<, >$. or $\neq$), standard deviation, sample size, and the value of the parameter in H_a (or the difference between the value in H_0 and the value in H_a). The MINITAB power analysis for Example 6.9 when $\alpha = .05$ is displayed in Figure 6.21. The power of the test (.516) is highlighted on the printout.

We have shown that the probability of committing a Type II error, β, is inversely related to α (Example 6.9) and that the value of β decreases as the value of μ_a moves farther from the null hypothesis value (sewer pipe example). The sample size n also affects β. Remember that the standard deviation of the sampling distribution of $\bar{x}$ is inversely proportional to the square root of the sample size ($\sigma_{\bar{x}} = \sigma/\sqrt{n}$). Thus, as illustrated in Figure 6.22, the variability of both the null and alternative sampling

Power and Sample Size

```
1-Sample Z Test

Testing mean = null (versus not = null)
Calculating power for mean = null + difference
Alpha = 0.05  Assumed standard deviation = 0.5
```

FIGURE 6.21

MINITAB Power Analysis
for Example 6.9

```
               Sample
Difference      Size      Power
       0.1       100    0.516005
```

distributions is decreased as n is increased. If the value of α is specified and remains fixed, the value of β decreases as n increases, as illustrated in Figure 6.22. Conversely, the power of the test for a given alternative hypothesis is increased as the sample size is increased. The properties of β and power are summarized in the box.

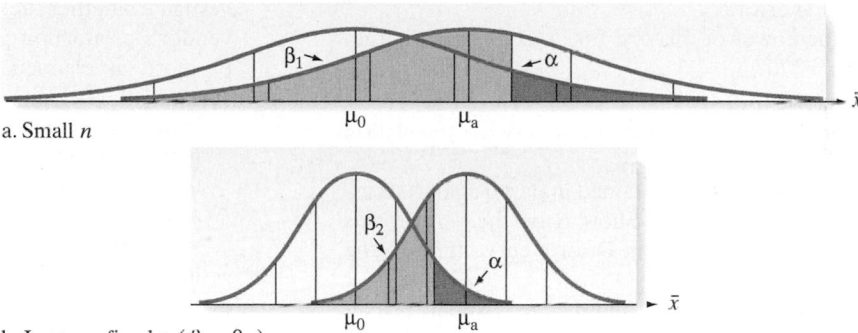

FIGURE 6.22

Relationship between α, β, and n

a. Small n

b. Large n, fixed α ($\beta_2 < \beta_1$)

Properties of β and Power

1. For fixed n and α, the value of β decreases and the power increases as the distance between the specified null value μ_0 and the specified alternative value μ_a increases (see Figure 6.19).

2. For fixed n and values of μ_0 and μ_a, the value of β increases and the power decreases as the value of α is decreased (see Figure 6.20).

3. For fixed α and values of μ_0 and μ_a, the value of β decreases and the power increases as the sample size n is increased (see Figure 6.22).

Exercises 6.76–6.85

Learning the Mechanics

6.76 a. List three factors that will increase the power of a test.
   b. What is the relationship between β, the probability of committing a Type II error, and the power of a test?

6.77 Suppose you want to test H_0: $\mu = 500$ against H_a: $\mu > 500$ using $\alpha = .05$. The population in question is normally distributed with standard deviation 100. A random sample of size $n = 25$ will be used.
   a. Sketch the sampling distribution of $\bar{x}$ assuming that H_0 is true.

   b. Find the value of $\bar{x}_0$, that value of $\bar{x}$ above which the null hypothesis will be rejected. Indicate the rejection region on your graph of part **a**. Shade the area above the rejection region and label it α.
   c. On your graph of part **a**, sketch the sampling distribution of $\bar{x}$ if $\mu = 550$. Shade the area under this distribution that corresponds to the probability that $\bar{x}$ falls in the nonrejection region when $\mu = 550$. Label this area β.
   d. Find β.
   e. Compute the power of this test for detecting the alternative H_a: $\mu = 550$.

6.78 Refer to Exercise 6.77.

    a. If $\mu = 575$ instead of 550, what is the probability that the hypothesis test will incorrectly fail to reject H_0? That is, what is β?

    b. If $\mu = 575$, what is the probability that the test will correctly reject the null hypothesis? That is, what is the power of the test?

    c. Compare β and the power of the test when $\mu = 575$ to the values you obtained in Exercise 6.77 for $\mu = 550$. Explain the differences.

6.79 It is desired to test $H_0: \mu = 75$ against $H_a: \mu < 75$ using $\alpha = .10$. The population in question is uniformly distributed with standard deviation 15. A random sample of size 49 will be drawn from the population.

    a. Describe the (approximate) sampling distribution of $\bar{x}$ under the assumption that H_0 is true.

    b. Describe the (approximate) sampling distribution of $\bar{x}$ under the assumption that the population mean is 70.

    c. If μ were really equal to 70, what is the probability that the hypothesis test would lead the investigator to commit a Type II error?

    d. What is the power of this test for detecting the alternative $H_a: \mu = 70$?

6.80 Refer to Exercise 6.79.

    a. Find β for each of the following values of the population mean: 74, 72, 70, 68, and 66.

    b. Plot each value of β you obtained in part **a** against its associated population mean. Show β on the vertical axis and μ on the horizontal axis. Draw a curve through the five points on your graph.

    c. Use your graph of part **b** to find the approximate probability that the hypothesis test will lead to a Type II error when $\mu = 73$.

    d. Convert each of the β values you calculated in part **a** to the power of the test at the specified value of μ. Plot the power on the vertical axis against μ on the horizontal axis. Compare the graph of part **b** to the *power curve* of this part.

    e. Examine the graphs of parts **b** and **d**. Explain what they reveal about the relationships among the distance between the true mean μ and the null hypothesized mean μ_0, the value of β, and the power.

6.81 Suppose you want to conduct the two-tailed test of $H_0: \mu = 30$ against $H_a: \mu \neq 30$ using $\alpha = .05$. A random sample of size 121 will be drawn from the population in question. Assume the population has a standard deviation equal to 1.2.

    a. Describe the sampling distribution of $\bar{x}$ under the assumption that H_0 is true.

    b. Describe the sampling distribution of $\bar{x}$ under the assumption that $\mu = 29.8$.

    c. If μ were really equal to 29.8, find the value of β associated with the test.

    d. Find the value of β for the alternative $H_a: \mu = 30.4$.

Applying the Concepts—Intermediate

6.82 **Square-footage of new California homes.** The average size of single-family homes built in the United States is 2,230 square feet, an increase of over 200 square feet a decade earlier (*Wall Street Journal Interactive Edition*, Jan. 7, 2000). A random sample of 100 new homes sold in California

yielded the following size information: $\bar{x} = 2{,}347$ square feet and $s = 257$ square feet.

    a. Assume the average size of U.S. homes is known with certainty. Do the sample data provide sufficient evidence to conclude that the mean size of California homes built exceeds the national average? Test using $\alpha = .01$.

    b. Suppose the actual mean size of new California homes was 2,330 square feet. What is the power of the test in part **a** to detect this 100-square-foot difference?

    c. If the California mean were actually 2,280 square feet, what is the power of the test in part **a** to detect this 50-square-foot difference?

6.83 **Manufacturers that practice sole sourcing.** If a manufacturer (the vendee) buys all items of a particular type from a particular vendor, the manufacturer is practicing *sole sourcing* (Schonberger and Knod, *Operations Management*, 1994). As part of a sole-sourcing arrangement, a vendor agrees to periodically supply its vendee with sample data from its production process. The vendee uses the data to investigate whether the mean length of rods produced by the vendor's production process is truly 5.0 millimeters (mm) or more, as claimed by the vendor and desired by the vendee.

    a. If the production process has a standard deviation of .01 mm, the vendor supplies $n = 100$ items to the vendee, and the vendee uses $\alpha = .05$ in testing $H_0: \mu = 5.0$ mm against $H_a: \mu < 5.0$ mm, what is the probability that the vendee's test will fail to reject the null hypothesis when in fact $\mu = 4.9975$ mm? What is the name given to this type of error?

    b. Refer to part **a**. What is the probability that the vendee's test will reject the null hypothesis when in fact $\mu = 5.0$? What is the name given to this type of error?

    c. What is the power of the test to detect a departure of .0025 mm below the specified mean rod length of 5.0 mm?

6.84 **Fuel economy of the Honda Civic.** According to the Environmental Protection Agency (EPA) *Fuel Economy Guide*, the 2006 Honda Civic automobile obtains a mean of 38 miles per gallon (mpg) on the highway. Suppose Honda claims that the EPA has underestimated the Civic's mileage. To support its assertion, the company selects 36 model 2006 Civic cars and records the mileage obtained for each car over a driving course similar to the one used by the EPA. The following data resulted: $\bar{x} = 40.3$ mpg, $s = 6.4$ mpg.

    a. If Honda wishes to show that the mean mpg for 2006 Civic autos is greater than 38 mpg, what should the alternative hypothesis be? The null hypothesis?

    b. Do the data provide sufficient evidence to support the auto manufacturer's claim? Test using $\alpha = .05$. List any assumptions you make in conducting the test.

    c. Calculate the power of the test for the mean values of 38.5, 39.0, 39.5, 40.0, and 40.5, assuming $s = 6.4$ is a good estimate of σ.

    d. Plot the power of the test on the vertical axis against the mean on the horizontal axis. Draw a curve through the points.

    e. Use the power curve of part **d** to estimate the power for the mean value $\mu = 39.75$. Calculate the power for this value of μ, and compare it to your approximation.

f. Use the power curve to approximate the power of the test when $\mu = 43$. If the true value of the mean mpg for this model is really 43, what (approximately) are the chances that the test will fail to reject the null hypothesis that the mean is 38?

6.85 Solder-joint inspections. Refer to Exercise 6.30 (p. 359), in which the performance of a particular type of laser-based inspection equipment was investigated. Assume that the standard deviation of the number of solder joints inspected on each run is 1.2. If $\alpha = .05$ is used in conducting the hypothesis test of interest using a sample of 48 circuit boards, and if the true mean number of solder joints that can be inspected is really equal to 9.5, what is the probability that the test will result in a Type II error?

6.7 Test of Hypothesis about a Population Variance (Optional)

Although many practical problems involve inferences about a population mean (or proportion), it is sometimes of interest to make an inference about a population variance, σ^2. To illustrate, a quality control supervisor in a cannery knows that the exact amount each can contains will vary since there are certain uncontrollable factors that affect the amount of fill. The mean fill per can is important, but equally important is the variation of fill. If σ^2, the variance of the fill, is large, some cans will contain too little and others too much. Suppose regulatory agencies specify that the standard deviation of the amount of fill should be less than .1 ounce. To determine whether the process is meeting this specification, the supervisor randomly selects 10 cans and weighs the contents of each. The results are given in Table 6.6.

 FILL AMOUNTS

TABLE 6.6　Fill Weights (in Ounces) of 10 Cans

16.00	16.06	15.95	16.04	16.10	16.05	16.02	16.03	15.99	16.02

Do these data provide sufficient evidence to indicate that the variability is as small as desired? To answer this question, we need a procedure for testing a hypothesis about σ^2.

Intuitively, it seems that we should compare the sample variance σ^2 to the hypothesized value of σ^2 (or s to σ) in order to make a decision about the population's variability. The quantity

$$\frac{(n-1)s^2}{\sigma^2}$$

has been shown to have a sampling distribution called a **chi-square** (χ^2) **distribution** when the population from which the sample is taken is *normally distributed*. Several chi-square distributions are shown in Figure 6.23.

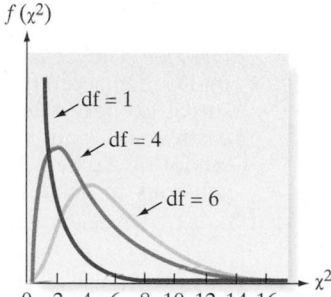

$f(\chi^2)$

df = 1
df = 4
df = 6

0　2　4　6　8　10 12 14 16　χ^2

FIGURE 6.23
Several χ^2 probability distributions

The upper-tail areas for this distribution have been tabulated and are given in Table VI of Appendix B, a portion of which is reproduced in Table 6.7. The table gives the values of χ^2, denoted as χ^2_α, that locate an area of α in the upper tail of the chi-square distribution; that is, $P(\chi^2 > \chi^2_\alpha) = \alpha$. In this case, as with the t-statistic, the shape of the chi-square distribution depends on the degrees of freedom associated with s^2, namely $(n-1)$. Thus, for $n = 10$ and an upper-tail value $\alpha = .05$, you will have $n - 1 = 9$ df and $\chi^2_{.05} = 16.9190$ (highlighted area in Table 6.7). To further illustrate the use of Table VI, we return to the can-filling example.

**TABLE 6.7 Reproduction of Part of Table VI in Appendix B:
Critical Values of Chi Square**

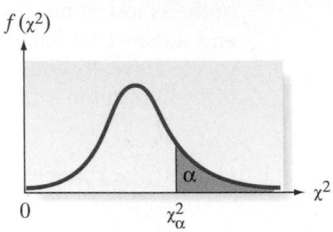

$f(\chi^2)$

Degrees of Freedom	$\chi^2_{.100}$	$\chi^2_{.050}$	$\chi^2_{.025}$	$\chi^2_{.010}$	$\chi^2_{.005}$
1	2.70554	3.84146	5.02389	6.63490	7.87944
2	4.60517	5.99147	7.37776	9.21034	10.5966
3	6.25139	7.81473	9.34840	11.3449	12.8381
4	7.77944	9.48773	11.1433	13.2767	14.8602
5	9.23635	11.0705	12.8325	15.0863	16.7496
6	10.6446	12.5916	14.4494	16.8119	18.5476
7	12.0170	14.0671	16.0128	18.4753	20.2777
8	13.3616	15.5073	17.5346	20.0902	21.9550
9	14.6837	16.9190	19.0228	21.6660	23.5893
10	15.9871	18.3070	20.4831	23.2093	25.1882
11	17.2750	19.6751	21.9200	24.7250	25.7569
12	18.5494	21.0261	23.3367	26.2170	28.2995
13	19.8119	22.3621	24.7356	27.6883	29.8194
14	21.0642	23.6848	26.1190	29.1413	31.3193
15	22.3072	24.9958	27.4884	30.5779	32.8013
16	23.5418	26.2862	28.8454	31.9999	34.2672
17	24.7690	27.5871	30.1910	33.4087	35.7185
18	25.9894	28.8693	31.5264	34.8053	37.1564
19	27.2036	30.1435	32.8523	36.1908	38.5822

Now Work Exercise 6.86

Biography

**FRIEDRICH R. HELMERT
(1843–1917)**

Helmert Transformations

German Friedrich Helmert studied engineering sciences and mathematics at Dresden University, where he earned his Ph.D., then accepted a position as a professor of geodesy—the scientific study of the earth's size and shape—at the technical school in Aachen. Helmert's mathematical solutions to geodesy problems led him to several statistics-related discoveries. His greatest statistical contribution occurred in 1876, when he was the first to prove that the sampling distribution of the sample variance, s^2, is a chi-square distribution. Helmert used a series of mathematical transformations to obtain the distribution of s^2—transformations that have since been named "Helmert transformations" in his honor. Later in life, Helmert was appointed professor of advanced geodesy at prestigious University of Berlin and director of the Prussian Geodetic Institute.

EXAMPLE 6.10

Conducting a Test for the Variance, σ^2, of Fill Weights

Problem Refer to the fill weights for the sample of ten 16-ounce cans in Table 6.6. Do the data provide sufficient evidence to indicate that the true standard deviation σ of the fill measurements of all 16-ounce cans is less than .1 ounce?

Solution Here, we want to test whether $\sigma < .1$. Since the null and alternative hypotheses must be stated in terms of σ^2 rather than σ, we want to test the null hypothesis that $\sigma^2 = (.1)^2 = .01$ against the alternative that $\sigma^2 < .01$. Therefore, the elements of the test are

H_0: $\sigma^2 = .01$ (Fill variance equals .01 —i.e., process specifications are not met)

H_a: $\sigma^2 < .01$ (Fill variance is less than .01 —i.e., process specifications are met)

Test statistic: $\chi^2 = \dfrac{(n-1)s^2}{\sigma^2}$

Assumption: The distribution of the amounts of fill is approximately normal.

Rejection region: The smaller the value of s^2 we observe, the stronger the evidence in favor of H_a. Thus, we reject H_0 for "small values" of the test statistic. With $\alpha = .05$ and 9 df, the χ^2 value for rejection is found in Table VI and pictured in Figure 6.24. We will reject H_0 if $\chi^2 < 3.32511$.

(Remember that the area given in Table VI is the area to the *right* of the numerical value in the table. Thus, to determine the lower-tail value, which has $\alpha = .05$ to its *left*, we used the $\chi^2_{.95}$ column in Table VI.)

FIGURE 6.24

Rejection region for Example 6.10

An Excel/PHStat2 analysis of the data in Table 6.6 is displayed in Figure 6.25. The value of s shown on the printout is $s = .04115$. Substituting into the formula for the test statistic, we have

$$\chi^2 = \frac{(n-1)s^2}{\sigma^2} = \frac{9(.04115)^2}{.01} = 1.524$$

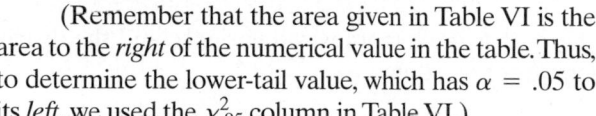

Chi-Square Test of Variance		
Data		
Null Hypothesis	$\sigma\mathbin{\char`\^}2=$	0.01
Level of Significance		0.05
Sample Size		10
Sample Standard Deviation		0.04115
Intermediate calculations		
Degrees of Freedom		9
Half Area		0.025
Chi-Square Statistic		1.62099025
Lower-Tail Test Results		
Lower Critical Value		3.32511514
p-Value		0.003035148
Reject the null hypothesis		

FIGURE 6.25

Excel/PHStat2 test for variance of fill weights

Since the test statistic falls into the rejection region, we reject H_0 in favor of H_a — that is, the supervisor can conclude that the variance σ^2 of the population of all amounts of fill is less than .01 ($\sigma < .1$) with probability of a Type I error equal to $\alpha = .05$. If this procedure is repeatedly used, it will incorrectly reject H_0 only 5% of the time. Thus, the quality control supervisor is confident in the decision that the cannery is operating within the desired limits of variability.

Look Back Note that both the test statistic (1.524) and the lower-tailed p-value of the test (.003) are shown at the bottom of the printout, Figure 6.25. Since $\alpha = .05$ exceeds the p-value, our decision to reject H_0 is confirmed.

Now Work Exercise 6.94

One-tailed and two-tailed tests of hypothesis for σ^2 are given in the following box.*

---

*A confidence interval for σ^2 can also be formed using the chi-square distribution with $(n-1)$ degrees of freedom. A $(1 - \alpha)100\%$ confidence interval is

$$\frac{(n-1)s^2}{\chi^2_{\alpha/2}} < \sigma^2 < \frac{(n-1)s^2}{\chi^2_{(1-\alpha/2)}}$$

Test of a Hypothesis about σ^2

One-Tailed Test	Two-Tailed Test
$H_0: \sigma^2 = \sigma_0^2$	$H_0: \sigma^2 = \sigma_0^2$
$H_a: \sigma^2 < \sigma_0^2$ (or $H_a: \sigma^2 > \sigma_0^2$)	$H_a: \sigma^2 \neq \sigma_0^2$
Test statistic: $\chi^2 = \dfrac{(n-1)s^2}{\sigma_0^2}$	Test statistic: $\chi^2 = \dfrac{(n-1)s^2}{\sigma_0^2}$
Rejection region: $\chi^2 < \chi^2_{(1-\alpha)}$	Rejection region: $\chi^2 < \chi^2_{(1-\alpha/2)}$ or $\chi^2 > \chi^2_{(\alpha/2)}$
(or $\chi^2 > \chi^2_\alpha$ when $H_a: \sigma^2 > \sigma_0^2$)	

where σ_0^2 is the hypothesized variance and the distribution of χ^2 is based on $(n-1)$ degrees of freedom.

Conditions Required for a Valid Hypothesis Test for s^2

1. A random sample is selected from the target population.
2. The population from which the sample is selected has a distribution that is approximately normal.

Caution

The procedure for conducting a hypothesis test for σ^2 in the above examples requires an assumption regardless of whether the sample size n is large or small. We must assume that the population from which the sample is selected has an approximate normal distribution. Unlike small sample tests for μ based on the t-statistic, *slight to moderate departures from normality will render the chi-square test invalid.*

Exercises 6.86–6.97

Learning the Mechanics

6.86 Let χ_0^2 be a particular value of χ^2. Find the value of χ_0^2
NW such that

   a. $P(\chi^2 > \chi_0^2) = .10$ for $n = 12$
   b. $P(\chi^2 > \chi_0^2) = .05$ for $n = 9$
   c. $P(\chi^2 > \chi_0^2) = .025$ for $n = 5$

6.87 A random sample of n observations is selected from a normal population to test the null hypothesis that $\sigma^2 = 25$. Specify the rejection region for each of the following combinations of H_a, α, and n:

   a. $H_a: \sigma^2 \neq 25; \alpha = .05; n = 16$
   b. $H_a: \sigma^2 > 25; \alpha = .01; n = 23$
   c. $H_a: \sigma^2 > 25; \alpha = .10; n = 15$
   d. $H_a: \sigma^2 < 25; \alpha = .01; n = 13$
   e. $H_a: \sigma^2 \neq 25; \alpha = .10; n = 7$
   f. $H_a: \sigma^2 < 25; \alpha = .05; n = 25$

6.88 A random sample of seven measurements gave $\bar{x} = 9.4$ and $s^2 = 4.84$.

   a. What assumptions must you make concerning the population in order to test a hypothesis about σ^2?
   b. Suppose the assumptions in part **a** are satisfied. Test the null hypothesis, $\sigma^2 = 1$, against the alternative hypothesis, $\sigma^2 > 1$. Use $\alpha = .05$.

   c. Test the null hypothesis that $\sigma^2 = 1$ against the alternative hypothesis that $\sigma^2 \neq 1$. Use $\alpha = .05$.

6.89 Refer to Exercise 6.88. Suppose we had $n = 100$, $\bar{x} = 9.4$, and $s^2 = 4.84$.

   a. Test the null hypothesis, $H_0: \sigma^2 = 1$, against the alternative hypothesis, $H_a: \sigma^2 > 1$.
   b. Compare your test result with that of Exercise 6.88.

6.90 A random sample of $n = 7$ observations from a normal population produced the following measurements: 4, 0, 6, 3, 3, 5, 9. Do the data provide sufficient evidence to indicate that $\sigma^2 < 1$? Test using $\alpha = .05$.

Applying the Concepts—Basic

6.91 Latex allergy in health care workers. Refer to the *Current Allergy & Clinical Immunology* (Mar. 2004) study of $n = 46$ hospital employees who were diagnosed with a latex allergy from exposure to the powder on latex gloves, Exercise 6.21 (p. 358). Recall that the number of latex gloves used per week by the sampled workers is summarized as follows: $\bar{x} = 19.3$ and $s = 11.9$. Let σ^2 represent the variance in the number of latex gloves used per week by all hospital employees. Consider testing $H_0: \sigma^2 = 100$ against $H_a: \sigma^2 = 100$.

a. Give the rejection region for the test at a significance level of $\alpha = .01$.

b. Calculate the value of the test statistic.

c. Use the results, parts **a** and **b**, to make the appropriate conclusion.

6.92 A new dental bonding agent. Refer to the *Trends in Biomaterials & Artificial Organs* (Jan. 2003) study of a new dental bonding adhesive (called *Smartbond*), Exercise 6.52 (p. 371). Recall that tests on a sample of 10 extracted teeth bonded with the new adhesive resulted in a mean breaking strength (after 24 hours) of $\bar{x} = 5.07$ Mpa and a standard deviation of $s = 46$ Mpa. The manufacturer must demonstrate that the breaking strength variance of the new adhesive is less than the variance of the standard composite adhesive, $\sigma^2 = .25$.

a. Set up the null and alternative hypothesis for the test.

b. Find the rejection region for the test using $\alpha = .01$.

c. Compute the test statistic.

d. Give the appropriate conclusion for the test.

e. What conditions are required for the test results to be valid?

⊚ **TEES**

6.93 Golf tees produced from an injection mold. Refer to Exercise 6.25 (p. 358) and the weights of tees produced by an injection mold process. If operating correctly, the process will produce tees with a weight variance of .000004 (ounces)^2. If the weight variance differs from .000004, the injection molder is out of control.

a. Set up the null and alternative hypothesis for testing whether the injection mold process is out of control.

b. Use the data saved in the TEES file to conduct the test, part **a**. Use $\alpha = .01$.

c. What conditions are required for inferences derived from the test to be valid? Are they reasonably satisfied?

Applying the Concepts—Intermediate

6.94 Point spreads of NFL games. Refer to the *Chance* (Fall 1998) study of point-spread errors in NFL games, Exercise 6.27 (p. 359). Recall that the difference between the actual game outcome and the point spread established by oddsmakers—the point-spread error—was calculated for 240 NFL games. The results are summarized as follows: $\bar{x} = -1.6$, $s = 13.3$. Suppose the researcher wants to know whether the true stan-

dard deviation of the point-spread errors exceeds 15. Conduct the analysis using $\alpha = .10$.

6.95 Do ball-bearings conform to specifications? It is essential in the manufacture of machinery to utilize parts that conform to specifications. In the past, diameters of the ball-bearings produced by a certain manufacturer had a variance of .00156. To cut costs, the manufacturer instituted a less expensive production method. The variance of the diameters of 100 randomly sampled bearings produced by the new process was .00211. Do the data provide sufficient evidence to indicate that diameters of ball-bearings produced by the new process are more variable than those produced by the old process?

⊚ **GASTURBINE**

6.96 Cooling method for gas turbines. Refer to the *Journal of Engineering for Gas Turbines and Power* (Jan. 2005) study of the performance of augmented gas turbine engines, Exercise 6.26 (p. 358). Recall that performance for each in a sample of 67 gas turbines was measured by heat rate (kilojoules per kilowatt per hour). The data are saved in the **GASTURBINE** file. Suppose that standard gas turbines have heat rates with a standard deviation of 1,500 kJ/kWh. Is there sufficient evidence to indicate that the heat rates of the augmented gas turbine engine are more variable than the heat rates of the standard gas turbine engine? Test using $\alpha = .05$.

Applying the Concepts—Advanced

6.97 Why do small firms export? Refer to the *Journal of Small Business Management* (Vol. 40, 2002) study of what motivates small firms to export, Exercise 6.31 (p. 359). Recall that in a survey of 137 exporting firms, each CEO was asked to respond to the statement "Management believes that the firm can achieve economies of scale by exporting" on a scale of 1 (strongly disagree) to 5 (strongly agree). Summary statistics for the $n = 137$ scale scores were reported as $\bar{x} = 3.85$ and $s = 1.5$.

a. Explain why the researcher will be unable to conclude that the true mean scale score exceeds 3.5 (as in Exercise 6.31) if the standard deviation of the scale scores is too large.

b. Give the largest value of the true standard deviation, σ, for which you will reject the null hypothesis $H_0: \mu = 3.5$ in favor of the alternative hypothesis $H_a: \mu > 3.5$ using $\alpha = .01$.

c. Based on the study results, is there evidence (at $\alpha = .01$) to indicate that σ is smaller than the value you determined in part **b**?

KEY TERMS

[Note: Starred (*) items are from the optional sections in this chapter.]

Alternative (research) hypothesis   346
*Chi-square distribution   387
Conclusion   350
Level of significance   350
Lower-tailed test   350

*Null distribution   379
Null hypothesis   346
Observed significance level (*p*-value)   360
One-tailed test   353
*Power of the test   382
Rejection region   347

Test statistic   346
Two-tailed test   353
Type I error   346
Type II error   348
Upper-tailed test   353

GUIDE TO SELECTING A ONE-SAMPLE HYPOTHESIS TEST

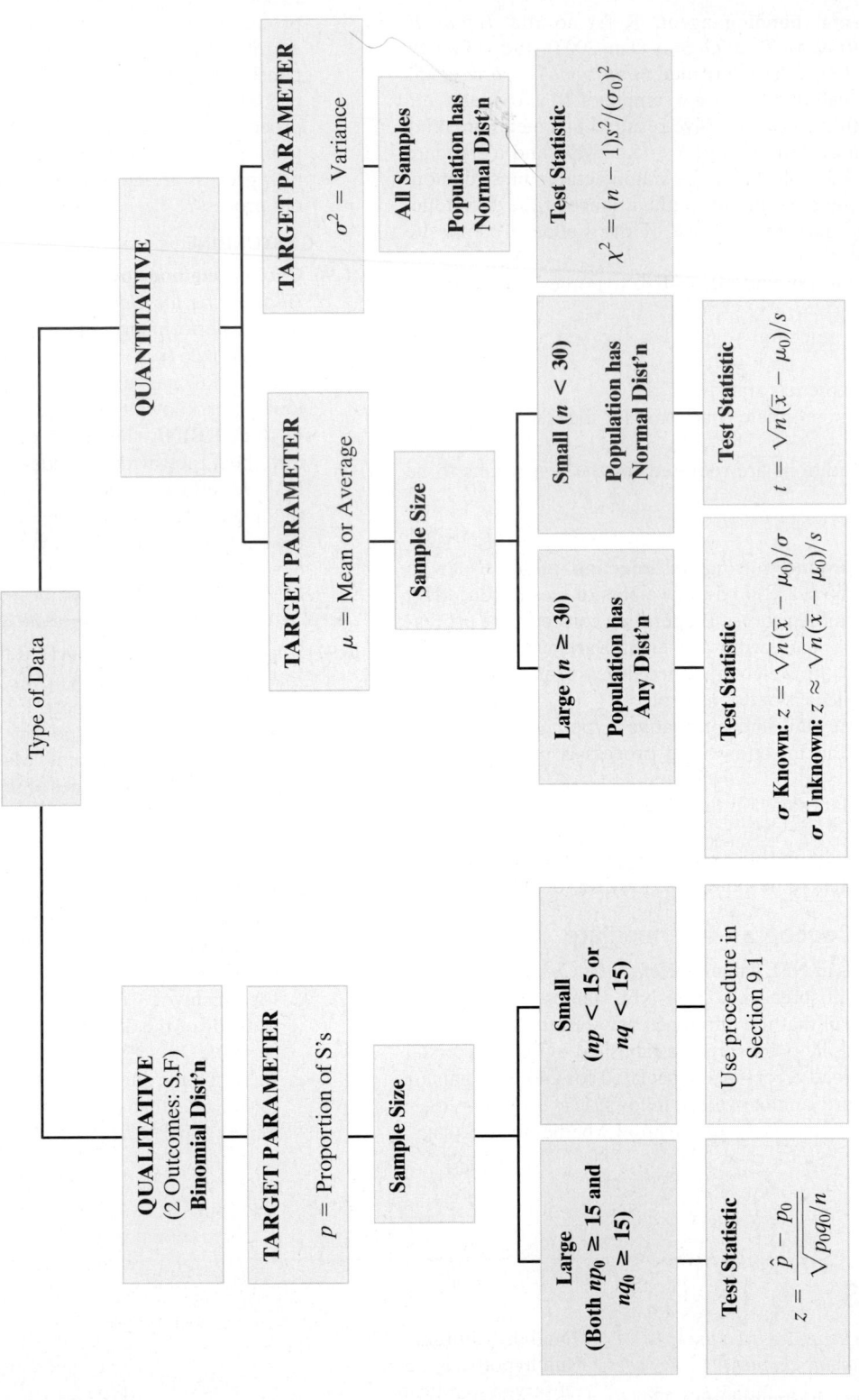

CHAPTER NOTES

Key Words for Identifying the Target Parameter:

μ—Mean, Average
p—Proportion, Fraction, Percentage, Rate, Probability
σ^2—Variance, Variability, Spread

Key Symbols

μ	Population mean
p	Population proportion, P(Success), in binomial trial
σ^2	Population variance
$\bar{x}$	Sample mean (estimator of μ)
$\hat{p}$	Sample proportion (estimator of p)
s^2	Sample variance (estimator of σ^2)
H_0	Null hypothesis
H_a	Alternative hypothesis
α	Probability of a Type I error
β	Probability of a Type II error
χ^2	Chi-square (sampling distribution of s^2 for normal data)

Elements of a Hypothesis Test:

1. *Null hypothesis* (H_0)
2. *Alternative hypothesis* (H_a)
3. *Test statistic* (z, t, or χ^2)
4. *Significance level* (α)
5. *p-value*
6. *Conclusion*

Type I Error = Reject H_0 when H_0 is true
(occurs with probability α)
Type II Error = Accept H_0 when H_0 is false
(occurs with probability β)
Power of a Test = P(Reject H_0 when H_0 is false)
$= 1 - \beta$

Forms of Alternative Hypothesis:

Lower-tailed: H_a: $\mu_0 < 50$
Upper-tailed: H_a: $\mu_0 > 50$
Two-tailed: H_a: $\mu_0 \neq 50$

Using p-values to Decide:

1. Choose significance level (α)
2. Obtain p-value of the test
3. If $\alpha > p$-value, Reject H_0

SUPPLEMENTARY EXERCISES 6.98–6.130

Note: List the assumptions necessary for the valid implementation of the statistical procedures you use in solving all these exercises. Starred (*) exercises refer to the optional sections in this chapter.

Learning the Mechanics

6.98 Specify the differences between a large-sample and small-sample test of hypothesis about a population mean μ. Focus on the assumptions and test statistics.

6.99 *Complete the following statement:* The smaller the p-value associated with a test of hypothesis, the stronger the support for the _____ hypothesis. Explain your answer.

6.100 Which of the elements of a test of hypothesis can and should be specified *prior* to analyzing the data that are to be utilized to conduct the test?

6.101 If you select a very small value for α when conducting a hypothesis test, will β tend to be big or small? Explain.

6.102 If the rejection of the null hypothesis of a particular test would cause your firm to go out of business, would you want α to be small or large? Explain.

6.103 A random sample of 20 observations selected from a normal population produced $\bar{x} = 72.6$ and $s^2 = 19.4$
 a. Test H_0: $\mu = 80$ against H_a: $\mu < 80$. Use $\alpha = .05$.
 b. Test H_0: $\mu = 80$ against H_a: $\mu \neq 80$. Use $\alpha = .01$.

6.104 A random sample of 175 measurements possessed a mean $\bar{x} = 8.2$ and a standard deviation $s = .79$.
 a. Test H_0: $\mu = 8.3$ against H_a: $\mu \neq 8.3$. Use $\alpha = .05$.
 b. Test H_0: $\mu = 8.4$ against H_a: $\mu \neq 8.4$. Use $\alpha = .05$.
 *c. Test H_0: $\sigma = 1$ against H_a: $\sigma \neq 1$. Use $\alpha = .05$.

 *d. Find the power of the test, part **a**, if $\mu_a = 8.5$.

6.105 A random sample of $n = 200$ observations from a binomial population yields $\hat{p} = .29$.

a. Test H_0: $p = .35$ against H_a: $p < .35$. Use $\alpha = .05$.
b. Test H_0: $p = .35$ against H_a: $p \neq .35$. Use $\alpha = .05$.

6.106 A t-test is conducted for the null hypothesis H_0: $\mu = 10$ versus the alternative H_a: $\mu > 10$ for a random sample of $n = 17$ observations. The test results are $t = 1.174$, p-value $= .1288$.
a. Interpret the p-value.
b. What assumptions are necessary for the validity of this test?
c. Calculate and interpret the p-value assuming the alternative hypothesis was instead H_a: $\mu \neq 10$.

*6.107 A random sample of 41 observations from a normal population possessed a mean $\bar{x} = 88$ and a standard deviation $s = 6.9$.
a. Test H_0: $\sigma^2 = 30$ against H_a: $\sigma^2 > 30$. Use $\alpha = .05$.
b. Test H_0: $\sigma^2 = 30$ against H_a: $\sigma^2 \neq 30$. Use $\alpha = .05$.

Applying the Concepts—Basic

6.108 Relating employment status to mental health A study reported in the *Journal of Occupational and Organizational Psychology* (Dec. 1992) investigated the relationship of employment status to mental health. Each in a sample of 49 unemployed men was given a mental health examination using the General Health Questionnaire (GHQ). The GHQ is a widely recognized measure of present mental health, with lower values indicating better mental health. The mean and standard deviation of the GHQ scores were $\bar{x} = 10.94$ and $s = 5.10$, respectively.
a. A GHQ score of 10 is generally considered to be a value that divides the mentally stable from the unstable. Specify the appropriate null and alternative hypotheses if we wish to test the research hypothesis that the mean GHQ score for all unemployed men exceeds 10. Is the test one-tailed or two-tailed? Why?
b. If we specify $\alpha = .05$, what is the appropriate rejection region for this test?
c. Conduct the test, and state your conclusion clearly in the language of this exercise.
d. Find and interpret the p-value of the test.

6.109 Survey of online shoppers. Creative Good, a New York consulting firm, claimed that 39% of shoppers fail in their attempts to purchase merchandise online because Web sites are too complex (*Forbes*, Dec. 13, 1999). Another consulting firm asked a random sample of 60 online shoppers to each test a different randomly selected e-commerce Web site. Only 15 reported sufficient frustration with their sites to deter making a purchase.
a. Do these data provide sufficient evidence to reject the claim made by Creative Good? Test using $\alpha = .01$.
b. Find the observed significance level of the test and interpret it in the context of the problem.

6.110 Quality of Cable-TV news. In a survey of 500 television viewers with access to cable TV, each was asked whether they agreed with the statement, "Overall, I find the quality of news on cable networks (such as CNN, FOXNews, CNBC, and MSNBC) to be better than news on the ABC, CBS, and NBC networks." A total of 248 viewers agreed with the statement (*Cabletelevision Advertising Bureau*, May 2002).
Note: The survey respondents were contacted via e-mail on the Internet.

a. Identify the population parameter of interest in the survey.
b. Give a point estimate of the population parameter.
c. Set up H_0 and H_a for testing whether the true percentage of TV viewers who find cable news to be better quality than network news differs from 50%.
d. Conduct the test, part **c**, using $\alpha = .10$ Make the appropriate conclusion in the words of the problem.
e. What conditions are required for the inference, part **d**, to be valid? Do they appear to be satisfied?

6.111 Beta-value of a stock. The "beta coefficient" of a stock is a measure of the stock's volatility (or risk) relative to the market as a whole. Stocks with beta coefficients greater than 1 generally bear greater risk (more volatility) than the market, whereas stocks with beta coefficients less than 1 are less risky (less volatile) than the overall market (Alexander, Sharpe, and Bailey, *Fundamentals of Investments,* 2000). A random sample of 15 high-technology stocks was selected at the end of 2006, and the mean and standard deviation of the beta coefficients were calculated: $\bar{x} = 1.23$, $s = .37$
a. Set up the appropriate null and alternative hypotheses to test whether the average high-technology stock is riskier than the market as a whole.
b. Establish the appropriate test statistic and rejection region for the test. Use $\alpha = .10$.
c. What assumptions are necessary to ensure the validity of the test?
d. Calculate the test statistic and state your conclusion.
e. What is the approximate p-value associated with this test? Interpret it.
*f. Conduct a test to determine if the variance of the stock beta values differs from .15. Use $\alpha = .05$.

6.112 Sleep apnea in truck drivers. Refer to the *Chest* (May 1995) study of obstructive sleep apnea, Exercise 5.98 (p. 336). Recall that the disorder causes a person to stop breathing and awaken briefly during a sleep cycle. Stanford University researchers found that 124 of 159 commercial truck drivers suffered from obstructive sleep apnea.
a. Sleep researchers theorize that 25% of the general population suffers from obstructive sleep apnea. Use a test of hypothesis (at $\alpha = .10$) to determine whether this percentage differs for commercial truck drivers.
b. Find the observed significance level of the test and interpret its value.
c. In part **b** of Exercise 5.98, you used a 90% confidence interval to make the inference of part **a.** Explain why these two inferences must necessarily agree.

⚙ **FLALAW**

6.113 Top Florida law schools. Refer to Exercise 5.88 (p. 335) and the data on $n = 26$ law firms in Florida listed in *Florida Trend* magazine (April 2002). Recall that you found a 90% confidence interval for μ, the mean number of offices operated by all Florida law firms.
a. Use the data saved in the **FLALAW** file to conduct a test (at $\alpha = .10$) of H_0: $\mu = 5$ versus H_a: $\mu \neq 5$.
b. Does the inference, part **a**, agree with the inference you made using the confidence interval in Exercise 5.88?

Applying the Concepts—Intermediate

6.114 Consumers' use of discount coupons. In 1894, druggist Asa Candler began distributing handwritten tickets to his customers for free glasses of Coca-Cola at his soda fountain. That was the genesis of the discount coupon. In 1975 it was estimated that 65% of U.S. consumers regularly used discount coupons when shopping. In a more recent consumer survey, 77% said they regularly redeem coupons (Mediamark Research, Inc.). Assume the recent survey consisted of a random sample of 1,000 shoppers.
  a. Does the survey provide sufficient evidence that the percentage of shoppers using cents-off coupons exceeds 65%? Test using $\alpha = .05$.
  b. Is the sample size large enough to use the inferential procedures presented in this section? Explain.
  c. Find the observed significance level for the test you conducted in part **a**, and interpret its value.

6.115 Errors in medical tests. Medical tests have been developed to detect many serious diseases. A medical test is designed to minimize the probability that it will produce a "false positive" or a "false negative." A *false positive* refers to a positive test result for an individual who does not have the disease, whereas a false negative is a negative test result for an individual who does have the disease.
  a. If we treat a medical test for a disease as a statistical test of hypothesis, what are the null and alternative hypotheses for the medical test?
  b. What are the Type I and Type II errors for the test? Relate each to false positives and false negatives.
  c. Which of the errors has graver consequences? Considering this error, is it more important to minimize α or β? Explain.

6.116 Drivers use of the Lincoln Tunnel. The Lincoln Tunnel (under the Hudson River) connects suburban New Jersey to midtown Manhattan. On Mondays at 8:30 A.M., the mean number of cars waiting in line to pay the Lincoln Tunnel toll is 1,220. Because of the substantial wait during rush hour, the Port Authority of New York and New Jersey is considering raising the amount of the toll between 7:30 and 8:30 A.M. to encourage more drivers to use the tunnel at an earlier or later time (*Newark Star-Ledger*, Aug. 27, 1995). Suppose the Port Authority experiments with peak-hour pricing for 6 months, increasing the toll from $4 to $7 during the rush hour peak. On 10 different workdays at 8:30 A.M. aerial photographs of the tunnel queues are taken and the number of vehicles counted. The results follow:

TUNNEL

| 1,260 | 1,052 | 1,201 | 942 | 1,062 | 999 | 931 | 849 | 867 | 735 |

Analyze the data for the purpose of determining whether peak-hour pricing succeeded in reducing the average number of vehicles attempting to use the Lincoln Tunnel during the peak rush hour.

6.117 Post-traumatic stress disorder. Most major corporations have psychologists available to help employees who suffer from stress. One problem that is difficult to diagnose is post-traumatic stress disorder (PTSD). Researchers studying PTSD often use as subjects former prisoners of war (POWs). *Psychological Assessment* (Mar. 1995) published the results of a study of World War II aviators who were captured by German forces after they were shot down. Having located a total of 239 World War II aviator POW survivors, the researchers asked each veteran to participate in the study; 33 responded to the letter of invitation. Each of the 33 POW survivors was administered the Minnesota Multiphasic Personality Inventory, one component of which measures the level of PTSD. [*Note:* The higher the score, the higher the level of PTSD.] The aviators produced a mean PTSD score of $\bar{x} = 9.00$ and a standard deviation of $s = 9.32$.
  a. Set up the null and alternative hypotheses for determining whether the true mean PTSD score of all World War II aviator POWs is less than 16. [*Note:* The value, 16, represents the mean PTSD score established for Vietnam POWs.]
  b. Conduct the test, part **a**, using $\alpha = .10$. What are the practical implications of the test?
  c. Discuss the representativeness of the sample used in the study and its ramifications.

6.118 Improving the productivity of chickens. Refer to the *Applied Animal Behaviour Science* (Oct. 2000) study of the color of string preferred by pecking domestic chickens, Exercise 5.96 (p. 336). Recall that $n = 72$ chickens were exposed to blue string and the number of pecks each chicken took at the string over a specified time interval had a mean of $\bar{x} = 1.13$ pecks and a standard deviation of $s = 2.21$ pecks. Also recall that previous research has shown that $\mu = 7.5$ pecks if chickens are exposed to white string.
  a. Conduct a test (at $\alpha = .01$) to determine if the true mean number of pecks at blue string is less than $\mu = 7.5$ pecks.
  b. In Exercise 5.96, you used a 99% confidence interval as evidence that chickens are more apt to peck at white string than blue string. Do the test results, part **a**, support this conclusion? Explain.

6.119 Are manufacturers satisfied with trade promotions? Sales promotions that are used by manufacturers to entice retailers to carry, feature, or push the manufacturer's products are called *trade promotions*. A survey of 250 manufacturers conducted by Cannondale Associates, a sales and marketing consulting firm, found that 91% of the manufacturers believe their spending for trade promotions is inefficient (*Potentials in Marketing*, June 1995). Is this sufficient evidence to reject a previous claim by the American Marketing Association that no more than half of all manufacturers are dissatisfied with their trade promotion spending?
  a. Conduct the appropriate hypothesis test at $\alpha = .02$. Begin your analysis by determining whether the sample size is large enough to apply the testing methodology presented in this chapter.
  b. Report the observed significance level of the test and interpret its meaning in the context of the problem.
  *****c.** Calculate β, the probability of a Type II error, if in fact 55% of all manufacturers are dissatisfied with their trade promotion spending.

6.120 Arresting shoplifters. Shoplifting in the United States costs retailers about $15 billion a year. Despite the seriousness of the problem, Shoplifters Alternative of Jericho, New York, claims that only 50% of all shoplifters are turned over to police (*Athens Daily News,* Dec. 12, 1999). A random sample of 40 U.S. retailers were questioned concerning the disposition of the most recent shoplifter they apprehended. A total of 24 were turned over to police. Do these data provide sufficient evidence to contradict Shoplifters Alternative?

a. Conduct a hypothesis test to answer the question of interest. Use $\alpha = .05$.

b. Is the sample size large enough to use the inferential procedure of part **a**?

c. Find the observed significance level of the hypothesis test in part **a**. Interpret the value.

d. For what values of α would the observed significance level be sufficient to reject the null hypothesis of the test you conducted in part **b**?

*6.121 **Arresting shoplifters (cont'd).** Refer to Exercise 6.120.

a. Describe a Type II error in terms of this application.

b. Calculate the probability β of a Type II error for this test assuming that the true fraction of shoplifters turned over to the police is $p = .55$.

c. Suppose the number of retailers sampled is increased from 40 to 100. How does this affect the probability of a Type II error for $p = .55$?

6.122 **Frequency marketing programs by restaurants.** To instill customer loyalty, airlines, hotels, rental car companies, and credit card companies (among others) have initiated *frequency marketing programs* that reward their regular customers. More than 80 million people are members of the frequent flier programs of the airline industry (*www.frequentflier.com*). A large fast-food restaurant chain wished to explore the profitability of such a program. They randomly selected 12 of their 1,200 restaurants nationwide and instituted a frequency program that rewarded customers with a $5.00 gift certificate after every 10 meals purchased at full price. They ran the trial program for 3 months. The restaurants not in the sample had an average increase in profits of $1,047.34 over the previous 3 months, whereas the restaurants in the sample had the following changes in profit:

PROFIT

$2,232.90	$545.47	$3,440.70	$1,809.10
$6,552.70	$4,798.70	$2,965.00	$2,610.70
$3,381.30	$1,591.40	$2,376.20	−$2,191.0

Note that the last number is negative, representing a decrease in profits.

a. Specify the appropriate null and alternative hypotheses for determining whether the mean profit change for restaurants with frequency programs is significantly greater (in a statistical sense) than $1,047.34.

b. Conduct the test of part **b** using $\alpha = .05$. Does it appear that the frequency program would be profitable for the company if adopted nationwide?

6.123 **EPA limits on vinyl chloride.** The EPA sets an airborne limit of 5 parts per million (ppm) on vinyl chloride, a colorless gas used to make plastics, adhesives, and other chemicals. It is both a carcinogen and a mutagen (New Jersey Department of Health, *Hazardous Substance Fact Sheet,* 2005). A major plastics manufacturer, attempting to

control the amount of vinyl chloride its workers are exposed to, has given instructions to halt production if the mean amount of vinyl chloride in the air exceeds 3.0 ppm. A random sample of 50 air specimens produced the following statistics: $\bar{x} = 3.1$ ppm, $s = .5$ ppm.

a. Do these statistics provide sufficient evidence to halt the production process? Use $\alpha = .01$.

b. If you were the plant manager, would you want to use a large or a small value for α for the test in part **a**? Explain.

c. Find the p-value for the test and interpret its value.

*6.124 **EPA limits vinyl chloride (cont'd).** Refer to Exercise 6.123.

a. In the context of the problem, define a Type II error.

b. Calculate β for the test described in part **a** of Exercise 6.123, assuming that the true mean is $\mu = 3.1$ ppm.

c. What is the power of the test to detect a departure from the manufacturer's 3.0 ppm limit when the mean is 3.1 ppm?

d. Repeat parts **b** and **c** assuming that the true mean is 3.2 ppm. What happens to the power of the test as the plant's mean vinyl chloride level departs further from the limit?

*6.125 **EPA limits on vinyl chloride (cont'd).** Refer to Exercises 6.123 and 6.124.

a. Suppose an α value of .05 is used to conduct the test. Does this change favor halting production? Explain.

b. Determine the value of β and the power for the test when $\alpha = .05$ and $\mu = 3.1$.

c. What happens to the power of the test when α is increased?

6.126 **Evaluating a measuring instrument.** One way of evaluating a measuring instrument is to repeatedly measure the same item and compare the average of these measurements to the item's known measured value. The difference is used to assess the instrument's accuracy (*Quality Progress,* Jan. 1993). To evaluate a particular Metlar scale, an item whose weight is known to be 16.01 ounces is weighed five times by the same operator. The measurements, in ounces, are as follows:

METLAR

15.99	16.00	15.97	16.01	15.96

a. In a statistical sense, does the average measurement differ from 16.01? Conduct the appropriate hypothesis test at $\alpha = .05$. What does your analysis suggest about the accuracy of the instrument?

b. List any assumptions you make in conducting the hypothesis test, part **a**.

*c. Evaluate the instrument's precision by testing whether the standard deviation of the weight measurements is greater than .01. Use $\alpha = .05$.

6.127 **Testing the validity of a TV advertisement.** The manufacturer of an over-the-counter analgesic claims that its product brings pain relief to headache sufferers in less than 3.5 minutes, on average. In order to be able to make this claim in its television advertisements, the manufacturer was required by a particular television network to present statistical evidence in support of the claim. The manufacturer

Summary of First-Round NCAA Tournament Games, 1985–1997

Matchup (Seeds)	Number of Games	Number Won by Favorite (Higher Seed)	Margin of Victory (Points)	
			Mean	Standard Deviation
1 vs 16	52	52	22.9	12.4
2 vs 15	52	49	17.2	11.4
3 vs 14	52	41	10.6	12.0
4 vs 13	52	42	10.0	12.5
5 vs 12	52	37	5.3	10.4
6 vs 11	52	36	4.3	10.7
7 vs 10	52	35	3.2	10.5
8 vs 9	52	22	−2.1	11.0

Source: Stern, H. S., and Mock, B. "College Basketball Upsets: Will a 16-Seed Ever Beat a 1-Seed?" *Chance,* Vol. 11, No. 1, Winter 1998, p. 29 (Table 3).

reported that for a random sample of 50 headache sufferers, the mean time to relief was 3.3 minutes and the standard deviation was 1.1 minutes.

a. Do these data support the manufacturer's claim? Test using $\alpha = .05$.

b. Report the *p*-value of the test.

c. In general, do large *p*-values or small *p*-values support the manufacturer's claim? Explain.

Applying the Concepts—Advanced

6.128 NCAA "March Madness". For 3 weeks each March, the National Collegiate Athletic Association (NCAA) holds its annual men's basketball championship tournament. The 64 best college basketball teams in the nation play a single-elimination tournament—a total of 63 games—to determine the NCAA champion. Tournament followers, from hardcore gamblers to the casual fan who enters the office betting pool, have a strong interest in handicapping the games. To provide insight into this phenomenon, statisticians Hal Stern and Barbara Mock analyzed data from 13 previous NCAA tournaments and published their results in *Chance* (Winter 1998). The results of first-round games are summarized in the table above.

a. A common perception among fans, media, and gamblers is that the higher seeded team has a better than 50–50 chance of winning a first-round game. Is there evidence to support this perception? Conduct the appropriate test for each matchup. What trends do you observe?

b. Is there evidence to support the claim that a 1-, 2-, 3-, or 4-seeded team will win by an average of more than 10 points in first-round games? Conduct the appropriate test for each matchup.

c. Is there evidence to support the claim that a 5-, 6-, 7-, or 8-seeded team will win by an average of less than five points in first-round games? Conduct the appropriate test for each matchup.

*d. For each matchup, test the null hypothesis that the standard deviation of the victory margin is 11 points.

e. The researchers also calculated the difference between the game outcome (victory margin, in points) and point spread established by Las Vegas oddsmakers for a sample of 360 recent NCAA tournament games. The mean difference is .7 and the standard deviation of the difference is 11.3. If the true mean difference is 0, then the point spread can be considered a good predictor of the game outcome. Use this sample information to test the hypothesis that the point spread, on average, is a good predictor of the victory margin in NCAA tournament games.

6.129 Factors that inhibit learning in marketing. What factors inhibit the learning process in the classroom? To answer this question, researchers at Murray State University surveyed 40 students from a senior-level marketing class (*Marketing Education Review,* Fall 1994). Each student was given a list of factors and asked to rate the extent to which each factor inhibited the learning process in courses offered in their department. A 7-point rating scale was used, where 1 = "not at all" and 7 = "to a great extent." The factor with the highest rating was instructor-related: "Professors who place too much emphasis on a single right answer rather than overall thinking and creative ideas." Summary statistics for the student ratings of this factor are: $\bar{x} = 4.70$, $s = 1.62$.

a. Conduct a test to determine if the true mean rating for this instructor-related factor exceeds 4. Use $\alpha = .05$. Interpret the test results.

b. Examine the results of the study from a practical view, then discuss why "statistically significant" does not always imply "practically significant."

c. Because the variable of interest, rating, is measured on a 7-point scale, it is unlikely that the population of ratings will be normally distributed. Consequently, some analysts may perceive the test, part **a**, to be invalid and search for alternative methods of analysis. Defend or refute this argument.

Critical Thinking Challenge

TAMALES

6.130 The Hot Tamale Caper. "Hot Tamales" are chewy, cinnamon-flavored candies. A bulk vending machine is known to dispense, on average, 15 Hot Tamales per bag with a standard deviation of 3 per bag. *Chance* (Fall 2000) published an article on a classroom project in which students were required to purchase bags of Hot Tamales from the machine and count the number of candies per bag. One student group claimed they purchased five bags that had the following candy counts: 25, 23, 21, 21, and 20. There was some question as to whether the students had fabricated the data. Use a hypothesis test to gain insight into whether or not the data collected by the students are fabricated. Use a level of significance that gives the benefit of the doubt to the students.

REFERENCES

Alexander, G. J., Sharpe, W.F., and Bailey, J. *Fundamentals of Investments,* 3rd ed. Upper Saddle River, N.J.: Prentice Hall, 2000.

Schonberger, R. J., and Knod Jr., E. M. *Operations Management,* 5th ed. Burr Ridge, III.: Irwin, 1994.

Snedecor, G. W., and Cochran, W. G. *Statistical Methods,* 7th ed. Ames: Iowa State University Press, 1980.

Stevenson, W. J. *Production/Operations Management,* 6th ed. Chicago: Irwin, 2000.

Wackerly, D., Mendenhall, W., and Scheaffer, R. *Mathematical Statistics with Applications,* 6th ed. North Scituate, Mass.: Duxbury, 2002.

Using Technology

6.1 Tests of Hypothesis Using SPSS

SPSS can be used to tests hypotheses about a population mean and a population proportion but cannot currently conduct a test for a population variance. To generate a test for the mean, first access the SPSS spreadsheet file that contains the sample data. Next, click on the "Analyze" button on the SPSS menu bar, then click on "Compare Means" and "One-Sample T Test", as shown in Figure 6.S.1. The resulting dialog box appears as shown in Figure 6.S.2. Specify the quantitative variable of interest in the "Test Variable(s)" box and the value of μ_0 for the null hypothesis in the "Test Value" box, then click "OK". SPSS will automatically conduct a two-tailed test of hypothesis.

Important Note: The SPSS one-sample *t*-procedure uses the *t*-statistic to conduct the test of hypothesis. When the sample size *n* is small, this is the appropriate method. When the sample size *n* is large, the *t*-value will be approximately equal to the large-sample *z*-value and the resulting test will still be valid.

To generate a test for a proportion, first access the SPSS spreadsheet file that contains the sample data. Next, click on the "Analyze" button on the SPSS menu bar, then click on "Nonparametric Tests" and "Binomial", as shown in Figure 6.S.3. The resulting dialog box appears as shown in Figure 6.S.4. Specify the binomial variable of interest in the "Test Variable List" box and the value of p_0 for the null hypothesis in the "Test Proportion" box.

Figure 6.S.1

SPSS menu options for a test about μ

Important Note: SPSS requires the binomial variable to be entered as a quantitative variable. Typically, this is accomplished by entering two numerical values (e.g., 0 and 1) for the two outcomes of the variable. If the data have been entered in this fashion, then select the "Get from data" option in the "Define Dichotomy" area of the dialog box. You can also create the two outcome values for a quantitative variable by selecting the "Cut point" option in the "Define Dichotomy" area and specifying a numerical value. All values of the variables less than or equal to the cut point value are assigned to one group (success) and all other values are assigned to the other group (failure). Once the dichotomy is defined, click "OK". SPSS will automatically conduct a two-tailed test of hypothesis for the proportion.

Figure 6.S.2

SPSS *t* test dialog box

Figure 6.S.3
SPSS menu options for a test about p

Figure 6.S.4
SPSS binomial test dialog box

6.2 Tests of Hypothesis Using MINITAB

MINITAB can be used to obtain one-sample tests for both a population mean and a population proportion but cannot currently produce a test for a population variance. To generate a hypothesis test for the mean using a previously created sample data set, first access the MINITAB data worksheet. Next, click on the "Stat" button on the MINITAB menu bar, then click on "Basic Statistics" and "1-Sample t", as shown in Figure 6.M.1. The resulting dialog box appears as shown in Figure 6.M.2. Click on "Samples in Columns", then specify the quantitative variable of interest in the open box. Specify the value of μ_0 for the null hypothesis in the "Test mean" box. Now, click on the "Options" button at the bottom of the dialog box and specify the form of the alternative hypothesis as shown in Figure 6.M.3. Click "OK" to return to the "1-Sample t" dialog box, then click "OK" again to produce the hypothesis test.

Figure 6.M.1
MINITAB menu options for a test about μ

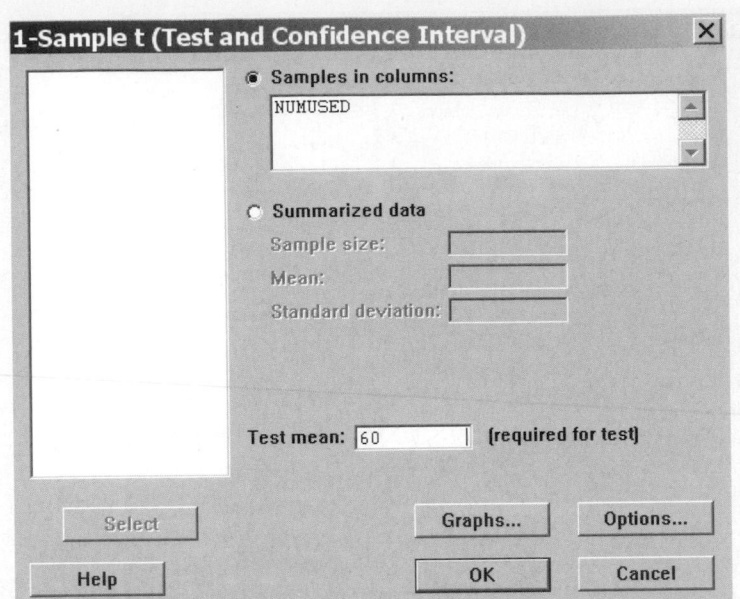

Figure 6.M.2
MINITAB one-sample *t* dialog box

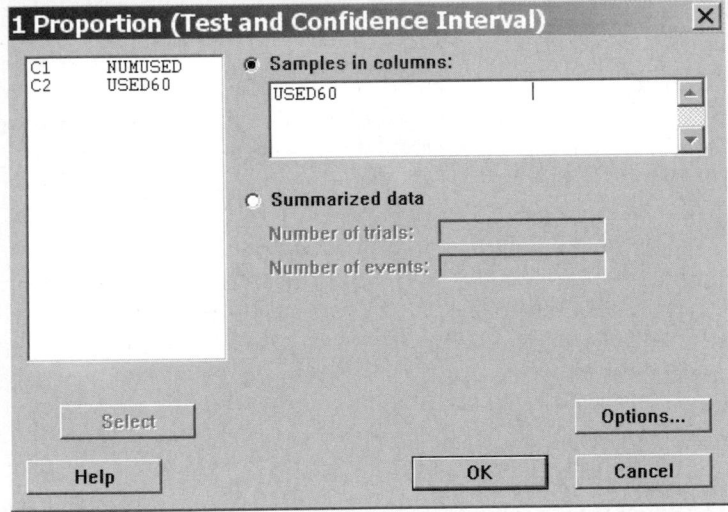

Figure 6.M.4
MINITAB 1-proportion dialog box

Figure 6.M.3
MINITAB one-sample *t* options dialog box

If you want to produce a test for the mean from summary information (e.g., the sample mean, sample standard deviation, and sample size), then click on "Summarized data" in the "1-Sample t" dialog box, enter the values of the summary statistics and μ_0, then click "OK".

Important Note: The MINITAB one-sample *t*-procedure uses the *t*-statistic to generate the hypothesis test. When the sample size *n* is small, this is the appropriate method. When the sample size *n* is large, the *t*-value will be approximately equal to the large-sample *z*-value and the resulting test will still be valid. If you have a large sample and you know the value of the population standard deviation σ (which is rarely the case), then select "1-sample Z" from the "Basic Statistics" menu options (see Figure 6.M.1) and make the appropriate selections.

To generate a test for a population proportion using a previously created sample data set, first access the MINITAB data worksheet. Next, click on the "Stat" button on the MINITAB menu bar, then click on "Basic Statistics" and "1 Proportion" (see Figure 6.M.1). The resulting dialog box appears as shown in Figure 6.M.4. Click on "Samples in Columns", then specify the qualitative variable of interest in the open box. Now, click on the "Options" button at the bottom of the dialog box and specify the null hypothesis value p_0 and the form of the alternative hypothesis in the resulting dialog box, as shown in Figure 6.M.5. Also, check the "Use test and interval based on normal distribution" box at the bottom. Click "OK" to return to the "1-Proportion" dialog box, then click "OK" again to produce the test results.

If you want to produce a confidence interval for a proportion from summary information (e.g., the number of successes and the sample size), then click on "Summarized data" in the "1-Proportion" dialog box (see Figure 6.M.4). Enter the value for the number of trials (i.e., the sample size) and the number of events (i.e., the number of successes), then click "OK".

6.3 Tests of Hypothesis Using Excel/PHStat2

Excel with the PHStat2 add-in can be used to obtain one-sample tests for population means, proportions, and variances. To generate a test of hypothesis for the mean using a previously created sample data set, first access the Excel worksheet. Next, click on the "PHStat" button on the

Figure 6.M.5
MINITAB 1-proportion options

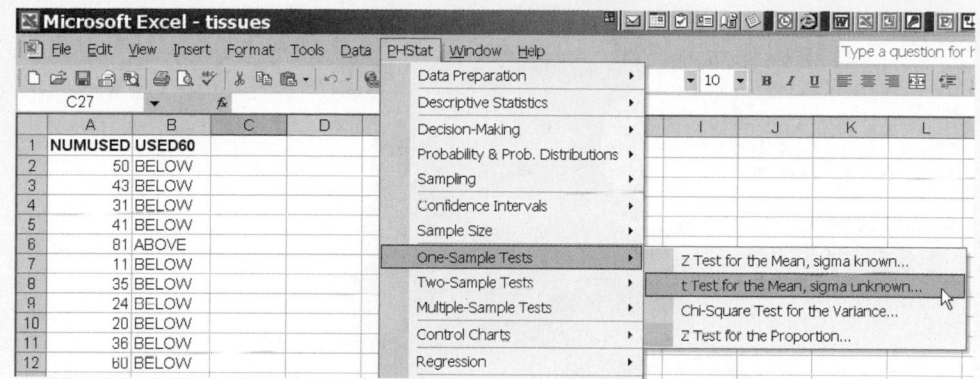

Figure 6.E.1

Excel/PHStat2 menu options for a test about μ

Excel menu bar, then click on "One-Sample Tests" and "t Test for the Mean, sigma unknown," as shown in Figure 6.E.1. The resulting dialog box appears as shown in Figure 6.E.2. Specify the value of μ_0 for the null hypothesis, the level of significance α, and the form of the alternative hypothesis (upper-, lower-, or two-tailed test), then click on "Sample Statistics Unknown" and specify the cell range for the quantitative variable of interest (see Figure 6.E.2). Click "OK" to produce the test results.

If you want to produce a test for the mean from summary information (e.g., the sample mean, sample standard deviation, and sample size), then click on "Sample Statistics Known" on the dialog box shown in Figure 6.E.2. Enter the values of the summary statistics, then click "OK".

Important Note: The Excel/PHStat2 one-sample 7 outlined above uses the *t*-statistic to generate the hypothesis test when σ is unknown. When the sample size *n* is small, this is the appropriate method. When the sample size *n* is large, the *t*-value will be approximately equal to the large-sample *z*-value and the resulting interval will still be valid. If you have a large sample and you know the value of the population standard deviation σ (which is rarely the case), then select "Z Test for the Mean, sigma known" from the "One-Sample Tests" menu options (see Figure 6.E.1) and make the appropriate selections.

To generate a test for a population proportion using Excel, you must first determine the sample size and the number of successes in the sample of interest. Next, click on the "PHStat" button on the Excel menu bar, then click on "One-Sample Tests" and "Z Test for the Proportion" (see Figure 6.E.1). The resulting dialog box appears as shown in Figure 6.E.3. Specify the null hypothesis value p_0 level of significance α, number of successes, sample size, and the form of the alternative hypothesis (upper-, lower-, or two tailed test), then click "OK" to produce the test results. To generate a test for a population variance using Excel, you must first determine the sample standard deviation for the variable of interest. Next, click on the "PHStat" button on the Excel menu bar, then click on "One-Sample Tests" and "Chi-Square Test for the Variance" (see Figure 6.E.1). The resulting dialog box appears as shown in Figure 6.E.4. Specify the null hypothesis value of the variance σ_0^2, level of significance α, sample size, sample standard deviation, and the form of the alternative hypothesis (upper-, lower-, or two-tailed test), then click "OK" to produce the test results.

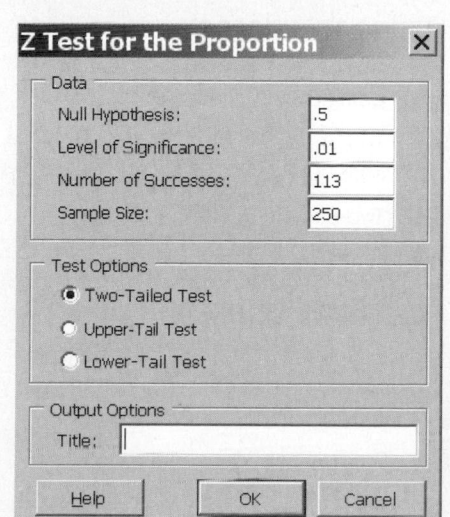

Figure 6.E.2

Excel *t*-test for mean dialog box

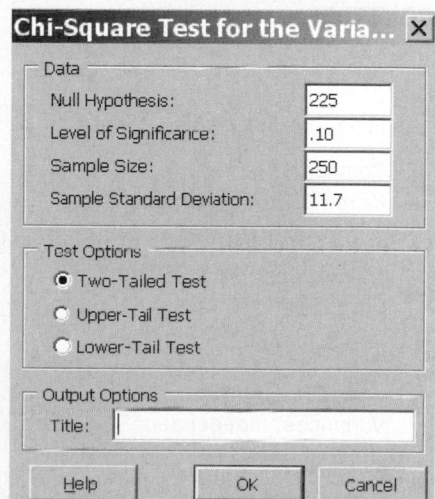

Figure 6.E.3

Excel test for proportion dialog box

Figure 6.E.4

Excel test for variance dialog box

7

Inferences Based on Two Samples

Confidence Intervals and Tests of Hypotheses

CONTENTS

7.1 Identifying the Target Parameter

7.2 Comparing Two Population Means: Independent Sampling

7.3 Comparing Two Population Means: Paired Difference Experiments

7.4 Comparing Two Population Proportions: Independent Sampling

7.5 Determining the Sample Size

7.6 Comparing Two Population Variances: Independent Sampling (Optional)

STATISTICS IN ACTION

The Effect of Self-Managed Work Teams on Family Life

USING TECHNOLOGY

7.1 Two-Sample Inferences Using SPSS

7.2 Two-Sample Inferences Using MINITAB

7.3 Two-Sample Inferences Using Excel/PHStat2

WHERE WE'VE BEEN

■ Explored two methods for making statistical inferences: *confidence intervals* and *tests of hypotheses*

■ Studied confidence intervals and tests for a single population mean μ, a single population proportion p, and a single population variance σ^2

■ Learned how to select the sample size necessary to estimate a population parameter with a specified margin of error

WHERE WE'RE GOING

■ Learn how to compare two populations using confidence intervals and tests of hypotheses.

■ Apply these inferential methods to problems where we want to compare two population means, two population proportions, or two population variances.

■ Determine the sizes of the samples necessary to estimate the difference between two population parameters with a specified margin of error.

STATISTICS IN ACTION

The Effect of Self-Managed Work Teams on Family Life

To improve quality, productivity, and timeliness, more and more American industries are adopting a new participative management style. This new approach utilizes self-managed work teams (SMWTs). A team typically consists of 5 to 15 workers who are collectively responsible for making decisions and performing all tasks related to a particular project. For example, a SMWT may be responsible for scheduling work hours, interfacing with customers, disciplining team members, and participating in hiring. Past studies revealed that SMWTs have positive impacts on both a firm's performance and employee attitudes.

SMWTs require that employees be trained in interpersonal skills such as listening, decision making, and conflict resolution. Consequently, SMWTs can have potential positive spillover effects on a worker's family life. Researchers L. Stanley-Stevens (Tarleton State University), D. E. Yeatts, and R. R. Seward (both University of North Texas) investigated the connection between SMWT work characteristics and workers' perceptions of positive spillover into family life (*Quality Management Journal*, Summer 1995).

Survey data were collected from 114 AT&T employees who work in one of fifteen SMWTs at an AT&T technical division. The workers were divided into two groups: (1) those who reported positive spillover of work skills to family life and (2) those who did not report positive work spillover. The two groups were compared on a variety of job and demographic characteristics, several of which are shown in Table SIA7.1. All but the demographic characteristics were measured on a 7-point scale, ranging from 1 = "strongly disagree" to 7 = "strongly agree"; thus, the larger the number, the more of the characteristic indicated.

The researchers' objectives were to compare the two groups of workers on each characteristic. In particular, they want to know which job-related characteristics are most highly associated with positive work spillover. From summary information provided in the *Quality Management Journal* article, we constructed a data set that represents the results of a survey similar to the one described above. The file named **SPILLOVER** includes the values of the variables listed in Table SIA7.1 for each of the 114 survey participants. We apply the statistical methodology presented in this chapter to this data set in several Statistics in Action Revisited examples.

Statistics in Action Revisited

- Comparing Means for the Two SMWT Survey Groups (p. 417)
- Comparing Proportions for the Two SMWT Survey Groups (p. 440)

 SPILLOVER

TABLE SIA7.1 Variables Measured in the SMWT Survey

Characteristic	Variable
Information flow	Use of creative ideas (7-point scale)
Information flow	Utilization of information (7-point scale)
Decision making	Participation in decisions regarding personnel matters (7-point scale)
Job	Good use of skills (7-point scale)
Job	Task identity (7-point scale)
Demographic	Age (years)
Demographic	Education (years)
Demographic	Gender (male or female)
Comparison	Group (positive spillover or no spillover)

7.1 Identifying the Target Parameter

Many experiments involve a comparison of two populations. For instance, a realtor may want to estimate the difference in mean sales price between city and suburban homes. A consumer group might test whether two major brands of food freezers differ in the average amount of electricity they use. A television market researcher wants to estimate the difference in the proportions of younger and older viewers who regularly watch a popular TV program. A golf ball supplier may be interested in comparing the variability in the distance that two competing brands of golf balls travel when struck with the same club. In this chapter, we consider techniques for using two samples to compare the populations from which they were selected.

The same procedures that are used to estimate and test hypotheses about a single population can be modified to make inferences about two populations. As in Chapters 5 and 6, the methodology used will depend on the sizes of the samples and the parameter of interest (i.e., the *target parameter*). Some key words and the type of data associated with the parameters covered in this chapter are listed in the box.

Determining the Target Parameter

Parameter	Key Words or Phrases	Type of Data
$\mu_1 - \mu_2$	Mean difference; difference in averages	Quantitative
$p_1 - p_2$	Difference between proportions, percentages, fractions, or rates; compare proportions	Qualitative
$(\sigma_1)^2/(\sigma_2)^2$	Ratio of variances; difference in variability or spread; compare variation	Quantitative

---

You can see that the key words *difference* and *compare* help identify the fact that two populations are to be compared. For the examples given above, the words *mean* in *mean sales price* and *average* in *average amount of electricity* imply that the target parameter is the difference in population means, $\mu_1 - \mu_2$. The word *proportions* in *proportions of younger and older adults* indicates that the target parameter is the difference in proportions, $p_1 - p_2$. Finally, the key word *variability* in *variability in the distance* identifies the ratio of population variances, $(\sigma_1)^2/(\sigma_2)^2$, as the target parameter.

As with inferences about a single population, the type of data (quantitative or qualitative) collected on the two samples is also indicative of the target parameter. With quantitative data, you are likely to be interested in comparing the means or variances of the data. With qualitative data with two outcomes (success or failure), a comparison of the proportions of successes is likely to be of interest.

We consider methods for comparing two population means in Sections 7.2 and 7.3. A comparison of population proportions is presented in Section 7.4 and population variances in optional Section 7.6. We show how to determine the sample sizes necessary for reliable estimates of the target parameters in Section 7.5.

7.2 Comparing Two Population Means: Independent Sampling

In this section we develop both large-sample and small-sample methodologies for comparing two population means. In the large-sample case, we use the z-statistic, while in the small-sample case we use the t-statistic.

Large Samples

EXAMPLE 7.1

Comparing Mean
Prices of Japanese and
U.S. Cars—A Large
Sample Confidence
Interval for $\mu_1 - \mu_2$

Problem In recent years, the United States and Japan have engaged in intense negotiations regarding restrictions on trade between the two countries. One of the claims made repeatedly by U.S. officials is that many Japanese manufacturers price their goods higher in Japan than in the United States, in effect subsidizing low prices in the United States by extremely high prices in Japan. According to the U.S. argument, Japan accomplishes this by keeping competitive U.S. goods from reaching the Japanese marketplace.

An economist decided to test the hypothesis that higher retail prices are being charged for Japanese automobiles in Japan than in the United States. She obtained independent random samples of 50 retail sales in the United States and 50 retail sales in Japan over the same time period and for the same model of automobile, converted the Japanese sales prices from yen to dollars using current conversion rates. The data, saved in the **AUTOSTUDY** file, are listed in Table 7.1. Form a 95% confidence interval for the difference between the population mean retail prices of this automobile model for the two countries. Interpret the result.

 AUTOSTUDY

TABLE 7.1 Automobile Retail Prices (thousands of dollars)

USA Sales:	18.2	16.2	17.2	18.7	18.4	16.6	14.9	16.8	12.1	10.8
	18.5	15.5	16.2	16.3	18.2	19.5	13.2	16.8	12.9	17.2
	18.2	16.3	16.8	16.4	18.6	15.6	17.1	18.1	18.9	19.0
	17.3	18.8	14.9	16.7	20.3	17.1	14.6	17.2	13.0	18.4
	16.9	13.3	16.3	15.9	16.6	17.6	16.0	17.1	14.6	18.0
Japan Sales:	18.5	14.0	18.2	21.1	13.9	18.7	14.9	16.4	16.3	18.0
	16.8	19.8	17.3	16.6	14.9	16.3	16.5	15.4	17.6	20.1
	16.4	18.0	17.5	18.4	19.8	14.8	18.2	16.7	20.2	16.2
	20.4	17.9	15.5	15.4	17.7	17.1	17.9	17.4	18.2	16.2
	18.5	16.9	17.6	14.4	21.6	18.6	16.2	14.3	12.5	20.0

Solution Recall that the general form of a large-sample confidence interval for a single mean μ is $\bar{x} \pm z_{\alpha/2}\sigma_{\bar{x}}$—that is, we add and subtract $z_{\alpha/2}$ standard deviations of the sample estimate, $\bar{x}$, to the value of the estimate. We employ a similar procedure to form the confidence interval for the difference between two population means.

Let μ_1 represent the mean of the population of retail sales prices for this car model sold in the United States. Let μ_2 be similarly defined for retail sales in Japan. We wish to form a confidence interval for $(\mu_1 - \mu_2)$. An intuitively appealing estimator for $(\mu_1 - \mu_2)$ is the difference between the sample means, $(\bar{x}_1 - \bar{x}_2)$. Thus, we will form the confidence interval of interest by

$$(\bar{x}_1 - \bar{x}_2) \pm z_{\alpha/2}\sigma_{(\bar{x}_1 - \bar{x}_2)}$$

Assuming the two samples are independent, the standard deviation of the difference between the sample means is

$$\sigma_{(\bar{x}_1 - \bar{x}_2)} = \sqrt{\frac{\sigma_1^2}{n_1} + \frac{\sigma_2^2}{n_2}} \approx \sqrt{\frac{s_1^2}{n_1} + \frac{s_2^2}{n_2}}$$

Summary statistics for the car sales data are displayed in the SPSS printout, Figure 7.1. Note that $\bar{x}_1 = \$16,596$, $\bar{x}_2 = \$17,236$, $s_1 = \$1,981$, and $s_2 = \$1,974$. Using these values

Group Statistics

	COUNTRY	N	Mean	Std. Deviation	Std. Error Mean
PRICE	USA	50	16596.00	1981.440	280.218
	JAPAN	50	17236.00	1974.093	279.179

Independent Samples Test

		Levene's Test for Equality of Variances		t-test for Equality of Means					95% Confidence Interval of the Difference	
		F	Sig.	t	df	Sig. (2-tailed)	Mean Difference	Std. Error Difference	Lower	Upper
PRICE	Equal variances assumed	.118	.732	-1.618	98	.109	-640.000	395.554	-1424.964	144.964
	Equal variances not assumed			-1.618	97.999	.109	-640.000	395.554	-1424.964	144.964

FIGURE 7.1

SPSS summary statistics and confidence interval for automobile price study

and noting that $\alpha = .05$ and $z_{.025} = 1.96$, we find that the 95% confidence interval is, approximately,

$$(16{,}596 - 17{,}236) \pm 1.96\sqrt{\frac{(1{,}981)^2}{50} + \frac{(1{,}974)^2}{50}} = -640 \pm (1.96)(396)$$

$$= -640 \pm 776$$

or $(-1416, 136)$. This interval is also given at the bottom of Figure 7.1. (Differences in the results are due to rounding.)

Using this estimation procedure over and over again for different samples, we know that approximately 95% of the confidence intervals formed in this manner will enclose the difference in population means $(\mu_1 - \mu_2)$. Therefore, we are highly confident that the difference in mean retail prices in the United States and Japan is between $-\$1{,}416$ and $\$136$. Since 0 falls in this interval, it is possible for the difference to be 0 (i.e., for $\mu_1 = \mu_2$); thus, the economist cannot conclude that a significant difference exists between the mean retail prices in the two countries.

Look Back If the confidence interval for $(\mu_1 - \mu_2)$ contains all positive numbers [e.g., $(527, 991)$], then we would conclude that the difference between the means is positive and that $\mu_1 > \mu_2$. Alternatively, if the interval contains all negative numbers [e.g., $(-722, -145)$], then we would conclude that the difference between the means is negative and that $\mu_1 < \mu_2$.

Now Work Exercise 7.3a

The justification for the procedure used in Example 7.1 to estimate $(\mu_1 - \mu_2)$ relies on the properties of the sampling distribution of $(\bar{x}_1 - \bar{x}_2)$. The performance of the estimator in repeated sampling is pictured in Figure 7.2, and its properties are summarized in the box.

Properties of the Sampling Distribution of $(\bar{x}_1 - \bar{x}_2)$

1. The mean of the sampling distribution $(\bar{x}_1 - \bar{x}_2)$ is $(\mu_1 - \mu_2)$.
2. If the two samples are independent, the standard deviation of the sampling distribution is

$$\sigma_{(\bar{x}_1 - \bar{x}_2)} = \sqrt{\frac{\sigma_1^2}{n_1} + \frac{\sigma_2^2}{n_2}}$$

where σ_1^2 and σ_2^2 are the variances of the two populations being sampled and n_1 and n_2 are the respective sample sizes. We also refer to $\sigma_{(\bar{x}_1 - \bar{x}_2)}$ as the **standard error** of the statistic $(\bar{x}_1 - \bar{x}_2)$.

Continued

FIGURE 7.2
Sampling distribution of
$(\bar{x}_1 - \bar{x}_2)$

3. The sampling distribution of $(\bar{x}_1 - \bar{x}_2)$ is approximately normal for *large samples* by the Central Limit Theorem.

In Example 7.1, we noted the similarity in the procedures for forming a large-sample confidence interval for one population mean and a large-sample confidence interval for the difference between two population means. When we are testing hypotheses, the procedures are again very similar. The general large-sample procedures for forming confidence intervals and testing hypotheses about $(\mu_1 - \mu_2)$ are summarized in the following boxes.

Large Sample Confidence Interval for $(\mu_1 - \mu_2)$

$$(\bar{x}_1 - \bar{x}_2) \pm z_{\alpha/2}\sigma_{(\bar{x}_1 - \bar{x}_2)} = (\bar{x}_1 - \bar{x}_2) \pm z_{\alpha/2}\sqrt{\frac{\sigma_1^2}{n_1} + \frac{\sigma_2^2}{n_2}}$$

Large-Sample Test of Hypothesis for $(\mu_1 - \mu_2)$

One-Tailed Test	Two-Tailed Test
$H_0: (\mu_1 - \mu_2) = D_0$	$H_0: (\mu_1 - \mu_2) = D_0$
$H_a: (\mu_1 - \mu_2) < D_0$	$H_a: (\mu_1 - \mu_2) \neq D_0$
[or $H_a: (\mu_1 - \mu_2) > D_0$]	

where D_0 = Hypothesized difference between the means (this difference is often hypothesized to be equal to 0)

Test statistic:

$$z = \frac{(\bar{x}_1 - \bar{x}_2) - D_0}{\sigma_{(\bar{x}_1 - \bar{x}_2)}} \quad \text{where} \quad \sigma_{(\bar{x}_1 - \bar{x}_2)} = \sqrt{\frac{\sigma_1^2}{n_1} + \frac{\sigma_2^2}{n_2}}$$

Rejection region: $z < -z_\alpha$ *Rejection region:* $|z| > z_{\alpha/2}$
[or $z > z_\alpha$ when
$H_a: (\mu_1 - \mu_2) > D_0$]

Conditions Required for Valid Large-Sample Inferences about $\mu_1 - \mu_2$

1. The two samples are randomly selected in an independent manner from the two target populations.
2. The sample sizes, n_1 and n_2, are both large (i.e., $n_1 \geq 30$ and $n_2 \geq 30$). [Due to the Central Limit Theorem, this condition guarantees that the sampling distribution of $(\bar{x}_1 - \bar{x}_2)$ will be approximately normal regardless of the shapes of the underlying probability distributions of the populations. Also, s_1^2 and s_2^2 will provide good approximations to σ_1^2 and σ_2^2 when the samples are both large.]

EXAMPLE 7.2

Comparing Mean Prices of Japanese and U.S. Cars with a Large-Sample Test for $\mu_1 - \mu_2$

Problem   Refer to the study of retail prices of an automobile sold in the United States and Japan, Example 7.1. Another way to compare the mean retail prices for the two countries is to conduct a test of hypothesis. Use the information on the SPSS printout, Figure 7.1, to conduct the test. Use $\alpha = .05$.

Solution   Again, we let μ_1 and μ_2 represent the population mean retail sales prices in the United States and Japan, respectively. If the claim made by the U.S. government is true, then the mean retail price in Japan will exceed the mean in the United States [i.e., $\mu_1 < \mu_2$ or $(\mu_1 - \mu_2) < 0$]. Thus, the elements of the test are as follows:

$$H_0: (\mu_1 - \mu_2) = 0 \text{ (i.e., } \mu_1 = \mu_2; \text{ note that } D_0 = 0 \text{ for this hypothesis test)}$$

$$H_a: (\mu_1 - \mu_2) < 0 \text{ (i.e., } \mu_1 < \mu_2)$$

$$\textit{Test statistic: } z = \frac{(\bar{x}_1 - \bar{x}_2) - D_0}{\sigma_{(\bar{x}_1 - \bar{x}_2)}} = \frac{\bar{x}_1 - \bar{x}_2 - 0}{\sigma_{(\bar{x}_1 - \bar{x}_2)}}$$

$$\textit{Rejection region: } z < -z_{.05} = -1.645 \qquad \text{(see Figure 7.3)}$$

Substituting the summary statistics given in Figure 7.1 into the test statistic, we obtain

$$z = \frac{(\bar{x}_1 - \bar{x}_2) - 0}{\sigma_{(\bar{x}_1 - \bar{x}_2)}} = \frac{(16{,}596 - 17{,}236)}{\sqrt{\dfrac{\sigma_1^2}{n_1} + \dfrac{\sigma_2^2}{n_2}}}$$

$$\approx \frac{-640}{\sqrt{\dfrac{s_1^2}{n_1} + \dfrac{s_2^2}{n_2}}} = \frac{-640}{\sqrt{\dfrac{(1{,}981)^2}{50} + \dfrac{(1{,}974)^2}{50}}} = \frac{-640}{396} = -1.62$$

[Note: This value of the test statistic is shown (highlighted) at the bottom of the SPSS printout, Figure 7.1 (p. 406)]

As you can see in Figure 7.3, the calculated z value does not fall in the rejection region. Therefore, the samples do not provide sufficient evidence, at $\alpha = .05$, for the economist to conclude that the mean retail price in Japan exceeds that in the United States.

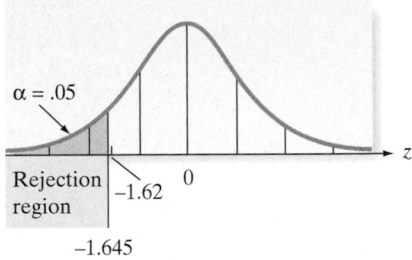

FIGURE 7.3
Rejection region for Example 7.2

Look Back   First, note that this conclusion agrees with the inference drawn from the 95% confidence interval in Example 7.1. Generally, however, a confidence interval will provide more information on the difference in means than a test. A test can only detect whether or not a difference between the means exists, while the confidence interval provides information on the magnitude of the difference. Second, a one-tailed hypothesis test and a confidence interval (which is two-tailed) may not always agree. However, a two-tailed test of hypothesis and a confidence interval will *always* give the same inference about the target parameter as long as the value of α is the same for both.

EXAMPLE 7.3

The p-Value of a Test for $\mu_1 - \mu_2$

Problem   Find the observed significance level for the test in Example 7.2. Interpret the result.

Solution   The alternative hypothesis in Example 7.2, $H_a: (\mu_1 - \mu_2) < 0$, required a lower one-tailed test using

$$z = \frac{\bar{x}_1 - \bar{x}_2}{\sigma_{(\bar{x}_1 - \bar{x}_2)}}$$

as a test statistic. Since the approximate z-value calculated from the sample data was -1.62, the observed significance level (p-value) for the lower-tailed test is the probability of observing a value of z more contradictory to the null hypothesis as $z = -1.62$; that is,

$$p\text{-value} = P(z < -1.62)$$

This probability is computed assuming H_0 is true and is equal to the shaded area shown in Figure 7.4.

The tabulated area corresponding to $z = 1.62$ in Table IV of Appendix B is .4474. Therefore, the observed significance level of the test is

$$p\text{-value} \approx .5 - .4474 = .0526$$

Since our selected α value, .05, is less than this p-value, we have insufficient evidence to reject $H_0: (\mu_1 - \mu_2) = 0$ in favor of $H_a: (\mu_1 - \mu_2) < 0$.

FIGURE 7.4
The observed significance level for Example 7.2

Look Back The p-value of the test is more easily obtained from a statistical software package. A MINITAB printout for the hypothesis test is displayed in Figure 7.5. The one-tailed p-value, highlighted on the printout, is .054, which agrees (except for rounding) with our approximated p-value.

FIGURE 7.5
MINITAB analysis for comparing U.S. and Japan mean auto prices

```
Two-Sample T-Test and CI: USA, JAPAN

Two-sample T for USA vs JAPAN

          N    Mean   StDev  SE Mean
USA      50   16596    1981      280
JAPAN    50   17236    1974      279


Difference = mu (USA) - mu (JAPAN)
Estimate for difference:  -640.000
95% upper bound for difference:  16.838
T-Test of difference = 0 (vs <): T-Value = -1.62  P-Value = 0.054  DF = 98
Both use Pooled StDev = 1977.7703
```

Now Work Exercise 7.3b

Small Samples

When comparing two population means with small samples (say, $n_1 < 30$ and $n_2 < 30$), the methodology of the previous three examples is invalid. The reason? When the sample sizes are small, estimates of σ_1^2 and σ_2^2 are unreliable and the Central Limit Theorem (which guarantees that the z statistic is normal) can no longer be applied. But as in the case of a single mean (Section 6.4), we use the familiar Student's t-distribution described in Chapter 5.

To use the t-distribution, both sampled populations must be approximately normally distributed with equal population variances, and the random samples must be selected independently of each other. The normality and equal variances assumptions imply relative frequency distributions for the populations that would appear as shown in Figure 7.6.

Since we assume the two populations have equal variances ($\sigma_1^2 = \sigma_2^2 = \sigma^2$), it is reasonable to use the information contained in both samples to

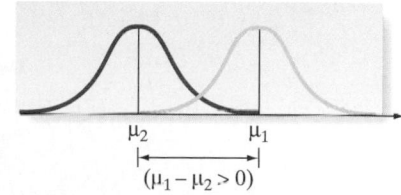

FIGURE 7.6
Assumptions for the two-sample t: (1) normal populations, (2) equal variances

construct a **pooled sample estimator of σ^2** for use in confidence intervals and test statistics. Thus, if s_1^2 and s_2^2 are the two sample variances (both estimating the variance σ^2 common to both populations), the pooled estimator of σ^2, denoted as s_p^2, is

$$s_p^2 = \frac{(n_1 - 1)s_1^2 + (n_2 - 1)s_2^2}{(n_1 - 1) + (n_2 - 1)} = \frac{(n_1 - 1)s_1^2 + (n_2 - 1)s_2^2}{n_1 + n_2 - 2}$$

or

$$s_p^2 = \frac{\overbrace{\sum(x_1 - \bar{x}_1)^2}^{\text{From sample 1}} + \overbrace{\sum(x_2 - \bar{x}_2)^2}^{\text{From sample 2}}}{n_1 + n_2 - 2}$$

where x_1 represents a measurement from sample 1 and x_2 represents a measurement from sample 2. Recall that the term *degrees of freedom* was defined in Section 5.2 as 1 less than the sample size. Thus, in this case, we have $(n_1 - 1)$ degrees of freedom for sample 1 and $(n_2 - 1)$ degrees of freedom for sample 2. Since we are pooling the information on σ^2 obtained from both samples, the degrees of freedom associated with the pooled variance s_p^2 is equal to the sum of the degrees of freedom for the two samples, namely, the denominator of s_p^2; that is, $(n_1 - 1) + (n_2 - 1) = n_1 + n_2 - 2$.

Note that the second formula given for s_p^2 shows that the pooled variance is simply a *weighted average* of the two sample variances, s_1^2 and s_2^2. The weight given each variance is proportional to its degrees of freedom. If the two variances have the same number of degrees of freedom (i.e., if the sample sizes are equal), then the pooled variance is a simple average of the two sample variances. The result is an average or "pooled" variance that is a better estimate of σ^2 than either s_1^2 or s_2^2 alone.

Biography

BRADLEY EFRON (1938–PRESENT)

The Bootstrap Method

Bradley Efron was raised in St. Paul, Minnesota, the son of a truck driver who was the amateur statistician for his bowling and baseball leagues. Efron received a BS in mathematics from California Institute of Technology in 1960, but, by his own admission, had no talent for modern abstract math. His interest in the science of statistics developed after reading a book, cover to cover, by Harold Cramer. Efron went to the University of Stanford to study statistics and earned his PhD there in 1964. He has been a faculty member in Stanford's Department of Statistics since 1966. Over his career, Efron has received numerous awards and prizes for his contributions to modern statistics, including the MacArthur Prize Fellow (1983), the American Statistical Association Wilks Medal (1990), and the Parzen Prize for Statistical Innovation (1998). In 1979, Efron invented a method—called the *bootstrap*—of estimating and testing population parameters in situations where either the sampling distribution is unknown or the assumptions are violated. The method involves repeatedly taking samples of size n (with replacement) from the original sample and calculating the value of the point estimate. Efron showed that the sampling distribution of the estimator is simply the frequency distribution of the bootstrap estimates.

Both the confidence interval and the test of hypothesis procedures for comparing two population means with small samples are summarized in the accompanying boxes.

Small-Sample Confidence Interval for $(\mu_1 - \mu_2)$ (Independent Samples)

$$(\bar{x}_1 - \bar{x}_2) \pm t_{\alpha/2}\sqrt{s_p^2\left(\frac{1}{n_1} + \frac{1}{n_2}\right)}$$

Continued

where $s_p^2 = \dfrac{(n_1 - 1)s_1^2 + (n_2 - 1)s_2^2}{n_1 + n_2 - 2}$

and $t_{\alpha/2}$ is based on $(n_1 + n_2 - 2)$ degrees of freedom.

Small-Sample Test of Hypothesis for $(\mu_1 - \mu_2)$ (Independent Samples)

One-Tailed Test	Two-Tailed Test
$H_0: (\mu_1 - \mu_2) = D_0$	$H_0: (\mu_1 - \mu_2) = D_0$
$H_a: (\mu_1 - \mu_2) < D_0$	$H_a: (\mu_1 - \mu_2) \neq D_0$
[or $H_a: (\mu_1 - \mu_2) > D_0$]	

$$\text{Test statistic: } t = \frac{(\bar{x}_1 - \bar{x}_2) - D_0}{\sqrt{s_p^2\left(\dfrac{1}{n_1} + \dfrac{1}{n_2}\right)}}$$

Rejection region: $t < -t_\alpha$	Rejection regions: $\lvert t \rvert > t_{\alpha/2}$
[or $t > t_\alpha$ when $H_a:(\mu_1 - \mu_2) > D_0$]	

where t_α and $t_{\alpha/2}$ are based on $(n_1 + n_2 - 2)$ degrees of freedom.

Conditions Required for Valid Small-Sample Inferences about $(\mu_1 - \mu_2)$

1. The two samples are randomly selected in an independent manner from the two target populations.
2. Both sampled populations have distributions that are approximately normal.
3. The population variances are equal (i.e., $\sigma_1^2 = \sigma_2^2$).

EXAMPLE 7.4

Comparing Manager Performance with a Small-Sample Confidence Interval for $(\mu_1 - \mu_2)$

Problem Behavioral researchers have developed an index designed to measure managerial success. The index (measured on a 100-point scale) is based on the manager's length of time in the organization and his or her level within the firm; the higher the index, the more successful the manager. Suppose a researcher wants to compare the average success index for two groups of managers at a large manufacturing plant. Managers in group 1 engage in a high volume of interactions with people outside the manager's work unit. (Such interactions include phone and face-to-face meetings with customers and suppliers, outside meetings, and public relations work.) Managers in group 2 rarely interact with people outside their work unit. Independent random samples of 12 and 15 managers are selected from groups 1 and 2, respectively, and the success index of each is recorded. The results of the study are given in Table 7.2.

a. Use the data in the table to estimate the true mean difference between the success indexes of managers in the two groups. Use a 95% confidence interval.
b. Interpret the interval, part a.
c. What assumptions must be made in order that the estimate be valid? Are they reasonably satisfied?

Solution

a. For this experiment, let μ_1 and μ_2 represent the mean success index of group 1 and group 2 managers, respectively. Then, the objective is to obtain a 95% confidence interval for $(\mu_1 - \mu_2)$.

MANSUCCESS

TABLE 7.2 Managerial Success Indexes for Two Groups of Managers

GROUP 1						GROUP 2					
Interaction with Outsiders						Few Interactions					
65	58	78	60	68	69	62	53	36	34	56	50
66	70	53	71	63	63	42	57	46	68	48	42
						52	53	43			

```
Two-sample T for SUCCESS

GROUP    N    Mean   StDev   SE Mean
1       12   65.33    6.61      1.9
2       15   49.47    9.33      2.4


Difference = mu (1) - mu (2)
Estimate for difference:  15.8667
95% CI for difference:  (9.2883, 22.4451)
T-Test of difference = 0 (vs not =): T-Value = 4.97   P-Value = 0.000   DF = 25
Both use Pooled StDev = 8.2472
```

FIGURE 7.7
MINITAB printout for Example 7.4

The first step in constructing the confidence interval is to obtain summary statistics (e.g., $\bar{x}$ and s) on the success index for each group of managers. The data of Table 7.2 were entered into a computer, and MINITAB was used to obtain these descriptive statistics. The MINITAB printout appears in Figure 7.7. Note that $\bar{x}_1 = 65.33$, $s_1 = 6.61$, $\bar{x}_2 = 49.47$, and $s_2 = 9.33$.

Next, we calculate the pooled estimate of variance:

$$s_p^2 = \frac{(n_1 - 1)s_1^2 + (n_2 - 1)s_2^2}{n_1 + n_2 - 2}$$

$$= \frac{(12 - 1)(6.61)^2 + (15 - 1)(9.33)^2}{12 + 15 - 2} = 67.97$$

where s_p^2 is based on $(n_1 + n_2 - 2) = (12 + 15 - 2) = 25$ degrees of freedom. Also, we find $t_{\alpha/2} = t_{.025} = 2.06$ (based on 25 degrees of freedom) from Table V of Appendix B.

Finally, the 95% confidence interval for $(\mu_1 - \mu_2)$, the difference between mean managerial success indexes for the two groups, is

$$(\bar{x}_1 - \bar{x}_2) \pm t_{\alpha/2}\sqrt{s_p^2\left(\frac{1}{n_1} + \frac{1}{n_2}\right)} = 65.33 - 49.47 \pm t_{.025}\sqrt{67.97\left(\frac{1}{12} + \frac{1}{15}\right)}$$

$$= 15.86 \pm (2.06)(3.19)$$

$$= 15.86 \pm 6.57$$

or (9.29, 22.43). This interval agrees (except for rounding) with the one shown at the bottom of the MINITAB printout, Figure 7.7.

b. Notice that the confidence interval includes only positive differences. Consequently, we are 95% confident that $(\mu_1 - \mu_2)$ exceeds 0. In fact, we estimate the mean success index, μ_1, for managers with a high volume of outsider interaction (group 1) to

FIGURE 7.8

MINITAB normal probability plots for manager success index

be anywhere between 9.29 and 22.43 points higher than the mean success index, μ_2, of managers with few interactions (group 2).

c. To properly use the small-sample confidence interval, the following assumptions must be satisfied:

1. The samples of managers are randomly and independently selected from the populations of group 1 and group 2 managers.
2. The success indexes are normally distributed for both groups of managers.
3. The variance of the success indexes are the same for the two populations, (i.e., $\sigma_1^2 = \sigma_2^2$).

The first assumption is satisfied, based on the information provided about the sampling procedure in the problem description. To check the plausibility of the remaining two assumptions, we resort to graphical methods. Figure 7.8 is a MINITAB printout that displays normal probability plots for the success indexes of the two samples of managers. The near straight-line trends on both plots indicate that the success index distributions are approximately mound shaped and symmetric. Consequently, each sample data set appears to come from a population that is approximately normal.

One way to check assumption #3 is to test the null hypothesis $H_0: \sigma_1^2 = \sigma_2^2$. This test is covered in optional Section 7.6. Another approach is to examine box plots for the sample data. Figure 7.9 is a MINITAB printout that shows side-by-side vertical box plots for the success indexes in the two samples. Recall, from Section 2.9 that the box plot represents the "spread" of a data set. The two box plots appear to have about the same spread; thus, the samples appear to come from populations with approximately the same variance.

Boxplot of SUCCESS vs GROUP

FIGURE 7.9

MINITAB box plots for Manager Success Index

Look Back All three assumptions appear to be reasonably satisfied for this application of the small-sample confidence interval.

Now Work Exercise 7.7

The two-sample t-statistic is a powerful tool for comparing population means when the assumptions are satisfied. It has also been shown to retain its usefulness when the sampled populations are only approximately normally distributed. And when the sample sizes are equal, the assumption of equal population variances can be relaxed — that is, if $n_1 = n_2$, then σ_1^2 and σ_2^2 can be quite different and the test statistic will still possess, approximately, a Student's t-distribution. In the case where $\sigma_1^2 \neq \sigma_2^2$ and $n_1 \neq n_2$, an approximate small-sample confidence interval or test can be obtained by modifying the degrees of freedom associated with the t-distribution.

The next box gives the approximate small-sample procedures to use when the assumption of equal variances is violated. The test for the "unequal sample sizes" case is based on Satterhwaite's (1946) approximation.

Approximate Small-Sample Procedures when $\sigma_1^2 \neq \sigma_2^2$

1. **Equal sample sizes ($n_1 = n_2 = n$)**

   Confidence interval: $(\bar{x}_1 - \bar{x}_2) \pm t_{\alpha/2}\sqrt{(s_1^2 + s_2^2)/n}$

   Test statistic for H_0: $(\mu_1 - \mu_2) = 0$: $t = (\bar{x}_1 - \bar{x}_2)/\sqrt{(s_1^2 + s_2^2)/n}$

   where t is based on $\nu = n_1 + n_2 - 2 = 2(n - 1)$ degrees of freedom.

2. **Unequal sample sizes ($n_1 \neq n_2$)**

   Confidence interval: $(\bar{x}_1 - \bar{x}_2) \pm t_{\alpha/2}\sqrt{(s_1^2/n_1) + (s_2^2/n_2)}$

   Test statistic for H_0: $(\mu_1 - \mu_2) = 0$: $t = (\bar{x}_1 - \bar{x}_2)/\sqrt{(s_1^2/n_1) + (s_2^2/n_2)}$ where t is based on degrees of freedom equal to

   $$\nu = \frac{(s_1^2/n_1 + s_2^2/n_2)^2}{\dfrac{(s_1^2/n_1)^2}{n_1 - 1} + \dfrac{(s_2^2/n_2)^2}{n_2 - 1}}$$

Note: The value of ν will generally not be an integer. Round ν down to the nearest integer to use the t-table.

When the assumptions are clearly not satisfied, you can select larger samples from the populations or you can use other available statistical tests (nonparametric statistical tests, which are described in Chapter 14).

What Should You Do if the Assumptions Are Not Satisfied?

Answer: If you are concerned that the assumptions are not satisfied, use the Wilcoxon rank sum test for independent samples to test for a shift in population distributions. See Chapter 14.

Confidence Interval for $\mu_1 - \mu_2$

Using the TI-83/TI-84 Graphing Calculator

Step 1   *Enter the data (Skip to Step 2 if you have summary statistics, not raw data)*

Press **STAT** and select **1:Edit**
Note: If the lists already contain data, clear the old data. Use the up
ARROW to highlight 'L1'.
Press **CLEAR ENTER**.
Use the up **ARROW** to highlight 'L2'.

Press **CLEAR ENTER**.
Use the **ARROW** and **ENTER** keys to enter the first data set into **L1.**
Use the **ARROW** and **ENTER** keys to enter the second data set into **L2.**

Step 2   *Access the Statistical Tests Menu*

Press **STAT**.
Arrow right to **TESTS**.
Arrow down to **2-SampTInt**.
Press **ENTER**.

Step 3   *Choose "**Data**" or "**Stats**". ("Data" is selected when you have entered the raw data into the Lists. "Stats" is selected when you are given only the means, standard deviations, and sample sizes.)*

Press **ENTER**.
If you selected "Data", set **List1** to **L1** and **List2** to **L2**.
Set **Freq1** to **1** and set **Freq2** to **1**.
Set **C-Level** to the confidence level.
If you are assuming that the two populations have equal variances, select **Yes** for **Pooled**.
If you are not assuming equal variances, select **No**.
Press **ENTER**.
Arrow down to "**Calculate**".
Press **ENTER**.

If you selected "Stats", enter the means, standard deviations, and sample sizes.
Set **C-Level** to the confidence level.
If you are assuming that the two populations have equal variances, select **Yes** for **Pooled**.
If you are not assuming equal variances, select **No**.
Press **ENTER**.
Arrow down to "**Calculate**".
Press **ENTER**.

(The accompanying screen is set up for an example with a mean of 100, a standard deviation of 10 and a sample size of 15 for the first data set and a mean of 105, a standard deviation of 12 and a sample size of 18 for the second data set.)

The confidence interval will be displayed with the degrees of freedom, the sample statistics and the pooled standard deviation (when appropriate).

Example   Compute a 95% confidence interval for the $\mu_1 - \mu_2$ using the following data. In this example, assume the population variances are equal.

Group 1: 65 58 78 60 68 69 66 70 53 71 63 63

Group 2: 62 53 36 34 56 50 42 57 46 68 48 42 52 53 43

As you can see from the screens, the
95% confidence interval for $\mu_1 - \mu_2$ is (**9.2883, 22.445**).
You will also notice the output includes the means, standard deviations, sample sizes and the pooled standard deviation.

Hypothesis Test for $\mu_1 - \mu_2$

Using the TI-83/TI-84 Graphing Calculator

Step 1 *Enter the data (Skip to Step 2 if you have summary statistics, not raw data)*

Press **STAT** and select **1:Edit**.
Note: If the lists already contain data, clear the old data. Use the up **ARROW** to highlight 'L1'.
Press **CLEAR ENTER**.
Use the up **ARROW** to highlight '**L2**'.
Press **CLEAR ENTER**.
Use the **ARROW** and **ENTER** keys to enter the first data set into **L1.**
Use the **ARROW** and **ENTER** keys to enter the second data set into **L2.**

Step 2 *Access the Statistical Tests Menu*

Press **STAT**.
Arrow right to **TESTS**.
Arrow down to **2-SampTTest**.
Press **ENTER**.

Step 3 *Choose "**Data**" or "**Stats**". ("Data" is selected when you have entered the raw data into the Lists. "Stats" is selected when you are given only the means, standard deviations, and sample sizes.)*

Press **ENTER**.
If you selected "Data", set **List1** to **L1** and **List2** to **L2**.
Set **Freq1** to **1** and set **Freq2** to **1**.
Use the **ARROW** to highlight the appropriate alternative hypothesis.
Press **ENTER**.
If you are assuming that the two populations have equal variances, select **Yes** for **Pooled**.
If you are not assuming equal variances, select **No**.
Press **ENTER**.
Arrow down to "**Calculate**".
Press **ENTER**.

If you selected "Stats", enter the means, standard deviations, and sample sizes.
Use the **ARROW** to highlight the appropriate alternative hypothesis.
Press **ENTER**.
If you are assuming that the two populations have equal variances, select **Yes** for **Pooled**.
If you are not assuming equal variances, select **No**.
Press **ENTER**.
Arrow down to "**Calculate**".
Press **ENTER**.

(The screen below is set up for an example with a mean of 100, a standard deviation of 10 and a sample size of 15 for the first data set and a mean of 120, a standard deviation of 12 and a sample size of 18 for the second data set.)

The results of the hypothesis test will be displayed with the *p*-value, degrees of freedom, the sample statistics and the pooled standard deviation (when appropriate).

Example   Test the hypotheses: vs. using the following data. In this example, assume the population variances are equal.

Group 1: 65 58 78 60 68 69 66 70 53 71 63 63

Group 2: 62 53 36 34 56 50 42 57 46 68 48 42 52 53 43

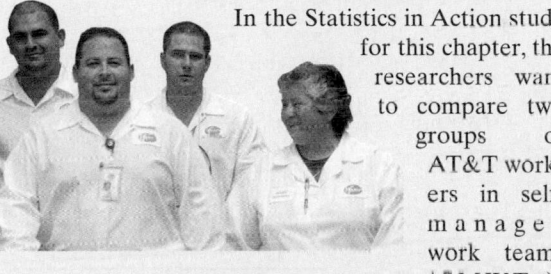

As you can see from the screens, $t = 4.967$ and the *p*-value is 0.00002. You will also notice the output includes the means, standard deviations, sample sizes and the pooled standard deviation.

STATISTICS IN ACTION REVISITED

Comparing Means for the Two SMWT Survey Groups

In the Statistics in Action study for this chapter, the researchers want to compare two groups of AT&T workers in self-managed work teams (SMWTs). Group 1 ($n_1 = 47$) were those employees who reported positive spillover of work skills to family life. Group 2 ($n_2 = 67$) were those employees who did not report positive work spillover. The researchers collected data on seven quantitative variables and one qualitative variable for each worker. The quantitative variables (listed in Table SIA7.1, p. 403) are Use of creative ideas, Utilization of information, Participation in decisions regarding personnel matters, Good use of skills, Task identity, Age, and Education. (*Reminder:* Age and Education are measured in years, while the other quantitative variables are measured on a 7-point scale.) These data are saved in the **SPILLOVER** file.

Recall that the researchers' objectives were to compare the two groups of workers on each characteristic. They accomplished this by conducting a two-tailed test of the null hypothesis, $H_0: (\mu_1 - \mu_2) = 0$, for each quantitative variable. Since both samples are large, ($n_1 = 47$ and $n_2 = 67$), the large-sample *z*-test is appropriate. We conducted these tests using SPSS.

The output is shown in Figure SIA7.1. (*Note:* The large-sample test results are provided in the row labeled "Equal variances not assumed" on the SPSS printout.)

The two-tailed *p*-values of the tests are highlighted on Figure SIA7.1. The only variables that show a significant difference at $\alpha = .05$ are Use of creative ideas (*p*-value = .000) and Good use of skills (*p*-value = .000). The two demographic variables, Age and Education, are clearly nonsignificant (*p*-values of .460 and .534, respectively), as are Utilization of information (*p*-value = .136) and Participation in decisions regarding personnel matters (*p*-value = .135). Although not significant at $\alpha = .05$, Task identity (*p*-value = .087), shows a significant difference at $\alpha = .10$.

In the cases of the significant variables, Use of creative ideas and Good use of skills, and the borderline significant variable Task identity, the estimate of the mean difference ($\mu_1 - \mu_2$) is positive—that is, for these variables the mean for the positive work spillover group is significantly larger than the mean for the nonspillover group. Consequently, the researchers concluded that Use of creative ideas and Good use of skills were the characteristics most highly associated with positive work spillover, followed by Task identity.

After reading this section, you now know that these conclusions can be readily obtained by examining the 95% confidence intervals for ($\mu_1 - \mu_2$) shown in the last column of the SPSS printout. Only the variables Use of creative ideas and Good use of skills have a confidence interval with all positive numbers.

Continued

Independent Samples Test

| | | Levene's Test for Equality of Variances | | t-test for Equality of Means | | | | | | |
| | | F | Sig. | t | df | Sig. (2-tailed) | Mean Difference | Std. Error Difference | 95% Confidence Interval of the Difference | |
									Lower	Upper
CREATIVE	Equal variances assumed	16.479	.000	8.565	112	.000	.81	.094	.621	.994
	Equal variances not assumed			8.847	108.727	.000	.81	.091	.627	.988
INFO	Equal variances assumed	6.501	.012	1.437	112	.153	.56	.387	-.210	1.323
	Equal variances not assumed			1.503	110.916	.136	.56	.370	-.177	1.289
DECPERS	Equal variances assumed	.059	.808	1.514	112	.133	.57	.378	-.177	1.323
	Equal variances not assumed			1.506	97.314	.135	.57	.380	-.182	1.328
SKILLS	Equal variances assumed	.139	.710	4.812	112	.000	1.03	.214	.606	1.454
	Equal variances not assumed			4.766	95.741	.000	1.03	.216	.601	1.459
TASKID	Equal variances assumed	27.854	.000	1.902	112	.060	.57	.299	-.024	1.163
	Equal variances not assumed			1.738	66.922	.087	.57	.328	-.085	1.224
AGE	Equal variances assumed	2.923	.090	.702	112	.484	.95	1.360	-1.740	3.649
	Equal variances not assumed			.742	111.872	.460	.95	1.287	-1.595	3.504
EDYRS	Equal variances assumed	4.430	.038	-.600	112	.549	-.14	.231	-.597	.319
	Equal variances not assumed			-.623	109.709	.534	-.14	.223	-.580	.303

Figure SIA7.1

SPSS comparison of two SMWT groups

Exercises 7.1–7.24

Learning the Mechanics

7.1 The purpose of this exercise is to compare the variability of $\bar{x}_1$ and $\bar{x}_2$ with the variability of $(\bar{x}_1 - \bar{x}_2)$.

a. Suppose the first sample is selected from a population with mean $\mu_1 = 150$ and variance $\sigma_1^2 = 900$. Within what range should the sample mean vary about 95% of the time in repeated samples of 100 measurements from this distribution? That is, construct an interval extending 2 standard deviations of $\bar{x}_1$ on each side of μ_1.

b. Suppose the second sample is selected independently of the first from a second population with mean $\mu_2 = 150$ and variance $\sigma_2^2 = 1,600$. Within what range should the sample mean vary about 95% of the time in repeated samples of 100 measurements from this distribution? That is, construct an interval extending 2 standard deviations of $\bar{x}_2$ on each side of μ_2.

c. Now consider the difference between the two sample means $(\bar{x}_1 - \bar{x}_2)$. What are the mean and standard deviation of the sampling distribution of $(\bar{x}_1 - \bar{x}_2)$?

d. Within what range should the difference in sample means vary about 95% of the time in repeated independent samples of 100 measurements each from the two populations?

e. What, in general, can be said about the variability of the difference between independent sample means relative to the variability of the individual sample means?

7.2 Independent random samples of 64 observations each are chosen from two normal populations with the following means and standard deviations:

Population 1	Population 2
$\mu_1 = 12$	$\mu_2 = 10$
$\sigma_1 = 4$	$\sigma_2 = 3$

Let $\bar{x}_1$ and $\bar{x}_2$ denote the two sample means.

a. Give the mean and standard deviation of the sampling distribution of $\bar{x}_1$.

b. Give the mean and standard deviation of the sampling distribution of $\bar{x}_2$.

c. Suppose you were to calculate the difference $(\bar{x}_1 - \bar{x}_2)$ between the sample means. Find the mean and standard deviation of the sampling distribution of $(\bar{x}_1 - \bar{x}_2)$.

d. Will the statistic $(\bar{x}_1 - \bar{x}_2)$ be normally distributed? Explain.

7.3 In order to compare the means of two populations, inde-
NW pendent random samples of 400 observations are selected from each population, with the following results:

Sample 1	Sample 2
$\bar{x}_1 = 5,275$	$\bar{x}_2 = 5,240$
$s_1 = 150$	$s_2 = 200$

a. Use a 95% confidence interval to estimate the difference between the population means $(\mu_1 - \mu_2)$. Interpret the confidence interval.

b. Test the null hypothesis $H_0: (\mu_1 - \mu_2) = 0$ versus the alternative hypothesis $H_a: (\mu_1 - \mu_2) \neq 0$. Give the significance level of the test, and interpret the result.

c. Suppose the test in part **b** was conducted with the alternative hypothesis H_a: $(\mu_1 - \mu_2) > 0$. How would your answer to part **b** change?

d. Test the null hypothesis H_0: $(\mu_1 - \mu_2) = 25$ versus H_a: $(\mu_1 - \mu_2) \neq 25$. Give the significance level, and interpret the result. Compare your answer to the test conducted in part **b**.

e. What assumptions are necessary to ensure the validity of the inferential procedures applied in parts **a–d**?

7.4 To use the t-statistic to test for a difference between the means of two populations, what assumptions must be made about the two populations? About the two samples?

7.5 Two populations are described in each of the following cases. In which cases would it be appropriate to apply the small-sample t-test to investigate the difference between the population means?

a. Population 1: Normal distribution with variance σ_1^2. Population 2: Skewed to the right with variance $\sigma_2^2 = \sigma_1^2$.

b. Population 1: Normal distribution with variance σ_1^2. Population 2: Normal distribution with variance $\sigma_2^2 \neq \sigma_1^2$.

c. Population 1: Skewed to the left with variance σ_1^2. Population 2: Skewed to the left with variance $\sigma_2^2 = \sigma_1^2$.

d. Population 1: Normal distribution with variance σ_1^2. Population 2: Normal distribution with variance $\sigma_2^2 = \sigma_1^2$.

e. Population 1: Uniform distribution with variance σ_1^2. Population 2: Uniform distribution with variance $\sigma_2^2 = \sigma_1^2$.

7.6 Assume that $\sigma_1^2 = \sigma_2^2 = \sigma^2$. Calculate the pooled estimator of σ^2 for each of the following cases:

a. $s_1^2 = 120$, $s_2^2 = 100$, $n_1 = n_2 = 25$

b. $s_1^2 = 12$, $s_2^2 = 20$, $n_1 = 20$, $n_2 = 10$

c. $s_1^2 = .15$, $s_2^2 = .20$, $n_1 = 6$, $n_2 = 10$

d. $s_1^2 = 3,000$, $s_2^2 = 2,500$, $n_1 = 16$, $n_2 = 17$

Note that the pooled estimate is a weighted average of the sample variances. To which of the variances does the pooled estimate fall nearer in each of the above cases?

7.7 Independent random samples from normal populations **NW** produced the results shown in the next table.

⊙ **LM7_7**

Sample 1	Sample 2
1.2	4.2
3.1	2.7
1.7	3.6
2.8	3.9
3.0	

a. Calculate the pooled estimate of σ^2.

b. Do the data provide sufficient evidence to indicate that $\mu_2 > \mu_1$? Test using $\alpha = .10$.

c. Find a 90% confidence interval for $(\mu_1 - \mu_2)$.

d. Which of the two inferential procedures, the test of hypothesis in part **b** or the confidence interval in part **c**, provides more information about $(\mu_1 - \mu_2)$?

7.8 Two independent random samples have been selected—100 observations from population 1 and 100 from population 2. Sample means $\bar{x}_1 = 15.5$ and $\bar{x}_2 = 26.6$ were obtained.

From previous experience with these populations, it is known that the variances are $\sigma_1^2 = 9$ and $\sigma_2^2 = 16$.

a. Find $\sigma_{(\bar{x}_1 - \bar{x}_2)}$.

b. Sketch the approximate sampling distribution for $(\bar{x}_1 - \bar{x}_2)$ assuming $(\mu_1 - \mu_2) = 10$.

c. Locate the observed value of $(\bar{x}_1 - \bar{x}_2)$ on the graph you drew in part **b**. Does it appear that this value contradicts the null hypothesis H_0: $(\mu_1 - \mu_2) = 10$?

d. Use the z-table on the inside of the front cover to determine the rejection region for the test of H_0: $(\mu_1 - \mu_2) = 10$ against H_0: $(\mu_1 - \mu_2) \neq 10$. Use $\alpha = .05$.

e. Conduct the hypothesis test of part **d** and interpret your result.

f. Construct a 95% confidence interval for $(\mu_1 - \mu_2)$. Interpret the interval.

g. Which inference provides more information about the value of $(\mu_1 - \mu_2)$—the test of hypothesis in part **e** or the confidence interval in part **f**?

7.9 Independent random samples of $n_1 = 233$ and $n_2 = 312$ are selected from two populations and used to test the hypothesis H_0: $(\mu_1 - \mu_2) = 0$ against the alternative H_a: $(\mu_1 - \mu_2) \neq 0$.

a. The two-tailed p-value of the test is .1150. Interpret this result.

b. If the alternative hypothesis had been H_a: $(\mu_1 - \mu_2) < 0$, how would the p-value change? Interpret the p-value for this one-tailed test.

7.10 Independent random samples from approximately normal populations produced the results shown below:

⊙ **LM7_10**

Sample 1				Sample 2			
52	33	42	44	52	43	47	56
41	50	44	51	62	53	61	50
45	38	37	40	56	52	53	60
44	50	43		50	48	60	55

a. Do the data provide sufficient evidence to conclude that $(\mu_2 - \mu_1) > 10$? Test using $\alpha = .01$.

b. Construct a 98% confidence interval for $(\mu_2 - \mu_1)$. Interpret your result.

7.11 Independent random samples selected from two normal populations produced the sample means and standard deviations shown below.

Sample 1	Sample 2
$n_1 = 17$	$n_2 = 12$
$\bar{x}_1 = 5.4$	$\bar{x}_2 = 7.9$
$s_1 = 3.4$	$s_2 = 4.8$

a. Conduct the test H_0: $(\mu_1 - \mu_2) = 0$ against H_a: $(\mu_1 - \mu_2) \neq 0$. Interpret the results.

b. Estimate $(\mu_1 - \mu_2)$ using a 95% confidence interval.

Applying the Concepts—Basic

⊙ **DIAMONDS**

7.12 Diamonds sold at retail. Refer to the data for 308 diamonds saved in the **DIAMONDS** file. Two quantitative variables in the data set are number of carats and selling price. One of the qualitative variables is the independent certification body that assessed each of the stones. Three certification bodies were used: GIA, IGI, and HRD. The MINITAB printout shown below gives the means and standard deviations of the quantitative variables for each certification body.

Descriptive Statistics: CARAT, PRICE

Variable	CERT	N	Mean	StDev
CARAT	GIA	151	0.6723	0.2456
	HRD	79	0.8129	0.1831
	IGI	78	0.3665	0.2163
PRICE	GIA	151	5310	3247
	HRD	79	7181	2898
	IGI	78	2267	2121

a. Construct a 95% confidence interval for the difference between the mean carat size of diamonds certified by GIA and the mean carat size of diamonds certified by HRD.

b. Interpret the result, part **a.** Specifically, which (if either) of the two population means compared is larger and by how much?

c. Construct a 95% confidence interval for the difference between the mean carat size of diamonds certified by GIA and the mean carat size of diamonds certified by IGI.

d. Interpret the result, part **c.** Specifically, which (if either) of the two population means is larger and by how much?

e. Construct a 95% confidence interval for the difference between the mean selling price of diamonds certified by HRD and the mean selling price of diamonds certified by IGI.

f. Interpret the result, part **e.** Specifically, which (if either) of the two population means is larger and by how much?

7.13 **Children's recall of TV ads.** Marketing professors at Robert Morris and Kent St. Universities examined children's recall and recognition of television advertisements. (*Journal of Advertising,* Spring 2006.) Two groups of children were shown a 60-second commercial for Sunkist FunFruit Rock-n-Roll Shapes. One group (the A/V group) was shown the ad with both audio and video; the second group (the video-only group) was shown only the video portion of the commercial. Following the viewing, the children were asked to recall 10 specific items from the ad. The number of the 10 items recalled correctly by each child is summarized in the table. The researchers theorized that "children who receive an audiovisual presentation will have the same level of mean recall of ad information as those who receive only the visual aspects of the ad."

Video Only Group	A/V Group
$n_1 = 20$	$n_2 = 20$
$\bar{x}_1 = 3.70$	$\bar{x}_2 = 3.30$
$s_1 = 1.98$	$s_2 = 2.13$

Source: Maher, J. K., Hu, M. Y., and Kolbe, R. H. "Children's Recall of Television Ad Elements." *Journal of Advertising,* Vol. 35, No. 1, Spring 2006 (Table 1).

a. Set up the appropriate null and alternative hypotheses to test the researchers' theory.

b. Find the value of the test statistic.

c. Give the rejection region for $\alpha = .10$.

d. Make the appropriate inference. What can you say about the researchers' theory?

e. The researchers' reported the *p*-value of the test as *p*-value = .542. Interpret this result.

f. What conditions are required for the inference to be valid?

7.14 **Rating service at five-star hotels.** A study published in *The Journal of American Academy of Business, Cambridge* (March 2002) examined whether the perception of service quality at five-star hotels in Jamaica differed by gender. Hotel guests were randomly selected from the lobby and restaurant areas and asked to rate ten service-related items (e.g., "The personal attention you received from our employees"). Each item was rated on a 5-point scale (1 = "much worse than I expected," 5 = "much better than I expected"), and the sum of the items for each guest was determined. A summary of the guest scores are provided in the next table.

Gender	Sample Size	Mean Score	Standard Deviation
Males	127	39.08	6.73
Females	114	38.79	6.94

a. Construct a 90% confidence interval for the difference between the population mean service-rating scores given by male and female guests at Jamaican five-star hotels.

b. Use the interval, part **a**, to make an inference about whether the perception of service quality at five-star hotels in Jamaica differs by gender.

7.15 **Financial incentives for college students.** Do students who play virtual-reality educational software games perform better in school? If so, software designers will use this information to create more attractive and motivating educational software. In a study published in *Educational Technology & Society* (April 2005), a class of 90 elementary schoolchildren were randomly divided into two groups of 45. One group used a virtual-reality game called VR-ENGAGE to learn about geography. The other group learned geography on the computer with a simple user interface. All students were given an exam at the beginning and the end of the learning period. The difference in test scores was used to find the percentage improvement in scores for each student. The following table summarizes the results for the two groups.

	VR-ENGAGE	Simple User Interface
n:	45	45
$\bar{x}$:	43.15	32.48
s:	12.57	9.26

Source: Virvou, M., Katsionis, G., and Manos, K. "Combining Software Games with Education: Evaluation of Its Educational Effectiveness." *Educational Technology & Society,* Vol. 8, No. 2, April 2005 (Table 2).

a. Visually inspect the summary results. Does it appear that the mean improvement in scores for the virtual-reality group is greater than the mean for the simple user interface group?

b. Conduct an analysis (either a confidence interval or a test of hypothesis) at $\alpha = .05$ to support your observation in part **a**.

7.16 Turnover rates in the United States and Japan. High job turnover rates are often associated with high product defect rates, since high turnover rates mean more inexperienced workers who are unfamiliar with the company's product lines (Stevenson, *Production/Operations Management*, 2000). In a recent study, five Japanese and five U.S. plants that manufacture air conditioners were randomly sampled; their turnover rates are listed in the table.

🔅 **TURNOVER**

U.S. Plants	Japanese Plants
7.11%	3.52%
6.06	2.02
8.00	4.91
6.87	3.22
4.77	1.92

a. Do the data provide sufficient evidence to indicate that the mean annual percentage turnover for U.S. plants exceeds the corresponding mean percentage for Japanese plants? Test using $\alpha = .05$.

b. Find and interpret the observed significance level of the test you conducted in part **a.**

c. List any assumptions you made in conducting the hypothesis test of part **a.** Comment on their validity for this application.

Applying the Concepts—Intermediate

7.17 Patent infringement case. *Chance* (Fall 2002) described a lawsuit where Intel Corp. was charged with infringing on a patent for an invention used in the automatic manufacture of computer chips. In response, Intel accused the inventor of adding material to his patent notebook after the patent was witnessed and granted. The case rested on whether a patent witness' signature was written on top of key text in the notebook, or under the key text. Intel hired a physicist who used an X-ray beam to measure the relative concentration of certain elements (e.g., nickel, zinc, potassium) at several spots on the notebook page. The zinc measurements for three notebook locations—on a text line, on a witness line, and on the intersection of the witness and text line—are provided in the table.

🔅 **PATENT**

Text line:	.335	.374	.440			
Witness line:	.210	.262	.188	.329	.439	.397
Intersection:	.393	.353	.285	.295	.319	

a. Use a test or a confidence interval (at $\alpha = .05$) to compare the mean zinc measurement for the text line with the mean for the intersection.

b. Use a test or a confidence interval (at $\alpha = .05$) to compare the mean zinc measurement for the witness line with the mean for the intersection.

c. From the results, parts **a** and **b,** what can you infer about the mean zinc measurements at the three notebook locations?

d. What assumptions are required for the inferences to be valid? Are they reasonably satisfied?

7.18 Computer-mediated communication study. Computer-mediated communication (CMC) is a form of interaction that heavily involves technology (e.g., instant-messaging, e-mail). A study was conducted to compare relational intimacy in people interacting via CMC to people meeting face-to-face (FTF); (*Journal of Computer-Mediated Communication*, April 2004). Participants were 48 undergraduate students, of which half were randomly assigned to the CMC group and half assigned to the FTF group. Each group was given a task that required communication with their group members. Those in the CMC group used the "chat" mode of instant-messaging software; those in the FTF group met in a conference room. The variable of interest, relational intimacy score, was measured (on a 7-point scale) for each participant after each of three different meeting sessions. Scores for the first meeting session are given below. The researchers hypothesized that, after the first meeting, the mean relational intimacy score for participants in the CMC group will be lower than the mean relational intimacy score for participants in the FTF group. Test the researchers' hypothesis using $\alpha = .10$.

🔅 **INTIMACY**

CMC:	4 3 3 4 3 3 3 3 4 4 3 4
	3 3 2 4 2 4 5 4 4 4 5 3

FTF:	5 4 4 4 3 3 3 4 3 3 3 3
	4 4 4 4 4 3 3 3 4 4 2 4

Note: Data simulated from descriptive statistics provided in article.

7.19 Ingratiatory behavior toward supervisors. *Ingratiation* is defined as a class of strategic behaviors designed to make others believe in the attractiveness of one's personal qualities. In organizational settings, individuals use such behaviors to influence superiors in order to attain personal goals. An index that measures ingratiatory behavior, called the Measure of Ingratiatory Behaviors in Organizational Settings (MIBOS) Index, was applied independently to a sample of managers employed by four manufacturing companies in the southeastern United States and to clerical personnel from a large university in the northwestern United States (*Journal of Applied Psychology*, Dec. 1998). Scores are reported on a five-point scale with higher scores indicating more extensive ingratiatory behavior. Summary statistics are shown in the table.

Managers	Clerical Personnel
$n_1 = 288$	$n_2 = 110$
$\bar{x}_1 = 2.41$	$\bar{x}_2 = 1.90$
$s_1 = .74$	$s_2 = .59$

Source: Harrison, Allison W., Hochwarter, Wayne A., Perrewe, Pamela L., and Ralston, David A. "The Ingratiation Construct: An Assessment of the Validity of the Measure of Ingratiatory Behaviors in Organization Settings (MIBOS)." *Journal of Applied Psychology*, Vol. 86, No. 6, Dec. 1998, pp. 932–943.

a. Specify the null and alternative hypotheses you would use to test for a difference in ingratiatory behavior between managers and clerical personnel.

b. Conduct the test of part **a** using $\alpha = .05$. Interpret the results of the test in the context of the problem.

c. Construct a 95% confidence interval for $(\mu_1 - \mu_2)$ and interpret the result. Your conclusion should agree with your answer in part **b.**

7.20 Should you purchase the lecture notes? Some college professors make bound lecture notes available to their classes in an effort to improve teaching effectiveness. *Marketing Educational Review* (Fall 1994) published a study of business students' opinions of lecture notes. Two groups of students were surveyed—86 students enrolled in a promotional strategy class that required the purchase of lecture notes, and 35 students enrolled in a sales/retailing elective that did not offer lecture notes. At the end of the semester, the students were asked to respond to the statement, "Having a copy of the lecture notes was [would be] helpful in understanding the material." Responses were measured on a 9-point semantic difference scale, where 1 = "strongly disagree" and 9 = "strongly agree." A summary of the results is reported in the table.

Classes Buying Lecture Notes	Classes Not Buying Lecture Notes
$n_1 = 86$	$n_2 = 35$
$\bar{x}_1 = 8.48$	$\bar{x}_2 = 7.80$
$s_1^2 = 0.94$	$s_2^2 = 2.99$

Source: Gray, J. I., and Abernathy, A. M. "Pros and Cons of Lecture Notes and Handout Packages: Faculty and Student Opinions," *Marketing Education Review*, Vol. 4, No. 3, Fall 1984, p. 25 (Table 4). American Marketing Association.

a. Describe the two populations involved in the comparison.
b. Do the samples provide sufficient evidence to conclude that there is a difference in the mean responses of the two groups of students? Test using $\alpha = .01$.
c. Construct a 99% confidence interval for $(\mu_1 - \mu_2)$. Interpret the result.
d. Would a 95% confidence interval for $(\mu_1 - \mu_2)$ be narrower or wider than the one you found in part **c**? Why?

7.21 Comparing purchasers and nonpurchasers of toothpaste. Marketing strategists would like to predict consumer response to new products and their accompanying promotional schemes. Consequently, studies that examine the differences between buyers and nonbuyers of a product are of interest. One classic study conducted by Shuchman and Riesz (*Journal of Marketing Research,* Feb. 1975) was aimed at characterizing the purchasers and nonpurchasers of Crest toothpaste. The researchers demonstrated that both the mean household size (number of persons) and mean household income were significantly larger for purchasers than for nonpurchasers. A similar study utilized independent random samples of size 20 and yielded the data shown in the next table on the age of the householder primarily responsible for buying toothpaste.
a. Do the data present sufficient evidence to conclude there is a difference in the mean age of purchasers and nonpurchasers? Use $\alpha = .10$.
b. What assumptions are necessary in order to answer part **a**?

c. Find the observed significance level for the test and interpret its value.
d. Calculate and interpret a 90% confidence interval for the difference between the mean ages of purchasers and nonpurchasers.

CREST

Purchasers						Nonpurchasers					
34	35	23	44	52	46	28	22	44	33	55	63
28	48	28	34	33	52	45	31	60	54	53	58
41	32	34	49	50	45	52	52	66	35	25	48
29	59					59	61				

7.22 Bacteria counts at a plant's liquid waste discharge. Suppose you manage a plant that purifies its liquid waste and discharges the water into a local river. An EPA inspector has collected water specimens of the discharge of your plant and also water specimens in the river upstream from your plant. Each water specimen is divided into five parts, the bacteria count is read on each, and the median count for each specimen is reported. The bacteria counts for each of six specimens are reported in the following table for the two locations.

BACTERIA

Plant Discharge			Upstream		
30.1	36.2	33.4	29.7	30.3	26.4
28.2	29.8	34.9	27.3	31.7	32.3

a. Why might the bacteria counts shown here tend to be approximately normally distributed?
b. What are the appropriate null and alternative hypotheses to test whether the mean bacteria count for the plant discharge exceeds that for the upstream location? Be sure to define any symbols you use.
c. Conduct the test, part **b**. Carefully interpret the results.

d. What assumptions are necessary to ensure the validity of this test?

GASTURBINE

7.23 Cooling method for gas turbines. Refer to the *Journal of Engineering for Gas Turbines and Power* (Jan. 2005) study of gas turbines augmented with high-pressure inlet fogging, Exercise 6.26 (p. 358). The researchers classified gas turbines into three categories: traditional, advanced, and aeroderivative. Summary statistics on heat rate (kilojoules per kilowatt per hour) for each of the three types of gas turbines in the sample are shown in the MINITAB printout below.
a. Is there sufficient evidence of a difference between the mean heat rates of traditional augmented gas turbines and aeroderivative augmented gas turbines? Test using $\alpha = .05$.

MINITAB Output for Exercise 7.23

Descriptive Statistics: HEATRATE

```
Variable   ENGINE        N    Mean   StDev   Minimum   Maximum
HEATRATE   Advanced     21    9764     639      9105     11588
           Aeroderiv     7   12312    2652      8714     16243
           Traditional  39   11544    1279     10086     14796
```

b. Is there sufficient evidence of a difference between the mean heat rates of advanced augmented gas turbines and aeroderivative augmented gas turbines? Test using $\alpha = .05$.

Applying the Concepts—Advanced

7.24 CareerBank.com annual salary survey. CareerBank.com conducts an annual salary survey of accounting, finance, and banking professionals. For the 2004 survey, data were collected for 2,800 responses submitted online by professionals across the country who voluntarily responded to CareerBank.com's Web-based survey. Salary comparisons were made by gender, education, and marital status. Some of the results are shown in the accompanying table.

a. Suppose you want to make an inference about the difference between the mean salaries of male and female accounting/finance/banking professionals at a 95% level of confidence. Why is this impossible to do using the information in the table?

b. Give values of the missing standard deviations that would lead you to conclude that the mean salary for males is significantly higher than the mean salary for females at a 95% level of confidence.

c. In your opinion, are the sample standard deviations, part **b**, reasonable values for the salary data? Explain.

d. How does the data-collection method impact any inferences derived from the data?

	Males	Females
Mean Salary	$69,848	$52,012
Number of Respondents	1,400	1,400

7.3 Comparing Two Population Means: Paired Difference Experiments

Suppose you want to compare the mean daily sales of two restaurants located in the same city. If you were to record the restaurants' total sales for each of 12 randomly selected days during a 6-month period, the results might appear as shown in Table 7.3. Do these data provide evidence of a difference between the mean daily sales of the two restaurants?

We want to test the null hypothesis that the mean daily sales, μ_1 and μ_2, for the two restaurants are equal against the alternative hypothesis that they differ; that is,

$$H_0: (\mu_1 - \mu_2) = 0$$
$$H_a: (\mu_1 - \mu_2) \neq 0$$

One way to conduct this test is to use the t-statistic for two independent samples (Section 7.2). The analysis is shown on the Excel printout, Figure 7.10. The test statistic, $t = .384$, is highlighted on the printout as well as the p-value of the test, p-value $= .705$. At $\alpha = .10$, the p-value exceeds α. Thus, from *this* analysis we might conclude that insufficient evidence exists to infer that there is a difference in mean daily sales for the two restaurants.

RESTSALES

TABLE 7.3 Daily Sales for Two Restaurants

Day	Restaurant 1 x_1	Restaurant 2 x_2
1 (Wednesday)	$1,005	$ 918
2 (Saturday)	2,073	1,971
3 (Tuesday)	873	825
4 (Wednesday)	1,074	999
5 (Friday)	1,932	1,827
6 (Thursday)	1,338	1,281
7 (Thursday)	1,449	1,302
8 (Monday)	759	678
9 (Friday)	1,905	1,782
10 (Monday)	693	639
11 (Saturday)	2,106	2,049
12 (Tuesday)	981	933

	A	B
1	t Test for Differences In Two Means	
2		
3	Data	
4	Hypothesized Difference	0
5	Level of Significance	0.05
6	Population 1 Sample	
7	Sample Size	12
8	Sample Mean	1349
9	Sample Standard Deviation	530.07
10	Population 2 Sample	
11	Sample Size	12
12	Sample Mean	1267
13	Sample Standard Deviation	516.04
14		
15	Intermediate Calculations	
16	Population 1 Sample Degrees of Freedom	11
17	Population 2 Sample Degrees of Freedom	11
18	Total Degrees of Freedom	22
19	Pooled Variance	273635.7
20	Difference in Sample Means	82
21	t Test Statistic	0.383975
22		
23	Two-Tail Test	
24	Lower Critical Value	-2.07388
25	Upper Critical Value	2.073875
26	p-Value	0.704683
27	Do not reject the null hypothesis	

FIGURE 7.10

EXCEL/PHStat2 analysis of daily restaurant sales

If you carefully examine the data in Table 7.3, however, you will find this conclusion difficult to accept. The sales of restaurant 1 exceed those of restaurant 2 *for every one of the randomly selected 12 days.* This, in itself, is strong evidence to indicate that μ_1 differs from μ_2, and we will subsequently confirm this fact. Why, then, was the *t*-test unable to detect this difference? The answer is, *The independent samples* t-*test is not a valid procedure to use with this set of data.*

The *t*-test is inappropriate because the assumption of independent samples is invalid. We have randomly chosen *days,* and thus, once we have chosen the sample of days for restaurant 1, we have *not* independently chosen the sample of days for restaurant 2. The dependence between observations within days can be seen by examining the pairs of daily sales, which tend to rise and fall together as we go from day to day. This pattern provides strong visual evidence of a violation of the assumption of independence required for the two-sample *t*-test of Section 7.2. Note also that

$$s_p^2 = \frac{(n_1 - 1)s_1^2 + (n_2 - 1)s_2^2}{n_1 + n_2 - 2}$$

$$= \frac{(12 - 1)(530.07)^2 + (12 - 1)(516.04)^2}{12 + 12 - 2} = 273{,}635.7.$$

Thus, there is a *large variation within samples* (reflected by the large value of s_p^2) in comparison to the relatively *small difference between the sample means.* Because s_p^2 is so large, the *t*-test of Section 7.2 is unable to detect a possible difference between μ_1 and μ_2.

We now consider a valid method of analyzing the data of Table 7.3. In Table 7.4, we add the column of differences between the daily sales of the two restaurants, $d = x_1 - x_2$. We can regard these daily differences in sales as a random sample of all daily differences, past and present. Then we can use this sample to make inferences about the mean of the population of differences, μ_d, which is equal to the difference $(\mu_1 - \mu_2)$—that is, the mean of the population (and sample) of differences equals the difference between the population (and sample) means. Thus, our test becomes

$$H_0: \mu_d = 0 \text{ [i.e., } (\mu_1 - \mu_2) = 0]$$
$$H_a: \mu_d \neq 0 \text{ [i.e., } (\mu_1 - \mu_2) \neq 0]$$

The test statistic is a one-sample *t* (Section 6.4), since we are now analyzing a single sample of differences for small *n:*

$$Test\ statistic: t = \frac{\bar{d} - 0}{s_d/\sqrt{n_d}}$$

TABLE 7.4 Daily Sales and Differences for Two Restaurants

Day	Restaurant 1 x_1	Restaurant 2 x_2	Difference $d = x_1 - x_2$
1 (Wednesday)	$1,005	$ 918	$ 87
2 (Saturday)	2,073	1,971	102
3 (Tuesday)	873	825	48
4 (Wednesday)	1,074	999	75
5 (Friday)	1,932	1,827	105
6 (Thursday)	1,338	1,281	57
7 (Thursday)	1,449	1,302	147
8 (Monday)	759	678	81
9 (Friday)	1,905	1,782	123
10 (Monday)	693	639	54
11 (Saturday)	2,106	2,049	57
12 (Tuesday)	981	933	48

where $\bar{d}$ = Sample mean difference

s_d = Sample standard deviation of differences

n_d = Number of differences = number of pairs

Assumptions: The population of differences in daily sales is approximately normally distributed. The sample differences are randomly selected from the population differences. [*Note:* We do not need to make the assumption that $\sigma_1^2 = \sigma_2^2$.

Rejection region: At significance level $\alpha = .05$, we will reject H_0 if $|t| > t_{.05}$, where $t_{.05}$ is based on $(n_d - 1)$ degrees of freedom.

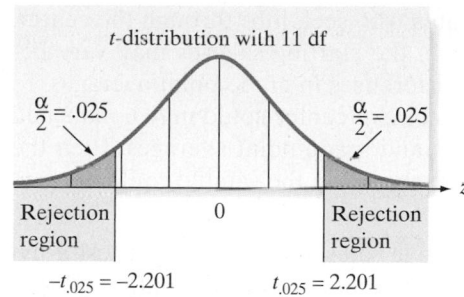

FIGURE 7.11

Rejection region for restaurant sales example

Referring to Table V in Appendix B, we find the *t*-value corresponding to $\alpha = .025$ and $n_d - 1 = 12 - 1 = 11$ df to be $t_{.025} = 2.201$. Then we will reject the null hypothesis if $|t| > 2.201$ (see Figure 7.11). Note that the number of degrees of freedom has decreased from $n_1 + n_2 - 2 = 22$ to 11 when we use the paired difference experiment rather than the two independent random samples design.

Summary statistics for the $n = 12$ differences are shown on the MINITAB printout, Figure 7.12. Note that $\bar{d} = 82.0$ and $s_d = 32.0$ (rounded). Substituting these values into the formula for the test statistic, we have

$$t = \frac{\bar{d} - 0}{s_d/\sqrt{n_d}} = \frac{82}{32/\sqrt{12}} = 8.88$$

Because this value of t falls in the rejection region, we conclude (at $\alpha = .05$) that the difference in population mean daily sales for the two restaurants differs from 0. We can reach the same conclusion by noting that the *p*-value of the test, highlighted in Figure 7.12, is approximately 0. The fact that $(\bar{x}_1 - \bar{x}_2) = \bar{d} = \$82.00$ strongly suggests that the mean daily sales for restaurant 1 exceeds the mean daily sales for restaurant 2.

```
Paired T for SALES1 - SALES2

                 N     Mean    StDev   SE Mean
SALES1          12   1349.00   530.07   153.02
SALES2          12   1267.00   516.04   148.97
Difference      12   82.0000   31.9886    9.2343


95% CI for mean difference: (61.6754, 102.3246)
T-Test of mean difference = 0 (vs not = 0): T-Value = 8.88   P-Value = 0.000
```

FIGURE 7.12

MINITAB analysis of differences in daily restaurant sales

> **Now Work Exercise 7.26a, b**

This kind of experiment, in which observations are paired and the differences are analyzed, is called a **paired difference experiment**. In many cases, a paired difference experiment can provide more information about the difference between population means than an independent samples experiment. The idea is to compare population means by comparing the differences between pairs of experimental units (objects, people, etc.) that were very similar prior to the experiment. The differencing removes sources of variation that tend to inflate σ^2. For instance, in the restaurant example, the day-to-day variability in daily sales is removed by analyzing the differences between the restaurants' daily sales. Making comparisons within groups of similar experimental units is called **blocking**, and the paired difference experiment is an example of a **randomized block experiment**. In our example, the days represent the blocks.

Some other examples for which the paired difference experiment might be appropriate are the following:

1. Suppose you want to estimate the difference $(\mu_1 - \mu_2)$ in mean price per gallon between two major brands of premium gasoline. If you choose two independent random samples of stations for each brand, the variability in price due to geographic location may be large. To eliminate this source of variability, you could choose pairs of stations of similar size, one station for each brand, in close geographic proximity and use the sample of differences between the prices of the brands to make an inference about $(\mu_1 - \mu_2)$.

2. A college placement center wants to estimate the difference $(\mu_1 - \mu_2)$ in mean starting salaries for men and women graduates who seek jobs through the center. If it independently samples men and women, the starting salaries may vary because of their different college majors and differences in grade point averages. To eliminate these sources of variability, the placement center could match male and female job seekers according to their majors and grade point averages. Then the differences between the starting salaries of each pair in the sample could be used to make an inference about $(\mu_1 - \mu_2)$.

3. To compare the performance of two automobile salespeople, we might test a hypothesis about the difference $(\mu_1 - \mu_2)$ in their respective mean monthly sales. If we randomly choose n_1 months of salesperson 1's sales and independently choose n_2 months of salesperson 2's sales, the month-to-month variability caused by the seasonal nature of new car sales might inflate s_p^2 and prevent the two-sample t-statistic from detecting a difference between μ_1 and μ_2, if such a difference actually exists. However, by taking the difference in monthly sales for the two salespeople for each of n months, we eliminate the month-to-month variability (seasonal variation) in sales, and the probability of detecting a difference between μ_1 and μ_2, if a difference exists, is increased.

The hypothesis-testing procedures and the method of forming confidence intervals for the difference between two means using a paired difference experiment are summarized in the following boxes for both large and small n.

Paired Difference Test of Hypothesis for $\mu_d = (\mu_1 - \mu_2)$

One-Tailed Test	Two-Tailed Test
H_0: $\mu_d = D_0$	H_0: $\mu_d = D_0$
H_a: $\mu_d < D_0$	H_a: $\mu_d \neq D_0$
[or H_a: $\mu_d > D_0$]	

Large Sample

Test statistic: $z = \dfrac{\bar{d} - D_0}{\sigma_d/\sqrt{n_d}} \approx \dfrac{\bar{d} - D_0}{s_d/\sqrt{n_d}}$

Rejection region: $z < -z_\alpha$ Rejection region: $|z| > z_{\alpha/2}$
[or $z > z_\alpha$ when H_a: $\mu_d > D_0$]

Small Sample

Test statistic: $t = \dfrac{\bar{d} - D_0}{s_d/\sqrt{n_d}}$

Rejection region: $t < -t_\alpha$ Rejection region: $|t| > t_{\alpha/2}$
[or $t > t_\alpha$ when H_a: $\mu_d > D_0$]

where t_α and $t_{\alpha/2}$ are based on $(n_d - 1)$ degrees of freedom

Paired Difference Confidence Interval for $\mu_d = (\mu_1 - \mu_2)$

Large Sample

$$\bar{d} \pm z_{\alpha/2}\frac{\sigma_d}{\sqrt{n_d}} \approx \bar{d} \pm z_{\alpha/2}\frac{s_d}{\sqrt{n_d}}$$

Small Sample

$$\bar{d} \pm t_{\alpha/2}\frac{s_d}{\sqrt{n_d}}$$

where $t_{\alpha/2}$ is based on $(n_d - 1)$ degrees of freedom.

Conditions Required for Valid Large-Sample Inferences about μ_d

1. A random sample of differences is selected from the target population of differences.
2. The sample size n_d is large (i.e., $n_d \geq 30$); due to the Central Limit Theorem, this condition guarantees that the test statistic will be approximately normal regardless of the shape of the underlying probability distribution of the population).

Conditions Required for Valid Small-Sample Inferences about μ_d

1. A random sample of differences is selected from the target population of differences.
2. The population of differences has a distribution that is approximately normal.

Now Work Exercise 7.25

EXAMPLE 7.5

Using a Confidence Interval for μ_d to Compare Mean Salaries of Males and Females

Problem An experiment is conducted to compare the starting salaries of male and female college graduates who find jobs. Pairs are formed by choosing a male and a female with the same major and similar grade point averages (GPAs). Suppose a random sample of 10 pairs is formed in this manner and the starting annual salary of each person is recorded. The results are shown in Table 7.5. Compare the mean starting salary, μ_1, for males to the mean starting salary, μ_2, for females using a 95% confidence interval. Interpret the results

Solution Since the data on annual salary are collected in pairs of males and females matched on GPA and major, a paired difference experiment is performed. To conduct the analysis, we first compute the differences between the salaries, as shown in Table 7.5. Summary statistics for these $n = 10$ differences are displayed in the MINITAB printout, Figure 7.13.

The 95% confidence interval for $\mu_d = (\mu_1 - \mu_2)$ for this small sample is

$$\bar{d} \pm t_{\alpha/2}\frac{s_d}{\sqrt{n_d}}$$

GRADPAIRS

TABLE 7.5 Data on Annual Salaries for Matched Pairs of College Graduates

Pair	Male x_1	Female x_2	Difference $d = x_1 - x_2$
1	$29,300	$28,800	$500
2	41,500	41,600	−100
3	40,400	39,800	600
4	38,500	38,500	0
5	43,500	42,600	900
6	37,800	38,000	$−200
7	69,500	69,200	300
8	41,200	40,100	1,100
9	38,400	38,200	200
10	59,200	58,500	700

```
Paired T for MALE - FEMALE

                N      Mean    StDev   SE Mean
MALE           10   43930.0  11665.1   3688.8
FEMALE         10   43530.0  11616.9   3673.6
Difference     10   400.000  434.613   137.437


95% CI for mean difference: (89.096, 710.904)
T-Test of mean difference = 0 (vs not = 0): T-Value = 2.91   P-Value = 0.017
```

FIGURE 7.13

MINITAB analysis of salary differences

where $t_{\alpha/2} = t_{.025} = 2.262$ (obtained from Table V, Appendix B) is based on $n_d - 1 = 9$ degrees of freedom. Substituting the values of $\bar{d} = 400$ and $s_d = 434.6$ shown on the printout, we obtain

$$\bar{d} \pm t_{.025}\frac{s_d}{\sqrt{n_d}} = 400 \pm 2.262\left(\frac{434.6}{\sqrt{10}}\right)$$

$$= 400 \pm 310.87 \approx 400 \pm 311 = (\$89, \$711)$$

[*Note:* This interval is also shown on the MINITAB printout, Figure 7.13.] Our interpretation is that the true mean difference between the starting salaries of males and females falls between $89 and $711, with 95% confidence. Since the interval falls above 0, we infer that $\mu_1 - \mu_2 > 0$; that is, that the mean salary for males exceeds the mean salary for females.

Look Back Remember that $\mu_d = \mu_1 - \mu_2$. So, if $\mu_d > 0$, then $\mu_1 > \mu_2$. Alternatively, if $\mu_d < 0$, then $\mu_1 < \mu_2$.

Now Work Exercise 7.33

To measure the amount of information about $(\mu_1 - \mu_2)$ gained by using a paired difference experiment in Example 7.5 rather than an independent samples experiment, we can compare the relative widths of the confidence intervals obtained by the two methods. A 95% confidence interval for $(\mu_1 - \mu_2)$ using the paired difference experiment is, from Example 7.5, ($89, $711). If we analyzed the same data as though this were

Group Statistics

	GENDER	N	Mean	Std. Deviation	Std. Error Mean
SALARY	M	10	43930.00	11665.148	3688.844
	F	10	43530.00	11616.946	3673.601

Independent Samples Test

		Levene's Test for Equality of Variances		t-test for Equality of Means							
										95% Confidence Interval of the Difference	
		F	Sig.	t	df	Sig. (2-tailed)	Mean Difference	Std. Error Difference	Lower	Upper
SALARY	Equal variances assumed	.000	.991	.077	18	.940	400.00	5206.046	-10537.5	11337.50
	Equal variances not assumed			.077	18.000	.940	400.00	5206.046	-10537.5	11337.51

FIGURE 7.14

SPSS analysis of salaries, assuming independent samples

an independent samples experiment,* we would first obtain the descriptive statistics shown in the SPSS printout, Figure 7.14.

Then we substitute the sample means and standard deviations shown on the printout into the formula for a 95% confidence interval for $(\mu_1 - \mu_2)$ using independent samples:

$$(\bar{x}_1 - \bar{x}_2) \pm t_{.025}\sqrt{s_p^2\left(\frac{1}{n_1} + \frac{1}{n_2}\right)}$$

where

$$s_p^2 = \frac{(n_1 - 1)s_1^2 + (n_2 - 1)s_2^2}{n_1 + n_2 - 2}$$

SPSS performed these calculations and obtained the interval ($10,537.50, $11,337.50). This interval is highlighted in Figure 7.14.

Notice that the independent samples interval includes 0. Consequently, if we were to use this interval to make an inference about $(\mu_1 - \mu_2)$, we would incorrectly conclude that the mean starting salaries of males and females do not differ! You can see that the confidence interval for the independent sampling experiment is about five times wider than for the corresponding paired difference confidence interval. Blocking out the variability due to differences in majors and grade point averages significantly increases the information about the difference in male and female mean starting salaries by providing a much more accurate (smaller confidence interval for the same confidence coefficient) estimate of $(\mu_1 - \mu_2)$.

You may wonder whether conducting a paired difference experiment is always superior to an independent samples experiment. The answer is, Most of the time, but not always. We sacrifice half the degrees of freedom in the t-statistic when a paired difference design is used instead of an independent samples design. This is a loss of information, and unless this loss is more than compensated for by the reduction in variability obtained by blocking (pairing), the paired difference experiment will result in a net loss of information about $(\mu_1 - \mu_2)$. Thus, we should be convinced that the pairing will significantly reduce variability before performing the paired difference experiment. Most of the time this will happen.

---

*This is done only to provide a measure of the increase in the amount of information obtained by a paired design in comparison to an unpaired design. Actually, if an experiment is designed using pairing, an unpaired analysis would be invalid because the assumption of independent samples would not be satisfied.

One final note: The pairing of the observations is determined before the experiment is performed (that is, by the *design* of the experiment). A paired difference experiment is *never* obtained by pairing the sample observations after the measurements have been acquired.

What Do You Do When the Assumption of a Normal Distribution for the Population of Differences Is Not Satisfied?

Answer: Use the Wilcoxon signed rank test for the paired difference design (Chapter 14).

ACTIVITY 7.1: *Box Office Receipts:* Comparing Population Means

Use the Internet to find the daily box office receipts for two different hit movies during the first eight weeks after their releases. In this activity, you will compare the mean daily box office receipts of these movies in two different ways.

1. Independently select random samples of size $n = 30$ from the data sets for each of the movies' daily box office receipts. Find the mean and standard deviation of each sample. Then find a confidence interval for the difference of the means.

2. Now pair the data for the two movies by day, that is, the box office receipts for the day of release for each movie are paired, the box office receipts for each movie's second day are paired, etc. Calculate the difference in box office receipts for each day

and select a random sample of size $n = 30$ from the daily differences. Then find a confidence interval for the sample mean.

3. Compare the confidence intervals from Exercises 1 and 2. Explain how the sampling for the paired difference experiment is different from the independent sampling. How might this sampling technique yield a better comparison of the two means in the box office example?

4. Compute the actual means for the daily box office receipts for each of the movies and then find the difference of the means. Does the difference of the means lie in both confidence intervals you found? Is the exact difference remarkably closer to one of the estimates? Explain.

Confidence Interval for a Paired Difference Mean

Using the TI-83/TI-84 Graphing Calculator

Note: There is no paired difference option on the calculator. These instructions demonstrate how to calculate the differences and then use the 1-sample *t*-interval.

Step 1   *Enter the data and calculate the differences.*

Press **STAT** and select **1:Edit**.
Note: If the lists already contain data, clear the old data. Use the up **ARROW** to highlight 'L1'.
Press **CLEAR ENTER**.
Use the up **ARROW** to highlight 'L2'.
Press **CLEAR ENTER**.
Use the **ARROW** and **ENTER** keys to enter the first data set into **L1**.
Use the **ARROW** and **ENTER** keys to enter the second data set into **L2**.
The differences will be calculated in **L3**.
Use the up **ARROW** to highlight 'L3'.
Press **CLEAR**. This will clear any old data, but **L3** will remain highlighted.
To enter the equation L3 = L1 − L2, use the following keystrokes:
Press **2ND '1'** (this will enter L1)
Press the **MINUS** button

Press 2ND '2' (this will enter L2)
(Notice the equation at the bottom of the screen.)
Press **ENTER** (the differences should be calculated in L3).

Step 2   *Access the Statistical Tests Menu*

Press **STAT**.
Arrow right to **TESTS**.
Arrow down to **TInterval (even for large sample case).**
Press **ENTER**.

L1	L2	**L3**	3
65	62	3	
58	53	5	
78	36	42	
60	34	26	
68	56	12	
69	50	19	
66	42	24	

L3 =L1−L2

```
EDIT CALC TESTS
2↑T-Test…
3:2-SampZTest…
4:2-SampTTest…
5:1-PropZTest…
6:2-PropZTest…
7:ZInterval…
8↓TInterval…
```

Step 3   *Choose "Data"*

Press **ENTER**.
Set **List** to **L3**.
Set **Freq** to **1**.
Set **C-Level** to the confidence level.
Arrow down to **"Calculate"**.
Press **ENTER**.

```
TInterval
 Inpt:DATA Stats
 List:L3
 Freq:1
 C-Level:.95
 Calculate
```

The confidence interval will be displayed with the mean, standard deviation, and sample size of the differences.

Hypothesis Test for a Paired Difference Mean

Using the TI-83/TI-84 Graphing Calculator

Note: There is no paired difference option on the calculator. These instructions demonstrate how to calculate the differences and then use the 1-sample *t*-test.

Step 1   *Enter the data and calculate the differences.*

Press **STAT** and select **1:Edit**.
Note: If the lists already contain data, clear the old data. Use the up **ARROW** to highlight 'L1'.
Press **CLEAR ENTER**.
Use the up **ARROW** to highlight 'L2'.
Press **CLEAR ENTER**.
Use the **ARROW** and **ENTER** keys to enter the first data set into **L1.**
Use the **ARROW** and **ENTER** keys to enter the second data set into **L2.**
The differences will be calculated in **L3**.
Use the up **ARROW** to highlight 'L3'.
Press **CLEAR**. This will clear any old data, but **L3** will remain highlighted.
To enter the equation L3 = L1 − L2, use the following keystrokes:
Press 2ND '1' (this will enter L1)
Press the **MINUS** button
Press 2ND '2' (this will enter L2)

Continued

(Notice the equation at the bottom of the screen.)
Press **ENTER** (the differences should be calculated in L3)

L1	L2	**L3**	3
65	62	3	
58	53	5	
78	36	42	
60	34	26	
68	56	12	
69	50	19	
66	42	24	

L3 =L₁-L₂

```
EDIT CALC TESTS
1:Z-Test…
2:T-Test…
3:2-SampZTest…
4:2-SampTTest…
5:1-PropZTest…
6:2-PropZTest…
7↓ZInterval…
```

Step 2   *Access the Statistical Tests Menu*

Press **STAT**.
Arrow right to **TESTS**.
Arrow down to **T-Test (even for large sample case)**.
Press **ENTER**.

Step 3   *Choose "Data"*

Press **ENTER**.
Enter the values for the hypothesis test where μ_0 = the value for μ_d in the null hypothesis.
Set **List** to **L3**.
Set **Freq** to **1**.
Use the **ARROW** to highlight the appropriate alternative hypothesis.
Press **ENTER**.
Arrow down to "**Calculate**".
Press **ENTER**.

The test statistic and the p-value will be displayed, as well as the sample mean, standard deviation, and sample size of the differences.

Exercises 7.25–7.40

Learning the Mechanics

7.25 A paired difference experiment yielded n_d pairs of observations. In each case, what is the rejection region for testing H_0: $\mu_d > 2$?
  a. $n_d = 12, \alpha = .05$
  b. $n_d = 24, \alpha = .10$
  c. $n_d = 4, \alpha = .025$
  d. $n_d = 80, \alpha = .01$

7.26 The data for a random sample of six paired observations
NW are shown in the table.

⊙ **LM7_26**

Pair	Sample from Population 1 (Observation 1)	Sample from Population 2 (Observation 2)
1	7	4
2	3	1
3	9	7
4	6	2
5	4	4
6	8	7

  a. Calculate the difference between each pair of observations by subtracting observation 2 from observation 1. Use the differences to calculate $\bar{d}$ and s_d^2.

  b. If μ_1 and μ_2 are the means of populations 1 and 2, respectively, express μ_d in terms of μ_1 and μ_2.
  c. Form a 95% confidence interval for μ_D.
  d. Test the null hypothesis H_0: $\mu_d = 0$ against the alternative hypothesis H_a: $\mu_d \neq 0$. Use $\alpha = .05$.

7.27 The data for a random sample of 10 paired observations are shown in the next table.

⊙ **LM7_27**

Pair	Sample from Population 1	Sample from Population 2
1	19	24
2	25	27
3	31	36
4	52	53
5	49	55
6	34	34
7	59	66
8	47	51
9	17	20
10	51	55

  a. If you wish to test whether these data are sufficient to indicate that the mean for population 2 is larger than that for population 1, what are the appropriate null and alternative hypotheses? Define any symbols you use.

b. Conduct the test, part **a**, using $\alpha = .10$.

c. Find a 90% confidence interval for μ_d. Interpret this result.

d. What assumptions are necessary to ensure the validity of this analysis?

7.28 A paired difference experiment produced the following results:

$$n_d = 38 \quad \bar{x}_1 = 92 \quad \bar{x}_2 = 95.5 \quad \bar{d} = -3.5 \quad s_d^2 = 21$$

a. Determine the values of z for which the null hypothesis, $\mu_1 - \mu_2 = 0$, would be rejected in favor of the alternative hypothesis, $\mu_1 - \mu_2 < 0$. Use $\alpha = .10$.

b. Conduct the paired difference test described in part **a**. Draw the appropriate conclusions.

c. What assumptions are necessary so that the paired difference test will be valid?

d. Find a 90% confidence interval for the mean difference μ_D.

e. Which of the two inferential procedures, the confidence interval of part **d** or the test of hypothesis of part **b**, provides more information about the differences between the population means?

7.29 A paired difference experiment yielded the following results:

$$n_d = 40, \quad \Sigma d = 468, \quad \Sigma d^2 = 6,880.$$

a. Test $H_0: \mu_d = 10$ against $H_a: \mu_d \neq 10$, where $\mu_d = (\mu_1 - \mu_2)$. Use $\alpha = .05$.

b. Report the p-value for the test you conducted in part **a**. Interpret the p-value.

c. Do you need to assume that the population of differences is normally distributed? Explain.

Applying the Concepts—Basic

7.30 Salaries of technology professionals. The data in the table, obtained from *Business Week's* (June, 22, 2006) technology section, represents typical salaries of technology professionals in 13 metropolitan areas for 2003 and 2005. Suppose you want to determine if the mean salary of technology professionals at all U.S. metropolitan areas has increased between 2003 and 2005.

TECHPRO

Metro Area	2003 Salary ($ thousands)	2005 Salary ($ thousands)
Silicon Valley	87.7	85.9
New York	78.6	80.3
Washington, D.C.	71.4	77.4
Los Angeles	70.8	77.1
Denver	73.0	77.1
Boston	76.3	80.1
Atlanta	73.6	73.2
Chicago	71.1	73.0
Philadelphia	69.5	69.8
San Diego	69.0	77.1
Seattle	71.0	66.9
Dallas-Ft. Worth	73.0	71.0
Detroit	62.3	64.1

Source: Dice, Inc.; www.businessweek.com, June 22, 2006.

a. Set up the null and alternative hypothesis for the test.

b. Calculate the difference between the 2003 and 2005 salaries for each metropolitan area.

c. Find the mean and standard deviation of the differences, part **b**.

d. Use the results, part **c**, to calculate the test statistic.

e. Find the rejection region for the test at $\alpha = .10$.

f. Make the appropriate conclusion.

g. What conditions are required for the inference in part **f** to be valid? Are these conditions reasonably satisfied?

7.31 Visual search and memory study. When searching for an item (e.g., a roadside traffic sign, a misplaced file, or a tumor in a mammogram), common sense dictates that you will not reexamine items previously rejected. However, researchers at Harvard Medical School found that a visual search has no memory (*Nature*, Aug. 6, 1998). In their experiment, nine subjects searched for the letter "T" mixed among several letters "L." Each subject conducted the search under two conditions: random and static. In the random condition, the location of the letters were changed every 111 milliseconds; in the static condition, the location of the letters remained unchanged. In each trial, the reaction time (i.e., the amount of time it took the subject to locate the target letter) was recorded in milliseconds.

a. One goal of the research is to compare the mean reaction times of subjects in the two experimental conditions. Explain why the data should be analyzed as a paired-difference experiment.

b. If a visual search had no memory, then the mean reaction times in the two conditions will not differ. Specify H_0 and H_a for testing the "no memory" theory.

c. The test statistic was calculated as $t = 1.52$ with p-value $= .15$. Make the appropriate conclusion.

7.32 Life expectancy of Oscar winners. Movie actors who win an Oscar usually can command a greater fee for their next motion picture. Does winning an Academy of Motion Picture Arts and Sciences award (a.k.a., an Oscar) lead to long-term mortality for movie actors? In an article in the *Annals of Internal Medicine* (May 15, 2001), researchers sampled 762 Academy Award winners and matched each one with another actor of the same sex who was in the same winning film and was born in the same era. The life expectancy (age) of each pair of actors was compared.

a. Explain why the data should be analyzed as a paired difference experiment.

b. Set up the null hypothesis for a test to compare the mean life expectancies of Academy Award winners and nonwinners.

c. The sample mean life expectancies of Academy Award winners and nonwinners were reported as 79.7 years and 75.8 years, respectively. The p-value for comparing the two population means was reported as $p = .003$. Interpret this value in the context of the problem.

7.33 Testing electronic circuits. Japanese researchers have developed a compression/depression method of testing electronic circuits based on Huffman coding (*IEICE Transactions on Information & Systems*, Jan. 2005). The new method is designed to reduce the time required for input decompression and output compression—called the *compression ratio*. Experimental results were obtained by testing a sample of 11 benchmark circuits (all of different sizes) from a SUN Blade 1000 workstation. Each circuit was tested using the standard compression/depression method and the new Huffman-based coding method and the compression ratio recorded. The data are given in the next table (p. 434). Compare the two methods with a 95% confidence interval. Which method has the smaller mean compression ratio?

434 Chapter 7 Inferences Based on Two Samples

CIRCUITS

Circuit	Standard Method	Huffman-coding Method
1	.80	.78
2	.80	.80
3	.83	.86
4	.53	.53
5	.50	.51
6	.96	.68
7	.99	.82
8	.98	.72
9	.81	.45
10	.95	.79
11	.99	.77

Source: Ichihara, H., Shintani, M., and Inoue, T. "Huffman-Based Test Response Coding." *IEICE Transactions on Information & Systems,* Vol. E88-D, No. 1, Jan. 2005 (Table 3).

CRASH

7.34 NHTSA new car crash tests. Refer to the National Highway Traffic Safety Administration (NHTSA) crash test data for new cars saved in the **CRASH** file. Crash-test dummies were placed in the driver's seat and front passenger's seat of a new car model, and the car was steered by remote control into a head-on collision with a fixed barrier while traveling at 35 miles per hour. Two of the variables measured for each of the 98 new cars in the data set are (1) the severity of the driver's chest injury and (2) the severity of the passenger's chest injury. (The more points assigned to the chest injury rating, the more severe the injury.) Suppose the NHTSA wants to determine whether the true mean driver chest injury rating exceeds the true mean passenger chest injury rating, and if so, by how much.
 a. State the parameter of interest to the NHTSA.
 b. Explain why the data should be analyzed as matched pairs.
 c. Find a 99% confidence interval for the true difference between the mean chest injury ratings of drivers and front-seat passengers.
 d. Interpret the interval, part **c**. Does the true mean driver chest injury rating exceed the true mean passenger chest injury rating? If so, by how much?
 e. What conditions are required for the analysis to be valid? Do these conditions hold for this data?

Applying the Concepts—Intermediate

7.35 Taking "power naps" during work breaks. Lack of sleep costs companies about $18 billion a year in lost productivity, according to the National Sleep Foundation. Companies are waking up to the problem, however. Some even have quiet rooms available for study or sleep. "Power naps" are in vogue (*Athens Daily News,* Jan. 9, 2000). A major airline recently began encouraging reservation agents to nap during their breaks. The table in the next column lists the number of complaints received about each of a sample of 10 reservation agents during the 6 months before naps were encouraged and during the 6 months after the policy change.
 a. Do the data present sufficient evidence to conclude that the new napping policy reduced the mean number of customer complaints about reservation agents? Test using $\alpha = .05$.
 b. What assumptions must hold to ensure the validity of the test?

c. What variables, not controlled in the study, could lead to an invalid conclusion?

POWERNAP

Operator	Before Policy	After Policy
1	10	5
2	3	0
3	16	7
4	11	4
5	8	6
6	2	4
7	1	2
8	14	3
9	5	5
10	6	1

7.36 Computer-mediated communication study. Refer to the *Journal of Computer-Mediated Communication* (Apr. 2004) study to compare relational intimacy in people interacting via computer-mediated communication (CMC) to people meeting face-to-face (FTF), Exercise 7.18 (p. 421). Recall that a relational intimacy score was measured (on a 7-point scale) for each participant after each of three different meeting sessions. The researchers also hypothesized that the mean relational intimacy score for participants in the CMC group will significantly increase between the first and third meetings, but the difference between the first and third meetings will not significantly change for participants in the FTF group.
 a. For the CMC group comparison, give the null and alternative hypotheses of interest.
 b. The researchers made the comparison, part **a**, using a paired *t*-test. Explain why the data should be analyzed as matched pairs.
 c. For the CMC group comparison, the reported test statistic was $t = 3.04$ with *p*-value = .003. Interpret these results. Is the researchers' hypothesis supported?
 d. For the FTF group comparison, give the null and alternative hypotheses of interest.
 e. For the FTF group comparison, the reported test statistic was $t = .39$ with *p*-value = .70. Interpret these results. Is the researchers' hypothesis supported?

7.37 Evaluating customer interest with a pupillometer. A *pupillometer* is a device used to observe changes in pupil dilations as the eye is exposed to different visual stimuli. Since there is a direct correlation between the amount an individual's pupil dilates and his or her interest in the stimuli, marketing organizations sometimes use pupillometers to help them evaluate potential consumer interest in new products, alternative package designs, and other factors (*Optical Engineering,* Mar. 1995). The Design and Market Research Laboratories of the Container Corporation of America used a pupillometer to evaluate consumer reaction to different silverware patterns for a client. Suppose 15 consumers were chosen at random, and each was shown two silverware patterns. Their pupillometer readings (in millimeters) are shown in the table at the top of p. 435.
 a. What are the appropriate null and alternative hypotheses to test whether the mean amount of pupil dilation differs for the two patterns? Define any symbols you use.
 b. Conduct the test, part **a**. Interpret the results.
 c. Is the paired difference design used for this study preferable to an independent samples design? For independent samples, we could select 30 consumers, divide them

into two groups of 15, and show each group a different pattern. Explain your preference.

PUPILL

Consumer	Pattern 1	Pattern 2
1	1.00	.80
2	.97	.66
3	1.45	1.22
4	1.21	1.00
5	.77	.81
6	1.32	1.11
7	1.81	1.30
8	.91	.32
9	.98	.91
10	1.46	1.10
11	1.85	1.60
12	.33	.21
13	1.77	1.50
14	.85	.65
15	.15	.05

7.38 Sensor motion of a robot. Refer to *The International Journal of Robotics Research* (Dec. 2004) study of the sensor motion of a robotic arm with a mounted camera, Exercise 2.110 (p. 100). Recall that the variable of interest is the error of estimating arm translation (measured in centimeters). Data for 10 experiments (in which the perturbation of camera intrinsics and projections were varied) are repeated in the accompanying table. Suppose two methods were used to measure translation error. Is there sufficient evidence (at $\alpha = .10$) to indicate that the mean translation error for method 1 differs from the mean translation error for method 2?

SENSOR

Trial	TRANSLATION ERROR (cm)	
	Method 1	Method 2
1	1.0	2.1
2	1.3	1.8
3	3.0	2.6
4	1.5	1.4
5	1.3	1.7
6	22.9	20.5
7	21.0	23.2
8	34.4	30.7
9	29.8	30.6
10	17.7	16.4

Adapted from: Strelow, D., and Singh, S. "Motion Estimation Form Image and Inertial Measurements." *The International Journal of Robotics Research,* Vol. 23, No. 12, Dec. 2004 (Table 4).

7.39 Evaluating a new drug. Merck Research Labs conducted an experiment to evaluate the effect of a new drug using the single-T swim maze. Nineteen impregnated dam rats were captured and allocated a dosage of 12.5 milligrams of the drug. One male and one female rat pup were randomly selected from each resulting litter to perform in the swim maze. Each pup was placed in the water at one end of the maze and allowed to swim until it escaped at the opposite end. If the pup failed to escape after a certain period of time, it was placed at the beginning of the maze and given another chance. The experiment was repeated until each pup accomplished three successful escapes. The next table reports the number of swims required by each pup to per-

form three successful escapes. Is there sufficient evidence of a difference between the mean number of swims required by male and female pups? Conduct the test (at $\alpha = .10$). Comment on the assumptions required for the test to be valid.

RATPUPS

Litter	Male	Female	Litter	Male	Female
1	8	5	11	6	5
2	8	4	12	6	3
3	6	7	13	12	5
4	6	3	14	3	8
5	6	5	15	3	4
6	6	3	16	8	12
7	3	8	17	3	6
8	5	10	18	6	4
9	4	4	19	9	5
10	4	4			

Source: Thomas E. Bradstreet, Merck Research Labs, BL 3–2, West Point, PA 19486.

Applying the Concepts—Advanced

7.40 Alcoholic fermentation in wines. Determining alcoholic fermentation in wine is critical to the wine-making process. Must/wine density is a good indicator of the fermentation point, because the density value decreases as sugars are converted into alcohol. For decades, winemakers have measured must/wine density with a hydrometer. Although accurate, the hydrometer employs a manual process that is very time-consuming. Consequently, large wineries are searching for more rapid measures of density measurement. An alternative method utilizes the hydrostatic balance instrument (similar to the hydrometer but digital). A winery in Portugal collected the must/wine density measurements for white wine samples randomly selected from the fermentation process for a recent harvest. For each sample, the density of the wine at 20°C was measured with both the hydrometer and the hydrostat balance. The densities for 40 wine samples are saved in the **WINE40** file. The first five and last five observations are shown in the table. The winery will use the alternative method of measuring wine density only if it can be demonstrated that the mean difference between the density measurements of the two methods does not exceed .002. Perform the analysis for the winery. Provide the winery with a written report of your conclusions.

WINE40 (first and last 5 observations)

Sample	Hydrometer	Hydrostatic
1	1.08655	1.09103
2	1.00270	1.00272
3	1.01393	1.01274
4	1.09467	1.09634
5	1.10263	1.10518
·	·	·
·	·	·
36	1.08084	1.08097
37	1.09452	1.09431
38	0.99479	0.99498
39	1.00968	1.01063
40	1.00684	1.00526

Source: Cooperative Cellar of Borba (*Adega Cooperativa de Borba*), Portugal.

7.4 Comparing Two Population Proportions: Independent Sampling

Suppose a personal water craft (PWC) manufacturer wants to compare the potential market for its products in the northeastern United States to the market in the southeastern United States. Such a comparison would help the manufacturer decide where to concentrate sales efforts. Using telephone directories, the company randomly chooses 1,000 households in the southeast (SE) and 1,000 households in the northeast (NE) and determines whether each household plans to buy a PWC within the next 5 years. The objective is to use this sample information to make an inference about the difference $(p_1 - p_2)$ between the proportion p_1 of *all* households in the SE and the proportion p_2 of *all* households in the NE that plan to purchase a PWC within 5 years.

The two samples represent independent binomial experiments. (See Section 4.3 for the characteristics of binomial experiments.) The binomial random variables are the numbers x_1 and x_2 of the 1,000 sampled households in each area that indicate they will purchase a PWC within 5 years. The results are summarized in Table 7.6.

TABLE 7.6 Results of Telephone Survey

SE	NE
$n_1 = 1{,}000$	$n_2 = 1{,}000$
$x_1 = 42$	$x_2 = 24$

We can now calculate the sample proportions $\hat{p}_1$ and $\hat{p}_2$ of the households in the SE and NE, respectively, that are prospective buyers:

$$\hat{p}_1 = \frac{x_1}{n_1} = \frac{42}{1{,}000} = .042$$

$$\hat{p}_2 = \frac{x_2}{n_2} = \frac{24}{1{,}000} = .024$$

The difference between the sample proportions $(\hat{p}_1 - \hat{p}_2)$ makes an intuitively appealing point estimator of the difference between the population parameters $(p_1 - p_2)$. For our example, the estimate is

$$(\hat{p}_1 - \hat{p}_2) = .042 - .024 = .018$$

To judge the reliability of the estimator $(\hat{p}_1 - \hat{p}_2)$, we must observe its performance in repeated sampling from the two populations—that is, we need to know the sampling distribution of $(\hat{p}_1 - \hat{p}_2)$. The properties of the sampling distribution are given in the next box. Remember that $\hat{p}_1$ and $\hat{p}_2$ can be viewed as means of the number of successes per trial in the respective samples, so the Central Limit Theorem applies when the sample sizes are large.

Properties of the Sampling Distribution of $(\hat{p}_1 - \hat{p}_2)$

1. The mean of the sampling distribution of $(\hat{p}_1 - \hat{p}_2)$ is $(p_1 - p_2)$; that is,

$$E(\hat{p}_1 - \hat{p}_2) = p_1 - p_2$$

Thus, $(\hat{p}_1 - \hat{p}_2)$ is an unbiased estimator of $(p_1 - p_2)$.

2. The standard deviation of the sampling distribution of $(\hat{p}_1 - \hat{p}_2)$ is

$$\sigma_{(\hat{p}_1 - \hat{p}_2)} = \sqrt{\frac{p_1 q_1}{n_1} + \frac{p_2 q_2}{n_2}}$$

3. If the sample sizes n_1 and n_2 are large (see Section 5.4 for a guideline), the sampling distribution of $(\hat{p}_1 - \hat{p}_2)$ is approximately normal.

Since the distribution of $(\hat{p}_1 - \hat{p}_2)$ in repeated sampling is approximately normal, we can use the z statistic to derive confidence intervals for $(p_1 - p_2)$ or to test a hypothesis about $(p_1 - p_2)$.

For the PWC example, a 95% confidence interval for the difference $(p_1 - p_2)$ is

$$(\hat{p}_1 - \hat{p}_2) \pm 1.96\sigma_{(\hat{p}_1 - \hat{p}_2)} \quad \text{or} \quad (\hat{p}_1 - \hat{p}_2) \pm 1.96\sqrt{\frac{p_1 q_1}{n_1} + \frac{p_2 q_2}{n_2}}$$

The quantities $p_1 q_1$ and $p_2 q_2$ must be estimated in order to complete the calculation of the standard deviation $\sigma_{(\hat{p}_1 - \hat{p}_2)}$ and hence the calculation of the confidence interval. In Section 5.4 we showed that the value of pq is relatively insensitive to the value chosen to approximate p. Therefore, $\hat{p}_1 \hat{q}_1$ and $\hat{p}_2 \hat{q}_2$ will provide satisfactory estimates to approximate $p_1 q_1$ and $p_2 q_2$, respectively. Then

$$\sqrt{\frac{p_1 q_1}{n_1} + \frac{p_2 q_2}{n_2}} \approx \sqrt{\frac{\hat{p}_1 \hat{q}_1}{n_1} + \frac{\hat{p}_2 \hat{q}_2}{n_2}}$$

and we will approximate the 95% confidence interval by

$$(\hat{p}_1 - \hat{p}_2) \pm 1.96\sqrt{\frac{\hat{p}_1 \hat{q}_1}{n_1} + \frac{\hat{p}_2 \hat{q}_2}{n_2}}$$

Substituting the sample quantities yields

$$(.042 - .024) \pm 1.96\sqrt{\frac{(.042)(.958)}{1{,}000} + \frac{(.024)(.976)}{1{,}000}}$$

or $.018 \pm .016$. Thus, we are 95% confident that the interval from .002 to .034 contains $(p_1 - p_2)$.

We infer that there are between .2% and 3.4% more households in the southeast than in the northeast that plan to purchase PWCs in the next 5 years.

Now Work Exercise 7.47

The general form of a confidence interval for the difference $(p_1 - p_2)$ between population proportions is given in the following box.

Large-Sample $(1 - \alpha)$% Confidence Interval for $(p_1 - p_2)$

$$(\hat{p}_1 - \hat{p}_2) \pm z_{\alpha/2}\sigma_{(\hat{p}_1 - \hat{p}_2)} = (\hat{p}_1 - \hat{p}_2) \pm z_{\alpha/2}\sqrt{\frac{p_1 q_1}{n_1} + \frac{p_2 q_2}{n_2}}$$

$$\approx (\hat{p}_1 - \hat{p}_2) \pm z_{\alpha/2}\sqrt{\frac{\hat{p}_1 \hat{q}_1}{n_1} + \frac{\hat{p}_2 \hat{q}_2}{n_2}}$$

Conditions Required for Valid Large-Sample Inferences about $(p_1 - p_2)$

1. The two samples are randomly selected in an independent manner from the two target populations.
2. The sample sizes, n_1 and n_2, are both large so that the sampling distribution of $(\hat{p}_1 - \hat{p}_2)$ will be approximately normal. (This condition will be satisfied if both $n_1 \hat{p}_1 \geq 15, n_1 \hat{q}_1 \geq 15$, and $n_2 \hat{p}_2 \geq 15, n_2 \hat{q}_2 \geq 15$.)

The z statistic,

$$z = \frac{(\hat{p}_1 - \hat{p}_2) - (p_1 - p_2)}{\sigma_{(\hat{p}_1 - \hat{p}_2)}}$$

is used to test the null hypothesis that $(p_1 - p_2)$ equals some specified difference, say D_0. For the special case where $D_0 = 0$—that is, where we want to test the null hypothesis $H_0: (p_1 - p_2) = 0$ (or, equivalently, $H_0: p_1 = p_2$)—the best estimate of $p_1 = p_2 = p$ is obtained by dividing the total number of successes $(x_1 + x_2)$ for the two samples by the total number of observations $(n_1 + n_2)$; that is,

$$\hat{p} = \frac{x_1 + x_2}{n_1 + n_2} \quad \text{or} \quad \hat{p} = \frac{n_1 \hat{p}_1 + n_2 \hat{p}_2}{n_1 + n_2}$$

The second equation shows that $\hat{p}$ is a weighted average of $\hat{p}_1$ and $\hat{p}_2$, with the larger sample receiving more weight. If the sample sizes are equal, then $\hat{p}$ is a simple average of the two sample proportions of successes.

We now substitute the weighted average $\hat{p}$ for both p_1 and p_2 in the formula for the standard deviation of $(\hat{p}_1 - \hat{p}_2)$:

$$\sigma_{(\hat{p}_1 - \hat{p}_2)} = \sqrt{\frac{p_1 q_1}{n_1} + \frac{p_2 q_2}{n_2}} \approx \sqrt{\frac{\hat{p}\hat{q}}{n_1} + \frac{\hat{p}\hat{q}}{n_2}} = \sqrt{\hat{p}\hat{q}\left(\frac{1}{n_1} + \frac{1}{n_2}\right)}$$

The test is summarized in the next box.

Large-Sample Test of Hypothesis About $(p_1 - p_2)$

One-Tailed Test	Two-Tailed Test
$H_0: (p_1 - p_2) = 0$*	$H_0: (p_1 - p_2) = 0$
$H_a: (p_1 - p_2) < 0$	$H_a: (p_1 - p_2) \neq 0$
[or $H_a: (p_1 - p_2) > 0$]	

$$\text{Test statistic: } z = \frac{(\hat{p}_1 - \hat{p}_2)}{\sigma_{(\hat{p}_1 - \hat{p}_2)}}$$

Rejection region: $z < -z_\alpha$	Rejection region: $|z| > z_{\alpha/2}$
[or $z > z_\alpha$ when $H_a: (p_1 - p_2) > 0$]	

$$\text{Note: } \sigma_{(\hat{p}_1 - \hat{p}_2)} = \sqrt{\frac{p_1 q_1}{n_1} + \frac{p_2 q_2}{n_2}} \approx \sqrt{\hat{p}\hat{q}\left(\frac{1}{n_1} + \frac{1}{n_2}\right)}, \text{ where } \hat{p} = \frac{x_1 + x_2}{n_1 + n_2}.$$

EXAMPLE 7.6

Comparing Repair Rates of Two Car Models Using a Large-Sample Test about $p_1 - p_2$

Problem   A consumer advocacy group wants to determine whether there is a difference between the proportions of the two leading automobile models that need major repairs (more than \$500) within 2 years of their purchase. A sample of 400 two-year owners of model 1 is contacted, and a sample of 500 two-year owners of model 2 is contacted. The numbers x_1 and x_2 of owners who report that their cars needed major repairs within the first 2 years are 53 and 78, respectively. Test the null hypothesis that no difference exists between the proportions in populations 1 and 2 needing major repairs against the alternative that a difference does exist. Use $\alpha = .10$.

---

*The test can be adapted to test for a difference $D_0 \neq 0$. Because most applications call for a comparison of p_1 and p_2, implying $D_0 = 0$, we will confine our attention to this case.

Solution   If we define p_1 and p_2 as the true proportions of model 1 and model 2 owners, respectively, whose cars need major repairs within 2 years, the elements of the test are

$$H_0: (p_1 - p_2) = 0$$

$$H_a: (p_1 - p_2) \neq 0$$

$$\text{Test statistic: } z = \frac{(\hat{p}_1 - \hat{p}_2) - 0}{\sigma_{(\hat{p}_1 - \hat{p}_2)}}$$

Rejection region ($\alpha = .10$): $|z| > z_{\alpha/2} = z_{.05} = 1.645$ (see Figure 7.15)

We now calculate the sample proportions of owners who need major car repairs,

$$\hat{p}_1 = \frac{x_1}{n_1} = \frac{53}{400} - .1325$$

$$\hat{p}_2 = \frac{x_2}{n_2} = \frac{78}{500} = .1560$$

Then

$$z = \frac{(\hat{p}_1 - \hat{p}_2) - 0}{\sigma_{(\hat{p}_1 - \hat{p}_2)}} \approx \frac{(\hat{p}_1 - \hat{p}_2)}{\sqrt{\hat{p}\hat{q}\left(\dfrac{1}{n_1} + \dfrac{1}{n_2}\right)}}$$

Observed
$z = -.99$

FIGURE 7.15
Rejection region for Example 7.6

where

$$\hat{p} = \frac{x_1 + x_2}{n_1 + n_2} - \frac{53 + 78}{400 + 500} = .1456$$

Note that $\hat{p}$ is a weighted average of $\hat{p}_1$ and $\hat{p}_2$, with more weight given to the larger sample of model 2 owners.

Thus, the computed value of the test statistic is

$$z = \frac{.1325 - .1560}{\sqrt{(.1456)(.8544)\left(\dfrac{1}{400} + \dfrac{1}{500}\right)}} = \frac{-.0235}{.0237} = -.99$$

The samples provide insufficient evidence at $\alpha = .10$ to detect a difference between the proportions of the two models that need repairs within 2 years. Even though 2.35% more sampled owners of model 2 found they needed major repairs, this difference is less than 1 standard deviation ($z = -.99$) from the hypothesized zero difference between the true proportions.

EXAMPLE **7.7**

Finding the Observed Significance Level of a Test for $p_1 - p_2$

Problem   Use a statistical software package to conduct the test in Example 7.6. Find and interpret the p-value of the test.

Solution   We entered the sample sizes (n_1 and n_2) and number of successes (x_1 and x_2) into Excel with the PHStat2 add-in and obtained the printout shown in Figure 7.16. The test statistic for this two-tailed test is shaded on the printout as well as the observed significance level (p-value). Note that p-value = .3205 is less than $\alpha = .10$. Consequently, there is no evidence of a difference between the true population proportions.

Z Test for Differences in Two Proportions	
Data	
Hypothesized Difference	0
Level of Significance	0.1
Group 1	
Number of Successes	53
Sample Size	400
Group 2	
Number of Successes	78
Sample Size	500
Intermediate Calculations	
Group 1 Proportion	0.1325
Group 2 Proportion	0.156
Difference in Two Proportions	-0.0235
Average Proportion	0.145555556
Z Test Statistic	-0.993356864
Two-Tailed Test	
Lower Critical Value	-1.644853476
Upper Critical Value	1.644853476
p-Value	0.320536082
Do not reject the null hypothesis	

FIGURE 7.16

Excel/PHStat2 printout for test of two proportions

STATISTICS IN ACTION REVISITED

Comparing Proportions for the Two SMWT Survey Groups

In the first Statistics in Action Revisited application in this chapter (p. 417), we demonstrated how researchers compared the means of several quantitative variables for two groups of AT&T workers. Recall that group 1 workers ($n_1 = 47$) were those employees who reported positive spillover of work skills to family life, and group 2 workers ($n_2 = 67$) were those employees who did not report positive work spillover. The researchers also collected data on the qualitative variable, Gender, for each worker, and wanted to know whether the proportion of male workers in the two groups differed.

An analysis of the Gender variable in the **SPILLOVER** file is shown in the MINITAB printout, Figure SIA7.2. Summary information given at the top of the printout shows that 39 of the 47 workers (83%) in the spillover group (group 1) were males, while 59 of the 67 workers (88%) in the nonspillover group (group 2) were males. A confidence interval for $(p_2 - p_1)$ and the results of a two-tailed test of the null hypothesis, $H_0: (p_2 - p_1) = 0$, are shown at the bottom of the printout. [*Note:* MINITAB orders the groups alphabetically. Since "NOSPILL" precedes "SPILLOV", population 1 in the MINITAB analysis is group 2 and population 2 is group 1.] The 95% confidence interval is $(-.08, .18)$ and the p-value for the hypothesis test is p-value = .453. Both of these results led the researchers to conclude that there is no significant difference between the proportions of males in the two SMWT groups.

Test and CI for Two Proportions: GENDER, GROUP

```
Event = MALE


GROUP      X    N   Sample p
NOSPILL   59   67   0.880597
SPILLOV   39   47   0.829787


Difference = p (NOSPILL) - p (SPILLOV)
Estimate for difference:  0.0508098
95% CI for difference:  (-0.0817519, 0.183371)
Test for difference = 0 (vs not = 0):  Z = 0.75  P-Value = 0.453
```

Figure SIA7.2
MINITAB comparison of SMWT groups for gender

Confidence Interval for ($p_1 - p_2$)

Using the TI-83/TI-84 Graphing Calculator

Step 1 *Access the Statistical Tests Menu*

Press **STAT**.
Arrow right to **TESTS**.
Arrow down to **2-PropZInt**.
Press **ENTER**.

Step 2 *Enter the values from the sample information and **the confidence level**.*

where x_1 = number of successes in the first sample
n_1 = sample size for the first sample
x_2 = number of successes in the second sample
n_2 = sample size for the second sample

Set **C-Level** to the confidence level.
Arrow down to "**Calculate**".
Press **ENTER**.

Example Find a 95% Confidence Interval for the difference in the proportions of two leading automobile models that need major repairs.

Model 1: A sample of 400 owners is contacted. Fifty-three owners report that their cars needed major repairs within the first two years.

Model 2: A sample of 500 owners is contacted. Seventy-eight owners report that their cars needed major repairs within the first two years.

The screens for this example are shown below.

```
EDIT CALC TESTS
1:Z-Test...
2:T-Test...
3:2-SampZTest...
4:2-SampTTest...
5:1-PropZTest...
6:2-PropZTest...
7↓ZInterval...
```

```
2-PropZInt
 (-.0695,.02249)
 p̂₁=.1325
 p̂₂=.156
 n₁=400
 n₂=500
```

The 95% confidence interval for the difference in the two proportions is (−.0695, .02249).

Hypothesis Test for $(p_1 - p_2)$

Using the TI-83/TI-84 Graphing Calculator

Step 1 *Access the Statistical Tests Menu*

Press **STAT**.
Arrow right to **TESTS**.
Arrow down to **2-PropZTest**.
Press **ENTER**.

Step 2 *Enter the values from the sample information and **select the alternative hypothesis**.*

where x_1 = number of successes in the first sample
n_1 = sample size for the first sample
x_2 = number of successes in the second sample
n_2 = sample size for the second sample

Use the **ARROW** to highlight the appropriate alternative hypothesis.
Press **ENTER**.
Arrow down to "**Calculate**".
Press **ENTER**.

Example Test the hypothesis that no difference exists between the proportions of two leading automobile models that need major repairs.

Model 1: A sample of 400 owners is contacted. Fifty-three owners report that their cars needed major repairs within the first two years.

Model 2: A sample of 500 owners is contacted. Seventy-eight owners report that their cars needed major repairs within the first two years.

The screens for this example are shown below.

```
2-PropZInt
 (-.0695,.02249)
 p̂1=.1325
 p̂2=.156
 n1=400
 n2=500
```

```
2-PropZTest
 p1≠p2
 z=-.9933568641
 p=.3205360811
 p̂1=.1325
 p̂2=.156
↓p̂=.1455555556
```

Since the p-value (.3205) is greater than α (.10), do not reject the null hypothesis. There is not sufficient evidence to detect a difference between the population proportions.

Exercises 7.41–7.57

Learning the Mechanics

7.41 Consider making an inference about $p_1 - p_2$, where there are x_1 successes in n_1 binomial trials and x_2 successes in n_2 binomial trials.

a. Describe the distributions of x_1 and x_2.

b. Explain why the Central Limit Theorem is important in finding an approximate distribution for $(\hat{p}_1 - \hat{p}_2)$.

7.42 For each of the following values of α, find the values of z for which H_0: $(p_1 - p_2) = 0$ would be rejected in favor of H_a: $(p_1 - p_2) < 0$.

a. $\alpha = .01$

b. $\alpha = .025$

c. $\alpha = .05$

d. $\alpha = .10$

7.43 In each case, determine whether the sample sizes are large enough to conclude that the sampling distribution of $(\hat{p}_1 - \hat{p}_2)$ is approximately normal.

a. $n_1 = 12, n_2 = 14, \hat{p}_1 = .42, \hat{p}_2 = .57$

b. $n_1 = 12, n_2 = 14, \hat{p}_1 = .92, \hat{p}_2 = .86$

c. $n_1 = n_2 = 30, \hat{p}_1 = .70, \hat{p}_2 = .73$

d. $n_1 = 100, n_2 = 250, \hat{p}_1 = .93, \hat{p}_2 = .97$

e. $n_1 = 125, n_2 = 200, \hat{p}_1 = .08, \hat{p}_2 = .12$

7.44 Construct a 95% confidence interval for $(p_1 - p_2)$ in each of the following situations:

a. $n_1 = 400, \hat{p}_1 = .65; n_2 = 400, \hat{p}_2 = .58$

b. $n_1 = 180, \hat{p}_1 = .31; n_2 = 250, \hat{p}_2 = .25$

c. $n_1 = 100, \hat{p}_1 = .46; n_2 = 120, \hat{p}_2 = .61$

ACTIVITY 7.2: *Keep the Change:* Inferences Based on Two Samples

In this activity, you will compare the mean amounts transferred for two different Bank of America customers as well as design some studies that might help the marketing department determine where to allocate more of its advertising budget. You will be working with data sets from Activity 1.1, *Keep the Change: Collecting Data* on page 16.

1. You will need to work with another student in the class on this exercise. Each of you should use your data set *Amounts Transferred* from the Chapter 1 Activity as a random sample from a theoretically larger set of all your amounts ever transferred. Then the means and standard deviations of your data sets will be the sample means and standard deviations. Write a confidence interval for the difference of the two means at the 95% level. Does the interval contain 0? Are your mean amounts transferred significantly different? Explain.

2. Design a study to determine whether there is a significant difference in the mean amount of Bank

of America matches for customers in California enrolled in the program and the mean amount of Bank of America matches for customers in Florida enrolled in the program. Be specific about sample sizes, tests used, and how a conclusion will be reached. How might the results of this study help Bank of America estimate costs in the program?

3. Design a study to determine whether there is a significant difference in the percentage of Bank of America customers in California enrolled in the program and the percentage of Bank of America customers in Florida enrolled in the program. Be specific about sample sizes, tests used, and how a conclusion will be reached. How might the results of this study help Bank of America's marketing department?

Keep the results from this activity for use in other activities.

7.45 Independent random samples, each containing 800 observations, were selected from two binomial populations. The samples from populations 1 and 2 produced 320 and 400 successes, respectively.
   a. Test $H_0: (p_1 - p_2) = 0$ against $H_a: (p_1 - p_2) > 0$. Use $\alpha = .05$.
   b. Test $H_0: (p_1 - p_2) = 0$ against $H_a: (p_1 - p_2) \neq 0$. Use $\alpha = .01$.
   c. Test $H_0: (p_1 - p_2) = 0$ against $H_a: (p_1 - p_2) < 0$. Use $\alpha = .01$.
   d. Form a 90% confidence interval for $(p_1 - p_2)$.

7.46 Random samples of size $n_1 = 55$ and $n_2 = 65$ were drawn from populations 1 and 2, respectively. The samples yielded $\hat{p}_1 = .7$ and $\hat{p}_2 = .6$. Test $H_0: (p_1 - p_2) = 0$ against $H_a: (p_1 - p_2) > 0$ using $\alpha = .05$.

Applying the Concepts—Basic

7.47 **The "winner's curse" in auction bidding.** In auction bidding, the "winner's curse" is the phenomenon of the winning (or highest) bid price being above the expected value of the item being auctioned. *The Review of Economics and Statistics* (Aug. 2001) published a study on whether bid experience impacts the likelihood of the winner's curse occurring. Two groups of bidders in a sealed-bid auction were compared: (1) super-experienced bidders and (2) less-experienced bidders. In the super-experienced group, 29 of 189 winning bids were above the item's expected value; in the less-experienced group, 32 of 149 winning bids were above the item's expected value.
   a. Find an estimate of p_1, the true proportion of super-experienced bidders who fall prey to the winner's curse.

b. Find an estimate of p_2, the true proportion of less-experienced bidders who fall prey to the winner's curse.
   c. Construct a 90% confidence interval for $p_1 - p_2$.
   d. Give a practical interpretation of the confidence interval, part **c.** Make a statement about whether bid experience impacts the likelihood of the winner's curse occurring.

7.48 **Planning habits survey.** *American Demographics* (Jan. 2002) reported the results of a survey on the planning habits of men and women. In response to the question, "What is your preferred method of planning and keeping track of meetings, appointments, and deadlines?", 56% of the men and 46% of the women answered, "Keep them in my head." A nationally representative sample of 1,000 adults participated in the survey; therefore, assume that 500 were men and 500 were women.
   a. Set up the null and alternative hypotheses for testing whether the percentage of men who prefer keeping track of appointments in their head is larger than the corresponding percentage of women.
   b. Compute the test statistic for the test.
   c. Give the rejection region for the test using $\alpha = .01$.
   d. Find the p-value for the test.
   e. Make the appropriate conclusion.

7.49 **Likelihood of getting a routine medical checkup.** Who is more likely to get a routine medical checkup, employed or unemployed people? To answer this question, a team of physicians and public health professors collected data on a sample of over 2,200 individuals (*American Journal of*

Public Health, Jan. 2002). Of the 1,140 individuals who were employed, 642 visited a physician for a routine checkup within the past year. In contrast, 740 of the 1,106 unemployed individuals had a routine medical checkup within the past year.

a. Specify the parameter of interest to the research team.

b. Set up the null and alternative hypotheses for testing whether there is a difference between the percentages of employed and unemployed people who had a recent routine medical checkup.

c. Compute the test statistic for the test.

d. Give the rejection region for the test using $\alpha = .01$.

e. The research team reported the p-value for the test as ≈ 0. Do you agree?

f. Make the appropriate conclusion.

7.50 Electronic versus printed surveys. The rapid evolution of computer hardware and software has made it easy for businesses to conduct computer-based and Web-based (i.e., electronic) surveys. Professors at Michigan State and DePaul Universities collaborated on a study designed to compare the response rates of electronic surveys and traditional print surveys (Decision Sciences Institute, *Decision Line,* July 2001). The two surveys were developed for customers who had purchased products over the Internet from a leading retailer of office supplies. Of the 631 customers mailed the printed survey, 261 returned usable responses. Of the 414 customers who were sent a computer disk with the electronic survey, 155 returned usable responses.

a. Estimate the difference between the response rates of the two survey types using a 90% confidence interval. Interpret the result.

b. If the difference in response rates is 5% or less, the researchers will infer that there is no "practical" difference in response rates for the two surveys. Are the researchers able to make this inference? Explain.

7.51 Racial profiling by the LAPD. *Racial profiling* is a term used to describe any police action that relies on ethnicity rather than behavior to target suspects engaged in criminal activities. Does the Los Angeles Police Department (LAPD) invoke racial profiling in stops and searches of LA drivers? This question was addressed in *Chance* (Spring 2006).

a. Data on stops and searches of both African Americans and white drivers from January through June 2005 are summarized in the accompanying table. Conduct a test (at $\alpha = .05$) to determine if there is a disparity in the proportions of African American and white drivers who are searched by the LA police after being stopped.

b. The LAPD defines a '*hit rate*' as the proportion of searches that result in a discovery of criminal activity. Use the data in the table to estimate the disparity in the hit rates for African American and white drivers using a 95% confidence interval. Interpret the results.

Race	Number Stopped	Number Searched	Number of "Hits"
African American	61,688	12,016	5,134
White	106,892	5,312	3,006

Source: Khadjavi, L. S. "Driving While Black in the City of Angels." *Chance,* Vol. 19, No. 2, Spring 2006 (Tables 1 and 2).

Applying the Concepts—Intermediate

7.52 Career success expectations. In evaluating the usefulness and validity of a questionnaire, researchers often pretest the questionnaire on different independently selected samples of respondents. Knowledge of the differences and similarities of the samples and their respective populations is important for interpreting the questionnaire's validity. *Educational and Psychological Measurement* (Feb. 1998) reported on a newly developed questionnaire for measuring the career success expectations of employees. The instrument was tested on the two independent samples described in the following table.

	Managers and Professionals	Part-Time MBA Students
Sample size	162	109
Gender (% males)	95.0	68.9
Marital status (% married)	91.2	53.4

Source: Stephens, Gregory K., Szajna, Bernadette, and Broome, Kirk M., "The Career Success Expectation Scale: An Exploratory and Confirmatory Factor Analysis." *Educational and Psychological Measurement,* Vol. 58, No. 1, Feb. 1998, pp. 129–141.

a. Does the population of managers and professionals from which the sample was drawn consist of more males than the part-time MBA population does? Conduct the appropriate test using $\alpha = .05$.

b. Describe any assumptions you made in conducting the test of part **a** and why you made them.

c. Does the population of managers and professionals consist of more married individuals than the part-time MBA population does? Conduct the appropriate hypothesis test using $\alpha = .01$.

d. What assumptions must hold for the test of part **c** to be valid?

7.53 Gambling in public high schools. With the rapid growth in legalized gambling in the United States, there is concern that the involvement of youth in gambling activities is also increasing. University of Minnesota professor Randy Stinchfield compared the rates of gambling among Minnesota public school students between 1992 and 1998 (*Journal of Gambling Studies,* Winter 2001). Based on survey data, the table shows the percentages of ninth-grade boys who gambled weekly or daily on any game (e.g., cards, sports betting, lotteries) for the 2 years.

	1992	1998
Number of ninth-grade boys in survey	21,484	23,199
Number who gambled weekly/daily	4,684	5,313

a. Are the percentages of ninth-grade boys who gambled weekly or daily on any game in 1992 and 1998 significantly different? (Use $\alpha = .01$.)

b. Professor Stinchfield states that "because of the large sample sizes, even small differences may achieve statistical significance, so interpretations of the differences should include a judgment regarding the magnitude of the difference and its public health significance." Do you agree with this statement? If not, why not? If so, obtain a measure of the magnitude of the difference between 1992 and 1998 and attach a measure of reliability to the difference.

SWDEFECTS

7.54 Predicting software defects. Refer to the PROMISE Software Engineering Repository data on 498 modules of software code written in "C" language for a NASA space-craft instrument, saved in the **SWDEFECTS** file. (See Exercise 3.61, p. 168.) Recall that the software code in each module was evaluated for defects; 49 were classified as "true" (i.e., module has defective code), and 449 were classified as "false" (i.e., module has correct code). Consider these to be independent random samples of soft-ware code modules. Researchers predicted the defect sta-tus of each module using the simple algorithm, "If number of lines of code in the module exceeds 50, predict the module to have a defect." The SPSS printout below shows the number of modules in each of the two samples that were predicted to have defects (PRED_LOC = "yes") and predicted to have no defects (PRED_LOC = "no"). Now, define the *accuracy rate* of the algorithm as the proportion of modules that were correctly predicted. Compare the accuracy rate of the algorithm when applied to modules with defective code to the accuracy rate of the algorithm when applied to modules with correct code. Use a 99% confidence interval.

7.55 Ages of commercial product managers. *Industrial Marketing Management* (Vol. 25, 1996) published a study that examined the demographics, decision-making roles, and time demands of product managers. Independent samples of $n_1 = 93$ consumer/commercial product man-agers and $n_2 = 212$ industrial product managers took part in the study. In the consumer/commercial group, 40% of the product managers are 40 years of age or older; in the industrial group, 54% are 40 or more years old. Make an inference about the difference between the true propor-tions of consumer/commercial and industrial product managers who are at least 40 years old. Justify your choice of method (confidence interval or hypothesis test) and α level. Do industrial product managers tend to be older than consumer/commercial product managers?

7.56 Children's ability to recognize cigarette advertisements. Should marketers use ads that appeal to children to sell adult products? One controversial advertisement campaign was Camel cigarettes' use of the cartoon character "Joe Camel" as its brand symbol. (The Federal Trade Commission eventually banned ads featuring Joe Camel because they supposedly encouraged young people to smoke.) Lucy L. Henke, a marketing professor at the University of New Hampshire, assessed young children's abilities to recognize cigarette brand advertising symbols. She found that 15 out of 28 children under the age of 6, and 46 out of 55 children age 6 and over recognized Joe Camel, the brand symbol of Camel cigarettes (*Journal of Advertising*, Winter 1995).

a. Use a 95% confidence interval to estimate the propor-tion of all children that recognize Joe Camel. Interpret the interval.

b. Do the data indicate that recognition of Joe Camel in-creases with age? Test using $\alpha = .05$.

Applying the Concepts—Advanced

7.57 Food craving study. Do you have an insatiable craving for chocolate or some other food? Since many North Americans apparently do, psychologists are designing sci-entific studies to examine the phenomenon. According to the *New York Times* (Feb. 22, 1995), one of the largest stud-ies of food cravings involved a survey of 1,000 McMaster University (Canada) students. The survey revealed that 97% of the women in the study acknowledged specific food cravings while only 67% of the men did.

a. How large do n_1 and n_2 need to be to conclude that the true proportion of women who acknowledge having food cravings exceeds the corresponding proportion of men? Assume $\alpha = .01$.

b. Why is it dangerous to conclude from the study that women have a higher incidence of food cravings than men?

SPSS Output for Exercise 7.54

DEFECT * PRED_LOC Crosstabulation

Count

		PRED_LOC		Total
		no	yes	
DEFECT	false	400	49	449
	true	29	20	49
Total		429	69	498

7.5 Determining the Sample Size

You can find the appropriate sample size to estimate the difference between a pair of parameters with a specified margin of error (ME) and degree of reliability by using the method described in Section 5.5—that is, to estimate the difference between a pair of parameters correct to within *ME* units with confidence level $(1 - \alpha)$, let $z_{\alpha/2}$ standard deviations of the sampling distribution of the estimator equal ME. Then solve for the sample size. To do this, you have to solve the problem for a specific ratio between n_1 and n_2. Most often, you will want to have equal sample sizes—that is, $n_1 = n_2 = n$. We will illustrate the procedure with two examples.

EXAMPLE 7.8

Finding the Sample Sizes for Estimating $\mu_1 - \mu_2$: Comparing Mean Crop Yields

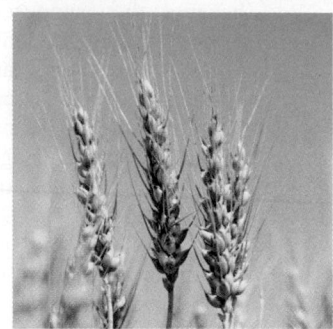

Problem New fertilizer compounds are often advertised with the promise of increased crop yields. Suppose we want to compare the mean yield μ_1 of wheat when a new fertilizer is used to the mean yield μ_2 with a fertilizer in common use. The estimate of the difference in mean yield per acre is to be correct to within .25 bushel with a confidence coefficient of .95. If the sample sizes are to be equal, find $n_1 = n_2 = n$, the number of one-acre plots of wheat assigned to each fertilizer.

Solution To solve the problem, you need to know something about the variation in the bushels of yield per acre. Suppose from past records you know the yields of wheat possess a range of approximately 10 bushels per acre. You could then approximate $\sigma_1 = \sigma_2 = \sigma$ by letting the range equal 4σ. Thus,

$$4\sigma \approx 10 \text{ bushels}$$
$$\sigma \approx 2.5 \text{ bushels}$$

The next step is to solve the equation

$$z_{\alpha/2}\sigma_{(\bar{x}_1 - \bar{x}_2)} = \text{ME} \qquad \text{or} \qquad z_{\alpha/2}\sqrt{\frac{\sigma_1^2}{n_1} + \frac{\sigma_2^2}{n_2}} = \text{ME}$$

for n, where $n = n_1 = n_2$. Since we want the estimate to lie within ME = .25 of $(\mu_1 - \mu_2)$ with confidence coefficient equal to .95, we have $z_{\alpha/2} = z_{.025} = 1.96$. Then, letting $\sigma_1 = \sigma_2 = 2.5$ and solving for n, we have

$$1.96\sqrt{\frac{(2.5)^2}{n} + \frac{(2.5)^2}{n}} = .25$$

$$1.96\sqrt{\frac{2(2.5)^2}{n}} = .25$$

$$n = 768.32 \approx 769 \text{ (rounding up)}$$

Consequently, you will have to sample 769 acres of wheat for each fertilizer to estimate the difference in mean yield per acre to within .25 bushel.

Look Back Since $n = 769$ would necessitate extensive and costly experimentation, you might decide to allow a larger margin of error (say, ME = .50 or ME = 1) in order to reduce the sample size, or you might decrease the confidence coefficient. The point is that we can obtain an idea of the experimental effort necessary to achieve a specified precision in our final estimate by determining the approximate sample size *before* the experiment is begun.

Now Work Exercise 7.58a

EXAMPLE **7.9**

Finding the Sample
Sizes for Estimating
$p_1 - p_2$: Comparing
Defect Rates of Two
Machines

Problem   A production supervisor suspects a difference exists between the proportions p_1 and p_2 of defective items produced by two different machines. Experience has shown that the proportion defective for each of the two machines is in the neighborhood of .03. If the supervisor wants to estimate the difference in the proportions to within .005 using a 95% confidence interval, how many items must be randomly sampled from the production of each machine? (Assume that the supervisor wants $n_1 = n_2 = n$.)

Solution   In this sampling problem, the margin of error is ME = .005, and for the specified level of reliability, $(1 - \alpha) = .95$, $z_{\alpha/2} = z_{.025} = 1.96$. Then, letting $p_1 = p_2 = .03$ and $n_1 = n_2 = n$, we find the required sample size per machine by solving the following equation for n:

$$z_{\alpha/2}\sigma_{(\hat{p}_1 - \hat{p}_2)} = \text{ME}$$

or

$$z_{\alpha/2}\sqrt{\frac{p_1 q_1}{n_1} + \frac{p_2 q_2}{n_2}} = ME$$

$$1.96\sqrt{\frac{(.03)(.97)}{n} + \frac{(.03)(.97)}{n}} = .005$$

$$1.96\sqrt{\frac{2(.03)(.97)}{n}} = .005$$

$$n = 8{,}943.2$$

Look Back   This large n will likely result in a tedious sampling procedure. If the supervisor insists on estimating $(p_1 - p_2)$ correct to within .005 with 95% confidence, approximately 9,000 items will have to be inspected for each machine.

Now Work Exercise 7.61a

You can see from the calculations in Example 7.9 that $\sigma_{(\hat{p}_1 - \hat{p}_2)}$ (and hence the solution, $n_1 = n_2 = n$) depends on the actual (but unknown) values of p_1 and p_2. In fact, the required sample size $n_1 = n_2 = n$ is largest when $p_1 - p_2 = .5$. Therefore, if you have no prior information on the approximate values of p_1 and p_2, use $p_1 = p_2 = .5$ in the formula for $\sigma_{(\hat{p}_1 - \hat{p}_2)}$. If p_1 and p_2 are in fact close to .5, then the values of n_1 and n_2 that you have calculated will be correct. If p_1 and p_2 differ substantially from .5, then your solutions for n_1 and n_2 will be larger than needed. Consequently, using $p_1 = p_2 = .5$ when solving for n_1 and n_2 is a conservative procedure because the sample sizes n_1 and n_2 will be at least as large as (and probably larger than) needed.

The procedures for determining sample sizes necessary for estimating $(\mu_1 - \mu_2)$ or $(p_1 - p_2)$ for the case $n_1 = n_2$ are given in the following boxes.

Determination of Sample Size for Estimating $\mu_1 - \mu_2$

To estimate $(\mu_1 - \mu_2)$ with a given margin of error ME and with confidence level $(1 - \alpha)$, use the following formula to solve for equal sample sizes that will achieve the desired reliability:

$$n_1 = n_2 = \frac{(z_{\alpha/2})^2(\sigma_1^2 + \sigma_2^2)}{(\text{ME})^2}$$

Continued

You will need to substitute estimates for the values of σ_1^2 and σ_2^2 before solving for the sample size. These estimates might be sample variances s_1^2 and s_2^2 from prior sampling (e.g., a pilot sample), or from an educated (and conservatively large) guess based on the range—that is, $s \approx R/4$.

Determination of Sample Size for Estimating $p_1 - p_2$

To estimate $(p_1 - p_2)$ with a given margin of error ME and with confidence level $(1 - \alpha)$, use the following formula to solve for equal sample sizes that will achieve the desired reliability:

$$n_1 = n_2 = \frac{(z_{\alpha/2})^2(p_1 q_1 + p_2 q_2)}{(\text{ME})^2}$$

You will need to substitute estimates for the values of p_1 and p_2 before solving for the sample size. These estimates might be based on prior samples, obtained from educated guesses or, most conservatively, specified as $p_1 = p_2 = .5$.

Exercises 7.58–7.68

Learning the Mechanics

7.58 Find the appropriate values of n_1 and n_2 (assume $n_1 = n_2$) needed to estimate $(\mu_1 - \mu_2)$ with:

NW **a.** A margin of error equal to 3.2 with 95% confidence. From prior experience it is known that $\sigma_1 \approx 15$ and $\sigma_2 \approx 17$.

b. A margin of error equal to 8 with 99% confidence. The range of each population is 60.

c. A 90% confidence interval of width 1.0. Assume that $\sigma_1^2 \approx 5.8$ and $\sigma_2^2 \approx 7.5$.

7.59 Suppose you want to estimate the difference between two population means correct to within 1.8 with a 95% confidence interval. If prior information suggests that the population variances are approximately equal to $\sigma_1^2 = \sigma_2^2 = 14$ and you want to select independent random samples of equal size from the populations, how large should the sample sizes, n_1 and n_2, be?

7.60 Enough money has been budgeted to collect independent random samples of size $n_1 = n_2 = 100$ from populations 1 and 2 in order to estimate $(\mu_1 - \mu_2)$. Prior information indicates that $\sigma_1 = \sigma_2 = 10$. Have sufficient funds been allocated to construct a 90% confidence interval for $(\mu_1 - \mu_2)$ of width 5 or less? Justify your answer.

7.61 Assuming that $n_1 = n_2$, find the sample sizes needed to estimate $(p_1 - p_2)$ for each of the following situations:

NW **a.** Margin of error = .01 with 99% confidence. Assume that $p_1 \approx .4$ and $p_2 \approx .7$.

b. A 90% confidence interval of width .05. Assume that there is no prior information available to obtain approximate values of p_1 and p_2.

c. Margin of error = .03 with 90% confidence. Assume that $p_1 \approx .2$ and $p_2 \approx .3$.

Applying the Concepts—Basic

7.62 Bacteria counts at a plant's liquid waste discharge. Refer to the EPA study of average bacteria counts in water specimens at two river locations, Exercise 7.22 (p. 422). How many water specimens need to be sampled at each location in order for a 95% confidence interval for the true mean difference in bacteria counts to yield an estimate that lies within 1.5 bacteria of the true difference? Assume equal sample sizes will be collected at each location.

7.63 Electronic versus printed surveys. Refer to the *Decision Line* (July 2001) study designed to compare the response rates of electronic surveys and traditional print surveys, Exercise 7.50 (p. 444). Recall that the two surveys were developed for customers who had purchased products over the Internet from a leading retailer of office supplies. How many customers should be sampled to estimate the difference between the response rates of the two survey types to within .01 using a 90% confidence interval? Assume the same number of customers should be sampled for each survey.

7.64 Conducting a political poll. A pollster wants to estimate the difference between the proportions of men and women who favor a particular national candidate using a 90% confidence interval of width .04. Suppose the pollster has no prior information about the proportions. If equal numbers of men and women are to be polled, how large should the sample sizes be?

Applying the Concepts—Intermediate

7.65 Life expectancies of working women and housewives. Is housework hazardous to your health? A study in the *Public Health Reports* (July–Aug. 1992) compares the life expectancies of 25-year-old white women in the labor force to those who are housewives. How large a sample would have to be taken from each group in order to be 95% confident that the estimate of difference in average life expectancies for the two groups is within 1 year of the true difference in average life expectancies? Assume that equal sample sizes will be selected from the two groups and that the standard deviation for both groups is approximately 15 years.

7.66 **Users of home shopping services.** All cable companies carry at least one home shopping channel. Who uses these home shopping services? Are the shoppers primarily men or women? Suppose you want to estimate the difference in the proportions of men and women who say they have used or expect to use televised home shopping using an 80% confidence interval of width .06 or less.

a. Approximately how many people should be included in your samples?

b. Suppose you want to obtain individual estimates for the two proportions of interest. Will the sample size found in part **a** be large enough to provide estimates of each proportion correct to within .02 with probability equal to .90? Justify your response.

7.67 **AMA survey on corporate downsizing.** According to a national survey of 1,441 firms by the *American Management*

Association, downsizing is no longer the dominant theme in the workplace. But are there regional differences in this phenomenon? Is there more growth in jobs in the Sunbelt than the Rustbelt? Assuming equal sample sizes for the two regions, how large would the samples need to be to estimate the difference in the proportion of firms that plan to add new jobs in the next year in the two regions? A 90% confidence interval of width no more than .10 is desired.

7.68 **Average housing space per person.** Even though Japan is an economic superpower, Japanese workers are in many ways worse off than their U.S. and European counterparts. For example, a decade ago the estimated average housing space per person (in square feet) was 665.2 in the United States, and only 269 in Japan (*Minneapolis Star-Tribune*, Jan. 31, 1993). Suppose a team of economists and sociologists from the United Nations plans to reestimate the difference in the mean housing space per person for U.S. and Japanese workers. Assume that equal sample sizes will be used for each country and that the standard deviation is 35 square feet for Japan and 80 for the United States. How many people should be sampled in each country to estimate the difference to within 10 square feet with 95% confidence?

7.6 Comparing Two Population Variances: Independent Sampling (Optional)

Many times it is of practical interest to use the techniques developed in this chapter to compare the means or proportions of two populations. However, there are also important instances when we wish to compare two population variances. For example, when two devices are available for producing precision measurements (scales, calipers, thermometers, etc.), we might want to compare the variability of the measurements of the devices before deciding which one to purchase. Or when two standardized tests can be used to rate job applicants, the variability of the scores for both tests should be taken into consideration before deciding which test to use.

For problems like these we need to develop a statistical procedure to compare population variances. The common statistical procedure for comparing population variances, σ_1^2 and σ_2^2, makes an inference about the ratio σ_1^2/σ_2^2. In this section, we will show how to test the null hypothesis that the ratio σ_1^2/σ_2^2 equals 1 (the variances are equal) against the alternative hypothesis that the ratio differs from 1 (the variances differ):

$$H_0: \frac{\sigma_1^2}{\sigma_2^2} = 1 \qquad (\sigma_1^2 = \sigma_2^2)$$

$$H_a: \frac{\sigma_1^2}{\sigma_2^2} \neq 1 \qquad (\sigma_1^2 \neq \sigma_2^2)$$

To make an inference about the ratio σ_1^2/σ_2^2, it seems reasonable to collect sample data and use the ratio of the sample variances, s_1^2/s_2^2. We will use the test statistic

$$F = \frac{s_1^2}{s_2^2}$$

To establish a rejection region for the test statistic, we need to know the sampling distribution of s_1^2/s_2^2. As you will subsequently see, the sampling distribution of s_1^2/s_2^2 is based on two of the assumptions already required for the t-test:

1. The two sampled populations are normally distributed.

2. The samples are randomly and independently selected from their respective populations.

When these assumptions are satisfied and when the null hypothesis is true (that is, $\sigma_1^2 = \sigma_2^2$), the sampling distribution of $F = s_1^2/s_2^2$ is the **F-distribution** with $(n_1 - 1)$ numerator degrees of freedom and $(n_2 - 1)$ denominator degrees of freedom, respectively. The shape of the F-distribution depends on the degrees of freedom associated with s_1^2 and s_2^2— that is, on $(n_1 - 1)$ and $(n_2 - 1)$. An F-distribution with 7 and 9 df is shown in Figure 7.17. As you can see, the distribution is skewed to the right, since s_1^2/s_2^2 cannot be less than 0 but can increase without bound.

FIGURE 7.17

An F-distribution with 7 numerator and 9 denominator degrees of freedom

We need to be able to find F values corresponding to the tail areas of this distribution in order to establish the rejection region for our test of hypothesis because we expect the ratio F of the sample variances to be either very large or very small when the population variances are unequal. The upper-tail F values for $\alpha = .10, .05, .025,$ and $.01$ can be found in Tables VII, VIII, IX, and X of Appendix B. Table VIII is partially reproduced in Table 7.7. It gives F values that correspond to $\alpha = .05$ upper-tail areas for different degrees of freedom ν_1 for the numerator sample variance, s_1^2, whereas the rows correspond to the degrees of freedom ν_2 for the denominator sample variance, s_2^2. Thus, if the numerator degrees of freedom is $\nu_1 = 7$ and the denominator degrees of freedom is $\nu_2 = 9$, we look in the seventh column and ninth row to find $F_{.05} = 3.29$. As shown in Figure 7.18, $\alpha = .05$ is the tail area to the right of 3.29 in the F-distribution with 7 and 9 df—that is, if $\sigma_1^2 = \sigma_2^2$, then the probability that the F statistic will exceed 3.29 is $\alpha = .05$.

FIGURE 7.18

An F-distribution for $\nu_1 = 7$ and $\nu_2 = 9$ df; $\alpha = .05$

Biography

TABLE 7.7 Reproduction of Part of Table VIII in Appendix B: Percentage Points of the F-Distribution, $\alpha = .05$

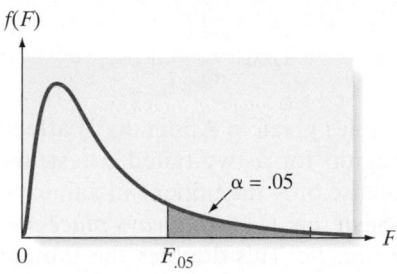

$f(F)$

$\alpha = .05$

$0 \quad F_{.05}$

	NUMERATOR DEGREES OF FREEDOM								
ν_1 / ν_2	1	2	3	4	5	6	7	8	9
1	161.4	199.5	215.7	224.6	230.2	234.0	236.8	238.9	240.5
2	18.51	19.00	19.16	19.25	19.30	19.33	19.35	19.37	19.38
3	10.13	9.55	9.28	9.12	9.01	8.94	8.89	8.85	8.81
4	7.71	6.94	6.59	6.39	6.26	6.16	6.09	6.04	6.00
5	6.61	5.79	5.41	5.19	5.05	4.95	4.88	4.82	4.77
6	5.99	5.14	4.76	4.53	4.39	4.28	4.21	4.15	4.10
7	5.59	4.74	4.35	4.12	3.97	3.87	3.79	3.73	3.68
8	5.32	4.46	4.07	3.84	3.69	3.58	3.50	3.44	3.39
9	5.12	4.26	3.86	3.63	3.48	3.37	3.29	3.23	3.18
10	4.96	4.10	3.71	3.48	3.33	3.22	3.14	3.07	3.02
11	4.84	3.98	3.59	3.36	3.20	3.09	3.01	2.95	2.90
12	4.75	3.89	3.49	3.25	3.11	3.00	2.91	2.85	2.80
13	4.67	3.81	3.41	3.18	3.03	2.92	2.83	2.77	2.71
14	4.60	3.74	3.34	3.11	2.96	2.85	2.76	2.70	2.65

Denominator Degrees of Freedom

Now Work Exercise 7.69

EXAMPLE 7.10

Comparing Paper Mill Production Variation Using an F-Test

Problem A manufacturer of paper products wants to compare the variation in daily production levels at two paper mills. Independent random samples of days are selected from each mill and the production levels (in units) recorded. The data are shown in Table 7.8. Do these data provide sufficient evidence to indicate a difference in the variability of production levels at the two paper mills? (Use $\alpha = .10$.)

Solution Let

σ_1^2 = Population variance of production levels at mill 1

σ_2^2 = Population variance of production levels at mill 2

PAPERMILLS

TABLE 7.8 Production Levels at Two Paper Mills

Mill 1:	34	18	28	21	32	40	22	23	22	29
	25	10	38							
Mill 2:	31	13	27	19	22	18	23	22	21	13
	18	15	24	13	19	18	19	23		

The hypotheses of interest, then, are

$$H_0: \frac{\sigma_1^2}{\sigma_2^2} = 1 \qquad (\sigma_1^2 = \sigma_2^2)$$

$$H_a: \frac{\sigma_1^2}{\sigma_2^2} \neq 1 \qquad (\sigma_1^2 \neq \sigma_2^2)$$

The nature of the F-tables given in Appendix B affects the form of the test statistic. To form the rejection region for a two-tailed F-test, we want to make certain that the upper tail is used, because only the upper-tail values of F are shown in Tables VII, VIII, IX, and X. To accomplish this, *we will always place the larger sample variance in the numerator of the F-test statistic.* This doubles the tabulated value for α, since we double the probability that the F-ratio will fall in the upper tail by always placing the larger sample variance in the numerator—that is, we establish a one-tailed rejection region by putting the larger variance in the numerator rather than establishing rejection regions in both tails.

Thus, for our example, we have a numerator s_1^2 with df $= \nu_1 = n_1 - 1 = 12$ and a denominator s_2^2 with df $= \nu_2 = n_2 - 1 = 17$. Therefore, the test statistic will be

$$F = \frac{\text{Larger sample variance}}{\text{Smaller sample variance}} = \frac{s_1^2}{s_2^2}$$

and we will reject $H_0: \sigma_1^2 = \sigma_2^2$ for $\alpha = .10$ when the calculated value of F exceeds the tabulated value:

$$F_{\alpha/2} = F_{.05} = 2.38 \quad \text{(see Figure 7.19)}$$

To calculate the value of the test statistic, we require the sample variances. Summary statistics for the data in Table 7.9 are shown on the MINITAB printout, Figure 7.20. The sample standard deviations (shaded) are $s_1 = 8.36$ and $s_2 = 4.85$. Therefore,

$$F = \frac{s_1^2}{s_2^2} = \frac{(8.36)^2}{(4.85)^2} = 2.97$$

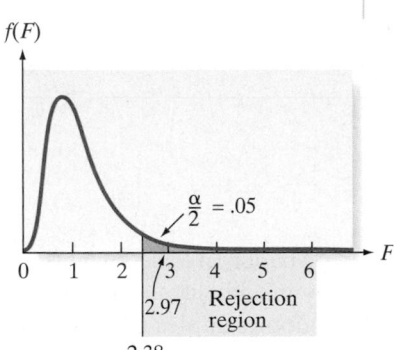

$f(F)$

$\frac{\alpha}{2} = .05$

Rejection region

2.97

2.38

FIGURE 7.19

Rejection region for Example 7.10

When we compare this result to the rejection region shown in Figure 7.19, we see that $F = 2.97$ falls in the rejection region. Therefore, the data provide sufficient evidence to indicate that the population variances differ. It appears that the variation in production levels at mill 1 tends to be higher than the variation at mill 2.

Look Back What would you have concluded if the value of F calculated from the samples had not fallen in the rejection region? Would you conclude that the null hypothesis of equal variances is true? No, because then you risk the possibility of a Type II error (accepting H_0 if H_a is true) without knowing the value of β, the probability of accepting $H_0: \sigma_1^2 = \sigma_2^2$ if in fact it is false. Since we will not consider the calculation of β for specific alternatives in this text, when the F statistic does not fall in the rejection region, we simply conclude that insufficient sample evidence exists to refute the null hypothesis that $\sigma_1^2 = \sigma_2^2$.

Descriptive Statistics: LEVEL

FIGURE 7.20

MINITAB summary statistics for data in Table 7.9

Variable	MILL	N	Mean	SE Mean	StDev	Minimum	Maximum
LEVEL	1	13	26.31	2.32	8.36	10.00	40.00
	2	18	19.89	1.14	4.85	13.00	31.00

Now Work Exercise 7.74a

The F-test for equal population variances is summarized in the following boxes.*

F-Test for Equal Population Variances

One-Tailed Test	Two-Tailed Test
$H_0: \sigma_1^2 = \sigma_2^2$	$H_0: \sigma_1^2 = \sigma_2^2$
$H_a: \sigma_1^2 < \sigma_2^2$ (or $H_a: \sigma_1^2 > \sigma_2^2$)	$H_a: \sigma_1^2 \neq \sigma_2^2$

Test statistic:

$$F = \frac{s_2^2}{s_1^2}$$

$$\left(\text{or } F = \frac{s_1^2}{s_2^2} \text{ when } H_a: \sigma_1^2 > \sigma_2^2 \right)$$

Test statistic:

$$F = \frac{\text{Larger sample variance}}{\text{Smaller sample variance}}$$

$$= \frac{s_1^2}{s_2^2} \text{ when } s_1^2 > s_2^2$$

$$\left(\text{or } \frac{s_2^2}{s_1^2} \text{ when } s_2^2 > s_1^2 \right)$$

Rejection region:

$$F > F_\alpha$$

Rejection region:

$$F > F_{\alpha/2}$$

where F_α and $F_{\alpha/2}$ are based on $\nu_1 =$ numerator degrees of freedom and $\nu_2 =$ denominator degrees of freedom; ν_1 and ν_2 are the degrees of freedom for the numerator and denominator sample variances, respectively.

Conditions Required for a Valid F-Test for Equal Variances

1. Both sampled populations are normally distributed.
2. The samples are random and independent.

EXAMPLE 7.11

The Observed Significance Level of an F-Test

Problem   Find the p-value for the test in Example 7.10 using the F-tables in Appendix B. Compare this to the exact p-value obtained from a computer printout.

Solution   Since the observed value of the F statistic in Example 7.10 was 2.97, the observed significance level of the test would equal the probability of observing a value of F at least as contradictory to $H_0: \sigma_1^2 = \sigma_2^2$ as $F = 2.97$, if in fact H_0 is true. Since we give the F-tables in Appendix B only for values of α equal to .10, .05, .025, and .01, we can only approximate the observed significance level. Checking Tables IX and X, we find $F_{.025} = 2.82$ and $F_{.01} = 3.46$. Since the observed value of F exceeds $F_{.025}$ but is less than $F_{.01}$, the observed significance level for the test is less than $2(.025) = .05$, but greater than $2(.01) = .02$—that is,

$$.02 < p\text{-value} < .05$$

The exact p-value of the test is shown on the MINITAB printout, Figure 7.21. This value (highlighted), is .04.

Look Back   We double the α value shown in Table IX and X because this is a two-tailed test.

---

*Although a test of a hypothesis of equality of variances is the most common application of the F-test, it can also be used to test a hypothesis that the ratio between the population variances is equal to some specified value, $H_0: \sigma_1^2/\sigma_2^2 = k$. The test is conducted in exactly the same way as specified in the box, except that we use the test statistic

$$F = \frac{s_1^2}{s_2^2}\left(\frac{1}{k}\right)$$

Test for Equal Variances: LEVEL versus MILL

```
95% Bonferroni confidence intervals for standard deviations

MILL   N    Lower     StDev    Upper
   1  13  5.73182   8.36047  14.9507
   2  18  3.49950   4.84936   7.7455


F-Test (normal distribution)
Test statistic = 2.97, p-value = 0.040


Levene's Test (any continuous distribution)
Test statistic = 3.78, p-value = 0.062
```

FIGURE 7.21

MINITAB F-test for equal variances

Now Work Exercise 7.74b

As a final example of an application, consider the comparison of population variances as a check of the assumption $\sigma_1^2 = \sigma_2^2$ needed for the two-sample t-test. Rejection of the null hypothesis $\sigma_1^2 = \sigma_2^2$ would indicate that the assumption is invalid. [*Note:* Nonrejection of the null hypothesis does *not* imply that the assumption is valid.] We illustrate with an example.

EXAMPLE 7.12

Checking the Assumption of Equal Variances

Problem In Example 7.4 (Section 7.2) we used the two-sample t-statistic to compare the success indexes of two groups of managers. The data are repeated in Table 7.9 for convenience. The use of the t-statistic was based on the assumption that the population variances of the managerial success indexes were equal for the two groups. Conduct a test of hypothesis to check this assumption at $\alpha = .10$.

 MANSUCCESS

TABLE 7.9 Managerial Success Indexes for Two Groups of Managers

GROUP 1						GROUP 2					
Interaction with Outsiders						Few Interactions					
65	58	78	60	68	69	62	53	36	34	56	50
66	70	53	71	63	63	42	57	46	68	48	42
						52	53	43			

Solution We want to test

$$H_0: \sigma_1^2 = \sigma_2^2$$
$$H_a: \sigma_1^2 \neq \sigma_2^2$$

This F-test is shown on the Excel printout, Figure 7.22. Both the test statistic, $F = 1.99$, and two-tailed p-value, .2553, are highlighted on the printout. Since $\alpha = .10$ is less than the p-value, we do not reject the null hypothesis that the population variances of the success indexes are equal. It is here that the temptation to misuse the F-test is strongest. *We cannot conclude that the data justify the use of the* t-*statistic*. This is equivalent to accepting H_0, and we have repeatedly warned against this conclusion because the probability of a Type II error, β, is unknown. The α level of .10 protects us only against rejecting H_0 if it is true. This use of the F-test may prevent us from abusing the t procedure when we

F Test for Differences in Two Variances	
Data	
Level of Significance	0.05
Population 1 Sample	
Sample Size	15
Sample Standard Deviation	9.334
Population 2 Sample	
Sample Size	12
Sample Standard Deviation	6.61
Intermediate Calculations	
F-Test Statistic	1.994035
Population 1 Sample Degrees of Freedom	14
Population 2 Sample Degrees of Freedom	11
Two-Tailed Test	
Lower Critical Value	0.323144
Upper Critical Value	3.358821
p-Value	0.255307
Do not reject the null hypothesis	

FIGURE 7.22

Excel/PHStat2 *F*-test for testing assumption of equal variances

obtain a value of F that leads to a rejection of the assumption that $\sigma_1^2 = \sigma_2^2$. But when the F-statistic does not fall in the rejection region, we know little more about the validity of the assumption than before we conducted the test.

Now Work Exercise 7.82

What Do You Do If the Assumption of Normal Population Distributions Is Not Satisfied?

Answer: The F-test is much less robust (i.e., much more sensitive) to departures from normality than the t-test for comparing the population means (Section 7.2). If you have doubts about the normality of the population frequency distributions, use a **nonparametric method** (e.g., *Levene's test*) for comparing the two population variances. This method can be found in the nonparametric statistics texts listed in the references for Chapter 14.

Hypothesis Test for (σ_1^2/σ_2^2)

Using the TI-83/TI-84 Graphing Calculator

Step 1   *Enter the data (Skip to Step 2 if you have summary statistics, not raw data).*

Press **STAT** and select **1:Edit**.
Note: If the lists already contain data, clear the old data. Use the up **ARROW** to highlight '**L1**'.
Press **CLEAR ENTER**.
Use the up **ARROW** to highlight '**L2**'.
Press **CLEAR ENTER**.
Use the **ARROW** and **ENTER** keys to enter the first data set into **L1**.
Use the **ARROW** and **ENTER** keys to enter the second data set into **L2**.

Step 2   *Access the Statistical Tests Menu*

Press **STAT**.
Arrow right to **TESTS**.
Arrow down to **2-SampFTest**.
Press **ENTER**.

Step 3 *Choose "**Data**" or "**Stats**". ("Data" is selected when you have entered the raw data into the Lists. "Stats" is selected when you are given only the means, standard deviations, and sample sizes.)*

Press **ENTER**.
If you selected "Data".
Set **List1** to **L1** and **List2** to **L2**.
Set **Freq1** to **1** and set **Freq2** to **1**.
Use the **ARROW** to highlight the appropriate alternative hypothesis.
Press **ENTER**.
Arrow down to "**Calculate**".
Press **ENTER**.

```
2-SampFTest
 Inpt:DATA Stats
 List1:L1
 List2:L2
 Freq1:1
 Freq2:1
 σ1:≠σ2 <σ2 >σ2
 Calculate Draw
```

If you selected "Stats", enter the standard deviations and sample sizes.
Use the **ARROW** to highlight the appropriate alternative hypothesis.
Press **ENTER**
Arrow down to "**Calculate**"
Press **ENTER**

```
2-SampFTest
 Inpt:Data Stats
 Sx1:10
 n1:23
 Sx2:12
 n2:33
 σ1:≠σ2 <σ2 >σ2
 Calculate Draw
```

The results of the hypothesis test will be displayed with the *p*-value, and the input data used.

Example Test the hypotheses: $H_0: \sigma_1^2 = \sigma_2^2$ vs. $H_a: \sigma_1^2 \neq \sigma_2^2$ using the data shown below.

Group 1: standard deviation = 10; $n = 23$

Group 2: standard deviation = 12; $n = 33$

```
2-SampFTest
 σ1≠σ2
 F=.6944444444
 p=.3759305952
 Sx1=10
 Sx2=12
 ↓n1=23
 ■
```

As you can see from the screens, $F = .6944$ and the *p*-value is .3759. Since this *p*-value is large, you ***do not reject*** the null hypothesis. You will also notice the output includes the standard deviations and sample sizes.

Exercises 7.69–7.83

Learning the Mechanics

7.69 Use Tables VII, VIII, IX, and X of Appendix B to find each
NW of the following *F*-values:
 a. $F_{.05}$ where $\nu_1 = 9$ and $\nu_2 = 6$
 b. $F_{.01}$ where $\nu_1 = 18$ and $\nu_2 = 14$
 c. $F_{.025}$ where $\nu_1 = 11$ and $\nu_2 = 4$
 d. $F_{.10}$ where $\nu_1 = 20$ and $\nu_2 = 5$

7.70 Given ν_1 and ν_2, find the following probabilities:
 a. $\nu_1 = 2, \nu_2 = 30, P(F \geq 5.39)$
 b. $\nu_1 = 24, \nu_2 = 10, P(F < 2.74)$
 c. $\nu_1 = 7, \nu_2 = 1, P(F \leq 236.8)$
 d. $\nu_1 = 40, \nu_2 = 40, P(F > 2.11)$

7.71 For each of the following cases, identify the rejection region that should be used to test $H_0: \sigma_1^2 = \sigma_2^2$ against $H_a: \sigma_1^2 > \sigma_2^2$. Assume $\nu_1 = 30$ and $\nu_2 = 20$.
 a. $\alpha = .10$
 b. $\alpha = .05$
 c. $\alpha = .025$
 d. $\alpha = .01$

7.72 For each of the following cases, identify the rejection region that should be used to test $H_0: \sigma_1^2 = \sigma_2^2$ against $H_a: \sigma_1^2 \neq \sigma_2^2$. Assume $\nu_1 = 10$ and $\nu_2 = 12$.
 a. $\alpha = .20$
 b. $\alpha = .10$
 c. $\alpha = .05$
 d. $\alpha = .02$

7.73 Specify the appropriate rejection region for testing $H_0: \sigma_1^2 = \sigma_2^2$ in each of the following situations:
 a. $H_a: \sigma_1^2 > \sigma_2^2; \alpha = .05, n_1 = 25, n_2 = 20$
 b. $H_a: \sigma_1^2 < \sigma_2^2; \alpha = .05, n_1 = 10, n_2 = 15$
 c. $H_a: \sigma_1^2 \neq \sigma_2^2; \alpha = .10, n_1 = 21, n_2 = 31$
 d. $H_a: \sigma_1^2 < \sigma_2^2; \alpha = .01, n_1 = 31, n_2 = 41$
 e. $H_a: \sigma_1^2 \neq \sigma_2^2; \alpha = .05, n_1 = 7, n_2 = 16$

7.74 Independent random samples were selected from each of
NW two normally distributed populations, $n_1 = 12$ from population 1 and $n_2 = 27$ from population 2. The means and variances for the two samples are shown in the table.

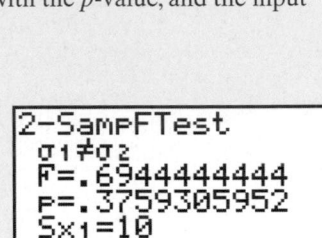

Sample 1	Sample 2
$n_1 = 12$	$n_2 = 27$
$\bar{x}_1 = 31.7$	$\bar{x}_2 = 37.4$
$s_1^2 = 3.87$	$s_2^2 = 8.75$

 a. Test the null hypothesis $H_0: \sigma_1^2 = \sigma_2^2$ against the alternative hypothesis $H_a: \sigma_1^2 \neq \sigma_2^2$. Use $\alpha = .10$.
 b. Find and interpret the approximate *p*-value of the test.

7.75 Independent random samples were selected from each of two normally distributed populations, $n_1 = 6$ from population 1 and $n_2 = 5$ from population 2. The data are shown in the next table.

LM7_75

Sample 1	Sample 2
3.1	2.3
4.4	1.4
1.2	3.7
1.7	8.9
.7	5.5
3.4	

a. Test $H_0: \sigma_1^2 = \sigma_2^2$ against $H_a: \sigma_1^2 < \sigma_2^2$. Use $\alpha = .01$.

b. Find and interpret the approximate p-value of the test.

Applying the Concepts—Basic

DIAMONDS

7.76 **Diamonds sold at retail.** Refer to Exercise 7.12 (p. 419) and the data saved in the **DIAMONDS** file. MINITAB descriptive statistics for carat size and selling price of the 308 diamonds are reproduced in the following printout. The diamonds are grouped according to the independent certification body (GIA, IGI, or HRD) that assessed the stones.

```
Descriptive Statistics: CARAT, PRICE

Variable   CERT   N    Mean     StDev
CARAT      GIA    151  0.6723   0.2456
           HRD    79   0.8129   0.1831
           IGI    78   0.3665   0.2163

PRICE      GIA    151  5310     3247
           HRD    79   7181     2090
           IGI    78   2267     2121
```

a. Conduct a test to determine whether the variation in carat size differs for diamonds certified by GIA and diamonds certified by HRD. Use $\alpha = .05$.

b. Conduct a test to determine whether the variation in carat size differs for diamonds certified by GIA and diamonds certified by IGI. Use $\alpha = .05$.

c. Conduct a test to determine whether the variation in selling price differs for diamonds certified by HRD and diamonds certified by IGI. Use $\alpha = .05$.

d. Use a statistical software package (and the data in the **DIAMONDS** file) to determine whether the assumption of normally distributed data for each certification group is reasonably satisfied.

7.77 **Rating service at five-star hotels.** Refer to *The Journal of American Academy of Business, Cambridge* (March 2002) study of how guests perceive the service quality at five-star hotels in Jamaica, Exercise 7.14 (p. 420). A summary of the guest perception scores, by gender, are reproduced in the next table. Let σ_M^2 and σ_F^2 represent the true variances in scores for male and female guests, respectively.

a. Set up H_0 and H_a for determining whether σ_M^2 is less than σ_F^2.

b. Find the test statistic for the test.

c. Give the rejection region for the test if $\alpha = .10$.

d. Find the approximate p-value of the test.

e. Make the appropriate conclusion in the words of the problem.

f. What conditions are required for the test results to be valid?

Gender	Sample size	Mean score	Standard deviation
Males	127	39.08	6.73
Females	114	38.79	6.94

7.78 **Mental health of workers and the unemployed.** A study in the *Journal of Occupational and Organizational Psychology* (Dec. 1992) investigated the relationship of employment status and mental health. A sample of working and unemployed people was selected, and each person was given a mental health examination using the General Health Questionnaire (GHQ), a widely recognized measure of mental health. Although the article focused on comparing the mean GHQ levels, a comparison of the variability of GHQ scores for employed and unemployed men and women is of interest as well.

a. In general terms, what does the amount of variability in GHQ scores tell us about the group?

b. What are the appropriate null and alternative hypotheses to compare the variability of the mental health scores of the employed and unemployed groups? Define any symbols you use.

c. The standard deviation for a sample of 142 employed men was 3.26, while the standard deviation for 49 unemployed men was 5.10. Conduct the test you set up in part **b** using $\alpha = .05$. Interpret the results.

d. What assumptions are necessary to ensure the validity of the test?

Applying the Concepts—Intermediate

7.79 **Analyzing human inspection errors.** Tests of product quality using human inspectors can lead to serious inspection error problems (*Journal of Quality Technology*, Apr. 1986). To evaluate the performance of inspectors in a new company, a quality manager had a sample of 12 novice inspectors evaluate 200 finished products. The same 200 items were evaluated by 12 experienced inspectors. The quality of each item—whether defective or nondefective—was known to the manager. The table lists the number of inspection errors (classifying a defective item as nondefective or vice versa) made by each inspector.

INSPECT

Novice Inspectors				Experienced Inspectors			
30	35	26	40	31	15	25	19
36	20	45	31	28	17	19	18
33	29	21	48	24	10	20	21

a. Prior to conducting this experiment, the manager believed the variance in inspection errors was lower for experienced inspectors than for novice inspectors. Do the sample data support her belief? Test using $\alpha = .05$.

b. What is the appropriate p-value of the test you conducted in part **a**?

7.80 Patent infringement case. Refer to the *Chance* (Fall 2002) description of a patent infringement case against Intel Corp., Exercise 7.17 (p. 421). The zinc measurements for three locations on the original inventor's notebook—on a text line, on a witness line, and on the intersection of the witness and text line—are reproduced in the table.

PATENT

Text line:	.335	.374	.440			
Witness line:	.210	.262	.188	.329	.439	.397
Intersection:	.393	.353	.285	.295	.319	

a. Use a test (at $\alpha = .05$) to compare the variation in zinc measurements for the text line with the corresponding variation for the intersection.

b. Use a test (at $\alpha = .05$) to compare the variation in zinc measurements for the witness line with the corresponding variation for the intersection.

c. From the results, parts **a** and **b**, what can you infer about the variation in zinc measurements at the three notebook locations?

d. What assumptions are required for the inferences to be valid? Are they reasonably satisfied? (You checked these assumptions when answering Exercise 7.17d.)

7.81 "Just-in-time" deliveries from factories to foxholes. Following the Persian Gulf War, the Pentagon changed its logistics processes to be more corporate-like. The extravagant "just-in-case" mentality was replaced with "just-in-time" systems. Emulating Federal Express and United Parcel Service, deliveries from factories to foxholes are now expedited using bar codes, laser cards, radio tags, and databases to track supplies. The following table contains order-to-delivery times (in days) for a sample of shipments from the United States to the Persian Gulf in 1991 and a sample of shipments to Bosnia in 1995.

ORDTIMES

Persian Gulf	Bosnia
28.0	15.1
20.0	6.4
26.5	5.0
10.6	11.4
9.1	6.5
35.2	6.5
29.1	3.0
41.2	7.0
27.5	5.5

Source: Adapted from Crock, S. "The Pentagon Goes to B-School." *Business Week,* December 11, 1995, p. 98.

a. Is there sufficient evidence to indicate that the variances in order-to-delivery times for Persian Gulf and Bosnia shipments differ? Use $\alpha = .05$.

b. Given your answer to part **a**, is it appropriate to construct a paired-difference confidence interval for the difference between the mean order-to-delivery times? Explain.

GASTURBINE

7.82 Cooling method for gas turbines. Refer to the *Journal of Engineering for Gas Turbines and Power* (Jan. 2005) study of gas turbines augmented with high-pressure inlet fogging, Exercise 7.23 (p. 422). Heat rate data (kilojoules per kilowatt per hour) for each of three types of gas turbines (advanced, aeroderivative, traditional) are saved in the **GASTURBINE** file. In order to compare the mean heat rates of two types of gas turbines, you assumed that the heat rate variances were equal.

a. Conduct a test (at $\alpha = .05$) for equality of heat rate variances for traditional and aeroderivative augmented gas turbines. Use the result to make a statement about the validity of the inference derived in Exercise 7.23a.

b. Conduct a test (at $\alpha = .05$) for equality of heat rate variances for advanced and aeroderivative augmented gas turbines. Use the result to make a statement about the validity of the inference derived in Exercise 7.23b.

7.83 Variability of math achievement scores. The *American Educational Research Journal* (Fall 1998) published a study to compare the mathematics achievement test scores of male and female students. The researchers hypothesized that the distribution of test scores for males is more variable than the corresponding distribution for females. Use the summary information in the table to test this claim at $\alpha = .01$.

	Males	Females
Sample size	1,764	1,739
Mean	48.9	48.4
Standard deviation	12.96	11.85

Source: Bielinski, J., and Davison, M. L. "Gender Differences by Item Difficulty Interactions in Multiple-Choice Mathematics Items." *American Educational Research Journal,* Vol. 35, No. 3, Fall 1998, p. 464 (Table 1).

KEY TERMS

Note: Starred (*) items are from the optional section in this chapter.

Blocking   425

*F-distribution   450
*Nonparametric method   455
Paired difference experiment   425

Pooled sample estimate of variance   410
Randomized block experiment   425
Standard error   406

GUIDE TO SELECTING A TWO-SAMPLE HYPOTHESIS & CONFIDENCE INTERVAL

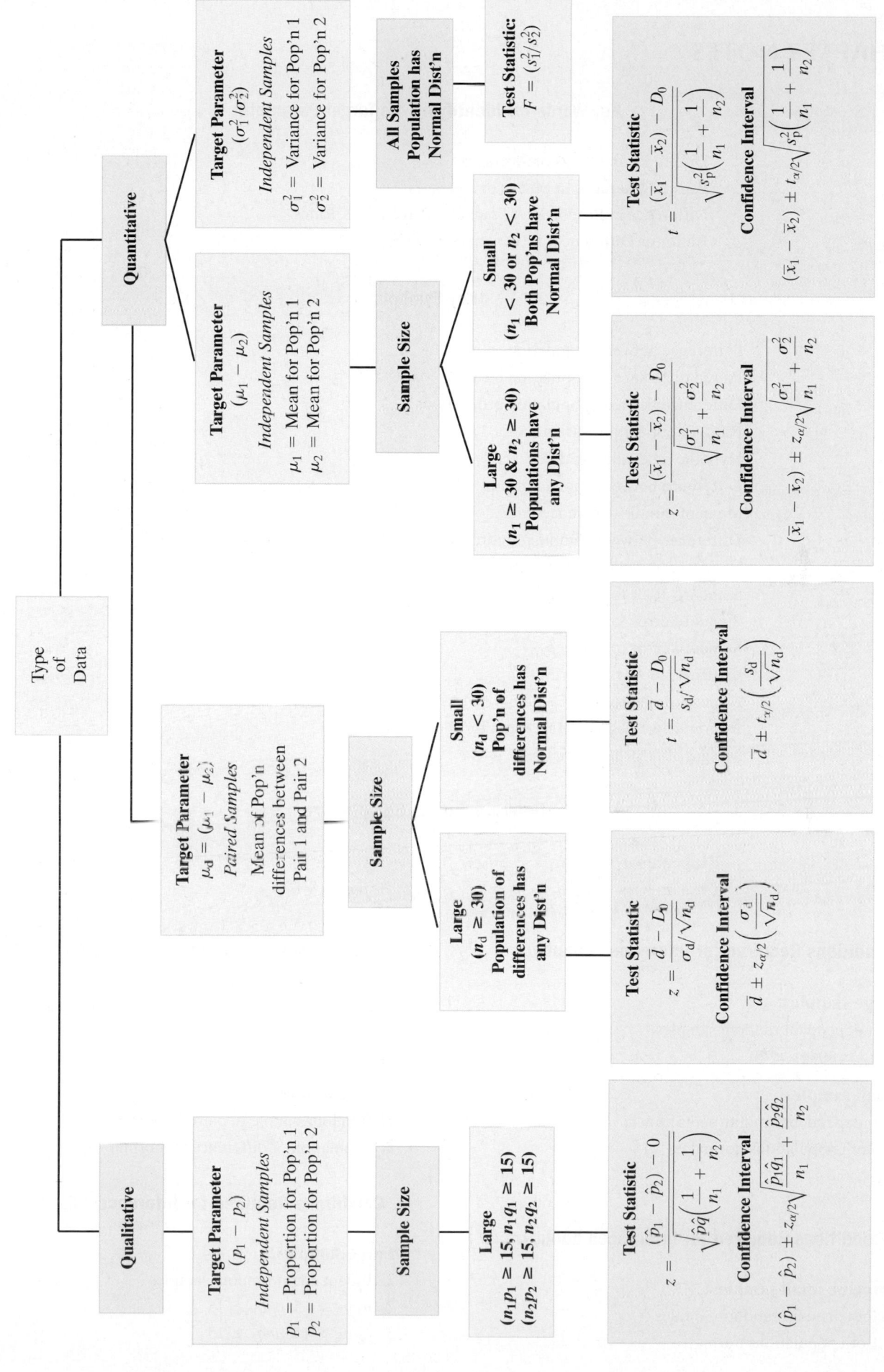

Type of Data

Quantitative

Target Parameter
(σ_1^2/σ_2^2)
Independent Samples
σ_1^2 = Variance for Pop'n 1
σ_2^2 = Variance for Pop'n 2

All Samples Population has Normal Dist'n

Test Statistic:
$F = (s_1^2/s_2^2)$

Target Parameter
$(\mu_1 - \mu_2)$
Independent Samples
μ_1 = Mean for Pop'n 1
μ_2 = Mean for Pop'n 2

Sample Size

Small
($n_1 < 30$ or $n_2 < 30$)
Both Pop'ns have Normal Dist'n

Test Statistic
$$t = \frac{(\bar{x}_1 - \bar{x}_2) - D_0}{\sqrt{s_p^2\left(\dfrac{1}{n_1} + \dfrac{1}{n_2}\right)}}$$
Confidence Interval
$$(\bar{x}_1 - \bar{x}_2) \pm t_{\alpha/2}\sqrt{s_p^2\left(\dfrac{1}{n_1} + \dfrac{1}{n_2}\right)}$$

Large
($n_1 \geq 30$ & $n_2 \geq 30$)
Populations have any Dist'n

Test Statistic
$$z = \frac{(\bar{x}_1 - \bar{x}_2) - D_0}{\sqrt{\dfrac{\sigma_1^2}{n_1} + \dfrac{\sigma_2^2}{n_2}}}$$
Confidence Interval
$$(\bar{x}_1 - \bar{x}_2) \pm z_{\alpha/2}\sqrt{\dfrac{\sigma_1^2}{n_1} + \dfrac{\sigma_2^2}{n_2}}$$

Target Parameter
$\mu_d = (\mu_1 - \mu_2)$
Paired Samples
Mean of Pop'n differences between Pair 1 and Pair 2

Sample Size

Small
($n_d < 30$)
Pop'n of differences has Normal Dist'n

Test Statistic
$$t = \frac{\bar{d} - D_0}{s_d/\sqrt{n_d}}$$
Confidence Interval
$$\bar{d} \pm t_{\alpha/2}\left(\dfrac{s_d}{\sqrt{n_d}}\right)$$

Large
($n_d \geq 30$)
Population of differences has any Dist'n

Test Statistic
$$z = \frac{\bar{d} - D_0}{\sigma_d/\sqrt{n_d}}$$
Confidence Interval
$$\bar{d} \pm z_{\alpha/2}\left(\dfrac{\sigma_d}{\sqrt{n_d}}\right)$$

Qualitative

Target Parameter
$(p_1 - p_2)$
Independent Samples
p_1 = Proportion for Pop'n 1
p_2 = Proportion for Pop'n 2

Sample Size

Large
($n_1 p_1 \geq 15, n_1 q_1 \geq 15$)
($n_2 p_2 \geq 15, n_2 q_2 \geq 15$)

Test Statistic
$$z = \frac{(\hat{p}_1 - \hat{p}_2) - 0}{\sqrt{\hat{p}\hat{q}\left(\dfrac{1}{n_1} + \dfrac{1}{n_2}\right)}}$$
Confidence Interval
$$(\hat{p}_1 - \hat{p}_2) \pm z_{\alpha/2}\sqrt{\dfrac{\hat{p}_1\hat{q}_1}{n_1} + \dfrac{\hat{p}_2\hat{q}_2}{n_2}}$$

459

CHAPTER NOTES

Key Words for Identifying the Target Parameter

$\mu_1 - \mu_2$	Difference in Means or Averages
μ_d	Paired Difference in Means or Averages
$p_1 - p_2$	Difference in Proportions, Fractions, Percentages, Rates
σ_1^2/σ_2^2	Ratio (or Difference) in Variances, Spreads

Key Symbols

$\mu_1 - \mu_2$	Difference between population means
μ_d	Paired difference in population means
$p_1 - p_2$	Difference between population proportions
σ_1^2/σ_2^2	Ratio of population variances
D_0	Hypothesized value of difference
$\bar{x}_1 - \bar{x}_2$	Difference between sample means
$\bar{d}$	Mean of sample differences
$\hat{p}_1 - \hat{p}_2$	Difference between sample proportions
s_1^2/s_2^2	Ratio of sample variances
$\sigma_{(\bar{x}_1 - \bar{x}_2)}$	Standard error for $\bar{x}_1 - \bar{x}_2$
$\sigma_{\bar{d}}$	Standard error for $\bar{d}$
$\sigma_{(\hat{p}_1 - \hat{p}_2)}$	Standard error for $\hat{p}_1 - \hat{p}_2$
F_α	Critical value for F-distribution
v_1	Numerator degrees of freedom for F-distribution
v_2	Denominator degrees of freedom for F-distribution
ME	Margin of error in estimation

Determining the Sample Size

Estimating $\mu_1 - \mu_2$: $n_1 = n_2 = (z_{\alpha/2})^2 (\sigma_1^2 + \sigma_2^2)/(\text{ME})^2$

Estimating $p_1 - p_2$: $n_1 = n_2 = (z_{\alpha/2})^2 (p_1 q_1 + p_2 q_2)/(\text{ME})^2$

Conditions Required for Inferences about $\mu_1 - \mu_2$

Large samples:
1. Independent random samples
2. $n_1 \geq 30, n_2 \geq 30$

Small samples:
1. Independent random samples
2. Both populations normal
3. $\sigma_1^2 = \sigma_2^2$

Conditions Required for Inferences about σ_1^2/σ_2^2

Large or small samples:
1. Independent random samples
2. Both populations normal

Conditions Required for Inferences about μ_d

Large samples:
1. Random sample of paired differences
2. $n_d \geq 30$

Small samples:
1. Random sample of paired differences
2. Population of differences is normal

Conditions Required for Inferences about $p_1 - p_2$

Large samples:
1. Independent random samples
2. $n_1 p_1 \geq 15, n_1 q_1 \geq 15$
3. $n_2 p_2 \geq 15, n_2 q_2 \geq 15$

Using a Confidence Interval for $(\mu_1 - \mu_2)$ or $(p_1 - p_2)$ to Determine whether a Difference Exists:

1. If the confidence interval includes all *positive* numbers $(+, +)$: $\rightarrow$ Infer $\mu_1 > \mu_2$ or $p_1 > p_2$
2. If the confidence interval includes all *negative* numbers $(-, -)$: $\rightarrow$ Infer $\mu_1 < \mu_2$ or $p_1 < p_2$
3. If the confidence interval includes 0 $(-, +)$: $\rightarrow$ Infer "no evidence of a difference"

SUPPLEMENTARY EXERCISES 7.84–7.115

Starred (*) exercises refer to the optional section in this chapter.

Learning the Mechanics

7.84 List the assumptions necessary for each of the following inferential techniques:
a. Large-sample inferences about the difference $(\mu_1 - \mu_2)$ between population means using a two-sample z-statistic
b. Small-sample inferences about $(\mu_1 - \mu_2)$ using an independent samples design and a two-sample t-statistic
c. Small-sample inferences about $(\mu_1 - \mu_2)$ using a paired difference design and a single-sample t-statistic to analyze the differences
d. Large-sample inferences about the differences $(p_1 - p_2)$ between binomial proportions using a two-sample z-statistic
*e. Inferences about the ratio σ_1^2/σ_2^2 of two population variances using an F-test.

7.85 Independent random samples were selected from two normally distributed populations with means μ_1 and μ_2, respectively. The sample sizes, means, and variances are shown in the following table.

Sample 1	Sample 2
$n_1 = 12$	$n_2 = 14$
$\bar{x}_1 = 17.8$	$\bar{x}_2 = 15.3$
$s_1^2 = 74.2$	$s_2^2 = 60.5$

a. Test $H_0: (\mu_1 - \mu_2) = 0$ against $H_a: (\mu_1 - \mu_2) > 0$. Use $\alpha = .05$.
b. Form a 99% confidence interval for $(\mu_1 - \mu_2)$.
c. How large must n_1 and n_2 be if you wish to estimate $(\mu_1 - \mu_2)$ to within 2 units with 99% confidence? Assume that $n_1 = n_2$.

7.86 Two independent random samples were selected from normally distributed populations with means and variances (μ_1, σ_1^2) and (μ_2, σ_2^2), respectively. The sample sizes, means, and variances are shown in the following table.

Sample 1	Sample 2
$n_1 = 20$	$n_2 = 15$
$\bar{x}_1 = 123$	$\bar{x}_2 = 116$
$s_1^2 = 31.3$	$s_2^2 = 120.1$

a. * Test $H_0: \sigma_1^2 = \sigma_2^2$ against $H_a: \sigma_1^2 \neq \sigma_2^2$. Use $\alpha = .05$.
b. Would you be willing to use a small sample t-test to test the null hypothesis $H_0: (\mu_1 - \mu_2) = 0$ against the alternative hypothesis $H_a: (\mu_1 - \mu_2) \neq 0$? Why?

7.87 Two independent random samples are taken from two populations. The results of these samples are summarized in the next table.

Sample 1	Sample 2
$n_1 = 135$	$n_2 = 148$
$\bar{x}_1 = 12.2$	$\bar{x}_2 = 8.3$
$s_1^2 = 2.1$	$s_2^2 = 3.0$

a. Form a 90% confidence interval for $(\mu_1 - \mu_2)$.
b. Test $H_0: (\mu_1 - \mu_2) = 0$ against $H_a: (\mu_1 - \mu_2) \neq 0$. Use $\alpha = .01$.
c. What sample sizes would be required if you wish to estimate $(\mu_1 - \mu_2)$ to within .2 with 90% confidence? Assume that $n_1 = n_2$.

7.88 Independent random samples were selected from two binomial populations. The sizes and number of observed successes for each sample are shown in the following table.

Sample 1	Sample 2
$n_1 = 200$	$n_2 = 200$
$x_1 = 110$	$x_2 = 130$

a. Test $H_0: (p_1 - p_2) = 0$ against $H_a: (p_1 - p_2) < 0$. Use $\alpha = .10$.
b. Form a 95% confidence interval for $(p_1 - p_2)$.
c. What sample sizes would be required if we wish to use a 95% confidence interval of width .01 to estimate $(p_1 - p_2)$?

7.89 A random sample of five pairs of observations were selected, one of each pair from a population with mean μ_1, the other from a population with mean μ_2. The data are shown in the accompanying table.

LM7_89

Pair	Value from Population 1	Value from Population 2
1	28	22
2	31	27
3	24	20
4	30	27
5	22	20

a. Test the null hypothesis $H_0: \mu_D = 0$ against $H_a: \mu_d \neq 0$, where $\mu_d = \mu_1 - \mu_2$. Use $\alpha = .05$.
b. Form a 95% confidence interval for μ_d.
c. When are the procedures you used in parts **a** and **b** valid?

Applying the Concepts—Basic

7.90 **Financial incentives for college students.** A study reported in *Inside Higher Education News* (May 22, 2006) found that financial incentives can improve low-income college students' grades and retention. As part of their "Opening

Doors" program, a Louisiana community college offered to pay students $1,000 per semester on condition that they maintain at least half-time enrollment and at least a 2.0 grade-point average (GPA).

a. About 61% of Opening Doors students enrolled full time as opposed to about 52% of traditional students. Identify the target parameter for this comparison.

b. The mean GPA of Opening Doors students was 2.3 as compared to the mean GPA of 2.1 for traditional students. Identify the target parameter for this comparison.

7.91 Determining the target parameter. For each of the following studies, give the parameter of interest and state any assumptions that are necessary for the inferences to be valid.

a. To investigate a possible link between jet lag and memory impairment, a University of Bristol (England) neurologist recruited 20 female flight attendants who worked flights across several time zones. Half of the attendants had only a short recovery time between flights and half had a long recovery time between flights. The average size of the right temporal lobe of the brain for the short-recovery group was significantly smaller than the average size of the right temporal lobe of the brain for the long-recovery group (*Tampa Tribune*, May 23, 2001).

b. In a study presented at the March 2001 meeting of the Association for the Advancement of Applied Sport Psychology, researchers revealed that the proportion of athletes who have a good self-image of their body is 20% higher than the corresponding proportion of nonathletes.

c. A University of Florida animal sciences professor has discovered that feeding chickens corn oil causes them to produce larger eggs (*UF News*, April 11, 2001). The weight of eggs produced by each of a sample of chickens on a regular feed diet was recorded. Then, the same chickens were fed a diet supplemented by corn oil, and the weight of eggs produced by each was recorded. The mean weight of the eggs produced with corn oil was 3 grams heavier than the mean weight produced with the regular diet.

OILSPILL

7.92 Hull failures of oil tankers. Refer to the *Marine Technology* (Jan. 1995) study of major oil spills from tankers and carriers, Exercise 2.135 (p. 117). The data for the 50 recent spills are saved in the **OILSPILL** file.

a. Construct a 90% confidence interval for the difference between the mean spillage amount of accidents caused by collision and the mean spillage amount of accidents caused by fire/explosion. Interpret the result.

b. Conduct a test of hypothesis to compare the mean spillage amount of accidents caused by grounding to the corresponding mean of accidents caused by hull failure. Use $\alpha = .05$.

c. Refer to parts **a** and **b**. State any assumptions required for the inferences derived from the analyses to be valid. Are these assumptions reasonably satisfied?

*d. Conduct a test of hypothesis to compare the variation in spillage amounts for accidents caused by collision and accidents caused by grounding. Use $\alpha = .02$.

7.93 Analysis of distances to work for men and women. Research reported in the *Professional Geographer* (May 1992) examines the hypothesis that the disproportionate housework responsibility of women in two-income households is a major factor in determining the proximity of a woman's place of employment. The distance to work for both men and women in two-income households was reported for random samples of both central city and suburban residences:

	CENTRAL CITY RESIDENCE		SUBURBAN RESIDENCE	
	Men	Women	Men	Women
n	159	119	138	93
$\overline{x}$	7.4	4.5	9.3	6.6
s	6.3	4.2	7.1	5.6

a. For central city residences, calculate a 99% confidence interval for the difference in average distance to work for men and women in two-income households. Interpret the interval.

b. Repeat part **a** for suburban residences.

c. Interpret the confidence intervals. Do they indicate that women tend to work closer to home than men?

d. What assumptions have you made to assure the validity of the confidence intervals constructed in parts **a** and **b?**

7.94 Durability of shock absorbers. A manufacturer of automobile shock absorbers was interested in comparing the durability of its shocks with that of the shocks produced by its biggest competitor. To make the comparison, one of the manufacturer's and one of the competitor's shocks were randomly selected and installed on the rear wheels of each of six cars. After the cars had been driven 20,000 miles, the strength of each test shock was measured, coded, and recorded. Results of the examination are shown in the table.

SHOCKABS

Car Number	Manufacturer's Shock	Competitor's Shock
1	8.8	8.4
2	10.5	10.1
3	12.5	12.0
4	9.7	9.3
5	9.6	9.0
6	13.2	13.0

a. Explain why the data are collected as matched pairs.

b. Do the data present sufficient evidence to conclude that there is a difference in the mean strength of the two types of shocks after 20,000 miles of use? Use $\alpha = .05$.

c. Find the approximate observed significance level for the test, and interpret its value.

d. What assumptions are necessary to apply a paired difference analysis to the data?

e. Construct a 95% confidence interval for μ_d. Interpret the confidence interval.

f. Suppose the data are based on independent random samples. Construct a 95% confidence interval for $(\mu_1 - \mu_2)$. Interpret your result.

g. Compare the confidence intervals you obtained in parts **e** and **f**. Which is wider? To what do you attribute the difference in width? Assuming in each case that the appropriate assumptions are satisfied, which interval provides you with more information about $(\mu_1 - \mu_2)$? Explain.

h. Are the results of an unpaired analysis valid if the data come from a paired experiment?

7.95 GPAs of traditional and nontraditional college students. Nontraditional university students, generally defined as those at least 25 years old, comprise an increasingly large proportion of undergraduate student bodies at most universities. A study reported in the *College Student Journal* (Dec. 1992) compared traditional and nontraditional students on a number of factors, including grade point average (GPA). The following table summarizes the information from the sample.

GPA	Traditional Students	Nontraditional Students
n	94	73
$\bar{x}$	2.90	3.50
s	.50	.50

a. What are the appropriate null and alternative hypotheses if we want to test whether the mean GPAs of traditional and nontraditional students differ?

b. Conduct the test using $\alpha = .01$, and interpret the result.

c. What assumptions are necessary to ensure the validity of the test?

7.96 **How concerned are you with product tampering?** A study in the *Journal of Psychology and Marketing* (Jan. 1992) investigates the degree to which American consumers are concerned about product tampering. Large random samples of male and female consumers were asked to rate their concern about product tampering on a scale of 1 (little or no concern) to 9 (very concerned).

a. What are the appropriate null and alternative hypotheses to determine whether a difference exists in the mean level of concern about product tampering between men and women? Define any symbols you use.

b. The *p*-value of the test is .008. Interpret this result.

c. What assumptions are necessary to ensure the validity of this test?

7.97 **Ages of cable-TV shoppers.** Refer to the International Association for Time Use Research study on cable TV viewers who purchase items from one of the home shopping channels, Exercise 6.44 (p. 366). The 1,600 sampled viewers described their motivation for watching cable TV shopping networks by giving their level of agreement (on a 5-point scale, where 1 = strongly disagree and 5 = strongly agree) with the statement, "I have nothing else to do." The researcher wanted to compare the mean responses of viewers who watch the shopping network at noon with those viewers who do not watch at noon.

a. Give the null and alternative hypotheses for determining whether the mean response of noontime watchers differs from the mean response of non-noontime watchers.

b. The researcher found the *p*-value for the test, part **a**, to be .02. Interpret this result, assuming $\alpha = .05$.

c. Interpret the result, part **b**, assuming $\alpha = .01$.

d. The sample means for noontime watchers and non-watchers were found to be 3.3 and 3.4, respectively. Comment on the "practical significance" of this result.

7.98 **Would you vote for a woman president?** *Working Women* (June 1999) published the results of a 1999 Gallup poll that found that 92% of adult Americans would vote for a woman president. In 1975, a similar poll found that only 73% would vote for a woman.

a. Let p_{1999} and p_{1975} represent the population parameters of interest for this study. In the words of the problem, define these parameters.

b. Assume the sample sizes were 2,000 in 1999 and 1,500 in 1975. Are these sample sizes large enough to conclude that the sampling distribution of $(p_{1999} - p_{1975})$ is approximately normally distributed? Justify your answer.

c. Construct a 90% confidence interval for $(p_{1999} - p_{1975})$. Interpret your confidence interval in the context of the problem.

d. Rework part **b** under the assumption that the sample sizes for 1999 and 1975 are 20 and 50, respectively.

7.99 **Would you vote for a woman president? (cont'd)** Refer to Exercise 7.98. Suppose you want to make a similar comparison for the years 2000 and 2003. How many adults should be sampled each year to estimate the difference in percentages who would vote for a woman president to within 3% with 90% confidence? Assume equal sample sizes will be collected.

7.100 **Job satisfaction study.** Does the time of day during which one works affect job satisfaction? A study in the *Journal of Occupational Psychology* (Sept. 1991) examined differences in job satisfaction between day-shift and night-shift nurses. Nurses' satisfaction with their hours of work, free time away from work, and breaks during work were measured. The following table shows the mean scores for each measure of job satisfaction (higher scores indicate greater satisfaction), along with the observed significance level comparing the means for the day-shift and night-shift samples:

	MEAN SATISFACTION		
	Day Shift	Night Shift	*p* Value
Satisfaction with:			
Hours of work	3.91	3.56	.813
Free time	2.55	1.72	.047
Breaks	2.53	3.75	.0073

a. Specify the null and alternative hypotheses if we wish to test whether a difference in job satisfaction exists between day-shift and night-shift nurses on each of the three measures. Define any symbols you use.

b. Interpret the *p*-value for each of the tests. (Each of the *p*-values in the table is two-tailed.)

c. Assume that each of the tests is based on small samples of nurses from each group. What assumptions are necessary for the tests to be valid?

7.101 **Comparing unemployment rates.** An economist wants to investigate the difference in unemployment rates between an urban industrial community and a university community in the same state. She interviews 525 potential members of the workforce in the industrial community and 375 in the university community. Of these, 47 and 22, respectively, are unemployed. Use a 95% confidence interval to estimate the difference in unemployment rates in the two communities.

Applying the Concepts—Intermediate

7.102 **Sampling plan for a movie promotion.** Advertising companies often try to characterize the average user of a client's product so ads can be targeted at particular segments of the buying community. A new movie is about to be released, and the advertising company wants to determine whether to aim the ad campaign at people under or over 25 years of age. It plans to arrange an advance showing of the movie to an audience from each group, then obtain an opinion about the movie from each individual. How many individuals should be included in each sample if the advertising company wants to estimate the difference in the proportions of viewers in each age group who will like the movie to within .05 with 90% confidence? Assume the sample size for each group will be the same and about half of each group will like the movie.

7.103 Solid-waste generation rates. The *International Journal of Environmental Health Research* (Vol. 4, 1994) reported on the solid-waste generation rates (in kilograms per capita per day) for samples of cities from industrialized and middle-income countries. The data are provided in the table.

⊙ **SOLWASTE**

Industrialized Countries		Middle-Income Countries	
New York (USA)	2.27	Singapore	0.87
Phoenix (USA)	2.31	Hong Kong	0.85
London (UK)	2.24	Medellin (Colombia)	0.54
Hamburg (Germany)	2.18	Kano (Nigeria)	0.46
Rome (Italy)	2.15	Manila (Philippines)	0.50
		Cairo (Egypt)	0.50
		Tunis (Tunisia)	0.56

a. Based on only a visual inspection of the data, does it appear that the mean waste generation rates of cities in industrialized and middle-income countries differ?

b. Conduct a test of hypothesis (at $\alpha = .05$) to support your observation in part **a**.

*c. In order to conduct the two-sample *t*-test in part **b** it was necessary to assume that the two population variances were equal. Test this assumption at $\alpha = .05$.

*d. What does your test indicate about the appropriateness of applying a two-sample *t*-test?

7.104 Killing moths with carbon dioxide. A University of South Florida biologist conducted an experiment to determine whether increased levels of carbon dioxide kill leaf- eating moths (*USF Magazine,* Winter 1999). Moth larvae were placed in open containers filled with oak leaves. Half the containers had normal carbon dioxide levels while the other half had double the normal level of carbon dioxide. Ten percent of the larvae in the containers with high carbon dioxide levels died, compared to 5% in the containers with normal levels. Assume that 80 moth larvae were placed, at random, in each of the two types of containers. Do the experimental results demonstrate that an increased level of carbon dioxide is effective in killing a higher percentage of leaf-eating moth larvae? Test using $\alpha = .01$.

7.105 Length of TV commercials. Rutgers professor Carol Byrd-Bredbenner studied the trend in prime-time television food advertising (*Nutrition & Food Science,* Vol. 30, 2000). Independent random samples of prime-time TV commercials for food products were recorded in 1992 and 1998, and the length of each commercial (in seconds) was determined. The results are summarized in the next table. Use the tools of this section to determine if a trend exists over the 6-year period.

Year	Number of Commercials	Mean Length	Standard Deviation
1992	105	24.52	7.32
1998	106	24.21	8.21

7.106 Switching college majors. When female undergraduates switch from science, mathematics, and engineering (SME) majors into disciplines that are not science based, such as journalism, marketing, and sociology, are their reasons different from those of their male counterparts? This question was investigated in *Science Education* (July 1995). A sample of 335 junior/senior undergraduates—172 females and 163 males—at two large research universities were identified as "switchers"—that is, they left a declared SME major for a non-SME major. Each student listed one or more factors that contributed to their switching decision.

a. Of the 172 females in the sample, 74 listed lack or loss of interest in SME (i.e., "turned off" by science) as a major factor, compared to 72 of the 163 males. Conduct a test (at $\alpha = .10$) to determine whether the proportion of female switchers who give "lack of interest in SME" as a major reason for switching differs from the corresponding proportion of males.

b. Thirty-three of the 172 females in the sample admitted they were discouraged or lost confidence due to low grades in SME during their early years, compared to 44 of 163 males. Construct a 90% confidence interval for the difference between the proportions of female and male switchers who lost confidence due to low grades in SME. Interpret the result.

7.107 State SAT scores. Refer to Exercise 2.29 (p. 60) and the data on average SAT scores for each of the 50 states and District of Columbia for the years 1990 and 2005. The data are saved in the **SATSCORES** file. (The first five observations and last two observations in the data set are shown in the table.)

⊙ **SATSCORES**

State	1990	2005
Alabama	1079	1126
Alaska	1015	1042
Arizona	1041	1056
Arkansas	1077	1115
California	1002	1026
⋮	⋮	⋮
Wisconsin	1111	1191
Wyoming	1072	1087

Source: College Entrance Examination Board, 2006.

a. In Exercise 2.29b, you computed the *paired differences* of SAT scores by subtracting the 1990 score from the 2005 score for each state. Find the mean of these 50 paired differences. This value is μ_d, the mean difference in SAT scores for the population of 50 states (and District of Columbia).

b. Explain why there is no need to employ the confidence interval or test procedures of this section to make an inference about μ_d.

c. Now, suppose the 50 paired differences of part **a** represent a sample of SAT score differences for 50 randomly selected high school students. Use the data in the **SATSCORES** file to make an inference about whether the true mean SAT score of high school students in 2005 differs from the true mean in 1999. Use a confidence level of .90.

7.108 Environmental impact study. Some power plants are located near rivers or oceans so that the available water can be used for cooling the condensers. Suppose that, as part of an environmental impact study, a power company wants to estimate the difference in mean water temperature between the discharge of its plant and the offshore waters. How many sample measurements must be taken at each site in order to estimate the true difference between means to within .2°C with 95% confidence? Assume that the range in readings will be about 4°C at each site and the same number of readings will be taken at each site.

7.109 Rat damage to sugarcane fields. Poisons are used to prevent rat damage in sugarcane fields. The U.S. Department of Agriculture is investigating whether the rat poison should be located in the middle of the field or on the outer perimeter. One way to answer this question is to determine where the greater amount of damage occurs. If damage is measured by the proportion of cane stalks that have been damaged by rats, how many stalks from each section of the field should be sampled in order to estimate the true difference between proportions of stalks damaged in the two sections to within .02 with 95% confidence?

*7.110 Instrument precision. When new instruments are developed to perform chemical analyses of products (food, medicine, etc.), they are usually evaluated with respect to two criteria: accuracy and precision. *Accuracy* refers to the ability of the instrument to identify correctly the nature and amounts of a product's components. *Precision* refers to the consistency with which the instrument will identify the components of the same material. Thus, a large variability in the identification of a single batch of a product indicates a lack of precision. Suppose a pharmaceutical firm is considering two brands of an instrument designed to identify the components of certain drugs. As part of a comparison of precision, 10 test-tube samples of a well-mixed batch of a drug are selected and then 5 are analyzed by instrument A and 5 by instrument B. The data shown below are the percentages of the primary component of the drug given by the instruments. Do these data provide evidence of a difference in the precision of the two machines? Use $\alpha = .10$.

⚙ **INSTRAB**

Instrument A	Instrument B
43	46
48	49
37	43
52	41
45	48

7.111 National Academy of Science study. Operation Crossroads was a 1946 military exercise in which atomic bombs were detonated over empty target ships in the Pacific Ocean. The Navy assigned sailors to wash down the test ships immediately after the atomic blasts. The National Academy of Science reported "that the overall death rate among Operation Crossroads sailors was 4.6% higher than among a comparable group of sailors....

However, this increase was not statistically significant" (*Tampa Tribune,* Oct. 30, 1996).
a. Describe the parameter of interest in the National Academy of Science study.
b. Interpret the statement, "This increase was not statistically significant."

7.112 Underwriting bonds. One way corporations raise money for expansion is to issue *bonds*, loan agreements to repay the purchaser a specified amount with a fixed rate of interest paid periodically over the life of the bond. The sale of bonds is usually handled by an underwriting firm. Does it pay for companies to shop around for an underwriter? The reason for the question is that the price of a bond may rise or fall after its issuance. Therefore, whether a corporation receives the market price for a bond depends on the skill of its underwriter (Radcliffe, 1994). The mean change in the prices of 27 bonds handled over a 12-month period by one underwriter and in the prices of 23 bonds handled by another are shown below.

	Underwriter 1	Underwriter 2
Sample size	27	23
Sample mean	−.0491	−.0307
Sample variance	.009800	.002465

a. Do the data provide sufficient evidence to indicate a difference in the mean change in bond prices handled by the two underwriters? Test using $\alpha = .05$.
b. Find a 95% confidence interval for the mean difference for the two underwriters, and interpret it.

Applying the Concepts—Advanced

7.113 Impact of gender on advertising. How does gender affect the type of advertising that proves to be most effective? An article in the *Journal of Advertising Research* (May/June 1990) makes reference to numerous studies that conclude males tend to be more competitive with others than with themselves. To apply this conclusion to advertising, the author creates two ads promoting a new brand of soft drink.

Ad 1: Four men are shown competing in racquetball
Ad 2: One man is shown competing against himself in racquetball

The author hypothesized that the first ad will be more effective when shown to males. To test this hypothesis, 43 males were shown both ads and asked to measure their attitude toward the advertisement (Aad), their attitude toward the brand of soft drink (Ab), and their intention to purchase the soft drink (Intention). Each variable was measured using a 7-point scale, with higher scores indicating a more favorable attitude. The results are shown in the following table. Do you agree with the author's hypothesis?

	SAMPLE MEANS		
	Aad	Ab	Intention
Ad 1	4.465	3.311	4.366
Ad 2	4.150	2.902	3.813
Level of significance	$p = .091$	$p = .032$	$p = .050$

7.114 Salaries of postgraduates. Refer to the *Economics of Education Review* (Vol. 21, 2002) study of the relationship between education level and earnings, Exercise 6.29 (p. 359). A National Adult Literacy Survey revealed that males with a postgraduate degree had a sample mean salary of \$61,340 (with standard error $s_{\bar{x}_M} = \$2,185$), while females with a postgraduate degree had a sample mean salary of \$32,227 (with standard error $s_{\bar{x}_F} = \$932$). Let μ_M represent the population mean salary of all males with postgraduate degrees and μ_F represent the population mean salary of all females with postgraduate degrees.

a. Set up the null and alternative hypotheses for determining whether μ_M exceeds μ_F.

b. Calculate the test statistic for the test, part **a**. [*Note:* $s_{\bar{x}_M - \bar{x}_F} = \sqrt{(s_{\bar{x}_M}^2 + s_{\bar{x}_F}^2)}$.]

c. Find the rejection region for the test using $\alpha = .01$.

d. Use the results, parts **b** and **c**, to make the appropriate conclusion.

Critical Thinking Challenge

7.115 Facility layout study. Facility layout and material flowpath design are major factors in the productivity analysis of automated manufacturing systems. Facility layout is concerned with the location arrangement of machines and buffers for work-in-process. Flowpath design is concerned with the direction of manufacturing material flows (e.g., unidirectional or bidirectional; Lee, Lei, and Pinedo, *Annals of Operations Research*, 1997). A manufacturer of printed circuit boards (PCBs) is interested in evaluating two alternative existing layout and flowpath designs. The output of each design was monitored for 8 consecutive working days. Design 2 appears to be superior to Design 1. Do you agree? Explain fully.

⚙ **FLOWPATH**

Working Days	Design 1	Design 2
8/16	1,220 units	1,273 units
8/17	1,092 units	1,363 units
8/18	1,136 units	1,342 units
8/19	1,205 units	1,471 units
8/20	1,086 units	1,299 units
8/23	1,274 units	1,457 units
8/24	1,145 units	1,263 units
8/25	1,281 units	1,368 units

REFERENCES

Freedman, D., Pisani, R., and Purves, R. *Statistics*. New York: W. W. Norton and Co., 1978.

Gibbons, J. D. *Nonparametric Statistical Inference,* 2nd ed. New York: McGraw-Hill, 1985.

Hollander, M., and Wolfe, D. A. *Nonparametric Statistical Methods.* New York: Wiley, 1973.

Lee, C. F., Finnerty, J. E., and Norton, E. A. *Foundations of Financial Management.* Minneapolis/St. Paul: West Publishing Co., 1997.

Mendenhall, W., Beaver, R. J., and Beaver, B. M. *Introduction to Probability and Statistics,* 11th ed. North Scituate, Mass.: Duxbury, 2002.

Satterthwaite, F. W. "An Approximate Distribution of Estimates of Variance Components." *Biometrics Bulletin,* Vol. 2, 1946, pp. 110–114.

Snedecor, G. W., and Cochran, W. *Statistical Methods,* 7th ed. Ames: Iowa State University Press, 1980.

Steel, R. G. D., and Torrie, J. H. *Principles and Procedures of Statistics,* 2nd ed. New York: McGraw-Hill, 1980.

Stevenson, William J. *Production/Operations Management,* 6th ed. Chicago: Irwin, 2000.

Twomey, David P. *Labor and Employment Law,* 9th ed. Cincinnati: South-Western Publishing Co., 1994.

Using Technology

7.1 Two Sample Inferences Using SPSS

SPSS can be used to make two-sample inferences about $\mu_1 - \mu_2$ for independent samples and μ_d for paired samples but cannot currently conduct analyses about $p_1 - p_2$ or an F-test to compare population variances.

To carry out an analysis for $\mu_1 - \mu_2$, first access the SPSS spreadsheet file that contains the sample data. The data file should contain one quantitative variable (which the means will be calculated on) and one qualitative variable with either two numerical coded values (e.g., 1 and 2) or two short categorical levels (e.g., "yes" and "no"). These two values represent the two groups or populations to be compared. Next, click on the "Analyze" button on the SPSS menu bar, then click on "Compare Means" and "Independent-Samples T Test," as shown in Figure 7.S.1.

The resulting dialog box appears as shown in Figure 7.S.2. Specify the quantitative variable of interest in the "Test Variable(s)" box and the qualitative variable in the "Grouping Variable" box. Click the "Define Groups" button, and specify the values of the two groups in the resulting dialog box (see Figure 7.S.3). Then click "Continue" to return to the

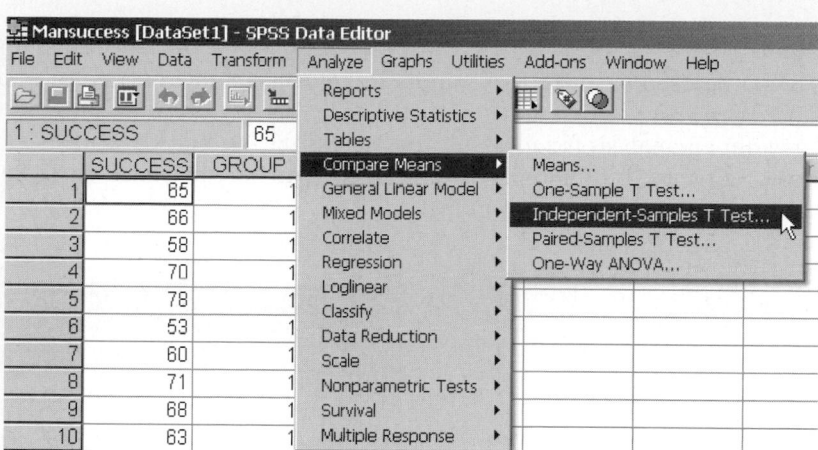

Figure 7.S.1

SPSS menu options for inferences about $\mu_1 - \mu_2$

Figure 7.S.2

SPSS Independent-Samples T Test dialog box

Figure 7.S.3

SPSS Define Groups dialog box

Figure 7.S.4

SPSS options dialog box

"Independent-Samples T Test" dialog screen. Without any further menu selections, SPSS will automatically conduct a two-tailed test of the null hypothesis, H_0: $\mu_1 - \mu_2 = 0$. If you want to generate a confidence interval for $\mu_1 - \mu_2$, click the "Options" button and specify the confidence level on the resulting menu screen, as shown in Figure 7.S.4. Click "Continue" to return to the "T Test" dialog box, then click "OK" to generate the SPSS printout.

Important Note: The SPSS two-sample t-procedure uses the t-statistic to conduct the test of hypothesis. When the sample sizes are small, this is the appropriate method. When the sample sizes are large, the t-value will be approximately equal to the large-sample z-value and the resulting test will still be valid.

To carry out an analysis of μ_d for matched pairs, first access the SPSS spreadsheet file that contains the sample data. The data file should contain two quantitative variables—one with the data values for the first group (or population) and one with the data values for the second group. (*Note:* The sample size should be the same for each group.) Next, click on the "Analyze" button on the SPSS menu bar, then click on "Compare Means" and "Paired-Samples T Test" (see Figure 7.S.1). The resulting dialog box appears as shown in Figure 7.S.5.

Specify the two quantitative variables of interest in the "Paired Variables" box, as shown in Figure 7.S.5. Without any further menu selections, SPSS will automatically conduct a two-tailed test of the null hypothesis, H_0: $\mu_d = 0$. If you want to generate a confidence interval for μ_d, click the "Options" button and specify the confidence level on the resulting menu screen (as shown in Figure 7.S.4). Click "Continue" to return to the "Paired-Samples" dialog box, then click "OK" to generate the SPSS printout.

Figure 7.S.5

SPSS Paired-Samples dialog box

Note: Although SPSS cannot perform an F-test to compare two variances, it will automatically provide a nonparametric test (e.g., Levene's test) for equal variances when you choose to do an independent samples t-test for $\mu_1 - \mu_2$.

7.2 Two-Sample Inferences Using MINITAB

MINITAB can be used to make two-sample inferences about $\mu_1 - \mu_2$ for independent samples, μ_d for paired samples, $p_1 - p_2$ and σ_1^2/σ_2^2.

To carry out an analysis for $\mu_1 - \mu_2$, first access the MINITAB worksheet that contains the sample data. Next, click on the "Basic Statistics" button on the MINITAB menu bar, then click on "2-Sample t", as shown in Figure 7.M.1. The resulting dialog box appears as shown in Figure 7.M.2.

Figure 7.M.1

MINITAB menu options for inferences about $\mu_1 - \mu_2$

Figure 7.M.2

MINITAB 2-Sample *T* dialog box

If the worksheet contains data for one quantitative variable (which the means will be computed on) and one qualitative variable (which represents the two groups or populations), select "Samples in one column," then specify the quantitative variable in the "Samples" area and the qualitative variable in the "Subscripts" area. (See Figure 7.M.2.)

If the worksheet contains the data for the first sample in one column and the data for the second sample in another column, select "Samples in different columns," then specify the "First" and "Second" variables. Alternatively, if you have only summarized data (i.e., sample sizes, sample means, and sample standard deviations), select "Summarized data" and enter these summarized values in the appropriate boxes.

Once you have made the appropriate menu selection, click the "Options" button on the MINITAB "2-Sample T" dialog box. Specify the confidence level for a confidence interval, the null hypothesized value of the difference, $\mu_1 - \mu_2$, and the form of the alternative hypothesis (lower tailed, two tailed, or upper tailed) in the resulting dialog box, as shown in Figure 7.M.3. Click "OK" to return to the "2-Sample T" dialog box, then click "OK" again to generate the MINITAB printout.

Figure 7.M.3
MINITAB options dialog box

Important Note: The MINITAB two-sample *t*-procedure uses the *t*-statistic to conduct the test of hypothesis. When the sample sizes are small, this is the appropriate method. When the sample sizes are large, the *t*-value will be approximately equal to the large-sample *z*-value and the resulting test will still be valid.

To carry out an analysis of μ_d for matched pairs, first access the MINITAB worksheet that contains the sample data. The data file should contain two quantitative variables—one with the data values for the first group (or population) and one with the data values for the second group. (*Note:* The sample size should be the same for each group.) Next, click on the "Basic Statistics" button on the MINITAB menu bar, then click on "Paired t" (see Figure 7.M.1). The resulting dialog box appears as shown in Figure 7.M.4. Select the "Samples in columns" option and specify the two quantitative variables of interest in the "First sample" and "Second sample" boxes, as shown in Figure 7.M.4. [Alternatively, if you have only summarized data of the paired differences, select the "Summarized data (differences)" option and enter the sample size, sample mean, and sample standard deviation in the appropriate boxes.]

Figure 7.M.4
MINITAB paired-samples dialog box

Next, click the "Options" button and specify the confidence level for a confidence interval, the null hypothesized value of the difference, μ_d, and the form of the alternative hypothesis (lower tailed, two tailed, or upper tailed) in the resulting dialog box. (See Figure 7.M.3.) Click "OK" to return to the "Paired t" dialog box, then click "OK" again to generate the MINITAB printout.

To analyze the difference between two proportions, $p_1 - p_2$, first access the MINITAB worksheet that contains the sample data. Next, click on the "Basic Statistics" button on the MINITAB menu bar, then click on "2 Proportions," as shown in Figure 7.M.1. The resulting dialog box appears as shown in Figure 7.M.5. Select the data option ("Samples in one column" or "Samples in different columns" or "Summarized data") and make the appropriate menu choices. (Figure 7.M.5 shows the menu options when you select "Summarized data.")

Next, click the "Options" button and specify the confidence level for a confidence interval, the null hypothesized value of the difference, and the form of the alternative hypothesis (lower tailed, two tailed, or upper tailed) in the resulting dialog box, as shown in Figure 7.M.6. (If you desire a pooled estimate of *p* for the test, be sure to check the appropriate box.) Click "OK" to return to the "2 Proportions" dialog box, then click "OK" again to generate the MINITAB printout.

Figure 7.M.5
MINITAB 2 proportions
dialog box

Figure 7.M.6
MINITAB 2 Proportions options box

Figure 7.M.7
MINITAB 2 Variances dialog box

To carry out an analysis for the ratio of two variances, σ_1^2/σ_2^2, first access the MINITAB worksheet that contains the sample data. Next, click on the "Basic Statistics" button on the MINITAB menu bar, then click on "2 Variances," as shown in Figure 7.M.1. The resulting dialog box appears as shown in Figure 7.M.7. The menu selections and options are similar to those for the two-sample t-test. Once the selections are made, click "OK" to produce the MINITAB F-test printout.

7.3 Two Sample Inferences Using Excel/PHStat2

Excel with the PHStat2 add-in can be used to make two-sample inferences about $\mu_1 - \mu_2$ for independent samples, μ_d for paired samples, $p_1 - p_2$, and σ_1^2/σ_2^2.

To conduct a hypothesis test for $\mu_1 - \mu_2$, first compute summary statistics for the data (e.g., sample sizes, sample means, and sample standard deviations for the two samples). Now, click on the "PHStat" button on the Excel main menu bar, then click on "Two-Sample Tests" and "t Test for Differences in Two Means," as shown in Figure 7.E.1. The resulting dialog box appears as shown in Figure 7.E.2.

Specify the null hypothesized value of the difference, $\mu_1 - \mu_2$, the level of significance, α, the summary statistics for the two samples, and the form of the alternative hypothesis (lower tailed, two tailed, or upper tailed) in the resulting dialog box, as shown in Figure 7.E.2. Click "OK" to generate the Excel printout.

Figure 7.E.1

Excel/PHStat2 menu options for inferences about $\mu_1 - \mu_2$

Figure 7.E.2

Excel/PHStat2 two-sample t-test dialog box

To conduct a paired difference analysis for μ_d, first compute the differences between the two paired values on the Excel workbook. Then carry out a t-test for a single mean. Consult the Excel "Using Technology" section of Chapter 6 (p. 400) to see the menu screens and selections for this analysis.

To conduct a large-sample hypothesis test for $p_1 - p_2$, first compute summary statistics for the data (e.g., sample sizes and sample number of successes for the two samples). Now, click on the "PHStat" button on the Excel main menu bar, then click on "Two-Sample Tests" and "Z Test for Differences in Two Proportions" (see in Figure 7.E.1). The resulting dialog box appears as shown in Figure 7.E.3. Specify the null hypothesized value of the difference, $p_1 - p_2$, the level of significance, α, the summary statistics for the two samples, and the form of the alternative hypothesis (lower tailed, two tailed, or upper tailed) in the resulting dialog box, as shown in Figure 7.E.3. Click "OK" to generate the Excel printout.

To conduct an F-test for the ratio of two variances, σ_1^2/σ_2^2, first compute summary statistics for the data (e.g., sample sizes and sample standard deviations for the two samples). Now, click on the "PHStat" button on the Excel main menu bar, then click on "Two-Sample Tests" and "F Test for Differences in Two Variances" (see in Figure 7.E.1). The resulting

Figure 7.E.3
Excel/PHStat2 two-
proportions test dialog box

dialog box appears as shown in Figure 7.E.4. Specify the null hypothesized value of the ratio, σ_1^2/σ_2^2, the level of significance, α, the summary statistics for the two samples, and the form of the alternative hypothesis (lower tailed, two tailed, or upper tailed) in the resulting dialog box, as shown in Figure 7.E.4. Click "OK" to generate the Excel printout.

Figure 7.E.4
Excel/PHStat2 F-test dialog
box

Real-World Case
The Kentucky Milk Case—Part II

(A Case Covering Chapters 5–7)

In The Kentucky Milk Case—Part I, you used graphical and numerical descriptive statistics to investigate bid collusion in the Kentucky school milk market. This case expands your previous analyses, incorporating inferential statistical methodology. The three areas of your focus are described below. (See page 128 for the file layout of the **MILK** data.) Again, you should prepare a professional document that presents the results of the analyses and any implications regarding collusionary practices in the tri-county Kentucky milk market.

1. *Incumbency rates.* Recall from Part I that market allocation (where the same dairy controls the same school districts year after year) is a common form of collusive behavior in bid-rigging conspiracies. Market allocation is typically gauged by the incumbency rate for a market in a given school year—defined as the percentage of school districts that are won by the same milk vendor who won the previous year. Past experience with milk bids in a competitive market reveals that a "normal" incumbency rate is about .7—that is, 70% of the school districts are expected to purchase their milk from the same vendor who supplied the milk the previous year. In the 13-district tri-county Kentucky market, 13 ven-

dor transitions potentially exist each year. Over the 1985–1988 period (when bid collusion was alleged to have occurred), there are 52 potential vendor transitions. Based on the actual number of vendor transitions that occurred each year and over the 1985–1988 period, make an inference regarding bid collusion.

2. *Bid price dispersion.* Recall that in competitive sealed-bid markets, more dispersion or variability among the bids is observed than in collusive markets. (This is due to conspiring vendors sharing information about their bids.) Consequently, if collusion exists, the variation in bid prices in the tri-county market should be significantly smaller than the corresponding variation in the surrounding market. For each milk product, conduct an analysis to compare the bid price variances of the two markets each year. Make the appropriate inferences.

3. *Average winning bid price.* According to collusion theorists, the mean winning bid price in the "rigged" market will exceed the mean winning bid price in the competitive market for each year in which collusion occurs. In addition, the difference between the competitive average and the "rigged" average tends to grow over time when collusionary tactics are employed over several consecutive years. For each milk product, conduct an analysis to compare the winning bid price means of the tri-county and surrounding markets each year. Make the appropriate inferences.

CHAPTER

8

Design of Experiments and Analysis of Variance

CONTENTS

STATISTICS IN ACTION

USING TECHNOLOGY

WHERE WE'VE BEEN

- Presented methods for estimating and testing hypotheses about a single population mean.

- Presented methods for comparing two population means.

WHERE WE'RE GOING

- Discuss the critical elements in the design of a sampling experiment.

- Learn how to set up three of the more popular experimental designs for comparing more than two population means: *completely randomized, randomized block,* and *factorial designs.*

- Show how to analyze data collected from a designed experiment using a technique called an *analysis of variance.*

STATISTICS IN ACTION

The Ethics of Downsizing

A major strategic alternative for many U.S. firms is to reduce the size of their workforce (i.e. to downsize). DuPont, Upjohn Company, AT&T, and IBM are just a few of the many major U.S. firms that have recently downsized. Although it may be in the best interest of the firm's shareholders to delay informing employees of the downsizing decision, top management is morally obligated to communicate to employees all aspects of the downsizing process, including when it will occur and how it will affect jobs. When full disclosure of downsizing by top management does not occur, employees are likely to perceive this as an ethical violation of their rights.

W. E. Hopkins (Colorado State University) and S. A. Hopkins (University of Denver) investigated the ethics of downsizing decisions from the employee's perspective and published their results in the *Journal of Business Ethics* (Vol. 18, 1999). The researchers surveyed a sample of 209 employees who were enrolled in an Executive MBA Program or weekend program at one of three Colorado universities. These individuals were divided into five distinct groups, depending on their job situation at a previous or current firm. The groups are fully described in Table SIA8.1.

Each of the 209 employees completed a questionnaire on his or her ethical perceptions of

downsizing. One item on the questionnaire, the focus of this Statistics in Action, asked employees to respond to the statement, "It is unethical for a downsizing decision to be announced or implemented on or prior to a major holiday (e.g., Christmas, Thanksgiving, etc.)." Responses were measured using a 5-point Likert scale, where 1 = strongly agree, 2 = agree, 3 = neutral, 4 = disagree, and 5 = strongly disagree. Data on both the qualitative variable Group and the quantitative variable Ethics response are saved in the **DOWNSIZE** file. The researchers used the data to test three hypotheses.

Hypothesis 1: Survivors', Casualties', and Implementors/casualties' perceptions of the ethics statement on downsizing will not differ significantly.

Hypothesis 2: Formulators' and Implementors/ survivors' perceptions of the ethics statement on downsizing will not differ significantly.

Hypothesis 3: Survivors', Casualties', and Implementors/casualties' perceptions of the ethics statement on downsizing will differ significantly from Formulators' and Implementors/survivors' perceptions.

We test the researchers' hypotheses by applying the statistical methodology of this chapter to the **DOWNSIZE** data in the following Statistics in Action Revisited sections.

Statistics in Action Revisited

- Testing for Differences in the Mean Ethics Responses of the Five Downsize Groups (p. 494)

- Ranking the Mean Ethics Responses for the Five Downsize Groups (p. 504).

 DOWNSIZE

TABLE SIA8.1 Employee Groups for Ethics of Downsizing Study

Group	Number	Description
Casualties	47	Nonmanagerial personnel who have been laid off at least once
Survivors	71	Nonmanagerial personnel who have worked for a firm that downsized but were never laid off
Implementors/casualties	27	Managers/supervisors who have been laid off at least once but now implement downsizing decisions
Implementors/survivors	33	Managers/supervisors who implement downsizing decisions for their current firm and worked for a firm that downsized but were never laid off
Formulators	31	CEOs who have actually made a decision to downsize and presided over its implementation

Most of the data analyzed in previous chapters were collected in *observational* sampling experiments rather than *designed* sampling experiments. In *observational studies,* the analyst has little or no control over the variables under study and merely observes their values. In contrast, *designed experiments* are those in which the analyst attempts to control the levels of one or more variables to determine their effect on a variable of interest. Although many practical business situations do not present the opportunity for such control, it is instructive, even for observational experiments, to have a working knowledge of the analysis and interpretation of data that result from designed experiments and to know the basics of how to design experiments when the opportunity arises.

We first present the basic elements of an experimental design in Section 8.1. We then discuss three of the simpler, and more popular, experimental designs in Sections 8.2 8.4. and 8.5. In Section 8.3 we show how to rank the population means, from smallest to largest.

8.1 Elements of a Designed Experiment

Certain elements are common to almost all designed experiments, regardless of the specific area of application. For example, the *response* is the variable of interest in the experiment. The response might be the SAT scores of a high school senior, the total sales of a firm last year, or the total income of a particular household this year. The response is also called the *dependent variable, y.* We use these terms interchangeably in this chapter.

> **Definition 8.1**
>
> The **response variable** is the variable of interest to be measured in the experiment. We also refer to the response as the **dependent variable.**

The intent of most statistical experiments is to determine the effect of one or more variables on the response. These variables, which we called the *independent variables* in regression analysis, are often referred to as the *factors* in a designed experiment. Like independent variables, factors are either *quantitative* or *qualitative,* depending on whether the variable is measured on a numerical scale or not. For example, we might want to explore the effect of the qualitative factor Gender on the response SAT score. In other words, we want to compare the SAT scores of male and female high school seniors. Or, we might wish to determine the effect of the quantitative factor Number of salespeople on the response Total sales for retail firms. Often two or more factors are of interest. For example, we might want to determine the effect of the quantitative factor Number of wage earners and the qualitative factor Location on the response Household income.

> **Definition 8.2**
>
> **Factors** are those variables whose effect on the response is of interest to the experimenter. **Quantitative factors** are measured on a numerical scale, whereas **qualitative factors** are those that are not (naturally) measured on a numerical scale. Factors are also referred to as **independent variables.**

Levels are the values of the factors that are utilized in the experiment. The levels of qualitative factors are usually nonnumerical. For example, the levels of Gender are Male and Female, and the levels of Location might be North, East, South, and West.* The levels of quantitative factors are numerical values. For example, the Number of salespeople

---

*The levels of a qualitative variable may bear numerical labels. For example, the Locations could be numbered 1, 2, 3 and 4. However, in such cases the numerical labels for a qualitative variable will usually be codes representing nonnumerical levels.

may have levels 1, 3, 5, 7, and 9. The factor Years of education may have levels 8, 12, 16, and 20.

> **Definition 8.3**
>
> **Factor levels** are the values of the factor utilized in the experiment.

When a *single factor* is employed in an experiment, the *treatments* of the experiment are the levels of the factor. For example, if the effect of the factor Gender on the response SAT score is being investigated, the treatments of the experiment are the two levels of Gender—Female and Male. Or, if the effect of the Number of wage earners on Household income is the subject of the experiment, the numerical values assumed by the quantitative factor Number of wage earners are the treatments. If *two or more factors* are utilized in an experiment, the treatments are the factor-level combinations used. For example, if the effects of the factors Gender and GPA on the response SAT score are being investigated, the treatments are the combinations of the levels of Gender and GPA used; thus (Female, 2.61), (Male, 3.43), and (Female, 3.82) would all be treatments.

> **Definition 8.4**
>
> The **treatments** of an experiment are the factor-level combinations utilized.

The objects on which the response variable and factors are observed are the *experimental units*. For example, SAT score, High school GPA, and Gender are all variables that can be observed on the same experimental unit—a high school senior. Or, the Total sales, the Earnings per share, and the Number of salespeople can be measured on a particular firm in a particular year, and the firm-year combination is the experimental unit. The Total income, the Number of female wage earners, and the Location can be observed for a household at a particular point in time, and the household-time combination is the experimental unit. Every experiment, whether observational or designed, has experimental units on which the variables are observed. However, the identification of the experimental units is more important in designed experiments, when the experimenter must actually sample the experimental units and measure the variables.

> **Definition 8.5**
>
> An **experimental unit** is the object on which the response and factors are observed or measured.*

When the specification of the treatments and the method of assigning the experimental units to each of the treatments are controlled by the analyst, the experiment is said to be *designed*. In contrast, if the analyst is just an observer of the treatments on a sample of experimental units, the experiment is *observational*. For example, if you give one randomly selected group of employees a training program and withhold it from another randomly selected group in order to evaluate the effect of the training on worker productivity, then you are designing an experiment. If, on the other hand, you compare the productivity of employees with college degrees with the productivity of employees without college degrees, the experiment is observational.

> **Definition 8.6**
>
> A **designed experiment** is one for which the analyst controls the specification of the treatments and the method of assigning the experimental units to each treatment. An **observational experiment** is one for which the analyst simply observes the treatments and the response on a sample of experimental units.

---

*Recall (Chapter 1) that the set of all experimental units is the population.

Biography

The diagram in Figure 8.1 provides an overview of the experimental process and a summary of the terminology introduced in this section. Note that the experimental unit is at the core of the process. The method by which the sample of experimental units is selected from the population determines the type of experiment. The level of every factor (the treatment) and the response are all variables that are observed or measured on each experimental unit.

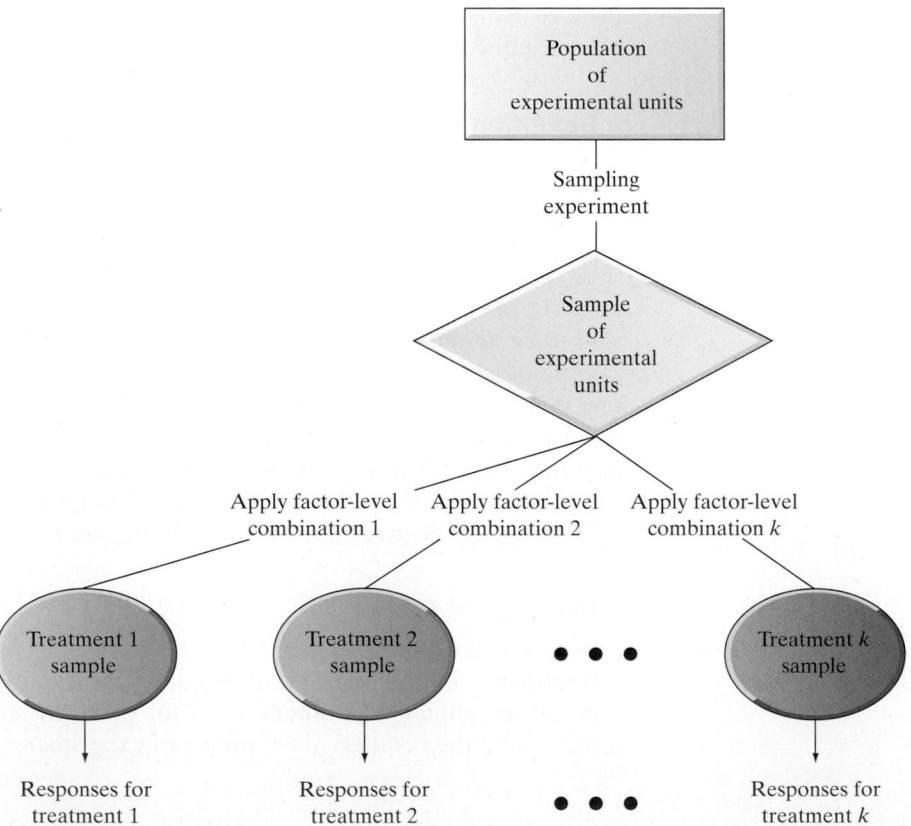

FIGURE 8.1

Sampling experiment: Process and terminology

EXAMPLE 8.1

The Key Elements of a Designed Experiment to Test Golf Ball Brands

Problem The USGA (United States Golf Association) regularly tests golf equipment to ensure that it conforms to USGA standards. Suppose it wishes to compare the mean distance traveled by four different brands of golf balls when struck by a driver (the club used to maximize distance). The following experiment is conducted: 10 balls of each brand are randomly selected. Each is struck by "Iron Byron" (the USGA's golf robot named for the famous golfer, Byron Nelson) using a driver, and the distance traveled is recorded. Identify each of the following elements in this experiment: response, factors, factor types, levels, treatments, and experimental units.

Solution The response is the variable of interest, Distance traveled. The only factor being investigated is Brand of golf ball, and it is nonnumerical and therefore qualitative. The four brands (say A, B, C, and D) represent the levels of this factor. Since only one factor is utilized, the treatments are the four levels of this factor—that is, the four brands. The experimental unit is a golf ball; more specifically, it is a golf ball at a particular position in the striking sequence, since the distance traveled can be recorded only when the ball is struck, and we would expect the distance to be different (due to random factors such as wind resistance, landing place, and so forth) if the same ball is struck a second time. Note that 10 experimental units are sampled for each treatment, generating a total of 40 observations.

Look Back This experiment, like many real applications, is a blend of designed and observational: The analyst cannot control the assignment of the brand to each golf ball (observational), but he or she can control the assignment of each ball to the position in the striking sequence (designed).

Now Work Exercise 8.5

EXAMPLE 8.2

A Two-Factor Experiment to Test Golf Ball Brands

Problem Suppose the USGA is also interested in comparing the mean distances the four brands of golf balls travel when struck by a five-iron and by a driver. Ten balls of each brand are randomly selected, five to be struck by the driver, and five by the five-iron. Identify the elements of the experiment, and construct a schematic diagram similar to Figure 8.1 to provide an overview of this experiment.

Solution The response is the same as in Example 8.1—Distance traveled. The experiment now has two factors, Brand of golf ball and Club utilized. There are four levels of Brand (A, B, C, and D) and two of Club (driver and five—iron, or 1 and 5). Treatments are factor-level combinations of golf ball and hitting position. Note that five experimental units are sampled per treatment, generating 40 observations. The experiment is summarized in Figure 8.2.

Look Back Whenever there are two or more factors in an experiment, remember to combine the levels of the factors—one level from each factor—to obtain the treatments.

Now Work Exercise 8.8

Our objective in designing an experiment is usually to maximize the amount of information obtained about the relationship between the treatments and the response. Of course, we are almost always subject to constraints on budget, time, and even the availability of experimental units. Nevertheless, designed experiments are generally preferred to observational experiments. Not only do we have better control of the amount and quality of the information collected, but we also avoid the biases inherent in observational experiments in the selection of the experimental units representing each treatment. Inferences based on observational experiments always carry the implicit

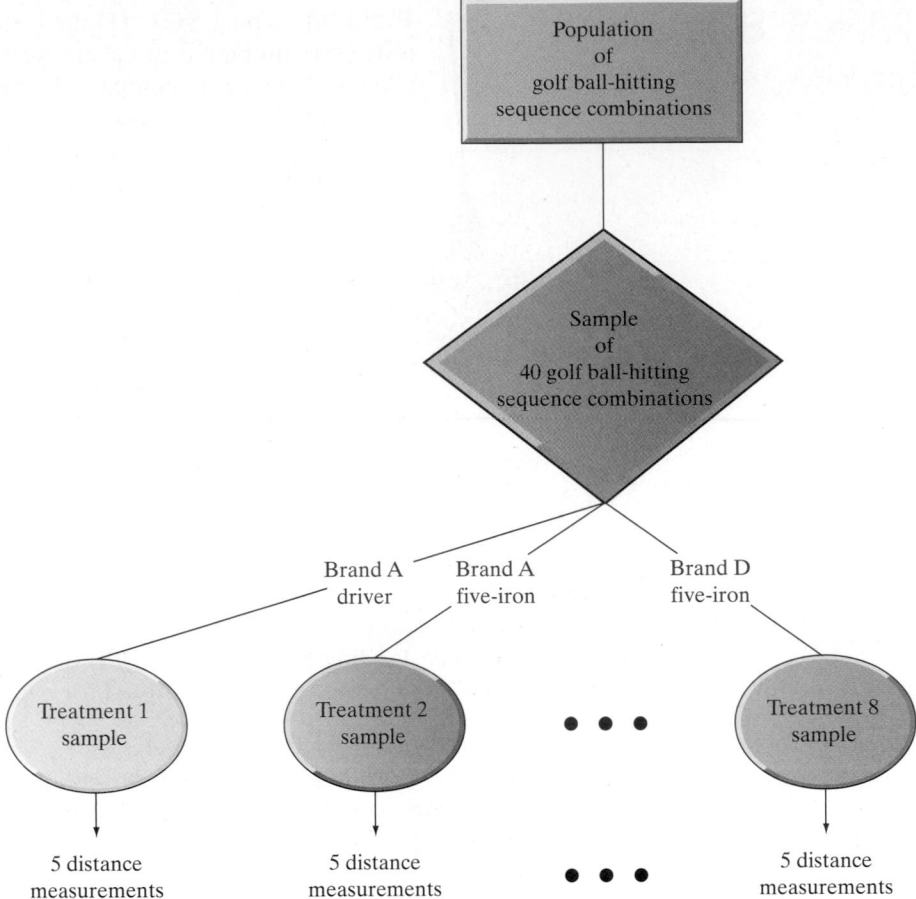

FIGURE 8.2

Two-factor golf experiment
summary: Example 8.2

assumption that the sample has no hidden bias that was not considered in the statistical
analysis. Better understanding of the potential problems with observational experiments
is a by-product of our study of experimental design in the remainder of this chapter.

Exercises 8.1–8.13

Learning the Mechanics

8.1   What are the treatments for a designed experiment that utilizes one qualitative factor with four levels—A, B, C, and D?

8.2   What are the treatments for a designed experiment with
two factors, one qualitative with two levels (A and B) and
one quantitative with five levels (50, 60, 70, 80, and 90)?

8.3   What is the difference between an observational and a designed experiment?

8.4   What are the experimental units on which each of the following responses are observed?
   a. College GPA
   b. Household income
   c. Gasoline mileage rating for an automobile model
   d. Number of defective sectors on a computer diskette
   e. December unemployment rate for a state

Applying the Concepts—Basic

8.5   **Identifying the type of experiment.** Brief descriptions of a
NW   number of experiments are given next. Determine whether
each is observational or designed, and explain your reasoning.

a. An economist obtains the unemployment rate and gross
state product for a sample of states over the past 10
years, with the objective of examining the relationship
between the unemployment rate and the gross state
product by census region.

b. A manager in a paper production facility installs one
of three incentive programs in each of nine plants to
determine the effect of each program on productivity.

c. A marketer of personal computers runs ads in each of
four national publications for one quarter and keeps
track of the number of sales that are attributable to each
publication's ad.

d. An electric utility engages a consultant to monitor the
discharge from its smokestack on a monthly basis over a
1-year period in order to relate the level of sulfur dioxide in the discharge to the load on the facility's generators.

e. Intrastate trucking rates are compared before and after
governmental deregulation of prices charged, with the
comparison also taking into account distance of haul,
goods hauled, and the price of diesel fuel

ACTIVITY 8.1: Designed Versus Observational Experiments

In this Activity, you will revisit Activity 7.1 (p. 430) and Activity 7.2 (p. 443) and consider two new, but similar, experiments.

1. Explain why each of the situations in *Box Office Receipts: Comparing Population Means* on page 430 and *Keep the Change: Inferences Based on Two Samples* on page 443 are observational experiments. What key elements of a designed experiment are missing in each situation?

2. A movie company wishes to measure the effect of advertising on box office receipts. Thirty U.S. cities with similar demographics are chosen for an experiment. The thirty cities are randomly divided into three groups of ten cities. In each city a trailer for a new film will be run on local cable during prime time in the week leading up to the release of the film. In the first group of ten cities the trailer will be run 500 times, in the second group the trailer will be run 1,000 times, and in the third group it will be run 1,500 times. The company will collect the box office receipts for the opening weekend of the film in each city and compare the mean box office receipts.

   Explain why this is a designed experiment. Identify the factor and the response variable. Is the factor quantitative or qualitative? Identify the factor levels and the experimental units. What part of choosing the cities is not necessarily random? Explain why it might be difficult to randomize this part of the experiment.

3. Suppose Bank of America wants to determine whether email and postcard reminders of the benefits of the *Keep the Change* program result in customers using their debit cards more often. A random sample of customers is chosen and split into four groups. The customers in one group are sent an email reminder, those in the second group are sent a postcard, the customers in the third group are sent both, and those in the last group neither. The bank keeps track of how many more times each customer uses his debit card in the two weeks after the reminders are sent as compared to the two weeks before the reminders are sent. The means for the four groups are compared.

   Explain why this is a designed experiment. Identify the factors and the response variable. Is the factor quantitative or qualitative? Identify the factor levels, the treatments, and the experimental units. Comparing this experiment to that in Exercise 2, why is it more realistic to choose a random sample for the experiment?

8.6 Credit card market shares. Refer to the CardWeb.com, Inc., study of credit card purchases, Exercise 1.14 (p. 25). Recall that the company tracked credit card purchases made by cardholders and measured two variables: (1) the type of credit card used (VISA, MasterCard, American Express, or Discover), and (2) the amount (in dollars) of the purchase. Suppose we want to compare the mean purchase amounts of VISA, MasterCard, American Express, and Discover cardholders. Identify each of the following elements for this study:
   a. Response variable   b. Factor(s)
   c. Treatments   d. Experimental units

8.7 CT scanning for lung cancer. Refer to Exercise 1.22 (p. 26) and the University of South Florida clinical trial of 50,000 smokers to compare the effectiveness of computed tomography (CT) scans with X-rays for detecting lung cancer (*Todays' Tomorrows*, Fall 2002). Recall that each participating smoker will be randomly assigned to one of two screening methods, CT or chest X-ray, and the age (in years) at which the scanning method first detects a tumor will be determined. One goal of the study is to compare the mean ages when cancer is first detected of the two screening methods
   a. Identify the response variable of the study.
   b. Identify the experimental units of the study.
   c. Identify the factor(s) in the study.
   d. Identify the treatments in the study.

Applying the Concepts—Intermediate

8.8 Value perceptions of consumers. Refer to the *Journal of Consumer Research* (Sept. 1996) study of whether between-store comparisons result in greater perceptions of value by consumers than within-store comparisons, Example 1.7 (p. 19). Recall that 50 consumers were randomly selected from all consumers in a designated market area to participate in the study. The researchers randomly assigned 25 consumers to read a within-store price promotion advertisement ("was $100, now $80") and 25 consumers to read a between-store price promotion ("$100 there, $80 here"). The consumers then gave their opinion on the value of the discount offer on a 10-point scale (where 1 = lowest value and 10 = highest value). The goal is to compare the average discount values of the two groups of consumers.
   a. What is the response variable for this study?
   b. What are the treatments for this study?
   c. What is the experimental unit for this study?

8.9 Value perceptions of consumers (cont'd). Refer to Exercise 8.8. In addition to the factor, Type of advertisement (within-store price promotion and between-store price promotion), the researchers also investigated the impact of a second factor, Location where ad is read (at home or in the store). About half of the consumers who were assigned to the within-store price promotion read the ad at home, and the other half read the ad in the store. Similarly, about half of the consumers who were assigned to the between-store price promotion read the ad at home, and the other half read the ad in the store. In this second experiment, the goal is to compare the average discount values of the groups of consumers created by combining Type of advertisement with Location.
   a. How many treatments are involved in this experiment?
   b. Identify the treatments.

8.10 Baker's versus brewer's yeast. The *Electronic Journal of Biotechnology* (Dec. 15, 2003) published an article on a comparison of two yeast extracts—baker's yeast and brewer's yeast. Brewer's yeast is a surplus by-product obtained from a brewery; hence it is less expensive than primary-grown baker's yeast. Samples of both yeast extracts were prepared at four different temperatures (45, 48, 51, and 54°C), and the autolysis yield (recorded as a percentage) was measured for each of the yeast-temperature combinations. The goal of the analysis is to investigate the impact of yeast extract and temperature on mean autolysis yield.
  a. Identify the factors (and factor levels) in the experiment.
  b. Identify the response variable.
  c. How many treatments are included in the experiment?
  d. What type of experimental design is employed?

8.11 Exam performance study. In *Teaching of Psychology* (August 1998), a study investigated whether final exam performance is affected by whether or not students take a practice test. Students in an introductory psychology class at Pennsylvania State University were initially divided into three groups based on their class standing: Low, Medium, or High. Within each group, the students were randomly assigned to either attend a review session or take a practice test prior to the final exam. Thus, six groups were formed: (Low, Review), (Low, Practice exam), (Medium, Review), (Medium, Practice exam), (High, Review), and (High, Practice exam). One goal of the study was to compare the mean final exam scores of the six groups of students.
  a. What is the experimental unit for this study?
  b. Is the study a designed experiment? Why?
  c. What are the factors in the study?
  d. Give the levels of each factor.
  e. How many treatments are in the study? Identify them.
  f. What is the response variable?

Applying the Concepts—Advanced

8.12 Ethics of salespeople. Within marketing, the area of personal sales has long suffered from a poor ethical image, particularly in the eyes of college students. An article in *Journal of Business Ethics* (Vol. 15, 1996) investigated whether such opinions by college students are a function of the type of sales job (high tech versus low tech) and/or the sales task (new account development versus account maintenance). Four different samples of college students were confronted with the four different situations (new account development in a high-tech sales task; new account development in a low-tech sales task; account maintenance in a high-tech sales task; and account maintenance in a low-tech sales task), and were asked to evaluate the ethical behavior of the salesperson on a 7-point scale ranging from 1 (not a serious ethical violation) to 7 (a very serious ethical violation). Identify each of the following elements of the experiment:
  a. Response   **b.** Factor(s) and factor level(s)
  c. Treatments   **d.** Experimental units

8.13 Testing a new pain-reliever tablet. Paracetamol is the active ingredient in drugs designed to relieve mild to moderate pain and fever. To save costs, pharmaceutical companies are looking to produce paracetamol tablets from locally available materials. The properties of paracetamol tablets derived from khaya gum were studied in the *Tropical Journal of Pharmaceutical Research* (June 2003). Three factors believed to impact the properties of paracetamol tablets are (1) the nature of the binding agent, (2) the concentration of the binding agent, and (3) the relative density of the tablet. In the experiment, binding agent was set at two levels (khaya gum and PVP), binding concentration at two levels (.5% and 4.0%), and relative density at two levels (low and high). One of the dependent variables investigated in the study was tablet dissolution time (i.e., the amount of time [in minutes] for 50% of the tablet to dissolve). The goal of the study was to determine the effect of binding agent, binding concentration, and relative density on mean dissolution time.
  a. Identify the dependent (response) variable in the study.
  b. What are the factors investigated in the study? Give the levels of each.
  c. How many treatments are possible in the study? List them.

8.2 The Completely Randomized Design: Single Factor

The simplest experimental design, a *completely randomized design,* consists of the *independent random selection* of experimental units representing each treatment. For example, we could independently select random samples of 20 female and 15 male high school seniors to compare their mean SAT scores. Or, we could independently select random samples of 30 households from each of four census districts to compare the mean income per household among the districts. In both examples, our objective is to compare treatment means by selecting random, independent samples for each treatment.

> **DEFINITION 8.7**
>
> A **completely randomized design** is a design for which independent random samples of experimental units are selected for each treatment.*

*We use *completely randomized* design to refer to both designed and observational experiments. Thus, the only requirement is that the experimental units to which treatments are applied (designed) or on which treatments are observed (observational) are independently selected for each treatment.

EXAMPLE 8.3

Assigning Treatments in a Completely Randomized Design to Compare Bottled Water Brands.

Problem Suppose we want to compare the taste preferences of consumers for three different brands of bottled water (say, Brands A, B, and C) using a random sample of 15 bottled water consumers. Set up a completely randomized design for this purpose—that is, assign the treatments to the experimental units for this design.

Solution In this study, the experimental units are the 15 consumers, and the treatments are the three brands of bottled water. One way to set up the completely randomized design is to randomly assign one of the three brands to each consumer to taste. Then we could measure (say, on a 1-to 10-point scale) the taste preference of each consumer. A good practice is to assign the same number of consumers to each brand—in this case, five consumers to each of the three brands. (When an equal number of experimental units are assigned to each treatment, we call the design a *balanced design*.)

A random number table (Table I, Appendix B) or computer software can be used to make the random assignments. Figure 8.3 is a MINITAB worksheet showing the random assignments made with the MINITAB "Random Data" function. You can see that MINITAB randomly assigned consumers numbered 2, 11, 1, 13, and 3 to taste Brand A, consumers numbered 15, 14, 7, 10, and 8 to taste Brand B, and consumers numbered 6, 5, 12, 9, and 4 to taste Brand C.

CRD3brands.MTW *

↓	C1 Consumer	C2 BrandA	C3 BrandB	C4 BrandC	C5
1	1	2	15	6	
2	2	11	14	5	
3	3	1	7	12	
4	4	13	10	9	
5	5	3	8	4	
6	6				
7	7				
8	8				
9	9				
10	10				
11	11				
12	12				
13	13				
14	14				
15	15				
16					

FIGURE 8.3
MINITAB random assignments of consumers to brands

Look Back In some experiments, it will not be possible to randomly assign treatments to the experimental units—the units will already be associated with one of the treatments. (For example, if the treatments are "Male" and "Female," you cannot change a person's gender.) In this case, a completely randomized design is one where you select independent random samples of experimental units from each treatment.

The objective of a completely randomized design is usually to compare the treatment means. If we denote the true, or population, means of the k treatments as $\mu_1, \mu_2, \ldots, \mu_k$, then we will test the null hypothesis that the treatment means are all equal against the alternative that at least two of the treatment means differ:

$$H_0: \mu_1 = \mu_2 = \cdots = \mu_k$$
$$H_a: \text{At least two of the } k \text{ treatment means differ}$$

The μs might represent the means of *all* female and male high school seniors' SAT scores or the means of *all* households' income in each of four census regions.

To conduct a statistical test of these hypotheses, we will use the means of the independent random samples selected from the treatment populations using the completely randomized design—that is, we compare the k sample means, $\bar{x}_1, \bar{x}_2, \ldots, \bar{x}_k$.

For example, suppose you select independent random samples of five female and five male high school seniors and obtain sample mean SAT scores of 550 and 590, respectively. Can we conclude that males score 40 points higher, on average, than females? To answer this question, we must consider the amount of sampling variability among the experimental units (students). If the scores are as depicted in the dot plot shown in Figure 8.4, then the difference between the means is small relative to the sampling variability of the scores within the treatments, Female and Male. We would be inclined not to reject the null hypothesis of equal population means in this case.

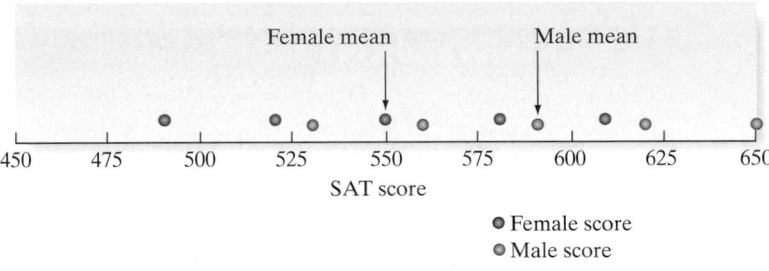

FIGURE 8.4

Dot plot of SAT scores: Difference between means dominated by sampling variability

In contrast, if the data are as depicted in the dot plot of Figure 8.5, then the sampling variability is small relative to the difference between the two means. We would be inclined to favor the alternative hypothesis that the population means differ in this case.

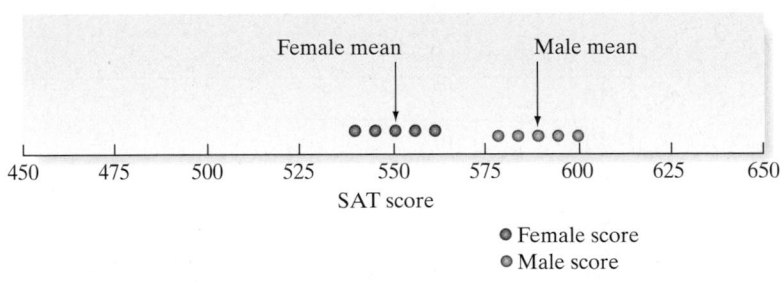

FIGURE 8.5

Dot plot of SAT scores: Difference between means large relative to sampling variability

Now Work Exercise 8.16a

You can see that the key is to compare the difference between the treatment means to the amount of sampling variability. To conduct a formal statistical test of the hypotheses requires numerical measures of the difference between the treatment means and the sampling variability within each treatment. The variation between the treatment means is measured by the **Sum of Squares for Treatments** (SST), which is calculated by squaring the distance between each treatment mean and the overall mean of *all* sample measurements, multiplying each squared distance by the number of sample measurements for the treatment and adding the results over all treatments:

$$\text{SST} = \sum_{i=1}^{k} n_i(\bar{x}_i - \bar{x})^2 = 5(550 - 570)^2 + 5(590 - 570)^2 = 4{,}000$$

where we use $\bar{x}$ to represent the overall mean response of all sample measurements— that is, the mean of the combined samples. The symbol n_i is used to denote the sample size for the ith treatment. You can see that the value of SST is 4,000 for the two samples of five female and five male SAT scores depicted in Figures 8.4 and 8.5.

Next, we must measure the sampling variability within the treatments. We call this the **Sum of Squares for Error** (SSE) because it measures the variability around the treatment means that is attributed to sampling error. Suppose the 10 measurements in the first dot plot (Figure 8.4) are 490, 520, 550, 580, and 610 for females, and 530, 560, 590, 620, and 650 for males. Then the value of SSE is computed by summing the squared distance between each response measurement and the corresponding treatment mean, and then adding the squared differences over all measurements in the entire sample:

$$\text{SSE} = \sum_{j=1}^{n_1} (x_{1j} - \bar{x}_1)^2 + \sum_{j=1}^{n_2} (x_{2j} - \bar{x}_2)^2 + \cdots + \sum_{j=1}^{n_k} (x_{kj} - \bar{x}_k)^2$$

where the symbol x_{1j} is the jth measurement in sample 1, x_{2j} is the jth measurement in sample 2, and so on. This rather complex-looking formula can be simplified by recalling the formula for the sample variance, s^2, given in Chapter 2:

$$s^2 = \sum_{i=1}^{n} \frac{(x_i - \bar{x})^2}{n - 1}$$

Note that each sum in SSE is simply the numerator of s^2 for that particular treatment. Consequently, we can rewrite SSE as

$$\text{SSE} = (n_1 - 1)s_1^2 + (n_2 - 1)s_2^2 + \cdots + (n_k - 1)s_k^2$$

where $s_1^2, s_2^2, \ldots, s_k^2$ are the sample variances for the k treatments. For our samples of SAT scores, we find $s_1^2 = 2{,}250$ (for females) and $s_2^2 = 2{,}250$ (for males); then we have

$$\text{SSE} = (5 - 1)(2{,}250) + (5 - 1)(2{,}250) = 18{,}000$$

To make the two measurements of variability comparable, we divide each by the degrees of freedom to convert the sums of squares to mean squares. First, the **Mean Square for Treatments** (MST), which measures the variability among the treatment means, is equal to

$$\text{MST} = \frac{\text{SST}}{k - 1} = \frac{4{,}000}{2 - 1} = 4{,}000$$

where the number of degrees of freedom for the k treatments is $(k - 1)$ Next, the **Mean Square for Error** (MSE), which measures the sampling variability within the treatments, is

$$\text{MSE} = \frac{\text{SSE}}{n - k} = \frac{18{,}000}{10 - 2} = 2{,}250$$

Finally, we calculate the ratio of MST to MSE—an **F statistic:**

$$F = \frac{\text{MST}}{\text{MSE}} = \frac{4{,}000}{2{,}250} = 1.78$$

Values of the F statistic near 1 indicate that the two sources of variation, between treatment means and within treatments, are approximately equal. In this case, the difference between the treatment means may well be attributable to sampling error, which provides little support for the alternative hypothesis that the population treatment means differ. Values of F well in excess of 1 indicate that the variation among treatment means well exceeds that within means and therefore support the alternative hypothesis that the population treatment means differ.

When does F exceed 1 by enough to reject the null hypothesis that the means are equal? This depends on the degrees of freedom for treatments and for error, and on the value of α selected for the test. We compare the calculated F value to a table F value (Tables VII–X of Appendix B) with $v_1 = (k - 1)$ degrees of freedom in the numerator and $v_2 = (n - k)$ degrees of freedom in the denominator and corresponding to a Type I error probability of α. For the SAT score example, the F statistic has $v_1 = (2 - 1) = 1$ numerator degree of freedom and $v_2 = (10 - 2) = 8$ denominator degrees of freedom. Thus, for $\alpha = .05$, we find (Table VIII of Appendix B)

$$F_{.05} = 5.32$$

The implication is that MST would have to be 5.32 times greater than MSE before we could conclude at the .05 level of significance that the two population treatment means differ. Since the data yielded $F = 1.78$, our initial impressions for the dot plot in Figure 8.4 are confirmed—there is insufficient information to conclude that the mean SAT scores differ for the populations of female and male high school seniors. The rejection region and the calculated F value are shown in Figure 8.6.

FIGURE 8.6
Rejection region and calculated F values for SAT score samples

In contrast, consider the dot plot in Figure 8.5. Since the means are the same as in the first example, 550 and 590, respectively, the variation between the means is the same, $MST = 4,000$. But the variation within the two treatments appears to be considerably smaller. The observed SAT scores are 540, 545, 550, 555, and 560 for females, and 580, 585, 590, 595, and 600 for males. These values yield $s_1^2 = 62.5$ and $s_2^2 = 62.5$. Thus, the variation within the treatments is measured by

$$\text{SSE} = (5 - 1)(62.5) + (5 - 1)(62.5) = 500$$

$$\text{MSE} = \frac{\text{SSE}}{n - k} = \frac{500}{8} = 62.5$$

Then the F-ratio is

$$F = \frac{\text{MST}}{\text{MSE}} = \frac{4,000}{62.5} = 64.0$$

Again, our visual analysis of the dot plot is confirmed statistically: $F = 64.0$ well exceeds the tabled F value, 5.32, corresponding to the .05 level of significance. We would therefore reject the null hypothesis at that level and conclude that the SAT mean score of males differs from that of females.

Now Work Exercise 8.16b–h

Recall that we performed a hypothesis test for the difference between two means in Section 7.2, using a two-sample t-statistic for two independent samples. When two independent samples are being compared, the t- and F-tests are equivalent. To see this, recall the formula

$$t = \frac{\bar{x}_1 - \bar{x}_2}{\sqrt{s_p^2 \left(\frac{1}{n_1} + \frac{1}{n_2} \right)}} = \frac{590 - 550}{\sqrt{(62.5)\left(\frac{1}{5} + \frac{1}{5} \right)}} = \frac{40}{5} = 8$$

where we used the fact that $s_p^2 = \text{MSE}$, which you can verify by comparing the formulas. Note that the calculated F for these samples ($F = 64$) equals the square of the calculated t for the same samples ($t = 8$) Likewise, the tabled F value (5.32) equals the square of the tabled t-value at the two-sided .05 level of significance ($t_{.025} = 2.306$ with 8 df). Since both the rejection region and the calculated values are related in the same way, the tests are equivalent. Moreover, the assumptions that must be met to ensure the validity of the t- and F-tests are the same:

1. The probability distributions of the populations of responses associated with each treatment must all be normal.

2. The probability distributions of the populations of responses associated with each treatment must have equal variances.

3. The samples of experimental units selected for the treatments must be random and independent.

In fact, the only real difference between the tests is that the F-test can be used to compare *more than two* treatment means, whereas the t-test is applicable to two samples only. The F-test is summarized in the accompanying box.

ANOVA F-Test to Compare k Treatment Means:
Completely Randomized Design

$$H_0: \mu_1 = \mu_2 = \cdots = \mu_k$$

H_a: At least two treatment means differ

$$\text{Test statistic: } F = \frac{\text{MST}}{\text{MSE}}$$

Rejection region: $F > F_\alpha$, where F_α is based on $(k - 1)$ numerator degrees of freedom (associated with MST) and $(n - k)$ denominator degrees of freedom (associated with MSE).

Conditions Required for a Valid ANOVA F-test:
Completely Randomized Design

1. The samples are randomly selected in an independent manner from the k treatment populations. (This can be accomplished by randomly assigning the experimental units to the treatments.)

2. All k sampled populations have distributions that are approximately normal.

3. The k population variances are equal (i.e., $\sigma_1^2 = \sigma_2^2 = \sigma_3^2 = \ldots = \sigma_k^2$).

Computational formulas for MST and MSE are given in Appendix C. We will rely on some of the many statistical software packages available to compute the F statistic, concentrating on the interpretation of the results rather than their calculations.

EXAMPLE 8.4

Conducting an
ANOVA *F*-Test to
Compare Golf Ball
Brands

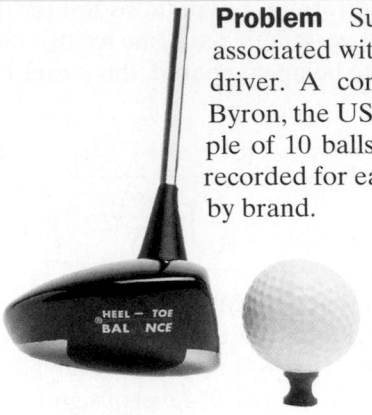

Problem   Suppose the USGA wants to compare the mean distances associated with four different brands of golf balls when struck with a driver. A completely randomized design is employed, with Iron Byron, the USGA's robotic golfer, using a driver to hit a random sample of 10 balls of each brand in a random sequence. The distance is recorded for each hit, and the results are shown in Table 8.1, organized by brand.

a. Set up the test to compare the mean distances for the four brands. Use $\alpha = .10$.

b. Use Excel to obtain the test statistic and *p*-value. Interpret the results.

GOLFCRD

TABLE 8.1   Results of Completely Randomized Design: Iron Byron Driver

	Brand A	Brand B	Brand C	Brand D
	251.2	263.2	269.7	251.6
	245.1	262.9	263.2	248.6
	248.0	265.0	277.5	249.4
	251.1	254.5	267.4	242.0
	260.5	264.3	270.5	246.5
	250.0	257.0	265.5	251.3
	253.9	262.8	270.7	261.8
	244.6	264.4	272.9	249.0
	254.6	260.6	275.6	247.1
	248.8	255.9	266.5	245.9
Sample Means	250.8	261.1	270.0	249.3

Solution

a. To compare the mean distances of the four brands, we first specify the hypotheses to be tested. Denoting the population mean of the *i*th brand by μ_j, we test

$$H_0: \mu_1 = \mu_2 = \mu_3 = \mu_4$$

H_a: The mean distances differ for at least two of the brands

The test statistic compares the variation among the four treatment (Brand) means to the sampling variability within each of the treatments.

$$\text{Test statistic: } F = \frac{MST}{MSE}$$

Rejection region: $F > F_\alpha = F_{.10}$

with $v_1 = (k - 1) = 3$ df and $v_2 = (n - k) = 36$ df

From Table VII of Appendix B, we find $F_{.10} \approx 2.25$ for 3 and 36 df. Thus, we will reject H_0 if $F > 2.25$. (See Figure 8.7.)

The assumptions necessary to ensure the validity of the test are as follows:

1. The samples of 10 golf balls for each brand are selected randomly and independently.
2. The probability distributions of the distances for each brand are normal.
3. The variances of the distance probability distributions for each brand are equal.

FIGURE 8.7

F-test for completely randomized design: Golf ball experiment

b. The Excel printout for the data in Table 8.1 resulting from this completely randomized design is given in Figure 8.8. At the bottom of the printout the Total Sum of Squares is designated **Total,** and it is partitioned into the **Between Groups** (i.e., Brand) and the **Within Groups** (i.e., Error) sum of squares. The **Sum of Squares** column is headed **SS.**

The values of the mean squares, MST and MSE (highlighted on the printout), are 931.4629 and 21.17503, respectively. The *F*-ratio, 43.98875, also highlighted on the printout, exceeds the tabled value of 2.25. We therefore reject the null hypothesis at the .10 level of significance, concluding that at least two of the brands differ with respect to mean distance traveled when struck by the driver.

Anova: Single Factor

SUMMARY

Groups	Count	Sum	Average	Variance
BrandA	10	2507.8	250.78	22.42178
BrandB	10	2610.6	261.06	14.94711
BrandC	10	2699.5	269.95	20.25833
BrandD	10	2493.2	249.32	27.07289

ANOVA

Source of Variation	SS	df	MS	F	P-value	F crit
Between Groups	2794.389	3	931.4629	43.98875	3.97E-12	2.242608
Within Groups	762.301	36	21.17503			
Total	3556.69	39				

FIGURE 8.8

Excel printout for ANOVA of golf ball distance data

Look Back We can also arrive at the appropriate conclusion by noting that the observed significance level of the *F*-test (highlighted on the printout) is approximately 0. This implies that we would reject the null hypothesis that the means are equal at any reasonably-selected α level.

[*Note:* Excel uses exponential notation to display the *p*-value. The value 3.97E-12 is equal to .00000000000397.]

Now Work Exercise 8.21

The results of an **analysis of variance** (ANOVA) can be summarized in a simple tabular format similar to that obtained from the Excel printout in Example 8.4. The general form of the table is shown in Table 8.2, where the symbols df, SS, and MS stand for

TABLE 8.2 General ANOVA Summary Table for a Completely Randomized Design

Source	df	SS	MS	F
Treatments	$k - 1$	SST	$MST = \dfrac{SST}{k-1}$	$\dfrac{MST}{MSE}$
Error	$n - k$	SSE	$MSE = \dfrac{SSE}{n-k}$	
Total	$n - 1$	SS(Total)		

TABLE 8.3 ANOVA Summary Table for Example 8.4

Source	df	SS	MS	F	p-Value
Brands	3	2,794.39	931.46	43.99	.0000
Error	36	762.30	21.18		
Total	39	3,556.69			

degrees of freedom, Sum of Squares, and Mean Square, respectively. Note that the two sources of variation, Treatments and Error, add to the Total Sum of Squares, SS(Total). The ANOVA summary table for Example 8.3 is given in Table 8.3, and the partitioning of the Total Sum of Squares into its two components is illustrated in Figure 8.9.

Suppose the *F*-test results in a rejection of the null hypothesis that the treatment means are equal. Is the analysis complete? Usually, the conclusion that at least two of the treatment means differ leads to other questions. Which of

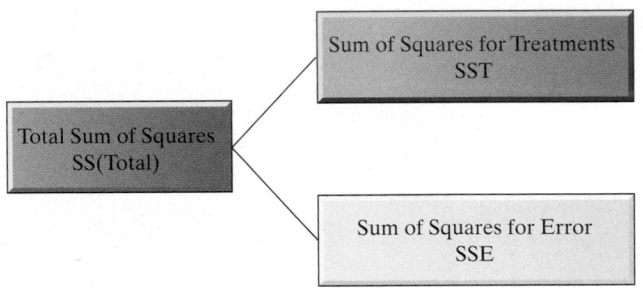

FIGURE 8.9
Partitioning of the Total Sum of Squares for the completely randomized design

the means differ, and by how much? For example, the *F*-test in Example 8.4 leads to the conclusion that at least two of the brands of golf balls have different mean distances traveled when struck with a driver. Now the question is, which of the brands differ? How are the brands ranked with respect to mean distance?

One way to obtain this information is to construct a confidence interval for the difference between the means of any pair of treatments using the method of Section 7.2. For example, if a 95% confidence interval for $(\mu_A - \mu_C)$ in Example 8.4 is found to be $(-24, -13)$, we are confident that the mean distance for Brand C exceeds the mean for Brand A (since all differences in the interval are negative). Constructing these confidence intervals for all possible brand pairs will allow you to rank the brand means. A method for conducting these *multiple comparisons*—one that controls for Type I errors—is presented in Section 8.3.

EXAMPLE 8.5

Checking the ANOVA Assumptions

Refer to the completely randomized design ANOVA conducted in Example 8.4. Are the assumptions required for the test approximately satisfied?

Solution The assumptions for the test are repeated below.

1. The samples of golf balls for each brand are selected randomly and independently.
2. The probability distributions of the distances for each brand are normal.
3. The variances of the distance probability distributions for each brand are equal.

Analysis of Variance

Using the TI-83/TI-84 Graphing Calculator
Computing a One-Way ANOVA

Step 1   *Enter each data set into its own list (i.e., sample 1 into L1, sample 2 into L2, sample 3 into L3, etc.).*

Step 2   *Access the Statistical Test Menu*

Press **STAT**
Arrow right to **TESTS**
Arrow down to **ANOVA(**
Press **ENTER**
Type in each List name separated by commas *(e.g., L1, L2, L3, L4)*
Press **ENTER**

Step 3   *View Display*

The calculator will display the *F*-test statistic, as well as the *p*-value, the Factor degrees of freedom, sum of squares, mean square, and by arrowing down, the Error degrees of freedom, sum of squares, mean square, and the pooled standard deviation.

Example   Below are four different samples. At the $\alpha = .05$ level of significance, test whether the four population means are equal. The null hypothesis will be $H_0: \mu_1 = \mu_2 = \mu_3 = \mu_4$. The alternative hypothesis is H_a. At least one mean is different.

SAMPLE1	SAMPLE2	SAMPLE3	SAMPLE4
60	59	55	58
61	52	55	58
56	51	52	55

The screens for this example are shown below.

As you can see from the screen, the *p*-value is 0.1598 which is **not less than** 0.05; therefore we should **not reject** H_0. The differences are not significantly different.

Since the sample consisted of 10 randomly selected balls of each brand and the robotic golfer Iron Byron was used to drive all the balls, the first assumption of independent random samples is satisfied. To check the next two assumptions, we will employ two graphical methods presented in Chapter 2: histograms and box plots. A MINITAB histogram of driving distances for each brand of golf ball is shown in Figure 8.10, followed by SPSS box plots in Figure 8.11.

The normality assumption can be checked by examining the histograms in Figure 8.10. With only 10 sample measurements for each brand, however, the displays are not very informative. More data would need to be collected for each brand before we could assess whether the distances come from normal distributions. Fortunately, analysis of variance has been shown to be a very **robust method** when the assumption of normality is not satisfied exactly—that is, *moderate departures from normality do not have much effect on the significance level of the ANOVA F-test or on confidence coefficients.* Rather

FIGURE 8.10

MINITAB histograms for golf ball distances

FIGURE 8.11

SPSS box plots for golf ball distances

than spend the time, energy, or money to collect additional data for this experiment in order to verify the normality assumption, we will rely on the robustness of the ANOVA methodology.

Box plots are a convenient way to obtain a rough check on the assumption of equal variances. With the exception of a possible outlier for Brand D, the box plots in Figure 8.11 show that the spread of the distance measurements is about the same for each brand. Since the sample variances appear to be the same, the assumption of equal population variances for the brands is probably satisfied. Although robust with respect to the normality assumption, ANOVA is *not robust* with respect to the equal variances assumption. Departures from the assumption of equal population variances can affect the associated measures of reliability (e.g., *p*-values and confidence levels). Fortunately, the effect is slight when the sample sizes are equal, as in this experiment.

Now Work Exercise 8.30

Although graphs can be used to check the ANOVA assumptions, as in Example 8.5, no measures of reliability can be attached to these graphs. When you have a plot that is unclear as to whether or not an assumption is satisfied, you can use formal statistical tests, which are beyond the scope of this text. (Consult the references for information on these tests.) When the validity of the ANOVA assumptions is in doubt, nonparametric statistical methods are useful.

What Do You Do when the Assumptions Are Not Satisfied for the Analysis of Variance for a Completely Randomized Design?

Answer: Use a nonparametric statistical method such as the Kruskal-Wallis *H*-Test of Section 14.5.

The procedure for conducting an analysis of variance for a completely randomized design is summarized in the following box. Remember that the hallmark of this design is independent random samples of experimental units associated with each treatment. However, designs with dependent samples may be more appropriate in certain situations. Consult the references for information on the use of these designs.

Steps for Conducting an ANOVA for a Completely Randomized Design

1. Be sure the design is truly completely randomized, with independent random samples for each treatment.

2. Check the assumptions of normality and equal variances.

3. Create an ANOVA summary table that specifies the variability attributable to treatments and error, making sure that it leads to the calculation of the *F* statistic for testing the null hypothesis that the treatment means are equal in the population. Use a statistical software program to obtain the numerical results. If no such package is available, use the calculation formulas in Appendix C.

4. If the *F*-test leads to the conclusion that the means differ,

   a. Conduct a multiple comparisons procedure for as many of the pairs of means as you wish to compare (see Section 8.3). Use the results to summarize the statistically significant differences among the treatment means.

   b. If desired, form confidence intervals for one or more individual treatment means.

5. If the *F*-test leads to the nonrejection of the null hypothesis that the treatment means are equal, consider the following possibilities:

   a. The treatment means are equal—that is, the null hypothesis is true.

   b. The treatment means really differ, but other important factors affecting the response are not accounted for by the completely randomized design. These

Continu

factors inflate the sampling variability, as measured by MSE, resulting in smaller values of the F statistic. Either increase the sample size for each treatment, or use a different experimental design (as in Section 8.4) that accounts for the other factors affecting the response.

Note: Be careful not to automatically conclude that the treatment means are equal since the possibility of a Type II error must be considered if you accept H_0.

STATISTICS IN ACTION REVISITED

Testing for Differences in the Mean Ethics Responses of the Five Downsize Groups

University professors W. E. Hopkins and S. A. Hopkins surveyed 209 employees and measured their "ethics scores" (i.e., their responses [on a 5-point scale] to the statement "It is unethical for a downsizing decision to be announced or implemented on or prior to a major holiday [e.g., Christmas, Thanksgiving, etc.]"). The employees were divided into five distinct groups: (1) Casualties, (2) Survivors, (3) Implementors/casualties, (4) Implementors/survivors, and (5) Formulators. (See Table SIA8.1.) The researchers used the data to test three hypotheses.

H_1: Survivors', Casualties', and Implementors/casualties' perceptions of the ethics statement on downsizing will not differ significantly.

H_2: Formulators' and Implementors/survivors' perceptions of the ethics statement on downsizing will not differ significantly.

H_3: Survivors', Casualties', and Implementors/casualties' perceptions of the ethics statement on downsizing will differ significantly from Formulators' and Implementors/survivors' perceptions.

If we let μ_j represent the true mean ethics score for all employees in Group j, then we can restate these hypotheses as follows:

$$H_1: \mu_1 = \mu_2 = \mu_3$$

$$H_2: \mu_4 = \mu_5$$

$$H_3: (\mu_4, \mu_5) \neq (\mu_1, \mu_2, \mu_3)$$

Initially, the researchers conducted an analysis of variance for a completely randomized design on the data. The dependent variable is Ethics score, the treatments are the five employee groups, and the null hypothesis is $H_0: \mu_1 = \mu_2 = \mu_3 = \mu_4 = \mu_5$. The MINITAB printout of the ANOVA is displayed in Figure SIA8.1. The observed significance level of the test (highlighted on the printout) is p-value $= .000$. For any α-level we select (.01, .05, or .10), there is sufficient evidence to reject the null hypothesis. Consequently, the researchers concluded that the mean ethics scores of the five groups of employees were significantly different.

Should the researchers conclude that hypotheses H_1, H_2, and H_3 are supported? Possibly, but not based solely on the results of the ANOVA F-test. Remember, the alternative hypothesis (H_a) for this test states that at least two of the five population means are different, but it does not indicate which means in particular are different. In order to test hypotheses H_1, H_2, and H_3, we will need to rank the treatment means using a procedure that provides a measure of reliability. We present such a method in the next section.

We should, however, check that the assumptions required for the F-test (normal populations with equal variances) are reasonably satisfied. MINITAB histograms and box plots for the data are shown in Figures SIA8.2 and SIA8.3. First, notice the nonsymmetrical shapes in the histograms, Figure SIA8.2. These graphs do not appear to support the assumption of normality for each treatment group. However, this assumption does not need to be satisfied exactly for the ANOVA to yield valid results. Second, examine the variability in the data shown on the box plots, Figure SIA8.3. It appears that the spread of the ethics scores for groups 1, 2, and 3 is much tighter than the spread for groups 4 and 5. Consequently, it is unlikely that the assumption of equal variances for the five treatment groups is satisfied. The researchers should consider running a nonparametric analysis of the data—an analysis that does not rely on the assumptions of normality and equal variances.

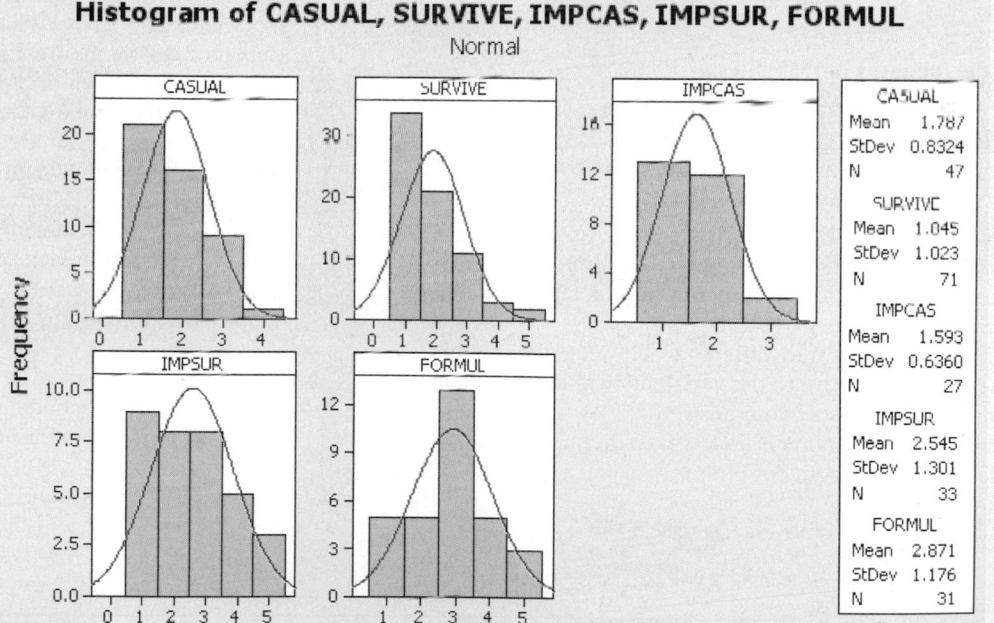

One-way ANOVA: CASUAL, SURVIVE, IMPCAS, IMPSUR, FORMUL

```
Source    DF      SS      MS      F       P
Factor     4    40.84   10.21   9.85   0.000
Error    204   211.35    1.04
Total    208   252.19


S = 1.018    R-Sq = 16.19%    R-Sq(adj) = 14.55%



                              Individual 95% CIs For Mean Based on
                              Pooled StDev
Level      N    Mean   StDev    +---------+---------+---------+---------
CASUAL    47   1.787   0.832          (----*----)
SURVIVE   71   1.845   1.023           (---*---)
IMPCAS    27   1.593   0.636    (------*------)
IMPSUR    33   2.545   1.301                      (----*-----)
FORMUL    31   2.871   1.176                          (-----*-----)
                                +---------+---------+---------+---------
                              1.20      1.80      2.40      3.00


Pooled StDev = 1.018
```

Figure SIA8.1
MINITAB ANOVA on the downsize data set

Histogram of CASUAL, SURVIVE, IMPCAS, IMPSUR, FORMUL
Normal

```
CASUAL              SURVIVE
Mean   1.787       Mean   1.845
StDev  0.8324      StDev  1.023
N      47          N      71

IMPCAS             IMPSUR
Mean   1.593       Mean   2.545
StDev  0.6360      StDev  1.301
N      27          N      33

FORMUL
Mean   2.871
StDev  1.176
N      31
```

Figure SIA8.2
MINITAB box histograms of the downsize data

Continued

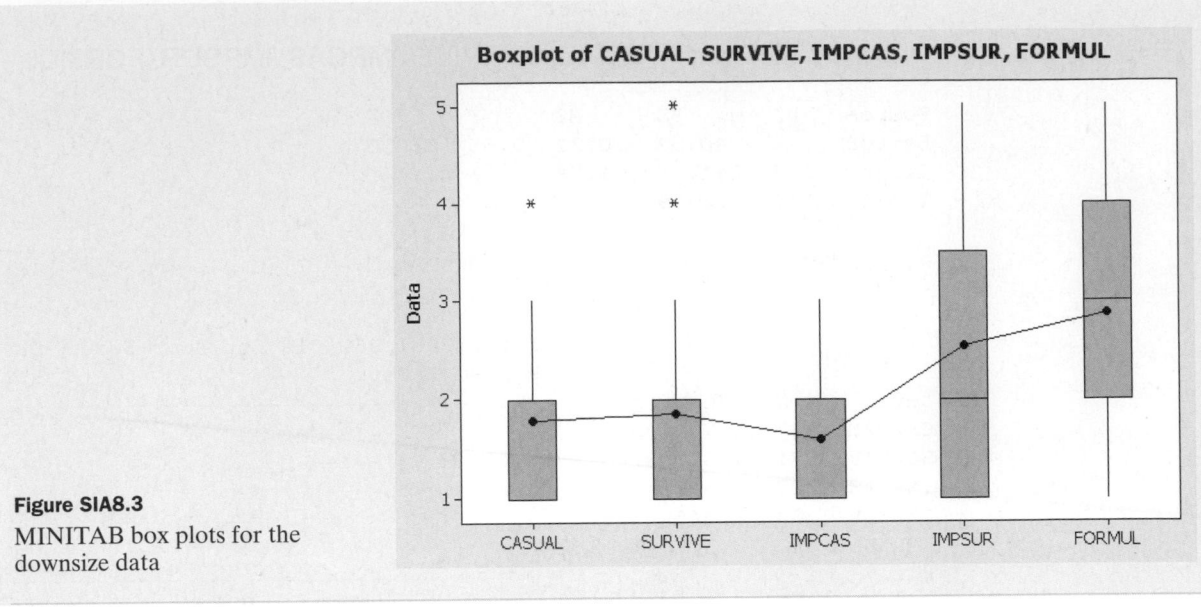

Figure SIA8.3
MINITAB box plots for the downsize data

Exercises 8.14–8.32

Learning the Mechanics

8.14 Use Tables VII, VIII, IX, and X of Appendix B to find each of the following F values:

    a. $F_{.05}, v_1 = 4, v_2 = 4$

    b. $F_{.01}, v_1 = 4, v_2 = 4$

    c. $F_{.10}, v_1 = 30, v_2 = 40$

    d. $F_{.025}, v_1 = 15, v_2 = 12$

8.15 Find the following probabilities:

    a. $P(F \le 3.48)$ for $v_1 = 5, v_2 = 9$

    b. $P(F > 3.09)$ for $v_1 = 15, v_2 = 20$

    c. $P(F > 2.40)$ for $v_1 = 15, v_2 = 15$

    d. $P(F \le 1.83)$ for $v_1 = 8, v_2 = 40$

8.16 Consider dot plots 1 and 2 shown below. Assume that the two samples represent independent, random samples corresponding to two treatments in a completely randomized design.

    a. In which plot is the difference between the sample means small relative to the variability within the sample observations? Justify your answer.

    b. Calculate the treatment means (i.e., the means of samples 1 and 2, for both dot plots).

c. Use the means to calculate the Sum of Squares for Treatments (SST) for each dot plot.

d. Calculate the sample variance for each sample and use these values to obtain the Sum of Squares for Error (SSE) for each dot plot.

e. Calculate the Total Sum of Squares [SS(Total)] for the two dot plots by adding the Sums of Squares for Treatments and Error. What percentage of SS(Total) is accounted for by the treatments—that is, what percentage of the Total Sum of Squares is the Sum of Squares for Treatments—in each case?

f. Convert the Sum of Squares for Treatments and Error to mean squares by dividing each by the appropriate number of degrees of freedom. Calculate the F-ratio of the Mean Square for Treatments (MST) to the Mean Square for Error (MSE) for each dot plot.

g. Use the F-ratios to test the null hypothesis that the two samples are drawn from populations with equal means. Use $\alpha = .05$.

h. What assumptions must be made about the probability distributions corresponding to the responses for each treatment in order to ensure the validity of the F-tests conducted in part **g**?

Dot Plots for Exercise 8.16

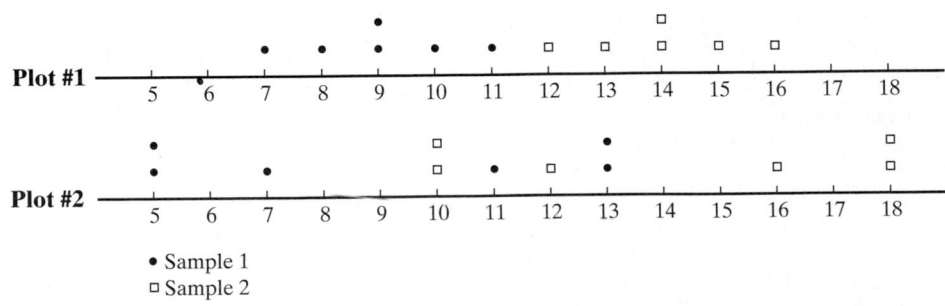

    • Sample 1

    □ Sample 2

8.17 Refer to Exercise 8.16. Conduct a two-sample t-test (Section 7.2) of the null hypothesis that the two treatment means are equal for each dot plot. Use $\alpha = .05$ and two-tailed tests. In the course of the test, compare each of the following with the F-tests in Exercise 8.16:

a. The pooled variances and the MSEs

b. The t- and F-test statistics

c. The tabled values of t and F that determine the rejection regions

d. The conclusions of the t- and F-tests

e. The assumptions that must be made in order to ensure the validity of the t- and F-tests

8.18 Refer to Exercises 8.16 and 8.17. Complete the following ANOVA table for each of the two dot plots:

Source	df	SS	MS	F
Treatments				
Error				
Total				

8.19 Suppose the Total Sum of Squares for a completely randomized design with $k = 6$ treatments and $n = 36$ total measurements (six per treatment) is equal to 500. In each of the following cases, conduct an F-test of the null hypothesis that the mean responses for the five treatments are the same. Use $\alpha = .10$.

a. Sum of Squares for Treatments (SST) is 20% of SS(Total)

b. SST is 50% of SS(Total)

c. SST is 80% of SS(Total)

d. What happens to the F-ratio as the percentage of the Total Sum of Squares attributable to treatments is increased?

8.20 A partially completed ANOVA table for a completely randomized design is shown here:

Source	df	SS	MS	F
Treatments	6	17.5	—	—
Error		—	—	
Total	41	46.5		

a. Complete the ANOVA table.

b. How many treatments are involved in the experiment?

c. Do the data provide sufficient evidence to indicate a difference among the population means? Test using $\alpha = .10$.

d. Find the approximate observed significance level for the test in part **c,** and interpret it.

e. Suppose that $\bar{x}_1 = 3.7$ and $\bar{x}_2 = 4.1$. Do the data provide sufficient evidence to indicate a difference between μ_1 and μ_2? Assume that there are six observations for each treatment. Test using $\alpha = .10$.

f. Refer to part **e.** Find a 90% confidence interval for $(\mu_1 - \mu_2)$. [Hint: Use $s = \sqrt{MSE}$ as an estimate of both σ_1 and σ_2.]

g. Refer to part **e.** Find a 90% confidence interval for μ_1. [Hint: Use $s = \sqrt{MSE}$ as an estimate of σ_1.]

8.21 The data in the next table resulted from an experiment that
NW utilized a completely randomized design.

LM8_21

Treatment 1	Treatment 2	Treatment 3
3.8	5.4	1.3
1.2	2.0	0.7
4.1	4.8	2.2
5.5	3.8	
2.3		

a. Use statistical software (or the appropriate calculation formulas in Appendix C) to complete the following ANOVA table:

Source	df	SS	MS	F
Treatments	—	—	—	—
Error	—	—	—	
Total	—	—		

b. Test the null hypothesis that $\mu_1 = \mu_2 = \mu_3$, where μ_i represents the true mean for treatment i, against the alternative that at least two of the means differ. Use $\alpha = .01$.

Applying the Concepts—Basic

8.22 College tennis recruiting with a team Web site. Most university athletic programs now have a Web site with information on individual sports and a Prospective Student Athlete Form that allows high school athletes to submit their academic and sports achievements directly to the college coach. *The Sport Journal* (Winter 2004) published a study of how important team Web sites are to the recruitment of college tennis players. A survey was conducted of NCAA tennis coaches, of which 53 were from Division I schools, 20 were from Division II schools, and 53 were from Division III schools. Coaches were asked to respond to a series of statements, including "the Prospective Student-Athlete Form on the Web site contributes very little to the recruiting process." Responses were measured on a 7-point scale (where $1 =$ strongly disagree and $7 =$ strongly agree). In order to compare the mean responses of tennis coaches from the three NCAA divisions, the data were analyzed with a completely randomized design ANOVA.

a. Identify the experimental unit, dependent (response) variable, factor, and treatments for this study.

b. Give the null and alternative hypothesis for the ANOVA F-test.

c. The observed significance level of the test was found to be p-value $< .003$. What conclusion can you draw if you want to test at $\alpha = .05$?

TVADRECALL

8.23 Study of recall of TV commercials. Television advertisers seek to promote their products on TV programs that attract the most viewers. Do TV shows with violence and sex impair memory for commercials? To answer this question, Iowa state professors B. Bushman and A. Bonacci conducted a designed experiment in which 324 adults were randomly assigned to one of three viewer groups, 108 in each group (*Journal of Applied Psychology*, June 2002). One group watched a TV program (e.g., *Tour of Duty*) with a violent content code (V) rating; the second group viewed a show (e.g., *Strip Mall*) with a sex content code (S) rating; and, the last group watched a neutral TV program (e.g., *Candid Camera*) with neither a V nor an S rating. Nine commercials were imbedded into each TV show. After viewing the program, each participant was scored on their recall of the brand names in the commercial messages, with scores ranging from 0 (no brands recalled) to 9 (all brands recalled). The data (simulated from information provided in the article) are saved in the **TVADRECALL** file. The researchers compared the mean recall scores of the three viewing groups with an analysis of variance for a completely randomized design.

a. Identify the experimental units in the study.
b. Identify the dependent (response) variable in the study.
c. Identify the factor and treatments in the study.
d. The sample mean recall scores for the three groups were $\bar{x}_v = 2.08$, $\bar{x}_s = 1.71$, and $\bar{x}_{\text{Neutral}} = 3.17$. Explain why one should not draw an inference about differences in the population mean recall scores based on only these summary statistics.
e. An ANOVA on the data in the **TVADRECALL** file yielded the results shown in the following MINITAB printout. Locate the test statistic and *p*-value on the printout.
f. Interpret the results, part **e**, using $\alpha = .01$. What can the researchers conclude about the three groups of TV ad viewers?

One-way ANOVA: VIOLENT, SEX, NEUTRAL

Source	DF	SS	MS	F	P
Factor	2	123.27	61.63	20.45	0.000
Error	321	967.35	3.01		
Total	323	1090.62			

S = 1.736   R-Sq = 11.30%   R-Sq(adj) = 10.75%

8.24 Robots trained to behave like ants. Robotic researchers investigated whether robots could be trained to behave like ants in an ant colony (*Nature*, Aug. 2000). Robots were

trained and randomly assigned to "colonies" (i.e., groups) consisting of 3, 6, 9, or 12 robots. The robots were assigned the task of foraging for "food" and to recruit another robot when they identified a resource-rich area. One goal of the experiment was to compare the mean energy expended (per robot) of the four different colony sizes.

a. What type of experimental design was employed?
b. Identify the treatments and the dependent variable.
c. Set up the null and alternative hypothesis of the test.
d. The following ANOVA results were reported: $F = 7.70$, numerator df $= 3$, denominator df $= 56$, *p*-value $< .001$. Conduct the test at a significance level of $\alpha = .05$ and interpret the result.

8.25 Most powerful women in America. Refer to Fortune (Nov. 14, 2005) magazine's study of the most powerful women in America, Exercise 2.45 (p. 72). Recall that the data on age (in years) and title of each of the 50 women in the survey are stored in the **WPOWER50** file. (The first five and last two observations of the data are listed in the accompanying table.) Suppose you want to compare the average ages of all powerful American women in four groups based on their position (title) within the firm: Group 1 (CEO); Group 2 (Chairman, President, CFO, COO, or CRO); Group 3 (EVP, SVP, and Vice Chair); and Group 4 (Founder, Treasurer, Executive).

WPOWER50

Rank	Name	Age	Company	Title
1	Meg Whitman	49	eBay	CEO/Chairman
2	Anne Mulcahy	52	Xerox	CEO/Chairman
3	Brenda Barnes	51	Sara Lee	CEO/President
4	Oprah Winfrey	51	Harpo	Chairman
5	Andrea Jung	47	Avon	CEO/Chairman
⋮	⋮	⋮	⋮	
49	Safra Catz	43	Oracle	President
50	Kathy Cassidy	51	General Electric	Treasurer

Source: *Fortune*, Nov. 14, 2005.

a. Give the null and alternative hypothesis to be tested.
b. An EXCEL analysis of variance printout for the test, part **a**, is shown below. Locate the sample means for the

	A	B	C	D	E	F	G
1	Anova: Single Factor						
2							
3	SUMMARY						
4	Groups	Count	Sum	Average	Variance		
5	GROUP1	15	766	51.06667	27.20952		
6	GROUP2	18	866	48.11111	31.39869		
7	GROUP3	14	694	49.57143	12.26374		
8	GROUP4	3	168	56	49		
9							
10							
11	ANOVA						
12	Source of Variation	SS	df	MS	F	P-value	F crit
13	Between Groups	191.1403	3	63.71344	2.5004	0.071175	2.806843
14	Within Groups	1172.14	46	25.4813			
15							
16	Total	1363.28	49				

Excel Output for Exercise 8.25

four groups on the printout. Why is it insufficient to make a decision about the null hypothesis based solely on these sample means?

c. Locate the test statistic and *p*-value on the printout. Use this information to make the appropriate conclusion at $\alpha = .10$.

d. Use the data in the **WPOWER50** file to determine whether the ANOVA assumptions are reasonably satisfied.

8.26 Study of mutual fund performance. Mutual funds are classified as large-cap funds, medium-cap funds, or small-cap funds, depending on the capitalization of the companies in the fund. Hawaii Pacific University researchers S. Shi and M. Seiler investigated whether the average performance of a mutual fund is related to capitalization size (*American Business Review,* Jan. 2002). Independent random samples of 30 mutual funds were selected from each of the three fund groups and the 90-day rate of return determined for each fund. The data for the 90 funds were subjected to an analysis of variances, with the results shown in the ANOVA summary table.

Source	df	SS	MS	F	p-value
Fund group	2	409.566	204.783	6.965	.002
Error	87	2,557.860	29.401		
Total	89	2,967.426			

Source: S. W. W. Shi, and M. J. Seiler, "Growth and Value Style Comparison of U.S. Stock Mutual Funds." *American Business Review,* January, 2002 (Table 3).

a. State the null and alternative hypotheses for the ANOVA.

b. Give the rejection region for the test using $\alpha = .01$.

c. Make the appropriate conclusion using either the test statistic or the *p*-value.

Applying the Concepts—Intermediate

8.27 Income and road rage. The phenomenon of road rage has received much media attention in recent years. Is a driver's propensity to engage in road rage related to his or her income? Researchers at Mississippi State University attempted to answer this question by conducting a survey of a representative sample of over 1,000 U.S. adult drivers (*Accident Analysis and Prevention,* Vol. 34, 2002). Based on how often each driver engaged in certain road rage behaviors (e.g., making obscene gestures at, tailgating, and thinking about physically hurting another driver), a road rage score was assigned. (Higher scores indicate a greater pattern of road rage behavior.) The drivers were also grouped by annual income: under $30,000, between $30,000 and $60,000, and over $60,000. The data were subjected to an analysis of variance, with the results summarized in the table. Fully interpret the results. Is a driver's propensity to engage in road rage related to his or her income?

Income Group	Sample Size	Mean Road Rage Score
Under $30,000	379	4.60
$30,000 to $60,000	392	5.08
Over $60,000	267	5.15

ANOVA Results:	F − value = 3.90	p − value < .01

Source: Wells-Parker, E. et al. "An Exploratory Study of the Relationship between Road Rage and Crash Experience in a Representative Sample of US Drivers." *Accident Analysis and Prevention,* Vol. 34, 2002 (Table 2).

8.28 Safety of nuclear power plants. Researchers at Pennsylvania State University and Iowa State University jointly studied the attitudes of three groups of professionals that influence U.S. policy governing new technologies: scientists, journalists, and federal government policymakers (*American Journal of Political Science,* Jan. 1998). Random samples of 100 scientists, 100 journalists, and 100 government officials were asked about the safety of nuclear power plants. Responses were made on a 7-point scale, where 1 = very unsafe and 7 = very safe. The mean safety scores for the groups are scientists, 4.1; journalists, 3.7; government officials, 4.2.

a. Identify the response variable for this study.

b. How many treatments are included in this study? Describe them.

c. Specify the null and alternative hypotheses that should be used to investigate whether there are differences in the attitudes of scientists, journalists, and government officials regarding the safety of nuclear power plants.

d. The MSE for the sample data is 2.355. At least how large must MST be in order to reject the null hypothesis of the test of part **a** using $\alpha = .05$?

e. If the MST = 11.280, what is the approximate *p*-value of the test of part **a**?

DDT

8.29 Contamination of fish near a power plant's discharge. Refer to the U.S. Army Corps of Engineers data on contaminated fish saved in the **DDT** file. Recall that species (channel catfish, largemouth bass, or smallmouth buffalofish), length (in centimeters), weight (in grams), and DDT level (in parts per million) were measured for each of 144 captured fish.

a. Is there sufficient evidence to indicate differences among the mean lengths of the three fish species? Test using $\alpha = .05$.

b. Is there sufficient evidence to indicate differences among the mean weights of the three fish species? Test using $\alpha = .05$.

c. Is there sufficient evidence to indicate differences among the mean DDT levels of the three fish species? Test using $\alpha = .05$.

d. Check any assumptions required for the methodology used in parts **a–c** to be valid.

DIAMONDS

8.30 Diamonds sold at retail. Refer to the *Journal of Statistics Education* study of 308 diamonds for sale on the open market, Exercise 2.25 (p. 59). Recall that the **DIAMONDS** file contains information on the quantitative variables, size (number of carats) and price (in dollars), and on the qualitative variables, color (D, E, F, G, H, and I), clarity (IF, VS1, VS2, VVS1, and VVS2), and independent certification group (GIA, HRD, or IGI). Select one of the quantitative variables and one of the qualitative variables.

a. Set up the null and alternative hypotheses for determining whether the means of the quantitative variable differ for the levels of the qualitative variable.

b. Use the data in the **DIAMONDS** file to conduct the test, part **a**, at $\alpha = 10$. State the conclusion in the words of the problem.

c. Check any assumptions required for the methodology used in part **b** to be valid.

8.31 Effectiveness of sales closing techniques. Industrial sales professionals have long debated the effectiveness of various sales closing techniques. University of Akron researchers S. Hawes, J. Strong, and B. Winick investigated the impact of five different closing techniques and a no-close condition on the level of a sales prospect's trust in the salesperson (*Industrial Marketing Management,* Sept. 1996). Two of the five closing techniques were the *assumed close* and the *impending event technique.* In the former, the salesperson simply writes up the order or behaves as if the sale has been made. In the latter, the salesperson encourages the buyer to buy now before some future event occurs that makes the terms of the sale less favorable for the buyer. Sales scenarios were presented to a sample of 237 purchasing executives. Each subject received one of the five closing techniques or a scenario in which no close was achieved. After reading the sales scenario, each executive was asked to rate their level of trust in the salesperson on a 7-point scale. The table reports the six treatments employed in the study and the number of subjects receiving each treatment.

Treatments: Closing Techniques	Sample Size
1. No close	38
2. Impending event	36
3. Social validation	29
4. If-then	42
5. Assumed close	36
6. Either-or	56

a. The investigator's hypotheses were

   H_0: The salesperson's level of prospect trust is not influenced by the choice of closing method.

   H_a: The salesperson's level of prospect trust is influenced by the choice of closing method.

   Rewrite these hypotheses in the form required for an analysis of variance.

b. The researchers reported the ANOVA F statistic as $F = 2.21$. Is there sufficient evidence to reject H_0 at $\alpha = .05$?

c. What assumptions must be met in order for the test of part **a** to be valid?

d. Would you classify this experiment as observational or designed? Explain.

Applying the Concepts—Advanced

8.32 Activities of entrepreneurs at start-up. On average, over a million new businesses are started in the United States every year. An article in the *Journal of Business Venturing* (Vol. 11, 1996) reported on the activities of entrepreneurs during the organization creation process. Among the questions investigated were what activities and how many activities do entrepreneurs initiate in attempting to establish a new business? A total of 71 entrepreneurs were interviewed and divided into three groups: those who were successful in founding a new firm (34), those still actively trying to establish a firm (21), and those who tried to start a new firm but eventually gave up (16). The total number of activities undertaken (i.e., developed a business plan, sought funding, looked for facilities, etc.) by each group over a specified time period during organization creation was measured and the following incomplete ANOVA table produced:

Source	df	SS	MS	F
Groups	—	128.70	—	—
Error	—	27,124.52	—	

Source: Carter, N., Garner, W., and Reynolds, P. "Exploring Start-up Event Sequences." *Journal of Business Venturing,* Vol. 11, 1996, p. 159.

a. Complete the ANOVA table.

b. Do the data provide sufficient evidence to indicate that the total number of activities undertaken differed among the three groups of entrepreneurs? Test using $\alpha = .05$.

c. What is the *p*-value of the test you conducted in part **b**?

d. One of the conclusions of the study was that the behaviors of entrepreneurs who have successfully started a new company can be differentiated from the behaviors of entrepreneurs who failed. Do you agree? Justify your answer.

e. Classify this study as observational or experimental. How does this impact the strength of the conclusions drawn from the study?

8.3 Multiple Comparisons of Means

Consider a completely randomized design with three treatments, A, B, and C. Suppose we determine that the treatment means are statistically different via the ANOVA *F*-test of Section 8.2. To complete the analysis, we want to rank the three treatment means. As mentioned in Section 8.2, we start by placing confidence intervals on the difference between various pairs of treatment means in the experiment. In the three-treatment experiment, for example, we would construct confidence intervals for the following differences: $\mu_A - \mu_B$, $\mu_A - \mu_C$, and $\mu_B - \mu_C$.

Determining the Number of Pairwise Comparisons of Treatment Means

In general, if there are k treatment means, there are

$$c = \frac{k(k-1)}{2}$$

pairs of means that can be compared.

If we want to have $100(1 - \alpha)\%$ confidence that each of the c confidence intervals contains the true difference it is intended to estimate, we must use a smaller value of α for each individual confidence interval than we would use for a single interval. For example, suppose we want to rank the means of the three treatments, A, B, and C, with 95% confidence that all three confidence intervals comparing the means contain the true differences between the treatment means. Then each individual confidence interval will need to be constructed using a level of significance smaller than $\alpha = .05$ in order to have 95% confidence that the three intervals collectively include the true differences.*

To make **multiple comparisons of a set of treatment means,** we can use a number of procedures that, under various assumptions, ensure that the overall confidence level associated with all the comparisons remains at or above the specified $100(1 - \alpha)\%$ level. Three widely used techniques are the Bonferroni, Scheffé, and Tukey methods. For each of these procedures, the risk of making a Type I error applies to the comparisons of the treatment means in the experiment; thus, the value of α selected is called an **experimentwise error rate** (in contrast to a **comparisonwise error rate**).

The choice of a multiple comparisons method in ANOVA will depend on the type of experimental design used and the comparisons of interest to the analyst. For example, **Tukey** (1949) developed his procedure specifically for pairwise comparisons when the sample sizes of the treatments are equal. The **Bonferroni method** (see Miller, 1981), like the Tukey procedure, can be applied when pairwise comparisons are of interest; however, Bonferroni's method does not require equal sample sizes. **Scheffé** (1953) developed a more general procedure for comparing all possible linear combinations of treatment means (called *contrasts*). Consequently, when making pairwise comparisons, the confidence intervals produced by Scheffé's method will generally be wider than the Tukey or Bonferroni confidence intervals.

Biography

CARLO E. BONFERRONI (1892–1960)

Bonferroni Inequalities

During his childhood years in Turin, Italy, Carlo Bonferroni developed an aptitude for mathematics while studying music. He went on to obtain a degree in mathematics at the University of Turin. Bonferroni's first appointment as a professor of mathematics was at the University of Bari in 1923. Ten years later, he became chair of financial mathematics at the University of Florence, where he remained until his death. Bonferroni was a prolific writer, authoring over 65 research papers and books. His interest in statistics included various methods of calculating a mean and a correlation coefficient. Among statisticians, however, Bonferroni is most well known for developing his Bonferroni inequalities in probability theory in 1935. Later, other statisticians proposed using these inequalities for finding simultaneous confidence intervals, which led to the development of the Bonferroni multiple comparisons method in ANOVA. Bonferroni balanced these scientific accomplishments with his music, becoming an excellent pianist and composer.

The formulas for constructing confidence intervals for differences between treatment means using the Tukey, Bonferroni, or Scheffé method are beyond the scope of this text. However, these procedures (and many others) are available in the ANOVA programs of most statistical software packages. The programs generate a confidence interval for the difference between two treatment means for all possible pairs of treatments, based on the experimentwise error rate (α) selected by the analyst.

---

*The reason each interval must be formed at a higher confidence level than that specified for the collection of intervals can be demonstrated as follows:

$$P\{\text{At least one of } c \text{ intervals fails to contain the true difference}\}$$

$$= 1 - P\{\text{All } c \text{ intervals contain the true differences}\}$$

$$= 1 - (1 - \alpha)^c \geq \alpha$$

Thus, to make this probability of at least one failure equal to α, we must specify the individual levels of significance to be less than α.

EXAMPLE 8.6

Ranking Treatment Means in the Golf Ball Experiment

Problem   Refer to the completely randomized design of Example 8.4, in which we concluded that at least two of the four brands of golf balls are associated with different mean distances traveled when struck with a driver.

a. Use Tukey's multiple comparisons procedure to rank the treatment means with an overall confidence level of 95%.

b. Estimate the mean distance traveled for balls manufactured by the brand with the highest rank.

Solution

a. To rank the treatment means with an overall confidence level of .95, we require the experimentwise error rate of $\alpha = .05$. The confidence intervals generated by Tukey's method appear at the top of the SPSS printout, Figure 8.12. [Note: SPSS uses the number 1 for Brand A, 2 for Brand B, etc.] For any pair of means, μ_i and μ_j, SPSS computes two confidence intervals—one for $(\mu_i - \mu_j)$ and one for $(\mu_j - \mu_i)$. Only one of these intervals is necessary to decide whether the means differ significantly.

In this example, we have $k = 4$ brand means to compare. Consequently, the number of relevant pairwise comparisons—that is, the number of nonredundant

Multiple Comparisons

Dependent Variable: DISTANCE
Tukey HSD

(I) BRANDNUM	(J) BRANDNUM	Mean Difference (I-J)	Std. Error	Sig.	95% Confidence Interval Lower Bound	95% Confidence Interval Upper Bound
1	2	-10.2800*	2.0579	.000	-15.822	-4.738
	3	-19.1700*	2.0579	.000	-24.712	-13.628
	4	1.4600	2.0579	.893	-4.082	7.002
2	1	10.2800*	2.0579	.000	4.738	15.822
	3	-8.8900*	2.0579	.001	-14.432	-3.348
	4	11.7400*	2.0579	.000	6.198	17.282
3	1	19.1700*	2.0579	.000	13.628	24.712
	2	8.8900*	2.0579	.001	3.348	14.432
	4	20.6300*	2.0579	.000	15.088	26.172
4	1	-1.4600	2.0579	.893	-7.002	4.082
	2	-11.7400*	2.0579	.000	-17.282	-6.198
	3	-20.6300*	2.0579	.000	-26.172	-15.088

*. The mean difference is significant at the .05 level.

DISTANCE

Tukey HSD[a]

BRANDNUM	N	Subset for alpha = .05 — 1	Subset for alpha = .05 — 2	Subset for alpha = .05 — 3
4	10	249.320		
1	10	250.780		
2	10		261.060	
3	10			269.950
Sig.		.893	1.000	1.000

Means for groups in homogeneous subsets are displayed.
  a. Uses Harmonic Mean Sample Size = 10.000.

FIGURE 8.12
SPSS printout of Tukey's multiple comparisons for the golf ball data

TABLE 8.4 Pairwise Comparisons for Example 8.6

Brand Comparison	Confidence Interval
$(\mu_A - \mu_B)$	$(-15.82, -4.74)$
$(\mu_A - \mu_C)$	$(-24.71, -13.63)$
$(\mu_A - \mu_D)$	$(-4.08, 7.00)$
$(\mu_B - \mu_C)$	$(-14.43, -3.35)$
$(\mu_B - \mu_D)$	$(6.20, 17.28)$
$(\mu_C - \mu_D)$	$(15.09, 26.17)$

Brand	Sample Mean
C	270.0
B	261.1
A	250.8
D	249.3

FIGURE 8.13

Summary of Tukey multiple comparisons

confidence intervals—is $c = 4(3)/2 = 6$. These six intervals, highlighted in Figure 8.12, are given in Table 8.4.

We are 95% confident that the intervals *collectively* contain all the differences between the true brand mean distances. Note that intervals that contain 0, such as the (Brand A–Brand D) interval from -4.08 to 7.00, do not support a conclusion that the true brand mean distances differ. If both endpoints of the interval are positive, as with the (Brand B–Brand D) interval from 6.20 to 17.28, the implication is that the first brand (B) mean distance exceeds the second (D). Conversely, if both endpoints of the interval are negative, as with the (Brand A–Brand C) interval from -24.71 to -13.63, the implication is that the second brand (C) mean distance exceeds the first brand (A) mean distance.

A convenient summary of the results of the Tukey multiple comparisons is a listing of the brand means from highest to lowest, with a solid line connecting those that are *not* significantly different. This summary is shown in Figure 8.13. A similar summary is shown at the bottom of the SPSS printout, Figure 8.12. The interpretation is that brand C's mean distance exceeds all others; brand B's mean exceeds that of brands A and D; and the means of brands A and D do not differ significantly. All these inferences are made simultaneously with 95% confidence, the overall confidence level of the Tukey multiple comparisons.

b. Brand C is ranked highest; thus, we want a confidence interval for μ_C. Since the samples were selected independently in a completely randomized design, a confidence interval for an individual treatment mean is obtained with the one-sample t confidence interval of Section 5.3, using the mean square for error, MSE, as the measure of sampling variability for the experiment. A 95% confidence interval on the mean distance traveled by brand C (apparently the "longest ball" of those tested), is

$$\bar{x}_C \pm t_{.025}\sqrt{\frac{MSE}{n}}$$

where $n = 10$, $t_{.025} \approx 2$ (based on 36 degrees of freedom), and MSE $= 21.175$ (obtained from the Excel printout, Figure 8.8). Substituting, we obtain

$$270.0 \pm (2)\sqrt{\frac{21.175}{10}}$$

$$270.0 \pm 2.9 \text{ or } (267.1, 272.9)$$

Thus, we are 95% confident that the true mean distance traveled for brand C is between 267.1 and 272.9 yards, when hit with a driver by Iron Byron.

Look Back The easiest way to create a summary table like the one in Figure 8.13 is to first list the treatment means in rank order. Begin with the largest mean and compare it to (in order) the second largest mean, the third largest mean, and so on, by examining the appropriate confidence intervals shown on the computer printout. If a confidence interval contains 0, then connect the two means with a line. (These two means are not significantly different.) Continue in this manner by comparing the second largest mean with the third largest, fourth largest, and so on, until all possible $c = (k)(k + 1)/2$ comparisons are made.

Now Work Exercise 8.39 ▬

Remember that the Tukey method—designed for comparing pairs of treatment means with equal sample sizes—is just one of numerous multiple comparisons procedures available. Another technique may be more appropriate for the experimental design you employ. Consult the references for details on these other methods and when they should be applied. Guidelines for using the Tukey, Bonferroni, and Scheffé methods are given in the box.

Guidelines for Selecting a Multiple Comparisons Method in ANOVA

Method	Treatment Sample Sizes	Types of Comparisons
Tukey	Equal	Pairwise
Bonferroni	Equal or unequal	Pairwise
Scheffé	Equal or unequal	General contrasts

Note: For equal sample sizes and pairwise comparisons, Tukey's method will yield simultaneous confidence intervals with the smallest width and the Bonferroni intervals will have smaller widths than the Scheffé intervals.

STATISTICS IN ACTION REVISITED

Ranking the Mean Ethics Responses for the Five Downsize Groups

In the previous Statistics in Action Revisited (p. 494), we used an ANOVA to test the null hypothesis that the mean ethics scores of five groups of employees are equal. Recall that these five groups were named (1) Casualties, (2) Survivors, (3) Implementors/casualties, (4) Implementors/survivors, and (5) Formulators. The ANOVA F-test resulted in a rejection of the null hypothesis, leading the researchers to conclude that the mean ethics scores of the five groups were significantly different. Now we follow up the ANOVA with multiple comparisons of the treatment (group) means. Since the group sample sizes are unequal, we employ the Bonferroni method.

The SPSS printout for this analysis, using an experimentwise error rate of .05, is displayed in Figure SIA8.4. The relevant confidence intervals for all possible differences between treatment means are highlighted on the printout. Note that there are $c = (k)(k - 1)/2 = (5)(4)/2 = 10$ comparisons of interest. Significant differences are indicated on the SPSS printout with an asterisk (*) in the "Mean Difference" column; these differences are associated with confidence intervals that do not include 0. The results show that groups 4 and 5 both have significantly larger mean scores than those for groups 1, 2, and 3. Also, there is no significant difference between the mean scores for groups 4 and 5; and there are no significant differences among mean scores for groups 1, 2, and 3. Consequently, we can rank the group means as shown in Table SIA8.2.

The researchers' original hypotheses about the five groups are repeated here. You can see that the rankings in Table SIA8.2 provide full support for these hypotheses.

H_1: Survivors', Casualties', and Implementors/casualties' perceptions of the ethics statement on downsizing will not differ significantly (i.e., no differences among groups 1, 2, and 3).

H_2: Formulators' and Implementors/survivors' perceptions of the ethics statement on downsizing will not

Multiple Comparisons

Dependent Variable: ETHICS
Bonferroni

(I) GROUPNUM	(J) GROUPNUM	Mean Difference (I-J)	Std. Error	Sig.	95% Confidence Interval	
					Lower Bound	Upper Bound
1	2	-.06	.191	1.000	-.60	.49
	3	.19	.246	1.000	-.50	.89
	4	-.76*	.231	.012	-1.41	-.10
	5	-1.08*	.236	.000	-1.75	-.42
2	1	.06	.191	1.000	-.49	.60
	3	.25	.230	1.000	-.40	.91
	4	-.70*	.214	.013	-1.31	-.09
	5	-1.03*	.219	.000	-1.65	-.40
3	1	-.19	.246	1.000	-.89	.50
	2	-.25	.230	1.000	-.91	.40
	4	-.95*	.264	.004	-1.70	-.20
	5	-1.28*	.268	.000	-2.04	-.52
4	1	.76*	.231	.012	.10	1.41
	2	.70*	.214	.013	.09	1.31
	3	.95*	.264	.004	.20	1.70
	5	-.33	.255	1.000	-1.05	.40
5	1	1.08*	.236	.000	.42	1.75
	2	1.03*	.219	.000	.40	1.65
	3	1.28*	.268	.000	.52	2.04
	4	.33	.255	1.000	-.40	1.05

*. The mean difference is significant at the .05 level.

Figure SIA8.4
SPSS Bonferroni multiple comparisons of means for the five treatment groups

TABLE SIA8.2 Ranking of Group Means Based on the Bonferroni Analysis

1.59	1.79	1.84	2.54	2.87
Implementors/casualties	Casualties	Survivors	Implementors/survivors	Formulators
Group 3	**Group 1**	**Group 2**	**Group 4**	**Group 5**

differ significantly (i.e., no difference between group 4 and group 5).

H_3: Survivors', Casualties', and Implementors/casualties' perceptions of the ethics statement on

downsizing will differ significantly from Formulators' and Implementors/survivors' perceptions (i.e., groups 4 and 5 are different from groups 1, 2, and 3).

Exercises 8.33–8.45

Learning the Mechanics

8.33 Consider a completely randomized design with k treatments. Assume all pairwise comparisons of treatment means are to be made using a multiple comparisons procedure. Determine the total number of pairwise comparisons for the following values of k.

a. $k = 3$ **b.** $k = 5$
c. $k = 4$ **d.** $k = 10$

8.34 Define an experimentwise error rate.

8.35 Define a comparisonwise error rate.

8.36 Consider a completely randomized design with five treatments, A, B, C, D, and E. The ANOVA F-test revealed significant differences among the means. A multiple comparisons procedure was used to compare all possible pairs of treatment means at $\alpha = .05$. The ranking of the five treatment means is summarized below. Identify which pairs of means are significantly different.

a. A C E B D
b. A C E B D
c. A C E B D
d. A C E B D

Applying the Concepts—Basic

8.37 College tennis recruiting with a team Web site. Refer to the *Sport Journal* (Winter 2004) study to compare the attitudes of Division I, Division II, and Division III college tennis coaches toward team Web sites as recruiting tools, Exercise 8.22 (p. 497). The mean responses (measured on a 7-point scale) to the statement, "the Prospective Student-Athlete Form on the Web site contributes very little to the recruiting process," are listed and ranked below. The results were obtained using a multiple comparisons procedure with an experiment wise error rate of .05. Interpret the results practically.

Mean:	4.51	3.60	3.21
Division:	I	II	III

8.38 Robots trained to behave like ants. Refer to the *Nature* (Aug. 2000) study of robots trained to behave like ants, Exercise 8.24 (p. 498). Multiple comparisons of mean energy expended for the four colony sizes were conducted using an experimentwise error rate of .05. The results are summarized below.

Sample mean:	.97	.95	.93	.80
Group Size:	3	6	9	12

a. How many pairwise comparisons are conducted in this analysis?

b. Interpret the results shown in the table.

8.39 Study of mutual fund performance. Refer to the *American Business Review* (Jan. 2002) comparison of large-cap, medium-cap, and small-cap mutual funds, Exercise 8.26 (p. 499). Using an experimentwise error rate of .05, Tukey confidence intervals for the difference between mean rates of return for all possible pairs of fund types are given below.

Comparison	Tukey confidence interval
$\mu_{Large} - \mu_{Medium}$	$(-.1847, 5.3807)$
$\mu_{Large} - \mu_{Small}$	$(2.4426, 8.0080)$
$\mu_{Medium} - \mu_{Small}$	$(-.1554, 5.4100)$

a. Why is the Tukey multiple comparisons method preferred over another method?

b. Is there a significant difference between the treatment means for large-cap and medium-cap mutual funds? Explain.

c. Is there a significant difference between the treatment means for large-cap and small-cap mutual funds? Explain.

d. Is there a significant difference between the treatment means for medium-cap and small-cap mutual funds? Explain.

e. Use your answers to parts **b–d** to rank the treatment means.

f. Give a measure of reliability for the inference in part **e**.

8.40 Safety of nuclear power plants. Refer to the *American Journal of Political Science* (Jan. 1998) study of the attitudes of three groups of professionals (scientists, journalists, and federal government policymakers) regarding the safety of nuclear power plants, Exercise 8.28 (p. 499). The mean safety scores for the groups were:

Government officials	4.2
Scientists	4.1
Journalists	3.7

a. Determine the number of pairwise comparisons of treatment means that can be made in this study.

b. Using an experimentwise error rate of $\alpha = .05$, Tukey's minimum significant difference for comparing means is .23—that is, if the difference between the sample means exceeds .23, the treatment means are statistically different. Use this information to conduct a multiple comparisons procedure of the safety score means. Fully interpret the results.

Applying the Concepts—Intermediate

🔘 **TVADRECALL**

8.41 Study of recall of TV commercials. Refer to the *Journal of Applied Psychology* (June 2002) completely randomized design study to compare the mean commercial recall scores of viewers of three TV programs, Exercise 8.23 (p. 497). Recall that one program had a violent content code (V) rating, one had a sex content code (S) rating, and one was a neutral TV program. The researchers conducted multiple comparisons of the three mean recall scores using Tukey's method.

a. How many pairwise comparisons are made in this study?

b. The multiple comparison results, using an experimentwise error rate of .05, are shown in the MINITAB printout on p. 507. Locate the confidence interval for the comparison of the V and S groups. Interpret this result, practically.

c. Repeat part **b** for the remaining comparisons. Which of the groups has the largest mean recall score?

d. In the journal article, the researchers concluded that "memory for [television] commercials is impaired after watching violent or sexual programming." Do you agree?

8.42 Income and road rage. Refer to the *Accident Analysis and Prevention* (Vol. 34, 2002) study of road rage, Exercise 8.27 (p. 499). Recall that the mean road rage scores of drivers in the three income groups, under $30 thousand, between $30 and $60 thousand, and over $60 thousand, were 4.60, 5.08, and 5.15, respectively.

a. An experimentwise error rate of .01 was used to rank the three means. Give a practical interpretation of this error rate.

b. How many pairwise comparisons are necessary to compare the three means? List them.

c. A multiple comparisons procedure revealed that the means for the two income groups, $30,000–$60,000 and over $60,000, were not significantly different. All other pairs of means were found to be significantly different. Summarize these results in table form.

d. Which of the comparisons of part **b** will yield a confidence interval that does not contain 0?

🔘 **DDT**

8.43 Contamination of fish near a power plant's discharge. Refer to the U.S. Army Corps of Engineers data on conta-

MINITAB Output for Exercise 8.41

```
Tukey 95% Simultaneous Confidence Intervals
All Pairwise Comparisons

Individual confidence level = 98.01%
```

```
VIOLENT subtracted from:

          Lower   Center   Upper   -------+---------+---------+---------+--
SEX      -0.923   -0.370   0.183          (----*----)
NEUTRAL   0.530    1.083   1.636                      (----*----)
                                   -------+---------+---------+---------+--
                                      -1.2       0.0       1.2       2.4
```

```
SEX subtracted from:

          Lower   Center   Upper   -------+---------+---------+---------+--
NEUTRAL   0.901    1.454   2.007                    (---*----)
                                   -------+---------+---------+---------+--
                                      -1.2       0.0       1.2       2.4
```

minated fish saved in the **DDT** file. In Exercise 8.29 (p. 499) you ran ANOVAs to compare three species (channel catfish, largemouth bass, or smallmouth buffalofish) on the dependent variables length (in centimeters), weight (in grams), and DDT level (in parts per million). For those dependent variables that resulted in a significant ANOVA F-test, perform multiple comparisons of the treatment means. Use an experimentwise error rate of .05. Interpret the results practically.

DIAMONDS

8.44 Diamonds sold at retail. Refer to the *Journal of Statistics Education* data on diamonds for sale on the open market saved in the **DIAMONDS** file. In Exercise 8.30 (p. 499) you ran an ANOVA to compare levels of a qualitative variable (either Color, Clarity, or Certification group) on the mean of a quantitative variable (either carat size or price). Follow up the analysis with multiple comparisons of the treatment means. Use an experimentwise error rate of .05. Interpret the results practically.

8.45 Effectiveness of sales closing techniques. Refer to the *Industrial Marketing Management* (Sept. 1996) comparison of six sales closing techniques, Exercise 8.31 (p. 500). The "level of trust" means for prospects of salespeople using each of the six closing techniques are listed in the table. A multiple comparisons of means analysis was conducted (at $\alpha = .05$), with the results shown in the third column of the table. Fully interpret the results.

Treatments: Closing Technique	Mean Level of Trust	Differing Treatments
1. No close	4.67	1 from 5 and 6
2. Impending event	4.48	2 from 6
3. Social validation	4.40	No differences
4. If-then	4.33	No differences
5. Assumed close	4.04	5 from 1
6. Either-or	3.98	6 from 1 and 2

Source: Hawes, S. M., Strong, J. T., and Winick, B. S. "Do Closing Techniques Diminish Prospect Trust?" *Industrial Marketing Management,* Vol. 25, No. 5, Sept. 1996, p. 355.

8.4 The Randomized Block Design

If the completely randomized design results in nonrejection of the null hypothesis that the treatment means are equal because the sampling variability (as measured by MSE) is large, we may want to consider an experimental design that better controls the variability. In contrast to the selection of independent samples of experimental units specified by the completely randomized design, the *randomized block design* utilizes experimental units that are *matched sets*, assigning one from each set to each treatment. The matched sets of experimental units are called *blocks*. The theory behind the randomized block design is that the sampling variability of the experimental units in each block will be reduced, in turn reducing the measure of error, MSE.

Definition 8.8

The **randomized block design** consists of a two-step procedure:

1. Matched sets of experimental units, called **blocks,** are formed, each block consisting of k experimental units (where k is the number of treatments). The b blocks should consist of experimental units that are as similar as possible.

2. One experimental unit from each block is randomly assigned to each treatment, resulting in a total of $n = bk$ responses.

For example, if we wish to compare SAT scores of female and male high school seniors, we could select independent random samples of five females and five males, and analyze the results of the completely randomized design as outlined in Section 8.2. Or, we could select matched pairs of females and males according to their scholastic records, and analyze the SAT scores of the pairs. For instance, we could select pairs of students with approximately the same GPAs from the same high school. Five such pairs (blocks) are depicted in Table 8.5. Note that this is just a *paired difference experiment*, first discussed in Section 7.3.

TABLE 8.5 Randomized Block Design: SAT Score Comparison

Block	Female SAT Score	Male SAT Score	Block Mean
1 (School A, 2.75 GPA)	540	530	535
2 (School B, 3.00 GPA)	570	550	560
3 (School C, 3.25 GPA)	590	580	585
4 (School D, 3.50 GPA)	640	620	630
5 (School E, 3.75 GPA)	690	690	690
Treatment Mean	606	594	

As before, the variation between the treatment means is measured by squaring the distance between each treatment mean and the overall mean, multiplying each squared distance by the number of measurements for the treatment and summing over treatments:

$$\text{SST} = \sum_{i=1}^{k} b(\bar{x}_{T_i} - \bar{x})^2$$

$$= 5(606 - 600)^2 + 5(594 - 600)^2 = 360$$

where $\bar{x}_{T_i}$ represents the sample mean for the ith treatment, b (the number of blocks) is the number of measurements for each treatment, and k is the number of treatments.

The blocks also account for some of the variation among the different responses— that is, just as SST measures the variation between the female and male means, we can calculate a measure of variation among the five block means representing different schools and scholastic abilities. Analogous to the computation of SST, we sum the squares of the differences between each block mean and the overall mean, multiplying each squared difference by the number of measurements for each block, and sum over blocks to calculate the **Sum of Squares for Blocks** (SSB):

$$\text{SSB} = \sum_{i=1}^{b} k(\bar{x}_{B_i} - \bar{x})^2$$

$$= 2(535 - 600)^2 + 2(560 - 600)^2 + 2(585 - 600)^2$$
$$+ 2(630 - 600)^2 + 2(690 - 600)^2$$
$$= 30{,}100$$

where $\bar{x}_{B_i}$ represents the sample mean for the ith block and k (the number of treatments) is the number of measurements in each block. As we expect, the variation in SAT scores attributable to Schools and Levels of scholastic achievement is apparently large.

Now, we want to compare the variability attributed to treatments with that which is attributed to sampling variability. In a randomized block design, the sampling variability is measured by subtracting that portion attributed to treatments and blocks from the Total Sum of Squares, SS(Total). The total variation is the sum of squared differences of each measurement from the overall mean:

$$SS(\text{Total}) = \sum_{i=1}^{n}(x_i - \bar{x})^2$$
$$= (540 - 600)^2 + (530 - 600)^2 + (570 - 600)^2 + (550 - 600)^2$$
$$+ \cdots + (690 - 600)^2$$
$$= 30{,}600$$

Then the variation attributable to sampling error is found by subtraction:

$$SSE = SS(\text{Total}) - SST - SSB = 30{,}600 - 360 - 30{,}100 = 140$$

In summary, the Total Sum of Squares—30,600—is divided into three components: 360 attributed to treatments (Gender), 30,100 attributed to blocks (Scholastic ability), and 140 attributed to sampling error.

The mean squares associated with each source of variability are obtained by dividing the sum of squares by the appropriate number of degrees of freedom. The partitioning of the Total Sum of Squares and the total degrees of freedom for a randomized block experiment is summarized in Figure 8.14.

To determine whether we can reject the null hypothesis that the treatment means are equal in favor of the alternative that at least two of them differ, we calculate

$$MST = \frac{SST}{k - 1} = \frac{360}{2 - 1} = 360$$

$$MSE = \frac{SSE}{n - b - k + 1} = \frac{140}{10 - 5 - 2 + 1} = 35$$

The F-ratio that is used to test the hypothesis is

$$F = \frac{360}{35} - 10.29$$

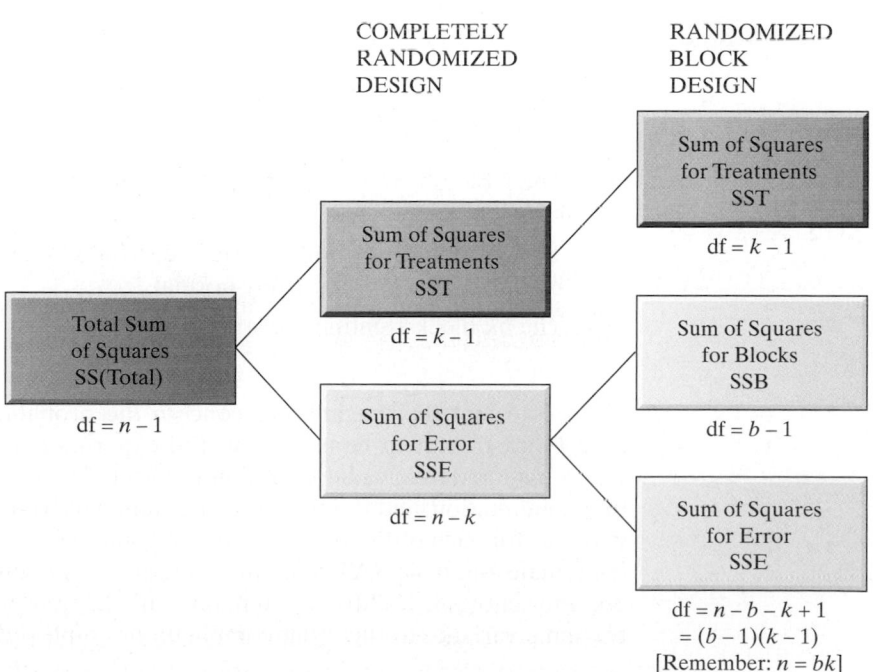

FIGURE 8.14

Partitioning of the total sum of squares for the randomized block design

Comparing this ratio to the tabled F value corresponding to $\alpha = .05$, $v_1 = (k - 1) = 1$ degree of freedom in the numerator, and $v_2 = (n - b - k + 1) = 4$ degrees of freedom in the denominator, we find that

$$F = 10.29 > F_{.05} = 7.71$$

which indicates that we should reject the null hypothesis and conclude that the mean SAT scores differ for females and males.

If you review Section 7.3, you will find that the analysis of a paired difference experiment results in a one-sample t-test on the differences between the treatment responses within each block. Applying the procedure to the differences between female and male scores in Table 8.5, we find

$$t = \frac{\bar{x}_d}{s_d/\sqrt{n_d}} = \frac{12}{\sqrt{70}/\sqrt{5}} = 3.207$$

At the .05 level of significance with $(n_d - 1) = 4$ degrees of freedom,

$$t = 3.21 > t_{.025} = 2.776$$

Since $t^2 = (3.207)^2 = 10.29$ and $t_{.025}^2 = (2.776)^2 = 7.71$, we find that the paired difference t-test and the ANOVA F-test are equivalent, with both the calculated test statistics and the rejection region related by the formula $F = t^2$. The difference between the tests is that the paired difference t-test can be used to compare only two treatments in a randomized block design, whereas the F-test can be applied to *two or more* treatments in a randomized block design. The F-test is summarized in the following box.

ANOVA *F*-Test to Compare *k* Treatment Means: Randomized Block Design

H_0: $\mu_1 = \mu_2 = \cdots = \mu_k$

H_a: At least two treatment means differ

Test statistic: $F = \dfrac{\text{MST}}{\text{MSE}}$

Rejection region: $F > F_\alpha$, where F_α is based on $(k - 1)$ numerator degrees of freedom and $(n - b - k + 1)$ denominator degrees of freedom.

Conditions Required for a Valid ANOVA *F*-test: Randomized Block Design

1. The b blocks are randomly selected, and all k treatments are applied (in random order) to each block.
2. The distributions of observations corresponding to all bk block-treatment combinations are approximately normal.
3. The bk block-treatment distributions have equal variances.

Note that the assumptions concern the probability distributions associated with each block-treatment combination. The experimental unit selected for each combination is assumed to have been randomly selected from all possible experimental units for that combination, and the response is assumed to be normally distributed with the same variance for each of the block-treatment combinations. For example, the F-test comparing female and male SAT score means requires the scores for each combination of gender and scholastic ability (e.g., females with 3.25 GPA) to be normally distributed with the same variance as the other combinations employed in the experiment.

The calculation formulas for randomized block designs are given in Appendix C. We will rely on statistical software packages to analyze randomized block designs and to obtain the necessary ingredients for testing the null hypothesis that the treatment means are equal.

EXAMPLE 8.7
Experimental Design Principles

Problem Refer to Examples 8.4–8.6. Suppose the USGA wants to compare the mean distances associated with the four brands of golf balls when struck by a driver but wishes to employ human golfers rather than the robot Iron Byron. Assume that 10 balls of each brand are to be utilized in the experiment.

  a. Explain how a completely randomized design could be employed.

  b. Explain how a randomized block design could be employed.

  c. Which design is likely to provide more information about the differences among the brand mean distances?

Solution

  a. Since the completely randomized design calls for independent samples, we can employ such a design by randomly selecting 40 golfers and then randomly assigning 10 golfers to each of the four brands. Finally, each golfer will strike the ball of the assigned brand, and the distance will be recorded. The design is illustrated in Figure 8.15(a).

  b. The randomized block design employs blocks of relatively homogeneous experimental units. For example, we could randomly select 10 golfers, and permit each golfer to hit four balls, one of each brand, in a random sequence. Then each golfer is a block, with each treatment (brand) assigned to each block (golfer). The design is summarized in Figure 8.15(b).

  c. Because we expect much more variability among distances generated by "real" golfers than by Iron Byron, we would expect the randomized block design to control the variability better than the completely randomized design—that is, with 40

BRAND

a. Completely randomized design

FIGURE 8.15

Illustration of completely randomized design and randomized block design: comparison of four golf ball brands

BRAND

		A	B	C	D
	1	Hit 3	Hit 1	Hit 4	Hit 2
	2	Hit 2	Hit 4	Hit 3	Hit 1
Golfers	⋮	⋮	⋮	⋮	⋮
	10	Hit 4	Hit 3	Hit 1	Hit 2

b. Randomized block design

different golfers, we would expect the sampling variability among the measured distances within each brand to be greater than that among the four distances generated by each of 10 golfers hitting one ball of each brand.

Now Work Exercise 8.50a,b

EXAMPLE 8.8

Comparing Golf Ball Brands with a Randomized Block Design

Problem   Refer to Example 8.7. Suppose the randomized block design of part **b** is employed, utilizing a random sample of 10 golfers, with each golfer using a driver to hit four balls, one of each brand, in a random sequence.

a. Set up a test of the research hypothesis that the brand mean distances differ. Use $\alpha = .05$.

b. The data for the experiment are given in Table 8.6. Use statistical software to analyze the data, and conduct the test set up in part **a**.

 GOLFRBD

TABLE 8.6   Distance Data for Randomized Block Design

Golfer (Block)	Brand A	Brand B	Brand C	Brand D
1	202.4	203.2	223.7	203.6
2	242.0	248.7	259.8	240.7
3	220.4	227.3	240.0	207.4
4	230.0	243.1	247.7	226.9
5	191.6	211.4	218.7	200.1
6	247.7	253.0	268.1	244.0
7	214.8	214.8	233.9	195.8
8	245.4	243.6	257.8	227.9
9	224.0	231.5	238.2	215.7
10	252.2	255.2	265.4	245.2
Sample Means	227.0	233.2	245.3	220.7

Solution

a. We want to test whether the data in Table 8.6 provide sufficient evidence to conclude that the brand mean distances differ. Denoting the population mean of the ith brand by μ_i, we test

$H_0: \mu_1 = \mu_2 = \mu_3 = \mu_4$

H_a: The mean distances differ for at least two of the brands

The test statistic compares the variation among the four treatment (brand) means to the sampling variability within each of the treatments.

Test statistic: $F = \dfrac{\text{MST}}{\text{MSE}}$

Rejection region: $F > F_\alpha = F_{.05}$, with $v_1 = (k - 1) = 3$ numerator degrees of freedom and $v_2 = (n - k - b + 1) = 27$ denominator degrees of freedom. From Table VIII of Appendix B, we find $F_{.05} = 2.96$. Thus, we will reject H_0 if $F > 2.96$.

The assumptions necessary to ensure the validity of the test are as follows: (1) The probability distributions of the distances for each brand–golfer combination are normal. (2) The variances of the distance probability distributions for each brand–golfer combination are equal.

FIGURE 8.16

MINITAB randomized block design ANOVA: golf ball brand comparison

Two-way ANOVA: DISTANCE versus BRAND, GOLFER

```
Source   DF      SS        MS      F       P
BRAND     3    3298.7   1099.55   54.31   0.000
GOLFER    9   12073.9   1341.54   66.26   0.000
Error    27     546.6     20.25
Total    39   15919.2

S = 4.499    R-Sq = 96.57%    R-Sq(adj) = 95.04%
```

b. MINITAB was used to analyze the data in Table 8.6, and the result is shown in Figure 8.16. The values of MST and MSE (highlighted on the printout) are 1,099.6 and 20.2, respectively. The F-ratio for Brand (also highlighted on the printout) is $F = 54.31$, which exceeds the tabled value of 2.96. We therefore reject the null hypothesis at the $\alpha = .05$ level of significance, concluding that at least two of the brands differ with respect to mean distance traveled when struck by the driver.

Look Back The result of part **b** is confirmed by noting that the observed significance level of the test, highlighted on the printout, is $p \approx 0$.

Now Work Exercise 8.50c

The results of an ANOVA can be summarized in a simple tabular format, similar to that utilized for the completely randomized design in Section 8.2. The general form of the table is shown in Table 8.7, and that for Example 8.8 is given in Table 8.8. Note that the randomized block design is characterized by three sources of variation—Treatments, Blocks, and Error—which sum to the Total Sum of Squares. We hope that employing blocks of experimental units will reduce the error variability, thereby making the test for comparing treatment means more powerful.

When the F-test results in the rejection of the null hypothesis that the treatment means are equal, we will usually want to compare the various pairs of treatment means to determine which specific pairs differ. We can employ a multiple comparisons procedure as in Section 8.3 The number of pairs of means to be compared will again be $c = k(k-1)/2$, where k is the number of treatment means. In Example 8.8, $c = 4(3)/2 = 6$; that is, there are six pairs of golf ball brand means to be compared.

TABLE 8.7 General ANOVA Summary Table for a Randomized Block Design

Source	df	SS	MS	F
Treatment	$k - 1$	SST	MST	MST/MSE
Block	$b - 1$	SSB	MSB	
Error	$n - k - b + 1$	SSE	MSE	
Total	$n - 1$	SS(Total)		

TABLE 8.8 ANOVA Table for Example 8.8

Source	df	SS	MS	F	p
Treatment (Brand)	3	3,298.7	1,099.6	54.31	.000
Block (Golfer)	9	12,073.9	1,341.5		
Error	27	546.6	20.2		
Total	39	15,919.2			

EXAMPLE 8.9

Ranking Golf Ball Brand Means in a Randomized Block Design

Problem Bonferroni's procedure is used to compare the mean distances of the four golf ball brands in Example 8.8. The resulting confidence intervals, with an experimentwise error rate of $\alpha = .05$, are shown in the SPSS printout, Figure 8.17. Interpret the results.

Multiple Comparisons

Dependent Variable: DISTANCE

Bonferroni

(I) BRAND	(J) BRAND	Mean Difference (I-J)	Std. Error	Sig.	95% Confidence Interval Lower Bound	95% Confidence Interval Upper Bound
A	B	-6.1300*	2.01222	.031	-11.8586	-.4014
	C	-18.2800*	2.01222	.000	-24.0086	-12.5514
	D	6.3200*	2.01222	.024	.5914	12.0486
B	A	6.1300*	2.01222	.031	.4014	11.8586
	C	-12.1500*	2.01222	.000	-17.8786	-6.4214
	D	12.4500*	2.01222	.000	6.7214	18.1786
C	A	18.2800*	2.01222	.000	12.5514	24.0086
	B	12.1500*	2.01222	.000	6.4214	17.8786
	D	24.6000*	2.01222	.000	18.8714	30.3286
D	A	-6.3200*	2.01222	.024	-12.0486	-.5914
	B	-12.4500*	2.01222	.000	-18.1786	-6.7214
	C	-24.6000*	2.01222	.000	-30.3286	-18.8714

Based on observed means.

*. The mean difference is significant at the .05 level.

FIGURE 8.17

SPSS listing of Bonferroni confidence intervals: follow-up to randomized block design ANOVA

Brand	Mean
C	245.3
B	233.2
A	227.0
D	220.7

FIGURE 8.18

Listing of brand means for randomized block design [Note: All differences are statistically significant.]

Solution Note that 12 confidence intervals are shown in Figure 8.17 rather than 6. Recall that SPSS computes intervals for both $\mu_j - \mu_i, i \neq j$. Only half of these are necessary to conduct the analysis, and these are highlighted on the printout. The intervals (rounded) are summarized below:

$$(A - B): \quad (-11.9, -.4)$$
$$(A - C): \quad (-24.0, -12.6)$$
$$(A - D): \quad (.6, 12.0)$$
$$(B - C): \quad (-17.9, -6.4)$$
$$(B - D): \quad (6.7, 18.2)$$
$$(C - D): \quad (18.9, 30.3)$$

Note that we are 95% confident that all the brand means differ because none of the intervals contains 0. The listing of the brand means in Figure 8.18 has no lines connecting them because there are no nonsignificant differences at the .05 level.

Now Work Exercise 8.50d

Unlike the completely randomized design, the randomized block design cannot, in general, be used to estimate individual treatment means. Whereas the completely randomized design employs a random sample for each treatment, the randomized block design does not necessarily employ a random sample of experimental units for each treatment. The experimental units within the blocks are assumed to be randomly selected, but the blocks themselves may not be randomly selected.

TABLE 8.9 ANOVA Table for Randomized Block Design: Test for Blocks Included

Source	df	SS	MS	F	p
Treatments (Brands)	3	3,298.7	1,099.6	54.31	.000
Blocks (Golfers)	9	12,073.9	1,341.5	66.26	.000
Error	27	546.6	20.2		
Total	39	15,919.2			

We can, however, test the hypothesis that the block means are significantly different. We simply compare the variability attributable to differences among the block means to that associated with sampling variability. The ratio of MSB to MSE is an F-ratio similar to that formed in testing treatment means. The F statistic is compared to a tabled value for a specific value of α, with numerator degrees of freedom $(b-1)$ and denominator degrees of freedom $(n-k-b+1)$. The test is usually given on the same printout as the test for treatment means. Refer to the MINITAB printout in Figure 8.18, and note that the test statistic for comparing the block means is

$$F = \frac{MSB}{MSE} = \frac{MS(\text{Golfers})}{MS(\text{Error})} = \frac{1,341.5}{20.2} = 66.26$$

with a p-value of .000. Since $\alpha = .05$ exceeds this p-value, we conclude that the block means are different. The results of the test are summarized in Table 8.9.

In the golf example, the test for block means confirms our suspicion that the golfers vary significantly; therefore, the use of the block design was a good decision. However, be careful not to conclude that the block design was a mistake if the F-test for blocks does not result in rejection of the null hypothesis that the block means are the same. Remember that the possibility of a Type II error exists, and we are not controlling its probability as we are the probability α of a Type I error. If the experimenter believes that the experimental units are more homogeneous within blocks than between blocks, then he or she should use the randomized block design regardless of the results of a single test comparing the block means.

The procedure for conducting an analysis of variance for a randomized block design is summarized in the next box. Remember that the hallmark of this design is the utilization of blocks of homogeneous experimental units in which each treatment is represented.

Steps for Conducting an ANOVA for a Randomized Block Design

1. Be sure the design consists of blocks (preferably, blocks of homogeneous experimental units) and that each treatment is randomly assigned to one experimental unit in each block.

2. If possible, check the assumptions of normality and equal variances for all block-treatment combinations. [*Note:* This may be difficult to do since the design will likely have only one observation for each block-treatment combination.]

3. Create an ANOVA summary table that specifies the variability attributable to Treatments, Blocks, and Error, and that leads to the calculation of the F statistic to test the null hypothesis that the treatment means are equal in the population. Use a statistical software package or the calculation formulas in Appendix C to obtain the necessary numerical ingredients.

4. If the F-test leads to the conclusion that the means differ, use the Bonferroni, Tukey, or similar procedure to conduct multiple comparisons of as many of the pairs of means as you wish. Use the results to summarize the statistically significant differences among the treatment means. Remember that, in general, the randomized block design cannot be used to form confidence intervals for individual treatment means.

5. If the *F*-test leads to the nonrejection of the null hypothesis that the treatment means are equal, several possibilities exist:

   a. The treatment means are equal—that is, the null hypothesis is true.

   b. The treatment means really differ, but other important factors affecting the response are not accounted for by the randomized block design. These factors inflate the sampling variability, as measured by MSE, resulting in smaller values of the *F* statistic. Either increase the sample size for each treatment or conduct an experiment that accounts for the other factors affecting the response (as in Section 8.5). Do not automatically reach the former conclusion, since the possibility of a Type II error must be considered if you accept H_0.

6. If desired, conduct the *F*-test of the null hypothesis that the block means are equal. Rejection of this hypothesis lends statistical support to the utilization of the randomized block design.

Note: It is often difficult to check whether the assumptions for a randomized block design are satisfied. When you feel these assumptions are likely to be violated, a nonparametric procedure is advisable.

What Do You Do when Assumptions Are Not Satisfied for the Analysis of Variance for a Randomized Block Design?

Answer: Use a nonparametric statistical method such as the Friedman F_r test of Section 14.6.

ACTIVITY 8.2: **Randomized Block Design**

In this Activity, you will revisit the Activity 8.1 (p. 481). For each of the designed experiments in Exercises 2 and 3 of Designed Versus Observational Experiments on page 481, you will rework the experiment to have a randomized block design. Explain how you will choose your experimental units from each population. Then describe the criteria you would use to split the experimental units into matched sets. How do you determine which experimental unit in each matched set receives each level of treatment? What data is collected and how is it compared? Do you believe that there is any benefit to the block design? Explain.

Exercises 8.46–8.57

Learning the Mechanics

8.46 A randomized block design yielded the following ANOVA table.

Source	df	SS	MS	F
Treatments	4	501	125.25	9.109
Blocks	2	225	112.50	8.182
Error	8	110	13.75	
Total	14	836		

a. How many blocks and treatments were used in the experiment?

b. How many observations were collected in the experiment?

c. Specify the null and alternative hypotheses you would use to compare the treatment means.

d. What test statistic should be used to conduct the hypothesis test of part **c**?

e. Specify the rejection region for the test of parts **c** and **d**. Use $\alpha = .01$.

f. Conduct the test of parts **c–e**, and state the proper conclusion.

g. What assumptions are necessary to ensure the validity of the test you conducted in part **f**?

8.47 An experiment was conducted using a randomized block design. The data from the experiment are displayed in the following table.

⊘ **LM8_47**

	BLOCK		
Treatment	1	2	3
1	2	3	5
2	8	6	7
3	7	6	5

a. Fill in the missing entries in the ANOVA table.

Source	df	SS	MS	F
Treatments	2	21.5555		
Blocks	2			
Error	4			
Total	8	30.2222		

b. Specify the null and alternative hypotheses you would use to investigate whether a difference exists among the treatment means.

c. What test statistic should be used in conducting the test of part **b?**

d. Describe the Type I and Type II errors associated with the hypothesis test of part **b.**

e. Conduct the hypothesis test of part **b** using $\alpha = .05$.

8.48 A randomized block design was used to compare the mean responses for three treatments. Four blocks of three homogeneous experimental units were selected, and each treatment was randomly assigned to one experimental unit within each block. The data are shown in the next table, and the SPSS ANOVA printout for this experiment is shown below.

⊘ **LM8_48**

Treatment	BLOCK			
	1	2	3	4
A	3.4	5.5	7.9	1.3
B	4.4	5.8	9.6	2.8
C	2.2	3.4	6.9	.3

a. Use the printout to fill in the entries in the following ANOVA table.

Source	df	SS	MS	F
Treatments				
Blocks				
Error				
Total				

b. Do the data provide sufficient evidence to indicate that the treatment means differ? Use $\alpha = .05$.

c. Do the data provide sufficient evidence to indicate that blocking was effective in reducing the experimental error? Use $\alpha = .05$.

d. Use the printout to rank the treatment means at $\alpha = .05$.

SPSS output for Exercise 8.48

Tests of Between-Subjects Effects

Dependent Variable: RESPONSE

Source	Type III Sum of Squares	df	Mean Square	F	Sig.
Corrected Model	83.781[a]	5	16.756	141.935	.000
Intercept	238.521	1	238.521	2020.412	.000
TRTMENT	12.032	2	6.016	50.958	.000
BLOCK	71.749	3	23.916	202.586	.000
Error	.708	6	.118		
Total	323.010	12			
Corrected Total	84.489	11			

a. R Squared = .992 (Adjusted R Squared = .985)

Multiple Comparisons

Dependent Variable: RESPONSE
Tukey HSD

(I) TRTMENT	(J) TRTMENT	Mean Difference (I-J)	Std. Error	Sig.	95% Confidence Interval	
					Lower Bound	Upper Bound
A	B	-1.125*	.2430	.009	-1.870	-.380
	C	1.325*	.2430	.004	.500	2.070
B	A	1.125*	.2430	.009	.380	1.870
	C	2.450*	.2430	.000	1.705	3.195
C	A	-1.325*	.2430	.004	-2.070	-.580
	B	-2.450*	.2430	.000	-3.195	-1.705

Based on observed means.

*. The mean difference is significant at the .05 level.

e. What assumptions are necessary to ensure the validity of the inferences made in parts **b, c,** and **d?**

8.49 Suppose an experiment utilizing a randomized block design has four treatments and nine blocks, for a total of $4 \times 9 = 36$ observations. Assume that the Total Sum of Squares for the response is SS(Total) = 500. For each of the following partitions of SS(Total), test the null hypothesis that the treatment means are equal, and test the null hypothesis that the block means are equal. Use $\alpha = .05$ for each test.

a. The Sum of Squares for Treatments (SST) is 20% of SS(Total), and the Sum of Squares for Blocks (SSB) is 30% of SS(Total).

b. SST is 50% of SS(Total), and SSB is 20% of SS(Total).

c. SST is 20% of SS(Total), and SSB is 50% of SS(Total).

d. SST is 40% of SS(Total), and SSB is 40% of SS(Total).

e. SST is 20% of SS(Total), and SSB is 20% of SS(Total).

Applying the Concepts—Basic

8.50 **Flower production of dwarf shrubs.** Dwarf shrubs are popu-
NW lar with model home landscapers. Stetson University researchers conducted an experiment to determine the effects of fire on the shrub's growth (*Florida Scientist,* Spring 1997). Twelve experimental plots of land were selected in a pasture where the shrub is abundant. Within each plot, three dwarf shrubs were randomly selected and treated as follows: one shrub was subjected to fire, another to clipping, and the third was left unmanipulated (a control). After 5 months, the number of flowers produced by each of the 36 shrubs was determined. The objective of the study was to compare the mean number of flowers produced by dwarf shrubs for the three treatments (fire, clipping, and control).

a. Identify the type of experimental design employed, including the treatments, response variable, and experimental units.

b. Illustrate the layout of the design using a graphic similar to Figure 8.15.

c. The ANOVA of the data resulted in a test statistic of $F = 5.42$ for treatments with an associated p-value of $p = .009$. Interpret this result.

d. The three treatment means were compared using Tukey's method at $\alpha = .05$. Interpret the results shown below.

Mean number of flowers	1.17	10.58	17.08
Treatment	Control	Clipping	Burning

8.51 **Rotary oil rigs.** An economist wants to compare the average monthly number of rotary oil rigs running in three states—California, Utah, and Alaska. In order to account for month-to-month variation, 3 months were randomly selected over a 2-year period, and the number of oil rigs running in each state in each month was obtained from data provided from *World Oil* (Jan. 2002) magazine. The data, reproduced in the accompanying table, were analyzed using a randomized block design.

⊙ **OILRIGS**

Month/Year	California	Utah	Alaska
Nov. 2000	27	17	11
Oct. 2001	34	20	14
Nov. 2001	36	15	14

a. Why is a randomized block design preferred over a completely randomized design for comparing the mean number of oil rigs running monthly in California, Utah, and Alaska?

b. Identify the treatments for the experiment.

c. Identify the blocks for the experiment.

d. State the null hypothesis for the ANOVA F-test.

e. Locate the test statistic and p-value on the MINITAB printout shown below. Interpret the results.

f. A Tukey multiple comparison of means (at $\alpha = .05$) is summarized in the SPSS printout at the top of p. 519. Which state(s) have the significantly largest mean number of oil rigs running monthly?

MINITAB output for Exercise 8.51

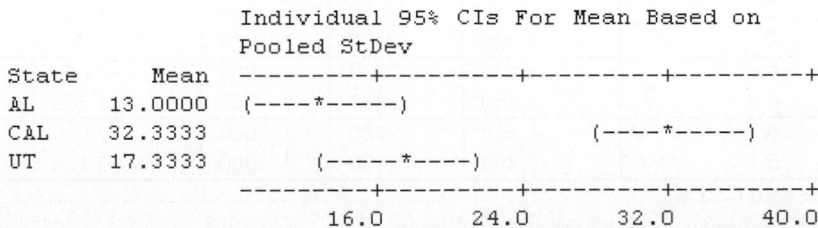

Two-way ANOVA: NumRigs versus State, Month/Year

```
Source        DF       SS       MS       F       P
State          2  617.556  308.778   38.07   0.002
Month/Year     2   30.889   15.444    1.90   0.262
Error          4   32.444    8.111
Total          8  680.889

S = 2.848    R-Sq = 95.23%    R-Sq(adj) = 90.47%


                 Individual 95% CIs For Mean Based on
                 Pooled StDev
State     Mean   ---------+---------+---------+---------+
AL     13.0000   (----*-----)
CAL    32.3333                               (----*-----)
UT     17.3333        (-----*----)
                 ---------+---------+---------+---------+
                     16.0      24.0      32.0      40.0
```

SPSS output for Exercise 8.51

NUMRIGS

Tukey HSD[a,b]

STATE	N	Subset 1	Subset 2
AL	3	13.00	
UT	3	17.33	
CAL	3		32.33
Sig.		.262	1.000

Means for groups in homogeneous subsets are displayed.
Based on Type III Sum of Squares
The error term is Mean Square(Error) = 8.111.

a. Uses Harmonic Mean Sample Size = 3.000.

b. Alpha = .05.

8.52 Effectiveness of geese decoys. What type of decoy should you purchase for hunting waterfowl? A study in the *Journal of Wildlife Management* (July 1995) compared the effectiveness of three different decoy types—taxidermy-mounted decoys, plastic shell decoys, and full-bodied plastic decoys—in attracting Canada geese to sunken pit blinds. In order to account for an extraneous source of variation, three pit blinds were used as blocks in the experiment. Thus, a randomized block design with three treatments (decoy types) and three blocks (pit blinds) was employed. The response variable was the percentage of a goose flock to approach within 46 meters of the pit blind on a given day. The data are given in the table* in the next column. A MINITAB printout of the analysis follows. Locate the p-value for treatments on the printout and interpret the result.

Two-way ANOVA: PERCENT versus DECOY, BLIND

```
Source   DF      SS       MS       F      P
DECOY     2   30.069   15.0344   0.61   0.589
BLIND     2   44.149   22.0744   0.89   0.479
Error     4   99.338   24.8344
Total     8  173.556

S = 4.983   R-Sq = 42.76%   R-Sq(adj) = 0.00%
```

*The actual design employed in the study was more complex than the randomized block design shown here. In the actual study, each number in the table represents the mean daily percentage of goose flocks attracted to the blind, averaged over 13–17 days.

DECOY

Blind	Shell	Full-Bodied	Taxidermy-Mounted
1	7.3	13.6	17.8
2	12.6	10.4	17.0
3	16.4	23.4	13.6

Source: Harrey, W. F., Hindman, L. J., and Rhodes. W. E. "Vulnerability of Canada Geese to Taxidermy-Mounted Decoys." *Journal of Wildlife Management,* Vol. 59, No. 3, July 1995, p. 475 (Table 1).

8.53 Participation in a company's walking program. A study was conducted to investigate the effect of prompting in a walking program instituted at a large corporation (*Health Psychology,* Mar. 1995). Five groups of walkers—27 in each group—agreed to participate by walking for 20 minutes at least one day per week over a 24-week period. The participants were prompted to walk each week via telephone calls, but different prompting schemes were used for each group. Walkers in the control group received no prompting phone calls; walkers in the "frequent/low" group received a call once a week with low structure (i.e., "just touching base"); walkers in the "frequent/high" group received a call once a week with high structure (i.e., goals are set); walkers in the "infrequent/low" group received a call once every 3 weeks with high structure; and walkers in the "infrequent/high" group received a call once every 3 weeks with high structure. The table below lists the number of participants in each group who actually walked the minimum requirement each week for weeks 1, 4, 8, 12, 16, and 24. The data were subjected to an analysis of variance for a randomized block design, with the five walker groups representing the treatments and the six time periods (weeks) representing the blocks.

WALKERS

Week	Control	Frequent/Low	Frequent/High	Infrequent/Low	Infrequent/High
1	7	23	25	21	19
4	2	19	25	10	12
8	2	18	19	9	9
12	2	7	20	8	2
16	2	18	18	8	7
24	1	17	17	7	6

Source: Lombard, D. N., et al. "Walking to Meet Health Guidelines: The Effect of Prompting Frequency and Prompt Structure." *Health Psychology,* Vol. 14, No. 2, Mar. 1995, p. 167 (Table 2). Copyright 1995 American Psychological Association.

Source	df	SS	MS	F	p-value
PROMPT	4	1185.000	—	—	0.0000
WEEK	—	386.400	77.28000	10.40	0.0001
Error	20	148.600	7.43000		
TOTAL	29	1720.00			

a. What is the purpose of blocking on weeks in this study?

b. Fill in the missing entries on the ANOVA summary table shown above.

c. Is there sufficient evidence of a difference in the mean number of walkers per week among the five walker groups? Use $\alpha = .05$.

d. Tukey's technique was used to compare all pairs of treatment means with an experimentwise error rate of $\alpha = .05$. The rankings are shown at the bottom of the page. Interpret these results.

e. What assumptions must hold to ensure the validity of the inferences in parts **c** and **d**?

Applying the Concepts—Intermediate

8.54 Reducing on-the-job stress. Plant therapists believe that plants can reduce on-the-job stress. A Kansas State University study was conducted to investigate this phenomenon. Two weeks prior to final exams, 10 undergraduate students took part in an experiment to determine what effect the presence of a live plant, a photo of a plant, or absence of a plant has on the student's ability to relax while isolated in a dimly lit room. Each student participated in three sessions—one with a live plant, one with a plant photo, and one with no plant (control).* During each session, finger temperature was measured at 1-minute intervals for 20 minutes. Since increasing finger temperature indicates an increased level of relaxation, the maximum temperature (in degrees) was used as the response variable. The data for the experiment are provided in the following table. Conduct an ANOVA and make the proper inferences at $\alpha = .10$.

PLANTS

Student	Live Plant	Plant Photo	No Plant (control)
1	91.4	93.5	96.6
2	94.9	96.6	90.5
3	97.0	95.8	95.4
4	93.7	96.2	96.7
5	96.0	96.6	93.5
6	96.7	95.5	94.8
7	95.2	94.6	95.7
8	96.0	97.2	96.2
9	95.6	94.8	96.0
10	95.6	92.6	96.6

Source: Elizabeth Schreiber. Department of Statistics, Kansas State University, Manhattan, Kansas

*The experiment is simplified for this exercise. The actual experiment involved 30 students who participated in 12 sessions.

8.55 Absentee rates at a jeans plant. A plant that manufactures denim jeans in the United Kingdom recently introduced a computerized automated handling system. The new system delivers garments to the assembly line operators by means of an overhead conveyor. While the automated system minimizes operator handling time, it inhibits operators from working ahead and taking breaks from their machine. A study in *New Technology, Work, and Employment* (July 2001) investigated the impact of the new handling system on worker absentee rates at the jeans plant. One theory is that the mean absentee rate will vary by day of the week, as operators decide to indulge in 1-day absences to relieve work pressure. Nine weeks were randomly selected and the absentee rate (percentage of workers absent) determined for each day (Monday through Friday) of the workweek. The data are listed in the table. Conduct a complete analysis of the data to determine whether the mean absentee rate differs across the 5 days of the workweek.

JEANS

Week	Mon	Tues	Wed	Thur	Fri
1	5.3	0.6	1.9	1.3	1.6
2	12.9	9.4	2.6	0.4	0.5
3	0.8	0.8	5.7	0.4	1.4
4	2.6	0.0	4.5	10.2	4.5
5	23.5	9.6	11.3	13.6	14.1
6	9.1	4.5	7.5	2.1	9.3
7	11.1	4.2	4.1	4.2	4.1
8	9.5	7.1	4.5	9.1	12.9
9	4.8	5.2	10.0	6.9	9.0

Source: Boggis, J. J. "The Eradication of Leisure." *New Technology, Work, and Employment,* Vol. 16, No. 2, July 2001 (Table 3).

8.56 Comparing two glaucoma drugs. Two drugs, A and B, used for the treatment of glaucoma (an eye disease) were tested for effectiveness on 10 diseased dogs. Drug A was administered to one eye (chosen randomly) of each dog and drug B to the other eye. Pressure measurements were taken 1 hour later on both eyeballs of each dog. The 10 diseased dogs serve as the blocks for comparing the two treatments, drugs A and B. Pressure measurements are given in the following table. (The smaller the measurement, the less serious the eye disease.)

EYEDOGS

Dog	Drug A	Drug B
1	.17	.15
2	.20	.18
3	.14	.13
4	.18	.18
5	.23	.19
6	.19	.12
7	.12	.07
8	.10	.09
9	.16	.14
10	.13	.08

Tukey Rankings for Exercise 8.53

Mean:	2.67	9.17	10.50	17.00	20.67
Prompt:	Control	Infr./High	Infr./Low	Frequent/Low	Frequent/High

a. Perform an analysis of variance for these data. Do the data provide sufficient evidence to indicate a difference in mean pressure readings for the two treatments (i.e., is one of the glaucoma drugs better than the other)? Use $\alpha = .05$.

b. What is the purpose of using the dogs as blocks in this experiment?

c. Recall that a randomized block design with $p = 2$ treatments is a paired difference experiment (Chapter 7). Analyze the data as a paired difference experiment using a t-test to compare the treatment means. Use $\alpha = .05$.

d. Compare the computed F and t values from parts **a** and **c**, and verify that $F = t^2$. Also verify that for the rejection region values of F and t, $F_\alpha = t_{\alpha/2}^2$.

e. Find the approximate observed significance level for the test in part **a** and interpret its value.

Applying the Concepts—Advanced

8.57 Anticorrosive behavior of steel coated with epoxy. Organic coatings that use epoxy resins are widely used for protecting steel and metal against weathering and corrosion. Researchers at National Technical University (Athens, Greece) examined the steel anticorrosive behavior of different epoxy coatings formulated with zinc pigments in an attempt to find the epoxy coating with the best corrosion inhibition (*Pigment & Resin Technology,* Vol. 32, 2003). The experimental units were flat, rectangular panels cut from steel sheets. Each panel was coated with one of four different coating systems, S1, S2, S3, and S4. Three panels were prepared for each coating system. (These panels are labeled S1-A, S1-B, S1-C, S2-A, S2-B, . . . , S4-C.) The characteristics of the four coating systems are listed below.

Each coated panel was immersed in deionized and deaerated water and then tested for corrosion. Since exposure time is likely to have a strong influence on anticorrosive behavior, the researchers attempted to remove this extraneous source of variation through the experimental design. Exposure times were fixed at 24 hours, 60 days, and 120 days. For each of the coating systems, one panel was exposed to water for 24 hours, one exposed to water for 60 days, and one exposed to water for 120 days in random order. The design is illustrated in the accompanying table.

DIAGRAM OF THE EXPERIMENTAL DESIGN

Exposure Time	Coating System/Panel Exposed
24 Hours	S1-A, S2-C, S3-C, S4-B
60 Days	S1-C, S2-A, S3-B, S4-A
120 Days	S1-B, S2-B, S3-A, S4-C

Following exposing, the corrosion rate (nanoamperes per square centimeter) was determined for each panel. The lower the corrosion rate, the greater the anticorrosion performance of the coating system. The data are shown in the next table. Are there differences among the epoxy treatment means? If so, which of the epoxy coating systems yields the lowest corrosion rate?

CORROSION RATES FOR EPOXY COATING EXPERIMENT

🔵 **EPOXY**

Exposure Time	System S1	System S2	System S3	System S4
24 hours	6.7	7.5	8.2	6.1
60 days	8.7	9.1	10.5	8.3
120 days	11.8	12.6	14.5	11.8

Source: Kouloumbi, N., et al. "Anticorrosion Performance of Epoxy Coatings on Steel Surface Exposed to Deionized Water." *Pigment & Resin Technology,* Vol. 32, No. 2, 2003 (Table II).

CHARACTERISTICS OF FOUR EPOXY COATING SYSTEMS

Coating System	1st Layer	2nd Layer
S1	Zinc dust	Epoxy paint, 100 micrometers thick
S2	Zinc phosphate	Epoxy paint, 100 micrometers thick
S3	Zinc phosphate with mica	Finish layer, 100 micrometers thick
S4	Zinc phosphate with mica	Finish layer, 200 micrometers thick

8.5 Factorial Experiments

All the experiments discussed in Sections 8.2–8.4 were **single-factor experiments.** The treatments were levels of a single factor, with the sampling of experimental units performed using either a completely randomized or a randomized block design. However, most responses are affected by more than one factor, and we will therefore often wish to design experiments involving more than one factor.

Consider an experiment in which the effects of two factors on the response are being investigated. Assume that factor A is to be investigated at a levels, and factor B at b levels. Recalling that treatments are factor-level combinations, you can see that the experiment has, potentially, ab treatments that could be included in the experiment. A *complete factorial experiment* is one in which all possible ab treatments are utilized.

> **Definition 8.9**
>
> A **complete factorial experiment** is one in which every factor-level combination is utilized—that is, the number of treatments in the experiment equals the total number of factor-level combinations.

For example, suppose the USGA wants to determine not only the relationship between distance and brand of golf ball, but also between distance and the club used to hit the ball. If they decide to use four brands and two clubs (say, driver and five-iron) in the experiment, then a complete factorial would call for utilizing all $4 \times 2 = 8$ Brand-Club combinations. This experiment is referred to more specifically as a **complete 4×2 factorial.** A layout for a two-factor factorial experiment (we are henceforth referring to a *complete factorial* when we use the term *factorial*) is given in Table 8.10. The factorial experiment is also referred to as a **two-way classification** because it can be arranged in the row-column format exhibited in Table 8.10.

TABLE 8.10 Schematic Layout of Two-Factor Factorial Experiment

	Level	\multicolumn{5}{c}{FACTOR *B* AT *b* LEVELS}
	Level	1	2	3	. . .	b
	1	Trt. 1	Trt. 2	Trt. 3	. . .	Trt. b
Factor A	2	Trt. $b + 1$	Trt. $b + 2$	Trt. $b + 3$	. . .	Trt. $2b$
at a Levels	3	Trt. $2b + 1$	Trt. $2b + 2$	Trt. $2b + 3$	. . .	Trt. $3b$
	⋮	⋮	⋮	⋮	. . .	⋮
	a	Trt. $(a - 1)b + 1$	Trt. $(a - 1)b + 2$	Trt. $(a - 1)b + 3$	. . .	Trt. ab

In order to complete the specification of the experimental design, the treatments must be assigned to the experimental units. If the assignment of the ab treatments in the factorial experiment is random and independent, the design is completely randomized. For example, if the machine Iron Byron is used to hit 80 golf balls, 10 for each of the eight Brand-Club combinations, in a random sequence, the design would be completely randomized. In the remainder of this section, we confine our attention to factorial experiments utilizing completely randomized designs.

If we utilize a completely randomized design to conduct a factorial experiment with ab treatments, we can proceed with the analysis in exactly the same way as we did in Section 8.2—that is, we calculate (or let the computer calculate) the measure of treatment mean variability (MST) and the measure of sampling variability (MSE) and use the F-ratio of these two quantities to test the null hypothesis that the treatment means are equal. However, if this hypothesis is rejected, so that we conclude some differences exist among the treatment means, important questions remain. Are both factors affecting the response, or only one? If both, do they affect the response independently, or do they interact to affect the response?

For example, suppose the distance data indicate that at least two of the eight treatment (Brand-Club combinations) means differ in the golf experiment. Does the brand of ball (factor A) or the club utilized (factor B) affect mean distance, or do both affect it? Several possibilities are shown in Figure 8.19. In Figure 8.19(a), the brand means are equal (only three are shown for the purpose of illustration), but the distances differ for the two levels of factor B (Club). Thus, there is no effect of Brand on distance, but a Club main effect is present. In Figure 8.19(b), the Brand means differ, but the Club means are equal for each Brand. Here a Brand main effect is present, but no effect of Club is present.

Figures 8.19(c) and 8.19(d) illustrate cases in which both factors affect the response. In Figure 8.19(c), the mean distances between clubs does not change for the three Brands, so that the effect of Brand on distance is independent of Club—that is, the two factors Brand and Club *do not interact*. In contrast, Figure 8.19(d) shows that the difference between mean distances between Clubs varies with Brand. Thus, the effect of Brand on distance depends on Club, and therefore the two factors *do interact*.

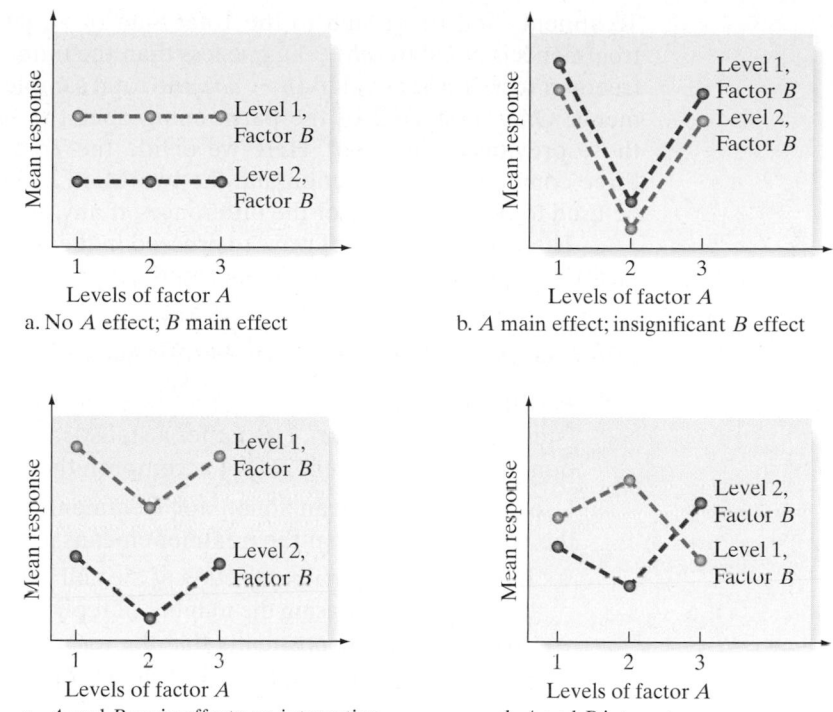

FIGURE 8.19

Illustration of possible treatment effects: Factorial experiment

a. No A effect; B main effect

b. A main effect; insignificant B effect

c. A and B main effects; no interaction

d. A and B interact

Now Work Exercise 8.67

In order to determine the nature of the treatment effect, if any, on the response in a factorial experiment, we need to break the treatment variability into three components: Interaction between Factors A and B, Main Effect of Factor A, and Main Effect of Factor B. The **Factor Interaction** component is used to test whether the factors combine to affect the response, while the **Factor Main Effect** components are used to determine whether the factors separately affect the response.

The partitioning of the Total Sum of Squares into its various components is illustrated in Figure 8.20. Notice that at stage 1, the components are identical to those in the one-factor, completely randomized designs of Section 8.2; the Sums of Squares for

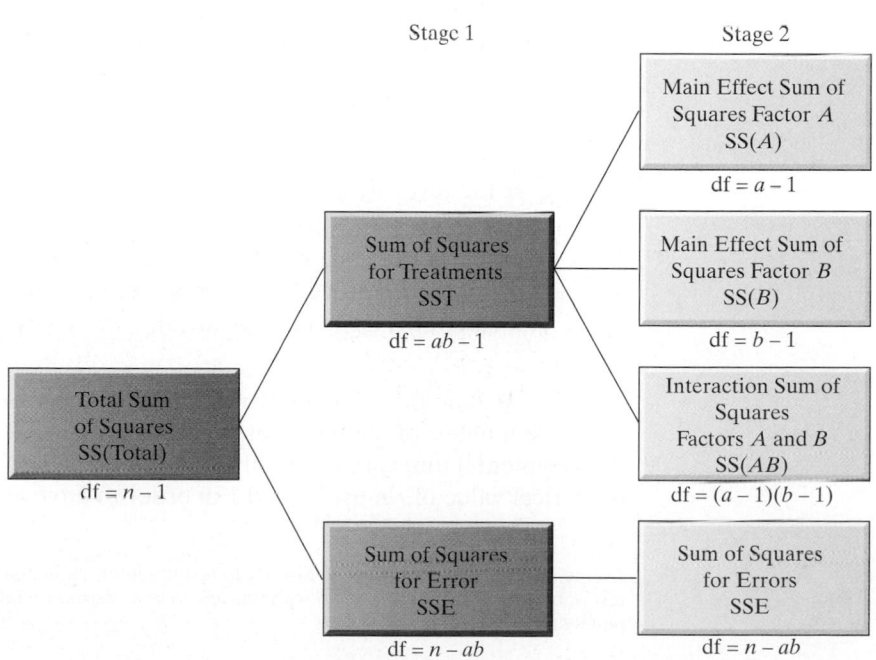

FIGURE 8.20

Partitioning the Total Sum of Squares for a two-factor factorial

Treatments and Error sum to the Total Sum of Squares. The degrees of freedom for treatments is equal to $(ab - 1)$, one less than the number of treatments. The degrees of freedom for error is equal to $(n - ab)$, the total sample size minus the number of treatments. Only at stage 2 of the partitioning does the factorial experiment differ from those previously discussed. Here we divide the Treatments Sum of Squares into its three components: Interaction and the two Main Effects. These components can then be used to test the nature of the differences, if any, among the treatment means.

There are a number of ways to proceed in the testing and estimation of factors in a factorial experiment. We present one approach in the next box.

Procedure for Analysis of Two-Factor Factorial Experiment

1. Partition the Total Sum of Squares into the Treatments and Error components (stage 1 of Figure 8.20). Use either a statistical software package or the calculation formulas in Appendix C to accomplish the partitioning.

2. Use the F-ratio of Mean Square for Treatments to Mean Square for Error to test the null hypothesis that the treatment means are equal.*

   a. If the test results in nonrejection of the null hypothesis, consider refining the experiment by increasing the number of replications or introducing other factors. Also consider the possibility that the response is unrelated to the two factors.

   b. If the test results in rejection of the null hypothesis, then proceed to step 3.

3. Partition the Treatments Sum of Squares into the Main Effect and Interaction Sum of Squares (stage 2 of Figure 8.20). Use either a statistical software package or the calculation formulas in Appendix C to accomplish the partitioning.

4. Test the null hypothesis that factors A and B do not interact to affect the response by computing the F-ratio of the Mean Square for Interaction to the Mean Square for Error.

   a. If the test results in nonrejection of the null hypothesis, proceed to step 5.

   b. If the test results in rejection of the null hypothesis, conclude that the two factors interact to affect the mean response. Then proceed to step 6a.

5. Conduct tests of two null hypotheses that the mean response is the same at each level of factor A and factor B. Compute two F-ratios by comparing the Mean Square for each Factor Main Effect to the Mean Square for Error.

   a. If one or both tests result in rejection of the null hypothesis, conclude that the factor affects the mean response. Proceed to step 6b.

   b. If both tests result in nonrejection, an apparent contradiction has occurred. Although the treatment means apparently differ (step 2 test), the interaction (step 4) and main effect (step 5) tests have not supported that result. Further experimentation is advised.

6. Compare the means:

   a. If the test for interaction (step 4) is significant, use a multiple comparisons procedure to compare any or all pairs of the treatment means.

   b. If the test for one or both main effects (step 5) is significant, use a multiple comparisons procedure to compare the pairs of means corresponding to the levels of the significant factor(s).

We assume the completely randomized design is a **balanced design,** meaning that the same number of observations are made for each treatment—that is, we assume that r experimental units are randomly and independently selected for each treatment. The numerical value of r must exceed 1 in order to have any degrees of freedom with which

*Some analysts prefer to proceed directly to test the interaction and main effect components, skipping the test of treatment means. We begin with this test to be consistent with our approach in the one-factor completely randomized design.

to measure the sampling variability. [Note that if $r = 1$, then $n = ab$, and the degrees of freedom associated with Error (Figure 8.20) is $df = n - ab = 0$]. The value of r is often referred to as the number of **replicates** of the factorial experiment since we assume that all ab treatments are repeated, or replicated, r times. Whatever approach is adopted in the analysis of a factorial experiment, several tests of hypotheses are usually conducted. The tests are summarized in the next box.

ANOVA Tests Conducted for Factorial Experiments: Completely Randomized Design, r Replicates per Treatment

Test for Treatment Means

H_0: No difference among the ab treatment means

H_a: At least two treatment means differ

Test statistic: $F = \dfrac{\text{MST}}{\text{MSE}}$

Rejection region: $F \geq F_\alpha$, based on $(ab - 1)$ numerator and $(n - ab)$ denominator degrees of freedom [Note: $n = abr$.]

Test for Factor Interaction

H_0: Factors A and B do not interact to affect the response mean

H_a: Factors A and B do interact to affect the response mean

Test statistic: $F = \dfrac{\text{MS}(AB)}{\text{MSE}}$

Rejection region: $F \geq F_\alpha$, based on $(a - 1)(b - 1)$ numerator and $(n - ab)$ denominator degrees of freedom

Test for Main Effect of Factor A

H_0: No difference among the a mean levels of factor A

H_a: At least two factor A mean levels differ

Test statistic: $F = \dfrac{\text{MS}(A)}{\text{MSE}}$

Rejection region: $F \geq F_\alpha$, based on $(a - 1)$ numerator and $(n - ab)$ denominator degrees of freedom

Test for Main Effect of Factor B

H_0: No difference among the b mean levels of factor B

H_a: At least two factor B mean levels differ

Test statistic: $F = \dfrac{\text{MS}(B)}{\text{MSE}}$

Rejection region: $F \geq F_\alpha$, based on $(b - 1)$ numerator and $(n - ab)$ denominator degrees of freedom

---

Conditions Required for Valid F-Tests in Factorial Experiments

1. The response distribution for each factor-level combination (treatment) is normal.
2. The response variance is constant for all treatments.
3. Random and independent samples of experimental units are associated with each treatment.

EXAMPLE 8.10

Conducting a
Factorial ANOVA of
the Golf Ball Brand
Data

Problem Suppose the USGA tests four different brands (A, B, C, D) of golf balls and two different clubs (driver, five-iron) in a completely randomized design. Each of the eight Brand-Club combinations (treatments) is randomly and independently assigned to four experimental units, each experimental unit consisting of a specific position in the sequence of hits by Iron Byron. The distance response is recorded for each of the 32 hits, and the results are shown in Table 8.11.

a. Use a statistical software package to partition the Total Sum of Squares into the components necessary to analyze this 4 × 2 factorial experiment.

b. Conduct the appropriate ANOVA tests and interpret the results of your analysis. Use $\alpha = .10$ for each test you conduct.

c. If appropriate, conduct multiple comparisons of the treatment means. Use an experimentwise error rate of .10. Illustrate the comparisons with a graph.

GOLFFAC1

TABLE 8.11 Distance Data for 4 × 2 Factorial Golf Experiment

		BRAND			
		A	B	C	D
Club	**Driver**	226.4	238.3	240.5	219.8
		232.6	231.7	246.9	228.7
		234.0	227.7	240.3	232.9
		220.7	237.2	244.7	237.6
	Five-Iron	163.8	184.4	179.0	157.8
		179.4	180.6	168.0	161.8
		168.6	179.5	165.2	162.1
		173.4	186.2	156.5	160.3

Solution

a. The SPSS printout that partitions the Total Sum of Squares [i.e., SS(Total)] for this factorial experiment is given in Figure 8.21. The value SS(Total) = 34,482.049, shown as "Corrected Total SS" at the bottom of the printout, is partitioned into the "Corrected Model" (i.e., Treatment) and Error Sums of Squares. Note that SST = 33,659.09 (with 7 degrees of freedom) and SSE = 822.24 (with 24 df) add to SS(Total) (with 31 df). The Treatment Sum of Squares, SST, is further divided into Main Effect (Brand and Club) and Interaction Sum of Squares. These values, highlighted on Figure 8.21, are SS(Brand) = 800.7 (with 3 df), SS(Club) = 32,093.1 (with 1 df), and SS(Brand × Club) = 766.0 (with 3 df).

Tests of Between-Subjects Effects

Dependent Variable: DISTANCE

Source	Type III Sum of Squares	df	Mean Square	F	Sig.
Corrected Model	33659.809a	7	4808.544	140.354	.000
Intercept	1306778.61	1	1306778.611	38142.98	.000
BRAND	800.736	3	266.912	7.791	.001
CLUB	32093.111	1	32093.111	936.752	.000
BRAND * CLUB	765.961	3	255.320	7.452	.001
Error	822.240	24	34.260		
Total	1341260.66	32			
Corrected Total	34482.049	31			

a. R Squared = .976 (Adjusted R Squared = .969)

FIGURE 8.21
SPSS ANOVA for factorial experiment on golf ball data

b. Once partitioning is accomplished, our first test is

H_0: The eight treatment means are equal

H_a: At least two of the eight means differ

Test statistic: $F = \dfrac{\text{MST}}{\text{MSE}} = 140.354$ (top line of printout)

Observed significance level: p = .000   (top line of printout)

Since $\alpha = .10$ exceeds p, we reject this null hypothesis and conclude that at least two of the Brand-Club combinations differ in mean distance.

After accepting the hypothesis that the treatment means differ, and therefore that the factors Brand and/or Club somehow affect the mean distance, we want to determine how the factors affect the mean response. We begin with a test of interaction between Brand and Club:

H_0: The factors Brand and Club do not interact to affect the mean response

H_a: Brand and Club interact to affect mean response

Test statistic: $F = \dfrac{\text{MS}(AB)}{\text{MSE}} = \dfrac{\text{MS}(\text{Brand} \times \text{Club})}{\text{MSE}}$

$= \dfrac{255.32}{34.26} = 7.452$ (bottom of printout)

Observed significance level: p = .001   (bottom of printout)

Since $\alpha = .10$ exceeds the p-value, we conclude that the factors Brand and Club interact to affect mean distance.

Because the factors interact, we do not test the main effects for Brand and Club. Instead, we compare the treatment means in an attempt to learn the nature of the interaction in part **c.**

c. Rather than compare all $8(7)/2 = 28$ pairs of treatment means, we test for differences only between pairs of brands within each club. That differences exist *between* clubs can be assumed. Therefore, only $4(3)/2 = 6$ pairs of means need to be compared for each club, or a total of 12 comparisons for the two clubs. The results of these comparisons using Tukey's method with an experimentwise error rate of $\alpha = .10$ for each club are displayed in the SPSS printout, Figure 8.22. For each club, the brand means are listed in descending order in Figure 8.22, and those not significantly different are listed in the same "Homogeneous Subset" column.

As shown in Figure 8.22, the picture is unclear with respect to Brand means. For the five-iron (top of Figure 8.22), the brand B mean significantly exceeds all other brands. However, when hit with a driver (bottom of Figure 8.22), brand B's mean is not significantly different from any of the other brands. The Club $\times$ Brand interaction can be seen in the SPSS plot of means in Figure 8.23. Note that the difference between the mean distances of the two clubs (driver and five-iron) varies depending on brand. The biggest difference appears for brand C while the smallest difference is for brand B.

Look Back Note the nontransitive nature of the multiple comparisons. For example, for the driver the brand C mean can be "the same" as the brand B mean, and the brand B mean can be "the same" as the brand D mean, and yet the brand C mean can significantly exceed the brand D mean. The reason lies in the definition of "the same"—we must be careful not to conclude two means are equal simply because they are placed in the same subgroup or connected by a vertical line. The line indicates only that *the connected means are not significantly different.* You should conclude (at the overall α level of significance) only that means not connected are different, while withholding judgment on those that are connected. The picture of which means differ and by how much will become clearer as we increase the number of replicates of the factorial experiment.

CLUB=5IRON

Tukey HSD[a,b]

BRAND	N	Subset 1	Subset 2
D	4	160.500	
C	4	167.175	
A	4	171.300	
B	4		182.675
Sig.		.103	1.000

Means for groups in homogeneous subsets are displayed.
Based on Type III Sum of Squares
The error term is Mean Square(Error) = 36.108.

a. Uses Harmonic Mean Sample Size = 4.000.

b. Alpha = .10.

CLUB=DRIVER

Tukey HSD[a,b]

BRAND	N	Subset 1	Subset 2
A	4	228.425	
D	4	229.750	
B	4	233.725	233.725
C	4		243.100
Sig.		.570	.146

Means for groups in homogeneous subsets are displayed.
Based on Type III Sum of Squares
The error term is Mean Square(Error) = 32.412.

a. Uses Harmonic Mean Sample Size = 4.000.

b. Alpha = .10.

FIGURE 8.22

SPSS ranking of brand means for each level of club

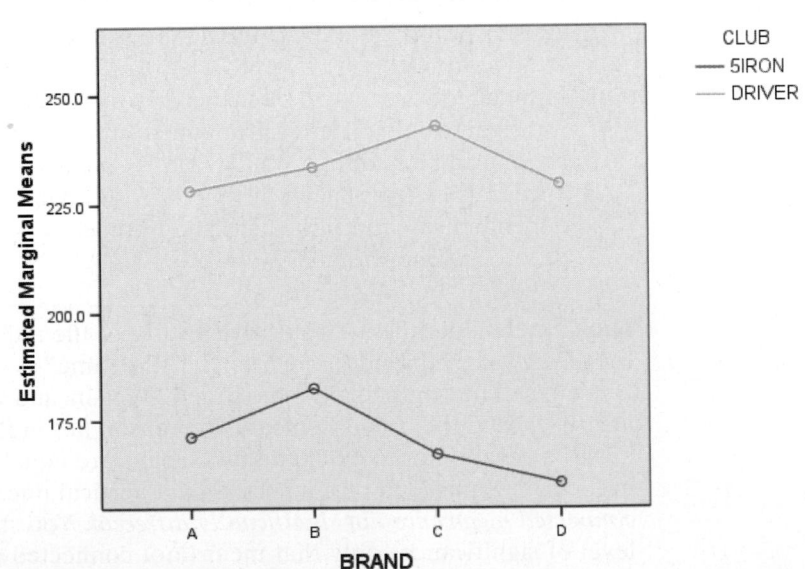

FIGURE 8.23

SPSS means plot for factorial golf ball experiment

Now Work Exercise 8.64

TABLE 8.12 General ANOVA Summary Table for a Two-Factor Factorial Experiment with *r* Replicates, where Factor A Has *a* levels and Factor B Has *b* Levels

Source	df	SS	MS	F
A	$a-1$	SSA	MSA	MSA/MSE
B	$b-1$	SSB	MSB	MSB/MSE
AB	$(a-1)(b-1)$	SSAB	MSAB	MSAB/MSE
Error	$ab(r-1)$	SSE	MSE	
Total	$n-1$	SS(Total)		

TABLE 8.13 ANOVA Summary Table for Example 8.10

Source	df	SS	MS	F
Brand	1	32,093.11	32,093.11	936.75
Club	3	800.74	266.91	7.79
Interaction	3	765.96	255.32	7.45
Error	24	822.24	34.26	
Total	31	34,482.05		

As with completely randomized and randomized block designs, the results of a factorial ANOVA are typically presented in an ANOVA summary table. Table 8.12 gives the general form of the ANOVA table, while Table 8.13 gives the ANOVA table for the golf ball data analyzed in Example 8.10. A two-factor factorial is characterized by four sources of variation—Factor A, Factor B, A × B interaction, and Error—which sum to the total Sum of Squares.

EXAMPLE 8.11

More Practice on Conducting a Factorial Analysis

Problem   Refer to Example 8.10. Suppose the same factorial experiment is performed on four other brands (E, F, G, and H), and the results are as shown in Table 8.14. Repeat the factorial analysis and interpret the results.

 GOLFFAC2

TABLE 8.14 Distance Data for Second Factorial Golf Experiment

		BRAND			
		E	F	G	H
Club	**Driver**	238.6	261.4	264.7	235.4
		241.9	261.3	262.9	239.8
		236.6	254.0	253.5	236.2
		244.9	259.9	255.6	237.5
	Five-Iron	165.2	179.2	189.0	171.4
		156.9	171.0	191.2	159.3
		172.2	178.0	191.3	156.6
		163.2	182.7	180.5	157.4

Solution   The MINITAB printout for the second factorial experiment is shown in Figure 8.24. Note that MINITAB (unlike SPSS) does not automatically conduct the *F*-test for treatment differences. Consequently, to conduct this test, we must first calculate the Sum of Squares for Treatments. Using the Sums of Squares for Brands, Clubs, and Interaction shown on the printout, we obtain

Two-way ANOVA: DISTANCE versus BRAND, CLUB

```
Source        DF        SS         MS         F       P
BRAND          3     3410.3     1136.8     46.21   0.000
CLUB           1    46443.9    46443.9   1887.94   0.000
Interaction    3      105.2       35.1      1.42   0.260
Error         24      590.4       24.6
Total         31    50549.8

S = 4.960    R-Sq = 98.83%    R-Sq(adj) = 98.49%
```

FIGURE 8.24
MINITAB Analysis for
Second Factorial Golf
Experiment

$$SS(\text{Treatments}) = SS(\text{Brands}) + SS(\text{Clubs}) + SS(\text{Interaction})$$
$$= 46{,}443.9 + 3{,}410.3 + 105.2 = 49{,}959.4$$

For this 4×2 factorial experiment there are 8 treatments. Then

$$MS(\text{Treatments}) = SS(\text{Treatments})/(8 - 1) = 49{,}959.4/7 = 7{,}137.1$$

The test statistic is

$$F = MS(\text{Treatments})/MSE = 7{,}137.1/24.6 = 290.1$$

Since this F-value exceeds the critical value of $F_{.10} = 1.98$ (obtained from Table VII, Appendix B), we reject the null hypothesis of no treatment differences and conclude that at least two of the Brand-Club combinations have significantly different mean distances.

Now, we test for interaction between Brand and Club:

$$F = \frac{MS(\text{Brand} \times \text{Club})}{MSE} = 1.42(\text{highlighted on the printout})$$

Since this F-ratio does not exceed the tabled value of $F_{.10} = 2.33$ with 3 and 24 df (obtained from Table VII, Appendix B) we cannot conclude at the .10 level of significance that the factors interact. In fact, note that the observed significance level (on the MINITAB printout) for the test of interaction is .26. Thus, at any level of significance lower than $\alpha = .26$, we could not conclude that the factors interact. We therefore test the main effects for Brand and Club.

We first test the Brand main effect:

H_0: No difference exists among the true Brand mean distances

H_a: At least two Brand mean distances differ

Test statistic: $F = \dfrac{MS(\text{Brand})}{MSE} = \dfrac{1{,}136.77}{24.60} = 46.21$ (highlighted on the printout)

Observed significance level: $p = .000$

Since $\alpha = .10$ exceeds the p-value, we conclude that at least two of the brand means differ. We will subsequently determine which brand means differ using Tukey's multiple comparisons procedure. But first, we want to test the Club main effect:

H_0: No differences exist between the Club mean distances

H_a: The Club mean distances differ

Test statistic: $F = \dfrac{MS(\text{Club})}{MSE} = \dfrac{46{,}443.9}{24.60} = 1{,}887.94$

Observed significance level: $p = .000$

Since $\alpha = .10$ exceeds the p-value, we conclude that the two clubs are associated with different mean distances. Since only two levels of Club were utilized in experiment, this

```
Tukey 90.0% Simultaneous Confidence Intervals
Response Variable DISTANCE
All Pairwise Comparisons among Levels of BRAND
BRAND = E   subtracted from:

BRAND   Lower   Center   Upper   ---------+---------+---------+-------
F       10.003  16.000   21.997                             (---*---)
G       15.153  21.150   27.147                                (---*---)
H       -9.235  -3.237    2.760                     (---*---)
                                  ---------+---------+---------+-------
                                        -16        0        16


BRAND = F   subtracted from:

BRAND   Lower   Center   Upper   ---------+---------+---------+-------
G       -0.85     5.15   11.15                          (---*---)
H      -25.23   -19.24  -13.24         (---*---)
                                  ---------+---------+---------+-------
                                        -16        0        16


BRAND = G   subtracted from:

BRAND   Lower   Center   Upper   ---------+---------+---------+-------
H      -30.38   -24.39  -18.39   (---*---)
                                  ---------+---------+---------+-------
                                        -16        0        16
```

FIGURE 8.25

MINITAB Tukey multiple comparisons for brand in second factorial golf experiment

F-test leads to the inference that the mean distance differs for two clubs. It is no surprise (to golfers) that the mean distance for balls hit with driver is significantly greater than the mean distance for those hit with the five-iron.

To determine which of the Brands' mean distances differ, we want to compare the $k = 4$ Brand means using Tukey's method at $\alpha = .10$. The results of these multiple comparisons are displayed in the MINITAB printout, Figure 8.25. MINITAB computes simultaneous 90% confidence intervals for the $c = (4)(3)/2 = 6$ possible comparisons of the form $\mu_i - \mu_j$. These intervals (highlighted on the printout) are summarized in Table 8.15. Any interval that does not include 0 implies a significant difference between the two treatment means. You can see that Brands G and F are associated with significantly greater mean distances than Brands E and H, but we cannot distinguish between Brands G and F or between Brands E and H.

Look Back Since the interaction between Brand and Club was not significant, we conclude that this difference among brands applies to both clubs. The sample means for all Club-Brand combinations are shown in Figure 8.26 and appear to support the conclusions of the tests and comparisons. Note that the Brand means maintain their relative positions for each Club—brands F and G dominate brands E and H for both the driver and five-iron.

TABLE 8.15 Summary of Tukey's Multiple Comparisons

Comparison	90% Confidence Interval	Inference
$\mu_F - \mu_E$	(10.00, 21.99)	$\mu_F > \mu_E$
$\mu_G - \mu_E$	(15.15, 27.15)	$\mu_G > \mu_E$
$\mu_H - \mu_E$	(-9.24, 2.76)	No significant difference
$\mu_G - \mu_F$	(-.85, 11.15)	No significant difference
$\mu_H - \mu_F$	(-25.23, -13.24)	$\mu_H < \mu_F$
$\mu_H - \mu_G$	(-30.38, -18.39)	$\mu_H < \mu_G$

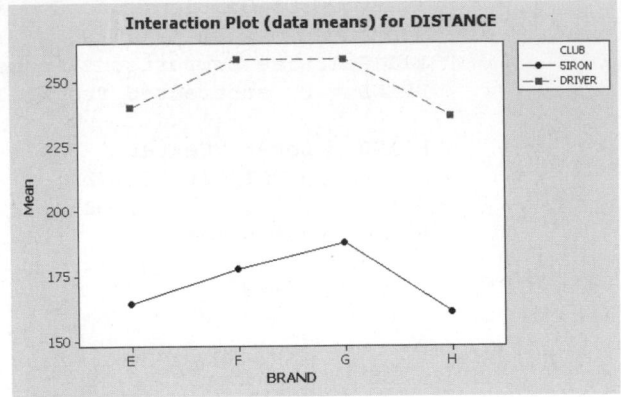

FIGURE 8.26
MINITAB means plot for second factorial golf ball experiment

Now Work Exercise 8.66

The analysis of factorial experiments can become complex if the number of factors is increased. Even the two-factor experiment becomes more difficult to analyze if some factor combinations have different numbers of observations than others. We have provided an introduction to these important experiments using two-factor factorials with equal numbers of observations for each treatment. Although similar principles apply to most factorial experiments, you should consult the references for this chapter at the end of the book if you need to design and analyze more complex factorials.

Exercises 8.58–8.72

Learning the Mechanics

8.58 Suppose you conduct a 4 × 3 factorial experiment.
  a. How many factors are used in the experiment?
  b. Can you determine the factor type(s)—qualitative or quantitative—from the information given? Explain.
  c. Can you determine the number of levels used for each factor? Explain.
  d. Describe a treatment for this experiment, and determine the number of treatments used.
  e. What problem is caused by using a single replicate of this experiment? How is the problem solved?

8.59 The partially completed ANOVA for a 3 × 4 factorial experiment with two replications is shown below.

Source	df	SS	MS	F
A	–	.8	—	—
B	–	5.3	—	—
AB	–	9.6	—	—
Error	–	—	—	
Total	–	17.0		

  a. Complete the ANOVA table.
  b. Which sums of squares are combined to find the Sum of Squares for Treatments? Do the data provide sufficient evidence to indicate that the treatment means differ? Use $\alpha = .05$.
  c. Does the result of the test in part **b** warrant further testing? Explain.
  d. What is meant by *factor interaction*, and what is the practical implication if it exists?

  e. Test to determine whether these factors interact to affect the response mean. Use $\alpha = .05$, and interpret the result.
  f. Does the result of the interaction test warrant further testing? Explain.

8.60 The partially complete ANOVA table given here is for a two-factor factorial experiment.

Source	df	SS	MS	F
Treatments	7	4.1	—	—
A	3	—	.75	—
B	1	.95	—	—
AB	—	—	.30	—
Error	—	—	—	
Total	23	6.5		

  a. Give the number of levels for each factor.
  b. How many observations were collected for each factor-level combination?
  c. Complete the ANOVA table.
  d. Test to determine whether the treatment means differ. Use $\alpha = .10$.
  e. Conduct the tests of factor interaction and main effects, each at the $\alpha = .10$ level of significance. Which of the tests are warranted as part of the factorial analysis? Explain.

8.61 The following two-way table gives data for a 2 × 3 factorial experiment with two observations for each factor-level combination.

LM8_61

	FACTOR B		
Level	1	2	3
Factor A 1	3.1, 4.0	4.6, 4.2	6.4, 7.1
2	5.9, 5.3	2.9, 2.2	3.3, 2.5

a. Identify the treatments for this experiment. Calculate and plot the treatment means, using the response variable as the y-axis and the levels of factor B as the x-axis. Use the levels of factor A as plotting symbols. Do the treatment means appear to differ? Do the factors appear to interact?

b. The MINITAB ANOVA printout for this experiment is shown below. Sum the appropriate sums of squares and test to determine whether the treatment means differ at the $\alpha = .05$ level of significance. Does the test support your visual interpretation from part **a?**

c. Does the result of the test in part **b** warrant a test for interaction between the two factors? If so, perform it using $\alpha = .05$.

d. Do the results of the previous tests warrant tests of the two factor main effects? If so, perform them using $\alpha = .05$.

e. Interpret the results of the tests. Do they support your visual interpretation from part **a?**

Two-way ANOVA: RESPONSE versus A, B

```
Source       DF      SS        MS       F       P
A             1    4.4408   4.44083   18.06   0.005
B             2    4.1267   2.06333    8.39   0.018
Interaction   2   18.0067   9.00333   36.62   0.000
Error         6    1.4750   0.24583
Total        11   28.0492

S = 0.4958   R-Sq = 94.74%   R-Sq(adj) = 90.36%
```

8.62 The next table gives data for a 2×2 factorial experiment with two observations per factor-level combination.

LM8_62

	FACTOR B	
Level	1	2
Factor A 1	29.6, 35.2	47.3, 42.1
2	12.9, 17.6	28.4, 22.7

a. Identify the treatments for this experiment. Calculate and plot the treatment means, using the response variable as the y-axis and the levels of factor B as the x-axis. Use the levels of factor A as plotting symbols. Do the treatment means appear to differ? Do the factors appear to interact?

b. Use the computational formulas in Appendix C to create an ANOVA table for this experiment.

c. Test to determine whether the treatment means differ at the $\alpha = .05$ level of significance. Does the test support your visual interpretation from part **a?**

d. Does the result of the test in part **b** warrant a test for interaction between the two factors? If so, perform it using $\alpha = .05$.

e. Do the results of the previous tests warrant tests of the two factor main effects? If so, perform them using $\alpha = .05$.

f. Interpret the results of the tests. Do they support your visual interpretation from part **a?**

g. Given the results of your tests, which pairs of means, if any, should be compared?

8.63 Suppose a 3×3 factorial experiment is conducted with three replications. Assume that SS(Total) $= 1,000$. For each of the following scenarios, form an ANOVA table, conduct the appropriate tests, and interpret the results.

a. The Sum of Squares of factor A main effect [SS(A)] is 20% of SS(Total), the Sum of Squares for factor B main effect [SS(B)] is 10% of SS(Total), and the Sum of Squares for interaction [SS(AB)] is 10% of SS(Total).

b. SS(A) is 10%, SS(B) is 10%, and SS(AB) is 50% of SS(Total).

c. SS(A) is 40%, SS(B) is 10%, and SS(AB) is 20% of SS(Total).

d. SS(A) is 40%, SS(B) is 40%, and SS(AB) is 10% of SS(Total).

Applying the Concepts—Basic

8.64 Baker's versus brewer's yeast. The *Electronic Journal of*
NW *Biotechnology* (Dec. 15, 2003) published an article on a comparison of two yeast extracts, baker's yeast and brewer's yeast. Brewer's yeast is a surplus by-product obtained from a brewery, hence it is less expensive than primary-grown baker's yeast. Samples of both yeast extracts were prepared at four different temperatures (45, 48, 51, and 54°C); thus, a 2×4 factorial design with yeast extract at two levels and temperature at four levels was employed. The response variable was the autolysis yield (recorded as a percentage).

a. How many treatments are included in the experiment?

b. An ANOVA found sufficient evidence of factor interaction at $\alpha = .05$. Interpret this result practically.

c. Give the null and alternative hypotheses for testing the main effects of yeast extract and temperature.

d. Explain why the tests, part **c,** should not be conducted.

e. Multiple comparisons of the four temperature means were conducted for each of the two yeast extracts. Interpret the results shown below.

Baker's yeast:	Mean yield (%):	41.1	47.5	48.6	50.3
	Temperature (°C):	54	45	48	51
Brewer's yeast:	Mean yield (%):	39.4	47.3	49.2	49.6
	Temperature (°C):	54	51	48	45

8.65 Removing bacteria from water. A coagulation-microfiltration process for removing bacteria from water was investigated in *Environmental Science & Engineering* (Sept. 1, 2000). Chemical engineers at Seoul National University performed a designed experiment to estimate the effect of both the level of the coagulant and acidity (pH) level on the coagulation efficiency of the process. Six levels of coagulant (5, 10, 20, 50, 100, and 200 milligrams per liter) and six pH levels (4.0, 5.0, 6.0, 7.0, 8.0, and 9.0) were employed. Water specimens collected from the Han River in Seoul, Korea, were placed in jars and each jar randomly assigned to receive one of the $6 \times 6 = 36$ combinations of coagulant level and pH level.

a. What type of experimental design was applied in this study?

b. Give the factors, factor levels, and treatments for the study.

8.66 Students' use of the computer. A computer lab at the
NW University of Oklahoma is open 24 hours a day, 7 days a week. In *Production and Inventory Management Journal* (3rd Qtr., 1999), S. Barmon investigated whether usage differed significantly (1) among the days of the week and (2) among the hours of the day. Using student log-on records, data on hourly student loads (number of users per hour) were collected during a 7-week period. A factorial ANOVA was used to analyze the data with the results presented in the table below.

Source	df	F	P
Model	167	25.06	.001
Error	1004		
Total	1171		

$R^2 = .8065$

Source	df	F	P
Day	6	68.39	.0001
Time	23	156.80	.0001
Day × Time	138	1.22	.0527

Source: Barman, S. "A Statistical Analysis of the Attendance Pattern of a Computer Laboratory." *Production and Inventory Management Journal,* Third Quarter, 1999, pp. 26–30.

a. Is this an observational or a designed experiment? Explain.

b. What are the two factors of the experiment and how many levels of each factor are used?

c. This is an a × b factorial experiment. What are *a* and *b*?

d. Conduct a test to determine whether any of the *a* × *b* treatment means significantly differ. Use $\alpha = .01$.

e. Specify the null and alternative hypotheses that should be used to test for an interaction effect between the two factors of the study.

f. Conduct the test of part **e** using $\alpha = .01$. Interpret your result in the context of the problem.

g. If appropriate, conduct main effects tests for both day and time. Use $\alpha = .01$. Interpret your results in the context of the problem.

8.67 Impact of paper color on exam scores. A study published in
NW *Teaching Psychology* (May 1998) examined how external clues influence student performance. Undergraduate students were randomly assigned to one of four different midterm examinations. Form 1 was printed on blue paper and contained difficult questions, while form 2 was also printed on blue paper but contained simple questions. Form 3 was printed on red paper, with difficult questions; form 4 was printed on red paper with simple questions. The researchers were interested in the impact that Color (red or blue) and Question (simple or difficult) had on mean exam score.

a. What experimental design was employed in this study? Identify the factors and treatments.

b. The researchers conducted an ANOVA and found a significant interaction between Color and Question (*p*-value < .03). Interpret this result.

c. The sample mean scores (percentage correct) for the four exam forms are listed in the table below. Plot the four means on a graph to illustrate the Color × Question interaction.

Form	Color	Question	Mean Score
1	Blue	Difficult	53.3
2	Blue	Simple	80.0
3	Red	Difficult	39.3
4	Red	Simple	73.6

Applying the Concepts—Intermediate

8.68 Factors that impact a customer's willingness to buy. Advancements in information technology have yielded services that compete against products with each providing roughly the same benefits to the consumer (e.g., home answering machines and voice-mail services). With the advent of such services, consumers also face different types of pricing schemes. Using a 2 × 2 factorial design, D. Fortin and T. Greenlee of the University of Rhode Island investigated the effects of the type of message retrieval system (answering machine vs. voice-mail service) and the type of pricing (lump sum amount for 5 years of use vs. monthly cost for 5 years of use) on consumers' willingness to buy (*Journal of Business Research,* Vol. 41, 1998). The first pricing option requires the consumer to do mental arithmetic to determine the total cost of the system; the second provides the true full cost. Thirty subjects were randomly assigned to each of the four treatments. Each was exposed to a purchase situation involving the relevant product or service and payment description and was asked to indicate his or her willingness to buy the item on a 5-point scale (1 = definitely would not buy; 5 = definitely would buy). The results are presented in the incomplete ANOVA table below.

a. Fill in the degrees of freedom (df) column in the ANOVA table.

b. Specify the null and alternative hypotheses that should be used in testing for interaction effects between type of message retrieval system and pricing option.

c. Conduct the test of part **b** using $\alpha = .05$. Interpret the results in the context of the problem.

d. Given the results of part **c,** is it advisable to conduct main effects tests? Why or why not? If so, perform the appropriate main effects tests using $\alpha = .05$.

Source	df	SS	MS	F
Type of message retrieval system	—	—	—	2.001
Pricing option	—	—	—	5.019
Type of system × Pricing option	—	—	—	4.986
Error	—	—	—	
Total	119	—		

Source: Adapted from Fortin, D., and Greenlee, T. "Using a Product/Service Evaluation Frame: An Experiment on the Economic Equivalence of Product versus Service Alternatives for Message Retrieval Systems." *Journal of Business Research,* Vol. 41, 1998, pp. 205–214.

8.69 Improving a can–filling process. *Quality Engineering* (Vol. 2, 1990) published the results of an experiment that was conducted by a dog food manufacturer to improve a filling process in which ground meat is packed into cans. The process uses a rotary filling machine with six cylinders, each of which dispenses ground meat. The company wanted to study the effects of differences in batches of meat and differences in cylinders on the weight of the final product. Five batches of meat were used in the experiment. Three filled cans were randomly selected from each cylinder while each batch was being run. The cans were weighed and the weights were recorded. To simplify the analysis, the weights were coded by subtracting 12 ounces from each weight. The coded data appear in the table below.

a. What type of experimental design was used by the dog food manufacturer?

b. Identify the factors used in the study and their levels.

c. How many different treatments were used in the experiment?

d. Analyze the data with an analysis of variance. Summarize the results in an ANOVA table.

e. In the context of the problem, explain what it means to say that batch and cylinder interact. Speculate on what could cause such an interaction.

f. Test for an interaction between batches and cylinders. Use $\alpha = .05$.

g. If appropriate, test for main effects using $\alpha = .05$.

DOGFOOD

		BATCH				
		1	2	3	4	5
Cylinder	**1**	1	4	6	3	1
		1	3	3	1	3
		2	5	7	3	3
	2	−1	−2	3	2	1
		3	1	1	0	0
		−1	0	5	1	1
	3	1	2	2	1	3
		1	0	4	3	3
		1	1	3	3	3
	4	−2	2	3	0	0
		3	0	3	0	1
		0	1	4	2	1
	5	1	2	0	1	−2
		1	1	1	0	3
		−1	5	2	−1	1
	6	0	0	3	3	3
		1	0	3	0	1
		1	3	4	2	2

Source: Griffith, B. A., Westman, A. E. R., and Lloyd, B. H. "Analysis of Variance." *Quality Engineering,* Vol 2. No. 2. 1990, pp. 195–226.

8.70 Manager's trust and job-related tension. Research published in *Accounting, Organizations and Society* (Vol. 19, 1994) investigated whether the effects of different performance evaluation styles (PES) on the level of job-related tension is affected by trust. Three performance evaluation styles were considered. Each is related to the way in which accounting information is used for the purpose of evaluation. The three styles are budget-constrained (BC), profit-conscious (PC), and the nonaccounting style (NA), which focuses on factors such as quality of output and attitude toward the job. A questionnaire was administered to 215 managers working in 18 Australian organizations. It measured the performance evaluation style of each manager's superior, the manager's job-related tension, and the manager's level of trust (low, medium, and high) in his or her supe-

rior. These data were used to produce the partial ANOVA table and table of treatment means shown next.

Source	df	SS	MS	F
PES	2	2.1774	—	—
Trust	—	7.6367	—	—
PES × Trust	4	1.7380	—	—
Error	206	—		
Total	214	161.1162		

		PERFORMANCE EVALUATION STYLE		
		BC	PC	NA
Trust	**Low**	3.2350 ($n = 32$)	3.111 ($n = 24$)	3.2290 ($n = 16$)
	Medium	2.7601 ($n = 26$)	2.8530 ($n = 31$)	2.6373 ($n = 14$)
	High	2.3067 ($n = 30$)	2.4436 ($n = 26$)	3.1810 ($n = 16$)

Source: Ross, A. "Trust as a Moderator of the Effect of Performance Evaluation Style on Job-Related Tension: A Research Note." *Accounting, Organizations and Society,* Vol. 19, No. 7, 1994, pp. 633 (Tables 3 and 4).

a. Describe the treatments of this study.

b. Complete the ANOVA table.

c. Investigate the presence of an interaction effect by conducting the appropriate hypothesis test using $\alpha = .05$.

d. Use a plot of treatment means to investigate the interaction effect. Interpret your results. Are your results of parts **c** and **d** consistent?

e. Explain why the F-tests for the two main effects are irrelevant given your answers to parts **c** and **d**.

Applying the Concepts—Advanced

8.71 Testing a new pain-reliever tablet. Refer to the *Tropical Journal of Pharmaceutical Research* (June 2003) study of the impact of binding agent, binding concentration, and relative density on the mean dissolution time of pain-relief tablets, Exercise 8.13 (p. 482). Recall that the binding agent was set at two levels (khaya gum and PVP), binding concentration at two levels (.5% and 4.0%), and relative density at two levels (low and high); thus, a $2 \times 2 \times 2$ factorial design was employed. The sample mean dissolution times for the treatments associated with the factors binding agent and relative density when the other factor (binding concentration) is held fixed at .5% are $\bar{x}_{Gum/Low} = 4.70$, $\bar{x}_{Gum/High} = 7.95$, $\bar{x}_{PVP/Low} = 3.00$, and $\bar{x}_{PVP/High} = 4.10$. Do the results suggest there is an interaction between binding agent and relative density? Explain.

8.72 On the trail of the cockroach. Knowledge of how cockroaches forage for food is valuable for companies that develop and manufacture roach bait and traps. Many entomologists believe, however, that the navigational behavior of cockroaches scavenging for food is random. D. Miller of Virginia Tech University challenged the "random-walk" theory by designing an experiment to test a cockroach's ability to follow a trail of their fecal material (*Explore,* Research at the University of Florida, Fall 1998). A methanol extract from roach feces—called a *pheromone*—was used to create a chemical trail. German cockroaches were released at the beginning of the trail, one at a time, and a video surveillance camera was used to monitor the roach's movements. In addition to the trail containing the fecal extract (the treatment), a trail using methanol only (the control) was created. To determine if trail-following ability differed among cockroaches of different age, sex, and reproductive status, four roach groups were utilized in the experiment: adult males, adult females, gravid (pregnant) females, and nymphs (immatures). Twenty roaches of each type were randomly assigned to the treatment trail and 10 of each type were randomly assigned to the control trail. Thus, a total of 120 roaches were used in the experiment. The movement pattern of each cockroach was measured (in "pixels") as the average trail deviation. The data for the 120 cockroaches in the study are stored in the data file named **ROACH**. (The first 5 and last 5 observations in the data set are listed here.) Conduct a complete analysis of the data. Determine whether roaches can distinguish between the fecal extract and control trail and whether trail-following ability differs according to age, sex, and reproductive status.

ROACH

Trail Deviation	Roach Group	Trail
3.1	Adult Male	Extract
42.0	Adult Male	Control
6.2	Adult Male	Extract
22.7	Adult Male	Control
34.0	Adult Male	Extract
⋮	⋮	⋮
23.8	Nymph	Extract
5.1	Nymph	Extract
3.8	Nymph	Extract
3.1	Nymph	Extract
2.8	Nymph	Extract

KEY TERMS

Analysis of variance (ANOVA)   489
Balanced design   525
Blocks   507
Bonferroni multiple comparisons procedure   501
Comparisonwise error rate   501
Complete factorial experiment   522
Completely randomized design   482
Dependent variable   476
Designed experiment   477
Experimental unit   477
Experimentwise error rate   501
Factorial experiments   521

Factor interaction   523
Factor levels   477
Factor main effect   523
Factors   476
F statistic   485
Independent variables   476
Mean square for error   485
Mean square for treatments   485
Multiple comparisons of means   501
Observational experiment   477
Qualitative factors   476
Quantitative factors   476
Randomized block design   508

Replicates of the experiment   525
Response variable   476
Robust method   492
Scheffé multiple comparisons procedure   501
Single-factor experiment   521
Sum of squares for blocks   508
Sum of squares for error   485
Sum of squares for treatments   484
Treatments   477
Tukey multiple comparisons procedure   501
Two-factor experiment   521

GUIDE TO SELECTING THE EXPERIMENTAL DESIGN

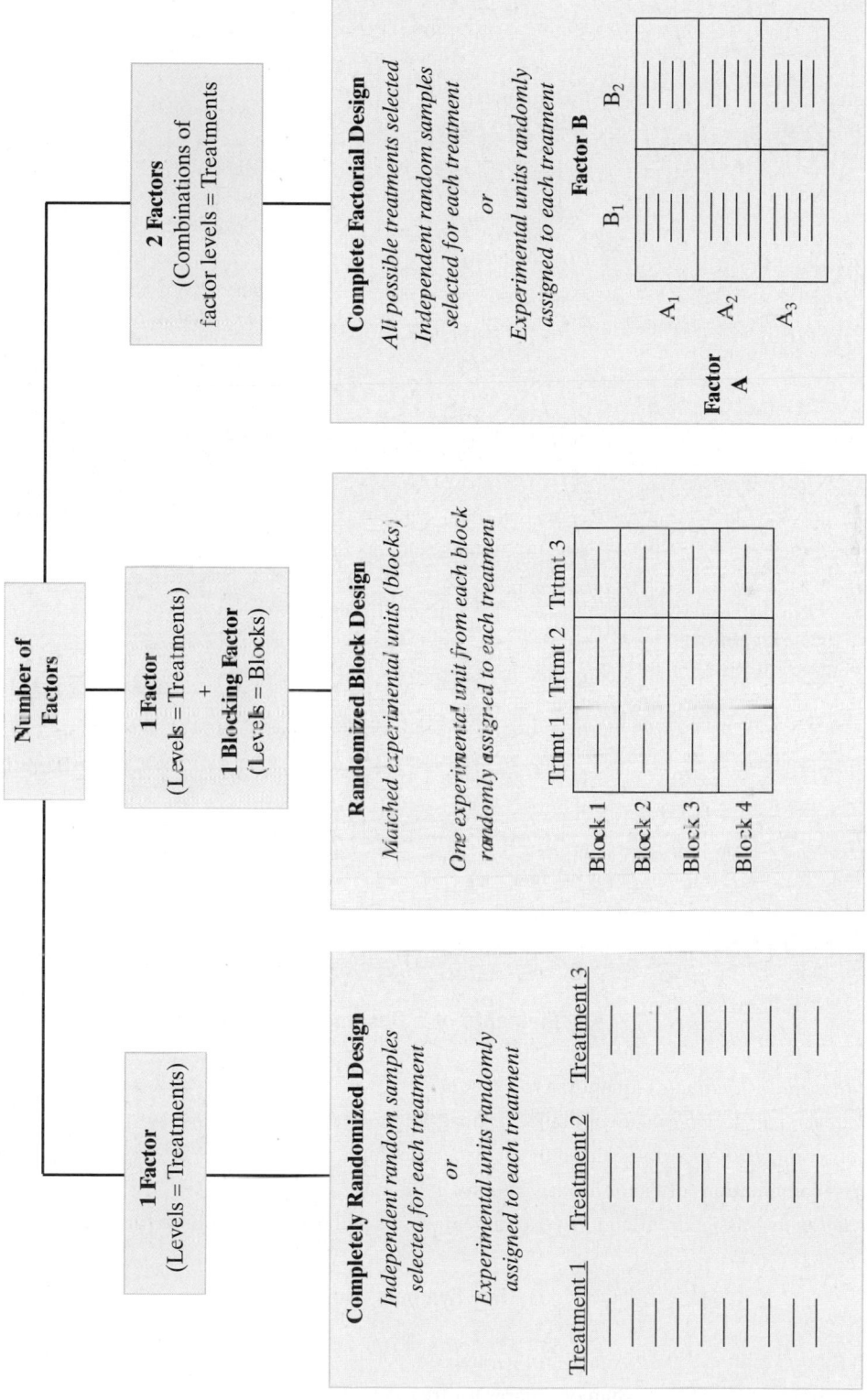

GUIDE TO CONDUCTING ANOVA *F*-TESTS

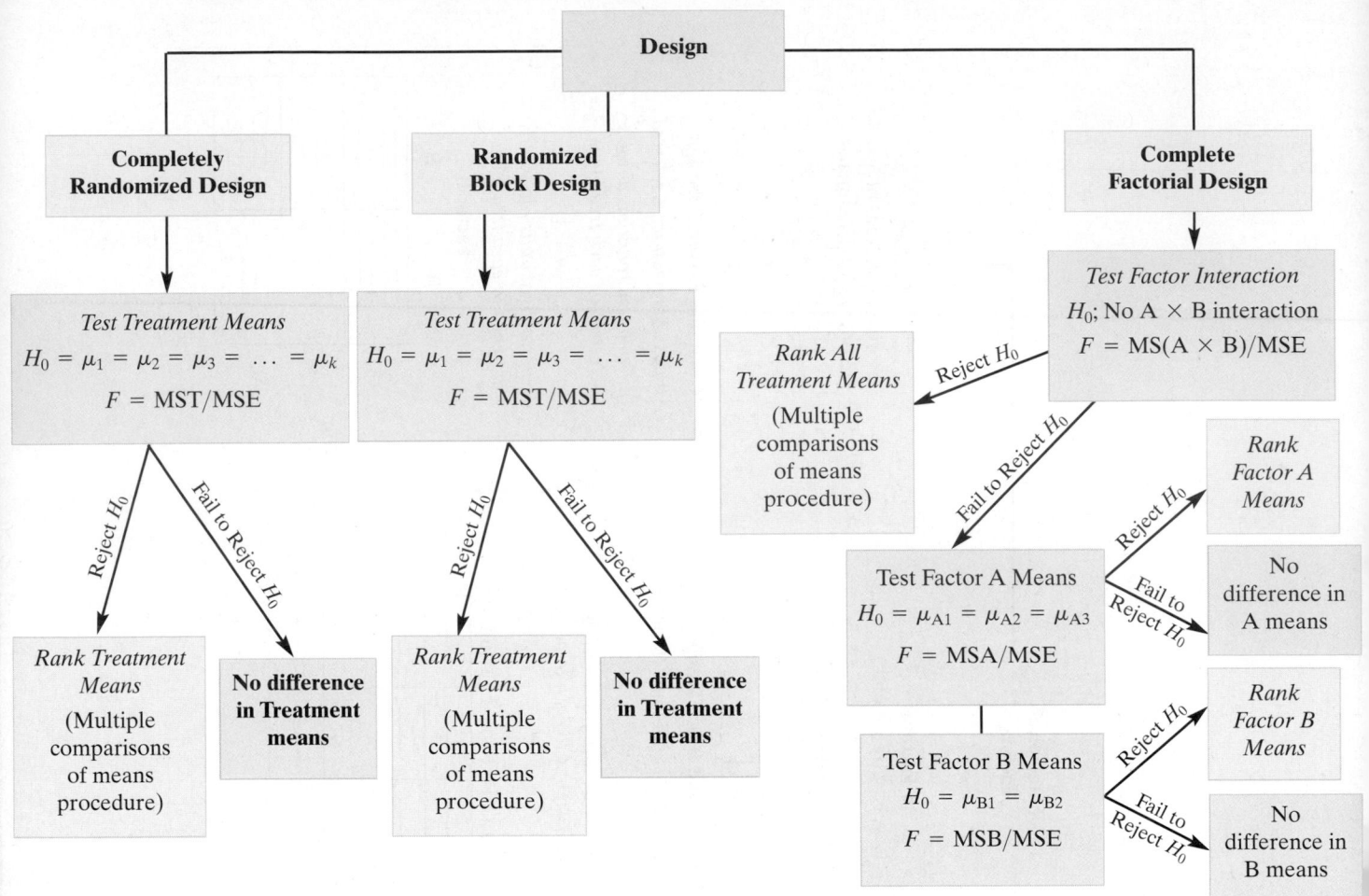

CHAPTER NOTES

Key Elements of a Designed Experiment:

(1) *Response (dependent) variable*—quantitative

(2) *Factors (independent variables)*—quantitative or qualitative

(3) *Factor levels (values of factors)*—selected by the experimenter

(4) *Treatments*—combinations of factor levels

(5) *Experimental units*—assign treatments to experimental units and measure response for each

Key Symbols/Notation

ANOVA	Analysis of variance
SST	Sum of squares for treatments
MST	Mean square for treatments
SSB	Sum of squares for blocks
MSB	Mean square for blocks

Continued

SSE	Sum of squares for error
MSE	Mean square for error
$a \times b$ factorial	Factorial design with one factor at a levels and the other factor at b levels
SS(A)	Sum of squares for main effect factor A
MS(A)	Mean square for main effect factor A
SS(B)	Sum of squares for main effect factor B
MS(B)	Mean square for main effect factor B
SS(AB)	Sum of squares for factor A $\times$ B interaction
MS(AB)	Mean square for factor A $\times$ B interaction

Balanced Design

Sample sizes for each treatment are equal

Tests for main effects in a factorial design

only appropriate if the test for factor interaction is nonsignificant

Conditions Required for Valid *F*-Test in a Completely Randomized Design

(1) All k treatment populations are approximately normal
(2) $\sigma_1^2 = \sigma_2^2 = \ldots = \sigma_k^2$

Conditions Required for Valid *F*-Tests in a Randomized Block Design

(1) All treatment-block populations are approximately normal
(2) All treatment-block populations have the same variance

Conditions Required for Valid *F*-Tests in a Complete Factorial Design

1. All treatment populations are approximately normal
2. All treatment populations have the same variance

Robust method

Slight to moderate departures from normality do not have impact on validity of the ANOVA results.

Experimentwise error rate

risk of making at least one Type I error when making multiple comparisons of means in ANOVA

Number of pairwise comparisons with k treatment means:

$$c = k(k - 1)/2$$

Multiple Comparisons of Means Methods

Tukey:
(1) Balanced design
(2) Pairwise comparisons of means

Bonferroni:
(1) Either balanced or unbalanced design
(2) Pairwise comparisons of means

Scheffé:
(1) Either balanced or unbalanced design
(2) General contrasts of means

SUPPLEMENTARY EXERCISES 8.73–8.95

Learning the Mechanics

8.73 Explain the difference between an experiment that utilizes a completely randomized design and one that utilizes a randomized block design.

8.74 What are the treatments in a two-factor experiment, with factor A at three levels and factor B at two levels?

8.75 Why does the experimentwise error rate of a multiple comparisons procedure differ from the significance level for each comparison (assuming the experiment has more than two treatments)?

8.76 A completely randomized design is utilized to compare four treatment means. The data are shown in the table.

⊙ **LM8_76**

Treatment 1	Treatment 2	Treatment 3	Treatment 4
8	6	9	12
10	9	10	13
9	8	8	10
10	8	11	11
11	7	12	11

  a. Given that SST = 36.95 and SS(Total) = 62.55, complete an ANOVA table for this experiment.

  b. Is there evidence that the treatment means differ? Use $\alpha = .10$.

  c. Place a 90% confidence interval on the mean response for treatment 4.

8.77 An experiment utilizing a randomized block design was conducted to compare the mean responses for four treatments—A, B, C, and D. The treatments were randomly assigned to the four experimental units in each of five blocks. The data are shown in the following table.

⊙ **EX10_77**

Treatment	BLOCK				
	1	2	3	4	5
A	8.6	7.5	8.7	9.8	7.4
B	7.3	6.3	7.3	8.4	6.3
C	9.1	8.3	9.0	9.9	8.2
D	9.3	8.2	9.2	10.0	8.4

  a. Given that SS(Total) = 22.31 and SS(Block) = 10.688 and SSE = .288, complete an ANOVA table for the experiment.

  b. Do the data provide sufficient evidence to indicate a difference among treatment means? Test using $\alpha = .05$.

  c. Does the result of the test in part **b** warrant further comparison of the treatment means? If so, how many pairwise comparisons need to be made?

  d. Is there evidence that the block means differ? Use $\alpha = .05$.

8.78 The next table shows a partially completed ANOVA table for a two-factor factorial experiment.
  a. Complete the ANOVA table.
  b. How many levels were used for each factor? How many treatments were used? How many replications were performed?

Source	df	SS	MS	F
A	3	2.6	—	—
B	5	9.2	—	—
$A \times B$	—	—	3.1	—
Error	—	18.7		
Total	47			

  c. Find the value of the Sum of Squares for Treatments. Test to determine whether the data provide evidence that the treatment means differ. Use $\alpha = .05$.

  d. Is further testing of the nature of factor effects warranted? If so, test to determine whether the factors interact. Use $\alpha = .05$. Interpret the result.

Applying the Concepts—Basic

8.79 **Strength of fiberboard boxes.** The *Journal of Testing and Evaluation* (July 1992) published an investigation of the mean compression strength of corrugated fiberboard shipping containers. Comparisons were made for boxes of five different sizes: A, B, C, D, and E. Twenty identical boxes of each size were tested and the peak compression strength (pounds) recorded for each box. The figure below shows the sample means for the five box types as well as the variation around each sample mean.
  a. Explain why the data is collected as a completely randomized design.
  b. Refer to box types B and D. Based on the graph, does it appear that the mean compressive strengths of these two box types are significantly different? Explain.
  c. Based on the graph, does it appear that the mean compressive strengths of all five box types are significantly different? Explain.

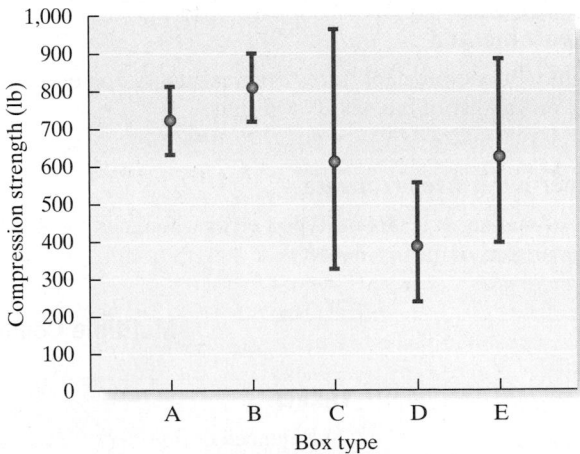

Source: Singh, S. P., et al. "Compression of Single-Wall Corrugated Shipping Containers Using Fixed and Floating Test Platens." *Journal of Testing and Evaluation,* Vol. 20, No. 4, July 1992, p. 319 (Figure 3). Copyright American Society for Testing and Materials. Reprinted with permission.

8.80 **Study on how to ask survey questions.** Marketing researchers generally agree that how you ask a question of consumers is as important as what you ask. An article in the *Journal of the Market Research Society* (July 1996) investigated the effects of positively versus negatively worded questions on consumer responses. Consumers were asked to express their level of agreement with positively worded statements on a scale of 1 (strongly disagree) to 5 (strongly agree). The scale values were reversed for negatively worded questions. A total of 154 subjects from the Midwest were randomly assigned to four treatment conditions defined by the two levels of the variables Involvement in Topic (high and low) and Question Wording (positive/negative). Each subject was asked to respond to a question (positively worded for one group and negatively worded for the other group). The 5-point scales described above were used. Those in the high-involvement condition received a question about the Gulf War; those in the low-involvement condition received a general question about shopping and products. The resulting data were analyzed using ANOVA.

a. What type of experimental design was used by the researcher?

b. Identify the factors used in the experiment. Are they quantitative or qualitative?

c. Describe the levels of each factor.

d. Describe the experiment's treatments.

e. What is the experiment's dependent variable?

8.81 **Fortune's E-50 list.** The Fortune E-50 is a listing of the top 50 electronic commerce and Internet-based companies, as determined by *Fortune* magazine each year. *Fortune* groups the companies into four categories: (1) e-companies, (2) Internet software and service, (3) Internet hardware, and (4) Internet communication. Consider a study to compare the mean rates of return for the stock of companies in the four *Fortune* categories. Since the age of an electronic commerce or Internet-based company may have an impact on rate of return, the study is designed to remove any age variation. Four 1-year-old companies, four 3-year-old companies, and four 5-year-old companies were selected; within each age group, one company was randomly selected from Category 1, one from Category 2, one from Category 3, and one from Category 4.

a. What type of experimental design is employed?

b. Indentify the key elements of the experiment (i.e., treatments, blocks, response variable, and experimental unit).

8.82 **Diversifying real estate holdings.** In forming real estate portfolios, investors may choose to diversify holdings across submarkets within the same metropolitan region. J. Rabianski and P. Cheng of Georgia State University investigated the appropriateness of this strategy for office properties (*Journal of Real Estate Portfolio Management,* Vol. 3, 1997). Using the office vacancy rate of a submarket as a proxy for total rate of return for the office submarket, the researchers compared submarkets within several U.S. metropolitan areas. The next table presents the mean vacancy rates of the eight office submarkets of Atlanta, Georgia, for a period of nine years. Quarterly vacancy rates were used in calculating the means.

a. Specify the null and alternative hypotheses to use in comparing the mean vacancy rates of the eight office-property submarkets of Atlanta.

b. The researchers reported on ANOVA *F* statistic of $F = 17.54$ for the Atlanta data. Conduct the hypothesis test you specified in part **a**. Draw the appropriate conclusions in the context of the problem.

c. Give the approximate *p*-value for the test you conducted in part **b**.

Submarket	Mean Vacancy Rate (%)
North Central	16.73
Northwest	16.81
Buckhead	16.85
Northeast	16.95
Midtown	19.75
North Lake	20.38
Downtown	20.73
South	28.26

Source: Adapted from Rabianski, J. S., and Cheng, P., "Intrametropolitan Spatial Diversification." *Journal of Real Estate Portfolio Management,* Vol.3.No.2, 1997, pp. 117–128.

d. What assumptions must be met to ensure the validity of the inference you made in part **b**? Which of these assumptions do you consider the most questionable in this application? Why?

e. The table gives the Bonferroni rankings of the means vacancy rates. (The vertical line connects means that are not significantly different at $\alpha = .10$.) Fully interpret the results.

8.83 **Leadership style and subordinate behavior.** Leadership acts occur when one person tries to influence the behavior of others toward the attainment of some goal. The effects of leadership style on the behavior of subordinates were investigated in *Accounting, Organizations and Society* (Vol. 20, 1995). Four types of leadership style were defined based on two variables: the degree of control applied (high or low) and the level of consideration shown for subordinates (high or low). A sample of 257 senior auditors in Big-Six accounting firms yielded the following distribution of leadership styles for the auditors' leaders:

Leadership Style	n
A. High control, Low consideration	51
B. Low control, Low consideration	63
C. High control, High consideration	79
D. Low control, High consideration	64
Total	257

All subjects were asked to indicate (confidentially) how frequently their auditing fieldwork had been intentionally substandard in a particular way. They were asked to respond using a scale that ranged from 1 (never) to 5 (always). These data are summarized in the following table. An ANOVA conducted to test for differences in the four treatment means yielded $F = 30.4$.

Leadership Style	Mean	Standard Deviation	Bonferroni Analysis: Significantly Smaller Means
A	4.27	1.13	B, C, D
B	2.83	1.18	D
C	2.54	1.24	None
D	2.87	1.31	None
Overall	2.87	1.42	

Source: Otley, D. T., and Pierce, B. J. "The Control Problem in Public Accounting Firms: An Empirical Study of the Impact of Leadership Style." *Accounting Organizations and Society,* Vol. 20, No. 5, 1995, pp. 405–420.

a. Do the data indicate that leadership style affects the behavior of subordinates? Test using $\alpha = .05$.

b. The Bonferroni multiple comparisons procedure was used to rank the four treatment means at an experiment-wise error rate of $\alpha = .05$. Carefully interpret the results shown in the table.

c. What assumptions must hold to ensure the validity of the Bonferroni procedure?

Applying the Concepts—Intermediate

8.84   A managerral decision problem. A direct-mail company assembles and stores paper products (envelopes, letters, brochures, order cards, etc.) for its customers. The company estimates the total number of pieces received in a shipment by estimating the weight per piece and then weighing the entire shipment. The company is unsure whether the sample of pieces used to estimate the mean weight per piece should be drawn from a single carton, or whether it is worth the extra time required to pull a few pieces from several cartons. To aid management in making a decision, eight brochures were pulled from each of five cartons of a typical shipment and weighed. The weights (in pounds) are shown in the table.

⊙ CARTONS

Carton 1	Carton 2	Carton 3	Carton 4	Carton 5
.01851	.01872	.01869	.01899	.01882
.01829	.01861	.01853	.01917	.01895
.01844	.01876	.01876	.01852	.01884
.01859	.01886	.01880	.01904	.01835
.01854	.01896	.01880	.01923	.01889
.01853	.01879	.01882	.01905	.01876
.01844	.01879	.01862	.01924	.01891
.01833	.01879	.01860	.01893	.01879

a. Identify the response, factor(s), treatments, and experimental units.

b. Do these data provide sufficient evidence to indicate differences in the mean weight per brochure among the five cartons?

c. What assumptions must be satisfied in order for the test of part **b** to be valid?

d. Use Tukey's method to compare all pairs of means, with $\alpha = .05$ as the overall level of significance.

e. Given the results, make a recommendation to management about whether to sample from one carton or from many cartons.

⊙ OILSPILL

8.85   Hull failures of oil tankers. Refer to the *Marine Technology* (Jan. 1995) study of major ocean oil spills by tanker vessels, Exercise 2.135 (p. 117). The spillage amounts (thousands of metric tons) and cause of accident for 48 tankers are saved in the **OILSPILL** file. Recall that the four accident causes are Collision, Grounding, Fire/explosion, and Hull failure. (*Note:* Delete the two observations with oil spills of unknown causes.)

a. Is there sufficient evidence to indicate differences among the mean spillage amounts for the four accident causes? Test using $\alpha = .01$. Be sure to check any assumptions required for the methodology used to be valid.

b. Conduct a follow-up analysis to rank the treatment means (use $\alpha = .01$).

8.86   Study of anticoagulant drugs. Three anticoagulant drugs are studied to compare their effectiveness in dissolving blood clots. Each of five subjects receives the drugs at equally spaced time intervals and in random order. Time periods between drug applications permit a drug to be passed out of a subject's body before the subject receives the next drug. After each drug is in the bloodstream, the length of time (in seconds) required for a cut of specified size to stop bleeding is recorded. The results are shown in the following table.

⊙ CLOTS

Person	DRUG		
	A	B	C
1	127.5	129.0	135.5
2	130.6	129.1	138.0
3	118.3	111.7	110.1
4	155.5	144.3	162.3
5	180.7	174.4	181.8

a. What type of experimental design was used in this study? Identify the response, factor(s), factor type(s), treatments, and experimental units.

b. Is there evidence of a difference in mean clotting time among the three drugs? Test using $\alpha = .10$.

c. What is the observed significance level of the test you conducted in part **a**? Interpret it.

d. Was blocking effective in reducing the variation among the data? That is, do the data support the contention that the mean clotting time varies from person to person?

e. If warranted, use a multiple comparisons technique to determine whether one of the drugs is most effective. Use an overall significance level of $\alpha = .10$.

8.87   Steel ingot quality study. A quality control supervisor measures the quality of a steel ingot on a scale of 0 to 10. He designs an experiment in which three different temperatures (ranging from 1,100 to 1,200°F) and five different pressures (ranging from 500 to 600 psi) are utilized, with 20 ingots produced at each Temperature-Pressure combination. Identify the following elements of the experiment:

a. Response   **b.** Factor(s) and factor type(s)

c. Treatments   **d.** Experimental units

8.88   Accountants' attitudes toward risk. Louisiana State University professor D. C. Kim investigated the effects of accountants' attitudes toward risk and recent budget-setting performance (relative to their colleagues) on their current budgetary decisions (*Accounting Review*, Apr. 1992). Eighty-one undergraduate students were used as subjects in the study. Using standard risk measurement methods, 40 subjects were found to be risk-seeking and 41 were risk-averse. Subjects were asked to play the role of an entry-level accountant in a public accounting firm. Each was asked to read a hypothetical audit engagement case. Each subject had either a case in which his or her recent performance at budgeting audit costs (billable hours) was either favorable or unfavorable relative to colleagues. After reading the case, each subject was asked to establish either a tight (risky) budget or a safe (riskless) budget and to indicate the strength of his or her preference for the budget. Subjects responded on an 11-point scale that varied from −5 (strong preference for a risky choice) to +5 (strong preference for a riskless choice). From these data, Kim generated the following partial ANOVA table:

Source	df	SS	MS	F
Recent performance (A)	1	243.2	—	—
Risk assessment (B)	1	57.8	—	—
AB	1	—	—	—
Error	77	670.8	—	
Total	80	976.3		

Source: Kim, D. C. "Risk Preferences in Participative Budgeting." *Accounting Review,* Vol. 67, Apr. 1992, pp. 303–318.

a. Complete the ANOVA table.

b. Do the data indicate that factors A and B interact? Test using $\alpha = .05$.

c. Does an individual's risk attitude affect his or her budgetary decisions? Test using $\alpha = .05$.

d. Does recent budgeting performance affect current budgeting decisions? Test using $\alpha = .01$.

8.89 **Product tampering study.** A study in the *Journal of Psychology and Marketing* (Jan. 1992) investigated consumer attitudes toward product tampering. One variable considered was the education level of the consumer. Consumers were divided into five educational classifications and asked to rate their concern about product tampering on a scale of 1 (little or no concern) to 9 (very concerned). The table gives the education levels and the means.

Education Level	Mean	Sample Size
Non–high school graduate	3.731	26
High school graduate	3.224	49
Some college completed	3.330	94
College graduate	3.167	60
Some postgraduate work	4.341	86

a. Identify the type of ANOVA design used in this experiment. Identify the treatments in this experiment.

b. The article compared the mean concern ratings for the five education levels. The F statistic for this test was reported to be 3.298. Conduct a test of hypothesis (at $\alpha = .05$) to determine whether the mean concern ratings differ for at least two of the education levels. [*Hint:* Calculate the degrees of freedom for Treatments and Error from the information given.]

c. Using $\alpha = .05$, a Bonferroni analysis yielded the result shown at the bottom of the page. Interpret the result.

8.90 **Protecting dental patients from radiation.** A composite of a metal powder mixed with a plastic resin was invented to stop a radiation beam used for skin or oral cancer therapy. A 2×2 factorial experiment with two replications was conducted in a dental research lab to measure the degree of radiation traveling through the composite when the density of the metal powder was either a heavy alloy or a light alloy and when a second layer of plastic under the composite was present or absent. The next table shows

the data collected. Use the techniques presented in this chapter to analyze these data, and make a recommendation regarding the preferred method of protecting patients from overexposure to potentially harmful radiation.

⊙ **RADIAT**

		ALLOY DENSITY	
		Heavy	Light
Second Plastic	**Present**	0.04, 0.02	0.46, 0.40
	Absent	0.38, 0.13	1.84, 2.29

Source: Personal Communication from F. Eichmiller, Paffenbarger Research Center, Gaithersburg, MD.

8.91 **Factors impacting on-the-job attitude.** Sixteen workers were randomly selected to participate in an experiment to determine the effects of work scheduling and method of payment on attitude toward the job. Two schedules were employed, the standard 8–5 workday and a modification whereby the worker could decide each day whether to start at 7:00 or 8:00 A.M.; in addition, the worker could choose between a half-hour or 1-hour lunch period each day. The two methods of payment were a standard hourly rate and a reduced hourly rate with an added piece rate based on the worker's production. Four workers were randomly assigned to each of the four scheduling-payment combinations, and each completed an attitude test after 1 month on the job. The test scores are shown in the following table.

⊙ **JOBATT**

		PAYMENT	
		Hourly Rate	Hourly and Piece Rate
Scheduling	**8–5**	54, 68, 55, 63	89, 75, 71, 83
	Worker-Modified Schedule	79, 65, 62, 74	83, 94, 91, 86

a. What type of experiment was performed? Identify the response, factor(s), factor type(s), treatments, and experimental units.

b. Is there evidence that the treatment means differ? Use $\alpha = .05$.

c. If the test in part **b** warrants further analysis, conduct the appropriate tests of interaction and main effects. Interpret your results.

d. What assumptions are necessary to ensure the validity of the inferences? State the assumptions in terms of this experiment.

8.92 **Testing the effectiveness of supermarket sales strategies.** Factorial designs are commonly employed in marketing research to evaluate the effectiveness of sales strategies. At one supermarket, two of the factors were Price level (regular, reduced price, cost to supermarket) and Display level (normal display space, normal display space plus end-of-aisle display, twice the normal display space). A

Multiple Comparisons for Exercise 8.89

Mean	3.167	3.224	3.330	3.731	4.3441
Education Level	College Graduate	High school graduate	Some college	Non–high school graduate	Postgraduate

3×3 complete factorial design was employed, where each treatment was applied three times to a particular product at a particular supermarket. The dependent variable of interest was unit sales for the week. (To minimize treatment carryover effects, each treatment was preceded and followed by a week in which the product was priced at its regular price and was displayed in its normal manner.) The table below reports the data collected.

a. How many treatments are considered in this study?

b. Do the data indicate that the mean sales differ among the treatments? Test using $\alpha = .10$.

c. Is the test of interaction between the factors Price and Display warranted as a result of the test in part **b**? If so, conduct the test using $\alpha = .10$.

d. Are the tests of the main effects for Price and Display warranted as a result of the previous tests? If so, conduct them using $\alpha = .10$.

e. Which pairs of treatment means should be compared as a result of the tests in parts **b–d**?

🔵 **SUPERMKT**

		PRICE		
		Regular	Reduced	Cost to Supermarket
	Normal	989	1,211	1,577
		1,025	1,215	1,559
		1,030	1,182	1,598
Display	**Normal Plus**	1,191	1,860	2,492
		1,233	1,910	2,527
		1,221	1,926	2,511
	Twice Normal	1,226	1,516	1,801
		1,202	1,501	1,833
		1,180	1,498	1,852

Applying the Concepts—Advanced

8.93 **Testing a new insect repellent.** Traditionally, people protect themselves from mosquito bites by applying insect repellent to their skin and clothing. Recent research suggests that permethrin, an insecticide with low toxicity to humans, can provide protection from mosquitoes. A study in the *Journal of the American Mosquito Control Association* (Mar. 1995) investigated whether a tent sprayed with a commercially available 1% permethrin formulation would protect people, both inside and outside the tent, against biting mosquitoes. Two canvas tents—one treated with permethrin, the other untreated—were positioned 25 meters apart on flat dry ground in an area infested with mosquitoes. Eight people participated in the experiment, with four randomly assigned to each tent. Of the four stationed at each tent, two were randomly assigned to stay inside the tent (at opposite corners) and two to stay outside the tent (at opposite corners). During a specified 20-minute period during the night, each person kept count of the number of mosquito bites received. The goal of the study was to determine the effect of both Tent type (treated or untreated) and Location (inside or outside the tent) on the mean mosquito bite count.

a. What type of design was employed in the study?

b. Identify the factors and treatments.

c. Identify the response variable.

d. The study found statistical evidence of interaction between Tent type and Location. Give a practical interpretation of this result.

8.94 **Improving the output of an industrial lathe.** *Quality Engineering* (Vol. 6, 1994) reported the results of an experiment that was designed to find ways to improve the output of an industrial lathe. The lathe is controlled by a computer that automatically feeds bar stock, cuts the stock, machines the surface finish, and releases the part. As it is machined, the bar stock spins and is held in place by a collet. The lathe operator sets the feed (the rate at which bars are machined) and the speed (spin rate). The product characteristic of interest is surface finish. It is measured on a gauge that records the vertical distance a probe travels as it moves along a given horizontal distance on the bar. The rougher the surface, the higher the gauge measurement. The factors that were manipulated in the experiment were speed, feed, collet tightness, and tool wear. The table below reports the factor-level settings and the resulting surface-finish measurements (H = High; L = Low).

a. What type of experimental design was used?

b. How many different treatments were applied?

🔵 **LATHE**

Speed	Feed	Collet Tightness	Surface Tool Wear	Finish
H	H	H	H	216
L	H	H	H	212
H	L	H	H	48
L	L	H	H	40
H	H	L	H	232
L	H	L	H	248
H	L	L	H	514
L	L	L	H	298
H	H	H	L	238
L	H	H	L	219
H	L	H	L	40
L	L	H	L	33
H	H	L	L	230
L	H	L	L	253
H	L	L	L	273
L	L	L	L	101
H	H	H	H	217
L	H	H	H	221
H	L	H	H	39
L	L	H	H	31
H	H	L	H	235
L	H	L	H	238
H	L	L	H	437
L	L	L	H	87
H	H	H	L	245
L	H	H	L	226
H	L	H	L	51
L	L	H	L	33
H	H	L	L	226
L	H	L	L	214
H	L	L	L	691
L	L	L	L	130

Source: Collins, W. H., and Colins, C. B. "Including Residual Analysis in Designed Experiments: Case Studies." *Quality Engineering*, Vol. 6, No. 4, 1994, pp. 547–565.

c. Perform an analysis of variance for these data.

d. Do significant interaction effects exist? Test using $\alpha = .05$. Interpret your results.

e. Is it necessary to perform main effect tests? Why or why not? If so, perform the tests using $\alpha = .05$.

f. What assumptions must hold to ensure the validity of your results in parts **c, d,** and **e?**

Critical Thinking Challenge

8.95 Exam performance study. Refer to the *Teaching of Psychology* (August 1998) study of whether a practice test helps students prepare for a final exam, Exercise 8.11 (p. 482). Recall that undergraduate students were grouped according to their class standing and whether they attended a review session or took a practice test prior to the final exam. The experimental design was a 3×2 factorial design, with Class Standing at 3 levels (low, medium, or high) and Exam Preparation at 2 levels (practice exam or review session). There were 22 students in each of the $3 \times 2 = 6$ treatment groups. After completing the final exam, each student rated their exam preparation on an 11-point scale ranging from 0 (not helpful at all) to 10 (extremely helpful). The data for this experiment (simulated from summary statistics provided in the article) are saved in the **PRACEXAM** file. The first 5 and last 5 observations in the data set are listed below. Conduct a complete analysis of variance of the helpfulness ratings data, including (if warranted) multiple comparisons of means. Do your findings support the research conclusion that "students at all levels of academic ability benefit from a . . . practice exam"?

PRACEXAM

Exam Preparation	Class Standing	Helpfulness Rating
PRACTICE	LOW	6
PRACTICE	LOW	7
PRACTICE	LOW	7
PRACTICE	LOW	5
PRACTICE	LOW	3
⋮	⋮	⋮
REVIEW	HI	5
REVIEW	HI	2
REVIEW	HI	5
REVIEW	HI	4
REVIEW	HI	3

Source: Balch, W. R. "Practice versus Review Exams and Final Exam Performance." *Teaching of Psychology,* Vol. 25, No. 3, August 1998 (adapted from Table 1).

REFERENCES

Cochran, W. G., and Cox, G. M. *Experimental Designs,* 2nd ed. New York: Wiley, 1957.

Hsu, J. C. *Multiple Comparisons: Theory and Methods.* London: Chapman & Hall, 1996.

Kramer, C. Y. "Extension of Multiple Range Tests to Group Means with Unequal Number of Replications." *Biometrics,* Vol. 12, 1956, pp. 307–310.

Mason, R. L., Gunst, R. F., and Hess, J. L. *Statistical Design and Analysis of Experiments.* New York: Wiley, 1989.

Mendenhall, W. *Introduction to Linear Models and the Design and Analysis of Experiments.* Belmont, Calif.: Wadsworth, 1968.

Miller, R. G., Jr. *Simultaneous Statistical Inference.* New York: Springer-Verlag, 1981.

Neter, J., Kutner, M., Nachtsheim, C., and Wasserman, W. *Applied Linear Statistical Models,* 4th ed. Homewood, Ill.: Richard D. Irwin, 1996.

Scheffe, H. "A Method for Judging All Contrasts in the Analysis of Variance," *Biometrica,* Vol. 40, 1953, pp. 87–104.

Scheffé, H. *The Analysis of Variance.* New York: Wiley, 1959.

Snedecor, G. W., and Cochran, W. G. *Statistical Methods,* 7th ed. Ames: Iowa State University Press, 1980.

Steele, R. G. D., and Torrie, J. H. *Principles and Procedures of Statistics: A Biometrical Approach,* 2nd ed. New York: McGraw-Hill, 1980.

Tukey, J. "Comparing Individual Means in the Analysis of Variance." *Biometrics,* Vol. 5, 1949, pp. 99–114.

Winer, B. J. *Statistical Principles in Experimental Design,* 2nd ed. New York: McGraw-Hill, 1971.

Using Technology

8.1 Analysis of Variance Using SPSS

SPSS can conduct ANOVAs for all three types of experimental designs discussed in this chapter: completely randomized, randomized block, and factorial designs.

Completely Randomized Design

To conduct a completely randomized design ANOVA, first access the SPSS spreadsheet file that contains the sample data. The data file should contain one quantitative variable (the response, or dependent, variable) and one factor variable with at least two levels. (These values must be numbers, e.g., 1, 2, 3, etc.) Next, click on the "Analyze" button on the SPSS menu bar, then click on "Compare Means" and "One-Way ANOVA", as shown in Figure 8.S.1.

Figure 8.S.1

SPSS menu options for one-way ANOVA

The resulting dialog box appears as shown in Figure 8.S.2. Specify the response variable in the "Dependent List" box and the factor variable in the "Factor" box. Click the "Post Hoc" button, and select a multiple comparisons method and experimentwise error rate in the resulting dialog box (see Figure 8.S.3). Then click "Continue" to return to the "One-Way ANOVA" dialog screen. Click "OK" to generate the SPSS printout.

Figure 8.S.2

SPSS one-way ANOVA dialog box

Randomized Block and Factorial Designs

To conduct either a randomized block or factorial design ANOVA, first access the SPSS spreadsheet file that contains the sample data. The data file should contain one quantitative variable (the response, or dependent, variable) and at least two other variables that represent the factors and/or blocks. Next, click on the "Analyze" button on the SPSS menu bar, then click on "General Linear Model" and "Univariate", as shown in Figure 8.S.4

The resulting dialog box appears as shown in Figure 8.S.5. Specify the response variable in the "Dependent Variable" box and the factor variable(s) and block variable in the "Fixed Factor(s)" box. Click the "Post Hoc" button, and select the factor variable of interest, a multiple comparisons method, and experimentwise error rate in the resulting dialog box (similar to Figure 8.S.3). Then click "Continue" to return to the "Two-Way ANOVA" dialog screen. Now click the "Model" button to specify the type of experimental design (randomized block or factorial) on the resulting

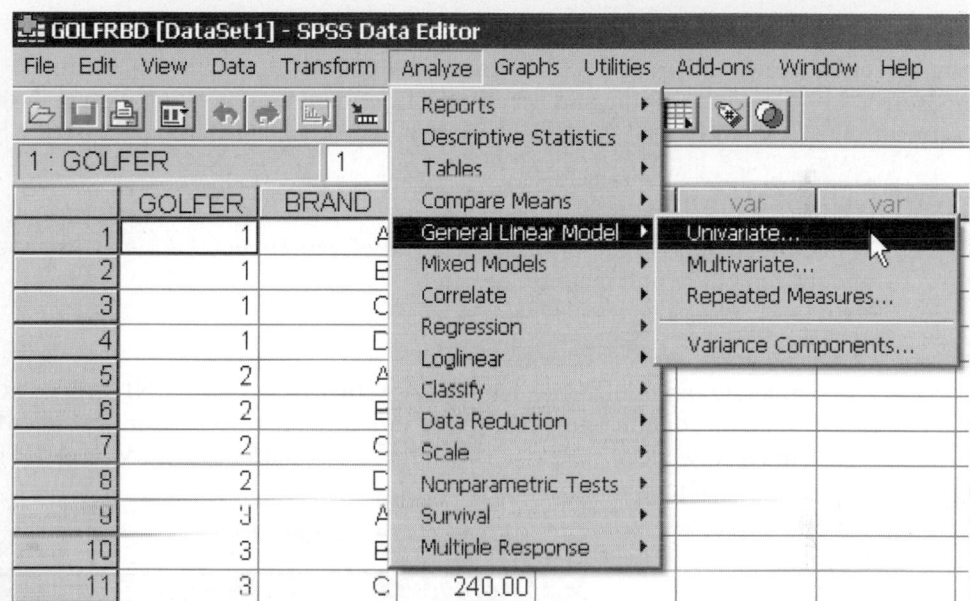

Figure 8.S.3
SPSS multiple comparisons
dialog box

Figure 8.S.4
SPSS menu options for two-
way ANOVA

Figure 8.S.5
SPSS two-way ANOVA dialog
box

Figure 8.S.6
SPSS design (model)
specification box

menu-screen as shown in Figure 8.S.6. For factorial designs, select the "Full Factorial" option; for randomized block designs, select the "Custom" option, and specify the treatment and blocking factors in the "Model" box. Click "Continue" to return to the "Two-Way ANOVA" dialog screen, then click "OK" to generate the SPSS printout.

8.2 Analysis of Variance Using MINITAB

MINITAB can conduct ANOVAs for all three types of experimental designs discussed in this chapter: completely randomized, randomized block, and factorial designs.

Completely Randomized Design

To conduct a completely randomized design ANOVA, first access the MINITAB worksheet file that contains the sample data. The data file should contain one quantitative variable (the response, or dependent, variable) and one qualitative factor variable with at least two levels. Next, click on the "Stat" button on the MINITAB menu bar, then click on "ANOVA" and "One-Way", as shown in Figure 8.M.1.

Figure 8.M.1
MINITAB menu options for
one-way ANOVA

The resulting dialog box appears as shown in Figure 8.M.2. Specify the response variable in the "Response" box and the factor variable in the "Factor" box. Click the "Comparisons" button, and select a multiple comparisons method and experimentwise error rate in the resulting dialog box (see Figure 8.M.3). Then click "OK" to return to the "One-Way ANOVA" dialog screen. Click "OK" to generate the MINITAB printout.

Figure 8.M.2
MINITAB one-way ANOVA dialog box

Figure 8.M.3
MINITAB multiple comparisons dialog box

Randomized Block and Factorial Designs

To conduct either a randomized block or factorial design ANOVA, first access the MINITAB worksheet file that contains the sample data. The data file should contain one quantitative variable (the response, or dependent, variable) and two other variables that represent the factors and/or blocks. Next, click on the "Stat" button on the MINITAB menu bar, then click on "ANOVA" and "Two-Way" (see Figure 8.M.1). The resulting dialog box appears as shown in Figure 8.M.4.

Specify the response variable in the "Response" box, the first factor variable in the "Row factor" box, and the second factor or block variable in the "Column factor" box. If the design is a randomized block, select the "Fit additive model" option as shown in Figure 8.M.4. If the design is factorial, leave the "Fit additive model" option unselected. Click "OK" to generate the MINITAB printout.

Note: Multiple comparisons of treatment means are obtained by selecting "Stat", then "ANOVA", then "General Linear Model".

Figure 8.M.4
MINITAB two-way ANOVA
dialog box

8.3 Analysis of Variance Using Excel/PHStat2

Excel can conduct ANOVAs for all three types of experimental designs discussed in this chapter: completely randomized, randomized block, and factorial designs.

Completely Randomized Design

To conduct a completely randomized design ANOVA, first access the Excel workbook file that contains the sample data. The file should contain k columns of data for the quantitative (response) variable, one for each of the k treatments. Next, click on the "Tools" button on the Excel main menu bar, then click on "Data Analysis", as shown in Figure 8.E.1.

Select "Anova: Single Factor" from the Data Analysis menu as shown in Figure 8.E.2 and click "OK". The resulting dialog box appears as shown in Figure 8.E.3.

Specify the "Input Range" of your data, select the "Grouped By: Columns" option, the value of α and, if the workbook contains labels, select "Labels in first row", as shown in Figure 8.E.3. Click "OK" to generate the Excel printout.

	A	B	C	D
1	**BrandA**	**BrandB**	**BrandC**	**BrandD**
2	251.2	263.2	269.7	251.6
3	245.1	262.9	263.2	248.6
4	248	265	277.5	249.4
5	251.1	254.5	267.4	242
6	260.5	264.3	270.5	246.5
7	250	257	265.5	251.3

Figure 8.E.1
Excel main menu options for data analysis

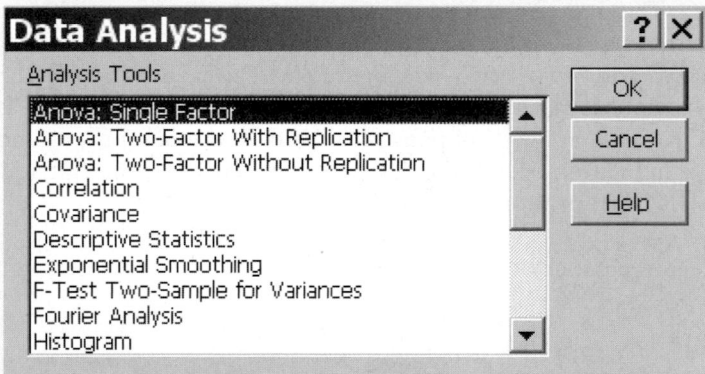

Figure 8.E.2
Excel data analysis menu
option for one-way ANOVA

Figure 8.E.3
Excel single factor ANOVA
dialog box

Note: Tukey's multiple comparisons method is available in Excel with the PHStat add-in *if you have access to a table of critical values of the Studentized range.* Click on the "PHStat" button on the Excel main menu bar, then click on "Multiple-Sample Tests" and "Tukey-Kramer Procedure". Enter the "Group Data Cell Range" and click "OK". PHStat will request that you fill in the critical value of the Studentized range (called the *Q-statistic*). Enter this value and press "Enter" to view the results.

Randomized Block Design

To conduct a randomized block design ANOVA, first access the Excel workbook file that contains the sample data. The file should contain k columns of data for the quantitative (response) variable, one for each of the k treatments, and b rows, one for each of the b blocks. Next, click on the "Tools" button on the Excel main menu bar, then click on "Data Analysis" (see Figure 8.E.1). Select "Anova: Two Factor Without Replication" from the Data Analysis menu (see Figure 8.E.2) and click "OK". The resulting dialog box appears as shown in Figure 8.E.4.

Specify the "Input Range" of your data, the value of α, and, if the workbook contains labels, select "Labels", as shown in Figure 8.E.4. Click "OK" to generate the Excel printout.

Note: Multiple comparisons of treatment means are unavailable in Excel for a randomized block design.

Figure 8.E.4

Excel two factor with replication ANOVA dialog box

Factorial Design

To conduct a two-factor factorial design ANOVA, first access the Excel workbook file that contains the sample data. The file should contain a columns of data for the quantitative (response) variable, one for each of the a levels of Factor A, and br rows, where b is the number of levels of factor B and r is the number of replicates. [Note: Place all the data for one level of Factor B in consecutive rows, followed by all the data for the next level of B, etc.] Next, click on the "Tools" button on the Excel main menu bar, then click on "Data Analysis" (see Figure 8.E.1). Select "Anova: Two Factor with Replication" from the Data Analysis menu (see Figure 8.E.2) and click "OK". The resulting dialog box appears as shown in Figure 8.E.5.

Specify the "Input Range" of your data, the number of "Rows per sample" (this is the number of replicates), and the value of α, as shown in Figure 8.E.5. Click "OK" to generate the Excel printout.

Note: Multiple comparisons of treatment means are unavailable in Excel for a factorial block design.

Figure 8.E.5

Excel two factor with replication ANOVA dialog box

CHAPTER

9

Categorical Data Analysis

CONTENTS

9.1 Categorical Data and the Multinomial Experiment

9.2 Testing Category Probabilities: One-Way Table

9.3 Testing Category Probabilities: Two-Way (Contingency) Table

9.4 A Word of Caution about Chi-Square Tests

STATISTICS IN ACTION

A Study of Coupon Users—Mail versus the Internet

USING TECHNOLOGY

9.1 Chi-Square Analyses Using SPSS

9.2 Chi-Square Analyses Using MINITAB

9.3 Chi-Square Analyses Using Excel/PHStat2

WHERE WE'VE BEEN

■ Presented methods for making inferences about the population proportion associated with a two-level qualitative variable (i.e., a binomial variable)

■ Presented methods for making inferences about the difference between two binomial proportions

WHERE WE'RE GOING

■ Discuss qualitative (i.e., categorical) data with more than two outcomes.

■ Present a *chi-square* hypothesis test for comparing the category proportions associated with a single qualitative variable—called a *one-way analysis.*

■ Present a *chi-square* hypothesis test for relating two qualitative variables—called a *two-way analysis.*

STATISTICS IN ACTION

A Study of Coupon Users—Mail versus the Internet

The service encounter is the critical interaction between a customer and the firm. In this encounter, the firm attempts to sell its services, to reinforce its offerings, and to satisfy the customer. A hot topic in marketing research is the exploration of a technology-based self-service (TBSS) encounter, where various technologies allow the customer to perform all or part of the service encounter. Examples of TBSS systems include ATMs, automated hotel checkout, banking by phone, self-scanning at retail stores, and transactions via the Internet such as Federal Express's package tracking and Charles Schwab's online brokerage services.

Marketing professor Dan Ladik (University of Suffolk) investigated a customer's motivation to use a TBSS and compared two customer segments—one that does not require any electronic technology use for service delivery and another that relies on the Internet for service delivery.

The self-service delivery system studied was one that distributes discount coupons via both the mail and the Internet. Ladik investigated whether there were differences in customer characteristics and customer satisfaction between the mail (nontechnology) coupon users and the Internet (TBSS) coupon users.

The data for the study were obtained from a national services firm that specializes in discount coupons. (For reasons of confidentiality, the firm is not named.) Both customers who use the nontechnology mail delivery method and customers who use the firm's Internet Web site to access the coupons were sampled. For this Statistics in Action problem, we will focus on a subset of the full data set—a sample of 440 coupon users. Using a questionnaire, several qualitative variables were measured for each user. These are listed in Table SIA 9.1. The data are saved in the **COUPONS** file.

In an attempt to answer the researcher's questions, we apply the statistical methodology presented in this chapter to this data set in two Statistics in Action Revisited examples.

Statistics in Action Revisited

- Testing Category Proportions for Customer Type in the Coupon Study (p. 559)
- Testing Whether Coupon Customer Characteristics Are Related to User Type (p. 572)

 COUPONS

TABLE SIA9.1 Qualitative Variables Measured in the Coupon Study

Variable Name	Levels (Possible Values)
Coupon user type	Mail, Internet, or both
Gender	Male or female
Education	High school, vo-tech/college, 4-year college degree, or graduate school
Work status	Full time, Part time, Not working, retired
Coupon satisfaction	Satisfied, unsatisfied, indifferent

9.1 Categorical Data and the Multinomial Experiment

Recall from Section 1.5 that observations on a qualitative variable can only be categorized. For example, consider the highest level of education attained by each in a group of salespersons. Level of education is a qualitative variable and each salesperson would fall in one and only one of the following five categories: some high school, high school diploma, some college, college degree, and graduate degree. The result of the categorization would be a count of the numbers of salespersons falling in the respective categories.

When the qualitative variable results in one of two responses (yes or no, success or failure, favor or do not favor, etc.), the data (i.e., the counts) can be analyzed using the binomial probability distribution discussed in Section 4.3. However, qualitative variables, such as level of education, that allow for more than two categories for a response are much more common, and these must be analyzed using a different method.

Qualitative data that fall in more than two categories often result from a **multinomial experiment.** The characteristics for a multinomial experiment with k outcomes are described in the box. You can see that the binomial experiment of Chapter 4 is a multinomial experiment with $k = 2$.

Properties of the Multinomial Experiment

1. The experiment consists of n identical trials.

2. There are k possible outcomes to each trial. These outcomes are called *classes, categories,* or *cells.*

3. The probabilities of the k outcomes, denoted by $p_1, p_2, \ldots, p_k$, remain the same from trial to trial, where $p_1 + p_2 + \cdots + p_k = 1$.

4. The trials are independent.

5. The random variables of interest are the *cell counts,* $n_1, n_2, \ldots, n_k$, of the number of observations that fall in each of the k classes.

EXAMPLE 9.1

Identifying a
Multinomial
Experiment

Problem Consider the problem of determining the highest level of education attained by each of $n = 100$ salespersons at a large company. Suppose we categorize level of education into one of five categories—some high school, high school diploma, some college, college degree, and graduate degree—and count the number of the 100 salespeople that fall into each category. Is this a multinomial experiment to a reasonable degree of approximation?

Solution Checking the five properties of a multinomial experiment shown in the box, we have the following:

1. The experiment consists of $n = 100$ identical trials, where each trial is to determine the highest level of education of a salesperson.

2. There are $k = 5$ possible outcomes to each trial corresponding to the five education-level categories.

3. The probabilities of the $k = 5$ outcomes, p_1, p_2, p_3, p_4, and p_5, remain (to a reasonable degree of approximation) the same from trial to trial, where p_i represents the true probability that a salesperson attains level of education i.

4. The trials are independent (i.e., the education level attained by one salesperson does not affect the level attained by any other salesperson).

5. We are interested in the count of the number of salespeople who fall into each of the five categories. These five *cell counts* are denoted n_1, n_2, n_3, n_4, and n_5.

Thus, the properties of a multinomial experiment are satisfied.

In this chapter, we are concerned with the analysis of categorical data—specifically, the data that represent the counts for each category of a multinomial experiment. In Section 9.2, we learn how to make inferences about category probabilities for data classified according to a single qualitative (or categorical) variable. Then, in Section 9.3, we consider inferences about category probabilities for data classified according to two qualitative variables. The statistic used for these inferences is one that possesses, approximately, the familiar chi-square distribution.

9.2 Testing Category Probabilities: One-Way Table

In this section, we consider a multinomial experiment with k outcomes that correspond to categories of a *single* qualitative variable. The results of such an experiment are summarized in a **one-way table.** The term *one-way* is used since only one variable is classified. Typically, we want to make inferences about the true proportions that occur in the k categories based on the sample information in the one-way table.

To illustrate, suppose a large supermarket chain conducts a consumer preference survey by recording the *brand of bread* purchased by customers in its stores. Assume the chain carries three brands of bread—two major brands (A and B) and its own store brand. The brand preferences of a random sample of 150 consumers are observed, and the number preferring each brand is tabulated; the resulting count data appear in Table 9.1.

TABLE 9.1   Results of Consumer Preference Survey

A	B	Store Brand
61	53	36

Note that our consumer-preference survey satisfies the properties of a multinomial experiment for the qualitative variable *brand of bread*. The experiment consists of randomly sampling $n = 150$ buyers from a large population of consumers containing an unknown proportion p_1 who prefer brand A, a proportion p_2 who prefer brand B, and a proportion p_3 who prefer the store brand. Each buyer represents a single trial that can result in one of three outcomes: The consumer prefers brand A, B, or the store brand with probabilities p_1, p_2, *and* p_3, respectively. (Assume that all consumers will have a preference.) The buyer preference of any single consumer in the sample does not affect the preference of another; consequently, the trials are independent. And, finally, you can see that the recorded data are the number of buyers in each of three consumer-preference categories. Thus, the consumer-preference survey satisfies the five properties of a multinomial experiment.

In the consumer-preference survey, and in most practical applications of the multinomial experiment, the k outcome probabilities $p_1, p_2, \ldots, p_k$ are unknown and we typically want to use the survey data to make inferences about their values. The unknown probabilities in the consumer-preference survey are

p_1 = Proportion of all buyers who prefer brand A

p_2 = Proportion of all buyers who prefer brand B

p_3 = Proportion of all buyers who prefer the store brand

For example, to decide whether the consumers have a preference for any of the brands, we will want to test the null hypothesis that the brands of bread are equally preferred (that is, $p_1 = p_2 = p_3 = \frac{1}{3}$) against the alternative hypothesis that one brand is preferred (that is, at least one of the probabilities p_1, p_2, and p_3 exceeds $\frac{1}{3}$). Thus, we want to test

H_0: $p_1 = p_2 = p_3 = \frac{1}{3}$ (no preference)

H_a: At least one of the proportions exceeds $\frac{1}{3}$ (a preference exists)

If the null hypothesis is true and $p_1 = p_2 = p_3 = 1/3$, the expected value (mean value) of the number of customers who prefer brand A is given by

$$E(n_1) = np_1 = (n)1/3 = (150)1/3 = 50$$

Similarly, $E(n_2) = E(n_3) = 50$ if the null hypothesis is true and no preference exists.

The following test statistic—the **chi-square test**—measures the degree of disagreement between the data and the null hypothesis:

$$\chi^2 = \frac{[n_1 - E(n_1)]^2}{E(n_1)} + \frac{[n_2 - E(n_2)]^2}{E(n_2)} + \frac{[n_3 - E(n_3)]^2}{E(n_3)}$$

$$= \frac{(n_1 - 50)^2}{50} + \frac{(n_2 - 50)^2}{50} + \frac{(n_3 - 50)^2}{50}$$

Note that the farther the observed numbers n_1 n_2, and n_3, are from their expected value (50), the larger χ^2 will become—that is, large values of χ^2 imply that the null hypothesis is false.

Biography

KARL PEARSON
(1895–1980)

The Father of Statistics

While attending college, London-born Karl Pearson exhibited a wide range of interests, including mathematics, physics, religion, history, socialism, and Darwinism. After earning a law degree at Cambridge University and a PhD in political science at the University of Heidelberg (Germany), Pearson become a professor of applied mathematics at University College in London. His 1892 book, *The Grammer of Science*, illustrated his conviction that statistical data analysis lies at the foundation of all knowledge; consequently, many consider Pearson to be the "father of statistics." A few of Pearson's many contributions to the field include introducing the term *standard deviation* and its associated symbol (σ), developing the distribution of the correlation coefficient, cofounding and editing the prestigious statistics journal *Biometrika*, and (what many consider his greatest achievement) creating the first chi-square "goodness-of-fit" test. Pearson inspired his students (including his son, Egon, and William Gossett) with his wonderful lectures and enthusiasm for statistics.

We have to know the distribution of χ^2 in repeated sampling before we can decide whether the data indicate that a preference exists. When H_0 is true, χ^2 can be shown to have (approximately) the familiar chi-square distribution of Section 6.7. For this one-way classification, the χ^2 distribution has $(k - 1)$ degrees of freedom.* The rejection region for the consumer-preference survey for $\alpha = .05$ and $k - 1 = 3 - 1 = 2$ df is

Rejection region: $\chi^2 > \chi^2_{.05}$

The value of $\chi^2_{.05}$ (found in Table VI of Appendix B) is 5.99147. (See Figure 9.1.) The computed value of the test statistic is

$$\chi^2 = \frac{(n_1 - 50)^2}{50} + \frac{(n_2 - 50)^2}{50} + \frac{(n_3 - 50)^2}{50}$$

$$= \frac{(61 - 50)^2}{50} + \frac{(53 - 50)^2}{50} + \frac{(36 - 50)^2}{50} = 6.52$$

Since the computed $\chi^2 = 6.52$ exceeds the critical value of 5.99147, we conclude at the $\alpha = .05$ level of significance that there does exist a consumer preference for one or more of the brands of bread.

Now that we have evidence to indicate that the proportions p_1, p_2, and p_3 are unequal, we can make inferences concerning their individual values using the methods of

---

*The derivation of the degrees of freedom for χ^2 involves the number of linear restrictions imposed on the count data. In the present case, the only constraint is that $\Sigma n_i = n$, where n (the sample size) is fixed in advance. Therefore, $df = k - 1$. For other cases, we will give the degrees of freedom for each usage of χ^2 and refer the interested reader to the references for more detail.

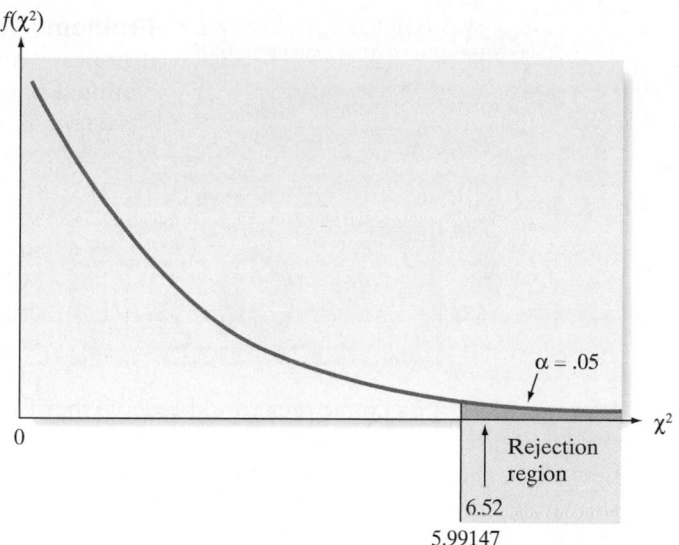

FIGURE 9.1

Rejection region for consumer-preference survey

Section 5.4. [*Note:* We cannot use the methods of Section 7.4 to compare two proportions because the cell counts are dependent random variables.] The general form for a test of a hypothesis concerning multinomial probabilities is shown in the next box.

A Test of a Hypothesis about Multinomial Probabilities: One-Way Table

$$H_0: p_1 = p_{1,0}, p_2 = p_{2,0}, \ldots, p_k = p_{k,0}$$

where $p_{1,0}, p_{2,0}, \ldots, p_{k,0}$ represent the hypothesized values of the multinomial probabilities

H_a: At least one of the multinomial probabilities does not equal its hypothesized value

$$\text{Test statistic: } \chi^2 = \sum \frac{[n_i - E(n_i)]^2}{E(n_i)}$$

where $E(n_i) = np_{i,0}$ is the **expected cell count**—that is, the expected number of outcomes of type i assuming that H_0 is true. The total sample size is n.

$$\text{Rejection region: } \chi^2 > \chi_\alpha^2$$

where χ_α^2 has $(k - 1)$ df.

Conditions Required for a Valid χ^2 Test: One-way Table

1. A multinomial experiment has been conducted. This is generally satisfied by taking a random sample from the population of interest.

2. The sample size n is large. This is satisfied if for every cell, the expected cell count $E(n_i)$ will be equal to 5 or more.*

---

*The assumption that all expected cell counts are at least 5 is necessary in order to ensure that the χ^2 approximation is appropriate. Exact methods for conducting the test of a hypothesis exist and may be used for small expected cell counts, but these methods are beyond the scope of this text.

EXAMPLE 9.2

Evaluating a Firm's
Merit-Increase Plan
Using a One-Way χ^2
Test

PAYPLAN

**TABLE 9.2 Distribution of
Pay Increases**

None	Standard	Merit
42	365	193

Problem A large firm has established what it hopes is an objective system of deciding on annual pay increases for its employees. The system is based on a series of evaluation scores determined by the supervisors of each employee. Employees with scores above 80 receive a merit pay increase, those with scores between 50 and 80 receive the standard increase, and those below 50 receive no increase. The firm designed the plan with the objective that, on the average, 25% of its employees would receive merit increases, 65% would receive standard increases, and 10% would receive no increase. After 1 year of operation using the new plan, the distribution of pay increases for the 600 company employees was as shown in Table 9.2. Test at the $\alpha = .01$ level to determine whether these data indicate that the distribution of pay increases differs significantly from the proportions established by the firm.

Solution Define the population proportions for the three pay increase categories to be

$$p_1 = \text{Proportion of employees who receive no pay increase}$$
$$p_2 = \text{Proportion of employees who receive a standard increase}$$
$$p_3 = \text{Proportion of employees who receive a merit increase}$$

Then the null hypothesis representing the distribution of percentages in the firm's proposed plan is

$$H_0: p_1 = .10, \ p_2 = .65, \ p_3 = .25$$

and the alternative is

$$H_a: \text{At least two of the proportions differ from the firm's proposed plan}$$

$$\text{Test statistic: } \chi^2 = \sum \frac{[n_i - E(n_i)]^2}{E(n_i)}$$

where

$$E(n_1) = np_{1,0} = 600(.10) = 60$$
$$E(n_2) = np_{2,0} = 600(.65) = 390$$
$$E(n_3) = np_{3,0} = 600(.25) = 150$$

Rejection region: For $\alpha = .01$ and df $= k - 1 = 2$, reject H_0 if $\chi^2 > \chi^2_{.01}$, where (from Table VI of Appendix B) $\chi^2_{.01} = 9.21034$.

We now calculate the test statistic:

$$\chi^2 = \frac{(42 - 60)^2}{60} + \frac{(365 - 390)^2}{390} + \frac{(193 - 150)^2}{150} = 19.33$$

This value exceeds the table value of $\chi^2(9.21034)$; therefore, the data provide strong evidence ($\alpha = .01$) that the company's actual pay plan distribution differs from its proposed plan.

The χ^2 test can also be conducted using statistical software. Figure 9.2 is an Excel printout of the analysis of the data in Table 9.2; note that the p-value of the test is .0000634908. Since $\alpha = .01$ exceeds this p-value, there is sufficient evidence to reject H_0.

	A	B	C
1			
2			
3	**CATEGORY**	**Observed**	**Expected**
4	None	42	60
5	Standard	365	390
6	Merit	193	150
7	TOTAL	600	
8			
9	Significance Level	0.05	
10	Number of categories	3	
11	Degrees of freedom	2	
12	**Chi-square test statistic**	19.32550222	
13	**p-value**	6.34908E-05	
14			

FIGURE 9.2
Excel chi-square analysis
of data in Table 9.2

Look Back Note that all the expected cell counts exceed 5. Consequently, the χ^2 test is appropriate.

Now Work Exercise 9.6

If we focus on one particular outcome of a multinomial experiment, we can use the methods developed in Section 5.4 for a binomial proportion to establish a confidence interval for any one of the multinomial probabilities.* For example, if we want a 95%; confidence interval for the proportion of the company's employees who will receive merit increases under the new system, we calculate

$$\hat{p}_3 \pm 1.96\sigma_{\hat{p}_3} \approx \hat{p}_3 \pm 1.96\sqrt{\frac{\hat{p}_3(1-\hat{p}_3)}{n}} \quad \text{where } \hat{p}_3 = \frac{n_3}{n} = \frac{193}{600} = .32$$

$$= .32 + 1.96\sqrt{\frac{(.32)(1-.32)}{600}} = .32 \pm .04$$

Thus, we estimate that between 28% and 36% of the firm's employees will qualify for merit increases under the new plan. It appears that the firm will have to raise the requirements for merit increases in order to achieve the stated goal of a 25% employee qualification rate.

STATISTICS IN ACTION REVISITED

Testing Category Proportions for Customer Type in the Coupon Study

In the research on a technology-based self-service (TBSS) encounter (p. 553), 440 users of a firm's discount coupons were sampled and given a questionnaire to complete. One of the variables of interest to the researcher was type of coupon user. Recall (from Table SIA9.1) that the customers received the coupons in one of three ways: only through the mail (non-technology user), only via the Internet (TBSS user), and via both the mail and Internet. What are the proportions of mail-only, Internet-only, and both users, and are these proportions statistically different?

---

*Note that focusing on one outcome has the effect of lumping the other $(k-1)$ outcomes into a single group. Thus, we obtain, in effect, two outcomes—or a binomial experiment.

To answer this question, we used SPSS to analyze the type of user variable in the **COUPONS** file. Figure SIA9.1 shows summary statistics and a graph to describe the three categories. From the summary table at the top of the printout, you can see that 262 (or 59.5%) of the customers are mail-only coupon users, 43 (or 9.8%) are Internet-only users, and the remainder (30.7%) use both mail and the Internet. These sample percentages are illustrated in the bar graph at the bottom of Figure SIA9.1. In this sample of customers, the majority (almost 60%) obtain their coupons strictly through the mail.

Is this sufficient evidence to indicate that the true proportions in the population of customers are different? Letting p_1, p_2, and p_3 represent the true proportions for the mail-only, Internet-only, and both categories, respectively, we tested H_0: $p_1 = p_2 = p_3 = 1/3$ using SPSS. The printout is displayed in Figure SIA9.2. The cell frequencies and expected numbers are shown in the top table of the figure, while the chi-square test statistic (164.895) and p-value (.000) are shown in the bottom table. At any reasonably selected α-level (say, $\alpha = .01$), the small p-value indicates that there is sufficient evidence to reject the null hypothesis and conclude that the true proportions associated with the three user type categories are indeed statistically different.

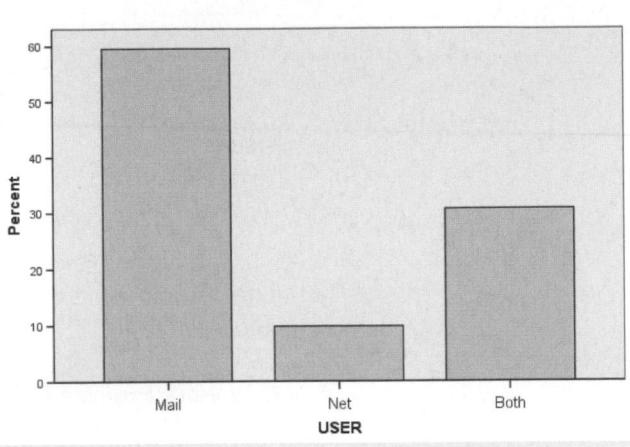

USER

		Frequency	Percent	Valid Percent	Cumulative Percent
Valid	Mail	262	59.5	59.5	59.5
	Net	43	9.8	9.8	69.3
	Both	135	30.7	30.7	100.0
	Total	440	100.0	100.0	

Figure SIA9.1
SPSS descriptive statistics and graph for type of coupon user

Chi-Square Test

Frequencies

USER

	Observed N	Expected N	Residual
Mail	262	146.7	115.3
Net	43	146.7	-103.7
Both	135	146.7	-11.7
Total	440		

Test Statistics

	USER
Chi-Square[a]	164.895
df	2
Asymp. Sig.	.000

a. 0 cells (.0%) have expected frequencies less than 5. The minimum expected cell frequency is 146.7.

Figure SIA9.2
SPSS chi-square test of user type categories

ACTIVITY 9.1: **Binomial versus Multinomial Experiments**

In this activity, you will study the difference between binomial and multinomial experiments.

1. A television station has hired an independent research group to determine whether television viewers in the area prefer its local news program to the news programs of two other stations in the same city. Explain why a multinomial experiment would be appropriate and design a poll that satisfies the five properties of a multinomial experiment. State the null and alternative hypotheses for the corresponding χ^2-test.

2. Suppose the television station believes that a majority of local viewers prefer its news program to those of its two competitors. Explain why a binomial experiment would be appropriate to support this claim and design a poll that satisfies the five properties of a binomial experiment. State the null and alternative hypotheses for the corresponding test.

3. Generalize the situations in Exercises 1 and 2 in order to describe conditions under which a multinomial experiment can be rephrased as a binomial experiment. Is there any advantage in doing so? Explain.

ACTIVITY 9.2: **Contingency Tables**

In this Activity, you will revisit Activity 3.1, *Exit Polls* (p. 160). For convenience the table shown in that activity is repeated here.

2004 Presidential Election, Vote by Gender

	Bush	Kerry	Other
Male (46%)	55%	44%	1%
Female (54%)	48%	51%	1%

Source: CNN.com

1. Determine whether the table above and the similar tables that you found for the activity on page 160 are contingency tables. If not, do you have enough

information to create a contingency table for the data? If you need more information, state specifically what information you need.

2. Choose one of your examples from the previous activity if it contains a contingency table or enough information to create one or use the Internet or some other source to find a new example with a contingency table given. Determine whether the conditions for a valid χ^2-test are met. If not, choose a different example where the conditions are met.

3. Perform an χ^2-test for independence for the example chosen in Exercise 2. Are the results what you would expect in the given situation? Explain.

Exercises 9.1–9.15

Learning the Mechanics

9.1 Find the rejection region for a one-dimensional χ^2 test of a null hypothesis concerning $p_1, p_2, \ldots, p_k$ if
a. $k = 3; \alpha = .05$
b. $k = 5; \alpha = .10$
c. $k = 4; \alpha = .01$

9.2 What are the characteristics of a multinomial experiment? Compare the characteristics to those of a binomial experiment.

9.3 What conditions must n satisfy to make the χ^2 test valid?

9.4 A multinomial experiment with $k = 3$ cells and $n = 320$ produced the data shown in the following one-way table. Do these data provide sufficient evidence to contradict the null hypothesis that $p_1 = .25$, $p_2 = .25$, and $p_3 = .50$? Test using $\alpha = .05$.

	CELL		
	1	2	3
n_i	78	60	182

9.5 A multinomial experiment with $k = 4$ cells and $n = 205$ produced the data shown in the following one-way table.

	CELL			
	1	2	3	4
n_i	43	56	59	47

a. Do these data provide sufficient evidence to conclude that the multinomial probabilities differ? Test using $\alpha = .05$.
b. What are the Type I and Type II errors associated with the test of part **a**?
c. Construct a 95% confidence interval for the multinomial probability associated with cell 3.

Applying the Concepts—Basic

9.6 **Location of major sports venues.** There has been a recent
NW trend for professional sports franchises in Major League Baseball (MLB), the National Football League (NFL), the National Basketball Association (NBA), and the National Hockey League (NHL) to build new stadiums and ballparks

in urban, downtown venues. An article in *Professional Geographer* (Feb. 2000) investigated whether there has been a significant suburban-to-urban shift in the location of major sport facilities. In 1985, 40% of all major sport facilities were located downtown, 30% in central city, and 30% in suburban areas. In contrast, of the 113 major sports franchises that existed in 1997, 58 were built downtown, 26 in a central city, and 29 in a suburban area.

a. Describe the qualitative variable of interest in the study. Give the levels (categories) associated with the variable.

b. Give the null hypothesis for a test to determine whether the proportions of major sports facilities in downtown, central city, and suburban areas in 1997 are the same as in 1985.

c. If the null hypothesis, part **b,** is true, how many of the 113 sports facilities in 1997 would you expect to be located in downtown, central city, and suburban areas, respectively?

d. Find the value of the chi-square statistic for testing the null hypothesis, part **b.**

e. Find the (approximate) *p*-value of the test and give the appropriate conclusion in the words of the problem. Assume $\alpha = .05$.

9.7 **"Made in the USA" survey.** Refer to the *Journal of Global Business* (Spring 2002) study of what "Made in the USA" on product labels means to the typical consumer, Exercise 2.8 (p. 48). Recall that 106 shoppers participated in the survey. Their responses, given as a percentage of U.S. labor and materials in four categories, are summarized in the table. Suppose a consumer advocate group claims that half of all consumers believe that "Made in the USA" means "100%" of labor and materials are produced in the United States, one-fourth believe that "75 to 99%" are produced in the United States, one-fifth believe that "50 to 74%" are produced in the United States, and 5 percent believe that "less than 50%" are produced in the United States.

Response to "Made in the USA"	Number of shoppers
100%	64
75 to 99%	20
50 to 74%	18
Less than 50%	4

Source: "'Made in the USA': Consumer perceptions, Deception and policy Alternatives." *Journal of Global Business,* Vol. 13, No. 24, Spring 2002 (Table 3).

a. Describe the qualitative variable of interest in the study. Give the levels (categories) associated with the variable.

b. What are the values of p_1, p_2, p_3, and p_4, the probabilities associated with the four response categories hypothesized by the consumer advocate group?

c. Give the null and alternative hypotheses for testing the consumer advocate group's claim.

d. Compute the test statistic for testing the hypotheses, part **c.**

e. Find the rejection region of the test at $\alpha = .10$.

f. State the conclusion in the words of the problem.

g. Find and interpret a 90% confidence interval for the true proportion of consumers who believe "Made in the USA" means "100%" of labor and materials are produced in the United States.

9.8 **Rankings of MBA programs.** Refer to the *Business Ethics* (Fall 2005) rankings of master's in business administration (MBA) programs worldwide, Exercise 2.14 (p. 49). Recall that each of 30 business schools was rated according to student exposure to social and environmental issues in the classroom. Ratings ranged from 1 star (lowest rated group) to 5 stars (highest rated group). A summary of the star ratings assigned to the 30 MBA programs is reproduced in the table.

a. Identify the categorical variable (and its levels) measured in this study.

b. How many of the sampled MBA programs would you expect to observe in each star rating category if there are no differences in the category proportions in the population of all MBA programs?

c. Specify the null and alternative hypotheses for testing whether there are differences in the star rating category proportions in the population of all MBA programs.

d. Calculate the χ^2 test statistic for testing the hypotheses in part **c.**

e. Give the rejection region for test using $\alpha = .05$.

f. Use the results, parts **d** and **e,** to make the appropriate conclusion.

g. Find and interpret a 95% confidence interval for the proportion of all MBA programs that are ranked in the three-star category.

Criteria	5 stars	4 stars	3 stars	2 stars	1 star	Total
Student Exposure	2	9	14	5	0	30

Source: Biello, D. "MBA programs for Social and Environmental Stewardship." *Business Ethics,* Fall 2005, p. 25.

9.9 **Survey on giving and volunteering.** The *National Tax Journal* (Dec. 2001) published a study of charitable givers based on data collected from the Independent Sector Survey on Giving and Volunteering. A total of 1,072 charitable givers reported that their charitable contributions were motivated by tax considerations. The number of these 1,072 givers in each of 10 household income categories is shown in the table below.

GIVERS

Household Income Group	Number of Charitable Givers
Under $10,000	42
$10,000–$20,000	93
$20,000–$30,000	99
$30,000–$40,000	153
$40,000–$50,000	91
$50,000–$60,000	114
$60,000–$70,000	157
$70,000–$80,000	101
$80,000–$100,000	95
Over $100,000	127

Source: Tiehen, L. "Tax policy and Charitable Contributions of Money." *National Tax Journal,* Vol. 54, No. 4, Dec. 2001, p. 717 (adapted from Table 5).

a. If the true proportions of charitable givers in each household income group are the same, how many of the 1,072 sampled givers would you expect to find in each income category?

b. Give the null hypothesis for testing whether true proportions of charitable givers in each household income group are the same.

c. Compute the chi-square test statistic for testing the null hypothesis, part **b**.

d. Find the rejection region for the test if $\alpha = .10$.

e. Give the appropriate conclusion for the test in the words of the problem.

Applying the Concepts—Intermediate

9.10 Top Internet search engines. Nielsen/NetRatings is a global leader in Internet media and market research. In May 2006, the firm reported on the "search" shares (i.e., percentage of all Internet searches) for the most popular search engines available on the Web. Google accounted for 50% of all searches, Yahoo! for 22%, MSN for 11%, and all other search engines for 17%. Suppose that in a random sample of 1,000 recent Internet searches, 487 used Google, 245 used Yahoo!, 121 used MSN, and 147 used another search engine.

a. Do the sample data disagree with the percentages reported by Nielsen/NetRatings? Test using $\alpha = .05$.

b. Find and interpret a 95% confidence interval for the percentage of all Internet searches that use the Google Search engine.

9.11 Opinions on national health insurance. In order to study consumer preferences for health care reform in the United States, researchers from the University of Michigan surveyed 500 U.S. households (*Journal of Consumer Affairs*, Winter 1999). Heads of household were asked whether they are in favor of, neutral about, or opposed to a national health insurance program in which all Americans are covered and costs are paid by tax dollars. The 434 useable responses are summarized in the table.

HEALTH

Favor	Neutral	Oppose
234	119	81

Source: Hong, G., and White-Means, S. "Consumer preferences for Health Care Reform." *Journal of Consumer Affairs*, Vol 33, No. 2, Winter 1999, pp. 237–253.

a. Is there sufficient evidence to conclude that opinions are not evenly divided on the issue of national health insurance? Conduct the appropriate test using $\alpha = .01$.

b. Construct a 95% confidence interval for the proportion of heads of household in the U.S. population who favor national health insurance.

9.12 Attitudes toward top corporate managers. Recent scandals involving large U.S. corporations (e.g., Enron, WorldCom, and Adelphia) apparently have had a major impact on the public's attitude toward business managers. In a 2002

Harris poll administered immediately after the Enron scandal, a national sample of 2,023 adults were asked to agree or disagree with the following statement: "Top company managers have become rich at the expense of ordinary workers" (*The Harris poll*, #55, Oct. 18, 2002). The response categories (and number of respondents in each) were strongly agree (1,173), somewhat agree (587), somewhat disagree (182), and strongly disagree (81). Suppose that prior to the Enron scandal the percentages of all U.S. adults falling into the four response categories were 45%, 35%, 15%, and 5%, respectively. Is there evidence to infer that the percentages of all U.S. adults falling into the four response categories changed after the Enron scandal? Test using $\alpha = .01$.

9.13 Management system failures. Refer to the *Process Safety Progress* (Dec. 2004) and U.S. Chemical Safety and Hazard Investigation Board study of industrial accidents caused by management system failures, Exercise 2.6 (p. 48). The table below gives a breakdown of the root causes of a sample of 83 incidents. Are there significant differences in the percentage of incidents in the four cause categories? Test using $\alpha = .05$.

MSFAIL

Management System Cause	Number of Incidents
Engineering & Design	27
Procedures & Practices	24
Management & Oversight	22
Training & Communication	10
TOTAL	83

Source: Blair, A. S. "Management System Failures Identified in Incidents Investigated by the U.S. Chemical Safety and Hazard Investigation Board." *Process Safety Progress*, Vol. 23, No. 4, Dec. 2004 (Table 1).

Applying the Concepts—Advanced

9.14 Analysis of a Scrabble game. In the board game Scrabble™, a player initially draws a "hand" of seven tiles at random from 100 tiles. Each tile has a letter of the alphabet and the player attempts to form a word from the letters in his/her hand. In *Chance* (Winter 2002), scientist C. J. Robinove investigated whether a handheld electronic version of the game, called ScrabbleExpress™, produces too few vowels in the 7-letter draws. For each of the 26 letters (and "blank" for any letter), the next table (p. 564) gives the true relative frequency of the letter in the board game as well as the frequency of occurrence of the letter in a sample of 700 tiles (i.e., 100 "hands") randomly drawn using the electronic game.

a. Do the data support the scientist's contention that ScrabbleExpress™ "presents the player with unfair word selection opportunities" that are not the same as the Scrabble™ board game? Test using $\alpha = .05$.

b. Estimate the true proportion of letters drawn in the electronic game that are vowels using a 95% confidence interval. Compare the results to the true relative frequency of a vowel in the board game.

⊙ **SCRABBLE**

Letter	Relative Frequency in Board Game	Frequency in Electronic Game
A	.09	39
B	.02	18
C	.02	30
D	.04	30
E	.12	31
F	.02	21
G	.03	35
H	.02	21
I	.09	25
J	.01	17
K	.01	27
L	.04	18
M	.02	31
N	.06	36
O	.08	20
P	.02	27
Q	.01	13
R	.06	27
S	.04	29
T	.06	27
U	.04	21
V	.02	33
W	.02	29
X	.01	15
Y	.02	32
Z	.01	14
# (blank)	.02	34
TOTAL		700

Source: Robinove, C. J. "Letter-Frequency Bias in an Electronic Scrabble Game." *Chance*, Vol. 15, No. 1, Winter 2002, p. 31 (Table 3).

9.15 Overloading in the trucking industry. Although illegal, overloading is common in the trucking industry. A state highway planning agency (Minnesota Department of Transportation) monitored the movements of overweight trucks on an interstate highway using an unmanned, computerized scale that is built into the highway. Unknown to the truckers, the scale weighed their vehicles as they passed over it. Each day's proportion of 1 week's total truck traffic (five-axle tractor truck semitrailers) is shown in the first table below. During the same week, the number of overweight trucks per day is given in the second table. The planning agency would like to know whether the number of overweight trucks per week is distributed over the 7 days of the week in direct proportion to the volume of truck traffic. Test using $\alpha = .05$.

⊙ **OVERLOAD**

Monday	.191
Tuesday	.198
Wednesday	.187
Thursday	.180
Friday	.155
Saturday	.043
Sunday	.046

Monday	90
Tuesday	82
Wednesday	72
Thursday	70
Friday	51
Saturday	18
Sunday	31

9.3 Testing Category Probabilities: Two-Way (Contingency) Table

In Section 9.1, we introduced the multinomial probability distribution and considered data classified according to a single qualitative criterion. We now consider multinomial experiments in which the data are classified according to two criteria—that is, *classification with respect to two qualitative factors.*

For example, consider a study in the *Journal of Marketing* (Fall 1992) on the impact of using celebrities in television advertisements. The researchers investigated the relationship between gender of a viewer and the viewer's brand awareness. Three hundred TV viewers were asked to identify products advertised by male celebrity spokespersons. The data are summarized in the **two-way table** shown in Table 9.3.

TABLE 9.3 Contingency Table for Marketing Example

		GENDER		
		Male	Female	Totals
Brand Awareness	**Could Identify Product**	95	41	136
	Could Not Identify Product	55	109	164
	Totals	150	150	300

This table is called a **contingency table;** it presents multinomial count data classified on two scales, or **dimensions, of classification**—namely, gender of viewer and brand awareness.

The symbols representing the cell counts for the multinomial experiment in Table 9.3 are shown in Table 9.4(a); and the corresponding cell, row, and column probabilities are shown in Table 9.4(b). Thus, n_{11} represents the number of viewers who are male and could identify the brand, and p_{11} represents the corresponding cell probability. Note the symbols for the row and column totals and also the symbols for the probability totals. The latter are called **marginal probabilities** for each row and column. The marginal probability p_{r1} is the probability that a TV viewer identifies the product; the marginal probability p_{c1} is the probability that the TV viewer is male. Thus,

$$p_{r1} = p_{11} + p_{12} \quad \text{and} \quad p_{c1} = p_{11} + p_{21}$$

Thus, we can see that this really is a multinomial experiment with a total of 300 trials, $(2)(2) = 4$ cells or possible outcomes, and probabilities for each cell as shown in Table 9.4(b). If the 300 TV viewers are randomly chosen, the trials are considered independent and the probabilities are viewed as remaining constant from trial to trial.

Suppose we want to know whether the two classifications, gender and brand awareness, are dependent—that is, if we know the gender of the TV viewer, does that information give us a clue about the viewer's brand awareness?

In a probabilistic sense, we know (Chapter 3) that independence of events A and B implies $P(AB) = P(A)P(B)$. Similarly, in the contingency table analysis, if the **two classifications are independent,** the probability that an item is classified in any particular cell of the table is the product of the corresponding marginal probabilities. Thus, under the hypothesis of independence, in Table 9.4(b), we must have

$$p_{11} = p_{r1}p_{c1}$$
$$p_{12} = p_{r1}p_{c2}$$

and so forth.

TABLE 9.4(a)   Observed Counts for Contingency Table 9.3

		GENDER		
		Male	Female	Totals
Brand Awareness	**Could Identify Product**	n_{11}	n_{12}	R_1
	Could Not Identify Product	n_{21}	n_{22}	R_2
	Totals	C_1	C_2	n

TABLE 9.4(b)   Probabilities for Contingency Table 9.3

		GENDER		
		Male	Female	Totals
Brand Awareness	**Could Identify Product**	p_{11}	p_{12}	p_{r1}
	Could Not Identify Product	p_{21}	p_{22}	p_{r2}
	Totals	p_{c1}	p_{c2}	1

To test the hypothesis of independence, we use the same reasoning employed in the one-dimensional tests of Section 9.2. First, we calculate the *expected*, or *mean*, *count in each cell* assuming that the null hypothesis of independence is true. We do this by noting that the expected count in a cell of the table is just the total number of multinomial trials, n, times the cell probability. Recall that n_{ij} represents the **observed count** in the cell located in the ith row and jth column. Then the expected cell count for the upper left-hand cell (first row, first column) is

$$E(n_{11}) = np_{11}$$

or, when the null hypothesis (the classifications are independent) is true,

$$E(n_{11}) = np_{r1}p_{c1}$$

Since these true probabilities are not known, we estimate p_{r1} and p_{c1} by the proportions $\hat{p}_{r1} = R_1/n$ and $\hat{p}_{c1} = C_1/n$, where R_1 and C_1 represent the totals for row 1 and column 1, respectively. Thus, the estimate of the expected value $E(n_{11})$ is

$$E_{11} = n\left(\frac{R_1}{n}\right)\left(\frac{C_1}{n}\right) = \frac{R_1 C_1}{n}$$

Similarly, for each i, j,

$$E_{ij} = \frac{(\text{Row total})(\text{Column total})}{\text{Total sample size}}$$

Thus,

$$E_{12} = \frac{R_1 C_1}{n}$$

$$E_{21} = \frac{R_2 C_1}{n}$$

$$E_{22} = \frac{R_2 C_2}{n}$$

Finding Expected Cell Counts for a Two-Way Contingency Table

The estimate of the expected number of observations falling into the cell in row i and column j is given by

$$E_{ij} = \frac{R_i C_j}{n}$$

where R_i = total for row i, C_j = total for column j, and n = sample size.

Using the data in Table 9.3, we find

$$E_{11} = \frac{R_1 C_1}{n} = \frac{(136)(150)}{300} = 68$$

$$E_{12} = \frac{R_1 C_2}{n} = \frac{(136)(150)}{300} = 68$$

$$E_{21} = \frac{R_2 C_1}{n} = \frac{(164)(150)}{300} = 82$$

$$E_{22} = \frac{R_2 C_2}{n} = \frac{(164)(150)}{300} = 82$$

The observed data and the estimated expected values (in parentheses) are shown in Table 9.5.

TABLE 9.5 Observed and Estimated Expected (in Parentheses) Counts

		GENDER		
		Male	Female	Totals
Brand Awareness	**Could Identify Product**	95 (68)	41 (68)	136
	Could Not Identify Product	55 (82)	109 (82)	164
	Totals	150	150	300

We now use the χ^2 statistic to compare the observed and expected (estimated) counts in each cell of the contingency table:

$$\chi^2 = \frac{[n_{11} - E_{11}]^2}{E_{11}} + \frac{[n_{12} - E_{12}]^2}{E_{12}} + \frac{[n_{21} - E_{21}]^2}{E_{21}} + \frac{[n_{22} - E_{22}]^2}{E_{22}}$$

$$= \sum \frac{[n_{ij} - E_{ij}]^2}{E_{ij}}$$

Note: The use of Σ in the context of a contingency table analysis refers to a sum over all cells in the table.

Substituting the data of Table 9.5 into this expression, we get

$$\chi^2 = \frac{(95 - 68)^2}{68} + \frac{(41 - 68)^2}{68} + \frac{(55 - 82)^2}{82} + \frac{(109 - 82)^2}{82} = 39.22$$

Large values of χ^2 imply that the observed counts do not closely agree and hence that the hypothesis of independence is false. To determine how large χ^2 must be before it is too large to be attributed to chance, we make use of the fact that the sampling distribution of χ^2 is approximately an χ^2 probability distribution when the classifications are independent.

When testing the null hypothesis of independence in a two-way contingency table, the appropriate degrees of freedom will be $(r - 1)(c - 1)$, where r is the number of rows and c is the number of columns in the table.

For the brand awareness example, the degrees of freedom for χ^2 are $(r - 1)(c - 1) = (2 - 1)(2 - 1) = 1$. Then, for $\alpha = .05$, we reject the hypothesis of independence when

$$\chi^2 > \chi^2_{.05} = 3.8146$$

Since the computed $\chi^2 = 39.22$ exceeds the value 3.84146, we conclude that viewer gender and brand awareness are dependent events.

The pattern of **dependence** can be seen more clearly by expressing the data as percentages. We first select one of the two classifications to be used as the base variable. In the preceding example, suppose we select gender of the TV viewer as the classificatory variable to be the base. Next, we represent the responses for each level of the second categorical variable (brand awareness in our example) as a percentage of the subtotal for the base variable. For example, from Table 9.5 we convert the response for males who identify the brand (95) to a percentage of the total number of male viewers (150)—that is,

$$(95/150)100\% = 63.3\%$$

The conversions of all Table 9.5 entries are similarly computed, and the values are shown in Table 9.6. The value shown at the right of each row is the row's total expressed as a percentage of the total number of responses in the entire table. Thus, the percentage of

TABLE 9.6 Percentage of TV Viewers Who Identify Brand, by Gender

		GENDER		
		Male	Female	Totals
Brand Awareness	**Could Identify Product**	63.3	27.3	45.3
	Could Not Identify Product	36.7	72.7	54.7
	Totals	100	100	100

TV viewers who identify the product is $\left(\frac{136}{300}\right)100\% = 45.3\%$ (rounded to the nearest percent).

If the gender and brand awareness variables are independent, then the percentages in the cells of the table are expected to be approximately equal to the corresponding row percentages. Thus, we would expect the percentages who identify the brand for each gender to be approximately 45% if the two variables are independent. The extent to which each gender's percentage departs from this value determines the dependence of the two classifications, with greater variability of the row percentages meaning a greater degree of dependence. A plot of the percentages helps summarize the observed pattern. In the SPSS bar graph in Figure 9.3, we show the gender of the viewer (the base variable) on the horizontal axis, and the percentages of TV viewers who identify the brand on the vertical axis. The "expected" percentage under the assumption of independence is shown as a dotted horizontal line.

Figure 9.3 clearly indicates the reason that the test resulted in the conclusion that the two classifications in the contingency table are dependent. The percentage of male TV viewers who identify the brand promoted by a male celebrity is more than twice as high as the percentage of female TV viewers who identify the brand.

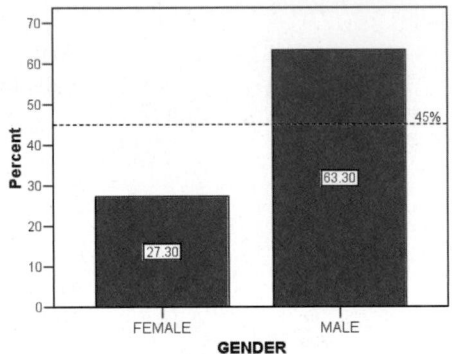

FIGURE 9.3
SPSS bar graph showing percentage of viewers who identified the TV product

Statistical measures of the degree of dependence and procedures for making comparisons of pairs of levels for classifications are available. They are beyond the scope of this text but can be found in the references. We will, however, utilize descriptive summaries such as Figure 9.3 to examine the degree of dependence exhibited by the sample data.

The general form of a two-way contingency table containing r rows and c columns (called an $r \times c$ contingency table) is shown in Table 9.7. Note that the observed count in the (ij) cell is denoted by n_{ij} the ith row total is R_i, the jth column total is C_j, and the total sample size is n. Using this notation, we give the general form of the contingency table test for independent classifications in the next box.

TABLE 9.7 General $r \times c$ Contingency Table

	Column	1	2	$\cdots$	c	Row Totals
Row	**1**	n_{11}	n_{12}	$\cdots$	n_{1c}	R_1
	2	n_{21}	n_{22}	$\cdots$	n_{2c}	R_2
	$\vdots$	$\vdots$	$\vdots$		$\vdots$	$\vdots$
	r	n_{r1}	n_{r2}	$\cdots$	n_{rc}	R_r
	Column Totals	C_1	C_2	$\cdots$	C_c	n

General Form of a Contingency Table Analysis: An χ^2-Test for Independence

H_0: The two classifications are independent.

H_a: The two classifications are dependent.

Test statistic: $\chi^2 = \sum \dfrac{[n_{ij} - E_{ij}]^2}{E_{ij}}$

where $E_{ij} = \dfrac{R_i C_j}{n}$

Rejection region: $\chi^2 > \chi_\alpha^2$, where χ_α^2 has $(r-1)(c-1)$df.

Conditions Required for a Valid χ^2-Test: Contingency Table

1. The n observed counts are a random sample from the population of interest. We may then consider this to be a multinomial experiment with $r \times c$ possible outcomes.

2. The sample size, n, will be large enough so that, for every cell, the expected count, E_{ij}, will be equal to 5 or more.

EXAMPLE 9.3

Conducting a Two-Way Analysis for a Brokerage Firm

Problem A large brokerage firm wants to determine whether the service it provides to affluent clients differs from the service it provides to lower-income clients. A sample of 500 clients is selected, and each client is asked to rate his or her broker. The results are shown in Table 9.8.

 BROKERAGE

TABLE 9.8 Survey Results (Observed Clients), Example 9.3.

		CLIENT'S INCOME			
		Under $30,000	$30,000–$60,000	Over $60,000	Totals
Broker Rating	Outstanding	48	64	41	153
	Average	98	120	50	268
	Poor	30	33	16	79
	Totals	176	217	107	500

a. Test to determine whether there is evidence that broker rating and customer income are independent. Use a $\alpha = .10$.

b. Plot the data and describe the patterns revealed. Is the result of the test supported by the plot?

Solution

a. The first step is to calculate estimated expected cell frequencies under the assumption that the classifications are independent. Rather than compute these values by hand, we resort to a computer. The MINITAB printout of the analysis of Table 9.8 is displayed in Figure 9.4. Each cell in Figure 9.4 contains the observed (top) and expected (bottom) frequency in that cell. Note that E_{11}, the estimated expected count for the Outstanding, Under $30,000 cell is 53.86. Similarly, the estimated

```
Rows: RATING    Columns: INCOME

                1:UND30K    2:30K-60K    3:OVR60K        All

1:OUTSTAN            48           64           41        153
                  27.27        29.49        38.32      30.60
                  53.86        66.40        32.74     153.00

2:AVERAGE           98          120           50        268
                  55.68        55.30        46.73      53.60
                  94.34       116.31        57.35     268.00

3:POOR              30           33           16         79
                  17.05        15.21        14.95      15.80
                  27.81        34.29        16.91      79.00

All                176          217          107        500
                 100.00       100.00       100.00     100.00
                 176.00       217.00       107.00     500.00


Cell Contents:      Count
                    % of Column
                    Expected count
```

Pearson Chi-Square = 4.278, DF = 4, P-Value = 0.370
Likelihood Ratio Chi-Square = 4.184, DF = 4, P-Value = 0.382

FIGURE 9.4

MINITAB contingency table analysis for brokerage data

expected count for the Outstanding, \$30,000–\$60,000 cell is $E_{12} = 66.40$. Since all the estimated expected cell frequencies are greater than 5, the χ^2 approximation for the test statistic is appropriate. Assuming the clients chosen were randomly selected from all clients of the brokerage firm, the characteristics of the multinomial probability distribution are satisfied. The null and alternative hypotheses we want to test are

> H_0: The rating a client gives his or her broker is independent of client's income
>
> H_a: Broker rating and client income are dependent

The test statistic, $\chi^2 = 4.278$, is highlighted at the bottom of the printout, as is the observed significance level (p-value) of the test. Since $\alpha = .10$ is less than $p = .370$, we fail to reject H_0. This survey does not support the firm's alternative hypothesis that affluent clients receive different broker service than lower-income clients.

b. The broker rating frequencies are expressed as percentages of income category frequencies and highlighted in the MINITAB printout, Figure 9.4. The expected percentages under the assumption of independence are shown in the "All" column of the printout. A MINITAB side-by-side bar graph of the data is shown in Figure 9.5. Note that the response percentages deviate only slightly from those expected under the assumption of independence, supporting the result of the test in part **a**—that is, neither the descriptive plot nor the statistical test provides evidence that the rating given the broker services depends on (varies with) the customer's income.

Now Work Exercise 9.21

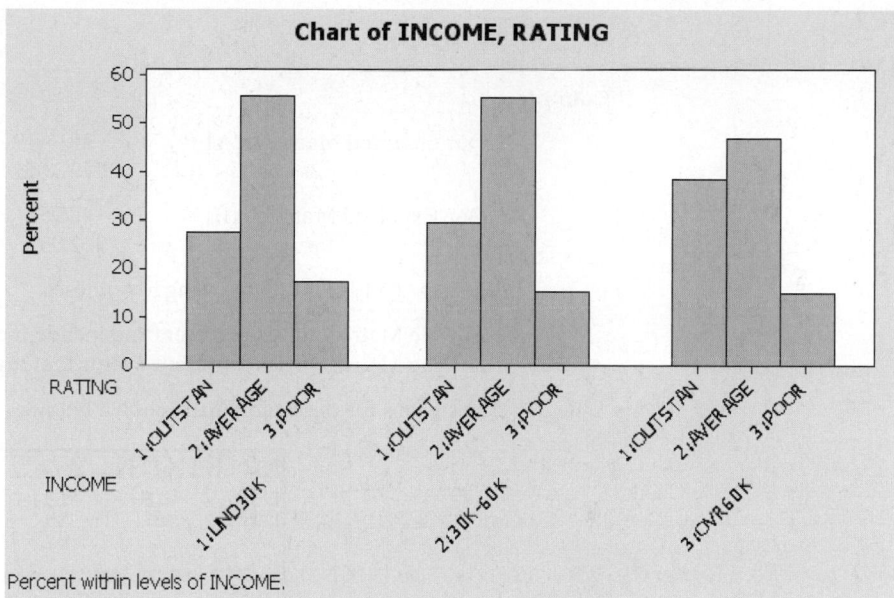

FIGURE 9.5
MINITAB side-by-side bar graph for brokerage data

Contingency Tables

Using the TI-83/TI-84 Graphing Calculator

Finding *p*-values for Contingency Tables

Step 1   *Access the Matrix menu to enter the observed values*

Press **2nd x⁻¹** for **MATRX** (Note: On the TI-83, press **MATRX**)
Arrow right to **EDIT**
Press **ENTER**
Use the **ARROW** key to enter the row and column dimensions of your observed Matrix
Use the **ARROW** key to enter your observed values into Matrix |A|

Step 2   *Access the Matrix menu to enter the expected values*

Press **2nd x⁻¹** for **MATRX** (Note: On the TI-83, press **MATRX**)
Arrow right to **EDIT**
Arrow down to **2:[B]**
Press **ENTER**
Use the **ARROW** key to enter the row and column dimensions of your expected matrix. (The dimensions will be the same as in Matrix A)
Use the **ARROW** key to enter your expected values into Matrix [B]

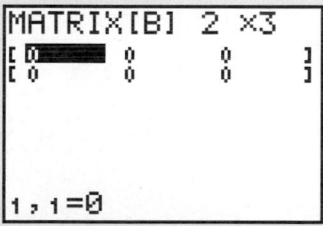

Step 3   *Access the Statistical Tests menu and perform the Chi-square test.*

Press **STAT**
Arrow right to **TESTS**
Arrow down to χ^2 **Test.**
Press **ENTER**
Arrow down to **Calculate**
Press **ENTER**

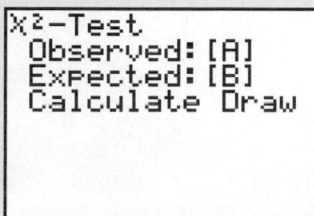

Continued

Step 4   *Reject H_0 if the p-value $< \alpha$*

Example

Our observed Matrix is [A] =

| 39 | 19 | 12 | 28 | 18 |
| 172 | 61 | 44 | 70 | 37 |

Our Expected Matrix is [B] =

| 48.952 | 18.56 | 12.992 | 22.736 | 12.76 |
| 162.05 | 61.44 | 43.008 | 75.264 | 42.24 |

Use $\alpha = .05$ to test the following hypotheses:

H_0: The Matrix entries represent Independent events.
H_a: The Matrix entries represent events that **are not** independent.

The screens for this example are shown below.

As you can see from the screen, the p-value is 0.1289. Since the p-value is **greater** than $\alpha = .05$, we **do not** reject H_0.

STATISTICS IN ACTION REVISITED

Testing Whether Coupon Customer Characteristics Are Related to User Type

In his study of a firm's discount coupon users (p. 553), marketing professor Dan Ladik wanted to know whether there are differences in customer characteristics (i.e., gender, education, work status, and satisfaction) among the three types of coupon users: mail-only (nontechnology) users, Internet-only (TBSS) users, and users of both mail and Internet coupons. One approach to analyzing these data is to determine whether each of the four customer characteristic variables is related to coupon user type. Since all the variables measured on the sample of 440 coupon users are qualitative, a contingency table analysis is appropriate.

Figures SIA9.3–SIA9.6(on pp. 573–575) show the SPSS contingency table analyses relating each customer

GENDER * USER Crosstabulation

			USER			
			Mail	Net	Both	Total
GENDER	Male	Count	84	7	31	122
		Expected Count	72.6	11.9	37.4	122.0
	Female	Count	178	36	104	318
		Expected Count	189.4	31.1	97.6	318.0
Total		Count	262	43	135	440
		Expected Count	262.0	43.0	135.0	440.0

Chi-Square Tests

	Value	df	Asymp. Sig. (2-sided)
Pearson Chi-Square	6.797[a]	2	.033
Likelihood Ratio	7.105	2	.029
Linear-by-Linear Association	4.371	1	.037
N of Valid Cases	440		

a. 0 cells (.0%) have expected count less than 5. The minimum expected count is 11.92.

Figure SIA9.3

SPSS contingency table analysis—gender versus user type

EDUC * USER Crosstabulation

			USER			
			Mail	Net	Both	Total
EDUC	HS	Count	34	7	19	60
		Expected Count	35.7	5.9	18.4	60.0
	VT/COLL	Count	96	20	62	178
		Expected Count	106.0	17.4	54.6	178.0
	COLL4	Count	85	9	38	132
		Expected Count	78.6	12.9	40.5	132.0
	GRAD	Count	47	7	16	70
		Expected Count	41.7	6.8	21.5	70.0
Total		Count	262	43	135	440
		Expected Count	262.0	43.0	135.0	440.0

Chi-Square Tests

	Value	df	Asymp. Sig. (2-sided)
Pearson Chi-Square	6.587[a]	6	.361
Likelihood Ratio	6.786	6	.341
Linear-by-Linear Association	3.546	1	.060
N of Valid Cases	440		

a. 0 cells (.0%) have expected count less than 5. The minimum expected count is 5.86.

Figure SIA9.4

SPSS contingency table analysis—education versus user type

Continued

COUPSAT * USER Crosstabulation

			Mail	Net	Both	Total
COUPSAT	Satisfied	Count	172	30	123	325
		Expected Count	193.5	31.8	99.7	325.0
		% within USER	65.6%	69.8%	91.1%	73.9%
	Indiff	Count	62	9	9	80
		Expected Count	47.6	7.8	24.5	80.0
		% within USER	23.7%	20.9%	6.7%	18.2%
	Unsatis	Count	28	4	3	35
		Expected Count	20.8	3.4	10.7	35.0
		% within USER	10.7%	9.3%	2.2%	8.0%
Total		Count	262	43	135	440
		Expected Count	262.0	43.0	135.0	440.0
		% within USER	100.0%	100.0%	100.0%	100.0%

The header USER spans Mail, Net, Both columns.

Chi-Square Tests

	Value	df	Asymp. Sig. (2-sided)
Pearson Chi-Square	30.418[a]	4	.000
Likelihood Ratio	34.934	4	.000
Linear-by-Linear Association	25.717	1	.000
N of Valid Cases	440		

a. 1 cells (11.1%) have expected count less than 5. The minimum expected count is 3.42.

Figure SIA9.5
SPSS contingency table analysis—satisfaction versus user type

characteristic to coupon user type. The p-values for the chi-square tests for the variables gender, education, satisfaction, and work status are .033, .361, .000, and .069, respectively. If we conduct each test at $\alpha = .01$ (we purposely chose a small α to minimize the chance of making a Type I error), the only significant result is for customer satisfaction—that is, the data provide evidence to indicate that the level of customer satisfaction depends on type of coupon user; however, there is not sufficient evidence to say that any of the other customer characteristics (gen-

der, education, or work status) are related to type of coupon user.

The column percentages highlighted in the contingency table of Figure SIA9.5 reveal the differences in satisfaction levels of the three user types. The percentages of satisfied customers for mail-only and Internet-only coupon users are 65.6% and 69.8%, respectively. However, for users of both mail and the Internet, 91.1% are satisfied. This information was used by the coupon firm to develop a marketing strategy aimed at mail-only and Internet-only coupon users.

Exercises 9.16–9.31

Learning the Mechanics

9.16 Find the rejection region for a test of independence of two classifications where the contingency table contains r rows and c columns.
  a. $r = 5, c = 5, \alpha = .05$
  b. $r = 3, c = 6, \alpha = .10$
  c. $r = 2, c = 3, \alpha = .01$

9.17 Consider the 2×3 (i.e., $r = 2$ and $c = 3$) contingency table shown on p. 575.
  a. Specify the null and alternative hypotheses that should be used in testing the independence of the row and column classifications.

WORK * USER Crosstabulation

			USER			
			Mail	Net	Both	Total
WORK	FULL	Count	148	29	90	267
		Expected Count	159.0	26.1	81.9	267.0
	PART	Count	31	8	13	52
		Expected Count	31.0	5.1	16.0	52.0
	NONE	Count	31	3	17	51
		Expected Count	30.4	5.0	15.6	51.0
	RETIRED	Count	52	3	15	70
		Expected Count	41.7	6.8	21.5	70.0
Total		Count	262	43	135	440
		Expected Count	262.0	43.0	135.0	440.0

Chi-Square Tests

	Value	df	Asymp. Sig. (2-sided)
Pearson Chi-Square	11.687[a]	6	.069
Likelihood Ratio	12.208	6	.057
Linear-by-Linear Association	5.619	1	.018
N of Valid Cases	440		

a. 1 cells (8.3%) have expected count less than 5. The minimum expected count is 4.98.

Figure SIA9.6
SPSS contingency table analysis—work status versus user type

LM9_17

		COLUMN		
		1	2	3
Row	1	9	34	53
	2	16	30	25

b. Specify the test statistic and the rejection region that should be used in conducting the hypothesis test of part **a.** Use $\alpha = .01$.
c. Assuming the row classification and the column classification are independent, find estimates for the expected cell counts.
d. Conduct the hypothesis test of part **a.** Interpret your result.

9.18 Refer to Exercise 9.17.
a. Convert the frequency responses to percentages by calculating the percentage of each column total falling in each row. Also convert the row totals to percentages of the total number of responses. Display the percentages in a table.
b. Create a bar graph with row 1 percentage on the vertical axis and column number on the horizontal axis. Show the row 1 total percentage as a horizontal line on the graph.

c. What pattern do you expect to see if the rows and columns are independent? Does the plot support the result of the test of independence in Exercise 9.17?

9.19 Test the null hypothesis of independence of the two classifications, A and B, of the 3×3 contingency table shown below. Test using $\alpha = .05$.

LM9_19

		B		
		B_1	B_2	B_3
A	A_1	40	72	42
	A_2	63	53	70
	A_3	31	38	30

9.20 Refer to Exercise 9.19.
a. Convert the responses to percentages by calculating the percentage of each B class total falling into each A classification.
b. Calculate the percentage of the total number of responses that constitute each of the A classification totals.
c. Create a bar graph with row A_1 percentage on the vertical axis and B classification on the horizontal axis. Does the graph support the result of the test of hypothesis in Exercise 9.19? Explain.

d. Repeat part **c** for the row A_2 percentages.

e. Repeat part **c** for the row A_3 percentages.

Applying the Concepts—Basic

9.21 **JAMA study of heart patients.** The *Journal of the American*
NW *Medical Association* (Apr. 18, 2001) published the results of a study of alcohol consumption in patients suffering from acute myocardial infarction (AMI). The patients were classified according to average number of alcoholic drinks per week and whether or not they had congestive heart failure. A summary of the results for 1,913 AMI patients is shown in the table.

⊙ **AMAAMI**

Congestive Heart Failure	ALCOHOL CONSUMPTION		
	Abstainers	Less than 7 drinks/week	7 or more drinks/week
Yes	146	106	29
No	750	590	292
Totals	896	696	321

Source: Mukamal, K. J., et al. "Prior Alcohol Consumption and Mortality Following Acute Myocardial Infarction." *Journal of the American Medical Association,* Vol. 285, No. 15, April 18, 2001 (Table 1).

a. Find the sample proportion of abstainers with congestive heart failure.

b. Find the sample proportion of moderate drinkers (patients who have less than 7 drinks per week) with congestive heart failure.

c. Find the sample proportion of heavy drinkers (patients who have 7 or more drinks per week) with congestive heart failure.

d. Compare the sample proportions, parts **a–c**. Does it appear that the proportion of AMI patients with congestive heart failure depends on alcohol consumption?

e. Give the null hypothesis for testing whether the proportion of AMI patients with congestive heart failure depends on alcohol consumption.

f. Use the MINITAB printout below to conduct the test, part **e**. Test at $\alpha = .05$.

9.22 **Survey on giving and volunteering.** Refer to the study of charitable givers published in the *National Tax Journal* (Dec. 2001), Exercise 9.9 (p. 562). In addition to the 1,072 charitable givers who reported that their charitable contributions were motivated by tax considerations, another 1,693 givers reported no tax motivation, giving a total sample of 2,765 charitable givers. Of the 1,072 who were motivated by tax considerations, 691 itemized deductions on their income tax returns. Of the 1,693 who were not motivated by tax considerations, 794 itemized deductions.

a. Consider the two categorical variables, tax motivation (yes or no) and itemize deductions (yes or no). Form a 2×2 contingency table for these variables.

b. Compute the expected cell counts for the contingency table, part **a**.

c. Compute the value of χ^2 for a test of independence.

d. At $\alpha = .05$, what inference can you make about whether the two variables, tax motivation and itemize deductions, are related for charitable givers?

e. Create a bar graph that will visually support your conclusion in part **d**.

9.23 **Are travel professionals equitably paid?** *Business Travel News* (July 17, 2006) reported the results of its annual Travel Manager Salary & Attitude survey. A total of 277 travel professionals, 103 males and 174 females, participated in the 2005 survey. One question asked for the travel professional's opinion on the fairness of his/her salary. Responses were classified as "salary too low," "equitable/fair," or "paid well." The table on page 577 gives a breakdown of the responses in each category by gender.

a. Find the proportion of male travel professionals who believe their salary is too low and compare it to the proportion of female travel professionals who believe their salary is too low.

b. Repeat part **a**, but compare the proportions who believe their salary is equitable/fair.

MINITAB Output for Exercise 9.21

```
Rows: FAILURE    Columns: ALCOHOL

             7ORMORE   ABSTAIN   LESS7      All

NO               292       750     590     1632
               273.8     764.4   593.8   1632.0

YES               29       146     106      281
                47.2     131.6   102.2    281.0

All              321       896     696     1913
               321.0     896.0   696.0   1913.0

Cell Contents:          Count
                        Expected count


Pearson Chi-Square = 10.197, DF = 2, P-Value = 0.006
Likelihood Ratio Chi-Square = 11.240, DF = 2, P-Value = 0.004
```

TRAVELPRO

	Males	Females
Salary too low	29	89
Equitable/fair	58	64
Paid well	16	21
TOTALS	103	174

c. Repeat part **a**, but compare the proportions who believe they are paid well.

d. Based on the comparisons, parts **a–c**, do you think opinion on the fairness of a travel professional's salary differs for males and females?

e. Refer to part **d**. Conduct the appropriate statistical test using $\alpha = .10$.

f. Construct and interpret a 90% confidence interval for the difference between the proportions of part **a**.

9.24 Dust plumes from farm equipment. Fugitive dust plumes generated by farm equipment can be hazardous to human health. In the *Journal of Agricultural, Biological, and Environmental Sciences* (Mar. 2001), environmental engineers developed a model for dust particle concentrations in plumes produced by a tractor operating in a wheat field. The tractor traveled along six parallel, equi-length paths in the field. A remote sensing instrument with a laser beam, placed at the edge of the field, measured the particulate matter in the dust every .5 seconds. Unfortunately, a few of the measurements were censored (i.e., higher than the signal level of the instrument). This usually occurred when the tractor was a short distance from the instrument's laser beam. The accompanying table shows the number of censored measurements for each of the six tractor lines.

a. Calculate and compare the sample proportion of censored measurements for the six tractor lines.

b. Do the data provide sufficient evidence to indicate that the proportion of censored measurements differs for the six tractor lines? Test using $\alpha = .01$.

c. Comment on the practical versus statistical significance of the test.

DUSTCENSOR

Tractor Line	Uncensored Measurements	Censored Measurements	TOTALS
1	6047	175	6222
2	4456	236	4692
3	6821	319	7140
4	5889	231	6120
5	9873	480	10,353
6	4607	187	4794
TOTALS	37,693	1628	39,321

Source: Johns, C., Holmen, B., Niemeier, A., and Shumway, R. "Nonlinear Regression for Modeling Censored One-Dimensional Concentration Profiles of Fugitive Dust Plumes." *Journal of Agricultural, Biological, and Environmental Sciences,* Vol. 6, No. 1, March 2001 (from data file provided by coauthor Brit Holmen).

Applying the Concepts—Intermediate

SWDEFECTS

9.25 Software defects. The PROMISE Software Engineering Repository at the University of Ottawa provides researchers with data sets for building predictive software models. (See Exercise 2.128, p. 115.) Data on 498 modules of software code written in "C" language for a NASA spacecraft instrument are saved in the **SWDEFECTS** file. Recall that each module was analyzed for defects and classified as "true" if it contained defective code and "false" if not. One algorithm for predicting whether or not a module has defects is "essential complexity" (denoted EVG), where a module with at least 15 subflow graphs with D-structured primes is predicted to have a defect. When the method predicts a defect, the predicted EVG value is "yes"; otherwise, it is "no." A contingency table for the two variables, actual defective status and predicted EVG, is shown in the SPSS printout on page 578. Interpret the results. Would you recommend the essential complexity algorithm as a predictor of defective software modules? Explain.

9.26 Pig farm study. An article in *Sociological Methods & Research* (May 2001) analyzed the data presented in the table. A sample of 262 Kansas pig farmers were classified according to their education level (college or not) and size of their pig farm (number of pigs). Conduct a test to determine whether a pig farmer's education level has an impact on the size of the pig farm. Use $\alpha = .05$ and support your answer with a graph.

PIGFARM

FARM SIZE	EDUCATION LEVEL		TOTALS
	No College	College	
< 1,000 pigs	42	53	95
1,000–2,000 pigs	27	42	69
2,000–5,000 pigs	22	20	42
> 5,000 pigs	27	29	56
TOTALS	118	144	262

Source: Agresti, A., and Liu, I. "Strategies for Modeling a Categorical Variable Allowing Multiple Category Choices." *Sociological Methods & Research,* Vol. 29, No. 4, May 2001 (Table 1).

9.27 Where do you get your travel information? In order to create a behavioral profile of pleasure travelers, M. Bonn (Florida State University), L. Forr (Georgia Southern University), and A. Susskind (Cornell University) interviewed 5,026 pleasure travelers in the Tampa Bay region (*Journal of Travel Research,* May 1999). Two of the characteristics they investigated were the travelers' education level and their use of the Internet to seek travel information. The table below summarizes the results of the interviews. The researchers concluded that travelers who use the Internet to search for travel information are likely to be people who are college educated. Do you agree? Test using $\alpha = .05$. What assumptions must hold to ensure the validity of your test?

NETRAVEL

Education	USE INTERNET	
	Yes	No
College Degree or More	1,072	1,287
Less than a College Degree	640	2,027

Source: Bonn, M., Furr, L., and Susskind, A. "Predicting a Behavioral Profile for Pleasure Travelers on the Basis of Internet Use Segmentation." *Journal of Travel Research,* Vol. 37, May 1999, pp. 333–340.

DEFECT * PRED_EVG Crosstabulation

Count

		PRED_EVG		Total
		no	yes	
DEFECT	false	441	8	449
	true	47	2	49
Total		488	10	498

Chi-Square Tests

	Value	df	Asymp. Sig. (2-sided)	Exact Sig. (2-sided)	Exact Sig. (1-sided)
Pearson Chi-Square	1.188[b]	1	.276		
Continuity Correction[a]	.306	1	.580		
Likelihood Ratio	.948	1	.330		
Fisher's Exact Test				.257	.257
N of Valid Cases	498				

a. Computed only for a 2x2 table

b. 1 cells (25.0%) have expected count less than 5. The minimum expected count is .98.

SPSS Output for Exercise 9.25

9.28 Ethical behavior of accountants. University of Louisville professor Julia Karcher conducted an experiment to investigate the ethical behavior of accountants (*Journal of Business Ethics,* Vol. 15, 1996). She focused on auditor abilities to detect ethical problems that may not be obvious. Seventy auditors from Big-Six accounting firms were given a detailed case study that contained several problems, including tax evasion by the client. In 35 of the cases, the tax evasion issue was severe; in the other 35 cases it was moderate. The auditors were asked to identify any problems they detected in the case. The following table summarizes the results for the ethical issue.

ACCETHIC

	SEVERITY OF ETHICAL ISSUE	
	Moderate	Severe
Ethical Issue Identified	27	26
Ethical Issue Not Identified	8	9

Source: Karcher, J. "Auditors' Ability to Discern the Presence of Ethical Problems." *Journal of Business Ethics,* Vol. 15, 1996, p. 1041 (Table V).

a. Did the severity of the ethical issue influence whether the issue was identified or not by the auditors? Test using $\alpha = .05$.

b. Suppose the left-hand column of the table contained the counts 35 and 0 instead of 27 and 8. Should the test of part **a** still be conducted? Explain.

c. Keeping the sample size the same, change the numbers in the contingency table so that the answer you would get for the question posed in part **a** changes.

9.29 Creating menus to influence others. Refer to the *Journal of Consumer Research* (Mar. 2003) study on influencing the choices of others by offering undesirable alternatives, Exercise 6.73 (p. 379). In another experiment conducted by the researcher, 96 subjects were asked to imagine that they had just moved to an apartment with two others and that they were shopping for a new appliance (e.g., television, microwave oven). Each subject was asked to create a menu of three brand choices for their roommates; then subjects were randomly assigned (in equal numbers) to one of three different "goal" conditions—(1) create the menu in order to influence roommates to buy a preselected brand, (2) create the menu in order to influence roommates to buy a brand of your choice, and (3) create the menu with no intent to influence roommates. The researcher theorized that the menus created to influence others will likely include undesirable alternative brands. Consequently, the number of menus in each goal condition that was consistent with the theory was determined. The data are summarized in the table at the top of page 579. Analyze the data for the purpose of determining whether the proportion of subjects who select menus consistent with the theory depends on goal condition. Use $\alpha = .01$.

9.30 Flight response of geese to helicopter traffic. Offshore oil drilling near an Alaskan estuary has led to increased air traffic—mostly large helicopters—in the area. The U.S. Fish and Wildlife Service commissioned a study to investigate the impact these helicopters have on the flocks of Pacific brant geese that inhabit the estuary in fall before migrating (*Statistical Case Studies: A Collaboration between Academe and Industry,* 1998). Two large helicopters were flown repeatedly over the estuary at different altitudes and lateral distances from the flock. The flight responses of the geese

⊙ **MENU3**

Goal Condition	Number Consistent with Theory	Number Not Consistent with Theory	Totals
Influence/preselected brand	15	17	32
Influence/own brand	14	18	32
No influence	3	29	32

Source: Hamilton, R. W. "Why Do People Suggest What They Do Not Want? Using Context Effects to Influence Others' Choices." *Journal of Consumer Research,* Vol. 29, March 2003 (Table 2).

(recorded as "low" or "high"), altitude (hundreds of meters), and lateral distance (hundreds of meters) for each of the 464 helicopter overflights were recorded and are saved in the **PACGEESE** file. (The data for the first 10 overflights are shown in the following table.)

⊙ **PACGEESE (First 10 observations shown)**

Overflight	Altitude	Lateral Distance	Flight Response
1	0.91	4.99	HIGH
2	0.91	8.21	HIGH
3	0.91	3.38	HIGH
4	9.14	21.08	LOW
5	1.52	6.60	HIGH
6	0.91	3.38	HIGH
7	3.05	0.16	HIGH
8	6.10	3.38	HIGH
9	3.05	6.60	HIGH
10	12.19	6.60	HIGH

Source: Erickson, W., Nick, T., and Ward, D. "Investigating Flight Response of Pacific Brant to Helicopters at Izembek Lagoon, Alaska, by Using Logistic Regression." *Statistical Case Studies: A Collaboration between Academe and Industry,* ASA-SIAM Series on Statistics and Applied Probability, 1998.)

a. The researchers categorized altitude as follows: less than 300 meters, 300–600 meters, and 600 or more meters. Summarize the data in the **PACGEESE** file by creating a contingency table for altitude category and flight response.

b. Conduct a test to determine if flight response of the geese depends on altitude of the helicopter. Test using $\alpha = .01$.

c. The researchers categorized lateral distance as follows: less than 1,000 meters, 1,000–2,000 meters, 2,000–3,000 meters, and 3,000 or more meters. Summarize the data in the **PACGEESE** file by creating a contingency table for lateral distance category and flight response.

d. Conduct a test to determine if flight response of the geese depends on lateral distance of helicopter from the flock. Test using $\alpha = .01$.

e. The current Federal Aviation Authority (FAA) minimum altitude standard for flying over the estuary is 2,000 feet (approximately 610 meters). Based on the results, parts **a–d**, what changes to the FAA regulations do you recommend in order to minimize the effects to Pacific brant geese?

Applying the Concepts—Advanced

9.31 Efficacy of an HIV vaccine. New, effective AIDS vaccines are now being developed using the process of "sieving"

(i.e., sifting out infections with some strains of HIV). Harvard School of Public Health statistician Peter Gilbert demonstrated how to test the efficacy of an HIV vaccine in *Chance* (Fall 2000). As an example, Gilbert reported the results of VaxGen's preliminary HIV vaccine trial using the following 2 × 2 table. The vaccine was designed to eliminate a particular strain of the virus, called the "MN strain." The trial consisted of 7 AIDS patients vaccinated with the new drug and 31 AIDS patients who were treated with a placebo (no vaccination). The table shows the number of patients who tested positive and negative for the MN strain in the trial follow-up period.

⊙ **VAXGEN1**

PATIENT GROUP	MN STRAIN		
	Positive	Negative	TOTALS
Unvaccinated	22	9	31
Vaccinated	2	5	7
TOTALS	24	14	38

Source: Gilbert, P. "Developing an AIDS Vaccine by Sieving." *Chance,* Vol. 13, No. 4, Fall 2000.

a. Conduct a test to determine whether the vaccine is effective in treating the MN strain of HIV. Use $\alpha = .05$.

b. Are the assumptions for the test, part **a**, satisfied? What are the consequences if the assumptions are violated?

c. In the case of a 2 × 2 contingency table, R. A. Fisher (1935) developed a procedure for computing the exact *p*-value for the test (called *Fisher's exact test*). The method utilizes the *hypergeometric probability distribution* (a discrete probability distribution not covered in Chapter 4). Consider the hypergeometric probability

$$\frac{\binom{7}{2}\binom{31}{22}}{\binom{38}{24}}$$

This represents the probability that 2 out of 7 vaccinated AIDS patients test positive and 22 out of 31 unvaccinated patients test positive (i.e., the probability of the table result given the null hypothesis of independence is true). Compute this probability (called the *probability of the contingency table*).

d. Refer to part **c.** Two contingency tables (with the same marginal totals as the original table) that are more contradictory to the null hypothesis of independence than the observed table follow (p. 580). First, explain why

GROUP * MNSTRAIN Crosstabulation

			MNSTRAIN		Total
			NEG	POS	
GROUP	UNVAC	Count	9	22	31
		Expected Count	11.4	19.6	31.0
	VACC	Count	5	2	7
		Expected Count	2.6	4.4	7.0
Total		Count	14	24	38
		Expected Count	14.0	24.0	38.0

Chi-Square Tests

	Value	df	Asymp. Sig. (2-sided)	Exact Sig. (2-sided)	Exact Sig. (1-sided)
Pearson Chi-Square	4.411[b]	1	.036		
Continuity Correction[a]	2.777	1	.096		
Likelihood Ratio	4.289	1	.038		
Fisher's Exact Test				.077	.050
N of Valid Cases	38				

a. Computed only for a 2x2 table

b. 2 cells (50.0%) have expected count less than 5. The minimum expected count is 2.58.

SPSS Output for Exercise 9.31

these tables provide more evidence to reject H_0 than the original table; then compute the probability of each table using the hypergeometric formula.

e. The p-value of Fisher's exact test is the probability of observing a result at least as contradictory to the null hypothesis as the observed contingency table, given the same marginal totals. Sum the probabilities of parts **c** and **d** to obtain the p-value of Fisher's exact test. (To verify your calculations, check the p-value at the bottom of the accompanying SPSS printout.) Interpret this value in the context of the vaccine trial.

VAXGEN2

	MN STRAIN		
PATIENT GROUP	Positive	Negative	TOTALS
Unvaccinated	23	8	31
Vaccinated	1	6	7
TOTALS	24	14	38

VAXGEN3

	MN STRAIN		
PATIENT GROUP	Positive	Negative	TOTALS
Unvaccinated	24	7	31
Vaccinated	0	7	7
TOTALS	24	14	38

9.4 A Word of Caution about Chi-Square Tests

Because the χ^2 statistic for testing hypotheses about multinomial probabilities is one of the most widely applied statistical tools, it is also one of the most abused statistical procedures. Consequently, the user should always be certain that the experiment satisfies the assumptions given with each procedure. Furthermore, the user should be certain that the sample is drawn from the correct population—that is, from the population about which the inference is to be made.

The use of the χ^2 probability distribution as an approximation to the sampling distribution for χ^2 should be avoided when the expected counts are very small. The approximation can become very poor when these expected counts are small, and thus the true α level may be quite different from the tabled value. As a rule of thumb, an expected cell count of at least 5 means that the χ^2 probability distribution can be used to determine an approximate critical value.

If the χ^2 value does not exceed the established critical value of χ^2 *do not accept the hypothesis of independence.* You would be risking a Type II error (accepting H_0 if it is false), and the probability β of committing such an error is unknown. The usual alternative hypothesis is that the classifications are dependent. Because the number of ways in which two classifications can be dependent is virtually infinite, it is difficult to calculate one or even several values of β to represent such a broad alternative hypothesis. Therefore, we avoid concluding that two classifications are independent, even when χ^2 is small.

Finally, if a contingency table χ^2 value does exceed the critical value, we must be careful to avoid inferring that a *causal* relationship exists between the classifications. Our alternative hypothesis states that the two classifications are statistically dependent—and a statistical dependence does not imply causality. Therefore, *the existence of a causal relationship cannot be established by a contingency table analysis.*

KEY TERMS

Categories   554
Cell   554
Cell counts   554
Chi-square test   556
Classes   554

Contingency table   564
Dependence   567
Dimensions of classification   564
Expected cell count   557
Independence of two classifications   565

Marginal probabilities   565
Multinomial experiment   554
Observed cell count   566
One-way table   555
Two-way table   564

CATEGORICAL DATA ANALYSIS GUIDE

CHAPTER NOTES

Multinomial Data:

Qualitative data that fall into more than two categories (or classes)

Properties of a Multinomial Experiment:

(1) n identical trials

(2) k possible outcomes to each trial

(3) probabilities of the k outcomes ($p_1, p_2, \ldots, p_k$) remain same from trial to trial, where $p_1 + p_2 + \ldots + p_k = 1$

(4) trials are independent

(5) variables of interest: *cell counts* (i.e., number of observations falling into each outcome category), denoted $n_1, n_2, \ldots, n_k$

Key Symbols/Notation

$p_{i,0}$	Value of multinomial probability p_i hypothesized in H_0
χ^2	Chi-square test statistic used in analysis of categorical data
n_i	Number of observed outcomes in cell i of a one-way table
E_i	Expected number of outcomes in cell i of a one-way table
p_{ij}	Probability of an outcome in row i and column j of a two-way table
n_{ij}	Number of observed outcomes in row i and column j of a two-way table
E_{ij}	Expected number of outcomes in row i and column j of a two-way table
R_i	Total number of outcomes in row i of a two-way table
C_j	Total number of outcomes in column j of a two-way table

One-Way Table

Summary table for a *single* qualitative variable

Two-Way (Contingency) Table

Summary table for *two* qualitative variables

Chi-Square (χ^2) Statistic

used to test category probabilities in one-way and two-way tables at the top of p. 583

Chi-square tests for independence

should **not** be used to *infer a causal relationship between 2 QLs*

Conditions Required for Valid χ^2-Tests

(1) multinomial experiment

(2) sample size n is large (expected cell counts are all greater than or equal to 5)

SUPPLEMENTARY EXERCISES 9.32–9.50

Learning the Mechanics

9.32 A random sample of 250 observations was classified according to the row and column categories shown in the table at the top of p. 583.

a. Do the data provide sufficient evidence to conclude that the rows and columns are dependent? Test using $\alpha = .05$.

b. Would the analysis change if the row totals were fixed before the data were collected?

c. Do the assumptions required for the analysis to be valid differ according to whether the row (or column) totals are fixed? Explain.

d. Convert the table entries to percentages by using each column total as a base and calculating each row response as a percentage of the corresponding column total. In addition, calculate the row totals and convert them to percentages of all 250 observations.

e. Create a bar graph with row 1 percentage on the vertical axis against the column number on the horizontal axis.

Draw horizontal lines corresponding to the row 1 percentages. Does the graph support the result of the test conducted in part **a**?

LM9_32

		Column		
		1	2	3
Row	1	20	20	10
	2	10	20	70
	3	20	50	30

9.33 A random sample of 150 observations was classified into the categories shown in the table below.

LM9_33

	Category				
	1	2	3	4	5
n_i	28	35	33	25	29

a. Do the data provide sufficient evidence that the categories are not equally likely? Use $\alpha = .10$.

b. Form a 90% confidence interval for p_2, the probability that an observation will fall in category 2.

Applying the Concepts—Basic

9.34 **Consumers' least favorite vegetables.** *Bon Appetit* magazine polled 200 of its readers concerning which of the four vegetables—brussel sprouts, okra, lima beans, and cauliflower—is their least favorite. The results (adapted from *Adweek*, Feb. 21, 2000) are presented in the table. Let p_1, p_2, p_3, and p_4 represent the proportions of all *Bon Appetit* readers who indicate brussel sprouts, okra, lima beans, and cauliflower, respectively, as their least favorite vegetable.

BONAPP

Brussel Sprouts	Okra	Lima Beans	Cauliflower
46	76	44	34

a. If, in general, *Bon Appetit* readers do not have a preference for their least favorite vegetable, what are the values of p_1, p_2, p_3, and p_4?

b. Specify the null and alternative hypotheses that should be used to determine whether *Bon Appetit* readers have a preference for one of the vegetables as "least favorite."

c. Conduct the test you described in part **b** using $\alpha = .05$. Report your conclusion in the context of the problem.

d. What assumptions must hold to ensure the validity of the test you conducted in part **c**? Which, if any, of these assumptions may be a concern in this application?

9.35 **Consumer privacy survey.** *Inc. Technology* (Mar. 18, 1997) reported the results of an Equifax/Harris Consumer Privacy Survey in which 328 Internet users indicated their level of agreement with the following statement: "The government needs to be able to scan Internet messages and user communications to prevent fraud and other crimes." The number of users in each response category is summarized below.

GOVWEB

Agree Strongly	Agree Somewhat	Disagree Somewhat	Disagree Strongly
59	108	82	79

a. Specify the null and alternative hypotheses you would use to determine if the opinions of Internet users are evenly divided among the four categories.

b. Conduct the test of part **a** using $\alpha = .05$.

c. In the context of this exercise, what is a Type I error? A Type II error?

d. What assumptions must hold in order to ensure the validity of the test you conducted in part **b**?

9.36 **Physical fitness and employee stress.** Research has indicated that the stress produced by today's lifestyles results in health problems for a large proportion of society. An article in the *International Journal of Sports psychology* (July–Sept. 1990) evaluated the relationship between physical fitness and stress. Five hundred forty-nine employees of companies that participate in the Health Examination Program offered by Health Advancement Services (HAS) were classified into three groups of fitness levels: good, average, and poor. Each person was tested for signs of stress. The next table reports the results for the three groups.

Fitness Level	Number with No Stress	Number with Signs of Stress
Poor	204	38
Average	184	28
Good	85	10

a. Do the data provide evidence to indicate that the likelihood for stress is dependent on an employee's fitness level?

b. In the context of this problem, specify the Type I and Type II errors associated with the test of part **a**.

c. Construct a graph that helps to interpret the result of the test in part **a**.

9.37 **Seat belt use study.** The *American Journal of Public Health* (July 1995) reported on a population-based study of trauma in Hispanic children. One of the objectives of the study was to compare the use of protective devices in motor vehicles used to transport Hispanic and non-Hispanic white children. On the basis of data collected from the San Diego County Regionalized Trauma System, 792 children treated for injuries sustained in vehicular accidents were classified according to ethnic status (Hispanic or non-Hispanic white) and seat belt usage (worn or not worn) during the accident. The data are summarized in the table below.

TRAUMA

	Hispanic	Non-Hispanic White	Totals
Seatbelts worn	31	148	179
Seatbelts not worn	283	330	613
Totals	314	478	792

Source: Matteneci, R. M. et al. "Trauma among Hispanic Children: A Population-Based Study in a Regionalized System of Trauma Care." *American Journal of Public Health*, Vol. 85, No. 7, July 1995, p. 1007 (Table 2).

a. Of the injured Hispanic children, what proportion were not wearing seat belts during the accident?

b. Of the injured non-Hispanic white children, what proportion were not wearing seat belts during the accident?

c. Compare the two sample proportions, parts **a** and **b**. Do you think the true population proportions differ?

d. Conduct a test to determine whether seat belt usage in motor vehicle accidents depends on ethnic status in the San Diego County Regionalized Trauma System. Use $\alpha = .01$.

e. Construct a 99% confidence interval for the difference between the proportions, parts **a** and **b**. Interpret the interval.

9.38 **Colors of M&M's candies.** M&M's plain chocolate candies come in six different colors: dark brown, yellow, red, orange, green, and blue. According to the manufacturer (Mars, Inc.), the color ratio in each large production batch is 30% brown, 20% yellow, 20% red, 10% orange, 10% green, and 10% blue. To test this claim, a professor at Carleton College (Minnesota) had students count the colors of M&M's found in "fun size" bags of the candy (*Teaching Statistics*, Spring 1993). The results for 370 M&M's are displayed in the table.

M&M

Brown	Yellow	Red	Orange	Green	Blue	Total
84	79	75	49	36	47	370

Source: Johnson, R.W. "Testing Colour proportions of M&M's." *Teaching Statistics,* Vol. 15, No. 1, Spring 1993, p. 2 (Table 1).

a. Assuming the manufacturer's stated percentages are accurate, calculate the expected numbers falling into the six categories.

b. Calculate the value of χ^2 for testing the manufacturer's claim.

c. Conduct a test to determine whether the true percentages of the colors produced differ from the manufacturer's stated percentages. Use $\alpha = .05$.

Applying the Concepts—Intermediate

9.39 **Instructional technology in the classroom.** In education, the term *instructional technology* refers to products such as computers, spreadsheets, CD-ROMs, videos, and presentation software. How frequently do professors use instructional technology in the classroom? To answer this question, researchers at Western Michigan University surveyed 306 of their fellow faculty (*Educational Technology,* Mar.–Apr. 1995). Responses to the frequency-of-technology use in teaching were recorded as "weekly to every class," "once a semester to monthly," or "never." The faculty responses (number in each response category) for the three technologies are summarized in the next table.

a. Determine whether the percentages in the three frequency-of-use response categories differ for computer spreadsheets. Use $\alpha = .01$.

b. Repeat part **a** for word processing.

c. Repeat part **a** for statistical software.

d. Construct a 99% confidence interval for the true percentage of faculty who never use computer spreadsheets in the classroom. Interpret the interval.

TECHUSE

Technology	Weekly	Once a Semester/ Monthly	Never
Computer spreadsheets	58	67	181
Word processing	168	61	77
Statistical software	37	82	187

9.40 **Insider ownership and firm size.** Because shareholders control the firm, they can transfer wealth from the firm's bondholders to themselves through several different dividend strategies. This potential conflict of interest between shareholders and bondholders can be reduced through the use of debt covenants. Accountants E. Griner and H. Huss of Georgia State University investigated the effects of insider ownership and the size of the firm on the types of debt covenants required by a firm's bondholders (*Journal of Applied Business Research,* Vol. 11, 1995). As part of the study, they examined a sample of 31 companies whose bondholders required covenants based on tangible assets rather than on liquidity or net assets or retained earnings. Characteristics of those 31 firms are summarized below. The objective of the study is to determine if there is a relationship between the extent of insider ownership and the size of the firm for firms with tangible asset covenants.

INSIDOWN

		SIZE	
		Small	Large
Inside Ownership	**Low**	3	17
	High	8	3

Source: Griner, E., and Huss, H. "Firm Size. Insider Ownership, and Accounting-Based Debt Covenants." *Journal of Applied Business Research,* Vol. 11, No. 4, 1995, p. 7 (Table 4).

a. Assuming the null hypothesis of independence is true, how many firms are expected to fall in each cell of the table above?

b. The researchers were unable to use the chi-square test to analyze the data. Show why.

c. A test of the null hypothesis can be conducted using *Fisher's exact test.* (See Exercise 9.31, p. 579.) This method calculates the exact probability (p-value) of observing sample results at least as contradictory to the null hypothesis as those observed for the researchers' data. The researchers reported the p-value for this test as .0043. Interpret this result.

d. Investigate the nature of the dependence exhibited by the contingency table by plotting the appropriate contingency table percentages. Describe what you find.

9.41 **Dosing errors at hospitals.** Each year, approximately 1.3 million Americans suffer adverse drug effects (ADEs)—that is, unintended injuries caused by prescribed medication. A study in the *Journal of the American Medical Association* (July 5, 1995) identified the cause of 247 ADEs that occurred at two Boston hospitals. The researchers found that dosing errors (that is, wrong dosage prescribed and/or dispensed) were the most common. The next table summarizes the proximate cause of 95 ADEs that resulted from a dosing error. Conduct a test (at $\alpha = .10$) to determine whether the true percentages of ADEs in the five "cause" categories are different.

ADE

Wrong Dosage Cause	Number of ADEs
(1) Lack of knowledge of drug	29
(2) Rule violation	17
(3) Faulty dose checking	13
(4) Slips	9
(5) Other	27

9.42 Occupations of fathers and sons. An economist was interested in knowing whether sons have a tendency to choose the same occupation as their fathers. To investigate this question, 500 males were polled and each questioned concerning his occupation and the occupation of his father. A summary of the numbers of father-son pairs falling in each occupational category is shown in the table at the bottom of the page. Do the data provide sufficient evidence at $\alpha = .05$ to indicate a dependence between a son's choice of occupation and his father's occupation?

9.43 Performance of solder joint inspectors. Westinghouse Electric Company has experimented with different means of evaluating the performance of solder joint inspectors. One approach involves comparing an individual inspector's classifications with those of the group of experts that comprise Westinghouse's Work Standards Committee. In one experiment conducted by Westinghouse, 153 solder connections were evaluated by the committee and 111 were classified as acceptable. An inspector evaluated the same 153 connections and classified 124 as acceptable. Of the items rejected by the inspector, the committee agreed with 19.

a. Construct a contingency table that summarizes the classifications of the committee and the inspector.

b. Based on a visual examination of the table you constructed in part **a**, does it appear that there is a relationship between the inspector's classifications and the committee's? Explain. (A graph of the percentage rejected by committee and inspector will aid your examination.)

c. Conduct a chi-square test of independence for these data. Use $\alpha = .05$. Carefully interpret the results of your test in the context of the problem.

9.44 Firms that practice TQM. To better understand whether and how Total Quality Management (TQM) is practiced in U.S. companies, University of Scranton researchers N. Tamimi and R. Sebastianelli interviewed one manager in each of a sample of 86 companies in Pennsylvania, New York, and New Jersey (*Production and Inventory Management Journal*, 1996). Concerning whether or not the firms were involved with TQM, the following data were obtained:

TQM

	Service Firms	Manufacturing Firms
Number practicing TQM	34	23
Number not practicing TQM	18	11
Total	52	34

Source: Adapted from Tamimi, N., and Sebastianelli, R. "How Firms Define and Measure Quality." *Production and Inventory Management Journal*, Third Quarter, 1996, p. 35.

a. The researchers concluded that "manufacturing firms were not significantly more likely to be involved with TQM than service firms." Do you agree? Test using $\alpha = .05$.

b. Find and interpret the approximate p-value for the test you conducted in part **a**.

c. What assumptions must hold in order for your test of part **a** and your p-value of part **b** to be valid?

9.45 Peanut butter market shares. Data from supermarket scanners are used by researchers to understand the purchasing patterns and preferences of consumers. Researchers frequently study the purchases of a sample of households, called a *scanner panel*. When shopping, these households present a magnetic identification card that permits their purchase data to be identified and aggregated. Marketing researchers recently studied the extent to which panel households' purchase behavior is representative of the population of households shopping at the same stores (*Marketing Research*, Nov. 1996). The table at the top of p. 586 reports the peanut butter purchase data collected by A. C. Nielsen Company for a panel of 2,500 households in Sioux Falls, SD, over a 102-week period. The market share percentages in the right column are derived from all peanut butter purchases at the same 15 stores at which the panel shopped during the same 102-week period.

a. Do the data provide sufficient evidence to conclude that the purchases of the household panel are not representative of the population of households? Test using $\alpha = .05$.

b. What assumptions must hold to ensure the validity of the testing procedure you used in part **a**?

c. Find the approximate p-value for the test of part **a** and interpret it in the context of the problem.

FATHSON

		SON			
		Professional or Business	Skilled	Unskilled	Farmer
Father	**Professional or Business**	55	38	7	0
	Skilled	79	71	25	0
	Unskilled	22	75	38	10
	Farmer	15	23	10	32

SCANNER

Brand	Size	Number of Purchases by Household Panel	Market Shares
Jif	18 oz.	3,165	20.10%
Jif	28	1,892	10.10
Jif	40	726	5.42
Peter Pan	10	4,079	16.01
Skippy	18	6,206	28.65
Skippy	28	1,627	12.38
Skippy	40	1,420	7.32
Total		19,115	

Source: Gupta, S., et. al. "Do Household Scanner Data Provide Representative Inferences from Brand Choices? A Comparison with Store Data." *Journal of Marketing Research,* Vol. 33, Nov. 1996, p. 393 (Table 6).

9.46 **Multiple sclerosis drug.** Interferons are proteins produced naturally by the human body that help fight infections and regulate the immune system. A drug developed from interferons, called Avonex, is now available for treating patients with multiple sclerosis (MS). In a clinical study, 85 MS patients received weekly injections of Avonex over a 2-year period. The number of exacerbations (i.e., flare-ups of symptoms) was recorded for each patient and is summarized in the accompanying table. For MS patients who take a placebo (no drug) over a similar two-week period, it is known from previous studies that 26% will experience no exacerbations, 30% one exacerbation, 11% two exacerbations, 14% three exacerbations, and 19% four or more exacerbations.

AVONEX

Number of Exacerbations	Number of Patients
0	32
1	26
2	15
3	6
4 or more	6

Source: Biogen, Inc., 1997.

a. Conduct a test to determine whether the exacerbation distribution of MS patients who take Avonex differs from the percentages reported for placebo patients. Test using $\alpha = .05$.

b. Find a 95% confidence interval for the true proportion of Avonex MS patients who are exacerbation–free during a 2-year period.

c. Refer to part **b.** Is there evidence that Avonex patients are more likely to have no exacerbations than placebo patients? Explain.

9.47 **Thumbs up or thumbs down.** For over 20 years, movie critics Gene Siskel (formerly of the *Chicago Tribune*) and Roger Ebert (*Chicago Sun-Times*) rated the latest film releases on national television's *Sneak Previews.* Since Siskel's death in 1999, Ebert has teamed with Richard Roeper (*New York Times Syndicate*) to rate movies on the syndicated TV-show *Ebert & Roeper at the Movies.* Ebert's and Roeper's ratings ("thumbs up" or "thumbs down") for 218 films released in 2003 are saved in the **THUMBSUP** file. Data for the first and last five movies in the file are shown in the table. Conduct a test to determine whether the movie reviews of the two critics are independent. Use $\alpha = .05$.

THUMBSUP

Movie	Ebert Rating	Roeper Rating
Terminator 3	DOWN	UP
Finding Nemo	UP	UP
2 Fast 2 Furious	UP	DOWN
Hulk	UP	UP
Matrix Reloaded	UP	UP
.	.	.
Daredevil	UP	UP
Just Married	DOWN	DOWN
Sonny	DOWN	DOWN
Narc	UP	DOWN
City of God	UP	UP

Source: www.movies.com.

9.48 **"Fitness for use" of gasoline filters.** Product or service quality is often defined as *fitness for use.* This means the product or service meets the customer's needs. Generally speaking, fitness for use is based on five quality characteristics: technological (e.g., strength, hardness), psychological (taste, beauty), time-oriented (reliability), contractual (guarantee provisions), and ethical (courtesy, honesty). The quality of a service may involve all these characteristics, while the quality of a manufactured product generally depends on technological and time-oriented characteristics (Schroeder, *Operations Management,* 1993). After a barrage of customer complaints about poor quality, a manufacturer of gasoline filters for cars had its quality inspectors sample 600 filters—200 per work shift—and check for defects. The data in the table resulted.

FILTER

Shift	Defectives Produced
First	25
Second	35
Third	80

a. Do the data indicate that the quality of the filters being produced may be related to the shift producing the filter? Test using $\alpha = .05$.

b. Estimate the proportion of defective filters produced by the first shift. Use a 95% confidence interval.

Applying the Concepts—Advanced

9.49 **Goodness-of-fit test.** A statistical analysis is to be done on a set of data consisting of 1,000 monthly salaries. The analysis requires the assumption that the sample was drawn from a normal distribution. A preliminary test, called the χ^2 *goodness-of-fit test,* can be used to help determine whether it is reasonable to assume that the sample is from a normal distribution. Suppose the mean and standard deviation of the 1,000 salaries are hypothesized to be $1,200 and $200, respectively. Using the standard normal table, we can approximate the probability of a salary being in the intervals listed in the next table (top, p. 587). The third column represents the expected number of the 1,000 salaries to be found in each interval if the sample was drawn from a normal distribution with $\mu = \$1,200$ and $\Sigma = \$200$. Suppose the last column contains the actual observed frequencies in the sample. Large differences between the observed

Table for Exercise 9.49

Interval	Probability	Expected Frequency	Observed Frequency
Less than $800	.023	23	26
Between $800 & $1,000	.136	136	146
Between $1,000 & $1,200	.341	341	361
Between $1,200 & $1,400	.341	341	311
Between $1,400 & $1,600	.136	136	143
Above $1,600	.023	23	13

and expected frequencies cast doubt on the normality assumption.

a. Compute the χ^2 statistic based on the observed and expected frequencies—just as you did in Section 9.2.

b. Find the tabulated χ^2 value when $\alpha = .05$ and there are 5 degrees of freedom. (There are $k - 1 = 5$ df associated with this χ^2 statistic.)

c. Based on the χ^2 statistic and the tabulated χ^2 value, is there evidence that the salary distribution is non-normal?

d. Find an approximate observed significance level for the test in part **c**.

Critical Thinking Challenge

9.50 **A "rigged" election?** *Chance* (Spring 2004) presented data from a recent election held to determine the board of directors of a local community. There were 27 candidates for the board, and each of 5,553 voters was allowed to choose 6 candidates. The claim was that "a fixed vote with fixed percentages (was) assigned to each and every candi-

date making it impossible to participate in an honest election." Votes were tallied in six time periods: after 600 total votes were in, after 1,200, after 2,444, after 3,444, after 4,444, and after 5,553 votes. The data for three of the candidates (Smith, Coppin, and Montes) are shown in the following table. A residential organization believes that "there was nothing random about the count and tallies each time period and specific unnatural or rigged percentages were being assigned to each and every candidate." Give your opinion. Is the probability of a candidate receiving votes independent of the time period? If so, does this imply a rigged election?

RIGVOTE

Time Period	1	2	3	4	5	6
Votes for Smith	208	208	451	392	351	410
Votes for Coppin	55	51	109	98	88	104
Votes for Montes	133	117	255	211	186	227
Total Votes	600	600	1,244	1,000	1,000	1,109

Source: Gelman, A. "55,000 Residents Desperately Need Your Help!" *Chance,* Vol. 17, No. 2, Spring 2004 (Figures 1 and 5).

REFERENCES

Agresti, A. *Categorical Data Analysis.* New York: Wiley, 1990.

Cochran, W. G. "The χ^2 Test of Goodness of Fit." *Annals of Mathematical Statistics,* 1952, 23.

Conover, W. J. *Practical Nonparametric Statistics,* 2nd ed. New York: Wiley, 1980.

DeGroot, M. H., Fienberg, S. E., and Kadane, J. B., eds. *Statistics and the Law.* New York: Wiley, 1986.

Fisher, R. A. "The Logic of Inductive Inference (with Discussion)." *Journal of the Royal Statistical Society,* Vol. 98, 1935, pp. 39–82.

Hollander, M., and Wolfe, D. A. *Nonparametric Statistical Methods.* New York: Wiley, 1973.

Savage, I. R. "Bibliography of Nonparametric Statistics and Related Topics." *Journal of the American Statistical Association,* 1953, 48.

Schroeder, R. G. *Operations Management,* 4th ed. New York: McGraw-Hill, 1993.

Using Technology

9.1 Chi-Square Analyses Using SPSS

SPSS can conduct chi-square tests for both one-way and two-way (contingency) tables.

One-Way Table

To conduct a chi-square test for a one-way table, first access the SPSS spreadsheet file that contains the variable with category values for each of the *n* observations in the data set. (*Note:* SPSS requires that these categories be specified numerically, e.g., 1, 2, 3, etc.) Next, click on the "Analyze" button on the SPSS menu bar, then click on "Nonparametric Tests" and "Chi- Square", as shown in Figure 9.S.1.

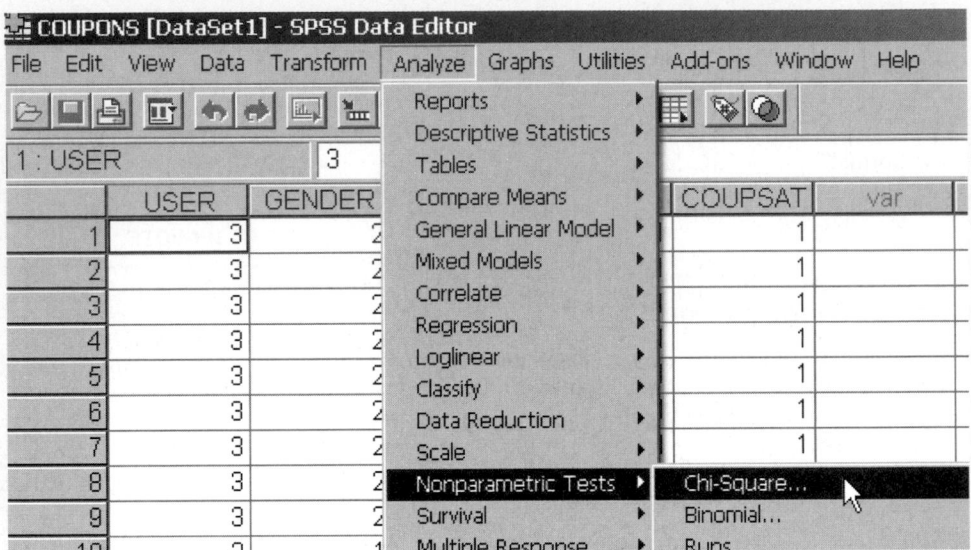

Figure 9.S.1
SPSS menu options for one-way chi-square analysis

The resulting dialog box appears as shown in Figure 9.S.2. Specify the qualitative variable of interest in the "Test Variable List" box. If you want to test for equal cell probabilities in the null hypothesis, then select the "All categories equal" option under the "Expected Values" box (as shown in Figure 9.S.2). If the null hypothesis specifies unequal cell probabilities, then select the "Values" option under the "Expected Values" box. Enter the hypothesized cell probabilities in the adjacent box, one at a time, clicking "Add" after each specification. Click "OK" to generate the SPSS printout.

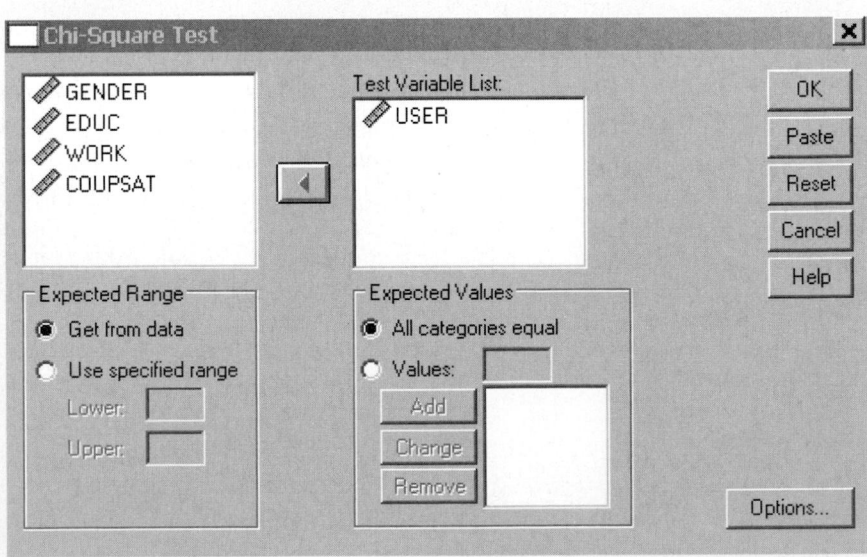

Figure 9.S.2
SPSS one-way chi-square dialog box

Two-Way Table

To conduct a chi-square test for a two-way (contingency) table, first access the SPSS spreadsheet file that contains the sample data. The data file should contain two qualitative variables, with category values for each of the *n* observations in the data set. Next, click on the "Analyze" button on the SPSS menu bar, then click on "Descriptive Statistics" and "Crosstabs", as shown in Figure 9.S.3.

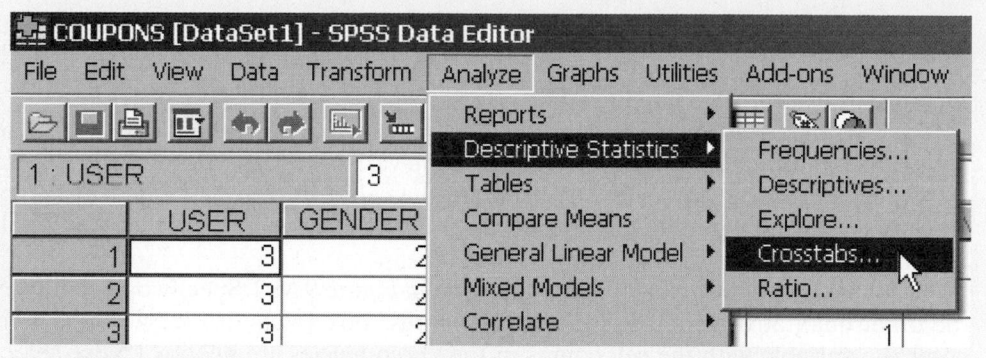

Figure 9.S.3

SPSS menu options for two-way chi-square analysis

The resulting dialog box appears as shown in Figure 9.S.4. Specify one qualitative variable in the "Row(s)" box and the other qualitative variable in the "Column(s)" box. Click the "Statistics" button and select the "Chi-square" option, as shown in Figure 9.S.5. Click "Continue" to return to the "Crosstabs" dialog box. If you want the contingency table to include expected values, row percentages, and/or column percentages, click the "Cells" button and make the appropriate menu selections. When you return to the "Crosstabs" menu screen, click "OK" to generate the SPSS printout.

Note: If your SPSS spreadsheet contains summary information (i.e., the cell counts for the contingency table) rather than the actual categorical data values for each observation, you must weight each observation in your data file by the cell count for that observation prior to running the chi-square analysis. Do this by selecting the "Data" button on the SPSS menu bar, then click on "Weight Cases" and specify the variable that contains the cell counts.

Figure 9.S.4

SPSS crosstabs dialog box

Figure 9.S.5

SPSS statistics menu selections for the two-way analysis

9.2 Chi-Square Analyses Using MINITAB

MINITAB can conduct chi-square tests for two-way (contingency) tables but cannot currently produce a chi-square test for a one-way table.

To conduct a chi-square test for a two-way table, first access the MINITAB worksheet file that contains the sample data. The data file should contain two qualitative variables, with category values for each of the n observations in the data set. Alternatively, the worksheet can contain the cell counts for each of the categories of the two qualitative variables. Next, click on the "Stat" button on the MINITAB menu bar, then click on "Tables" and "Cross Tabulation and Chi-Square", as shown in Figure 9.M.1.

The resulting dialog box appears as shown in Figure 9.M.2. Specify one qualitative variable in the "For rows" box and the other qualitative variable in the "For columns" box. [*Note:* If your worksheet contains cell counts for the categories, enter the variable with the cell counts in the "Frequencies are in" box.] Next, select the summary statistics (e.g., counts, percentages) you want to display in the contingency table. Then click the "Chi-square" button. The resulting dialog box is shown in Figure 9.M.3. Select "Chi-Square analysis" and "Expected cell counts" and click "OK". When you return to the "Cross Tabulation" menu screen, click "OK" to generate the MINITAB printout.

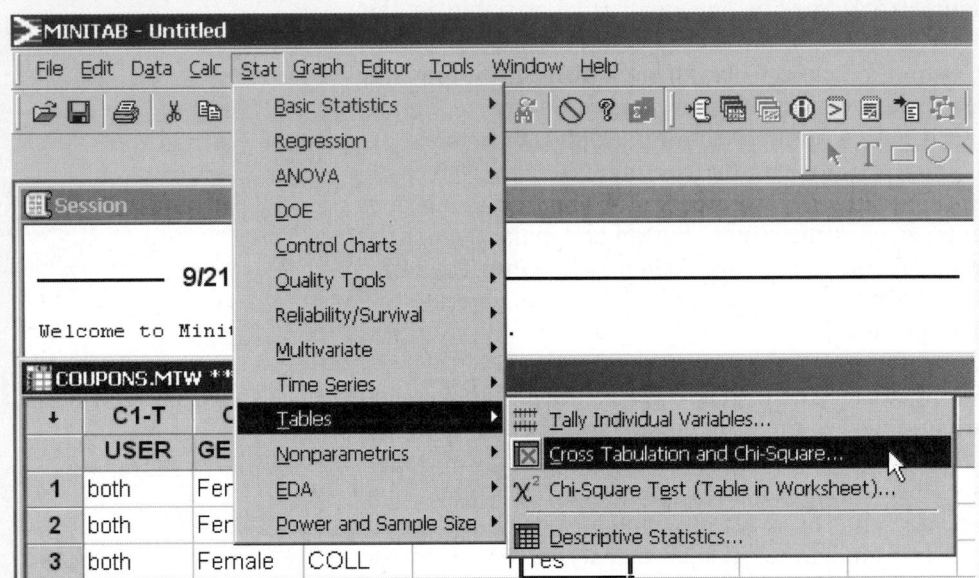

Figure 9.M.1
MINITAB menu options for two-way chi-square analysis

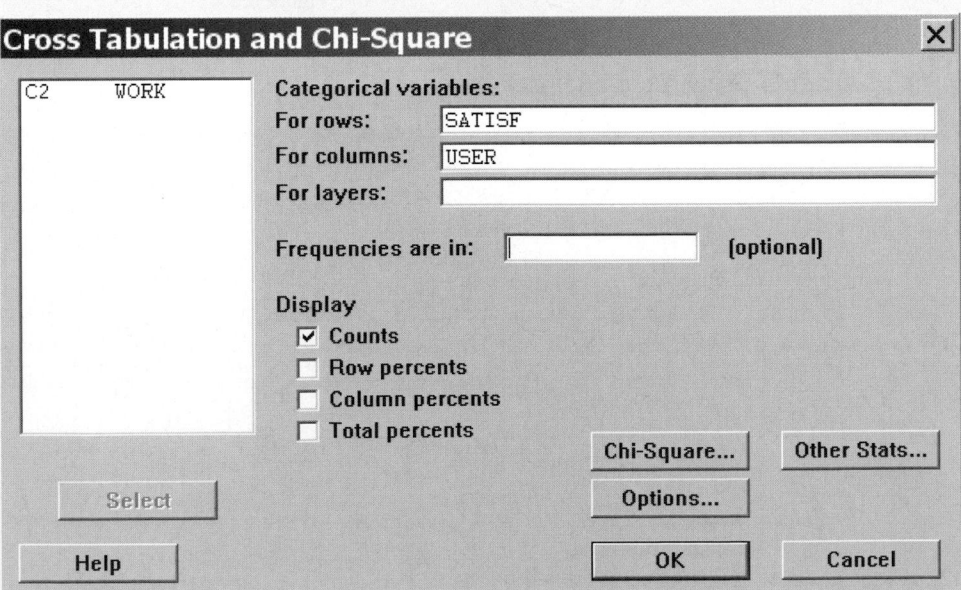

Figure 9.M.2
MINITAB cross tabulation dialog box

Figure 9.M.3
MINITAB chi-square dialog
box

Note: If your MINITAB worksheet contains only the cell counts for the contingency table in columns, click the "Chi-Square Test (Table in Worksheet)" menu option (see Figure 9.M.1) and specify the columns in the "Columns containing the table" box. Click "OK" to produce the MINITAB printout.

9.3 Chi-Square Analyses Using Excel/PHStat2

Excel can conduct chi-square tests for both one-way and two-way (contingency) tables; however, you must have previously computed the cell counts for the table.

One-Way Table

To conduct a chi-square test for a one-way table, first create a workbook with columns representing the levels of the qualitative variable, the cell counts, and the expected cell counts, as shown in Figure 9.E.1. The *p*-value of the chi-square test is found using the formula

$$= CHITEST(range\ of\ cell\ counts,\ range\ of\ expected\ cell\ counts)$$

Figure 9.E.1
Excel workbook format for
one-way chi-square analysis

Microsoft Excel - coupons

B9   =CHITEST(B2:B5,C2:C5)

	A	B	C	D	E
1	LEVEL	Number	Expected		
2	1	20	25		
3	2	40	25		
4	3	30	25		
5	4	10	25		
6	TOTAL	100			
7					
8	Chi-square	19.99774			
9	p-value	0.00017			
10	df	3			
11					

(This formula is shown in the formula area of the Excel workbook, Figure 9.E.1.) Once the *p*-value is computed, the value of chi-square test statistic is found using the formula

$$= CHIINV(cell\ with\ p\text{-}value, cell\ with\ degrees\ of\ freedom)$$

Two-Way Table

To conduct a chi-square test for a two-way (contingency), click "PHStat" from the Excel menu bar, then select "Multiple-Sample Tests" and "Chi-Square Test", as shown in Figure 9.E.2. On the resulting dialog box, specify the significance level (α), number of rows and number of columns for the contingency table, as shown in Figure 9.E.3, then click "OK". The Excel workbook shown in Figure 9.E.4 will appear.

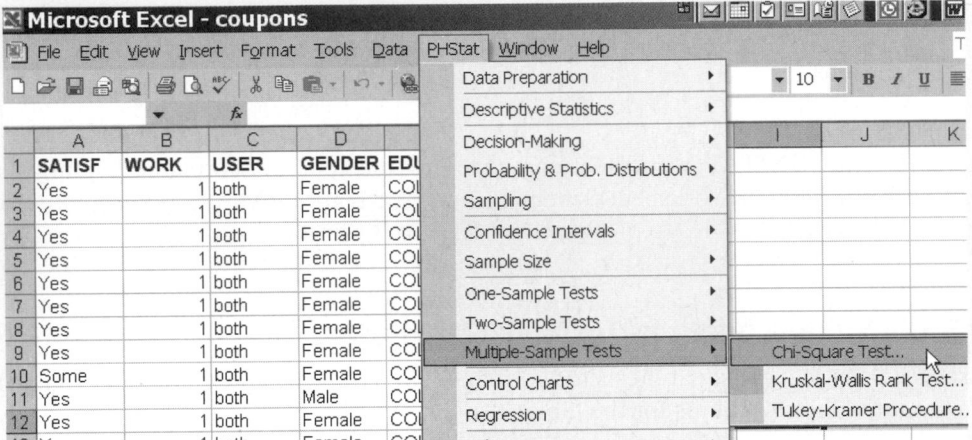

Figure 9.E.2

Excel menu selections for a two-way chi-square analysis

Enter the cell counts in the appropriate cells of the contingency table shown at the top of the workbook. Once the cell counts have been entered, the value of the chi-square test statistic and *p*-value of the test will appear at the bottom of the Excel workbook.

Figure 9.E.3

Excel/PHStat2 two-way chi-square dialog box

	A	B	C	D	E	F
1	**Chi-Square Test**					
2						
3	**Observed Frequencies**					
4		**Column variable**				
5	**Row variable**	**C1**	**C2**	**C3**	**Total**	
6	**R1**	22	45	21	88	
7	**R2**	11	17	15	43	
8	**Total**	33	62	36	131	
9						
10	Expected Frequencies					
11		Column variable				
12	Row variable	C1	C2	C3	Total	
13	R1	22.16794	41.64885	24.18321	88	
14	R2	10.83206	20.35115	11.81679	43	
15	Total	33	62	36	131	
16						
17	**Data**					
18	**Level of Significance**	0.05				
19	Number of Rows	2				
20	Number of Columns	3				
21	Degrees of Freedom	2				
22						
23	**Results**					
24	**Critical Value**	5.991476				
25	**Chi-Square Test Statistic**	2.101829				
26	*p*-**Value**	0.349618				
27	**Do not reject the null hypothesis**					
28						

Figure 9.E.4

Excel workbook format for two-way chi-square analysis

Real-World Case
Discrimination in the Workplace

(A Case Covering Chapters 8–9)

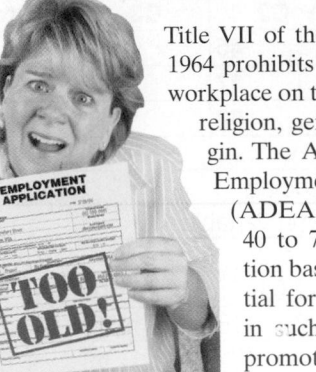

Title VII of the Civil Rights Act of 1964 prohibits discrimination in the workplace on the basis of race, color, religion, gender, or national origin. The Age Discrimination in Employment Act of 1967 (ADEA) protects workers age 40 to 70 against discrimination based on age. The potential for discrimination exists in such processes as hiring, promotion, compensation, and termination.

In 1971 the U.S. Supreme Court established that employment discrimination cases fall into two categories: **disparate treatment** and **disparate impact.** In the former, the issue is whether the employer intentionally discriminated against a worker. For example, if the employer considered an individual's race in deciding whether to terminate him, the case is one of disparate treatment. In a disparate impact case, the issue is whether employment practices have an adverse impact on a protected group or class of people, even when the employer does not intend to discriminate.

Part I: Downsizing at a Computer Firm

Disparate impact cases almost always involve the use of statistical evidence and expert testimony by professional statisticians. Attorneys for the plaintiffs frequently use hypothesis test results in the form of *p*-values in arguing the case for their clients.

Table C4.1 was recently introduced as evidence in a race case that resulted from a round of layoffs during the downsizing of a division of a computer manufacturer. The company had selected 51 of the division's 1,215 employees to lay off. The plaintiffs—in this case 15 of the 20 African

Americans who were laid off—were suing the company for $20 million in damages.

The company's lawyers argued that the selections followed from a performance-based ranking of all employees. The plaintiffs' legal team and their expert witnesses, citing the results of a statistical test of hypothesis, argued that layoffs were a function of race.

The validity of the plaintiffs' interpretation of the data is dependent on whether the assumptions of the test are met in this situation. In particular, like all hypothesis tests presented in this text, the assumption of random sampling must hold. If it does not, the results of the test may be due to the violation of this assumption rather than to discrimination. In general, the appropriateness of the testing procedure is dependent on the test's ability to capture the relevant aspects of the employment process in question (DeGroot, Fienberg, and Kadane, *Statistics and the Law*, 1986).

Prepare a document to be submitted as evidence in the case (i.e., an exhibit), in which you evaluate the validity of the plaintiffs' interpretation of the data. Your evaluation should be based in part on your knowledge of the processes companies use to lay off employees and how well those processes are reflected in the hypothesis-testing procedure employed by the plaintiffs.

Part II: Age Discrimination—You Be the Judge

In 1996, as part of a significant restructuring of product lines, AJAX Pharmaceuticals (a fictitious name for a real company) laid off 24 of 55 assembly-line workers in its Pittsburgh manufacturing plant. Citing the ADEA, 11 of the laid-off workers claimed they were discriminated against on the basis of age and sued AJAX for $5,000,000. Management disputed the claim, saying that since the workers were essentially interchangeable, they had used random sampling to choose the 24 workers to be terminated.

Table C4.2 lists the 55 assembly-line workers and identifies which were terminated and which remained active. Plaintiffs are denoted by an asterisk. These data were used by both the plaintiffs and the defendants to determine whether the layoffs had an adverse impact on workers age 40 and over and to establish the credibility of management's random sampling claim.

Using whatever statistical methods you think are appropriate, build a case that supports the plaintiffs' position. (Call documents related to this issue Exhibit A.) Similarly, build a case that supports the defendants' position. (Call these documents Exhibit B.) Then discuss which of the two cases is more convincing and why. [*Note:* The data for this case are available in the **DISCRIM** file, described in the table.]

💿 LAYOFFS

TABLE C4.1 Summary of Downsizing Data for Race Case

		DECISION	
		Retained	Laid off
Race	**White**	1,051	31
	Black	113	20

Source: Confidential personal communication with P. George Benson.

TABLE C4.2 Data for Age Discrimination Case

Employee	Yearly Wages	Age	EmploymentStatus
*Adler, C. J.	$41,200	45	Terminated
Alario, B. N.	39,565	43	Active
Anders, J. M.	30,980	41	Active
Bajwa, K. K.	23,225	27	Active
Barny, M. L.	21,250	26	Active
*Berger, R. W.	41,875	45	Terminated
Brenn, L. O.	31,225	41	Active
Cain, E. J.	30,135	36	Terminated
Carle, W. J.	29,850	32	Active
Castle, A. L.	21,850	22	Active
Chan, S. D.	43,005	48	Terminated
Cho, J. Y.	34,785	41	Active
Cohen, S. D.	25,350	27	Active
Darel, F. E.	36,300	42	Active
*Davis, D. E.	40,425	46	Terminated
*Dawson, P. K.	39,150	42	Terminated
Denker, U. H.	19,435	19	Active
Dorando, T. R.	24,125	28	Active
Dubois, A. G.	30,450	40	Active
England, N.	24,750	25	Active
Estis, K. B.	22,755	23	Active
Fenton, C. K.	23,000	24	Active
Finer, H. R.	42,000	46	Terminated
*Frees, O. C.	44,100	52	Terminated
Gary, J. G.	44,975	55	Terminated
Gillen, D. J.	25,900	27	Active
Harvey, D. A.	40,875	46	Terminated
Higgins, N. M.	38,595	41	Active
*Huang, T. J.	42,995	48	Terminated
Jatho, J. A.	31,755	40	Active
Johnson, C. H.	29,540	32	Active
Jurasik, T. B.	34,300	41	Active
Klein, K. L.	43,700	51	Terminated
Lang, T. F.	19,435	22	Active
Liao, P. C.	28,750	32	Active
*Lostan, W. J.	44,675	52	Terminated
Mak, G. L.	35,505	38	Terminated
Maloff, V. R.	33,425	38	Terminated
McCall, R. M.	31,300	36	Terminated
*Nadeau, S. R.	42,300	46	Terminated
*Nguyen, O. L.	43,625	50	Terminated
Oas, R. C.	37,650	42	Active
*Patel, M. J.	38,400	43	Terminated
Porter, K. D.	32,195	35	Terminated
Rosa, L. M.	19,435	21	Active
Roth, J. H	32,785	39	Terminated
Sayino, G. L.	37,900	42	Active
Scott, I. W.	29,150	30	Terminated
Smith, E. E.	35,125	41	Active
Teel, Q. V.	27,655	33	Active
*Walker, F. O.	42,545	47	Terminated
Wang, T. G.	22,200	32	Active
Yen, D. O.	40,350	44	Terminated
Young, N. L.	28,305	34	Active
Zeitels, P. W.	36,500	42	Active

*Denotes plaintiffs

 DISCRIM (Number of observations: 55)

Variable	Type
LASTNAME	QL
WAGES	QN
AGE	QN
STATUS	QL

CHAPTER 10

Simple Linear Regression

WHERE WE'VE BEEN

- Presented methods for estimating and testing population parameters (e.g., the mean, proportion, and variance) for a single sample.

- Extended these methods to allow for a comparison of population parameters for multiple samples.

WHERE WE'RE GOING

- Introduce the straight-line (*simple linear regression*) model as a means of relating one quantitative variable to another quantitative variable.

- Introduce the *correlation coefficient* as a means of relating one quantitative variable to another quantitative variable.

- Assess how well the simple linear regression model fits the sample data.

- Utilize the simple linear regression model for predicting the value of one variable from a specified value of another variable.

STATISTICS IN ACTION

An MBA's Work-Life Balance

If you graduate with a master of business administration (MBA) degree, how much will you value a healthy balance between work and home life over high pay? According to the Aspen Institute's Business and Society Program's 2003 study of MBA students, over half (53%) feel that work-life balance is one of the most important factors, if not the most important factor, in job selection. Attitudes such as these have led many business schools to offer courses that assist MBA students with developing good work-life balance habits.

The importance of having employees with a healthy work-life balance has been recognized by U.S. companies for decades. A positive outlook on life, as well as good mental and physical health, allows employees to reach their full potential; whereas, those employees who struggle balancing work and life tend to be less productive and more prone to absenteeism. Most large companies have developed work-life balance programs for their employees. Nevertheless, recent studies have discovered a low utilization rate for these company programs. In this era of corporate downsizing and outsourcing, employees live in fear of losing their high-paying jobs — hence, they tend to work harder and longer hours. Clearly, the desire for a balanced life is in conflict with these on-the-job pressures.

For this Statistics in Action, we explore the work-life balance issue among employed MBA alumni. Background information and the data for the study are obtained from a *Graduate Management Admission Council (GMAC) Research Re-*port (Oct. 13, 2005) titled "Work-Life Balance: An MBA Alumni Report." Twice a year, the GMAC conducts a survey of MBA alumni to assess the performance of graduate management schools, monitor alumni educational needs, and measure job placement, satisfaction, and turnover. For the April 2005 survey, over 2,000 recent MBA graduates answered a series of questions on work-life balance. (For example, one question asked alumni to state their level of agreement with the statement "My personal and work demands are overwhelming.") Based on these responses, the GMAC determined a work-life balance scale score for each MBA alumni. Scores ranged from 0 to 100, with lower scores indicating a higher imbalance between work and life. Many other variables, including salary and average number of hours worked per week, were also measured.

The data for the work-life balance study is saved in the **GMAC** file. In the Statistics in Action Revisited sections of this chapter, we examine the relationship between the work-life balance score and these other variables to provide insight into the work-life balance issue.

 GMAC

Statistics in Action Revisited

- Estimating a Straight-Line Regression Model for the Work-Life Balance Data (p. 607)
- Assessing How Well the Straight-Line Regression Model Fits the Work-Life Balance Data (p. 624)
- Using the Coefficient of Correlation and Coefficient of Determination to Assess the Work-Life Balance Data (p. 634)
- Predicting Work-Life Balance Score Using the Straight-Line Model (p. 643)

In Chapters 5–8 we described methods for making inferences about population means. The mean of a population was treated as a *constant,* and we showed how to use sample data to estimate or to test hypotheses about this constant mean. In many applications, the mean of a population is not viewed as a constant, but rather as a variable. For example, the mean sale price of residences sold this year in a large city might be treated as a variable that depends on the square feet of living space in the residence. For example, the relationship might be

$$\text{Mean sale price} = \$30{,}000 + \$60 \text{ (Square feet)}$$

597

This formula implies that the mean sale price of 1,000-square-foot homes is $90,000, the mean sale price of 2,000-square-foot homes is $150,000, and the mean sale price of 3,000-square-foot homes is $210,000.

In this chapter we discuss situations in which the mean of the population is treated as a variable, dependent on the value of another variable. The dependence of residential sale price on the square feet of living space is one illustration. Other examples include the dependence of mean sales revenue of a firm on advertising expenditure, the dependence of mean starting salary of a college graduate on the student's GPA, and the dependence of mean monthly production of automobiles on the total number of sales in the previous month.

We begin our discussion with the simplest of all models relating a population mean to another variable, *the straight-line model.* We show how to use the sample data to estimate the straight-line relationship between the mean value of one variable, *y*, as it relates to a second variable, *x*. The methodology of estimating and using a straight-line relationship is referred to as *simple linear regression analysis.*

10.1 Probabilistic Models

An important consideration in merchandising a product is the amount of money spent on advertising. Suppose you want to model the monthly sales revenue of an appliance store as a function of the monthly advertising expenditure. The first question to be answered is this: "Do you think an exact relationship exists between these two variables?" That is, do you think it is possible to state the exact monthly sales revenue if the amount spent on advertising is known? We think you will agree with us that this is *not* possible for several reasons. Sales depend on many variables other than advertising expenditure—for example, time of year, the state of the general economy, inventory, and price structure. Even if many variables are included in a model (the topic of Chapter 11), it is still unlikely that we would be able to predict the monthly sales *exactly.* There will almost certainly be some variation in monthly sales due strictly to *random phenomena* that cannot be modeled or explained.

If we were to construct a model that hypothesized an exact relationship between variables, it would be called a **deterministic model.** For example, if we believe that *y*, the monthly sales revenue, will be exactly 15 times *x*, the monthly advertising expenditure, we write

$$y = 15x$$

This represents a *deterministic relationship* between the variables *y* and *x*. It implies that *y* can always be determined exactly when the value of *x* is known. *There is no allowance for error in this prediction.*

If, on the other hand, we believe there will be unexplained variation in monthly sales—perhaps caused by important but unincluded variables or by random phenomena—we discard the deterministic model and use a model that accounts for this **random error.** This **probabilistic model** includes both a deterministic component and a random error component. For example, if we hypothesize that the sales *y* is related to advertising expenditure *x* by

$$y = 15x + \text{Random error}$$

we are hypothesizing a *probabilistic relationship* between *y* and *x*. Note that the deterministic component of this probabilistic model is 15*x*.

Figure 10.1(a) shows the possible values of *y* and *x* for five different months, when the model is deterministic. All the pairs of (x, y) data points must fall exactly on the line because a deterministic model leaves no room for error.

Figure 10.1(b) shows a possible set of points for the same values of *x* when we are using a probabilistic model. Note that the deterministic part of the model (the straight line itself) is the same. Now, however, the inclusion of a random error component allows the monthly sales to vary from this line. Since we know that the sales revenue does vary

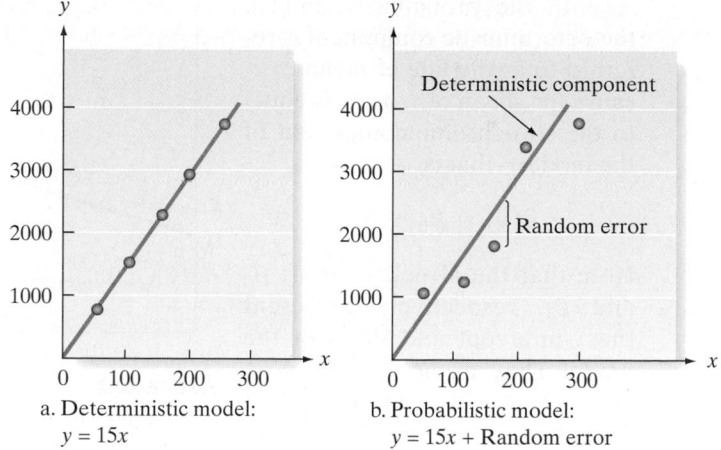

FIGURE 10.1

Possible sales revenues, y, for five different months, x

a. Deterministic model:
$y = 15x$

b. Probabilistic model:
$y = 15x +$ Random error

randomly for a given value of x, the probabilistic model provides a more realistic model for y than does the deterministic model.

General Form of Probabilistic Models

$$y = \text{Deterministic component} + \text{Random error}$$

where y is the variable of interest. We always assume that the mean value of the random error equals 0. This is equivalent to assuming that the mean value of y, $E(y)$, equals the deterministic component of the model; that is,

$$E(y) = \text{Deterministic component}$$

In this chapter we present the simplest of probabilistic models—the **straight-line model**—which derives its name from the fact that the deterministic portion of the model graphs as a straight line. Fitting this model to a set of data is an example of **regression analysis,** or **regression modeling.** The elements of the straight-line model are summarized in the next box.

A First-Order (Straight-Line) Probabilistic Model

$$y = \beta_0 + \beta_1 x + \varepsilon$$

where

$y =$ **Dependent** *or* **response variable** (variable to be modeled)

$x =$ **Independent** *or* **predictor variable** (variable used as a predictor of y)*

$E(y) = \beta_0 + \beta_1 x =$ Deterministic component

ε (epsilon) $=$ Random error component

β_0 (beta zero) $=$ **y-intercept of the line,** that is, the point at which the line *intercepts or cuts through the y-axis* (see Figure 10.2)

β_1 (beta one) $=$ **Slope of the line,** that is, the change (amount of increase or decrease) in the deterministic component of y for every 1-unit increase in x.

[*Note:* A *positive* slope implies that $E(y)$ *increases* by the amount β_1 (see Figure 10.2). A *negative* slope implies that $E(y)$ *decreases* by the amount β_1.]

---

*The word *independent* should not be interpreted in a probabilistic sense, as defined in Chapter 3. The phrase *independent variable* is used in regression analysis to refer to a predictor variable for the response y.

In the probabilistic model, the deterministic component is referred to as the **line of means,** because the mean of y, $E(y)$, is equal to the straight-line component of the model—that is,

$$E(y) = \beta_0 + \beta_1 x$$

Note that the Greek symbols β_0 and β_1, respectively, represent the y-intercept and slope of the model. They are population parameters that will be known only if we have access to the entire population of (x, y) measurements.

FIGURE 10.2
The straight-line model

Together with a specific value of the independent variable x, they determine the mean value of y, which is just a specific point on the line of means (Figure 10.2).

Biography

FRANCIS GALTON
(1822–1911)

The Law of Universal Regression

Francis Galton was the youngest of seven children born to a middle-class English family of Quaker faith. A cousin of Charles Darwin, Galton attended Trinity College (Cambridge, England) to study medicine. Due to the death of his father, Galton was unable to obtain his degree. His competence in both medicine and mathematics, however, led Galton to pursue a career as a scientist. Galton made major contributions to the fields of genetics, psychology, meteorology, and anthropology. Some consider Galton to be the first social scientist for his applications of the novel statistical concepts of the time—in particular, regression and correlation. While studying natural inheritance in 1886, Galton collected data on heights of parents and adult children. He noticed the tendency for tall (or short) parents to have tall (or short) children but that the children were not as tall (or short), on average, as their parents. Galton called this phenomenon the "law of universal regression," for the average heights of adult children tended to "regress" to the mean of the population. Galton, with the help of his friend and disciple, Karl Pearson, applied the straight-line model to the height data, and the term *regression* model was coined.

The values of β_0 and β_1 will be unknown in almost all practical applications of regression analysis. The process of developing a model, estimating the unknown parameters, and using the model can be viewed as the five-step procedure shown in the next box.

Step 1: Hypothesize the deterministic component of the model that relates the mean, $E(y)$, to the independent variable x (Section 10.1).

Step 2: Use the sample data to estimate unknown parameters in the model (Section 10.2).

Step 3: Specify the probability distribution of the random error term and estimate the standard deviation of this distribution (Sections 10.3 and 10.4).

Step 4: Statistically evaluate the usefulness of the model (Sections 10.5, 10.6, and 10.7).

Step 5: When satisfied that the model is useful, use it for prediction, estimation, and other purposes (Section 10.8).

Exercises 10.1–10.9

Learning the Mechanics

10.1 In each case, graph the line that passes through the given points.
    a. $(1, 1)$ and $(5, 5)$ **b.** $(0, 3)$ and $(3, 0)$
    c. $(-1, 1)$ and $(4, 2)$ **d.** $(-6, -3)$ and $(2, 6)$

10.2 Give the slope and y-intercept for each of the lines graphed in Exercise 10.1.

10.3 The equation for a straight line (deterministic model) is

$$y = \beta_0 + \beta_1 x$$

If the line passes through the point $(-2, 4)$, then $x = -2$, $y = 4$ must satisfy the equation; that is,

$$4 = \beta_0 + \beta_1(-2)$$

Similarly, if the line passes through the point $(4, 6)$, then $x = 4$, $y = 6$ must satisfy the equation; that is,

$$6 = \beta_0 + \beta_1(4)$$

Use these two equations to solve for β_0 and β_1; then find the equation of the line that passes through the points $(-2, 4)$ and $(4, 6)$.

10.4 Refer to Exercise 10.3. Find the equations of the lines that pass through the points listed in Exercise 10.1.

10.5 Plot the following lines:
    a. $y = 4 + x$ **b.** $y = 5 - 2x$ **c.** $y = -4 + 3x$
    d. $y = -2x$ **e.** $y = x$ **f.** $y = .50 + 1.5x$

10.6 Give the slope and y-intercept for each of the lines defined in Exercise 10.5.

10.7 Why do we generally prefer a probabilistic model to a deterministic model? Give examples for which the two types of models might be appropriate.

10.8 What is the line of means?

10.9 If a straight-line probabilistic relationship relates the mean $E(y)$ to an independent variable x, does it imply that every value of the variable y will always fall exactly on the line of means? Why or why not?

10.2 Fitting the Model: The Least Squares Approach

After the straight-line model has been hypothesized to relate the mean $E(y)$ to the independent variable x, the next step is to collect data and to estimate the (unknown) population parameters, the y-intercept β_0 and the slope β_1.

To begin with a simple example, suppose an appliance store conducts a 5-month experiment to determine the effect of advertising on sales revenue. The results are shown in Table 10.1. (The number of measurements and the measurements themselves are unrealistically simple in order to avoid arithmetic confusion in this introductory example.) This set of data will be used to demonstrate the five-step procedure of regression modeling given in Section 10.1. In this section we hypothesize the deterministic component of the model and estimate its unknown parameters (steps 1 and 2). The model assumptions and the random error component (step 3) are the subjects of Sections 10.3 and 10.4, whereas Sections 10.5–10.7 assess the utility of the model (step 4). Finally, we use the model for prediction and estimation (step 5) in Section 10.8.

Step 1: *Hypothesize the deterministic component of the probabilistic model.* As stated before, we will consider only straight-line models in this chapter. Thus, the complete model to relate mean sales revenue $E(y)$ to advertising expenditure x is given by

$$E(y) = \beta_0 + \beta_1 x$$

 ADSALES

TABLE 10.1 Advertising–Sales Data

Month	Advertising Expenditure, x ($100s)	Sales Revenue, y ($1,000s)
1	1	1
2	2	1
3	3	2
4	4	2
5	5	4

Step 2: *Use sample data to estimate unknown parameters in the model.* This step is the subject of this section—namely, how can we best use the information in the sample of five observations in Table 10.1 to estimate the unknown y-intercept β_0 and slope β_1?

To determine whether a linear relationship between y and x is plausible, it is helpful to plot the sample data in a **scattergram** (or **scatterplot**). Recall (Section 2.9) that a scattergram locates each of the five data points on a graph, as shown in Figure 10.3. Note that the scattergram suggests a general tendency for y to increase as x increases. If you place a ruler on the scattergram, you will see that a line may be drawn through three of the five points, as shown in Figure 10.4. To obtain the equation of this visually fitted line, note that the line intersects the y-axis at $y = -1$, so the y-intercept is -1. Also, y increases exactly 1 unit for every 1-unit increase in x, indicating that the slope is $+1$. Therefore, the equation is

$$\tilde{y} = -1 + 1(x) = -1 + x$$

where $\tilde{y}$ is used to denote the predicted y from the visual model.

FIGURE 10.3
Scattergram for data in Table 10.1

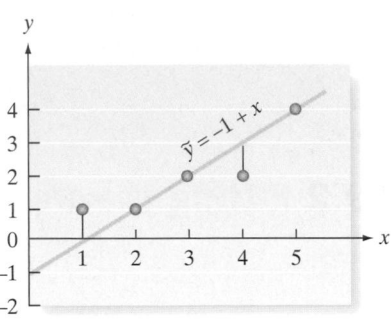

FIGURE 10.4
Visual straight line fitted to the data in Figure 10.3

One way to decide quantitatively how well a straight line fits a set of data is to note the extent to which the data points deviate from the line. For example, to evaluate the model in Figure 10.4, we calculate the magnitude of the *deviations* (i.e., the differences between the observed and the predicted values of y). These deviations, or **errors of prediction,** are the vertical distances between observed and predicted values (see Figure 10.4). The observed and predicted values of y, their differences, and their squared differences are shown in Table 10.2. Note that the *sum of errors* equals 0 and the *sum of squares of the errors* (SSE), which gives greater emphasis to large deviations of the points from the line, is equal to 2.

You can see by shifting the ruler around the graph that it is possible to find many lines for which the sum of errors is equal to 0, but it can be shown that there is one (and only one) line for which the SSE is a *minimum*. This line is called the **least squares line,** the **regression line,** or the **least squares prediction equation.** The methodology used to obtain this line is called the **method of least squares.**

Now Work Exercise 10.12a–d

To find the least squares prediction equation for a set of data, assume that we have a sample of n data points consisting of pairs of values of x and y, say (x_1, y_1),

TABLE 10.2 Comparing Observed and Predicted Values for the Visual Model

x	y	$\tilde{y} = -1 + x$	$(y - \tilde{y})$	$(y - \tilde{y})^2$
1	1	0	$(1 - 0) = 1$	1
2	1	1	$(1 - 1) = 0$	0
3	2	2	$(2 - 2) = 0$	0
4	2	3	$(2 - 3) = -1$	1
5	4	4	$(4 - 4) = 0$	0
			Sum of errors = 0	Sum of squared errors (SSE) = 2

$(x_2, y_2), \ldots, (x_n, y_n)$. For example, the $n = 5$ data points shown in Table 10.2 are $(1, 1)$, $(2, 1)$, $(3, 2)$, $(4, 2)$, and $(5, 4)$. The fitted line, which we will calculate based on the five data points, is written as

$$\hat{y} = \hat{\beta}_0 + \hat{\beta}_1 x$$

The "hats" indicate that the symbols below them are estimates: $\hat{y}$ (y-hat) is an estimator of the mean value of y, $E(y)$, and a predictor of some future value of y; and $\hat{\beta}_0$ and $\hat{\beta}_1$ are estimators of β_0 and β_1, respectively.

For a given data point, say the point (x_i, y_i), the observed value of y is y_i and the predicted value of y would be obtained by substituting x_i into the prediction equation:

$$\hat{y}_i = \hat{\beta}_0 + \hat{\beta}_1 x_i$$

And the deviation of the ith value of y from its predicted value is

$$(y_i - \hat{y}_i) = [y_i - (\hat{\beta}_0 + \hat{\beta}_1 x_i)]$$

Then the sum of squares of the deviations of the y-values about their predicted values for all the n points is

$$SSE = \sum [y_i - (\hat{\beta}_0 + \hat{\beta}_1 x_i)]^2$$

The quantities $\hat{\beta}_0$ and $\hat{\beta}_1$ that make the SSE a minimum are called the **least squares estimates** of the population parameters β_0 and β_1, and the prediction equation $\hat{y} = \hat{\beta}_0 + \hat{\beta}_1 x$ is called the *least squares line*.

Definition 10.1

The **least squares line** $\hat{y} = \hat{\beta}_0 + \hat{\beta}_1 x$ is one that has the following two properties:

1. the sum of the errors (SE) equals 0
2. the sum of squared errors (SSE) is smaller than for any other straight-line model

---

The values of $\hat{\beta}_0$ and $\hat{\beta}_1$ that minimize the SSE are (proof omitted) given by the formulas in the box.*

Formulas for the Least Squares Estimates

Slope: $\hat{\beta}_1 = \dfrac{SS_{xy}}{SS_{xx}}$

y-intercept: $\hat{\beta}_0 = \bar{y} - \hat{\beta}_1 \bar{x}$

where $SS_{xy} = \sum (x_i - \bar{x})(y_i - \bar{y}) = \sum x_i y_i - \dfrac{\left(\sum x_i\right)\left(\sum y_i\right)}{n}$

$SS_{xx} = \sum (x_i - \bar{x})^2 = \sum x_i^2 - \dfrac{\left(\sum x_i\right)^2}{n}$

n = Sample size

---

*Students who are familiar with calculus should note that the values of β_0 and β_1 that minimize $SSE = \sum (y_i - \hat{y}_i)^2$ are obtained by setting the two partial derivatives $\partial SSE/\partial \beta_0$ and $\partial SSE/\partial \beta_1$ equal to 0. The solutions to these two equations yield the formulas shown in the box. Furthermore, we denote the *sample* solutions to the equations by $\hat{\beta}_0$ and $\hat{\beta}_1$, where the "hat" denotes that these are sample estimates of the true population intercept β_0 and true population slope β_1.

EXAMPLE 10.1

Applying the Method of Least Squares to the Sales–Advertising Data

Problem Refer to the monthly sales-advertising data presented in Table 10.1. Consider the straight-line model, $E(y) = \beta_0 + \beta_1 x$, where y = sales revenue (thousands of dollars) and x = advertising expenditure (hundreds of dollars).

a. Use the method of least squares to estimate the values of β_0 and β_1.

b. Predict the sales revenue when advertising expenditure is $200 (i.e., when $x = 2$).

c. Find SSE for the analysis.

d. Give practical interpretations to β_0 and β_1.

Solution

a. Preliminary computations for finding the least squares line for the advertising-sales data are presented in Table 10.3. We can now calculate

$$SS_{xy} = \sum x_i y_i - \frac{\left(\sum x_i\right)\left(\sum y_i\right)}{5} = 37 - \frac{(15)(10)}{5} = 37 - 30 = 7$$

$$SS_{xx} = \sum x_i^2 - \frac{\left(\sum x_i\right)^2}{5} = 55 - \frac{(15)^2}{5} = 55 - 45 = 10$$

Then the slope of the least squares line is

$$\hat{\beta}_1 = \frac{SS_{xy}}{SS_{xx}} = \frac{7}{10} = .7$$

and the y-intercept is

$$\hat{\beta}_0 = \bar{y} - \hat{\beta}_1\bar{x} = \frac{\sum y_i}{5} - \hat{\beta}_1\frac{\sum x_i}{5}$$

$$= \frac{10}{5} - (.7)\left(\frac{15}{5}\right) = 2 - (.7)(3) = 2 - 2.1 = -.1$$

The least squares line is thus

$$\hat{y} = \hat{\beta}_0 + \hat{\beta}_1 x = -.1 + .7x$$

The graph of this line is shown in Figure 10.5.

TABLE 10.3 Preliminary Computations for Advertising–Sales Example

x_i	y_i	x_i^2	$x_i y_i$
1	1	1	1
2	1	4	2
3	2	9	6
4	2	16	8
5	4	25	20
Totals $\sum x_i = 15$	$\sum y_i = 10$	$\sum x_i^2 = 55$	$\sum x_i y_i = 37$

FIGURE 10.5

The line $\hat{y} = -.1 + .7x$ fitted to the data

b. The predicted value of y for a given value of x can be obtained by substituting into the formula for the least squares line. Substituting $x = 2$ into the least squares equation yields

$$\hat{y} = -.1 + .7x = -.1 + .7(2) = 1.3$$

Thus, when advertising expenditure is $200, we predict monthly sales revenue to be $1,300. We show how to find a prediction interval for y in Section 10.8.

c. The observed and predicted values of y, the deviations of the y values about their predicted values, and the squares of these deviations are shown in Table 10.4. Note that the sum of squares of the deviations, SSE, is 1.10, and (as we would expect) this is less than the SSE $= 2.0$ obtained in Table 10.2 for the visually fitted line.

d. The estimated y-intercept, $\hat{\beta}_0 = -.1$, appears to imply that the estimated mean sales revenue is equal to $-.1$, or $-$100$, when the advertising expenditure, x, is equal to $0. Since negative sales revenues are not possible, this seems to make the model nonsensical. However, *the model parameters should be interpreted only within the sampled range of the independent variable*—in this case, for advertising expenditures between $100 and $500. Thus, the y-intercept—which is, by definition, at $x = 0$ ($0 advertising expenditure)—is not within the range of the sampled values of x and is not subject to meaningful interpretation.

The slope of the least squares line, $\hat{\beta}_1 = .7$, implies that for every unit increase of x, the mean value of y is estimated to increase by .7 unit. In terms of this example, for every $100 increase in advertising, the mean sales revenue is estimated to increase by $700 *over the sampled range of advertising expenditures from $100 to $500*. Thus, the model does not imply that increasing the advertising expenditures from $500 to $1,000 will result in an increase in mean sales of $3,500, because the range of x in the sample does not extend to $1,000 ($x = 10$). Be careful to interpret the estimated parameters only within the sampled range of x.

Look Back The calculations required to obtain $\hat{\beta}_0$, $\hat{\beta}_1$, and SSE in simple linear regression, although straightforward, can become rather tedious. Even with the use of a pocket calculator, the process is laborious and susceptible to error, especially when the sample size is large. Fortunately, the use of a statistical software package can significantly reduce

TABLE 10.4 Comparing Observed and Predicted Values for the Least Squares Prediction Equation

x	y	$\hat{y} = -.1 + .7x$	$(y - \hat{y})$	$(y - \hat{y})^2$
1	1	.6	$(1 - .6) = .4$	.16
2	1	1.3	$(1 - 1.3) = -.3$	.09
3	2	2.0	$(2 - 2.0) = 0$	.00
4	2	2.7	$(2 - 2.7) = -.7$	.49
5	4	3.4	$(4 - 3.4) = .6$	.36
			Sum of errors $= 0$	SSE $= 1.10$

Model Summary

Model	R	R Square	Adjusted R Square	Std. Error of the Estimate
1	.904[a]	.817	.756	.606

a. Predictors: (Constant), ADVEXP_X

ANOVA[b]

Model		Sum of Squares	df	Mean Square	F	Sig.
1	Regression	4.900	1	4.900	13.364	.035[a]
	Residual	1.100	3	.367		
	Total	6.000	4			

a. Predictors: (Constant), ADVEXP_X

b. Dependent Variable: SALES_Y

Coefficients[a]

Model		Unstandardized Coefficients		Standardized Coefficients	t	Sig.
		B	Std. Error	Beta		
1	(Constant)	-.100	.635		-.157	.885
	ADVEXP_X	.700	.191	.904	3.656	.035

a. Dependent Variable: SALES_Y

FIGURE 10.6a

SPSS printout for the advertising–sales regression

Regression Analysis: SALES_Y versus ADVEXP_X

```
The regression equation is
SALES_Y = - 0.100 + 0.700 ADVEXP_X


Predictor      Coef   SE Coef      T       P
Constant    -0.1000    0.6351   -0.16   0.885
ADVEXP_X     0.7000    0.1915    3.66   0.035


S = 0.605530    R-Sq = 81.7%    R-Sq(adj) = 75.6%


Analysis of Variance

Source          DF      SS       MS       F      P
Regression       1   4.9000   4.9000   13.36  0.035
Residual Error   3   1.1000   0.3667
Total            4   6.0000
```

FIGURE 10.6b

MINITAB printout for the advertising-sales regression

the labor involved in regression calculations. The SPSS, MINITAB, and Excel outputs for the simple linear regression of the data in Table 10.1 are displayed in Figures 10.6(a)–(c). The values of $\hat{\beta}_0$ and $\hat{\beta}_1$ are highlighted on the printouts. These values, $\hat{\beta}_0 = -.1$ and $\hat{\beta}_1 = .7$, agree exactly with our hand-calculated values. The value of SSE = 1.10 is also highlighted on the printouts.

	A	B	C	D	E	F	G
1	Regression Analysis						
2							
3	*Regression Statistics*						
4	Multiple R	0.903696114					
5	R Square	0.816666667					
6	Adjusted R Square	0.755555556					
7	Standard Error	0.605530071					
8	Observations	5					
9							
10	ANOVA						
11		*df*	*SS*	*MS*	*F*	*Significance F*	
12	Regression	1	4.9	4.9	13.36363636	0.035352847	
13	Residual	3	1.1	0.366666667			
14	Total	4	6				
15							
16		*Coefficients*	*Standard Error*	*t Stat*	*P-value*	*Lower 95%*	*Upper 95%*
17	Intercept	-0.1	0.635085296	-0.157459164	0.88488398	-2.12112675	1.92112675
18	ADVEXP_X	0.7	0.191485422	3.655630775	0.035352847	0.090607356	1.309392644
19							

FIGURE 10.6C

Excel printout for the advertising–sales regression

Now Work Exercise 10.14d,e

Interpreting the Estimates of β_0 and β_1 in Simple Linear Regression

y-intercept: $\hat{\beta}_0$ represents the predicted value of y when $x = 0$ (*Caution:* This value will not be meaningful if the value $x = 0$ is nonsensical or outside the range of the sample data.)

slope: $\hat{\beta}_1$ represents the increase (or decrease) in y for every 1-unit increase in x (*Caution:* This interpretation is only valid for x-values within the range of the sample data.)

Even when the interpretations of the estimated parameters in a simple linear regression are meaningful, we need to remember that they are only estimates based on the sample. As such, their values will typically change in repeated sampling. How much confidence do we have that the estimated slope, $\hat{\beta}_1$, accurately approximates the true slope, β_1? This requires statistical inference, in the form of confidence intervals and tests of hypotheses, which we address in Section 10.5.

To summarize, we defined the best-fitting straight line to be the one that minimizes the sum of squared errors around the line, and we called it the *least squares line*. We should interpret the least squares line only within the sampled range of the independent variable. In subsequent sections we show how to make statistical inferences about the model.

STATISTICS IN ACTION REVISITED

Estimating a Straight-Line Regression Model for the Work-Life Balance Data

We return to the *Graduate Management Admission Council (GMAC) Research Report* on the work-life balance of MBA alumni (p. 597). In the GMAC's April 2005 survey, 2,087 recent MBA graduates answered a series of questions on work-life balance. Two variables of interest to the GMAC were work-life balance score (measured on a scale of 0 to 100, with lower scores indicating a higher imbalance between work and life) and average number of hours worked per week. The data for these variables for the 2,087 respondents are saved in the **GMAC** file. The first 15 observations are listed in Table SIA10.1.

Continued

Now let x = average number of hours worked per week and y = work-life balance scale score for each MBA alumnus. One way to investigate the link between these two variables is to fit the straight-line model, $E(y) = \beta_0 + \beta_1 x$, to the data in Table SIA10.1.

A MINITAB scatterplot of the data is shown in Figure SIA10.1. The least squares line, obtained from the MINITAB regression printout shown in Figure SIA10.2, is also displayed on the scatterplot. Although the least squares line has a slight downward trend, the variation of the data points around the line is large. It does not appear that number of hours worked per week (x) will be a very good predictor of work-life balance score (y). In fact, the estimated slope (obtained from Figure SIA10.2) is $\beta_1 = -.35$. Thus, for every 1-hour increase in number of weekly hours worked, we estimate that an MBA alumnus' work-life balance score will decrease only .35 point. In the Statistics in Action Revisited sections that follow, we will provide a measure of reliability to this inference and investigate the work-life balance issue further.

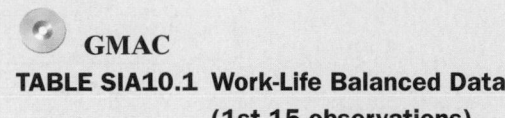

GMAC

TABLE SIA10.1 Work-Life Balanced Data (1st 15 observations)

WLB-Score	Hours
75.22	50
64.98	45
49.62	50
44.51	55
70.10	50
54.74	60
55.98	55
21.24	60
59.86	50
70.10	50
29.00	70
64.98	45
36.75	40
35.45	40
45.75	50

Figure SIA10.1

MINITAB scatterplot of work-life balance data

Figure SIA10.2

MINITAB simple linear regression for work-life balance data

Regression Analysis: WLB-SCORE versus HOURS

```
The regression equation is
WLB-SCORE = 62.5 - 0.347 HOURS


Predictor       Coef   SE Coef         T       P
Constant      62.499     1.414     44.22   0.000
HOURS       -0.34673   0.02761    -12.56   0.000


S = 12.2845    R-Sq = 7.0%    R-Sq(adj) = 7.0%


Analysis of Variance

Source            DF        SS       MS        F       P
Regression         1     23803    23803   157.73   0.000
Residual Error  2085    314647      151
Total           2086    338451
```

Simple Linear Regression

Using the TI-83/TI-84 Graphing Calculator

I. Finding the least squares regression equation

Step 1 *Enter the data*

Press **STAT** and select **1:Edit**
Note: If a list already contains data, clear the old data.
Use the up arrow to highlight the list name, "**L1**" or "**L2**".
Press **CLEAR ENTER**.
Enter your *x*-data in **L1** and your *y*-data in **L2**.

Step 2 *Find the equation*

Press **STAT** and highlight **CALC**
Press **4** for **LinReg(ax + b)**
Press **ENTER**
The screen will show the values for *a* and *b* in the equation $y = ax + b$.

Example The figures below show a table of data entered on the TI-84/TI-83 and the
regression equation obtained using the steps given above.

II. Finding *r* and r^2

If *r* and r^2 do not already appear on the LinReg screen from part I,

Step 1 *Turn the diagnostics feature on*

Press **2nd 0** for **CATALOG**
Press the **ALPHA** key and x^{-1} for **D**
Press the down **ARROW** until **DiagnosticsOn** is highlighted
Press **ENTER** twice

Step 2 *Find the regression equation as shown in part I above*

The values for r and r^2 will appear on the screen as well.

Example The figure below shows the output with the **DiagnosticsOn.**

```
LinReg
 y=ax+b
 a=2.495967742
 b=63.3391129
 r²=.9620199454
 r=.9808261545
```

III. Graphing the least squares line with the scatterplot

Step 1 *Enter the data as shown in part I above*

Step 2 *Set up the data plot*

Press **Y=** and **CLEAR** all functions from the Y registers
Press **2nd Y=** for **STAT PLOT**

Continued

Press **1** for **Plot1**
Set the cursor so that **ON** is flashing and press **ENTER**.
For **Type**, use the **ARROW** and **ENTER** keys to highlight and select the scatterplot (first icon in the first row).
For **Xlist**, choose the column containing the *x*-data.
For **Ylist**, choose the column containing the *y*-data.

Step 3 *Find the regression equation and store the equation in Y1*

Press **STAT** and highlight **CALC**
Press **4** for **LinReg(ax + b)** (Note: Don't press ENTER here because you want to store the regression equation in Y1)
Press **VARS**
Use the right arrow to highlight **Y-VARS**
Press **ENTER** to select **1:Function**
Press **ENTER** to select **1:Y1**
Press **ENTER**

Step 4 *View the scatterplot and regression line*

Press **ZOOM** and then press **9** to select **9:ZoomStat**

You should see the data graphed along with the regression line.

Example The figure shows a graph of the scatterplot and least squares line obtained using the steps given above.

ACTIVITY 10.1: *Keep the Change:* Least Squares Models

In this activity, you will once again use data collected in Activity 1.1 *Keep the Change: Collecting Data* (p. 16). For each student in your class, collect the sum of the data set *Purchase Totals*, the sum of the data set *Amounts Transferred*, and the number of purchases (the number of data items in the set *Purchase Totals*).

1. For each student in your class, form an ordered pair

(Sum of Purchase Totals, Sum of Amounts Transferred)

Use these ordered pairs to create a scattergram. Then use the ordered pairs to find the values of $\hat{\beta}_0$ and $\hat{\beta}_1$ in the least squares line for the data.

2. Suppose that three customers have made only one debit-card purchase each, as shown in the following table.

Customer	Purchases	Actual Amount Transferred	Estimated Amount Transferred	Difference
A	$ 3.49			
B	$ 30.49			
C	$300.49			

Complete the table by first finding the actual amount that will be transferred for each customer. Then use the least squares line $y = \hat{\beta}_0 + \hat{\beta}_1 x$ from Exercise 1 to estimate the amount transferred. Finally, calculate the difference between the actual and estimated amounts for each customer.

3. Based on your results in Exercise 2, comment on the usefulness of using your model from Exercise 1 to estimate the transferred amounts. Do you believe that the least squares model is an appropriate model in this situation? Explain.

4. For each student in your class, form an ordered pair

(Number of Purchases, Sum of Amounts Transferred)

Use these ordered pairs to create a scattergram. Then use the ordered pairs to find the values of $\hat{\beta}_0$ and $\hat{\beta}_1$ in the least squares line for the data. Create your own hypothetical data as in Exercise 2 to test your model. Do you believe that this model is more or less useful than the model in Exercise 1? Explain.

Exercises 10.10–10.23

Learning the Mechanics

10.10 The following table is similar to Table 10.3. It is used for making the preliminary computations for finding the least squares line for the given pairs of x and y values.

x_i	y_i	x_i^2	$x_i y_i$
7	2		
4	4		
6	2		
2	5		
1	7		
1	6		
3	5		

Totals	$\sum x_i =$	$\sum y_i =$	$\sum x_i^2 =$	$\sum x_i y_i =$

   a. Complete the table.   **b.** Find SS_{xy}.
   c. Find SS_{xx}.   **d.** Find $\hat{\beta}_1$.
   e. Find $\bar{x}$ and $\bar{y}$.   **f.** Find $\hat{\beta}_0$.
   g. Find the least squares line.

10.11 Refer to Exercise 10.10. After the least squares line has been obtained, the table below (which is similar to Table 10.4) can be used for (1) comparing the observed and the predicted values of y, and (2) computing SSE.

x	y	$\hat{y}$	$(y - \hat{y})$	$(y - \hat{y})^2$
7	2			
4	4			
6	2			
2	5			
1	7			
1	6			
3	5			

$$\sum(y - \hat{y}) = \qquad SSE = \sum(y - \hat{y})^2 -$$

   a. Complete the table.
   b. Plot the least squares line on a scattergram of the data. Plot the following line on the same graph: $\hat{y} = 14 - 2.5x$
   c. Show that SSE is larger for the line in part **b** than it is for the least squares line.

10.12 Construct a scattergram for the data in the following table.
NW

x	.5	1	1.5
y	2	1	3

   a. Plot the following two lines on your scattergram:

$$y = 3 - x \quad \text{and} \quad y = 1 + x$$

   b. Which of these lines would you choose to characterize the relationship between x and y? Explain.
   c. Show that the sum of errors for both of these lines equals 0.
   d. Which of these lines has the smaller SSE?
   e. Find the least squares line for the data and compare it to the two lines described in part **a.**

10.13 Consider the following pairs of measurements:

   ⊘ **LM10_13**

x	8	5	4	6	2	5	3
y	1	3	6	3	7	2	5

   a. Construct a scattergram for these data.
   b. What does the scattergram suggest about the relationship between x and y?
   c. Find the least squares estimates of β_0 and β_1.
   d. Plot the least squares line on your scattergram. Does the line appear to fit the data well? Explain.

APPLET Applet Exercise 10.1

Use the applet entitled *Regression by Eye* to explore the relationship between the pattern of data in a scattergram and the corresponding least squares model.
   a. Run the applet several times. For each time, attempt to move the green line into a position that appears to minimize the vertical distances of the points from the line. Then click *Show regression line* to see the actual regression line. How close is your line to the actual line? Click *New data* to reset the applet.
   b. Click the trash can to clear the graph. Use the mouse to place five points on the scattergram that are approximately in a straight line. Then move the green line to approximate the regression line. Click *Show regression line* to see the actual regression line. How close were you this time?
   c. Continue to clear the graph and plot sets of five points with different patterns among the points. Use the green line to approximate the regression line. How close do you come to the actual regression line each time?
   d. Based on your experiences with the applet, explain why we need to use more reliable methods of finding the regression line than just "eyeing" it.

Applying the Concepts—Basic

⊘ **DIAMONDS**

10.14 Characteristics of diamonds sold at retail. Refer to the *Journal of Statistics Education* data on 308 diamonds for sale on the open market, saved in the **DIAMONDS** file. In Exercise 2.115 (p. 105), you related the size of the diamond (number of carats) to the asking price (dollars) using a scatterplot.
   a. Write the equation of a straight-line model relating asking price (y) to number of carats (x).
   b. A MINITAB simple linear regression printout for the data is shown on p. 612. Find the equation of the least squares line.
NW   **c.** Give a practical interpretation of the y-intercept of the least squares line. If a practical interpretation is not possible, explain why.
NW   **d.** Give a practical interpretation of the slope of the least squares line. Over what range of x is the interpretation meaningful?
   e. Use the least squares line to predict the asking price of a .52-carat diamond.

10.15 State SAT scores. Refer to the data on average state SAT scores for 1990 and 2005, Exercise 2.29 (p. 60). The first five observations and last two observations in the **SATSCORES** file are reproduced in the next table. In Exercise 2.113 you examined the relationship between the 1990 SAT score and the 2005 SAT score with a scatterplot.

MINITAB Output for Exercise 10.14

Regression Analysis: PRICE versus CARAT

```
The regression equation is
PRICE = - 2298 + 11599 CARAT


Predictor      Coef    SE Coef       T       P
Constant     -2298.4     158.5   -14.50   0.000
CARAT        11598.9     230.1    50.41   0.000


S = 1117.56    R-Sq = 89.3%    R-Sq(adj) = 89.2%


Analysis of Variance

Source            DF          SS          MS        F       P
Regression         1  3173248722  3173248722  2540.73   0.000
Residual Error   306   382178624     1248950
Total            307  3555427347
```

a. Write the equation of a straight-line model relating 2005 SAT score (y) to 1990 SAT score (x).

b. An SPSS simple linear regression printout for the data is shown below. Find the least squares prediction equation.

c. Give a practical interpretation of the y-intercept of the least squares line. If a practical interpretation is not possible, explain why.

d. Give a practical interpretation of the slope of the least squares line. Over what range of x is the interpretation meaningful?

⊙ **SATSCORES**

State	1990	2005
Alabama	1079	1126
Alaska	1015	1042
Arizona	1041	1056
Arkansas	1077	1115
California	1002	1026
.	.	.
.	.	.
.	.	.
Wisconsin	1111	1191
Wyoming	1072	1087

Source: College Entrance Examination Board, 2006.

10.16 Extending the life of an aluminum smelter pot. An investigation of the properties of bricks used to line aluminum smelter pots was published in *The American Ceramic Society Bulletin* (Feb. 2005). Six different commercial bricks were evaluated. The life length of a smelter pot depends on the porosity of the brick lining (the less porosity, the longer the life); consequently, the researchers measured the apparent porosity of each brick specimen, as well as the mean pore diameter of each brick. The data are given in the accompanying table.

⊙ **SMELTPOT**

Brick	Apparent Porosity (%)	Mean Pore Diameter (micrometers)
A	18.8	12.0
B	18.3	9.7
C	16.3	7.3
D	6.9	5.3
E	17.1	10.9
F	20.4	16.8

Source: Bonadia, P., et al. "Aluminosilicate Refractories for Aluminum Cell Linings." *The American Ceramic Society Bulletin*, Vol. 84, No. 2, Feb., 2005 (Table II).

a. Find the least squares line relating porosity (y) to mean pore diameter (x).

b. Interpret the y-intercept of the line.

c. Interpret the slope of the line.

d. Predict the apparent porosity percentage for a brick with a mean pore diameter of 10 micrometers.

10.17 Drug controlled-release rate study. Researchers at Dow Chemical Co. investigated the effect of tablet surface area and volume on the rate at which a drug is released in a controlled-release dosage (*Drug Development and*

Coefficients[a]

Model		Unstandardized Coefficients		Standardized Coefficients	t	Sig.
		B	Std. Error	Beta		
1	(Constant)	-43.308	58.216		-.744	.460
	SAT1990	1.073	.056	.940	19.275	.000

a. Dependent Variable: SAT2005

SPSS Output for Exercise 10.15

Industrial Pharmacy, Vol. 28, 2002). Six similarly shaped tablets were prepared with different weights and thicknesses, and the ratio of surface area to volume was measured for each. Using a dissolution apparatus, each tablet was placed in 900 milliliters of deionized water, and the diffusional drug release rate (percentage of drug released divided by the square root of time) was determined. The experimental data are listed in the table.

⊙ DOWDRUG

Drug Release Rate (% released/$\sqrt{time}$)	Surface Area to Volume (mm^2/mm^3)
60	1.50
48	1.05
39	.90
33	.75
30	.60
29	.65

Source: Reynolds, T., Mitchell, S., and Balwinski, K. "Investigation of the Effect of Tablet Surface Area/Volume on Drug Release from Hydroxypropylmethylcellulose Controlled-Release Matrix Tablets." *Drug Development and Industrial Pharmacy*, Vol. 28, No. 4, 2002 (Figure 3).

a. Fit the simple linear model, $E(y) = \beta_0 + \beta_1 x$, where y = drug release rate and x = surface area to volume ratio.

b. Interpret the estimates of β_0 and β_1.

c. Predict the drug release rate for a tablet that has a surface area/volume ratio of .50.

d. Comment on the reliability of the prediction in part **c**.

Applying the Concepts—Intermediate

10.18 Sweetness of orange juice. The quality of the orange juice produced by a manufacturer (e.g., Minute Maid, Tropicana) is constantly monitored. There are numerous sensory and chemical components that combine to make the best-tasting orange juice. For example, one manufacturer has developed a quantitative index of the "sweetness" of orange juice. (The higher the index, the sweeter the juice.) Is there a relationship between the sweetness index and a chemical measure such as the amount of water soluble pectin (parts per million) in the orange juice? Data collected on these two variables for 24 production runs at a juice manufacturing plant are shown in the table in the next column. Suppose a manufacturer wants to use simple linear regression to predict the sweetness (y) from the amount of pectin (x).

⊙ OJUICE

Run	Sweetness Index	Pectin (ppm)
1	5.2	220
2	5.5	227
3	6.0	259
4	5.9	210
5	5.8	224
6	6.0	215
7	5.8	231
8	5.6	268
9	5.6	239
10	5.9	212
11	5.4	410
12	5.6	256
13	5.8	306
14	5.5	259
15	5.3	284
16	5.3	383
17	5.7	271
18	5.5	264
19	5.7	227
20	5.3	263
21	5.9	232
22	5.8	220
23	5.8	246
24	5.9	241

Note: The data in the table are authentic. For confidentiality reasons, the manufacturer cannot be disclosed.

a. Find the least squares line for the data.

b. Interpret $\hat{\beta}_0$ and $\hat{\beta}_1$ in the words of the problem.

c. Predict the sweetness index if amount of pectin in the orange juice is 300 ppm. [*Note:* A measure of reliability of such a prediction is discussed in Section 10.8]

10.19 Most generous philanthropists. Over the past 5 years, Intel Corp. founder Gordon Moore donated over 7 million dollars to environmental causes while Microsoft founder Bill Gates donated over 5 million dollars to health, education, and libraries. These two entrepreneurs were the top two givers in *Business Week's* (Nov. 28, 2005) annual list of the 50 Most Generous Philanthropists. Data on total amount pledged and remaining net worth (in millions of dollars) for the 50 top givers are saved in the **TOPGIVERS** file. (The data for the first 10 names on the list are given in the table below.)

⊙ TOPGIVERS (1st 10 donors listed)

Donor	Company/Background	Pledged ($ millions)	Net Worth ($ millions)
Gordon Moore	Intel	7,046	4,600
Bill Gates	Microsoft	5,458	51,000
Warren Buffett	Berkshire Hathaway	2,622	40,000
George Soros	Investor	2,367	7,200
Eli Broad	SunAmerica	1,475	5,500
James Stowers	American Century	1,205	716
Walton Family	Wal-Mart	1,100	82,700
Alfred Mann	Medical devices	993	2,100
Michael Dell	Dell	933	18,000
George Kaiser	Oil and gas	617	4,500

Source: Business Week, Nov. 28, 2005, p. 61.

a. Propose a straight-line model relating amount pledged (y) to net worth (x).

b. Fit the model to the data in the **TOPGIVERS** file using the method of least squares.

c. Graph the least squares line on a scattergram of the data. Is there visual evidence of a linear relationship between the two variables? Is the relationship positive or negative?

d. Interpret the estimates of the y-intercept and slope in the words of the problem.

10.20 FCAT scores and poverty. In the state of Florida, elementary school performance is based on the average score obtained by students on a standardized exam, called the Florida Comprehensive Assessment Test (FCAT). An analysis of the link between FCAT scores and sociodemographic factors was published in the *Journal of Educational and Behavioral Statistics* (Spring 2004). Data on average math and reading FCAT scores of third-graders, as well as the percentage of students below the poverty level, for a sample of 22 Florida elementary schools are listed in the table.

a. Propose a straight-line model relating math score (y) to percentage (x) of students below the poverty level.

b. Fit the model to the data in the **FCAT** file using the method of least squares.

c. Graph the least squares line on a scattergram of the data. Is there visual evidence of a relationship between the two variables? Is the relationship positive or negative?

d. Interpret the estimates of the y-intercept and slope in the words of the problem.

e. Now consider a model relating reading score (y) to percentage (x) of students below the poverty level. Repeat parts **a–d** for this model.

FCAT

Elementary School	FCAT-Math Math	FCAT-Reading	% Below Poverty
1	166.4	165.0	91.7
2	159.6	157.2	90.2
3	159.1	164.4	86.0
4	155.5	162.4	83.9
5	164.3	162.5	80.4
6	169.8	164.9	76.5
7	155.7	162.0	76.0
8	165.2	165.0	75.8
9	175.4	173.7	75.6
10	178.1	171.0	75.0
11	167.1	169.4	74.7
12	177.0	172.9	63.2
13	174.2	172.7	52.9
14	175.6	174.9	48.5
15	170.8	174.8	39.1
16	175.1	170.1	38.4
17	182.8	181.4	34.3
18	180.3	180.6	30.3
19	178.8	178.0	30.3
20	181.4	175.9	29.6
21	182.8	181.6	26.5
22	186.1	183.8	13.8

Source: Tekwe, C.D., et al. "An Empirical Comparison of Statistical Models for Value-Added Assessment of School Performance." *Journal of Educational and Behavioral Statistics*, Vol. 29, No. 1, Spring 2004 (Table 2).

10.21 Retaliation against company "whistle-blowers." Individuals who report perceived wrongdoing of a corporation or public agency are known as *whistle-blowers.* Two researchers developed an index to measure the extent of retaliation against a whistle-blower (*Journal of Applied Psychology*, 1986). The index was based on the number of forms of reprisal actually experienced, the number of forms of reprisal threatened, and the number of people within the organization (e.g., coworkers or immediate supervisor) who retaliated against them. The table below lists the retaliation index (higher numbers indicate more extensive retaliation) and salary for a sample of 15 whistle-blowers from federal agencies.

a. Construct a scattergram for the data. Does it appear that the extent of retaliation increases, decreases, or stays the same with an increase in salary? Explain.

b. Use the method of least squares to fit a straight line to the data.

c. Graph the least squares line on your scattergram. Does the least squares line support your answer to the question in part **a?** Explain.

RETAL

Retaliation Index	Salary	Retaliation Index	Salary
301	$62,000	535	$19,800
550	36,500	455	44,000
755	21,600	615	46,600
327	24,000	700	15,100
500	30,100	650	70,000
377	35,000	630	21,000
290	47,500	360	16,900
452	54,000		

Source: Data adapted from Near, J. P., and Miceli, M. P. "Retaliation against Whistle Blowers: Predictors and Effects." *Journal of Applied Psychology*, Vol. 71, No. 1, 1986, pp. 137–145.

d. Interpret the y-intercept, $\hat{\beta}_0$, of the least squares line in terms of this application. Is the interpretation meaningful?

e. Interpret the slope, $\hat{\beta}_1$, of the least squares line in terms of this application. Over what range of x is this interpretation meaningful?

10.22 Survey of the top business schools. Each year, the *Wall Street Journal* and *Harris Interactive* track the opinions and experiences of college recruiters for large corporations and summarize the results in the Business School Survey. In 2005, the survey included rankings of 76 business schools. Survey data for the top 10 business schools are given in the table at the top of p. 615.

a. Select one of the variables as the dependent variable, y, and another as the independent variable, x. Use your knowledge of the subject area and common sense to help you select the variables.

b. Fit the simple linear model, $E(y) = \beta_0 + \beta_1 x$, to the data in the **BSCHOOL** file. Interpret the estimates of the slope and y-intercept.

Applying the Concepts—Advanced

10.23 Spreading rate of spilled liquid. Refer to the *Chemical Engineering Progress* (Jan. 2005) study of the rate at which a spilled volatile liquid will spread across a surface, Exercise 2.118 (p. 105). Recall that a DuPont Corp. engi-

BSCHOOL

School	Enrollment (# full-time students)	Annual Tuition ($)	Mean GMAT	% with Job Offer	Ave. Salary ($)
Dartmouth	503	38,400	704	—	119,800
Michigan	1873	33,076	690	91	105,986
Carnegie Mellon	661	38,800	691	93	95,531
Northwestern	2650	38,844	700	94	117,060
Yale	468	36,800	696	86	104,018
Pennsylvania	1840	40,458	716	92	117,471
Cal., Berkeley	1281	21,512	701	92	112,699
Columbia	1796	38,290	709	95	126,319
North Carolina	855	16,375	652	86	92,565
Southern Cal.	1588	37,558	685	82	88,839

Source: The Wall Street Journal, Sep. 21, 2005.

neer calculated the mass (in pounds) of a 50-gallon methanol spill after a period of time ranging from 0 to 60 minutes. Do the data (at right) indicate that the mass of the spill tends to diminish as time increases? If so, how much will the mass diminish each minute?

LIQUIDSPILL

Time (minutes)	Mass (pounds)	Time (minutes)	Mass (pounds)
0	6.64	22	1.86
1	6.34	24	1.60
2	6.04	26	1.37
4	5.47	28	1.17
6	4.94	30	0.98
8	4.44	35	0.60
10	3.98	40	0.34
12	3.55	45	0.17
14	3.15	50	0.06
16	2.79	55	0.02
18	2.45	60	0.00
20	2.14		

Source. Barry, J. "Estimating Rates of Spreading and Evaporation of Volatile Liquids." Chemical Engineering Progress, Vol. 101, No. 1, Jan., 2005.

10.3 Model Assumptions

In Section 10.2 we assumed that the probabilistic model relating the firm's sales revenue y to the advertising dollars is

$$y = \beta_0 + \beta_1 x + \varepsilon$$

We also recall that the least squares estimate of the deterministic component of the model, $\beta_0 + \beta_1 x$, is

$$\hat{y} = \hat{\beta}_0 + \hat{\beta}_1 x = -.1 + .7x$$

Now we turn our attention to the random component ε of the probabilistic model and its relation to the errors in estimating β_0 and β_1. We will use a probability distribution to characterize the behavior of ε. We will see how the probability distribution of ε determines how well the model describes the relationship between the dependent variable y and the independent variable x.

Step 3 in a regression analysis requires us to specify the probability distribution of the random error ε. We will make four basic assumptions about the general form of this probability distribution:

Assumption 1: The mean of the probability distribution of ε is 0—that is, the average of the values of ε over an infinitely long series of experiments is 0 for each setting of the independent variable x. This assumption implies that the mean value of y, $E(y)$, for a given value of x is $E(y) = \beta_0 + \beta_1 x$.

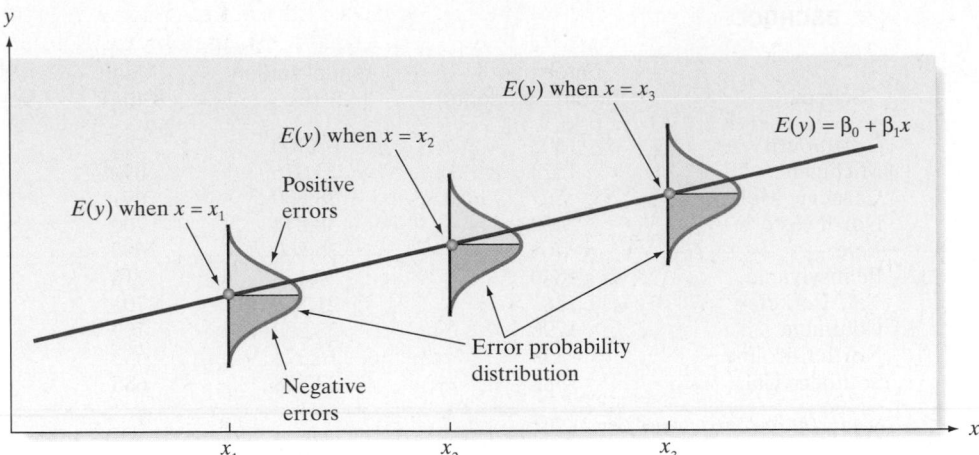

FIGURE 10.7
The probability distribution
of ε

Assumption 2: The variance of the probability distribution of ε is constant for all settings of the independent variable x. For our straight-line model, this assumption means that the variance of ε is equal to a constant, say σ^2, for all values of x.

Assumption 3: The probability distribution of ε is normal.

Assumption 4: The values of ε associated with any two observed values of y are independent—that is, the value of ε associated with one value of y has no effect on the values of ε associated with other y values.

The implications of the first three assumptions can be seen in Figure 10.7, which shows distributions of errors for three values of x, namely, x_1, x_2, and x_3. Note that the relative frequency distributions of the errors are normal with a mean of 0 and a constant variance σ^2. (All the distributions shown have the same amount of spread or variability.) The straight line shown in Figure 10.7 is the line of means. It indicates the mean value of y for a given value of x. We denote this mean value as $E(y)$. Then, the line of means is given by the equation

$$E(y) = \beta_0 + \beta_1 x$$

These assumptions make it possible for us to develop measures of reliability for the least squares estimators and to develop hypothesis tests for examining the usefulness of the least squares line. We have various techniques for checking the validity of these assumptions, and we have remedies to apply when they appear to be invalid. Several of these remedies are discussed in Chapter 11. Fortunately, the assumptions need not hold exactly in order for least squares estimators to be useful. The assumptions will be satisfied adequately for many applications encountered in practice.

10.4 An Estimator of σ^2

It seems reasonable to assume that the greater the variability of the random error ε (which is measured by its variance σ^2), the greater will be the errors in the estimation of the model parameters β_0 and β_1 and in the error of prediction when $\hat{y}$ is used to predict y for some value of x. Consequently, you should not be surprised, as we proceed through this chapter, to find that σ^2 appears in the formulas for all confidence intervals and test statistics that we will be using.

In most practical situations, σ^2 is unknown and we must use our data to estimate its value. The best estimate of σ^2, denoted by s^2, is obtained by dividing the sum of squares of the deviations of the y values from the prediction line,

$$\text{SSE} = \sum (y_i - \hat{y}_i)^2$$

by the number of degrees of freedom associated with this quantity. We use 2 df to estimate the two parameters β_0 and β_1 in the straight-line model, leaving $(n - 2)$ df for the error variance estimation.

Estimation of σ^2 for a (First-Order) Straight-Line Model

$$s^2 = \frac{\text{SSE}}{\text{Degrees of freedom for error}} = \frac{SSE}{n - 2}$$

where $\text{SSE} = \sum(y_i - \hat{y}_i)^2 = \text{SS}_{yy} - \hat{\beta}_1 \text{SS}_{xy}$

$$\text{SS}_{yy} = \sum(y_i - \bar{y})^2 = \sum y_i^2 - \frac{\left(\sum y_i\right)^2}{n}$$

To estimate the standard deviation σ of ε, we calculate

$$s = \sqrt{s^2} = \sqrt{\frac{\text{SSE}}{n - 2}}$$

We will refer to s as the **estimated standard error of the regression model.**

Warning

When performing these calculations, you may be tempted to round the calculated values of SS_{yy}, $\hat{\beta}_1$, and SS_{xy}. Be certain to carry at least six significant figures for each of these quantities to avoid substantial errors in calculation of the SSE.

EXAMPLE 10.2

Estimating σ for the Sales-Advertising Regression

Problem   Refer to Example 10.1 and the simple linear regression of the sales–advertising data in Table 10.3.

a.   Compute an estimate of σ.

b.   Give a practical interpretation of the estimate.

Solution

a.   We previously calculated SSE = 1.10 for the least squares line $\hat{y} = -.1 + .7x$. Recalling that there were $n = 5$ data points, we have $n - 2 = 5 - 2 = 3$ df for estimating σ^2. Thus,

$$s^2 = \frac{\text{SSE}}{n - 2} = \frac{1.10}{3} = .367$$

is the estimated variance, and

$$s = \sqrt{.367} = .61$$

is the standard error of the regression model.

b.   You may be able to grasp s intuitively by recalling the interpretation of a standard deviation given in Chapter 2 and remembering that the least squares line estimates the mean value of y for a given value of x. Since s measures the spread of the distribution of y values about the least squares line, we should not be surprised to find that most of the observations lie within $2s$, or $2(.61) = 1.22$, of the least squares line. For this simple example (only five data points), all five sales revenue values

Regression Analysis: SALES_Y versus ADVEXP_X

```
The regression equation is
SALES_Y = - 0.100 + 0.700 ADVEXP_X


Predictor       Coef   SE Coef       T      P
Constant     -0.1000    0.6351   -0.16  0.885
ADVEXP_X      0.7000    0.1915    3.66  0.035


S = 0.605530    R-Sq = 81.7%    R-Sq(adj) = 75.6%


Analysis of Variance

Source           DF       SS       MS      F      P
Regression        1   4.9000   4.9000  13.36  0.035
Residual Error    3   1.1000   0.3667
Total             4   6.0000
```

FIGURE 10.8

MINITAB printout for the advertising–sales regression

fall within $2s$ (or \$1,220) of the least squares line. In Section 10.8, we use s to evaluate the error of prediction when the least squares line is used to predict a value of y to be observed for a given value of x.

Look Back: The values of s^2 and s can also be obtained from a simple linear regression printout. The MINITAB printout for the advertising–sales example is reproduced in Figure 10.8. The value of s^2 is highlighted at the bottom of the printout in the **MS** (Mean Square) column in the row labeled **Residual Error.** (In regression, the estimate of σ^2 is called Mean Square for Error, or MSE.) The value, $s^2 = .3667$, agrees with the one calculated by hand. The value of s is also highlighted in Figure 10.8. This value, $s = .60553$, agrees (except for rounding) with our hand-calculated value.

Now Work Exercise 10.28

Interpretation of s, the Estimated Standard Deviation of ε

We expect most ($\approx 95\%$) of the observed y values to lie within $2s$ of their respective least squares predicted values, $\hat{y}$.

Exercises 10.24–10.34

Learning the Mechanics

10.24 Visually compare the scattergrams shown below. If a least squares line were determined for each data set, which do you think would have the smallest variance, s^2? Explain.

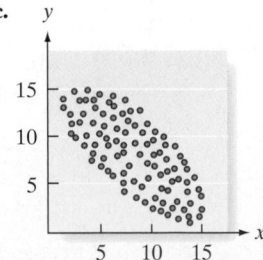

10.25 Suppose you fit a least squares line to 26 data points and the calculated value of SSE is 8.34.

  a. Find s^2, the estimator of σ^2 (the variance of the random error term ε).

  b. What is the largest deviation that you might expect between any one of the 26 points and the least squares line?

10.26 Calculate SSE and s^2 for each of the following cases:

  a. $n = 20$, $SS_{yy} = 95$, $SS_{xy} = 50$, $\hat{\beta}_1 = .75$

  b. $n = 40$, $\Sigma y^2 = 860$, $\Sigma y = 50$, $SS_{xy} = 2{,}700$
  $\hat{\beta}_1 = .2$

  c. $n = 10$, $\Sigma(y_i - \bar{y})^2 = 58$, $SS_{xy} = 91$, $SS_{xx} = 170$

10.27 Refer to Exercises 10.10 and 10.13. Calculate SSE, s^2, and s for the least squares lines obtained in these exercises. Interpret the standard error of the regression model, s, for each.

Applying the Concepts—Basic

DIAMONDS

10.28 Characteristics of diamonds sold at retail. Refer to the simple linear regression relating y = asking price (dollars) to
NW x = number of carats for diamonds sold on the open market, Exercise 10.14 (p. 611).

  a. Locate the values of SSE, s^2, and s on the MINITAB printout shown on p. 612.

  b. Give a practical interpretation of the value of s.

SAT SCORES

10.29 State SAT scores. Refer to the simple linear regression relating $y = 2005$ SAT score to $x = 1990$ SAT score, Exercise 10.15 (p. 611). A portion of the SPSS printout of the analysis is shown below.

  a. Locate the values of SSE, s^2, and s on the SPSS printout.

  b. Give a practical interpretation of the value of s.

DOWDRUG

10.30 Drug controlled-release rate study. Refer to simple linear regression relating the drug release rate (y) to surface area-to-volume ratio (x), Exercise 10.17 (p. 612).

  a. Find the value of s for the straight-line model.

  b. Give a practical interpretation of the value of s.

Applying the Concepts—Intermediate

OJUICE

10.31 Sweetness of orange juice. Refer to the study of the quality of orange juice produced at a juice manufacturing plant, Exercise 10.18 (p. 613). Recall that simple linear regression was used to predict the sweetness index (y) from the amount of pectin (x) in the orange juice.

  a. Find the values of SSE, s^2, and s for this regression.

  b. Explain why it is difficult to give a practical interpretation to s^2.

  c. Give a practical interpretation of the value of s.

10.32 Hospital charges vs. length of stay. *Statistical Bulletin* (Oct.–Dec. 1999) reported the average hospital charge and the average length of hospital stay for patients undergoing radical prostatectomies in a sample of 12 states. The data are listed in the accompanying table.

HOSPITAL

State	Average Hospital Charge ($)	Average Length of Stay (days)
Massachusetts	11,680	3.64
New Jersey	11,630	4.20
Pennsylvania	9,850	3.84
Minnesota	9,950	3.11
Indiana	8,490	3.86
Michigan	9,020	3.54
Florida	13,820	4.08
Georgia	8,440	3.57
Tennessee	8,790	3.80
Texas	10,400	3.52
Arizona	12,860	3.77
California	16,740	3.78

Source: Statistical Bulletin, Vol. 80, No. 4, Oct.–Dec. 1999, p. 13.

  a. Plot the data on a scattergram.

  b. Use the method of least squares to model the relationship between average hospital charge (y) and length of hospital stay (x).

Model Summary

Model	R	R Square	Adjusted R Square	Std. Error of the Estimate
1	.940[a]	.883	.881	23.420

a. Predictors: (Constant), SAT1990

ANOVA[b]

Model		Sum of Squares	df	Mean Square	F	Sig.
1	Regression	203794.5	1	203794.464	371.535	.000[a]
	Residual	26877.46	49	548.520		
	Total	230671.9	50			

a. Predictors: (Constant), SAT1990

b. Dependent Variable: SAT2005

SPSS Output for Exercise 10.29

c. Find the estimated standard error of the regression model and interpret its value in the context of the problem.

d. For a hospital stay of length $x = 4$ days, find $\hat{y} \pm 2s$.

e. What fraction of the states in the sample have average hospital charges within $\pm 2s$ of the least squares line?

⊘ **FCAT**

10.33 FCAT scores and poverty. Refer to the *Journal of Educational and Behavioral Statistics* (Spring 2004) study of scores on the Florida Comprehensive Assessment Test (FCAT), Exercise 10.20 (p. 614).

a. Consider the simple linear regression relating math score (y) to percentage (x) of students below the poverty level. Find and interpret the value of s for this regression.

b. Consider the simple linear regression relating reading score (y) to percentage (x) of students below the poverty level. Find and interpret the value of s for this regression.

c. Which dependent variable, math score or reading score, can be more accurately predicted by percentage (x) of students below the poverty level? Explain.

Applying the Concepts—Advanced

10.34 Life tests of cutting tools. To improve the quality of the output of any production process, it is necessary first to understand the capabilities of the process (Gitlow, *et al.*, *Quality Management: Tools and Methods for Improvement*, 1995). In a particular manufacturing process, the useful life of a cutting tool is related to the speed at which the tool is operated. The data in the table below were derived from life tests for the two different brands of cutting tools currently used in the production process. For which brand would you feel more confident in using the least squares line to predict useful life for a given cutting speed? Explain.

⊘ **CUTTOOLS**

Cutting Speed (meters per minute)	USEFUL LIFE (HOURS)	
	Brand A	Brand B
30	4.5	6.0
30	3.5	6.5
30	5.2	5.0
40	5.2	6.0
40	4.0	4.5
40	2.5	5.0
50	4.4	4.5
50	2.8	4.0
50	1.0	3.7
60	4.0	3.8
60	2.0	3.0
60	1.1	2.4
70	1.1	1.5
70	.5	2.0
70	3.0	1.0

10.5 Assessing the Utility of the Model: Making Inferences about the Slope β_1

Now that we have specified the probability distribution of ε and found an estimate of the variance σ^2, we are ready to make statistical inferences about the model's usefulness for predicting the response y. This is step 4 in our regression modeling procedure.

Refer again to the data of Table 10.1 and suppose the appliance store's sales revenue is *completely unrelated* to the advertising expenditure. What could be said about the values of β_0 and β_1 in the hypothesized probabilistic model

$$y = \beta_0 + \beta_1 x + \varepsilon$$

if x contributes no information for the prediction of y? The implication is that the mean of y—that is, the deterministic part of the model $E(y) = \beta_0 + \beta_1 x$—does not change as x changes. In the straight-line model, this means that the true slope, β_1, is equal to 0 (see Figure 10.9). Alternatively, if there is a positive linear relationship between x and y, then the slope β_1 will be positive. Therefore, to test the null hypothesis that the linear model contributes no information for the prediction of y against the alternative hypothesis that the slope is positive, we test

$$H_0: \beta_1 = 0 \text{ against } H_a: \beta_1 > 0$$

If the data support the alternative hypothesis, we will conclude that the slope is positive and that x does contribute information for the prediction of y using the straight-line model (although the true relationship between $E[y]$ and x could be more complex than a straight line). Thus, in effect, this is a test of the usefulness of the hypothesized model.

The appropriate test statistic is found by considering the sampling distribution of $\hat{\beta}_1$, the least squares estimator of the slope β_1, as shown in the following box.

FIGURE 10.9

Graph of the straight-line model when slope is zero, i.e., $y = \beta_0 + \epsilon$

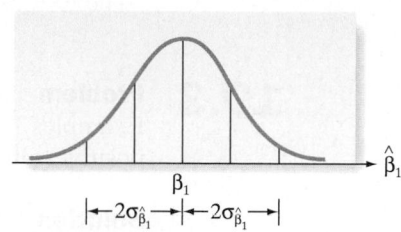

FIGURE 10.10

Sampling distribution of $\hat{\beta}_1$

Sampling Distribution of $\hat{\beta}_1$

If we make the four assumptions about ϵ (see Section 10.3), the sampling distribution of the least squares estimator $\hat{\beta}_1$ of the slope will be normal with mean β_1 (the true slope) and standard deviation

$$\sigma_{\hat{\beta}_1} = \frac{\sigma}{\sqrt{SS_{xx}}} \quad \text{(see Figure 10.10)}$$

We estimate $\sigma_{\hat{\beta}_1}$ by $s_{\hat{\beta}_1} = \dfrac{s}{\sqrt{SS_{xx}}}$ and refer to this quantity as the **estimated standard error of the least squares slope $\hat{\beta}_1$.**

Since σ is usually unknown, the appropriate test statistic is a t-statistic, formed as follows:

$$t = \frac{\hat{\beta}_1 - \text{Hypothesized value of } \beta_1}{s_{\hat{\beta}_1}} \qquad \text{where } s_{\hat{\beta}_1} = \frac{s}{\sqrt{SS_{xx}}}$$

Thus,

$$t = \frac{\hat{\beta}_1 - 0}{s/\sqrt{SS_{xx}}}$$

Note that we have substituted the estimator s for σ and then formed the estimated standard error $s_{\hat{\beta}_1}$ by dividing s by $\sqrt{SS_{xx}}$. The number of degrees of freedom associated with this t-statistic is the same as the number of degrees of freedom associated with s. Recall that this number is $(n - 2)$ df when the hypothesized model is a straight line (see Section 10.4). The setup of our test of the usefulness of the straight-line model is summarized in the boxes.

A Test of Model Utility: Simple Linear Regression

One-Tailed Test	Two-Tailed Test
$H_0: \beta_1 = 0$	$H_0: \beta_1 = 0$
$H_a: \beta_1 < 0 \ (\text{or } H_a: \beta_1 > 0)$	$H_a: \beta_1 \neq 0$

$$\text{Test statistic: } t = \frac{\hat{\beta}_1}{s_{\hat{\beta}_1}} = \frac{\hat{\beta}_1}{s/\sqrt{SS_{xx}}}$$

Rejection region: $t < -t_\alpha$	Rejection region: $|t| > t_{\alpha/2}$
(or $t > t_\alpha$ when $H_a: \beta_1 > 0$)	

where t_α and $t_{\alpha/2}$ are based on $(n - 2)$ degrees of freedom

> **Conditions Required for a Valid Test: Simple Linear Regression**
>
> The four assumptions about ε listed in Section 10.3.

EXAMPLE 10.3
Testing the Slope, β_1, of the Sales–Advertising Line

Problem   Refer to the simple linear regression analysis of the sales–advertising data, Examples 10.1 and 10.2. Conduct a test (at $\alpha = .05$) to determine if sales revenue (y) is positively linearly related to advertising expenditure (x).

Solution   As stated previously, we want to test $H_0: \beta_1 = 0$ against $H_a: \beta_1 > 0$. For this example, $n = 5$. Thus t will be based on $n - 2 = 3$ df and the rejection region (at $\alpha = .05$) will be

$$t > t_{.05} = 2.353$$

We previously calculated $\hat{\beta}_1 = .7$, $s = .61$, and $SS_{xx} = 10$. Thus, the test statistic is

$$t = \frac{\hat{\beta}_1}{s/\sqrt{SS_{xx}}} = \frac{.7}{.61/\sqrt{10}} = \frac{.7}{.19} = 3.7$$

Since this calculated t-value falls in the rejection region (see Figure 10.11), we reject the null hypothesis and conclude that the slope β_1 is greater than 0. The sample evidence indicates that advertising expenditure x is positively linearly related to sales revenue y.

[*Note:* We can reach the same conclusion by using the observed significance level (p-value) of the test from a computer printout. The MINITAB printout for the advertising–sales example is reproduced in Figure 10.12. The test statistic and *two-tailed* p-value are highlighted on the printout. The appropriate *one-tailed* p-value is obtained by dividing the value shown on the printout (.035) by 2; that is, one-tailed

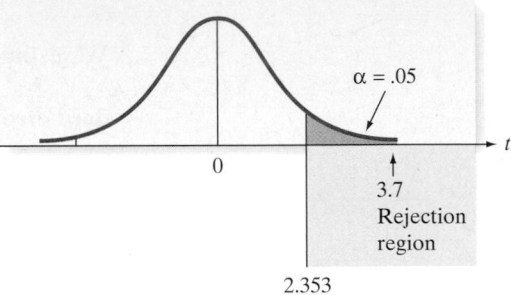

FIGURE 10.11
Rejection region and calculated t-value for testing $H_0: \beta_1 = 0$ versus $H_a: \beta_1 \neq 0$

p-value = (two-tailed p-value)/2 = .035/2 = .0175. (See the next box.) Since the p-value is smaller than $\alpha = .05$, we will reject H_0.]

Regression Analysis: SALES_Y versus ADVEXP_X

```
The regression equation is
SALES_Y = - 0.100 + 0.700 ADVEXP_X


Predictor      Coef   SE Coef      T       P
Constant    -0.1000    0.6351   -0.16   0.885
ADVEXP_X     0.7000    0.1915    3.66   0.035


S = 0.605530    R-Sq = 81.7%    R-Sq(adj) = 75.6%


Analysis of Variance

Source          DF      SS       MS      F      P
Regression       1   4.9000   4.9000   13.36  0.035
Residual Error   3   1.1000   0.3667
Total            4   6.0000
```

FIGURE 10.12
MINITAB printout for the advertising–sales regression

Look Back What conclusion can be drawn if the calculated t-value does not fall in the rejection region or if the observed significance level of the test exceeds α? We know from previous discussions of the philosophy of hypothesis testing that such a t-value does *not* lead us to accept the null hypothesis—that is, we do not conclude that $\beta_1 = 0$. Additional data might indicate that β_1 differs from 0, or a more complex relationship may exist between x and y, requiring the fitting of a model other than the straight-line model. We discuss several such models in Chapter 11.

Now Work Exercise 10.39

Interpreting p-Values for β Coefficients in Regression

Almost all statistical computer software packages report a *two-tailed p*-value for each of the β parameters in the regression model. For example, in simple linear regression, the p-value for the two-tailed test $H_0: \beta_1 = 0$ versus $H_a: \beta_1 \neq 0$ is given on the printout. If you want to conduct a *one-tailed* test of hypothesis, you will need to adjust the p-value reported on the printout as follows:

$$Upper\text{-}tailed\ test\ (H_a: \beta_1 > 0): \quad p\text{-value} = \begin{cases} p/2 & \text{if } t > 0 \\ 1 - p/2 & \text{if } t < 0 \end{cases}$$

$$Lower\text{-}tailed\ test\ (H_a: \beta_1 < 0): \quad p\text{-value} = \begin{cases} p/2 & \text{if } t < 0 \\ 1 - p/2 & \text{if } t > 0 \end{cases}$$

where p is the p-value reported on the printout and t is the value of the test statistic.

Another way to make inferences about the slope β_1 is to estimate it using a confidence interval. This interval is formed as shown in the next box.

A $100(1 - \alpha)\%$ Confidence Interval for the Simple Linear Regression Slope β_1

$$\hat{\beta}_1 \pm t_{\alpha/2} s_{\hat{\beta}_1}$$

where the estimated standard error $\hat{\beta}_1$ is calculated by

$$s_{\hat{\beta}_1} = \frac{s}{\sqrt{SS_{xx}}}$$

and $t_{\alpha/2}$ is based on $(n - 2)$ degrees of freedom.

Conditions Required for a Valid Confidence Interval: Simple Linear Regression

The four assumptions about ε listed in Section 10.3.

In the advertising–sales example, $t_{\alpha/2}$ is based on $(n - 2) = 3$ degrees of freedom. For $\alpha = .05, t_{.025} = 3.182$. Therefore, a 95% confidence interval for the slope β_1, the expected change in sales revenue for a \$100 increase in advertising expenditure, is

$$\hat{\beta}_1 \pm (t_{.025}) s_{\hat{\beta}_1} = .7 \pm 3.182\left(\frac{s}{\sqrt{SS_{xx}}}\right) = .7 \pm 3.182\left(\frac{.61}{\sqrt{10}}\right) = .7 \pm .61$$

Thus, the interval estimate of the slope parameter β_1 is .09 to 1.31. [*Note*: This interval can also be obtained using statistical software and is highlighted on the SPSS printout, Figure 10.13.] In terms of this example, the implication is that we can be 95% confident

FIGURE 10.13

SPSS printout with 95% confidence intervals for the sales–advertising regression βs

Coefficients[a]

Model		Unstandardized Coefficients		Standardized Coefficients	t	Sig.	95% Confidence Interval for B	
		B	Std. Error	Beta			Lower Bound	Upper Bound
1	(Constant)	-.100	.635		-.157	.885	-2.121	1.921
	ADVEXP_X	.700	.191	.904	3.656	.035	.091	1.309

a. Dependent Variable: SALES_Y

that the *true* mean increase in monthly sales revenue per additional $100 of advertising expenditure is between $90 and $1,310. This inference is meaningful only over the sampled range of x—that is, from $100 to $500 of advertising expenditures.

> **Now Work Exercise 10.37c**

Since all the values in this interval are positive, it appears that β_1 is positive and that the mean of y, $E(y)$, increases as x increases. However, the rather large width of the confidence interval reflects the small number of data points (and, consequently, a lack of information) in the experiment. Particularly bothersome is the fact that the lower end of the confidence interval implies that we are not even recovering our additional expenditure, since a $100 increase in advertising may produce as little as a $90 increase in mean sales. If we wish to tighten this interval, we need to increase the sample size.

STATISTICS IN ACTION REVISITED

Assessing How Well the Straight-Line Regression Model Fits the Work-Life Balance Data

In the previous Statistics in Action Revisited, we fit the straight-line model, $E(y) = \beta_0 + \beta_1 x$, where x = average number of hours worked per week and y = work-life balance scale score for each MBA alumnus. The SPSS regression printout for the analysis is shown in Figure SIA10.3. The two-tailed p-value for testing the null hypothesis, H_0: $\beta_1 = 0$ (highlighted on the printout) is p-value ≈ 0. Consequently, for any reasonably chosen value of α, there is sufficient evidence to reject H_0 and conclude that work-life balance score is linearly related to average number of hours worked per week.

This result seemingly contradicts the inference drawn from a scatterplot of the data shown in Figure

Model Summary

Model	R	R Square	Adjusted R Square	Std. Error of the Estimate
1	.265[a]	.070	.070	12.28455

a. Predictors: (Constant), HOURS

ANOVA[b]

Model		Sum of Squares	df	Mean Square	F	Sig.
1	Regression	23803.05	1	23803.051	157.730	.000[a]
	Residual	314647.5	2085	150.910		
	Total	338450.5	2086			

a. Predictors: (Constant), HOURS
b. Dependent Variable: WLBSCORE

Coefficients[a]

Model		Unstandardized Coefficients		Standardized Coefficients	t	Sig.	95% Confidence Interval for B	
		B	Std. Error	Beta			Lower Bound	Upper Bound
1	(Constant)	62.499	1.414		44.215	.000	59.726	65.271
	HOURS	-.347	.028	-.265	-12.559	.000	-.401	-.293

a. Dependent Variable: WLBSCORE

Figure SIA10.3
SPSS simple linear regression for work-life balance data

SIA10.1 (p. 608). Recall that the variation of the data points around the least squares line is very large, implying that number of hours worked per week (x) will not be a very good predictor of work-life balance score (y). This apparent contradiction is due to the extremely large sample size ($n = 2,087$) for the data. The test of hypothesis for the slope will likely result in a rejection of the null hypothesis for extremely large n values, even in cases where there is a very weak linear relationship between y and x. We can gain further insight into this phenomenon by examining two other statistics: the 95% confidence interval for the slope, β_1, and the estimated standard deviation of the model, s.

The 95% confidence for β_1, highlighted on the SPSS printout, is $(-.401, -.293)$. With 95% confidence, we can state that for every 1-hour increase in number of weekly hours worked, an MBA alumnus' work-life balance score will decrease between .29 and

.40 point—that is, the decrease will not even be a half of a point! What about a 10-hour increase in number of hours worked? Multiplying the endpoints of the interval by 10, we see that this large increase in x only leads to a decrease in work-life balance score between 2.9 and 4.0 points.

The model standard deviation, also highlighted on the SPSS printout, is $s = 12.3$. Our interpretation is that the straight-line model can predict work-life balance score (y) to within about $2s = 24.6$ points of its true value. This is a potentially large error of prediction, considering that the work-life balance scale ranges from 0 to 100 points.

Although the hypothesis test for the slope is *statistically significant*, both the confidence interval for the slope and the model standard deviation indicate the model may not be *practically significant* (i.e., not of value in actual practice).

Exercises 10.35–10.50

Learning the Mechanics

10.35 Construct both a 95% and a 90% confidence interval for β_1 for each of the following cases:
   a. $\hat{\beta}_1 = 31, s = 3, SS_{xx} = 35, n = 10$
   b. $\hat{\beta}_1 = 64, SSE = 1,960, SS_{xx} = 30, n = 14$
   c. $\hat{\beta}_1 = -8.4, SSE = 146, SS_{xx} = 64, n = 20$

10.36 Consider the following pairs of observations:

x	1	4	3	2	5	6	0
y	1	3	3	1	4	7	2

   a. Construct a scattergram for the data.
   b. Use the method of least squares to fit a straight line to the seven data points in the table.
   c. Plot the least squares line on your scattergram of part **a.**
   d. Specify the null and alternative hypotheses you would use to test whether the data provide sufficient evidence to indicate that x contributes information for the (linear) prediction of y.
   e. What is the test statistic that should be used in conducting the hypothesis test of part **d?** Specify the degrees of freedom associated with the test statistic.
   f. Conduct the hypothesis test of part **d** using $\alpha = .05$.

10.37 Refer to Exercise 10.36. Construct an 80% and a 98% confidence interval for β_1.

10.38 Do the accompanying data provide sufficient evidence to conclude that a straight line is useful for characterizing the relationship between x and y?

x	4	2	4	3	2	4
y	1	6	5	3	2	4

Applying the Concepts—Basic

DIAMONDS

10.39 Characteristics of diamonds sold at retail. Refer to the
NW MINITAB simple linear regression analysis relating

y = asking price (dollars) to x = number of carats for diamonds sold on the open market, Exercise 10.14 (p. 611).
   a. Give the null and alternative hypotheses for determining whether a positive linear relationship exists between y and x.
   b. Locate the p-value of the test on the MINITAB printout. Interpret the result if $\alpha = .01$.
   c. Find a 99% confidence interval for the slope, β_1. Interpret the result.

SATSCORES

10.40 State SAT Scores. Refer to the SPSS simple linear regression relating y = average state SAT score in 2005 with x = average state SAT score in 1990, Exercise 10.15 (p. 611).
   a. Give the null and alternative hypotheses for determining whether a positive linear relationship exists between y and x.
   b. Locate the p-value of the test on the SPSS printout. Interpret the result if $\alpha = .05$.
   c. Find a 95% confidence interval for the slope, β_1. Interpret the result.

DOWDRUG

10.41 Drug controlled-release rate study. Refer to the simple linear regression analysis relating y = drug release rate to x = surface area-to-volume, Exercise 10.17 (p. 612). Use the results of the regression to form a 90% confidence interval the slope, β_1. Interpret the result.

OJUICE

10.42 Sweetness of orange juice. Refer to the simple linear regression relating y = sweetness index of an orange juice sample with x = amount of water soluble pectin, Exercise 10.18 (p. 613). Use the results of the regression to form a 95% confidence interval the slope, β_1. Interpret the result.

Applying the Concepts—Intermediate

BSCHOOL

10.43 Survey of the top business schools. Refer to the *Wall Street Journal* (Sep. 25, 2005) Business School Survey, Exercise

10.22 (p. 614). If you pay more in tuition to go to a top business school, will it necessarily result in a higher probability of a job offer upon graduation? Let y = percentage of graduates with job offers and x = tuition cost, then fit the simple linear model, $E(y) = \beta_0 + \beta_1 x$, to the data in the **BSCHOOL** file. Is there sufficient evidence (at $\alpha = .10$) of a positive linear relationship between y and x?

LIQUIDSPILL

10.44 Spreading rate of spilled liquid. Refer to the *Chemical Engineering Progress* (Jan. 2005) study of the rate at which a spilled volatile liquid will spread across a surface, Exercise 10.23 (p. 614). For the data in the **LIQUIDSPILL** file, let y = mass of the spill and x = elapsed time of the spill.
  a. Is there sufficient evidence (at $\alpha = .05$) to indicate that the mass of the spill tends to diminish linearly as time increases?
  b. Give an interval estimate (with 95% confidence) of the decrease in spill mass for each minute of elapsed time.

10.45 Married tennis players and their rankings. *Tennis* magazine (Feb. 2000) claims that "tennis players who tie the knot often see their games unravel." The table below lists a sample of former players and their rankings on their wedding days and on their first anniversaries.
  a. Construct a scattergram for these data. Does it tend to support or refute the magazine's claim? Justify your answer.
  b. Use the method of least squares to construct a model of the relationship between wedding day ranking (x) and first anniversary ranking (y).
  c. Does the linear model you developed in part **b** contribute information for predicting players' rankings on their first anniversaries? Test at $\alpha = .05$.

TENLOVE

Player	Ranking on Wedding Day	Ranking on First Anniversary
Arthur Ashe	12	130
Jonathan Stark	67	165
Richey Reneberg	28	97
Paul Haarhuis	28	73
Richard Fromberg	40	79
Byron Black	44	77
Sabine Appelmans	16	49
Petr Korda	7	11
Dominique Van Roost	43	46
Ivan Lendl	1	3
John McEnroe	7	9
Stefan Edberg	2	3
Chris Evert	4	4
Mats Wilander	3	3
Sandrine Testud	14	12
Zina Garrison	6	4
Yevgeny Kafelnikov	8	4
Boris Becker	11	3
Michael Stich	15	6
Julie Halard-Decugis	32	15
Todd Woodbridge	71	27
Jason Stoltenberg	82	31

Source: Tennis, Feb. 2000, p. 14.

  d. If there were no changes whatsoever in the rankings of the sample of players after getting married, what would the true values of β_0 and β_1 be?

10.46 Do New Jersey banks serve minority communities? Financial institutions have a legal and social responsibility to serve all communities. Do banks adequately serve both inner-city and suburban neighborhoods, both poor and wealthy communities? In New Jersey, banks have been charged with withdrawing from urban areas with a high percentage of minorities. To examine this charge, a regional New Jersey newspaper, the *Asbury Park Press*, compiled county by county data on the number (y) of people in each county per branch bank in the county and the percentage (x) of the population in each county that is minority. These data for each of New Jersey's 21 counties are provided in the table below.

NJBANKS

County	Number of People per Bank Branch	Percentage of Minority Population
Atlantic	3,073	23.3
Bergen	2,095	13.0
Burlington	2,905	17.8
Camden	3,330	23.4
Cape May	1,321	7.3
Cumberland	2,557	26.5
Essex	3,474	48.8
Gloucester	3,068	10.7
Hudson	3,683	33.2
Hunterdon	1,998	3.7
Mercer	2,607	24.9
Middlesex	3,154	18.1
Monmouth	2,609	12.6
Morris	2,253	8.2
Ocean	2,317	4.7
Passaic	3,307	28.1
Salem	2,511	16.7
Somerset	2,333	12.0
Sussex	2,568	2.4
Union	3,048	25.6
Warren	2,349	2.8

Source: D'Ambrosio, P., and Chambers, S. "No Checks and Balances." *Asbury Park Press,* September 10, 1995.

  a. Plot the data in a scattergram. What pattern, if any, does the plot reveal?
  b. Consider the linear model $E(y) = \beta_0 + \beta_1 x$. If, in fact, the charge against the New Jersey banks is true, then an increase in the percentage of minorities (x) will lead to a decrease in the number of bank branches in a county and therefore will result in an increase in the number of people (y) per branch. Will the value of β_1 be positive or negative in this situation?
  c. Do these data support or refute the charge made against the New Jersey banking community? Test using $\alpha = .01$.

10.47 Predicting water erosion of soils. The U.S. Department of Agriculture has developed and adopted the Universal Soil Loss Equation (USLE) for predicting water erosion of soils. In geographical areas where runoff from melting snow is common, the USLE requires an accurate estimate of snowmelt runoff erosion. An article in the *Journal of Soil and Water Conservation* (Mar.–Apr. 1995) used sim-

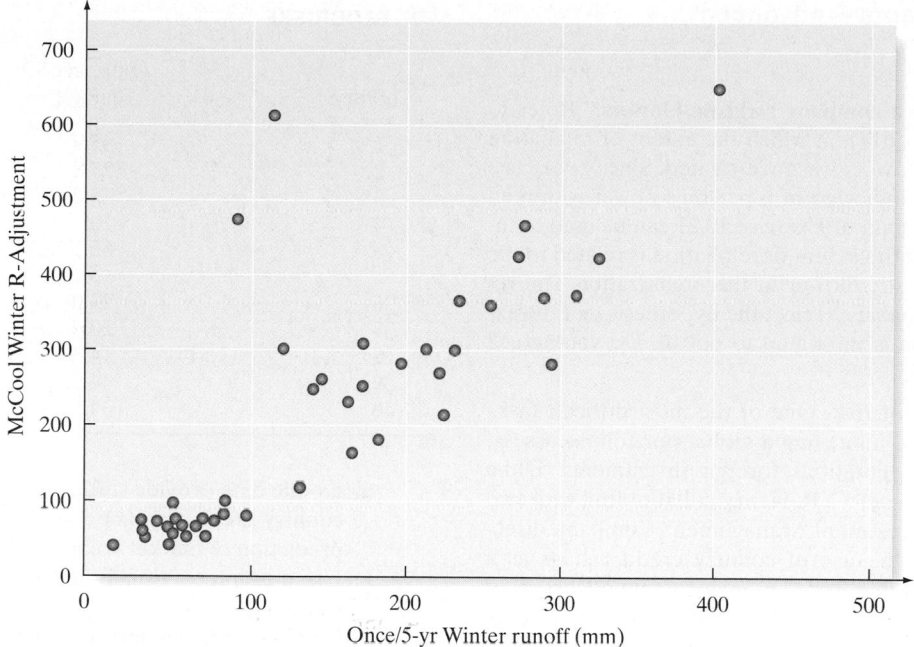

McCool Winter R-Adjustment (y-axis)

Once/5-yr Winter runoff (mm) (x-axis)

Scattergram for Exercise 10.47

ple linear regression to develop a snowmelt erosion index. Data for 54 climatological stations in Canada were used to model the McCool winter-adjusted rainfall erosivity index, y, as a straight-line function of the once-in-5-year snowmelt runoff amount, x (measured in millimeters).

a. The data points are plotted in the scattergram shown above. Is there visual evidence of a linear trend?

b. The data for seven stations were removed from the analysis due to lack of snowfall during the study period. Why is this strategy advisable?

c. The simple linear regression on the remaining $n - 47$ data points yielded the following results:

$$\hat{y} = -6.72 + 1.39x; \quad s_{\hat{\beta}_1} = .06$$

Use this information to construct a 90% confidence interval for β_1.

d. Interpret the interval, part **c.**

10.48 Evaluating managerial success. H. Mintzberg's classic book *The Nature of Managerial Work* (1973) identified the roles found in all managerial jobs. An observational study of 19 managers from a medium-sized manufacturing plant extended Mintzberg's work by investigating which activities *successful* managers actually perform (*Journal of Applied Behavioral Science,* Aug. 1985). To measure success, the researchers devised an index based on the manager's length of time in the organization and his or her level within the firm; the higher the index, the more successful the manager. The next table presents data (which are representative of the data collected by the researchers) that can be used to determine whether managerial success is related to the extensiveness of a manager's network-building interactions with people outside the manager's work unit. Such interactions include phone and face-to-face meetings with customers and suppliers, attending outside meetings, and doing public relations work.

MANAGERS

Manager	Manager Success Index, y	Number of Interactions with Outsiders, x
1	40	12
2	73	71
3	95	70
4	60	81
5	81	43
6	27	50
7	53	42
8	66	18
9	25	35
10	63	82
11	70	20
12	47	81
13	80	40
14	51	33
15	32	45
16	50	10
17	52	65
18	30	20
19	42	21

a. Construct a scattergram for the data.

b. Find the prediction equation for managerial success.

c. Find s for your prediction equation. Interpret the standard deviation s in the context of this problem.

d. Plot the least squares line on your scattergram of part **a.** Does it appear that the number of interactions with outsiders contributes information for the prediction of managerial success? Explain.

e. Conduct a formal statistical hypothesis test to answer the question posed in part **d.** Use $\alpha = .05$.

f. Construct a 95% confidence interval for β_1. Interpret the interval in the context of the problem.

Applying the Concepts—Advanced

RETAL

10.49 Retaliation against company "whistle-blowers." Refer to Exercise 10.21 (p. 614), in which the extent of retaliation against whistle-blowers was investigated. Since salary is a reasonably good indicator of a person's power within an organization, the data of Exercise 10.21 can be used to investigate whether the extent of retaliation is related to the power of the whistle-blower in the organization. The researchers were unable to reject the hypothesis that the extent of retaliation is unrelated to power. Do you agree? Test using $\alpha = .05$.

10.50 Foreign investment risk. One of the most difficult tasks of developing and managing a global portfolio is assessing the risks of potential foreign investments. Duke University researcher C. R. Henry collaborated with two First Chicago Investment Management Company directors to examine the use of country credit ratings as a means of evaluating foreign investments (*Journal of Portfolio Management,* Winter 1995). To be effective, such a measure should help explain and predict the volatility of the foreign market in question. Data on annualized risk (y) and average credit rating (x) for 40 fictitious countries (based on the study results) are saved in the **GLOBRISKF** file. (The first and last five countries are shown in the table.)

GLOBRISKF

Country	Annualized Risk (%)	Average Credit Rating
1	85.9	30.7
2	25.8	77.1
3	25.2	82.7
4	20.9	77.3
5	63.7	35.1
⋮	⋮	⋮
36	73.0	31.5
37	20.7	86.5
38	14.3	95.3
39	44.9	43.9
40	34.5	23.4

a. Do the data provide sufficient evidence to conclude that country credit risk (x) contributes information for the prediction of market volatility (y)?

b. Use a graph to visually locate any unusual data points (outliers).

c. Eliminate the outlier(s), part **b**, from the data set and rerun the simple linear regression analysis. Note any dramatic changes in the results.

10.6 The Coefficient of Correlation

Recall (from optional Section 2.10) that a **bivariate relationship** describes a relationship between two variables, x and y. Scattergrams are used to graphically describe a bivariate relationship. In this section we will discuss the concept of **correlation** and show how it can be used to measure the linear relationship between two variables x and y. A numerical descriptive measure of the linear association between x and y is provided by the *coefficient of correlation, r.*

Definition 10.2

The **coefficient of correlation,** * r, is a measure of the strength of the *linear* relationship between two variables x and y. It is computed (for a sample of n measurements on x and y) as follows:

$$r = \frac{SS_{xy}}{\sqrt{SS_{xx}SS_{yy}}}$$

Note that the computational formula for the correlation coefficient r given in Definition 10.2 involves the same quantities that were used in computing the least squares prediction equation. In fact, since the numerators of the expressions for $\hat{\beta}_1$ and r are identical, you can see that $r = 0$ when $\hat{\beta}_1 = 0$ (the case where x contributes no information for the prediction of y) and that r is positive when the slope is positive and negative when the slope is negative. Unlike $\hat{\beta}_1$, the correlation coefficient r is *scaleless* and assumes a value between -1 and $+1$, regardless of the units of x and y.

A value of r near or equal to 0 implies little or no linear relationship between y and x. In contrast, the closer r comes to 1 or -1, the stronger the linear relationship between

*The value of r is often called the *Pearson correlation coefficient* to honor its developer, Karl Pearson. (See Biography, p. 556).

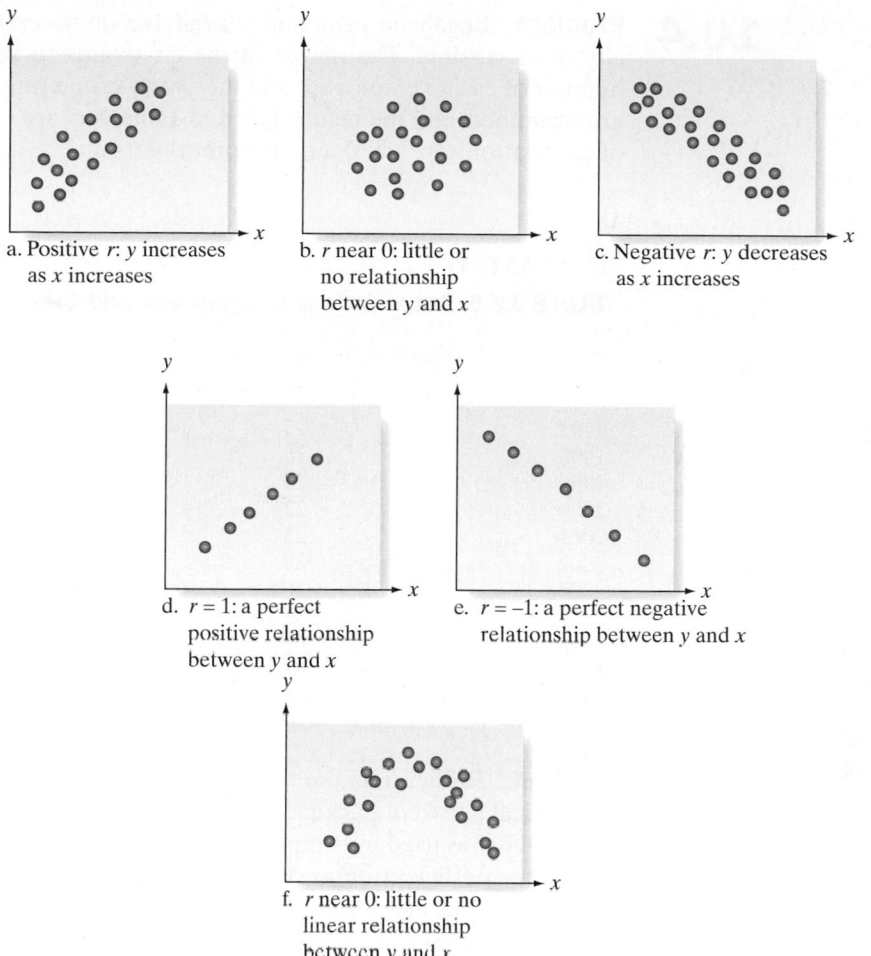

FIGURE 10.14

Values of r and their implications

a. Positive r: y increases as x increases

b. r near 0: little or no relationship between y and x

c. Negative r: y decreases as x increases

d. $r = 1$: a perfect positive relationship between y and x

e. $r = -1$: a perfect negative relationship between y and x

f. r near 0: little or no linear relationship between y and x

y and x. And if $r = 1$ or $r = -1$, all the sample points fall exactly on the least squares line. Positive values of r imply a positive linear relationship between y and x; that is, y increases as x increases. Negative values of r imply a negative linear relationship between y and x; that is, y decreases as x increases. Each of these situations is portrayed in Figure 10.14.

Now Work Exercise 10.52

We demonstrate how to calculate the coefficient of correlation r using the data in Table 10.1 for the advertising–sales example. The quantities needed to calculate r are SS_{xy}, SS_{xx}, and SS_{yy}. The first two quantities have been calculated previously and are repeated here for convenience:

$$SS_{xy} = 7 \qquad SS_{xx} = 10 \qquad SS_{yy} = \sum y^2 - \frac{\left(\sum y\right)^2}{n}$$

$$= 26 - \frac{(10)^2}{5} = 26 - 20 = 6$$

We now find the coefficient of correlation:

$$r = \frac{SS_{xy}}{\sqrt{SS_{xx}SS_{yy}}} = \frac{7}{\sqrt{(10)(6)}} = \frac{7}{\sqrt{60}} = .904$$

The fact that r is positive and near 1 in value indicates that the sales revenue y tends to increase as advertising expenditure x increases—*for this sample of five months.* This is the same conclusion we reached when we found the calculated value of the least squares slope to be positive.

EXAMPLE 10.4

Relating Crime Rate and Casino Employment Using the Correlation Coefficient

Problem Legalized gambling is available on several riverboat casinos operated by a city in Mississippi. The mayor of the city wants to know the correlation between the number of casino employees and the yearly crime rate. The records for the past 10 years are examined, and the results listed in Table 10.5 are obtained. Calculate the coefficient of correlation r for the data. Interpret the result.

 CASINO

TABLE 10.5 Data on Casino Employees and Crime Rate, Example 10.4

Year	Number of Casino Employees, x (thousands)	Crime Rate, y (number of crimes per 1,000 population)
1997	15	1.35
1998	18	1.63
1999	24	2.33
2000	22	2.41
2001	25	2.63
2002	29	2.93
2003	30	3.41
2004	32	3.26
2005	35	3.63
2006	38	4.15

Solution Rather than use the computing formula given in Definition 10.2, we resort to a statistical software package. The data of Table 10.5 were entered into a computer and MINITAB was used to compute r. The MINITAB printout is shown in Figure 10.15.

The coefficient of correlation, highlighted at the top on the printout, is $r = .987$. Thus, the size of the casino workforce and crime rate in this city are very highly correlated—at least over the past 10 years. The implication is that a strong positive linear relationship exists between these variables (see the scatterplot at the bottom of Figure 10.15). We must be careful, however, not to jump to any unwarranted conclusions. For instance, the mayor may be tempted to conclude that hiring more casino workers next

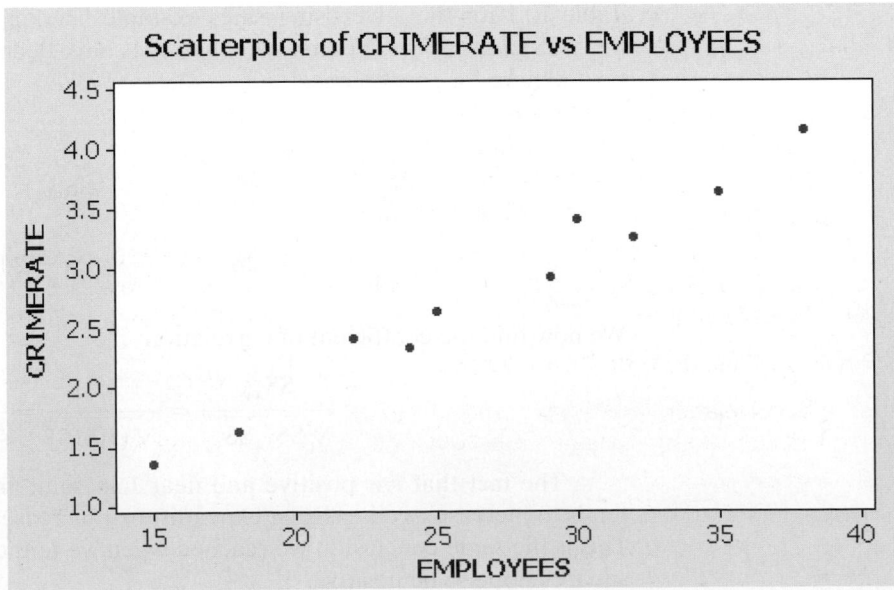

Correlations: EMPLOYEES, CRIMERAT

```
Pearson correlation of EMPLOYEES and CRIMERAT = 0.987
P-Value = 0.000
```

FIGURE 10.15
MINITAB correlation printout for Example 10.4

year will increase the crime rate—that is, that there is a *causal relationship* between the two variables. However, high correlation does not imply causality. The fact is, many things have probably contributed both to the increase in the casino workforce and to the increase in crime rate. The city's tourist trade has undoubtedly grown since legalizing riverboat casinos, and it is likely that the casinos have expanded both in services offered and in number. *We cannot infer a causal relationship on the basis of high sample correlation. When a high correlation is observed in the sample data, the only safe conclusion is that a linear trend may exist between x and y.*

Look Back Another variable, such as the increase in tourism, may be the underlying cause of the high correlation between x and y.

Now Work Exercise 10.60 a,b

Warning

When using the sample correlation coefficient, r, to infer the nature of the relationship between x and y, two caveats exist: (1) A *high correlation* does not necessarily imply that a causal relationship exists between x and y—only that a linear trend may exist; (2) a *low correlation* does not necessarily imply that x and y are unrelated—only that x and y are not strongly linearly related.

Keep in mind that the correlation coefficient r measures the linear correlation between x values and y values in the sample, and a similar linear coefficient of correlation exists for the population from which the data points were selected. The **population correlation coefficient** is denoted by the symbol ρ (rho). As you might expect, ρ is estimated by the corresponding sample statistic, r. Or, instead of estimating ρ, we might want to test the null hypothesis $H_0: \rho = 0$ against $H_a: \rho \neq 0$—that is, we can test the hypothesis that x contributes no information for the prediction of y by using the straight-line model against the alternative that the two variables are at least linearly related.

However, we already performed this *identical* test in Section 10.5 when we tested $H_0: \beta_1 = 0$ against $H_a: \beta_1 \neq 0$—that is, the null hypothesis $H_0: \rho = 0$ is equivalent to the hypothesis $H_0: \beta_1 = 0$.* When we tested the null hypothesis $H_0: \beta_1 = 0$ in connection with the advertising–sales example, the data led to a rejection of the null hypothesis at the $\alpha = .05$ level. This rejection implies that the null hypothesis of a 0 linear correlation

---

ACTIVITY 10.2: *Keep the Change:* Correlation Coefficients

In this activity, you will use data collected in Activity 1.1, *Keep the Change: Collecting Data* (p. 16) and the results from Activity 10.1, *Keep the Change: Least Squares Models* on (p. 610) to study the strength of a linear relationship.

1. For each of the least squares models in Exercises 1 and 4 in the Activity on page 610, calculate the corresponding correlation coefficient. Do these values support your conclusion about which model is more useful? Explain.

2. For each purchase in your original data set *Purchase Totals*, form the ordered pair

   (Purchase Total, Amount Transferred)

Calculate the correlation coefficient and discuss the strength of the linear relationship between the

two variables. Explain why you might expect the slope of the corresponding least squares line to be close to zero. Find the least squares model and comment on its usefulness. Does the model produce estimated values that are meaningless for large purchase totals? Explain.

3. For each student in your class, form an ordered pair

   (Sum of Amounts Transferred, Bank Matching)

Calculate the correlation coefficient. How strong is the linear relationship between the two variables? Find the least squares model. Is the slope $\hat{\beta}_1$ approximately 13 and the y-intercept $\hat{\beta}_0$ approximately 0? Explain why the line should have this slope and y-intercept. How good are the estimates given by the model in this situation?

---

*The correlation test statistic that is equivalent to $t = \hat{\beta}_1/s_{\hat{\beta}_1}$ is $t = \dfrac{r}{\sqrt{(1 - r^2)/(n - 2)}}$.

between the two variables (sales revenue and advertising expenditure) can also be rejected at the $\alpha = .05$ level. The only real difference between the least squares slope $\hat{\beta}_1$ and the coefficient of correlation r is the measurement scale. Therefore, the information they provide about the usefulness of the least squares model is to some extent redundant. For this reason, we will use the slope to make inferences about the existence of a positive or negative linear relationship between two variables.

10.7 The Coefficient of Determination

Another way to measure the usefulness of the model is to measure the contribution of x in predicting y. To accomplish this, we calculate how much the errors of prediction of y were reduced by using the information provided by x. To illustrate, consider the sample shown in the scattergram of Figure 10.16(a). If we assume that x contributes no information for the prediction of y, the best prediction for a value of y is the sample mean $\bar{y}$, which is shown as the horizontal line in Figure 10.16(b). The vertical line segments in Figure 10.16(b) are the deviations of the points about the mean $\bar{y}$. Note that the sum of squares of deviations for the prediction equation $\hat{y} = \bar{y}$ is

$$SS_{yy} = \sum (y_i - \bar{y})^2$$

Now suppose you fit a least squares line to the same set of data and locate the deviations of the points about the line as shown in Figure 10.16(c). Compare the deviations about the prediction lines in Figures 10.16(b) and 10.16(c). You can see that

1. If x contributes little or no information for the prediction of y, the sums of squares of deviations for the two lines,

a. Scattergram of data

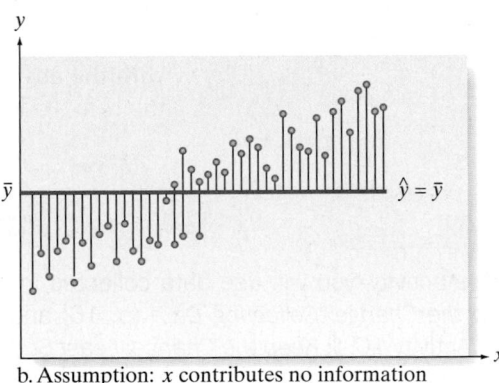

b. Assumption: x contributes no information for predicting y, $\hat{y} = \bar{y}$

c. Assumption: x contributes information for predicting y, $\hat{y} = \hat{\beta}_0 + \hat{\beta}_1 x$

FIGURE 10.16

A comparison of the sum of squares of deviations for two models

$$SS_{yy} = \sum(y_i - \bar{y})^2 \quad \text{and} \quad SSE = \sum(y_i - \hat{y}_i)^2$$

will be nearly equal.

2. If x does contribute information for the prediction of y, the SSE will be smaller than SS_{yy}. In fact, if all the points fall on the least squares line, then SSE $= 0$.

Then the reduction in the sum of squares of deviations that can be attributed to x, expressed as a proportion of SS_{yy}, is

$$\frac{SS_{yy} - SSE}{SS_{yy}}$$

Note that SS_{yy} is the "total sample variation" of the observations around the mean $\bar{y}$ and that SSE is the remaining "unexplained sample variability" after fitting the line $\hat{y}$. Thus, the difference $(SS_{yy} - SSE)$ is the "explained sample variability" attributable to the linear relationship with x. Then a verbal description of the proportion is

$$\frac{SS_{yy} - SSE}{SS_{yy}} = \frac{\text{Explained sample variability}}{\text{Total sample variability}}$$

$$= \text{Proportion of total sample variability explained by the linear relationship}$$

In simple linear regression, it can be shown that this proportion—called the *coefficient of determination*—is equal to the square of the simple linear coefficient of correlation r.

Definition 10.3

The **coefficient of determination** is

$$r^2 = \frac{SS_{yy} - SSE}{SS_{yy}} = 1 - \frac{SSE}{SS_{yy}}$$

It represents the proportion of the total sample variability around $\bar{y}$ that is explained by the linear relationship between y and x. (In simple linear regression, it may also be computed as the square of the coefficient of correlation r.)

Note that r^2 is always between 0 and 1, because r is between -1 and $+1$. Thus, an r^2 of .60 means that the sum of squares of deviations of the y values about their predicted values has been reduced 60% by the use of the least squares equation $\hat{y}$, instead of $\bar{y}$, to predict y.

EXAMPLE 10.5

Obtaining the Value of r^2 for the Sales-Appraisal Data

Problem Calculate the coefficient of determination for the advertising–sales example. The data are repeated in Table 10.6 for convenience. Interpret the result.

Solution From previous calculations,

$$SS_{yy} = 6 \quad \text{and} \quad SSE = \sum(y - \hat{y})^2 = 1.10$$

Then, from Definition 10.3, the coefficient of determination is given by

$$r^2 = \frac{SS_{yy} - SSE}{SS_{yy}} = \frac{6.0 - 1.1}{6.0} = \frac{4.9}{6.0} = .82$$

ADSALES

TABLE 10.6 Advertising Expenditure Sales Revenue Data

Advertising Expenditure, x ($100s)	Sales Revenue, y ($1,000s)
1	1
2	1
3	2
4	2
5	4

Model Summary

Model	R	R Square	Adjusted R Square	Std. Error of the Estimate
1	.904ª	.817	.756	.606

a. Predictors: (Constant), ADVEXP_X

FIGURE 10.17
Portion of SPSS printout for advertising–sales regression

Another way to compute r^2 is to recall (Section 10.6) that $r = .904$. Then we have $r^2 = (.904)^2 = .82$. A third way to obtain r^2 is from a computer printout. This value is highlighted on the SPSS printout reproduced in Figure 10.17. Our interpretation is as follows: We know that using advertising expenditure, x, to predict y with the least squares line

$$\hat{y} = -.1 + .7x$$

accounts for 82% of the total sum of squares of deviations of the five sample y values about their mean. Or, stated another way, 82% of the sample variation in sales revenue (y) can be "explained" by using advertising expenditure (x) in a straight-line model.

Now Work Exercise 10.56a ─── ■

> **Practical Interpretation of the Coefficient of Determination, r^2**
>
> About $100(r^2)\%$ of the sample variation in y (measured by the total sum of squares of deviations of the sample y values about their mean $\bar{y}$) can be explained by (or attributed to) using x to predict y in the straight-line model.

STATISTICS IN ACTION REVISITED

Using the Coefficient of Correlation and Coefficient of Determination to Assess the Work-Life Balance Data

In the previous Statistics in Action Revisited (p. 624), we discovered that an MBA alumnus' average number of hours worked per week (x) was statistically useful, but not practically useful, for predicting work-life balance score (y) in a straight-line model. Both the coefficients of correlation and determination (highlighted on the MINITAB printouts in Figure SIA10.4) also support this conclusion. The correlation coefficient value, $r = -.265$ although statistically significantly different from 0, indicates a fairly weak negative linear relationship between the variables. The coefficient of determination, $r^2 = .07$, implies that only 7% of the sample variation in work-life balance score can be explained by the straight-line model.

Regression Analysis: WLB-SCORE versus HOURS

```
The regression equation is
WLB-SCORE = 62.5 - 0.347 HOURS


Predictor         Coef   SE Coef        T       P
Constant        62.499     1.414    44.22   0.000
HOURS          -0.34673   0.02761   -12.56   0.000


S = 12.2845    R-Sq = 7.0%    R-Sq(adj) = 7.0%


Analysis of Variance

Source             DF       SS       MS        F       P
Regression          1    23803    23803   157.73   0.000
Residual Error   2085   314647      151
Total            2086   338451
```

Figure SIA10.4
MINITAB printouts with coefficients of correlation and determination for the work-life balance data

Correlations: WLB-SCORE, HOURS

```
Pearson correlation of WLB-SCORE and HOURS = -0.265
P-Value = 0.000
```

Simple Linear Regression

Using the TI-83/TI-84 Graphing Calculator
Finding r and r^2

Step 1   *Enter the data*

Press **STAT** and select **1:Edit**
Note: If a list already contains data, clear the old data. Use the up arrow to highlight the list name, **L.1** or **L.2'**
Press **CLEAR ENTER.**
Enter your x-data in **L1** and your y-data in **L2.**

Step 2   *Turn the diagnostics feature on*

Press **2nd 0** for **CATALOG**
Press the key for **D**
Press the down arrow key until **Diagnostics On** is highlighted
Press **ENTER** twice

Step 3   *Find the equation*

Press **STAT** and highlight **CALC**
Press 4 for LinReg (**ax + b**)
Press **ENTER**
The screen will show the values for *a* and *b* in the equation y = ax + b.
The values for *r* and r^2 will appear on the screen as well.

Example   The figure shows the form of the output with the **DiagnosticsOn.**

```
LinReg
y=ax+b
a=2.495967742
b=63.3391129
r²=.9620199454
r=.9808261545
```

Exercises 10.51–10.65

Learning the Mechanics

10.51 Describe the slope of the least squares line if
 a. $r = .7$ **b.** $r = -.7$ **c.** $r = 0$ **d.** $r^2 = .64$

10.52 Explain what each of the following sample correlation co-
NW efficients tells you about the relationship between the x and y values in the sample:
 a. $r = 1$ **b.** $r = -1$ **c.** $r = 0$
 d. $r = -.90$ **e.** $r = .10$ **f.** $r = -.88$

10.53 Calculate r^2 for the least squares line in each of the following exercises. Interpret their values.
 a. Exercise 10.10   **b.** Exercise 10.13

10.54 Construct a scattergram for each data set. Then calculate r and r^2 for each data set. Interpret their values.

a.

x	−2	−1	0	1	2
y	−2	1	2	5	6

b.

x	−2	−1	0	1	2
y	6	5	3	2	0

c.

x	1	2	2	3	3	3	4
y	2	1	3	1	2	3	2

d.

x	0	1	3	5	6
y	0	1	2	1	0

APPLET **Applet Exercise 10.2**

Use the applet entitled *Correlation by Eye* to explore the relationship between the pattern of data in a scattergram and the corresponding correlation coefficient.
 a. Run the applet several times. Each time, guess the value of the correlation coefficient. Then click *Show r* to see the actual correlation coefficient. How close is your value to the actual value of r? Click *New data* to reset the applet.
 b. Click the trash can to clear the graph. Use the mouse to place five points on the scattergram that are approximately in a straight line. Then guess the value of the correlation coefficient. Click *Show r* to see the actual correlation coefficient. How close were you this time?
 c. Continue to clear the graph and plot sets of five points with different patterns among the points. Guess the value of r. How close do you come to the actual value of r each time?
 d. Based on your experiences with the applet, explain why we need to use more reliable methods of finding the correlation coefficient than just "eyeing" it.

Applying the Concepts—Basic

10.55 "Metaskills" and career management. In today's business environment, effective management of one's own career requires a skill set that includes adaptability, tolerance for ambiguity, self-awareness, and identify change. Management professors at Pace University (New York) used correlation coefficients to investigate the relationship between these "metaskills" and effective career management (*International Journal of Manpower*, Aug. 2000). Data were collected for 446 business graduates who had all completed a management "metaskills" course. Two of the many variables measured were self-knowledge skill level (x) and goalsetting ability (y). The correlation coefficient for these two variables was $r = .70$.
 a. Give a practical interpretation of the value of r.
 b. The p-value for a test of no correlation between the two variables was reported as p-value = .001. Interpret this result.
 c. Find the coefficient of determination, r^2, and interpret the result.

DIAMONDS

10.56 Characteristic of diamonds sold at retail. Refer to the MINITAB simple linear regression analysis relating $y =$ asking price (dollars) to $x =$ number of carats for diamonds sold on the open market, Exercise 10.14 (p. 611).
 NW **a.** Locate the coefficient of determination, r^2, on the MINITAB printout and interpret the result.
 b. Find the value of the coefficient of correlation, r, from the value of r^2 and the sign of the estimated slope. Interpret the result.

OJUICE

10.57 Sweetness of orange juice. Refer to the simple linear regression relating $y =$ sweetness index of an orange juice sample with $x =$ amount of water soluble pectin, Exercise 10.18 (p. 613). Find and interpret the coefficient of determination, r^2, and the coefficient of correlation, r.

10.58 Sports news on local TV broadcasts. *The Sports Journal* (Winter 2004) published the results of a study conducted to assess the factors that impact the time allotted to sports news on local television news broadcasts. Information on total time (in minutes) allotted to sports and audience ratings of the TV news broadcast (measured on a 100-point scale) was obtained from a national sample of 163 news directors. A correlation analysis on the data yielded $r = .43$.
 a. Interpret the value of the correlation coefficient, r.
 b. Find and interpret the value of the coefficient of determination, r^2.

Applying the Concepts—Intermediate

10.59 Salary linked to height. Are short people short-changed when it comes to salary? According to business professors T. A. Judge (University of Florida) and D. M. Cable (University of North Carolina), tall people tend to earn more money over their career than short people (*Journal of Applied Psychology*, June 2004). Using data collected from participants in the National Longitudinal Surveys begun in 1979, the researchers computed the correlation between average earnings from 1985–2000 (in dollars) and height (in inches) for several occupations. The results are given in the next table (p. 637).
 a. Interpret the value of r for people in sales occupations.
 b. Compute r^2 for people in sales occupations. Interpret the result.
 c. Give H_0 and H_a for testing whether average earnings and height are positively correlated.
 d. The test statistic for testing H_0 and H_a in part **c** is

$$t = \frac{r\sqrt{n-2}}{\sqrt{1-r^2}}.$$

Compute this value for people in sales occupations.

e. Use the result, part **d**, to conduct the test at $\alpha = .01$. Give the appropriate conclusion.

f. Select another occupation and repeat parts **a–e**.

Occupation	Correlation, r	Sample Size, n
Sales	.41	117
Managers	.35	455
Blue Collar	.32	349
Service Workers	.31	265
Professional/Technical	.30	453
Clerical	.25	358
Crafts/Forepersons	.24	250

Source: Judge, T. A., and Cable, D. M. "The Effect of Physical Height on Workplace Success and Income: Preliminary Test of a Theoretical Model." *Journal of Applied Psychology*, Vol. 89, No. 3, June 2004 (Table 5).

10.60 The Forbes 400. The *Forbes 400* is an annual ranking of the 400 wealthiest people in the United States. The top 15 billionaires on this list for 2006 are described in the table at the bottom of the page.

NW a. Construct a scattergram for these data. What does the plot suggest about the relationship between age and net worth of billionaires?

NW b. Find the coefficient of correlation and explain what it tells you about the relationship between age and net worth.

c. If the correlation coefficient of part **b** had the opposite sign, how would that change your interpretation of the relationship between age and net worth?

d. Find the coefficient of determination for a straight-line model relating net worth (y) to age (x). Interpret the result in the words of the problem.

BSCHOOL

10.61 Survey of the top business schools. Refer to the *Wall Street Journal* (Sep. 25, 2005) Business School Survey, Exercise

10.22 (p. 614). Find and interpret r and r^2 for the simple linear regression relating y = percentage of graduates with job offers and x = tuition cost, then fit the simple linear model.

LIQUIDSPILL

10.62 Spreading rate of spilled liquid. Refer to the *Chemical Engineering Progress* (Jan. 2005) study of the rate at which a spilled volatile liquid will spread across a surface, Exercise 10.23 (p. 614). Find and interpret r and r^2 for the simple linear regression y = mass of the spill and x = elapsed time of the spill.

10.63 Foreign vs. U.S. stock rates of return. If the economies of the world were tightly interconnected, the stock markets of different countries would move together. If they did, there would be no reason for investors to diversify their stock portfolios with stocks from a variety of countries (Sharpe, Alexander, and Bailey, *Investments*, 1999). The table below lists the correlations of returns on stocks in each of six countries with the returns of U.S. stocks.

Country	Correlation between Foreign and U.S. Stocks
Australia	.48
Canada	.74
France	.50
Germany	.43
Japan	.41
U.K.	.58

Source: Sharpe, W. F., Alexander, G. J., and Bailey, Jeffery V. *Investments.* Upper Saddle River, N.J.: Prentice Hall, 1999, p. 887.

a. Interpret the Australia/U.S. correlation. What does it suggest about the linear relationship between the stocks of the two countries?

b. Sketch a scattergram that is roughly consistent with the magnitude of the France/U.S. correlation.

c. Why must we be careful not to conclude from the information in the table that the country that is most tightly integrated with the United States is Canada?

FORBES400

Rank	Name	Net Worth ($ billions)	Age	Marital Status	Residence	Source of Wealth
1	Gates, Bill	53.0	50	married	Medina, WA	Microsoft
2	Buffett, Warren	46.0	76	widowed	Omaha, NE	Berkshire
3	Adelson, Sheldon	20.5	73	married	Las Vegas, NV	gambling
4	Ellison, Lawrence	19.5	62	married	Redwood, CA	Oracle
5	Allen, Paul	16.0	53	single	Seattle, WA	Microsoft
6	Walton, Jim	15.7	58	married	Bentonville, AR	Wal-Mart
7	Walton, Christy	15.6	51	widowed	Jackson, WY	Wal-Mart
8	Walton, S. Robson	15.6	62	married	Bentonville, AR	Wal-Mart
9	Dell, Michael	15.5	41	married	Austin, TX	Dell Computer
10	Walton, Alice	15.5	57	divorced	Fort Worth, TX	Wal-Mart
11	Walton, Helen	15.3	86	widowed	Bentonville, AR	Wal-Mart
12	Brin, Sheldon	14.1	23	single	Palo Alto, CA	Google
13	Page, Larry	14.0	33	single	San Francisco, CA	Google
14	Taylor, Jack	13.9	84	married	St. Louis, MO	Enterprise Rent-A-Car
15	Ballmer, Steve	13.6	50	married	Bellevue, WA	Microsoft

Source: Forbes, Sept. 21, 2006.

10.64 Snow geese feeding trial. Researchers at the University of Toronto conducted a series of experiments to investigate whether a commercially sold pet food could serve as a substitute diet for baby snow geese (*Journal of Applied Ecology*, Vol. 32, 1995). Goslings were deprived of food until their guts were empty, then were allowed to feed for 6 hours on a diet of plants or Purina Duck Chow. For each feeding trial, the change in the weight of the gosling after 2.5 hours was recorded as a percentage of initial weight. Two other variables recorded were digestion efficiency (measured as a percentage) and amount of acid-detergent fiber in the digestive tract (also measured as a percentage). The data for 42 feeding trials are saved in the **SNOWGEES** file. (The first and last five observations are shown in the table at the bottom of the page.)

a. The researchers were interested in the correlation between weight change (y) and digestion efficiency (x). Plot the data for these two variables in a scattergram. Do you observe a trend?

b. Find the coefficient of correlation relating weight change y to digestion efficiency x. Interpret this value.

c. Conduct a test (at $\alpha = .01$) to determine whether weight change y is correlated with digestion efficiency x.

d. Repeat parts **b** and **c**, but exclude the data for trials that used duck chow from the analysis. What do you conclude?

e. The researchers were also interested in the correlation between digestion efficiency (y) and acid-detergent fiber (x). Repeat parts **a–d** for these two variables.

Applying the Concepts—Advanced

10.65 Attitudes toward quality management. Studies of Asian (particularly Japanese) and U.S. managers in the 1970s and 1980s found sharp differences of opinion and attitude toward quality management. Do these differences continue to exist? To find out, two California State University researchers (B. F. Yavas and T. M. Burrows) surveyed 100 U.S. and 96 Asian managers in the electronics manufacturing industry (*Quality Management Journal*, Fall 1994). The table (next column) gives the percentages of U.S. and Asian managers who agree with each of 13 randomly selected statements regarding quality. (For example, one statement is "Quality is a problem in my company." Another is "Improving quality is expensive.")

QLAGREE

Statement	PERCENTAGE OF MANAGERS WHO AGREE	
	United States	Asian
1	36	38
2	31	42
3	28	43
4	27	48
5	78	58
6	74	49
7	43	46
8	50	56
9	31	65
10	66	58
11	18	21
12	61	69
13	53	45

Source: Yavas, B. F., and Burrows, T. M. "A Comparative Study of Attitudes of U.S. and Asian Managers toward Product Quality." *Quality Management Journal,* Fall 1994, p. 49 (Table 5).

a. Find the coefficient of correlation r for these data.

b. Interpret r in the context of the problem.

c. Refer to part **b**. Using the coefficient of correlation r to make inferences about the difference in attitudes between U.S. and Asian managers regarding quality can be misleading. The value of r measures the strength of the linear relationship between two variables; it does not account for a difference between the means of the variables. To illustrate this, examine the hypothetical data in the following table. Show that $r \approx 1$, but the Asian percentage is approximately 30 points higher for each quality statement. Would you conclude that the attitudes of U.S. and Asian managers are similar?

QLAGREE2

Quality Statement	HYPOTHETICAL PERCENTAGE OF MANAGERS WHO AGREE	
	United States	Asian
1	20	50
2	30	65
3	40	70
4	50	80
5	55	90

SNOWGEESE

Feeding Trial	Diet	Weight Change (%)	Digestion Efficiency (%)	Acid-Detergent Fiber (%)
1	Plants	−6	0	28.5
2	Plants	−5	2.5	27.5
3	Plants	−4.5	5	27.5
4	Plants	0	0	32.5
5	Plants	2	0	32
⋮	⋮	⋮	⋮	⋮
38	Duck Chow	9	59	8.5
39	Duck Chow	12	52.5	8
40	Duck Chow	8.5	75	6
41	Duck Chow	10.5	72.5	6.5
42	Duck Chow	14	69	7

Source: Gadallah, F. L., and Jefferies, R. L. "Forage Quality in Brood Rearing Areas of the Lesser Snow Goose and the Growth of Captive Goslings." *Journal of Applied Biology,* Vol. 32, No. 2, 1995, pp. 281–282 (adapted from Figures 2 and 3).

10.8 Using the Model for Estimation and Prediction

If we are satisfied that a useful model has been found to describe the relationship between x and y, we are ready for step 5 in our regression modeling procedure: using the model for estimation and prediction.

The most common uses of a probabilistic model for making inferences can be divided into two categories. The first is the use of the model for estimating the mean value of y, $E(y)$, *for a specific value of* x.

For our advertising–sales example, we may want to estimate the mean sales revenue for *all* months during which $400 ($x = 4$) is expended on advertising.

The second use of the model entails predicting a new individual y *value for a given* x.

That is, if we decide to expend $400 in advertising next month, we may want to predict the firm's sales revenue for that month.

In the first case, we are attempting to estimate the mean value of y for a very large number of experiments at the given x value. In the second case, we are trying to predict the outcome of a single experiment at the given x value. Which of these model uses—estimating the mean value of y or predicting an individual new value of y (for the same value of x)—can be accomplished with the greater accuracy?

Before answering this question, we first consider the problem of choosing an estimator (or predictor) of the mean (or a new individual) y value. We will use the least squares prediction equation

$$\hat{y} = \hat{\beta}_0 + \hat{\beta}_1 x$$

both to estimate the mean value of y and to predict a specific new value of y for a given value of x. For our example, we found

$$\hat{y} = -.1 + .7x$$

so that the estimated mean sales revenue for all months when $x = 4$ (advertising is $400) is

$$\hat{y} = -.1 + .7(4) = 2.7$$

or $2,700. (Recall that the units of y are thousands of dollars.) The same value is used to predict a new y value when $x = 4$—that is, both the estimated mean and the predicted value of y are $\hat{y} = 2.7$ when $x = 4$, as shown in Figure 10.18.

The difference between these two model uses lies in the relative accuracy of the estimate and the prediction. These accuracies are best measured by using the sampling errors of the least squares line when it is used as an estimator and as a predictor, respectively. These errors are reflected in the standard deviations given in the next box.

FIGURE 10.18
Estimated mean value and predicted individual value of sales revenue y for $x = 4$

Sampling Errors for the Estimator of the Mean of y and the Predictor of an Individual New Value of y

1. The standard deviation of the sampling distribution of the estimator $\hat{y}$ of the mean value of y at a specific value of x, say x_p, is

$$\sigma_{\hat{y}} = \sigma \sqrt{\frac{1}{n} + \frac{(x_p - \bar{x})^2}{SS_{xx}}}$$

where σ is the standard deviation of the random error ε. We refer to $\sigma_{\hat{y}}$ as the standard error of $\hat{y}$.

2. The standard deviation of the prediction error for the predictor $\hat{y}$ of an individual new y value at a specific value of x is

$$\sigma_{(y-\hat{y})} = \sigma\sqrt{1 + \frac{1}{n} + \frac{(x_p - \bar{x})^2}{SS_{xx}}}$$

where σ is the standard deviation of the random error ε. We refer to $\sigma_{(y-\hat{y})}$ as the standard error of the prediction.

The true value of σ is rarely known, so we estimate σ by s and calculate the estimation and prediction intervals as shown in the next two boxes.

A 100$(1 - \alpha)$% Confidence Interval for the Mean Value of y at $x = x_p$

$$\hat{y} \pm t_{\alpha/2}(\text{Estimated standard error of } \hat{y})$$

or

$$\hat{y} \pm t_{\alpha/2}s\sqrt{\frac{1}{n} + \frac{(x_p - \bar{x})^2}{SS_{xx}}}$$

where $t_{\alpha/2}$ is based on $(n - 2)$ degrees of freedom.

A 100$(1 - \alpha)$% Prediction Interval* for an Individual New Value of y at $x = x_p$

$$\hat{y} \pm t_{\alpha/2}(\text{Estimated standard error of prediction})$$

or

$$\hat{y} \pm t_{\alpha/2}s\sqrt{1 + \frac{1}{n} + \frac{(x_p - \bar{x})^2}{SS_{xx}}}$$

where $t_{\alpha/2}$ is based on $(n - 2)$ degrees of freedom.

EXAMPLE 10.6

Estimating the Mean of y for the Sales-Appraisal Application

Problem Refer to the sales-appraisal simple linear regression in previous examples. Find a 95% confidence interval for the mean monthly sales when the appliance store spends $400 on advertising.

Solution For a $400 advertising expenditure, $x = 4$ and the confidence interval for the mean value of y is

$$\hat{y} \pm t_{\alpha/2}s\sqrt{\frac{1}{n} + \frac{(x_p - \bar{x})^2}{SS_{xx}}} = \hat{y} \pm t_{.025}s\sqrt{\frac{1}{5} + \frac{(4 - \bar{x})^2}{SS_{xx}}}$$

where $t_{.025}$ is based on $n - 2 = 5 - 2 = 3$ degrees of freedom. Recall that $\hat{y} = 2.7$, $s = .61$, $\bar{x} = 3$, and $SS_{xx} = 10$. From Table V in Appendix B, $t_{.025} = 3.182$. Thus, we have

---

*The term *prediction interval* is used when the interval formed is intended to enclose the value of a random variable. The term *confidence interval* is reserved for estimation of population parameters (such as mean).

$$2.7 \pm (3.182)(.61)\sqrt{\frac{1}{5} + \frac{(4-3)^2}{10}} = 2.7 \pm (3.182)(.61)(.55)$$
$$= 2.7 \pm (3.182)(.34)$$
$$= 2.7 \pm 1.1 = (1.6, 3.8)$$

Therefore, when the store spends $400 a month on advertising, we are 95% confident that the mean sales revenue is between $1,600 and $3,800.

Look Back Note that we used a small amount of data (small in size) for purposes of illustration in fitting the least squares line. The interval would probably be narrower if more information had been obtained from a larger sample.

Now Work Exercise 10.66a–d

EXAMPLE 10.7

Predicting an Individual value of y for the Sales-Appraisal Application

Problem Refer, again, to the sales-appraisal regression. Predict the monthly sales for next month, if $400 is spent on advertising. Use a 95% prediction interval.

Solution To predict the sales for a particular month for which $x_p = 4$, we calculate the 95% prediction interval as

$$\hat{y} \pm t_{\alpha/2}s\sqrt{1 + \frac{1}{n} + \frac{(x_p - \bar{x})^2}{SS_{xx}}} = 2.7 \pm (3.182)(.61)\sqrt{1 + \frac{1}{5} + \frac{(4-3)^2}{10}}$$
$$= 2.7 \pm (3.182)(.61)(1.14)$$
$$= 2.7 \pm (3.182)(.70)$$
$$= 2.7 \pm 2.2 = (.5, 4.9)$$

Therefore, we predict with 95% confidence that the sales revenue next month (a month in which we spend $400 in advertising) will fall in the interval from $500 to $4,900.

Look Back Like the confidence interval for the mean value of y, the prediction interval for y is quite large. This is because we have chosen a simple example (only five data points) to fit the least squares line. The width of the prediction interval could be reduced by using a larger number of data points.

Now Work Exercise 10.66e

Both the confidence interval for $E(y)$ and prediction interval for y can be obtained using a statistical software package. Figure 10.19 is a MINITAB printout showing the confidence interval and prediction interval for the data in the advertising-sales example. The 95% confidence interval for $E(y)$ when $x = 4$, highlighted under "95% CI" in Figure 10.19, is $(1.645, 3.755)$. The 95% prediction interval for y when $x = 4$, highlighted in Figure 10.19 under "95% PI", is $(.503, 4.897)$. Both intervals agree with the ones computed in Examples 10.6–10.7.

```
Predicted Values for New Observations

New
Obs    Fit   SE Fit      95% CI            95% PI
 1    2.700   0.332   (1.645, 3.755)   (0.503, 4.897)
```

FIGURE 10.19
MINITAB printout giving 95% confidence interval for $E(y)$ and 95% prediction interval for y

```
Values of Predictors for New Observations

New
Obs   ADVEXP_X
 1      4.00
```

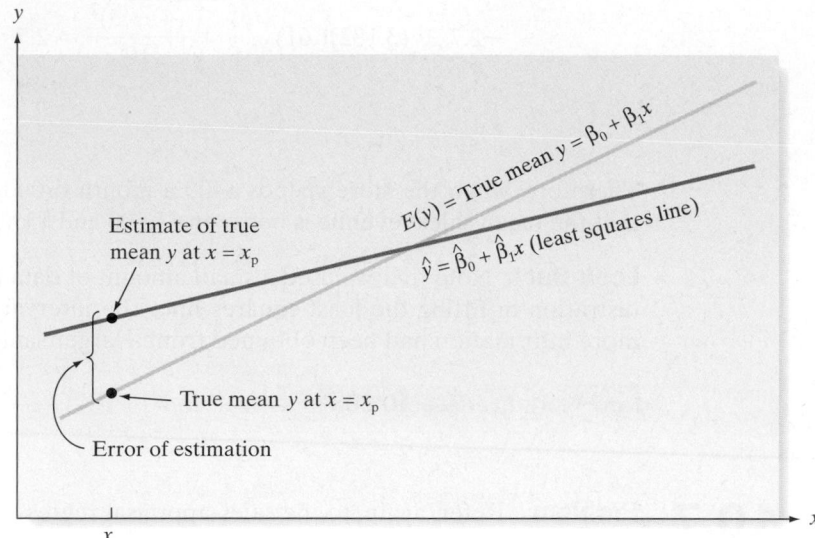

FIGURE 10.20

Error of estimating the mean value of y for a given value of x

Note that the prediction interval for an individual new value of y is *always* wider than the corresponding confidence interval for the mean value of y. Will this always be true? The answer is yes. The error in estimating the mean value of y, $E(y)$, for a given value of x, say x_p, is the distance between the least squares line and the true line of means, $E(y) = \beta_0 + \beta_1 x$. This error, $[\hat{y} - E(y)]$, is shown in Figure 10.20. In contrast, *the error* $(y_p - \hat{y})$ *in predicting some future value of* y *is the sum of two errors*—the error of estimating the mean of y, $E(y)$, plus the random error that is a component of the value of y to be predicted (see Figure 10.21). Consequently, the error of predicting a particular value of y will be larger than the error of estimating the mean value of y for a particular value of x. Note from their formulas that both the error of estimation and the error of prediction take their smallest values when $x_p = \bar{x}$. The farther x_p lies from $\bar{x}$, the larger will be the errors of estimation and prediction. You can see why this is true by noting the deviations for different values of x_p between the line of means $E(y) = \beta_0 + \beta_1 x$ and the predicted line of means $\hat{y} = \hat{\beta}_0 + \hat{\beta}_1 x$ shown in Figure 10.21. The deviation is larger at the extremes of the interval where the largest and smallest values of x in the data set occur.

Both the confidence intervals for mean values and the prediction intervals for new values are depicted over the entire range of the regression line in Figure 10.22. You can see that the confidence interval is always narrower than the prediction interval and that they are both narrowest at the mean $\bar{x}$, increasing steadily as the distance $|x - \bar{x}|$

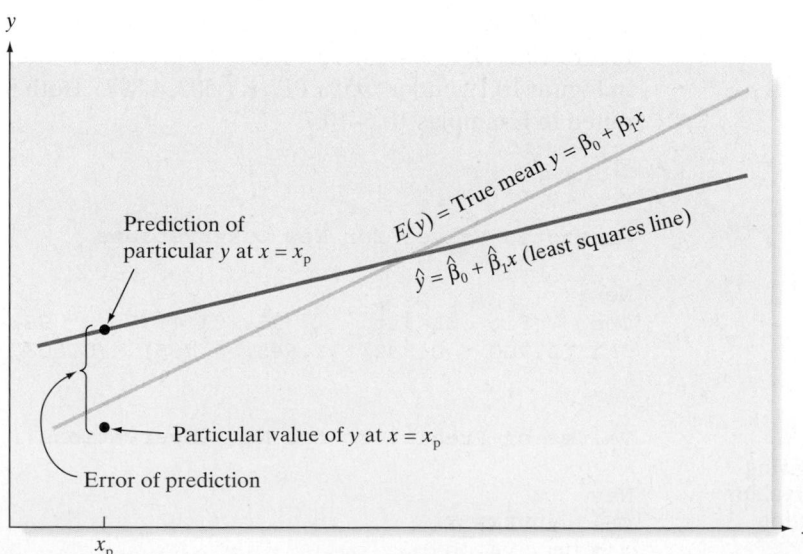

FIGURE 10.21

Error of predicting a future value of y for a given value of x

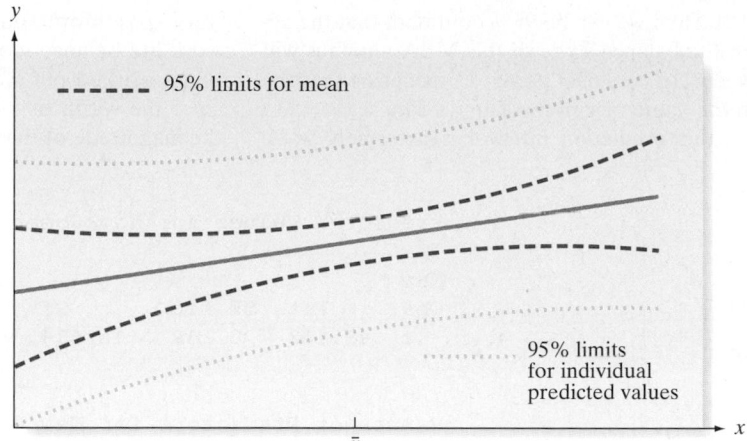

FIGURE 10.22

Confidence intervals for mean values and prediction intervals for new values

increases. In fact, when x is selected far enough away from $\bar{x}$ so that it falls outside the range of the sample data, it is dangerous to make any inferences about $E(y)$, or y.

Caution

Using the least squares prediction equation to estimate the mean value of y or to predict a particular value of y for values of x that fall *outside the range* of the values of x contained in your sample data may lead to errors of estimation or prediction that are much larger than expected. Although the least squares model may provide a very good fit to the data over the range of x values contained in the sample, it could give a poor representation of the true model for values of x outside this region.

The confidence interval width grows smaller as n is increased; thus, in theory, you can obtain as precise an estimate of the mean value of y as desired (at any given x) by selecting a large enough sample. The prediction interval for a new value of y also grows smaller as n increases, but there is a lower limit on its width. If you examine the formula for the prediction interval, you will see that the interval can get no smaller than $\hat{y} \pm z_{\alpha/2}\sigma$.* Thus, the only way to obtain more accurate predictions for new values of y is to reduce the standard deviation of the regression model, σ. This can be accomplished only by improving the model, either by using a curvilinear (rather than linear) relationship with x or by adding new independent variables to the model, or both. Methods of improving the model are discussed in Chapter 11.

Now Work Exercise 10.66f

STATISTICS IN ACTION REVISITED

Predicting Work-Life Balance Score Using the Straight-Line Model

In the two previous Statistics in Action Revisited sections, we recommended that the straight-line model for work-life balance score (y) as a function of hours worked per week (x) not be used in practice. We il-

lustrate this point further by showing the inaccuracy of using x to predict y with the model.

The MINITAB printout shown in Figure SIA10.5 gives a 95% prediction interval for the work-life balance score of an MBA alumnus who works, on average, $x = 50$ hours per week. The highlighted interval is

Continued

---

*The result follows from the facts that, for large n, $t_{\alpha/2} \approx z_{\alpha/2}$, $s \approx \sigma$, and the last two terms under the radical in the standard error of the predictor are approximately 0.

(21.1, 69.3). Thus, we can be 95% confident that the actual work-life balance score of this MBA alumnus will fall between 21.1 and 69.3 points. Considering that the range on the value of y in the sample data set is 8.5 to 75 points, this prediction interval is extremely wide.

Very little information is gained on an MBA alumnus' work-life balance score given we know the number of hours worked per week. This result is not surprising, since the width of the prediction interval depends on the magnitude of the model standard deviation, s.

```
Predicted Values for New Observations

New
Obs    Fit   SE Fit      95% CI             95% PI
  1  45.162  0.269  (44.634, 45.689)  (21.065, 69.259)


Values of Predictors for New Observations

New
Obs  HOURS
  1   50.0
```

Figure SIA10.5

MINITAB prediction interval for work-life balance model

Exercises 10.66–10.76

Learning the Mechanics

10.66 Consider the following pairs of measurements:

NW

LM10_66

x	−2	0	2	4	6	8	10
y	0	3	2	3	8	10	11

a. Construct a scattergram for these data.
b. Find the least squares line, and plot it on your scattergram.
c. Find s^2. s
d. Find a 90% confidence interval for the mean value of y when $x = 3$. Plot the upper and lower bounds of the confidence interval on your scattergram.
e. Find a 90% prediction interval for a new value of y when $x = 3$. Plot the upper and lower bounds of the prediction interval on your scattergram.
f. Compare the widths of the intervals you constructed in parts **d** and **e**. Which is wider and why?

10.67 Consider the pairs of measurements shown in the table. For these data, $SS_{xx} = 38.9000$, $SS_{yy} = 33.600$, $SS_{xy} = 32.8$ and $\hat{y} = -.414 + .843x$.

LM10_67

x	4	6	0	5	2	3	2	6	2	1
y	3	5	−1	4	3	2	0	4	1	1

a. Construct a scattergram for these data.
b. Plot the least squares line on your scattergram.
c. Use a 95% confidence interval to estimate the mean value of y when $x_p = 6$. Plot the upper and lower bounds of the interval on your scattergram.
d. Repeat part **c** for $x_p = 3.2$ and $x_p = 0$.
e. Compare the widths of the three confidence intervals you constructed in parts **c** and **d** and explain why they differ.

10.68 Refer to Exercise 10.67.
a. Using no information about x, estimate and calculate a 95% confidence interval for the mean value of y. [*Hint:* Use the one-sample t methodology of Section 5.4.]
b. Plot the estimated mean value and the confidence interval as horizontal lines on your scattergram.
c. Compare the confidence intervals you calculated in parts **c** and **d** of Exercise 10.67 with the one you calculated in part **a** of this exercise. Does x appear to contribute information about the mean value of y?
d. Check the answer you gave in part **c** with a statistical test of the null hypothesis $H_0: \beta_1 = 0$ against $H_a: \beta_1 \neq 0$. Use $\alpha = .05$.

10.69 In fitting a least squares line to $n = 10$ data points, the following quantities were computed:

$$SS_{xx} = 32$$
$$\bar{x} = 3$$
$$SS_{yy} = 26$$
$$\bar{y} = 4$$
$$SS_{xy} = 28$$

a. Find the least squares line.
b. Graph the least squares line.
c. Calculate SSE.
d. Calculate s^2.
e. Find a 95% confidence interval for the mean value of y when $x_p = 2.5$.
f. Find a 95% prediction interval for y when $x_p = 4$.

Applying the Concepts—Basic

DIAMONDS

10.70 Characteristics of diamonds sold at retail. Refer to the MINITAB simple linear regression analysis relating

```
Predicted Values for New Observations

New
Obs     Fit  SE Fit       95% CI            95% PI
  1  3733.1    68.6  (3598.1, 3868.1)  (1529.8, 5936.3)


Values of Predictors for New Observations

New
Obs   CARAT
  1   0.520
```

MINITAB output for Exercise 10.70

y = asking price (dollars) to x = number of carats for diamonds sold on the open market, Exercise 10.14 (p. 611). The portion of the MINITAB printout giving a 95% confidence interval for $E(y)$ and a 95% prediction interval for y when $x = .52$ is shown above.

a. Locate and interpret the 95% confidence interval for $E(y)$.

b. Locate and interpret the 95% prediction interval for y.

DOWDRUG

10.71 Drug controlled-release rate study. Refer to the *Drug Development and Industrial Pharmacy* (Vol. 28, 2002) drug controlled-release rate study, Exercise 10.17 (p. 612). Recall that data for six drug tablets were used to fit the simple linear model, $E(y) = \beta_0 + \beta_1 x$, where y = drug release rate and x = surface-area-to-volume ratio. In Exercise 10.17c you used the model to predict the drug release rate for tablet that has a surface area/volume ratio of .50. An Excel/PHStat2 printout giving the associated 90% prediction interval is shown at right. Give a practical interpretation for the prediction interval.

10.72 Sweetness of orange juice. Refer to the simple linear regression of sweetness index y and amount of pectin x for $n = 24$ orange juice samples, Exercise 10.18 (p. 613). A 90% confidence interval for the mean sweetness index, $E(y)$, for each of the first 12 runs is shown on the SPSS spreadsheet below. Select an observation and interpret this interval.

	A	B
1	**Confidence Interval Estimate**	
2		
3	**Data**	
4	X Value	0.5
5	Confidence Level	90%
6		
7	Intermediate Calculations	
8	Sample Size	6
9	Degrees of Freedom	4
10	t Value	2.131846
11	Sample Mean	0.908333
12	Sum of Squared Difference	0.557083
13	Standard Error of the Estimate	2.013046
14	h Statistic	0.465969
15	Predicted Y (YHat)	25.16754
16		
17	**For Average Y**	
18	Interval Half Width	2.929463
19	Confidence Interval Lower Limit	22.2381
20	Confidence Interval Upper Limit	28.097
21		
22	**For Individual Response Y**	
23	Interval Half Width	5.196035
24	Prediction Interval Lower Limit	19.9715
25	Prediction Interval Upper Limit	30.3636

Excel/PHStat2 output for Exercise 10.71

	run	sweet	pectin	lower90m	upper90m
1	1	5.2	220	5.64898	5.83848
2	2	5.5	227	5.63898	5.81613
3	3	6.0	259	5.57819	5.72904
4	4	5.9	210	5.66194	5.87173
5	5	5.8	224	5.64337	5.82560
6	6	6.0	215	5.65564	5.85493
7	7	5.8	231	5.63284	5.80379
8	8	5.6	268	5.55553	5.71011
9	9	5.6	239	5.61947	5.78019
10	10	5.9	212	5.65946	5.86497
11	11	5.4	410	5.05526	5.55416
12	12	5.6	256	5.58517	5.73592

SPSS Output for Exercise 10.72

Applying the Concepts—Intermediate

LIQUIDSPILL

10.73 Spreading rate of spilled liquid. Refer to the *Chemical Engineering Progress* (Jan. 2005) study of the rate at which a spilled volatile liquid will spread across a surface, Exercises 10.23 (p. 614). Recall that simple linear regression was used to model y = mass of the spill as a function of x = elapsed time of the spill.

a. Find a 99% confidence interval for the mean mass of all spills with an elapsed time of 15 minutes. Interpret the result.

b. Find a 99% prediction interval for the mass of a single spill with an elapsed time of 15 minutes. Interpret the result.

c. Compare the intervals, parts **a** and **b**. Which interval is wider? Will this always be the case? Explain.

10.74 Forecasting managerial needs. Managers are an important part of any organization's resource base. Accordingly, the organization should be just as concerned about forecasting its future managerial needs as it is with forecasting its needs for, say, the natural resources used in its production process (Northcraft and Neale, *Organizational Behavior: A Management Challenge*, 1994). A common forecasting procedure is to model the relationship between sales and the number of managers needed, since the demand for managers is the result of the increases and decreases in the demand for products and services that a firm offers its customers. To develop this relationship, the data shown in the table below are collected from a firm's records.

MANAGERS2

Units Sold, x	Managers, y	Units Sold, x	Managers, y
5	10	30	22
4	11	31	25
8	10	36	30
7	10	38	30
9	9	40	31
15	10	41	31
20	11	51	32
21	17	40	30
25	19	48	32
24	21	47	32

a. Test the usefulness of the model. Use $\alpha = .05$. State your conclusion in the context of the problem.

b. The company projects that it will sell 39 units next month. Use the least squares model to construct a 90% prediction interval for the number of managers needed next month.

c. Interpret the interval in part **b**. Use the interval to determine the reliability of the firm's projection.

10.75 Predicting quit rates in manufacturing. The reasons given by workers for quitting their jobs generally fall into one of two categories: (1) worker quits to seek or take a different job, or (2) worker quits to withdraw from the labor force. Economic theory suggests that wages and quit rates are related. The next table lists quit rates (quits per 100 employees) and the average hourly wage in a sample of 15 manufacturing industries. Consider the simple linear regression of quit rate y on average wage x.

QUITTERS

Industry	Quit Rate, y	Average Wage, x
1	1.4	$ 8.20
2	.7	10.35
3	2.6	6.18
4	3.4	5.37
5	1.7	9.94
6	1.7	9.11
7	1.0	10.59
8	.5	13.29
9	2.0	7.99
10	3.8	5.54
11	2.3	7.50
12	1.9	6.43
13	1.4	8.83
14	1.8	10.93
15	2.0	8.80

a. Do the data present sufficient evidence to conclude that average hourly wage rate contributes useful information for the prediction of quit rates? What does your model suggest about the relationship between quit rates and wages?

b. Find a 95% prediction interval for the quit rate in an industry with an average hourly wage of $9.00. Interpret the result.

c. Find a 95% confidence interval for the mean quit rate for industries with an average hourly wage of $9.00. Interpret this result.

Applying the Concepts—Advanced

CUTTOOLS

10.76 Life tests of cutting tools. Refer to the data saved in the **CUTTOOLS** file, Exercise 10.34 (p. 620).

a. Use a 90% confidence interval to estimate the mean useful life of a brand A cutting tool when the cutting speed is 45 meters per minute. Repeat for brand B. Compare the widths of the two intervals and comment on the reasons for any difference.

b. Use a 90% prediction interval to predict the useful life of a brand A cutting tool when the cutting speed is 45 meters per minute. Repeat for brand B. Compare the widths of the two intervals to each other and to the two intervals you calculated in part **a**. Comment on the reasons for any differences.

c. Note that the estimation and prediction you performed in parts **a** and **b** were for a value of x that was not included in the original sample—that is, the value $x = 45$ was not part of the sample. However, the value is within the range of x values in the sample, so the regression model spans the x value for which the estimation and prediction were made. In such situations, estimation and prediction represent *interpolations*. Suppose you were asked to predict the useful life of a brand A cutting tool for a cutting speed of $x = 100$ meters per minute. Since the given value of x is outside the range of the sample x values, the prediction is an example of *extrapolation*. Predict the useful life of a brand A cutting tool that is operated at 100 meters per minute, and construct a 95% confidence interval for the actual useful life of the tool. What additional assumption do you have to make in order to ensure the validity of an extrapolation?

10.9 A Complete Example

In the preceding sections, we have presented the basic elements necessary to fit and use a straight-line regression model. In this section we will assemble these elements by applying them in an example with the aid of a computer.

Suppose a fire insurance company wants to relate the amount of fire damage in major residential fires to the distance between the burning house and the nearest fire station. The study is to be conducted in a large suburb of a major city; a sample of 15 recent fires in this suburb is selected. The amount of damage, y, and the distance between the fire and the nearest fire station, x, are recorded for each fire. The results are given in Table 10.7.

Step 1: First, we hypothesize a model to relate fire damage, y, to the distance from the nearest fire station, x. We hypothesize a straight-line probabilistic model:

$$y = \beta_0 + \beta_1 x + \epsilon$$

Step 2: Next, we enter the data of Table 10.7 into a computer and use a statistical software package to estimate the unknown parameters in the deterministic component of the hypothesized model. The Excel printout for the simple linear regression analysis is shown in Figure 10.23. The least squares estimates of the slope β_1 and intercept β_0, highlighted on the printout, are

FIREDAM

TABLE 10.7 Fire Damage Data

Distance from Fire Station, x (miles)	Fire Damage, y (thousands of dollars)
3.4	26.2
1.8	17.8
4.6	31.3
2.3	23.1
3.1	27.5
5.5	36.0
.7	14.1
3.0	22.3
2.6	19.6
4.3	31.3
2.1	24.0
1.1	17.3
6.1	43.2
4.8	36.4
3.8	26.1

FIGURE 10.23

Excel printout for fire damage regression analysis

Regression Analysis

Regression Statistics	
Multiple R	0.960977715
R Square	0.923478169
Adjusted R Square	0.917591874
Standard Error	2.316046184
Observations	15

ANOVA

	df	SS	MS	F	Significance F
Regression	1	841.766358	841.766350	156.8861596	1.2478E-08
Residual	13	69.75097535	5.365459643		
Total	14	911.5173333			

	Coefficients	Standard Error	t Stat	P-value	Lower 95%	Upper 95%
Intercept	10.27792855	1.420277811	7.236562082	6.58556E-06	7.209605476	13.34625162
DISTANCE	4.919330727	0.392747749	12.52542054	1.2478E-08	4.070850963	5.767810491

FIGURE 10.24
MINITAB scatterplot with least squares line for fire damage regression analysis

$$\hat{\beta}_1 = 4.919331$$

$$\hat{\beta}_0 = 10.277929$$

and the least squares equation is (rounded)

$$\hat{y} = 10.278 + 4.919x$$

This prediction equation is graphed in the MINITAB scatterplot, Figure 10.24.

The least squares estimate of the slope, $\hat{\beta}_1 = 4.919$, implies that the estimated mean damage increases by \$4,919 for each additional mile from the fire station. This interpretation is valid over the range of x, or from .7 to 6.1 miles from the station. The estimated y-intercept, $\hat{\beta}_0 = 10.278$, has the interpretation that a fire 0 miles from the fire station has an estimated mean damage of \$10,278. Although this would seem to apply to the fire station itself, remember that the y-intercept is meaningfully interpretable only if $x = 0$ is within the sampled range of the independent variable. Since $x = 0$ is outside the range in this case, $\hat{\beta}_0$ has no practical interpretation.

Step 3: Now we specify the probability distribution of the random error component ϵ. The assumptions about the distribution are identical to those listed in Section 10.3. Although we know that these assumptions are not completely satisfied (they rarely are for practical problems), we are willing to assume they are approximately satisfied for this example. The estimate of the standard deviation σ of ϵ, highlighted on the Excel printout (Fig. 10.23) is

$$s = 2.31635$$

This implies that most of the observed fire damage (y) values will fall within approximately $2s = 4.64$ thousand dollars of their respective predicted values when using the least squares line. [Note: A more precise prediction interval for y is given in Step 5.]

Step 4: We can now check the usefulness of the hypothesized model—that is, whether x really contributes information for the prediction of y using the straight-line model. First, test the null hypothesis that the slope β_1 is 0—that is, that there is no linear relationship between fire damage and the distance from the nearest fire station, against the alternative hypothesis that fire damage increases as the distance increases. We test

$$H_0: \beta_1 = 0$$

$$H_a: \beta_1 > 0$$

The two-tailed observed significance level for testing $H_a: \beta_1 \neq 0$, highlighted on the printout, is approximately 0. When we divide this value in half, the p-value for our one-tailed test is also approximately 0. This small p-value leaves little doubt that mean fire damage and distance between the fire and station are at least linearly related, with mean fire damage increasing as the distance increases.

We gain additional information about the relationship by forming a 95% confidence interval for the slope β_1. The lower and upper endpoints of this interval are highlighted on the Excel printout shown in Figure 10.23.

This yields the interval (4.070, 5.768). We estimate (with 95% confidence) that the interval from \$4,070 to \$5,768 encloses the mean increase (β_1) in fire damage per additional mile distance from the fire station.

Another measure of the utility of the model is the coefficient of determination, r^2. The value (highlighted on Figure 10.23) is $r^2 = .9235$, which implies that about 92% of the sample variation in fire damage (y) is explained by the distance (x) between the fire and the fire station.

The coefficient of correlation, r, that measures the strength of the linear relationship between y and x is not shown on the Excel printout and must be calculated. Using the facts that $r = \sqrt{r^2}$ in simple linear regression and that r and $\hat{\beta}_1$ have the same sign, we find

$$r = +\sqrt{r^2} = \sqrt{.9235} = .96$$

The high correlation confirms our conclusion that β_1 is greater than 0; it appears that fire damage and distance from the fire station are positively correlated. All signs point to a strong linear relationship between y and x.

Step 5: We are now prepared to use the least squares model. Suppose the insurance company wants to predict the fire damage if a major residential fire were to occur 3.5 miles from the nearest fire station. A 95% confidence interval for $E(y)$ and prediction interval for y when $x = 3.5$ are shown on the Excel printout, Figure 10.25.

Confidence Interval Estimate

Data	
X Value	3.5
Confidence Level	95%

Intermediate Calculations	
Sample Size	15
Degrees of Freedom	13
t Value	2.160368
Sample Mean	3.28
Sum of Squared Difference	34.784
Standard Error of the Estimate	2.316346
h Statistic	0.068058
Average Predicted Y (YHat)	27.49559

For Average Predicted Y (YHat)	
Interval Half Width	1.305483
Confidence Interval Lower Limit	26.1901
Confidence Interval Upper Limit	28.80107

For Individual Response Y	
Interval Half Width	5.171645
Prediction Interval Lower Limit	22.32394
Prediction Interval Upper Limit	32.66723

FIGURE 10.25
Excel/PHStat2 confidence/prediction interval for fire damage regression analysis

The predicted value (given in the middle of the printout) is $\hat{y} = 27.4956$, while the 95% prediction interval (highlighted) is (22.3239, 32.6672). Therefore, with 95% confidence we predict fire damage in a major residential fire 3.5 miles from the nearest station to be between $22,324 and $32,667.

Caution

We would not use this prediction model to make predictions for homes less than .7 mile or more than 6.1 miles from the nearest fire station. A look at the data in Table 10.7 reveals that all the x values fall between .7 and 6.1. It is dangerous to use the model to make predictions outside the region in which the sample data fall. A straight line might not provide a good model for the relationship between the mean value of y and the value of x when stretched over a wider range of x values.

KEY TERMS

Bivariate relationship   628
Coefficient of correlation   628
Coefficient of determination   633
Confidence interval for mean of y 640
Dependent variable   599
Deterministic model   598
Errors of prediction   602
Independent variable   599
Least squares estimates   603

Least squares line   602
Line of means   600
Method of least squares   602
Population correlation coefficient   631
Prediction interval for y 640
Predictor variable   599
Probabilistic model   598
Random error   598
Regression analysis   599

Response variable   599
Scattergram   602
Slope   599
Standard error of estimated slope   621
Standard error of regression model   617
Straight-line (first-order) model   599
y-intercept   599

GUIDE TO SIMPLE LINEAR REGRESSION

Step 1: Hypothesize the model:

$$E(y) = \beta_0 + \beta_1 x$$

Step 2: Estimate the β's

(Method of least squares)

Step 3: Assumptions on random error, ε

1) Mean $(\varepsilon) = 0$
2) Var$(\varepsilon) = \sigma^2$ is constant
3) ε has a normal distribution
4) ε's are independent

Step 4: Assess model adequacy

Test for zero slope: $H_0: \beta_1 = 0$
and/or
Confidence interval for slope, β_1

(Reject $H_0: \beta_1 = 0$ or
CI for β_1 does not include 0)
Model statistically useful

(Fail to reject $H_0: \beta_1 = 0$ or
CI for β_1 includes 0)
Model not statistically useful

Reformulate the model
(Return to Step 1)

Examine 2s and r^2

2s is "large" or r^2 is "small"
Model not practically useful

2s is "small and r^2 is "large"

Step 5: Estimation and/or Prediction

Confidence Interval for $E(y)$ given x

Prediction Interval for y given x

CHAPTER NOTES

Simple linear regression variables:

y = **Dependent** variable (quantitative)

x = **Independent** variable (quantitative)

Method of least squares properties:

1) average error of prediction = 0

2) sum of squared errors is minimum

Practical interpretation of y-intercept:

Predicted y-value when $x = 0$

(no practical interpretation if $x = 0$ is either nonsensical or outside range of sample data)

Practical interpretation of slope:

Increase (or decrease) in y for every 1-unit increase in x

First-order (straight-line) model:

$$E(y) = \beta_0 + \beta_1 x$$

where $E(y)$ = mean of y

β_0 = **y-intercept** of line (point where line intercepts y-axis)

β_1 = **slope** of line (change in y for every 1-unit change in x)

Coefficient of correlation, r:

1) ranges between -1 and $+1$

2) measures strength of *linear relationship* between y and x

Coefficient of determination, r^2:

1) ranges between 0 and 1

2) measures proportion of sample variation in y "explained" by the model

Practical interpretation of model standard deviation, s:

Ninety-five percent of y-values fall within 2s of their respected predicted values

Width of *confidence interval for* E(y) will always be **narrower** than width of *prediction interval for* y

Key Symbols/Notation

y	Dependent variable (variable to be predicted)
x	Independent variable (variable used to predict y)
$E(y)$	Expected (mean) of y
β_0	y-intercept of true line
β_1	slope of true line
$\hat{\beta}_0$	Least squares estimate of y-intercept
$\hat{\beta}_1$	Least squares estimate of slope
ε	Random error
$\hat{y}$	Predicted value of y for a given x-value
$(y - \hat{y})$	Estimated error of prediction
SSE	Sum of squared errors of prediction
r	Coefficient of correlation
r^2	Coefficient of determination
x_p	Value of x used to predict y
$r^2 = \dfrac{\text{SS}_{yy} - \text{SSE}}{\text{SS}_{yy}}$	Coefficient of determination
$\hat{y} \pm t_{\alpha/2} s \sqrt{\dfrac{1}{n} + \dfrac{(x_p - \overline{x})^2}{\text{SS}_{xx}}}$	$(1 - \alpha)$ 100% confidence interval for E(y) when $x = x_p$
$\hat{y} \pm t_{\alpha/2} s \sqrt{1 + \dfrac{1}{n} + \dfrac{(x_p - \overline{x})^2}{\text{SS}_{xx}}}$	$(1 - \alpha)$ 100% prediction interval for y when $x = x_p$

SUPPLEMENTARY EXERCISES 10.77–10.94

Learning the Mechanics

10.77 In fitting a least squares line to $n = 15$ data points, the following quantities were computed: $SS_{xx} = 55$, $SS_{yy} = 198$, $SS_{xy} = -88$, $\bar{x} = 1.3$, and $\bar{y} = 35$.
   a. Find the least squares line.
   b. Graph the least squares line.
   c. Calculate SSE.
   d. Calculate s^2.
   e. Find a 90% confidence interval for β_1. Interpret this estimate.
   f. Find a 90% confidence interval for the mean value of y when $x = 15$.
   g. Find a 90% prediction interval for y when $x = 15$.

10.78 Consider the following sample data:

y	5	1	3
x	5	1	3

   a. Construct a scattergram for the data.
   b. It is possible to find many lines for which $\Sigma(y - \hat{y}) = 0$. For this reason, the criterion $\Sigma(y - \hat{y}) = 0$ is not used for identifying the "best-fitting" straight line. Find two lines that have $\Sigma(y - \hat{y}) = 0$.
   c. Find the least squares line.
   d. Compare the value of SSE for the least squares line to that of the two lines you found in part **b**. What principle of least squares is demonstrated by this comparison?

10.79 Consider the following 10 data points:

   LM10_79

x	3	5	6	4	3	7	6	5	4	7
y	4	3	2	1	2	3	3	5	4	2

   a. Plot the data on a scattergram.
   b. Calculate the values of r and r^2.
   c. Is there sufficient evidence to indicate that x and y are linearly correlated? Test at the $\alpha = .10$ level of significance.

Applying the Concepts—Basic

10.80 Burnout of human services professionals. Emotional exhaustion, or *burnout*, is a significant problem for people with careers in the field of human services. Regression analysis was used to investigate the relationship between burnout and aspects of the human services professional's job and job-related behavior (*Journal of Applied Behavioral Science*, Vol. 22, 1986). Emotional exhaustion was measured with the Maslach Burnout Inventory, a questionnaire. One of the independent variables considered, called *concentration*, was the proportion of social contacts with individuals who belong to a person's work group. The next table lists the values of the emotional exhaustion index (higher values indicate greater exhaustion) and concentration for a sample of 25 human services professionals who work in a large public hospital. A MINITAB printout of the simple linear regression is provided.
   a. Construct a scattergram for the data. Do the variables x and y appear to be related?

   b. Find the correlation coefficient for the data and interpret its value. Does your conclusion mean that concentration causes emotional exhaustion? Explain.

   BURNOUT

Exhaustion Index, y	Concentration, x	Exhaustion Index, y	Concentration, x
100	20%	493	86%
525	60	892	83
300	38	527	79
980	88	600	75
310	79	855	81
900	87	709	75
410	68	791	77
296	12	718	77
120	35	684	77
501	70	141	17
920	80	400	85
810	92	970	96
506	77		

   c. Test the usefulness of the straight-line relationship with concentration for predicting burnout. Use $\alpha = .05$.
   d. Find the coefficient of determination for the model and interpret it.

```
The regression equation is
EXHAUST = - 29 + 8.87 CONCEN


Predictor    Coef    SE Coef      T       P
Constant    -29.5     106.7    -0.28   0.785
CONCEN      8.865     1.471     6.03   0.000


S = 174.207    R-Sq = 61.2%    R-Sq(adj) = 59.5%


Analysis of Variance

Source          DF       SS        MS       F      P
Regression       1   1102408   1102408   36.33  0.000
Residual Error  23    698009     30348
Total           24   1800417


Predicted Values for New Observations

New
Obs    Fit   SE Fit      95% CI            95% PI
 1   679.7    38.7   (599.7, 759.8)   (310.6, 1048.9)


Values of Predictors for New Observations

New
Obs  CONCEN
 1    80.0
```

MINITAB output for Exercise 10.80

e. Find a 95% confidence interval for the slope β_1. Interpret the result.

f. Use a 95% confidence interval to estimate the mean exhaustion level for all professionals who have 80% of their social contacts within their work groups. Interpret the interval.

10.81 Length of TV commercials. Refer to the *Nutrition & Food Science* (Vol. 30, 2000) study of the trend in prime-time television advertising, Exercise 7.105 (p. 464). The number of prime-time TV commercials for all products and for just food products for randomly selected hours during 1971, 1977, 1988, 1992, and 1998 was recorded. The rate of commercials per hour for each of these years is given in the table. The researchers were interested in modeling the rate of prime-time TV commercials per hour as a function of x = the number of years since 1970.

FOODADS

Year	Number of Years since 1970	Total Commercials (rate per hour)	Food Ads (rate per hour)
1971	1	—	5.4
1977	7	11	3.0
1988	18	26	6.5
1992	22	31	6.0
1998	28	40	6.0

Source: Byrd-Bredbenner, C., and Grasso, D. "Trends in US Prime-Time Television Food Advertising across Three Decades." *Nutrition & Food Science,* Vol. 30, No. 2, 2000, p. 61 (Table 1).

a. Graph the data for total TV commercials in a scatterplot. Do you detect a trend?

b. Fit a straight-line model for y = rate of total commercials per hour using the method of least squares.

c. Interpret the slope of the least squares line.

d. Interpret the y-intercept of the least squares line.

e. Repeat parts **a–d** for food commercials during prime time.

f. The researchers concluded that "the hourly rate for total commercials is increasing significantly by 1.4 commercials per hour each year." Do you agree with this statement? Explain.

g. The researchers also concluded that "the hourly rate for food advertisements is not changing over time in a statistically significant fashion." Do you agree with this statement? Explain.

h. Use simple linear regression to find a 95% prediction interval for rate of total number of prime-time TV commercials per hour in the year 2005.

i. Give a practical interpretation of the interval, part **h**.

j. Why might the inference made from the prediction interval be invalid? Explain.

10.82 Buying income of households. *Sales and Marketing Management* determined the "effective buying income" (EBI) of the average household in a state. Can the EBI be used to predict retail sales per household in the store-group category "eating and drinking places"?

a. Use the data for 13 states given in the next table to find the least squares line relating retail sales per household (y) to average household EBI (x).

b. Plot the least squares line, as well as the actual data points, on a scattergram.

c. Based on the graph, part **b**, give your opinion regarding the predictive ability of the least squares line.

d. Find a 95% confidence interval for the slope of the line.

e. Use the results, part **d**, to assess the adequacy of the straight-line model.

EBI

State	Average Household Buying Income ($)	Retail Sales: Eating and Drinking Places ($ per household)
Connecticut	60,998	2,553.8
New Jersey	63,853	2,154.8
Michigan	46,915	2,523.3
Minnesota	44,717	2,278.6
Florida	42,442	2,475.8
South Carolina	37,848	2,358.4
Mississippi	34,490	1,538.4
Oklahoma	34,830	2,063.1
Texas	44,729	2,363.5
Colorado	44,571	3,214.9
Utah	43,421	2,653.8
California	50,713	2,215.0
Oregon	40,597	2,144.0

Source: Sales and Marketing Management, 1995.

10.83 Document search performance. One of the most common types of "information retrieval" processes is document-database searching. An experiment was conducted to investigate the variables that influence search performance in the Medline database and retrieval system (*Journal of Information Science,* Vol. 21, 1995). Simple linear regression was used to model the fraction y of the set of potentially informative documents that are retrieved using Medline as a function of the number x of terms in the search query, based on a sample of $n = 124$ queries. The results are summarized below:

$$\hat{y} = .202 + .135x$$

$$t \text{ (for testing } H_0\text{: } \beta_1 = 0) = 4.98$$

$$\text{Two-tailed } p\text{-value} = .001$$

a. Is there sufficient evidence to indicate that x and y are linearly related? Test using $\alpha = .01$.

b. If appropriate, use the model to predict the fraction of documents retrieved for a search query with $x = 3$ terms.

c. The value of r was reported in the article as $r = .679$. Interpret this result.

d. Calculate the coefficient of determination, r^2, and interpret the result.

10.84 Computer anxiety. Many high school students experience "math anxiety," which has been shown to have a negative effect on their learning achievement. Does such an attitude carry over to learning computer skills? A researcher at Duquesne University investigated this question and published her results in *Educational Technology* (May–June 1995). A sample of 1,730 high school students—902 boys and 828 girls—from public schools in Pittsburgh, Pennsylvania, participated in the study. Using 5-point Likert scales, where 1 = "strongly disagree" and 5 = "strongly agree," the researcher measured the students' interest and confidence in both mathematics and computers.

a. For boys, math confidence and computer interest were correlated at $r = .14$. Fully interpret this result.

b. For girls, math confidence and computer interest were correlated at $r = .33$. Fully interpret this result.

MANAGERS

10.85 Evaluating managerial success. Refer to Exercise 10.48 (p. 627), in which managerial success, y, was modeled as a function of the number of contacts a manager makes with people outside his or her work unit, x, during a specific period of time. The data are saved in the **MANAGERS** file.

a. A particular manager was observed for 2 weeks, as in the *Journal of Applied Behavioral Science* study. She made 55 contacts with people outside her work unit. Predict the value of the manager's success index. Use a 90% prediction interval.

b. A second manager was observed for 2 weeks. This manager made 110 contacts with people outside his work unit. Why should caution be exercised in using the least squares model developed from the given data set to construct a prediction interval for this manager's success index?

c. In the context of this problem, determine the value of x for which the associated prediction interval for y is the narrowest.

Applying the Concepts—Intermediate

10.86 Maize rust study. Common maize rust is a serious disease of sweet corn. Researchers in New York state have developed an action threshold for initiation of fungicide applications based on a regression equation relating maize rust incidence to severity of the disease (*Phytopathology*, Vol. 80, 1990). In one particular field, data were collected on more than 100 plants of the sweet corn hybrid Jubilee. For each plant, incidence was measured as the percentage of leaves infected (x) and severity was calculated as the log (base 10) of the average number of infections per leaf (y). A simple linear regression analysis of the data produced the following results:

$$\hat{y} = -.939 + .020x$$
$$r^2 = .816$$
$$s = .288$$

a. Interpret the value of $\hat{\beta}_1$.

b. Interpret the value of r^2.

c. Interpret the value of s.

d. Calculate the value of r and interpret it.

e. Use the result, part **d**, to test the utility of the model. Use $\alpha = .05$. (Assume $n = 100$.)

f. Predict the severity of the disease when the incidence of maize rust for a plant is 80%. [*Note:* Take the antilog (base 10) of $\hat{y}$ to obtain the predicted average number of infections per leaf.]

10.87 Collecting Beanie Babies Refer to Exercise 2.134 (p. 116) and the data on 50 Beanie Babies collector's items, published in *Beanie World Magazine*. Can age (in months as of Sept. 1998) of a Beanie Baby be used to accurately predict its market value? Answer this question by conducting a complete simple linear regression analysis on the data

saved in the **BEANIE** file. (The first and last five observations are shown in the table.)

BEANIE

Name	Age (months) as of Sept. 1998	Value ($)
1. Ally the Alligator	52	55.00
2. Batty the Bat	12	12.00
3. Bongo the Brown Monkey	28	40.00
4. Blackie the Bear	52	10.00
5. Bucky the Beaver	40	45.00
⋮	⋮	⋮
46. Stripes the Tiger (Gold/Black)	40	400.00
47. Teddy the 1997 Holiday Bear	12	50.00
48. Tuffy the Terrier	17	10.00
49. Tracker the Basset Hound	5	15.00
50. Zip the Black Cat	28	40.00

Source: Beanie World Magazine, Sept. 1998.

10.88 Monetary values of NFL teams. Refer to the *Forbes* magazine (Sep. 1, 2005) report on the financial standings of each team in the National Football League (NFL), Exercise 2.143 (p. 118). The table listing the current value (without deduction for debt, except stadium debt) and operating income for each team is reproduced below.

NFLVALUE

Team	Current Value ($mil)	Operating Income ($mil)
Dallas Cowboys	1,063	54.3
Washington Redskins	1,264	53.8
New England Patriots	1,040	50.5
Denver Broncos	907	49.4
Cincinnati Bengals	716	45.6
Tampa Bay Buccaneers	877	45.4
San Francisco 49ers	699	43.6
New Orleans Saints	718	42.6
Houston Texans	946	41.3
Cleveland Browns	892	41.1
Chicago Bears	871	40.1
St. Louis Rams	757	39.8
Pittsburgh Steelers	820	36.5
Buffalo Bills	708	36.1
Green Bay Packers	849	35.4
Tennessee Titans	839	35.1
Jacksonville Jaguars	691	34.6
San Diego Chargers	678	32.8
Baltimore Ravens	864	32.7
Kansas City Chiefs	762	31
Atlanta Falcons	690	26.8
New York Giants	806	26.7
Philadelphia Eagles	952	24.5
Carolina Panthers	878	24.3
Indianapolis Colts	715	16.4
Arizona Cardinals	673	16.2
Miami Dolphins	856	15.8
Minnesota Vikings	658	15.6
Detroit Lions	780	15.4
Seattle Seahawks	823	14.4
New York Jets	739	12
Oakland Raiders	676	7.8

Source: Forbes, Dec. 1, 2005.

Trial Number	Static Weight of Truck, x (thousand pounds)	Weigh-in-Motion Reading Prior to Calibration Adjustment, y_1 (thousand pounds)	Weigh-in-Motion Reading After Calibration Adjustment, y_2 (thousand pounds)
1	27.9	26.0	27.8
2	29.1	29.9	29.1
3	38.0	39.5	37.8
4	27.0	25.1	27.1
5	30.3	31.6	30.6
6	34.5	36.2	34.3
7	27.8	25.1	26.9
8	29.6	31.0	29.6
9	33.1	35.6	33.0
10	35.5	40.2	35.0

Source: Adapted from data in Wright J. L., Owen, F., and Pena, D. "Status of MN/DOT's Weigh-in-Motion Program." St. Paul: Minnesota Department of Transportation, January 1983.

a. Propose a straight-line model relating an NFL team's current value (y) to its operating income (x).

b. Fit the model to the data using the method of least squares.

c. Interpret the least squares estimates of the slope and y-intercept in the words of the problem.

d. Statistically assess the adequacy of the model. Do you recommend using it to predict an NFL team's value?

10.89 Evaluating a truck weigh-in-motion program. The Minnesota Department of Transportation installed a state-of-the-art weigh-in-motion scale in the concrete surface of the eastbound lanes of Interstate 494 in Bloomington, Minnesota. After installation, a study was undertaken to determine whether the scale's readings correspond with the static weights of the vehicles being monitored. (Studies of this type are known as *calibration studies.*) After some preliminary comparisons using a two-axle, six-tire truck carrying different loads (see the table above), calibration adjustments were made in the software of the weigh-in-motion system and the scales were reevaluated.

a. Construct two scattergrams, one of y_1 versus x and the other of y_2 versus x.

b. Use the scattergrams of part **a** to evaluate the performance of the weigh-in-motion scale both before and after the calibration adjustment.

c. Calculate the correlation coefficient for both sets of data and interpret their values. Explain how these correlation coefficients can be used to evaluate the weigh-in-motion scale.

d. Suppose the sample correlation coefficient for y_2 and x was 1. Could this happen if the static weights and the weigh-in-motion readings disagreed? Explain.

10.90 Energy efficiency of buildings. Firms planning to build new plants or make additions to existing facilities have become very conscious of the energy efficiency of proposed new structures and are interested in the relation between yearly energy consumption and the number of square feet of building shell. The accompanying table lists the energy consumption in British thermal units (a BTU is the amount of heat required to raise 1 pound of water 1°F) for 22 buildings that were all subjected to the same climatic conditions. Consider a straight-line model relating BTU consumption, y, to building shell area, x.

a. Find the least squares estimates of the intercept β_0 and the slope β_1.

b. Investigate the usefulness of the model you developed in part **a**. Is yearly energy consumption positively linearly related to the shell area of the building? Test using $\alpha = .10$.

c. Find the observed significance level of the test of part **b**. Interpret its value.

d. Find the coefficient of determination r^2 and interpret its value.

e. A company wishes to build a new warehouse that will contain 8,000 square feet of shell area. Find the predicted value of energy consumption and associated 95% prediction interval. Comment on the usefulness of this interval.

f. The application of the model you developed in part **a** to the warehouse problem of part **e** is appropriate only if certain assumptions can be made about the new warehouse. What are these assumptions?

BTU/Year (thousands)	Shell Area (square feet)
3,870,000	30,001
1,371,000	13,530
2,422,000	26,060
672,200	6,355
233,100	4,576
218,900	24,680
354,000	2,621
3,135,000	23,350
1,470,000	18,770
1,408,000	12,220
2,201,000	25,490
2,680,000	23,680
337,500	5,650
567,500	8,001
555,300	6,147
239,400	2,660
2,629,000	19,240
1,102,000	10,700
423,500	9,125
423,500	6,510
1,691,000	13,530
1,870,000	18,860

10.91 Top Florida law firms. Refer to *Florida Trend Magazine's* (April 2002) data on law firms with headquarters in the state of Florida, Exercise 2.44 (p. 71). Data on the number of lawyers and number of law offices, saved in the **FLALAW** file, are reproduced in the table below. Suppose you want to predict the number of law offices (y) based on the number of lawyers (x) at the firm.

a. Use the method of least squares (and computer software) to find the best-fitting line to the data.

b. Evaluate the line by conducting a complete simple linear regression analysis.

c. A firm with 300 lawyers is planning on building its headquarters in Florida. How many law offices should the firm expect to build?

Applying the Concepts—Advanced

10.92 Regression through the origin. Sometimes it is known from theoretical considerations that the straight-line relationship between two variables, x and y, passes through the origin of the xy-plane. Consider the relationship between the total weight of a shipment of 50-pound bags of flour, y, and the number of bags in the shipment, x. Since a shipment containing $x = 0$ bags (i.e., no shipment at all) has a total weight of $y = 0$, a straight-line model of the relationship between x and y should pass through the point $x = 0$, $y = 0$. In such a case you could assume $\beta_0 = 0$ and characterize the relationship between x and y with the following model:

$$y = \beta_1 x + \varepsilon$$

The least squares estimate of β_1 for this model is

$$\hat{\beta}_1 = \frac{\sum x_i y_i}{\sum x_i^2}$$

From the records of past flour shipments, 15 shipments were randomly chosen and the data shown in the table below were recorded.

FLOUR2

Weight of Shipment	Number of 50-Pound Bags in Shipment
5,050	100
10,249	205
20,000	450
7,420	150
24,685	500
10,206	200
7,325	150
4,958	100
7,162	150
24,000	500
4,900	100
14,501	300
28,000	600
17,002	400
16,100	400

a. Find the least squares line for the given data under the assumption that $\beta_0 = 0$. Plot the least squares line on a scattergram of the data.

b. Find the least squares line for the given data using the model

FLALAW

Rank	Firm	Headquarters	Number of Lawyers	Number of Offices
1	Holland & Knight	Tallahassee	529	11
2	Akerman Senterfit	Orlando	355	9
3	Greenberg Traurig	Miami	301	6
4	Carlton Fields	Tampa	207	6
5	Gruden McClosky Smit	Ft. Lauder	175	9
6	Fowler White Boggs	Tampa	175	7
7	Foley & Lardner	Orlando	159	5
8	GrayHarris	Orlando	158	6
9	Broad and Cassel	Orlando	150	7
10	Shutts & Bowen	Miami	144	5
11	Steel Hector & Davis	Miami	141	5
12	Gunster Yoakley	WPalmBeach	140	6
13	Adorno & Zeder	Miami	105	4
14	Becker & Poliakoff	Ft. Lauder	100	12
15	Lowndes Drosdick	Orlando	100	1
16	Conroy Simberg Ganon	Hollywood	91	6
17	Stearns Weaver	Miami	85	3
18	Wicker Smith O'Hara	Miami	85	6
19	Rogers Towers Bailey	Jacksonville	80	2
20	Butler Burnette	Tampa	77	3
21	Bilzin Sumberg Dunn	Miami	70	1
22	Morgan Colling	Orlando	70	4
23	White & Case	Miami	70	1
24	Fowler White Burnett	Miami	64	4
25	Rissman Weisberg	Orlando	63	3
26	Rumberger Kirk	Orlando	63	4

Source: Florida Trend Magazine, April 2002, p. 105.

$$y = \beta_0 + \beta_1 x + \varepsilon$$

(i.e., do not restrict β_0 to equal 0). Plot this line on the same scatterplot you constructed in part **a.**

c. Refer to part **b.** Why might $\hat{\beta}_0$ be different from 0 even though the true value of β_0 is known to be 0?

d. The estimated standard error of $\hat{\beta}_0$ is equal to

$$s\sqrt{\frac{1}{n} + \frac{\bar{x}^2}{SS_{xx}}}$$

Use the t-statistic

$$t = \frac{\hat{\beta}_0 - 0}{s\sqrt{(1/n) + (\bar{x}^2/SS_{xx})}}$$

to test the null hypothesis $H_0: \beta_0 = 0$ against the alternative $H_a: \beta_0 \neq 0$. Use $\alpha = .10$. Should you include β_0 in your model?

Critical Thinking Challenges

10.93 Comparing cost functions. Managers are interested in modeling past cost behavior in order to make more accurate predictions of future costs. Models of past cost behavior are called *cost functions*. Factors that influence costs are called *cost drivers* (Horngren, Foster, and Datar, *Cost Accounting*, 1994). The cost data shown below are from a rug manufacturer. Indirect manufacturing labor costs consist of machine maintenance costs and setup labor costs. Machine-hours and direct manufacturing labor-hours are cost drivers. Your task is to estimate and compare two alternative cost functions for indirect manufacturing labor costs. In the first, machine-hours is the independent variable; in the second, direct manufacturing labor-hours is the independent variable. Prepare a report that compares the two cost functions and recommends which should be used to explain and predict indirect manufacturing labor costs. Be sure to justify your choice.

⊛ **RUG**

Week	Indirect Manufacturing Labor Costs	Machine-Hours	Direct Manufacturing Labor-Hours
1	$1,190	68	30
2	1,211	88	35
3	1,004	62	36
4	917	72	20
5	770	60	47
6	1,456	96	45
7	1,180	78	44
8	710	46	38
9	1,316	82	70
10	1,032	94	30
11	752	68	29
12	963	48	38

Source: Data and exercise adapted from Horngren, C. T., Foster, G., and Datar, S. M. *Cost Accounting*, Englewood Cliffs, N.J.: Prentice Hall, 1994.

10.94 Spall damage in bricks. A recent civil suit revolved around a 5-building brick apartment complex located in the Bronx, New York, which began to suffer *spalling* damage (i.e., a separation of some portion of the face of a brick from its body). The owner of the complex alleged that the bricks were defectively manufactured. The brick manufacturer countered that poor design and shoddy management led to the damage. To settle the suit, an estimate of the rate of damage per 1,000 bricks, called the *spall rate*, was required (*Chance*, Summer 1994). The owner estimated the spall rate using several *scaffold-drop* surveys. (With this method, an engineer lowers a scaffold down at selected places on building walls and counts the number of visible spalls for every 1,000 bricks in the observation area.) The brick manufacturer conducted its own survey by dividing the walls of the complex into 83 wall segments and taking a photograph of each wall segment. (The number of spalled bricks that could be made out from each photo was recorded and the sum over all 83 wall segments used as an estimate of total spall damage.) In this court case, the jury was faced with the following dilemma: The scaffold-drop survey provided the most accurate estimate of spall rates in a given wall segment. Unfortunately, the drop areas were not selected at random from the entire complex; rather, drops were made at areas with high spall concentrations, leading to an overestimate of the total damage. On the other hand, the photo survey was complete in that all 83 wall segments in the complex were checked for spall damage. But the spall rate estimated by the photos, at least in areas of high spall concentration, was biased low (spalling damage cannot always be seen from a photo), leading to an underestimate of the total damage.

⊛ **BRICKS**

Drop Location	Drop Spall Rate (per 1,000 bricks)	Photo Spall Rate (per 1,000 bricks)
1	0	0
2	5.1	0
3	6.6	0
4	1.1	.8
5	1.8	1.0
6	3.9	1.0
7	11.5	1.9
8	22.1	7.7
9	39.3	14.9
10	39.9	13.9
11	43.0	11.8

Source: Fairley, W. B., *et al.* "Bricks, Buildings, and the Bronx: Estimating Masonry Deterioration." *Chance*, Vol. 7. No. 3, Summer 1994, p. 36 (Figure 3). [*Note:* The data points are estimated from the points shown on a scatterplot.]

The data in the table are the spall rates obtained using the two methods at 11 drop locations. Use the data, as did expert statisticians who testified in the case, to help the jury estimate the true spall rate at a given wall segment. Then explain how this information, coupled with the data (not given here) on all 83 wall segments, can provide a reasonable estimate of the total spall damage (i.e., total number of damaged bricks).

REFERENCES

Chatterjee, S., and Price, B. *Regression Analysis by Example*, 2nd ed. New York: Wiley, 1991.

Draper, N., and Smith, H. *Applied Regression Analysis*, 3rd ed. New York: Wiley, 1987.

Gitlow, H., Oppenheim, A., and Oppenheim, R. *Quality Management: Tools and Methods for Improvement*, 2nd ed. Burr Ridge, Ill.: Irwin, 1995.

Graybill, F. *Theory and Application of the Linear Model*. North Scituate, Mass.: Duxbury, 1976.

Kleinbaum, D., and Kupper, L. *Applied Regression Analysis and Other Multivariable Methods*, 2nd ed. North Scituate, Mass.: Duxbury, 1997.

Mendenhall, W. *Introduction to Linear Models and the Design and Analysis of Experiments*, Belmont, Calif.: Wadsworth, 1968.

Mendenhall, W., and Sincich, T. *A Second Course in Statistics: Regression Analysis*, 6th ed. Upper Saddle River, N.J.: Prentice Hall, 2003.

Mintzberg, H. *The Nature of Managerial Work*. New York: Harper and Row, 1973.

Montgomery, D., Peck, E., and Vining, G. *Introduction to Linear Regression Analysis*, 3rd ed. New York: Wiley, 2001.

Mosteller, F., and Tukey, J. W. *Data Analysis and Regression: A Second Course in Statistics*. Reading, Mass.: Addison-Wesley, 1977.

Neter, J., Kutner, M., Nachtsheim, C., and Wasserman, W. *Applied Linear Statistical Models*, 4th ed. Hornewood, Ill.: Richard Irwin, 1996.

Rousseeuw, P. J., and Leroy, A. M. *Robust Regression and Outlier Detection*. New York: Wiley, 1987.

Weisburg, S. *Applied Linear Regression*, 2nd ed. New York: Wiley, 1985.

Using Technology

10.1 Simple Linear Regression Using SPSS

To conduct a simple linear regression analysis, first access the SPSS spreadsheet file that contains the two quantitative variables (dependent and independent variables). Next, click on the "Analyze" button on the SPSS menu bar, then click on "Regression" and "Linear", as shown in Figure 10.S.1. The resulting dialog box appears as shown in Figure 10.S.2.

Specify the dependent variable in the "Dependent" box and the independent variable in the "Independent(s)" box. Be sure to select "Enter" in the "Method" box.

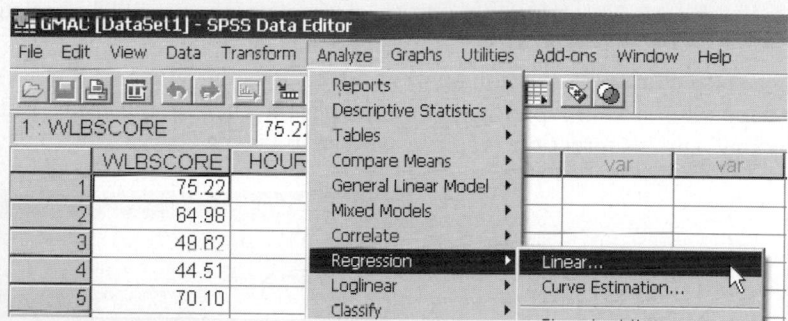

Figure 10.S.1
SPSS menu options for regression

Optionally, you can get SPSS to produce confidence intervals for the model parameters by clicking the "Statistics" button and checking the appropriate menu items in the resulting menu list. Also, you can obtain prediction intervals for y and confidence intervals for $E(y)$ by clicking the "Save" button and checking the appropriate items in the resulting menu list. (The prediction intervals will be added as new columns to the SPSS data spreadsheet.) To return to the main Regression dialog box from any of these optional screens, click "Continue". Click "OK" on the Regression dialog box to view the linear regression results.

Figure 10.S.2
SPSS linear regression dialog box

To obtain the correlation coefficient for the two quantitative variables, click on the "Analyze" button on the main menu bar, then click on "Correlate" (see Figure 10.S.1), and finally click on "Bivariate". The resulting dialog box appears in Figure 10.S.3. Enter the variables of interest in the "Variables" box, check the "Pearson" option, then click "OK" to obtain a printout of the correlation.

Figure 10.S.3
SPSS correlation dialog box

10.2 Simple Linear Regression Using MINITAB

To conduct a simple linear regression analysis, first access the MINITAB worksheet file that contains the two quantitative variables (dependent and independent variables). Next, click on the "Stat" button on the MINITAB menu bar, then click on "Regression" and "Regression" again, as shown in Figure 10.M.1.

Figure 10.M.1
MINITAB menu options for regression

Figure 10.M.2
MINITAB regression dialog
box

The resulting dialog box appears as shown in Figure 10.M.2. Specify the dependent variable in the "Response" box and the independent variable in the "Predictors" box.

Optionally, you can get MINITAB to produce prediction intervals for y and confidence intervals for $E(y)$ by clicking the "Options" button. The resulting dialog box is shown in Figure 10.M.3. Check "Confidence limits" and/or "Prediction limits", specify the "Confidence level", and enter the value of x in the "Prediction intervals for new observations" box. Click "OK" to return to the main Regression dialog box, then click "OK" again to produce the MINITAB simple linear regression printout.

Figure 10.M.3
MINITAB regression options

To obtain the correlation coefficient for the two quantitative variables, click on the "Stat" button on the MINITAB main menu bar, then click on "Basic Statistics", then click on "Correlation", as shown in Figure 10.M.4. The resulting dialog box appears in Figure 10.M.5. Enter the two variables of interest in the "Variables" box, then click "OK" to obtain a printout of the correlation.

Figure 10.M.4
MINITAB menu options for correlation

Figure 10.M.5
MINITAB correlation dialog box

10.3 Simple Linear Regression Using Excel/PHStat2

To conduct a simple linear regression analysis, first access the Excel worksheet file that contains the two quantitative variables (dependent and independent variables). Next, click "PHStat" from the Excel menu bar, then select "Regression" and "Simple Linear Regression", as shown in Figure 10.E.1. The resulting dialog box is shown in Figure 10.E.2. Specify the cell ranges for the *y* and *x* variables, the confidence level for confidence intervals for the model parameters, and select both the "Regression Statistics" and "ANOVA and Coefficients" table options.

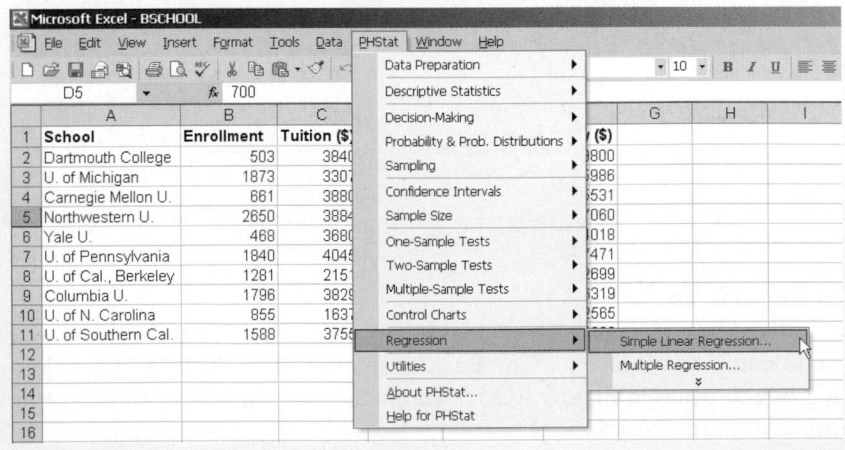

Figure 10.E.1
Excel/PHStat2 menu options for simple linear regression

Figure 10.E.2
Excel/PHStat2 simple linear
regression dialog box

Optionally, you can get Excel to produce prediction intervals for y and confidence intervals for $E(y)$ by selecting the "Confidence and Prediction Interval for X = " option, and entering the value of x of interest, as shown at the bottom of Figure 10.E.2. Click "OK" to produce the simple linear regression results. (The standard regression printout will appear in one worksheet and the confidence/prediction intervals will appear in a second worksheet.)

To obtain the correlation coefficient for the two quantitative variables, click on the "Tools" button on the MINITAB main menu bar, then click on "Data Analysis", and select the "Correlation" option. The resulting dialog box appears in Figure 10.E.3. Specify the cell range for the two variables of interest and select the "Grouped by: Columns" option. (*Note*: The two variables must be in adjacent columns in the Excel worksheet.) Click "OK" to obtain the value of the correlation coefficient on a separate worksheet.

Figure 10.E.3
Excel correlation dialog box

CHAPTER

11

Multiple Regression and Model Building

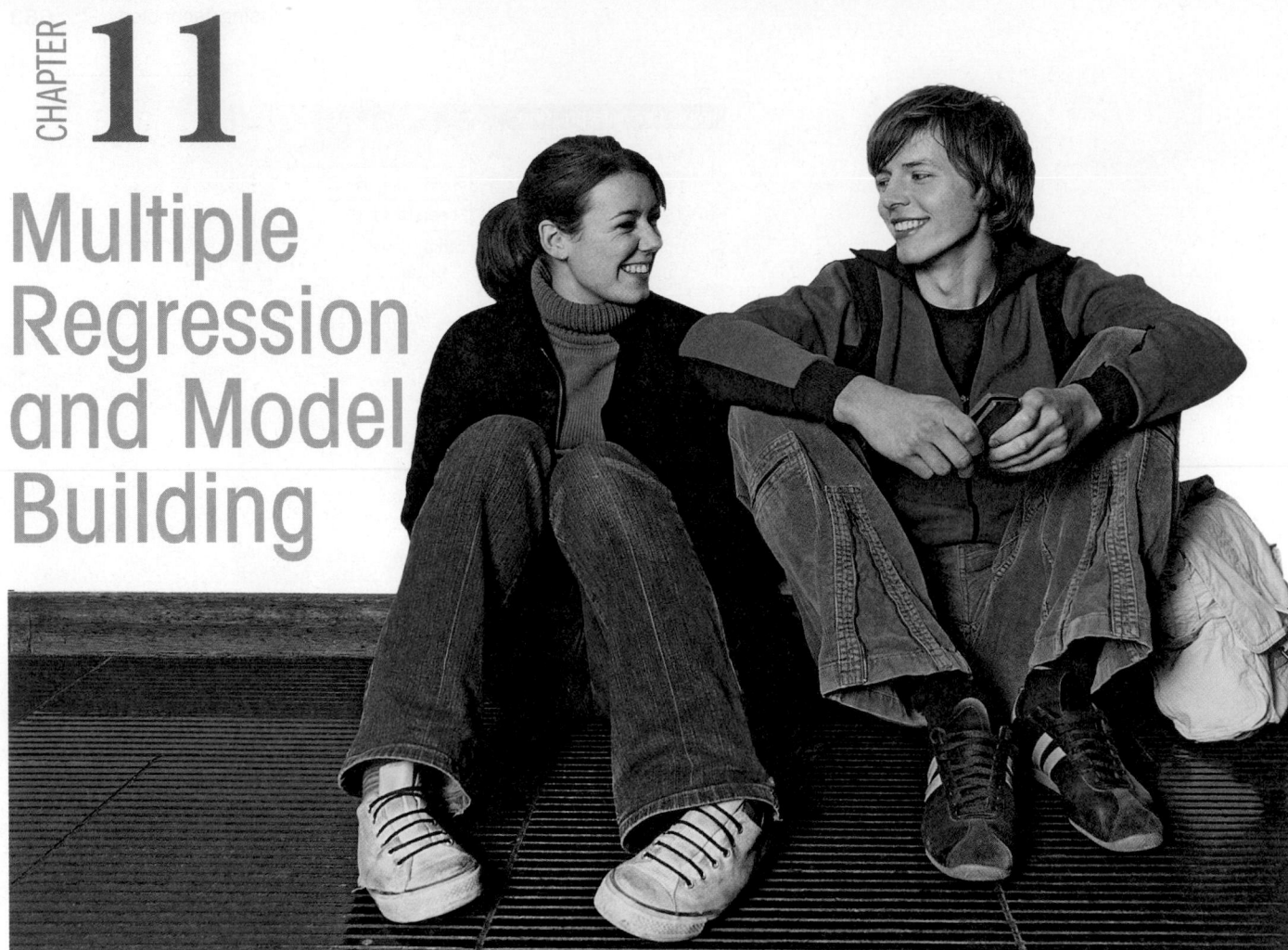

CONTENTS

STATISTICS IN ACTION

Bid-Rigging in the Highway Construction Industry

USING TECHNOLOGY

WHERE WE'VE BEEN

■ Introduced the straight-line model relating a dependent variable y to a single independent variable x.

■ Demonstrated how to estimate the parameters of the straight-line model using the method of least squares.

■ Showed how to statistically assess the adequacy of the model.

■ Showed how to use the model to estimate $E(y)$ and predict y for a given value of x.

WHERE WE'RE GOING

■ Introduce a *multiple regression* model as a means of relating a dependent variable y to two or more independent variables.

■ Present several different multiple regression models involving both quantitative and qualitative independent variables.

■ Assess how well the multiple regression model fits the sample data.

■ Show how an analysis of the model's *residuals* can aid in detecting violations of model assumptions and in identifying model modifications.

STATISTICS IN ACTION

Bid-Rigging in the Highway Construction Industry

In the United States, commercial contractors bid for the right to construct state highways and roads. A state government agency, usually the Department of Transportation (DOT), notifies various contractors of the state's intent to build a highway. Sealed bids are submitted by the contractors, and the contractor with the lowest bid (building cost) is awarded the road con-struction contract. The bidding process works extremely well in competitive markets but has the potential to increase construction costs if the markets are noncompetitive or if collusive practices are present. The latter occurred in the 1980s in Florida. Numerous road contractors either admitted or were found guilty of price fixing (i.e., setting the cost of construction above the fair, or competitive, cost through bid-rigging or other means).

This Statistics in Action involves data collected by the Florida attorney general shortly fol-lowing the price-fixing crisis. The attorney general's objective is to build a model for the cost (*y*) of a road construction contract awarded using the sealed-bid system. The **FLAG** file contains data for a sample of 235 road contracts. The variables measured for each contract are listed in Table SIA11.1. Ultimately, the attorney general wants to use the model to predict the costs of future road contracts in the state.

In several Statistics in Action Revisited sections (see below), we show how to analyze the data using a multiple regression analysis.

Statistics in Action Revisited

- A First-Order Model for Road Contract Cost (p. 690)
- Selecting the Independent Variables and Building a Model for Road Contract Cost (p. 740)
- A Residual Analysis for the Road Cost Model (p. 759)

FLAG

TABLE SIA11.1 Variables in the FLAG Data File

Variable Name	Type	Description
CONTRACT	Quantitative	Road contract number
COST	Quantitative	Low bid contract cost (thousands of dollars)
DOTEST	Quantitative	DOT engineer's cost estimate (thousands of dollars)
STATUS	Qualitative	Bid status (1 = fixed, 0 = competitive)
B2B1RAT	Quantitative	Ratio of second lowest bid to low bid
B3B1RAT	Quantitative	Ratio of third lowest bid to low bid
BHB1RAT	Quantitative	Ratio of highest bid to low bid
DISTRICT	Qualitative	Location of road (1 = South Florida, 0 = North Florida)
BTPRATIO	Quantitative	Ratio of number of bidders to number of plan holders
DAYSEST	Quantitative	DOT engineer's estimate of number of workdays required

11.1 Multiple Regression Models

Most practical applications of regression analysis utilize models that are more complex than the simple straight-line model. For example, a realistic probabilistic model for reac-tion time stimulus would include more than just the amount of a particular drug in the bloodstream. Factors such as age, a measure of visual perception, and sex of the subject are a few of the many variables that might be related to reaction time. Thus, we would want to incorporate these and other potentially important independent variables into the model in order to make accurate predictions.

665

Probabilistic models that include more than one independent variable are called **multiple regression models.** The general form of these models is

$$y = \beta_0 + \beta_1 x_1 + \beta_2 x_2 + \cdots + \beta_k x_k + \epsilon$$

The dependent variable y is now written as a function of k independent variables, $x_1, x_2, \ldots, x_k$. The random error term is added to make the model probabilistic rather than deterministic. The value of the coefficient β_i determines the contribution of the independent variable x_i, and β_0 is the y-intercept. The coefficients $\beta_0, \beta_1 \ldots, \beta_k$ are usually unknown because they represent population parameters.

At first glance it might appear that the regression model shown above would not allow for anything other than straight-line relationships between y and the independent variables, but this is not true. Actually, $x_1, x_2, \ldots, x_k$ can be functions of variables as long as the functions do not contain unknown parameters. For example, the reaction time, y, of a subject to a visual stimulus could be a function of the independent variables

$$x_1 = \text{Age of the subject}$$
$$x_2 = (\text{Age})^2 = x_1^2$$
$$x_3 = 1 \text{ if male subject, } 0 \text{ if female subject}$$

The x_2 term is called a **higher-order term,** since it is the value of a quantitative variable (x_1) squared (i.e., raised to the second power). The x_3 term is a **coded variable** representing a qualitative variable (gender). The multiple regression model is quite versatile and can be made to model many different types of response variables.

The General Multiple Regression Model

$$y = \beta_0 + \beta_1 x_1 + \beta_2 x_2 + \cdots + \beta_k x_k + \epsilon$$

where

y is the dependent variable

$x_1, x_2, \ldots, x_k$ are the independent variables

$E(y) = \beta_0 + \beta_1 x_1 + \beta_2 x_2 + \cdots + \beta_k x_k$ is the deterministic portion of the model

β_i determines the contribution of the independent variable x_i

Note: The symbols $x_1, x_2, \ldots, x_k$ may represent higher-order terms for quantitative predictors or terms that represent qualitative predictors.

As shown in the box, the steps used to develop the multiple regression model are similar to those used for the simple linear regression model.

Analyzing a Multiple Regression Model

Step 1 Hypothesize the deterministic component of the model. This component relates the mean, $E(y)$, to the independent variables $x_1, x_2, \ldots, x_k$. This involves the choice of the independent variables to be included in the model (Sections 11.2, 11.5–11.10).

Step 2 Use the sample data to estimate the unknown model parameters $\beta_0, \beta_1, \beta_2, \ldots, \beta_k$ in the model (Section 11.2).

Step 3 Specify the probability distribution of the random error term, ϵ, and estimate the standard deviation of this distribution, σ (Section 11.3).

Step 4 Check that the assumptions on ϵ are satisfied, and make model modifications if necessary (Section 11.11).

Step 5   Statistically evaluate the usefulness of the model (Sections 11.3).

Step 6   When satisfied that the model is useful, use it for prediction, estimation, and other purposes (Section 11.4).

The assumptions we make about the random error ε of the multiple regression model are also similar to those in a simple linear regression. These are summarized below.

Assumptions for Random Error ε

For any given set of values of $x_1, x_2, \ldots, x_k$, the random error ε has a probability distribution with the following properties:

1. Mean equal to 0
2. Variance equal to σ^2
3. Normal distribution
4. Random errors are independent (in a probabilistic sense)

Throughout this chapter, we introduce several different types of models that form the foundation of **model building** (or useful model construction). In the next several sections, we consider the most basic multiple regression model, called the *first-order model*.

11.2 The First-Order Model: Estimating and Interpreting the β Parameters

A model that includes only terms for *quantitative* independent variables, called a **first-order model,** is described in the box. Note that the first-order model does not include any higher-order terms (such as x_1^2).

A First-Order Model in Five Quantitative Independent Variables*

$$E(y) = \beta_0 + \beta_1 x_1 + \beta_2 x_2 + \beta_3 x_3 + \beta_4 x_4 + \beta_5 x_5$$

where $x_1, x_2, \ldots, x_5$ are all quantitative variables that *are not* functions of other independent variables.

Note: β_i represents the slope of the line relating y to x_i when all the other x's are held fixed.

The method of fitting first-order models—and multiple regression models in general—is identical to that of fitting the simple straight-line model: the method of least squares—that is, we choose the estimated model

$$\hat{y} = \hat{\beta}_0 + \hat{\beta}_1 x_1 + \cdots + \hat{\beta}_k x_k$$

that minimizes

$$SSE = \Sigma(y - \hat{y})^2$$

As in the case of the simple linear model, the sample estimates $\hat{\beta}_0, \hat{\beta}_1, \ldots, \hat{\beta}_k$ are obtained as a solution to a set of simultaneous linear equations.†

---

*The terminology *first order* is derived from the fact that each x in the model is raised to the first power.
†Students who are familiar with calculus should note that $\hat{\beta}_0, \hat{\beta}_1, \ldots, \hat{\beta}_k$ are the solutions to the set of equations $\partial SSE/\partial \hat{\beta}_0 = 0, \partial SSE/\partial \hat{\beta}_1 = 0, \ldots, \partial SSE/\partial \hat{\beta}_k = 0$. The solution is usually given in matrix form, but we do not present the details here. See the references for details.

The primary difference between fitting the simple and multiple regression models is computational difficulty. The $(k + 1)$ simultaneous linear equations that must be solved to find the $(k + 1)$ estimated coefficients $\hat{\beta}_0, \hat{\beta}_1, \ldots, \hat{\beta}_k$ are difficult (sometimes nearly impossible) to solve with a calculator. Consequently, we resort to the use of computers. Instead of presenting the tedious hand calculations required to fit the models, we present output from SPSS, MINITAB, and Excel.

Biography

GEORGE U. YULE (1871–1951)

Yule Processes

Born on a small farm in Scotland, George Yule received an extensive childhood education. After graduating from University College (London), where he studied civil engineering, Yule spent a year employed in engineering workshops. However, he made a career change in 1893, accepting a teaching position back at University College under the guidance of statistician Karl Pearson (see p. 556). Inspired by Pearson's work, Yule produced a series of important articles on the statistics of regression and correlation. Yule is considered the first to apply the method of least squares in regression analysis, and he developed the theory of multiple regression. He eventually was appointed a lecturer in statistics at Cambridge University and later became the president of the prestigious Royal Statistical Society. Yule made many other contributions to the field, including the invention of time series analysis and the development of Yule processes and the Yule distribution.

EXAMPLE 11.1

Fitting a 1st Order Multiple Regression Model for Sale Price of a Home

HOME FOR SALE

Problem   Suppose a property appraiser wants to model the relationship between the sale price of a residential property in a midsize city and the following three independent variables: (1) appraised land value of the property, (2) appraised value of improvements (i.e., home value) on the property, and (3) area of living space on the property (i.e., home size). Consider the first-order model

$$y = \beta_0 + \beta_1 x_1 + \beta_2 x_2 + \beta_3 x_3 + \epsilon$$

where

$$y = \text{Sale price (dollars)}$$
$$x_1 = \text{Appraised land value (dollars)}$$
$$x_2 = \text{Appraised improvements (dollars)}$$
$$x_3 = \text{Area (square feet)}$$

To fit the model, the appraiser selected a random sample of $n = 20$ properties from the thousands of properties that were sold in a particular year. The resulting data are given in Table 11.1.

a.   Use scattergrams to plot the sample data. Interpret the plots.

b.   Use the method of least squares to estimate the unknown parameters $\beta_0, \beta_1, \beta_2$, and β_3 in the model.

c.   Find the value of SSE that is minimized by the least squares method.

d.   Estimate σ, the standard deviation of the model, and interpret the result.

Solution

a.   MINITAB side-by-side scatterplots for examining the bivariate relationships between y and x_1, y and x_2, and y and x_3 are shown in Figure 11.1. Of the three variables, appraised improvements (x_2) appears to have the strongest linear relationship with sale price (y).

REALESTATE

TABLE 11.1 Real Estate Appraisal Data for 20 Properties

Property # (Obs.)	Sale Price, y	Land Value, x_1	Improvements Value, x_2	Area, x_3
1	68,900	5,960	44,967	1,873
2	48,500	9,000	27,860	928
3	55,500	9,500	31,439	1,126
4	62,000	10,000	39,592	1,265
5	116,500	18,000	72,827	2,214
6	45,000	8,500	27,317	912
7	38,000	8,000	29,856	899
8	83,000	23,000	47,752	1,803
9	59,000	8,100	39,117	1,204
10	47,500	9,000	29,349	1,725
11	40,500	7,300	40,166	1,080
12	40,000	8,000	31,679	1,529
13	97,000	20,000	58,510	2,455
14	45,500	8,000	23,454	1,151
15	40,900	8,000	20,897	1,173
16	80,000	10,500	56,248	1,960
17	56,000	4,000	20,859	1,344
18	37,000	4,500	22,610	988
19	50,000	3,400	35,948	1,076
20	22,400	1,500	5,779	962

Source: Alachua County (Florida) Property Appraisers Office.

FIGURE 11.1

MINITAB scatterplots for the data of Table 11.1

b. The model hypothesized above is fit to the data of Table 11.1 using MINITAB. The MINITAB printout is reproduced in Figure 11.2. The least squares estimates of the β parameters appear (highlighted) in the column labeled **Coef.**

You can see that $\hat{\beta}_0 = 1,470$, $\hat{\beta}_1 = .8145$, $\hat{\beta}_2 = .8204$, and $\hat{\beta}_3 = 13.529$. Therefore, the equation that minimizes SSE for this data set (i.e., the **least squares prediction equation**) is

$$\hat{y} = 1,470 + .8145x_1 + .8204x_2 + 13.53x_3$$

c. The minimum value of the SSE, highlighted in Figure 11.2, is SSE $= 1,003,491,259$.

d. Recall that the estimator of σ^2 for the straight-line model is $s^2 = \text{SSE}/(n - 2)$ and note that the denominator is (n − Number of estimated β parameters), which is ($n - 2$) in the straight-line model. Since we must estimate four parameters, $\beta_0, \beta_1, \beta_2,$ and β_3 for the first-order model, the estimator of σ^2 is

$$s^2 = \frac{SSE}{(n-4)} = \frac{SSE}{20 - 4} = \frac{1,003,491,259}{16} = 62,718,204$$

Regression Analysis: SALEPRIC versus LANDVAL, IMPROVAL, AREA

```
The regression equation is
SALEPRIC = 1470 + 0.814 LANDVAL + 0.820 IMPROVAL + 13.5 AREA


Predictor      Coef   SE Coef      T       P
Constant       1470      5746   0.26   0.801
LANDVAL      0.8145    0.5122   1.59   0.131
IMPROVAL     0.8204    0.2112   3.88   0.001
AREA         13.529     6.586   2.05   0.057


S = 7919.48    R-Sq = 89.7%    R-Sq(adj) = 87.8%


Analysis of Variance

Source           DF          SS          MS       F       P
Regression        3  8779676741  2926558914   46.66   0.000
Residual Error   16  1003491259    62718204
Total            19  9783168000
```

FIGURE 11.2

MINITAB analysis of sale price model

This value, often called the **mean square for error (MSE),** is highlighted at the bottom of the MINITAB printout in Figure 11.2. The estimate of σ, then, is

$$s = \sqrt{62{,}718{,}204} = 7{,}919.5$$

which is highlighted in the middle of the MINITAB printout in Figure 11.2. One useful interpretation of the estimated standard deviation s is that the interval $\pm 2s$ will provide a rough approximation to the accuracy with which the model will predict future values of y for given values of x. Thus, we expect the model to provide predictions of sale price to within about $\pm 2s = \pm 2(7{,}919.5) = \pm 15{,}839$ dollars.*

Look Back: As with simple linear regression, we will use the estimator of σ^2 both to check the utility of the model (Section 11.3) and to provide a measure of reliability of predictions and estimates when the model is used for those purposes (Section 11.4). Thus, you can see that the estimation of σ^2 plays an important part in the development of a regression model.

Now Work Exercise 11.2a–c

Estimator of σ^2 for a Multiple Regression Model with k Independent Variables

$$s^2 = \frac{\text{SSE}}{n - \text{Number of estimated } \beta \text{ parameters}} = \frac{\text{SSE}}{n - (k + 1)}$$

After obtaining the least squares prediction equation, the analyst will usually want to make meaningful interpretations of the β estimates. Recall that in the straight-line model (Chapter 10)

$$y = \beta_0 + \beta_1 x + \epsilon$$

β_0 represents the y-intercept of the line and β_1 represents the slope of the line. From our discussion in Chapter 10, β_1 has a practical interpretation — it represents the mean

*The $\pm 2s$ approximation will improve as the sample size is increased. We will provide more precise methodology for the construction of prediction intervals in Section 11.4.

change in y for every 1-unit increase in x. When the independent variables are quantitative, the β parameters in the first-order model specified in Example 11.1 have similar interpretations. The difference is that when we interpret the β that multiplies one of the variables (e.g., x_1), we must be certain to hold the values of the remaining independent variables (e.g., x_2, x_3) fixed.

To see this, suppose that the mean $E(y)$ of a response y is related to two quantitative independent variables, x_1 and x_2, by the first-order model

$$E(y) = 1 + 2x_1 + x_2$$

In other words, $\beta_0 = 1$, $\beta_1 = 2$, and $\beta_2 = 1$.

Now, when $x_2 = 0$, the relationship between $E(y)$ and x_1 is given by

$$E(y) = 1 + 2x_1 + (0) = 1 + 2x_1$$

A graph of this relationship (a straight line) is shown in Figure 11.3. Similar graphs of the relationship between $E(y)$ and x_1 for $x_2 = 1$,

$$E(y) = 1 + 2x_1 + (1) = 2 + 2x_1$$

and for $x_2 = 2$,

$$E(y) = 1 + 2x_1 + (2) = 3 + 2x_1$$

also are shown in Figure 11.3. Note that the slopes of the three lines are all equal to $\beta_1 = 2$, the coefficient that multiplies x_1.

Figure 11.3 exhibits a characteristic of all first-order models: If you graph $E(y)$ versus any one variable—say, x_1—for fixed values of the other variables, the result will always be a *straight line* with slope equal to β_1. If you repeat the process for other values of the fixed independent variables, you will obtain a set of *parallel* straight lines. This indicates that the effect of the independent variable x_i on $E(y)$ is independent of all the other independent variables in the model, and this effect is measured by the slope β_i (see the box on p. 667).

A three-dimensional graph of the model $E(y) = 1 + 2x_1 + x_2$ is shown in Figure 11.4. Note that the model graphs as a plane. If you slice the plane at a particular value of x_2 (say, $x_2 = 0$), you obtain a straight line relating $E(y)$ to x_1 (e.g., $E[y] = 1 + 2x_1$). Similarly, if you slice the plane at a particular value of x_1, you obtain a straight line relating $E(y)$ to x_2. Since it is more difficult to visualize three-dimensional and, in general, k-dimensional surfaces, we will graph all the models presented in this chapter in two dimensions. *The key to obtaining these graphs is to hold fixed all but one of the independent variables in the model.*

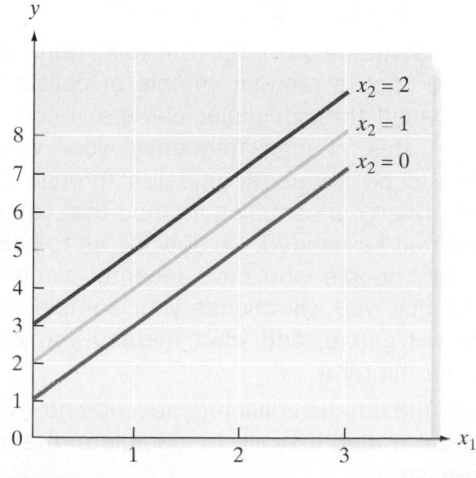

FIGURE 11.3

Graphs of $E(y) = 1 + 2x_1 + x_2$ for $x_2 = 0, 1, 2$

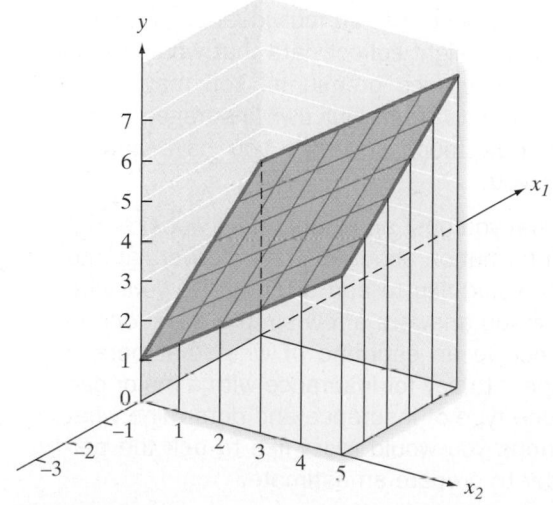

FIGURE 11.4

The plane $E(y) = 1 + 2x_1 + x_2$

EXAMPLE 11.2

Interpreting the β Estimates of the Home Sales Price Model

Problem Refer to the first-order model for sale price y considered in Example 11.1. Interpret the estimates of the β parameters in the model.

Solution The least squares prediction equation, as given in Example 11.1, is $\hat{y} = 1{,}470 + .8145x_1 + .8204x_2 + 13.53x_3$. We know that with first-order models, β_1 represents the slope of the $y - x_1$ line for fixed x_2 and x_3—that is, β_1 measures the change in $E(y)$ for every 1-unit increase in x_1 when all other independent variables in the model are held fixed. Similar statements can be made about β_2 and β_3; e.g., β_2 measures the change in $E(y)$ for every 1-unit increase in x_1 when all other x's in the model are held fixed. Consequently, we obtain the following interpretations:

1. $\hat{\beta}_1 = .8145$: We estimate the mean sale price of a property, $E(y)$, to increase .8145 dollar for every $1 increase in appraised land value (x_1) when both appraised improvements (x_2) and area (x_3) are held fixed.

2. $\hat{\beta}_2 = .8204$: We estimate the mean sale price of a property, $E(y)$, to increase .8204 dollar for every $1 increase in appraised improvements (x_2) when both appraised land value (x_1) and area (x_3) are held fixed.

3. $\hat{\beta}_3 = 13.53$: We estimate the mean sale price of a property, $E(y)$, to increase $13.53 for each additional square foot of living area (x_3) when both appraised land value (x_1) and appraised improvements (x_2) are held fixed.

The value $\hat{\beta}_0 = 1{,}470$ does not have a meaningful interpretation in this example. To see this, note that $\hat{y} = \hat{\beta}_0$ when $x_1 = x_2 = x_3 = 0$. Thus, $\hat{\beta}_0 = 1{,}470$ represents the estimated mean sale price when the values of all the independent variables are set equal to 0. Since a residential property with these characteristics—appraised land value of $0, appraised improvements of $0, and 0 square feet of living area—is not practical, the value of $\hat{\beta}_0$ has no meaningful interpretation.

Look Back In general, $\hat{\beta}_0$ will not have a practical interpretation unless it makes sense to set the values of the x's simultaneously equal to 0.

Now Work Exercise 11.12a,b

ACTIVITY 11.1: *Insurance Premiums:* Collecting Data for Several Variables

Premiums for life insurance, health insurance, homeowners insurance, and car insurance are based on more than one factor. In this activity, you will consider factors that influence the price that an individual pays for insurance and how you might collect data that would be useful in studying insurance premiums. You may wish to look over statements from your own insurance policies to determine how much coverage you have and how much it costs you.

1. Suppose that you host an independent website that provides information about insurance coverage and costs. You would like to add a feature to your site where a person answers a few simple questions in order to receive an estimate of what that person should expect to pay for insurance with a major carrier. Pick one type of insurance and determine what five questions you would most like to ask the person in order to prepare an estimate.

2. Use your five questions from Exercise 1 to define five independent variables. What is the dependent variable in this situation? What would a first-order model for this situation look like?

3. The estimates provided on your website will be based upon a random sample of policies recently purchased through major carriers. Because insurance rates change frequently, your website will need to be frequently updated through new samples. Design a sampling method that can easily be repeated as needed. Be specific as to how you will identify people who have recently purchased policies, how you will choose your sample, what data you will gather, and what method you will use to gather the data.

4. Once the data is collected, describe how you will organize it and use it to complete the model in Exercise 3.

Caution

The interpretation of the β parameters in a multiple regression model will depend on the terms specified in the model. The interpretations above are for a first-order linear model only. In practice, you should be sure that a first-order model is the correct model for $E(y)$ before making these β interpretations. (We discuss alternative models for $E(y)$ in Sections 11.5–11.8.)

11.3 Inferences about the β Parameters and the Overall Model Utility

Inferences about the individual β parameters in a model are obtained using either a confidence interval or a test of hypothesis, as outlined in the following two boxes.*

A 100$(1 - \alpha)$% Confidence Interval for a β Parameter

$$\hat{\beta}_i \pm t_{\alpha/2}s_{\hat{\beta}_i},$$

where $t_{\alpha/2}$ is based on $n - (k + 1)$ degrees of freedom and

n = Number of observations

$k + 1$ = Number of β parameters in the model

Test of an Individual Parameter Coefficient in the Multiple Regression Model

One-Tailed Test	Two-Tailed Test
$H_0: \beta_i = 0$	$H_0: \beta_i = 0$
$H_a: \beta_i < 0$ [or $H_a: \beta_i > 0$]	$H_a: \beta_i \neq 0$

Test statistic: $t = \dfrac{\hat{\beta}_i}{s_{\hat{\beta}_i}}$

Rejection region: $t < -t_\alpha$ [or $t > t_\alpha$ when $H_a: \beta_i > 0$]	Rejection region: $|t| > t_{\alpha/2}$

where t_α and $t_{\alpha/2}$ are based on $n - (k + 1)$ degrees of freedom and

n = Number of observations

$k + 1$ = Number of β parameters in the model

Conditions Required for Valid Inferences about the β Parameters

The four assumptions about the probability distribution for the random error ϵ. (p. 667).

We illustrate these methods with another example.

---

*The formulas for computing $\hat{\beta}_i$ and its standard error are so complex, the only reasonable way to present them is by using matrix algebra. We do not assume a prerequisite of matrix algebra for this text, and, in any case, we think the formulas can be omitted in an introductory course without serious loss. They are programmed into almost all statistical software packages with multiple regression routines and are presented in some of the texts listed in the references.

EXAMPLE 11.3

Making Inferences about the β Parameters in a Model for Price of an Antique Clock

Problem   A collector of antique grandfather clocks knows that the price received for the clocks increases linearly with the age of the clocks. Moreover, the collector hypothesizes that the auction price of the clocks will increase linearly as the number of bidders increases. Thus, the following first-order model is hypothesized:

$$y = \beta_0 + \beta_1 x_1 + \beta_2 x_2 + \epsilon$$

where

y = Auction price
x_1 = Age of clock (years)
x_2 = Number of bidders

A sample of 32 auction prices of grandfather clocks, along with their age and the number of bidders, is given in Table 11.2. The model $y = \beta_0 + \beta_1 x_1 + \beta_2 x_2 + \epsilon$ is fit to the data, and the Excel printout is shown in Figure 11.5.

a. Test the hypothesis that the mean auction price of a clock increases as the number of bidders increases when age is held constant, that is, test $\beta_2 > 0$. Use $\alpha = .05$.

b. Form a 90% confidence interval for β_1 and interpret the result.

Solution

a. The hypotheses of interest concern the parameter β_2. Specifically,

$$H_0: \beta_2 = 0$$
$$H_a: \beta_2 > 0$$

The test statistic is a t-statistic formed by dividing the sample estimate $\hat{\beta}_2$ of the parameter β_2 by estimated standard error of $\hat{\beta}_2$ (denoted $s_{\hat{\beta}_2}$). These estimates as well as the calculated t-value are highlighted at the bottom of the Excel printout. These values yield the following:

$$\text{Test statistic: } t = \frac{\hat{\beta}_2}{s_{\hat{\beta}_2}} = \frac{85.953}{8.729} = 9.85$$

 GFCLOCKS

TABLE 11.2 Auction Price Data

Age, x_1	Number of Bidders, x_2	Auction Price, y	Age, x_1	Number of Bidders, x_2	Auction Price, y
127	13	$1,235	170	14	$2,131
115	12	1,080	182	8	1,550
127	7	845	162	11	1,884
150	9	1,522	184	10	2,041
156	6	1,047	143	6	845
182	11	1,979	159	9	1,483
156	12	1,822	108	14	1,055
132	10	1,253	175	8	1,545
137	9	1,297	108	6	729
113	9	946	179	9	1,792
137	15	1,713	111	15	1,175
117	11	1,024	187	8	1,593
137	8	1,147	111	7	785
153	6	1,092	115	7	744
117	13	1,152	194	5	1,356
126	10	1,336	168	7	1,262

Regression Analysis

Regression Statistics	
Multiple R	0.94463957
R Square	0.892343916
Adjusted R Square	0.884919359
Standard Error	133.4846678
Observations	32

ANOVA

	df	SS	MS	F	Significance F
Regression	2	4283062.96	2141531.48	120.1881617	9.21636E-15
Residual	29	516726.5399	17818.15655		
Total	31	4799789.5			

	Coefficients	Standard Error	t Stat	P-value	Lower 90.0%	Upper 90.0%
Intercept	-1338.95134	173.8094707	-7.703558013	1.70581E-08	-1634.275722	-1043.62696
AGE	12.7405741	0.904740307	14.08203331	1.69276E-14	11.20330533	14.27784287
NUMBIDS	85.95298437	8.728523289	9.847368395	9.34495E-11	71.12211393	100.7838548

FIGURE 11.5

Excel analysis of auction price model for grandfather clocks

The rejection region for the test is found in exactly the same way as the rejection regions for the t-tests in previous chapters—that is, we consult Table V in Appendix B to obtain an upper-tail value of t. This is a value t_α such that $P(t > t_\alpha) = \alpha$. We can then use this value to construct rejection regions for either one-tailed or two-tailed tests.

For $\alpha = .05$ and $n - (k + 1) = 32 - (2 + 1) = 29$ df, the critical t-value obtained from Table V is $t_{.05} = 1.699$. Therefore,

Rejection region: $t > 1.699$ (see Figure 11.6)

Since the test statistic value, $t = 9.85$, falls in the rejection region, we have sufficient evidence to reject H_0. Thus, the collector can conclude that the mean auction price of a clock increases as the number of bidders increases, when age is held constant. Note that the observed significance level of the test is also given on the printout. Since p-value ≈ 0, any nonzero α (e.g., $\alpha = .01$) will lead us to reject H_0.

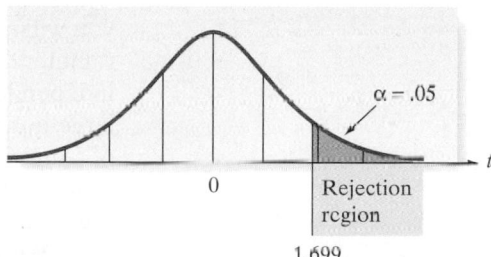

FIGURE 11.6

Rejection region for H_0: $\beta_2 = 0$ vs. H_a: $\beta_2 > 0$

b. A 90% confidence interval for β_1 is (from the box):

$$\hat{\beta}_1 \pm t_{\alpha/2} s_{\hat{\beta}_1} = \hat{\beta}_1 \pm t_{.05} s_{\hat{\beta}_1}$$

Substituting $\hat{\beta}_1 = 12.74$, $s_{\hat{\beta}_1} = .905$ (both obtained from the Excel printout, Figure 11.5) and $t_{.05} = 1.699$ (from part **a**) into the equation, we obtain

$$12.74 \pm 1.699(.905) = 12.74 \pm 1.54$$

or (11.20, 14.28). This interval is also shown on the Excel printout, Figure 11.5). Thus, we are 90% confident that β_1 falls between 11.20 and 14.28. Since β_1 is the slope of the line relating auction price (y) to age of the clock (x_1), we conclude that price increases between $11.20 and $14.28 for every 1-year increase in age, holding number of bidders (x_2) constant.

Look Back When interpreting the β multiplied by one x, be sure to hold fixed the values of the other x's in the model.

Now Work Exercise 11.12c,d

There are caveats with conducting t-tests on individual β parameters in a model for the purposes of determining which x's are useful for predicting y. Several of these are listed next.

Caution

It is dangerous to conduct t-tests on the individual β parameters in a *first-order linear model* for the purpose of determining which independent variables are useful for predicting y and which are not. If you fail to reject H_0: $\beta_i = 0$, several conclusions are possible:

1. There is no relationship between y and x_i.
2. A straight-line relationship between y and x exists (holding the other x's in the model fixed), but a Type II error occurred.
3. A relationship between y and x_i (holding the other x's in the model fixed) exists but is more complex than a straight-line relationship (e.g., a curvilinear relationship may be appropriate). The most you can say about a β parameter test is that there is either sufficient (if you reject H_0: $\beta_i = 0$) or insufficient (if you do not reject H_0: $\beta_i = 0$) evidence of a *linear* (*straight-line*) relationship between y and x_i.

In addition, conducting t-tests on each β parameter in a model is *not* the best way to determine whether the overall model is contributing information for the prediction of y. If we were to conduct a series of t-tests to determine whether the independent variables are contributing to the predictive relationship, we would be very likely to make one or more errors in deciding which terms to retain in the model and which to exclude.

For example, suppose you fit a first-order model in 10 quantitative x variables and decide to conduct t-tests on all 10 of the individual β's in the model, each at $\alpha = .05$. Even if all the β parameters (except β_0) are equal to 0, approximately 40% of the time you will incorrectly reject the null hypothesis at least once and conclude that some β parameter differs from 0.* Thus, in multiple regression models for which a large number of independent variables are being considered, conducting a series of t-tests may include a large number of insignificant variables and exclude some useful ones. To test the utility of a multiple regression model, we need a *global test* (one that encompasses all the β parameters). We would also like to find some statistical quantity that measures how well the model fits the data.

We commence with the easier problem—finding a measure of how well a linear model fits a set of data. For this we use the multiple regression equivalent of r^2, the coefficient of determination for the straight-line model (Chapter 10), as shown in the box.

Definition 11.1

The **multiple coefficient of determination, R^2,** is defined as

$$R^2 = 1 - \frac{\text{SSE}}{\text{SS}_{yy}} = \frac{\text{SS}_{yy} - \text{SSE}}{\text{SS}_{yy}} = \frac{\text{Explained variablilty}}{\text{Total variability}}$$

Just as for the simple linear model, R^2 represents the fraction of the sample variation of the y values (measured by SS_{yy}) that is explained by the least squares prediction equation. Thus, $R^2 = 0$ implies a complete lack of fit of the model to the data, and $R^2 = 1$ implies a perfect fit with the model passing through every data point. In general, the larger the value of R^2, the better the model fits the data.

---

*The proof of this result (assuming independence of tests) proceeds as follows:
$P(\text{Reject } H_0 \text{ at least once}|\beta_1 = \beta_2 = \cdots = \beta_{10} = 0)$
$= 1 - P(\text{Reject } H_0 \text{ no times}|\beta_1 = \beta_2 = \cdots = \beta_{10} = 0)$
$\leq 1 - [P(\text{Accept } H_0: \beta_1 = 0|\beta_1 = 0) \cdot P(\text{Accept } H_0: \beta_2 = 0|\beta_2 = 0) \cdot \cdots \cdot P(\text{Accept } H_0: \beta_{10} = 0|\beta_{10} = 0)]$
$= 1 - [(1 - \alpha)^{10}] = 1 - (.05)^{10} = .401$
For dependent tests, the Bonferroni inequality states that
$P(\text{Reject } H_0 \text{ at least once}|\beta_1 = \beta_2 = \cdots = \beta_{10} = 0) \leq 10(\alpha) = 10(.05) = .50.$

Regression Analysis: SALEPRIC versus LANDVAL, IMPROVAL, AREA

```
The regression equation is
SALEPRIC = 1470 + 0.814 LANDVAL + 0.820 IMPROVAL + 13.5 AREA


Predictor      Coef    SE Coef      T       P
Constant       1470       5746   0.26   0.801
LANDVAL      0.8145     0.5122   1.59   0.131
IMPROVAL     0.8204     0.2112   3.88   0.001
AREA         13.529      6.586   2.05   0.057


S = 7919.48    R-Sq = 89.7%    R-Sq(adj) = 87.8%


Analysis of Variance

Source            DF           SS          MS       F      P
Regression         3   8779676741  2926558914   46.66  0.000
Residual Error    16   1003491259    62718204
Total             19   9783168000
```

FIGURE 11.7

MINITAB analysis of sale price model

To illustrate, the value $R^2 = .897$ for the sale price model of Example 11.1 is indicated in Figure 11.7. This high value of R^2 implies that using the independent variables land value, appraised improvements, and home size in a first-order model explains 89.7% of the total *sample variation* (measured by SS_{yy}) of sale price y. Thus, R^2 is a sample statistic that tells how well the model fits the data and thereby represents a measure of the usefulness of the entire model.

A large value of R^2 computed from the *sample* data does not necessarily mean that the model provides a good fit to all of the data points in the *population*. For example, a first-order linear model that contains three parameters will provide a perfect fit to a sample of three data points and R^2 will equal 1. Likewise, you will always obtain a perfect fit ($R^2 = 1$) to a set of n data points if the model contains exactly n parameters. Consequently, if you want to use the value of R^2 as a measure of how useful the model will be for predicting y, it should be based on a sample that contains substantially more data points than the number of parameters in the model.

Caution

In a multiple regression analysis, use the value of R^2 as a measure of how useful a linear model will be for predicting y only if the sample contains substantially more data points than the number of β parameters in the model.

As an alternative to using R^2 as a measure of model adequacy, the *adjusted multiple coefficient of determination*, denoted R_a^2, is often reported. The formula for R_a^2 is shown in the box.

Definition 11.2

The **adjusted multiple coefficient of determination** is given by

$$R_a^2 = 1 - \left[\frac{(n-1)}{n-(k+1)} \right]\left(\frac{SSE}{SS_{yy}} \right)$$

$$= 1 - \left[\frac{(n-1)}{n-(k+1)} \right](1 - R^2)$$

Note: $R_a^2 \leq R^2$

R^2 and R_a^2 have similar interpretations. However, unlike R^2, R_a^2 takes into account ("adjusts" for) both the sample size n and the number of β parameters in the model. R_a^2 will always be smaller than R^2, and more importantly, cannot be "forced" to 1 by simply adding more and more independent variables to the model. Consequently, analysts prefer the more conservative R_a^2 when choosing a measure of model adequacy. In Figure 11.7, note that $R_a^2 = .878$, a value only slightly smaller than R^2.

Despite their utility, R^2 and R_a^2 are only sample statistics. Therefore, it is dangerous to judge the global usefulness of the model based solely on these values. A better method is to conduct a test of hypothesis involving *all* the β parameters (except β_0) in a model. In particular, for the general multiple regression model $E(y) = \beta_0 + \beta_1 x_1 + \beta_2 x_2 + \cdots + \beta_k x_k$, we would test

$$H_0\colon \beta_1 = \beta_2 = \cdots = \beta_k = 0$$
$$H_a\colon \text{At least one of the coefficients is nonzero}$$

The test statistic used to test this hypothesis is an F-statistic, and several equivalent versions of the formula can be used (although we will usually rely on the computer to calculate the F-statistic):

$$\textit{Test statistic: } F = \frac{(SS_{yy} - SSE)/k}{SSE/[n - (k + 1)]}$$

$$= \frac{\text{Mean Square (Model)}}{\text{Mean Square (Error)}} = \frac{R^2/k}{(1 - R^2)/[n - (k + 1)]}$$

These formulas indicate that the F-statistic is the ratio of the *explained* variability divided by the model degrees of freedom to the *unexplained* variability divided by the error degrees of freedom. Thus, the larger the proportion of the total variability accounted for by the model, the larger the F-statistic.

To determine when the ratio becomes large enough that we can confidently reject the null hypothesis and conclude that the model is more useful than no model at all for predicting y, we compare the calculated F-statistic to a tabulated F value with k df in the numerator and $[n - (k + 1)]$ df in the denominator. Recall that tabulations of the F-distribution for various values of α are given in Tables VII, VIII, IX, and X of Appendix B.

Rejection region: $F > F_\alpha$, where F is based on k numerator and

$n - (k + 1)$ denominator degrees of freedom.

The analysis of variance F-test for testing the usefulness of the model is summarized in the next box.

Testing Global Usefulness of the Model: The Analysis of Variance *F*-Test

$H_0\colon \beta_1 = \beta_2 = \cdots = \beta_k = 0$ (All model terms are unimportant for predicting y)

$H_a\colon$ At least one $\beta_i \neq 0$ (At least one model term is useful for predicting y)

$$\textit{Test statistic: } F = \frac{(SS_{yy} - SSE)/k}{SSE/[n - (k + 1)]} = \frac{R^2/k}{(1 - R^2)/[n - (k + 1)]}$$

$$= \frac{\text{Mean Square (Model)}}{\text{Mean Square (Error)}}$$

where n is the sample size and k is the number of terms in the model.

Rejection region: $F > F_\alpha$, with k numerator degrees of freedom and $[n - (k + 1)]$ denominator degrees of freedom.

> **Conditions Required for the Global F-Test in Regression to Be Valid**
>
> The standard regression assumptions about the random error component (Section 11.1).

Caution

A rejection of the null hypothesis $H_0: \beta_1 = \beta_2 = \cdots = \beta_k$ in the global F-test leads to the conclusion [with $100(1 - \alpha)\%$ confidence] that the model is statistically useful. However, statistically "useful" does not necessarily mean "best." Another model may prove even more useful in terms of providing more reliable estimates and predictions. This global F-test is usually regarded as a test that the model *must* pass to merit further consideration.

EXAMPLE 11.4

Assessing the Overall Adequacy of the Clock Auction Price Model

Problem   Refer to Example 11.3, in which an antique collector modeled the auction price y of grandfather clocks as a function of the age of the clock, x_1, and the number of bidders, x_2. Recall that the hypothesized first-order model is

$$y = \beta_0 + \beta_1 x_1 + \beta_2 x_2 + \epsilon$$

a. Find and interpret the adjusted coefficient of determination R_a^2 on the Excel printout, Figure 11.5.

b. Conduct the global F-test of model usefulness at the $\alpha = .05$ level of significance.

Solution

a. The R_a^2 value (highlighted in Figure 11.5) is .885. This implies that the least squares model has explained about 88.5% of the total sample variation in y values (auction prices), after adjusting for sample size and number of independent variables in the model.

b. The elements of the global test of the model follow:

$H_0: \beta_1 = \beta_2 = 0$ (*Note:* $k = 2$)

H_a: At least one of the two model coefficients is nonzero

Test statistic: $F = \dfrac{\text{MS(Model)}}{\text{MSE}} = \dfrac{2{,}141{,}531}{17{,}818} = 120.19$ (see Figure 11.5)

p-value ≈ 0

Conclusion: Since $\alpha = .05$ exceeds the observed significance level, $(p \approx 0)$, the data provide strong evidence that at least one of the model coefficients is nonzero. The overall model appears to be statistically useful for predicting auction prices.

Look Back   Can we be sure that the best prediction model has been found if the global F-test indicates that a model is useful? Unfortunately, we cannot. The addition of other independent variables may improve the usefulness of the model. (See the box above.) We consider more complex multiple regression models in Sections 11.5–11.8.

Now Work Exercise 11.11d–h

In this section, we discussed several different statistics for assessing the utility of a multiple regression model: t-tests on individual β parameters, R^2, R_a^2, and the global F-test. Both R^2 and R_a^2 are indicators of how well the prediction equation fits the data. Intuitive evaluations of the contribution of the model based on R^2 must be examined with care. Unlike R_a^2, the value of R^2 increases as more and more variables are added to the model. Consequently, you could force R^2 to take a value very close to 1 even though the model contributes no information for the prediction of y. In fact, R^2 equals 1 when the number of terms in the model (including β_0) equals the number of data points. Therefore, you should not rely solely on the value of R^2 (or even R_a^2) to tell you whether the model is useful for predicting y.

Conducting t-tests on all of the individual β parameters is also not the best method of testing the global utility of the model, since these multiple tests result in a high probability of making at least one Type I error. Use the F-test for testing the global utility of the model.

After we have determined that the overall model is useful for predicting y using the F-test, we may elect to conduct one or more t-tests on the individual β parameters. However, the test (or tests) to be conducted should be decided *a priori*—that is, prior to fitting the model. Also, we should limit the number of t-tests conducted to avoid the potential problem of making too many Type I errors. Generally, the regression analyst will conduct t-tests only on the "most important" β's. We provide insight in identifying the most important β's in a linear model in Sections 11.5–11.18.

Recommendation for Checking the Utility of a Multiple Regression Model

1. First, conduct a test of overall model adequacy using the F-test—that is, test

$$H_0: \beta_1 = \beta_2 = \cdots = \beta_k = 0$$

If the model is deemed adequate (that is, if you reject H_0), then proceed to step 2. Otherwise, you should hypothesize and fit another model. The new model may include more independent variables or higher-order terms.

2. Conduct t-tests on those β parameters in which you are particularly interested (that is, the "most important" β's). These usually involve only the β's associated with higher-order terms (x_2, x_1x_2, etc.). However, it is a safe practice to limit the number of β's that are tested. Conducting a series of t-tests leads to a high overall Type I error rate α.

Exercises 11.1–11.24

Learning the Mechanics

11.1 Write a first-order model relating $E(y)$ to
  a. two quantitative independent variables.
  b. four quantitative independent variables.
  c. five quantitative independent variables.

11.2 MINITAB was used to fit the model
NW $E(y) = \beta_0 + \beta_1x_1 + \beta_2x_2$ to $n = 20$ data points, and the printout shown was obtained.
  a. What are the sample estimates of β_0, β_1, and β_2?
  b. What is the least squares prediction equation?
  c. Find SSE, MSE, and s. Interpret the standard deviation in the context of the problem.
  d. Test $H_0: \beta_1 = 0$ against $H_a: \beta_1 \neq 0$. Use $\alpha = .05$.
  e. Use a 95% confidence interval to estimate β_2.
  f. Find R^2 and R_a^2 and interpret these values.
  g. Find the test statistic for testing $H_0: \beta_1 = \beta_2 = 0$.
  h. Find the observed significance level of the test, part **g**. Interpret the result.

11.3 Suppose you fit the multiple regression model

$$y = \beta_0 + \beta_1x_1 + \beta_2x_2 + \beta_3x_3 + \epsilon$$

to $n = 30$ data points and obtain the following result:

$$\hat{y} = 3.4 - 4.6x_1 + 2.7x_2 + .93x_3$$

```
The regression equation is
Y = 506.35 - 941.9 X1 - 429.1 X2


Predictor      Coef    SE Coef       T       P
Constant     506.346    45.17    11.21   0.000
X1          -941.900   275.08    -3.42   0.003
X2          -429.060   379.83    -1.13   0.274


S = 94.251    R-Sq = 45.9%    R-Sq(adj) = 39.6%


Analysis of Variance

Source           DF       SS      MS       F       P
Regression        2   128329   64165    7.22   0.005
Residual Error   17   151016    8883
Total            19   279345
```

MINITAB Output for Exercise 11.2

The estimated standard errors of $\hat{\beta}_2$ and $\hat{\beta}_3$ are 1.86 and .29, respectively.
  a. Test the null hypothesis $H_0: \beta_2 = 0$ against the alternative hypothesis $H_a: \beta_2 \neq 0$. Use $\alpha = .05$.

b. Test the null hypothesis H_0: $\beta_3 = 0$ against the alternative hypothesis H_a: $\beta_3 \neq 0$. Use $\alpha = .05$.

c. The null hypothesis H_0: $\beta_2 = 0$ is not rejected. In contrast, the null hypothesis H_0: $\beta_3 = 0$ is rejected. Explain how this can happen even though $\hat{\beta}_2 > \hat{\beta}_3$.

11.4 Suppose you fit the first-order multiple regression model

$$y = \beta_0 + \beta_1 x_1 + \beta_2 x_2 + \epsilon$$

to $n = 25$ data points and obtain the prediction equation

$$\hat{y} = 6.4 + 3.1x_1 + .92x_2$$

The estimated standard deviations of the sampling distributions of $\hat{\beta}_1$ and $\hat{\beta}_2$ are 2.3 and .27, respectively.

a. Test H_0: $\beta_1 = 0$ against H_a: $\beta_1 > 0$. Use $\alpha = .05$.

b. Test H_0: $\beta_2 = 0$ against H_a: $\beta_2 \neq 0$. Use $\alpha = .05$.

c. Find a 90% confidence interval for β_1. Interpret the interval.

d. Find a 99% confidence interval for β_2. Interpret the interval.

11.5 How is the number of degrees of freedom available for estimating σ^2 (the variance of ϵ) related to the number of independent variables in a regression model?

11.6 Consider the first-order model equation in three quantitative independent variables

$$E(y) = 1 + 2x_1 + x_2 - 3x_3$$

a. Graph the relationship between y and x_1 for $x_2 = 1$ and $x_3 = 3$.

b. Repeat part **a** for $x_2 = -1$ and $x_3 = 1$.

c. How do the graphed lines in parts **a** and **b** relate to each other? What is the slope of each line?

d. If a linear model is first-order in three independent variables, what type of geometric relationship will you obtain when $E(y)$ is graphed as a function of one of the independent variables for various combinations of values of the other independent variables?

11.7 Suppose you fit the first-order model

$$y = \beta_0 + \beta_1 x_1 + \beta_2 x_2 + \beta_3 x_3 + \beta_4 x_4 + \beta_5 x_5 + \epsilon$$

to $n = 30$ data points and obtain

$$\text{SSE} = .33 \quad R^2 = .92$$

a. Do the values of SSE and R^2 suggest that the model provides a good fit to the data? Explain.

b. Is the model of any use in predicting y? Test the null hypothesis H_0: $\beta_1 = \beta_2 = \beta_3 = \beta_4 = \beta_5 = 0$ against the alternative hypothesis H_a: At least one of the parameters $\beta_1, \beta_2, \ldots, \beta_5$ is nonzero. Use $\alpha = .05$.

11.8 If the analysis of variance F-test leads to the conclusion that at least one of the model parameters is nonzero, can you conclude that the model is the best predictor for the dependent variable y? Can you conclude that all of the terms in the model are important for predicting y? What is the appropriate conclusion?

Applying the Concepts—Basic

11.9 Highway crash data analysis. Researchers at Montana State University have written a tutorial on an empirical method for analyzing before and after highway crash data

(Montana Department of Transportation, Research Report, May 2004). The initial step in the methodology is to develop a Safety Performance Function (SPF)—a mathematical model that estimates crash occurrence for a given roadway segment. Using data collected for over 100 roadway segments, the researchers fit the model, $E(y) = \beta_0 + \beta_1 x_1 + \beta_2 x_2$, where $y =$ number of crashes per 3 years, $x_1 =$ roadway length (miles), and $x_2 =$ AADT = average annual daily traffic (number of vehicles). The results are shown in the following tables.

INTERSTATE HIGHWAYS

Variable	Parameter Estimate	Standard Error	t-value
Intercept	1.81231	.50568	3.58
Length (x_1)	.10875	.03166	3.44
AADT (x_2)	.00017	.00003	5.19

NON-INTERSTATE HIGHWAYS

Variable	Parameter Estimate	Standard Error	t-value
Intercept	1.20785	.28075	4.30
Length (x_1)	.06343	.01809	3.51
AADT (x_2)	.00056	.00012	4.86

a. Give the least squares prediction equation for the interstate highway model.

b. Give practical interpretations of the β estimates, part **a**.

c. Refer to part **a**. Find a 99% confidence interval for β_1 and interpret the result.

d. Refer to part **a**. Find a 99% confidence interval for β_2 and interpret the result.

e. Repeat parts **a–d** for the non-interstate highway model.

11.10 Trust in e-retailers. Electronic commerce (or "e-commerce") describes the use of electronic networks to simplify a business operation. With e-commerce, retailers now can advertise and sell their products easily over the Web. In *Internet Research: Electronic Networking Applications and Policy* (Vol. 11, 2001), Canadian researchers investigated the factors that impact the level of trust in Web e-retailers. Five quantitative independent variables were used to model level of trust (y):

$x_1 =$ ease of navigation on the Web site

$x_2 =$ consistency of the Web site

$x_3 =$ ease of learning the Web interface

$x_4 =$ perception of the interface design

$x_5 =$ level of support available to the user

a. Write a first-order model for level of trust as a function of the five independent variables.

b. The model, part **a**, was fit to data collected for $n = 66$ visitors to e-retailers' Web sites and yielded a coefficient of determination of $R^2 = .58$. Interpret this result.

c. Compute the F-statistic used to test the global utility of the model.

d. Using $\alpha = .10$, give the appropriate conclusion for the test, part **c**.

11.11 Novelty of a vacation destination. Many tourists choose a
NW vacation destination based on the newness or uniqueness (i.e., the novelty) of the itinerary. Texas A&M University

professor J. Petrick investigated the relationship between novelty and vacationing golfers' demographics (*Annals of Tourism Research*, Vol. 29, 2002). Data were obtained from a mail survey of 393 golf vacationers to a large coastal resort in the southeastern United States. Several measures of novelty level (on a numerical scale) were obtained for each vacationer, including "change from routine," "thrill," "boredom-alleviation," and "surprise." The researcher employed four independent variables in a regression model to predict each of the novelty measures. The independent variables were x_1 = number of rounds of golf per year, x_2 = total number of golf vacations taken, x_3 = number of years played golf, and x_4 = average golf score.

a. Give the hypothesized equation of a first-order model for y = change from routine.

b. A test of $H_0: \beta_3 = 0$ versus $H_a: \beta_3 < 0$ yielded a p-value of .005. Interpret this result if $\alpha = .01$.

c. The estimate of β_3 was found to be negative. Based on this result (and the result of part **b**), the researcher concluded that "those who have played golf for more years are less apt to seek change from their normal routine in their golf vacations." Do you agree with this statement? Explain.

d. The regression results for three dependent novelty measures, based on data collected for $n = 393$ golf vacationers, are summarized in the table below. Give the null hypothesis for testing the overall adequacy of the first-order regression model.

e. Give the rejection region for the test, part **d**, for $\alpha = .01$.

f. Use the test statistics reported in the table and the rejection region from part **e** to conduct the test for each of the dependent measures of novelty.

g. Verify that the p-values reported in the table support your conclusions in part **f**.

h. Interpret the values of R^2 reported in the table.

Dependent Variable	F-value	p-value	R^2
Thrill	5.56	<.001	.055
Change from routine	3.02	.018	.030
Surprise	3.33	.011	.023

Source: Petrick, J. F. "An Examination of Golf Vacationers' Novelty." *Annals of Tourism Research*, Vol. 29, 2002.

11.12 Predicting runs scored in baseball. In *Chance* (Fall 2000), statistician Scott Berry built a multiple regression model for predicting total number of runs scored by a Major League Baseball team during a season. Using data on all teams from 1990–1998 (a sample of $n = 234$), the results in the next table were obtained.

a. Write the least squares prediction equation for y = total number of runs scored by a team in a season.

b. Interpret, practically, the β estimates in the model.

c. Conduct a test of $H_0: \beta_7 = 0$ against $H_a: \beta_7 < 0$ at $\alpha = .05$. Interpret the results.

d. Form a 95% confidence interval for β_5. Interpret the results.

e. Predict the number of runs scored by your favorite Major League Baseball team last year. How close is the predicted value to the actual number of runs scored by your team? (*Note:* You can find data on your favorite team on the Internet at www.majorleaguebaseball.com.)

Independent Variable	β Estimate	Standard Error
Intercept	3.70	15.00
Walks (x_1)	.34	.02
Singles (x_2)	.49	.03
Doubles (x_3)	.72	.05
Triples (x_4)	1.14	.19
Home Runs (x_5)	1.51	.05
Stolen Bases (x_6)	.26	.05
Caught Stealing (x_7)	−.14	.14
Strikeouts (x_8)	−.10	.01
Outs (x_9)	−.10	.01

Source: Berry, S. M. "A Statistician Reads the Sports Pages: Modeling Offensive Ability in Baseball." *Chance*, Vol. 13, No. 4, Fall 2000 (Table 2).

11.13 Factors that identify urban counties. In a study of urban and rural counties in the western United States published in *Professional Geographer* (Feb. 2000), University of Nevada (Reno) researchers asked a sample of 256 county commissioners to rate their "home" county on a scale of 1 (most rural) to 10 (most urban). The urban/rural rating (y) was used as the dependent variable in a first-order multiple regression model with six independent variables: total county population (x_1), population density (x_2), population concentration (x_3), population growth (x_4), proportion of county land in farms (x_5), and 5-year change in agricultural land base (x_6). Some of the regression results are shown in the table.

Independent Variable	β Estimate	p-value
x_1: Total population	0.110	0.045
x_2: Population density	0.065	0.230
x_3: Population concentration	0.540	0.000
x_4: Population growth	−0.009	0.860
x_5: Farm land	−0.150	0.003
x_6: Agricultural change	−0.027	0.580

Overall model:
$R^2 = .44$ $R_a^2 = .43$ $F = 32.47$ p-value $< .001$

Source: Berry, K. A., et al. "Interpreting What Is Rural and Urban for Western U.S. Counties." *Professional Geographer*, Vol. 52, No. 1, Feb. 2000 (Table 2).

a. Interpret the estimate of the β's for y.

b. Give the null hypothesis for testing overall model adequacy.

c. Conduct the test, part **b**, at $\alpha = .01$ and give the appropriate conclusion.

d. Interpret the values of R^2 and R_a^2.

e. Give the null hypothesis for testing the contribution of population growth (x_4) to the model.

f. Conduct the test, part **e**, at $\alpha = .01$ and give the appropriate conclusion.

11.14 Global warming and foreign investments. Scientists believe that a major cause of global warming is higher levels of carbon dioxide (CO_2) in the atmosphere. In the *Journal of World-Systems Research* (Summer 2003), sociologists examined the impact of foreign investment dependence on CO_2 emissions in $n = 66$ developing countries. In particular, the researchers modeled the level of CO_2 emissions in 1996 based on foreign investments made 16 years earlier and several other independent variables. The variables and the model results are listed in the next table.

$y = \ln(\text{level of CO}_2 \text{ emissions in 1996})$	β Estimate	t-value	p-value
$x_1 = \ln(\text{foreign investments in 1980})$	.79	2.52	$< .05$
$x_2 = \text{gross domestic investment in 1980})$	.01	.13	$> .10$
$x_3 = \text{trade exports in 1980}$	$-.02$	-1.66	$> .10$
$x_4 = \ln(\text{GNP in 1980})$	$-.44$	$-.97$	$> .10$
$x_5 = \text{agricultural production in 1980}$	$-.03$	$-.66$	$> .10$
$x_6 = 1$ if African country, 0 if not	-1.19	-1.52	$> .10$
$x_7 = \ln(\text{level of CO}_2 \text{ emissions in 1980})$	.56	3.35	$< .001$

$R^2 = .31$

Source: Grimes, P., and Kentor, J. "Exporting the Greenhouse: Foreign Capital Penetration and CO$_2$ Emissions 1980–1996." *Journal of World-Systems Research,* Vol. IX, No. 2, Summer 2003 (Table 1).

a. Interpret the value of R^2.
b. Use the value of R^2 to test the null hypothesis, $H_0: \beta_1 = \beta_2 = \cdots = \beta_7 = 0$, at $\alpha = .01$.
c. What null hypothesis would you test to determine if foreign investments in 1980 is a statistically useful predictor of CO$_2$ emissions in 1996?
d. Conduct the test, part c, at $\alpha = .05$.

Applying the Concepts—Intermediate

11.15 Incomes of Mexican street vendors. Detailed interviews were conducted with over 1,000 street vendors in the city of Puebla, Mexico, in order to study the factors influencing vendors' incomes (*World Development,* Feb. 1998). Vendors were defined as individuals working in the street and included vendors with carts and stands on wheels and excluded beggars, drug dealers, and prostitutes. The researchers collected data on gender, age, hours worked per day, annual earnings, and education level. A subset of these data appear in the table.

⊙ STREETVN

Vendor Number	Annual Earnings, y	Age, x_1	Hours Worked per Day, x_2
21	$2841	29	12
53	1876	21	8
60	2934	62	10
184	1552	18	10
263	3065	40	11
281	3670	50	11
354	2005	65	5
401	3215	44	8
515	1930	17	8
633	2010	70	6
677	3111	20	9
710	2882	29	9
800	1683	15	5
914	1817	14	7
997	4066	33	12

Source: Adapted from Smith, Paula A., and Metzger, Michael R. "The Return to Education: Street Vendors in Mexico." *World Development,* Vol. 26, No. 2, Feb. 1998, pp. 289–296.

a. Write a first-order model for mean annual earnings, $E(y)$, as a function of age (x_1) and hours worked (x_2).
b. Fit the model to the data and give the least squares prediction equation.
c. Interpret the estimated β coefficients in your model.
d. Is age x_1 a statistically useful predictor of annual earnings? Test using $\alpha = .01$.

e. Construct a 95% confidence interval for β_2. Interpret the interval in the words of the problem.
f. Find and interpret the value of R^2.
g. Find and interpret the value of R_a^2. Explain the relationship between R^2 and R_a^2.
h. Conduct a test of the global utility of the model at $\alpha = .01$.

11.16 Contamination from a plant's discharge. Refer to the U.S. Army Corps of Engineers data on fish contaminated from the toxic discharges of a chemical plant located on the banks of the Tennessee River in Alabama. Recall that the engineers measured the length (in centimeter), weight (in grams), and DDT level (in parts per million) for 144 captured fish. In addition, the number of miles upstream from the river was recorded. The data are saved in the **DDT** file. (The first and last five observations are shown in the accompanying table.)

⊙ DDT

River	Mile	Species	Length	Weight	DDT
FC	5	CHANNELCATFISH	42.5	732	10.00
FC	5	CHANNELCATFISH	44.0	795	16.00
FC	5	CHANNELCATFISH	41.5	547	23.00
FC	5	CHANNELCATFISH	39.0	465	21.00
FC	5	CHANNELCATFISH	50.5	1252	50.00
⋮	⋮	⋮	⋮	⋮	⋮
TR	345	LARGEMOUTHBASS	23.5	358	2.00
TR	345	LARGEMOUTHBASS	30.0	856	2.20
TR	345	LARGEMOUTHBASS	29.0	793	7.40
TR	345	LARGEMOUTHBASS	17.5	173	0.35
TR	345	LARGEMOUTHBASS	36.0	1433	1.90

a. Fit the first-order model, $E(y) = \beta_0 + \beta_1 x_1 + \beta_2 x_2 + \beta_3 x_3$, to the data, where $y = $ DDT level, $x_1 = $ mile, $x_2 = $ length, and $x_3 = $ weight. Report the least squares prediction equation.
b. Find the estimate of the standard deviation of ε for the model and give a practical interpretation of its value.
c. Conduct a test of the global utility of the model. Use $\alpha = .05$.
d. Do the data provide sufficient evidence to conclude that DDT level increases as length increases? Report the observed significance level of the test and reach a conclusion using $\alpha = .05$.
e. Find and interpret a 95% confidence interval for β_3.

GASTURBINE (Data for first and last 5 gas turbines shown)

RPM	CP Ratio	Inlet Temp.	Exhaust Temp.	Air Flow	Heat Rate
27245	9.2	1134	602	7	14622
14000	12.2	950	446	15	13196
17384	14.8	1149	537	20	11948
11085	11.8	1024	478	27	11289
14045	13.2	1149	553	29	11964
⋮					
18910	14.0	1066	532	8	12766
3600	35.0	1288	448	152	8714
3600	20.0	1160	456	84	9469
16000	10.6	1232	560	14	11948
14600	13.4	1077	536	20	12414

Source: Bhargava, R., and Meher-Homji, C. B. "Parametric Analysis of Existing Gas Turbines with Inlet Evaporative and Overspray Fogging." *Journal of Engineering for Gas Turbines and Power*, Vol. 127, No. 1, Jan. 2005.

11.17 Cooling method for gas turbines. Refer to the *Journal of Engineering for Gas Turbines and Power* (Jan. 2005) study of a high-pressure inlet fogging method for a gas turbine engine, Exercise 6.26 (p. 358). Recall that the heat rate (kilojoules per kilowatt per hour) was measured for each in a sample of 67 gas turbines augmented with high-pressure inlet fogging. In addition, several other variables were measured, including cycle speed (revolutions per minute), inlet temperature (°C), exhaust gas temperature (°C), cycle pressure ratio, and air mass flow rate (kilograms per second). The data are saved in the **GASTURBINE** file. (The first and last 5 observations are listed in the table above.)

a. Write a first-order model for heat rate (y) as a function of speed, inlet temperature, exhaust temperature, cycle pressure ratio, and air flow rate.

b. Fit the model to the data using the method of least squares.

c. Give practical interpretations of the β estimates.

d. Find the model standard deviation, s, and interpret its value.

e. Conduct a test for overall model utility using $\alpha = .01$.

f. Find and interpret R_a^2.

g. Is there sufficient evidence (at $\alpha = .01$) to indicate that heat rate (y) is linearly related to inlet temperature?

11.18 Snow geese feeding trial. Refer to the *Journal of Applied Ecology* (Vol. 32, 1995) study of the feeding habits of baby snow geese, Exercise 10.64 (p. 638). The data on gosling weight change, digestion efficiency, acid-detergent fiber (all measured as percentages), and diet (plants or duck chow) for 42 feeding trials are saved in the **SNOWGEESE** file. (The first and last five observations are shown in the table below.) The botanists were interested in predicting weight change (y) as a function of the other variables. Consider the first-order model $E(y) = \beta_0 + \beta_1 x_1 + \beta_2 x_2$, where x_1 is digestion efficiency and x_2 is acid-detergent fiber.

a. Find the least squares prediction equation for weight change, y.

b. Interpret the β-estimates in the equation, part **a**.

c. Conduct a test to determine if digestion efficiency, x_1, is a useful linear predictor of weight change. Use $\alpha = .01$.

d. Form a 99% confidence interval for β_2. Interpret the result.

e. Find and interpret R^2 and R_a^2. Which statistic is the preferred measure of model fit? Explain.

f. Is the overall model statistically useful for predicting weight change? Test using $\alpha = .05$.

11.19 Extracting water from oil. In the oil industry, water that mixes with crude oil during production and transportation

SNOWGEESE

Feeding Trial	Diet	Weight Change (%)	Digestion Efficiency (%)	Acid-Detergent Fiber (%)
1	Plants	−6	0	28.5
2	Plants	−5	2.5	27.5
3	Plants	−4.5	5	27.5
4	Plants	0	0	32.5
5	Plants	2	0	32
⋮	⋮	⋮	⋮	
38	Duck Chow	9	59	8.5
39	Duck Chow	12	52.5	8
40	Duck Chow	8.5	75	6
41	Duck Chow	10.5	72.5	6.5
42	Duck Chow	14	69	7

Source: Gadallah, F. L., and Jefferies, R. L. "Forage Quality in Brood Rearing Areas of the Lesser Snow Goose and the Growth of Captive Goslings." *Journal of Applied Biology*, Vol. 32, No. 2, 1995, pp. 281–282 (adapted from Figures 2 and 3).

⊙ WATEROIL

Experiment Number	Voltage, y (kw/cm)	Disperse Phase Volume, x_1 (%)	Salinity, x_2 (%)	Temperature, x_3 (°C)	Time Delay, x_4 (hours)	Surfactant Concentration, x_5 (%)	Span: Triton, x_6	Solid Particles, x_7 (%)
1	.64	40	1	4	.25	2	.25	.5
2	.80	80	1	4	.25	4	.25	2
3	3.20	40	4	4	.25	4	.75	.5
4	.48	80	4	4	.25	2	.75	2
5	1.72	40	1	23	.25	4	.75	2
6	.32	80	1	23	.25	2	.75	.5
7	.64	40	4	23	.25	2	.25	2
8	.68	80	4	23	.25	4	.25	.5
9	.12	40	1	4	24	2	.75	2
10	.88	80	1	4	24	4	.75	.5
11	2.32	40	4	4	24	4	.25	2
12	.40	80	4	4	24	2	.25	.5
13	1.04	40	1	23	24	4	.25	.5
14	.12	80	1	23	24	2	.25	2
15	1.28	40	4	23	24	2	.75	.5
16	.72	80	4	23	24	4	.75	2
17	1.08	0	0	0	0	0	0	0
18	1.08	0	0	0	0	0	0	0
19	1.04	0	0	0	0	0	0	0

Source: Førdedal, H. et al. "A Multivariate Analysis of W/O Emulsions in High External Electric Fields as Studied by Means of Dielectric Time Domain Spectroscopy." *Journal of Colloid and Interface Science,* Vol. 173, No. 2, Aug. 1995, p. 398 (Table 2).

must be removed. Chemists have found that the oil can be extracted from the water/oil mix electrically. Researchers at the University of Bergen (Norway) conducted a series of experiments to study the factors that influence the voltage (y) required to separate the water from the oil (*Journal of Colloid and Interface Science*, Aug. 1995). The seven independent variables investigated in the study are listed in the table above. (Each variable was measured at two levels—a "low" level and a "high" level.) Sixteen water/oil mixtures were prepared using different combinations of the independent variables; then each emulsion was exposed to a high electric field. In addition, three mixtures were tested when all independent variables were set to 0. The data for all 19 experiments are also given in the table.

a. Propose a first-order model for y as a function of all seven independent variables.

b. Use a statistical software package to fit the model to the data in the table.

c. Fully interpret the β estimates.

d. Evaluate the overall utility of the model at $\alpha = .10$.

11.20 Study of fees charged by auditors. External auditors are hired to review and analyze the financial and other records of an organization and to attest to the integrity of the organization's financial statements. In recent years, the fees charged by auditors have come under increasing scrutiny. S. Butterworth and K. A. Houghton, two University of Melbourne (Australia) researchers, investigated the effects of seven variables on the logarithm of the fee charged by auditors (*Journal of Business Finance and Accounting*, April 1995). The multiple regression model $E(y) = \beta_0 + \beta_1 x_1 + \beta_2 x_2 + \beta_3 x_3 + \cdots + \beta_7 x_7$ was fit to data collected for $n = 268$ companies. The results are summarized in the table on p. 686.

a. Write the least squares prediction equation.

b. Assess the overall fit of the model.

c. Interpret the estimate of β_3.

d. The researchers hypothesized the direction of the effect of each independent variable on audit fees. These hypotheses are given in the "Expected Sign of β" column in the table on p. 686. (For example, if the expected sign is negative, the alternative hypothesis is H_a: $\beta_i < 0$.) Interpret the results of the hypothesis test for β_4. Use $\alpha = .05$.

e. The main objective of the analysis was to determine whether new auditors charge less than incumbent auditors in a given year. If this hypothesis is true, then the true value of β_1 is negative. Is there evidence to support this hypothesis? Explain.

11.21 Occupational safety study. An important goal in occupational safety is "active caring." Employees demonstrate active caring (AC) about the safety of their coworkers when they identify environmental hazards and unsafe work practices and then implement appropriate corrective actions for these unsafe conditions or behaviors. Three factors hypothesized to increase the propensity for an employee to actively care for safety are (1) high self-esteem, (2) optimism, and (3) group cohesiveness. *Applied & Preventive Psychology* (Winter 1995) attempted to establish empirical support for the AC hypothesis by fitting the model $E(y) = \beta_0 + \beta_1 x_1 + \beta_2 x_2 + \beta_3 x_3$, where

y = AC score (active caring score, 15-point scale)

x_1 = Self-esteem score

x_2 = Optimism score

x_3 = Group cohesion score

The regression analysis, based on data collected for $n = 31$ hourly workers at a large fiber-manufacturing plant, yielded a multiple coefficient of determination of $R^2 = .362$.

Results for Exercise 11.20

Independent Variable	Expected Sign of β	β Estimate	t Value	Level of Significance (p-Value)
Constant	−	−4.30	−3.45	.001 (two-tailed)
$x_1 = \begin{cases} 1 \text{ if auditee changed auditors after one year} \\ 0 \text{ if not} \end{cases}$	+	−.002	−0.049	.961 (one-tailed)
x_2 = Logarithm of auditee's total assets	+	.336	9.94	.000 (one-tailed)
x_3 = Number of subsidiaries of auditee	+	.384	7.63	.000 (one-tailed)
$x_4 = \begin{cases} 1 \text{ if auditee receives an audit qualification} \\ 0 \text{ if not} \end{cases}$	+	.067	1.76	.079 (one-tailed)
$x_5 = \begin{cases} 1 \text{ if auditee in mining industry} \\ 0 \text{ if not} \end{cases}$	−	−.143	−4.05	.000 (one-tailed)
$x_6 = \begin{cases} 1 \text{ if auditee is a member of a "Big 8" firm} \\ 0 \text{ if not} \end{cases}$	+	.081	2.18	.030 (one-tailed)
x_7 = Logarithm of dollar-value of non-audit services provided by auditor	+/−	.134	4.54	.000 (two-tailed)

$R^2 = .712$ $\qquad\qquad F = 111.1$

Source: Butterworth, S., and Houghton, K. A. "Auditor Switching: The Pricing of Audit Services." *Journal of Business Finance and Accounting,* Vol. 22, No. 3, April 1995, p. 334 (Table 4).

  a. Interpret the value of R^2.
  b. Use the R^2 value to test the global utility of the model. Use $\alpha = .05$.

11.22 R^2 and model fit. Because the coefficient of determination R^2 always increases when a new independent variable is added to the model, it is tempting to include many variables in a model to force R^2 to be near 1. However, doing so reduces the degrees of freedom available for estimating σ^2, which adversely affects our ability to make reliable inferences. Suppose you want to use 18 economic indicators to predict next year's gross domestic product (GDP). You fit the model

$$y = \beta_0 + \beta_1 x_1 + \beta_2 x_2 + \cdots + \beta_{17} x_{17} + \beta_{18} x_{18} + \epsilon$$

where y = GDP and $x_1, x_2, \ldots, x_{18}$ are the economic indicators. Only 20 years of data ($n = 20$) are used to fit the model, and you obtain $R^2 = .95$. Test to see whether this impressive-looking R^2 is large enough for you to infer that the model is useful—that is, that at least one term in the model is important for predicting GDP. Use $\alpha = .05$.

Applying the Concepts—Advanced

11.23 Bordeaux wine sold at auction. The vineyards in the Bordeaux region of France are known for producing ex-cellent red wines. However, the uncertainty of the weather during the growing season, the phenomenon that wine tastes better with age, and the fact that some Bordeaux vineyards produce better wines than others, encourages speculation concerning the value of a case of wine produced by a certain vineyard during a certain year (or vintage). As a result, many wine experts attempt to predict the auction price of a case of Bordeaux wine. The publishers of a newsletter titled *Liquid Assets: The International Guide to Fine Wine* discussed a multiple regression approach to predicting the London auction price of red Bordeaux wine in *Chance* (Fall 1995). The natural logarithm of the price y (in dollars) of a case containing a dozen bottles of red wine was modeled as a function of weather during growing season and age of vintage using data collected for the vintages of 1952–1980. Three models were fit to the data. The results of the regressions are summarized in the table below.

  a. For each model, conduct a t-test (at $\alpha = .05$) for each of the β parameters in the model. Interpret the results.
  b. When the natural log of y is used as a dependent variable, the antilogarithm of a β coefficient minus 1—that is $e^{\beta_i} - 1$—represents the percentage change in y for every 1-unit increase in the associated x value. Use this information to interpret the β estimates of each model.

Independent Variables	BETA ESTIMATES (STANDARD ERRORS)		
	Model 1	Model 2	Model 3
x_1 = Vintage year	.0354 (.0137)	.0238 (.00717)	.0240 (.00747)
x_2 = Average growing season temperature (°C)	(not included)	.616 (.0952)	.608 (.116)
x_3 = Sept./Aug. rainfall (cm)	(not included)	−.00386 (.00081)	−.00380 (.00095)
x_4 = Rainfall in months preceding vintage (cm)	(not included)	.0001173 (.000482)	.00115 (.000505)
x_5 = Average Sept. temperature (°C)	(not included)	(not included)	.00765 (.565)
	$R^2 = .212$	$R^2 = .828$	$R^2 = .828$
	$s = .575$	$s = .287$	$s = .293$

Source: Ashenfelter, O., Ashmore, D., and LaLonde, R. "Bourdeaux Wine Vintage Quality and Weather." *Chance,* Vol. 8, No. 4, Fall 1995, p. 116 (Table 2).

SHIPDEPT

Week	Labor, y (hrs.)	Pounds Shipped, x_1 (1,000s)	Percentage of Units Shipped by Truck, x_2	Average Shipment Weight, x_3 (lbs.)
1	100	5.1	90	20
2	85	3.8	99	22
3	108	5.3	58	19
4	116	7.5	16	15
5	92	4.5	54	20
6	63	3.3	42	26
7	79	5.3	12	25
8	101	5.9	32	21
9	88	4.0	56	24
10	71	4.2	64	29
11	122	6.8	78	10
12	85	3.9	90	30
13	50	3.8	74	28
14	114	7.5	89	14
15	104	4.5	90	21
16	111	6.0	40	20
17	110	8.1	55	16
18	100	2.9	64	19
19	82	4.0	35	23
20	85	4.8	58	25

c. Based on the values of R^2 and s, which of the three models would you recommend for predicting Bordeaux wine prices? Explain.

11.24 Cost analysis for a shipping department. Multiple regression is used by accountants in cost analysis to shed light on the factors that cause costs to be incurred and the magnitudes of their effects. The independent variables of such a regression model are the factors believed to be related to cost, the dependent variable. In some instances, however, it is desirable to use physical units instead of cost as the dependent variable in a cost analysis. This would be the case if most of the cost associated with the activity of interest is a function of some physical unit, such as hours of labor. The advantage of this approach is that the regression model will provide estimates of the number of labor hours required under different circumstances, and these hours can then be costed at the current labor rate (Horngren, Foster, and Datar, 1994). The sample data shown in the table above have been collected from a firm's accounting and production records to provide cost information about the firm's shipping department. Consider the model $y = \beta_0 + \beta_1 x_1 + \beta_2 x_2 + \beta_3 x_3 + \epsilon$.

a. Find the least squares prediction equation.
b. Use an F-test to investigate the usefulness of the model specified in part **a**. Use $\alpha = .01$, and state your conclusion in the context of the problem.
c. Test $H_0: \beta_2 = 0$ versus $H_a: \beta_2 \neq 0$ using $\alpha = .05$. What do the results of your test suggest about the magnitude of the effects of x_2 on labor costs?
d. Find R^2, and interpret its value in the context of the problem.
e. If shipping department employees are paid $7.50 per hour, how much less, on average, will it cost the company per week if the average number of pounds per shipment increases from a level of 20 to 21? Assume that x_1 and x_2 remain unchanged. Your answer is an estimate of what is known in economics as the *expected marginal cost associated with a 1-pound increase in x_3.*
f. With what approximate precision can this model be used to predict the hours of labor? [*Note:* The precision of multiple regression predictions is discussed in Section 11.4.]
g. Can regression analysis alone indicate what factors *cause* costs to increase? Explain.

11.4 Using the Model for Estimation and Prediction

In Section 10.8 we discussed the use of the least squares line for estimating the mean value of y, $E(y)$, for some particular value of x, say $x = x_p$. We also showed how to use the same fitted model to predict, when $x = x_p$, some new value of y to be observed in the future. Recall that the least squares line yielded the same value for both the estimate of $E(y)$ and the prediction of some future value of y—that is, both are the result of substituting x_p into the prediction equation $\hat{y} = \hat{\beta}_0 + \hat{\beta}_1 x$ and calculating $\hat{y}_p$. There the equivalence ends. The confidence interval for the mean $E(y)$ is narrower than the prediction interval for y because of the additional uncertainty attributable to the random error ϵ when predicting some future value of y.

	PROPERTY	LANDVAL	IMPROVAL	AREA	PREDICT	LLMean95	ULMean95	LLPred95	ULPred95
1	1	5960	44967	1873	68557	59404	77709	49435	87678
2	2	9000	27860	928	44213	37904	50522	26278	62148
3	3	9500	31439	1126	50235	45338	55132	32747	67723
4	4	10000	39592	1265	59212	54285	64139	41715	76709
5	5	18000	72827	2214	105834	95659	116009	86203	125465
6	6	8500	27317	912	43144	36932	49355	25243	61044
7	7	8000	29856	899	44644	38243	51044	26677	62611
8	8	23000	47752	1803	83774	71575	95972	63021	104526
9	9	8100	39117	1204	56449	50998	61901	38798	74101
10	10	9000	29349	1725	56217	48550	63884	37760	74673
11	11	7300	40166	1080	54981	47863	62099	36746	73216
12	12	8000	31679	1529	54662	49555	59770	37114	72211
13	13	20000	58510	2455	98977	88619	109336	79250	118704
14	14	8000	23454	1151	42800	37649	47951	25239	60361
15	15	8000	20897	1173	41000	35078	46922	23198	58802
16	16	10500	56248	1960	82687	74643	90731	64071	101303
17	17	4000	20859	1344	40024	32814	47235	21753	58296
18	18	4500	22610	988	37052	31827	42278	19469	54635
19	19	3400	35948	1076	48290	40504	56076	29784	66796
20	20	1500	5779	962	20448	11231	29664	1296	39600
21	21	15000	50000	1800	79061	73381	84742	61338	96785

FIGURE 11.8

SPSS spreadsheet with 95% confidence intervals for sale price model

These same concepts carry over to the multiple regression model. Consider, again, the first-order model relating sale price of a residential property to land value (x_1), improvements (x_2), and home size (x_3). Suppose we want to estimate the mean sale price for a given property with $x_1 = \$15,000$, $x_2 = \$50,000$, and $x_3 = 1,800$ square feet. Assuming that the first-order model represents the true relationship between sale price and the three independent variables, we want to estimate

$$E(y) = \beta_0 + \beta_1 x_1 + \beta_2 x_2 + \beta_3 x_3 = \beta_0 + \beta_1(15,000) + \beta_2(50,000) + \beta_3(1,800)$$

Substituting into the least squares prediction equation, we find the estimate of $E(y)$ to be

$$\hat{y} = \hat{\beta}_0 + \hat{\beta}_1(15,000) + \hat{\beta}_2(50,000) + \hat{\beta}_3(1,800)$$
$$= 1,470.27 + .814(15,000) + .820(50,000) + 13.529(1,800) = 79,061.4$$

To form a confidence interval for the mean, we need to know the standard deviation of the sampling distribution for the estimator $\hat{y}$. For multiple regression models, the form of this standard deviation is rather complex. However, the regression routines of statistical computer software packages allow us to obtain the confidence intervals for mean values of y for any given combination of values of the independent variables. A portion of the SPSS output for the sale price example is shown in Figure 11.8.

In addition to the 95% confidence interval for the mean (highlighted under the "LLMean95" and "ULMean95" columns), the SPSS printout gives the selected x-values (highlighted at the bottom of the printout), and the value of $\hat{y} = 79,061$ (highlighted under PREDICT). From the 95% confidence interval for the mean, (73,381, 84,742), we can infer (with 95% confidence) that the mean sale price for all properties with $x_1 = \$15,000$, $x_2 = \$50,000$, and $x_3 = 1,800$ square feet will fall between \$73,381 and \$84,742.

If we were interested in predicting the sale price for a particular (single) property with $x_1 = \$15,000$, $x_2 = \$50,000$, and $x_3 = 1,800$ square feet, we would use $\hat{y} = \$79,061$ as the predicted value. However, the prediction interval for a new value of y is wider than the confidence interval for $E(y)$. The 95% prediction interval (highlighted on the SPSS printout under "LLPred95" and "ULPred95") is (61,338, 96,785). Thus, with 95% confidence, we conclude that the sale price for an individual property with the characteristics $x_1 = \$15,000$, $x_2 = \$50,000$, and $x_3 = 1,800$ square feet will fall between \$61,338 and \$96,785.

EXAMPLE 11.5

Estimating $E(y)$ and Predicting y

Problem Refer to Examples 11.3–11.4 and the first-order model, $E(y) = \beta_0 + \beta_1 x_1 + \beta_2 x_2$, where y = auction price of a grandfather clock, x_1 = age of the clock, and x_2 = number of bidders.

a. Estimate the average auction price for all 150-year-old clocks sold at an auction with 10 bidders using a 95% confidence interval. Interpret the result.

b. Suppose you want to predict the auction price for one clock that is 50 years old and has 2 bidders. How should you proceed?

Solution

a. Here, the key words *average* and *for all* imply we want to estimate the mean of y, $E(y)$. We want a 95% confidence interval for $E(y)$ when $x_1 = 150$ years and $x_2 = 10$ bidders. A MINITAB printout for this analysis is shown in Figure 11.9. The confidence interval (highlighted under "95% CI") is (1381.4, 1481.9). Thus, we are 95% confident that the mean auction price for all 150-year-old clocks sold at an auction with 10 bidders lies between $1,381.4 and $1,481.9.

b. Now, we want to predict the auction price, y, for a single ("one") grandfather clock when $x_1 = 50$ years and $x_2 = 2$ bidders. Consequently, we desire a 95% prediction interval for y. However, before we form this prediction interval, we should check to make sure that the selected values of the independent variables, $x_1 = 50$ and $x_2 = 2$, are both reasonable and within their respective sample ranges. If you examine the sample data shown in Table 11.2 (p. 674), you will see that the range for age is $108 \le x_1 \le 194$, and the range for number of bidders is $5 \le x_2 \le 15$. Thus, both selected values fall well *outside* their respective ranges. Recall the *Caution* box in Section 10.8 (p. 643) warning about the dangers of using the model to predict y for a value of an independent variable that is not within the range of the sample data. This may lead to an unreliable prediction. If we want to make such a prediction, we would need to collect additional data on clocks with these characteristics (i.e., $x_1 = 50$ years and $x_2 = 2$ bidders) and then refit the model.

Regression Analysis: PRICE versus AGE, NUMBIDS

```
The regression equation is
PRICE = - 1339 + 12.7 AGE + 86.0 NUMBIDS


Predictor      Coef   SE Coef       T      P
Constant    -1339.0     173.8   -7.70  0.000
AGE         12.7406    0.9047   14.08  0.000
NUMBIDS      85.953     8.729    9.85  0.000


S = 133.485   R-Sq = 89.2%   R-Sq(adj) = 88.5%

Analysis of Variance

Source           DF        SS       MS       F      P
Regression        2   4283063  2141531  120.19  0.000
Residual Error   29    516727    17818
Total            31   4799790


Predicted Values for New Observations

New
Obs     Fit   SE Fit       95% CI             95% PI
  1  1431.7     24.6   (1381.4, 1481.9)   (1154.1, 1709.3)

Values of Predictors for New Observations

New
Obs   AGE   NUMBIDS
  1   150      10.0
```

FIGURE 11.9

MINITAB printout with 95% confidence intervals for grandfather clock model

Now Work Exercise 11.25

STATISTICS IN ACTION REVISITED

A First-Order Model for Road Contract Cost

The Florida Attorney General wants to develop a model for the cost (y) of a road construction contract awarded using the sealed-bid system and to use the model to predict the costs of future road contracts in the state. In addition to contract cost, the FLAG file contains data on eight potential predictor variables for a sample of 235 road contracts. (See Table SIA11.1 on p. 665.) MINITAB scatterplots (with the dependent variable, COST, plotted against each of the potential predictors) for the data are shown in Figure SIA11.1. From the scatterplots, it appears that the DOT engineer's cost estimate (DOTEST) and estimate of work days (DAYSEST) would be good predictors of contract cost. [In a future Statistics in Action Revisited section (p. 740), we will learn that

the two best predictors of contract cost are actually DOTEST and the fixed or competitive status (STATUS) of the contract.] However, in this section, we will fit the first-order regression model using all eight independent variables.

The MINITAB printout for the regression analysis is shown in Figure SIA11.2. The global F-statistic ($F = 1166.68$) and associated p-value (.000) shown on the printout indicate that the overall model is statistically useful for predicting construction cost. The value of R^2 indicates that the model can explain 97.6% of the sample variation in contract cost. Both of these results provide strong statistical support for using the model for estimation and prediction.

[*Note:* Not all of the independent variables have statistically significant t-values. However, we caution against dropping the insignificant variables from the model at this stage. One reason (discussed in this sec-

Figure SIA11.1

MINITAB scatterplots for FLAG data

Matrix Plot of COST vs STATUS, DISTRICT

Figure SIA11.1 (cont'd)

```
The regression equation is
COST = 124 + 0.906 DOTEST - 147 B2B1RAT - 84 B3B1RAT - 59.1 BHB1RAT + 148 STA>>
       + 37.8 DISTRICT + 218 BTPRATIO + 0.344 DAYSEST


Predictor      Coef   SE Coef       T       P
Constant      123.9     426.8    0.29   0.772
DOTEST      0.90647   0.01659   54.64   0.000
B2B1RAT      -147.1     419.0   -0.35   0.726
B3B1RAT       -83.8     245.4   -0.34   0.733
BHB1RAT      -59.09     54.90   -1.00   0.283
STATUS       148.16     51.48    2.88   0.004
DISTRICT      37.75     43.07    0.88   0.382
BTPRATIO      217.6     139.6    1.56   0.120
DAYSEST      0.3439    0.1803    1.91   0.058


S = 304.589   R-Sq = 97.6%   R-Sq(adj) = 97.6%


Analysis of Variance

Source          DF          SS         MS        F      P
Regression       8   865907936  108238492  1166.68  0.000
Residual Error 226    20967037      92774
Total          234   886874973
```

Figure SIA11.2

MINITAB regression output for first-order model of road construction cost

tion) is that performing a large number of *t*-tests will yield an inflated probability of at least one Type I error. In later sections of this chapter, we develop other reasons for why the multiple *t*-test approach is not a good strategy for determining which independent variables to keep in the model.]

The MINITAB printout shown in Figure SIA11.3 gives a 95% prediction interval for cost and a 95% confidence interval for the mean cost for the *x*-values associated with the last observation (contract) in the FLAG file. These *x*-values are engineer's cost estimate (DOTEST) = 497 thousand dollars, ratio of second

Continued

```
Predicted Values for New Observations

New
Obs    Fit   SE Fit       95% CI            95% PI
  1  433.7    48.0    (339.2, 528.2)   (-173.9, 1041.2)


Values of Predictors for New Observations

New
Obs  DOTEST  B2B1RAT  B3B1RAT  BHB1RAT    STATUS   DISTRICT  BTPRATIO  DAYSEST
  1     497     1.07     1.08     1.19  0.000000       1.00     0.500     90.0
```

Figure SIA11.3
MINITAB printout with 95% confidence and prediction intervals

lowest bid to lowest bid (B2B1RAT) = 1.07, ratio of third lowest bid to lowest bid (B3B1RAT) = 1.08, ratio of highest bid to lowest bid (BHB1RAT) = 1.19, competitive bid (STATUS = 0), south Florida contract (DISTRICT = 1), bidders to planholders ratio (BTPRATIO) = 0.5, and estimated work days (DAYSEST) = 90. The 95% confidence interval of (339.2, 528.2) implies that for all road contracts with these x-values, the mean contract cost falls between 339.2 and 528.2 thousand dollars, with 95% confidence.

The 95% prediction interval of $(-173.9, 1041.2)$ implies that for an individual road contract with these x-values, the contract cost falls between 0 (since cost cannot be negative) and 1,041.2 thousand dollars, with 95% confidence. Note the wide range of the prediction interval. This is due to the large magnitude of the model standard deviation, $s = 305$ thousand dollars. Although the model is deemed statistically useful for predicting contract cost, it may not be "practically" useful. To reduce the magnitude of s, we will need to improve the model's predictive ability. (We consider such a model in the next Statistics in Action Revisited section.)

Exercises 11.25–11.31

Applying the Concepts—Basic

⊙ **STREETVN**

11.25 Incomes of Mexican street vendors. Refer to the *World*
NW *Development* (Feb. 1998) study of street vendors' earnings, y, Exercise 11.15 (p. 683). The SPSS spreadsheet below shows both a 95% prediction interval for y (right side) and a 95% confidence interval for $E(y)$ (left side) for a 45-year-old vendor who works 10 hours a day (i.e., for $x_1 = 45$ and $x_2 = 10$).
 a. Interpret the 95% prediction interval for y in the words of the problem.
 b. Interpret the 95% confidence interval for $E(y)$ in the words of the problem.
 c. Note that the interval of part **a** is wider than the interval of part **b**. Will this always be true? Explain.

⊙ **DDT**

11.26 Chemical plant contamination. Refer to Exercise 11.16 (p. 683) and the U.S. Army Corps of Engineers data on contaminated fish. You fit the first-order model,

$E(y) = \beta_0 + \beta_1 x_1 + \beta_2 x_2 + \beta_3 x_3$, to the data, where y = DDT level (parts per million), x_1 = number of miles upstream, x_2 = length (centimeters), and x_3 = weight (in grams). Use the Excel printout at the top of p. 693 to predict, with 90% confidence, the DDT level of a fish caught 100 miles upstream with a length of 40 centimeters and a weight of 800 grams. Interpret the result.

⊙ **GASTURBINE**

11.27 Cooling method for gas turbines. Refer to the *Journal of Engineering for Gas Turbines and Power* (Jan. 2005) study of a high-pressure inlet fogging method for a gas turbine engine, Exercise 11.17 (p. 684). Recall that you fit a first-order model for heat rate (y) as a function of speed (x_1), inlet temperature (x_2), exhaust temperature (x_3), cycle pressure ratio (x_4), and air flow rate (x_5) to data saved in the **GASTURBINE** file. A MINITAB printout with both a 95% confidence interval for $E(y)$ and prediction interval for y for selected values of the x's is shown on p. 693.
 a. Interpret the 95% prediction interval for y in the words of the problem.

age	hours	ci95low	ci95upp	pi95low	pi95upp
45	10	2620.25197	3414.87349	1759.74674	4275.37871

SPSS Output for Exercise 11.25

For Average Predicted Y (YHat)		Confidence and Prediction Estimate Intervals	
Interval Half Width	27.58531		
Confidence Interval Lower Limit	-15.8394	Data	
Confidence Interval Upper Limit	39.33117	Confidence Level	90%
			1
For Individual Response Y		MILE given value	100
Interval Half Width	163.7415	LENGTH given value	40
Prediction Interval Lower Limit	-151.996	WEIGHT given value	800
Prediction Interval Upper Limit	175.4874		

Excel/PHStat2 Output for Exercise 11.26

```
Predicted Values for New Observations

New
Obs      Fit   SE Fit       95% CI              95% PI
  1  12632.5    237.3   (12157.9, 13107.1)   (11599.6, 13665.5)


Values of Predictors for New Observations

New
Obs   RPM   INLET-TEMP   EXH-TEMP   CPRATIO   AIRFLOW
  1  7500         1000        525      13.5      10.0
```

MINITAB Output for Exercise 11.27

b. Interpret the 95% confidence interval for $E(y)$ in the words of the problem.

c. Will the confidence interval for $E(y)$ always be narrower than the prediction interval for y? Explain.

Applying the Concepts—Intermediate

11.28 California rain levels. An article published in *Geography* (July 1980) used multiple regression to predict annual rainfall levels in California. Data on the average annual precipitation (*y*), altitude (x_1), latitude (x_2), and distance from the Pacific coast (x_3) were collected for 30 meteorological stations scattered throughout California. The first 10 observations are listed in the table below. Consider the first-order model $y = \beta_0 + \beta_1x_1 + \beta_2x_2 + \beta_3x_3 + \epsilon$.

a. Fit the model to the data and give the least squares prediction equation.

b. Is there evidence that the first-order model is useful for predicting annual precipitation *y*? Test using $\alpha = .05$.

c. Predict, with 95% confidence, the average annual precipitation for the Giant Forest meteorological station (station #9).

SNOWGEESE

11.29 Snow geese feeding trial. Refer to the *Journal of Applied Ecology* study of the feeding habits of baby snow geese, Exercise 11.18 (page 684). You fit the first-order model relating gosling weight change *y* to digestion efficiency x_1 and acid-detergent fiber x_2. Estimate, with 95% confidence, the mean weight change for all snow geese with $x_1 = 5\%$ and $x_2 = 30\%$.

11.30 Extracting water from oil. Refer to Exercise 11.19 (p. 684). The researchers concluded that "in order to break a water-

CALIRAIN (Data for 1st 10 stations listed)

Station	Avg. Annual Precipitation, *y* (inches)	Altitude, x_1 (feet)	Latitude, x_2 (degrees)	Distance from Coast, x_3 (miles)
1. Eureka	39.57	43	40.8	1
2. Red Bluff	23.27	341	40.2	97
3. Thermal	18.20	4152	33.8	70
4. Fort Bragg	37.48	74	39.4	1
5. Soda Springs	49.26	6752	39.3	150
6. San Francisco	21.82	52	37.8	5
7. Sacramento	18.07	25	38.5	80
8. San Jose	14.17	95	37.4	28
9. Giant Forest	42.63	6360	36.6	145
10. Salinas	13.85	74	36.7	12

Source: Taylor, P. J. "A Pedagogic Application of Multiple Regression Analysis." *Geography*, July 1980, Vol. 65, pp. 203–212.

oil mixture with the lowest possible voltage, the volume fraction of the disperse phase x_1 should be high, while the salinity x_2 and the amount of surfactant x_5 should be low." Use this information and the first-order model of Exercise 11.19 to find a 95% prediction interval for this "low" voltage y. Interpret the interval.

11.31 Boiler drum production. In a production facility, an accurate estimate of man-hours needed to complete a task is crucial to management in making such decisions as the proper number of workers to hire, an accurate deadline to quote a client, or cost-analysis decisions regarding budgets. A manufacturer of boiler drums wants to use regression to predict the number of man-hours needed to erect the drums in future projects. To accomplish this, data for 35 boilers were collected. In addition to man-hours (y), the variables measured were boiler capacity ($x_1 =$ lb/hr), boiler design pressure ($x_2 =$ pounds per square inch or psi), boiler type ($x_3 = 1$ if industry field erected, 0 if utility field erected), and drum type ($x_4 = 1$ if steam, 0 if mud). The data are saved in the **BOILERS** file. (The first and last five observations are listed in the accompanying table.)

a. Fit the model $E(y) = \beta_0 + \beta_1 x_1 + \beta_2 x_2 + \beta_3 x_3 + \beta_4 x_4$ to the data. Give the estimates of the β's.

b. Conduct a test for the global utility of the model. Use $\alpha = .01$.

c. Find a 95% confidence interval for $E(y)$ when $x_1 = 150,000$, $x_2 = 500$, $x_3 = 1$, and $x_4 = 0$. Interpret the result.

BOILERS

Man-Hours, y	Boiler Capacity, x_1	Design Pressure, x_2	Boiler Type, x_3	Drum Type, x_4
3,137	120,000	375	1	1
3,590	65,000	750	1	1
4,526	150,000	500	1	1
10,825	1,073,877	2,170	0	1
4,023	150,000	325	1	1
⋮	⋮	⋮	⋮	⋮
4,206	441,000	410	1	0
4,006	441,000	410	1	0
3,728	627,000	1,525	0	0
3,211	610,000	1,500	0	0
1,200	30,000	325	1	0

Source: Dr. Kelly Uscategui, University of Connecticut

11.5 Model Building: Interaction Models

In Section 11.2, we demonstrated the relationship between $E(y)$ and the independent variables in a first-order model. When $E(y)$ is graphed against any one variable (say, x_1) for fixed values of the other variables, the result is a set of *parallel* straight lines (see Figure 11.3, p. 671). When this situation occurs (as it always does for a first-order model), we say that the relationship between $E(y)$ and any one independent variable *does not depend* on the values of the other independent variables in the model.

However, if the relationship between $E(y)$ and x_1 does, in fact, depend on the values of the remaining x's held fixed, then the first-order model is not appropriate for predicting y. In this case, we need another model that will take into account this dependence. Such a model includes the *cross products* of two or more x's.

For example, suppose that the mean value $E(y)$ of a response y is related to two quantitative independent variables, x_1 and x_2, by the model

$$E(y) = 1 + 2x_1 - x_2 + x_1 x_2$$

A graph of the relationship between $E(y)$ and x_1 for $x_2 = 0, 1$, and 2 is displayed in Figure 11.10.

Note that the graph shows three nonparallel straight lines. You can verify that the slopes of the lines differ by substituting each of the values $x_2 = 0, 1$, and 2 into the equation. For $x_2 = 0$:

$$E(y) = 1 + 2x_1 - (0) + x_1(0) = 1 + 2x_1 \quad \text{(slope = 2)}$$

FIGURE 11.10

Graphs of $1 + 2x_1 - x_2 + x_1x_2$ for $x_2 = 0, 1, 2$

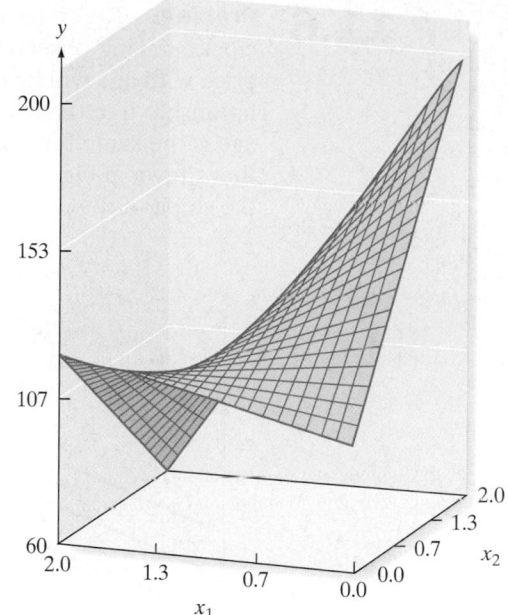

FIGURE 11.11

Computer-generated graph for an interaction model

For $x_2 = 1$,

$$E(y) = 1 + 2x_1 - (1) + x_1(1) = 3x_1 \qquad (\text{slope} = 3)$$

For $x_2 = 2$,

$$E(y) = 1 + 2x_1 - (2) + x_1(2) = -1 + 4x_1 \qquad (\text{slope} = 4)$$

Note that the slope of each line is represented by $\beta_1 + \beta_3 x_2 = 2 + x_2$. Thus, the effect on $E(y)$ of a change in x_1 (i.e., the slope) now *depends* on the value of x_2. When this situation occurs, we say that x_1 and x_2 **interact**. The cross-product term, x_1x_2, is called an **interaction term**, and the model $E(y) = \beta_0 + \beta_1x_1 + \beta_2x_2 + \beta_3x_1x_2$ is called an **interaction model** with two quantitative variables.

An Interaction Model Relating $E(y)$ to Two Quantitative Independent Variables

$$E(y) = \beta_0 + \beta_1x_1 + \beta_2x_2 + \beta_3x_1x_2$$

where

$(\beta_1 + \beta_3x_2)$ represents the change in $E(y)$ for every 1-unit increase in x_1, holding x_2 fixed

$(\beta_2 + \beta_3x_1)$ represents the change in $E(y)$ for every 1-unit increase in x_2, holding x_1 fixed

---

A three-dimensional graph (generated by computer) of an interaction model in two quantitative x's is shown in Figure 11.11. Unlike the flat planar surface displayed in Figure 11.4, the interaction model traces a ruled surface (twisted plane) in three-dimensional space. If we slice the twisted plane at a fixed value of x_2, we obtain a straight line relating $E(y)$ to x_1; however, the slope of the line will change as we change the value of x_2. Consequently, an interaction model is appropriate when the linear relationship between y and one independent variable depends on the value of another independent variable. The next example illustrates this idea.

EXAMPLE 11.6

Fitting an Interaction Model.

Problem Refer to Examples 11.3 and 11.4. Suppose the collector of grandfather clocks, having observed many auctions, believes that the *rate of increase* of the auction price with age will be driven upward by a large number of bidders. Thus, instead of a relationship like that shown in Figure 11.12(a), in which the rate of increase in price with age is the same for any number of bidders, the collector believes the relationship is like that shown in Figure 11.12(b). Note that as the number of bidders increases from 5 to 15, the slope of the price versus age line increases.

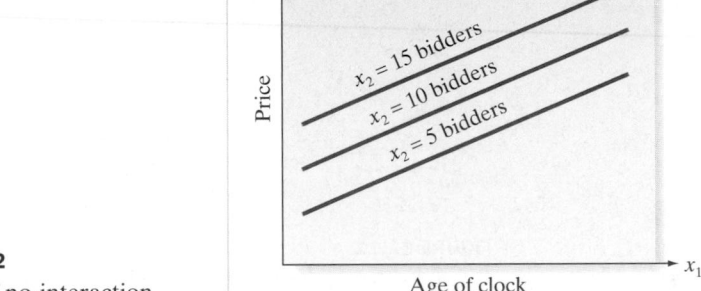

FIGURE 11.12

Examples of no-interaction and interaction models

a. No interaction between x_1 and x_2

b. Interaction between x_1 and x_2

Consequently, the interaction model is proposed:

$$y = \beta_0 + \beta_1 x_1 + \beta_2 x_2 + \beta_3 x_1 x_2 + \epsilon$$

The 32 data points listed in Table 11.2 were used to fit the model with interaction. A portion of the MINITAB printout is shown in Figure 11.13.

a. Test the overall utility of the model using the global F-test at $\alpha = .05$.

b. Test the hypothesis (at $\alpha = .05$) that the price-age slope increases as the number of bidders increases—that is, that age and number of bidders, x_2, interact positively.

c. Estimate the change in auction price of a 150-year-old grandfather clock, y, for each additional bidder.

Solution

a. The global F-test is used to test the null hypothesis

$$H_0: \beta_1 = \beta_2 = \beta_3 = 0$$

The test statistic and p-value of the test (highlighted on the MINITAB printout) are $F = 193.04$ and p-value $= 0$, respectively. Since $\alpha = .05$ exceeds the p-value, there is sufficient evidence to conclude that the model fit is a statistically useful predictor of auction price, y.

b. The hypotheses of interest to the collector concern the interaction parameter β_3. Specifically,

$$H_0: \beta_3 = 0$$
$$H_a: \beta_3 > 0$$

Since we are testing an individual β parameter, a t-test is required. The test statistic and two-tailed p-value (highlighted on the printout) are $t = 6.11$ and p-value $= 0$, respectively. The upper-tailed p-value, obtained by dividing the two-tailed p-value in half, is $0/2 = 0$. Since $\alpha = .05$ exceeds the p-value, the collector

Regression Analysis: PRICE versus AGE, NUMBIDS, AGEBID

```
The regression equation is
PRICE = 320 + 0.88 AGE - 93.3 NUMBIDS + 1.30 AGEBID


Predictor    Coef   SE Coef      T       P
Constant    320.5     295.1    1.09   0.287
AGE         0.878     2.032    0.43   0.669
NUMBIDS    -93.26     29.89   -3.12   0.004
AGEBID     1.2978    0.2123    6.11   0.000


S = 88.9145    R-Sq = 95.4%    R-Sq(adj) = 94.9%


Analysis of Variance

Source          DF       SS       MS       F       P
Regression       3  4578427  1526142  193.04   0.000
Residual Error  28   221362     7906
Total           31  4799790
```

FIGURE 11.13

MINITAB printout for interaction model of auction price

can reject H_0 and conclude that the rate of change of the mean price of the clocks with age increases as the number of bidders increases; that is, x_1 and x_2 interact positively. Thus, it appears that the interaction term should be included in the model.

c. To estimate the change in auction price, y, for every 1-unit increase in number of bidders, x_2, we need to estimate the slope of the line relating y to x_2 when the age of the clock, x_1, is 150 years old. An analyst who is not careful may estimate this slope as $\hat{\beta}_2 = -93.26$. Although the coefficient of x_2 is negative, this does *not* imply that auction price decreases as the number of bidders increases. Since interaction is present, the rate of change (slope) of mean auction price with the number of bidders *depends* on x_1, the age of the clock. Thus, the estimated rate of change of y for a unit increase in x_2 (one new bidder) for a 150-year-old clock is

$$\text{Estimated slope of the } y \text{ versus } x_2 \text{ line} = \hat{\beta}_2 + \hat{\beta}_3 x_1$$
$$= -93.26 + 1.30(150) - 101.74$$

In other words, we estimate that the auction price of a 150-year-old clock will *increase* by about \$101.74 for every additional bidder.

Look Back Although the rate of increase will vary as x_1 is changed, it will remain positive for the range of values of x_1 included in the sample. Extreme care is needed in interpreting the signs and sizes of coefficients in a multiple regression model.

Now Work Exercise 11.36

Example 11.6 illustrates an important point about conducting t-tests on the β parameters in the interaction model. The "most important" β parameter in this model is the interaction β, β_3. [Note that this β is also the one associated with the highest-order term in the model, $x_1 x_2$.* Consequently, we will want to test $H_0: \beta_3 = 0$ after we have determined that the overall model is useful for predicting y. Once interaction is detected (as in Example 11.6), however, tests on the first-order terms x_1 and x_2 should *not* be

---

*The order of a term is equal to the sum of the exponents of the quantitative variables included in the term. Thus, when x_1 and x_2 are both quantitative variables, the cross-product, $x_1 x_2$, is a second-order term.

conducted since they are meaningless tests; the presence of interaction implies that both x's are important.

Caution

Once interaction has been deemed important in the model $E(y) = \beta_0 + \beta_1 x_1 + \beta_2 x_2 + \beta_3 x_1 x_2$, do not conduct t-tests on the β coefficients of the first-order terms x_1 and x_2. These terms should be kept in the model regardless of the magnitude of their associated p-values shown on the printout.

Exercises 11.32–11.44

Learning the Mechanics

11.32 Write an interaction model relating the mean value of y, $E(y)$ to
  a. two quantitative independent variables
  b. three quantitative independent variables [*Hint:* Include all possible two-way cross-product terms.]

11.33 Suppose the true relationship between $E(y)$ and the quantitative independent variables x_1 and x_2 is

$$E(y) = 3 + x_1 + 2x_2 - x_1 x_2$$

  a. Describe the corresponding three-dimensional response surface.
  b. Plot the linear relationship between y and x_2 for $x_2 = 0, 1, 2$, where $0 \le x_2 \le 5$.
  c. Explain why the lines you plotted in part **b** are not parallel.
  d. Use the lines you plotted in part **b** to explain how changes in the settings of x_1 and x_2 affect $E(y)$.
  e. Use your graph from part **b** to determine how much $E(y)$ changes when x_1 is changed from 2 to 0 and x_2 is simultaneously changed from 4 to 5.

11.34 Suppose you fit the interaction model

$$y = \beta_0 + \beta_1 x_1 + \beta_2 x_2 + \beta_3 x_1 x_2 + \epsilon$$

to $n = 32$ data points and obtain the following results:

$$SS_{yy} = 479 \qquad SSE = 21 \qquad \hat{\beta}_3 = 10 \qquad s_{\hat{\beta}_3} = 4$$

  a. Find R^2 and interpret its value.
  b. Is the model adequate for predicting y? Test at $\alpha = .05$.

  c. Use a graph to explain the contribution of the $x_1 x_2$ term to the model.
  d. Is there evidence that x_1 and x_2 interact? Test at $\alpha = .05$.

11.35 The MINITAB printout below was obtained from fitting the model

$$y = \beta_0 + \beta_1 x_1 + \beta_2 x_2 + \beta_3 x_1 x_2 + \epsilon$$

to $n = 15$ data points.
  a. What is the prediction equation for the response surface?
  b. Describe the geometric form of the response surface of part **a**.
  c. Plot the prediction equation for the case when $x_2 = 1$. Do this twice more on the same graph for the cases when $x_2 = 3$ and $x_2 = 5$.
  d. Explain what it means to say that x_1 and x_2 interact. Explain why your graph of part **c** suggests that x_1 and x_2 interact.
  e. Specify the null and alternative hypotheses you would use to test whether x_1 and x_2 interact.
  f. Conduct the hypothesis test of part **e** using $\alpha = .01$.

```
The regression equation is
Y = -2.55 + 3.82 X1 + 2.63 X2 -1.29 X1X2


Predictor    Coef   SE Coef      T       P
Constant   -2.550     1.142   -2.23   0.043
X1          3.815     0.529    7.22   0.000
X2          2.630     0.344    7.64   0.000
X1X2       -1.285     0.159   -8.06   0.000


S = 0.713     R-Sq = 85.6%    R-Sq(adj) = 81.6%


Analysis of Variance

Source          DF       SS       MS       F       P
Regression       3   33.149   11.050   21.75   0.000
Residual Error  11    5.587    0.508
Total           14   38.736
```

MINITAB Output for Exercise 11.35

Applying the Concepts—Basic

11.36 Role of retailer interest on shopping behavior. Retail inter-
NW est is defined by marketers as the level of interest a consumer has in a given retail store. Marketing professors at the
University of Tennessee at Chattanooga and the University
of Alabama investigated the role of retailer interest in consumers' shopping behavior (*Journal of Retailing*, Summer
2006). Using survey data collected for $n = 375$ consumers,
the professors developed an interaction model for
y = willingness of the consumer to shop at a retailer's store
in the future (called *repatronage intentions*) as a function of
x_1 = consumer satisfaction and x_2 = retailer interest. The
regression results are shown below.

Variable	$\hat{\beta}$	t-value	p-value
Satisfaction (x_1)	.426	7.33	<.01
Retailer interest (x_2)	.044	0.85	>.10
Interaction $(x_1 x_2)$	−.157	−3.09	<.01

$R^2 = .65$, $F = 226.35$, p-value < .001

a. Is the overall model statistically useful for predicting y?
Test using $\alpha = .05$.
b. Conduct a test for interaction at $\alpha = .05$.
c. Use the β-estimates to sketch the estimated relationship
between repatronage intentions (y) and satisfaction (x_1)
when retailer interest is $x_2 = 1$ (a low value).
d. Repeat part **c** when retailer interest is $x_2 = 7$ (a high
value).
e. Sketch the two lines, parts **c** and **d**, on the same graph to
illustrate the nature of the interaction.

11.37 Defects in nuclear missile housing parts. The technique of
multivariable testing (MVT) was discussed in the *Journal
of the Reliability Analysis Center* (First Quarter, 2004).
MVT was shown to improve the quality of carbon-foam
rings used in nuclear missile housings. The rings are produced via a casting process that involves mixing ingredients, oven curing, and carving the finished part. One type
of defect analyzed was number y of black streaks in the
manufactured ring. Two variables found to impact the
number of defects were turntable speed (revolutions per
minute), x_1, and cutting-blade position (inches from center), x_2.
a. The researchers discovered "an interaction between
blade position and turntable speed." Hypothesize a regression model for $E(y)$ that incorporates this interaction.
b. The researchers reported a positive linear relationship
between number of defects (y) and turntable speed (x_1)
but found that the slope of the relationship was much
steeper for lower values of cutting-blade position (x_2).
What does this imply about the interaction term in the
model, part **a**? Explain.

11.38 Consumer behavior while waiting in line. While waiting in
a long line for service (e.g., to use an ATM or at the post
office), at some point you may decide to leave the queue.
The *Journal of Consumer Research* (Nov. 2003) published
a study of consumer behavior while waiting in a queue. A
sample of $n = 148$ college students were asked to imagine
that they were waiting in line at a post office to mail a

package and that the estimated waiting time is 10 minutes
or less. After a 10-minute wait, students were asked about
their level of negative feelings (annoyed, anxious) on a
scale of 1 (strongly disagree) to 9 (strongly agree). Before
answering, however, the students were informed about
how many people were ahead of them and behind them in
the line. The researchers used regression to relate negative
feelings score (y) to number ahead in line (x_1) and number behind in line (x_2).
a. The researchers fit an interaction model to the data.
Write the hypothesized equation of this model.

b. In the words of the problem, explain what it means to
say that "x_1 and x_2 interact to effect y."
c. A t-test for the interaction β in the model resulted in a
p-value greater than .25. Interpret this result.

d. From their analysis, the researchers concluded that "the
greater the number of people ahead, the higher the negative feeling score" and "the greater the number of people behind, the lower the negative feeling score." Use
this information to determine the signs of β_1 and β_2 in
the model.

Applying the Concepts—Intermediate

📀 **STREETVN**

11.39 Incomes of Mexican street vendors. Refer to the *World
Development* (Feb. 1998) study of street vendors in the
city of Puebla, Mexico, Exercise 11.15 (p. 683). Recall
that the vendors' mean annual earnings, $E(y)$, was modeled as a first-order function of age (x_1) and hours
worked (x_2). Now, consider the interaction model
$E(y) = \beta_0 + \beta_1 x_1 + \beta_2 x_2 + \beta_3 x_1 x_2$.
a. Find the least squares prediction equation.
b. What is the estimated slope relating annual earnings (y)
to age (x_1) when number of hours worked (x_2) is 10?
Interpret the result.
c. What is the estimated slope relating annual earnings (y)
to hours worked (x_2) when age (x_1) is 40? Interpret the
result.
d. Give the null hypothesis for testing whether age (x_1) and
hours worked (x_2) interact.
e. Find the p-value of the test, part **d**.
f. Refer to part **e**. Give the appropriate conclusion in the
words of the problem.

11.40 Factors that impact an auditor's judgment. A study was
conducted to determine the effects of linguistic delivery
style and client credibility on auditors' judgments
(*Advances in Accounting and Behavioral Research*,
2004). Two hundred auditors from Big 5 accounting firms
were asked to assume that he or she was an audit team
supervisor of a new manufacturing client and was performing an analytical review of the client's financial
statement. The researchers gave the auditors different
information on the client's credibility and linguistic delivery style of the client's explanation. Each auditor then
provided an assessment of the likelihood that the client-
provided explanation accounts for the fluctuation in the
financial statement. The three variables of interest—
credibility (x_1), linguistic delivery style (x_2), and likelihood

(*y*)—were all measured on a numerical scale. Regression analysis was used to fit the interaction model, $y = \beta_0 + \beta_1 x_1 + \beta_2 x_2 + \beta_3 x_1 x_2 + \varepsilon$. The results are summarized in the table below.

a. Interpret the phrase "client credibility and linguistic delivery style interact" in the words of the problem.

b. Give the null and alternative hypotheses for testing the overall adequacy of the model.

c. Conduct the test, part **b**, using the information in the table.

d. Give the null and alternative hypotheses for testing whether client credibility and linguistic delivery style interact.

e. Conduct the test, part **d**, using the information in the table.

f. The researchers estimated the slope of the Likelihood–Linguistic Delivery Style line at a low level of client credibility ($x_1 = 22$). Obtain this estimate and interpret it in the words of the problem.

g. The researchers also estimated the slope of the Likelihood–Linguistic Delivery Style line at a high level of client credibility ($x_1 = 46$). Obtain this estimate and interpret it in the words of the problem.

GASTURBINE

11.41 Cooling method for gas turbines. Refer to the *Journal of Engineering for Gas Turbines and Power* (Jan. 2005) study of a high-pressure inlet fogging method for a gas turbine engine, Exercise 11.17 (p. 684). Recall that you fit a first-order model for heat rate (*y*) as a function of speed (x_1), inlet temperature (x_2), exhaust temperature (x_3), cycle pressure ratio (x_4), and air flow rate (x_5) to data saved in the **GASTURBINE** file.

a. Researchers hypothesize that the linear relationship between heat rate (*y*) and temperature (both inlet and exhaust) depends on air flow rate. Write a model for heat rate that incorporates the researchers' theories.

b. Use statistical software to fit the interaction model, part **a**, to the data in the **GASTURBINE** file. Give the least squares prediction equation.

c. Conduct a test (at $\alpha = .05$) to determine whether inlet temperature and air flow rate interact to effect heat rate.

d. Conduct a test (at $\alpha = .05$) to determine whether exhaust temperature and air flow rate interact to effect heat rate.

e. Practically interpret the results of the tests, parts **c** and **d**.

11.42 Therapists' reactions to child-abuse reports. Licensed therapists are mandated by law to report child abuse by their clients. This requires the therapist to breach confidentiality and possibly lose the client's trust. A national survey of licensed psychotherapists was conducted to in-

vestigate clients' reactions to legally mandated child-abuse reports (*American Journal of Orthopsychiatry*, Jan. 1997). The sample consisted of 303 therapists who had filed a child-abuse report against one of their clients. The researchers were interested in finding the best predictors of a client's reaction (*y*) to the report, where *y* is measured on a 30-point scale. (The higher the value, the more favorable the client's response to the report.) The independent variables found to have the most predictive power are listed here.

x_1: Therapist's age (years)
x_2: Therapist's gender (1 if male, 0 if female)
x_3: Degree of therapist's role strain (25-point scale)
x_4: Strength of client-therapist relationship (40-point scale)
x_5: Type of case (1 if family, 0 if not)
$x_1 x_2$: Age × Gender interaction

a. Hypothesize a first-order model relating *y* to each of the five independent variables.

b. Give the null hypothesis for testing the contribution of x_4, strength of client-therapist relationship, to the model.

c. The test statistic for the test, part **b**, was $t = 4.408$ with an associated *p*-value of .001. Interpret this result.

d. The estimated β coefficient for the $x_1 x_2$ interaction term was positive and highly significant ($p < .001$). According to the researchers, "this interaction suggests that ... as the age of the therapist increased, ... male therapists were less likely to get negative client reactions than were female therapists." Do you agree?

e. For this model, $R^2 = .2946$. Interpret this value.

WATEROIL

11.43 Extracting water from oil. Refer to the *Journal of Colloid and Interface Science* study of water/oil mixtures, Exercise 11.19. (p. 684). Recall that three of the seven variables used to predict voltage (*y*) were volume (x_1), salinity (x_2), and surfactant concentration (x_5). The model the researchers fit is

$$E(y) = \beta_0 + \beta_1 x_1 + \beta_2 x_2 + \beta_3 x_5 + \beta_4 x_1 x_2 + \beta_5 x_1 x_5.$$

a. Note that the model includes interaction between disperse phase volume (x_1) and salinity (x_2) as well as interaction between disperse phase volume (x_1) and surfactant concentration (x_5). Discuss how these interaction terms affect the hypothetical relationship between *y* and x_1. Draw a sketch to support your answer.

b. Fit the interaction model to the data in the **WATEROIL** file. Does this model appear to fit the data better than the first-order model in Exercise 11.19? Explain.

c. Interpret the β estimates of the interaction model.

Results for Exercise 11.40

	Beta Estimate	Std Error	*t*-Statistic	*p*-Value
Constant	15.865	10.980	1.445	0.150
Client credibility (x_1)	0.037	0.339	0.110	0.913
Linguistic delivery style (x_2)	−0.678	0.328	−2.064	0.040
Interaction ($x_1 x_2$)	0.036	0.009	4.008	<0.005

F-statistic = 55.35 ($p < 0.0005$): Adjusted R^2 = .450

Variable	β Estimate	Standard Error	Two-Tailed p-Value
TV news exposure (x_1)	.02	.01	.03
Political knowledge (x_2)	.07	.03	.03
Gender (x_3)	.67	.11	$< .001$
Race (x_4)	$-.76$	.13	$< .001$
Partisanship (x_5)	.07	.01	$< .001$
Defense spending (x_6)	.20	.02	$< .001$
Education (x_7)	.07	.02	$< .001$
Knowledge $\times$ gender (x_2x_3)	$-.09$	.04	.02
Knowledge $\times$ race (x_2x_4)	.10	.06	.08

Source: Iyengar, S., and Simon, A. "News Coverage of the Gulf Crisis and Public Opinion." *Communication Research*, Vol. 20, No. 3, June 1993, p. 380 (Table 2).

11.44 Media coverage of a war. Does extensive media coverage of a military crisis influence public opinion on how to respond to the crisis? Political scientists at UCLA researched this question and reported their results in *Communication Research* (June 1993). The military crisis of interest was the 1990 Persian Gulf War, precipitated by Iraq's leader Saddam Hussein's invasion of Kuwait. The researchers used multiple regression analysis to model the level y of support Americans had for a military (rather than a diplomatic) response to the crisis. Values of y ranged from 0 (preference for a diplomatic response) to 4 (preference for a military response). The following independent variables were used in the model:

x_1 = Level of TV news exposure in a selected week (number of days)

x_2 = Knowledge of seven political figures (1 point each correct answer)

x_3 = Gender (1 if male, 0 if female)

x_4 = Race (1 if nonwhite, 0 if white)

x_5 = Partisanship (0–6 scale, where 0 = strong Democrat and 6 = strong Republican)

x_6 = Defense spending attitude (1–7 scale, where 1 = greatly decrease spending and 7 = greatly increase spending)

x_7 = Education level (1–7 scale, where 1 = less than eight grades and 7 = college)

Data from a survey of 1,763 U.S. citizens were used to fit the model

$$E(y) = \beta_0 + \beta_1x_1 + \beta_2x_2 + \beta_3x_3 + \beta_4x_4 +$$
$$\beta_5x_5 + \beta_6x_6 + \beta_7x_7 + \beta_8x_2x_3 + \beta_9x_2x_4$$

The regression results are shown in the table above.

a. Interpret the β estimate for the variable x_1, TV news exposure.

b. Conduct a test to determine whether an increase in TV news exposure is associated with an increase in support for a military resolution of the crisis. Use $\alpha = .05$.

c. Is there sufficient evidence to indicate that the relationship between support for a military resolution (y) and gender (x_3) depends on political knowledge (x_2)? Test using $\alpha = .05$.

d. Is there sufficient evidence to indicate that the relationship between support for a military resolution (y) and race (x_4) depends on political knowledge (x_2)? Test using $\alpha = .05$.

e. The coefficient of determination for the model was $R^2 = .194$. Interpret this value.

f. Use the value of R^2, part **e**, to conduct a global test for model utility. Use $\alpha = .05$.

11.6 Model Building: Quadratic and Other Higher-Order Models

All of the models discussed in the previous sections proposed straight-line relationships between $E(y)$ and each of the independent variables in the model. In this section, we consider models that allow for curvature in the relationships. Each of these models is a **second-order model** because it will include an x^2 term.

First, we consider a model that includes only one independent variable x. The form of this model, called the **quadratic model,** is

$$y = \beta_0 + \beta_1x + \beta_2x^2 + \epsilon$$

The term involving x^2, called a **quadratic term** (or **second-order term**), enables us to hypothesize curvature in the graph of the response model relating y to x. Graphs of the quadratic model for two different values of β_2 are shown in Figure 11.14. When the curve opens upward, the sign of β_2 is positive (see Figure 11.14a); when the curve opens downward, the sign of β_2 is negative (see Figure 11.14b).

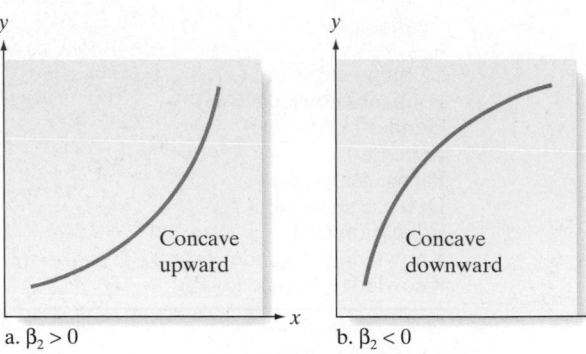

FIGURE 11.14
Graphs for two quadratic
models

a. $\beta_2 > 0$ b. $\beta_2 < 0$

**A Quadratic (Second-Order) Model in a Single Quantitative
Independent Variable**

$$E(y) = \beta_0 + \beta_1 x + \beta_2 x^2$$

where

    β_0 is the y-intercept of the curve

    β_1 is a shift parameter

    β_2 is the rate of curvature

EXAMPLE 11.7

Analyzing a
Quadratic Model for
Electrical Usage

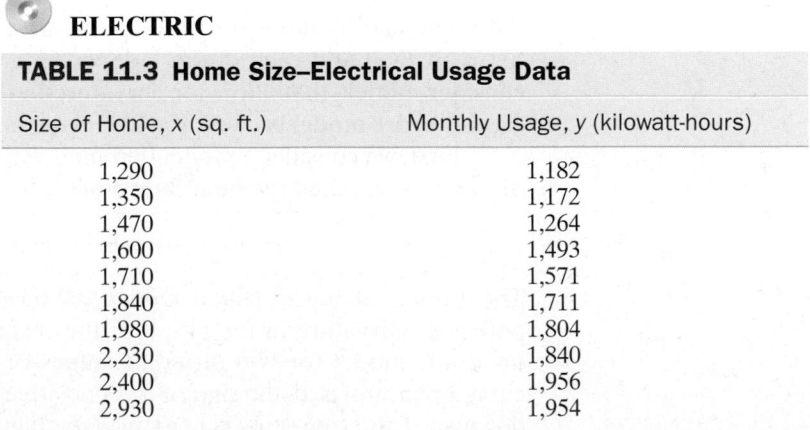

Problem In all-electric homes, the amount of electricity expended
is of interest to consumers, builders, and groups involved with energy conservation. Suppose we wish to investigate the monthly electrical usage, y, in all-electric homes and its relationship to the
size, x, of the home. Moreover, suppose we think that monthly
electrical usage in all-electric homes is related to the size of the
home by the quadratic model

$$y = \beta_0 + \beta_1 x + \beta_2 x^2 + \epsilon$$

To fit the model, the values of y and x are collected for 10 homes during a particular
month. The data are shown in Table 11.3.

a. Construct a scatterplot for the data. Is there evidence to support the use of a quadratic model?

⊙ ELECTRIC

TABLE 11.3 Home Size–Electrical Usage Data

Size of Home, x (sq. ft.)	Monthly Usage, y (kilowatt-hours)
1,290	1,182
1,350	1,172
1,470	1,264
1,600	1,493
1,710	1,571
1,840	1,711
1,980	1,804
2,230	1,840
2,400	1,956
2,930	1,954

b. Use the method of least squares to estimate the unknown parameters β_0, β_1, and β_2 in the quadratic model.

c. Graph the prediction equation and assess how well the model fits the data, both visually and numerically.

d. Interpret the β estimates.

e. Is the overall model useful (at $\alpha = .01$) for predicting electrical usage y?

f. Is there sufficient evidence of downward curvature in the electrical usage–home size relationship? Test using $\alpha = .01$.

Solution

a. A MINITAB scattergram for the data of Table 11.3 is shown in Figure 11.15. The figure illustrates that the electrical usage appears to increase in a curvilinear manner with the size of the home. This provides some support for the inclusion of the quadratic term x^2 in the model.

b. We used Excel to fit the model to the data in Table 11.3. Part of the Excel regression output is displayed in Figure 11.16. The least squares estimates of the β para-

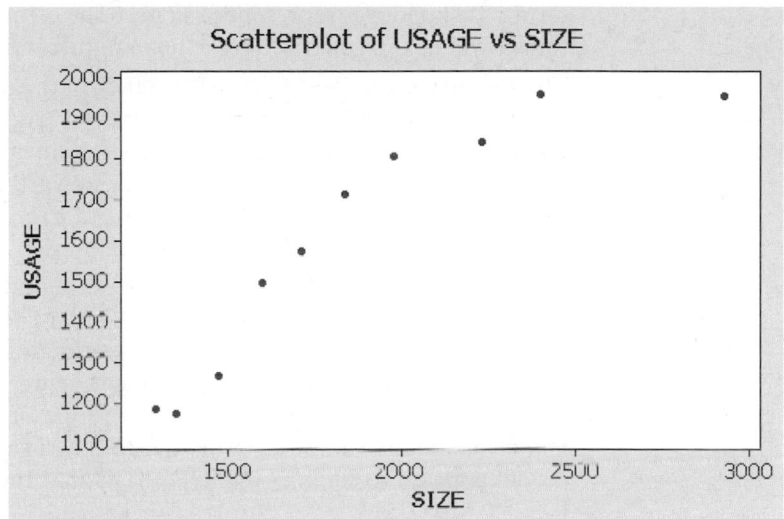

FIGURE 11.15

MINITAB scatterplot for electrical usage data

Regression Analysis						
Regression Statistics						
Multiple R	0.990901117					
R Square	0.981885024					
Adjusted R Square	0.976709317					
Standard Error	46.80133336					
Observations	10					
ANOVA						
	df	*SS*	*MS*	*F*	*Significance F*	
Regression	2	831069.5464	415534.7732	189.7103041	8.00078E-07	
Residual	7	15332.55363	2190.364804			
Total	9	846402.1				
	Coefficients	*Standard Error*	*t Stat*	*P-value*	*Lower 95%*	*Upper 95%*
Intercept	-1216.143887	242.8063685	-5.008698472	0.001550025	-1790.289304	-641.9984703
SIZE	2.398930177	0.245835602	9.758269998	2.51335E-05	1.817621767	2.980238587
SIZESQ	-0.00045004	5.90766E-05	-7.617907059	0.000124415	-0.000589734	-0.000310346

FIGURE 11.16

Excel regression output for electrical usage model

meters (highlighted) are $\hat{\beta}_0 = -1{,}216.1$, $\hat{\beta}_1 = 2.3989$, and $\hat{\beta}_2 = -.00045$. Therefore, the equation that minimizes the SSE for the data is

$$\hat{y} = -1{,}216.1 + 2.3989x - .00045x^2$$

c. Figure 11.17 is a MINITAB graph of the least squares prediction equation. Note that the graph provides a good fit to the data of Table 11.3. A numerical measure of fit is obtained with the adjusted coefficient of determination, R_a^2. This value (highlighted on Figure 11.16) is $R_a^2 = .9767$. This implies that almost 98% of the sample variation in electrical usage (y) can be explained by the quadratic model (after adjusting for sample size and degrees of freedom).

d. The interpretation of the estimated coefficients in a quadratic model must be undertaken cautiously. First, the estimated y-intercept, $\hat{\beta}_0$, can be meaningfully interpreted only if the range of the independent variable includes zero—that is, if $x = 0$ is included in the sampled range of x. Although $\hat{\beta}_0 = -1{,}216.1$ seems to imply that the estimated electrical usage is negative when $x = 0$, this zero point is not in the range of the sample (the lowest value of x is 1,290 square feet), and the value is nonsensical (a home with 0 square feet); thus the interpretation of $\hat{\beta}_0$ is not meaningful.

The estimated coefficient of x is $\hat{\beta}_1 = 2.3989$, but in the presence of the quadratic term x^2, it no longer represents a slope.* The estimated coefficient of the first-order term x will not, in general, have a meaningful interpretation in the quadratic model.

The sign of the coefficient, $\hat{\beta}_2 = -.00045$, of the quadratic term, x^2, is the indicator of whether the curve is concave downward (mound-shaped) or concave upward (bowl-shaped). A negative $\hat{\beta}_2$ implies downward concavity, as in this example (Figure 11.17), and a positive $\hat{\beta}_2$ implies upward concavity. Rather than interpreting the numerical value of $\hat{\beta}_2$ itself, we utilize a graphical representation of the model, as in Figure 11.17, to describe the model.

Note that Figure 11.17 implies that the estimated electrical usage is leveling off as the home sizes increase beyond 2,500 square feet. In fact, the convexity of the model would lead to decreasing usage estimates if we were to display the model out to 4,000 square feet and beyond (see Figure 11.18). However, model interpretations are not meaningful outside the range of the independent variable, which has a maximum value of 2,930 square feet in this example. Thus, although the model appears to support the hypothesis that the *rate of increase* per square foot

FIGURE 11.17

MINITAB plot of least squares model for electrical usage

*For students with knowledge of calculus, note that the slope of the quadratic model is the first derivative $\partial y / \partial x = \beta_1 + 2\beta_2 x$. Thus, the slope varies as a function of x, rather than the constant slope associated with the straight-line model.

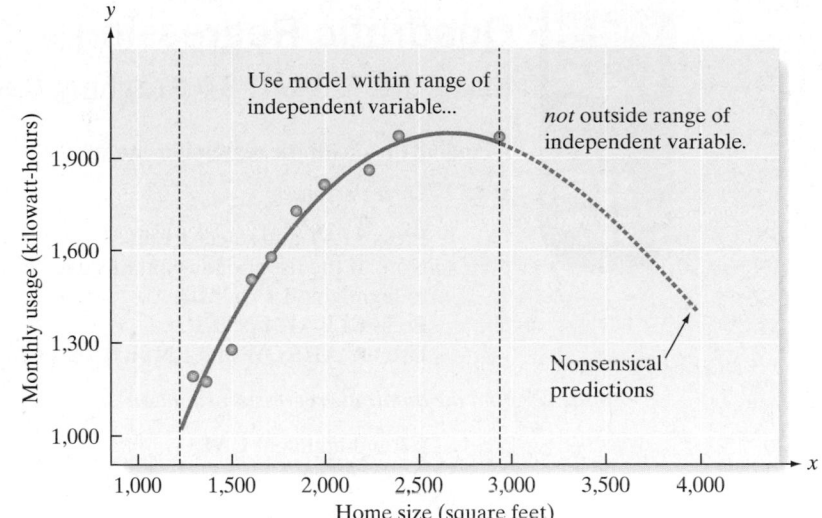

FIGURE 11.18

Potential misuse of quadratic model

decreases for the home sizes near the high end of the sampled values, the conclusion that usage will actually begin to decrease for very large homes would be a *misuse* of the model, since no homes of 3,000 square feet or more were included in the sample.

e. To test whether the quadratic model is statistically useful, we conduct the global *F*-test:

H_0: $\beta_1 = \beta_2 = 0$

H_a: At least one of the above coefficients is nonzero

From the Excel printout, Figure 11.16, the test statistic (highlighted) is $F = 189.710$ with an associated *p*-value of 0. For any reasonable α we reject H_0 and conclude that the overall model is a useful predictor of electrical usage, *y*.

f. Figure 11.17 shows concave downward curvature in the relationship between size of a home and electrical usage in the sample of 10 data points. To determine if this type of curvature exists in the population, we want to test

H_0: $\beta_2 = 0$ (no curvature in the response curve)

H_a: $\beta_2 < 0$ (downward concavity exists in the response curve)

The test statistic for testing β_2 highlighted on the printout, is $t = -7.618$ and the associated two-tailed *p*-value is .00012. Since this is a one-tailed test, the appropriate *p*-value is $(.00012)/2 = .00006$. Now $\alpha = .01$ exceeds this *p*-value. Thus, there is very strong evidence of downward curvature in the population—that is, electrical usage increases more slowly per square foot for large homes than for small homes.

Look Back Note that the Excel printout in Figure 11.16 also provides the *t*-test statistic and corresponding two-tailed *p*-values for the tests of H_0: $\beta_0 = 0$ and H_0: $\beta_1 = 0$. Since the interpretation of these parameters is not meaningful for this model, the tests are not of interest.

Now Work Exercise 11.50

When two or more quantitative independent variables are included in a second-order model, we can incorporate squared terms for each *x* in the model, as well as the interaction between the two independent variables. A model that includes all possible second-order terms in two independent variables—called a **complete second-order model**—is given in the box (p. 707).

Quadratic Regression

Using the TI-83/TI-84 Graphing Calculator

I. Finding the quadratic regression equation

Step 1   *Enter the data*

Press **STAT** and select **1:Edit**
Note: If the list already contains data, clear the old data. Use the up arrow to highlight "**L1**" or "**L2**".
Press **CLEAR ENTER**.
Use the **ARROW** and **ENTER** keys to enter the data set into **L1** and **L2.**

Step 2   *Find the quadratic regression equation*

Press **STAT** and highlight **CALC**
Press **5** for **QuadReg**
Press **ENTER**
The screen will show the values for a, b, and c in the equation
If the diagnostics are on, the screen will also give the value for r^2
To turn the diagnostics feature on:
Press **2nd 0** for **CATALOG**
Press the **ALPHA** key and x^{-1} for **D**
Press the down **ARROW** until **DiagnosticsOn** is highlighted
Press **ENTER** twice

II. Graphing the quadratic curve with the scatterplot

Step 1   *Enter the data as shown in part I above*

Step 2   *Set up the data plot*

Press **Y=** and **CLEAR** all functions from the Y registers
Press **2nd Y=** for **STAT PLOT**
Press **1** for **Plot1**
Set the cursor so that **ON** is flashing and press **ENTER**.
For **Type**, use the **ARROW** and **ENTER** keys to highlight and select the scatterplot (first icon in the first row).
For **Xlist**, choose the column containing the *x*-data.
For **Freq,** choose the column containing the *y*-data.

Step 3   *Find the regression equation and store the equation in Y1*

Press **STAT** and highlight **CALC**
Press **5** for **QuadReg** (Note: Don't press ENTER here because you want to store the regression equation in Y1)
Press **VARS**
Use the right arrow to highlight **Y-VARS**
Press **ENTER** to select **1:Function**
Press **ENTER** to select **1:Y1**
Press **ENTER**

Step 4   *View the scatterplot and regression line*

Press **ZOOM** and then press **9** to select **9:ZoomStat**

Example   The figures on the right show a table of data entered on the TI-84/TI-83, the quadratic regression equation and the graph obtained using the steps given above.

Complete Second-Order Model with Two Quantitative Independent Variables

$$E(y) = \beta_0 + \beta_1 x_1 + \beta_2 x_2 + \beta_3 x_2 x_2 + \beta_4 x_1^2 + \beta_5 x_2^2$$

Comments on the Parameters

β_0: y-intercept, the value of $E(y)$ when $x_1 = x_2 = 0$

β_1, β_2: Changing β_1 and β_2 causes the surface to shift along the x_1- and x_2-axes

β_3: Controls the rotation of the surface

β_4, β_5: Signs and values of these parameters control the type of surface and the rates of curvature.

Three types of surfaces are produced by a second-order model:* a **paraboloid** that opens upward (Figure 11.19a), a paraboloid that opens downward (Figure 11.19b), and a **saddle-shaped surface** (Figure 11.19c).

A complete second-order model is the three-dimensional equivalent of a quadratic model in a single quantitative variable. Instead of tracing parabolas, it traces paraboloids and saddle surfaces. Since only a portion of the complete surface is used to fit the data, this model provides a very large variety of gently curving surfaces that can be used to fit data. It is a good choice for a model if you expect curvature in the response surface relating $E(y)$ to x_1 and x_2.

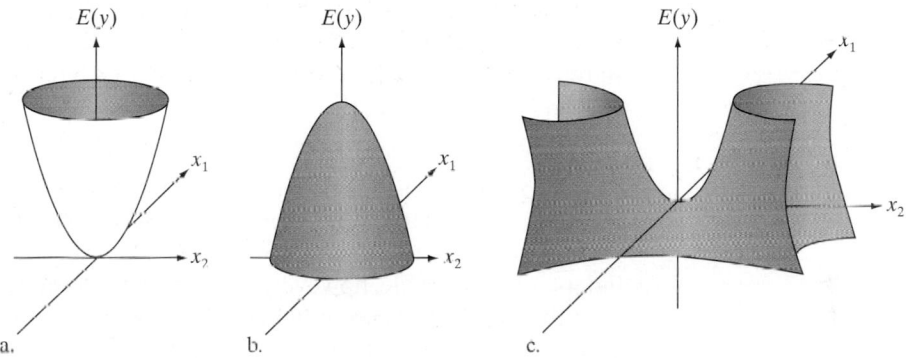

FIGURE 11.19
Graphs for three second-order surfaces

EXAMPLE 11.8

A More Complex Second-Order Model for Hours Worked per Week

Problem A social scientist would like to relate the number of hours worked per week (outside the home) by a married woman to the number of years of formal education she has completed and the number of children in her family.

a. Identify the dependent variable and the independent variables.

b. Write the first-order model for this example.

c. Modify the model in part **b** to include an interaction term.

d. Write a complete second-order model for $E(y)$.

Solution

a. The dependent variable is

$$y = \text{Number of hours worked per week by a married woman}$$

---

*The saddle-shaped surface (Figure 11.19c) is produced when $\beta_3^2 > 4\beta_4\beta_5$; the paraboloid opens upward (Figure 11.19a) when $\beta_4 + \beta_5 > 0$ and opens downward (Figure 11.19b) when $\beta_4 + \beta_5 < 0$.

The two independent variables, both quantitative in nature, are

$$x_1 = \text{Number of years of formal education completed by the woman}$$
$$x_2 = \text{Number of children in the family}$$

b. The first-order model is

$$E(y) = \beta_0 + \beta_1 x_1 + \beta_2 x_2$$

This model would probably not be appropriate in this situation because x_1 and x_2 may interact and/or curvature terms corresponding to x_1^2 and x_2^2 may be needed to obtain a good model for $E(y)$.

c. Adding the interaction term, we obtain

$$E(y) = \beta_0 + \beta_1 x_1 + \beta_2 x_2 + \beta_3 x_1 x_2$$

This model should be better than the model in part **b,** since we have now allowed for interaction between x_1 and x_2.

d. The complete second-order model is

$$E(y) = \beta_0 + \beta_1 x_1 + \beta_2 x_2 + \beta_3 x_1 x_2 + \beta_4 x_1^2 + \beta_5 x_2^2$$

Since it would not be surprising to find curvature in the response surface, the complete second-order model would be preferred to the models in parts **b** and **c.**

Look Back How can we tell whether the complete second-order model really does provide better predictions of hours worked than the models in parts **b** and **c?** The answers to these and similar questions are examined in Section 11.9.

Most relationships between $E(y)$ and two or more quantitative independent variables are second-order and require the use of either the interactive or the complete second-order model to obtain a good fit to a data set. As in the case of a single quantitative independent variable, however, the curvature in the response surface may be very slight over the range of values of the variables in the data set. When this happens, a first-order model may provide a good fit to the data.

Exercises 11.45–11.58

Learning the Mechanics

11.45 Write a second-order model relating the mean of y, $E(y)$, to
  a. one quantitative independent variable
  b. two quantitative independent variables
  c. three quantitative independent variables [*Hint:* Include all possible two-way cross-product terms and squared terms.]

11.46 Suppose you fit the second-order model

$$y = \beta_0 + \beta_1 x + \beta_2 x^2 + \epsilon$$

to $n = 25$ data points. Your estimate of β_2 is $\hat{\beta}_2 = .47$, and the estimated standard error of the estimate is .15.
  a. Test $H_0: \beta_2 = 0$ against $H_a: \beta_2 \neq 0$. Use $\alpha = .05$.
  b. Suppose you want to determine only whether the quadratic curve opens upward; that is, as x increases, the slope of the curve increases. Give the test statistic and the rejection region for the test for $\alpha = .05$. Do the data support the theory that the slope of the curve increases as x increases? Explain.

11.47 Suppose you fit the quadratic model

$$E(y) = \beta_0 + \beta_1 x + \beta_2 x^2$$

to a set of $n = 20$ data points and found $R^2 = .91$, $SS_{yy} = 29.94$, and SSE $= 2.63$.
  a. Is there sufficient evidence to indicate that the model contributes information for predicting y? Test using $\alpha = .05$.
  b. What null and alternative hypotheses would you test to determine whether upward curvature exists?
  c. What null and alternative hypotheses would you test to determine whether downward curvature exists?

11.48 Consider the following quadratic models:
  (1) $y = 1 - 2x + x^2$
  (2) $y = 1 + 2x + x^2$
  (3) $y = 1 + x^2$
  (4) $y = 1 - x^2$
  (5) $y = 1 + 3x^2$

```
The regression equation is
Y = -24.56 + 1.12 X1 + 27.99 X2 - 0.54 X1X2 - 0.004 X1SQ + 0.002 X2SQ


Predictor        Coef     SE Coef        T        P
Constant      -24.563       6.531    -3.76    0.001
X1            1.19848      0.1103    10.86    0.000
X2             27.988      79.489     0.35    0.727
X1X2          -0.5397      1.0338    -0.52    0.605
X1SQ          -0.0043      0.0004   -10.74    0.000
X2SQ           0.0020      0.0033     0.60    0.550


S = 2.762    R-Sq = 79.7%    R-Sq(adj) = 76.6%

Analysis of Variance

Source          DF        SS        MS        F        P
Regression       5    989.30    197.86    25.93    0.000
Residual Error  33    251.81      7.63
Total           38   1241.11
```

MINITAB Output for Exercise 11.49

a. Graph each of the quadratic models, side by side, on the same sheet of graph paper.
b. What effect does the first-order term ($2x$) have on the graph of the curve?
c. What effect does the second-order term (x^2) have on the graph of the curve?

11.49 MINITAB was used to fit the complete second-order model

$$E(y) = \beta_0 + \beta_1 x_1 + \beta_2 x_2 + \beta_3 x_1 x_2 + \beta_4 x_1^2 + \beta_5 x_2^2$$

to $n = 39$ data points. The printout is shown above.
a. Is there sufficient evidence to indicate that at least one of the parameters, $\beta_1, \beta_2, \beta_3, \beta_4$, and β_5 is non zero? Test using $\alpha = .05$.
b. Test $H_0: \beta_4 = 0$ against $H_a: \beta_4 \neq 0$. Use $\alpha = .01$.
c. Test $H_0: \beta_5 = 0$ against $H_a: \beta_5 \neq 0$. Use $\alpha = .01$.
d. Use graphs to explain the consequences of the tests in parts **b** and **c**.

Applying the Concepts—Basic

11.50 Catalytic convertors in cars. A quadratic model was applied to motor vehicle toxic emissions data collected between 1984 and 1999 in Mexico City (*Environmental Science & Engineering*, Sept. 1, 2000). The following equation was used to predict the percentage (y) of motor vehicles without catalytic converters in the Mexico City fleet for a given year (x):
$\hat{y} = 325{,}790 - 321.67x + .0794x^2$.
a. Explain why the value, $\hat{\beta}_0 = 325{,}790$, has no practical interpretation.
b. Explain why the value, $\hat{\beta}_1 = -321.67$ should not be interpreted as a slope.
c. Examine the value of $\hat{\beta}_2$ to determine the nature of the curvature (upward or downward) in the sample data.
d. The researchers used the model to estimate "that just after the year 2021 the fleet of cars with catalytic converters will completely disappear." Comment on the danger of using the model to predict y in the year 2021.

11.51 Testing tires for wear. Underinflated or overinflated tires can increase tire wear. A new tire was tested for wear at different pressures with the results shown in the following table.

TIRES

Pressure, x (pounds per square inch)	Mileage, y (thousands)
30	29
31	32
32	36
33	38
34	37
35	33
36	26

a. Plot the data on a scattergram.
b. If you were given only the information for $x = 30, 31, 32, 33$, what kind of model would you suggest? For $x = 33, 34, 35, 36$? For all the data?

11.52 Estimating change-point dosage. A standard method for studying toxic substances and their effects on humans is to observe the responses of rodents exposed to various doses of the substance over time. In the *Journal of Agricultural, Biological, and Environmental Statistics* (June 2005), researchers used least squares regression to estimate the *change-point* dosage—defined as the largest dose level that has no adverse effects. Data were obtained from a dose-response study of rats exposed to the toxic substance aconiazide. A sample of 50 rats was evenly divided into five dosage groups: 0, 100, 200, 500, and 750 milligrams per kilograms of body weight. The dependent variable y measured was the weight change (in grams) after a 2-week exposure. The researchers fit the quadratic model $E(y) = \beta_0 + \beta_1 x + \beta_2 x^2$, where x = dosage level, with the following results: $\hat{y} = 10.25 + .0053x - .0000266x^2$.

a. Construct a rough sketch of the least squares prediction equation. Describe the nature of the curvature in the estimated model.

b. Estimate the weight change (y) for a rat given a dosage of 500 mg/kg of aconiazide.

c. Estimate the weight change (y) for a rat given a dosage of 0 mg/kg of aconiazide. (This dosage is called the *control* dosage level.)

d. Of the five dosage groups in the study, find the largest dosage level x that yields an estimated weight change that is closest to, but below the estimated weight change for the control group. This value is the *change-point* dosage.

11.53 Oil evaporation study. The *Journal of Hazardous Materials* (July 1995) presented a literature review of models designed to predict oil spill evaporation. One model discussed in the article used boiling (x_1) and API specific gravity (x_2) to predict the molecular weight (y) of the oil that is spilled. A complete second-order model for y was proposed.

a. Write the equation of the model.

b. Identify the terms in the model that allow for curvilinear relationships.

Applying the Concepts—Intermediate

11.54 Revenues of popular movies. The *Internet Movie Database* (www.imdb.com) monitors the gross revenues for all major motion pictures. The accompanying table gives both the domestic (United States and Canada) and international gross revenues for a sample of 15 popular movies.

IMDB

Movie Title (year)	Domestic Gross ($ millions)	International Gross ($ millions)
Titanic (1997)	600.7	1,234.6
E.T. (1982)	439.9	321.8
Pirates of the Caribbean:		
Dead Man's Chest (2006)	420.3	631.0
Jurassic Park (1993)	356.8	563.0
Lion King (1994)	328.4	455.0
Harry Potter and the		
Sorcerer's Stone (2001)	317.6	651.1
Sixth Sense (1999)	293.5	368.0
Jaws (1975)	260.0	210.6
Ghost (1990)	217.6	300.0
Saving Private Ryan (1998)	216.1	263.2
Gladiator (2000)	187.7	268.6
Dances with Wolves (1990)	184.2	240.0
The Exorcist (1973)	204.6	153.0
My Big Fat Greek Wedding (2002)	241.4	115.1
Rocky IV (1985)	127.9	172.6

Source: The Internet Movie Database (www.imdb.com).

a. Write a first-order model for foreign gross revenues (y) as a function of domestic gross revenues (x).

b. Write a second-order model for international gross revenues y as a function of domestic gross revenues x.

c. Construct a scattergram for these data. Which of the models from parts **a** and **b** appears to be the better choice for explaining the variation in foreign gross revenues?

d. Fit the model of part **b** to the data and investigate its usefulness. Is there evidence of a curvilinear relationship between international and domestic gross revenues? Try using $\alpha = .05$.

e. Based on your analysis in part **d,** which of the models from parts **a** and **b** better explains the variation in international gross revenues? Compare your answer to your preliminary conclusion from part **c.**

11.55 Automobile assembly time study. Running a manufacturing operation efficiently requires knowledge of the time it takes employees to manufacture the product; otherwise the cost of making the product cannot be determined. Furthermore, management would not be able to establish an effective incentive plan for its employees because it would not know how to set work standards (Chase and Aquilano, *Production and Operations Management*, 1992). Estimates of production time are frequently obtained using time studies. The data in the table below came from a recent time study of a sample of 15 employees performing a particular task on an automobile assembly line.

ASSEMBLY

Time to Assemble, y (minutes)	Months of Experience, x
10	24
20	1
15	10
11	15
11	17
19	3
11	20
13	9
17	3
18	1
16	7
16	9
17	7
18	5
10	20

a. Fit the model $y = \beta_0 + \beta_1 x + \beta_2 x^2 + \epsilon$ and give the least squares prediction equation.

b. Plot the fitted equation on a scattergram of the data. Is there sufficient evidence to support the inclusion of the quadratic term in the model? Explain.

c. Test the null hypothesis that $\beta_2 = 0$ against the alternative that $\beta_2 \neq 0$. Use $\alpha = .01$. Does the quadratic term make an important contribution to the model?

d. Your conclusion in part **c** should have been to drop the quadratic term from the model. Do so and fit the "reduced model," $y = \beta_0 + \beta_1 x + \epsilon$, to the data.

e. Define β_1 in the context of this exercise. Find a 90% confidence interval for β_1 in the reduced model of part **d.**

11.56 Optimizing semiconductor material processing. Fluorocarbon plasmas are used in the production of semiconductor materials. In the *Journal of Applied Physics* (Dec. 1, 2000), electrical engineers at Nagoya University (Japan) studied the kinetics of fluorocarbon plasmas in order to optimize material processing. In one portion of the study, the surface production rate of fluorocarbon radicals emitted from the production process was measured at various points in time (in milliseconds) after the radio frequency power was turned off. The data are given in the next table (p. 711). Consider a model relating surface production rate (y) to time (x).

RADICALS

Rate	Time
1.00	0.1
0.80	0.3
0.40	0.5
0.20	0.7
0.05	0.9
0.00	1.1
−0.05	1.3
−0.02	1.5
0.00	1.7
−0.10	1.9
−0.15	2.1
−0.05	2.3
−0.13	2.5
−0.08	2.7
0.00	2.9

Source: Takizawa, K., et al. "Characteristics of C_3 Radicals in High-Density C_4F_8 Plasmas Studied by Laser-Induced Fluorescence Spectroscopy." *Journal of Applied Physics,* Vol. 88, No. 11, Dec. 1, 2000 (Figure 7).

a. Graph the data in a scattergram. What trend do you observe?

b. Fit a quadratic model to the data. Give the least squares prediction equation.

c. Is there sufficient evidence of upward curvature in the relationship between surface production rate and time after turnoff? Use $\alpha = .05$.

11.57 Strength of manufactured plastic. The amount of pressure used to produce a certain plastic is thought to be related to the strength of the plastic. Researchers hypothesize that, below a certain level, increases in pressure increase the strength of the plastic; at some point, however, additional increases in pressure will have a detrimental effect on its strength. Write a model in which the relationship of the plastic strength y to pressure x reflects this hypothesis. Sketch the model.

11.58 Orange juice demand study. A chilled orange juice warehousing operation in New York City was experiencing too many out-of-stock situations with its 96-ounce containers. To better understand current and future demand for this product, the company examined the last 40 days of sales, which are shown in the next table. One of the company's objectives is to model demand, y, as a function of sale day, x (where $x = 1, 2, 3, \ldots, 40$).

a. Construct a scatterplot for these data.

b. Does it appear that a second-order model might better explain the variation in demand than a first-order model? Explain.

c. Fit a first-order model to these data.

d. Fit a second-order model to these data.

e. Compare the results in parts **c** and **d** and decide which model better explains variation in demand. Justify your choice.

NYJUICE

Sale Day, x	Demand for 96 oz. Containers, y (in cases)
1	4,581
2	4,239
3	2,754
4	4,501
5	4,016
6	4,680
7	4,950
8	3,303
9	2,367
10	3,055
11	4,248
12	5,067
13	5,201
14	5,133
15	4,211
16	3,195
17	5,760
18	5,661
19	6,102
20	6,099
21	5,902
22	2,295
23	2,682
24	5,787
25	3,339
26	3,798
27	2,007
28	6,282
29	3,267
30	4,779
31	9,000
32	9,531
33	3,915
34	8,964
35	6,984
36	6,660
37	6,921
38	10,005
39	10,153
40	11,520

Source: Personal communication from Rick Campbell, Dave Metzler, and Tom Nelson, Rutgers University.

11.7 Model Building: Qualitative (Dummy) Variable Models

Multiple regression models can also be written to include **qualitative** (or **categorical**) independent variables. Qualitative variables, unlike quantitative variables, cannot be measured on a numerical scale. Therefore, we must code the values of the qualitative variable (called **levels**) as numbers before we can fit the model. These coded qualitative variables are called **dummy** (or **indicator**) **variables** since the numbers assigned to the various levels are arbitrarily selected.

To illustrate, suppose a female executive at a certain company claims that male executives earn higher salaries, on average, than female executives with the same education, experience, and responsibilities. To support her claim, she wants to model the salary y of an executive using a qualitative independent variable representing the gender of an executive (male or female).

A convenient method of coding the values of a qualitative variable at two levels involves assigning a value of 1 to one of the levels and a value of 0 to the other. For example, the dummy variable used to describe gender could be coded as follows:

$$x = \begin{cases} 1 & \text{if male} \\ 0 & \text{if female} \end{cases}$$

The choice of which level is assigned to 1 and which is assigned to 0 is arbitrary. The model then takes the following form:

$$E(y) = \beta_0 + \beta_1 x$$

The advantage of using a 0–1 coding scheme is that the β coefficients are easily interpreted. The model above allows us to compare the mean executive salary $E(y)$ for males with the corresponding mean for females.

$$\begin{aligned} \text{Males } (x = 1): \quad E(y) &= \beta_0 + \beta_1(1) = \beta_0 + \beta_1 \\ \text{Females } (x = 0): \quad E(y) &= \beta_0 + \beta_1(0) = \beta_0 \end{aligned}$$

These two means are illustrated in the bar graph in Figure 11.20.

First note that β_0 represents the mean salary for females (say, μ_F). When a 0–1 coding convention is used, β_0 will always represent the mean response associated with the level of the qualitative variable assigned the value 0 (called the **base level**). The difference between the mean salary for males and the mean salary for females, $\mu_M - \mu_F$, is represented by β_1—that is,

$$\mu_M - \mu_F = (\beta_0 + \beta_1) - (\beta_0) = \beta_1$$

This difference is shown in Figure 11.20.* With a 0–1 coding convention, β_1 will always represent the difference between the mean response for the level assigned the value 1 and the mean for the base level. Thus, for the executive salary model, we have

$$\beta_0 = \mu_F$$
$$\beta_1 = \mu_M - \mu_F$$

Now carefully examine the model with a single qualitative independent variable at two levels, because we will use exactly the same pattern for any number of levels. Moreover, the interpretation of the parameters will always be the same.

One level (say, level A) is selected as the base level. Then for the 0–1 coding† for the dummy variables,

$$\mu_A = \beta_0$$

The coding for all dummy variables is as follows: To represent the mean value of y for a particular level, let that dummy variable equal 1; otherwise, the dummy variable is set equal to 0. Using this system of coding,

$$\mu_B = \beta_0 + \beta_1$$
$$\mu_C = \beta_0 + \beta_2$$

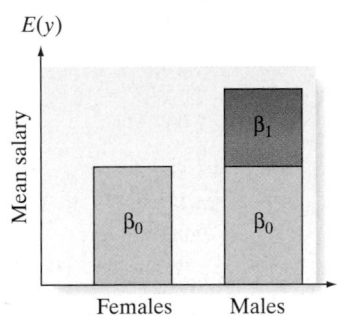

$E(y)$

Mean salary

β_1

β_0 β_0

Females   Males

FIGURE 11.20

Bar graph comparing $E(y)$ for males and females

---

*Note that β_1 could be negative. If β_1 were negative, the height of the bar corresponding to males would be *reduced* (rather than increased) from the height of the bar for females by the amount β_1. Figure 11.20 is constructed assuming that β_1 is a positive quantity.

†You do not have to use a 0–1 system of coding for the dummy variables. Any two-value system will work, but the interpretation given to the model parameters will depend on the code. Using the 0–1 system makes the model parameters easy to interpret.

and so on. Because $\mu_A = \beta_0$, any other model parameter will represent the difference between means for that level and the base level:

$$\beta_1 = \mu_B - \mu_A$$
$$\beta_2 = \mu_C - \mu_A$$

and so on. Consequently, each β multiplied by a dummy variable represents the difference between $E(y)$ at one level of the qualitative variable and $E(y)$ at the base level.

Procedure for Writing a Model with One Qualitative Independent Variable with k Levels

Always use a number of dummy variables that is one less than the number of levels of the qualitative variable. Thus, for a qualitative variable with k levels, use $k - 1$ dummy variables:

$$y = \beta_0 + \beta_1 x_1 + \beta_2 x_2 + \cdots + \beta_{k-1} x_{k-1} + \varepsilon$$

where x_i is the dummy variable for level $i + 1$ and

$$x_i = \begin{cases} 1 & \text{if } y \text{ is observed at level } i + 1 \\ 0 & \text{otherwise} \end{cases}$$

Then, for this system of coding

$$\mu_A = \beta_0 \qquad \text{and} \qquad \beta_1 = \mu_B - \mu_A$$
$$\mu_B = \beta_0 + \beta_1 \qquad\qquad \beta_2 = \mu_C - \mu_A$$
$$\mu_C = \beta_0 + \beta_2 \qquad\qquad \beta_3 = \mu_D - \mu_A$$
$$\mu_D = \beta_0 + \beta_3 \qquad\qquad \vdots$$

EXAMPLE 11.9

A Model with One Qualitative Independent Variable

Problem   Suppose an economist wants to compare the mean dollar amounts owed by delinquent credit card customers in three different socioeconomic classes: (1) lower class, (2) middle class, and (3) upper class. A sample of 10 customers with delinquent accounts is selected from each group, and the amount owed by each is recorded, as shown in Table 11.4.

 DELINQUENT

TABLE 11.4 Dollars Owed, Example 11.9

Group 1 (lower class)	Group 2 (middle class)	Group 3 (upper class)
$148	$513	$335
76	264	643
393	433	216
520	94	536
236	535	128
134	327	723
55	214	258
166	135	380
415	280	594
153	304	465

a. Hypothesize a regression model for amount owed (y) using socioeconomic class as an independent variable.

b. Interpret the β's in the model.

c. Use the model to determine if the mean dollar amounts owed by customers differ significantly for the three socioeconomic groups at $\alpha = .05$.

Solution

a. Note that socioeconomic status (low, middle, upper class) is a qualitative variable (measured on an ordinal scale). For a 3-level qualitative variable, we need two dummy variables in the regression model. The model relating $E(y)$ to this single qualitative variable, socioeconomic group, is

$$E(y) = \beta_0 + \beta_1 x_1 + \beta_2 x_2$$

where (arbitrarily)

$$x_1 = \begin{cases} 1 & \text{if Group 2} \\ 0 & \text{if not} \end{cases} \qquad x_2 = \begin{cases} 1 & \text{if Group 3} \\ 0 & \text{if not} \end{cases}$$

b. For this model

$$\beta_0 = \mu_1$$
$$\beta_1 = \mu_2 - \mu_1$$
$$\beta_2 = \mu_3 - \mu_1$$

where $\mu_1, \mu_2,$ and μ_3 are the mean responses for socioeconomic groups 1, 2, and 3, respectively—that is, β_0 represents the mean amount owed for group 1 (lower class), β_1 represents the mean difference in amounts owed for group 2 (middle) and group 1 (lower), and β_2 represents the mean difference in amounts owed for group 3 (upper) and group 1 (lower).

c. Testing the null hypothesis that the means for the three groups are equal—that is, $\mu_1 = \mu_2 = \mu_3$—is equivalent to testing

$$H_0: \beta_1 = \beta_2 = 0$$

You can see this by observing that if $\beta_1 = \mu_2 - \mu_1 = 0$, then $\mu_1 = \mu_2$. Similarly, if $\beta_2 = \mu_3 - \mu_1 = 0$, then $\mu_3 = \mu_1$. Thus, if H_0 is true, then $\mu_1, \mu_2,$ and μ_3 must be equal. The alternative hypothesis is

H_a: At least one of the parameters, β_1 and β_2, differs from 0 which implies that at least two of the three means ($\mu_1, \mu_2,$ and μ_3) differ.

To test this hypothesis, we conduct the global F-test for the model. The MINITAB printout for fitting the model,

$$E(y) = \beta_0 + \beta_1 x_1 + \beta_2 x_2$$

is shown in Figure 11.21. The value of the F-statistic for testing the adequacy of the model, $F = 3.48$, and the observed significance level of the test, p-value $= .045$, are both highlighted. Since $\alpha = .05$ exceeds the p-value, we reject H_0 and conclude that at least one of the parameters, β_1 and β_2, differs from 0. Or, equivalently, we conclude that the data provide sufficient evidence to indicate that the mean indebtedness does vary from one socioeconomic group to another.

Look Back This global F-test is equivalent to the analysis of variance F-test for a completely randomized design of Chapter 8.

Regression Analysis: AMOUNT versus X1, X2

```
The regression equation is
AMOUNT = 230 + 80.3 X1 + 198 X2


Predictor      Coef    SE Coef      T       P
Constant     229.60      53.43    4.30   0.000
X1            80.30      75.56    1.06   0.297
X2           198.20      75.56    2.62   0.014


S = 168.948    R-Sq = 20.5%    R-Sq(adj) = 14.6%


Analysis of Variance

Source            DF      SS       MS      F       P
Regression         2   198772    99386   3.48   0.045
Residual Error    27   770671    28543
Total             29   969443
```

FIGURE 11.21
MINITAB regression printout
for dummy variable model

Now Work Exercise 11.67

Caution

A common mistake by regression analysts is to use a single dummy variable x for a qualitative variable at k levels, where $x = 1, 2, 3, \ldots, k$. Such a regression model will have unestimable β's and β's that are difficult to interpret. Remember, when modeling $E(y)$ with a single qualitative independent variable, the number of 0–1 dummy variables to include in the model will always be one less than the number of levels of the qualitative variable.

Exercises 11.59–11.71

Learning the Mechanics

11.59 Write a regression model relating the mean value of y to a qualitative independent variable that can assume two levels. Interpret all the terms in the model.

11.60 Write a regression model relating $E(y)$ to a qualitative independent variable that can assume three levels. Interpret all the terms in the model.

11.61 The following model was used to relate $E(y)$ to a single qualitative variable with four levels:

$$E(y) = \beta_0 + \beta_1 x_1 + \beta_2 x_2 + \beta_3 x_3$$

where

$$x_1 = \begin{cases} 1 \text{ if level 2} \\ 0 \text{ if not} \end{cases}$$

$$x_2 = \begin{cases} 1 \text{ if level 3} \\ 0 \text{ if not} \end{cases}$$

$$x_3 = \begin{cases} 1 \text{ if level 4} \\ 0 \text{ if not} \end{cases}$$

This model was fit to $n = 30$ data points and the following result was obtained:

$$\hat{y} = 10.2 - 4x_1 + 12x_2 + 2x_3$$

a. Use the least squares prediction equation to find the estimate of $E(y)$ for each level of the qualitative independent variable.

b. Specify the null and alternative hypotheses you would use to test whether $E(y)$ is the same for all four levels of the independent variable.

11.62 MINITAB (see printout on p. 716) was used to fit the following model to $n = 15$ data points:

$$y = \beta_0 + \beta_1 x_1 + \beta_2 x_2 + \epsilon$$

where

$$x_1 = \begin{cases} 1 \text{ if level 2} \\ 0 \text{ if not} \end{cases}$$

$$x_2 = \begin{cases} 1 \text{ if level 3} \\ 0 \text{ if not} \end{cases}$$

a. Report the least squares prediction equation.
b. Interpret the values of β_1 and β_2.
c. Interpret the following hypotheses in terms of $\mu_1, \mu_2,$ and μ_3:

$H_0: \beta_1 = \beta_2 = 0$
$H_a:$ At least one of the parameters β_1 and β_2 differs from 0

d. Conduct the hypothesis test of part **c**.

```
The regression equation is
Y = 80.0 + 16.8 X1 + 40.4 X2


Predictor      Coef    SE Coef      T       P
Constant     80.000      4.082   19.60   0.000
X1           16.800      5.774    2.91   0.013
X2           40.400      5.774    7.00   0.000


S = 9.129      R-Sq = 80.5%   R-Sq(adj) = 77.2%

Analysis of Variance

Source           DF       SS       MS       F       P
Regression        2   4118.9   2059.5   24.72   0.000
Residual Error   12   1000.0     83.3
Total            14   5118.9
```

MINITAB Output for
Exercise 11.62

Applying the Concepts—Basic

11.63 Accuracy of software effort estimates. Periodically, software engineers must provide estimates of their effort in developing new software. In the *Journal of Empirical Software Engineering* (Vol. 9, 2004), multiple regression was used to predict the accuracy of these effort estimates. The dependent variable, defined as the relative error in estimating effort,

$$y = (\text{Actual effort} - \text{Estimated effort})/(\text{Actual effort})$$

was determined for each in a sample of $n = 49$ software development tasks. Several qualitative independent variables were evaluated as potential predictors of relative error. Some of these variables are described in the table.

Estimator role (Developer or Project leader)
Task complexity (Low, Medium, or High)
Contract type (Fixed price or Hourly rate)
Customer priority (Time-of-delivery, Cost, or Quality)

---

a. Write a model for $E(y)$ as a function of estimator role. Interpret the β's.
b. Write a model for $E(y)$ as a function of task complexity. Interpret the β's.
c. Write a model for $E(y)$ as a function of contract type. Interpret the β's.
d. Write a model for $E(y)$ as a function of customer priority. Interpret the β's.

11.64 Comparing private and public college tuition. According to the *Chronicle of Higher Education Almanac,* 4-year private colleges charge, on average, five times as much for tuition and fees than 4-year public colleges. In order to estimate the true difference in the mean amounts charged for the 2006–2007 academic year, random samples of 40 private colleges and 40 public colleges were contacted and questioned about their tuition structures.
a. Which of the procedures described in Chapter 7 could be used to estimate the difference in mean charges between private and public colleges?
b. Propose a regression model involving the qualitative independent variable Type of college that could be used to investigate the difference between the means. Be sure to specify the coding scheme for the dummy variable in the model.

c. Explain how the regression model you developed in part **b** could be used to estimate the difference between the population means.

11.65 Improving SAT scores. Refer to the *Chance* (Winter 2001) study of students who paid a private tutor (or coach) to help them improve their Standardized Admission Test (SAT) scores, Exercise 2.84 (p. 86). Multiple regression was used to estimate the effect of coaching on SAT–Mathematics scores. Data on 3,492 students (573 of whom were coached) were used to fit the model, $E(y) = \beta_0 + \beta_1 x_1 + \beta_2 x_2$, where $y = $ SAT–Math score, $x_1 = $ score on PSAT, and $x_2 = \{1$ if student was coached, 0 if not$\}$.
a. The fitted model had an adjusted R^2 value of .76. Interpret this result.
b. The estimate of β_2 in the model was 19, with a standard error of 3. Use this information to form a 95% confidence interval for β_2. Interpret the interval.
c. Based on the interval, part **b**, what can you say about the effect of coaching on SAT–Math scores?

11.66 Study of entry-level job preferences. *Benefits Quarterly* (First Quarter, 1995) published a study of entry-level job preferences. Several independent variables were used to model the job preferences (measured on a 10-point scale) of 164 business school graduates, including the following qualitative variables:
a. Flextime of the position applied for (yes/no)
b. Level of day care support required (none, referral, or on-premise)
c. Spousal transfer support required (none, counseling, or active search)
d. Marital status of applicant (married/not)
e. Gender of applicant (male/female)
For each of the above qualitative variables, hypothesize a model for job preference (y) as a function of that variable. Interpret the β's in each model.

Applying the Concepts—Intermediate

⊙ TVADRECALL

11.67 Study of recall of TV commercials. Refer to the *Journal of Applied Psychology* (June 2002) study of recall of television commercials, Exercise 8.23 (p. 497). Participants were assigned to watch one of three types of TV programs, with nine commercials embedded in each show. Group V watched a TV program (e.g., *Tour of Duty*) with a violent content code rating; group S viewed a show (e.g., *Strip Mall*) with a sex content code rating; and group N watched a neutral TV program (e.g., *Candid Camera*) with neither a V nor an S rating. The dependent variable measured for each participant was a score (y) on their recall of the brand names in the commercial messages, with scores ranging from 0 (no brands recalled) to 9 (all brands recalled). The data are saved in the **TVADRECALL** file.

a. Write a model for $E(y)$ as a function of viewer group.
b. Fit the model, part **a**, to the data saved in the **TVADRECALL** file. Give the least squares prediction equation.
c. Conduct a test of overall model utility at $\alpha = .01$. Interpret the results. Show that the results agree with the analysis conducted in Exercise 8.23.
d. The sample mean recall scores for the three groups were $\bar{y}_V = 2.08, \bar{y}_S = 1.71$, and $\bar{y}_N = 3.17$. Show how to find these sample means using only the β- estimates obtained in part **b**.

11.68 Deferred tax allowance study. A study was conducted to identify accounting choice variables that influence a manager's decision to change the level of the deferred tax asset allowance at the firm (*The Engineering Economist*, Jan./Feb., 2004). Data were collected for a sample of 329 firms that reported deferred tax assets in 2000. The dependent variable of interest (DTVA) is measured as the change in the deferred tax asset valuation allowance divided by the deferred tax asset. The independent variables used as predictors of DTVA are listed as follows:

LEVERAGE: x_1 = ratio of debt book value to shareholder's equity
BONUS: x_2 = 1 if firm maintains a management bonus plan, 0 if not
MVALUE: x_3 = market value of common stock
BBATH: x_4 = 1 if operating earnings negative and lower than last year, 0 if not
EARN: x_5 = change in operating earnings divided by total assets

A first-order model was fit to the data with the following results (p-values in parentheses):

$$R_a^2 = .280$$

$$\hat{y} = .044 + .006x_1 - .035x_2 - .001x_3 + .296x_4 + .010x_5,$$
$$\quad (.070) \quad (.228) \quad (.157) \quad (.678) \quad (.001) \quad (.869)$$

a. Interpret the estimate of the β-coefficient for x_4.
b. The "Big Bath" theory proposed by the researchers states that the mean DTVA for firms with negative earnings and earnings lower than last year will exceed the mean DTVA of other firms. Is there evidence to support this theory? Test using $\alpha = .05$.
c. Interpret the value of R_a^2.

11.69 Comparing mosquito repellents. Which insect repellents protect best against mosquitoes? *Consumer Reports* (June 2000) tested 14 products that all claim to be an effective mosquito repellent. Each product was classified as either lotion/cream or aerosol/spray. The cost of the product (in dollars) was divided by the amount of the repellent needed to cover exposed areas of the skin (about 1/3 ounce) to

obtain a cost-per-use value. Effectiveness was measured as the maximum number of hours of protection (in half-hour increments) provided when human testers exposed their arms to 200 mosquitoes. The data from the report are listed in the table.

REPELLENT

Insect Repellent	Type	Cost/ Use	Maximum Protection
Amway Hour Guard 12	Lotion/Cream	$2.08	13.5 hours
Avon Skin-So-Soft	Aerosol/Spray	0.67	0.5
Avon BugGuard Plus	Lotion/Cream	1.00	2.0
Ben's Backyard Formula	Lotion/Cream	0.75	7.0
Bite Blocker	Lotion/Cream	0.46	3.0
BugOut	Aerosol/Spray	0.11	6.0
Cutter Skinsations	Aerosol/Spray	0.22	3.0
Cutter Unscented	Aerosol/Spray	0.19	5.5
Muskoll Ultra6Hours	Aerosol/Spray	0.24	6.5
Natrapel	Aerosol/Spray	0.27	1.0
Off! Deep Woods	Aerosol/Spray	1.77	14.0
Off! Skintastic	Lotion/Cream	0.67	3.0
Sawyer Deet Formula	Lotion/Cream	0.36	7.0
Repel Permanone	Aerosol/Spray	2.75	24.0

Source: "Buzz Off." *Consumer Reports,* June 2000.

a. Suppose you want to use repellent type to model the cost-per-use (y). Create the appropriate number of dummy variables for repellent type and write the model.
b. Fit the model, part **a**, to the data.
c. Give the null hypothesis for testing whether repellent type is a useful predictor of cost-per-use (y).
d. Conduct the test, part **c**, and give the appropriate conclusion. Use $\alpha = .10$.
e. Repeat parts **a–d** if the dependent variable is maximum number of hours of protection (y).

11.70 REIT equity study. Robert Johnson (Association for Investment Management and Research) and Gerald Jensen (Northern Illinois University) examined effects of the Federal Reserve's monetary policies on the rates of returns to different types of real estate assets (*Real Estate Finance*, Spring 1999). They employed the following model for the monthly rate of return (y) for the asset:

$$E(y) = \beta_0 + \beta_1 x$$

where $x = \begin{cases} 1 \text{ if the Fed's monetary policy is restrictive} \\ 0 \text{ if the Fed's monetary policy is expansive} \end{cases}$

In one part of the study, they fit this model using monthly rate of return data from 1972–1997 for an equity REIT (real estate investment trust) index and, for comparison purposes, to a Treasury Bill (T-Bill) index. They obtained the results (t statistics shown in parentheses) shown in the accompanying table.

Index	Estimate of β_0	Estimate of β_1	F-Value	R^2
T-Bills	0.04742 (30.94)	0.001948 (8.14)	66.24	0.1819
Equity REIT	0.01863 (6.19)	−0.01582 (−3.46)	11.98	0.0387

Source: Johnson, Robert R., and Jensen, Gerald R. "Federal Reserve Monetary Policy and Real Estate Investment Trust Returns." *Real Estate Finance*, Vol. 16, No. 1, Spring 1999, pp. 52–59.

a. Evaluate the usefulness of each fitted model. Draw conclusions in the context of the problem.

b. Interpret the estimated value of β_1 in each model.

c. Predict the mean monthly rate of return for the equity REIT index when the Federal Reserve's monetary policy is restrictive. Repeat for an expansive policy.

Applying the Concepts—Advanced

11.71 As large U.S. companies flattened their management hierarchies during the 1990s, many of the middle managers who were laid off gave up on "corporate life" and started their own companies or bought franchise operations. This talent migration, along with the fact that most new jobs in the United States were being created by small businesses, cast entrepreneurism into the national spotlight. The businesses listed in the table were among the fastest growing in the franchise industry.

a. Propose a regression model that will enable you to compare the mean number of new franchises for the four types of franchises (food, cleaning, accounting/consulting, hospitality).

b. Without the aid of a computer, find estimates of the β's in the model.

c. Use a statistical software package to fit the model, part **a,** to the data. Interpret the regression results. Specifically, are there differences in the mean number of franchises for the four franchise types?

⊘ FRANCHISE

Franchise	Type	Number of New Franchises
Blimpie	Food	330
Tower Cleaning	Cleaning	55
CleanNet USA	Cleaning	430
KFC	Food	169
Comprehensive Business Services	Accounting/Consulting	58
Jani-King	Cleaning	451
Coverall Cleaning Concepts	Cleaning	435
McDonald's	Food	744
Applebee's	Food	124
Padgett Business Services	Accounting/Consulting	47
Super 8 Motels	Hospitality	181
General Business Services	Accounting/Consulting	44
LedgerPlus	Accounting/Consulting	79
Sonic Drive In	Food	73
Pizza Inn	Food	39
Holiday Inn Worldwide	Hospitality	150
Choice Hotels Int'l	Hospitality	93
Merry Maids	Cleaning	102
Checkers Drive-In	Food	45

Source: Entrepreneur, Apr. 1996, p. 150.

11.8 Model Building: Models with Both Quantitative and Qualitative Variables (Optional)

Suppose you want to relate the mean monthly sales $E(y)$ of a company to monthly advertising expenditure x for three different advertising media (say newspaper, radio, and television) and you wish to use first-order (straight-line) models to model the responses for all three media. Graphs of these three relationships might appear as shown in Figure 11.22.

Since the lines in Figure 11.22 are hypothetical, a number of practical questions arise. Is one advertising medium as effective as any other? That is, do the three mean sales lines differ for the three advertising media? Do the increases in mean sales per dollar input in advertising differ for the three advertising media? That is, do the slopes of the three lines differ? Note that the two practical questions have been rephrased into questions about the parameters that define the three lines of Figure 11.22. To answer them, we must write a single regression model that will characterize the three lines of Figure 11.22 and that, by testing hypotheses about the lines, will answer the questions.

The response described previously, monthly sales, is a function of *two* independent variables, one quantitative (advertising expenditure x_1) and one qualita-

$E(y)$

Television
Newspaper
Radio

Mean monthly sales

0   5   10 15 20 25 30 35 40 x
Monthly advertising expenditure
(thousands of dollars)

FIGURE 11.22

Graphs of the relationship between mean sales $E(y)$ and advertising expenditure x

tive (type of medium). We will proceed, in stages, to build a model relating $E(y)$ to these variables and will show graphically the interpretation we would give to the model at each stage. This will help you to see the contributions of the various terms in the model.

1. The straight-line relationship between mean sales $E(y)$ and advertising expenditure is the same for all three media—that is, a single line will describe the relationship between $E(y)$ and advertising expenditure x_1 for all the media (see Figure 11.23).

$$E(y) = \beta_0 + \beta_1 x \qquad \text{where } x_1 = \text{Advertising expenditure}$$

2. The straight lines relating mean sales $E(y)$ to advertising expenditure x_1 differ from one medium to another, but the rate of increase in mean sales per increase in dollar advertising expenditure x_1 is the same for all media—that is, the lines are parallel but possess different y-intercepts (see Figure 11.24).

$$E(y) = \beta_0 + \beta_1 x_1 + \beta_2 x_2 + \beta_3 x_3$$

where

$$x_1 = \text{Advertising expenditure}$$

$$x_2 = \begin{cases} 1 & \text{if radio medium} \\ 0 & \text{if not} \end{cases}$$

$$x_3 = \begin{cases} 1 & \text{if television medium} \\ 0 & \text{if not} \end{cases}$$

Notice that this model is essentially a combination of a first-order model with a single quantitative variable and the model with a single qualitative variable:

First-order model with a single
quantitative variable: $E(y) = \beta_0 + \beta_1 x_1$

Model with single qualitative
variable at three levels: $E(y) = \beta_0 + \beta_2 x_2 + \beta_3 x_3$

where x_1, x_2, and x_3 are as just defined. The model described here implies no interaction between the two independent variables, which are advertising expenditure x_1 and the qualitative variable (type of advertising medium). The change in $E(y)$ for a 1-unit increase in x_1 is identical (the slopes of the lines are equal) for all three advertising media. The terms corresponding to each of the independent variables are called **main effect terms** because they imply no interaction.

3. The straight lines relating mean sales $E(y)$ to advertising expenditure x_1 differ for the three advertising media—that is, both the line intercepts and the slopes differ (see Figure 11.25).

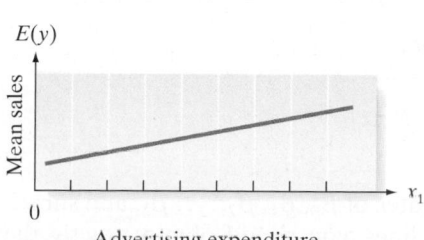

FIGURE 11.23

The relationship between $E(y)$ and x_1 is the same for all media

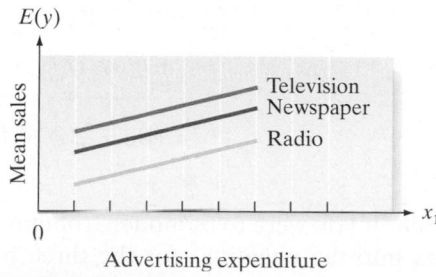

FIGURE 11.24

Parallel response lines for the three media

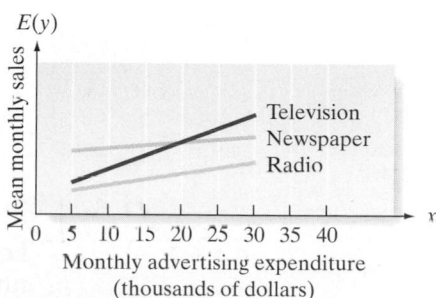

FIGURE 11.25

Different response lines for the three media

As you will see, this interaction model is obtained by adding terms involving the cross-product terms, one each from each of the two independent variables:

$$E(y) = \overbrace{\beta_0 + \beta_1 x_1}^{\substack{\text{Main effect,} \\ \text{advertising} \\ \text{expenditure}}} + \overbrace{\beta_2 x_2 + \beta_3 x_3}^{\substack{\text{Main effect,} \\ \text{type of} \\ \text{medium}}} + \overbrace{\beta_4 x_1 x_2 + \beta_5 x_1 x_3}^{\text{Interaction}}$$

Note that each of the preceding models is obtained by adding terms to model 1, the single first-order model used to model the responses for all three media. Model 2 is obtained by adding the main effect terms for type of medium, the qualitative variable. Model 3 is obtained by adding the interaction terms to model 2.

EXAMPLE 11.10

Interpreting the β's in a Model with Mixed Independent Variables

Problem   Substitute the appropriate values of the dummy variables in model 3 (above) to obtain the equations of the three response lines in Figure 11.25.

Solution   The complete model that characterizes the three lines in Figure 11.25 is

$$E(y) = \beta_0 + \beta_1 x_1 + \beta_2 x_2 + \beta_3 x_3 + \beta_4 x_1 x_2 + \beta_5 x_1 x_3$$

where

$$x_1 = \text{Advertising expenditure}$$

$$x_2 = \begin{cases} 1 & \text{if radio medium} \\ 0 & \text{if not} \end{cases}$$

$$x_3 = \begin{cases} 1 & \text{if television medium} \\ 0 & \text{if not} \end{cases}$$

Examining the coding, you can see that $x_2 = x_3 = 0$ when the advertising medium is newspaper. Substituting these values into the expression for $E(y)$, we obtain the newspaper medium line:

$$E(y) = \beta_0 + \beta_1 x_1 + \beta_2(0) + \beta_3(0) + \beta_4 x_1(0) + \beta_5 x_1(0) = \beta_0 + \beta_1 x_1$$

Similarly, we substitute the appropriate values of x_2 and x_3 into the expression for $E(y)$ to obtain the radio medium line ($x_2 = 1, x_3 = 0$):

$$E(y) = \beta_0 + \beta_1 x_1 + \beta_2(1) + \beta_3(0) + \beta_4 x_1(1) + \beta_5 x_1(0)$$

$$= \underbrace{(\beta_0 + \beta_2)}_{\text{y-intercept}} + \underbrace{(\beta_1 + \beta_4)}_{\text{Slope}} x_1$$

and the television medium line: ($x_2 = 0, x_3 = 1$):

$$E(y) = \beta_0 + \beta_1 x_1 + \beta_2(0) + \beta_3(1) + \beta_4 x_1(0) + \beta_5 x_1(1)$$

$$= \underbrace{(\beta_0 + \beta_3)}_{\text{y-intercept}} + \underbrace{(\beta_1 + \beta_5)}_{\text{Slope}} x_1$$

Look Back   If you were to fit model 3, obtain estimates of $\beta_0, \beta_1, \beta_2, \ldots, \beta_5$, and substitute them into the equations for the three media lines, you would obtain exactly the same prediction equations as you would obtain if you were to fit three separate straight lines, one to each of the three sets of media data. You may ask why we would not fit the three lines separately. Why bother fitting a model that combines all three lines (model 3) into the same equation? The answer is that you need to use this procedure if you wish to use statistical tests to compare the three media lines. We need to be able to express a practical question about the lines in terms of a hypothesis that a set of parameters in the model equals 0. (We demonstrate this procedure in the next section.) You could not do this if you were to perform three separate regression analyses and fit a line to each set of media data.

Now Work Exercise 11.72

EXAMPLE 11.11

Testing for Two Different Slopes for Productivity

Problem An industrial psychologist conducted an experiment to investigate the relationship between worker productivity and a measure of salary incentive for two manufacturing plants; one plant had union representation, and the other plant had nonunion representation. The productivity y per worker was measured by recording the number of machined castings that a worker could produce in a 4-week period of 40 hours per week. The incentive was the amount x_1 of bonus (in cents per casting) paid for all castings produced in excess of 1,000 per worker for the 4-week period. Nine workers were selected from each plant, and three from each group of nine were assigned to receive a 20¢ bonus per casting, three a 30¢ bonus, and three a 40¢ bonus. The productivity data for the 18 workers, three for each plant type and incentive combination, are shown in Table 11.5.

 CASTING

TABLE 11.5 Productivity Data for Example 11.11

Type of Plant	INCENTIVE		
	20¢/casting	30¢/casting	40¢/casting
Union	1,435 1,512 1,491	1,583 1,529 1,610	1,601 1,574 1,636
Nonunion	1,575 1,512 1,488	1,635 1,589 1,661	1,645 1,616 1,689

a. Write a model for mean productivity, $E(y)$, assuming that the relationship between $E(y)$ and incentive, x_1, is first-order.

b. Fit the model and graph the prediction equations for the union and nonunion plants.

c. Do the data provide sufficient evidence to indicate that the rate of increase of worker productivity is different for union and nonunion plants? Test at $\alpha = .10$.

Solution

a. If we assume that a first-order model* is adequate to detect a change in mean productivity as a function of incentive x_1, then the model that produces two straight lines, one for each plant, is

$$E(y) = \beta_0 + \beta_1 x_1 + \beta_2 x_2 + \beta_3 x_1 x_2$$

where

$$x_1 = \text{Incentive} \qquad x_2 = \begin{cases} 1 & \text{if nonunion plant} \\ 0 & \text{if union plant} \end{cases}$$

---

*Although the model contains a term involving $x_1 x_2$, it is first order (graphs as a straight line) in the quantitative variable x_1. The variable x_2 is a dummy variable that introduces or deletes terms in the model. The order of a model is determined only by the quantitative variables that appear in the model.

Model Summary

Model	R	R Square	Adjusted R Square	Std. Error of the Estimate
1	.843[a]	.711	.649	40.839

a. Predictors: (Constant), INC_PDUM, INCENTIV, PDUMMY

ANOVA[b]

Model		Sum of Squares	df	Mean Square	F	Sig.
1	Regression	57332.39	3	19110.796	11.459	.000[a]
	Residual	23349.22	14	1667.802		
	Total	80681.61	17			

a. Predictors: (Constant), INC_PDUM, INCENTIV, PDUMMY

b. Dependent Variable: CASTINGS

Coefficients[a]

Model		Unstandardized Coefficients		Standardized Coefficients	t	Sig.
		B	Std. Error	Beta		
1	(Constant)	1365.833	51.836		26.349	.000
	INCENTIV	6.217	1.667	.758	3.729	.002
	PDUMMY	47.778	73.308	.357	.652	.525
	INC_PDUM	.033	2.358	.008	.014	.989

a. Dependent Variable: CASTINGS

FIGURE 11.26
SPSS printout of the complete model for the casting data

b. The SPSS printout for the regression analysis is shown in Figure 11.26. Reading the parameter estimates highlighted at the bottom of the printout, you can see that

$$\hat{y} = 1{,}365.833 + 6.217x_1 + 47.778x_2 + .033x_1x_2$$

The prediction equation for the union plant can be obtained (see the coding) by substituting $x_2 = 0$ into the general prediction equation. Then

$$\hat{y} = \hat{\beta}_0 + \hat{\beta}_1x_1 + \hat{\beta}_2(0) + \hat{\beta}_3x_1(0) = \hat{\beta}_0 + \hat{\beta}_1x_1$$
$$= 1{,}365.833 + 6.217x_1$$

Similarly, the prediction equation for the nonunion plant can be obtained by substituting $x_2 = 1$ into the general prediction equation. Then

$$\hat{y} = \hat{\beta}_0 + \hat{\beta}_1x_1 + \hat{\beta}_2x_2 + \hat{\beta}_3x_1x_2$$
$$= \hat{\beta}_0 + \hat{\beta}_1x_1 + \hat{\beta}_2(1) + \hat{\beta}_3x_1(1)$$

$$= \underbrace{(\beta_0 + \beta_2)}_{y\text{-intercept}} + \underbrace{(\beta_1 + \beta_3)}_{Slope}x_1$$

$$= (1{,}365.833 + 47.778) + (6.217 + .033)x_1$$
$$= 1{,}413.611 + 6.250x_1$$

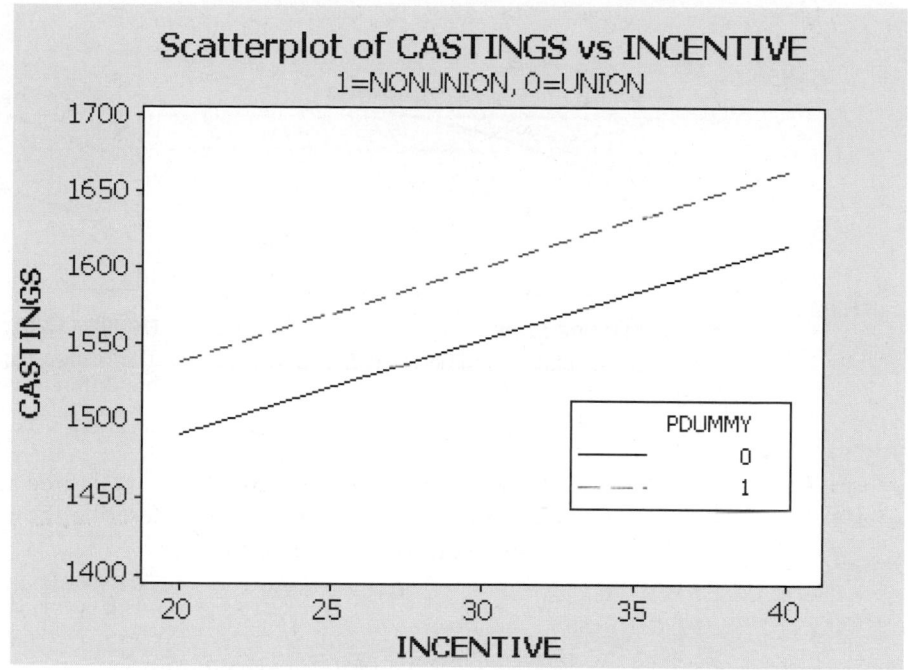

FIGURE 11.27

MINITAB plot of prediction equations for the two productivity lines

A MINITAB graph of these prediction equations is shown in Figure 11.27. Note that the slopes of the two lines are nearly identical (6.217 for union and 6.250 for nonunion).

c. If the rate of increase of productivity with incentive (i.e., the slope) for nonunion plants is different than the corresponding slope for union plants, then the interaction β (i.e., β_3) will differ from 0. Consequently, we want to test

$$H_0: \beta_3 = 0$$
$$H_a: \beta_3 \neq 0$$

This test is conducted using the t-test of Section 11.3. From the SPSS printout, the test statistic and corresponding p-value are

$$t = .014 \qquad p = .989$$

Since $\alpha = .10$ is less than the p-value, we fail to reject H_0. There is insufficient evidence to conclude that the union and nonunion shapes differ. Thus, the test supports our observation of two nearly identical slopes in part **b.**

Look Back Since interaction is not significant, we will drop the $x_1 x_2$ term from the model and use the simpler model, $E(y) = \beta_0 + \beta_1 x_1 + \beta_2 x_2$, to predict productivity.

Now Work Exercise 11.79

Models with both quantitative and qualitative x's may also include higher-order (e.g., second-order) terms. In the problem of relating mean monthly sales $E(y)$ of a company to monthly advertising expenditure x_1 and Type of Medium, suppose we think that the relationship between $E(y)$ and x_1 is curvilinear. We will construct the model, stage by stage, to enable you to compare the procedure with the stage-by-stage construction of the first-order model in the beginning of this section. The graphical interpretations will help you understand the contributions of the model terms.

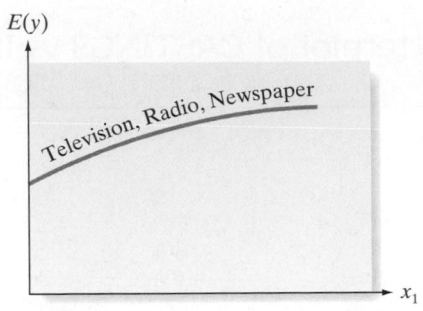

FIGURE 11.28
The relationship between $E(y)$ and x_1 is the same for all media

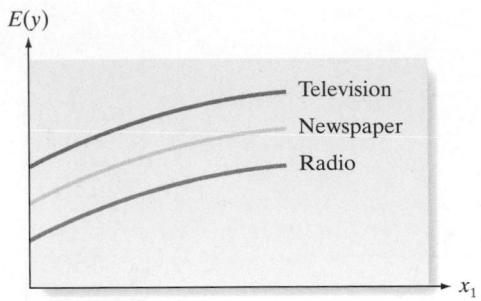

FIGURE 11.29
The response curves have the same shapes but different y-intercepts

1. The mean sales curves are identical for all three advertising media—that is, a single second-order curve will suffice to describe the relationship between $E(y)$ and x_1 for all the media (see Figure 11.28):

$$E(y) = \beta_0 + \beta_1 x_1 + \beta_2 x_1^2$$

where $x_1 = $ Advertising expenditure

2. The response curves possess the same shapes but different y-intercepts (see Figure 11.29):

$$E(y) = \beta_0 + \beta_1 x_1 + \beta_2 x_1^2 + \beta_3 x_2 + \beta_4 x_3$$

where

$$x_1 = \text{Advertising expenditure}$$

$$x_2 = \begin{cases} 1 & \text{if radio medium} \\ 0 & \text{if not} \end{cases}$$

$$x_3 = \begin{cases} 1 & \text{if television medium} \\ 0 & \text{if not} \end{cases}$$

3. The response curves for the three advertising media are different (i.e., Advertising expenditure and Type of medium interact), as shown in Figure 11.30:

$$E(y) = \beta_0 + \beta_1 x_1 + \beta_2 x_1^2 + \beta_3 x_2 + \beta_4 x_3 + \beta_5 x_1 x_2 + \beta_6 x_1 x_3 + \beta_7 x_1^2 x_2 + \beta_8 x_1^2 x_3$$

Now that you know how to write a model with two independent variables—one qualitative and one quantitative—we ask, Why do it? Why not write a separate second-order model for each type of medium where $E(y)$ is a function of only advertising expenditure? As stated earlier, one reason we wrote the single model representing all three response curves is so that we can test to determine whether the curves are different. We illustrate this procedure in Section 11.9. A second reason for writing a single model is that we obtain a pooled estimate of σ^2, the variance of the random error component ϵ. If

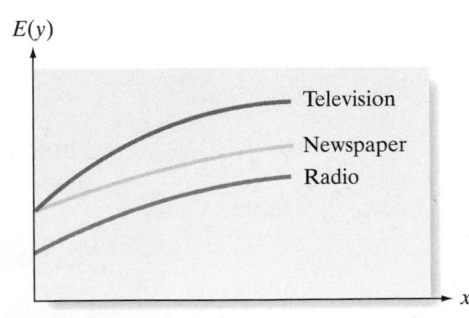

FIGURE 11.30
The response curves for the three media differ

the variance of ϵ is truly the same for each type of medium, the pooled estimate is superior to three separate estimates calculated by fitting a separate model for each type of medium.

Exercises 11.72–11.83

Learning the Mechanics

11.72 Consider a multiple regression model for a response y,
NW with one quantitative independent variable x_1, and one
qualitative variable at three levels.
  a. Write a first-order model that relates the mean response
  $E(y)$ to the quantitative independent variable.
  b. Add the main effect terms for the qualitative independent variable to the model of part **a.** Specify the coding
  scheme you use.
  c. Add terms to the model of part **b** to allow for interaction
  between the quantitative and qualitative independent
  variables.
  d. Under what circumstances will the response lines of the
  model in part **c** be parallel?
  e. Under what circumstances will the model in part **c** have
  only one response line?

11.73 Refer to Exercise 11.72.
  a. Write a complete second-order model that relates $E(y)$
  to the quantitative variable.
  b. Add the main effect terms for the qualitative variable
  (at three levels) to the model of part **a.**
  c. Add terms to the model of part **b** to allow for interaction
  between the quantitative and qualitative independent
  variables.
  d. Under what circumstances will the response curves of
  the model have the same shape but different y-inter-
  cepts?
  e. Under what circumstances will the response curves of
  the model be parallel lines?
  f. Under what circumstances will the response curves of
  the model be identical?

11.74 Consider the model:

$$y = \beta_0 + \beta_1 x_1 + \beta_2 x_2 + \beta_3 x_3 + \epsilon$$

where x_1 is a quantitative variable and x_2 and x_3 are
dummy variables describing a qualitative variable at three
levels using the coding scheme

$$x_2 = \begin{cases} 1 & \text{if level 2} \\ 0 & \text{otherwise} \end{cases} \qquad x_3 = \begin{cases} 1 & \text{if level 3} \\ 0 & \text{otherwise} \end{cases}$$

The resulting least squares prediction equation is

$$\hat{y} = 44.8 + 2.2x_1 + 9.4x_2 + 15.6x_3$$

  a. What is the response line (equation) for $E(y)$ when
  $x_2 = x_3 = 0$? When $x_2 = 1$ and $x_3 = 0$? When $x_2 = 0$
  and $x_3 = 1$?
  b. What is the least squares prediction equation associated
  with level 1? Level 2? Level 3? Plot these on the same
  graph.

11.75 Consider the model:

$$y = \beta_0 + \beta_1 x_1 + \beta_2 x_1^2 + \beta_3 x_2 + \beta_4 x_3 +$$
$$\beta_5 x_1 x_2 + \beta_6 x_1 x_3 + \beta_7 x_1^2 x_2 + \beta_8 x_1^2 x_3 + \epsilon$$

where x_1 is a quantitative variable and

$$x_2 = \begin{cases} 1 & \text{if level 2} \\ 0 & \text{otherwise} \end{cases} \qquad x_3 = \begin{cases} 1 & \text{if level 3} \\ 0 & \text{otherwise} \end{cases}$$

The resulting least squares prediction equation is

$$\hat{y} = 48.8 - 3.4x_1 + .07x_1^2 - 2.4x_2 - 7.5x_3 +$$
$$3.7x_1 x_2 + 2.7x_1 x_3 - .02x_1^2 x_2 - .04x_1^2 x_3$$

  a. What is the equation of the response curve for $E(y)$
  when $x_2 = 0$ and $x_3 = 0$? When $x_2 = 1$ and $x_3 = 0$?
  When $x_2 = 0$ and $x_3 = 1$?
  b. On the same graph, plot the least squares prediction equation associated with level 1, with level 2, and with level 3.

11.76 Write a model that relates $E(y)$ to two independent variables—one quantitative and one qualitative at four levels.
Construct a model that allows the associated response
curves to be second-order but does not allow for interaction between the two independent variables.

Applying the Concepts—Basic

⊘ **DDT**

11.77 Chemical plant contamination. Refer to Exercise 11.16
(p. 683) and the model relating the mean DDT level $E(y)$
of contaminated fish to x_1 = miles captured upstream,
x_2 = length, and x_3 = weight. Now consider a model for
$E(y)$ as a function of both weight and species (channel catfish, largemouth bass, and smallmouth buffalo).
  a. Set up the appropriate dummy variables for species.
  b. Write the equation of a model that proposes parallel
  straight-line relationships between mean DDT level
  $E(y)$ and weight, one line for each species.
  c. Write the equation of a model that proposes nonparallel
  straight-line relationships between mean DDT level
  $E(y)$ and weight, one line for each species.
  d. Fit the model, part **b,** to the data saved in the **DDT** file.
  Give the least squares prediction equation.
  e. Refer to part **d.** Interpret the value of the least squares estimate of the beta coefficient multiplied by weight.
  f. Fit the model, part **c,** to the data saved in the **DDT** file.
  Give the least squares prediction equation.
  g. Refer to part **f.** Find the estimated slope of the line relating DDT level (y) to weight for the channel catfish
  species.

⊘ **SNOWGEESE**

11.78 Snow geese feeding trial. Refer to the *Journal of Applied
Ecology* study of feeding habits of baby snow geese,
Exercise 11.18 (p. 684).
  a. Write a first-order model relating gosling weight change
  (y) to digestion efficiency (x_1) and diet (plants or duck
  chow) that allows for different slopes for each diet.
  b. Fit the model, part **a,** to the data saved in the
  SNOWGEESE file and give the least squares prediction
  equation.
  c. Find the estimated slope of the line for goslings fed a
  diet of plants. Interpret its value.
  d. Find the estimated slope of the line for goslings fed a
  diet of duck chow. Interpret its value.
  e. Conduct a test to determine whether the slopes associated with the two diets are significantly different. Use
  $\alpha = .05$

11.79 Smoking and resting energy. The influence of cigarette smoking on resting energy expenditure (REE) in normal-weight and obese smokers was investigated (*Health Psychology*, Mar. 1995). The researchers hypothesized that the relationship between a smoker's REE and length of time since smoking differs for normal-weight and obese smokers. Consequently, the interaction model was examined:

$$E(y) = \beta_0 + \beta_1 x_1 + \beta_2 x_2 + \beta_3 x_1 x_2$$

where

y = REE, measured in kilocalories per day

x_1 = Time, in minutes after smoking, of metabolic energy reading (levels = 10, 20, and 30 minutes)

$$x_2 = \begin{cases} 1 & \text{if normal weight} \\ 0 & \text{if obese} \end{cases}$$

a. Give the equation of the hypothesized line relating mean REE to time after smoking for obese smokers. What is the slope of the line?

b. Repeat part **a** for normal-weight smokers.

c. A test for interaction resulted in an observed significance level of .044. Interpret this value.

Applying the Concepts—Intermediate

11.80 "Sun Safety" study. Numerous "sun safety" products exist on the market to prevent excessive exposure to solar radiation. But many people do not practice "sun safety" or recognize the effectiveness of these products. A group of University of Arizona researchers examined the feasibility of educating preschool (4- to 5-year-old) children about sun safety (*American Journal of Public Health*, July 1995). A sample of 122 preschool children was divided into two groups, the control group and the intervention group. Children in the intervention group received a *Be Sun Safe* curriculum in preschool, while the control group did not. All children were tested for their knowledge, comprehension, and application of sun safety at two points in time: prior to the sun safety curriculum (pretest, x_1) and 7 weeks following the curriculum (posttest, y).

a. Write a first-order model for mean posttest score, $E(y)$, as a function of pretest score, x_1 and group. Assume that no interaction exists between pretest score and group.

b. For the model, part **a**, show that the slope of the line relating posttest score to pretest score is the same for both groups of children.

c. Repeat part **a**, but assume that pretest score and group interact.

d. For the model, part **c**, show that the slope of the line relating posttest score to pretest score differs for the two groups of children.

11.81 Recently sold single-family homes. The National Association of Realtors maintains a database consisting of sales information on homes sold in the United States. The next table lists the sale prices for a sample of 28 recently sold single-family homes. The table also identifies the region of the country in which the home is located and the total number of homes sold in the region during the month the home sold.

a. Propose a complete second-order model for the sale price of a single-family home as a function of region and sales volume.

b. Give the equation of the curve relating sale price to sales volume for homes sold in the West.

c. Repeat part **b** for homes sold in the Northwest.

d. Which β's in the model, part **a**, allow for differences among the mean sale prices for homes in the four regions?

e. Fit the model, part **a**, to the data using an available statistical software package. Is the model statistically useful for predicting sale price? Test using $\alpha = .01$.

NAR

Home Price	Region	Sales Volume
$218,200	NE	55,156
235,900	NE	61,025
192,888	NE	48,991
200,990	NE	55,156
345,300	NE	60,324
178,999	NE	51,446
240,855	NW	61,025
183,200	NW	94,166
165,225	NW	92,063
160,633	NW	89,485
173,900	NW	91,772
241,000	NW	99,025
188,950	NW	94,166
192,880	NW	95,688
193,000	S	155,666
211,980	S	160,000
179,500	S	153,540
185,650	S	148,668
250,900	S	163,210
190,990	S	141,822
242,790	S	163,611
258,900	W	109,083
202,420	W	101,111
365,900	W	116,983
219,900	W	108,773
228,250	W	105,106
235,300	W	107,839
269,800	W	109,026

Source: Adapted from National Association of Realtors, www.realtor.org.

11.82 Entrepreneurial networks and company growth. California State University at Long Beach researcher E. L. Hansen used multiple regression analysis to investigate the link between entrepreneurial networks and new organization growth (*Entrepreneurship Theory and Practice*, Summer 1995). The dependent variable, initial new organization growth (y), is defined as the monthly payroll of the firm at the end of its first year in business. One independent variable considered in the model (and found to be statistically significant) is entrepreneurial action set size (x_1), defined as the number of people in the entrepreneur's social network who are directly or indirectly involved with the founding of the new organization. A second independent variable considered in the study was a dummy variable that represented the technology level of the new firm, where

$$x_2 = \begin{cases} 1 & \text{if high-tech firm} \\ 0 & \text{if low-tech firm} \end{cases}$$

a. Write a first-order model for new firm growth (y) as a function of entrepreneurial action set size (x_1) and technology level (x_2). Assume that the effect of size

⊘ **VOLATILEF**

Country	Volatility (standard deviation of return), y	Credit Rating, x_1	Developed (D) or Emerging (E), x_2
1	56.9	9.5	E
2	25.1	72.4	D
3	28.4	58.2	E
4	56.2	9.9	E
5	21.5	92.1	D
6	21.8	90.3	D
7	31.5	47.3	E
8	23.5	80.4	D
9	23.3	81.5	D
10	49.1	15.3	E
11	56.1	10.0	E
12	21.4	92.8	D
13	37.9	31.2	E
14	25.5	70.3	E
15	33.0	43.0	E
16	25.5	70.6	D
17	47.4	17.0	E
18	29.8	53.0	D
19	39.8	27.6	E
20	24.6	74.9	D
21	61.7	7.2	E
22	23.4	81.1	D
23	22.6	85.8	D
24	24.5	75.3	D
25	46.3	18.2	E
26	47.5	16.9	E
27	22.0	89.0	D
28	21.5	91.9	D
29	38.1	30.7	E
30	37.4	32.2	E

on new firm growth is independent of technology level.

b. In terms of the β's of the model, part **a,** give the slope of the line relating new firm growth y to size x_1 for high-tech firms.

c. Repeat part **a,** but assume that the rate of change of new firm growth y with size x_1 depends on technology level x_2.

d. In terms of the β's of the model, part **c,** give the slope of the line relating new firm growth y to size x_1 for high-tech firms.

11.83 Volatility of foreign stocks. The relationship between country credit ratings and the volatility of the countries' stock markets was examined in the *Journal of Portfolio Management* (Spring 1996). The researchers point out that this volatility can be explained by two factors: the countries' credit ratings and whether the countries in question have developed or emerging markets. The table above gives the volatility (measured as the standard deviation of stock returns), credit rating (measured as a percentage),

and market type (developed or emerging) for a sample of 30 fictitious countries based on the study results.

a. Write a model that describes the relationship between volatility (y) and credit rating (x_1) as two nonparallel lines, one for each type of market. Specify the dummy variable coding scheme you use.

b. Plot volatility y against credit rating x_1 for all the developed markets in the sample. On the same graph, plot y against x_1 for all emerging markets in the sample. Does it appear that the model specified in part **a** is appropriate? Explain.

c. Fit the model, part **a,** to the data using a statistical software package. Report the least squares prediction equation for each of the two types of markets.

d. Plot the two prediction equations of part **c** on a scattergram of the data.

e. Is there evidence to conclude that the slope of the linear relationship between volatility y and credit rating x_1 depends on market type? Test using $\alpha = .01$.

11.9 Model Building: Comparing Nested Models (Optional)

To be successful model builders, we require a statistical method that will allow us to determine (with a high degree of confidence) which one among a set of candidate models best fits the data. In this section, we present such a technique for *nested models*.

> **Definition 11.3**
>
> Two models are **nested** if one model contains all the terms of the second model and at least one additional term. The more complex of the two models is called the **complete (or full)** model, and the simpler of the two is called the **reduced** model.

To illustrate the concept of nested models, consider the straight-line interaction model for the mean auction price $E(y)$ of a grandfather clock as a function of two quantitative variables: age of the clock (x_1) and number of bidders (x_2). The interaction model, fit in Example 11.6, is

$$E(y) = \beta_0 + \beta_1 x_1 + \beta_2 x_2 + \beta_3 x_1 x_2$$

If we assume that the relationship between auction price (y), age (x_1), and bidders (x_2) is curvilinear, then the complete second-order model is more appropriate:

$$E(y) = \overbrace{\beta_0 + \beta_1 x_1 + \beta_2 x_2 + \beta_3 x_1 x_2}^{\text{Terms in interaction model}} + \overbrace{\beta_4 x_1^2 + \beta_5 x_2^2}^{\text{Quadratic terms}}$$

Note that the curvilinear model contains quadratic terms for x_1 and x_2, as well as the terms in the interaction model. Therefore, the models are nested models. In this case, the interaction model is nested within the more complex curvilinear model. Thus, the curvilinear model is the *complete* model and the interaction model is the *reduced* model.

Suppose we want to know whether the more complex curvilinear model contributes more information for the prediction of y than the straight-line interaction model. This is equivalent to determining whether the quadratic terms β_4 and β_5 should be retained in the model. To test whether these terms should be retained, we test the null hypothesis

$$H_0: \beta_4 = \beta_5 = 0 \text{ (i.e., quadratic terms are not important for predicting } y)$$

against the alternative hypothesis

H_a: At least one of the parameters β_4 and β_5 is nonzero (i.e., at least one of the quadratic terms is useful for predicting y)

Note that the terms being tested are those additional terms in the complete (curvilinear) model that are not in the reduced (straight-line interaction) model.

In Section 11.3, we presented the t-test for a single β coefficient and the global F-test for *all* the β parameters (except β_0) in the model. We now need a test for a *subset* of the β parameters in the complete model. The test procedure is intuitive. First, we use the method of least squares to fit the reduced model and calculate the corresponding sum of squares for error, SSE_R (the sum of squares of the deviations between observed and predicted y-values). Next, we fit the complete model and calculate its sum of squares for error, SSE_C. Then we compare SSE_R to SSE_C by calculating the difference, $\text{SSE}_R - \text{SSE}_C$. If the additional terms in the complete model are significant, then SSE_C should be much smaller than SSE_R, and the difference $\text{SSE}_R - \text{SSE}_C$ will be large.

Since SSE will always decrease when new terms are added to the model, the question is whether the difference $\text{SSE}_R - \text{SSE}_C$ is large enough to conclude that it is due to more than just an increase in the number of model terms and to chance. The formal statistical test utilizes an F-statistic, as shown in the box.

When the assumptions listed in Section 11.1 about the random error term are satisfied, this F-statistic has an F-distribution with v_1 and v_2 df. Note that v_1 is the number of β parameters being tested, and v_2 is the number of degrees of freedom associated with s^2 in the complete model.

F-Test for Comparing Nested Models

Reduced model: $E(y) = \beta_0 + \beta_1 x_1 + \cdots + \beta_g x_g$

Complete model: $E(y) = \beta_0 + \beta_1 x_1 + \cdots + \beta_g x_g + \beta_{g+1} x_{g+1} + \cdots + \beta_k x_k$

$H_0: \beta_{g+1} = \beta_{g+2} = \cdots = \beta_k = 0$

H_a: At least one of the β parameters under test is nonzero.

Test statistic: $F = \dfrac{(\text{SSE}_R - \text{SSE}_C)/(k - g)}{\text{SSE}_C/[n - (k + 1)]}$

$= \dfrac{(\text{SSE}_R - \text{SSE}_C)/\#\beta\text{'s tested in } H_0}{\text{MSE}_C}$

where

SSE_R = Sum of squared errors for the reduced model

SSE_C = Sum of squared errors for the complete model

MSE_C = Mean square error (s^2) for the complete model

$k - g$ = Number of β parameters specified in H_0 (i.e., number of β parameters tested)

$k + 1$ = Number of β parameters in the complete model (including β_0)

n = Total sample size

Rejection region: $F > F_\alpha$

where F is based on $v_1 = k - g$ numerator degrees of freedom and $v_2 = n - (k + 1)$ denominator degrees of freedom.

EXAMPLE 11.12

Analyzing a Complete Second-Order Model for Product Quality

Problem Many companies manufacture products (e.g., steel, paint, gasoline) that are at least partially chemically produced. In many instances, the quality of the finished product is a function of the temperature and pressure at which the chemical reactions take place. Suppose you want to model the quality y of a product as a function of the temperature x_1 and the pressure x_2 at which it is produced. Four inspectors independently assign a quality score between 0 and 100 to each product, and then the quality y is calculated by averaging the four scores. An experiment is conducted by varying temperature between 80°F and 100°F and pressure between 50 and 60 pounds per square inch (psi). The resulting data are given in Table 11.6.

a. Fit a complete second-order model to the data.

b. Sketch the fitted model in three dimensions.

c. Do the data provide sufficient evidence to indicate that the second-order terms, β_3, β_4, and β_5, contribute information for the prediction of y?

Solution

a. The complete second-order model is

$$E(y) = \beta_0 + \beta_1 x_1 + \beta_2 x_2 + \beta_3 x_1 x_2 + \beta_4 x_1^2 + \beta_5 x_2^2$$

The data in Table 11.6 were used to fit this model, and the MINITAB output is shown in Figure 11.31.

QUALITY

TABLE 11.6 Temperature (x_1), Pressure (x_2), and Quality of the Finished Product (y)

x_1 (°F)	x_2 (psi)	y	x_1 (°F)	x_2 (psi)	y	x_1 (°F)	x_2 (psi)	y
80	50	50.8	90	50	63.4	100	50	46.6
80	50	50.7	90	50	61.6	100	50	49.1
80	50	49.4	90	50	63.4	100	50	46.4
80	55	93.7	90	55	93.8	100	55	69.8
80	55	90.9	90	55	92.1	100	55	72.5
80	55	90.9	90	55	97.4	100	55	73.2
80	60	74.5	90	60	70.9	100	60	38.7
80	60	73.0	90	60	68.8	100	60	42 5
80	60	71.2	90	60	71.3	100	60	41.4

```
The regression equation is
QUALITY = - 5128 + 31.1 TEMP + 140 PRES - 0.145 TEM_PRES - 0.133 TEMPSQ
          - 1.14 PRESSQ


Predictor        Coef    SE Coef        T       P
Constant       -5127.9      110.3   -46.49   0.000
TEMP            31.096      1.344    23.13   0.000
PRES           139.747      3.140    44.50   0.000
TEM_PRES     -0.145500   0.009692   -15.01   0.000
TEMPSQ       -0.133389   0.006853   -19.46   0.000
PRESSQ        -1.14422    0.02741   -41.74   0.000


S = 1.67870   R-Sq = 99.3%   R-Sq(adj) = 99.1%


Analysis of Variance

Source          DF       SS       MS       F       P
Regression       5   8402.3   1680.5  596.32   0.000
Residual Error  21     59.2      2.8
Total           26   8461.4
```

FIGURE 11.31

MINITAB printout of complete second-order model for product quality

The least squares prediction equation is

$$\hat{y} = -5,128 + 31.1x_1 + 139.75x_2 - .146x_1x_2 - .133x_1^2 - 1.14x_2^2$$

b. A three-dimensional graph of this prediction model, called a **response surface,** is shown in Figure 11.32. Note that the quality seems to be greatest for temperatures of about 85–90°F and for pressures of about 55–57 pounds per square inch.* Further experimentation in these ranges might lead to a more precise determination of the optimal temperature–pressure combination.

c. To determine whether the data provide sufficient information to indicate that the second-order terms contribute information for the prediction of y, we wish to test

$$H_0: \beta_3 = \beta_4 = \beta_5 = 0$$

*Students with knowledge of calculus should note that we can solve for the exact temperature and pressure that maximize quality in the least squares model by solving $\partial\hat{y}/\partial x_1 = 0$ and $\partial\hat{y}/\partial x_2 = 0$ for x_1 and x_2. Sample estimates of these estimated optimal values are $x_1 = 86.25°F$ and $x_2 = 55.58$ psi.

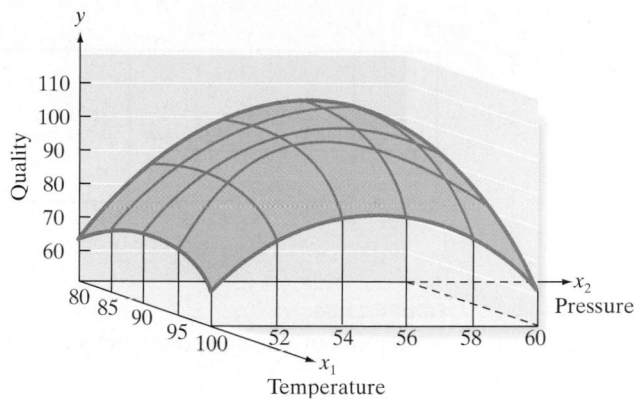

FIGURE 11.32

Plot of second-order least squares model for Example 11.12

against the alternative hypothesis

H_a: At least one of the parameters, β_3, β_4, β_5, differs from 0

The first step in conducting the test is to drop the second-order terms out of the complete (second-order) model and fit the reduced model

$$E(y) = \beta_0 + \beta_1 x_1 + \beta_2 x_2$$

to the data. The MINITAB printout for this model is shown in Figure 11.33.

You can see that the sums of squares for error, highlighted in Figures 11.31 and 11.33 for the complete and reduced models, respectively, are

$$\text{SSE}_C = 59.2$$
$$\text{SSE}_R = 6{,}671.5$$

and that s^2 for the complete model (also highlighted in Figure 11.31) is

$$s^2 = \text{MSE}_C = 2.8$$

Recall that $n = 27$, $k = 5$, and $g = 2$. Therefore, the calculated value of the F statistic, based on $v_1 = (k - g) = 3$ numerator df and $v_2 = [n - (k + 1)] = 21$ denominator df, is

```
The regression equation is
QUALITY = 106 - 0.916 TEMP + 0.788 PRES


Predictor       Coef   SE Coef        T       P
Constant      106.09     55.95     1.90   0.070
TEMP         -0.9161    0.3930    -2.33   0.028
PRES          0.7878    0.7860     1.00   0.326


S = 16.6727    R-Sq = 21.2%    R-Sq(adj) = 14.6%


Analysis of Variance

Source            DF        SS       MS       F       P
Regression         2    1789.9    895.0    3.22   0.058
Residual Error    24    6671.5    278.0
Total             26    8461.4
```

FIGURE 11.33

MINITAB printout of first-order model for quality

Model Summary

Model	R	R Square	Adjusted R Square	Std. Error of the Estimate	Change Statistics R Square Change	F Change	df1	df2	Sig. F Change
1	.460[a]	.212	.146	16.673	.212	3.220	2	24	.058
2	.996[b]	.993	.991	1.679	.781	782.143	3	21	.000

a. Predictors: (Constant), PRESSURE, TEMP

b. Predictors: (Constant), PRESSURE, TEMP, TEM_PRES, TEMPSQ, PRESSQ

FIGURE 11.34

SPSS printout showing nested model F-test for product quality model

$$F = \frac{(SSE_R - SSE_C)/(k - g)}{SSE_C/[n - (k + 1)]} = \frac{(SSE_R - SSE_C)/(k - g)}{MSE_C}$$

where $v_1 = (k - g)$ is equal to the number of parameters involved in H_0. Therefore,

$$\text{Test statistic: } F = \frac{(6{,}671.5 - 59.2)/3}{2.8} = 787.2$$

The final step in the test is to compare this computed value of F with the tabulated value based on $v_1 = 3$ and $v_2 = 21$ df. If we choose $\alpha = .05$, then $F_{.05} = 3.07$ and the rejection region is

$$\text{Rejection region: } F > 3.07.$$

Since the computed value of F falls in the rejection region (i.e., it exceeds $F_{.05} = 3.07$), we reject H_0 and conclude that at least one of the second-order terms contributes information for the prediction of y. The second-order model appears to provide better predictions of y than a first-order model.

Look Back Some statistical software packages will perform the desired nested model F-test if requested. The test statistic and p-value for the test above are highlighted on the SPSS printout, Figure 11.34.

Now Work Exercise 11.88

The nested model F-test can be used to determine whether *any* subset of terms should be included in a complete model by testing the null hypothesis that a particular set of β parameters simultaneously equals 0. For example, we may want to test to determine whether a set of interaction terms for quantitative variables or a set of main effect terms for a qualitative variable should be included in a model. If we reject H_0, the complete model is the better of the two nested models.

Suppose the F-test in Example 11.12 yielded a test statistic that did not fall in the rejection region. Although we must be cautious about accepting H_0, most practitioners of regression analysis adopt the principle of *parsimony*—that is, in situations where two competing models are found to have essentially the same predictive power (as in this case), the model with the fewer number of β's (i.e., the more parsimonious model) is selected. Based on this principle, we would drop the three second-order terms and select the straight-line (reduced) model over the second-order (complete) model.

Definition 11.4

A **parsimonious model** is a general linear model with a small number of β parameters. In situations where two competing models have essentially the same predictive power (as determined by an F-test), choose the more parsimonious of the two.

When the candidate models in model building are nested models, the F-test developed in this section is the appropriate procedure to apply to compare the models. However, if the models are not nested, this F-test is not applicable. In this situation, the analyst must base the choice of the best model on statistics such as R_a^2 and s. It is important to remember that decisions based on these and other numerical descriptive measures of model adequacy cannot be supported with a measure of reliability and are often very subjective in nature.

Exercises 11.84–11.95

Learning the Mechanics

11.84 Explain why the F-test used to compare complete and reduced models is a one-tailed, upper-tailed test.

11.85 Determine which pairs of the following models are "nested" models. For each pair of nested models, identify the complete and reduced model.
   a. $E(y) = \beta_0 + \beta_1 x_1 + \beta_2 x_2$
   b. $E(y) = \beta_0 + \beta_1 x_1$
   c. $E(y) = \beta_0 + \beta_1 x_1 + \beta_2 x_1^2$
   d. $E(y) = \beta_0 + \beta_1 x_1 + \beta_2 x_2 + \beta_3 x_1 x_2$
   e. $E(y) = \beta_0 + \beta_1 x_1 + \beta_2 x_2 + \beta_3 x_1 x_2 + \beta_4 x_1^2 + \beta_5 x_2^2$

11.86 Suppose you fit the regression model

$$y = \beta_0 + \beta_1 x_1 + \beta_2 x_2 + \beta_3 x_1 x_2 + \beta_4 x_1^2 + \beta_5 x_2^2 + \epsilon$$

to $n = 30$ data points and you wish to test

$$H_0: \beta_3 = \beta_4 = \beta_5 = 0$$

   a. State the alternative hypothesis H_a.
   b. Give the reduced model appropriate for conducting the test.
   c. What are the numerator and denominator degrees of freedom associated with the F-statistic?
   d. Suppose the SSE's for the reduced and complete models are $\text{SSE}_R = 1,250.2$ and $\text{SSE}_C = 1,125.2$. Conduct the hypothesis test and interpret the results of your test. Test using $\alpha = .05$.

11.87 The complete model

$$y = \beta_0 + \beta_1 x_1 + \beta_2 x_2 + \beta_3 x_3 + \beta_4 x_4 + \epsilon$$

was fit to $n = 20$ data points, with SSE = 152.66. The reduced model, $y = \beta_0 + \beta_1 x_1 + \beta_2 x_2 + \epsilon$, was also fit, with SSE = 160.44.
   a. How many β parameters are in the complete model? The reduced model?
   b. Specify the null and alternative hypotheses you would use to investigate whether the complete model contributes more information for the prediction of y than the reduced model.
   c. Conduct the hypothesis test of part **d.** Use $\alpha = .05$.

Applying the Concepts—Basic

11.88 **Mental health of a community.** An article in the
NW *Community Mental Health Journal* (Aug. 2000) used multiple regression analysis to model the level of community adjustment of clients of the Department of Mental Health and Addiction Services in Connecticut. The dependent variable, community adjustment (y), was measured quantitatively based on staff ratings of the clients. (Lower scores indicate better adjustment.) The complete model

was a first-order model with 21 independent variables. The independent variables were categorized as Demographic (4 variables), Diagnostic (7 variables), Treatment (4 variables), and Community (6 variables).
   a. Write the equation of $E(y)$ for the complete model.
   b. Give the null hypothesis for testing whether the 7 Diagnostic variables contribute information for the prediction of y.
   c. Give the equation of the reduced model appropriate for the test, part **b.**
   d. The test, part **b,** resulted in a test statistic of $F = 59.3$ and p-value < .0001. Interpret this result in the words of the problem.

GASTURBINE

11.89 **Cooling method for gas turbines.** Refer to the *Journal of Engineering for Gas Turbines and Power* (Jan. 2005) study of a high-pressure inlet fogging method for a gas turbine engine, Exercise 11.17 (p. 684). Consider a model for heat rate (kilojoules per kilowatt per hour) of a gas turbine as a function of cycle speed (revolutions per minute) and cycle pressure ratio. The data are saved in the **GASTURBINE** file.
   a. Write a complete second-order model for heat rate (y).
   b. Give the null and alternative hypotheses for determining whether the curvature terms in the complete second-order model are statistically useful for predicting heat rate (y).
   c. For the test in part **b,** identify the "complete" and "reduced" model.
   d. Portions of the MINITAB printouts for the two models are shown at the top of p. 734. Find the values of SSE_R, SSE_C, and MSE_C on the printouts.
   e. Compute the value of the test statistics for the test of part **b.**
   f. Find the rejection region for the test of part **b** using $\alpha = .10$.
   g. State the conclusion of the test in the words of the problem.

BEANIE

11.90 **Collecting Beanie Babies.** Refer to Exercise 10.87 (p. 655) and the data on the values of 50 Beanie Babies collector's items, published in *Beanie World Magazine*. Suppose we want to predict the market value of a Beanie Baby using age (in months as of Sept. 1998) and whether the Beanie Baby has been retired or is current (i.e., still in production).
   a. Write a complete second-order model for market value as a function of age and current/retired status.
   b. Specify the null hypothesis for testing whether the quadratic terms in the model, part **a,** are important for predicting market value.

Complete Model

```
The regression equation is
HEATRATE = 15583 + 0.078 RPM - 523 CPRATIO + 0.00445 RPM_CPR - 0.000000 RPMSQ
           + 8.84 CPRSQ


S = 563.513    R-Sq = 88.5%    R-Sq(adj) = 87.5%


Analysis of Variance


Source            DF         SS         MS       F       P
Regression         5  148526859   29705372   93.55   0.000
Residual Error    61   19370350     317547
Total             66  167897208
```

Reduced Model

```
The regression equation is
HEATRATE = 12065 + 0.170 RPM - 146 CPRATIO - 0.00242 RPM_CPR


S = 633.842    R-Sq = 84.9%    R-Sq(adj) = 84.2%


Analysis of Variance


Source            DF         SS         MS        F       P
Regression         3  142586570   47528857   118.30   0.000
Residual Error    63   25310639     401756
Total             66  167897208
```

MINITAB Output for Exercise 11.89

c. Specify the null hypothesis for testing whether the interaction terms in the model, part **a,** are important for predicting market value.

d. Fit the three models of parts **a–c** to the data saved in the **BEANIE** file. Conduct the tests specified in parts **b** and **c.** Interpret the results.

Applying the Concepts—Intermediate

11.91 Improving SAT scores. Refer to the *Chance* (Winter 2001) study of students who paid a private tutor (or coach) to help them improve their Standardized Admission Test (SAT) scores, Exercise 11.65 (p. 716). Recall that the base-line model, $E(y) = \beta_0 + \beta_1 x_1 + \beta_2 x_2$, where y = SAT–Math score, x_1 = score on PSAT, and x_2 = {1 if student was coached, 0 if not}, had the following results: $R_a^2 = .76$, $\beta_2 = 19$, and $s_{\hat{\beta}_2} = 3$. As an alternative model, the researcher added several "control" variables, including dummy variables for student ethnicity (x_3, x_4, and x_5), a socioeconomic status index variable (x_6), two variables that measured high school performance (x_7 and x_8), the number of math courses taken in high school (x_9), and the overall GPA for the math courses (x_{10}).

a. Write the hypothesized equation for $E(y)$ for the alternative model.

b. Give the null hypothesis for a nested model F-test comparing the initial and alternative models.

c. The nested model F-test, part **b,** was statistically significant at $\alpha = .05$. Practically interpret this result.

d. The alternative model, part **a,** resulted in $R_a^2 = .79$, $\beta_2 = 14$, and $s_{\hat{\beta}_2} = 3$. Interpret the value of R_a^2.

e. Refer to part **d.** Find and interpret a 95% confidence interval for β_2.

f. The researcher concluded that "the estimated effect of SAT coaching decreases from the baseline model when control variables are added to the model." Do you agree? Justify your answer.

g. As a modification to the model of part **a,** the researcher added all possible interactions between the coaching variable (x_2) and the other independent variables in the model. Write the equation for $E(y)$ for this modified model.

h. Give the null hypothesis for comparing the models, parts **a** and **g.** How would you perform this test?

11.92 "Sun Safety" Study. Refer to the *American Journal of Public Health* study of preschool children's awareness of sun safety, Exercise 11.80 (p. 726). Consider the first-order, interaction model

$$E(y) = \beta_0 + \beta_1 x_1 + \beta_2 x_2 + \beta_3 x_1 x_2$$

where

y = sun safety posttest score

x_1 = sun safety pretest score

$x_2 = \begin{cases} 1 \text{ if in the } BeSunSafe \text{ intervention group} \\ 0 \text{ if in the control group} \end{cases}$

a. Assuming interaction exists, give the reduced model for testing whether the mean posttest scores differ for the intervention and control groups.

b. When sun safety knowledge was used as the dependent variable, the test of part **a** resulted in a p-value of .03. Interpret this result.

c. When sun safety comprehension was used as the dependent variable, the test of part **a** resulted in a p-value of .033. Interpret this result.

d. When sun safety application was used as the dependent variable, the test of part **a** resulted in a p-value of .322. Interpret this result.

11.93 Gas as a waste encapsulant. Since glass is not subject to radiation damage, encapsulation of waste in glass is considered to be one of the most promising solutions to the problem of low-level nuclear waste in the environment. However, chemical reactions may weaken the glass. This concern led to a study undertaken jointly by the Department of Materials Science and Engineering at the University of Florida and the U.S. Department of Energy to assess the utility of glass as a waste encapsulant.* Corrosive chemical solutions (called *corrosion baths*) were prepared and applied directly to glass samples containing one of three types of waste (TDS-3A, FE, and AL); the chemical reactions were observed over time. A few of the key variables measured were

y = Amount of silicon (in parts per million) found in solution at end of experiment. (This is both a measure of the degree of breakdown in the glass and a proxy for the amount of radioactive species released into the environment.)

x_1 = Temperature (°C) of the corrosion bath

x_2 = 1 if waste type TDS-3A, 0 if not

x_3 = 1 if waste type FE, 0 if not

(Waste type AL is the base level.) Suppose we want to model amount y of silicon as a function of temperature (x_1) and type of waste (x_2, x_3).

a. Write a model that proposes parallel straight-line relationships between amount of silicon and temperature, one line for each of the three waste types.

b. Add terms for the interaction between temperature and waste type to the model of part **a**.

c. Refer to the model of part **b**. For each waste type, give the slope of the line relating amount of silicon to temperature.

d. Explain how you could test for the presence of temperature–waste type interaction.

11.94 Emotional distress in firefighters. The *Journal of Human Stress* (Summer 1987) reported on a study of "psychological response of firefighters to chemical fire." It is thought that the following complete second-order model will be adequate to describe the relationship between emotional distress and years of experience for two

groups of firefighters—those exposed to a chemical fire and those unexposed.

$$E(y) = \beta_0 + \beta_1 x_1 + \beta_2 x_1^2 + \beta_3 x_2 + \beta_4 x_1 x_2 + \beta_5 x_1^2 x_2$$

where

y = Emotional distress

x_1 = Experience (years)

x_2 = 1 if exposed to chemical fire, 0 if not

a. What hypothesis would you test to determine whether the *rate* of increase of emotional distress with experience is different for the two groups of firefighters?

b. What hypothesis would you test to determine whether there are differences in mean emotional distress levels that are attributable to exposure group?

c. The second-order model, fit to a sample of 200 firefighters resulted in SSE = 783.90. The reduced model, $E(y) = \beta_0 + \beta_1 x_1 + \beta_2 x_1^2$, fit to the same data, resulted in SSE = 795.23. Is there sufficient evidence to support the claim that the mean emotional distress levels differ for the two groups of firefighters? Use $\alpha = .05$.

Applying the Concepts—Advanced

11.95 Modeling monthly collision claims. A medium-sized automobile insurance company is interested in developing a regression model to help predict the monthly collision claims of its policyholders. A company analyst has proposed modeling monthly collision claims (y) in the Middle Atlantic States as a function of the percentage of claims by drivers under age 30 (x_1) and the average daily temperature during the month (x_2). She believes that as the percentage of claims by drivers under age 30 increases, claims will rise since younger drivers are usually involved in more serious accidents than older drivers. She also believes that claims will rise as the average daily temperature decreases, since lower temperatures are associated with icy, hazardous driving conditions. In order to develop a preliminary model, data were collected for the state of New Jersey over a 3-year period. The data are saved in the **NJCLAIMS** file. (The first and last five observations are listed in the table on p. 736.)

a. Use a statistical software package to fit the complete second-order model

$$E(y) = \beta_0 + \beta_1 x_1 + \beta_2 x_2 + \beta_3 x_1 x_2 + \beta_4 x_1^2 + \beta_5 x_2^2$$

b. Test the hypothesis $H_0: \beta_4 = \beta_5 = 0$ using $\alpha = .05$. Interpret the results in practical terms.

c. Do the results support the analysts' beliefs? Explain. (You may need to conduct further tests of hypotheses to answer this question.)

*The background information for this exercise was provided by Dr. David Clark, Department of Materials Science and Engineering, University of Florida.

⊙ **NJCLAIMS** (First and last 5 months listed)

Month	Monthly Collision Claims, y ($)	Percentage of Monthly Claimants under the Age of 30, x_1	Newark, N.J., Average Daily Temperature during the Month, x_2 (°F)
1	116,250	50.0	31.5
2	217,180	60.8	33.0
3	43,436	45.1	45.0
4	159,265	56.4	53.9
5	130,308	53.3	63.9
⋮	⋮	⋮	⋮
44	136,528	53.1	76.6
45	193,608	59.8	68.6
46	38,722	45.6	62.4
47	212,309	63.9	50.0
48	118,796	52.3	42.3

Sources: Anonymous insurance company; New Jersey Department of Insurance; Weather of U.S. Cities, 4th ed., Gale Research Inc., Detroit, 1992.

11.10 Model Building: Stepwise Regression (Optional)

Consider the problem of predicting the salary y of an executive. Perhaps the biggest problem in building a model to describe executive salaries is choosing the important independent variables to be included in the model. The list of potentially important independent variables is extremely long (e.g., age, experience, tenure, education level, etc.), and we need some objective method of screening out those that are not important.

The problem of deciding which of a large set of independent variables to include in a model is a common one. Trying to determine which variables influence the profit of a firm, affect blood pressure of humans, or are related to a student's performance in college are only a few examples.

A systematic approach to building a model with a large number of independent variables is difficult because the interpretation of multivariable interactions and higher-order terms is tedious. We therefore turn to a screening procedure, available in most statistical software packages, known as **stepwise regression.**

The most commonly used stepwise regression procedure works as follows. The user first identifies the response, y, and the set of potentially important independent variables, $x_1, x_2, \ldots, x_k$, where k is generally large. [*Note:* This set of variables could include both first-order and higher-order terms. However, we may often include only the main effects of both quantitative variables (first-order terms) and qualitative variables (dummy variables), since the inclusion of second-order terms greatly increases the number of independent variables.] The response and independent variables are then entered into the computer software, and the stepwise procedure begins.

Step 1: The software program fits all possible one-variable models of the form

$$E(y) = \beta_0 + \beta_1 x_i$$

to the data, where x_i is the ith independent variable, $i = 1, 2, \ldots, k$. For each model, the test of the null hypothesis

$$H_0: \beta_1 = 0$$

against the alternative hypothesis

$$H_a: \beta_1 \neq 0$$

is conducted using the t-test (or the equivalent F-test) for a single β parameter. The independent variable that produces the largest (absolute) t-value is declared the best one-variable predictor of y.* Call this independent variable x_1.

Step 2: The stepwise program now begins to search through the remaining $(k - 1)$ independent variables for the best two-variable model of the form

$$E(y) = \beta_0 + \beta_1 x_1 + \beta_2 x_i$$

This is done by fitting all two-variable models containing x_1 and each of the other $(k - 1)$ options for the second variable x_i. The t-values for the test H_0: $\beta_2 = 0$ are computed for each of the $(k - 1)$ models (corresponding to the remaining independent variables, $x_i, i = 2, 3, \ldots, k$), and the variable having the largest t is retained. Call this variable x_2.

At this point, some software packages diverge in methodology. The better packages now go back and check the t-value of $\hat{\beta}_1$ after $\hat{\beta}_2 x_2$ has been added to the model. If the t-value has become nonsignificant at some specified α level (say $\alpha = .10$), the variable x_1 is removed and a search is made for the independent variable with a β parameter that will yield the most significant t-value in the presence of $\hat{\beta}_2 x_2$. Other packages do not recheck the significance of $\hat{\beta}_1$ but proceed directly to step 3.

The reason the t-value for x_1 may change from step 1 to step 2 is that the meaning of the coefficient $\hat{\beta}_1$ changes. In step 2, we are approximating a complex response surface in two variables with a plane. The best-fitting plane may yield a different value for $\hat{\beta}_1$ than that obtained in step 1. Thus, both the value of $\hat{\beta}_1$ and its significance usually changes from step 1 to step 2. For this reason, the software packages that recheck the t-values at each step are preferred.

Step 3: The stepwise procedure now checks for a third independent variable to include in the model with x_1 and x_2—that is, we seek the best model of the form

$$E(y) = \beta_0 + \beta_1 x_1 + \beta_2 x_2 + \beta_3 x_i$$

To do this, we fit all the $(k - 2)$ models using x_1, x_2, and each of the $(k - 2)$ remaining variables, x_i, as a possible x_3. The criterion is again to include the independent variable with the largest t-value. Call this best third variable x_3.

The better programs now recheck the t-values corresponding to the x_1 and x_2 coefficients, removing the variables with t-values that have become nonsignificant. This procedure is continued until no further independent variables can be found that yield significant t-values (at the specified α level) in the presence of the variables already in the model.

The result of the stepwise procedure is a model containing only those terms with t-values that are significant at the specified α level. Thus, in most practical situations, only several of the large number of independent variables remain. However, it is very important *not* to jump to the conclusion that all the independent variables important for predicting y have been identified or that the unimportant independent variables have been eliminated. Remember, the stepwise procedure is using only *sample estimates* of the true model coefficients (β's) to select the important variables. An extremely large number of single β parameter t-tests have been conducted, and the probability is very high that one or more errors have been made in including or excluding variables—that is, we have very probably included some unimportant independent variables in the model (Type I errors) and eliminated some important ones (Type II errors).

There is a second reason why we might not have arrived at a good model. When we choose the variables to be included in the stepwise regression, we may often omit

---

*Note that the variable with the largest t-value is also the one with the largest (absolute) Pearson product moment correlation, r (Section 10.6), with y.

high-order terms (to keep the number of variables manageable). Consequently, we may have initially omitted several important terms from the model. Thus, we should recognize stepwise regression for what it is: an objective screening procedure.

Successful model builders will now consider second-order terms (for quantitative variables) and other interactions among variables screened by the stepwise procedure. It would be best to develop this response surface model with a second set of data independent of that used for the screening, so the results of the stepwise procedure can be partially verified with new data. This is not always possible, however, because in many modeling situations only a small amount of data is available.

Do not be deceived by the impressive-looking t-values that result from the stepwise procedure—it has retained only the independent variables with the largest t-values. Also, be certain to consider second-order terms in systematically developing the prediction model. Finally, if you have used a first-order model for your stepwise procedure, remember that it may be greatly improved by the addition of higher-order terms.

Caution

Be wary of using the results of stepwise regression to make inferences about the relationship between $E(y)$ and the independent variables in the resulting first-order model. First, an extremely large number of t-tests have been conducted, leading to a high probability of making one or more Type I or Type II errors. Second, the stepwise model does not include any higher-order or interaction terms. Stepwise regression should be used only when necessary—that is, when you want to determine which of a large number of potentially important independent variables should be used in the model-building process.

EXAMPLE 11.13
Running a Stepwise Regression

Problem An international management consulting company develops multiple regression models for executive salaries of its client firms. The consulting company has found that models that use the natural logarithm of salary as the dependent variable have better predictive power than those using salary as the dependent variable.* A preliminary step in the construction of these models is the determination of the most important independent variables. For one firm, 10 potential independent variables (seven quantitative and three qualitative) were measured in a sample of 100 executives. The data, described in Table 11.7, are saved in the **EXECSAL** file. Since it would be very difficult to construct a complete second-order model with all of the 10 independent variables, use stepwise regression to decide which of the 10 variables should be included in the building of the final model for the natural log of executive salaries.

Solution We will use stepwise regression with the main effects of the 10 independent variables to identify the most important variables. The dependent variable y is the natural logarithm of the executive salaries. The MINITAB stepwise regression printout is shown in Figure 11.35.

Note that the first variable included in the model is x_1, years of experience. At the second step, x_3, a dummy variable for the qualitative variable, bonus eligibility or not, is brought into the model. In steps 3, 4, and 5, the variables x_4 (number of employees supervised), x_2 (years of education), and x_5 (corporate assets), respectively, are selected for model inclusion. MINITAB stops after five steps because no other independent vari-

---

*This is probably because salaries tend to be incremented in *percentages* rather than dollar values. When a response variable undergoes percentage changes as the independent variables are varied, the logarithm of the response variable will be more suitable as a dependent variable.

EXECSAL

TABLE 11.7 Independent Variables in the Executive Salary Example

Independent Variable	Description	Type
x_1	Experience (years)	Quantitative
x_2	Education (years)	Quantitative
x_3	Bonus eligibility (1 if yes, 0 if no)	Qualitative
x_4	Number of employees supervised	Quantitative
x_5	Corporate assets (millions of dollars)	Quantitative
x_6	Board member (1 if yes, 0 if no)	Qualitative
x_7	Age (years)	Quantitative
x_8	Company profits (past 12 months, millions of dollars)	Quantitative
x_9	Has international responsibility (1 if yes, 0 if no)	Qualitative
x_{10}	Company's total sales (past 12 months, millions of dollars)	Quantitative

```
Alpha-to-Enter: 0.15   Alpha-to-Remove: 0.15


Response is Y on 10 predictors, with N = 100


Step              1       2       3       4       5
Constant      11.091  10.968  10.783  10.278   9.962


X1             0.0278  0.0273  0.0273  0.0273  0.0273
T-Value         12.62   15.13   18.80   24.68   26.50
P-Value         0.000   0.000   0.000   0.000   0.000


X3                     0.197   0.233   0.232   0.225
T-Value                 7.10   10.17   13.30   13.74
P-Value                 0.000   0.000   0.000   0.000


X4                             0.00040 0.00055 0.00052
T-Value                         7.32    10.92   11.06
P-Value                         0.000   0.000   0.000


X2                                     0.0300  0.0291
T-Value                                 8.38    8.72
P-Value                                 0.000   0.000


X5                                             0.00196
T-Value                                          3.95
P-Value                                          0.000


S               0.161   0.131   0.106  0.0807  0.0751
R-Sq            61.90   74.92   83.91   90.75   92.06
R-Sq(adj)       61.51   74.40   83.41   90.36   91.64
Mallows C-p     343.9   195.5    93.8    16.8     3.6
```

FIGURE 11.35

MINITAB stepwise regression printout for executive salary data

ables met the criterion for admission into the model. As a default, MINITAB uses $\alpha = .15$ in the t-tests conducted. In other words, if the p-value associated with a β coefficient exceeds $\alpha = .15$, the variable is *not* included in the model.

The results of the stepwise regression suggest that we should concentrate on these five independent variables. Models with second-order terms and interactions should be proposed and evaluated to determine the best model for predicting executive salaries.

Now Work Exercise 11.97

Recommendation

Do *not* use the stepwise regression model as the final model for predicting y. Recall that the stepwise procedure tends to perform a large number of t-tests, inflating the overall probability of a Type I error, and does not automatically include higher-order terms (e.g., interactions and squared terms) in the final model. Use stepwise regression as a variable screening tool when there exists a large number of potential important independent variables. Then begin building models for y using the variables identified by stepwise.

STATISTICS IN ACTION REVISITED

Selecting the Independent Variables and Building a Model for Road Contract Cost

In the previous Statistics in Action Revisited section (p. 690), we used all eight of the independent variables in Table SIA11.1 to fit a first-order model for the cost (y) of a road construction contract awarded using the sealed-bid system. Although the model was deemed statistically useful for predicting y, the standard deviation of the model (s = 305 thousand dollars) was probably too large for the model to be "practically" useful.

A more complex model—one involving higher-order terms (interactions and squared terms)—needs to be considered. A complete second-order model involving all eight of the independent variables, however, would require over 100 terms! Consequently, we'll use stepwise regression to select the "best" subset of independent variables and then form a complete second-order model with just these variables.

Figure SIA11.4 is a MINITAB printout of the stepwise regression. You can see that the DOT engineer's cost estimate (DOTEST) is the first variable

```
Alpha-to-Enter: 0.15   Alpha-to-Remove: 0.15


Response is COST on 8 predictors, with N = 235


Step              1        2        3        4
Constant       20.91   -20.54   -55.22  -212.85


DOTEST        0.9263   0.9308   0.9110   0.9132
T-Value        93.89    95.52    56.86    57.11
P-Value        0.000    0.000    0.000    0.000


STATUS                    166      167      171
T-Value                  3.38     3.40     3.50
P-Value                 0.001    0.001    0.001


DAYSEST                           0.27     0.33
T-Value                           1.55     1.85
P-Value                          0.122    0.065


BTPRATIO                                    241
T-Value                                    1.81
P-Value                                   0.072


S                313      306      305      304
R-Sq           97.42    97.55    97.57    97.60
R-Sq(adj)      97.41    97.52    97.54    97.56
Mallows C-p     15.2      5.7      5.2      4.0
```

Figure SIA11.4

MINITAB stepwise regression for the road cost data

selected, followed by bid status (STATUS), estimated work days (DAYSEST), and bids-to-planholders ratio (BTPRATIO). Recall that MINITAB uses a default α level of .15. If we reduce the significance level for entry to $\alpha = .05$, only DOTEST and STATUS are selected since the p-values (highlighted on the printout) for DAYSEST and BTPRATIO are both greater than .05.

Since bid status is a qualitative variable ($x_2 = 1$ if fixed and 0 if competitive), a complete second-order model for contract cost (y) using DOTEST (x_1) and STATUS (x_2) is given by the equation

$$E(y) = \beta_0 + \beta_1 x_1 + \beta_2 (x_1)^2 + \beta_3 x_2 + \beta_4 x_1 x_2 + \beta_5 (x_1)^2 x_2$$

The MINITAB printout for this model is shown in Figure SIA11.5. Note that the global F-test for the model is statistically significant (p-value = .000), and

the model standard deviation, $s = 296.6$, is smaller than the standard deviation of the first-order model.

Are the second-order terms in the model, $\beta_2(x_1)^2$ and $\beta_5(x_1)^2 x_2$, necessary? If not, we can simplify the model by dropping these curvature terms. The hypothesis of interest is $H_0: \beta_2 = \beta_5 = 0$. To test this subset of β's, we compare the complete second-order model to a model without the curvilinear terms. The reduced model takes the form

$$E(y) = \beta_0 + \beta_1 x_1 + \beta_3 x_2 + \beta_4 x_1 x_2$$

The results of this nested model (or partial) F-test are shown at the bottom of the SPSS printout, Figure SIA11.6. The p-value of the test (highlighted on the SPSS printout) is .355. Since this p-value is greater than $\alpha = .05$, there is insufficient evidence to reject H_0—that is, there is no evidence to indicate that the two curvature terms are useful predictors of road construction

```
The regression equation is
COST = - 3.0 + 0.916 DOTEST + 0.000001 DOTEST2 - 36.7 STATUS + 0.324 STA_DOT
       - 0.000036 STA_DOT2


Predictor         Coef      SE Coef       T       P
Constant         -2.98        30.89    -0.10   0.923
DOTEST         0.91553      0.02917    31.39   0.000
DOTEST2     0.00000072   0.00000340     0.21   0.833
STATUS          -36.72        74.77    -0.49   0.624
STA_DOT         0.3242       0.1192     2.72   0.007
STA_DOT2   -0.00003576   0.00002470    -1.44   0.150


S = 296.646   R-Sq = 97.7%   R-Sq(adj) = 97.7%


Analysis of Variance

Source          DF         SS         MS         F       P
Regression       5  866723202  173344640   1969.85   0.000
Residual Error 229   20151771      87999
Total          234  886874973
```

Figure SIA11.5
MINITAB regression printout for the complete second-order model of contract cost

Model Summary

Model	R	R Square	Adjusted R Square	Std. Error of the Estimate	R Square Change	F Change	df1	df2	Sig. F Change
1	.988ᵃ	.977	.977	296.69515	.977	3281.312	3	231	.000
2	.989ᵇ	.977	.977	296.64238	.000	1.041	2	229	.355

a. Predictors: (Constant), STA_DOT, DOTEST, STATUS
b. Predictors: (Constant), STA_DOT, DOTEST, STATUS, DOTEST2, STA_DOT2

Figure SIA11.6
SPSS printout of test to compare the complete second-order model of contract cost to the reduced model

Continued

cost. Consequently, the reduced model is selected as the better predictor of cost.

The MINITAB printout for the reduced model is shown in Figure SIA11.7. The overall model is statistically useful (p-value $= .000$ for global F-test), explaining about 98% of the sample variation in contract costs. The model standard deviation, $s = 296.7$, implies that we can predict costs to within about 593 thousand dollars. Also, the t-test for the interaction term, $\beta_4 x_1 x_2$, is significant (p-value $= .000$), implying that the relationship between contract cost (y) and DOT cost estimate depends on bid status (fixed or competitive).

The nature of the interaction is illustrated in the MINITAB graph of the least squared prediction equation for the reduced model, Figure SIA11.8. You can see that the rate of increase of contract cost (y) with the DOT engineer's estimate of cost (x_1) is steeper for fixed contracts than for competitive contracts.

```
The regression equation is
COST = - 6.4 + 0.921 DOTEST + 28.7 STATUS + 0.163 STA_DOT


Predictor        Coef    SE Coef       T       P
Constant        -6.43      26.21   -0.25   0.806
DOTEST       0.921336   0.009723   94.75   0.000
STATUS          28.67      58.66    0.49   0.625
STA_DOT       0.16328    0.04043    4.04   0.000


S = 296.699   R-Sq = 97.7%   R-Sq(adj) = 97.7%


Analysis of Variance

Source           DF          SS          MS         F       P
Regression        3   866540004   288846668   3281.22   0.000
Residual Error  231    20334968       88030
Total           234   886874973
```

Figure SIA11.7
MINITAB regression printout for the reduced model of contract cost

Figure SIA11.8
MINITAB plot of least squares prediction equation for the reduced model of contract cost

Exercises 11.96–11.99

Learning the Mechanics

11.96 There are six independent variables, x_1, x_2, x_3, x_4, x_5, and x_6, that might be useful in predicting a response y. A total of $n = 50$ observations is available, and it is decided to employ stepwise regression to help in selecting the independent variables that appear to be useful. The computer fits all possible one-variable models of the form

$$E(y) = \beta_0 + \beta_1 x_i$$

where x_i is the ith independent variable, $i = 1, 2, \ldots, 6$. The information in the table is provided from the computer printout.

Independent Variable	$\hat{\beta}_i$	$s_{\hat{\beta}_i}$
x_1	1.6	.42
x_2	−.9	.01
x_3	3.4	1.14
x_4	2.5	2.06
x_5	−4.4	.73
x_6	.3	.35

a. Which independent variable is declared the best one-variable predictor of y? Explain.

b. Would this variable be included in the model at this stage? Explain.

c. Describe the next phase that a stepwise procedure would execute.

Applying the Concepts—Basic

11.97 Entry-level job preferences. *Benefits Quarterly* (First
NW Quarter, 1995) published a study of entry-level job preferences. A number of independent variables were used to model the job preferences (measured on a 10-point scale) of 164 business school graduates. Suppose stepwise regression is used to build a model for job preference score (y) as a function of the following independent variables:

$$x_1 = \begin{cases} 1 & \text{if flextime position} \\ 0 & \text{if not} \end{cases}$$

$$x_2 = \begin{cases} 1 & \text{if day care support required} \\ 0 & \text{if not} \end{cases}$$

$$x_3 = \begin{cases} 1 & \text{if spousal transfer support required} \\ 0 & \text{if not} \end{cases}$$

x_4 = Number of sick days allowed

$$x_5 = \begin{cases} 1 & \text{if applicant married} \\ 0 & \text{if not} \end{cases}$$

x_6 = Number of children of applicant

$$x_7 = \begin{cases} 1 & \text{if male applicant} \\ 0 & \text{if female applicant} \end{cases}$$

a. How many models are fit to the data in step 1? Give the general form of these models.

b. How many models are fit to the data in step 2? Give the general form of these models.

c. How many models are fit to the data in step 3? Give the general form of these models.

d. Explain how the procedure determines when to stop adding independent variables to the model.

e. Describe two major drawbacks to using the final stepwise model as the "best" model for job preference score y.

Applying the Concepts—Intermediate

11.98 Bus Rapid Transit study. Bus Rapid Transit (BRT) is a rapidly growing trend in the provision of public transportation in America. The Center for Urban Transportation Research (CUTR) at the University of South Florida conducted a survey of BRT customers in Miami (*Transportation Research Board* Annual Meeting, Jan. 2003). Data on the following variables (all measured on a 5-point scale, where 1 = very unsatisfied and 5 = very satisfied) were collected for a sample of over 500 bus riders: overall satisfaction with BRT (y), safety on bus (x_1), seat availability (x_2), dependability (x_3), travel time (x_4), cost (x_5), information/maps (x_6), convenience of routes (x_7), traffic signals (x_8), safety at bus stops (x_9), hours of service (x_{10}), and frequency of service (x_{11}). CUTR analysts used stepwise regression to model overall satisfaction (y).

a. How many models are fit at step 1 of the stepwise regression?

b. How many models are fit at step 2 of the stepwise regression?

c. How many models are fit at step 11 of the stepwise regression?

d. The stepwise regression selected the following eight variables to include in the model (in order of selection): x_{11}, x_4, x_2, x_7, x_{10}, x_1, x_9, and x_3. Write the equation for $E(y)$ that results from stepwise.

e. The model, part **d**, resulted in $R^2 = .677$. Interpret this value.

f. Explain why the CUTR analysts should be cautious in concluding that the "best" model for $E(y)$ has been found.

11.99 Adverse effects of hot-water runoff. A marine biologist was hired by the EPA to determine whether the hot-water runoff from a particular power plant located near a large gulf is having an adverse effect on the marine life in the area. The biologist's goal is to acquire a prediction equation for the number of marine animals located at certain designated areas, or stations, in the gulf. Based on past experience, the EPA considered the following environmental factors as predictors for the number of animals at a particular station:

x_1 = Temperature of water (TEMP)

x_2 = Salinity of water (SAL)

x_3 = Dissolved oxygen content of water (DO)

x_4 = Turbidity index, a measure of the turbidity of the water (TI)

x_5 = Depth of the water at the station (ST_DEPTH)

x_6 = Total weight of sea grasses in sampled area (TGRSWT)

As a preliminary step in the construction of this model, the biologist used a stepwise regression procedure to identify the most important of these six variables. A total of 716 samples were taken at different stations in the gulf, producing the SPSS printout shown below. (The response measured was y, the logarithm of the number of marine animals found in the sampled area.)

a. According to the SPSS printout, which of the six independent variables should be used in the model? (Use $\alpha = .10$.)

b. Are we able to assume that the marine biologist has identified all the important independent variables for the prediction of y? Why?

c. Using the variables identified in part **a**, write the first-order model with interaction that may be used to predict y.

d. How would the marine biologist determine whether the model specified in part **c** is better than the first-order model?

e. Note the small value of R^2. What action might the biologist take to improve the model?

Variables Entered/Removed[a]

Model	Variables Entered	Variables Removed	Method
1	ST_DEPTH	.	Stepwise (Criteria: Probability-of-F-to-enter <= .050, Probability-of-F-to-remove >= .100).
2	TGRSWT	.	Stepwise (Criteria: Probability-of-F-to-enter <= .050, Probability-of-F-to-remove >= .100).
3	TI	.	Stepwise (Criteria: Probability-of-F-to-enter <= .050, Probability-of-F-to-remove >= .100).

a. Dependent Variable: LOGNUM

Model Summary

Model	R	R Square	Adjusted R Square	Std. Error of the Estimate
1	.329[a]	.122	.121	.7615773
2	.427[b]	.182	.180	.7348470
3	.432[c]	.187	.184	.7348469

a. Predictors: (Constant), ST_DEPTH

b. Predictors: (Constant), ST_DEPTH, TGRSWT

c. Predictors: (Constant), ST_DEPTH, TGRSWT, TI

SPSS Output for Exercise 11.99

11.11 Residual Analysis: Checking the Regression Assumptions

When we apply regression analysis to a set of data, we never know for certain whether the assumptions of Section 11.1 are satisfied. How far can we deviate from the assumptions and still expect regression analysis to yield results that will have the reliability stated in this chapter? How can we detect departures (if they exist) from the assumptions, and what can we do about them? We provide some answers to these questions in this section.

Recall from Section 11.1 that for any given set of values of $x_1, x_2, \ldots, x_k$ we assume that the random error term ϵ has a normal probability distribution with mean equal to 0 and variance equal to σ^2. Also, we assume that the random errors are probabilistically independent. It is unlikely that these assumptions are ever satisfied exactly in a practical application of regression analysis. Fortunately, experience has shown that least squares regression analysis produces reliable statistical tests, confidence intervals, and prediction intervals as long as the departures from the assumptions are not too great. In this section we present some methods for determining whether the data indicate significant departures from the assumptions.

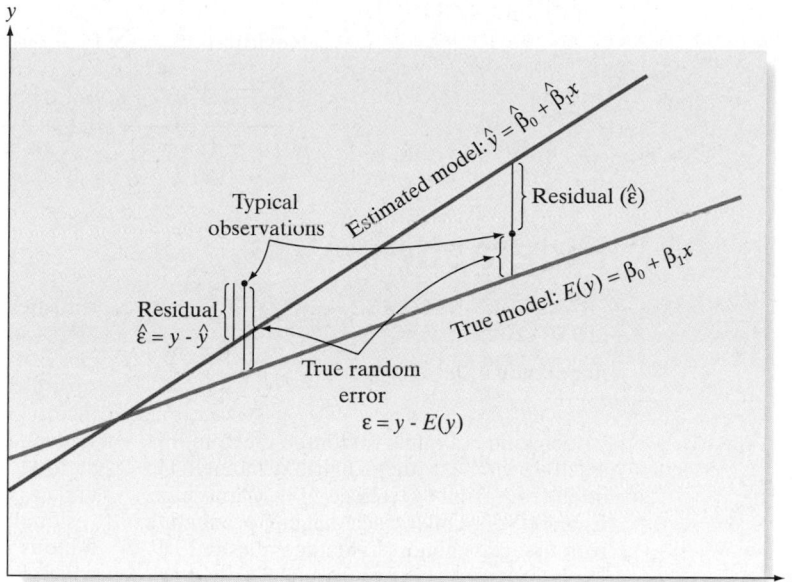

FIGURE 11.36

Actual random error ϵ and regression residual $\hat{\epsilon}$

Because the assumptions all concern the random error component, ϵ, of the model, the first step is to estimate the random error. Since the actual random error associated with a particular value of y is the difference between the actual y value and its unknown mean, we estimate the error by the difference between the actual y-value and the *estimated* mean. This estimated error is called the *regression residual*, or simply the **residual,** and is denoted by $\hat{\epsilon}$. The actual error ϵ and residual $\hat{\epsilon}$ are shown in Figure 11.36.

Definition 11.5

A **regression residual,** $\hat{\epsilon}$, is defined as the difference between an observed y value and its corresponding predicted value:

$$\hat{\epsilon} = (y - \hat{y}) = y - (\hat{\beta}_0 + \hat{\beta}_1 x_1 + \hat{\beta}_2 x_2 + \cdots + \hat{\beta}_k x_k)$$

Since the true mean of y (that is, the true regression model) is not known, the actual random error cannot be calculated. However, because the residual is based on the estimated mean (the least squares regression model), it can be calculated and used to estimate the random error and to check the regression assumptions. Such checks are generally referred to as **residual analyses.** Two useful properties of residuals are given in the next box.

Properties of Regression Residuals

1. The mean of the residuals is equal to 0. This property follows from the fact that the sum of the differences between the observed y values and their least squares predicted $\hat{y}$ values is equal to 0.

$$\sum(\text{Residuals}) = \sum(y - \hat{y}) = 0$$

2. The standard deviation of the residuals is equal to the standard deviation of the fitted regression model, s. This property follows from the fact that the sum of the squared residuals is equal to SSE, which when divided by the error degrees of freedom is equal to the variance of the fitted regression model, s^2. The square root of the variance is both the standard deviation of the residuals and the standard deviation of the regression model.

Continued

$$\sum (\text{Residuals})^2 = \sum (y - \hat{y})^2 = \text{SSE}$$

$$s = \sqrt{\frac{\sum(\text{Residuals})^2}{n - (k + 1)}} = \sqrt{\frac{\text{SSE}}{n - (k + 1)}}$$

Biography

FRANCIS J. ANSCOMBE (1918–2001)

Anscombe's Data

British citizen Frank Anscombe grew up in a small town near the English Channel. He attended Trinity College in Cambridge, England, on a merit scholarship, graduating with first class honors in mathematics in 1939. He later earned his master's degree in 1943. During World War II, Anscombe worked for the British Ministry of Supply, developing a mathematical solution for aiming antiaircraft rockets at German bombers and buzz bombs. Following the war, Anscombe worked at the Rothamsted Experimental Station, applying statistics to agriculture. There, he formed his appreciation for solving problems with social relevance. During his career as a professor of statistics, Anscombe served on the faculty of Cambridge, Princeton, and Yale Universities. He was a pioneer in the application of computers to statistical analysis and was one of the original developers of residual analysis in regression. Anscombe is famous for a paper he wrote in 1973, in which he showed that one regression model could be fit by four very different data sets ("Anscombe's data"). While Anscombe published 50 research articles on statistics, he also had serious interests in classical music, poetry, and art.

The following examples show how a graphical analysis of regression residuals can be used to verify the assumptions associated with the model and to support improvements to the model when the assumptions do not appear to be satisfied. Although the residuals can be calculated and plotted by hand, we rely on the statistical software for these tasks in the examples and exercises.

First, we demonstrate how a residual plot can detect a model in which the hypothesized relationship between $E(y)$ and an independent variable x is misspecified. The assumption of mean error of 0 is violated in these types of models.*

EXAMPLE 11.14
Analyzing the Residuals from the Electrical Usage Model

Problem   Refer to the problem of modeling the relationship between home size (x) and electrical usage (y) in Example 11.7 (p. 702). The data for $n = 10$ homes are repeated in Table 11.8. MINITAB printouts for a straight-line model and a quadratic model fitted to the data are shown in Figures 11.37(a) and 11.37(b), respectively. The residuals

 ELECTRIC

TABLE 11.8 Home Size–Electrical Usage Data

Size of Home, x (sq. ft.)	Monthly Usage, y (kilowatt-hours)
1,290	1,182
1,350	1,172
1,470	1,264
1,600	1,493
1,710	1,571
1,840	1,711
1,980	1,804
2,230	1,840
2,400	1,956
2,930	1,954

*For a misspecified model, the hypothesized mean of y, denoted by $E_h(y)$, will not equal the true mean of y, $E(y)$. Since $y = E_h(y) + \epsilon$, then $\epsilon = y - E_h(y)$ and $E(\epsilon) = E[y - E_h(y)] = E(y) - E_h(y) \neq 0$.

```
The regression equation is
USAGE = 579 + 0.540 SIZE


Predictor        Coef   SE Coef      T       P
Constant        578.9     167.0    3.47   0.008
SIZE          0.54030   0.08593    6.29   0.000


S = 133.438    R-Sq = 83.2%    R-Sq(adj) = 81.1%


Analysis of Variance

Source              DF        SS        MS       F       P
Regression           1    703957    703957   39.54   0.000
Residual Error       8    142445     17806
Total                9    846402


Obs   SIZE    USAGE     Fit  SE Fit  Residual  St Resid
  1   1290   1182.0  1275.9    66.0     -93.9     -0.81
  2   1350   1172.0  1308.3    62.1    -136.3     -1.15
  3   1470   1264.0  1373.2    55.0    -109.2     -0.90
  4   1600   1493.0  1443.4    48.6      49.6      0.40
  5   1710   1571.0  1502.8    44.7      60.2      0.54
  6   1840   1711.0  1573.1    42.3     137.9      1.09
  7   1980   1804.0  1648.7    43.1     155.3      1.23
  8   2230   1840.0  1783.8    51.8      56.2      0.46
  9   2400   1956.0  1875.7    61.5      80.3      0.68
 10   2930   1954.0  2162.0    99.6    -208.0     -2.34R
```

FIGURE 11.37a
MINITAB printout for
straight-line model of
electrical usage

R denotes an observation with a large standardized residual.

from these models are highlighted in the printouts. The residuals are then plotted on the vertical axis against the variable x, size of home, on the horizontal axis in Figures 11.38(a) and 11.38(b), respectively.

a. Verify that each residual is equal to the difference between the observed y value and the estimated mean value, $\hat{y}$.

b. Analyze the residual plots.

Solution

a. For the straight-line model the residual is calculated for the first y value as follows:

$$\hat{\epsilon} = (y - \hat{y}) = 1{,}182 - 1{,}275.9 = -93.9$$

where $\hat{y}$ is the first number in the column labeled **Fit** on the MINITAB printout in Figure 11.37(a). Similarly, the residual for the first y value using the quadratic model (Figure 11.37[b]) is

$$\hat{\epsilon} = 1{,}182 - 1{,}129.6 = 52.4$$

Both residuals agree (after rounding) with the first values given in the column labeled **Residual** in Figures 11.37(a) and 11.37(b), respectively. Although the residuals both correspond to the same observed y value, 1,182, they differ because the predicted mean value changes depending on whether the straight-line model or quadratic model is used. Similar calculations produce the remaining residuals.

```
The regression equation is
USAGE = - 1216 + 2.40 SIZE - 0.000450 SIZESQ


Predictor          Coef       SE Coef       T        P
Constant        -1216.1         242.8    -5.01    0.002
SIZE             2.3989        0.2458     9.76    0.000
SIZESQ      -0.00045004   0.00005908    -7.62    0.000


S = 46.8013    R-Sq = 98.2%    R-Sq(adj) = 97.7%


Analysis of Variance

Source          DF        SS       MS       F        P
Regression       2    831070   415535  189.71    0.000
Residual Error   7     15333     2190
Total            9    846402


Obs  SIZE   USAGE      Fit  SE Fit  Residual  St Resid
  1  1290  1182.0   1129.6    30.1      52.4      1.46
  2  1350  1172.0   1202.2    25.9     -30.2     -0.77
  3  1470  1264.0   1337.8    19.8     -73.8     -1.74
  4  1600  1493.0   1470.0    17.4      23.0      0.53
  5  1710  1571.0   1570.1    18.0       0.9      0.02
  6  1840  1711.0   1674.2    19.9      36.8      0.87
  7  1980  1804.0   1769.4    21.9      34.6      0.84
  8  2230  1840.0   1895.5    23.3     -55.5     -1.37
  9  2400  1956.0   1949.1    23.6       6.9      0.17
 10  2930  1954.0   1949.2    44.7       4.8      0.35 X
```

FIGURE 11.37b

MINITAB printout for quadratic model of electrical usage

X denotes an observation whose X value gives it large influence.

FIGURE 11.38a

MINITAB residual plot for straight-line model of electrical usage

b. The MINITAB plot of the residuals for the straight-line model (Figure 11.38a) reveals a nonrandom pattern. The residuals exhibit a curved shape, with the residuals for the small values of x below the horizontal 0 (mean of the residuals) line, the residuals corresponding to the middle values of x above the 0 line, and the residual

FIGURE 11.38b

MINITAB residual plot for quadratic model of electrical usage

for the largest value of x again below the 0 line. The indication is that the mean value of the random error ϵ *within* each of these ranges of x (small, medium, large) may not be equal to 0. Such a pattern usually indicates that curvature needs to be added to the model.

When the second-order term is added to the model, the nonrandom pattern disappears. In Figure 11.38(b), the residuals appear to be randomly distributed around the 0 line, as expected. Note, too, that the $\pm 2s$ standard deviation lines are at about ± 95 on the quadratic residual plot, compared to (about) ± 275 on the straight-line plot. The implication is that the quadratic model provides a considerably better model for predicting electrical usage.

Look Book The residual analysis verifies our conclusions from Example 11.7, where we found the t-test for the quadratic term, $\beta_2 x^2$, to be statistically significant.

Now Work Exercise 11.100a ▪

Residual analyses are also useful for detecting one or more observations that deviate significantly from the regression model. We expect approximately 95% of the residuals to fall within 2 standard deviations of the 0 line, and all or almost all of them to lie within 3 standard deviations of their mean of 0. Residuals that are extremely far from the 0 line, and disconnected from the bulk of the other residuals, are called *outliers* and should receive special attention from the regression analyst.

> **Definition 11.6**
>
> A residual that is larger than $3s$ (in absolute value) is considered to be an **outlier.**

EXAMPLE 11.15
Identifying Outliers

Problem Refer to Example 11.6 (page 696) in which we modeled the auction price y of a grandfather clock as a function of age x_1 and number of bidders x_2. The data for this example are repeated in Table 11.9, with one important difference: The auction price of the clock at the top of the second column has been changed from $2,131 to $1,131 (highlighted in Table 11.9). The interaction model

$$E(y) = \beta_0 + \beta_1 x_1 + \beta_2 x_2 + \beta_3 x_1 x_2$$

is again fit to these (modified) data, with the MINITAB printout shown in Figure 11.39. The residuals are shown highlighted in the printout and then plotted against the number of bidders, x_2, in Figure 11.40. Analyze the residual plot.

```
The regression equation is
PRICE = - 513 + 8.17 AGE + 19.9 NUMBIDS + 0.320 AGE_BIDS


Predictor      Coef   SE Coef      T       P
Constant     -512.8     665.9   -0.77   0.448
AGE           8.165     4.585    1.78   0.086
NUMBIDS       19.89     67.44    0.29   0.770
AGE_BIDS     0.3196    0.4790    0.67   0.510


S = 200.598   R-Sq = 72.9%   R-Sq(adj) = 70.0%


Analysis of Variance

Source             DF        SS       MS       F       P
Regression          3   3033587   1011196   25.13   0.000
Residual Error     28   1126703     40239
Total              31   4160290


Obs   AGE    PRICE      Fit   SE Fit   Residual   St Resid
  1   127   1235.0   1310.4    59.3      -75.4      -0.39
  2   115   1080.0   1105.9    62.1      -25.9      -0.14
  3   127    845.0    947.5    61.1     -102.5      -0.54
  4   150   1522.0   1322.5    37.1      199.5       1.01
  5   156   1047.0   1179.5    60.3     -132.5      -0.69
  6   182   1979.0   1831.9    82.9      147.1       0.81
  7   156   1822.0   1598.0    61.9      224.0       1.17
  8   132   1253.0   1185.8    39.7       67.2       0.34
  9   137   1297.0   1178.9    39.0      118.1       0.60
 10   113    946.0    913.9    58.6       32.1       0.17
 11   137   1713.0   1561.0    78.4      152.0       0.82
 12   117   1024.0   1072.6    53.1      -48.6      -0.25
 13   137   1147.0   1115.2    44.3       31.8       0.16
 14   153   1092.0   1149.2    59.0      -57.2      -0.30
 15   117   1152.0   1187.2    69.7      -35.2      -0.19
 16   126   1336.0   1117.6    43.4      218.4       1.12
 17   170   1131.0   1914.4   116.7     -783.4      -4.80R
 18   182   1550.0   1597.7    62.8      -47.7      -0.25
 19   162   1884.0   1598.3    57.0      285.7       1.49
 20   184   2041.0   1776.6    70.7      264.4       1.41
 21   143    845.0   1048.4    58.9     -203.4      -1.06
 22   159   1483.0   1421.8    40.6       61.2       0.31
 23   108   1055.0   1130.7    97.9      -75.7      -0.43
 24   175   1545.0   1522.7    55.4       22.3       0.12
 25   108    729.0    695.5    99.6       33.5       0.19
 26   179   1792.0   1642.7    57.6      149.3       0.78
 27   111   1175.0   1224.0   107.2      -49.0      -0.29
 28   187   1593.0   1651.3    68.6      -58.3      -0.31
 29   111    785.0    781.1    80.9        3.9       0.02
 30   115    744.0    822.7    75.5      -78.7      -0.42
 31   194   1356.0   1480.7   133.6     -124.7      -0.83 X
 32   168   1262.0   1374.0    57.7     -112.0      -0.58


R denotes an observation with a large standardized residual.
X denotes an observation whose X value gives it large influence.
```

FIGURE 11.39

MINITAB regression printout for altered grandfather clock data

GFCLOCKALT

TABLE 11.9 Altered Auction Price Data

Age, x_1 (years)	Number of Bidders, x_2	Auction Price, y ($)	Age, x_1 (years)	Number of Bidders, x_2	Auction Price, y ($)
127	13	1,235	170	14	1,131
115	12	1,080	182	8	1,550
127	7	845	162	11	1,884
150	9	1,522	184	10	2,041
156	6	1,047	143	6	845
182	11	1,979	159	9	1,483
156	12	1,822	108	14	1,055
132	10	1,253	175	8	1,545
137	9	1,297	108	6	729
113	9	946	179	9	1,792
137	15	1,713	111	15	1,175
117	11	1,024	187	8	1,593
137	8	1,147	111	7	785
153	6	1,092	115	7	744
117	13	1,152	194	5	1,356
126	10	1,336	168	7	1,262

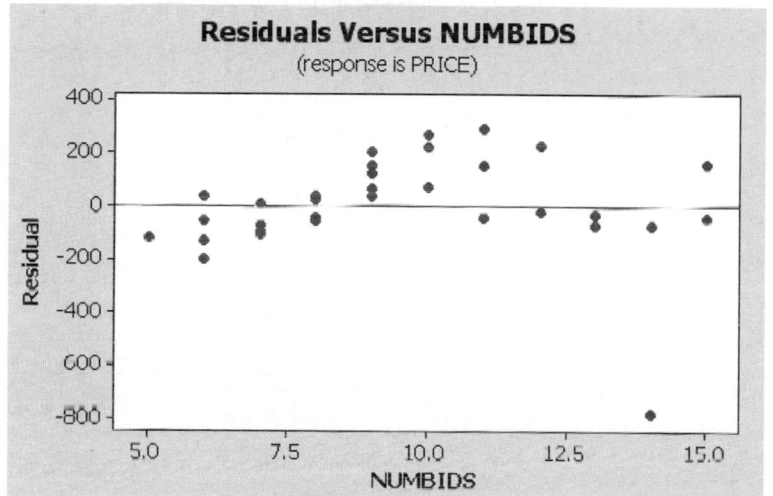

FIGURE 11.40

MINITAB residual plot for altered grandfather clock data

Solution The residual plot dramatically reveals the one altered measurement. Note that one of the two residuals at $x_2 = 14$ bidders falls more than 3 standard deviations below 0. Note that no other residual falls more than 2 standard deviations from 0.

What do we do with outliers once we identify them? First, we try to determine the cause. Were the data entered into the computer incorrectly? Was the observation recorded incorrectly when the data were collected? If so, we correct the observation and rerun the analysis. Another possibility is that the observation is not representative of the conditions we are trying to model. For example, in this case the low price may be attributable to extreme damage to the clock, or to a clock of inferior quality compared to the others. In these cases we probably would exclude the observation from the analysis. In many cases you may not be able to determine the cause of the outlier. Even so, you may want to rerun the regression analysis excluding the outlier in order to assess the effect of that observation on the results of the analysis.

```
The regression equation is
PRICE = 474 - 0.46 AGE - 114 NUMBIDS + 1.48 AGE_BIDS


Predictor      Coef    SE Coef       T       P
Constant      474.0      298.2     1.59   0.124
AGE           -0.465     2.107    -0.22   0.827
NUMBIDS     -114.12      31.23    -3.65   0.001
AGE_BIDS      1.4781     0.2295    6.44   0.000


S = 85.8286    R-Sq = 95.2%    R-Sq(adj) = 94.7%


Analysis of Variance

Source          DF         SS         MS        F       P
Regression       3    3933417    1311139   177.99   0.000
Residual Error  27     198897       7367
Total           30    4132314
```

FIGURE 11.41

MINITAB regression printout when outlier is deleted

FIGURE 11.42

MINITAB residual plot when outlier is deleted

Figure 11.41 shows the printout when the outlier observation is excluded from the grandfather clock analysis, and Figure 11.42 shows the new plot of the residuals against the number of bidders. Now only one of the residuals lies beyond 2 standard deviations from 0, and none of them lies beyond 3 standard deviations. Also, the model statistics indicate a much better model without the outlier. Most notably, the standard deviation (s) has decreased from 200.6 to 85.83, indicating a model that will provide more precise estimates and predictions (narrower confidence and prediction intervals) for clocks that are similar to those in the reduced sample.

Look Back Remember that if the outlier is removed from the analysis when in fact it belongs to the same population as the rest of the sample, the resulting model may provide misleading estimates and predictions.

Now Work Exercise 11.100c

Outlier analysis is another example of testing the assumption that the expected (mean) value of the random error ϵ is 0, since this assumption is in doubt for the error terms corresponding to the outliers. The next example in this section checks the assumption of the normality of the random error component.

EXAMPLE 11.16

Using Residuals to Check for Normal Errors

Problem   Refer to Example 11.15. Analyze the distribution of the residuals in the grandfather clock example, both before and after the outlier residual is removed. Determine whether the assumption of a normally distributed error term is reasonable.

Solution   A histogram and normal probability plot for the two sets of residuals are constructed using MINITAB and are shown in Figures 11.43 and 11.44. Note that the outlier appears to skew the histogram in Figure 11.43, whereas the histogram in Figure 11.44 appears to be more mound-shaped. Similarly, the pattern of residuals in the normal probability plot in Figure 11.44 (outlier deleted) is more nearly a straight line than the pattern in Figure 11.43 (outlier included). Although the graphs do not provide formal statistical tests of normality, they do provide a descriptive display. In this example the normality assumption appears to be more plausible after the outlier is removed. Consult the references for methods to conduct statistical tests of normality using the residuals.

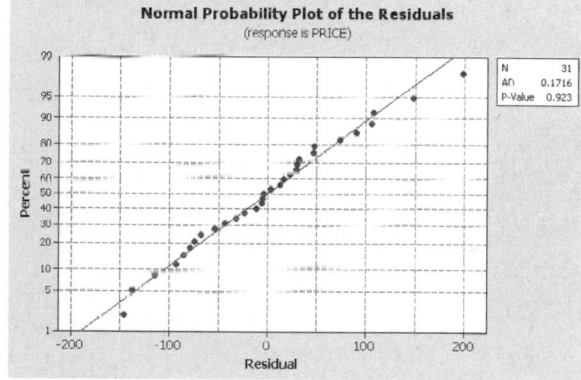

FIGURE 11.43
MINITAB graphs of regression residuals for grandfather clock model (outlier included)

FIGURE 11.44
MINITAB graphs of regression residuals for grandfather clock model (outlier deleted)

Now Work Exercise 11.100d

Of the four assumptions in Section 11.1, the assumption that the random error is normally distributed is the least restrictive when we apply regression analysis in practice—that is, moderate departures from a normal distribution have very little effect on the validity of the statistical tests, confidence intervals, and prediction intervals presented in this chapter. In this case, we say that regression analysis is **robust** with respect to nonnormal errors. However, great departures from normality cast doubt on any inferences derived from the regression analysis.

Residual plots can also be used to detect violations of the assumption of constant error variance. For example, a plot of the residuals versus the predicted value $\hat{y}$ may display one of the patterns shown in Figure 11.45. In these figures, the range in values of the residuals increases (or decreases) as $\hat{y}$ increases, thus indicating that the variance of the random error, ϵ, becomes larger (or smaller) as the estimate of $E(y)$ increases in value. Since $E(y)$ depends on the x values in the model, this implies that the variance of ϵ is not constant for all settings of the x's.

In the final example of this section, we demonstrate how to use this plot to detect a nonconstant variance and suggest a useful remedy.

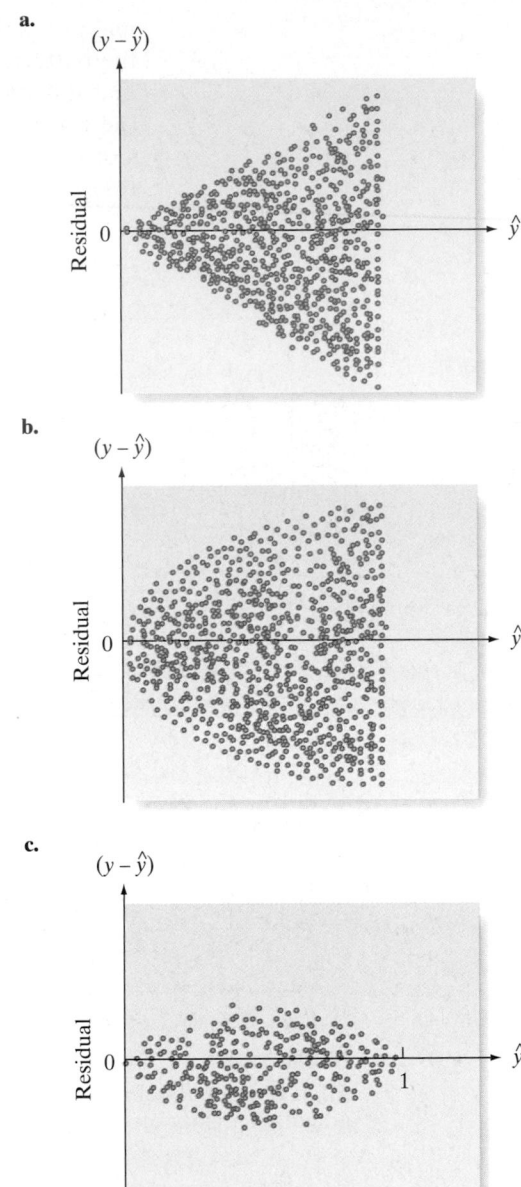

FIGURE 11.45
Residual plots showing changes in the variance of ϵ

**EXAMPLE
11.17**

Using Residuals to Check Equal Variances

Problem   The data in Table 11.10 are the salaries, y, and years of experience, x, for a sample of 50 social workers. The first-order model $E(y) = \beta_0 + \beta_1 x$ was fitted to the data using SPSS. The SPSS printout is shown in Figure 11.46, followed by a plot of the residuals versus $\hat{y}$ in Figure 11.47. Interpret the results. Make model modifications, if necessary.

Solution   The SPSS printout, Figure 11.46, suggests that the first-order model provides an adequate fit to the data. The R^2-value indicates that the model explains 78.7% of the sample variation in salaries. The t-value for testing β_1, 13.31, is highly significant (p-value ≈ 0) and indicates that the model contributes information for the prediction of

SOCWORK

TABLE 11.10 Salary Data for Example 11.17

Years of Experience, x	Salary, y	Years of Experience, x	Salary, y	Years of Experience, x	Salary, y
7	$26,075	21	$43,628	28	$99,139
28	79,370	4	16,105	23	52,624
23	65,726	24	65,644	17	50,594
18	41,983	20	63,022	25	53,272
19	62,308	20	47,780	26	65,343
15	41,154	15	38,853	19	46,216
24	53,610	25	66,537	16	54,288
13	33,697	25	67,447	3	20,844
2	22,444	28	64,785	12	32,586
8	32,562	26	61,581	23	71,235
20	43,076	27	70,678	20	36,530
21	56,000	20	51,301	19	52,745
18	58,667	18	39,346	27	67,282
7	22,210	1	24,833	25	80,931
2	20,521	26	65,929	12	32,303
18	49,727	20	41,721	11	38,371
11	33,233	26	82,641		

Model Summary[b]

Model	R	R Square	Adjusted R Square	Std. Error of the Estimate
1	.887[a]	.787	.782	8642.441

a. Predictors: (Constant), ESP

b. Dependent Variable: SALARY

ANOVA[b]

Model		Sum of Squares	df	Mean Square	F	Sig.
1	Regression	1.3E+10	1	1.324E+10	177.257	.000[a]
	Residual	3.6E+09	48	74691793.28		
	Total	1.7E+10	49			

a. Predictors: (Constant), ESP

b. Dependent Variable: SALARY

Coefficients[a]

Model		Unstandardized Coefficients		Standardized Coefficients	t	Sig.
		B	Std. Error	Beta		
1	(Constant)	11360.72	3160.317		3.597	.001
	ESP	2141.381	160.839	.887	13.314	.000

a. Dependent Variable: SALARY

FIGURE 11.46

SPSS regression printout for first-order model of salary

y. However, an examination of the residuals plotted against $\hat{y}$ (Figure 11.47) reveals a potential problem. Note the "cone" shape of the residual variability; the size of the residuals increases as the estimated mean salary increases, implying that the constant variance assumption is violated.

One way to stabilize the variance of ϵ is to refit the model using a transformation on the dependent variable *y*. With economic data (e.g., salaries) a useful **variance-stabilizing transformation** is the natural logarithm of *y*, denoted $\ln(y)$.* We fit the model

$$\ln(y) = \beta_0 + \beta_1 x + \epsilon$$

to the data of Table 11.10. Figure 11.48 shows the SPSS regression analysis printout for the $n = 50$ measurements, while Figure 11.49 shows a plot of the residuals from the log model.

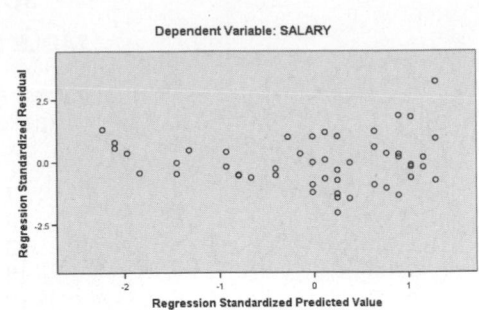

FIGURE 11.47
SPSS residual plot for first-order model of salary

Model Summary^b

Model	R	R Square	Adjusted R Square	Std. Error of the Estimate
1	.929^a	.864	.861	.1541127

a. Predictors: (Constant), ESP

b. Dependent Variable: LNSALARY

ANOVA^b

Model		Sum of Squares	df	Mean Square	F	Sig.
1	Regression	7.212	1	7.212	303.660	.000^a
	Residual	1.140	48	.024		
	Total	8.352	49			

a. Predictors: (Constant), ESP

b. Dependent Variable: LNSALARY

Coefficients^a

Model		Unstandardized Coefficients		Standardized Coefficients	t	Sig.
		B	Std. Error	Beta		
1	(Constant)	9.841	.056		174.631	.000
	ESP	.050	.003	.929	17.426	.000

a. Dependent Variable: LNSALARY

FIGURE 11.48
SPSS regression printout for model of log salary

---

*Other variance-stabilizing transformations that are used successfully in practice are $\sqrt{y}$ and $\sin^{-1}\sqrt{y}$. Consult the references for more details on these transformations.

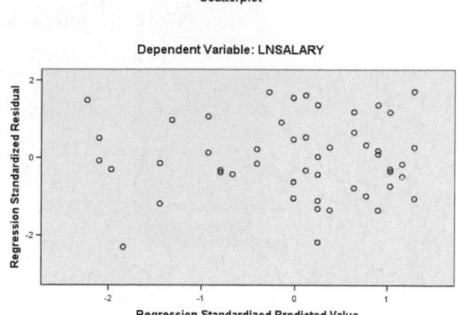

FIGURE 11.49
SPSS residual plot for model
of log salary

You can see that the logarithmic transformation has stabilized the error variances. Note that the cone shape is gone; there is no apparent tendency of the residual variance to increase as mean salary increases. We therefore are confident that inferences using the logarithmic model are more reliable than those using the untransformed model.

Now Work Exercise 11.100b

Residual analysis is a useful tool for the regression analyst, not only to check the assumptions, but also to provide information about how the model can be improved. A summary of the residual analyses presented in this section to check the assumption that the random error ϵ is normally distributed with mean 0 and constant variance is presented in the next box.

Steps in a Residual Analysis

1. Check for a misspecified model by plotting the residuals against each of the quantitative independent variables. Analyze each plot, looking for a curvilinear trend. This shape signals the need for a quadratic term in the model. Try a second order term in the variable against which the residuals are plotted.

2. Examine the residual plots for outliers. Draw lines on the residual plots at 2- and 3-standard-deviation distances below and above the 0 line. Examine residuals outside the 3-standard-deviation lines as potential outliers, and check to see that approximately 5% of the residuals exceed the 2-standard-deviation lines. Determine whether each outlier can be explained as an error in data collection or transcription, or corresponds to a member of a population different from that of the remainder of the sample, or simply represents an unusual observation. If the observation is determined to be an error, fix it or remove it. Even if you can't determine the cause; you may want to rerun the regression analysis without the observation to determine its effect on the analysis.

3. Check for nonnormal errors by plotting a frequency distribution of the residuals, using a stem-and-leaf display or a histogram. Check to see if obvious departures from normality exist. Extreme skewness of the frequency distribution may be due to outliers or could indicate the need for a transformation of the dependent variable. (Normalizing transformations are beyond the scope of this book, but you can find information in the references.)

4. Check for unequal error variances by plotting the residuals against the predicted values, $\hat{y}$. If you detect a cone-shaped pattern or some other pattern that indicates that the variance of ϵ is not constant, refit the model using an appropriate variance-stabilizing transformation on y, such as $\ln(y)$. (Consult the references for other useful variance-stabilizing transformations.)

Residuals

Using the TI-83/TI-84 Graphing Calculator

Plotting Residuals

When computing a regression equation on the TI-84/TI-83, the residuals are automatically computed and saved to a list called **RESID. RESID** can be found under the **LIST menu** (**2nd STAT**).

Step 1   *Enter the data*

> Press **STAT** and select **1:Edit**
> Note: If the list already contains data, clear the old data. Use the up arrow to highlight "**L1**" or "**L2**".
> Press **CLEAR ENTER.**
> Use the **ARROW** and **ENTER** keys to enter the data set into **L1** and **L2.**

Step 2   *Compute the regression equation*

> Press **STAT** and highlight **CALC**
> Press **4** for **LinReg(ax + b)**
> Press **ENTER**

Step 3   *Set up the data plot*

> Press **Y=** and **CLEAR** all functions from the Y registers
> Press **2nd Y=** for **STATPLOT**
> Press **1** for **Plot1**
> Set the cursor so that **ON** is flashing and press **ENTER.**
> For **Type**, use the **ARROW** and **ENTER** keys to highlight and select the scatterplot (first icon in the first row).
> Move the cursor to **Xlist** and choose the column containing the *x*-data.
> Move the cursor to **Ylist.** Press **2nd STAT** for **LIST.** Use the down arrow to highlight the listname **RESID** and press **ENTER**

Step 4   *View the scatterplot of the residuals*

> Press **ZOOM 9** for **ZoomStat**

Example   The figures below show a table of data entered on the TI-84/TI-83 and the scatterplot of the residuals obtained using the steps given above.

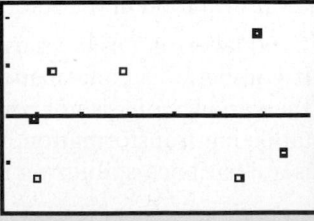

STATISTICS IN ACTION REVISITED

A Residual Analysis for the Road Cost Model

In the previous Statistics in Action Revisited section (p. 740), we found the interaction model, $E(y) = \beta_0 + \beta_1 x_1 + \beta_3 x_2 + \beta_4 x_1 x_2$, to be both a statistically and practically useful model for predicting the cost (y) of a road construction contract. Recall that the two independent variables are the DOT engineer's estimate of cost (x_1) and bid status, where $x_2 = 1$ if a fixed bid and $x_2 = 0$ if a competitive bid. Before actually using the model in practice, we need to examine the residuals to be sure that the standard regression assumptions are reasonably satisfied.

Figures SIA11.9 and SIA11.10 are MINITAB graphs of the residuals from the interaction model. The histogram shown in Figure SIA11.9 appears to be approximately normally distributed; consequently the assumption of normal errors is reasonably satisfied. The scatterplot of the residuals against $\hat{y}$ shown in Figure SIA11.10, however, shows a distinct "funnel" pattern; this indicates that the assumption of a constant error variance is likely to be violated. One way to modify the model to satisfy this assumption is to use a variance-stabilizing transformation (such as the natural log) on cost (y). When both the y and x variables in a regression equation are economic variables (prices, costs, salaries, etc.), it is often advantageous to transform the x-variable also. Consequently, we'll modify the model by making a log transform on both cost (y) and DOTEST (x_1).

Our modified (log-log) interaction model takes the form

$$E(y^*) = \beta_0 + \beta_1 x_1^* + \beta_2 x_2 + \beta_3(x_1^*)x_2$$

where $y^* = \ln(\text{COST})$ and $x_1^* = \ln(\text{DOTEST})$. The MINITAB printout for this model is shown in Figure SIA11.11, followed by graphs of the residuals in Figures SIA11.12 and SIA11.13. The histogram shown in Figure SIA11.12 is approximately normal, and more important, the scatterplot of the residuals shown in Figure SIA11.13 has no distinct trend. It appears that the log transformations successfully stabilized the error variance. Note, however, that the t-test for the interaction term in the model (highlighted in Figure SIA11.11) is no longer statistically significant (p-value = .420). Consequently, we will drop the interaction term from the model and use the simpler modified model,

$$E(y^*) = \beta_0 + \beta_1 x_1^* + \beta_2 x_2$$

to predict road contract cost.

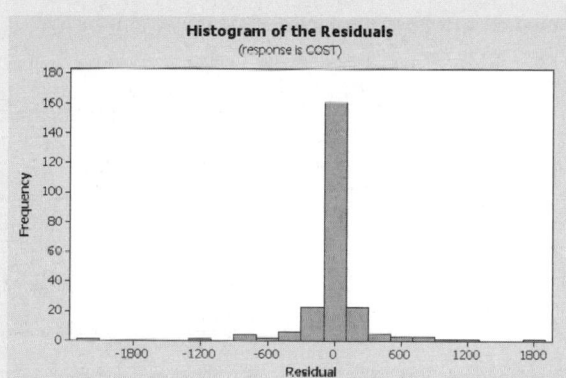

Figure SIA11.9

MINITAB histogram of residuals from interaction model for road cost

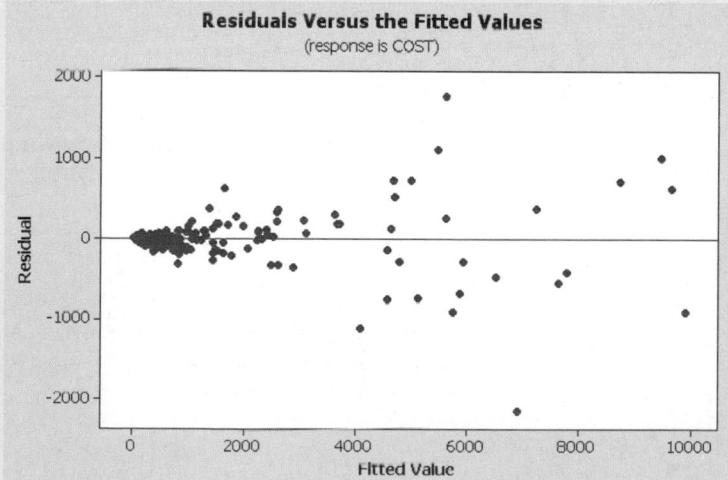

Figure SIA11.10

MINITAB plot of residuals versus predicted values from interaction model for road cost

Continued

```
The regression equation is
LNCOST = - 0.162 + 1.01 LNDOTEST + 0.324 STATUS - 0.0176 STA_LNDOT


Predictor       Coef    SE Coef       T       P
Constant    -0.16188    0.05193   -3.12   0.002
LNDOTEST     1.00780    0.00798  126.23   0.000
STATUS        0.3243     0.1356    2.39   0.018
STA_LNDOT   -0.01762    0.02181   -0.81   0.420


S = 0.154922   R-Sq = 98.8%   R-Sq(adj) = 98.7%


Analysis of Variance

Source            DF       SS       MS         F       P
Regression         3   439.64   146.55   6105.87   0.000
Residual Error   231     5.54     0.02
Total            234   445.18
```

Figure SIA11.11

MINITAB regression printout for modified (log-log) model of road construction cost

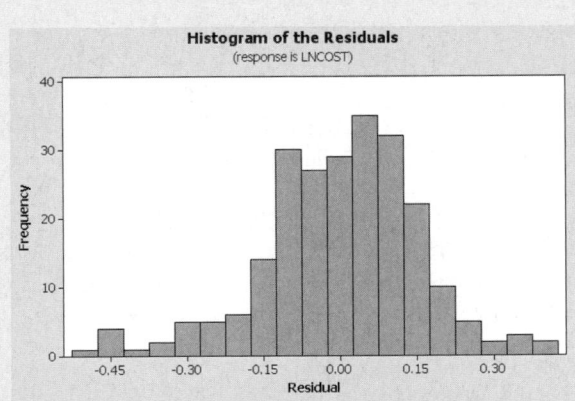

Figure SIA11.12

MINITAB histogram of residuals from modified (log-log) model for road construction cost

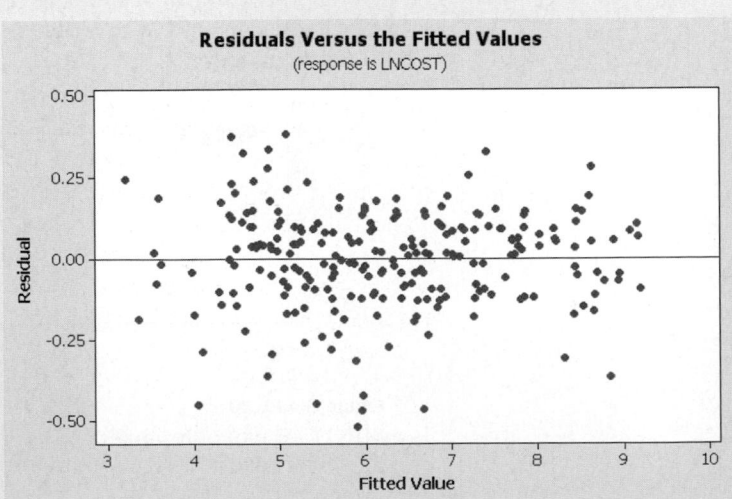

Figure SIA11.13

MINITAB plot of residuals versus predicted values from modified (log-log) model for road construction cost

11.12 Some Pitfalls: Estimability, Multicollinearity, and Extrapolation

You should be aware of several potential problems when constructing a prediction model for some response y. A few of the most important are discussed in this final section.

Problem 1   **Parameter Estimability**   Suppose you want to fit a model relating annual crop yield y to the total expenditure for fertilizer x. We propose the first-order model

$$E(y) = \beta_0 + \beta_1 x$$

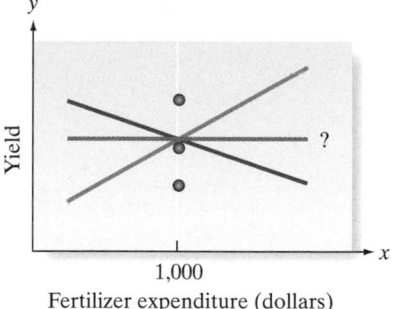

Now suppose we have three years of data and $1,000 is spent on fertilizer each year. The data are shown in Figure 11.50. You can see the problem: The parameters of the model cannot be estimated when all the data are concentrated at a single x value. Recall that it takes two points (x-values) to fit a straight line. Thus, the parameters are not estimable when only one x is observed.

A similar problem would occur if we attempted to fit the quadratic model

FIGURE 11.50

Yield and fertilizer expenditure data: Three years

$$E(y) = \beta_0 + \beta_1 x + \beta_2 x^2$$

to a set of data for which only one or two different x-values were observed (see Figure 11.51). At least three different x-values must be observed before a quadratic model can be fit to a set of data (that is, before all three parameters are estimable).

In general, the number of levels of observed x-values must be one more than the order of the polynomial in x that you want to fit.

For controlled experiments, the researcher can select one of the experimental designs in Chapter 8 that will permit estimation of the model parameters.

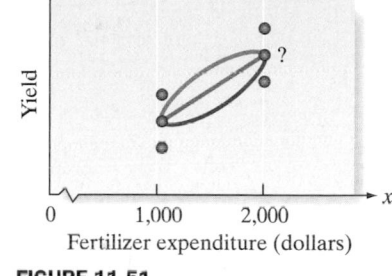

FIGURE 11.51

Only two x values observed: Quadratic model is not estimable

Even when the values of the independent variables cannot be controlled by the researcher, the independent variables are almost always observed at a sufficient number of levels to permit estimation of the model parameters. When the statistical software you use suddenly refuses to fit a model, however, the problem is probably inestimable parameters.

Problem 2   **Multicollinearity**   Often, two or more of the independent variables used in a regression model contribute redundant information—that is, the independent variables are correlated with each other. For example, suppose we want to construct a model to predict the gas mileage rating of a truck as a function of its load, x_1 (in tons), and the horsepower, x_2 (in foot-pounds per second), of its engine. We would expect heavy loads to require greater horsepower and to result in lower mileage ratings. Thus, although both x_1 and x_2 contribute information for the prediction of mileage rating, y, some of the information is overlapping because x_1 and x_2 are correlated.

When the independent variables are correlated, we say *multicollinearity* exists. In practice, it is not uncommon to observe correlations among the independent variables. However, a few problems arise when serious multicollinearity is present in the regression variables.

Definition 11.7

Multicollinearity exists when two or more of the independent variables used in regression are correlated.

First, high correlations among the independent variables increase the likelihood of rounding errors in the calculations of the β estimates, standard errors, and so forth. Second, and more important, the regression results may be confusing and misleading. Consider the model for gasoline mileage rating (y) of a truck:

$$E(y) = \beta_0 + \beta_1 x_1 + \beta_2 x_2$$

where x_1 = load and x_2 = horsepower. Fitting the model to a sample data set, we might find that the t-tests for testing β_1 and β_2 are both nonsignificant at the α = .05 level, while the F-test for H_0: $\beta_1 = \beta_2 = 0$ is highly significant (p = .001). The tests may seem to be contradictory, but really they are not. The t-tests indicate that the contribution of one variable, say x_1 = load, is not significant after the effect of x_2 = horsepower has been accounted for (because x_2 is also in the model). The significant F-test, on the other hand, tells us that at least one of the two variables is making a contribution to the prediction of y (i.e., either β_1 or β_2 or both differ from 0). In fact, both are probably contributing, but the contribution of one overlaps with that of the other.

Multicollinearity can also have an effect on the signs of the parameter estimates. More specifically, a value of β_i may have the opposite sign from what is expected. In the truck gasoline mileage example, we expect heavy loads to result in lower mileage ratings, and we expect higher horsepowers to result in lower mileage ratings; consequently, we expect the signs of both the parameter estimates to be negative. Yet we may actually see a positive value of β_1 and be tempted to claim that heavy loads result in *higher* mileage ratings. This is the danger of interpreting a β coefficient when the independent variables are correlated. Because the variables contribute redundant information, the effect of x_1 = load on y = mileage rating is measured only partially by β_1.

How can you avoid the problems of multicollinearity in regression analysis? One way is to conduct a designed experiment (Chapter 8) so that the levels of the x-variables are uncorrelated. Unfortunately, time and cost constraints may prevent you from collecting data in this manner. Consequently, most data are collected observationally. Since observational data frequently consist of correlated independent variables, you will need to recognize when multicollinearity is present and, if necessary, make modifications in the regression analysis.

Several methods are available for detecting multicollinearity in regression. A simple technique is to calculate the coefficient of correlation, r, between each pair of independent variables in the model and use the procedure outlined in Section 10.6 to test for significantly correlated variables. If one or more of the r-values is statistically different from 0, the variables in question are correlated, and a multicollinearity problem may exist.* Other indications of the presence of multicollinearity include those mentioned above—namely, nonsignificant t-tests for the individual parameter estimates when the F-test for overall model adequacy is significant, and estimates with opposite signs from what is expected.†

Detecting Multicollinearity in the Regression Model

1. Significant correlations between pairs of independent variables
2. Nonsignificant t-tests for all (or nearly all) of the individual β parameters when the F-test for overall model adequacy is significant
3. Signs opposite from what is expected in the estimated β parameters

---

*Remember that r measures only the pairwise correlation between x-values. Three variables, x_1, x_2, and x_3, may be highly correlated as a group but may not exhibit large pairwise correlations. Thus, multicollinearity may be present even when all pairwise correlations are not significantly different from 0.
†More formal methods for detecting multicollinearity, such as variance-inflation factors (VIFs), are available. Independent variables with a VIF of 10 or above are usually considered to be highly correlated with one or more of the other independent variables in the model. Calculation of VIFs are beyond the scope of this introductory text. Consult the chapter references for a discussion of VIFs and other formal methods of detecting multicollinearity.

**EXAMPLE
11.18**
Detecting
Multicollinearity

Problem   The Federal Trade Commission (FTC) annually ranks varieties of domestic cigarettes according to their tar, nicotine, and carbon monoxide contents. The U.S. Surgeon General considers each of these three substances hazardous to a smoker's health. Past studies have shown that increases in the tar and nicotine contents of a cigarette are accompanied by an increase in the carbon monoxide emitted from the cigarette smoke. Table 11.11 presents data on tar, nicotine, and carbon monoxide contents (in milligrams) and weight (in grams) for a sample of 25 (filter) brands tested in a recent year. Suppose we want to model carbon monoxide content, y, as a function of tar content, x_1, nicotine content, x_2, and weight, x_3, using the model

$$E(y) = \beta_0 + \beta_1 x_1 + \beta_2 x_2 + \beta_3 x_3$$

The model is fit to the 25 data points in Table 11.11, and a portion of the MINITAB printout is shown in Figure 11.52. Examine the printout. Do you detect any signs of multicollinearity?

Solution   First, note that the F-test for overall model utility is highly significant. The test statistic ($F = 78.98$) and observed significance level (p-value = .000) are highlighted on the MINITAB printout, Figure 11.52. Therefore, at, say $\alpha = .01$, we can conclude that at least one of the parameters, β_1, β_2, or β_3, in the model is nonzero. The t-tests for two of three individual β's, however, are nonsignificant. (The p-values for these tests are shaded on the printout.) Unless tar (x_1) is the only one of the three variables useful for predicting carbon monoxide content, these results are the first indication of a potential multicollinearity problem.

The negative values for β_2 and β_3 (highlighted on the printout) are a second clue to the presence of multicollinearity. From past studies, the FTC expects carbon monoxide content (y) to increase when either nicotine content (x_2) or weight (x_3) increases—

 FTC

TABLE 11.11 FTC Cigarette Data for Example 11.18

Tar (x_1)	Nicotine (x_2)	Weight (x_3)	Carbon Monoxide (y)
14.1	.86	.9853	13.6
16.0	1.06	1.0938	16.6
29.8	2.03	1.1650	23.5
8.0	.67	.9280	10.2
4.1	.40	.9462	5.4
15.0	1.04	.8885	15.0
8.8	.76	1.0267	9.0
12.4	.95	.9225	12.3
16.6	1.12	.9372	16.3
14.9	1.02	.8858	15.4
13.7	1.01	.9643	13.0
15.1	.90	.9316	14.4
7.8	.57	.9705	10.0
11.4	.78	1.1240	10.2
9.0	.74	.8517	9.5
1.0	.13	.7851	1.5
17.0	1.26	.9186	18.5
12.8	1.08	1.0395	12.6
15.8	.96	.9573	17.5
4.5	.42	.9106	4.9
14.5	1.01	1.0070	15.9
7.3	.61	.9806	8.5
8.6	.69	.9693	10.6
15.2	1.02	.9496	13.9
12.0	.82	1.1184	14.9

Source: Federal Trade Commission

Regression Analysis: CO versus TAR, NICOTINE, WEIGHT

```
The regression equation is
CO = 3.20 + 0.963 TAR - 2.63 NICOTINE - 0.13 WEIGHT


Predictor      Coef   SE Coef       T       P
Constant      3.202     3.462    0.93   0.365
TAR          0.9626    0.2422    3.97   0.001
NICOTINE     -2.632     3.901   -0.67   0.507
WEIGHT       -0.130     3.885   -0.03   0.974


S = 1.44573    R-Sq = 91.9%    R-Sq(adj) = 90.7%


Analysis of Variance

Source          DF      SS      MS      F      P
Regression       3  495.26  165.09  78.98  0.000
Residual Error  21   43.89    2.09
```

Correlations: TAR, NICOTINE, WEIGHT

```
             TAR  NICOTINE
NICOTINE   0.977
           0.000

WEIGHT     0.491     0.500
           0.013     0.011


Cell Contents: Pearson correlation
               P-Value
```

FIGURE 11.52
MINITAB printout for model
of CO content, Example 11.18

that is, the FTC expects *positive* relationships between y and x_2 and between y and x_3, not negative ones.

All signs indicate that a serious multicollinearity problem exists.

Look Back To confirm our suspicions, we had MINITAB produce the coefficient of correlation, r, for each of the three pairs of independent variables in the model. The resulting output is shown (highlighted) at the bottom of Figure 11.52. You can see that tar (x_1) and nicotine (x_2) are highly correlated ($r = .977$) while weight (x_3) is moderately correlated with the other two x's ($r \approx .5$). All three correlations have p-values of .01 or lower; consequently, all three are significantly different from 0 at, say, $\alpha = .05$.

Now Work Exercise 11.101

Once you have detected that multicollinearity exists, there are several alternative measures available for solving the problem. The appropriate measure to take depends on the severity of the multicollinearity and the ultimate goal of the regression analysis.

Some researchers, when confronted with highly correlated independent variables, choose to include only one of the correlated variables in the final model. If you are interested only in using the model for estimation and prediction (step 6), you may decide not to drop any of the independent variables from the model. In the presence of multicollinearity, we have seen that it is dangerous to interpret the individual β parameters. However, confidence intervals for $E(y)$ and prediction intervals for y generally remain unaffected *as long as the values of the x's used to predict y follow the same pattern of multicollinearity exhibited in the sample data*—that is, you must take strict care to ensure that the values of the x-variables fall within the range of the sample data.

Solutions to Some Problems Created by Multicollinearity in Regression*

1. Drop one or more of the correlated independent variables from the model. One way to decide which variables to keep in the model is to employ stepwise regression (Section 11.10).

2. If you decide to keep all the independent variables in the model,
   a. Avoid making inferences about the individual β parameters based on the t-tests.
   b. Restrict inferences about $E(y)$ and future y values to values of the x's that fall within the range of the sample data.

Problem 3   **Prediction Outside the Experimental Region**   Many research economists had developed highly technical models to relate the state of the economy to various economic indices and other independent variables. Many of these models were multiple regression models, where, for example, the dependent variable y might be next year's gross domestic product (GDP) and the independent variables might include this year's rate of inflation, this year's consumer price index (CPI), and so on. In other words, the model might be constructed to predict next year's economy using this year's knowledge.

Unfortunately, these models were almost all unsuccessful in predicting the recession in the early 1970s and the late 1990s. What went wrong? One of the problems was that many of the regression models were used to **extrapolate** (i.e., predict y-values of the independent variables that were outside the region in which the model was developed). For example, the inflation rate in the late 1960s, when the models were developed, ranged from 6% to 8%. When the double-digit inflation of the early 1970s became a reality, some researchers attempted to use the same models to predict future growth in GDP. As you can see in Figure 11.53, the model may be very accurate for predicting y when x is in the range of experimentation, but the use of the model outside that range is a dangerous practice.

Problem 4   **Correlated Errors**   Another problem associated with using a regression model to predict a variable y based on independent variables $x_1, x_2, \ldots, x_k$ arises from the fact that the data are frequently *time series* that is, the values of both the dependent and independent variables are observed sequentially over a period of time. The observations tend to be correlated over time, which in turn often causes the prediction errors of the regression model to be correlated. Thus, the assumption of independent errors is violated, and the model tests and prediction intervals are no longer valid. One solution to this problem is to construct a **time series model;** time series analysis is the subject of Chapter 13.

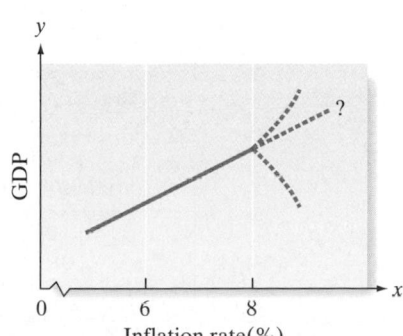

FIGURE 11.53

Using a regression model outside the experimental region

*Several other solutions are available. For example, in the case where higher-order regression models are fit, the analyst may want to code the independent variables so that higher-order terms (e.g., x^2) for a particular x-variable are not highly correlated with x. One transformation that works is $z = (x - \bar{x})/s$. Other, more sophisticated procedures for addressing multicollinearity (such as *ridge regression*) are beyond the scope of the text. Consult the references at the end of this chapter.

Exercises 11.100–11.109

Learning the Mechanics

11.100 Identify the problem(s) in each of the residual plots
NW shown at the bottom of the page.

11.101 Consider fitting the multiple regression model
NW

$$E(y) = \beta_0 + \beta_1 x_1 + \beta_2 x_2 + \beta_3 x_3 + \beta_4 x_4 + \beta_5 x_5$$

A matrix of correlations for all pairs of independent variables is given below. Do you detect a multicollinearity problem? Explain.

	x_1	x_2	x_3	x_4	x_5
x_1	—	.17	.02	−.23	.19
x_2		—	.45	.93	.02
x_3			—	.22	−.01
x_4				—	.86
x_5					—

Applying the Concepts—Basic

11.102 **Factors identifying urban counties.** Refer to the *Professional Geographer* (Feb. 2000) study of urban and rural counties in the western United States, Exercise 11.13 (p. 682). Recall that six independent variables—total county population (x_1), population density (x_2), population concentration (x_3), population growth (x_4), proportion of county land in farms (x_5), and 5-year change in agricultural land base (x_6)—were used to model the urban/rural rating (y) of a county. Prior to running the multiple regression analysis, the researchers were concerned about possible multi-

collinearity in the data. Below is a correlation matrix (i.e., a table of correlations between all pairs of the independent variables).

Independent variable	x_1	x_2	x_3	x_4	x_5
x_1: Total population					
x_2: Population density	.20				
x_3: Population concentration	.45	.43			
x_4: Population growth	−.05	−.14	−.01		
x_5: Farm land	−.16	−.15	−.07	−.20	
x_6: Agricultural change	−.12	−.12	−.22	−.06	−.06

Source: Berry, K. A. et al. "Interpreting What Is Rural and Urban for Western U.S. Counties." *Professional Geographer,* Vol. 52, No. 1, Feb. 2000 (Table 2).

a. Based on the correlation matrix, is there any evidence of extreme multicollinearity?
b. Refer to the multiple regression results in the table given in Exercise 11.13 (p. 682). Based on the reported tests, is there any evidence of extreme multicollinearity?

11.103 **Global warming and foreign investments.** Refer to the *Journal of World-Systems Research* (Summer 2003) study of the link between foreign investments and carbon dioxide emissions, Exercise 11.14 (p. 682). Recall that the researchers modeled the annual level (y) of CO_2 emissions as a function of seven independent variables for $n = 66$ developing countries. A matrix giving the correlation (r) for each pair of independent variables is shown on p. 767 (top). Identify the independent variables that are highly correlated. What problems may result from including these highly correlated variables in the regression model?

a.

b.

c.

d.

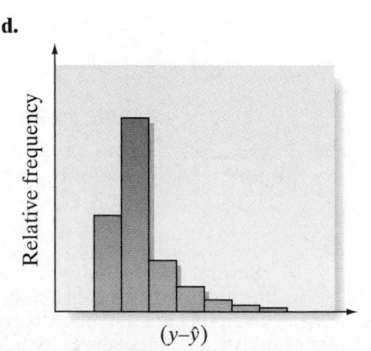

Residual plots for Exercise 11.100

Correlation matrix for Exercise 11.103

Independent Variable	x_2	x_3	x_4	x_5	x_6	$x_7 = $ ln (level of CO_2 emissions in 1980)
$x_1 = $ ln(foreign investments in 1980)	.13	.57	.30	−.38	.14	−.14
$x_2 = $ gross domestic investment in 1980		.49	.36	−.47	−.14	.25
$x_3 = $ trade exports in 1980			.43	−.47	−.06	−.07
$x_4 = $ ln(GNP in 1980)				−.84	−.53	.42
$x_5 = $ agricultural production in 1980					.45	−.50
$x_6 = $ 1 if African country, 0 if not						−.47

Source: Grimes, P., and Kentor, J. "Exporting the Greenhouse: Foreign Capital Penetration and CO_2 Emissions 1980–1996." *Journal of World-Systems Research,* Vol. IX, No. 2, Summer 2003 (Appendix B).

11.104 Passive exposure to smoke. Passive exposure to environmental tobacco smoke has been associated with growth suppression and an increased frequency of respiratory tract infections in normal children. Is this association more pronounced in children with cystic fibrosis? To answer this question, 43 children (18 girls and 25 boys) attending a 2-week summer camp for cystic fibrosis patients were studied (*The New England Journal of Medicine,* Sept. 20, 1990). Researchers investigated the correlation between a child's weight percentile (*y*) and the number of cigarettes smoked per day in the child's home (*x*). The table below lists the data for the 25 boys. Using simple linear regression, the researchers predicted the weight percentile for the last observation ($x = 44$ cigarettes) to be $\hat{y} = 29.63$. Given that the standard deviation of the model is $s = 24.68$, is this observation an outlier? Explain.

🌀 **CFSMOKE**

Weight Percentile, y	No. of Cigarettes Smoked per Day, x
6	0
6	15
2	40
8	23
11	20
17	7
24	3
25	0
17	25
25	20
25	15
31	23
35	10
43	0
49	0
50	0
49	22
46	30
54	0
58	0
62	0
66	0
66	23
83	0
87	44

Source: Rubin, B. K. "Exposure of Children with Cystic Fibrosis to Environmental Tobacco Smoke." *The New England Journal of Medicine,* Sept. 20, 1990, Vol. 323, No. 12, p. 85 (data extracted from Figure 3).

11.105 Passive exposure to smoke (cont'd). Refer to Exercise 11.104. Two residual plots for the simple linear regression model are shown below.
a. Which graph should be used to check for normal errors? Does the assumption of normality appear to be satisfied?
b. Which graph should be used to check for unequal error variances? Does the assumption of equal variances appear to be satisfied?

Applying the Concepts—Intermediate

11.106 Household food consumption. The data in the next table (p. 768) were collected for a random sample of 26 households in Washington, D.C. An economist wants to relate

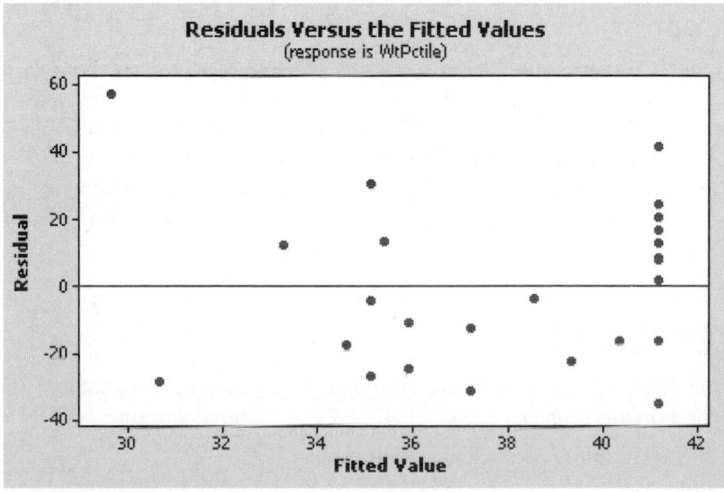

MINITAB Output for Exercise 11.105

DCFOOD

Household	Food Consumption ($1,000s)	Income ($1,000s)	Household Size	Household	Food Consumption ($1,000s)	Income ($1,000s)	Household Size
1	4.2	41.1	4	14	4.1	95.2	2
2	3.4	30.5	2	15	5.5	45.6	9
3	4.8	52.3	4	16	4.5	78.5	3
4	2.9	28.9	1	17	5.0	20.5	5
5	3.5	36.5	2	18	4.5	31.6	4
6	4.0	29.8	4	19	2.8	39.9	1
7	3.6	44.3	3	20	3.9	38.6	3
8	4.2	38.1	4	21	3.6	30.2	2
9	5.1	92.0	5	22	4.6	48.7	5
10	2.7	36.0	1	23	3.8	21.2	3
11	4.0	76.9	3	24	4.5	24.3	7
12	2.7	69.9	1	25	4.0	26.9	5
13	5.5	43.1	7	26	7.5	7.3	5

household food consumption, y, to household income, x_1, and household size, x_2, with the first-order model

$$E(y) = \beta_0 + \beta_1 x_1 + \beta_2 x_2$$

a. Fit the model to the data. Do you detect any signs of multicollinearity in the data? Explain.

b. Is there visual evidence (from a residual plot) that a second-order model may be more appropriate for predicting household food consumption? Explain.

c. Comment on the assumption of constant error variance, using a residual plot. Does it appear to be satisfied?

d. Are there any outliers in the data? If so, identify them.

e. Based on a graph of the residuals, does the assumption of normal errors appear to be reasonably satisfied? Explain.

11.107 Analysis of Tokyo urban air. Chemical engineers at Tokyo Metropolitan University analyzed urban air specimens for the presence of low-molecular-weight dicarboxylic acid (*Environmental Science & Engineering*, Oct. 1993). The dicarboxylic acid (as a percentage of total carbon) and oxidant concentrations for 19 air specimens collected from urban Tokyo are listed in the next table. Consider the straight-line model relating dicarboxylic acid percentage (y) to oxidant concentration (x). Conduct a complete residual analysis for the model.

DDT

11.108 Contamination from a plant's discharge. Refer to the U.S. Army Corps of Engineers data on fish contaminated from the toxic discharges of a chemical plant located on the banks of the Tennessee River in Alabama. In Exercise 11.16 (p. 683) you fit the first-order model, $E(y) = \beta_0 + \beta_1 x_1 + \beta_2 x_2 + \beta_3 x_3$, where $y = $ DDT

URBANAIR

Dicarboxylic Acid (%)	Oxidant (ppm)	Dicarboxylic Acid (%)	Oxidant (ppm)
.85	78	.50	32
1.45	80	.38	28
1.80	74	.30	25
1.80	78	.70	45
1.60	60	.80	40
1.20	62	.90	45
1.30	57	1.22	41
.20	49	1.00	34
.22	34	1.00	25
.40	36		

Source: Kawamura, K., and Ikushima, K. "Seasonal Changes in the Distribution of Dicarboxylic Acids in the Urban Atmosphere." *Environmental Science & Technology,* Vol. 27, No. 10, Oct. 1993, p. 2232 (data extracted from Figure 4).

level in captured fish, $x_1 = $ miles captured upstream, $x_2 = $ fish length, and $x_3 = $ fish weight. Conduct a complete residual analysis for the model. Do you recommend any model modifications be made? Explain.

GASTURBINE

11.109 Cooling method for gas turbines. Refer to the *Journal of Engineering for Gas Turbines and Power* (Jan. 2005) study of a high-pressure inlet fogging method for a gas turbine engine, Exercise 11.89 (p. 733). Now consider the interaction model for heat rate (y) of a gas turbine as a function of cycle speed (x_1) and cycle pressure ratio (x_2), $E(y) = \beta_0 + \beta_1 x_1 + \beta_2 x_2 + \beta_3 x_1 x_2$. Use the data saved in the **GASTURBINE** file to conduct a complete residual analysis for the model. Do you recommend making model modifications?

KEY TERMS

Note: Starred (*) items are from the optional sections in this chapter.

Adjusted multiple coefficient of determination 677
Base level 712

GUIDE TO MULTIPLE REGRESSION

CHAPTER NOTES

Multiple Regression Variables

y = **Dependent** variable (quantitative)

$x_1, x_2, \ldots, x_k$ are **independent** variables (quantitative or qualitative)

Quadratic Model in 1 Quantitative x

$$E(y) = \beta_0 + \beta_1 x + \beta_2 x^2$$

β_2 represents the rate of curvature in for x

($\beta_2 > 0$ implies *upward* curvature)

($\beta_2 < 0$ implies *downward* curvature)

Complete Second-Order Model in 2 Quantitative x's

$$E(y) = \beta_0 + \beta_1 x_1 + \beta_2 x_2 + \beta_3 x_1 x_2 + \beta_4 x_1^2 + \beta_5 x_2^2$$

β_4 represents the rate of curvature in for x_1, holding x_2 fixed

β_5 represents the rate of curvature in for x_2, holding x_1 fixed

Complete Second-Order Model in 1 Quantitative x and 1 Qualitative x (Two Levels, A and B)

$$E(y) = \beta_0 + \beta_1 x_1 + \beta_2 x_1^2 + \beta_3 x_2 + \beta_4 x_1 x_2 + \beta_5 x_1^2 x_2$$

$$x_2 = \{1 \text{ if level A}, 0 \text{ if level B}\}$$

Interaction between x_1 and x_2

Implies that the relationship between y and one x depends on the other x.

Parsimonious Model

A model with a small number of β parameters.

Recommendation for Assessing Model Adequacy

(1) Conduct global F-test; if significant then:

(2) Conduct t-tests on only the "most important" β's (*interaction* or *squared terms*)

(3) Interpret value of 2s

(4) Interpret value of R_a^2

Recommendation for Testing Individual β's

(1) If *curvature* (x^2) deemed important, do not conduct test for first-order (x) term in the model

(2) If *interaction* ($x_1 x_2$) deemed important, do not conduct tests for first-order terms (x_1 and x_2) in the model

Extrapolation

Occurs when you predict y for values of x's that are outside of range of sample data.

First-Order Model in k Quantitative x's

$$E(y) = \beta_0 + \beta_1 x_1 + \beta_2 x_2 + \cdots + \beta_k x_k$$

Each β_i represents the change in y for every 1-unit increase in x_i, holding all other x's fixed

Interaction Model in 2 Quantitative x's

$$E(y) = \beta_0 + \beta_1 x_1 + \beta_2 x_2 + \beta_3 x_1 x_2$$

($\beta_1 + \beta_3 x_2$) represents the change in y for every 1-unit increase in x_1, for fixed value of x_2

($\beta_2 + \beta_3 x_1$) represents the change in y for every 1-unit increase in x_2, for fixed value of x_1

Dummy Variable Model for 1 Qualitative x

$$E(y) = \beta_0 + \beta_1 x_1 + \beta_2 x_2 + \cdots + \beta_{k-1} x_{k-1}$$

$$x_1 = \{1 \text{ if level 1}, 0 \text{ if not}\}$$
$$x_2 = \{1 \text{ if level 2}, 0 \text{ if not}\}$$
$$x_{k-1} = \{1 \text{ if level } k-1, 0 \text{ if not}\}$$

$\beta_0 = E(y)$ for level k (base level) $= \mu_k$

$\beta_1 = \mu_1 - \mu_k$

$\beta_2 = \mu_2 - \mu_k$

Adjusted Coefficient of Determination, R_a^2

Cannot be "forced" to 1 by adding independent variables to the model.

Nested Models

Are models where one model (the *complete model*) contains all the terms of another model (the *reduced model*) plus at least one additional term.

Multicollinearity

Occurs when two or more x's are correlated.

Indicators of multicollinearity:

(1) Highly correlated x's

(2) Significant global F-test but all t-tests nonsignificant

(3) Signs on β's opposite from expected

Problems with Using Stepwise Regression Model as the "Final" Model

(1) *Extremely large number of t-tests* inflate overall probability of at least one Type I error

(2) *No higher-order terms* (interactions or squared terms) are included in the model

Analysis of Residuals	**Key Symbols**

Analysis of Residuals

(1) Detect **misspecified model**: *plot residuals vs. quantitative x* (look for trends, e.g., curvilinear trend)

(2) Detect **nonconstant error variance**: *plot residuals vs. $\hat{y}$* (look for patterns, e.g., cone shape)

(3) Detect **nonnormal errors**: *histogram, stem-leaf, or normal probability plot of residuals* (look for strong departures from normality)

(4) Identify **outliers**: *residuals greater than 3s in absolute value* (investigate outliers before deleting)

Key Symbols

x_1^2	Quadratic form for a quantitative x
$x_1 x_2$	Interaction term
MSE	Mean square for error (estimates σ^2)
$\hat{\epsilon}$	Estimated random error (residual)
SSE_R	Sum of squared errors, reduced model
SSE_C	Sum of squared errors, complete model
MSE_C	Mean squared error, complete model
$\ln(y)$	Natural logarithm of dependent variable

Key Formulas

$s^2 = MSE = \dfrac{SSE}{n - (k + 1)}$	Estimator of σ^2 for a model with k independent variables
$t = \dfrac{\hat{\beta}_i}{s_{\hat{\beta}_i}}$	Test statistic for testing H_0: β_i
$\hat{\beta}_i \pm (t_{\alpha/2}) s_{\hat{\beta}_i}$, where $t_{\alpha/2}$ depends on $n - (k + 1)$ df	$100(1 - \alpha)\%$ confidence interval for β_i
$R^2 = \dfrac{SS_{yy} - SSE}{SS_{yy}}$	Multiple coefficient of determination
$R_a^2 = 1 - \left[\dfrac{(n - 1)}{n - (k + 1)}\right](1 - R^2)$	Adjusted multiple coefficient of determination
$F = \dfrac{MS(Model)}{MSE} = \dfrac{R^2/k}{(1 - R^2)/[n - (k + 1)]}$	Test statistic for testing H_0: $\beta_1 = \beta_2 = \cdots = \beta_k = 0$
$F = \dfrac{(SSE_R - SSE_C)/\text{number of } \beta\text{'s tested}}{MSE_C}$	Test statistic for comparing reduced and complete models*
$y - \hat{y}$	Regression residual

SUPPLEMENTARY EXERCISES 11.110–11.146

Note: Starred (*) exercises refer to the optional sections in this chapter.

Learning the Mechanics

11.110 Suppose you fit the model

$$y = \beta_0 + \beta_1 x_1 + \beta_2 x_1^2 + \beta_3 x_2 + \beta_4 x_1 x_2 + \epsilon$$

to $n = 25$ data points with the following results:

$$\hat{\beta}_0 = 1.26 \quad \hat{\beta}_1 = -2.43 \quad \hat{\beta}_2 = .05 \quad \hat{\beta}_3 = .62 \quad \hat{\beta}_4 = 1.81$$
$$s_{\hat{\beta}_1} = 1.21 \quad s_{\hat{\beta}_2} = .16 \quad s_{\hat{\beta}_3} = .26 \quad s_{\hat{\beta}_4} = 1.49$$
$$SSE = .41 \quad R^2 = .83$$

a. Is there sufficient evidence to conclude that at least one of the parameters β_1, β_2, β_3, or β_4 is nonzero? Test using $\alpha = .05$.

b. Test H_0: $\beta_1 = 0$ against H_a: $\beta_1 < 0$. Use $\alpha = .05$.

c. Test H_0: $\beta_2 = 0$ against H_a: $\beta_2 > 0$. Use $\alpha = .05$.

d. Test H_0: $\beta_3 = 0$ against H_a: $\beta_3 \neq 0$. Use $\alpha = .05$.

11.111 When a multiple regression model is used for estimating the mean of the dependent variable and for predicting a new value of y, which will be narrower—the confidence interval for the mean or the prediction interval for the new y value? Why?

11.112 Suppose you have developed a regression model to explain the relationship between y and x_1, x_2, and x_3. The ranges of the variables you observed were as follows: $10 \le y \le 100$, $5 \le x_1 \le 55$, $.5 \le x_2 \le 1$, and $1{,}000 \le x_3 \le 2{,}000$. Will the error of prediction be smaller when you use the least squares equation to predict y when $x_1 = 30$, $x_2 = .6$, and $x_3 = 1{,}300$, or $x_1 = 60$, $x_2 = .4$, and $x_3 = 900$? Why?

11.113 Suppose you used MINITAB to fit the model

$$y = \beta_0 + \beta_1 x_1 + \beta_2 x_2 + \epsilon$$

to $n = 15$ data points and you obtained the printout shown on page 772.

a. What is the least squares prediction equation?

b. Find R^2 and interpret its value.

```
The regression equation is
Y  = 90.1 - 1.84 X1 + .285 X2


Predictor      Coef   SE Coef      T       P
Constant      90.10     23.10    3.90   0.002
X1            -1.836     0.367   -5.01   0.001
X2             0.285     0.231    1.24   0.465


S = 10.68       R-Sq = 91.6%    R-Sq(adj) = 90.2%

Analysis of Variance

Source            DF       SS       MS       F        P
Regression         2    14801     7400    64.91   0.001
Residual Error    12     1364      114
Total             14    16165
```

MINITAB Output for Exercise 11.113

c. Is there sufficient evidence to indicate that the model is useful for predicting y? Conduct an F-test using $\alpha = .05$.

d. Test the null hypothesis $H_0: \beta_1 = 0$ against the alternative hypothesis $H_a: \beta_1 \neq 0$. Test using $\alpha = .05$. Draw the appropriate conclusions.

e. Find the standard deviation of the regression model and interpret it.

11.114 The first-order model $E(y) = \beta_0 + \beta_1 x_1$ was fit to $n = 19$ data points. A residual plot for the model is provided below. Is the need for a quadratic term in the model evident from the residual plot? Explain.

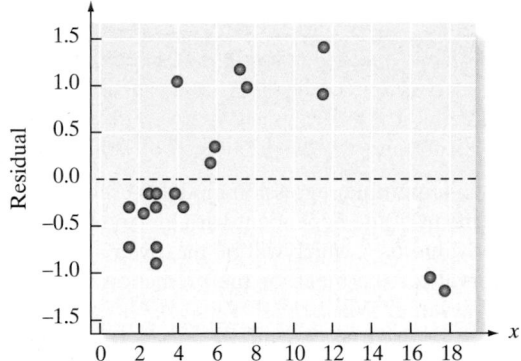

11.115 Why is the model building step the key to the success or failure of a regression analysis?

11.116 Suppose you fit the regression model

$$E(y) = \beta_0 + \beta_1 x_1 + \beta_2 x_2 + \beta_3 x_2^2 + \beta_4 x_1 x_2 + \beta_5 x_1 x_2^2$$

to $n = 35$ data points and wish to test the null hypothesis $H_0: \beta_4 = \beta_5 = 0$.

a. State the alternative hypothesis.

b. Explain in detail how to compute the F statistic needed to test the null hypothesis.

c. What are the numerator and denominator degrees of freedom associated with the F statistic in part **b?**

d. Give the rejection region for the test if $\alpha = .05$.

11.117 Write a model relating $E(y)$ to one qualitative independent variable that is at four levels. Define all the terms in your model.

11.118 It is desired to relate $E(y)$ to a quantitative variable x_1 and a qualitative variable at three levels.

a. Write a first-order model.

b. Write a model that will graph as three different second-order curves—one for each level of the qualitative variable.

11.119 Explain why stepwise regression is used. What is its value in the model-building process?

11.120 Consider relating $E(y)$ to two quantitative independent variables x_1 and x_2.

a. Write a first-order model for $E(y)$.

b. Write a complete second-order model for $E(y)$.

11.121 To model the relationship between y, a dependent variable, and x, an independent variable, a researcher has taken one measurement on y at each of three different x values. Drawing on his mathematical expertise, the researcher realizes that he can fit the second-order model

$$E(y) = \beta_0 + \beta_1 x + \beta_2 x^2$$

and it will pass exactly through all three points, yielding SSE = 0. The researcher, delighted with the "excellent" fit of the model, eagerly sets out to use it to make inferences. What problems will he encounter in attempting to make inferences?

Applying the Concepts—Basic

11.122 GPAs of business students. An Educational Testing Service (ETS) research scientist used multiple regression analysis to model y, the final grade point average (GPA) of business and management doctoral students (*Journal of Educational Statistics*, Spring 1993). A list of the potential independent variables measured for each doctoral student in the study follows:

(1) Quantitative Graduate Management Aptitude Test (GMAT) score

(2) Verbal GMAT score

(3) Undergraduate GPA

(4) First-year graduate GPA

(5) Student cohort (i.e., year in which student entered doctoral program: year 1, year 3, or year 5)

a. Identify the variables as quantitative or qualitative.

b. For each quantitative variable, give your opinion on whether the variable is positively or negatively related to final GPA.

c. For each of the qualitative variables, set up the appropriate dummy variable.

d. Write a first-order, main-effects model relating final GPA, y, to the five independent variables.

e. Interpret the β's in the model, part **d.**

f. Write a first-order model for final GPA, y, that allows for a different slope for each student cohort.

g. For each quantitative independent variable in the model, part **f,** give the slope of the line (in terms of the β's) for the year 1 cohort.

11.123 Comparing two orange juice extractors. The Florida Citrus Commission is interested in evaluating the performance of two orange juice extractors, brand A and brand B. It is believed that the size of the fruit used in the test may influence the juice yield (amount of juice per pound of oranges) obtained by the extractors. The commission wants to develop a regression model relating the mean juice yield $E(y)$ to the type of orange juice extractor (brand A or brand B) and the size of orange (diameter), x_1.

a. Identify the independent variables as qualitative or quantitative.

b. Write a model that describes the relationship between $E(y)$ and size of orange as two parallel lines, one for each brand of extractor.

c. Modify the model of part **b** to permit the slopes of the two lines to differ.

d. Sketch typical response lines for the model of part **b.** Do the same for the model of part **c.** Carefully label your graphs.

e. Specify the null and alternative hypotheses you would use to determine whether the model in part **c** provides more information for predicting yield than does the model in part **b.**

f. Explain how you would obtain the quantities necessary to compute the F-statistic that would be used in testing the hypotheses you described in part **e.**

11.124 Analysis of managers' salaries. Much research—and much litigation—has been conducted on the disparity between the salary levels of men and women. Research reported in *Work and Occupations* (Nov. 1992) analyzes the salaries for a sample of 191 Illinois managers using a regression analysis with the following independent variables:

$$x_1 = \text{Gender of manager} - \begin{cases} 1 & \text{if male} \\ 0 & \text{if not} \end{cases}$$

$$x_2 = \text{Race of manager} = \begin{cases} 1 & \text{if white} \\ 0 & \text{if not} \end{cases}$$

$x_3 = \text{Education level (in years)}$

$x_4 = \text{Tenure with firm (in years)}$

$x_5 = \text{Number of hours worked per week}$

The regression results are shown in the following table as they were reported in the article.

Variable	$\hat{\beta}$	p-Value
x_1	12.774	<.05
x_2	.713	>.10
x_3	1.519	<.05
x_4	.320	<.05
x_5	.205	<.05
Constant	15.491	—
$R^2 = .240$		$n = 191$

a. Write the hypothesized model that was used, and interpret each of the β parameters in the model.

b. Write the least squares equation that estimates the model in part **a,** and interpret each of the β estimates.

c. Interpret the value of R^2. Test to determine whether the model is useful for predicting annual salary. Test using $\alpha = .05$.

d. Test to determine whether the gender variable indicates that male managers are paid more than female managers, even after adjusting for and holding constant the other four factors in the model. Test using $\alpha = .05$. [*Note:* The p-values given in the table are two-tailed.]

e. Why would one want to adjust for these other factors before conducting a test for salary discrimination?

11.125 Determinants of area property crime levels. The *Journal of Quantitative Criminology* (Vol. 8, 1992) published a paper on the determinants of area property crime levels in the United Kingdom. Several multiple regression models for property crime prevalence, y, measured as the percentage of residents in a geographical area who were victims of at least one property crime, were examined. The results for one of the models, based on a sample of $n = 313$ responses collected for the British Crime Survey, are shown in the table on page 774. [*Note:* All variables except Density are expressed as a percentage of the base area.]

a. Test the hypothesis that the density (x_1) of a region is positively linearly related to crime prevalence (y), holding the other independent variables constant.

b. Do you advise conducting t-tests on each of the 18 independent variables in the model to determine which variables are important predictors of crime prevalence? Explain.

c. The model yielded $R^2 = .411$. Use this information to conduct a test of the global utility of the model. Use $\alpha = .05$

11.126 Accuracy of software effort estimates. Refer to the *Journal of Empirical Software Engineering* (Vol. 9, 2004) study of the accuracy of software effort estimates, Exercise 11.63 (p. 716). Recall that the dependent variable (y) is measured as relative error of the effort estimate of a software development task. A total of eight independent variables were evaluated as potential predictors of relative error. Each of these was formulated as a dummy variable, as shown in the second table on p.774.

a. The eight independent variables were entered into a stepwise regression, and the following two variables were selected for entry into the model: x_1 and x_8. Write the main effects model for $E(y)$ as a function of these two variables.

b. The stepwise regression yielded the following prediction equation:

$$\hat{y} = .12 - .28x_1 + .27x_8$$

Results for Exercise 11.125

Variable	β	t	p-value
x_1 = Density (population per hectare)	.331	3.88	$p < .01$
x_2 = Unemployed male population	−.121	−1.17	$p > .10$
x_3 = Professional population	−.187	−1.90	$.01 < p < .10$
x_4 = Population aged less than 5	−.151	−1.51	$p > .10$
x_5 = Population aged between 5 and 15	.353	3.42	$p < .01$
x_6 = Female population	.095	1.31	$p > .10$
x_7 = 10-year change in population	.130	1.40	$p > .10$
x_8 = Minority population	−.122	−1.51	$p > .10$
x_9 = Young adult population	.163	5.62	$p < .01$
x_{10} = 1 if North region, 0 if not	.369	1.72	$.01 < p < .10$
x_{11} = 1 if Yorkshire region, 0 if not	−.210	−1.39	$p > .10$
x_{12} = 1 if East Midlands region, 0 if not	−.192	−0.78	$p > .10$
x_{13} = 1 if East Anglia region, 0 if not	−.548	−2.22	$.01 < p < .10$
x_{14} = 1 if South East region, 0 if not	.152	1.37	$p > .10$
x_{15} = 1 if South West region, 0 if not	−.151	−0.88	$p > .10$
x_{16} = 1 if West Midlands region, 0 if not	−.308	−1.93	$.01 < p < .10$
x_{17} = 1 if North West region, 0 if not	.311	2.13	$.01 < p < .10$
x_{18} = 1 if Wales region, 0 if not	−.019	−0.08	$p > .10$

Source: Osborn, D. R., Tickett, A., and Elder, R. "Area Characteristics and Regional Variates as Determinants of Area Property Crime." *Journal of Quantitative Criminology,* Vol. 8, No. 3, 1992, Plenum Publishing Corp.

Give a practical interpretation of the β estimates multiplied by x_1 and x_8.

c. The researcher is concerned that the sign of $\hat{\beta}_1$ in the model is the opposite from what is expected. (The researcher expects a project leader to have a smaller relative error of estimation than a developer.) Give at least one reason why this phenomenon occurred.

Company role of estimator:	x_1 = 1 if developer, 0 if project leader
Task complexity:	x_2 = 1 if low, 0 if medium/high
Contract type:	x_3 = 1 if fixed price, 0 if hourly rate
Customer importance:	x_4 = 1 if high, 0 if low/medium
Customer priority:	x_5 = 1 if time-of-delivery, 0 if cost or quality
Level of knowledge:	x_6 = 1 if high, 0 if low/medium
Participation:	x_7 = 1 if estimator participates in work, 0 if not
Previous accuracy:	x_8 = 1 if more than 20% accurate, 0 if less than 20% accurate

11.127 Predicting distress job in EMS workers. The *Journal of Consulting and Clinical Psychology* (June 1995) reported on a study of emergency services (EMS) rescue workers who responded to the I-880 freeway collapse during the 1989 San Francisco earthquake. The goal of the study was to identify the predictors of symptomatic distress in the EMS workers. One of the distress variables studied was the Global Symptom Index (GSI). Several models for GSI, y, were considered based on the following independent variables:

x_1 = Critical Incident Exposure scale (CIE)
x_2 = Hogan Personality Inventory-Adjustment scale (HPI-A)
x_3 = Years of experience (EXP)
x_4 = Locus of Control scale (LOC)
x_5 = Social Support scale (SS)
x_6 = Dissociative Experiences scale (DES)
x_7 = Peritraumatic Dissociation Experiences Questionnaire, self-report (PDEQ-SR)

a. Write a first-order model for $E(y)$ as a function of the first five independent variables, x_1–x_5.

b. The model of part **a**, fitted to data collected for $n = 147$ EMS workers, yielded the following results: $R^2 = .469$, $F = 34.47$, p-value $< .001$. Interpret these results.

c. Write a first-order model for $E(y)$ as a function of all seven independent variables, x_1–x_7.

d. The model, part **c**, yielded $R^2 = .603$. Interpret this result.

e. The t-tests for testing the DES and PDEQ-SR variables both yielded a p-value of .001. Interpret these results.

11.128 Impact of the economy on suicide rates. Since the Great Depression of the 1930s, the link between the suicide rate and the state of the economy has been the subject of much research. Research exploring this link using regression analysis was reported in an article in the *Journal of Socio-Economics* (Spring 1992). The researchers collected data from a 45-year period on the following variables:

y = Suicide rate
x_1 = Unemployment rate
x_2 = Percentage of females in the labor force
x_3 = Divorce rate
x_4 = Logarithm of Gross National Product (GNP)
x_5 = Annual percent change in GNP

One of the models explored by the researchers was a multiple regression model relating y to linear terms in x_1 through x_5. The least squares model shown next resulted (the observed significance levels of the β estimates are shown in parentheses beneath the estimates):

$$\hat{y} = .002 + .0204x_1 - .0231x_2 + .0765x_3 + .2760x_4 + .0018x_5$$
$$\quad\quad (.002) \quad (.02) \quad (>.10) \quad (>.10) \quad (>.10)$$
$$R^2 = .45$$

a. Interpret the value of R^2. Is there sufficient evidence to indicate that the model is useful for predicting the suicide rate? Use $\alpha = .05$.

b. Interpret each of the coefficients in the model and each of the corresponding significance levels.

c. Is there sufficient evidence to indicate that the unemployment rate is a useful predictor of the suicide rate? Use $\alpha = .05$.

d. Discuss each of the following terms with respect to potential problems with the above model: curvature (second-order terms), interaction, and multicollinearity.

11.129 Prototyping new software. To meet the increasing demand for new software products, many systems development experts have adopted a prototyping methodology. The effects of prototyping on the system development life cycle (SDLC) was investigated in the *Journal of Computer Information Systems* (Spring 1993). A survey of 500 randomly selected corporate level MIS managers was conducted. Three potential independent variables were: (1) *importance* of prototyping to each phase of the SDLC; (2) degree of *support* prototyping provides for the SDLC; and (3) degree to which prototyping *replaces* each phase of the SDLC. The table below gives the pairwise correlations of the three variables in the survey data for one particular phase of the SDLC. Use this information to assess the degree of multicollinearity in the survey data. Would you recommend using all three independent variables in a regression analysis? Explain.

Variable Pairs	Correlation Coefficient, r
Importance–Replace	.2682
Importance–Support	.6991
Replace–Support	−.0531

Source: Hardgrave, B. C., Doke, E. R., and Swanson, N. E. "Prototyping Effects of the System Development Life Cycle: An Empirical Study." *Journal of Computer Information Systems,* Vol. 33, No. 3, Spring 1993, p. 16 (Table 1).

11.130 A CEO's impact on corporate profits. Can a corporation's annual profit be predicted from information about the company's chief executive officer (CEO)? *Forbes* (May 1999) presented data on company profit (in $ millions), CEO's annual income (in $ thousands), and percentage of the company's stock owned by the CEO. Consider a model relating company profit (y) to CEO income (x_1) and stock percentage (x_2). Explain what it means to say that "CEO income x_1 and stock percentage x_2 interact to affect company profit y."

11.131 Selecting sites of La Quinta Motor Inns. Location is one of the most important decisions for hotel chains and lodging firms. Researchers S. E. Kimes (Cornell University) and J. A. Fitzsimmons (University of Texas) studied the site selection process of La Quinta Motor Inns, a moderately priced hotel chain (*Interfaces*, Mar.–Apr. 1990). Using data collected on 57 mature inns owned by La Quinta, the researchers built a regression model designed to predict the profitability for sites under construction. The least squares model is given below:

$$\hat{y} = 39.05 - 5.41x_1 + 5.86x_2 - 3.09x_3 + 1.75x_4$$

where

y = operating margin (measured as a percentage)

x_1 = state population (in thousands) divided by the total number of inns in the state

x_2 = room rate ($) for the inn

x_3 = square root of the median income of the area (in $ thousands)

x_4 = number of college students within four miles of the inn

All variables were "standardized" to have a mean of 0 and a standard deviation of 1.

a. Interpret the β estimates of the model. Comment on the effect of each independent variable on operating margin, y. [*Note:* A profitable inn is defined as one with an operating margin of over 50%.]

b. The model yielded $R^2 = .51$. Give a descriptive measure of model adequacy.

c. Make an inference about model adequacy by conducting the appropriate test. Use $\alpha = .05$.

Applying the Concepts—Intermediate

11.132 Promotion of supermarket vegetables. A supermarket chain is interested in exploring the relationship between the sales of its store-brand canned vegetables (y), the amount spent on promotion of the vegetables in local newspapers (x_1), and the amount of shelf space allocated to the brand (x_2). One of the chain's supermarkets was randomly selected, and over a 20-week period x_1 and x_2 were varied, as reported in the table.

CANVEG

Week	Sales ($)	Advertising Expenditures ($)	Shelf Space (sq. ft.)
1	2,010	201	75
2	1,850	205	50
3	2,400	355	75
4	1,575	208	30
5	3,550	590	75
6	2,015	397	50
7	3,908	820	75
8	1,870	400	30
9	4,877	997	75
10	2,190	515	30
11	5,005	996	75
12	2,500	625	50
13	3,005	860	50
14	3,480	1,012	50
15	5,500	1,135	75
16	1,995	635	30
17	2,390	837	30
18	4,390	1,200	50
19	2,785	990	30
20	2,989	1,205	30

a. Fit the following model to the data:

$$y = \beta_0 + \beta_1 x_1 + \beta_2 x_2 + \beta_3 x_1 x_2 + \epsilon$$

b. Conduct an F-test to investigate the overall usefulness of this model. Use $\alpha = .05$.

c. Test for the presence of interaction between advertising expenditures and shelf space. Use $\alpha = .05$.

d. Explain what it means to say that advertising expenditures and shelf space interact.

e. Explain how you could be misled by using a first-order model instead of an interaction model to explain how advertising expenditures and shelf space influence sales.

11.133 Yield strength of steel alloy. Industrial engineers at the University of Florida used regression modeling as a tool to reduce the time and cost associated with developing new metallic alloys (*Modelling and Simulation in Materials Science and Engineering*, Vol. 13, 2005). To illustrate, the engineers built a regression model for the tensile yield strength (y) of a new steel alloy. The potential important predictors of yield strength are listed in the accompanying table.

x_1 = Carbon amount (% weight)
x_2 = Manganese amount (% weight)
x_3 = Chromium amount (% weight)
x_4 = Nickel amount (% weight)
x_5 = Molybdenum amount (% weight)
x_6 = Copper amount (% weight)
x_7 = Nitrogen amount (% weight)
x_8 = Vanadium amount (% weight)
x_9 = Plate thickness (millimeters)
x_{10} = Solution treating (milliliters)
x_{11} = Aging temperature (degrees, Celsius)

a. The engineers discovered that the variable Nickel (x_4) was highly correlated with the other potential independent variables. Consequently, Nickel was dropped from the model. Do you agree with this decision? Explain.

b. The engineers used stepwise regression on the remaining 10 potential independent variables in order to search for a parsimonious set of predictor variables. Do you agree with this decision? Explain.

c. The stepwise regression selected the following independent variables: x_1 = Carbon, x_2 = Manganese, x_3 = Chromium, x_5 = Molybdenum, x_6 = Copper, x_8 = Vanadium, x_9 = Plate thickness, x_{10} = Solution treating, and x_{11} = Aging temperature. All these variables were statistically significant in the stepwise model, with R^2 = .94. Consequently, the engineers used the estimated stepwise model to predict yield strength. Do you agree with this decision? Explain.

11.134 Fertilized watershed runoff and soil loss. Phosphorus used in soil fertilizers can contaminate freshwater sources during rainfall runoff. Consequently, it is important for water quality engineers to estimate the amount of dissolved phosphorus in the water. *Geoderma* (June 1995) presented an investigation of the relationship between soil loss and percentage of dissolved phosphorus in water samples collected at 20 fertilized watersheds in Oklahoma. The data are given in the next table.

a. Plot the data in a scattergram. Do you detect a linear or curvilinear trend?

b. Fit the quadratic model, $E(y) = \beta_0 + \beta_1 x + \beta_2 x^2$ to the data.

c. Conduct a test to determine if a curvilinear relationship exists between dissolved phosphorus percentage (y) and soil loss (x). Test using α = .05.

11.135 Modeling peak-hour roadway traffic. Traffic forecasters at the Minnesota Department of Transportation (MDOT) use regression analysis to estimate weekday peak-hour traffic volumes on existing and proposed roadways. In particular, they model y, the peak-hour volume (typically, the volume between 7:00 and 8:00 A.M.), as a function of x_1, the road's total volume for the day. For one project involving the redesign of a section of Interstate 494, the forecasters collected $n = 72$ observations of peak-hour traffic

⊘ **PHOSPHOR**

Watershed	Soil Loss, x (kilometers per half-acre)	Dissolved Phosphorus Percentage, y
1	18	42.3
2	17	50.2
3	35	52.7
4	16	77.1
5	14	36.8
6	54	17.5
7	153	66.4
8	81	67.5
9	183	28.9
10	284	15.1
11	767	20.1
12	148	38.3
13	649	5.6
14	479	8.6
15	1,371	5.5
16	9,150	4.6
17	15,022	2.2
18	69	77.9
19	4,392	7.8
20	312	42.9

Source: Sharpley, A. N., Robinson, J. S., and Smith, S. J. "Bioavailable Phosphorus Dynamics in Agricultural Soils and Effects on Water Quality." *Geoderma*, Vol. 67, No. 1–2, June 1995, p. 11 (Table 4).

volume and 24-hour weekday traffic volume using electronic sensors that count vehicles. The data are saved in the **MINNDOT** file. (The first and last five observations are listed in the table.)

⊘ **MINNDOT** (Selected observations)

Observation Number	Peak-Hour Volume	24-Hour Volume	I-35
1	1,990.94	20,070	0
2	1,989.63	21,234	0
3	1,986.96	20,633	0
4	1,986.96	20,676	0
5	1,983.78	19,818	0
⋮	⋮	⋮	
68	2,147.93	22,948	1
69	2,147.85	23,551	1
70	2,144.23	21,637	1
71	2,142.41	23,543	1
72	2,137.39	22,594	1

Source: John Sem, Director, Allan E. Pint, State Traffic Forecast Engineer; and James Page Sr., Transportation Planner, Traffic and Commodities Studies Section, Minnesota Department of Transportation, St. Paul, Minnesota.

a. Construct a scattergram for the data, plotting peak-hour volume y against 24-hour volume x_1. Note the isolated group of observations at the top of the scattergram. Investigators discovered that all of these data points were collected at the intersection of Interstate 35W and 46th Street. (These are observations 55–72 in the table.) While all other locations in the sample were three-lane highways, this location was unique in that the highway widens to four lanes just north of the electronic sensor. Consequently, the forecasters decided to include a dummy variable to account for a difference between the I-35W location and all other locations.

b. Knowing that peak-hour traffic volumes have a theoretical upper bound, the forecaster hypothesized that a second-order model should be used to explain the variation in y. Propose a complete second-order model for $E(y)$ as a function of 24-hour volume x_1 and the dummy variable for location.

c. Using an available statistical software package, fit the model of part **b** to the data. Interpret the results. Specifically, is the curvilinear relationship between peak-hour volume and 24-hour volume different at the two locations?

d. Conduct a residual analysis of the model, part **b.** Evaluate the assumptions of normality and constant error variance, and determine whether any outliers exist.

11.136 Predicting percentage of problem mortgages. *Best's Review* (June 1999) compared the mortgage loan portfolios for a sample of 25 life/health insurance companies. The information in the table (bottom of the page), saved in the **BESTINS** file, is extracted from the article. Suppose you want to model the percentage of problem mortgages (y) of a company as a function of total mortgage loans (x_1), percentage of invested assets (x_2), percentage of commercial mortgages (x_3), and percentage of residential mortgages (x_4).

a. Write a first-order model for $E(y)$.

b. Fit the model of part **a** to the data and evaluate its overall usefulness. Use $\alpha = .05$.

c. Interpret the β estimates in the fitted model.

d. Construct scattergrams of y versus each of the four independent variables in the model. Which variables warrant inclusion in the model as second-order (i.e., squared) terms?

e. Fit the model that results from your exploratory analysis in part **d** to the data. Evaluate its overall usefulness using $\alpha = .05$.

f. Do the one or more second-order terms of your model, part **e,** contribute information for the prediction of the percentage of problem mortgages? Test using $\alpha = .05$.

11.137 Impact of advertising on market share. The audience for a product's advertising can be divided into four segments according to the degree of exposure received as a result of the advertising. These segments are groups of consumers who receive very high (VH), high (H), medium (M), or low (L) exposure to the advertising. A company is interested in exploring whether its advertising effort affects its product's market share. Accordingly, the company identifies 24 sample groups of consumers who have been exposed to its advertising, six groups at each exposure level. Then, the company determines its product's market share within each group.

MKTSHR

Market Share within Group	Exposure Level
10.1	L
10.3	L
10.0	L
10.3	L
10.2	L
10.5	L
10.6	M
11.0	M
11.2	M
10.9	M
10.8	M
11.0	M
12.2	H
12.1	H
11.8	H
12.6	H
11.9	H
12.9	H
10.7	VH
10.8	VH
11.0	VH
10.5	VH
10.8	VH
10.6	VH

a. Write a regression model that expresses the company's market share as a function of advertising exposure level. Define all terms in your model, and list any assumptions you make about them.

b. Did you include interaction terms in your model? Why or why not?

c. The data in the table, saved in the **MKTSHR** file, were obtained by the company. Fit the model you constructed in part **a** to the data.

d. Is there evidence to suggest that the firm's expected market share differs for different levels of advertising exposure? Test using $\alpha = .05$.

11.138 Downtime of a production process. An operations manager is interested in modeling $E(y)$, the expected length of time per month (in hours) that a machine will be shut

BESTINS (Selected observations)

Company	Total Mortgage Loan, x_1	% Invested Assets, x_2	% Commercial Mortgages, x_3	% Residential Mortgages, x_4	% Problem Mortgages, y
TIAA Group	$18,803,163	20.7	100.0	0.0	11.4
Metropolitan Insurance	18,171,162	13.9	77.8	1.6	3.8
Prudential of Am Group	16,213,150	12.9	87.4	2.3	4.1
Principal Mutual IA	11,940,345	30.3	98.8	1.2	32.6
Northwestern Mutualk	10,834,616	17.8	99.5	0.0	2.2
⋮	⋮	⋮	⋮	⋮	⋮
State Farm Group	2,027,648	8.6	97.6	2.4	0.1
Pacific Mutual Life	1,945,392	9.7	96.4	3.6	6.1

Source: Best's Review (Life/Health), June 1999, p. 35.

down for repairs, as a function of the type of machine (001 or 002) and the age of the machine (in years). The manager has proposed the following model:

$$E(y) = \beta_0 + \beta_1 x_1 + \beta_2 x_1^2 + \beta_3 x_2$$

where

x_1 = Age of machine

x_2 = 1 if machine type 001, 0 if machine type 002

a. Use the data obtained on $n = 20$ machine breakdowns, shown below, to estimate the parameters of this model.

b. Do these data provide sufficient evidence to conclude that the second-order term (x_1^2) in the model proposed by the operations manager is necessary? Test using $\alpha = .05$.

c. Test the null hypothesis that $\beta_1 = \beta_2 = 0$ using $\alpha = .10$. Interpret the results of the test in the context of the problem.

⊙ **SHUTDOWN**

Downtime (hours per month)	Machine Age, x_1 (years)	Machine Type	x_2
10	1.0	001	1
20	2.0	001	1
30	2.7	001	1
40	4.1	001	1
9	1.2	001	1
25	2.5	001	1
19	1.9	001	1
41	5.0	001	1
22	2.1	001	1
12	1.1	001	1
10	2.0	002	0
20	4.0	002	0
30	5.0	002	0
44	8.0	002	0
9	2.4	002	0
25	5.1	002	0
20	3.5	002	0
42	7.0	002	0
20	4.0	002	0
13	2.1	002	0

11.139 **Forecasting daily admission of a water park.** To determine whether extra personnel are needed for the day, the owners of a water adventure park would like to find a model that would allow them to predict the day's attendance each morning before opening based on the day of the week and weather conditions. The model is of the form

$$E(y) = \beta_0 + \beta_1 x_1 + \beta_2 x_2 + \beta_3 x_3$$

where

y = Daily admission

$x_1 = \begin{cases} 1 & \text{if weekend} \\ 0 & \text{otherwise} \end{cases}$ (dummy variable)

$x_2 = \begin{cases} 1 & \text{if sunny} \\ 0 & \text{if overcast} \end{cases}$ (dummy variable)

x_3 = Predicted daily high temperature (°F)

These data were recorded for a random sample of 30 days, and a regression model was fitted to the data. The least squares analysis produced the following results:

$$\hat{y} = -105 + 25x_1 + 100x_2 + 10x_3$$

with

$$s_{\hat{\beta}_1} = 10 \qquad s_{\hat{\beta}_2} = 30 \qquad s_{\hat{\beta}_3} = 4 \qquad R^2 = .65$$

a. Interpret the estimated model coefficients.

b. Is there sufficient evidence to conclude that this model is useful for the prediction of daily attendance? Use $\alpha = .05$.

c. Is there sufficient evidence to conclude that the mean attendance increases on weekends? Use $\alpha = .10$.

d. Use the model to predict the attendance on a sunny weekday with a predicted high temperature of 95°F.

e. Suppose the 90% prediction interval for part **d** is (645, 1,245). Interpret this interval.

11.140 **Forecasting daily admission of a water park (cont'd).** Refer to Exercise 11.139. The owners of the water adventure park are advised that the prediction model could probably be improved if interaction terms were added. In particular, it is thought that the *rate* at which mean attendance increases as predicted high temperature increases will be greater on weekends than on weekdays. The following model is therefore proposed:

$$E(y) = \beta_0 + \beta_1 x_1 + \beta_2 x_2 + \beta_3 x_3 + \beta_4 x_1 x_3$$

The same 30 days of data used in Exercise 11.139 are again used to obtain the least squares model

$$\hat{y} = 250 - 700x_1 + 100x_2 + 5x_3 + 15x_1 x_3$$

with

$$s_{\hat{\beta}_4} = 3.0 \quad R^2 = .96$$

a. Graph the predicted day's attendance, y, against the day's predicted high temperature, x_3, for a sunny weekday and for a sunny weekend day. Plot both on the same paper for x_3 between 70 and 100°F. Note the increase in slope for the weekend day. Interpret this.

b. Do the data indicate that the interaction term is a useful addition to the model? Use $\alpha = .05$.

c. Use this model to predict the attendance for a sunny weekday with a predicted high temperature of 95°F.

d. Suppose the 90% prediction interval for part **c** is (800, 850). Compare this result with the prediction interval for the model without interaction in Exercise 11.139, part **e**. Do the relative widths of the confidence intervals support or refute your conclusion about the utility of the interaction term (part **b**)?

e. The owners, noting that the coefficient $\hat{\beta}_1 = -700$, conclude the model is ridiculous because it seems to imply that the mean attendance will be 700 less on weekends than on weekdays. Explain why this is *not* the case.

11.141 **Sale prices of apartments.** A Minneapolis, Minnesota, real estate appraiser used regression analysis to explore the relationship between the sale prices of apartment buildings and various characteristics of the buildings. The **MNSALES** file contains data for a random sample of 25 apartment buildings. *Note:* Physical condition of each apartment building is coded E (excellent), G (good), or F (fair).

MNSALES (Data for Exercise 11.141)

Code No.	Sale Price, y (\$)	No. of Apartments, x_1	Age of Structure, x_2 (years)	Lot Size, x_3 (sq. ft)	No. of On-Site Parking Spaces, x_4	Gross Building Area, x_5 (sq. ft)	Condition of Apartment *Building*
0229	90,300	4	82	4,635	0	4,266	F
0094	384,000	20	13	17,798	0	14,391	G
0043	157,500	5	66	5,913	0	6,615	G
0079	676,200	26	64	7,750	6	34,144	E
0134	165,000	5	55	5,150	0	6,120	G
0179	300,000	10	65	12,506	0	14,552	G
0087	108,750	4	82	7,160	0	3,040	G
0120	276,538	11	23	5,120	0	7,881	G
0246	420,000	20	18	11,745	20	12,600	G
0025	950,000	62	71	21,000	3	39,448	G
0015	560,000	26	74	11,221	0	30,000	G
0131	268,000	13	56	7,818	13	8,088	F
0172	290,000	9	76	4,900	0	11,315	E
0095	173,200	6	21	5,424	6	4,461	G
0121	323,650	11	24	11,834	8	9,000	G
0077	162,500	5	19	5,246	5	3,828	G
0060	353,500	20	62	11,223	2	13,680	F
0174	134,400	4	70	5,834	0	4,680	E
0084	187,000	8	19	9,075	0	7,392	G
0031	155,700	4	57	5,280	0	6,030	E
0019	93,600	4	82	6,864	0	3,840	F
0074	110,000	4	50	4,510	0	3,092	G
0057	573,200	14	10	11,192	0	23,704	E
0104	79,300	4	82	7,425	0	3,876	F
0024	272,000	5	82	7,500	0	9,542	E

Source: Robinson Appraisal Co., Inc., Mankato, Minnesota

a. Write a model that describes the relationship between sale price and number of apartment units as three parallel lines, one for each level of physical condition. Be sure to specify the dummy variable coding scheme you use.

b. Plot y against x_1 (number of apartment units) for all buildings in excellent condition. On the same graph, plot y against x_1 for all buildings in good condition. Do this again for all buildings in fair condition. Does it appear that the model you specified in part **a** is appropriate? Explain.

c. Fit the model from part **a** to the data. Report the least squares prediction equation for each of the three building condition levels.

d. Plot the three prediction equations of part **c** on a scattergram of the data.

e. Do the data provide sufficient evidence to conclude that the relationship between sale price and number of units differs depending on the physical condition of the apartments? Test using $\alpha = .05$.

f. Check the data set for multicollinearity. How does this impact your choice of independent variables to use in a model for sale price?

g. Conduct a complete residual analysis for the model to check the assumptions on ϵ.

11.142 Light output of a bulb. A firm that has developed a new type of lightbulb is interested in evaluating its performance in order to decide whether to market it. It is known that the light output of the bulb depends on the cleanliness of its surface area and the length of time the bulb has been in operation. Use the data in the next table and the procedures you learned in this chapter to build a regression model that relates drop in light output to bulb surface cleanliness and length of operation. Be sure to conduct a residual analysis also.

LTBULB

Drop in Light Output (% original output)	Bulb Surface (C = clean) (D = dirty)	Length of Operation (hours)
0	C	0
16	C	400
22	C	800
27	C	1,200
32	C	1,600
36	C	2,000
38	C	2,400
0	D	0
4	D	400
6	D	800
8	D	1,200
9	D	1,600
11	D	2,000
12	D	2,400

11.143 Forecasting a job applicant's merit rating. A large research and development firm rates the performance of each member of its technical staff on a scale of 0 to 100, and this merit rating is used to determine the size of the person's pay raise for the coming year. The firm's personnel department is interested in developing a regression model to help them forecast the merit rating that an applicant for a technical position will receive after being employed three years. The firm proposes to use the following second-order model to forecast the merit ratings of applicants who have just completed their graduate studies and have no prior related job experience:

$$E(y) = \beta_0 + \beta_1 x_1 + \beta_2 x_2 + \beta_3 x_1 x_2 + \beta_4 x_1^2 + \beta_5 x_2^2$$

where

y = Applicant's merit rating after 3 years

x_1 = Applicant's GPA in graduate school

x_2 = Applicant's total score (verbal plus quantitative) on the Graduate Record Examination (GRE)

The model, fit to data collected for a random sample of $n = 40$ employees, resulted in SSE = 1830.44 and SS(model) = 4911.5.

The reduced model $E(y) = \beta_0 + \beta_1 x_1 + \beta_2 x_2$ is also fit to the same data, resulting in SSE = 3197.16.

a. Identify the appropriate null and alternative hypotheses to test whether the complete (second-order) model contributes information for the prediction of y.

b. Conduct the test of hypothesis given in part **a.** Test using $\alpha = .05$. Interpret the results in the context of this problem.

c. Identify the appropriate null and alternative hypotheses to test whether the complete model contributes more information than the reduced (first-order) model for the prediction of y.

d. Conduct the test of hypothesis given in part **c.** Test using $\alpha = .05$. Interpret the results in the context of this problem.

e. Which model, if either, would you use to predict y? Explain.

11.144 Premarketing test of a new dog food. Researchers for a dog food company have developed a new puppy food they hope will compete with the major brands. One premarketing test involved the comparison of the new food with that of two competitors in terms of weight gain. Fifteen 8-week-old German shepherd puppies, each from a different litter, were divided into three groups of five puppies each. Each group was fed one of the three brands of food.

a. Set up a model that assumes the final weight y is linearly related to initial weight x but does not allow for differences among the three brands; that is, assume the

response curve is the same for the three brands of dog food. Sketch the response curve as it might appear.

b. Set up a model that assumes the final weight is linearly related to initial weight and allows the intercepts of the lines to differ for the three brands. In other words, assume that the initial weight and brand both affect final weight, but the two variables do not interact. Sketch typical response curves.

c. Now write the main effects with interaction model. For this model we assume the final weight is linearly related to initial weight, but both the slopes and the intercepts of the lines depend on the brand. Sketch typical response curves.

Critical Thinking Challenges

11.145 Developing a model for college GPA. Many colleges and universities develop regression models for predicting the GPA of incoming freshmen. This predicted GPA can then be used to make admission decisions. Although most models use many independent variables to predict GPA, we will illustrate by choosing two variables:

x_1 = Verbal score on college entrance examination (percentile)

x_2 = Mathematics score on college entrance examination (percentile)

The data in the table below are obtained for a random sample of 40 freshmen at one college. Use the data to develop a useful prediction equation for college freshman GPA (y). Be sure to conduct a residual analysis for the model.

11.146 IQs and "The Bell Curve." *The Bell Curve* (Free Press, 1994) written by Richard Herrnstein and Charles Murray (H&M), is a controversial book about race, genes, IQ, and economic mobility. The book heavily employs statistics and statistical methodology in an attempt to support the authors' positions on the relationships among these variables and their social consequences. The main theme of *The Bell Curve* can be summarized as follows:

(1) Measured intelligence (IQ) is largely genetically inherited.

(2) IQ is correlated positively with a variety of socioeconomic status success measures, such as prestigious job, high annual income, and high educational attainment.

⊚ COLLGPA

Verbal, x_1	Mathematics, x_2	GPA, y	Verbal, x_1	Mathematics, x_2	GPA, y	Verbal, x_1	Mathematics, x_2	GPA, y
81	87	3.49	83	76	3.75	97	80	3.27
68	99	2.89	64	66	2.70	77	90	3.47
57	86	2.73	83	72	3.15	49	54	1.30
100	49	1.54	93	54	2.28	39	81	1.22
54	83	2.56	74	59	2.92	87	69	3.23
82	86	3.43	51	75	2.48	70	95	3.82
75	74	3.59	79	75	3.45	57	89	2.93
58	98	2.86	81	62	2.76	74	67	2.83
55	54	1.46	50	69	1.90	87	93	3.84
49	81	2.11	72	70	3.01	90	65	3.01
64	76	2.69	54	52	1.48	81	76	3.33
66	59	2.16	65	79	2.98	84	69	3.06
80	61	2.60	56	78	2.58			
100	85	3.30	98	67	2.73			

(3) From 1 and 2, it follows that socioeconomic successes are largely genetically caused and therefore resistant to educational and environmental interventions (such as affirmative action).

The statistical methodology (regression) employed by the authors and the inferences derived from the statistics were critiqued in *Chance* (Summer 1995) and *The Journal of the American Statistical Association* (Dec. 1995). The following are just a few of the problems with H&M's use of regression that are identified:

Problem 1   H&M consistently use a trio of independent variables—IQ, socioeconomic status, and age—in a series of first-order models designed to predict dependent social outcome variables such as income and unemployment. (Only on a single occasion are interaction terms incorporated.) Consider, for example, the model

$$E(y) = \beta_0 + \beta_1 x_1 + \beta_2 x_2 + \beta_3 x_3$$

where y = income, x_1 = IQ, x_2 = socioeconomic status, and x_3 = age. H&M utilize t-tests on the individual β parameters to assess the importance of the independent variables. As with most of the models considered in *The Bell Curve*, the estimate of β_1 in the income model is positive and statistically significant at $\alpha = .05$, and the associated t value is larger (in absolute value) than the t-values associated with the other independent variables. Consequently, *H&M claim that IQ is a better predictor of income than the other two independent variables.* No attempt was made to determine whether the model was properly specified or whether the model provides an adequate fit to the data.

Problem 2   In an appendix, the authors describe multiple regression as a "mathematical procedure that yields coefficients for each of [the independent variables], indicating how much of a change in [the dependent variable] can be anticipated for a given change in any particular [independent] variable, with all the others held constant." Armed with this information and the fact that the estimate of β_1 in the model above is positive, *H&M infer that a high IQ necessarily implies (or causes) a high income, and a low IQ inevitably leads to a low income.* (Cause-and-effect inferences like this are made repeatedly throughout the book.)

Problem 3   The title of the book refers to the normal distribution and its well-known "bell-shaped" curve. There is a misconception among the general public that scores on intelligence tests (IQ) are normally distributed. In fact, most IQ scores have distributions that are decidedly skewed. Traditionally, psychologists and psychometricians have transformed these scores so that the resulting numbers have a precise normal distribution. H&M make a special point to do this. Consequently, *the measure of IQ used in all the regression models is normalized (i.e., transformed so that the resulting distribution is normal), despite the fact that regression methodology does not require predictor (independent) variables to be normally distributed.*

Problem 4   A variable that is not used as a predictor of social outcome in any of the models in *The Bell Curve* is level of education. H&M purposely omit education from the models, arguing that IQ causes education, not the other way around. Other researchers who have examined H&M's data report that *when education is included as an independent variable in the model, the effect of IQ on the dependent variable (say, income) is diminished.*

a. Comment on each of the problems identified. Why do each of these problems cast a shadow on the inferences made by the authors?

b. Using the variables specified in the model above, describe how you would conduct the multiple regression analysis. (Propose a more complex model and describe the appropriate model tests, including a residual analysis.)

REFERENCES

Barnett, V., and Lewis, T. *Outliers in Statistical Data.* New York: Wiley, 1978.

Belsley, D. A., Kuh, E., and Welsch, R. E. *Regression Diagnostics: Identifying Influential Data and Sources of Collinearity.* New York: Wiley, 1980.

Chase, R. B., and Aquilano, N. J. *Production and Operations Management*, 6th ed. Homewood, Ill.: Richard D. Irwin, 1992.

Chatterjee, S., and Price, B. *Regression Analysis by Example*, 2nd ed. New York: Wiley, 1991.

Draper, N., and Smith, H. *Applied Regression Analysis*, 2nd ed. New York: Wiley, 1981.

Graybill, F. *Theory and Application of the Linear Model.* North Scituate, Mass.: Duxbury, 1976.

Horngren, Charles T., Foster, George, and Datar, Srikant M. *Cost Accounting*, 8th ed. Englewood Cliffs, N.J.: Prentice Hall, 1994.

Mansfield, E. *Applied Microeconomics.* New York: Norton, 1994.

Mendenhall, W. *Introduction to Linear Models and the Design and Analysis of Experiments.* Belmont, Calif.: Wadsworth, 1968.

Mendenhall, W., and Sincich, T. *A Second Course in Statistics: Regression Analysis*, 6th ed. Upper Saddle River, N.J.: Prentice Hall, 2003.

Mosteller, F., and Tukey, J. W. *Data Analysis and Regression: A Second Course in Statistics.* Reading, Mass.: Addison-Wesley, 1977.

Neter, J., Kutner, M., Nachtshcim, C., and Wasserman, W. *Applied Linear Statistical Models*, 4th ed. Homewood, Ill.: Richard Irwin, 1996.

Rousseeuw, P. J. and Leroy, A. M. *Robust Regression and Outlier Detection.* New York: Wiley, 1987.

Weisberg, S. *Applied Linear Regression*, 2nd ed. New York: Wiley, 1985.

Using Technology

11.1 Multiple Regression Using SPSS

To conduct a multiple regression analysis, first access the SPSS spreadsheet file that contains the dependent and independent variables. Next, click on the "Analyze" button on the SPSS menu bar, then click on "Regression" and "Linear", as shown in Figure 11.S.1. The resulting dialog box appears as shown in Figure 11.S.2. Specify the dependent variable in the "Dependent" box and the independent variables in the "Independent(s)" box. [*Note*: If your model includes interaction and/or squared terms, you must create and add these higher-order variables to the SPSS spreadsheet file *prior* to running a regression analysis. You can do this by clicking the "Transform" button on the SPSS main menu and selecting the "Compute" option.] To perform a standard regression analysis, select "Enter" in the "Method" box. To perform a stepwise regression analysis, select "Stepwise" in the "Method" box.

Figure 11.S.1
SPSS menu options for regression

To perform a nested model *F*-test for additional model terms, click the "Next" button and enter the terms you want to test in the "Independent(s)" box. [*Note*: These terms, plus the terms you entered initially, form the complete model for the nested *F*-test.] Next, click the "Statistics" button and select "R squared change". Click "Continue" to return to the main SPSS regression dialog box.

To produce confidence intervals for the model parameters, click the "Statistics" button and check the appropriate menu items in the resulting menu list. To obtain prediction intervals for y and confidence intervals for $E(y)$, click the "Save" button, and check the appropriate items in the resulting menu list. (The prediction intervals will be added as new columns to the SPSS data spreadsheet.) Residual plots are obtained by clicking the "Plots" button and making the appropriate selections on the resulting menu. To return to the main Regression dialog box from any of these optional screens, click "Continue". Click "OK" on the Regression dialog box to view the multiple regression results.

Figure 11.S.2
SPSS linear regression dialog box

11.2 Multiple Regression Using MINITAB

To conduct a multiple regression analysis, first access the MINITAB worksheet file that contains the dependent and independent variables. Next, click on the "Stat" button on the MINITAB menu bar, then click on "Regression" and "Regression" again, as shown in Figure 11.M.1.

The resulting dialog box appears as shown in Figure 11.M.2. Specify the dependent variable in the "Response" box and the independent variables in the "Predictors" box. [*Note*: If your model includes interaction and/or squared terms, you must create and add these higher-order variables to the MINITAB worksheet *prior* to running a regression analysis. You can do this by clicking the "Calc" button on the MINITAB main menu and selecting the "Calculator" option.]

To produce prediction intervals for y and confidence intervals for $E(y)$, click the "Options" button and select the appropriate menu items in the resulting menu list. Residual plots are obtained by clicking the "Graphs" button and making the appropriate selections on the resulting menu. To return to the main Regression dialog box from any of these optional

Figure 11.M.1
MINITAB menu options for regression

Figure 11.M.2
MINITAB regression dialog box

screens, click "OK". When you have made all your selections, click "OK" on the main Regression dialog box to produce the MINITAB multiple regression printout.

To conduct a stepwise regression analysis, click on the "Stat" button on the main menu bar, then click on "Regression", and click on "Stepwise" (see Figure 11.M.1). The resulting dialog box appears in Figure 11.M.3. Specify the dependent variable in the "Response" box and the independent variables in the stepwise model in the "Predictors" box. As an option, you can select the value of α to use in the analysis by clicking on the "Methods" button and specifying the value. (The default is $\alpha = .15$.) Click "OK" to view the stepwise regression results.

Figure 11.M.3
MINITAB stepwise regression dialog box

11.3 Multiple Regression Using Excel/PHStat2

To conduct a multiple regression analysis, first access the Excel worksheet file that contains the dependent and independent variables. [*Note*: If your model includes interaction and/or squared terms, you must create and add these higher-order variables to the Excel worksheet *prior* to running a regression analysis.] Next, click "PHStat" from the Excel menu bar, then select "Regression" and "Multiple Regression", as shown in Figure 11.E.1. The resulting dialog box is shown in

Figure 11.E.1
Excel menu options for multiple regression

Figure 11.E.2. Specify the cell ranges for the y- and x-variables in the "Data" area of the Multiple Regression dialog box. [*Note*: The x-variables must be in adjacent columns on the EXCEL worksheet.]

Select the confidence level for confidence intervals for the model parameters, and select both the "Regression Statistics" and "ANOVA and Coefficients" table options. To produce graphs of the regression residual, select the "Residual Plots" option. To produce prediction intervals for y and confidence intervals for $E(y)$, select the "Confidence and Prediction Interval Estimates" option and specify the confidence level (as shown at the bottom of Figure 11.E.2). After making all your selections, click "OK" to produce the multiple regression results. [*Note*: The standard regression printout will appear in one worksheet and the confidence/prediction intervals will appear in a second worksheet. Also, on the second worksheet, you will be prompted to select specific values of the x's for predicting y.]

Figure 11.E.2
Excel/PHStat2 multiple regression dialog box

To conduct a stepwise regression analysis, click "PHStat" from the Excel menu bar, then select "Regression" and "Stepwise Regression" (see Figure 11.E.1). The resulting dialog box is shown in Figure 11.E.3. Specify the cell ranges for the y- and x-variables in the "Data" area of the Stepwise Regression dialog box. [*Note*: The x-variables must be in adjacent columns on the Excel worksheet.] As an option, you can select the p-value to use for variable entry and removal. (The default is p-value = .05.) Click "OK" to view the stepwise regression results.

Figure 11.E.3
Excel/PHStat2 stepwise regression dialog box

Real-World Case

The Condo Sales Case

(A Case Covering Chapters 10 and 11)

This case involves an investigation of the factors that affect the sale price of oceanside condominium units. It represents an extension of an analysis of the same data by Herman Kelting (1979). Although condo sale prices have increased dramatically over the past 20 years, the relationship between these factors and sale price remain about the same. Consequently, the data provide valuable insight into today's condominium sales market.

The sales data were obtained for a new oceanside condominium complex consisting of two adjacent and connected eight-floor buildings. The complex contains 200 units of equal size (approximately 500 square feet each). The locations of the buildings relative to the ocean, the swimming pool, the parking lot, etc., are shown in the accompanying figure. There are several features of the complex that you should note:

1. The units facing south, called *ocean view,* face the beach and ocean. In addition, units in building 1 have a good view of the pool. Units to the rear of the building, called *bay-view,* face the parking lot and an area of land that ultimately borders a bay. The view from the upper floors of these units is primarily of wooded, sandy terrain. The bay is very distant and barely visible.

2. The only elevator in the complex is located at the east end of building 1, as are the office and the game room. People moving to or from the higher floor units in building 2 would likely use the elevator and move through the passages to their units. Thus, units on the higher floors and at a greater distance from the elevator would be less convenient; they would require greater effort in moving baggage, groceries, and so on and would be farther away from the game room, the office, and the swimming pool. These units also possess an advantage: there would be the least amount of traffic through the hallways in the area and hence they are the most private.

3. Lower-floor oceanside units are most suited to active people; they open onto the beach, ocean, and pool. They are within easy reach of the game room, and they are easily reached from the parking area.

4. Checking the layout of the condominium complex, you discover that some of the units in the center of the com-

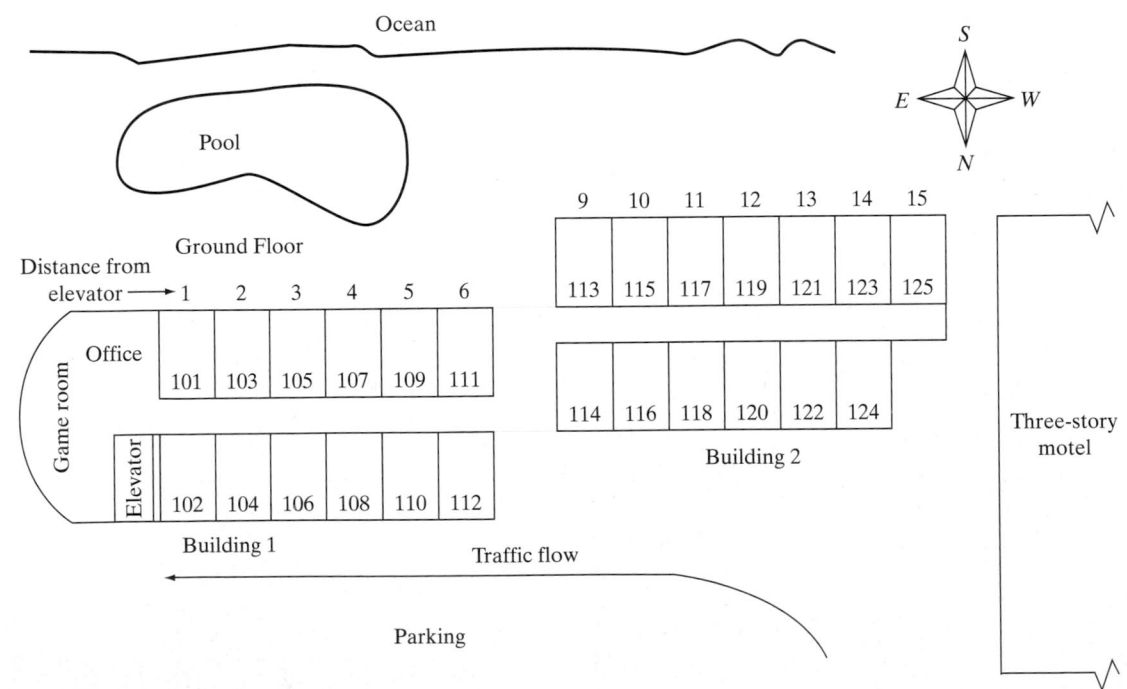

FIGURE C5.1
Layout of condominium complex

plex, units ending in numbers 11 and 14, have part of their view blocked.

5. The condominium complex was completed at the time of the 1975 recession; sales were slow and the developer was forced to sell most of the units at auction approximately 18 months after opening. Consequently, the auction data are completely buyer-specified and hence consumer-oriented in contrast to most other real estate sales data that are, to a high degree, seller and broker specified.

6. Many unsold units in the complex were furnished by the developer and rented prior to the auction. Consequently, some of the units bid on and sold at auction had furniture, others did not.

This condominium complex is obviously unique. For example, the single elevator located at one end of the complex produces a remarkably high level of both inconvenience and privacy for the people occupying units on the top floors in building 2. Consequently, the developer is unsure of how the height of the unit (floor number), distance of the unit from the elevator, presence or absence of an ocean view, etc., affect the prices of the units sold at auction. To investigate these relationships, the following data (saved in the **CONDO** data file) were recorded for each of the 106 units sold at the auction:

1. *Sale price.* Measured in hundreds of dollars (adjusted for inflation).

2. *Floor height.* The floor location of the unit; the variable levels are $1, 2, \ldots, 8$.

3. *Distance from elevator.* This distance, measured along the length of the complex, is expressed in number of condominium units. An additional two units of distance was added to the units in building 2 to account for the walking distance in the connecting area between the two buildings. Thus, the distance of unit 105

from the elevator would be 3, and the distance between unit 113 and the elevator would be 9. The variable levels are $1, 2, \ldots, 15$.

4. *View of ocean.* The presence or absence of an ocean view is recorded for each unit and specified with a dummy variable (1 if the unit possessed an ocean view and 0 if not). Note that units not possessing an ocean view would face the parking lot.

5. *End unit.* We expect the partial reduction of view of end units on the ocean side (numbers ending in 11) to reduce their sale price. The ocean view of these end units is partially blocked by building 2. This qualitative variable is also specified with a dummy variable (1 if the unit has a unit number ending in 11 and 0 if not).

6. *Furniture.* The presence or absence of furniture is recorded for each unit and is represented with a single dummy variable (1 if the unit was furnished and 0 if not).

Your objective for this case is to build a regression model that accurately predicts the sale price of a condominium unit sold at auction. Prepare a professional document that presents the results of your analysis. Include graphs that demonstrate how each of the independent variables in your model affects auction price. A layout of the **CONDO** data file is described below.

 CONDO (Number of Observation: 106)

Variable	Type
PRICE	QN
FLOOR	QN
DISTANCE	QN
VIEW	QL
ENDUNIT	QL
FURNISH	QL

Methods for Quality Improvement

CONTENTS

STATISTICS IN ACTION

Testing Jet Fuel Additive for Safety

USING TECHNOLOGY

WHERE WE'VE BEEN

- Presented methods for making inferences about populations based on sample data (Chapters 5–9) using confidence intervals and tests of hypotheses.

- Presented methods for modeling the relationships between variables (Chapters 10–11) using regression analysis.

WHERE WE'RE GOING

- Return to an examination of processes (i.e., actions/operations that transform inputs to outputs).

- Describe methods for improving processes and the quality of the output they produce.

- Present control charts for monitoring a process mean, variance, or proportion.

STATISTICS IN ACTION

Testing Jet Fuel Additive for Safety

The American Society of Testing and Materials (ASTM) International provides standards and guidelines for materials, products, systems, and services. The Federal Aviation Administration (FAA) has a huge conglomerate of testing requirements for jet fuel safety that are spelled out in ASTM methods. This Statistics in Action involves an engineering firm that is developing a new method of surfactant detection in jet fuel.

Surfactants (surface active agents) are basically soaps, which can form due to acids in the fuel but are more commonly caused by contamination from other products, such as engine cleaning additives. Although the surfactants do not directly cause problems, they reduce the ability of coalescing filters to remove water. Water in jet fuel carries bacteria that deposits in tanks and engine components, causing major corrosion and engine damage.

The standard test for surfactants (described in ASTM Rule D-3948) is to use a miniature filter (Filter-A) with a pumping mechanism (Pump-A). A water/fuel mixture is pumped through the filter at a specific rate, and the amount of water that passes through the filter is detected with an optical transmittance test. Test measurements will typically yield a result between 80 and 85.

In an attempt to improve the precision of the surfactant test, the engineering firm compared the standard test (Pump-A with Filter-A) to three other pumping mechanism and filter option combinations—Pump-A with Filter-B, Pump-B with Filter-A, and Pump-B with Filter-B. Each day, a routine batch of jet fuel was created by adding 0.4 ppm of a surfactant solution. Twelve samples of the fuel were randomly selected and randomly divided into four groups of three samples each. The three samples in a group were tested for surfactants using one of the four pump/filter combinations. Consequently, each day there were three test results for each pump/filter method. This pattern of sampling continued for over 100 days. The test measurements are saved in four **JETFUEL** files. (Data for the first five days of the sampling experiment are listed in Table SIA 12.1).

TABLE SIA12.1 Selected Data in the JETFUEL Files

	Weekday	Month	Day	Sample	Pump-B Filter-A	Pump-A Filter-A	Pump-B Filter-B	Pump-A Filter-B
JETFUELA-A	Tue	May	9	1	76	84	85	85
JETFUELA-B				2	81	91	84	84
				3	81	86	84	88
JETFUELB-A	Wed	May	10	1	84	92	87	92
				2	81	93	82	95
JETFUELB-B				3	86	94	85	90
	Thu	May	11	1	83	94	82	90
				2	82	96	85	87
				3	79	92	84	81
	Fri	May	12	1	81	96	81	90
				2	84	91	82	91
				3	83	96	88	92
	Mon	May	15	1	80	90	87	94
				2	88	92	85	94
				3	87	91	86	84

Continued

The firm wants to monitor the results of the surfactant tests and determine if one of the test methods yields the most stable process. In the Statistics in Action Revisited sections listed, we show how to analyze the data using methods for quality and process control.

Statistics in Action Revisited

- Monitoring the Mean of the Jet Fuel Surfactant Test Process (p. 818)
- Monitoring the Variation of the Jet Fuel Surfactant Test Process (p. 830)

Over the last two decades, U.S. firms have been seriously challenged by products of superior quality from overseas, particularly from Japan. Japan currently produces 25% of the cars sold in the United States. In 1989, for the first time, the top-selling car in the United States was made in Japan: the Honda Accord. Although it's an American invention, virtually all VCRs are produced in Japan. Only one U.S. firm still manufactures televisions; the rest are made in Japan.

To meet this competitive challenge, more and more U.S. firms—both manufacturing and service firms—have begun quality-improvement initiatives of their own. Many of these firms now stress **total quality management** (TQM) (i.e., the management of quality in all phases and aspects of their business, from the design of their products to production, distribution, sales, and service).

Broadly speaking, TQM is concerned with (1) finding out what it is that the customer wants, (2) translating those wants into a product or service design, and (3) producing a product or service that meets or exceeds the specifications of the design. In this chapter we focus primarily on the third of these three areas and its major problem—product and service variation.

Variation is inherent in the output of all production and service processes. No two parts produced by a given machine are the same; no two transactions performed by a given bank teller are the same. Why is this a problem? With variation in output comes variation in the quality of the product or service. If this variation is unacceptable to customers, sales are lost, profits suffer, and the firm may not survive.

The existence of this ever-present variation has made statistical methods and statistical training vitally important to industry. In this chapter we present some of the tools and methods currently employed by firms worldwide to monitor and reduce product and service variation.

12.1 Quality, Processes, and Systems

Quality

Before describing various tools and methods that can be used to monitor and improve the quality of products and services, we need to consider what is meant by the term *quality*. Quality can be defined from several different perspectives. To the engineers and scientists who design products, quality typically refers to the amount of some ingredient or attribute possessed by the product. For example, high-quality ice cream contains a large amount of butterfat. High-quality rugs have a large number of knots per square inch. A high-quality shirt or blouse has 22 to 26 stitches per inch.

To managers, engineers, and workers involved in the production of a product (or the delivery of a service), quality usually means conformance to requirements, or the degree to which the product or service conforms to its design specifications. For example, in order to fit properly, the cap of a particular molded plastic bottle must be between 1.0000 inch and 1.0015 inches in diameter. Caps that do not conform to this requirement are considered to be of inferior quality. For an example in a service operation, consider the service provided to customers in a fast-food restaurant. A particular restaurant has been designed to serve customers within 2 minutes of the time their order is placed. If it takes more than 2 minutes, the service does not conform to specifications and is considered to be of inferior quality. Using this production-based interpretation of quality, well-made products are high quality; poorly made products are low quality. Thus, a well-made Rolls-Royce and a well-made Chevrolet Nova are both high-quality cars.

Although quality can be defined from either the perspective of the designers or the producers of a product, in the final analysis both definitions should be derived from the needs and preferences of the *user* of the product or service. A firm that produces goods that no one wants to purchase cannot stay in business. We define *quality* accordingly.

Definition 12.1

The **quality** of a good or service is indicated by the extent to which it satisfies the needs and preferences of its users.

Consumers' needs and wants shape their perceptions of quality. Thus, to produce a high-quality product, it is necessary to study the needs and wants of consumers. This is typically one of the major functions of a firm's marketing department. Once the consumer research has been conducted, it is necessary to translate consumers' desires into a product design. This design must then be translated into a production plan and production specifications that, if properly implemented, will turn out a product with characteristics that will satisfy users' needs and wants. In short, consumer perceptions of quality play a role in all phases and aspects of a firm's operations.

But what product characteristics are consumers looking for? What is it that influences users' perceptions of quality? This is the kind of knowledge that firms need in order to develop and deliver high-quality goods and services. The basic elements of quality are summarized in the eight dimensions shown in the box.

The Eight Dimensions of Quality*

1. **Performance:** The primary operating characteristics of the product. For an automobile, these would include acceleration, handling, smoothness of ride, gas mileage, etc.

2. **Features:** The "bells and whistles" that supplement the product's basic functions. Examples include CD players and digital clocks on cars and the frequent-flyer mileage and free drinks offered by airlines.

3. **Reliability:** Reflects the probability that the product will operate properly within a given period of time.

4. **Conformance:** The extent or degree to which a product meets preestablished standards. This is reflected in, for example, a pharmaceutical manufacturer's concern that the plastic bottles it orders for its drugs have caps that are between 1.0000 and 1.0015 inches in diameter, as specified in the order.

5. **Durability:** The life of the product. If repair is possible, durability relates to the length of time a product can be used before replacement is judged to be preferable to continued repair.

6. **Serviceability:** The ease of repair, speed of repair, and competence and courtesy of the repair staff.

7. **Aesthetics:** How a product looks, feels, sounds, smells, or tastes.

8. **Other perceptions that influence judgments of quality:** Such factors as a firm's reputation and the images of the firm and its products that are created through advertising.

---

*Garvin, D. *Managing Quality*. New York: Free Press/Macmillan, 1988.

In order to design and produce products of high quality, it is necessary to translate the characteristics described in the box into product attributes that can be built into the product by the manufacturer—that is, user preferences must be interpreted in terms of product variables over which the manufacturer has control. For example, in considering the performance characteristics of a particular brand of wooden pencil, users may indicate a preference for being able to use the pencil for longer periods between sharpenings. The manufacturer may translate this performance characteristic into one or more measurable physical characteristics such as wood hardness, lead hardness, and lead composition. Besides being used to design high-quality products, such variables are used in the process of monitoring and improving quality during production.

Processes

Much of this textbook focuses on methods for using sample data drawn from a population to learn about that population. In this chapter and the next, however, our attention is not on populations but on processes—such as manufacturing processes—and the output that they generate. In general, a process is defined as follows:

Definition 12.2

A **process** is a series of actions or operations that transforms inputs to outputs. A process produces output over time.

Processes can be organizational or personal in nature. Organizational processes are those associated with organizations such as businesses and governments. Perhaps the best example is a manufacturing process, which consists of a series of operations, performed by people and machines, whereby inputs such as raw materials and parts are converted into finished products (the outputs). Examples include automobile assembly lines, oil refineries, and steel mills. Personal processes are those associated with your private life. The series of steps you go through each morning to get ready for school or work can be thought of as a process. Through turning off the alarm clock, showering, dressing, eating, and opening the garage door, you transform yourself from a sleeping person to one who is ready to interact with the outside world. Figure 12.1 presents a general description of a process and its inputs.

It is useful to think of processes as *adding value* to the inputs of the process. Manufacturing processes, for example, are designed so that the value of the outputs to potential customers exceeds the value of the inputs—otherwise the firm would have no demand for its products and would not survive.

Systems

To understand what causes variation in process output and how processes and their output can be improved, we must understand the role that processes play in *systems*.

Definition 12.3

A **system** is a collection or arrangement of interacting processes that has an ongoing purpose or mission. A system receives inputs from its environment, transforms those inputs to outputs, and delivers them to its environment. In order to survive, a system uses feedback (i.e., information) from its environment to understand and adapt to changes in its environment.

Figure 12.2 presents a model of a basic system. As an example of a system, consider a manufacturing company. It has a collection of interacting processes—marketing research, engineering, purchasing, receiving, production, sales, distribution, billing, and so on. Its mission is to make money for its owners, to provide high-quality working conditions for its employees, and to stay in business. The firm receives raw materials and parts (inputs) from outside vendors that, through its production processes, it transforms to fin-

INPUTS   **OUTPUTS**

FIGURE 12.1
Graphical depiction of a process and its inputs

ished goods (outputs). The finished goods are distributed to its customers. Through its marketing research, the firm "listens" to (receives feedback from) its customers and potential customers in order to change or adapt its processes and products to meet (or exceed) the needs, preferences, and expectations of the marketplace.

Since systems are collections of processes, the various types of system inputs are the same as those listed in Figure 12.1 for processes. System outputs are products or services. These outputs may be physical objects made, assembled, repaired, or moved by the system; or they may be symbolical, such as information, ideas, or knowledge. For example, a brokerage house supplies customers with information about stocks and bonds and the markets where they are traded.

Two important points about systems and the output of their processes are as follows: (1) No two items produced by a process are the same; (2) variability is an inherent characteristic of the output of all processes. This is illustrated in Figure 12.3. No two cars produced by the same assembly line are the same: No two windshields are the same; no two wheels are the same; no two tires are the same; no two hubcaps are the same. The same thing can be said for processes that deliver services. Consider the services offered at the teller windows of a bank to two customers waiting in two lines. Will they wait in line the same amount of time? Will they be serviced by tellers with the same degree of expertise and with the same personalities? Assuming the customers' transactions are the same, will they take the same amount of time to execute? The answer to all these questions is no

FIGURE 12.2
Model of a basic system

FIGURE 12.3
Output variation

Biography

**W. EDWARDS DEMING
(1900–1993)**

Deming's 14 Points

Born in Sioux City, Iowa, Ed Deming was raised on an Iowa farm until age 7, when his family moved to Wyoming. Because his parents emphasized the importance of education, Deming enrolled at the University of Wyoming in 1917, graduating 4 years later with a degree in electrical engineering. He eventually earned his PhD in mathematical physics from Yale University in 1928. Deming worked for both the U.S. Department of Agriculture and Census Bureau before becoming a statistics professor at New York University and Columbia University. While studying under W. A. Shewhart (see Biography, p. 804) in the 1930s, Deming become interested in the application of statistics to quality and process improvement for industry. He is probably most famous for his "14 Points for Management" (see accompanying box)—guidelines that transform the organizational climate to one in which process-management efforts can flourish. In 1950, the Japanese Union of Scientists and Engineers invited Deming to present a series of lectures on these ideas. His expertise and advice on quality-control methods helped to revolutionize Japan's industry, leading to the Japanese economic boom in the 20th century. (The *Deming Prize* is awarded every year to the corporation with the greatest accomplishment in quality improvement in the world.)

Deming's 14 Points: Guidelines for Quality Improvement

1. **Create constancy of purpose toward improvement of product and service, with the aim to become competitive and to stay in business, and to provide jobs.** The organization must have a clear goal or purpose. Everyone in the organization must be encouraged to work toward that goal day in and day out, year after year.

2. **Adopt the new philosophy.** Reject detection-rejection management in favor of a customer-oriented, preventative style of management in which never-ending quality improvement is the driving force.

3. **Cease dependence on inspection to achieve quality.** It is because of poorly designed products and excessive process variation that inspection is needed. If quality is designed into products and process management is used in their production, mass inspection of finished products will not be necessary.

4. **End the practice of awarding business on the basis of price tag.** Do not simply buy from the lowest bidder. Consider the quality of the supplier's products along with the supplier's price. Establish long-term relationships with suppliers based on loyalty and trust. Move toward using a single supplier for each item needed.

5. **Improve constantly and forever the system of production and service, to improve quality and productivity, and thus constantly decrease costs**.

6. **Institute training.** Workers are often trained by other workers who were never properly trained themselves. The result is excessive process variation and inferior products and services. This is not the workers' fault; no one has told them how to do their jobs well.

7. **Institute leadership.** Supervisors should help the workers to do a better job. Their job is to lead, not to order workers around or to punish them.

8. **Drive out fear, so that everyone may work effectively for the company.** Many workers are afraid to ask questions or to bring problems to the attention of management. Such a climate is not conducive to producing high-quality goods and services. People work best when they feel secure.

9. **Break down barriers between departments.** Everyone in the organization must work together as a team. Different areas within the firm should have complementary, not conflicting, goals. People across the organization must realize that they are all part of the same system. Pooling their resources to solve problems is better than competing against each other.

10. **Eliminate slogans, exhortations, and arbitrary numerical goals and targets for the workforce that urge the workers to achieve new levels of productivity and quality.** Simply asking the workers to improve their work is not enough; they must be shown *how* to improve it. Management must realize that significant improvements can be achieved only if management takes responsibility for quality and makes the necessary changes in the design of the system in which the workers operate.

11. **Eliminate numerical quotas.** Quotas are purely quantitative (e.g., number of pieces to produce per day); they do not take quality into consideration. When faced with quotas, people attempt to meet them at any cost, regardless of the damage to the organization.

12. **Remove barriers that rob employees of their pride of workmanship.** People must be treated as human beings, not commodities. Working conditions must be improved, including the elimination of poor supervision, poor product design, defective materials, and defective machines. These things stand in the way of workers' performing up to their capabilities and producing work they are proud of.

13. **Institute a vigorous program of education and self-improvement.** Continuous improvement requires continuous learning. Everyone in the organization must be trained in the modern methods of quality improvement, including statistical concepts and interdepartmental teamwork. Top management should be the first to be trained.

14. **Take action to accomplish the transformation.** Hire people with the knowledge to implement the 14 points. Build a critical mass of people committed to transforming the organization. Put together a top management team to lead the way. Develop a plan and an organizational structure that will facilitate the transformation.

In general, variation in output is caused by the six factors listed in the box.

The Six Major Sources of Process Variation

1. People
2. Machines
3. Materials
4. Methods
5. Measurement
6. Environment

Awareness of this ever-present process variation has made training in statistical thinking and statistical methods highly valued by industry. By **statistical thinking** we mean the knack of recognizing variation and exploiting it in problem solving and decision making. The remainder of this chapter is devoted to statistical tools for monitoring process variation.

12.2 Statistical Control

For the rest of this chapter we turn our attention to **control charts**—graphical devices used for monitoring process variation, for identifying when to take action to improve the process and for assisting in diagnosing the causes of process variation. Control charts, developed by Walter Shewhart of Bell Laboratories in the mid-1920s, are the tool of choice for continuously monitoring processes. Before we go into the details of control chart construction and use, however, it is important that you have a fuller understanding of process variation. To this end, we discuss patterns of variation in this section.

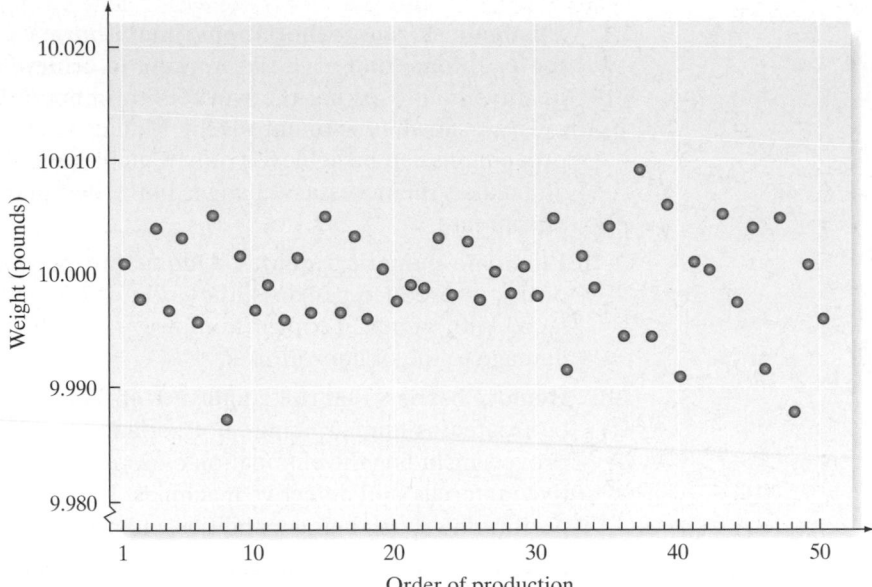

FIGURE 12.4

Time series plot of fill weights for 50 consecutively produced gallon cans of paint

As was discussed in Chapter 2, the proper graphical method for describing the variation of process output is a *time series plot*, sometimes called a **run chart.** Recall that in a time series plot, the measurements of interest are plotted against time or are plotted in the order in which the measurements were made, as in Figure 12.4. Whenever you face the task of analyzing data that were generated over time, your first reaction should be to plot them. The human eye is one of our most sensitive statistical instruments. Take advantage of that sensitivity by plotting the data and allowing your eyes to seek out patterns in the data.

Let's begin thinking about process variation by examining the plot in Figure 12.4 more closely. The measurements, taken from a paint manufacturing process, are the weights of 50 one-gallon cans of paint that were consecutively filled by the same filling head (nozzle). The weights were plotted in the order of production. Do you detect any systematic, persistent patterns in the sequence of weights? For example, do the weights tend to drift steadily upward or downward over time? Do they oscillate—high, then low, then high, then low, and so on?

To assist your visual examination of this or any other time series plot, Roberts (1991) recommends enhancing the basic plot in two ways. First, compute (or simply esti-

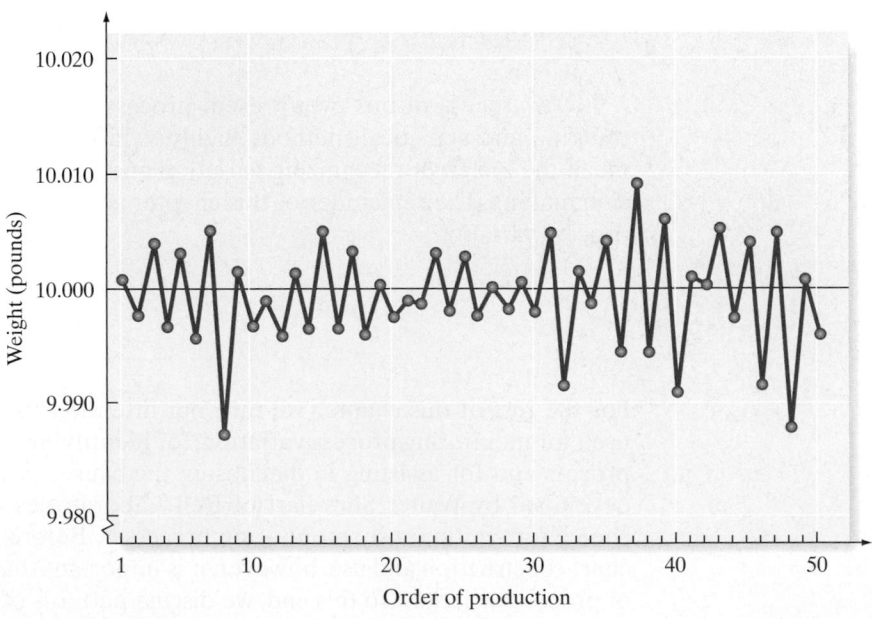

FIGURE 12.5

An enhanced version of the paint fill time series

mate) the mean of the set of 50 weights and draw a horizontal line on the graph at the level of the mean. This **centerline** gives you a point of reference in searching for patterns in the data. Second, using straight lines, connect each of the plotted weights in the order in which they were produced. This helps display the sequence of the measurements. Both enhancements are shown in Figure 12.5.

Now do you see a pattern in the data? Successive points alternate up and down, high then low, in an **oscillating sequence.** In this case, the points alternate above and below the centerline. This pattern was caused by a valve in the paint-filling machine that tended to stick in a partially closed position every other time it operated.

Other patterns of process variation are shown in Figure 12.6. We discuss several of them later.

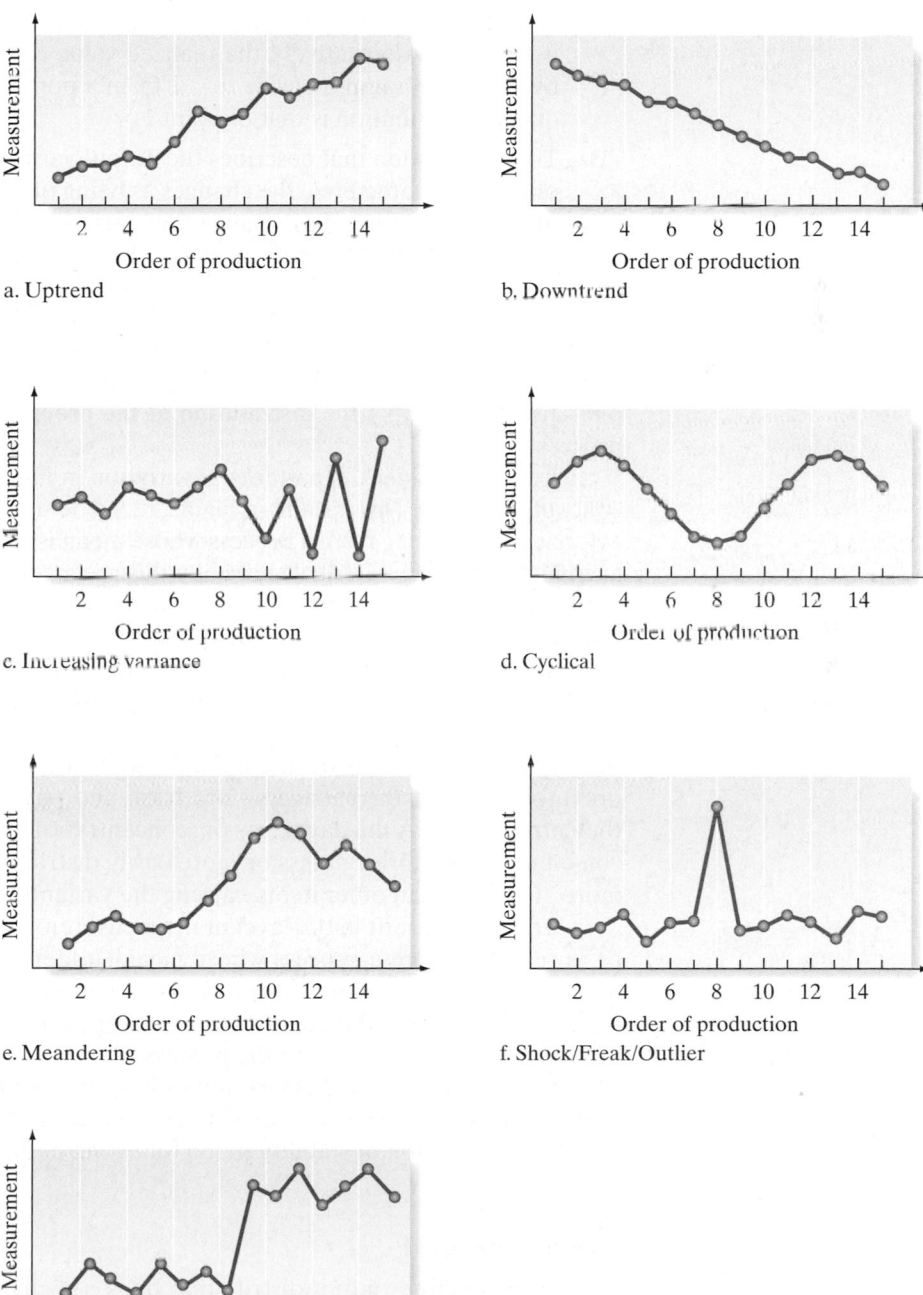

FIGURE 12.6

Patterns of process variation: Some examples

In trying to describe process variation and diagnose its causes, it helps to think of the sequence of measurements of the output variable (e.g., weight, length, number of defects) as having been generated in the following way:

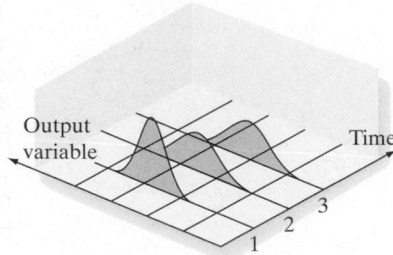

1. At any point in time, the output variable of interest can be described by a particular probability distribution (or relative frequency distribution). This distribution describes the possible values that the variable can assume and their likelihood of occurrence. Three such distributions are shown in Figure 12.7.

FIGURE 12.7
Distributions describing one output variable at three points in time

2. The particular value of the output variable that is realized at a given time can be thought of as being generated or produced according to the distribution described in point 1. (Alternatively, the realized value can be thought of as being generated by a random sample of size $n = 1$ from a population of values whose relative frequency distribution is that of point 1.)

3. The distribution that describes the output variable may change over time. For simplicity, we characterize the changes as being of three types: the mean (i.e., location) of the distribution may change; the variance (i.e., shape) of the distribution may change; or both. This is illustrated in Figure 12.8.

In general, when the output variable's distribution changes over time, we refer to this as a change in the *process*. Thus, if the mean shifts to a higher level, we say that the process mean has shifted. Accordingly, we sometimes refer to the distribution of the output variable as simply the **distribution of the process,** or the **output distribution of the process.**

Let's reconsider the patterns of variation in Figure 12.6 and model them using this conceptualization. This is done in Figure 12.9. The uptrend of Figure 12.6(a) can be characterized as resulting from a process whose mean is gradually shifting upward over time, as in Figure 12.9(a). Gradual shifts like this are a common phenomenon in manufacturing processes. For example, as a machine wears out (e.g., cutting blades dull), certain characteristics of its output gradually change.

The pattern of increasing dispersion in Figure 12.6(c) can be thought of as resulting from a process whose mean remains constant but whose variance increases over time, as shown in Figure 12.9(c). This type of deterioration in a process may be the result of worker fatigue. At the beginning of a shift, workers—whether they be typists, machine operators, waiters, or managers—are fresh and pay close attention to every item that they process. But as the day wears on, concentration may wane and the workers may become more and more careless or more easily distracted. As a result, some items receive more attention than other items, causing the variance of the workers' output to increase.

The sudden shift in the level of the measurements in Figure 12.6(g) can be thought of as resulting from a process whose mean suddenly increases but whose variance remains constant, as shown in Figure 12.9(g). This type of pattern may be caused by such things as a change in the quality of raw materials used in the process or bringing a new machine or new operator into the process.

One thing that all these examples have in common is that the distribution of the output variable *changes over time*. In such cases, we say the process lacks **stability.** We formalize the notion of stability in the following definition.

Definition 12.4

A process whose output distribution does *not* change over time is said to be in a state of **statistical control,** or simply **in control.** If it does change, it is said to be **out of statistical control,** or simply **out of control.**

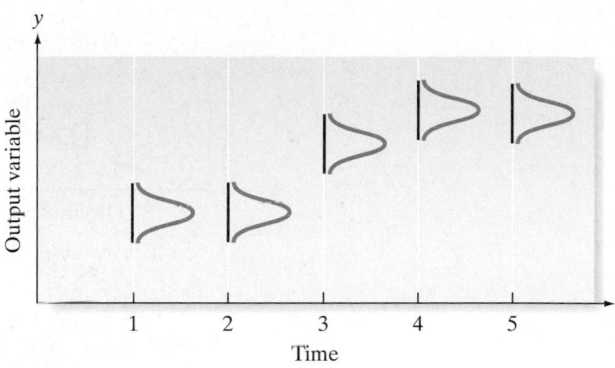

a. Change in mean (i.e., location)

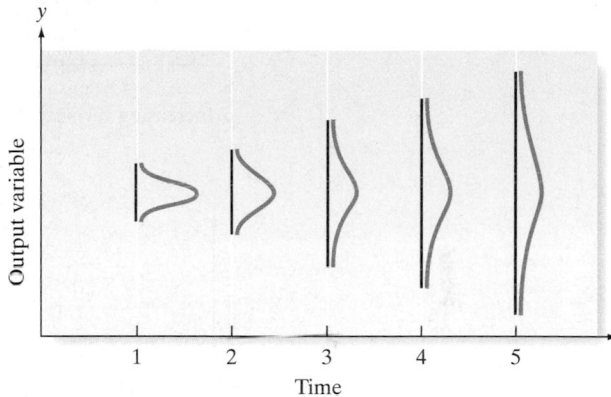

b. Change in variance (i.e., shape)

FIGURE 12.8

Types of changes in output variables

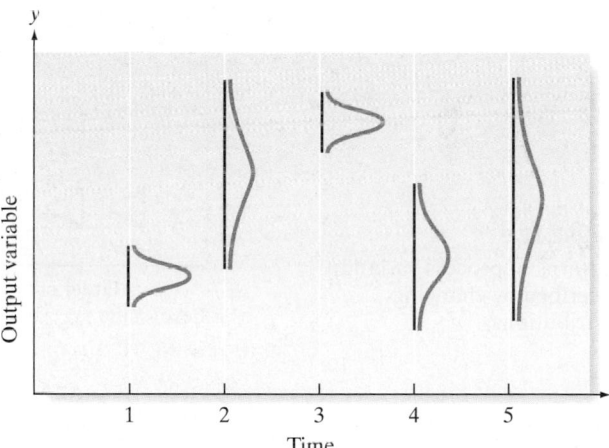

c. Change in mean and variance

Figure 12.10 illustrates a sequence of output distributions for both an in-control and an out-of-control process.

To see what the pattern of measurements looks like on a time series plot for a process that is in statistical control, consider Figure 12.11. These data are from the same paint-filling process we described earlier, but the sequence of measurements was made *after* the faulty valve was replaced. Notice that there are no discernible persistent, systematic patterns in the sequence of measurements such as those in Figures 12.5 and 12.6(a)–12.6(e). Nor are there level shifts or transitory shocks as in Figures 12.6(f)–12.6(g). This "patternless" behavior is called **random behavior. The output of**

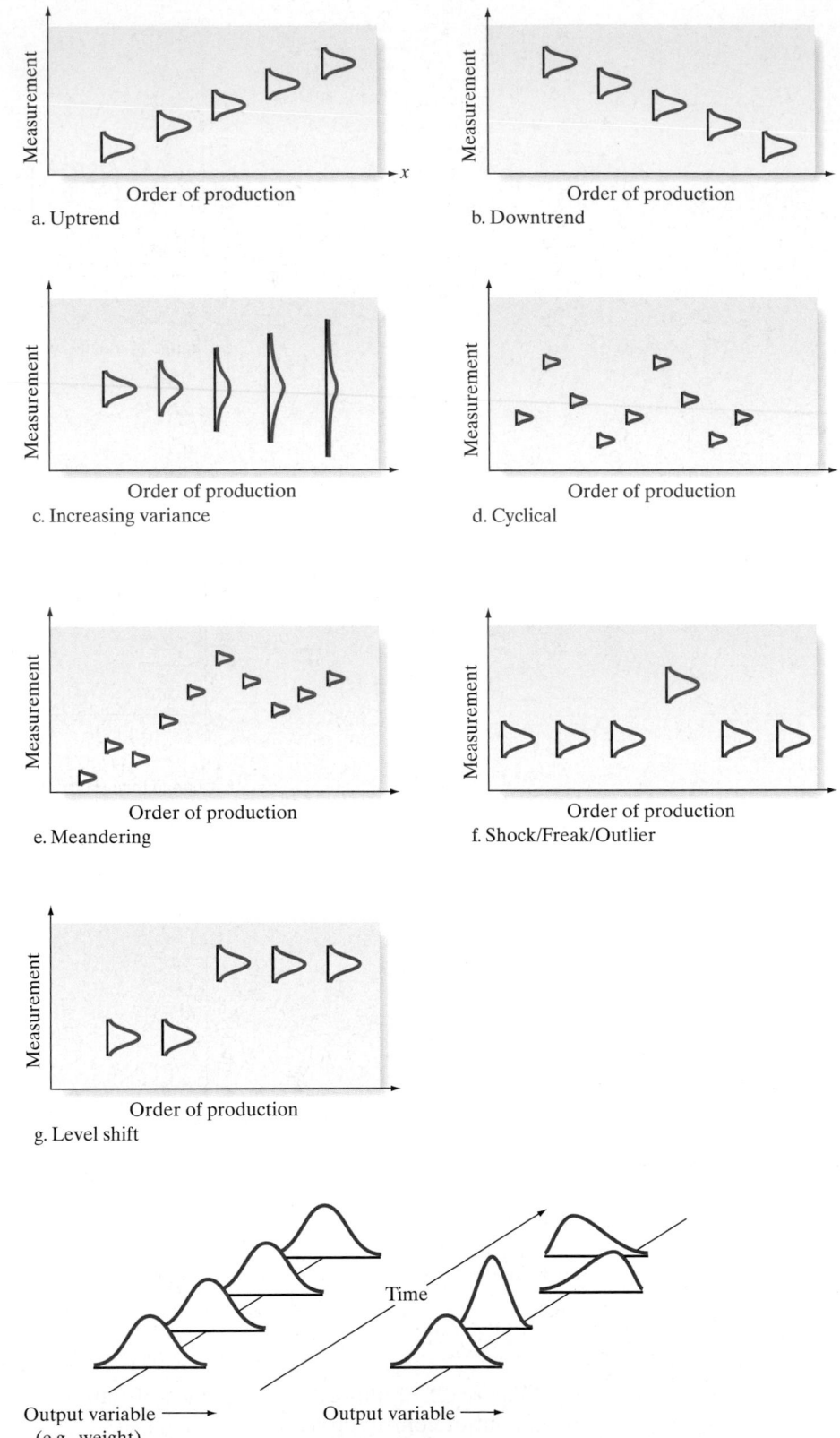

FIGURE 12.9

Patterns of process variation described by changing distributions

FIGURE 12.10

Comparison of in-control and out-of-control processes

processes that are in statistical control exhibits random behavior. Thus, even the output of stable processes exhibits variation.

If a process is in control and remains in control, its future will be like its past. Accordingly, the process is predictable, in the sense that its output will stay within certain limits. This cannot be said about an out-of-control process. As illustrated in Figure

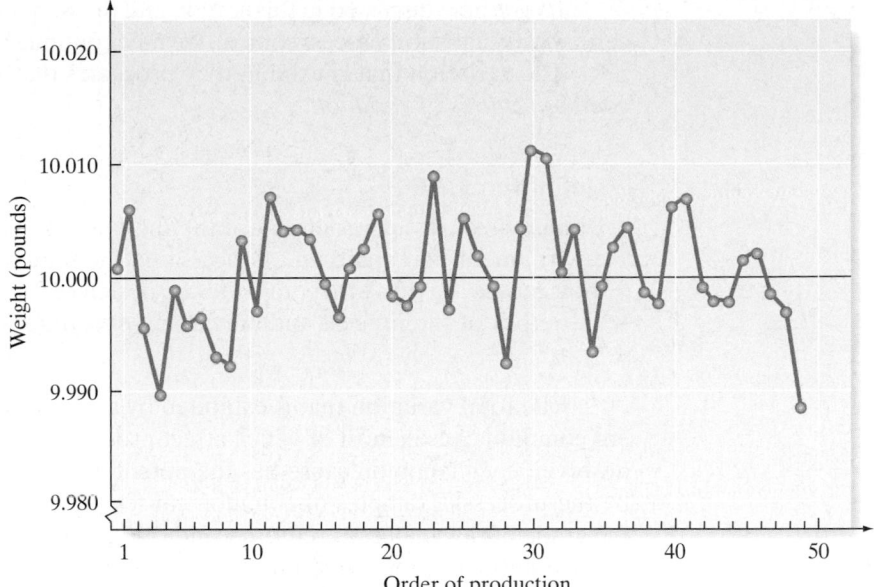

FIGURE 12.11

Time series plot of 50 consecutive paint can fills collected after replacing faulty valve

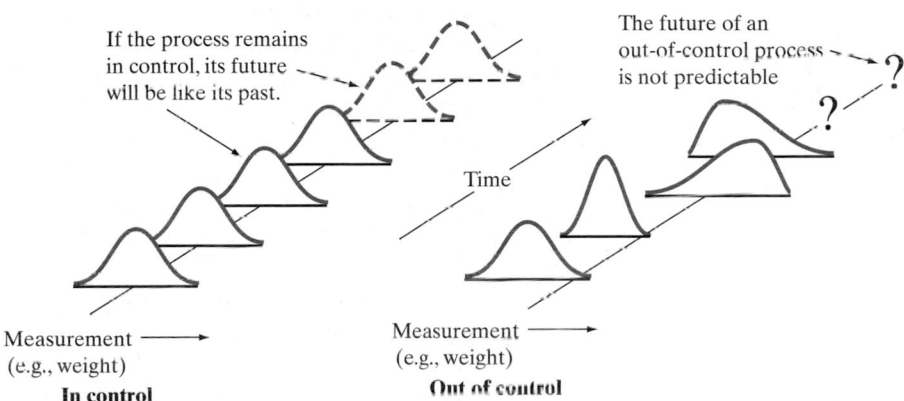

FIGURE 12.12

In-control processes are predictable; out-of-control processes are not

12.12, with most out-of-control processes, you have no idea what the future pattern of output from the process may look like.* You simply do not know what to expect from the process. Consequently, a business that operates out-of-control processes runs the risk of (1) providing inferior-quality products and services to its internal customers (people within the organization who use the outputs of the processes) and (2) selling inferior products and services to its external customers. In short, it risks losing its customers and threatens its own survival.

One of the fundamental goals of process management is to identify out-of-control processes, to take actions to bring them into statistical control, and to keep them in a state of statistical control. The series of activities used to attain this goal is referred to as *statistical process control*.

Definition 12.5

The process of monitoring and eliminating variation in order to *keep* a process in a state of statistical control or to *bring* a process into statistical control is called **statistical process control (SPC).**

---

*The output variables of in-control processes may follow approximately normal distributions, as in Figures 12.10 and 12.12, or they may not. But any in-control process will follow the *same* distribution over time. Do not misinterpret the use of normal distributions in many figures in this chapter as indicating that all in-control processes follow normal distributions.

Everything discussed in this section and the remaining sections of this chapter is concerned with statistical process control. We now continue our discussion of statistical control.

The variation that is exhibited by processes that are in control is said to be due to *common causes of variation*.

Definition 12.6

Common causes of variation are the methods, materials, machines, personnel, and environment that make up a process and the inputs required by the process. Common causes are thus attributable to the design of the process. Common causes affect all output of the process and may affect everyone who participates in the process.

The total variation that is exhibited by an in-control process is due to many different common causes, most of which affect process output in very minor ways. In general, however, each common cause has the potential to affect every unit of output produced by the process. Examples of common causes include the lighting in a factory or office, the grade of raw materials required, and the extent of worker training. Each of these factors can influence the variability of the process output. Poor lighting can cause workers to overlook flaws and defects that they might otherwise catch. Inconsistencies in raw materials can cause inconsistencies in the quality of the finished product. The extent of the training provided to workers can affect their level of expertise and, as a result, the quality of the products and services for which they are responsible.

Since common causes are, in effect, designed into a process, the level of variation that results from common causes is viewed as being representative of the capability of the process. If that level is too great (i.e., if the quality of the output varies too much), the process must be redesigned (or modified) to eliminate one or more common causes of variation. Since process redesign is the responsibility of management, the *elimination of common causes of variation is typically the responsibility of management*, not of the workers.

Processes that are out of control exhibit variation that is the result of both common causes and *special causes of variation*.

Definition 12.7

Special causes of variation (sometimes called **assignable causes**) are events or actions that are not part of the process design. Typically, they are transient, fleeting events that affect only local areas or operations within the process (e.g., a single worker, machine, or batch of materials) for a brief period of time. Occasionally, however, such events may have a persistent or recurrent effect on the process.

Examples of special causes of variation include a worker accidentally setting the controls of a machine improperly, a worker becoming ill on the job and continuing to work, a particular machine slipping out of adjustment, and a negligent supplier shipping a batch of inferior raw materials to the process.

In the latter case, the pattern of output variation may look like Figure 12.6(f). If instead of shipping just one bad batch the supplier continued to send inferior materials, the pattern of variation might look like Figure 12.6(g). The output of a machine that is gradually slipping out of adjustment might yield a pattern like Figure 12.6(a), 12.6(b), or 12.6(c). All these patterns owe part of their variation to common causes and part to the noted special causes. In general, we treat any pattern of variation other than a random pattern as due to both common and special causes.* Since the effects of special causes are frequently localized within a process, *special causes can often be diagnosed and elim-*

---

*For certain processes (e.g., those affected by seasonal factors), a persistent systematic pattern—such as the cyclical pattern of Figure 12.6(d)—is an inherent characteristic. In these special cases, some analysts treat the cause of the systematic variation as a common cause. This type of analysis is beyond the scope of this text. We refer the interested reader to Alwan and Roberts (1988).

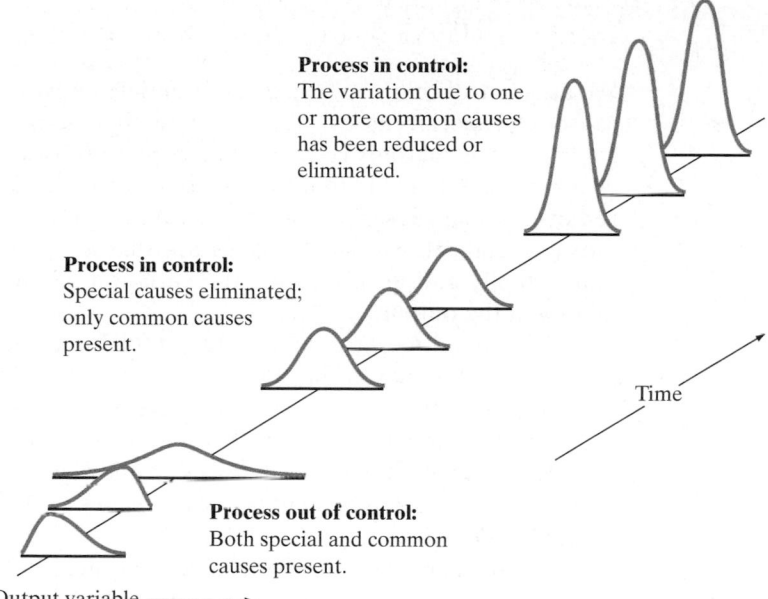

Process in control:
The variation due to one or more common causes has been reduced or eliminated.

Process in control:
Special causes eliminated; only common causes present.

Time

Process out of control:
Both special and common causes present.

FIGURE 12.13
The effects of eliminating causes of variation

Output variable ⟶

inated by workers or their immediate supervisor. Occasionally, they must be dealt with by management, as in the case of a negligent or deceitful supplier.

It is important to recognize that **most processes are not naturally in a state of statistical control.** As Deming (1986, p. 322) observed, *"Stability [i.e., statistical control] is seldom a natural state. It is an achievement, the result of eliminating special causes one by one . . . leaving only the random variation of a stable process"* (italics added).

Process improvement first requires the identification, diagnosis, and removal of special causes of variation. Removing all special causes puts the process in a state of statistical control. Further improvement of the process then requires the identification, diagnosis, and removal of common causes of variation. The effects on the process of the removal of special and common causes of variation are illustrated in Figure 12.13.

In the remainder of this chapter, we introduce you to some of the methods of statistical process control. In particular, we address how control charts help us determine whether a given process is in control.

ACTIVITY 12.1: *Quality Control: Consistency*

In some businesses, such as the food service industry, the consistency of a product contributes greatly to customer satisfaction. When a customer orders a particular menu item on a regular basis, he or she expects to receive a product which has approximately the same taste and appearance each time. The challenge for a national chain is not only to have a single worker be consistent but also to have thousands of workers nationwide produce the same menu item with little variation in taste and appearance.

1. The quality of some products, such as coffee and french fries, deteriorates quickly as the finished product is waiting to be purchased. Visit a coffee house or fast-food restaurant and ask specific questions about steps taken to guarantee a fresh product. If a customer complains that a product has been sitting too long, how have the employees been

instructed to respond? Is there a policy regarding how many complaints must be received before a product is thrown out and a new batch made?

2. Visit a popular national chain restaurant and ask about measures taken to ensure consistency of portion size, flavor, and attractiveness of menu items among restaurants in the chain. Be sure to ask about vendors who supply the components of a dish. Does the chain allow for regional variations in the menu? If so, to what degree? Does the national chain have a system in place to check for consistency? If so, how does it work?

3. Did either of the establishments you visited indicate the use of statistical methods in checking for quality? If so, what were the methods? Identify at least one way each of the two places you visited could use control charts to track the quality of a product.

12.3 The Logic of Control Charts

We use control charts to help us differentiate between process variation due to common causes and special causes—that is, we use them to determine whether a process is under statistical control (only common causes present) or not (both common and special causes present). Being able to differentiate means knowing when to take action to find and remove special causes and when to leave the process alone. If you take actions to remove special causes that do not exist—that is called *tampering with the process*—you may actually end up increasing the variation of the process and, thereby, hurting the quality of the output.

In general, control charts are useful for evaluating the past performance of a process and for monitoring its current performance. We can use them to determine whether a process was in control during, say, the past 2 weeks or to determine whether the process is remaining under control from hour to hour or minute to minute. In the latter case, our goal is the swiftest detection and removal of any special causes of variation that might arise. Keep in mind that **the primary goal of quality-improvement activities is variance reduction.**

In this chapter we show you how to construct and use control charts for both quantitative and qualitative quality variables. Important quantitative variables include such things as weight, width, and time. An important qualitative variable is product status: defective or nondefective.

An example of a control chart is shown in Figure 12.14. A control chart is simply a time series plot of the individual measurements of a quality variable (i.e., an output variable), to which a centerline and two other horizontal lines called **control limits** have been added. The centerline represents the mean of the process (i.e., the mean of the quality variable) *when the process is in a state of statistical control*. The **upper control limit** and the **lower control limit** are positioned so that *when the process is in control* the probability of an individual value of the output variable falling outside the control limits is very small. Most practitioners position the control limits a distance of 3 standard deviations from the centerline (i.e., from the process mean) and refer to them as **3-sigma limits.** If the process is in control and following a normal distribution, the probability of an individual measurement falling outside the control limits is .0027 (less than 3 chances in 1,000). This is shown in Figure 12.15.

Biography

WALTER A. SHEWHART (1891–1967)

Shewhart Charts

Illinois native Walter Shewhart earned his bachelor's degree from the University of Illinois, followed by his PhD in physics from the University of California in 1917. A short time later, Shewhart joined Bell Laboratories in New Jersey as an engineer, where he spent the majority of his career. Shewhart also served as a statistical consultant for the U.S. War Department, the United Nations, and the Indian government, as well as teaching at several prominent American universities. Shewhart's most important contribution to both statistics and industry was the development of the statistical control of quality. He first proposed the idea of a control chart in 1924—a procedure commonly called the "Shewhart procedure" or "Shewhart chart." While at Bell Laboratories, Shewhart taught and worked with statistics icon W. Edwards Deming. Shewhart's monumental work, *Economic Control of Quality of Manufactured Product*, published in 1931, is regarded as a complete and thorough exposition of the basic principles of quality control; consequently, he is regarded as the father of statistical quality control.

As long as the individual values stay between the control limits, the process is considered to be under control, meaning that no special causes of variation are influencing the output of the process. If one or more values fall outside the control limits, either a **rare event** has occurred or the process is out of control. Following the rare-event

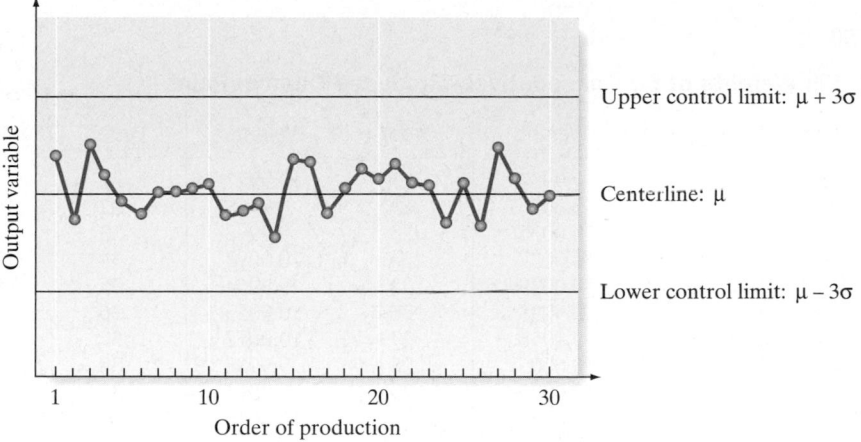

FIGURE 12.14

A control chart

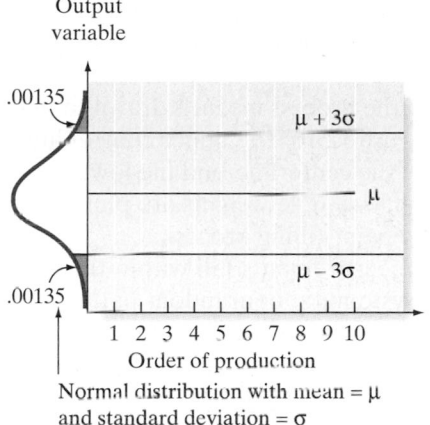

FIGURE 12.15

The probability of observing a measurement beyond the control limits when the process is in control

approach to inference described earlier in the text, such a result is interpreted as evidence that the process is out of control and that actions should be taken to eliminate the special causes of variation that exist.

Other evidence to indicate that the process is out of control may be present on the control chart. For example, if we observe any of the patterns of variation shown in Figure 12.6, we can conclude the process is out of control *even if all the points fall between the control limits*. In general, any persistent, systematic variation pattern (i.e., any nonrandom pattern) is interpreted as evidence that the process is out of control. We discuss this in detail in the next section.

In Chapter 6 we described how to make inferences about populations using hypothesis-testing techniques. What we do in this section should seem quite similar. Although our focus now is on making inferences about a *process* rather than a *population*, we are again testing hypotheses. In this case, we test

H_0: Process is under control

H_a: Process is out of control

Each time we plot a new point and see whether it falls inside or outside of the control limits, we are running a two-sided hypothesis test. The control limits function as the critical values for the test.

What we learned in Chapter 6 about the types of errors that we might make in running a hypothesis test holds true in using control charts as well. Any time we reject the hypothesis that the process is under control and conclude that the process is out of control, we run the risk of making a Type I error (rejecting the null hypothesis when the null is true). Anytime we conclude (or behave as if we conclude) that the process is in control, we run the risk of a Type II error (accepting the null hypothesis when the alternative is true). There is nothing magical or mystical about control charts. Just as in any hypothesis test, the conclusion suggested by a control chart may be wrong.

One of the main reasons that 3-sigma control limits are used (rather than 2-sigma or 1-sigma limits, for example) is the small Type I error probability associated with their use. The probability we noted previously of an individual measurement falling outside the control limits—.0027—is a Type I error probability. Since we interpret a sample point that falls beyond the limits as a signal that the process is out of control, the use of 3-sigma limits yields very few signals that are "false alarms."

To make these ideas more concrete, we will construct and interpret a control chart for the paint-filling process discussed in Section 12.2. Our intention is simply to help you better understand the logic of control charts. Structured, step-by-step descriptions of how to construct control charts will be given in later sections.

The sample measurements from the paint-filling process, presented in Table 12.1, were previously plotted in Figure 12.11. We use the mean and standard deviation of the sample, $\bar{x} = 9.9997$ and $s = .0053$, to estimate the mean and the standard deviation of

PAINT50

TABLE 12.1 Fill Weights of 50 Consecutively Produced Cans of Paint

Order	Weight	Order	Weight	Order	Weight	Order	Weight	Order	Weight
1	10.0008	11	9.9957	21	9.9977	31	10.0107	41	10.0054
2	10.0062	12	10.0076	22	9.9968	32	10.0102	42	10.0061
3	9.9948	13	10.0036	23	9.9982	33	9.9995	43	9.9978
4	9.9893	14	10.0037	24	10.0092	34	10.0038	44	9.9969
5	9.9994	15	10.0029	25	9.9964	35	9.9925	45	9.9969
6	9.9953	16	9.9995	26	10.0053	36	9.9983	46	10.0006
7	9.9963	17	9.9956	27	10.0012	37	10.0018	47	10.0011
8	9.9925	18	10.0005	28	9.9988	38	10.0038	48	9.9973
9	9.9914	19	10.0020	29	9.9914	39	9.9974	49	9.9958
10	10.0035	20	10.0053	30	10.0036	40	9.9966	50	9.9873

the process. Although these are estimates, in using and interpreting control charts we treat them *as if* they were the actual mean μ and standard deviation σ of the process. This is standard practice in control charting.

The centerline of the control chart, representing the process mean, is drawn so that it intersects the vertical axis at 9.9997, as shown in Figure 12.16. The upper control limit is drawn at a distance of $3s = 3(.0053) = .0159$ above the centerline, and the lower control limit is $3s = .0159$ below the centerline. Then the 50 sample weights are plotted on the chart in the order that they were generated by the paint-filling process.

As can be seen in Figure 12.16, all the weight measurements fall within the control limits. Further, there do not appear to be any systematic nonrandom patterns in the data such as displayed in Figures 12.5 and 12.6. Accordingly, we are unable to conclude that the process is out of control—that is, we are unable to reject the null hypothesis that the process is in control. However, instead of using this formal hypothesis-testing language in interpreting control chart results, we prefer simply to

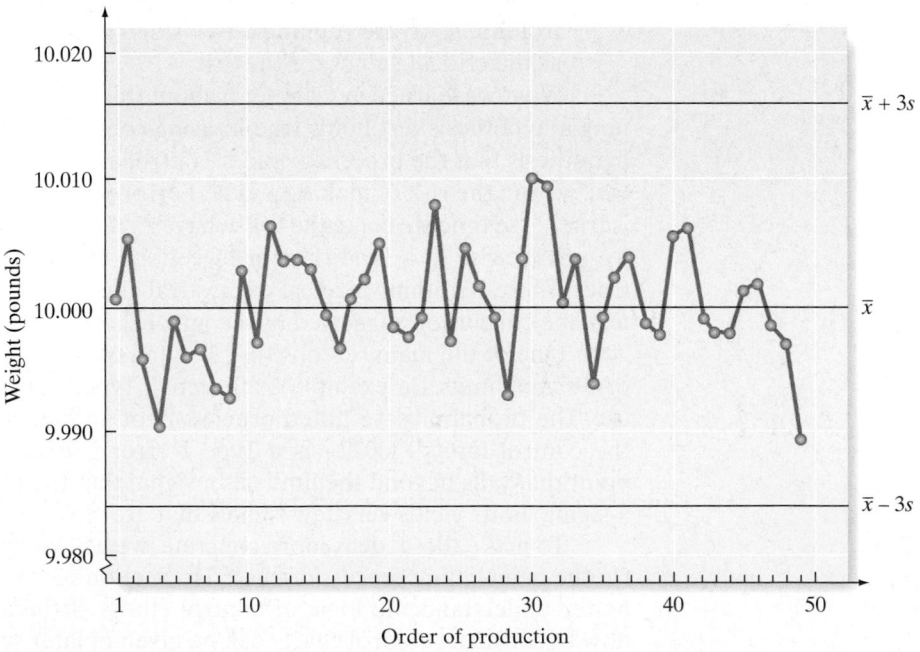

FIGURE 12.16

Control chart of fill weights for 50 consecutive paint can fills say that the data suggest or indicate that the process is in control. We do this, however, with the full understanding that the probability of a Type II error is generally unknown in control chart applications and that we might be wrong in our conclusion. What we are really saying when we conclude that the process is in control is that *the data indicate that it is better to behave as if the process were under control than to tamper with the process.*

We have portrayed the control chart hypothesis test as testing "in control" versus "out of control." Another way to look at it is this: When we compare the weight of an *individual* can of paint to the control limits, we are conducting the following two-tailed hypothesis test:

$$H_0: \mu = 9.9997$$

$$H_0: \mu \neq 9.9997$$

where 9.9997 is the centerline of the control chart. The control limits delineate the two rejection regions for this test. Accordingly, with each weight measurement that we plot and compare to the control limits, we are testing whether the process mean (the mean fill weight) has changed. Thus, what the control chart is monitoring is the mean of the process. **The control chart leads us to accept or reject statistical control on the basis of whether the mean of the process has changed or not.** This type of process instability is illustrated in the top graph of Figure 12.8. In the paint-filling process example, the process mean apparently has remained constant over the period in which the sample weights were collected.

Other types of control charts—one of which we will describe in Section 12.5—help us determine whether the *variance* of the process has changed, as in the middle and bottom graphs of Figure 12.8.

The control chart we have just described is called an **individuals chart,** or an **x-chart.** The term *individuals* refers to the fact that the chart uses individual measurements to monitor the process—that is, measurements taken from individual units of process output. This is in contrast to plotting sample means on the control chart—for example, as we do in the next section.

Students sometimes confuse control limits with product *specification limits.* We have already explained control limits, which are a function of the natural variability of the process. Assuming we always use 3-sigma limits, the position of the control limits is a function of the size of σ, the process standard deviation.

> **Definition 12.8**
>
> **Specification limits** are boundary points that define the acceptable values for an output variable (i.e., for a quality characteristic) of a particular product or service. They are determined by customers, management, and product designers. Specification limits may be two sided, with upper and lower limits, or one sided, with either an upper or a lower limit.

Process output that falls inside the specification limits is said to **conform to specifications.** Otherwise it is said to be **nonconforming.**

Unlike control limits, specification limits are not dependent on the process in any way. A customer of the paint-filling process may specify that all cans contain no more than 10.005 pounds of paint and no less than 9.995 pounds. These are specification limits. The customer has reasons for these specifications but may have no idea whether the supplier's process can meet them. Both the customer's specification limits and the control limits of the supplier's paint-filling process are shown in Figure 12.17. Do you think the customer will be satisfied with the quality of the product received? We don't. Although some cans are within the specification limits, most are not, as indicated by the shaded region on the figure.

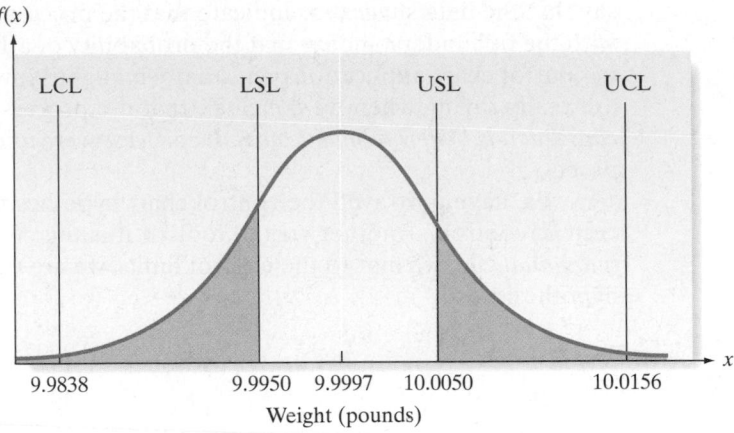

FIGURE 12.17

Comparison of control limits
and specification limits

LCL = Lower control limit
UCL = Upper control limit
LSL = Lower specification limit
USL = Upper specification limit

12.4 A Control Chart for Monitoring the Mean of a Process: The $\bar{x}$-Chart

In the last section, we introduced you to the logic of control charts by focusing on a chart that reflected the variation in individual measurements of process output. We used the chart to determine whether the process mean had shifted. The control chart we present in this section—the $\bar{x}$-**chart**—is also used to detect changes in the process mean, but it does so by monitoring the variation in the mean of samples that have been drawn from the process— that is, instead of plotting individual measurements on the control chart, in this case we plot sample means. Because of the additional information reflected in sample means (because each sample mean is calculated from n individual measurements), the $\bar{x}$-chart is more sensitive than the individuals chart for detecting changes in the process mean.

In practice, the $\bar{x}$-chart is rarely used alone. It is typically used in conjunction with a chart that monitors the variation of the process, usually a chart called an R-chart. The $\bar{x}$- and R-charts are the most widely used control charts in industry. Used in concert, these charts make it possible to determine whether a process has gone out of control because the variation has changed or because the mean has changed. We present the R-chart in the next section, at the end of which we discuss their simultaneous use. For now, we focus only on the $\bar{x}$-chart. **Consequently, we assume throughout this section that the process variation is stable.***

Figure 12.18 provides an example of an $\bar{x}$-chart. As with the individuals chart, the centerline represents the mean of the process, and the upper and lower control limits are positioned a distance of 3 standard deviations from the mean. However, since the chart is tracking sample means rather than individual measurements, the relevant standard deviation is the standard deviation of $\bar{x}$ not σ, the standard deviation of the output variable.

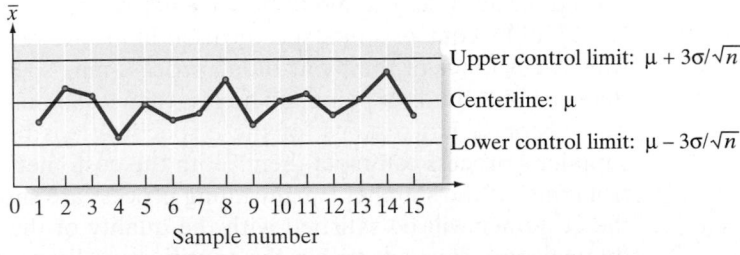

FIGURE 12.18

$\bar{x}$-chart

*To the instructor: Technically, the R-chart should be constructed and interpreted before the $\bar{x}$-chart. However, in our experience, students more quickly grasp control chart concepts if they are familiar with the underlying theory. We begin with $\bar{x}$-charts because their underlying theory was presented in Chapters 4–6.

If the process were in statistical control, the sequence of $\bar{x}$'s plotted on the chart would exhibit random behavior between the control limits. Only if a rare event occurred or if the process went out of control would a sample mean fall beyond the control limits.

To better understand the justification for having control limits that involve $\sigma_{\bar{x}}$, consider the following. The $\bar{x}$-chart is concerned with the variation in $\bar{x}$, which, as we saw in Chapter 4, is described by $\bar{x}$'s sampling distribution. But what is the sampling distribution of $\bar{x}$? If the process is in control and its output variable x is characterized at each point in time by a normal distribution with mean μ and standard deviation σ, the distribution of $\bar{x}$ (i.e., $\bar{x}$'s sampling distribution) also follows a normal distribution with mean μ at each point in time. But, as we saw in Chapter 4, its standard deviation is $\sigma_{\bar{x}} = \sigma/\sqrt{n}$. The control limits of the $\bar{x}$-chart are determined from and interpreted with respect to the sampling distribution of $\bar{x}$, not the distribution of x. These points are illustrated in Figure 12.19.*

In order to construct an $\bar{x}$-chart, you should have at least 20 samples of n items each, where $n \geq 2$. This will provide sufficient data to obtain reasonably good estimates of the mean and variance of the process. The centerline, which represents the mean of the process, is determined as follows:

$$Centerline: \bar{\bar{x}} = \frac{\bar{x}_1 + \bar{x}_2 + \cdots + \bar{x}_k}{k}$$

where k is the number of samples of size n from which the chart is to be constructed and $\bar{x}_i$ is the sample mean of the ith sample. Thus $\bar{\bar{x}}$ is an estimator of μ.

The control limits are positioned as follows:

$$Upper\ control\ limit: \bar{\bar{x}} + \frac{3\sigma}{\sqrt{n}}$$

$$Lower\ control\ limit: \bar{\bar{x}} - \frac{3\sigma}{\sqrt{n}}$$

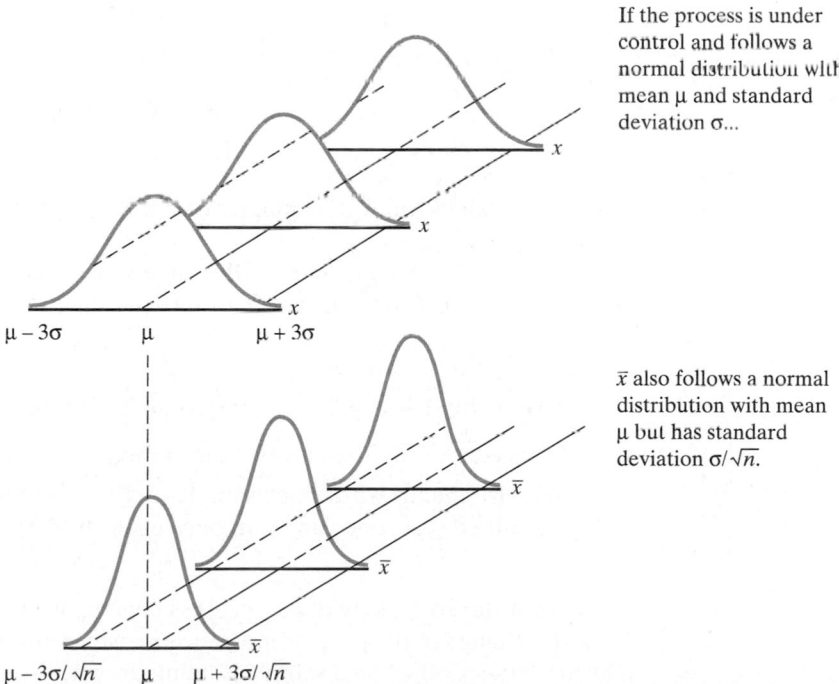

If the process is under control and follows a normal distribution with mean μ and standard deviation σ...

$\bar{x}$ also follows a normal distribution with mean μ but has standard deviation σ/√n.

FIGURE 12.19

The sampling distribution of $\bar{x}$

*The sampling distribution of $\bar{x}$ can also be approximated using the Central Limit Theorem (Chapter 4—that is, when the process is under control and $\bar{x}$ is to be computed from a large sample from the process ($n \geq 30$), the sampling distribution will be approximately normally distributed with the mean μ and standard deviation $\sigma/\sqrt{n}$. Even for samples as small as 4 or 5, the sampling distribution of $\bar{x}$ will be approximately normal as long as the distribution of x is reasonably symmetric and roughly bell shaped.

Since σ, the process standard deviation, is virtually always unknown, it must be estimated. This can be done in several ways. One approach involves calculating the standard deviations for each of the k samples and averaging them. Another involves using the sample standard deviation s from a large sample that was generated while the process was believed to be in control. We employ a third approach, however—the one favored by industry. It has been shown to be as effective as the other approaches for sample sizes of $n = 10$ or less, the sizes most often used in industry.

This approach utilizes the ranges of the k samples to estimate the process standard deviation, σ. Recall from Chapter 2 that the range, R, of a sample is the difference between the maximum and minimum measurements in the sample. It can be shown that dividing the mean of the k ranges, $\overline{R}$, by the constant d_2, obtains an unbiased estimator for σ. [For details, see Ryan (1989).] The estimator, denoted by $\hat{\sigma}$, is calculated as follows:

$$\hat{\sigma} = \frac{\overline{R}}{d_2} = \frac{R_1 + R_2 + \cdots + R_k}{k}\left(\frac{1}{d_2}\right)$$

where R_i is the range of the ith sample and d_2 is a constant that depends on the sample size. Values of d_2 for samples of size $n = 2$ to $n = 25$ can be found in Appendix B, Table XI.

Substituting $\hat{\sigma}$ for σ in the formulas for the upper control limit (UCL) and the lower control limit (LCL), we get

$$\text{UCL:} \overline{\overline{x}} + \frac{3\left(\dfrac{\overline{R}}{d_2}\right)}{\sqrt{n}} \qquad \text{LCL:} \overline{\overline{x}} - \frac{3\left(\dfrac{\overline{R}}{d_2}\right)}{\sqrt{n}}$$

Notice that $(\overline{R}/d_2)/\sqrt{n}$ is an estimator of $\sigma_{\overline{x}}$. The calculation of these limits can be simplified by creating the constant

$$A_2 = \frac{3}{d_2\sqrt{n}}$$

Then the control limits can be expressed as

$$\text{UCL:} \overline{\overline{x}} + A_2\overline{R}$$
$$\text{LCL:} \overline{\overline{x}} - A_2\overline{R}$$

where the values for A_2 for samples of size $n = 2$ to $n = 25$ can be found in Appendix B, Table XI.

The degree of sensitivity of the $\overline{x}$-chart to changes in the process mean depends on two decisions that must be made in constructing the chart.

The Two Most Important Decisions in Constructing an $\overline{x}$-Chart

1. The sample size, n, must be determined.
2. The frequency with which samples are to be drawn from the process must be determined (e.g., once an hour, once each shift, or once a day).

In order to quickly detect process change, we try to choose samples in such a way that the change in the process mean occurs *between* samples, not *within* samples (i.e., not during the period when a sample is being drawn). In this way, every measurement in the sample before the change will be unaffected by the change, and every measurement in the sample following the change will be affected. The result is that the $\overline{x}$ computed from the latter sample should be substantially different from that of the former sample—a signal that something has happened to the process mean.

Definition 12.9

Samples whose size and frequency have been designed to make it likely that process changes will occur between, rather than within, the samples are referred to as **rational subgroups.**

Rational Subgrouping Strategy

The samples (rational subgroups) should be chosen in a manner that

1. Gives the maximum chance for the *measurements* in each sample to be similar (i.e., to be affected by the same sources of variation)
2. Gives the maximum chance for the *samples* to differ (i.e., be affected by at least one different source of variation)

The following example illustrates the concept of *rational subgrouping.* An operations manager suspects that the quality of the output in a manufacturing process may differ from shift to shift because of the preponderance of newly hired workers on the night shift. The manager wants to be able to detect such differences quickly, using an x̄-chart. Following the rational subgrouping strategy, the control chart should be constructed with samples that are drawn *within* each shift. None of the samples should span shifts—that is, no sample should contain, say, the last three items produced by shift 1 and the first two items produced by shift 2. In this way, the measurements in each sample would be similar, but the x̄'s would reflect differences between shifts.

The secret to designing an effective x̄-chart is to anticipate the *types of special causes of variation* that might affect the process mean. Then purposeful rational subgrouping can be employed to construct a chart that is sensitive to the anticipated cause or causes of variation.

The preceding discussion and example focused primarily on the timing or frequency of samples. Concerning the size of the samples, practitioners typically work with samples of size $n = 4$ to $n = 10$ consecutively produced items. Using small samples of consecutively produced items helps to ensure that the measurements in each sample will be similar (i.e., affected by the same causes of variation).

Constructing an x̄-Chart: A Summary

1. Using a rational subgrouping strategy, collect at least 20 samples (subgroups), each of size $n \geq 2$.
2. Calculate the mean and range for each sample.
3. Calculate the mean of the sample means, $\bar{\bar{x}}$, and the mean of the sample ranges, $\bar{R}$:

$$\bar{\bar{x}} = \frac{\bar{x}_1 + \bar{x}_2 + \cdots + \bar{x}_k}{k} \qquad \bar{R} = \frac{R_1 + R_2 + \cdots + R_k}{k}$$

where

k = number of samples (i.e., subgroups)
$\bar{x}_i$ = sample mean for the ith sample
R_i = range of the ith sample

4. Plot the centerline and control limits:

$$Centerline: \bar{\bar{x}}$$
$$Upper\ control\ limit: \bar{\bar{x}} + A_2\bar{R}$$
$$Lower\ control\ limit: \bar{\bar{x}} - A_2\bar{R}$$

Continued

where A_2 is a constant that depends on n. Its values are given in Appendix B, Table XI, for samples of size $n = 2$ to $n = 25$.

5. Plot the k sample means on the control chart in the order that the samples were produced by the process.

When interpreting a control chart, it is convenient to think of the chart as consisting of six zones, as shown in Figure 12.20. Each zone is 1 standard deviation wide. The two zones within 1 standard deviation of the centerline are called **C zones;** the regions between 1 and 2 standard deviations from the centerline are called **B zones;** and the regions between 2 and 3 standard deviations from the centerline are called **A zones.** The box describes how to construct the *zone boundaries* for an $\bar{x}$-chart.

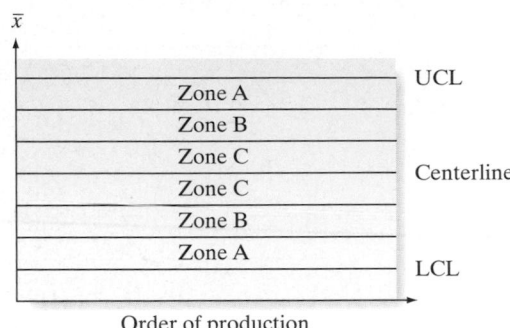

FIGURE 12.20
The zones of a control chart

Constructing Zone Boundaries for an $\bar{x}$-Chart

The zone boundaries can be constructed in either of the following ways:

1. Using the 3-sigma control limits:

$$Upper\ A{-}B\ boundary: \bar{\bar{x}} + \frac{2}{3}(A_2\bar{R})$$

$$Lower\ A{-}B\ boundary: \bar{\bar{x}} - \frac{2}{3}(A_2\bar{R})$$

$$Upper\ B{-}C\ boundary: \bar{\bar{x}} + \frac{1}{3}(A_2\bar{R})$$

$$Lower\ B{-}C\ boundary: \bar{\bar{x}} - \frac{1}{3}(A_2\bar{R})$$

2. Using the estimated standard deviation of $\bar{x}$, $(\bar{R}/d_2)/\sqrt{n}$:

$$Upper\ A{-}B\ boundary: \bar{\bar{x}} + 2\left[\frac{\left(\dfrac{\bar{R}}{d_2}\right)}{\sqrt{n}}\right]$$

$$Lower\ A{-}B\ boundary: \bar{\bar{x}} - 2\left[\frac{\left(\dfrac{\bar{R}}{d_2}\right)}{\sqrt{n}}\right]$$

$$Upper\ B{-}C\ boundary: \bar{\bar{x}} + \left[\frac{\left(\dfrac{\bar{R}}{d_2}\right)}{\sqrt{n}}\right]$$

$$Lower\ B{-}C\ boundary: \bar{\bar{x}} - \left[\frac{\left(\dfrac{\bar{R}}{d_2}\right)}{\sqrt{n}}\right]$$

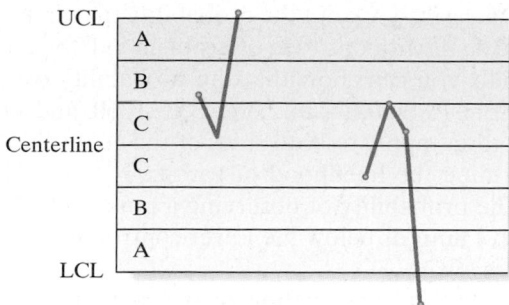

Rule 1: One point beyond Zone A

Rule 2: Nine points in a row in Zone C or beyond

Rule 3: Six points in a row steadily increasing or decreasing

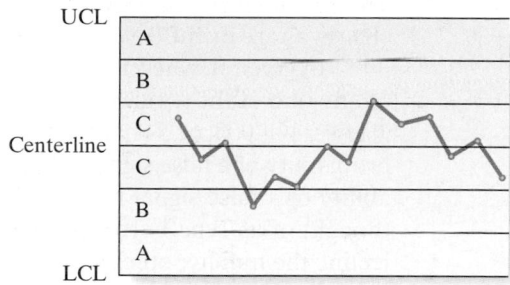

Rule 4: Fourteen points in a row alternating up and down

Rule 5: Two out of three points in a row in Zone A or beyond

Rule 6: Four out of five points in a row in Zone B or beyond

Rules 1, 2, 5, and 6 should be applied separately to the upper and lower halves of the control chart. Rules 3 and 4 should be applied to the whole chart.

FIGURE 12.21

Pattern-analysis rules for detecting the presence of special causes of variation

Practitioners use six simple rules that are based on these zones to help determine when a process is out of control. The six rules are summarized in Figure 12.21. They are referred to as **pattern-analysis rules.**

Rule 1 is the familiar point-beyond-the-control-limit rule that we have mentioned several times. The other rules all help to determine when the process is out of control *even though all the plotted points fall within the control limits*—that is, the other rules help to identify nonrandom patterns of variation that have not yet broken through the control limits (or may never break through).

All the patterns shown in Figure 12.21 are *rare events* under the assumption that the process is under control. To see this, let's assume that the process is under control and follows a normal distribution. We can then easily work out the probability that an individual point will fall in any given zone. (We dealt with this type of problem in Chapter 4.) Just focusing on one side of the centerline, you can show that the probability of a point falling beyond Zone A is .00135, in Zone A is .0214, in Zone B is .1360, and in Zone C is .3413. Of course, the same probabilities apply to both sides of the centerline.

From these probabilities we can determine the likelihood of various patterns of points. For example, let's evaluate Rule 1. The probability of observing a point outside the control limits (i.e., above the upper control limit or below the lower control limit) is .00135 + .00135 = .0027. This is clearly a rare event.

As another example, Rule 5 indicates that the observation of two out of three points in a row in Zone A or beyond is a rare event. Is it? The probability of being in Zone A or beyond is .00135 + .0214 = .02275. We can use the binomial distribution (Chapter 4) to find the probability of observing 2 out of 3 points in or beyond Zone A. The binomial probability $P(x = 2)$ when $n = 3$ and $p = .02275$ is .0015. Again, this is clearly a rare event.

In general, when the process is in control and normally distributed, the probability of any one of these rules *incorrectly* signaling the presence of special causes of variation is less than .005, or 5 chances in 1,000. If all of the first four rules are applied, the overall probability of a false signal is about .01. If all six of the rules are applied, the overall probability of a false signal rises to .02, or 2 chances in 100. These three probabilities can be thought of as Type I error probabilities. Each indicates the probability of incorrectly rejecting the null hypothesis that the process is in a state of statistical control.

Explanation of the possible causes of these nonrandom patterns is beyond the scope of this text. We refer the interested reader to AT&T's *Statistical Quality Control Handbook* (1956).

We use these rules again in the next section when we interpret the *R*-chart.

Interpreting an $\bar{x}$-Chart

1. The **process is out of control** if one or more sample means fall beyond the control limits or if any of the other five patterns of variation of Figure 12.21 are observed. Such signals are an indication that one or more special causes of variation are affecting the process mean. We must identify and eliminate them to bring the process into control.

2. The **process is treated as being in control** if none of the previously noted out-of-control signals are observed. Processes that are in control should not be tampered with. However, if the level of variation is unacceptably high, common causes of variation should be identified and eliminated.

Assumption: The variation of the process is stable. (If it were not, the control limits of the $\bar{x}$-chart would be meaningless, since they are a function of the process variation. The *R*-chart, presented in the next section, is used to investigate this assumption.)

In theory, the centerline and control limits should be developed using samples that were collected during a period in which the process was in control. Otherwise, they will not be representative of the variation of the process (or, in the present case, the variation of $\bar{x}$) when the process is in control. However, we will not know whether the process is in control until after we have constructed a control chart. Consequently, when a control chart is first constructed, the centerline and control limits are treated as **trial values.** If the chart indicates that the process was in control during the period when the sample data were collected, then the centerline and control limits become "official" (i.e., no longer treated as trial values). It is then appropriate to extend the control limits and the centerline to the right and to use the chart to monitor future process output.

However, if in applying the pattern-analysis rules of Figure 12.21 it is determined that the process was out of control while the sample data were being collected, the trial values (i.e., the trial chart) should, in general, not be used to monitor the process. The points on the control chart that indicate that the process is out of control should be investigated to see if any special causes of variation can be identified. A graphical method that can be used to facilitate this investigation—a *cause-and-effect diagram*—is described in optional Section 12.7. If special causes of variation are found, (1) they should be eliminated, (2) any points on the chart determined to have been influenced by the special causes—whether inside or outside the control limits—should be discarded, and (3) *new* trial centerline and control limits should be calculated from the remaining data. However, the new trial limits may still indicate that the process is out of control. If so, repeat these three steps until all points fall within the control limits.

If special causes cannot be found and eliminated, the severity of the out-of-control indications should be evaluated and a judgment made as to whether (1) the out-of-control points should be discarded anyway and new trial limits constructed, (2) the original trial limits are good enough to be made official, or (3) new sample data should be collected to construct new trial limits.

EXAMPLE 12.1

Creating and Interpreting an $\bar{x}$-Chart for a Paint-Filling Process

Problem Let's return to the paint-filling process described in Sections 12.2 and 12.3. Suppose instead of sampling 50 consecutive gallons of paint from the filling process to develop a control chart, it was decided to sample five consecutive cans once each hour for the next 25 hours. The sample data are presented in Table 12.2. This sampling strategy (rational subgrouping) was selected because several times a month the filling head in question becomes clogged. When that happens, the head dispenses less and less paint over the course of the day. However, the pattern of decrease is so irregular that minute-to-minute or even half-hour-to-half-hour changes are difficult to detect.

a. Explain the logic behind the rational subgrouping strategy that was used.

b. Construct an $\bar{x}$-chart for the process using the data in Table 12.2.

c. What does the chart suggest about the stability of the filling process (whether the process is in or out of statistical control)?

d. Should the control limits be used to monitor future process output?

Solution

a. The samples are far enough apart in time to detect hour-to-hour shifts or changes in the mean amount of paint dispensed, but the individual measurements that make up each sample are close enough together in time to ensure that the process has changed little, if at all, during the time the individual measurements were made. Overall, the rational subgrouping employed affords the opportunity for process changes to occur between samples and therefore show up on the control chart as differences between the sample means.

b. Twenty-five samples ($k = 25$ subgroups), each containing $n = 5$ cans of paint, were collected from the process. The first step after collecting the data is to calculate the 25 sample means and sample ranges needed to construct the $\bar{x}$-chart. The mean and range of the first sample are

$$\bar{x} = \frac{10.0042 + 9.9981 + 10.0010 + 9.9964 + 10.0001}{5} = 9.99996$$

$$R = 10.0042 - 9.9964 = .0078$$

All 25 means and ranges are displayed in Table 12.2.

PAINT125

TABLE 12.2 Twenty-Five Samples of Size 5 from the Paint-Filling Process

Sample	Measurements					Mean	Range
1	10.0042	9.9981	10.0010	9.9964	10.0001	9.99996	.0078
2	9.9950	9.9986	9.9948	10.0030	9.9938	9.99704	.0092
3	10.0028	9.9998	10.0086	9.9949	9.9980	10.00082	.0137
4	9.9952	9.9923	10.0034	9.9965	10.0026	9.99800	.0111
5	9.9997	9.9883	9.9975	10.0078	9.9891	9.99648	.0195
6	9.9987	10.0027	10.0001	10.0027	10.0029	10.00142	.0042
7	10.0004	10.0023	10.0024	9.9992	10.0135	10.00356	.0143
8	10.0013	9.9938	10.0017	10.0089	10.0001	10.00116	.0151
9	10.0103	10.0009	9.9969	10.0103	9.9986	10.00340	.0134
10	9.9980	9.9954	9.9941	9.9958	9.9963	9.99592	.0039
11	10.0013	10.0033	9.9943	9.9949	9.9999	9.99874	.0090
12	9.9986	9.9990	10.0009	9.9947	10.0008	9.99880	.0062
13	10.0089	10.0056	9.9976	9.9997	9.9922	10.00080	.0167
14	9.9971	10.0015	9.9962	10.0038	10.0022	10.00016	.0076
15	9.9949	10.0011	10.0043	9.9988	9.9919	9.99820	.0124
16	9.9951	9.9957	10.0094	10.0040	9.9974	10.00032	.0143
17	10.0015	10.0026	10.0032	9.9971	10.0019	10.00126	.0061
18	9.9983	10.0019	9.9978	9.9997	10.0029	10.00012	.0051
19	9.9977	9.9963	9.9981	9.9968	10.0009	9.99796	.0046
20	10.0078	10.0004	9.9966	10.0051	10.0007	10.00212	.0112
21	9.9963	9.9990	10.0037	9.9936	9.9962	9.99776	.0101
22	9.9999	10.0022	10.0057	10.0026	10.0032	10.00272	.0058
23	9.9998	10.0002	9.9978	9.9966	10.0060	10.00008	.0094
24	10.0031	10.0078	9.9988	10.0032	9.9944	10.00146	.0134
25	9.9993	9.9978	9.9964	10.0032	10.0041	10.00016	.0077

Next, we calculate the mean of the sample means and the mean of the sample ranges:

$$\overline{\overline{x}} = \frac{9.99996 + 9.99704 + \cdots + 10.00016}{25} = 9.9999$$

$$\overline{R} = \frac{.0078 + .0092 + \cdots + .0077}{25} = .010072$$

The centerline of the chart is positioned at $\overline{\overline{x}} = 9.9999$. To determine the control limits, we need the constant A_2, which can be found in Table XI of Appendix B. For $n = 5$, $A_2 = .577$. Then,

$$\text{UCL:} \overline{\overline{x}} + A_2\overline{R} = 9.9999 + .577(.010072) = 10.0058$$

$$\text{LCL:} \overline{\overline{x}} - A_2\overline{R} = 9.9999 - .577(.010072) = 9.9940$$

After positioning the control limits on the chart, we plot the 25 sample means in the order of sampling and connect the points with straight lines. The resulting trial $\overline{x}$-chart, shown in Figure 12.22, is produced using MINITAB.

c. To check the stability of the process, we use the six pattern-analysis rules for detecting special causes of variation, which were presented in Figure 12.21. To apply most of these rules requires identifying the A, B, and C zones of the control chart. These are indicated (with annotations) in Figure 12.22. We describe how they were constructed below.

The boundary between the A and B zones is 2 standard deviations from the centerline, and the boundary between the B and C zones is 1 standard deviation from the centerline. Thus, using $A_2\overline{R}$ and the 3-sigma limits previously calculated, we locate the A, B, and C zones above the centerline:

FIGURE 12.22

MINITAB $\bar{x}$-chart for the paint-filling process

$$\text{A–B boundary} = \bar{\bar{x}} + \tfrac{2}{3}(A_2\overline{R}) = 9.9999 + \tfrac{2}{3}(.577)(.010072) = 10.0039$$
$$\text{B–C boundary} = \bar{\bar{x}} + \tfrac{1}{3}(A_2\overline{R}) = 9.9999 + \tfrac{1}{3}(.577)(.010072) = 10.0019$$

Similarly, the zones below the centerline are located:

$$\text{A–B boundary} = \bar{\bar{x}} - \tfrac{2}{3}(A_2\overline{R}) = 9.9959$$
$$\text{B–C boundary} = \bar{\bar{x}} - \tfrac{1}{3}(A_2\overline{R}) = 9.9979$$

A careful comparison of the six pattern-analysis rules with the sequence of sample means yields no out-of-control signals. All points are inside the control limits, and there appear to be no nonrandom patterns within the control limits—that is, we can find no evidence of a shift in the process mean. Accordingly, we conclude that the process is in control.

d. Since the process was found to be in control during the period in which the samples were drawn, the trial control limits constructed in part **b** can be considered official. They should be extended to the right and used to monitor future process output.

Look Back Most statistical software (like MINITAB) will automatically calculate and plot the sample means and control limits. The amount of hand calculations needed to create an $\bar{x}$-chart is minimal.

Now Work Exercise 12.7

EXAMPLE 12.2

Monitoring Future Output with an $\bar{x}$-Chart

Problem   Ten new samples of size $n = 5$ were drawn from the paint-filling process of the previous example. The sample data, including sample means and ranges, are shown in Table 12.3. Investigate whether the process remained in control during the period in which the new sample data were collected.

Solution   We begin by simply extending the control limits, centerline, and zone boundaries of the control chart in Figure 12.22 to the right. Next, beginning with sample number 26, we plot the 10 new sample means on the control chart and connect them with straight lines. This extended version of the control chart, produced using MINITAB, is shown in Figure 12.23.

Now that the control chart has been prepared, we apply the six pattern-analysis rules for detecting special causes of variation (Figure 12.21) to the new sequence of sample means. First, notice that the mean for sample 32 falls below the lower control limit (Rule 1). Also, notice that six points in a row steadily decrease (samples 27–32). Rule 3 says that if we observe six points in a row steadily increasing or decreasing, that is an

PAINT125ADD

TABLE 12.3 Ten Additional Samples of Size 5 from the Paint-Filling Process

Sample	Measurements					Mean	Range
26	10.0019	9.9981	9.9952	9.9976	9.9999	9.99854	.0067
27	10.0041	9.9982	10.0028	10.0040	9.9971	10.00124	.0070
28	9.9999	9.9974	10.0078	9.9971	9.9923	9.99890	.0155
29	9.9982	10.0002	9.9916	10.0040	9.9916	9.99712	.0124
30	9.9933	9.9963	9.9955	9.9993	9.9905	9.99498	.0088
31	9.9915	9.9984	10.0053	9.9888	9.9876	9.99432	.0177
32	9.9912	9.9970	9.9961	9.9879	9.9970	9.99384	.0091
33	9.9942	9.9960	9.9975	10.0019	9.9912	9.99616	.0107
34	9.9949	9.9967	9.9936	9.9941	10.0071	9.99728	.0135
35	9.9943	9.9969	9.9937	9.9912	10.0053	9.99628	.0141

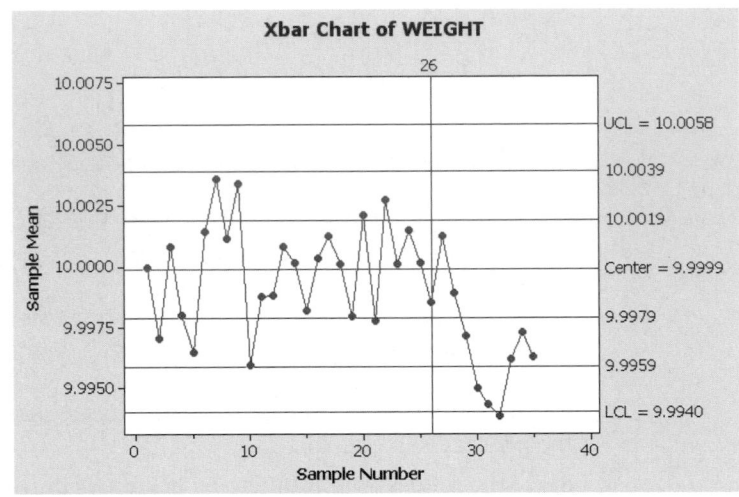

FIGURE 12.23
MINITAB extended $\bar{x}$-chart for the paint-filling process

indication of the presence of special causes of variation. Notice that if you apply the rules from left to right along the sequence of sample means, the decreasing pattern also triggers signals from Rules 5 (samples 29–31) and 6 (samples 28–32). These signals lead us to conclude that the process has gone out of control.

Look Back Apparently, the filling head began to clog about the time that either sample 26 or 27 was drawn from the process. As a result, the mean of the process (the mean fill weight dispensed by the process) began to decline.

Now Work Exercise 12.8

STATISTICS IN ACTION REVISITED

Monitoring the Mean of the Jet Fuel Surfactant Test Process

The engineering firm that tests for surfactants in jet fuel additive is experimenting with different pump and filter combinations—Pump-A with Filter-A (the standard test), Pump-A with Filter-B, Pump-B with Filter-A, and Pump-B with Filter-B. To monitor the test results, three fuel samples were tested each day by each of the four methods, for a period of over 100 consecutive days. A "safe" surfactant additive measurement should range between 80 and 90, and this range represents the specification limits of the process.

We analyzed the data in the **JETFUEL** files using MINITAB. Treating the three samples collected on the same day as a rational subgroup, four MINITAB $\bar{x}$-charts are produced (one for each pump/filter method) in Figures SIA12.1(a)—(d). As an option, MINITAB will highlight (in red) any sample means that match any of the six pattern-analysis rules for detecting special causes of variation. The number of the rule that is violated is shown next to the sample mean on the chart.

You can see that only one of the process means is "in control"—the mean for the Pump-B with Filter-B

Figure SIA12.1a

$\bar{x}$-chart for Pump-A with Filter-A (standard) method

Figure SIA12.1b

$\bar{x}$ chart for Pump-A with Filter-B method

Figure SIA12.1c

$\bar{x}$-chart for Pump-B with Filter-A method

Continued

test method—as shown in Figure SIA12.1(d). There is at least one pattern-analysis rule violated in each of the other three $\bar{x}$-charts. Also, each sample mean for Pump-B/Filter-B falls within the specification limits (80%–90%). In contrast, the other injection methods have several means that fall outside the specification limits of the process. Of the three nonstandard surfactant test methods, the Pump-B/Filter-B method appears to have the most promise. This analysis helped the company to focus on perfecting this method of surfactant testing in jet fuel.

Figure SIA12.1d
$\bar{x}$-chart for Pump-B with Filter-B method

Exercises 12.1–12.17

Learning the Mechanics

12.1 What is a control chart? Describe its use.

12.2 Explain why rational subgrouping should be used in constructing control charts.

12.3 When a control chart is first constructed, why are the centerline and control limits treated as trial values?

12.4 Which process parameter is an $\bar{x}$-chart used to monitor?

12.5 Even if all the points on an $\bar{x}$-chart fall between the control limits, the process may be out of control. Explain.

12.6 What must be true about the variation of a process before an $\bar{x}$-chart is used to monitor the mean of the process? Why?

12.7 Use the six pattern-analysis rules described in Figure 12.21
NW to determine whether the process being monitored with the $\bar{x}$-chart shown at top, right is out of statistical control.

12.8 Consider the $\bar{x}$-chart shown to the right.
NW **a.** Is the process affected by only special causes of variation, only common causes of variation, or both? Explain.
  b. The means for the next five samples in the process are 27, 29, 32, 36, and 34. Plot these points on an extended $\bar{x}$-chart. What does the pattern suggest about the process?

12.9 Use Table XI in Appendix B to find the value of A_2 for each of the following sample sizes.
  a. $n = 3$
  b. $n = 10$
  c. $n = 22$

$\bar{x}$-chart for Exercise 12.7

$\bar{x}$-chart for Exercise 12.8

12.10 Twenty-five samples of size $n = 5$ were collected to construct an $\bar{x}$-chart. The accompanying sample means and ranges were calculated for these data.

a. Calculate the mean of the sample means, $\bar{\bar{x}}$, and the mean of the sample ranges, $\bar{R}$.

b. Calculate and plot the centerline and the upper and lower control limits for the $\bar{x}$-chart.

c. Calculate and plot the A, B, and C zone boundaries of the $\bar{x}$-chart.

d. Plot the 25 sample means on the $\bar{x}$-chart and use the six pattern-analysis rules to determine whether the process is under statistical control.

LM12_10

Sample	$\bar{x}$	R	Sample	$\bar{x}$	R
1	80.2	7.2	14	83.1	10.2
2	79.1	9.0	15	79.6	7.8
3	83.2	4.7	16	80.0	6.1
4	81.0	5.6	17	83.2	8.4
5	77.6	10.1	18	75.9	9.9
6	81.7	8.6	19	78.1	6.0
7	80.4	4.4	20	81.4	7.4
8	77.5	6.2	21	81.7	10.4
9	79.8	7.9	22	80.9	9.1
10	85.3	7.1	23	78.4	7.3
11	77.7	9.8	24	79.6	8.0
12	82.3	10.7	25	81.6	7.6
13	79.5	9.2			

12.11 The data in the following table were collected for the purpose of constructing an $\bar{x}$-chart.

a. Calculate $\bar{x}$ and R for each sample.

b. Calculate $\bar{\bar{x}}$ and $\bar{R}$.

c. Calculate and plot the centerline and the upper and lower control limits for the $\bar{x}$-chart.

d. Calculate and plot the A, B, and C zone boundaries of the $\bar{x}$-chart.

e. Plot the 20 sample means on the $\bar{x}$-chart. Is the process in control? Justify your answer.

LM12_11

Sample	Measurements			
1	19.4	19.7	20.6	21.2
2	18.7	18.4	21.2	20.7
3	20.2	18.8	22.6	20.1
4	19.6	21.2	18.7	19.4
5	20.4	20.9	22.3	18.6
6	17.3	22.3	20.3	19.7
7	21.8	17.6	22.8	23.1
8	20.9	17.4	19.5	20.7
9	18.1	18.3	20.6	20.4
10	22.6	21.4	18.5	19.7
11	22.7	21.2	21.5	19.5
12	20.1	20.6	21.0	20.2
13	19.7	18.6	21.2	19.1
14	18.6	21.7	17.7	18.3
15	18.2	20.4	19.8	19.2
16	18.9	20.7	23.2	20.0
17	20.5	19.7	21.4	17.8
18	21.0	18.7	19.9	21.2
19	20.5	19.6	19.8	21.8
20	20.6	16.9	22.4	19.7

Applying the Concepts—Basic

12.12 CPU of a computer chip. The central processing unit (CPU) of a microcomputer is a computer chip containing millions of transistors. Connecting the transistors are slender circuit paths only .5 to .85 micron wide. To understand how narrow these paths are, consider that a micron is a millionth of a meter, and a human hair is 70 microns wide (*Compute*, 1992). A manufacturer of CPU chips knows that if the circuit paths are not .5–.85 micron wide, a variety of problems will arise in the chips' performance. The manufacturer sampled four CPU chips six times a day (every 90 minutes from 8:00 A.M. until 4:30 P.M.) for 5 consecutive days and measured the circuit path widths. These data and MINITAB were used to construct the $\bar{x}$-chart shown below.

a. Assuming that $\bar{R} = .335$, calculate the chart's upper and lower control limits, the upper and lower A–B boundaries, and the upper and lower B–C boundaries.

b. What does the chart suggest about the stability of the process used to put circuit paths on the CPU chip? Justify your answer.

c. Should the control limits be used to monitor future process output? Explain.

12.13 Cereal box manufacturing. A machine at K-Company fills boxes with bran flakes cereal. The target weight for the filled boxes is 24 ounces. The company would like to use an $\bar{x}$-chart to monitor the performance of the machine. To develop the control chart, the company decides to sample and weigh five boxes of cereal each day (at 8:00 and 11:00 A.M. and 2:00, 5:00, and 8:00 P.M.) for 20 consecutive days. The data are presented in the next table, along with an SPSS printout with summary statistics (p. 822).

a. Construct an $\bar{x}$-chart from the given data.

b. What does the chart suggest about the stability of the filling process (whether the process is in or out of statistical control)? Justify your answer.

c. Should the control limits be used to monitor future process output? Explain.

d. Two shifts of workers run the filling operation. Each day the second shift takes over at 3:00 P.M. Will the rational subgrouping strategy used by K-Company facilitate or hinder the identification of process variation caused by differences in the two shifts? Explain.

CEREAL

Day	Weight of Cereal Boxes (ounces)				
1	24.02	23.91	24.12	24.06	24.13
2	23.89	23.98	24.01	24.00	23.91
3	24.11	24.02	23.99	23.79	24.04
4	24.06	23.98	23.95	24.01	24.11
5	23.81	23.90	23.99	24.07	23.96
6	23.87	24.12	24.07	24.01	23.99
7	23.88	24.00	24.05	23.97	23.97
8	24.01	24.03	23.99	23.91	23.98
9	24.06	24.02	23.80	23.79	24.07
10	23.96	23.99	24.03	23.99	24.01
11	24.10	23.90	24.11	23.98	23.95
12	24.01	24.07	23.93	24.09	23.98
13	24.14	24.07	24.08	23.98	24.02
14	23.91	24.04	23.89	24.01	23.95
15	24.03	24.04	24.01	23.98	24.10
16	23.94	24.07	24.12	24.00	24.02
17	23.88	23.94	23.91	24.06	24.07
18	24.11	23.99	23.90	24.01	23.98
19	24.05	24.04	23.97	24.08	23.95
20	24.02	23.96	23.95	23.89	24.04

Case Summaries[a]

	DAY	MEANWT	RANGEWT
1	1	24.05	.22
2	2	23.96	.12
3	3	23.99	.32
4	4	24.02	.16
5	5	23.95	.26
6	6	24.01	.25
7	7	23.97	.17
8	8	23.98	.12
9	9	23.95	.28
10	10	24.00	.07
11	11	24.01	.21
12	12	24.02	.16
13	13	24.06	.16
14	14	23.96	.15
15	15	24.03	.12
16	16	24.03	.18
17	17	23.97	.19
18	18	24.00	.21
19	19	24.02	.13
20	20	23.97	.15

a. Limited to first 100 cases.

Applying the Concepts—Intermediate

12.14 Military aircraft bolts. A precision parts manufacturer produces bolts for use in military aircraft. Ideally, the bolts should be 37 centimeters in length. The company sampled four consecutively produced bolts each hour on the hour for 25 consecutive hours and measured them using a computerized precision instrument. The data are presented next.

BOLTS

Hour	Bolt Lengths (centimeters)			
1	37.03	37.08	36.90	36.88
2	36.96	37.04	36.85	36.98
3	37.16	37.11	36.99	37.01
4	37.20	37.06	37.02	36.98
5	36.81	36.97	36.91	37.10
6	37.13	36.96	37.01	36.89
7	37.07	36.94	36.99	37.00
8	37.01	36.91	36.98	37.12
9	37.17	37.03	36.90	37.01
10	36.91	36.99	36.87	37.11
11	36.88	37.10	37.07	37.03
12	37.06	36.98	36.90	36.99
13	36.91	37.22	37.12	37.03
14	37.08	37.07	37.10	37.04
15	37.03	37.04	36.89	37.01
16	36.95	36.98	36.90	36.99
17	36.97	36.94	37.14	37.10
18	37.11	37.04	36.98	36.91
19	36.88	36.99	37.01	36.94
20	36.90	37.15	37.09	37.00
21	37.01	36.96	37.05	36.96
22	37.09	36.95	36.93	37.12
23	37.00	37.02	36.95	37.04
24	36.99	37.07	36.90	37.02
25	37.10	37.03	37.01	36.90

a. What process is the manufacturer interested in monitoring?

b. Construct an $\bar{x}$-chart from the data.

c. Does the chart suggest that special causes of variation are present? Justify your answer.

d. Provide an example of a special cause of variation that could potentially affect this process. Do the same for a common cause of variation.

e. Should the control limits be used to monitor future process output? Explain.

12.15 Bayfield Mud Company case. In their text *Quantitative Analysis of Management* (1997), B. Render (Rollins College) and R. M. Stair (Florida State University) present the case of the Bayfield Mud Company. Bayfield supplies boxcars of 50-pound bags of mud treating agents to the Wet-Land Drilling Company. Mud treating agents are used to control the pH and other chemical properties of the cone during oil drilling operations. Wet-Land has complained to Bayfield that its most recent shipment of bags were underweight by about 5%. (The use of underweight bags may result in poor chemical control during drilling, which may hurt drilling efficiency resulting in serious economic consequences.) Afraid of losing a long-time customer, Bayfield immediately began investigating their production process. Management suspected that the causes of the problem were the recently added third shift and the fact that all 3 shifts were under pressure to increase output to meet increasing demand for the product. Their quality control staff began randomly sampling and weighing 6 bags of output each hour. The average weight of each sample over the last 3 days is recorded in the table on p. 823 along with the weight of the heaviest and lightest bag in each sample.

◉ **MUDBAGS**

Time	Average Weight (pounds)	Lightest	Heaviest	Time	Average Weight (pounds)	Lightest	Heaviest
6:00 A.M.	49.6	48.7	50.7	6:00 P.M	46.8	41.0	51.2
7:00	50.2	49.1	51.2	7:00	50.0	46.2	51.7
8:00	50.6	49.6	51.4	8:00	47.4	44.0	48.7
9:00	50.8	50.2	51.8	9:00	47.0	44.2	48.9
10:00	49.9	49.2	52.3	10:00	47.2	46.6	50.2
11:00	50.3	48.6	51.7	11:00	48.6	47.0	50.0
12 noon	48.6	46.2	50.4	12 midnight	49.8	48.2	50.4
1:00 P.M.	49.0	46.4	50.0	1:00 A.M.	49.6	48.4	51.7
2:00	49.0	46.0	50.6	2:00	50.0	49.0	52.2
3:00	49.8	48.2	50.8	3:00	50.0	49.2	50.0
4:00	50.3	49.2	52.7	4:00	47.2	46.3	50.5
5:00	51.4	50.0	55.3	5:00	47.0	44.1	49.7
6:00	51.6	49.2	54.7	6:00	48.4	45.0	49.0
7:00	51.8	50.0	55.6	7:00	48.8	44.8	49.7
8:00	51.0	48.6	53.2	8:00	49.6	48.0	51.8
9:00	50.5	49.4	52.4	9:00	50.0	48.1	52.7
10:00	49.2	46.1	50.7	10:00	51.0	48.1	55.2
11:00	49.0	46.3	50.8	11:00	50.4	49.5	54.1
12 midnight	48.4	45.4	50.2	12 noon	50.0	48.7	50.9
1:00 A.M.	47.6	44.3	49.7	1:00 P.M.	48.9	47.6	51.2
2:00	47.4	44.1	49.6	2:00	49.8	48.4	51.0
3:00	48.2	45.2	49.0	3:00	49.8	48.8	50.8
4:00	48.0	45.5	49.1	4:00	50.0	49.1	50.6
5:00	48.4	47.1	49.6	5:00	47.8	45.2	51.2
6:00	48.6	47.4	52.0	6:00	46.4	44.0	49.7
7:00	50.0	49.2	52.2	7:00	46.4	44.4	50.0
8:00	49.8	49.0	52.4	8:00	47.2	46.6	48.9
9:00	50.3	49.4	51.7	9:00	48.4	47.2	49.5
10:00	50.2	49.6	51.8	10:00	49.2	48.1	50.7
11:00	50.0	49.0	52.3	11:00	48.4	47.0	50.8
12 noon	50.0	48.8	52.4	12 midnight	47.2	46.4	49.2
1:00 P.M.	50.1	49.4	53.6	1:00 A.M.	47.4	46.8	49.0
2:00	49.7	48.6	51.0	2:00	48.8	47.2	51.4
3:00	48.4	47.2	51.7	3:00	49.6	49.0	50.6
4:00	47.2	45.3	50.9	4:00	51.0	50.5	51.5
5:00	46.8	44.1	49.0	5:00	50.5	50.0	51.9

Source: Kinard, J., Western Carolina University, as reported in Render, B., and Stair, Jr., R. *Quantitative Analysis for Management*, 6th ed. Upper Saddle River, N.J.: Prentice Hall, 1997.

a. Construct an x̄-chart for these data.
b. Is the process under statistical control?
c. Does it appear that management's suspicion about the third shift is correct? Explain?

12.16 Robotics clamp gap width. University of Waterloo (Canada) statistician S. H. Steiner applied control chart methodology to the manufacturing of a horseshoe-shaped metal fastener called a *robotics clamp* (*Applied Statistics*, Vol. 47, 1998). Users of the clamp were concerned with the width of the gap between the two ends of the fastener. Their preferred target width is .054 inches. An optical measuring device was used to measure the gap width of the fastener during the manufacturing process. The manufacturer sampled five finished clamps every 15 minutes throughout its 16-hour daily production schedule and optically measured the gap. Data for 4 consecutive hours of production are presented in the table at right.

a. Construct an x̄-chart from these data.

◉ **CLAMPGAP**

Time	Gap Width (thousandths of an inch)				
00:15	54.2	54.1	53.9	54.0	53.8
00:30	53.9	53.7	54.1	54.4	55.1
00:45	54.0	55.2	53.1	55.9	54.5
01:00	52.1	53.4	52.9	53.0	52.7
01:15	53.0	51.9	52.6	53.4	51.7
01:30	54.2	55.0	54.0	53.8	53.6
01:45	55.2	56.6	53.1	52.9	54.0
02:00	53.3	57.2	54.5	51.6	54.3
02:15	54.9	56.3	55.2	56.1	54.0
02:30	55.7	53.1	52.9	56.3	55.4
02:45	55.2	51.0	56.3	55.6	54.2
03:00	54.2	54.2	55.8	53.8	52.1
03:15	55.7	57.5	55.4	54.0	53.1
03:30	53.7	56.9	54.0	55.1	54.2
03:45	54.1	53.9	54.0	54.6	54.8
04:00	53.5	56.1	55.1	55.0	54.0

Source: Adapted from Steiner, Stefan, H. "Grouped Data Exponentially Weighted Moving Average Control Charts." *Applied Statistics—Journal of the Royal Statistical Society*, Vol. 47, Part 2, 1998, pp. 203–216.

b. Apply the pattern-analysis rules to the control chart. Does your analysis suggest that special causes of variation are present in the clamp manufacturing process? Which of the six rules led you to your conclusion?

c. Should the control limits be used to monitor future process output? Explain.

12.17 Filling vials of morphine. A pharmaceutical company produces vials filled with morphine (*Communications in Statistics*, Vol. 27, 1998). Most of the time the filling process remains stable, but once in a while the mean value shifts off the target of 52.00 grams. To monitor the process, one sample of size 3 is drawn from the process every 27 minutes. Measurements for 20 consecutive samples are shown in the accompanying table.

a. Construct an $\bar{x}$-chart for these data.

b. What does the $\bar{x}$-chart suggest about the stability of the process?

c. Is the process influenced by both common and special causes of variation? Explain.

d. Should the control limits and centerline of the $\bar{x}$-chart of part **a** be used to monitor future output of the morphine filling process? Explain.

● MORPHINE

Sample	Amount of Morphine in Vials (grams)		
1	51.60	52.35	52.00
2	52.10	53.00	51.90
3	51.75	51.85	52.05
4	52.10	53.50	53.95
5	52.00	52.35	52.40
6	51.70	52.10	51.90
7	52.00	51.50	52.35
8	52.25	52.40	52.05
9	52.00	51.60	51.80
10	52.15	51.65	51.40
11	51.20	52.15	52.35
12	52.00	52.35	51.85
13	51.60	52.15	52.00
14	51.40	52.35	52.10
15	52.90	53.75	54.25
16	54.30	53.90	54.15
17	53.85	53.65	54.90
18	54.25	53.55	54.05
19	54.00	53.60	53.95
20	53.80	54.50	54.20

Source: Adapted from Costa, A. F. B. "VSSI X Charts with Sampling at Fixed Times." *Communications in Statistics — Theory and Methods,* Vol. 27, No. 11 (1998), pp. 2853–2869.

12.5 A Control Chart for Monitoring the Variation of a Process: The R-Chart

Recall from Section 12.2 that a process may be out of statistical control because its mean or variance or both are changing over time (see Figure 12.8). The $\bar{x}$-chart of the previous section is used to detect changes in the process mean. The control chart we present in this section — the **R-chart** — is used to detect changes in process variation.

The primary difference between the $\bar{x}$-chart and the R-chart is that instead of plotting *sample means* and monitoring their variation, we plot and monitor the variation of *sample ranges*. Changes in the behavior of the sample range signal changes in the variation of the process.

We could also monitor process variation by plotting *sample standard deviations* — that is, we could calculate *s* for each-sample (i.e., each subgroup) and plot them on a control chart known as an **s-chart.** In this chapter, however, we focus on just the R-chart because (1) when using samples of size 9 or less, the s-chart and the R-chart reflect about the same information, and (2) the R-chart is used much more widely by practitioners than is the s-chart (primarily because the sample range is easier to calculate and interpret than the sample standard deviation). For more information about s-charts, see the references at the end of the book.

The underlying logic and basic form of the R-chart are similar to the $\bar{x}$-chart. In monitoring $\bar{x}$, we use the standard deviation of $\bar{x}$ to develop 3-sigma control limits. Now, since we want to be able to determine when R takes on unusually large or small values, we use the standard deviation of R, or σ_R, to construct 3-sigma control limits. The centerline of the $\bar{x}$-chart represents the process mean μ or, equivalently, the mean of the sampling distribution of $\bar{x}$, $\mu_{\bar{x}}$. Similarly, the centerline of the R-chart represents μ_R, the mean of the sampling distribution of R. These points are illustrated in the R-chart of Figure 12.24.

As with the $\bar{x}$-chart, you should have at least 20 samples of n items each ($n \geq 2$) to construct an R-chart. This will provide sufficient data to obtain reasonably good esti-

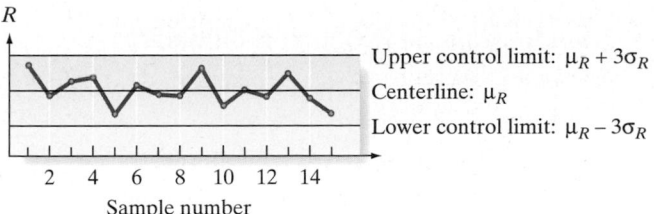

FIGURE 12.24
R-chart

mates of μ_R and σ_R. Rational subgrouping is again used for determining sample size and frequency of sampling.

The centerline of the *R*-chart is positioned as follows:

$$Centerline: \overline{R} = \frac{R_1 + R_2 + \cdots + R_k}{k}$$

where k is the number of samples of size n and R_i is the range of the ith sample. $\overline{R}$ is an estimate of μ_R.

In order to construct the control limits, we need an estimator of σ_R. The estimator recommended by Montgomery (1991) and Ryan (1989) is

$$\hat{\sigma}_R = d_3\left(\frac{\overline{R}}{d_2}\right)$$

where d_2 and d_3 are constants whose values depend on the sample size, n. Values for d_2 and d_3 for samples of size $n = 2$ to $n = 25$ are given in Table XI of Appendix B.

The control limits are positioned as follows:

$$Upper\ control\ limit: \overline{R} + 3\hat{\sigma}_R = \overline{R} + 3d_3\left(\frac{\overline{R}}{d_2}\right)$$

$$Lower\ control\ limit: \overline{R} - 3\hat{\sigma}_R = \overline{R} - 3d_3\left(\frac{\overline{R}}{d_2}\right)$$

Notice that $\overline{R}$ appears twice in each control limit. Accordingly, we can simplify the calculation of these limits by factoring out $\overline{R}$:

$$UCL: \overline{R}\left(1 + \frac{3d_3}{d_2}\right) = \overline{R}D_4 \qquad LCL: \overline{R}\left(1 - \frac{3d_3}{d_2}\right) = \overline{R}D_3$$

where

$$D_4 = \left(1 + \frac{3d_3}{d_2}\right) \qquad D_3 = \left(1 - \frac{3d_3}{d_2}\right)$$

The values for D_3 and D_4 have been tabulated for samples of size $n = 2$ to $n = 25$ and can be found in Appendix B, Table XI.

For samples of size $n = 2$ through $n = 6$, D_3 is negative, and the lower control limit falls below zero. Since the sample range cannot take on negative values, such a control limit is meaningless. Thus, when $n \le 6$, the *R*-chart contains only one control limit, the upper control limit.

Although D_3 is actually negative for $n \le 6$, the values reported in Table XI in Appendix B are all zeros. This has been done to discourage the inappropriate construction of negative lower control limits. If the lower control limit is calculated using $D_3 = 0$, you obtain $D_3\overline{R} = 0$. This should be interpreted as indicating that the *R*-chart has no lower 3-sigma control limit.

Constructing an *R*-Chart: A Summary

1. Using a rational subgrouping strategy, collect at least 20 samples (i.e., subgroups), each of size $n \geq 2$.
2. Calculate the range of each sample.
3. Calculate the mean of the sample ranges, $\overline{R}$:

$$\overline{R} = \frac{R_1 + R_2 + \cdots + R_k}{k}$$

where

k = The number of samples (i.e., subgroups)

R_i = The range of the ith sample

4. Plot the centerline and control limits:

Centerline: $\overline{R}$

Upper control limit: $\overline{R}D_4$

Lower control limit: $\overline{R}D_3$

where D_3 and D_4 are constants that depend on n. Their values can be found in Appendix B, Table XI. When $n \leq 6$, $D_3 = 0$, indicating that the control chart does not have a lower control limit.

5. Plot the k sample ranges on the control chart in the order that the samples were produced by the process.

We interpret the completed *R*-chart in basically the same way as we did the $\overline{x}$-chart. We look for indications that the process is out of control. Those indications include points that fall outside the control limits as well as any nonrandom patterns of variation that appear between the control limits. To help spot nonrandom behavior, we include the A, B, and C zones (described in the previous section) on the *R*-chart. The next box describes how to construct the zone boundaries for the *R*-chart. It requires only Rules 1 through 4 of Figure 12.21, because Rules 5 and 6 are based on the assumption that the statistic plotted on the control chart follows a normal (or nearly normal) distribution, whereas *R*'s distribution is skewed to the right.*

Constructing Zone Boundaries for an *R*-Chart

The simplest method of construction uses the estimator of the standard deviation of *R*, which is $\hat{\sigma}_R = d_3(\overline{R}/d_2)$:

$$\text{Upper A–B boundary: } \overline{R} + 2d_3\left(\frac{\overline{R}}{d_2}\right)$$

$$\text{Lower A–B boundary: } \overline{R} - 2d_3\left(\frac{\overline{R}}{d_2}\right)$$

$$\text{Upper B–C boundary: } \overline{R} + d_3\left(\frac{\overline{R}}{d_2}\right)$$

$$\text{Lower B–C boundary: } \overline{R} - d_3\left(\frac{\overline{R}}{d_2}\right)$$

Note: Whenever $n \leq 6$, the *R*-chart has no lower 3-sigma control limit. However, the lower A–B, B–C boundaries can still be plotted if they are nonnegative.

*Some authors (e.g., Kane, 1989) apply all six pattern-analysis rules as long as $n \geq 4$.

Interpreting an *R*-Chart

1. The **process is out of control** if one or more sample ranges fall beyond the control limits (Rule 1) or if any of the three patterns of variation described by Rules 2, 3, and 4 (Figure 12.21) are observed. Such signals indicate that one or more special causes of variation are influencing the *variation* of the process. These causes should be identified and eliminated to bring the process into control.

2. The **process is treated as being in control** if none of the noted out-of-control signals are observed. Processes that are in control should not be tampered with. However, if the level of variation is unacceptably high, common causes of variation should be identified and eliminated.

As with the $\bar{x}$-chart, the centerline and control limits should be developed using samples that were collected during a period in which the process was in control. Accordingly, when an *R*-chart is first constructed, the centerline and the control limits are treated as *trial values* (see Section 12.4) and are modified, if necessary, before being extended to the right and used to monitor future process output.

EXAMPLE 12.3

Creating and Interpreting an *R*-Chart for a Paint-Filling Process

Refer to Example 12.1.

Problem

a. Construct an *R*-chart for the paint-filling process.

b. What does the chart indicate about the stability of the filling process during the time when the data were collected?

c. Is it appropriate to use the control limits constructed in part **a** to monitor future process output?

Solution

a. The first step after collecting the data is to calculate the range of each sample. For the first sample the range is

$$R_1 = 10.0042 - 9.9964 = .0078$$

All 25 sample ranges appear in Table 12.2 (p. 816).

Next, calculate the mean of the ranges:

$$\bar{R} = \frac{.0078 + .0092 + \cdots + .0077}{25} = .010072$$

The centerline of the chart is positioned at $\bar{R} = .010072$. To determine the control limits, we need the constants D_3 and D_4, which can be found in Table XI of Appendix B. For $n = 5$, $D_3 = 0$ and $D_4 = 2.114$. Since $D_3 = 0$, the lower 3-sigma control limit is negative and is not included on the chart. The upper control limit is calculated as follows:

$$\text{UCL: } \bar{R}D_4 = (.010072)(2.114) = .02130$$

After positioning the upper control limit on the chart, we plot the 25 sample ranges in the order of sampling and connect the points with straight lines. The resulting trial *R*-chart, produced using MINITAB, is shown in Figure 12.25.

b. To facilitate our examination of the *R*-chart, we plot the four zone boundaries. Recall that in general the A–B boundaries are positioned 2 standard deviations from the centerline and the B–C boundaries are 1 standard deviation from the

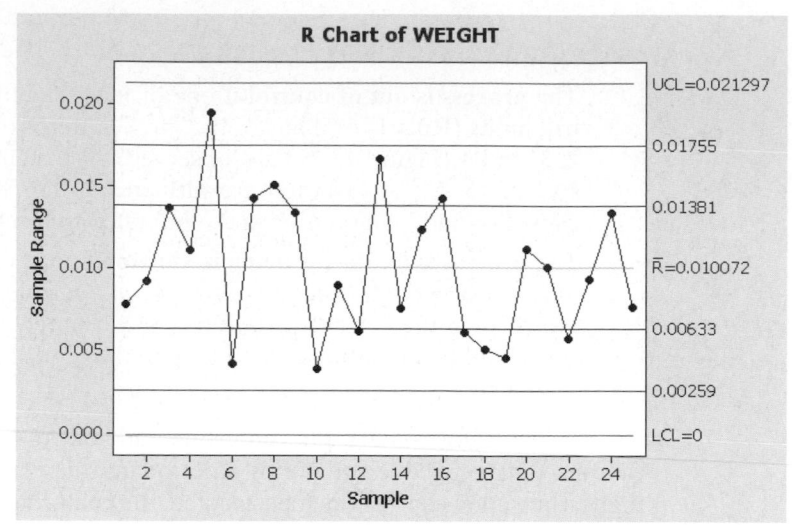

FIGURE 12.25

MINITAB R-chart for the paint-filling process

centerline. In the case of the R-chart, we use the estimated standard deviation of R, $\hat{\sigma}_R = d_3(\overline{R}/d_2)$, and calculate the boundaries:

$$Upper\ A\!-\!B\ boundary\!: \overline{R} + 2d_3\!\left(\frac{\overline{R}}{d_2}\right) = .01755$$

$$Lower\ A\!-\!B\ boundary\!: \overline{R} - 2d_3\!\left(\frac{\overline{R}}{d_2}\right) = .00259$$

$$Upper\ B\!-\!C\ boundary\!: \overline{R} + d_3\!\left(\frac{\overline{R}}{d_2}\right) = .01381$$

$$Lower\ B\!-\!C\ boundary\!: \overline{R} - d_3\!\left(\frac{\overline{R}}{d_2}\right) = .00633$$

where (from Table XI of Appendix B) for $n = 5$, $d_2 = 2.326$ and $d_3 = .864$. Notice in Figure 12.25 that the lower A zone is slightly narrower than the upper A zone. This occurs because the lower 3-sigma control limit (the usual lower boundary of the lower A zone) is negative.

All the plotted R values fall below the upper control limit. This is one indication that the process is under control (i.e., is stable). However, we must also look for patterns of points that would be unlikely to occur if the process were in control. To assist us with this process, we use pattern-analysis rules 1–4 (Figure 12.21). None of the rules signal the presence of special causes of variation. Accordingly, we conclude that it is reasonable to treat the process—in particular, the variation of the process—as being under control during the period in question. Apparently, no significant special causes of variation are influencing the variation of the process.

c. Yes. Since the variation of the process appears to be in control during the period when the sample data were collected, the control limits appropriately characterize the variation in R that would be expected when the process is in a state of statistical control.

Now Work Exercise 12.21

In practice, the $\overline{x}$-chart and the R-chart are not used in isolation, as our presentation so far might suggest. Rather, they are used together to monitor the mean (i.e., the location) of the process and the variation of the process simultaneously. In fact, many practitioners plot them on the same piece of paper.

One important reason for dealing with them as a unit is that the control limits of the $\bar{x}$-chart are a function of R—that is, the control limits depend on the variation of the process. (Recall that the control limits are $\bar{x} \pm A_2\bar{R}$.) Thus, if the process variation is out of control the control limits of the $\bar{x}$-chart have little meaning. This is because when the process variation is changing (as in the bottom two graphs of Figure 12.8), any single estimate of the variation (such as $\bar{R}$ or s) is not representative of the process. Accordingly, **the appropriate procedure is to first construct and then interpret the *R*-chart. If it indicates that the process variation is in control, then it makes sense to construct and interpret the $\bar{x}$-chart.**

Figure 12.26 is reprinted from Kaoru Ishikawa's classic text on quality-improvement methods, *Guide to Quality Control* (1986). It illustrates how particular changes in a process over time may be reflected in $\bar{x}$- and *R*-charts. At the top of the figure, running across the page, is a series of probability distributions A, B, and C that describe the process (i.e., the output variable) at different points in time. In practice, we never have this information. For this example, however, Ishikawa worked with a known process (i.e., with its given probabilistic characterization) to illustrate how sample data from a known process might behave.

The control limits for both charts were constructed from $k = 25$ samples of size $n = 5$. These data were generated by Distribution A. The 25 sample means and ranges were plotted on the $\bar{x}$- and *R*-charts, respectively. Since the distribution did not change over this period of time, it follows from the definition of statistical control that the process was under control. If you did not know this—as would be the case in practice—what would you conclude from looking at the control charts? (Remember, always interpret the *R*-chart before the $\bar{x}$-chart.) Both charts indicate that the process is under control. Accordingly, the control limits are made official and can be used to monitor future output, as is done next.

Toward the middle of the figure, the process changes. The mean shifts to a higher level. Now the output variable is described by Distribution B. The process is out of control. Ten new samples of size 5 are sampled from the process. Since the variation of the process has not changed, the *R*-chart should indicate that the variation remains stable. This is, in fact, the case. All points fall below the upper control limit. As we would hope, it is the $\bar{x}$-chart that reacts to the change in the mean of the process.

Then the process changes again (Distribution C). This time the mean shifts back to its original position, but the variation of the process increases. The process is still out of

FIGURE 12.26

Combined $\bar{x}$- and *R*-chart
Source: Reprinted from *Guide to Quality Control*, by Kaoru Ishikawa, © 1986 by Asian Productivity Organization, with permission of the publisher Asian Productivity Organization. Distributed in North America by Quality Resources, New York, NY.

control but this time for a different reason. Checking the R-chart first, we see that it has reacted as we would hope. It has detected the increase in the variation. Given this R-chart finding, the control limits of the $\bar{x}$-chart become inappropriate (as described before) and we would not use them. Notice, however, how the sample means react to the increased variation in the process. This increased variation in $\bar{x}$ is consistent with what we know about the variance of $\bar{x}$. It is directly proportional to the variance of the process, $\sigma_{\bar{x}}^2 = \sigma^2/n$.

Keep in mind that what Ishikawa did in this example is exactly the opposite of what we do in practice. In practice we use sample data and control charts to make inferences about changes in unknown process distributions. Here, for the purpose of helping you to understand and interpret control charts, known process distributions were changed to see what would happen to the control charts.

STATISTICS IN ACTION REVISITED

Monitoring the Variation of the Jet Fuel Surfactant Test Process

Recall (p. 818) that the engineering firm discovered that tests for surfactants in jet fuel additive using Pump-B with Filter-B yielded an "in-control" process mean. However, as discussed in this section, the variation of the process should be checked first before interpreting the $\bar{x}$-chart. Figure SIA12.2 is a MINITAB R-chart for the test results using Pump-B with Filter-B. As an option, we again instructed MINITAB to highlight (in red) any sample ranges that match any of the

four pattern-analysis rules for detecting special causes of variation given in this section. (If a rule is violated, the rule number will be shown next to the sample range on the chart.)

Figure SIA12.2 shows that the process variation is "in control"—none of the pattern-analysis rules for ranges are matched. Now that we've established the stability of the process variance, the $\bar{x}$-chart of Figure SIA12.1(d) can be meaningfully interpreted. Together, the $\bar{x}$-chart and R-chart helped the engineering firm establish the Pump-B with Filter-B surfactant test method as a viable alternative to the standard test, one which appears to have no special causes of variation present and with more precision than the standard.

[*Note:* Extensive testing done with the Navy concluded the improved precision of the "new" surfactant test was valid. However, the new test was unable to detect several light surfactants that can still cause problems in jet engines. The original test for surfactants in jet fuel additive remains the industry standard.]

Figure SIA12.2

R-chart for Pump-B with Filter-B method

Exercises 12.18–12.29

Learning the Mechanics

12.18 What characteristic of a process is an *R*-chart designed to monitor?

12.19 In practice, $\bar{x}$- and *R*-charts are used together to monitor a process. However, the *R*-chart should be interpreted before the $\bar{x}$-chart. Why?

12.20 Use Table XI in Appendix B to find the values of D_3 and D_4 for each of the following sample sizes.
  a. $n = 4$
  b. $n = 12$
  c. $n = 24$

12.21 Construct and interpret an *R*-chart for the data in Exercise
NW   12.10 (p. 821).
  a. Calculate and plot the upper control limit and, if appropriate, the lower control limit.
  b. Calculate and plot the A, B, and C zone boundaries on the *R*-chart.
  c. Plot the sample ranges on the *R*-chart and use pattern-analysis rules 1–4 of Figure 12.21 to determine whether the process is under statistical control.

12.22 Construct and interpret an *R*-chart for the data in Exercise 12.11 (p. 821).
  a. Calculate and plot the upper control limit and, if appropriate, the lower control limit.
  b. Calculate and plot the A, B, and C zone boundaries on the *R*-chart.
  c. Plot the sample ranges on the *R*-chart and determine whether the process is in control.

12.23 Construct and interpret an *R*-chart and an $\bar{x}$-chart from the sample data shown below. Remember to interpret the *R*-chart *before* the $\bar{x}$-chart.

Applying the Concepts—Basic

12.24 **CPU of a computer chip.** Refer to Exercise 12.12 (p. 821), where the desired circuit path widths were .5 to .85 micron. The manufacturer sampled four CPU chips six times a day (every 90 minutes from 8:00 A.M. until 4:30 P.M.) for 5 consecutive days. The path widths were measured and used to construct the MINITAB *R*-chart shown on p. 832.
  a. Calculate the chart's upper and lower control limits.
  b. What does the *R*-chart suggest about the presence of special causes of variation during the time when the data were collected?
  c. Should the control limit(s) be used to monitor future process output? Explain.
  d. How many different *R* values are plotted on the control chart? Notice how most of the *R* values fall along three horizontal lines. What could cause such a pattern?

12.25 **Cola bottle filling process.** A soft-drink bottling company is interested in monitoring the amount of cola injected into 16-ounce bottles by a particular filling head. The process is entirely automated and operates 24 hours a day. At 6:00 A.M. and 6:00 P.M. each day, a new dispenser of carbon dioxide capable of producing 20,000 gallons of cola is hooked up to the filling machine. In order to monitor the process using control charts, the company decided to sample five consecutive bottles of cola each hour beginning at 6:15 A.M. (i.e., 6:15 A.M., 7:15 A.M., 8:15 A.M., etc.). The data for the first day are given in the table on p. 833. An SPSS descriptive statistics printout is also provided on p. 832.
  a. Will the rational subgrouping strategy that was used enable the company to detect variation in fill caused by differences in the carbon dioxide dispensers? Explain.

LM12_23

Sample	Measurements							$\bar{x}$	R
	1	2	3	4	5	6	7		
1	20.1	19.0	20.9	22.2	18.9	18.1	21.3	20.07	4.1
2	19.0	17.9	21.2	20.4	20.0	22.3	21.5	20.33	4.4
3	22.6	21.4	21.4	22.1	19.2	20.6	18.7	20.86	3.9
4	18.1	20.8	17.8	19.6	19.8	21.7	20.0	19.69	3.9
5	22.6	19.1	21.4	21.8	18.4	18.0	19.5	20.11	4.6
6	19.1	19.0	22.3	21.5	17.8	19.2	19.4	19.76	4.5
7	17.1	19.4	18.6	20.9	21.8	21.0	19.8	19.80	4.7
8	20.2	22.4	22.0	19.6	19.6	20.0	18.5	20.33	3.9
9	21.9	24.1	23.1	22.8	25.6	24.2	25.2	23.84	3.7
10	25.1	24.3	26.0	23.1	25.8	27.0	26.5	25.40	3.9
11	25.8	29.2	28.5	29.1	27.8	29.0	28.0	28.20	3.4
12	28.2	27.5	29.3	30.7	27.6	28.0	27.0	28.33	3.7
13	28.2	28.6	28.1	26.0	30.0	28.5	28.3	28.24	4.0
14	22.1	21.4	23.3	20.5	19.8	20.5	19.0	20.94	4.3
15	18.5	19.2	18.0	20.1	22.0	20.2	19.5	19.64	4.0
16	21.4	20.3	22.0	19.2	18.0	17.9	19.5	19.76	4.1
17	18.4	16.5	18.1	19.2	17.5	20.9	19.6	18.60	4.4
18	20.1	19.8	22.3	22.5	21.8	22.7	23.0	21.74	3.2
19	20.0	17.5	21.0	18.2	19.5	17.2	18.1	18.79	3.8
20	22.3	18.2	21.5	19.0	19.4	20.5	20.0	20.13	4.1

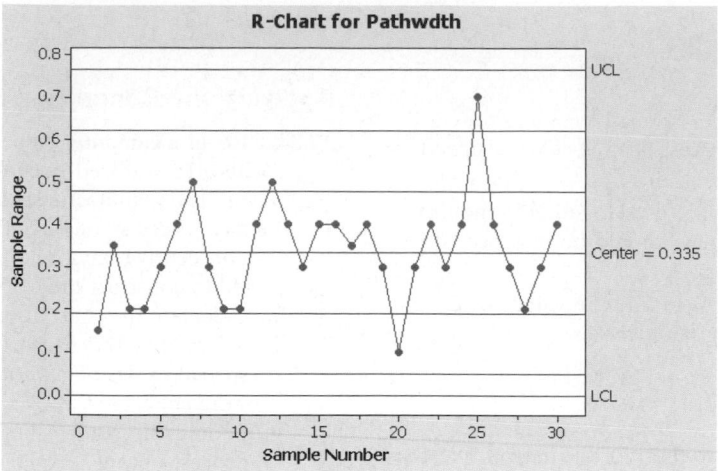

MINITAB Output for Exercise 12.24

b. Construct an *R*-chart from the data.

c. What does the *R*-chart indicate about the stability of the filling process during the time when the data were collected? Justify your answer.

d. Should the control limit(s) be used to monitor future process output? Explain.

e. Given your answer to part **c,** should an $\bar{x}$-chart be constructed from the given data? Explain.

Descriptive Statistics for 25 Cola Samples

	Count	Mean	Minimum	Maximum	Range
1	5	16.01	15.98	16.03	.05
2	5	16.00	15.97	16.03	.06
3	5	16.01	15.98	16.04	.06
4	5	16.00	15.98	16.03	.05
5	5	16.01	15.97	16.04	.07
6	5	16.01	15.97	16.04	.07
7	5	16.00	15.96	16.05	.09
8	5	16.01	15.97	16.05	.08
9	5	15.99	15.95	16.03	.08
10	5	16.01	15.95	16.06	.11
11	5	16.00	15.93	16.07	.14
12	5	16.02	15.94	16.08	.14
13	5	15.99	15.96	16.01	.05
14	5	16.00	15.98	16.02	.04
15	5	16.00	15.98	16.03	.05
16	5	16.00	15.97	16.02	.05
17	5	16.01	15.99	16.05	.06
18	5	16.01	15.98	16.04	.06
19	5	15.98	15.96	16.01	.05
20	5	16.01	15.96	16.04	.08
21	5	16.01	15.97	16.05	.08
22	5	16.01	15.95	16.07	.12
23	5	16.02	15.95	16.07	.12
24	5	15.99	15.93	16.08	.15

SPSS Output for Exercise 12.25

SECTION 12.5   A Control Chart for Monitoring the Variation of a Process: The *R*-Chart   **833**

COLAFILL

Sample	Measurements				
1	16.01	16.03	15.98	16.00	16.01
2	16.03	16.02	15.97	15.99	15.99
3	15.98	16.00	16.03	16.04	15.99
4	16.00	16.03	16.02	15.98	15.98
5	15.97	15.99	16.03	16.01	16.04
6	16.01	16.03	16.04	15.97	15.99
7	16.04	16.05	15.97	15.96	16.00
8	16.02	16.05	16.03	15.97	15.98
9	15.97	15.99	16.02	16.03	15.95
10	16.00	16.01	15.95	16.04	16.06
11	15.95	16.04	16.07	15.93	16.03
12	15.98	16.07	15.94	16.08	16.02
13	15.96	16.00	16.01	16.00	15.98
14	15.98	16.01	16.02	15.99	15.99
15	15.99	16.03	16.00	15.98	16.01
16	16.02	16.02	16.01	15.97	16.00
17	16.01	16.05	15.99	15.99	16.03
18	15.98	16.03	16.04	15.98	16.01
19	15.97	15.96	15.99	15.99	16.01
20	16.03	16.01	16.04	15.96	15.99
21	15.99	16.03	15.97	16.05	16.03
22	15.98	15.95	16.07	16.01	16.04
23	15.99	16.06	15.95	16.03	16.07
24	16.00	16.01	16.08	15.94	15.93

ATM

Week	Replacement Cycle Time (in days)				
1	7	10	6	6	10
2	7	12	8	8	6
3	7	8	7	11	6
4	8	8	12	11	12
5	3	8	4	7	7
6	6	10	11	5	7
7	5	12	11	8	7
8	7	12	8	7	6
9	8	10	12	10	5
10	12	8	6	6	8
11	10	9	9	5	4
12	3	10	7	6	8
13	9	9	8	7	2
14	7	10	18	20	8
15	8	18	15	18	21
16	10	22	16	8	7
17	3	18	4	8	12
18	11	7	8	17	19
19	10	8	19	20	25
20	6	3	18	18	7

Applying the Concepts—Intermediate

12.26 Replacement times for lost ATM cards. In an effort to reduce customer dissatisfaction with delays in replacing lost automated teller machine (ATM) cards, some retail banks monitor the time required to replace a lost ATM card. Called *replacement cycle time,* it is the elapsed time from when the customer contacts the bank about the loss until the customer receives a new card (*Management Science,* Sept. 1999). A particular retail bank monitors replacement cycle time for the first five requests each week for replacement cards. Variation in cycle times is monitored using an *R*-chart. Data for 20 weeks is presented above (at right).

a. Construct an *R*-chart for these data.

b. What does the *R*-chart suggest about the presence of special causes of variation in the process?

c. Should the control limits of your *R*-chart be used to monitor future replacement cycle times? Explain.

d. Given your conclusion in part **b** and the pattern displayed on the *R*-chart, discuss the possible future impact on the performance of the bank.

12.27 Bayfield Mud Company case. Refer to Exercise 12.15 (p. 822), in which the Bayfield Mud Company was concerned with discovering why their filling operation was producing underfilled bags of mud.

a. Construct an *R*-chart for the filling process.

b. According to the *R*-chart, is the process under statistical control? Explain.

c. Does the *R*-chart provide any evidence concerning the cause of Bayfield's underfilling problem? Explain.

12.28 Robotics clamp gap width. Refer to Exercise 12.16 (p. 823), in which a robotics clamp manufacturer was concerned about gap width.

a. Construct an *R*-chart for the gap width.

b. Which parameter of the manufacturing process does your *R*-chart provide information about?

c. What does the *R*-chart suggest about the presence of special causes of variation during the time when the data were collected?

Applying the Concepts—Advanced

12.29 Precision of scale weight measurements. The *Journal of Quality Technology* (July 1998) published an article examining the effects of the precision of measurement on the *R*-chart. The authors presented data from a British nutrition company that fills containers labeled "500 grams" with a powdered dietary supplement. Once every 15 minutes, five containers are sampled from the filling process and the fill weight is measured. The first table on p. 834 lists the measurements for 25 consecutive samples made with a scale that is accurate to .5 gram, followed by a second table that gives measurements for the same samples made with a scale that is accurate to only 2.5 grams. Throughout the time period over which the samples were drawn, it is known that the filling process was in statistical control with mean 500 grams and standard deviation 1 gram.

a. Construct an *R*-chart for the data that is accurate to .5 gram. Is the process under statistical control? Explain.

b. Given your answer to part **a,** is it appropriate to construct an $\bar{x}$-chart for the data? Explain.

c. Construct an *R*-chart for the data that is accurate to only 2.5 grams. What does it suggest about the stability of the filling process?

d. Based on your answers to parts **a** and **c,** discuss the importance of the accuracy of measurement instruments in evaluating the stability of production processes.

⊙ **FILLWT1**

Sample	Fill Weights Accurate to .5 Gram					Range
1	500.5	499.5	502.0	501.0	500.5	2.5
2	500.5	499.5	500.0	499.0	500.0	1.5
3	498.5	499.0	500.0	499.5	500.0	1.5
4	500.5	499.5	499.0	499.0	500.5	1.5
5	500.0	501.0	500.5	500.5	500.0	1.0
6	501.0	498.5	500.0	501.5	500.5	3.0
7	499.5	500.0	499.0	501.0	499.5	2.0
8	498.5	498.0	500.0	500.5	500.5	2.5
9	498.0	499.0	502.0	501.0	501.5	4.0
10	499.0	499.5	499.5	500.0	499.5	1.0
11	502.5	499.5	501.0	501.5	502.0	3.0
12	501.5	501.5	500.0	500.0	501.0	1.5
13	498.5	499.5	501.0	500.5	498.5	2.5
14	499.5	498.0	500.0	499.5	498.5	2.0
15	501.0	500.0	498.0	500.5	500.0	3.0
16	502.5	501.5	502.0	500.5	500.5	2.0
17	499.5	500.5	500.0	499.5	499.5	1.0
18	499.0	498.5	498.0	500.0	498.0	2.0
19	499.0	498.0	500.5	501.0	501.0	3.0
20	501.5	499.5	500.0	500.5	502.0	2.5
21	501.0	500.5	502.0	502.5	502.5	2.0
22	501.5	502.5	502.5	501.5	502.0	1.0
23	499.5	502.0	500.0	500.5	502.0	2.5
24	498.5	499.0	499.0	500.5	500.0	2.0
25	500.0	499.5	498.5	500.0	500.5	2.0

⊙ **FILLWT2**

Sample	Fill Weights Accurate to 2.5 Grams					Range
1	500.0	500.0	502.5	500.0	500.0	2.5
2	500.0	500.0	500.0	500.0	500.0	0.0
3	500.0	500.0	500.0	500.0	500.0	0.0
4	497.5	500.0	497.5	497.5	500.0	2.5
5	500.0	500.0	500.0	500.0	500.0	0.0
6	502.5	500.0	497.5	500.0	500.0	5.0
7	500.0	500.0	502.5	502.5	500.0	2.5
8	497.5	500.0	500.0	497.5	500.0	2.5
9	500.0	500.0	497.5	500.0	502.5	5.0
10	500.0	500.0	500.0	500.0	500.0	0.0
11	500.0	505.0	502.5	500.0	500.0	5.0
12	500.0	500.0	500.0	500.0	500.0	0.0
13	500.0	500.0	497.5	500.0	500.0	2.5
14	500.0	500.0	500.0	500.0	500.0	0.0
15	502.5	502.5	502.5	500.0	502.5	2.5
16	500.0	500.0	500.0	500.0	500.0	0.0
17	497.5	497.5	497.5	497.5	497.5	0.0
18	500.0	500.0	500.0	500.0	500.0	0.0
19	495.0	497.5	500.0	500.0	500.0	5.0
20	500.0	502.5	500.0	500.0	502.5	2.5
21	500.0	500.0	500.0	500.0	500.0	0.0
22	500.0	500.0	500.0	500.0	500.0	0.0
23	500.0	500.0	500.0	500.0	500.0	0.0
24	497.5	497.5	500.0	497.5	497.5	2.5
25	500.0	500.0	497.5	500.0	500.0	2.5

Source: Adapted from Tricker, A., Coates, E., and Okell, E. "The Effects on the *R*-chart of Precision of Measurement." *Journal of Quality Technology,* Vol. 30, No. 3, July 1998, pp. 232–239.

12.6 A Control Chart for Monitoring the Proportion of Defectives Generated by a Process: The p-Chart

Among the dozens of different control charts that have been proposed by researchers and practitioners, the $\bar{x}$- and R-charts are by far the most popular for use in monitoring *quantitative* output variables such as time, length, and weight. Among the charts developed for use with *qualitative* output variables, the chart we introduce in this section is the most popular. Called the **p-chart,** it is used when the output variable is categorical (i.e., measured on a nominal scale). With the p-chart, the proportion, p, of units produced by the process that belong to a particular category (e.g., defective or nondefective; successful or unsuccessful; early, on-time, or late) can be monitored.

The p-chart is typically used to monitor the proportion of defective units produced by a process (i.e., the proportion of units that do not conform to specification). This proportion is used to characterize a process in the same sense that the mean and variance are used to characterize a process when the output variable is quantitative. Examples of process proportions that are monitored in industry include the proportion of billing errors made by credit card companies; the proportion of nonfunctional semiconductor chips produced; and the proportion of checks that a bank's magnetic ink character-recognition system is unable to read.

As is the case for the mean and variance, the process proportion can change over time. For example, it can drift upward or downward or jump to a new level. In such cases, the process is out of control. **As long as the process proportion remains constant, the process is in a state of statistical control.**

As with the other control charts presented in this chapter, the p-chart has a center-line and control limits that are determined from sample data. After k samples of size n are drawn from the process, each unit is classified (e.g., defective or nondefective), the proportion of defective units in each sample—$\hat{p}$—is calculated, the centerline and control limits are determined using this information, and the sample proportions are plotted

FIGURE 12.27
p-Chart

on the *p*-chart. It is the variation in the $\hat{p}$'s over time that we monitor and interpret. Changes in the behavior of the $\hat{p}$'s signal changes in the process proportion, *p*.

The *p*-chart is based on the assumption that the number of defectives observed in each sample is a binomial random variable. What we have called the process proportion is really the binomial probability, *p*. (We discussed binomial random variables in Chapter 4.) When the process is in a state of statistical control, *p* remains constant over time. Variation in $\hat{p}$—as displayed on a *p*-chart—is used to judge whether *p* is stable.

To determine the centerline and control limits for the *p*-chart, we need to know $\hat{p}$'s sampling distribution. We described the sampling distribution of $\hat{p}$ in Section 5.4. Recall that

$$\hat{p} = \frac{\text{Number of defective items in the sample}}{\text{Number of items in the sample}} = \frac{x}{n}$$

$$\mu_{\hat{p}} = p$$

$$\sigma_{\hat{p}} = \sqrt{\frac{p(1-p)}{n}}$$

and that for large samples $\hat{p}$ is approximately normally distributed. Thus, if *p* were known, the centerline would be *p* and the 3-sigma control limits would be $p \pm 3\sqrt{p(1-p)/n}$. However, since *p* is unknown, it must be estimated from the sample data. The appropriate estimator is $\overline{p}$, the overall proportion of defective units in the *nk* units sampled:

$$\overline{p} = \frac{\text{Total number of defective units in all } k \text{ samples}}{\text{Total number of units sampled}}$$

To calculate the control limits of the *p*-chart, substitute $\overline{p}$ for *p* in the preceding expression for the control limits, as illustrated in Figure 12.27.

In constructing a *p*-chart, it is advisable to use a much larger sample size than is typically used for $\bar{x}$- and *R*-charts. Most processes that are monitored in industry have relatively small process proportions, often less than .05 (i.e., less than 5% of output is nonconforming). In those cases, if a small sample size is used, say *n* = 5, samples drawn from the process would likely not contain any nonconforming output. As a result, most, if not all, $\hat{p}$'s would equal zero.

We present a rule of thumb that can be used to determine a sample size large enough to avoid this problem. This rule will also help protect against ending up with a negative lower control limit, a situation that frequently occurs when both *p* and *n* are small. See Montgomery (1991) or Duncan (1986) for further details.

Sample-Size Determination for Monitoring a Process Proportion

Choose *n* such that $n > \dfrac{9(1 - p_0)}{p_0}$

where

   n = Sample size

   p_0 = An estimate (perhaps judgmental) of the process proportion *p*

For example, if p is thought to be about .05, the rule indicates that samples of at least size 171 should be used in constructing the p-chart:

$$n > \frac{9(1 - .05)}{.05} = 171$$

In the next three boxes, we summarize how to construct a p-chart and its zone boundaries and how to interpret a p-chart.

Constructing a p-Chart: A Summary

1. Using a rational subgrouping strategy, collect at least 20 samples, each of size

$$n > \frac{9(1 - p_0)}{p_0}$$

where p_0 is an estimate of p, the proportion defective (i.e., nonconforming) produced by the process. p_0 can be determined from sample data (i.e., $\hat{p}$) or may be based on expert opinion.

2. For each sample, calculate $\hat{p}$, the proportion of defective units in the sample:

$$\hat{p} = \frac{\text{Number of defective items in the sample}}{\text{Number of items in the sample}}$$

3. Plot the centerline and control limits:

$$\textit{Centerline: } \overline{p} = \frac{\text{Total number of defective units in all } k \text{ samples}}{\text{Total number of units in all } k \text{ samples}}$$

$$\textit{Upper control limit: } \overline{p} + 3\sqrt{\frac{\overline{p}(1 - \overline{p})}{n}}$$

$$\textit{Lower control limit: } \overline{p} - 3\sqrt{\frac{\overline{p}(1 - \overline{p})}{n}}$$

where k is the number of samples of size n and $\overline{p}$ is the overall proportion of defective units in the nk units sampled. $\overline{p}$ is an estimate of the unknown process proportion p.

4. Plot the k sample proportions on the control chart in the order that the samples were produced by the process.

As with the $\overline{x}$- and R-charts, the centerline and control limits should be developed using samples that were collected during a period in which the process was in control. Accordingly, when a p-chart is first constructed, the centerline and the control limits should be treated as *trial values* (see Section 12.4) and, if necessary, modified before being extended to the right on the control chart and used to monitor future process output.

Constructing Zone Boundaries for a p-Chart

$$\textit{Upper A–B boundary: } \overline{p} + 2\sqrt{\frac{\overline{p}(1 - \overline{p})}{n}}$$

$$\textit{Lower A–B boundary: } \overline{p} - 2\sqrt{\frac{\overline{p}(1 - \overline{p})}{n}}$$

$$\text{Upper } B-C \text{ boundary: } \overline{p} + \sqrt{\frac{\overline{p}(1-\overline{p})}{n}}$$

$$\text{Lower } B-C \text{ boundary: } \overline{p} - \sqrt{\frac{\overline{p}(1-\overline{p})}{n}}$$

Note: When the lower control limit is negative, it should not be plotted on the control chart. However, the lower zone boundaries can still be plotted if they are nonnegative.

Interpreting a *p*-Chart

1. The **process is out of control** if one or more sample proportions fall beyond the control limits (Rule 1) or if any of the three patterns of variation described by Rules 2, 3, and 4 (Figure 12.21) are observed. Such signals indicate that one or more special causes of variation are influencing the process proportion, *p*. These causes should be identified and eliminated in order to bring the process into control.

2. The **process is treated as being in control** if none of the above noted out-of-control signals are observed. Processes that are in control should not be tampered with. However, if the level of variation is unacceptably high, common causes of variation should be identified and eliminated.

EXAMPLE 12.4

Creating and Interpreting a *p*-Chart for an Order Assembly Process

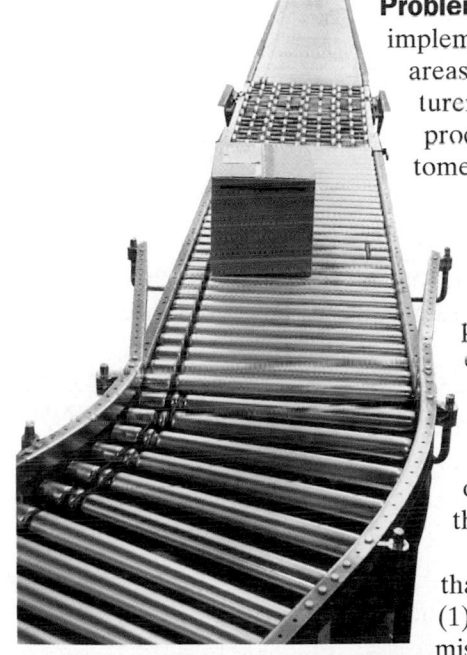

Problem A manufacturer of auto parts is interested in implementing statistical process control in several areas within its warehouse operation. The manufacturer wants to begin with the order assembly process. Too frequently orders received by customers contain the wrong items or too few items.

For each order received, parts are picked from storage bins in the warehouse, labeled, and placed on a conveyor belt system. Since the bins are spread over a 3-acre area, items that are part of the same order may be placed on different spurs of the conveyor belt system. Near the end of the belt system, all spurs converge and a worker sorts the items according to the order they belong to. That information is contained on the labels that were placed on the items by the pickers.

The workers have identified three errors that cause shipments to be improperly assembled: (1) pickers pick from the wrong bin, (2) pickers mislabel items, and (3) the sorter makes an error. The firm's quality manager has implemented a sampling program in which 90 assembled orders are sampled each day and checked for accuracy. An assembled order is considered nonconforming (defective) if it differs in any way from the order placed by the customer. To date, 25 samples have been evaluated. The resulting data are shown in Table 12.4.

a. Construct a *p*-chart for the order assembly operation.

b. What does the chart indicate about the stability of the process?

c. Is it appropriate to use the control limits and centerline constructed in part **a** to monitor future process output?

WAREHOUSE

TABLE 12.4 Twenty-Five Samples of Size 90 from the Warehouse Order Assembly Process

Sample	Size	Defective Orders	Sample Proportion
1	90	12	.13333
2	90	6	.06667
3	90	11	.12222
4	90	8	.08889
5	90	13	.14444
6	90	14	.15556
7	90	12	.13333
8	90	6	.06667
9	90	10	.11111
10	90	13	.14444
11	90	12	.13333
12	90	24	.26667
13	90	23	.25556
14	90	22	.24444
15	90	8	.08889
16	90	3	.03333
17	90	11	.12222
18	90	14	.15556
19	90	5	.05556
20	90	12	.13333
21	90	18	.20000
22	90	12	.13333
23	90	13	.14444
24	90	4	.04444
25	90	6	.06667
Totals	**2,250**	**292**	

Solution

a. The first step in constructing the p-chart after collecting the sample data is to calculate the sample proportion for each sample. For the first sample,

$$\hat{p} = \frac{\text{Number of defective items in the sample}}{\text{Number of items in the sample}} = \frac{12}{90} = .13333$$

All the sample proportions are displayed in Table 12.4. Next, calculate the proportion of defective items in the total number of items sampled:

$$\bar{p} = \frac{\text{Total number of defective items}}{\text{Total number of items sampled}} = \frac{292}{2,250} = .12978$$

The centerline is positioned at $\bar{p}$, and $\bar{p}$ is used to calculate the control limits:

$$\bar{p} \pm 3\sqrt{\frac{\bar{p}(1-\bar{p})}{n}} = .12978 \pm 3\sqrt{\frac{.12978(1-.12978)}{90}}$$

$$= .12978 \pm .10627$$

$$\text{UCL: } .23605$$

$$\text{LCL: } .02351$$

After plotting the centerline and the control limits, plot the 25 sample proportions in the order of sampling and connect the points with straight lines. The completed control chart, obtained using MINITAB, is shown in Figure 12.28.

FIGURE 12.28

MINITAB *p*-chart for the
order assembly process

b. To assist our examination of the control chart, we add the 1- and 2-standard-deviation zone boundaries. The boundaries are located by substituting $\bar{p} = .12978$ into the following formulas:

$$\text{Upper } A–B \text{ boundary: } \bar{p} + 2\sqrt{\frac{\bar{p}(1-\bar{p})}{n}} = .20063$$

$$\text{Lower } A–B \text{ boundary: } p - 2\sqrt{\frac{\bar{p}(1-\bar{p})}{n}} = .05893$$

$$\text{Upper } B–C \text{ boundary: } \bar{p} + \sqrt{\frac{\bar{p}(1-\bar{p})}{n}} = .16521$$

$$\text{Lower } B–C \text{ boundary: } \bar{p} - \sqrt{\frac{\bar{p}(1-\bar{p})}{n}} = .09435$$

Note that three of the sample proportions fall above the upper control limit (Rule 1); thus, there is strong evidence that the process is out of control. None of the nonrandom patterns of Rules 2, 3, and 4 (Figure 12.21) are evident. The process proportion appears to have increased dramatically somewhere around sample 12.

c. Because the process was apparently out of control during the period in which sample data were collected to build the control chart, it is not appropriate to continue using the chart. The control limits and centerline are not representative of the process when it is in control. The chart must be revised before it is used to monitor future output.

In this case, the three out-of-control points were investigated, and it was discovered that they occurred on days when a temporary sorter was working in place of the regular sorter. Actions were taken to ensure that in the future better-trained temporary sorters would be available.

Since the special cause of the observed variation was identified and eliminated, all sample data from the 3 days the temporary sorter was working were dropped from the data set and the centerline and control limits were recalculated:

$$\text{Centerline: } \bar{p} = \frac{223}{1980} = .11263$$

$$\text{Control limits: } \bar{p} \pm 3\sqrt{\frac{\bar{p}(1-\bar{p})}{n}} = .11263 \pm 3\sqrt{\frac{.11263(.88737)}{90}}$$

$$= .11263 \pm .09997$$

$$\text{UCL: } .21259 \qquad \text{LCL: } .01266$$

The revised zones are calculated by substituting $\bar{p} = .11263$ in the following formulas:

$$Upper\ A-B\ boundary: \bar{p} + 2\sqrt{\frac{\bar{p}(1-\bar{p})}{n}} = .17927$$

$$Upper\ B-C\ boundary: \bar{p} + \sqrt{\frac{\bar{p}(1-\bar{p})}{n}} = .14595$$

$$Lower\ A-B\ boundary: \bar{p} - 2\sqrt{\frac{\bar{p}(1-\bar{p})}{n}} = .04598$$

$$Lower\ B-C\ boundary: \bar{p} - \sqrt{\frac{\bar{p}(1-\bar{p})}{n}} = .07931$$

The revised control chart appears in Figure 12.29. Notice that now all sample proportions fall within the control limits. These limits can now be treated as official, extended to the right on the chart, and used to monitor future orders.

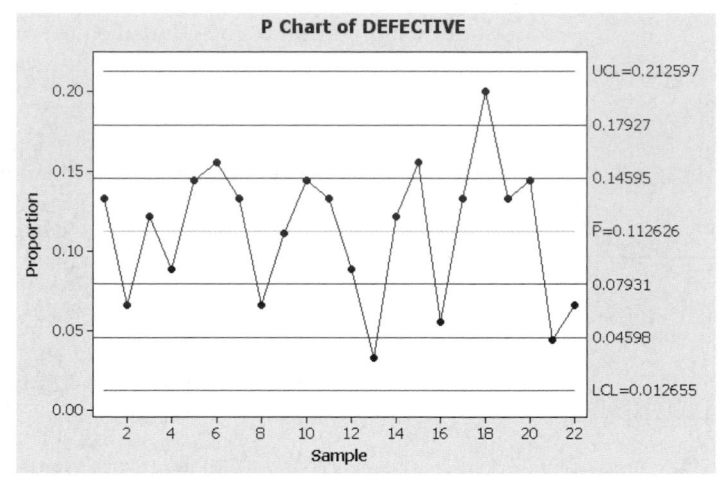

FIGURE 12.29

Revised MINITAB p-chart for the order assembly process

Now Work Exercise 12.33

Exercises 12.30–12.38

Learning the Mechanics

12.30 What characteristic of a process is a p-chart designed to monitor?

12.31 The proportion of defective items generated by a manufacturing process is believed to be 8%. In constructing a p-chart for the process, determine how large the sample size should be to avoid ending up with a negative lower control limit.

12.32 To construct a p-chart for a manufacturing process, 25 samples of size 200 were drawn from the process. The number of defectives in each sample is listed on p. 841.
  a. Calculate the proportion defective in each sample.
  b. Calculate and plot $\bar{p}$ and the upper and lower control limits for the p-chart.
  c. Calculate and plot the A, B, and C zone boundaries on the p-chart.

  d. Plot the sample proportions on the p-chart and connect them with straight lines.
  e. Use the pattern-analysis rules 1–4 for detecting the presence of special causes of variation (Figure 12.21) to determine whether the process is out of control.

12.33 To construct a p-chart, 20 samples of size 150 were drawn
NW from a process. The proportion of defective items found in each of the samples is listed in the second table on p.841.
  a. Calculate and plot the centerline and the upper and lower control limits for the p-chart.
  b. Calculate and plot the A, B, and C zone boundaries on the p-chart.
  c. Plot the sample proportions on the p-chart.
  d. Is the process under control? Explain.
  e. Should the control limits and centerline of part **a** be used to monitor future process output? Explain.

LM12_32

Sample	Sample Size	Defectives
1	200	16
2	200	14
3	200	9
4	200	11
5	200	15
6	200	8
7	200	12
8	200	16
9	200	17
10	200	13
11	200	15
12	200	10
13	200	9
14	200	12
15	200	14
16	200	11
17	200	8
18	200	7
19	200	12
20	200	15
21	200	9
22	200	16
23	200	13
24	200	11
25	200	10

LM12_33

Sample	Proportion Defective	Sample	Proportion Defective
1	.03	11	.07
2	.05	12	.04
3	.10	13	.06
4	.02	14	.05
5	.08	15	.07
6	.09	16	.06
7	.08	17	.07
8	.05	18	.02
9	.07	19	.05
10	.06	20	.03

12.34 In each of the following cases, use the sample size formula to determine a sample size large enough to avoid constructing a *p*-chart with a negative lower control limit.
   a. $p_0 = .01$ **b.** $p_0 = .05$ **c.** $p_0 = .10$ **d.** $p_0 = .20$

Applying the Concepts—Basic

12.35 Defective micron chips. A manufacturer produces micron chips for personal computers. From past experience, the production manager believes that 1% of the chips are defective. The company collected a sample of the first 1,000 chips manufactured after 4:00 P.M. every other day for a month. The chips were analyzed for defects; then these data and MINITAB were used to construct the *p*-chart shown below.
   a. From a statistical perspective, is a sample size of 1,000 adequate for constructing the *p*-chart? Explain.
   b. Calculate the chart's upper and lower control limits.
   c. What does the *p*-chart suggest about the presence of special causes during the time when the data were collected?
   d. Critique the rational subgrouping strategy used by the disk manufacturer.

12.36 Rubber company tire tests. Goodstone Tire & Rubber Company is interested in monitoring the proportion of defective tires generated by the production process at its Akron, Ohio, production plant. The company's chief engineer believes that the proportion is about 7%. Because the tires are destroyed during the testing process, the company would like to keep the number of tires tested to a minimum. However, the engineer would also like to use a *p*-chart with a positive lower control limit. A positive lower control limit makes it possible to determine when the process has generated an unusually small proportion of defectives. Such an occurrence is good news and would signal the engineer to look for causes of the superior performance. That information can be used to improve the production process. Using the sample size formula, the chief engineer recommended that the company randomly sample and test 120 tires from each day's production. To date, 20 samples have been taken. The data are presented on p. 842.
   a. Use the sample size formula to show how the chief engineer arrived at the recommended sample size of 120.

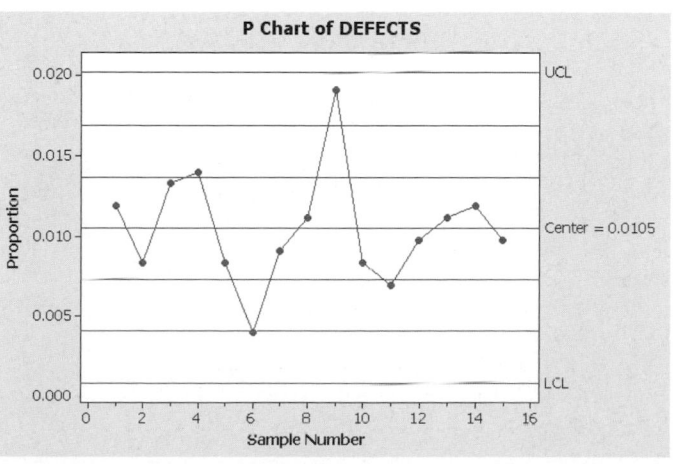

MINITAB Output for
Exercise 12.35

b. Construct a *p*-chart for the tire production process.

c. What does the chart indicate about the stability of the process? Explain.

d. Is it appropriate to use the control limits to monitor future process output? Explain.

e. Is the *p*-chart you constructed in part **b** capable of signaling hour-to-hour changes in *p*? Explain.

DEFTIRES

Sample	Sample Size	Defectives
1	120	11
2	120	5
3	120	4
4	120	8
5	120	10
6	120	13
7	120	9
8	120	8
9	120	10
10	120	11
11	120	10
12	120	12
13	120	8
14	120	6
15	120	10
16	120	5
17	120	10
18	120	10
19	120	3
20	120	8

Applying the Concepts—Intermediate

12.37 Monitoring newspaper typesetters. Accurate typesetting is crucial to the production of high-quality newspapers. The editor of the Morristown *Daily Tribune*, a weekly publication with circulation of 27,000, has instituted a process for monitoring the performance of typesetters. Each week 100 paragraphs of the paper are randomly sampled and read for accuracy. The number of paragraphs with errors is recorded in the following table for each of the last 30 weeks.

a. Construct a *p*-chart for the process.

b. Is the process under statistical control? Explain.

c. Should the control limits of part **a** be used to monitor future process output? Explain.

d. Suggest two methods that could be used to facilitate the diagnosis of causes of process variation.

TYPESET

Week	Paragraphs with Errors	Week	Paragraphs with Errors
1	2	16	2
2	4	17	3
3	10	18	7
4	4	19	3
5	1	20	2
6	1	21	3
7	13	22	7
8	9	23	4
9	11	24	3
10	0	25	2
11	3	26	2
12	4	27	0
13	2	28	1
14	2	29	3
15	8	30	4

Primary Source: Jerry Kinard, Western Carolina University.
Secondary Source: Render, B., and Stair, Jr., R. *Quantitative Analysis for Management,* 6th ed. Upper Saddle River, N. J.: Prentice Hall, 1997.

12.38 Quality of rewritable CDs. A Japanese compact disk (CD) manufacturer has a daily production rate of about 20,000 CD-RW (rewritable disks). Quality is monitored by randomly sampling 200 finished CDs every other hour from the production process and testing them for defects. If one or more defects are discovered, the CD is considered defective and is destroyed. The production process operates 20 hours per day, 7 days a week. The following table reports data for the last 3 days of production.

a. Construct a *p*-chart for the CD-RW production process.

b. What does it indicate about the stability of the process? Explain.

c. What advice can you give the manufacturer to assist them in their search for the special cause(s) of variation that is plaguing the process?

CDRW

Day	Hour	Number of Defectives	Day	Hour	Number of Defectives
1	1	13		6	3
	2	5		7	1
	3	2		8	2
	4	3		9	3
	5	2		10	1
	6	3	3	1	9
	7	1		2	5
	8	2		3	2
	9	1		4	1
	10	1		5	3
2	1	11		6	2
	2	6		7	4
	3	2		8	2
	4	3		9	1
	5	1		10	1

12.7 Diagnosing the Causes of Variation (Optional)

Statistical process control (SPC) consists of three major activities or phases: (1) monitoring process variation, (2) diagnosing causes of variation, and (3) eliminating those causes. A more detailed description of SPC is shown in Figure 12.30, which depicts SPC as a quality-improvement cycle. In the monitoring phase, statistical signals from the process are evaluated in order to uncover opportunities to improve the process. This is the phase we have dealt with in Sections 12.3–12.6. We turn our attention now to the diagnosis phase.

The diagnosis phase is the critical link in the SPC improvement cycle. The monitoring phase simply identifies *whether* problems exist; the diagnosis phase identifies *what* the problems are. If the monitoring phase detected the presence of special causes of variation (i.e., an out-of-control signal was observed on a control chart), the diagnosis phase is concerned with tracking down the underlying cause or causes. If no special causes were detected in the monitoring phase (i.e., the process is under statistical control) and further improvement in the process is desired, the diagnosis phase concentrates on uncovering common causes of variation.

It is important to recognize that the achievement of process improvement requires more than the application of statistical tools such as control charts. This is particularly evident in the diagnosis phase. The diagnosis of causes of variation requires expert knowledge about the process in question. Just as you would go to a physician to diagnose a pain in your back, you would turn to people who work in the process or to engineers or analysts with process expertise to help you diagnose the causes of process variation.

Several methods have been developed for assisting process experts with process diagnosis, including *flowcharting* and the simple but powerful graphical tool called *Pareto analysis* (Chapter 2). Another graphical method, the **cause-and-effect diagram,** is described in this section. (A fourth methodology, *experimental design,* is the topic of Chapter 8.)

The cause-and-effect diagram was developed by Kaoru Ishikawa of the University of Tokyo in 1943. As a result, it is also known as an *Ishikawa diagram.* The cause-and-effect diagram facilitates the construction of causal chains that explain the occurrence of events, problems, or conditions. It is often constructed through brainstorming sessions involving a small group of process experts. It has been employed for decades by Japanese firms but was not widely applied in the United States until the mid-1980s.

The basic framework of the cause-and-effect diagram is shown in Figure 12.31. In the right-hand box in the figure, we record the effect whose cause(s) we want to diagnose.

For instance, GOAL/QPC (a Massachusetts-based TQM consulting group) used the cause-and-effect diagram in Figure 12.32 to demonstrate why pizzas are delivered

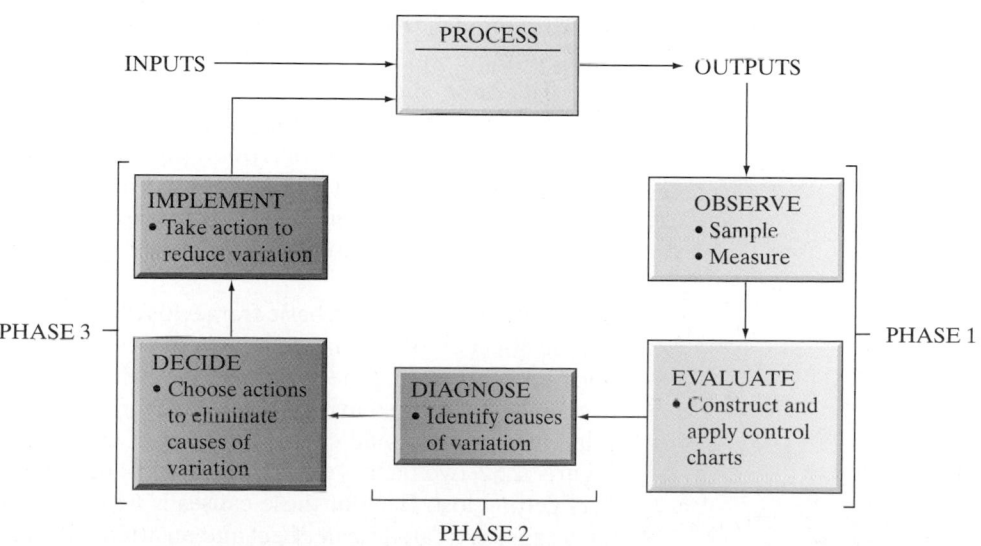

FIGURE 12.30

SPC viewed as a quality-improvement cycle

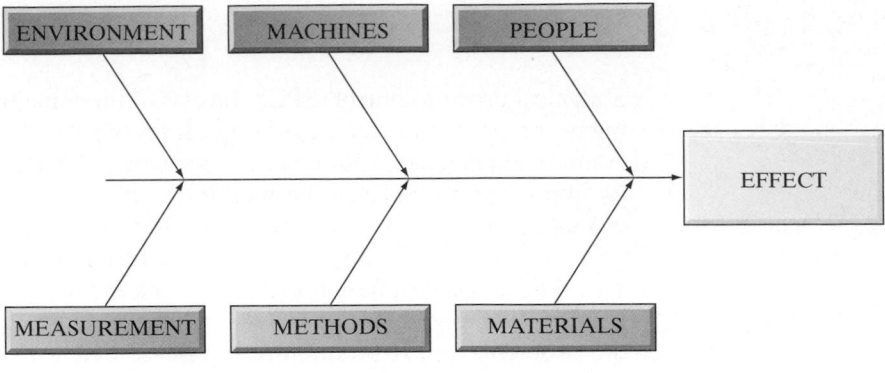

FIGURE 12.31

The basic framework for a cause-and-effect diagram

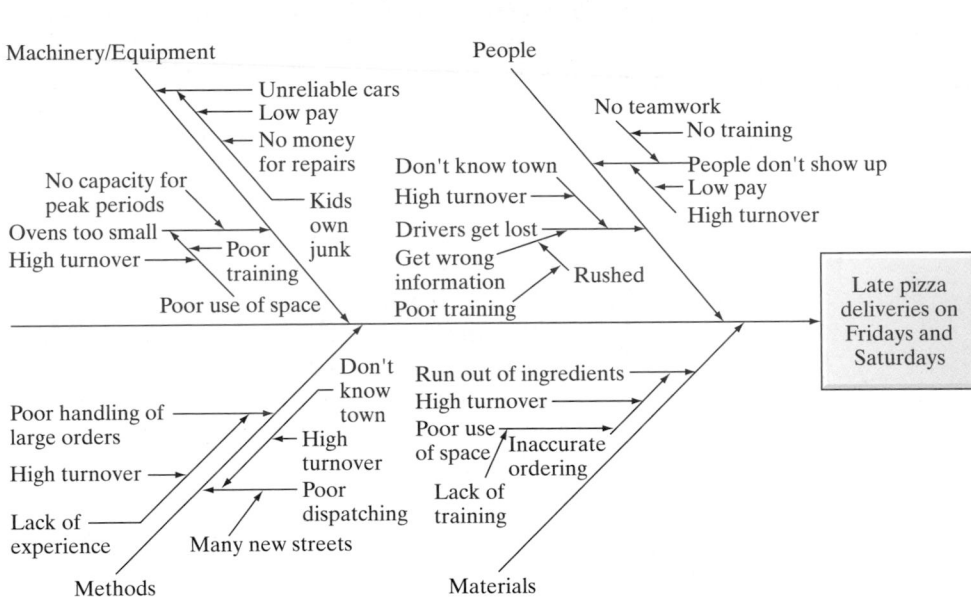

FIGURE 12.32

Cause-and-effect diagram for late pizza deliveries

Source: Reprinted with permission from The Memory Jogger™ II, GOAL/QPC, 13 Branch Street, Methuan, Massachusetts, 1994, p. 27.

late on Fridays and Saturdays. As a second example, Figure 12.33 displays the reasons for high variation in the fill weights of 20-pound bags of dry dog food.

Examining Figure 12.31, we see the branches of the cause-and-effect diagram, which represent the major factors that influence the process and that could be responsible for the effect. These are often taken to be the six universal sources of process variation that we described in Section 12.1: people, machines, materials, methods, measurement, and environment. Notice that in the examples of Figures 12.32 and 12.33 these categories were tailored to fit the process in question. The set of categories must be broad enough to include virtually all possible factors that could influence the process. It is less important how many categories are used or how you label the categories.

The cause-and-effect diagram is constructed using effect-to-cause reasoning—that is, you begin by specifying the effect of interest and then move backward to identify *potential* causes of the effect. After a potential cause has been identified, you treat it as an effect and try to find its cause, and so forth. The result is a **causal chain.** A completed cause-and-effect diagram typically contains many causal chains. These chains help us to track down causes whose eradication will reduce, improve, or eliminate the effect in question.

After setting up the basic framework for the cause-and-effect diagram and recording the effect of interest in the box on the right, you construct the causal chains, proceeding backward from general potential causes to increasingly specific causes. Begin by choosing one of the universal cause categories—say, people—and asking, "What factors related to people could cause the effect in question?" In the pizza delivery example of Figure 12.32, two factors were identified: (1) drivers not showing up for work and (2) drivers getting lost. Each of these causes is written on a twig of the People branch. Next, each cause is treated as an effect and an attempt is made to identify its cause—that is, we look for subcauses. For example, driver absenteeism was blamed on (1) high turnover

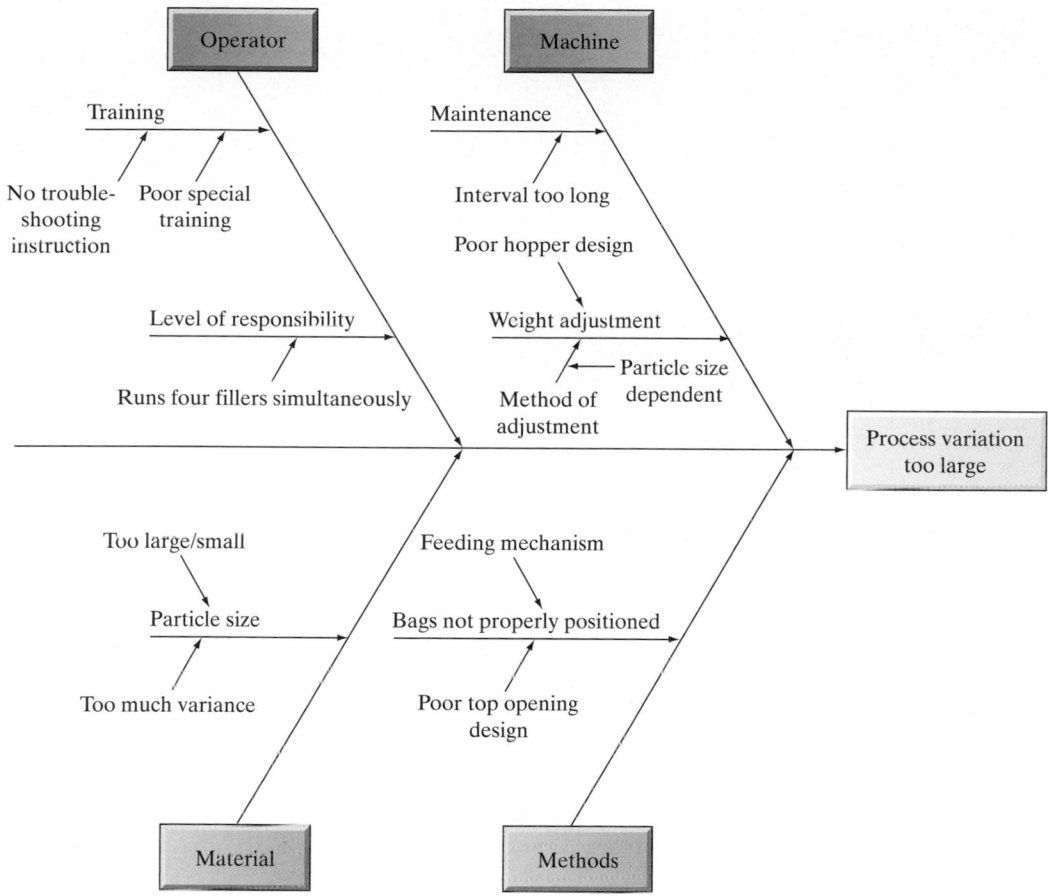

FIGURE 12.33

Cause-and-effect diagram for the filling process for 20-lb bags of dog food

Source: R. E. DeVor, T. Chang, and J. W. Southerland, *Statistical Quality Design and Control,* New York, Macmillan, 1992. © 1992. Reprinted by permission of Prentice Hall, Inc., Upper Saddle River, NJ.

and (2) no teamwork. The high turnover, in turn, was blamed on low pay, while lack of teamwork was blamed on insufficient training. Thus, the "No show" twig has both a "High turnover" twig and a "No teamwork" twig attached to it; and, each of these twigs has a cause twig attached. Multiple causal chains like this should be constructed for each branch of the cause-and-effect diagram.

Once completed, the various causal chains of the cause-and-effect diagram must be evaluated (often subjectively) to identify one or more factors thought most likely to be causes of the effect in question. Then actions can be chosen and implemented (see Figure 12.30) to eliminate the causes and improve the process.

Besides facilitating process diagnosis, cause-and-effect diagrams serve to document the causal factors that may potentially affect a process and to communicate that information to others in the organization. The cause-and-effect diagram is a very flexible tool that can be applied in a variety of situations. It can be used as a formal part of the SPC improvement cycle, as suggested above, or simply as a means of investigating the causes of organizational problems, events, or conditions. It can also help select the appropriate process variables to monitor with control charts.

12.8 Capability Analysis (Optional)

In the previous four sections, we pointed out that if a process were in statistical control, but the level of variation was unacceptably high, common causes of variation should be identified and eliminated. This was illustrated in Figure 12.13. In this optional section, we describe a methodology that can be used to help determine when such variation is unacceptably high. The methodology is called **capability analysis.** As we have seen, the

FIGURE 12.34

Output distributions of six different in-control processes, where LSL = lower specification limit and USL = upper specification limit

achievement of process stability is vitally important to process improvement efforts. But it is not an end in itself. A process may be in control but still not be capable of producing output that is acceptable to customers.

To see this, consider Figure 12.34. The figure displays six different in-control processes. Recall that if a process is under statistical control, its output distribution does not change over time and the process can be characterized by a single probability distribution, as in each of the panels of the figure. The upper and lower specification limits for the output of each of the six processes are also indicated on each panel, as is the target value for the output variable. Recall from Definition 12.8 that the specification limits are boundary points that define the acceptable values for an output variable.

The processes of panels **a, b,** and **c** produce a high percentage of items that are outside the specification limits. None of these processes is *capable* of satisfying its customers. In panel **a,** the process is centered on the target value, but the variation due to common causes is too high. In panel **b,** the variation is low relative to the width of the specification limits, but the process is off-center. In panel **c,** both problems exist: the variation is too high and the process is off-center. Thus, bringing a process into statistical control is not sufficient to guarantee the capability of the process.

All three processes in panels **d, e,** and **f** are capable. In each case, the process distribution fits comfortably between the specification limits. Virtually all of the individual items produced by these processes would be acceptable. However, any significant tightening of the specification limits—whether by customers or internal managers or engineers—would result in the production of unacceptable output and necessitate the initiation of process improvement activities to restore the process' capability. Further, even though a process is capable, continuous improvement of a process requires constant improvement of its capability.

When a process is known to be in control, the most direct way to assess its capability is to construct a frequency distribution (e.g. dot plot, histogram, or stem-and-leaf display) for a large sample of individual measurements (usually 50 or more) from the process. Then, add the specification limits and the target value for the output variable on

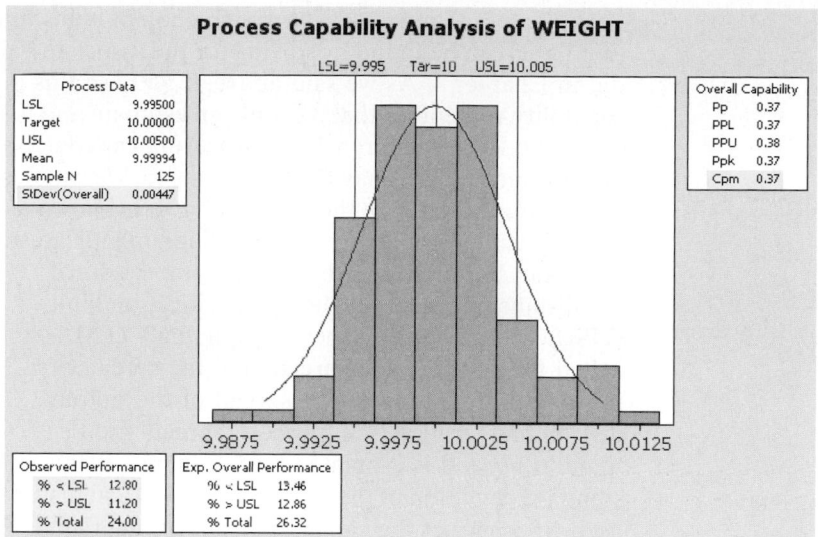

Process Capability Analysis of WEIGHT

LSL=9.995   Tar=10   USL=10.005

Process Data	
LSL	9.99500
Target	10.00000
USL	10.00500
Mean	9.99994
Sample N	125
StDev(Overall)	0.00447

Overall Capability	
Pp	0.37
PPL	0.37
PPU	0.38
Ppk	0.37
Cpm	0.37

9.9875   9.9925   9.9975   10.0025   10.0075   10.0125

Observed Performance	
% < LSL	12.80
% > USL	11.20
% Total	24.00

Exp. Overall Performance	
% < LSL	13.46
% > USL	12.86
% Total	26.32

FIGURE 12.35

MINITAB capability analysis diagram for the paint-filling process

the graph. This is called a **capability analysis diagram.** It is a simple visual tool for assessing process capability.

The MINITAB printout shown in Figure 12.35 is a capability analysis diagram for the paint-filling process found to be under statistical control in Examples 12.1 and 12.2. You can see that the process is roughly centered on the target of 10 pounds of paint but that a large number of paint cans fall outside the specification limits. This tells us that the process is not capable of satisfying customer requirements.

Most quality-management professionals and statisticians agree that the capability analysis diagram is the best way to describe the performance of an in-control process. However, many companies have found it useful to have a numerical measure of capability. The ability to summarize capability in a single number has the advantages of convenience, simplicity, and ease of communication. However, it also has the major disadvantage of potentially misleading those who use it. Just as when you characterize a data set by its mean and ignore its variation, the information you provide to your audience is incomplete and may adversely affect their actions and decisions. (A more thorough discussion about the dangers of numerical measures of capability is presented later in this section.)

There are several different approaches to quantifying capability. We will briefly describe two of them. The first (and most direct) consists of counting the number of items that fall outside the specification limits in the capability analysis diagram and reporting the percentage of such items in the sample. The original data set or a graphical technique that displays the individual measurements—such as a stem-and-leaf display or a dot plot—can be used to obtain the needed count. Or, you can use the capability analysis option of a statistical software package.

The desired information for the paint data is provided in the lower-left corner of the MINITAB printout, Figure 12.35. You can see that 24% of the 125 paint cans fall outside the specification limits (12.8% below 9.995 and 11.2% above 10.005). Thus, 24% of the 125 cans in the sample (i.e., 30 cans) are unacceptable.

When this percentage is used to characterize the capability of the process, the implication is that over time, if this process remains in control, roughly 24% of the paint cans will be unacceptable. Remember, however, that this percentage is only an estimate, a sample statistic, not a known parameter. It is based on a sample of size 125 and is subject to both sampling error and measurement error. We discussed such percentages and proportions in detail in Chapter 5.

If it is known that the process follows approximately a normal distribution, as is often the case, a similar approach to quantifying process capability can be used. In this case, the mean and standard deviation of the sample of measurements used to construct the capability analysis diagram can be taken as estimates of the mean and standard deviation of the process. Then, the fraction of items that would fall outside the specification limits can be found by solving for the associated area under the normal curve, as we did in Chapter 4. As we said above, if you use this percentage to characterize process capability, remember that it is only an estimate and is subject to sampling error.

The second approach to measuring capability is to construct a **capability index.** Several such indexes have been developed. We will describe one used for stable processes that are centered on the target value. It is known as the C_p **index.***

When the capability analysis diagram indicates that the process is centered, capability can be measured through a comparison of the distance between the upper specification limit (USL) and the lower specification limit (LSL), called the **specification spread,** and the spread of the output distribution. The spread of the output distribution—called the **process spread**—is defined as 6σ and is estimated by $6s$, where s is the standard deviation of the sample of measurements used to construct the capability analysis diagram. These two distances are illustrated in Figure 12.36. The ratio of these distances is the capability index known as C_p.

FIGURE 12.36
Process spread versus specification spread

Definition 12.10

The **capability index** for a process *centered on the desired mean* is

$$C_p = \frac{(\text{Specification spread})}{(\text{Process spread})} = \frac{(USL - LSL)}{6\sigma}$$

where σ is estimated by s, the standard deviation of the sample of measurements used to construct the capability analysis diagram.

Interpretation of Capability Index, C_p

C_p summarizes the performance of a stable, centered process relative to the specification limits. It indicates the extent to which the output of the process falls within the specification limits.

1. If $C_p = 1$ (specification spread = process spread), process is capable
2. If $C_p > 1$ (specification spread > process spread), process is capable
3. If $C_p < 1$ (specification spread < process spread), process is not capable

If the process follows a normal distribution,

$C_p = 1.00$ means about 2.7 units per 1,000 will be unacceptable
$C_p = 1.33$ means about 63 units per million will be unacceptable
$C_p = 1.67$ means about .6 units per million will be unacceptable
$C_p = 2.00$ means about 2 units per billion will be unacceptable

---

In manufacturing applications where the process follows a normal distribution (approximately), managers typically require a C_p of at least 1.33. With a C_p of 1.33, the process spread takes up only 75% of the specification spread, leaving a little wiggle room in case the process moves off center.

---

*For off-center processes, its sister index, C_{pk}, is used. Consult the chapter references for a description of C_{pk}.

EXAMPLE 12.5

Finding and Interpreting C_p for the Paint-Filling Process

Problem Let's return to the paint-filling process analyzed in Examples 12.1 and 12.3. Using 25 samples of size 5 (125 measurements), we constructed $\bar{x}$- and R-charts and concluded that the process was in a state of statistical control. The specification limits for the acceptable amount of paint fill per can are shown in the capability analysis diagram of Figure 12.35.

  a. Is it appropriate to construct a capability index for this process?

  b. Find C_p for this process and interpret its value.

Solution

  a. Since the process is stable (under control), its output distribution can be characterized by the same probability distribution at any point in time (see Figure 12.12). Accordingly, it is appropriate to assess the performance of the process using that distribution and related performance measures such as C_p.

  b. From Definition 12.10,

$$C_p = \frac{(\text{USL} - \text{LSL})}{6\sigma}$$

From the capability analysis diagram of Figure 12.35, we can see that the upper and lower specification limits are 10.005 pounds and 9.995 pounds, respectively. But what is σ? Since the output distribution will never be known exactly, neither will σ, the standard deviation of the output distribution. It must be estimated with s, the standard deviation of a large sample drawn from the process. In this case, we use the standard deviation of the 125 measurements used to construct the capability analysis diagram. This value, $s = .00447$, is highlighted in the upper left of the MINITAB printout, Figure 12.35. Then

$$C_p = \frac{(10.005 - 9.995)}{6(.00447)} = \frac{.01}{.02682} - .373$$

(This value of C_p is highlighted in the upper right corner of Figure 12.35.) Since C_p is less than 1.0, the process is not capable. The process spread is wider than the specification spread.

Look Back The C_p statistic confirms the results shown on the capability analysis diagram (Figure 12.35), where 24% of the sampled cans were found to be unacceptable.

Now Work Exercise 12.48

For two reasons, great care should be exercised in using and interpreting C_p. First, like the sample standard deviation, s, used in its computation, C_p is a statistic and is subject to sampling error—that is, the value of C_p will change from sample to sample. Thus, unless you understand the magnitude of the sampling error, you should be cautious in comparing the C_p's of different processes. Second, C_p does not reflect the shape of the output distribution. Distributions with different shapes can have the same C_p value. Accordingly, C_p should not be used in isolation, but in conjunction with the capability analysis diagram.

If a capability analysis study indicates that an in-control process is not capable, as in the paint-filling example, it is usually variation, rather than off-centeredness, that is the culprit. Thus, capability is typically achieved or restored by seeking out and eliminating common causes of variation.

Exercises 12.39–12.51

Learning the Mechanics

12.39 Explain why it is inappropriate to conduct a capability analysis study for a process that is not in statistical control.

12.40 Explain the difference between *process spread* and *specification spread*.

12.41 Describe two different ways to assess the capability of a process.

12.42 Why is it recommended to use and interpret C_p in conjunction with a capability analysis diagram rather than in isolation?

12.43 For a process that is in control and follows a normal distribution, interpret each of the following C_p values:
    a. 1.00   **b.** 1.33   **c.** .50   **d.** 2.00

12.44 Find the specification spread for each of the following:
    a. USL = 19.65, LSL = 12.45
    b. USL = .0010, LSL = .0008
    c. USL = 1.43, LSL = 1.27
    d. USL = 490, LSL = 486

12.45 Find (or estimate) the process spread for each of the following.
    a. $\sigma = 21$
    b. $\sigma = 5.2$
    c. $s = 110.06$
    d. $s = .0024$

12.46 Find the value of C_p for each of the following situations:
    a. USL = 1.0065, LSL = 1.0035, $s = .0005$
    b. USL = 22, LSL = 21, $s = .2$
    c. USL = 875, LSL = 870, $s = .75$

Applying the Concepts—Basic

12.47 Upper specification limit of a process. An in-control, centered process that follows a normal distribution has a $C_p = 2.0$. How many standard deviations away from the process mean is the upper specification limit?

12.48 Capability of an in-control process. A process is in control
NW with a normally distributed output distribution with mean 1,000 and standard deviation 100. The upper and lower specification limits for the process are 1,020 and 980, respectively.
    a. Assuming no changes in the behavior of the process, what percentage of the output will be unacceptable?
    b. Find and interpret the C_p value of the process.

Applying the Concepts—Intermediate

12.49 Cereal box filling process. The following table (top) shows the data on weights of cereal boxes from Exercise 12.13. Assume the specification limits for the weights are USL = 24.2 ounces and LSL = 23.8 ounces.
    a. Assuming the process is under control, construct a capability analysis diagram for the process.
    b. Is the process capable? Support your answer with a numerical measure of capability.

12.50 Military aircraft bolts. Refer to Exercise 12.14 (p. 822). The data on lengths of bolts used in military aircraft are reproduced to the right.

CEREAL

Day	Weight of Cereal Boxes (ounces)				
1	24.02	23.91	24.12	24.06	24.13
2	23.89	23.98	24.01	24.00	23.91
3	24.11	24.02	23.99	23.79	24.04
4	24.06	23.98	23.95	24.01	24.11
5	23.81	23.90	23.99	24.07	23.96
6	23.87	24.12	24.07	24.01	23.99
7	23.88	24.00	24.05	23.97	23.97
8	24.01	24.03	23.99	23.91	23.98
9	24.06	24.02	23.80	23.79	24.07
10	23.96	23.99	24.03	23.99	24.01
11	24.10	23.90	24.11	23.98	23.95
12	24.01	24.07	23.93	24.09	23.98
13	24.14	24.07	24.08	23.98	24.02
14	23.91	24.04	23.89	24.01	23.95
15	24.03	24.04	24.01	23.98	24.10
16	23.94	24.07	24.12	24.00	24.02
17	23.88	23.94	23.91	24.06	24.07
18	24.11	23.99	23.90	24.01	23.98
19	24.05	24.04	23.97	24.08	23.95
20	24.02	23.96	23.95	23.89	24.04

BOLTS

Hour	Bolt Lengths (centimeters)			
1	37.03	37.08	36.90	36.88
2	36.96	37.04	36.85	36.98
3	37.16	37.11	36.99	37.01
4	37.20	37.06	37.02	36.98
5	36.81	36.97	36.91	37.10
6	37.13	36.96	37.01	36.89
7	37.07	36.94	36.99	37.00
8	37.01	36.91	36.98	37.12
9	37.17	37.03	36.90	37.01
10	36.91	36.99	36.87	37.11
11	36.88	37.10	37.07	37.03
12	37.06	36.98	36.90	36.99
13	36.91	37.22	37.12	37.03
14	37.08	37.07	37.10	37.04
15	37.03	37.04	36.89	37.01
16	36.95	36.98	36.90	36.99
17	36.97	36.94	37.14	37.10
18	37.11	37.04	36.98	36.91
19	36.88	36.99	37.01	36.94
20	36.90	37.15	37.09	37.00
21	37.01	36.96	37.05	36.96
22	37.09	36.95	36.93	37.12
23	37.00	37.02	36.95	37.04
24	36.99	37.07	36.90	37.02
25	37.10	37.03	37.01	36.90

Management has specified upper and lower specification limits of 37 cm and 35 cm, respectively.

    a. Assuming the process is in control, construct a capability analysis diagram for the process.

b. Find the percentage of bolts that fall outside the specification limits.

c. Find the capability index, C_p.

d. Is the process capable? Explain.

12.51 New iron-making process. *Mining Engineering* (Oct. 2004) published a study of a new technology for producing high-quality iron nuggets directly from raw iron ore and coal. For one phase of the study, the percentage change in the carbon content of the produced nuggets was measured at 4-hour intervals for 33 consecutive intervals. The data for the 33 time intervals are listed in the table. Specifications state that the carbon content should be within 3.42 ± 0.3 percent.

a. Construct a capability analysis diagram for the iron-making process.

b. Determine the proportion of carbon measurements that fall outside specifications.

c. Find the capability index for the process and interpret its value.

CARBON

Interval	Carbon Change (%)	Interval	Carbon Change (%)
1	3.25	18	3.55
2	3.30	19	3.48
3	3.23	20	3.42
4	3.00	21	3.40
5	3.51	22	3.50
6	3.60	23	3.45
7	3.65	24	3.75
8	3.50	25	3.52
9	3.40	26	3.10
10	3.35	27	3.25
11	3.48	28	3.78
12	3.50	29	3.70
13	3.25	30	3.50
14	3.60	31	3.40
15	3.55	32	3.45
16	3.60	33	3.30
17	2.90		

Source: Hoffman, G., and Tsuge, O. "ITmk3—Application of a New Ironmaking Technology for the Iron Ore Mining Industry." *Mining Engineering*, Vol. 56, No. 9, October 2004 (Figure 5).

KEY TERMS

Note: Starred (*) items are from the optional sections in this chapter.

A zone 812
B zone 812
*capability analysis 845
*capability analysis diagram 847
*capability index 848
causal chain 844
*cause-and-effect diagram 843
centerline 797
common causes of variation 802
conform to specs 807
control chart 795
control limits 804
C zone 812
in control 798

individuals chart 807
lower control limit 804
nonconforming 807
oscillating sequence 797
out of control 798
output distribution 798
pattern-analysis rules 813
p-chart 834
process 792
*process spread 848
process variation 800
quality 791
random behavior 799
rare event 804
rational subgroups 811
R-chart 824

run chart 796
s-chart 824
special (assignable) causes of variation 802
specification limits 807
*specification spread 848
stability 798
statistical process control 801
statistical thinking 795
system 792
3-sigma limits 804
total quality management 790
trial values 814
upper control limit 804
x-chart 807
x̄-chart 808

GUIDE TO CONTROL CHARTS

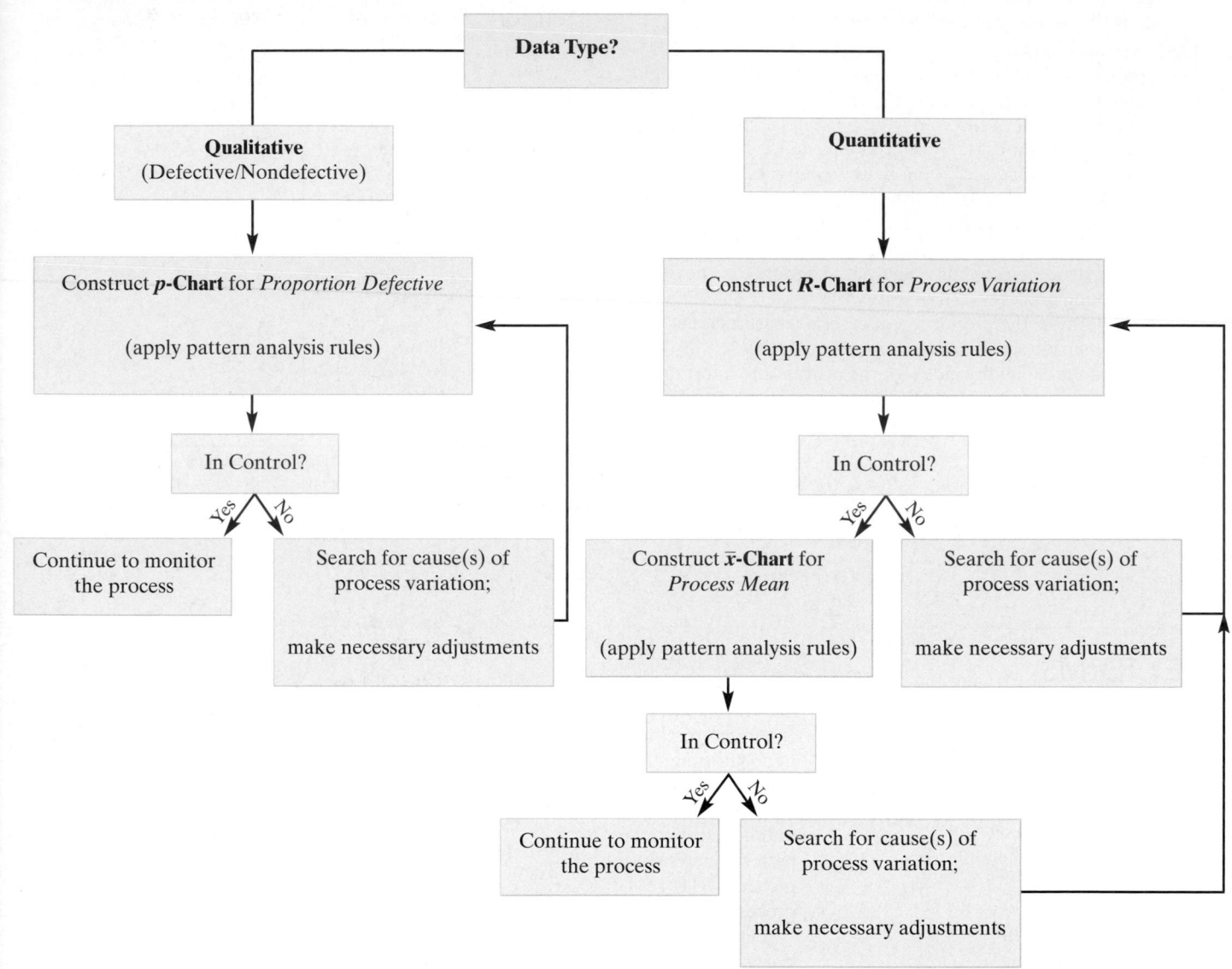

CHAPTER NOTES

		Key Formulas		
Control Chart	**Centerline**	**Control Limits**	**A–B Boundary**	**B–C Boundary**
$\bar{x}$-chart	$\bar{\bar{x}} = \dfrac{\sum\limits_{i=1}^{k} \bar{x}_i}{k}$	$\bar{\bar{x}} \pm A_2\bar{R}$ or $\bar{\bar{x}} \pm 2\dfrac{(\bar{R}/d_2)}{\sqrt{n}}$	$\bar{\bar{x}} \pm \dfrac{2}{3}(A_2\bar{R})$ or $\bar{\bar{x}} \pm \dfrac{(\bar{R}/d_2)}{\sqrt{n}}$	$\bar{\bar{x}} \pm \dfrac{1}{3}(A_2\bar{R})$
R-chart	$\bar{R} = \dfrac{\sum\limits_{i=1}^{k} R_i}{k}$	$(\bar{R}D_3, \bar{R}D_4)$	$\bar{R} \pm 2d_3\left(\dfrac{\bar{R}}{d_2}\right)$	$\bar{R} \pm d_3\left(\dfrac{\bar{R}}{d_2}\right)$
p-chart	$\bar{p} = \dfrac{\text{Total number defectives}}{\text{Total number units sampled}}$	$\bar{p} \pm 3\sqrt{\dfrac{\bar{p}(1-\bar{p})}{n}}$	$\bar{p} \pm 2\sqrt{\dfrac{\bar{p}(1-\bar{p})}{n}}$	$\bar{p} \pm \sqrt{\dfrac{\bar{p}(1-\bar{p})}{n}}$

Total Quality Management (TQM)

Involves the management of quality in all phases of a business

Statistical Process Control (SPC)

The process of monitoring and eliminating variation to keep a process in control

In-Control Process

—Has an output distribution that *does not change over time*

Out-of-Control Process

—Has an output distribution that *changes over time*

Dimensions of Quality

(1) Performance
(2) Features
(3) Reliability
(4) Conformance
(5) Durability
(6) Serviceability
(7) Aesthetics
(8) Reputation and Image

Major Sources of Process Variation

(1) People
(2) Machines
(3) Materials
(4) Methods
(5) Measurement
(6) Environment

Causes of Variation

(1) Common causes
(2) Special (assignable) causes

Types of Control Charts

(1) $\bar{x}$-**chart:** monitor the process mean
(2) *R*-**chart:** monitor the process variation
(3) *p*-**chart:** monitor the proportion of nonconforming items

Specification Limits

—Define acceptable values for an output variable

LSL = lower specification limit
USL = upper specification limit
$(USL - LSL)$ = specification spread

Capability Analysis

—Determines if process is capable of satisfying its customers

Capability Index (C_p)

—summarizes performance of a process relative to the specification limits

$$C_p = (USL - LSL)/6\sigma$$

Pattern-Analysis Rules

Determine whether a process is in or out of control

Rational Subgroups

Samples designed to make it more likely that process changes will occur between (rather than within) subgroups

Sample Size for *p*-Chart:

$$(n > 9(1 - p_0)/p_0),$$

where p_0 estimates true proportion defective

Cause-and-Effect Diagram

Facilitates process diagnosis and documents causal factors in a process

Key Symbols	
LCL	Lower control limit
UCL	Upper control limit
$\bar{\bar{x}}$	Average of the sample means
$\bar{R}$	Average of the sample ranges
A_2	Constant obtained from Table XI, Appendix B
D_3	Constant obtained from Table XI, Appendix B
D_4	Constant obtained from Table XI, Appendix B
d_2	Constant obtained from Table XI, Appendix B
d_3	Constant obtained from Table XI, Appendix B
$\hat{p}$	Estimated number of defectives in sample
$\bar{p}$	Overall proportion of defective units in all nk samples
p_0	Estimated overall proportion of defectives for entire process
SPC	Statistical process control
USL	Upper specification limit
LSL	Lower specification limit
C_p	Capability index

SUPPLEMENTARY EXERCISES 12.52–12.76

Note: Starred (*) exercises refer to the optional sections in this chapter.

Learning the Mechanics

12.52 Define *quality* and list its important dimensions.

12.53 What is a system? Give an example of a system with which you are familiar, and describe its inputs, outputs, and transformation process.

12.54 What is a process? Give an example of an organizational process and a personal process.

12.55 Select a personal process that you would like to better understand or to improve and construct a flowchart for it.

12.56 Describe the six major sources of process variation.

12.57 Suppose all the output of a process over the last year were measured and found to be within the specification limits required by customers of the process. Should you worry about whether the process is in statistical control? Explain.

* **12.58** Select a problem, event, or condition whose cause or causes you would like to diagnose. Construct a cause-and-effect diagram that would facilitate your diagnosis.

* **12.59** In estimating a population mean μ using a sample mean $\bar{x}$, why is it likely that $\bar{x} \neq \mu$? Construct a cause-and-effect diagram for the effect $\bar{x} \neq \mu$.

* **12.60** Construct a cause-and-effect diagram to help explain why customer waiting time at the drive-in window of a fast-food restaurant is a variable.

12.61 Processes that are in control are predictable; out-of-control processes are not. Explain.

12.62 Compare and contrast special and common causes of variation.

12.63 Explain the difference between control limits and specification limits.

* **12.64** Should control charts be used to monitor a process that is both in control and capable? Why or why not?

* **12.65** Under what circumstances is it appropriate to use C_p to assess capability?

12.66 A process is under control and follows a normal distribution with mean 100 and standard deviation 10. In constructing a standard $\bar{x}$-chart for this process, the control limits are set 3 standard deviations from the mean—that is, $100 \pm 3(10/\sqrt{n})$. The probability of observing an $\bar{x}$ outside the control limits is $(.00135 + .00135) = .0027$. Suppose it is desired to construct a control chart that signals the presence of a potential special cause of variation for less extreme values of $\bar{x}$. How many standard deviations from the mean should the control limits be set such that the probability of the chart falsely indicating the presence of a special cause of variation is .10 rather than .0027?

Applying the Concepts—Basic

12.67 **Weight of a product.** Consider the time series data for the weight of a manufactured product shown on p. 855 (top).
  a. Construct a time series plot. Be sure to connect the points and add a centerline.
  b. Which type of variation pattern in Figure 12.6 best describes the pattern revealed by your plot?

⊙ TIMEWT

Order of Production	Weight (grams)	Order of Production	Weight (grams)
1	6.0	9	6.5
2	5.0	10	9.0
3	7.0	11	3.0
4	5.5	12	11.0
5	7.0	13	3.0
6	6.0	14	12.0
7	8.0	15	2.0
8	5.0		

12.68 Lengths of pencils. The accompanying length measurements were made on 20 consecutively produced pencils.

⊙ PENCIL

Order of Production	Length (inches)	Order of Production	Length (inches)
1	7.47	11	7.57
2	7.48	12	7.56
3	7.51	13	7.55
4	7.49	14	7.58
5	7.50	15	7.56
6	7.51	16	7.59
7	7.48	17	7.57
8	7.49	18	7.55
9	7.48	19	7.56
10	7.50	20	7.58

a. Construct a time series plot. Be sure to connect the plotted points and add a centerline.

b. Which type of variation pattern in Figure 12.6 best describes the pattern shown in your plot?

12.69 Applying pattern-analysis rules. Use the appropriate pattern-analysis rules to determine whether the process being monitored by the control chart shown below is under the influence of special causes of variation.

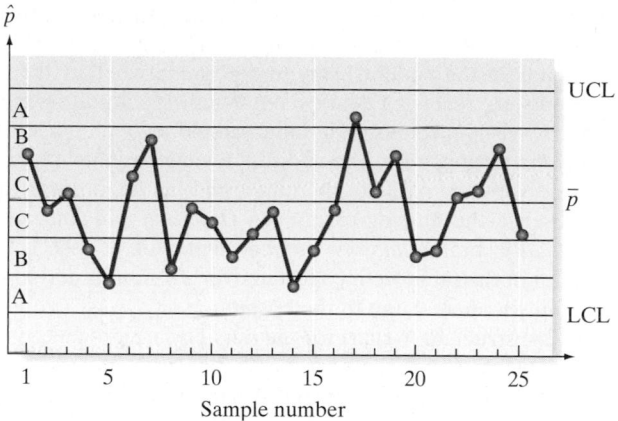

Applying the Concepts—Intermediate

12.70 Defective plastic mold. A company that manufactures plastic molded parts believes it is producing an unusually large number of defects. To investigate this suspicion, each shift drew seven random samples of 200 parts, visually inspected each part to determine whether it was defective, and tallied the primary type of defect present (Hart, 1992). These data are presented in the table below.

a. From a statistical perspective, are the number of samples and the sample size of 200 adequate for constructing a p-chart for these data? Explain.

b. Construct a p-chart for this manufacturing process.

⊙ MOLD

Sample	Shift	# of Defects	TYPE OF DEFECT Crack	Burn	Dirt	Blister	Trim
1	1	4	1	1	1	0	1
2	1	6	2	1	0	2	1
3	1	11	1	2	3	3	2
4	1	12	2	2	2	3	3
5	1	5	0	1	0	2	2
6	1	10	1	3	2	2	2
7	1	8	0	3	1	1	3
8	2	16	2	0	8	2	4
9	2	17	3	2	8	2	2
10	2	20	0	3	11	3	3
11	2	28	3	2	17	2	4
12	2	20	0	0	16	4	0
13	2	20	1	1	18	0	0
14	2	17	2	2	13	0	0
15	3	13	3	2	5	1	2
16	3	10	0	3	4	2	1
17	3	11	2	2	3	2	2
18	3	7	0	3	2	2	0
19	3	6	1	2	0	1	2
20	3	8	1	1	2	3	1
21	3	9	1	2	2	2	2

c. Should the control limits be used to monitor future process output? Explain.

d. Suggest a strategy for identifying the special causes of variation that may be present.

12.71 Monitoring quality of nursing care. A hospital uses control charts to monitor the quality of its nursing care. A set of 363 scoring criteria, or standards, are applied at critical points in the patients' stay to determine whether the patients are receiving beneficial nursing care. Auditors regularly visit each hospital unit, sample two patients, and evaluate their care. The auditors review patients' records; interview the patients, the nurse, and the head nurse; and observe the nursing care given (*International Journal of Quality and Reliability Management*, Vol. 9, 1992). The data in the table were collected over a 3-month period for a newly opened unit of the hospital.

a. Construct an R-chart for the nursing care process.

b. Construct an $\bar{x}$-chart for the nursing care process.

c. Should the control charts of parts **a** and **b** be used to monitor future process output? Explain.

d. The hospital would like all quality scores to exceed 335 (their specification limit). Over the 3-month period, what proportion of the sampled patients received care that did not conform to the hospital's requirements?

NURSING

Sample	Scores	Sample	Scores
1	345, 341	11	360, 355
2	331, 328	12	325, 335
3	343, 355	13	350, 348
4	351, 352	14	336, 337
5	360, 348	15	345, 329
6	342, 336	16	358, 351
7	328, 331	17	353, 352
8	344, 344	18	334, 340
9	359, 334	19	341, 335
10	346, 361	20	358, 345

12.72 Package sorting time. AirExpress, an overnight mail service, is concerned about the operating efficiency of the package-sorting departments at its Toledo, Ohio, terminal. The company would like to monitor the time it takes for packages to be put in outgoing delivery bins from the time they are received. The sorting department operates 6 hours per day, from 6:00 P.M. to midnight. The company randomly sampled four packages during each hour of operation during 4 consecutive days. The time for each package to move through the system, in minutes, is given in the next table (top, right).

a. Construct an $\bar{x}$-chart from these data. In order for this chart to be meaningful, what assumption must be made about the variation of the process? Why?

b. What does the chart suggest about the stability of the package-sorting process? Explain.

c. Should the control limits be used to monitor future process output? Explain.

12.73 Waiting times of airline passengers. Officials at Mountain Airlines are interested in monitoring the length of time customers must wait in line to check in at their airport counter in Reno, Nevada. In order to develop a control chart, five customers were sampled each day for 20 days. The data, in minutes, are presented at right.

TRANSIT

Sample	Transit Time (mins.)			
1	31.9	33.4	37.8	26.2
2	29.1	24.3	33.2	36.7
3	30.3	31.1	26.3	34.1
4	39.6	29.4	31.4	37.7
5	27.4	29.7	36.5	33.3
6	32.7	32.9	40.1	29.7
7	30.7	36.9	26.8	34.0
8	28.4	24.1	29.6	30.9
9	30.5	35.5	36.1	27.4
10	27.8	29.6	29.0	34.1
11	34.0	30.1	35.9	28.8
12	25.5	26.3	34.8	30.0
13	24.6	29.9	31.8	37.9
14	30.6	36.0	40.2	30.8
15	29.7	33.2	34.9	27.6
16	24.1	26.8	32.7	29.0
17	29.4	31.6	35.2	27.6
18	31.1	33.0	29.6	35.2
19	27.0	29.0	35.1	25.1
20	36.6	32.4	28.7	27.9
21	33.0	27.1	26.2	35.1
22	33.2	41.2	30.7	31.6
23	26.7	35.2	39.7	31.5
24	30.5	36.8	27.9	28.6

CHECKIN

Sample	Waiting Time (mins.)				
1	3.2	6.7	1.3	8.4	2.2
2	5.0	4.1	7.9	8.1	.4
3	7.1	3.2	2.1	6.5	3.7
4	4.2	1.6	2.7	7.2	1.4
5	1.7	7.1	1.6	.9	1.8
6	4.7	5.5	1.6	3.9	4.0
7	6.2	2.0	1.2	.9	1.4
8	1.4	2.7	3.8	4.6	3.8
9	1.1	4.3	9.1	3.1	2.7
10	5.3	4.1	9.8	2.9	2.7
11	3.2	2.9	4.1	5.6	.8
12	2.4	4.3	6.7	1.9	4.8
13	8.8	5.3	6.6	1.0	4.5
14	3.7	3.6	2.0	2.7	5.9
15	1.0	1.9	6.5	3.3	4.7
16	7.0	4.0	4.9	4.4	4.7
17	5.5	7.1	2.1	.9	2.8
18	1.8	5.6	2.2	1.7	2.1
19	2.6	3.7	4.8	1.4	5.8
20	3.6	.8	5.1	4.7	6.3

a. Construct an R-chart from these data.

b. What does the R-chart suggest about the stability of the process? Explain.

c. Explain why the R-chart should be interpreted prior to the $\bar{x}$-chart.

d. Construct an $\bar{x}$-chart from these data.

e. What does the $\bar{x}$-chart suggest about the stability of the process? Explain.

f. Should the control limits for the R-chart and $\bar{x}$-chart be used to monitor future process output? Explain.

12.74 Waiting times of airline passengers (cont'd). Consider the airline check-in process described in Exercise 12.73.

   a. Assume the process is under control and construct a capability analysis diagram for the process. Management has specified an upper specification limit of 5 minutes.

   b. Is the process capable? Justify your answer.

   c. If it is appropriate to estimate and interpret C_p for this process, do so. If it is not, explain why.

   d. Why didn't management provide a lower specification limit?

12.75 Credit histories with data-entry errors. A company called CRW runs credit checks for a large number of banks and insurance companies. Credit history information is typed into computer files by trained administrative assistants. The company is interested in monitoring the proportion of credit histories that contain one or more data-entry errors. Based on her experience with the data-entry operation, the director of the data processing unit believes that the proportion of histories with data-entry errors is about 6%. CRW audited 150 randomly selected credit histories each day for 20 days. The sample data are presented below.

🔘 **CRW**

Sample	Sample Size	Histories with Errors
1	150	9
2	150	11
3	150	12
4	150	8
5	150	10
6	150	6
7	150	13
8	150	9
9	150	11
10	150	5
11	150	7
12	150	6
13	150	12
14	150	10
15	150	11
16	150	7
17	150	6
18	150	12
19	150	14
20	150	10

   a. Use the sample size formula to show that a sample size of 150 is large enough to prevent the lower control limit of the p-chart they plan to construct from being negative.

   b. Construct a p-chart for the data-entry process.

   c. What does the chart indicate about the presence of special causes of variation? Explain.

   d. Provide an example of a special cause of variation that could potentially affect this process. Do the same for a common cause of variation.

   e. Should the control limits be used to monitor future credit histories produced by the data entry operation? Explain.

12.76 Defects in graphite shafts. Over the last year, a company that manufactures golf clubs has received numerous complaints about the performance of its graphite shafts and has lost several market share percentage points. In re-

sponse, the company decided to monitor its shaft production process to identify new opportunities to improve its product. The process involves pultrusion. A fabric is pulled through a thermosetting polymer bath and then through a long heated steel die. As it moves through the die, the shaft is cured. Finally, it is cut to the desired length. Defects that can occur during the process are internal voids, broken strands, gaps between successive layers, and microcracks caused by improper curing. The company's newly formed quality department sampled 10 consecutive shafts every 30 minutes, and nondestructive testing was used to seek out flaws in the shafts. The data from each 8-hour work shift were combined to form a shift sample of 160 shafts. Data on the proportion of defective shafts for 36 shift samples are presented in the table.

   a. Use the appropriate control chart to determine whether the process proportion remains stable over time.

🔘 **SHAFT1**

Shift Number	Number of Defective Shafts	Proportion of Defective Shafts
1	9	.05625
2	6	.03750
3	8	.05000
4	14	.08750
5	7	.04375
6	5	.03125
7	7	.04375
8	9	.05625
9	5	.03125
10	9	.05625
11	1	.00625
12	7	.04375
13	9	.05625
14	14	.08750
15	7	.04375
16	8	.05000
17	4	.02500
18	10	.06250
19	6	.03750
20	12	.07500
21	8	.05000
22	5	.03125
23	9	.05625
24	15	.09375
25	6	.03750
26	8	.05000
27	4	.02500
28	7	.04375
29	2	.01250
30	6	.03750
31	9	.05625
32	11	.06875
33	8	.05000
34	9	.05625
35	7	.04375
36	8	.05000

Source: Kolarik, W. *Creating Quality: Concepts, Systems, Strategies, and Tools.* New York: McGraw-Hill, 1995.

b. Does your control chart indicate that both common and special causes of variation are present? Explain.

c. Data on the types of flaws identified are also given. [*Note:* Each defective shaft may have more than one flaw.] To help diagnose the causes of variation in process output, construct a Pareto diagram for the types of shaft defects observed. Which are the "vital few"? The "trivial many"?

🔘 **SHAFT2**

Type of Defect	Number of Defects
Internal voids	11
Broken strands	96
Gaps between layer	72
Microcracks	150

REFERENCES

Alwan, L. C., and Roberts, H. V. "Time-Series Modeling for Statistical Process Control." *Journal of Business and Economic Statistics*, 1988, Vol. 6, pp. 87–95.

Banks, J. *Principles of Quality Control.* New York: Wiley, 1989.

Checkland, P. *Systems Thinking, Systems Practice.* New York: Wiley, 1981.

Deming, W. E. *Out of the Crisis.* Cambridge, Mass.: MIT Center for Advanced Engineering Study, 1986.

DeVor, R. E., Chang, T., and Southerland, J. W. *Statistical Quality Design and Control.* New York: Macmillan, 1992.

Duncan, A. J. *Quality Control and Industrial Statistics.* Homewood, Ill.: Irwin, 1986.

Feigenbaum, A. V. *Total Quality Control*, 3rd ed. New York: McGraw-Hill, 1983.

Garvin, D. A. *Managing Quality.* New York: Free Press/Macmillan, 1988.

Gitlow, H., Gitlow, S., Oppenheim, A., and Oppenheim, R. *Tools and Methods for the Improvement of Quality.* Homewood, Ill.: Irwin, 1989.

Grant, E. L., and Leavenworth, R. S. *Statistical Quality Control*, 6th ed. New York: McGraw-Hill, 1988.

Hart, Marilyn K. "Quality Tools for Improvement." *Production and Inventory Management Journal*, First Quarter 1992, Vol. 33, No. 1, p. 59.

Ishikawa, K. *Guide to Quality Control*, 2nd ed. White Plains, N.Y.: Kraus International Publications, 1986.

Joiner, B. L., and Goudard, M. A. "Variation, Management, and W. Edwards Deming." *Quality Process*, Dec. 1990, pp. 29–37.

Juran, J. M. *Juran of Planning for Quality.* New York: Free Press/Macmillan, 1988.

Juran, J. M., and Gryna, F. M., Jr. *Quality Planning Analysis*, 2nd ed. New York: McGraw-Hill, 1980.

Kane, V. E. *Defect Prevention.* New York: Marcel Dekker, 1989.

Latzko, W. J. *Quality and Productivity for Bankers and Financial Managers.* New York: Marcel Dekker, 1986.

Moen, R. D., Nolan, T. W., and Provost, L. P. *Improving Quality through Planned Experimentation.* New York: McGraw-Hill, 1991.

Montgomery, D. C. *Introduction to Statistical Quality Control*, 2nd ed. New York: Wiley, 1991.

Nelson, L. L. "The Shewhart Control Chart—Tests for Special Causes." *Journal of Quality Technology*, Oct. 1984, Vol. 16, No. 4, pp. 237–239.

Roberts, H. V. *Data Analysis for Managers*, 2nd ed. Redwood City, Calif.: Scientific Press, 1991.

Rosander, A. C. *Applications of Quality Control in the Service Industries.* New York: Marcel Dekker, 1985.

Rummler, G. A., and Brache, A. P. *Improving Performance: How to Manage the White Space on the Organization Chart.* San Francisco: Jossey-Bass, 1991.

Ryan, T. P. *Statistical Methods for Quality Improvement.* New York: Wiley, 1989.

Statistical Quality Control Handbook. Indianapolis, Ind.: AT&T Technologies, Select Code 700-444 (inquiries: 800-432-6600); originally published by Western Electric Company, 1956.

The Ernst and Young Quality Improvement Consulting Group. *Total Quality: An Executive's Guide for the 1990s.* Homewood, Ill.: Dow-Jones Irwin, 1990.

Wadsworth, H. M., Stephens, K. S., and Godfrey, A. B. *Modern Methods for Quality Control and Improvement.* New York: Wiley, 1986.

Walton, M. *The Deming Management Method.* New York: Dodd, Mead, & Company, 1986.

Wheeler, D. J., and Chambers, D. S. *Understanding Statistical Process Control.* Knoxville, Tenn.: Statistical Process Controls, Inc., 1986.

Using Technology

12.1 Control Charts Using SPSS

To create control charts for process data, first access the SPSS spreadsheet file that contains the quality data. Next, click on the "Graphs" button on the SPSS menu bar, then click on "Control", as shown in Figure 12.S.1. The resulting dialog box appears as shown in Figure 12.S.2.

Select the type of control chart you want to produce (x-bar, R- or p-chart) and whether the cases (rows) on the spreadsheet represent individual quality measurements ("Cases are units") or the subgroups ("Cases are subgroups"), then click the "Define" button on the Control Chart dialog box.

If you selected an x-bar or R-chart where cases are subgroups, the dialog box shown in Figure 12.S.3 will appear. If you selected an x-bar or R-chart where cases are individual units, the dialog box shown in Figure 12.S.4 will appear. Make the appropriate selections (process variables and subgroup variable), then click "OK" to produce the SPSS control chart. (As an option, you can conduct a capability analysis by clicking the "Statistics" button and making the appropriate menu selections [specification limits, target value, and C_p statistic].)

If you selected a p-chart on the Control Chart dialog box (Figure 12.S.2), the dialog box shown in Figure 12.S.5 will appear. Specify the variables that represent the number nonconforming and the subgroups, and specify the sample size. Click "OK" to view the SPSS control chart.

Figure 12.S.1
SPSS menu options for control charts

Figure 12.S.2
SPSS control chart dialog box

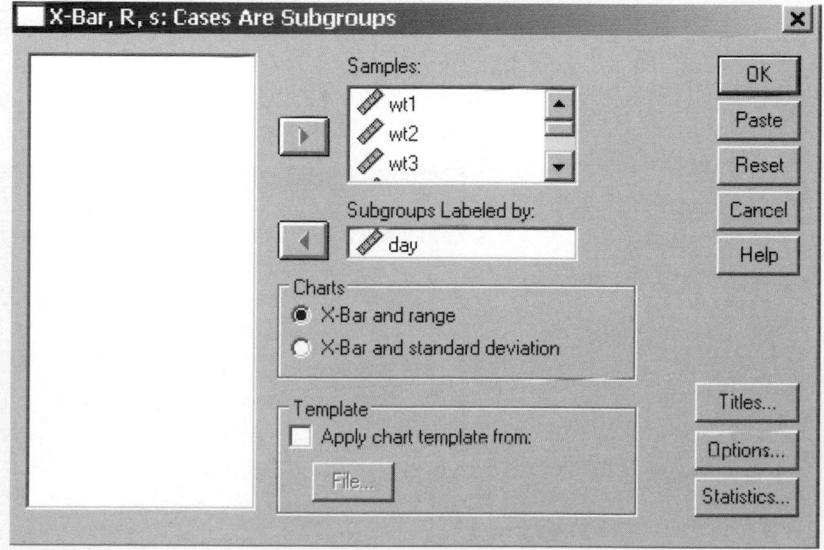

Figure 12.S.3
SPSS options for $\bar{x}$ and R-charts (cases are subgroups)

Figure 12.S.4
SPSS options for $\bar{x}$ and
R-charts (cases are units)

Figure 12.S.5
SPSS options for p-charts

12.2 Control Charts Using MINITAB

To create an $\bar{x}$-chart or R-chart for process data, first access the MINITAB worksheet file that contains the quality data. Next, click on the "Stat" button on the MINITAB menu bar, then click on "Control Charts", "Variables Charts for Subgroups", and either "Xbar" or "R", as shown in Figure 12.M.1. The resulting dialog box appears similar to the one shown in Figure 12.M.2.

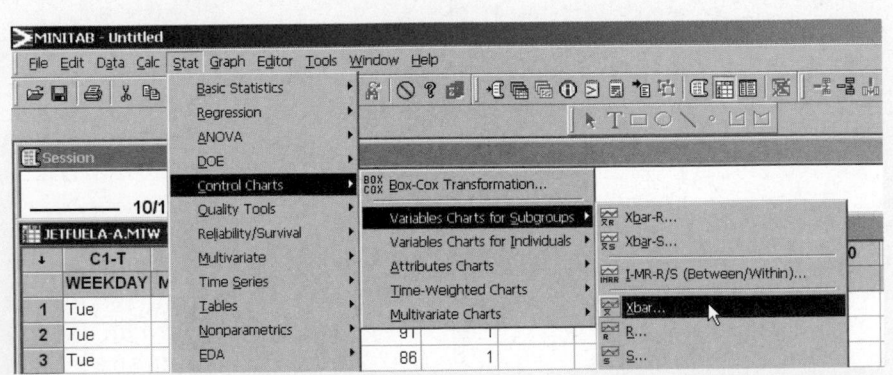

Figure 12.M.1
MINITAB menu options for
control charts

If each row on the worksheet represents an individual quality measurement, then specify "All observations for a chart are in one column:", as shown in Figure 12.M.2. Enter the quality variable in the next box, and specify the subgroup size.

If each row on the worksheet represents a subgroup, with columns representing the sample measurements, then specify "observations for a subgroup are in one row of columns:", as shown in Figure 12.M.3. Enter the columns with the sample measurements in the next box.

Figure 12.M.2
MINITAB $\bar{x}$-chart dialog box
(rows are individual units)

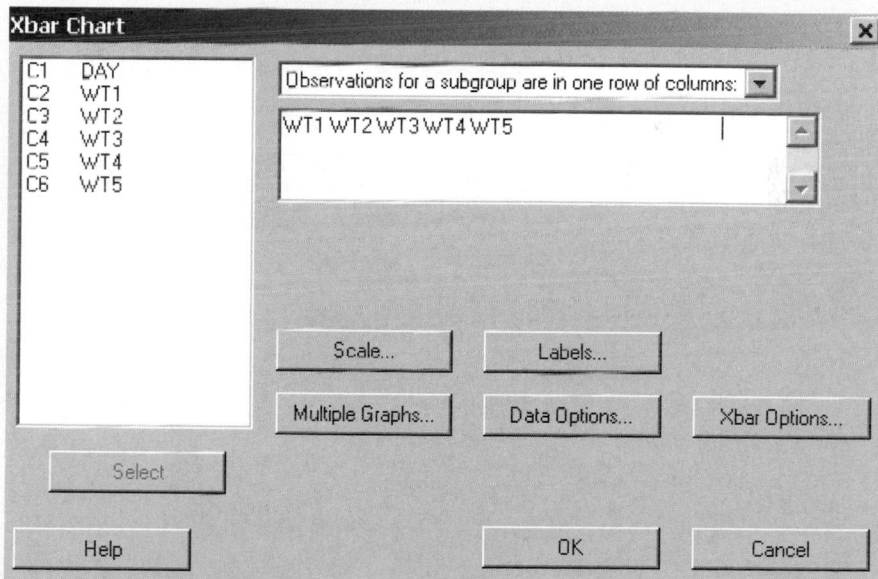

Figure 12.M.3
MINITAB $\bar{x}$-chart dialog box
(rows are subgroups)

If you want MINITAB to apply the pattern-analysis rules to the plotted points on the graph, click the "Xbar (or R) Options" button, click "Tests", and check the rules you want apply. Click "OK" to return to the Control Chart dialog box, then click "OK" again to produce the MINITAB control chart.

To create a p-chart for attribute data, click on the "Stat" button on the MINITAB menu bar, then click on "Control Charts" and "Attributes Charts" (see Figure 12.M.1). On the resulting menu, select "P". The resulting dialog box appears similar to the one shown in Figure 12.M.4. Specify the variable that represents the number of nonconforming items and specify the subgroup (sample) size. If you want MINITAB to apply the pattern-analysis rules to the plotted points on the graph, click the "P Chart Options" button, click "Tests", and check the rules you want to apply. Click "OK" to return to the Control Chart dialog box, then click "OK" again to produce the MINITAB control chart.

To create a capability analysis diagram, click on the "Stat" button on the MINITAB menu bar, then click on "Quality Tools", "Capability Analysis", and "Normal", as shown in Figure 12.M.5. The resulting dialog box appears similar to the one shown in Figure 12.M.6. Specify the quality variable of interest, subgroup size, and lower and upper specification limits on the menu screen. Click the "Options" button to specify the type of statistics (e.g., C_p and percents outside specification limits) to be displayed on the graph. Click "OK" to produce the MINITAB capability analysis diagram.

Figure 12.M.4
MINITAB *p*-chart dialog box

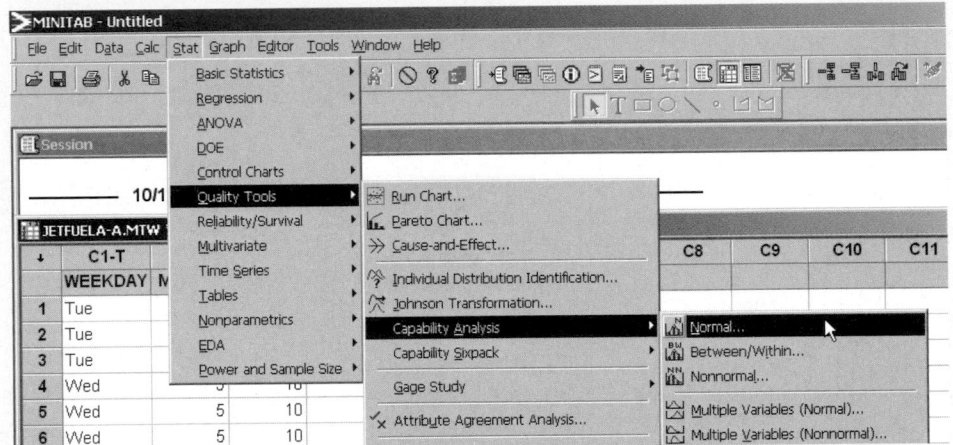

Figure 12.M.5
MINITAB menu options for capability analysis

Figure 12.M.6
MINITAB capability analysis dialog box

12.3 Control Charts Using Excel/PHStat2

To create an $\bar{x}$-chart or R-chart, first access the Excel workbook file that contains the quality data. The workbook should contain columns for the sample mean and sample range, with the rows representing each subgroup. Next, click on the "PHStat" button on the Excel menu bar, then click on "Control Charts", and "R & XBar Charts", as shown in Figure 12.E.1. The resulting dialog box appears similar to the one shown in Figure 12.E.2.

Specify the subgroup (sample) size, cell range for the sample ranges, and cell range for the sample means, as shown in Figure 12.E.2. Click "OK" to produce the Excel control charts.

To create a p-chart, first access the Excel workbook file that contains the attribute data. The workbook should contain a column for the number of nonconforming items (defects), with the rows representing each subgroup. Next, click on the "PHStat" button on the Excel menu bar, then click on "Control Charts", and "p Chart" (see Figure 12.E.1). The resulting dialog box appears similar to the one shown in Figure 12.E.3. Specify the cell range for the number of nonconforming items and the subgroup (sample) size, as shown in Figure 12.E.3. Click "OK" to produce the Excel control chart.

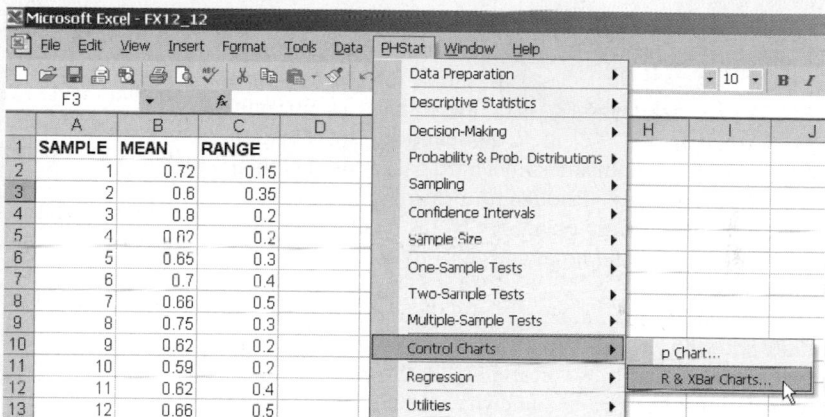

Figure 12.E.1

Excel menu options for control charts

Figure 12.E.2

Excel R and $\bar{x}$-charts dialog box

Figure 12.E.3

Excel p-chart dialog box

Real-World Case
The Gasket Manufacturing Case

(A Case Covering Chapter 12)

The Problem

A Midwestern manufacturer of gaskets for automotive and off-road vehicle applications was suddenly and unexpectedly notified by a major customer—a U.S. auto manufacturer—that they had significantly tightened the specification limits on the overall thickness of a hard gasket used in their automotive engines. Although the current specification limits were by and large being met by the gasket manufacturer, their product did not come close to meeting the new specification.

The gasket manufacturer's first reaction was to negotiate with the customer to obtain a relaxation of the new specification. When these efforts failed, the customer-supplier relationship became somewhat strained. The gasket manufacturer's next thought was that if they waited long enough, the automotive company would eventually be forced to loosen the requirements and purchase the existing product. However, as time went on, it became clear that this was not going to happen and that some positive steps would have to be taken to improve the quality of their gaskets. But what should be done? And by whom?

The Product

Figure C5.1 shows the product in question, a hard gasket. A hard gasket is comprised of two outer layers of soft gasket material and an inner layer consisting of a perforated piece of sheet metal. These three pieces are assembled, and some blanking and punching operations follow, after which metal rings are installed around the inside of the cylinder bore clearance holes and the entire outside periphery of the gasket. The quality characteristic of interest in this case is the assembly thickness.

The Process

An initial study by the staff engineers revealed that the variation in the thickness of soft gasket material—the two outer layers of the hard gasket—was large and undoubted-

ly responsible for much of the total variability in the final product. Figure C5.2 shows the roll mill process that fabricates the sheets of soft gasket material from which the two outer layers of the hard gasket are made. To manufacture a sheet of soft gasket material, an operator adds raw material, in a soft pelletlike form, to the gap—called the *knip*—between the two rolls. The larger roll rotates about its axis with no lateral movement; the smaller roll rotates and moves back and forth laterally to change the size of the knip. As the operator adds more and more material to the knip, the sheet is formed around the larger roll. When the smaller roll reaches a preset destination (i.e., final gap/sheet thickness), a bell rings and a red light goes on, telling the operator to stop adding raw material. The operator stops the rolls and cuts the sheet horizontally along the larger roll so that it may be pulled off the roll. The finished sheet, called a *pull*, is pulled onto a table where the operator checks its thickness with a micrometer. The operator can adjust the final gap if he or she believes that the sheets are coming out too thick or too thin relative to the prescribed nominal value (i.e., the target thickness).

Process Operation

Investigation revealed that the operator runs the process in the following way. After each sheet is made, the operator measures the thickness with a micrometer. The thickness values for three consecutive sheets are averaged and the average is plotted on a piece of graph paper that, at the start of the shift, has only a solid horizontal line drawn on it to indicate the target thickness value for the particular soft gasket sheet the operator is making. Periodically, the operator reviews these evolving data and makes a decision as to whether or not the process mean—the sheet thickness—needs to be adjusted. This can be accomplished by stopping the machine, loosening some clamps on the small roll, and jogging the small roll laterally in or out by a few thousandths of an inch—whatever the operator feels is needed. The clamps are tightened, the gap is checked with a taper gauge, and if adjusted properly, the operator begins to make sheets again. Typically, this adjustment process takes

FIGURE C5.1

A hard gasket for automotive applications

FIGURE C5.2

Roll mill for the manufacture of soft gasket material

10 to 15 minutes. The questions of when to make such adjustments and how much to change the roll gap for each adjustment are completely at the operator's discretion, based on the evolving plot of thickness averages.

Figure C5.3 shows a series of plots that detail the history of one particular work shift over which the operator made several process adjustments. (These data come from the same shift that the staff engineers used to collect data for a process capability study that is described later.) Figure C5.3(a) shows the process data after the first 12 sheets have been made—four averages of three successive sheet thicknesses. At this point the operator judged that the data were telling her that the process was running below the target, so she stopped the process and made an adjustment to slightly increase the final roll gap. She then proceeded to make more sheets. Figure C5.3(b) shows the state of the process somewhat later. Now it appeared to the operator that the sheets were coming out too thick, so she stopped and made another adjustment. As shown in Figure C5.3(c), the process seemed to run well for a while, but then an average somewhat below the target led the operator to believe that another adjustment was necessary. Figures C5.3(d) and C5.3(e) show points in time where other adjustments were made.

Figure C5.3(f) shows the complete history of the shift. A total of 24 × 3, or 72, sheets were made during this shift. When asked, the operator indicated that the history of this shift was quite typical of what happens on a day-to-day basis.

The Company's Stop-Gap Solution

While the staff engineers were studying the problem to formulate an appropriate action plan, something had to be done to make it possible to deliver hard gaskets within the new specification limits. Management decided to increase product inspection and, in particular, to grade each piece of material according to thickness so that the wide variation in thickness could be balanced out at the assembly process. Extra inspectors were used to grade each piece of soft gasket material. Sheets of the same thickness were shipped in separate bundles on pallets to a sister plant for assembly. Thick and thin sheets were selected as needed to make a hard gasket that met the specification. The process worked pretty well, and there was some discussion about making it permanent. However, some felt it was too costly and did not get at the root cause of the problem.

The Engineering Department's Analysis

Meanwhile, the staff engineers in the company were continuing to study the problem and came to the conclusion that the existing roll mill process equipment for making the soft gasket sheets simply was not capable of meeting the new specifications. This conclusion was reached as a result of the examination of production data and scrap logs over the past several months. They had researched some new equipment that had a track record for very good sheet-to-sheet consistency and had decided to write a proposal to replace the existing roll mills with this new equipment.

FIGURE C5.3

Process adjustment history over one shift

GASKET

TABLE C5.1 Measurements of Sheet Thickness

Sheet	Thickness (in.)	Sheet	Thickness (in.)	Sheet	Thickness (in.)
1	0.0440	25	0.0464	49	0.0427
2	0.0446	26	0.0457	50	0.0437
3	0.0437	27	0.0447	51	0.0445
4	0.0438	28	0.0451	52	0.0431
5	0.0425	29	0.0447	53	0.0448
6	0.0443	30	0.0457	54	0.0429
7	0.0453	31	0.0456	55	0.0425
8	0.0428	32	0.0455	56	0.0442
9	0.0433	33	0.0445	57	0.0432
10	0.0451	34	0.0448	58	0.0429
11	0.0441	35	0.0423	59	0.0447
12	0.0434	36	0.0442	60	0.0450
13	0.0459	37	0.0459	61	0.0443
14	0.0466	38	0.0468	62	0.0441
15	0.0476	39	0.0452	63	0.0450
16	0.0449	40	0.0456	64	0.0443
17	0.0471	41	0.0471	65	0.0423
18	0.0451	42	0.0450	66	0.0447
19	0.0472	43	0.0472	67	0.0429
20	0.0477	44	0.0465	68	0.0427
21	0.0452	45	0.0461	69	0.0464
22	0.0457	46	0.0462	70	0.0448
23	0.0459	47	0.0463	71	0.0451
24	0.0472	48	0.0471	72	0.0428

To strengthen the proposal, their boss asked them to include data that demonstrated the poor capability of the existing equipment. The engineers, confident that the equipment was not capable, selected what they thought was the best operator and the best roll mill (the plant has several roll mill lines) and took careful measurements of the thickness of each sheet made on an 8-hour shift. During that shift, a total of 72 sheets/pulls were made. This was considered quite acceptable since the work standard for the process is 70 sheets per shift. The measurements of the sheet thickness (in the order of manufacture) for the 72 sheets are given in Table C5.1. The engineers set out to use these data to conduct a process capability study.

Relying on a statistical methods course that one of the engineers had in college 10 years ago, the group decided to construct a frequency distribution from the data and use it to estimate the percentage of the measurements that fell within the specification limits. Their histogram is shown in Figure C5.4. Also shown in the figure are the upper and lower specification values. The dark shaded part of the histogram represents the amount of the product that lies outside of the specification limits. It is immediately apparent from the histogram that a large proportion of the output does not meet the customer's needs. Eight of the 72 sheets fall outside the specification limits. Therefore, in terms of percent conforming to specifications, the engineers estimated the process capability to be 88.8%. This was clearly unacceptable. This analysis confirmed the engineer's low opinion of the roll mill process equipment. They included it

FIGURE C5.4
Histogram of data from process capability study

in their proposal and sent their recommendation to replace the equipment to the president's office.

Your Assignment

You have been hired as an external consultant by the company's president, Marilyn Carlson. She would like you to critique the engineers' analysis, conclusion, and recommendations.

Suspecting that the engineers' work may be flawed, President Carlson would also like you to conduct your own study and make your own recommendations concerning how to resolve the company's problem. She would like you

GASKET

TABLE C5.2 Measurements of Sheet Thickness for a Shift Run with No Operator Adjustment

Sheet	Thickness (in.)	Sheet	Thickness (in.)	Sheet	Thickness (in.)
1	0.0440	25	0.0464	49	0.0427
1	.0445	25	.0443	49	.0445
2	.0455	26	.0450	50	.0471
3	.0457	27	.0441	51	.0465
4	.0435	28	.0449	52	.0438
5	.0453	29	.0448	53	.0445
6	.0450	30	.0467	54	.0472
7	.0438	31	.0465	55	.0453
8	.0459	32	.0449	56	.0444
9	.0428	33	.0448	57	.0451
10	.0449	34	.0461	58	.0455
11	.0449	35	.0439	59	.0435
12	.0467	36	.0452	60	.0443
13	.0433	37	.0443	61	.0440
14	.0461	38	.0434	62	.0438
15	.0451	39	.0454	63	.0444
16	.0455	40	.0456	64	.0444
17	.0454	41	.0459	65	.0450
18	.0461	42	.0452	66	.0467
19	.0455	43	.0447	67	.0445
20	.0458	44	.0442	68	.0447
21	.0445	45	.0457	69	.0461
22	.0445	46	.0454	70	.0450
23	.0451	47	.0445	71	.0463
24	.0436	48	.0451	72	.0456

to use the data reported in Table C5.1 along with the data of Table C5.2, which she ordered be collected for you. These data were collected in the same manner as the data in Table C5.1. However, they were collected during a period of time when the roll mill operator was instructed *not* to adjust the sheet thickness. In your analysis, if you choose to construct control charts, use the same three-measurement subgrouping that the operators use.

Prepare an in-depth written report for the president that responds to her requests. It should begin with an executive summary and include whatever tables and figures are needed to support your analysis and recommendations. [The data file for this case is named **GASKET.** The file contains three variables: sheet number, thickness, and a code for operator adjustments (A) or no adjustments (N).]

This case is based on the experiences of an actual company whose identity is disguised for confidentiality reasons. The case was originally written by DeVor, Chang, and Sutherland (*Statistical Quality Design and Control* [New York: Macmillan Publishing Co., 1992] pp. 298–329) and has been adapted to focus on the material presented in Chapter 12.

A

Basic Counting Rules

Sample points associated with many experiments have identical characteristics. If you can develop a counting rule to count the number of sample points, it can be used to aid in the solution of many probability problems. For example, many experiments involve sampling n elements from a population of N. Then, as explained in Section 3.1, we can use the formula

$$\binom{N}{n} = \frac{N!}{n!(N-n)!}$$

to find the number of different samples of n elements that could be selected from the total of N elements. This gives the number of sample points for the experiment.

Here, we give you a few useful counting rules. You should learn the characteristics of the situation to which each rule applies. Then, when working a probability problem, carefully examine the experiment to see whether you can use one of the rules.

Learning how to decide whether a particular counting rule applies to an experiment takes patience and practice. If you want to develop this skill, try to use the rules to solve some of the exercises in Chapter 3. Proofs of the rules below can be found in the text by W. Feller listed in the references to Chapter 3.

Multiplicative Rule

You have k sets of different elements, n_1 in the first set, n_2 in the second set, ..., and n_k in the kth set. Suppose you want to form a sample of k elements by *taking one element from each of the* k *sets*. The number of different samples that can be formed is the product

$$n_1 \cdot n_2 \cdot n_3 \cdot \cdots \cdot n_k$$

EXAMPLE A.1

Applying the Multiplicative Rule

Problem A product can be shipped by four airlines and each airline can ship via three different routes. How many distinct ways exist to ship the product?

Solution A method of shipment corresponds to a pairing of one airline and one route. Therefore, $k = 2$, the number of airlines is $n_1 = 4$, the number of routes is $n_2 = 3$, and the number of ways to ship the product is

$$n_1 \cdot n_2 = (4)(3) = 12$$

Look Back How the multiplicative rule works can be seen by using a tree diagram, introduced in Section 3.6. The airline choice is shown by three branching lines in Figure A.1.

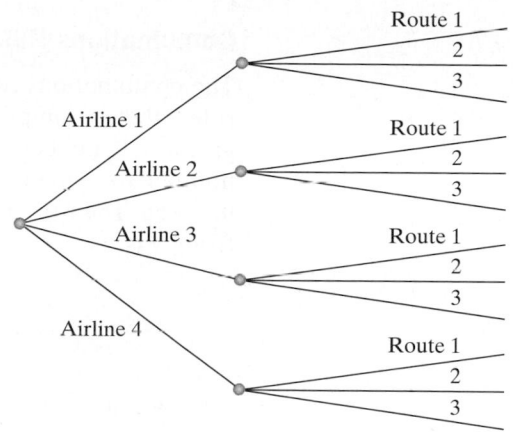

FIGURE A.1
Tree diagram for airline
example

EXAMPLE **A.2**
Applying the
Multiplicative Rule

Problem   You have 20 candidates for three different executive positions, E_1, E_2, and E_3. How many different ways could you fill the positions?

Solution   For this example, there are $k = 3$ sets of elements:

 Set 1: The candidates available to fill position E_1

 Set 2: The candidates remaining (after filling E_1) that are available to fill E_2

 Set 3: The candidates remaining (after filling E_1 and E_2) that are available to fill E_3

The numbers of elements in the sets are $n_1 = 20$, $n_2 = 19$, and $n_3 = 18$. Thus, the number of different ways to fill the three positions is

$$n_1 \cdot n_2 \cdot n_3 = (20)(19)(18) = 6,480$$

Partitions Rule

You have a *single* set of N distinctly different elements, and you want to partition it into k sets, the first set containing n_1 elements, the second containing n_2 elements, ..., and the kth containing n_k elements. The number of different partitions is

$$\frac{N!}{n_1!n_2! \cdot \cdots \cdot n_k!} \text{ where } n_1 + n_2 + n_3 + \cdots + n_k = N$$

EXAMPLE **A.3**
Applying the
Partitions Rule

Problem   You have 12 construction workers available for three job sites. Suppose you want to assign three workers to job 1, four to job 2, and five to job 3. How many different ways could you make this assignment?

Solution   For this example, $k = 3$ (corresponding to the $k = 3$ job sites), $N = 12$, and $n_1 = 3$, $n_2 = 4$, $n_3 = 5$. Then, the number of different ways to assign the workers to the job sites is

$$\frac{N!}{n_1!n_2!n_3!} = \frac{12!}{3!4!5!} = \frac{12 \cdot 11 \cdot 10 \cdot \cdots \cdot 3 \cdot 2 \cdot 1}{(3 \cdot 2 \cdot 1)(4 \cdot 3 \cdot 2 \cdot 1)(5 \cdot 4 \cdot 3 \cdot 2 \cdot 1)} = 27,720$$

Combinations Rule

The combinations rule given in Chapter 3 is a special case ($k = 2$) of the partitions rule—that is, sampling is equivalent to partitioning a set of N elements into $k = 2$ groups: elements that appear in the sample and those that do not. Let $n_1 = n$, the number of elements in the sample, and $n_2 = N - n$, the number of elements remaining. Then the number of different samples of n elements that can be selected from N is

$$\frac{N!}{n_1! n_2!} = \frac{N!}{n!(N-n)!} = \binom{N}{n}$$

This formula was given in Section 3.1.

EXAMPLE A.4

Applying the
Combinations Rule

Problem   How many samples of four firefighters can be selected from a group of 10?

Solution   We have $N = 10$ and $n = 4$; then

$$\binom{N}{n} = \binom{10}{4} = \frac{10!}{4!6!} = \frac{10 \cdot 9 \cdot 8 \cdot \,\cdots\, \cdot 3 \cdot 2 \cdot 1}{(4 \cdot 3 \cdot 2 \cdot 1)(6 \cdot 5 \cdot \,\cdots\, \cdot 2 \cdot 1)} = 210$$

TABLE I   Random Numbers

Row \ Column	1	2	3	4	5	6	7	8	9	10	11	12	13	14
1	10480	15011	01536	02011	81647	91646	69179	14194	62590	36207	20969	99570	91291	90700
2	22368	46573	25595	85393	30995	89198	27982	53402	93965	34095	52666	19174	39615	99505
3	24130	48360	22527	97265	76393	64809	15179	24830	49340	32081	30680	19655	63348	58629
4	42167	93093	06243	61680	07856	16376	39440	53537	71341	57004	00849	74917	97758	16379
5	37570	39975	81837	16656	06121	91782	60468	81305	49684	60672	14110	06927	01263	54613
6	77921	06907	11008	42751	27756	53498	18602	70659	90655	15053	21916	81825	44394	42880
7	99562	72905	56420	69994	98872	31016	71194	18738	44013	48840	63213	21069	10634	12952
8	96301	91977	05463	07972	18876	20922	94595	56869	69014	60045	18425	84903	42508	32307
9	89579	14342	63661	10281	17453	18103	57740	84378	25331	12566	58678	44947	05585	56941
10	85475	36857	53342	53988	53060	59533	38867	62300	08158	17983	16439	11458	18593	64952
11	28918	69578	88231	33276	70997	79936	56865	05859	90106	31595	01547	85590	91610	78188
12	63553	40961	48235	03427	49626	69445	18663	72695	52180	20847	12234	90511	33703	90322
13	09429	93969	52636	92737	88974	33488	36320	17617	30015	08272	84115	27156	30613	74952
14	10365	61129	87529	85689	48237	52267	67689	93394	01511	26358	85104	20285	29975	89868
15	07119	97336	71048	08178	77233	13916	47564	81056	97735	85977	29372	74461	28551	90707
16	51085	12765	51821	51259	77452	16308	60756	92144	49442	53900	70960	63990	75601	40719
17	02368	21382	52404	60268	89368	19885	55322	44819	01188	65255	64835	44919	05944	55157
18	01011	54092	33362	94904	31273	04146	18594	29852	71585	85030	51132	01915	92747	64951
19	52162	53916	46369	58586	23216	14513	83149	98736	23495	64350	94738	17752	35156	35749
20	07056	97628	33787	09998	42698	06691	76988	13602	51851	46104	88916	19509	25625	58104
21	48663	91245	85828	14346	09172	30168	90229	04734	59193	22178	30421	61666	99904	32812
22	54164	58492	22421	74103	47070	25306	76468	26384	58151	06646	21524	15227	96909	44592
23	32639	32363	05597	24200	13363	38005	94342	28728	35806	06912	17012	64161	18296	22851
24	29334	27001	87637	87308	58731	00256	45834	15398	46557	41135	10367	07684	36188	18510
25	02488	33062	28834	07351	19731	92420	60952	61280	50001	67658	32586	86679	50720	94953
26	81525	72295	04839	96423	24878	82651	66566	14778	76797	14780	13300	87074	79666	95725
27	29676	20591	68086	26432	46901	20849	89768	81536	86645	12659	92259	57102	80428	25280
28	00742	57392	39064	66432	84673	40027	32832	61362	98947	96067	64760	64584	96096	98253
29	05366	04213	25669	26422	44407	44048	37937	63904	45766	66134	75470	66520	34693	90449
30	91921	26418	64117	94305	26766	25940	39972	22209	71500	64568	91402	42416	07844	69618
31	00582	04711	87917	77341	42206	35126	74087	99547	81817	42607	43808	76655	62028	76630
32	00725	69884	62797	56170	86324	88072	76222	36086	84637	93161	76038	65855	77919	88006
33	69011	65795	95876	55293	18988	27354	26575	08625	40801	59920	29841	80150	12777	48501
34	25976	57948	29888	88604	67917	48708	18912	82271	65424	69774	33611	54262	85963	03547
35	09763	83473	73577	12908	30883	18317	28290	35797	05998	41688	34952	37888	38917	88050

(continued)

TABLE I   (continued)

Row \ Column	1	2	3	4	5	6	7	8	9	10	11	12	13	14
36	91576	42595	27953	30134	04024	86385	29880	99730	55536	84855	29080	09250	79656	73211
37	17955	56349	90999	49127	20044	59931	06115	20542	18059	02008	73708	83517	36103	42791
38	46503	18584	18845	49618	02304	51038	20655	58727	28168	15475	56942	53389	20562	87338
39	92157	89634	94824	78171	84610	82834	09922	25417	44137	48413	25555	21246	35509	20468
40	14577	62765	35605	81263	39667	47358	56873	56307	61607	49518	89656	20103	77490	18062
41	98427	07523	33362	64270	01638	92477	66969	98420	04880	45585	46565	04102	46880	45709
42	34914	63976	88720	82765	34476	17032	87589	40836	32427	70002	70663	88863	77775	69348
43	70060	28277	39475	46473	23219	53416	94970	25832	69975	94884	19661	72828	00102	66794
44	53976	54914	06990	67245	68350	82948	11398	42878	80287	88267	47363	46634	06541	97809
45	76072	29515	40980	07391	58745	25774	22987	80059	39911	96189	41151	14222	60697	59583
46	90725	52210	83974	29992	65831	38857	50490	83765	55657	14361	31720	57375	56228	41546
47	64364	67412	33339	31926	14883	24413	59744	92351	97473	89286	35931	04110	23726	51900
48	08962	00358	31662	25388	61642	34072	81249	35648	56891	69352	48373	45578	78547	81788
49	95012	68379	93526	70765	10592	04542	76463	54328	02349	17247	28865	14777	62730	92277
50	15664	10493	20492	38391	91132	21999	59516	81652	27195	48223	46751	22923	32261	85653
51	16408	81899	04153	53381	79401	21438	83035	92350	36693	31238	59649	91754	72772	02338
52	18629	81953	05520	91962	04739	13092	97662	24822	94730	06496	35090	04822	86774	98289
53	73115	35101	47498	87637	99016	71060	88824	71013	18735	20286	23153	72924	35165	43040
54	57491	16703	23167	49323	45021	33132	12544	41035	80780	45393	44812	12512	98931	91202
55	30405	83946	23792	14422	15059	45799	22716	19792	09983	74353	68668	30429	70735	25499
56	16631	35006	85900	98275	32388	52390	16815	69298	82732	38480	73817	32523	41961	44437
57	96773	20206	42559	78985	05300	22164	24369	54224	35083	19687	11052	91491	60383	19746
58	38935	64202	14349	82674	66523	44133	00697	35552	35970	19124	63318	29686	03387	59846
59	31624	76384	17403	53363	44167	64486	64758	75366	76554	31601	12614	33072	60332	92325
60	78919	19474	23632	27889	47914	02584	37680	20801	72152	39339	34806	08930	85001	87820
61	03931	33309	57047	74211	63445	17361	62825	39908	05607	91284	68833	25570	38818	46920
62	74426	33278	43972	10110	89917	15665	52872	73823	73144	88662	88970	74492	51805	99378
63	09066	00903	20795	95452	92648	45454	09552	88815	16553	51125	79375	97596	16296	66092
64	42238	12426	87025	14267	20979	04508	64535	31355	86064	29472	47689	05974	52468	16834
65	16153	08002	26504	41744	81959	65642	74240	56302	00033	67107	77510	70625	28725	34191
66	21457	40742	29820	96783	29400	21840	15035	34537	33310	06116	95240	15957	16572	06004
67	21581	57802	02050	89728	17937	37621	47075	42080	97403	48626	68995	43805	33386	21597
68	55612	78095	83197	33732	05810	24813	86902	60397	16489	03264	88525	42786	05269	92532
69	44657	66999	99324	51281	84463	60563	79312	93454	68876	25471	93911	25650	12682	73572
70	91340	84979	46949	81973	37949	61023	43997	15263	80644	43942	89203	71795	99533	50501

(continued)

TABLE I (continued)

Column / Row	1	2	3	4	5	6	7	8	9	10	11	12	13	14
71	91227	21199	31935	27022	84067	05462	35216	14486	29891	68607	41867	14951	91696	85065
72	50001	38140	66321	19924	72163	09538	12151	06878	91903	18749	34405	56087	82790	70925
73	65390	05224	72958	28609	81406	39147	25549	48542	42627	45233	57202	94617	23772	07896
74	27504	96131	83944	41575	10573	08619	64482	73923	36152	05184	94142	25299	84387	34925
75	37169	94851	39117	89632	00959	16487	65536	49071	39782	17095	02330	74301	00275	48280
76	11508	70225	51111	38351	19444	66499	71945	05422	13442	78675	84081	66938	93654	59894
77	37449	30362	06694	54690	04052	53115	62757	95348	78662	11163	81651	50245	34971	52924
78	46515	70331	85922	38329	57015	15765	97161	17869	45349	61796	66345	81073	49106	79860
79	30986	81223	42416	58353	21532	30502	32305	86482	05174	07901	54339	58861	74818	46942
80	63798	64995	46583	09785	44160	78128	83991	42865	92520	83531	80377	35909	81250	54238
81	82486	84846	99254	67632	43218	50076	21361	64816	51202	88124	41870	52689	51275	83556
82	21885	32906	92431	09060	64297	51674	64126	62570	26123	05155	59194	52799	28225	85762
83	60336	98782	07408	53458	13564	59089	26445	29789	85205	41001	12535	12133	14645	23541
84	43937	46891	24010	25560	86355	33941	25786	54990	71899	15475	95434	98227	21824	19585
85	97656	63175	89303	16275	07100	92063	21942	18611	47348	20203	18534	03862	78095	50136
86	03299	01221	05418	38982	55758	92237	26759	86367	21216	98442	08303	56613	91511	75928
87	79626	06486	03574	17668	07785	76020	79924	25651	83325	88428	85076	72811	22717	50585
88	85636	68335	47539	03129	65651	11977	02510	26113	99447	68645	34327	15152	55230	93448
89	18039	14367	64337	06177	12143	46609	32989	74014	64708	00533	35398	58408	13261	47908
90	08362	15656	60627	36478	65648	16764	53412	09013	07832	41574	17639	82163	60859	75567
91	79556	29068	04142	16268	15387	12856	66227	38358	22478	73373	88732	09443	82558	05250
92	92608	82674	27072	32534	17075	27698	98204	63863	11951	34648	88022	56148	34925	57031
93	23982	25835	40055	67006	12293	02753	14827	23235	35071	99704	37543	11601	35503	85171
94	09915	96306	05908	97901	28395	14186	00821	80703	70426	75647	76310	88717	37890	40129
95	59037	33300	26695	62247	69927	76123	50842	43834	86654	70959	79725	93872	28117	19233
96	42488	78077	69882	61657	34136	79180	97526	43092	04098	73571	80799	76536	71255	64239
97	46764	86273	63003	93017	31204	36692	40202	35275	57306	55543	53203	18098	47625	88684
98	03237	45430	55417	63282	90816	17349	88298	90183	36600	78406	06216	95787	42579	90730
99	86591	81482	52667	61582	14972	90053	89534	76036	49199	43716	97548	04379	46370	28672
100	38534	01715	94964	87288	65680	43772	39560	12918	86537	62738	19636	51132	25739	56947

Source: Abridged from W. H. Beyer (ed.). CRC Standard Mathematical Tables, 24th edition. (Cleveland: The Chemical Rubber Company), 1976. Reproduced by permission of the publisher.

TABLE II Binomial Probabilities

Tabulated values are $\sum_{x=0}^{k} p(x)$. (Computations are rounded at the third decimal place.)

a. $n = 5$

k \ p	.01	.05	.10	.20	.30	.40	.50	.60	.70	.80	.90	.95	.99
0	.951	.774	.590	.328	.168	.078	.031	.010	.002	.000	.000	.000	.000
1	.999	.977	.919	.737	.528	.337	.188	.087	.031	.007	.000	.000	.000
2	1.000	.999	.991	.942	.837	.683	.500	.317	.163	.058	.009	.001	.000
3	1.000	1.000	1.000	.993	.969	.913	.812	.663	.472	.263	.081	.023	.001
4	1.000	1.000	1.000	1.000	.998	.990	.969	.922	.832	.672	.410	.226	.049

b. $n = 6$

k \ p	.01	.05	.10	.20	.30	.40	.50	.60	.70	.80	.90	.95	.99
0	.941	.735	.531	.262	.118	.047	.016	.004	.001	.000	.000	.000	.000
1	.999	.967	.886	.655	.420	.233	.109	.041	.011	.002	.000	.000	.000
2	1.000	.998	.984	.901	.744	.544	.344	.179	.070	.017	.001	.000	.000
3	1.000	1.000	.999	.983	.930	.821	.656	.456	.256	.099	.016	.002	.000
4	1.000	1.000	1.000	.998	.989	.959	.891	.767	.580	.345	.114	.033	.001
5	1.000	1.000	1.000	1.000	.999	.996	.984	.953	.882	.738	.469	.265	.059

c. $n = 7$

k \ p	.01	.05	.10	.20	.30	.40	.50	.60	.70	.80	.90	.95	.99
0	.932	.698	.478	.210	.082	.028	.008	.002	.000	.000	.000	.000	.000
1	.998	.956	.850	.577	.329	.159	.063	.019	.004	.000	.000	.000	.000
2	1.000	.996	.974	.852	.647	.420	.227	.096	.029	.005	.000	.000	.000
3	1.000	1.000	.997	.967	.874	.710	.500	.290	.126	.033	.003	.000	.000
4	1.000	1.000	1.000	.995	.971	.904	.773	.580	.353	.148	.026	.004	.000
5	1.000	1.000	1.000	1.000	.996	.981	.937	.841	.671	.423	.150	.044	.002
6	1.000	1.000	1.000	1.000	1.000	.998	.992	.972	.918	.790	.522	.302	.068

(continued)

TABLE II   (*continued*)

d. *n* = 8

k \ p	.01	.05	.10	.20	.30	.40	.50	.60	.70	.80	.90	.95	.99
0	.923	.663	.430	.168	.058	.017	.004	.001	.000	.000	.000	.000	.000
1	.997	.943	.813	.503	.255	.106	.035	.009	.001	.000	.000	.000	.000
2	1.000	.994	.962	.797	.552	.315	.145	.050	.011	.001	.000	.000	.000
3	1.000	1.000	.995	.944	.806	.594	.363	.174	.058	.010	.000	.000	.000
4	1.000	1.000	1.000	.990	.942	.826	.637	.406	.194	.056	.005	.000	.000
5	1.000	1.000	1.000	.999	.989	.950	.855	.685	.448	.203	.038	.006	.000
6	1.000	1.000	1.000	1.000	.999	.991	.965	.894	.745	.497	.187	.057	.003
7	1.000	1.000	1.000	1.000	1.000	.999	.996	.983	.942	.832	.570	.337	.077

e. *n* = 9

k \ p	.01	.05	.10	.20	.30	.40	.50	.60	.70	.80	.90	.95	.99
0	.914	.630	.387	.134	.040	.010	.002	.000	.000	.000	.000	.000	.000
1	.997	.929	.775	.436	.196	.071	.020	.004	.000	.000	.000	.000	.000
2	1.000	.992	.947	.738	.463	.232	.090	.025	.004	.000	.000	.000	.000
3	1.000	.999	.992	.914	.730	.483	.254	.099	.025	.003	.000	.000	.000
4	1.000	1.000	.999	.980	.901	.733	.500	.267	.099	.020	.001	.000	.000
5	1.000	1.000	1.000	.997	.975	.901	.746	.517	.270	.086	.008	.001	.000
6	1.000	1.000	1.000	1.000	.996	.975	.910	.768	.537	.262	.053	.008	.000
7	1.000	1.000	1.000	1.000	1.000	.996	.980	.929	.804	.564	.225	.071	.003
8	1.000	1.000	1.000	1.000	1.000	1.000	.998	.990	.960	.866	.613	.370	.086

f. *n* = 10

k \ p	.01	.05	.10	.20	.30	.40	.50	.60	.70	.80	.90	.95	.99
0	.904	.599	.349	.107	.028	.006	.001	.000	.000	.000	.000	.000	.000
1	.996	.914	.736	.376	.149	.046	.011	.002	.000	.000	.000	.000	.000
2	1.000	.988	.930	.678	.383	.167	.055	.012	.002	.000	.000	.000	.000
3	1.000	.999	.987	.879	.650	.382	.172	.055	.011	.001	.000	.000	.000
4	1.000	1.000	.998	.967	.850	.633	.377	.166	.047	.006	.000	.000	.000
5	1.000	1.000	1.000	.994	.953	.834	.623	.367	.150	.033	.002	.000	.000
6	1.000	1.000	1.000	.999	.989	.945	.828	.618	.350	.121	.013	.001	.000
7	1.000	1.000	1.000	1.000	.998	.988	.945	.833	.617	.322	.070	.012	.000
8	1.000	1.000	1.000	1.000	1.000	.998	.989	.954	.851	.624	.264	.086	.004
9	1.000	1.000	1.000	1.000	1.000	1.000	.999	.994	.972	.893	.651	.401	.096

(continued)

TABLE II *(continued)*

g. *n* = 15

k \ p	.01	.05	.10	.20	.30	.40	.50	.60	.70	.80	.90	.95	.99
0	.860	.463	.206	.035	.005	.000	.000	.000	.000	.000	.000	.000	.000
1	.990	.829	.549	.167	.035	.005	.000	.000	.000	.000	.000	.000	.000
2	1.000	.964	.816	.398	.127	.027	.004	.000	.000	.000	.000	.000	.000
3	1.000	.995	.944	.648	.297	.091	.018	.002	.000	.000	.000	.000	.000
4	1.000	.999	.987	.838	.515	.217	.059	.009	.001	.000	.000	.000	.000
5	1.000	1.000	.998	.939	.722	.403	.151	.034	.004	.000	.000	.000	.000
6	1.000	1.000	1.000	.982	.869	.610	.304	.095	.015	.001	.000	.000	.000
7	1.000	1.000	1.000	.996	.950	.787	.500	.213	.050	.004	.000	.000	.000
8	1.000	1.000	1.000	.999	.985	.905	.696	.390	.131	.018	.000	.000	.000
9	1.000	1.000	1.000	1.000	.996	.966	.849	.597	.278	.061	.002	.000	.000
10	1.000	1.000	1.000	1.000	.999	.991	.941	.783	.485	.164	.013	.001	.000
11	1.000	1.000	1.000	1.000	1.000	.998	.982	.909	.703	.352	.056	.005	.000
12	1.000	1.000	1.000	1.000	1.000	1.000	.996	.973	.873	.602	.184	.036	.000
13	1.000	1.000	1.000	1.000	1.000	1.000	1.000	.995	.965	.833	.451	.171	.010
14	1.000	1.000	1.000	1.000	1.000	1.000	1.000	1.000	.995	.965	.794	.537	.140

h. *n* = 20

k \ p	.01	.05	.10	.20	.30	.40	.50	.60	.70	.80	.90	.95	.99
0	.818	.358	.122	.012	.001	.000	.000	.000	.000	.000	.000	.000	.000
1	.983	.736	.392	.069	.008	.001	.000	.000	.000	.000	.000	.000	.000
2	.999	.925	.677	.206	.035	.004	.000	.000	.000	.000	.000	.000	.000
3	1.000	.984	.867	.411	.107	.016	.001	.000	.000	.000	.000	.000	.000
4	1.000	.997	.957	.630	.238	.051	.006	.000	.000	.000	.000	.000	.000
5	1.000	1.000	.989	.804	.416	.126	.021	.002	.000	.000	.000	.000	.000
6	1.000	1.000	.998	.913	.608	.250	.058	.006	.000	.000	.000	.000	.000
7	1.000	1.000	1.000	.968	.772	.416	.132	.021	.001	.000	.000	.000	.000
8	1.000	1.000	1.000	.990	.887	.596	.252	.057	.005	.000	.000	.000	.000
9	1.000	1.000	1.000	.997	.952	.755	.412	.128	.017	.001	.000	.000	.000
10	1.000	1.000	1.000	.999	.983	.872	.588	.245	.048	.003	.000	.000	.000
11	1.000	1.000	1.000	1.000	.995	.943	.748	.404	.113	.010	.000	.000	.000
12	1.000	1.000	1.000	1.000	.999	.979	.868	.584	.228	.032	.000	.000	.000
13	1.000	1.000	1.000	1.000	1.000	.994	.942	.750	.392	.087	.002	.000	.000
14	1.000	1.000	1.000	1.000	1.000	.998	.979	.874	.584	.196	.011	.000	.000
15	1.000	1.000	1.000	1.000	1.000	1.000	.994	.949	.762	.370	.043	.003	.000
16	1.000	1.000	1.000	1.000	1.000	1.000	.999	.984	.893	.589	.133	.016	.000
17	1.000	1.000	1.000	1.000	1.000	1.000	1.000	.996	.965	.794	.323	.075	.001
18	1.000	1.000	1.000	1.000	1.000	1.000	1.000	.999	.992	.931	.608	.264	.017
19	1.000	1.000	1.000	1.000	1.000	1.000	1.000	1.000	.999	.988	.878	.642	.182

(continued)

TABLE II   (*continued*)

i. $n = 25$

k \ p	.01	.05	.10	.20	.30	.40	.50	.60	.70	.80	.90	.95	.99
0	.778	.277	.072	.004	.000	.000	.000	.000	.000	.000	.000	.000	.000
1	.974	.642	.271	.027	.002	.000	.000	.000	.000	.000	.000	.000	.000
2	.998	.873	.537	.098	.009	.000	.000	.000	.000	.000	.000	.000	.000
3	1.000	.966	.764	.234	.033	.002	.000	.000	.000	.000	.000	.000	.000
4	1.000	.993	.902	.421	.090	.009	.000	.000	.000	.000	.000	.000	.000
5	1.000	.999	.967	.617	.193	.029	.002	.000	.000	.000	.000	.000	.000
6	1.000	1.000	.991	.780	.341	.074	.007	.000	.000	.000	.000	.000	.000
7	1.000	1.000	.998	.891	.512	.154	.022	.001	.000	.000	.000	.000	.000
8	1.000	1.000	1.000	.953	.677	.274	.054	.004	.000	.000	.000	.000	.000
9	1.000	1.000	1.000	.983	.811	.425	.115	.013	.000	.000	.000	.000	.000
10	1.000	1.000	1.000	.994	.902	.586	.212	.034	.002	.000	.000	.000	.000
11	1.000	1.000	1.000	.998	.956	.732	.345	.078	.006	.000	.000	.000	.000
12	1.000	1.000	1.000	1.000	.983	.846	.500	.154	.017	.000	.000	.000	.000
13	1.000	1.000	1.000	1.000	.994	.922	.655	.268	.044	.002	.000	.000	.000
14	1.000	1.000	1.000	1.000	.998	.966	.788	.414	.098	.006	.000	.000	.000
15	1.000	1.000	1.000	1.000	1.000	.987	.885	.575	.189	.017	.000	.000	.000
16	1.000	1.000	1.000	1.000	1.000	.996	.946	.726	.323	.047	.000	.000	.000
17	1.000	1.000	1.000	1.000	1.000	.999	.978	.846	.488	.109	.002	.000	.000
18	1.000	1.000	1.000	1.000	1.000	1.000	.993	.926	.659	.220	.009	.000	.000
19	1.000	1.000	1.000	1.000	1.000	1.000	.998	.971	.807	.383	.033	.001	.000
20	1.000	1.000	1.000	1.000	1.000	1.000	1.000	.991	.910	.579	.098	.007	.000
21	1.000	1.000	1.000	1.000	1.000	1.000	1.000	.998	.967	.766	.236	.034	.000
22	1.000	1.000	1.000	1.000	1.000	1.000	1.000	1.000	.991	.902	.463	.127	.002
23	1.000	1.000	1.000	1.000	1.000	1.000	1.000	1.000	.998	.973	.729	.358	.026
24	1.000	1.000	1.000	1.000	1.000	1.000	1.000	1.000	1.000	.996	.928	.723	.222

TABLE III   Poisson Probabilities

Tabulated values are $\sum_{x=0}^{k} p(x)$. *(Computations are rounded at the third decimal place.)*

λ \ k	0	1	2	3	4	5	6	7	8	9
.02	.980	1.000								
.04	.961	.999	1.000							
.06	.942	.998	1.000							
.08	.923	.997	1.000							
.10	.905	.995	1.000							
.15	.861	.990	.999	1.000						
.20	.819	.982	.999	1.000						
.25	.779	.974	.998	1.000						
.30	.741	.963	.996	1.000						
.35	.705	.951	.994	1.000						
.40	.670	.938	.992	.999	1.000					
.45	.638	.925	.989	.999	1.000					
.50	.607	.910	.986	.998	1.000					
.55	.577	.894	.982	.998	1.000					
.60	.549	.878	.977	.997	1.000					
.65	.522	.861	.972	.996	.999	1.000				
.70	.497	.844	.966	.994	.999	1.000				
.75	.472	.821	.959	.993	.999	1.000				
.80	.449	.809	.953	.991	.999	1.000				
.85	.427	.791	.945	.989	.998	1.000				
.90	.407	.772	.937	.987	.998	1.000				
.95	.387	.754	.929	.981	.997	1.000				
1.00	.368	.736	.920	.981	.996	.999	1.000			
1.1	.333	.699	.900	.974	.995	.999	1.000			
1.2	.301	.663	.879	.966	.992	.998	1.000			
1.3	.273	.627	.857	.957	.989	.998	1.000			
1.4	.247	.592	.833	.946	.986	.997	.999	1.000		
1.5	.223	.558	.809	.934	.981	.996	.999	1.000		

(continued)

TABLE III   (*continued*)

λ \ k	0	1	2	3	4	5	6	7	8	9
1.6	.202	.525	.783	.921	.976	.994	.999	1.000		
1.7	.183	.493	.757	.907	.970	.992	.998	1.000		
1.8	.165	.463	.731	.891	.964	.990	.997	.999	1.000	
1.9	.150	.434	.704	.875	.956	.987	.997	.999	1.000	
2.0	.135	.406	.677	.857	.947	.983	.995	.999	1.000	
2.2	.111	.355	.623	.819	.928	.975	.993	.998	1.000	
2.4	.091	.308	.570	.779	.904	.964	.988	.997	.999	1.000
2.6	.074	.267	.518	.736	.877	.951	.983	.995	.999	1.000
2.8	.061	.231	.469	.692	.848	.935	.976	.992	.998	.999
3.0	.050	.199	.423	.647	.815	.916	.966	.988	.996	.999
3.2	.041	.171	.380	.603	.781	.895	.955	.983	.994	.998
3.4	.033	.147	.340	.558	.744	.871	.942	.977	.992	.997
3.6	.027	.126	.303	.515	.706	.844	.927	.969	.988	.996
3.8	.022	.107	.269	.473	.668	.816	.909	.960	.984	.994
4.0	.018	.092	.238	.433	.629	.785	.889	.949	.979	.992
4.2	.015	.078	.210	.395	.590	.753	.867	.936	.972	.989
4.4	.012	.066	.185	.359	.551	.720	.844	.921	.964	.985
4.6	.010	.056	.163	.326	.513	.686	.818	.905	.955	.980
4.8	.008	.048	.143	.294	.476	.651	.791	.887	.944	.975
5.0	.007	.040	.125	.265	.440	.616	.762	.867	.932	.968
5.2	.006	.034	.109	.238	.406	.581	.732	.845	.918	.960
5.4	.005	.029	.095	.213	.373	.546	.702	.822	.903	.951
5.6	.004	.024	.082	.191	.342	.512	.670	.797	.886	.941
5.8	.003	.021	.072	.170	.313	.478	.638	.771	.867	.929
6.0	.002	.017	.062	.151	.285	.446	.606	.744	.847	.916

λ \ k	10	11	12	13	14	15	16
2.8	1.000						
3.0	1.000						
3.2	1.000						
3.4	.999	1.000					
3.6	.999	1.000					
3.8	.998	.999	1.000				
4.0	.997	.999	1.000				
4.2	.996	.999	1.000				
4.4	.994	.998	.999	1.000			
4.6	.992	.997	.999	1.000			
4.8	.990	.996	.999	1.000			
5.0	.986	.995	.998	.999	1.000		
5.2	.982	.993	.997	.999	1.000		
5.4	.977	.990	.996	.999	1.000		
5.6	.972	.988	.995	.998	.999	1.000	
5.8	.965	.984	.993	.997	.999	1.000	
6.0	.957	.980	.991	.996	.999	.999	1.000

(continued)

TABLE III   (continued)

k λ	0	1	2	3	4	5	6	7	8	9
6.2	.002	.015	.054	.134	.259	.414	.574	.716	.826	.902
6.4	.002	.012	.046	.119	.235	.384	.542	.687	.803	.886
6.6	.001	.010	.040	.105	.213	.355	.511	.658	.780	.869
6.8	.001	.009	.034	.093	.192	.327	.480	.628	.755	.850
7.0	.001	.007	.030	.082	.173	.301	.450	.599	.729	.830
7.2	.001	.006	.025	.072	.156	.276	.420	.569	.703	.810
7.4	.001	.005	.022	.063	.140	.253	.392	.539	.676	.788
7.6	.001	.004	.019	.055	.125	.231	.365	.510	.648	.765
7.8	.000	.004	.016	.048	.112	.210	.338	.481	.620	.741
8.0	.000	.003	.014	.042	.100	.191	.313	.453	.593	.717
8.5	.000	.002	.009	.030	.074	.150	.256	.386	.523	.653
9.0	.000	.001	.006	.021	.055	.116	.207	.324	.456	.587
9.5	.000	.001	.004	.015	.040	.089	.165	.269	.392	.522
10.0	.000	.000	.003	.010	.029	.067	.130	.220	.333	.458

	10	11	12	13	14	15	16	17	18	19
6.2	.949	.975	.989	.995	.998	.999	1.000			
6.4	.939	.969	.986	.994	.997	.999	1.000			
6.6	.927	.963	.982	.992	.997	.999	.999	1.000		
6.8	.915	.955	.978	.990	.996	.998	.999	1.000		
7.0	.901	.947	.973	.987	.994	.998	.999	1.000		
7.2	.887	.937	.967	.984	.993	.997	.999	.999	1.000	
7.4	.871	.926	.961	.980	.991	.996	.998	.999	1.000	
7.6	.854	.915	.954	.976	.989	.995	.998	.999	1.000	
7.8	.835	.902	.945	.971	.986	.993	.997	.999	1.000	
8.0	.816	.888	.936	.966	.983	.992	.996	.998	.999	1.000
8.5	.763	.849	.909	.949	.973	.986	.993	.997	.999	.999
9.0	.706	.803	.876	.926	.959	.978	.989	.995	.998	.999
9.5	.645	.752	.836	.898	.940	.967	.982	.991	.996	.998
10.0	.583	.697	.792	.864	.917	.951	.973	.986	.993	.997

	20	21	22							
8.5	1.000									
9.0	1.000									
9.5	.999	1.000								
10.0	.998	.999	1.000							

(continued)

TABLE III   *(continued)*

λ \ k	0	1	2	3	4	5	6	7	8	9
10.5	.000	.000	.002	.007	.021	.050	.102	.179	.279	.397
11.0	.000	.000	.001	.005	.015	.038	.079	.143	.232	.341
11.5	.000	.000	.001	.003	.011	.028	.060	.114	.191	.289
12.0	.000	.000	.001	.002	.008	.020	.046	.090	.155	.242
12.5	.000	.000	.000	.002	.005	.015	.035	.070	.125	.201
13.0	.000	.000	.000	.001	.004	.011	.026	.054	.100	.166
13.5	.000	.000	.000	.001	.003	.008	.019	.041	.079	.135
14.0	.000	.000	.000	.000	.002	.006	.014	.032	.062	.109
14.5	.000	.000	.000	.000	.001	.004	.010	.024	.048	.088
15.0	.000	.000	.000	.000	.001	.003	.008	.018	.037	.070

λ \ k	10	11	12	13	14	15	16	17	18	19
10.5	.521	.639	.742	.825	.888	.932	.960	.978	.988	.994
11.0	.460	.579	.689	.781	.854	.907	.944	.968	.982	.991
11.5	.402	.520	.633	.733	.815	.878	.924	.954	.974	.986
12.0	.347	.462	.576	.682	.772	.844	.899	.937	.963	.979
12.5	.297	.406	.519	.628	.725	.806	.869	.916	.948	.969
13.0	.252	.353	.463	.573	.675	.764	.835	.890	.930	.957
13.5	.211	.304	.409	.518	.623	.718	.798	.861	.908	.942
14.0	.176	.260	.358	.464	.570	.669	.756	.827	.883	.923
14.5	.145	.220	.311	.413	.518	.619	.711	.790	.853	.901
15.0	.118	.185	.268	.363	.466	.568	.664	.749	.819	.875

λ \ k	20	21	22	23	24	25	26	27	28	29
10.5	.997	.999	.999	1.000						
11.0	.995	.998	.999	1.000						
11.5	.992	.996	.998	.999	1.000					
12.0	.988	.994	.987	.999	.999	1.000				
12.5	.983	.991	.995	.998	.999	.999	1.000			
13.0	.975	.986	.992	.996	.998	.999	1.000			
13.5	.965	.980	.989	.994	.997	.998	.999	1.000		
14.0	.952	.971	.983	.991	.995	.997	.999	.999	1.000	
14.5	.936	.960	.976	.986	.992	.996	.998	.999	.999	1.000
15.0	.917	.947	.967	.981	.989	.994	.997	.998	.999	1.000

(continued)

TABLE III (*continued*)

λ \ k	4	5	6	7	8	9	10	11	12	13
16	.000	.001	.004	.010	.022	.043	.077	.127	.193	.275
17	.000	.001	.002	.005	.013	.026	.049	.085	.135	.201
18	.000	.000	.001	.003	.007	.015	.030	.055	.092	.143
19	.000	.000	.001	.002	.004	.009	.018	.035	.061	.098
20	.000	.000	.000	.001	.002	.005	.011	.021	.039	.066
21	.000	.000	.000	.000	.001	.003	.006	.013	.025	.043
22	.000	.000	.000	.000	.001	.002	.004	.008	.015	.028
23	.000	.000	.000	.000	.000	.001	.002	.004	.009	.017
24	.000	.000	.000	.000	.000	.000	.001	.003	.005	.011
25	.000	.000	.000	.000	.000	.000	.001	.001	.003	.006

	14	15	16	17	18	19	20	21	22	23
16	.368	.467	.566	.659	.742	.812	.868	.911	.942	.963
17	.281	.371	.468	.564	.655	.736	.805	.861	.905	.937
18	.208	.287	.375	.469	.562	.651	.731	.799	.855	.899
19	.150	.215	.292	.378	.469	.561	.647	.725	.793	.849
20	.105	.157	.221	.297	.381	.470	.559	.644	.721	.787
21	.072	.111	.163	.227	.302	.384	471	.558	.640	.716
22	.048	.077	.117	.169	.232	.306	.387	.472	.556	.637
23	.031	.052	.082	.123	.175	.238	.310	.389	.472	.555
24	.020	.034	.056	.087	.128	.180	.243	.314	.392	.473
25	.012	.022	.038	.060	.092	.134	.185	.247	.318	.394

	24	25	26	27	28	29	30	31	32	33
16	.978	.987	.993	.996	.998	.999	.999	1.000		
17	.959	.975	.985	.991	.995	.997	.999	.999	1.000	
18	.932	.955	.972	.983	.990	.994	.997	.998	.999	1.000
19	.893	.927	.951	.969	.980	.988	.993	.996	.998	.999
20	.843	.888	.922	.948	.966	.978	.987	.992	.995	.997
21	.782	.838	.883	.917	.944	.963	.976	.985	.991	.994
22	.712	.777	.832	.877	.913	.940	.959	.973	.983	.989
23	.635	.708	.772	.827	.873	.908	.936	.956	.971	.981
24	.554	.632	.704	.768	.823	.868	.904	.932	.953	.969
25	.473	.553	.629	.700	.763	.818	.863	.900	.929	.950

	34	35	36	37	38	39	40	41	42	43
19	.999	1.000								
20	.999	.999	1.000							
21	.997	.998	.999	.999	1.000					
22	.994	.996	.998	.999	.999	1.000				
23	.988	.993	.996	.997	.999	.999	1.000			
24	.979	.987	.992	.995	.997	.998	.999	.999	1.000	
25	.966	.978	.985	.991	.991	.997	.998	.999	.999	1.000

TABLE IV   Normal Curve Areas

z	.00	.01	.02	.03	.04	.05	.06	.07	.08	.09
.0	.0000	.0040	.0080	.0120	.0160	.0199	.0239	.0279	.0319	.0359
.1	.0398	.0438	.0478	.0517	.0557	.0596	.0636	.0675	.0714	.0753
.2	.0793	.0832	.0871	.0910	.0948	.0987	.1026	.1064	.1103	.1141
.3	.1179	.1217	.1255	.1293	.1331	.1368	.1406	.1443	.1480	.1517
.4	.1554	.1591	.1628	.1664	.1700	.1736	.1772	.1808	.1844	.1879
.5	.1915	.1950	.1985	.2019	.2054	.2088	.2123	.2157	.2190	.2224
.6	.2257	.2291	.2324	.2357	.2389	.2422	.2454	.2486	.2517	.2549
.7	.2580	.2611	.2642	.2673	.2704	.2734	.2764	.2794	.2823	.2852
.8	.2881	.2910	.2939	.2967	.2995	.3023	.3051	.3078	.3106	.3133
.9	.3159	.3186	.3212	.3238	.3264	.3289	.3315	.3340	.3365	.3389
1.0	.3413	.3438	.3461	.3485	.3508	.3531	.3554	.3577	.3599	.3621
1.1	.3643	.3665	.3686	.3708	.3729	.3749	.3770	.3790	.3810	.3830
1.2	.3849	.3869	.3888	.3907	.3925	.3944	.3962	.3980	.3997	.4015
1.3	.4032	.4049	.4066	.4082	.4099	.4115	.4131	.4147	.4162	.4177
1.4	.4192	.4207	.4222	.4236	.4251	.4265	.4279	.4292	.4306	.4319
1.5	.4332	.4345	.4357	.4370	.4382	.4394	.4406	.4418	.4429	.4441
1.6	.4452	.4463	.4474	.4484	.4495	.4505	.4515	.4525	.4535	.4545
1.7	.4554	.4564	.4573	.4582	.4591	.4599	.4608	.4616	.4625	.4633
1.8	.4641	.4649	.4656	.4664	.4671	.4678	.4686	.4693	.4699	.4706
1.9	.4713	.4719	.4726	.4732	.4738	.4744	.4750	.4756	.4761	.4767
2.0	.4772	.4778	.4783	.4788	.4793	.4798	.4803	.4808	.4812	.4817
2.1	.4821	.4826	.4830	.4834	.4838	.4842	.4846	.4850	.4854	.4857
2.2	.4861	.4864	.4868	.4871	.4875	.4878	.4881	.4884	.4887	.4890
2.3	.4893	.4896	.4898	.4901	.4904	.4906	.4909	.4911	.4913	.4916
2.4	.4918	.4920	.4922	.4925	.4927	.4929	.4931	.4932	.4934	.4936
2.5	.4938	.4940	.4941	.4943	.4945	.4946	.4948	.4949	.4951	.4952
2.6	.4953	.4955	.4956	.4957	.4959	.4960	.4961	.4962	.4963	.4964
2.7	.4965	.4966	.4967	.4968	.4969	.4970	.4971	.4972	.4973	.4974
2.8	.4974	.4975	.4976	.4977	.4977	.4978	.4979	.4979	.4980	.4981
2.9	.4981	.4982	.4982	.4983	.4984	.4984	.4985	.4985	.4986	.4986
3.0	.4987	.4987	.4987	.4988	.4988	.4989	.4989	.4989	.4990	.4990
3.1	.49903	.49906	.49910	.49913	.49916	.49918	.49921	.49924	.49926	.48829
3.2	.49931	.49934	.49936	.49938	.49940	.49942	.49944	.49946	.49948	.49950
3.3	.49952	.49953	.49955	.49957	.49958	.49960	.49961	.49962	.49964	.49965
3.4	.49966	.49968	.49969	.49970	.49971	.49972	.49973	.49974	.49975	.49976
3.5	.49977	.49978	.49978	.49979	.49980	.49981	.49981	.49982	.49983	.49983
3.6	.49984	.49985	.49985	.49986	.49986	.49987	.49987	.49988	.49988	.49989
3.7	.49989	.49990	.49990	.49990	.49991	.49991	.49992	.49992	.49992	.49992
3.8	.49993	.49993	.49993	.49994	.49994	.49994	.49994	.49995	.49995	.49995
3.9	.49995	.49995	.49996	.49996	.49996	.49996	.49996	.49996	.49997	.49997

Source: Abridged from Table I of A. Hald, *Statistical Tables and Formulas* (New York: Wiley), 1952. Reproduced by permission of A. Hald.

TABLE V   Critical Values of *t*

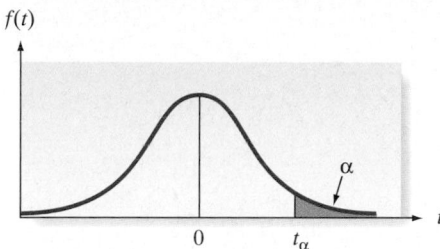

Degrees of Freedom	$t_{.100}$	$t_{.050}$	$t_{.025}$	$t_{.010}$	$t_{.005}$	$t_{.001}$	$t_{.0005}$
1	3.078	6.314	12.706	31.821	63.657	318.31	636.62
2	1.886	2.920	4.303	6.965	9.925	22.326	31.598
3	1.638	2.353	3.182	4.541	5.841	10.213	12.924
4	1.533	2.132	2.776	3.747	4.604	7.173	8.610
5	1.476	2.015	2.571	3.365	4.032	5.893	6.869
6	1.440	1.943	2.447	3.143	3.707	5.208	5.959
7	1.415	1.895	2.365	2.998	3.499	4.785	5.408
8	1.397	1.860	2.306	2.896	3.355	4.501	5.041
9	1.383	1.833	2.262	2.821	3.250	4.297	4.781
10	1.372	1.812	2.228	2.764	3.169	4.144	4.587
11	1.363	1.796	2.201	2.718	3.106	4.025	4.437
12	1.356	1.782	2.179	2.681	3.055	3.930	4.318
13	1.350	1.771	2.160	2.650	3.012	3.852	4.221
14	1.345	1.761	2.145	2.624	2.977	3.787	4.140
15	1.341	1.753	2.131	2.602	2.947	3.733	4.073
16	1.337	1.746	2.120	2.583	2.921	3.686	4.015
17	1.333	1.740	2.110	2.567	2.898	3.646	3.965
18	1.330	1.734	2.101	2.552	2.878	3.610	3.922
19	1.328	1.729	2.093	2.539	2.861	3.579	3.883
20	1.325	1.725	2.086	2.528	2.845	3.552	3.850
21	1.323	1.721	2.080	2.518	2.831	3.527	3.819
22	1.321	1.717	2.074	2.508	2.819	3.505	3.792
23	1.319	1.714	2.069	2.500	2.807	3.485	3.767
24	1.318	1.711	2.064	2.492	2.797	3.467	3.745
25	1.316	1.708	2.060	2.485	2.787	3.450	3.725
26	1.315	1.706	2.056	2.479	2.779	3.435	3.707
27	1.314	1.703	2.052	2.473	2.771	3.421	3.690
28	1.313	1.701	2.048	2.467	2.763	3.408	3.674
29	1.311	1.699	2.045	2.462	2.756	3.396	3.659
30	1.310	1.697	2.042	2.457	2.750	3.385	3.646
40	1.303	1.684	2.021	2.423	2.704	3.307	3.551
60	1.296	1.671	2.000	2.390	2.660	3.232	3.460
120	1.289	1.658	1.980	2.358	2.617	3.160	3.373
∞	1.282	1.645	1.960	2.326	2.576	3.090	3.291

TABLE VI   Critical Values of χ^2

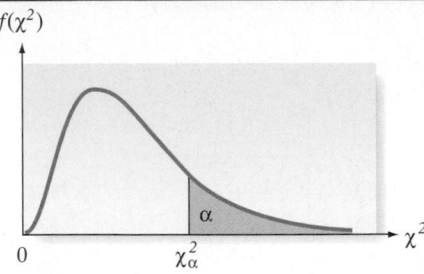

Degrees of Freedom	$\chi^2_{.995}$	$\chi^2_{.990}$	$\chi^2_{.975}$	$\chi^2_{.950}$	$\chi^2_{.900}$
1	.0000393	.0001571	.0009821	.0039321	.0157908
2	.0100251	.0201007	.0506356	.102587	.210720
3	.0717212	.114832	.215795	.351846	.584375
4	.206990	.297110	.484419	.710721	1.063623
5	.411740	.554300	.831211	1.145476	1.61031
6	.675727	.872085	1.237347	1.63539	2.20413
7	.989265	1.239043	1.68987	2.16735	2.83311
8	1.344419	1.646482	2.17973	2.73264	3.48954
9	1.734926	2.087912	2.70039	3.32511	4.16816
10	2.15585	2.55821	3.24697	3.94030	4.86518
11	2.60321	3.05347	3.81575	4.57481	5.57779
12	3.07382	3.57056	4.40379	5.22603	6.30380
13	3.56503	4.10691	5.00874	5.89186	7.04150
14	4.07468	4.66043	5.62872	6.57063	7.78953
15	4.60094	5.22935	6.26214	7.26094	8.54675
16	5.14224	5.81221	6.90766	7.96164	9.31223
17	5.69724	6.40776	7.56418	8.67176	10.0852
18	6.26481	7.01491	8.23075	9.39046	10.8649
19	6.84398	7.63273	8.90655	10.1170	11.6509
20	7.43386	8.26040	9.59083	10.8508	12.4426
21	8.03366	8.89720	10.28293	11.5913	13.2396
22	8.64272	9.54249	10.9823	12.3380	14.0415
23	9.26042	10.19567	11.6885	13.0905	14.8479
24	9.88623	10.8564	12.4011	13.8484	15.6587
25	10.5197	11.5240	13.1197	14.6114	16.4734
26	11.1603	12.1981	13.8439	15.3791	17.2919
27	11.8076	12.8786	14.5733	16.1513	18.1138
28	12.4613	13.5648	15.3079	16.9279	18.9392
29	13.1211	14.2565	16.0471	17.7083	19.7677
30	13.7867	14.9535	16.7908	18.4926	20.5992
40	20.7065	22.1643	24.4331	26.5093	29.0505
50	27.9907	29.7067	32.3574	34.7642	37.6886
60	35.5346	37.4848	40.4817	43.1879	46.4589
70	43.2752	45.4418	48.7576	51.7393	55.3290
80	51.1720	53.5400	57.1532	60.3915	64.2778
90	59.1963	61.7541	65.6466	69.1260	73.2912
100	67.3276	70.0648	74.2219	77.9295	82.3581

(continued)

TABLE VI (continued)

Degrees of Freedom	$\chi^2_{.100}$	$\chi^2_{.050}$	$\chi^2_{.025}$	$\chi^2_{.010}$	$\chi^2_{.005}$
1	2.70554	3.84146	5.02389	6.63490	7.87944
2	4.60517	5.99147	7.37776	9.21034	10.5966
3	6.25139	7.81473	9.34840	11.3449	12.8381
4	7.77944	9.48773	11.1433	13.2767	14.8602
5	9.23635	11.0705	12.8325	15.0863	16.7496
6	10.6446	12.5916	14.4494	16.8119	18.5476
7	12.0170	14.0671	16.0128	18.4753	20.2777
8	13.3616	15.5073	17.5346	20.0902	21.9550
9	14.6837	16.9190	19.0228	21.6660	23.5893
10	15.9871	18.3070	20.4831	23.2093	25.1882
11	17.2750	19.6751	21.9200	24.7250	26.7569
12	18.5494	21.0261	23.3367	26.2170	28.2995
13	19.8119	22.3621	24.7356	27.6883	29.8194
14	21.0642	23.6848	26.1190	29.1413	31.3193
15	22.3072	24.9958	27.4884	30.5779	32.8013
16	23.5418	26.2962	28.8454	31.9999	34.2672
17	24.7690	27.5871	30.1910	33.4087	35.7185
18	25.9894	28.8693	31.5264	34.8053	37.1564
19	27.2036	30.1435	32.8523	36.1908	38.5822
20	28.4120	31.4104	34.1696	37.5662	39.9968
21	29.6151	32.6705	35.4789	38.9321	41.4010
22	30.8133	33.9244	36.7807	40.2894	42.7956
23	32.0069	35.1725	38.0757	41.6384	44.1813
24	33.1963	36.4151	39.3641	42.9798	45.5585
25	34.3816	37.6525	40.6465	44.3141	46.9278
26	35.5631	38.8852	41.9232	45.6417	48.2899
27	36.7412	40.1133	43.1944	46.9630	49.6449
28	37.9159	41.3372	44.4607	48.2782	50.9933
29	39.0875	42.5569	45.7222	49.5879	52.3356
30	40.2560	43.7729	46.9792	50.8922	53.6720
40	51.8050	55.7585	59.3417	63.6907	66.7659
50	63.1671	67.5048	71.4202	76.1539	79.4900
60	74.3970	79.0819	83.2976	88.3794	91.9517
70	85.5271	90.5312	95.0231	100.425	104.215
80	96.5782	101.879	106.629	112.329	116.321
90	107.565	113.145	118.136	124.116	128.299
100	118.498	124.342	129.561	135.807	140.169

TABLE VII   Percentage Points of the *F*-distribution, $\alpha = .10$

ν_1		NUMERATOR DEGREES OF FREEDOM							
ν_2	**1**	**2**	**3**	**4**	**5**	**6**	**7**	**8**	**9**
1	39.86	49.50	53.59	55.83	57.24	58.20	58.91	59.44	59.86
2	8.53	9.00	9.16	9.24	9.29	9.33	9.35	9.37	9.38
3	5.54	5.46	5.39	5.34	5.31	5.28	5.27	5.25	5.24
4	4.54	4.32	4.19	4.11	4.05	4.01	3.98	3.95	3.94
5	4.06	3.78	3.62	3.52	3.45	3.40	3.37	3.34	3.32
6	3.78	3.46	3.29	3.18	3.11	3.05	3.01	2.98	2.96
7	3.59	3.26	3.07	2.96	2.88	2.83	2.78	2.75	2.72
8	3.46	3.11	2.92	2.81	2.73	2.67	2.62	2.59	2.56
9	3.36	3.01	2.81	2.69	2.61	2.55	2.51	2.47	2.44
10	3.29	2.92	2.73	2.61	2.52	2.46	2.41	2.38	2.35
11	3.23	2.86	2.66	2.54	2.45	2.39	2.34	2.30	2.27
12	3.18	2.81	2.61	2.48	2.39	2.33	2.28	2.24	2.21
13	3.14	2.76	2.56	2.43	2.35	2.28	2.23	2.20	2.16
14	3.10	2.73	2.52	2.39	2.31	2.24	2.19	2.15	2.12
15	3.07	2.70	2.49	2.36	2.27	2.21	2.16	2.12	2.09
16	3.05	2.67	2.46	2.33	2.24	2.18	2.13	2.09	2.06
17	3.03	2.64	2.44	2.31	2.22	2.15	2.10	2.06	2.03
18	3.01	2.62	2.42	2.29	2.20	2.13	2.08	2.04	2.00
19	2.99	2.61	2.40	2.27	2.18	2.11	2.06	2.02	1.98
20	2.97	2.59	2.38	2.25	2.16	2.09	2.04	2.00	1.96
21	2.96	2.57	2.36	2.23	2.14	2.08	2.02	1.98	1.95
22	2.95	2.56	2.35	2.22	2.13	2.06	2.01	1.97	1.93
23	2.94	2.55	2.34	2.21	2.11	2.05	1.99	1.95	1.92
24	2.93	2.54	2.33	2.19	2.10	2.04	1.98	1.94	1.91
25	2.92	2.53	2.32	2.18	2.09	2.02	1.97	1.93	1.89
26	2.91	2.52	2.31	2.17	2.08	2.01	1.96	1.92	1.88
27	2.90	2.51	2.30	2.17	2.07	2.00	1.95	1.91	1.87
28	2.89	2.50	2.29	2.16	2.06	2.00	1.94	1.90	1.87
29	2.89	2.50	2.28	2.15	2.06	1.99	1.93	1.89	1.86
30	2.88	2.49	2.28	2.14	2.05	1.98	1.93	1.88	1.85
40	2.84	2.44	2.23	2.09	2.00	1.93	1.87	1.83	1.79
60	2.79	2.39	2.18	2.04	1.95	1.87	1.82	1.77	1.74
120	2.75	2.35	2.13	1.99	1.90	1.82	1.77	1.72	1.68
∞	2.71	2.30	2.08	1.94	1.85	1.77	1.72	1.67	1.63

Source: From M. Merrington, and C. M. Thompson. "Tables of Percentage Points of the Inverted Beta (*F*)-Distribution." *Biometrika*, 1943, 33, 73–88. Reproduced by permission of the *Biometrika* Trustees.

(continued)

TABLE VII   (*continued*)

ν_2 \ ν_1	10	12	15	20	24	30	40	60	120	∞
	\multicolumn{10}{c}{**NUMERATOR DEGREES OF FREEDOM**}
1	60.19	60.71	61.22	61.74	62.00	62.26	62.53	62.79	63.06	63.33
2	9.39	9.41	9.42	9.44	9.45	9.46	9.47	9.47	9.48	9.49
3	5.23	5.22	5.20	5.18	5.18	5.17	5.16	5.15	5.14	5.13
4	3.92	3.90	3.87	3.84	3.83	3.82	3.80	3.79	3.78	3.76
5	3.30	3.27	3.24	3.21	3.19	3.17	3.16	3.14	3.12	3.10
6	2.94	2.90	2.87	2.84	2.82	2.80	2.78	2.76	2.74	2.72
7	2.70	2.67	2.63	2.59	2.58	2.56	2.54	2.51	2.49	2.47
8	2.54	2.50	2.46	2.42	2.40	2.38	2.36	2.34	2.32	2.29
9	2.42	2.38	2.34	2.30	2.28	2.25	2.23	2.21	2.18	2.16
10	2.32	2.28	2.24	2.20	2.18	2.16	2.13	2.11	2.08	2.06
11	2.25	2.21	2.17	2.12	2.10	2.08	2.05	2.03	2.00	1.97
12	2.19	2.15	2.10	2.06	2.04	2.01	1.99	1.96	1.93	1.90
13	2.14	2.10	2.05	2.01	1.98	1.96	1.93	1.90	1.88	1.85
14	2.10	2.05	2.01	1.96	1.94	1.91	1.89	1.86	1.83	1.80
15	2.06	2.02	1.97	1.92	1.90	1.87	1.85	1.82	1.79	1.76
16	2.03	1.99	1.94	1.89	1.87	1.84	1.81	1.78	1.75	1.72
17	2.00	1.96	1.91	1.86	1.84	1.81	1.78	1.75	1.72	1.69
18	1.98	1.93	1.89	1.84	1.81	1.78	1.75	1.72	1.69	1.66
19	1.96	1.91	1.86	1.81	1.79	1.76	1.73	1.70	1.67	1.63
20	1.94	1.89	1.84	1.79	1.77	1.74	1.71	1.68	1.64	1.61
21	1.92	1.87	1.83	1.78	1.75	1.72	1.69	1.66	1.62	1.59
22	1.90	1.86	1.81	1.76	1.73	1.70	1.67	1.64	1.60	1.57
23	1.89	1.84	1.80	1.74	1.72	1.69	1.66	1.62	1.59	1.55
24	1.88	1.83	1.78	1.73	1.70	1.67	1.64	1.61	1.57	1.53
25	1.87	1.82	1.77	1.72	1.69	1.66	1.63	1.59	1.56	1.52
26	1.86	1.81	1.76	1.71	1.68	1.65	1.61	1.58	1.54	1.50
27	1.85	1.80	1.75	1.70	1.67	1.64	1.60	1.57	1.53	1.49
28	1.84	1.79	1.74	1.69	1.66	1.63	1.59	1.56	1.52	1.48
29	1.83	1.78	1.73	1.68	1.65	1.62	1.58	1.55	1.51	1.47
30	1.82	1.77	1.72	1.67	1.64	1.61	1.57	1.54	1.50	1.46
40	1.76	1.71	1.66	1.61	1.57	1.54	1.51	1.47	1.42	1.38
60	1.71	1.66	1.60	1.54	1.51	1.48	1.44	1.40	1.35	1.29
120	1.65	1.60	1.55	1.48	1.45	1.41	1.37	1.32	1.26	1.19
∞	1.60	1.55	1.49	1.42	1.38	1.34	1.30	1.24	1.17	1.00

DENOMINATOR DEGREES OF FREEDOM

TABLE VIII   Percentage Points of the *F*-distribution, $\alpha = .05$

	ν_1	NUMERATOR DEGREES OF FREEDOM								
ν_2		1	2	3	4	5	6	7	8	9
1		161.4	199.5	215.7	224.6	230.2	234.0	236.8	238.9	240.5
2		18.51	19.00	19.16	19.25	19.30	19.33	19.35	19.37	19.38
3		10.13	9.55	9.28	9.12	9.01	8.94	8.89	8.85	8.81
4		7.71	6.94	6.59	6.39	6.26	6.16	6.09	6.04	6.00
5		6.61	5.79	5.41	5.19	5.05	4.95	4.88	4.82	4.77
6		5.99	5.14	4.76	4.53	4.39	4.28	4.21	4.15	4.10
7		5.59	4.74	4.35	4.12	3.97	3.87	3.79	3.73	3.68
8		5.32	4.46	4.07	3.84	3.69	3.58	3.50	3.44	3.39
9		5.12	4.26	3.86	3.63	3.48	3.37	3.29	3.23	3.18
10		4.96	4.10	3.71	3.48	3.33	3.22	3.14	3.07	3.02
11		4.84	3.98	3.59	3.36	3.20	3.09	3.01	2.95	2.90
12		4.75	3.89	3.49	3.26	3.11	3.00	2.91	2.85	2.80
13		4.67	3.81	3.41	3.18	3.03	2.92	2.83	2.77	2.71
14		4.60	3.74	3.34	3.11	2.96	2.85	2.76	2.70	2.65
15		4.54	3.68	3.29	3.06	2.90	2.79	2.71	2.64	2.59
16		4.49	3.63	3.24	3.01	2.85	2.74	2.66	2.59	2.54
17		4.45	3.59	3.20	2.96	2.81	2.70	2.61	2.55	2.49
18		4.41	3.55	3.16	2.93	2.77	2.66	2.58	2.51	2.46
19		4.38	3.52	3.13	2.90	2.74	2.63	2.54	2.48	2.42
20		4.35	3.49	3.10	2.87	2.71	2.60	2.51	2.45	2.39
21		4.32	3.47	3.07	2.84	2.68	2.57	2.49	2.42	2.37
22		4.30	3.44	3.05	2.82	2.66	2.55	2.46	2.40	2.34
23		4.28	3.42	3.03	2.80	2.64	2.53	2.44	2.37	2.32
24		4.26	3.40	3.01	2.78	2.62	2.51	2.42	2.36	2.30
25		4.24	3.39	2.99	2.76	2.60	2.49	2.40	2.34	2.28
26		4.23	3.37	2.98	2.74	2.59	2.47	2.39	2.32	2.77
27		4.21	3.35	2.96	2.73	2.57	2.46	2.37	2.31	2.25
28		4.20	3.34	2.95	2.71	2.56	2.45	2.36	2.29	2.24
29		4.18	3.33	2.93	2.70	2.55	2.43	2.35	2.28	2.22
30		4.17	3.32	2.92	2.69	2.53	2.42	2.33	2.27	2.21
40		4.08	3.23	2.84	2.61	2.45	2.34	2.25	2.18	2.12
60		4.00	3.15	2.76	2.53	2.37	2.25	2.17	2.10	2.04
120		3.92	3.07	2.68	2.45	2.29	2.17	2.09	2.02	1.96
∞		3.84	3.00	2.60	2.37	2.21	2.10	2.01	1.94	1.88

Source: From M. Merrington, and C. M. Thompson. "Tables of Percentage Points of the Inverted Beta (*F*)-Distribution." *Biometrika,* 1943, 33, 73–88. Reproduced by permission of the *Biometrika* Trustees.

(continued)

TABLE VIII   (*continued*)

ν_2 \ ν_1	NUMERATOR DEGREES OF FREEDOM									
	10	**12**	**15**	**20**	**24**	**30**	**40**	**60**	**120**	**∞**
1	241.9	243.9	245.9	248.0	249.1	250.1	251.1	252.2	253.3	254.3
2	19.40	19.41	19.43	19.45	19.45	19.46	19.47	19.48	19.49	19.50
3	8.79	8.74	8.70	8.66	8.64	8.62	8.59	8.57	8.55	8.53
4	5.96	5.91	5.86	5.80	5.77	5.75	5.72	5.69	5.66	5.63
5	4.74	4.68	4.62	4.56	4.53	4.50	4.46	4.43	4.40	4.36
6	4.06	4.00	3.94	3.87	3.84	3.81	3.77	3.74	3.70	3.67
7	3.64	3.57	3.51	3.44	3.41	3.38	3.34	3.30	3.27	3.23
8	3.35	3.28	3.22	3.15	3.12	3.08	3.04	3.01	2.97	2.93
9	3.14	3.07	3.01	2.94	2.90	2.86	2.83	2.79	2.75	2.71
10	2.98	2.91	2.85	2.77	2.74	2.70	2.66	2.62	2.58	2.54
11	2.85	2.79	2.72	2.65	2.61	2.57	2.53	2.49	2.45	2.40
12	2.75	2.69	2.62	2.54	2.51	2.47	2.43	2.38	2.34	2.30
13	2.67	2.60	2.53	2.46	2.42	2.38	2.34	2.30	2.25	2.21
14	2.60	2.53	2.46	2.39	2.35	2.31	2.27	2.22	2.18	2.13
15	2.54	2.48	2.40	2.33	2.29	2.25	2.20	2.16	2.11	2.07
16	2.49	2.42	2.35	2.28	2.24	2.19	2.15	2.11	2.06	2.01
17	2.45	2.38	2.31	2.23	2.19	2.15	2.10	2.06	2.01	1.96
18	2.41	2.34	2.27	2.19	2.15	2.11	2.06	2.02	1.97	1.92
19	2.38	2.31	2.23	2.16	2.11	2.07	2.03	1.98	1.93	1.88
20	2.35	2.28	2.20	2.12	2.08	2.04	1.99	1.95	1.90	1.84
21	2.32	2.25	2.18	2.10	2.05	2.01	1.96	1.92	1.87	1.81
22	2.30	2.23	2.15	2.07	2.03	1.98	1.94	1.89	1.84	1.78
23	2.27	2.20	2.13	2.05	2.01	1.96	1.91	1.86	1.81	1.76
24	2.25	2.18	2.11	2.03	1.98	1.94	1.89	1.84	1.79	1.73
25	2.24	2.16	2.09	2.01	1.96	1.92	1.87	1.82	1.77	1.71
26	2.22	2.15	2.07	1.99	1.95	1.90	1.85	1.80	1.75	1.69
27	2.20	2.13	2.06	1.97	1.93	1.88	1.84	1.79	1.73	1.67
28	2.19	2.12	2.04	1.96	1.91	1.87	1.82	1.77	1.71	1.65
29	2.18	2.10	2.03	1.94	1.90	1.85	1.81	1.75	1.70	1.64
30	2.16	2.09	2.01	1.93	1.89	1.84	1.79	1.74	1.68	1.62
40	2.08	2.00	1.92	1.84	1.79	1.74	1.69	1.64	1.58	1.51
60	1.99	1.92	1.84	1.75	1.70	1.65	1.59	1.53	1.47	1.39
120	1.91	1.83	1.75	1.66	1.61	1.55	1.50	1.43	1.35	1.25
∞	1.83	1.75	1.67	1.57	1.52	1.46	1.39	1.32	1.22	1.00

DENOMINATOR DEGREES OF FREEDOM

TABLE IX   Percentage Points of the *F*-distribution, $\alpha = .025$

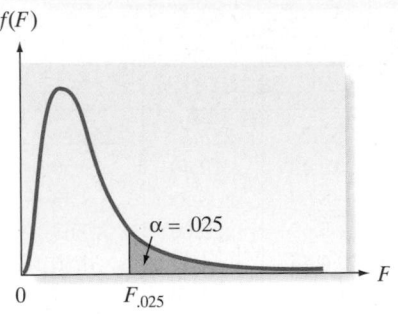

	ν_1	NUMERATOR DEGREES OF FREEDOM								
	ν_2	1	2	3	4	5	6	7	8	9
	1	647.8	799.5	864.2	899.6	921.8	937.1	948.2	956.7	963.3
	2	38.51	39.00	39.17	39.25	39.30	39.33	39.36	39.37	39.39
	3	17.44	16.04	15.44	15.10	14.88	14.73	14.62	14.54	14.47
	4	12.22	10.65	9.98	9.60	9.36	9.20	9.07	8.98	8.90
	5	10.01	8.43	7.76	7.39	7.15	6.98	6.85	6.76	6.68
	6	8.81	7.26	6.60	6.23	5.99	5.82	5.70	5.60	5.52
	7	8.07	6.54	5.89	5.52	5.29	5.12	4.99	4.90	4.82
	8	7.57	6.06	5.42	5.05	4.82	4.65	4.53	4.43	4.36
	9	7.21	5.71	5.08	4.72	4.48	4.32	4.20	4.10	4.03
DENOMINATOR DEGREES OF FREEDOM	10	6.94	5.46	4.83	4.47	4.24	4.07	3.95	3.85	3.78
	11	6.72	5.26	4.63	4.28	4.04	3.88	3.76	3.66	3.59
	12	6.55	5.10	4.47	4.12	3.89	3.73	3.61	3.51	3.44
	13	6.41	4.97	4.35	4.00	3.77	3.60	3.48	3.39	3.31
	14	6.30	4.86	4.24	3.89	3.66	3.50	3.38	3.29	3.21
	15	6.20	4.77	4.15	3.80	3.58	3.41	3.29	3.20	3.12
	16	6.12	4.69	4.08	3.73	3.50	3.34	3.22	3.12	3.05
	17	6.04	4.62	4.01	3.66	3.44	3.28	3.16	3.06	2.98
	18	5.98	4.56	3.95	3.61	3.38	3.22	3.10	3.01	2.93
	19	5.92	4.51	3.90	3.56	3.33	3.17	3.05	2.96	2.88
	20	5.87	4.46	3.86	3.51	3.29	3.13	3.01	2.91	2.84
	21	5.83	4.42	3.82	3.48	3.25	3.09	2.97	2.87	2.80
	22	5.79	4.38	3.78	3.44	3.22	3.05	2.93	2.84	2.76
	23	5.75	4.35	3.75	3.41	3.18	3.02	2.90	2.81	2.73
	24	5.72	4.32	3.72	3.38	3.15	2.99	2.87	2.78	2.70
	25	5.69	4.29	3.69	3.35	3.13	2.97	2.85	2.75	2.68
	26	5.66	4.27	3.67	3.33	3.10	2.94	2.82	2.73	2.65
	27	5.63	4.24	3.65	3.31	3.08	2.92	2.80	2.71	2.63
	28	5.61	4.22	3.63	3.29	3.06	2.90	2.78	2.69	2.61
	29	5.59	4.20	3.61	3.27	3.04	2.88	2.76	2.67	2.59
	30	5.57	4.18	3.59	3.25	3.03	2.87	2.75	2.65	2.57
	40	5.42	4.05	3.46	3.13	2.90	2.74	2.62	2.53	2.45
	60	5.29	3.93	3.34	3.01	2.79	2.63	2.51	2.41	2.33
	120	5.15	3.80	3.23	2.89	2.67	2.52	2.39	2.30	2.22
	∞	5.02	3.69	3.12	2.79	2.57	2.41	2.29	2.19	2.11

(continued)

TABLE IX   (continued)

ν_2 \ ν_1	NUMERATOR DEGREES OF FREEDOM									
	10	**12**	**15**	**20**	**24**	**30**	**40**	**60**	**120**	**∞**
1	968.6	976.7	984.9	993.1	997.2	1,001	1,006	1,010	1,014	1,018
2	39.40	39.41	39.43	39.45	39.46	39.46	39.47	39.48	39.49	39.50
3	14.42	14.34	14.25	14.17	14.12	14.08	14.04	13.99	13.95	13.90
4	8.84	8.75	8.66	8.56	8.51	8.46	8.41	8.36	8.31	8.26
5	6.62	6.52	6.43	6.33	6.28	6.23	6.18	6.12	6.07	6.02
6	5.46	5.37	5.27	5.17	5.12	5.07	5.01	4.96	4.90	4.85
7	4.76	4.67	4.57	4.47	4.42	4.36	4.31	4.25	4.20	4.14
8	4.30	4.20	4.10	4.00	3.95	3.89	3.84	3.78	3.73	3.67
9	3.96	3.87	3.77	3.67	3.61	3.56	3.51	3.45	3.39	3.33
10	3.72	3.62	3.52	3.42	3.37	3.31	3.26	3.20	3.14	3.08
11	3.53	3.43	3.33	3.23	3.17	3.12	3.06	3.00	2.94	2.88
12	3.37	3.28	3.18	3.07	3.02	2.96	2.91	2.85	2.79	2.72
13	3.25	3.15	3.05	2.95	2.89	2.84	2.78	2.72	2.66	2.60
14	3.15	3.05	2.95	2.84	2.79	2.73	2.67	2.61	2.55	2.49
15	3.06	2.96	2.86	2.76	2.70	2.64	2.59	2.52	2.46	2.40
16	2.99	2.89	2.79	2.68	2.63	2.57	2.51	2.45	2.38	2.32
17	2.92	2.82	2.72	2.62	2.56	2.50	2.44	2.38	2.32	2.25
18	2.87	2.77	2.67	2.56	2.50	2.44	2.38	2.32	2.26	2.19
19	2.82	2.72	2.62	2.51	2.45	2.39	2.33	2.27	2.20	2.13
20	2.77	2.68	2.57	2.46	2.41	2.35	2.29	2.22	2.16	2.09
21	2.73	2.64	2.53	2.42	2.37	2.31	2.25	2.18	2.11	2.04
22	2.70	2.60	2.50	2.39	2.33	2.27	2.21	2.14	2.08	2.00
23	2.67	2.57	2.47	2.36	2.30	2.24	2.18	2.11	2.04	1.97
24	2.64	2.54	2.44	2.33	2.27	2.21	2.15	2.08	2.01	1.94
25	2.61	2.51	2.41	2.30	2.24	2.18	2.12	2.05	1.98	1.91
26	2.59	2.49	2.39	2.28	2.22	2.16	2.09	2.03	1.95	1.88
27	2.57	2.47	2.36	2.25	2.19	2.13	2.07	2.00	1.93	1.85
28	2.55	2.45	2.34	2.23	2.17	2.11	2.05	1.98	1.91	1.83
29	2.53	2.43	2.32	2.21	2.15	2.09	2.03	1.96	1.89	1.81
30	2.51	2.41	2.31	2.20	2.14	2.07	2.01	1.94	1.87	1.79
40	2.39	2.29	2.18	2.07	2.01	1.94	1.88	1.80	1.72	1.64
60	2.27	2.17	2.06	1.94	1.88	1.82	1.74	1.67	1.58	1.48
120	2.16	2.05	1.94	1.82	1.76	1.69	1.61	1.53	1.43	1.31
∞	2.05	1.94	1.83	1.71	1.64	1.57	1.48	1.39	1.27	1.00

DENOMINATOR DEGREES OF FREEDOM

TABLE X   Percentage Points of the *F*-distribution, $\alpha = .01$

	NUMERATOR DEGREES OF FREEDOM								
ν_1 / ν_2	1	2	3	4	5	6	7	8	9
1	4,052	4,999.5	5,403	5,625	5,764	5,859	5,928	5,982	6,022
2	98.50	99.00	99.17	99.25	99.30	99.33	99.36	99.37	99.39
3	34.12	30.82	29.46	28.71	28.24	27.91	27.67	27.49	27.35
4	21.20	18.00	16.69	15.98	15.52	15.21	14.98	14.80	14.66
5	16.26	13.27	12.06	11.39	10.97	10.67	10.46	10.29	10.16
6	13.75	10.92	9.78	9.15	8.75	8.47	8.26	8.10	7.98
7	12.25	9.55	8.45	7.85	7.46	7.19	6.99	6.84	6.72
8	11.26	8.65	7.59	7.01	6.63	6.37	6.18	6.03	5.91
9	10.56	8.02	6.99	6.42	6.06	5.80	5.61	5.47	5.35
10	10.04	7.56	6.55	5.99	5.64	5.39	5.20	5.06	4.94
11	9.65	7.21	6.22	5.67	5.32	5.07	4.89	4.74	4.63
12	9.33	6.93	5.95	5.41	5.06	4.82	4.64	4.50	4.39
13	9.07	6.70	5.74	5.21	4.86	4.62	4.44	4.30	4.19
14	8.86	6.51	5.56	5.04	4.69	4.46	4.28	4.14	4.03
15	8.68	6.36	5.42	4.89	4.56	4.32	4.14	4.00	3.89
16	8.53	6.23	5.29	4.77	4.44	4.20	4.03	3.89	3.78
17	8.40	6.11	5.18	4.67	4.34	4.10	3.93	3.79	3.68
18	8.29	6.01	5.09	4.58	4.25	4.01	3.84	3.71	3.60
19	8.18	5.93	5.01	4.50	4.17	3.94	3.77	3.63	3.52
20	8.10	5.85	4.94	4.43	4.10	3.87	3.70	3.56	3.46
21	8.02	5.78	4.87	4.37	4.04	3.81	3.64	3.51	3.40
22	7.95	5.72	4.82	4.31	3.99	3.76	3.59	3.45	3.35
23	7.88	5.66	4.76	4.26	3.94	3.71	3.54	3.41	3.30
24	7.82	5.61	4.72	4.22	3.90	3.67	3.50	3.36	3.26
25	7.77	5.57	4.68	4.18	3.85	3.63	3.46	3.32	3.22
26	7.72	5.53	4.64	4.14	3.82	3.59	3.42	3.29	3.18
27	7.68	5.49	4.60	4.11	3.78	3.56	3.39	3.26	3.15
28	7.64	5.45	4.57	4.07	3.75	3.53	3.36	3.23	3.12
29	7.60	5.42	4.54	4.04	3.73	3.50	3.33	3.20	3.09
30	7.56	5.39	4.51	4.02	3.70	3.47	3.30	3.17	3.07
40	7.31	5.18	4.31	3.83	3.51	3.29	3.12	2.99	2.89
60	7.08	4.98	4.13	3.65	3.34	3.12	2.95	2.82	2.72
120	6.85	4.79	3.95	3.48	3.17	2.96	2.79	2.66	2.56
∞	6.63	4.61	3.78	3.32	3.02	2.80	2.64	2.51	2.41

(DENOMINATOR DEGREES OF FREEDOM)

(continued)

TABLE X   (continued)

ν_2 \ ν_1	10	12	15	20	24	30	40	60	120	∞
1	6,056	6,106	6,157	6,209	6,235	6,261	6,287	6,313	6,339	6,366
2	99.40	99.42	99.43	99.45	99.46	99.47	99.47	99.48	99.49	99.50
3	27.23	27.05	26.87	26.69	26.60	26.50	26.41	26.32	26.22	26.13
4	14.55	14.37	14.20	14.02	13.93	13.84	13.75	13.65	13.56	13.46
5	10.05	9.89	9.72	9.55	9.47	9.38	9.29	9.20	9.11	9.02
6	7.87	7.72	7.56	7.40	7.31	7.23	7.14	7.06	6.97	6.88
7	6.62	6.47	6.31	6.16	6.07	5.99	5.91	5.82	5.74	5.65
8	5.81	5.67	5.52	5.36	5.28	5.20	5.12	5.03	4.95	4.86
9	5.26	5.11	4.96	4.81	4.73	4.65	4.57	4.48	4.40	4.31
10	4.85	4.71	4.56	4.41	4.33	4.25	4.17	4.08	4.00	3.91
11	4.54	4.40	4.25	4.10	4.02	3.94	3.86	3.78	3.69	3.60
12	4.30	4.16	4.01	3.86	3.78	3.70	3.62	3.54	3.45	3.36
13	4.10	3.96	3.82	3.66	3.59	3.51	3.43	3.34	3.25	3.17
14	3.94	3.80	3.66	3.51	3.43	3.35	3.27	3.18	3.09	3.00
15	3.80	3.67	3.52	3.37	3.29	3.21	3.13	3.05	2.96	2.87
16	3.69	3.55	3.41	3.26	3.18	3.10	3.02	2.93	2.84	2.75
17	3.59	3.46	3.31	3.16	3.08	3.00	2.92	2.83	2.75	2.65
18	3.51	3.37	3.23	3.08	3.00	2.92	2.84	2.75	2.66	2.57
19	3.43	3.30	3.15	3.00	2.92	2.84	2.76	2.67	2.58	2.49
20	3.37	3.23	3.09	2.94	2.86	2.78	2.69	2.61	2.52	2.42
21	3.31	3.17	3.03	2.88	2.80	2.72	2.64	2.55	2.46	2.36
22	3.26	3.12	2.98	2.83	2.75	2.67	2.58	2.50	2.40	2.31
23	3.21	3.07	2.93	2.78	2.70	2.62	2.54	2.45	2.35	2.26
24	3.17	3.03	2.89	2.74	2.66	2.58	2.49	2.40	2.31	2.21
25	3.13	2.99	2.85	2.70	2.62	2.54	2.45	2.36	2.27	2.17
26	3.09	2.96	2.81	2.66	2.58	2.50	2.42	2.33	2.23	2.13
27	3.06	2.93	2.78	2.63	2.55	2.47	2.38	2.29	2.20	2.10
28	3.03	2.90	2.75	2.60	2.52	2.44	2.35	2.26	2.17	2.06
29	3.00	2.87	2.73	2.57	2.49	2.41	2.33	2.23	2.14	2.03
30	2.98	2.84	2.70	2.55	2.47	2.39	2.30	2.21	2.11	2.01
40	2.80	2.66	2.52	2.37	2.29	2.20	2.11	2.02	1.92	1.80
60	2.63	2.50	2.35	2.20	2.12	2.03	1.94	1.84	1.73	1.60
120	2.47	2.34	2.19	2.03	1.95	1.86	1.76	1.66	1.53	1.38
∞	2.32	2.18	2.04	1.88	1.79	1.70	1.59	1.47	1.32	1.00

NUMERATOR DEGREES OF FREEDOM (column headers); DENOMINATOR DEGREES OF FREEDOM (ν_2, rows)

TABLE XI   Control Chart Constants

Number of Observations in Subgroup, n	A_2	d_2	d_3	D_3	D_4
2	1.880	1.128	.853	.000	3.267
3	1.023	1.693	.888	.000	2.574
4	.729	2.059	.880	.000	2.282
5	.577	2.326	.864	.000	2.114
6	.483	2.534	.848	.000	2.004
7	.419	2.704	.833	.076	1.924
8	.373	2.847	.820	.136	1.864
9	.337	2.970	.808	.184	1.816
10	.308	3.078	.797	.223	1.777
11	.285	3.173	.787	.256	1.744
12	.266	3.258	.778	.283	1.717
13	.249	3.336	.770	.307	1.693
14	.235	3.407	.762	.328	1.672
15	.223	3.472	.755	.347	1.653
16	.212	3.532	.749	.363	1.637
17	.203	3.588	.743	.378	1.622
18	.194	3.640	.738	.391	1.608
19	.187	3.689	.733	.403	1.597
20	.180	3.735	.729	.415	1.585
21	.173	3.778	.724	.425	1.575
22	.167	3.819	.720	.434	1.566
23	.162	3.858	.716	.443	1.557
24	.157	3.895	.712	.451	1.548
25	.153	3.931	.709	.459	1.541

Source: ASTM Manual on the Presentation of Data and Control Chart Analysis, Philadelphia, PA: American Society for Testing Materials, pp. 134–136, 1976.

TABLE XII   Critical Values for the Durbin-Watson d Statistic, $\alpha = .05$

	$k = 1$		$k = 2$		$k = 3$		$k = 4$		$k = 5$	
n	d_L	d_U	d_L	d_U	d_L	d_U	d_L	d_U	d_L	d_U
15	1.08	1.36	.95	1.54	.82	1.75	.69	1.97	.56	2.21
16	1.10	1.37	.98	1.54	.86	1.73	.74	1.93	.62	2.15
17	1.13	1.38	1.02	1.54	.90	1.71	.78	1.90	.67	2.10
18	1.16	1.39	1.05	1.53	.93	1.69	.92	1.87	.71	2.06
19	1.18	1.40	1.08	1.53	.97	1.68	.86	1.85	.75	2.02
20	1.20	1.41	1.10	1.54	1.00	1.68	.90	1.83	.79	1.99
21	1.22	1.42	1.13	1.54	1.03	1.67	.93	1.81	.83	1.96
22	1.24	1.43	1.15	1.54	1.05	1.66	.96	1.80	.96	1.94
23	1.26	1.44	1.17	1.54	1.08	1.66	.99	1.79	.90	1.92
24	1.27	1.45	1.19	1.55	1.10	1.66	1.01	1.78	.93	1.90
25	1.29	1.45	1.21	1.55	1.12	1.66	1.04	1.77	.95	1.89
26	1.30	1.46	1.22	1.55	1.14	1.65	1.06	1.76	.98	1.88
27	1.32	1.47	1.24	1.56	1.16	1.65	1.08	1.76	1.01	1.86
28	1.33	1.48	1.26	1.56	1.18	1.65	1.10	1.75	1.03	1.85
29	1.34	1.48	1.27	1.56	1.20	1.65	1.12	1.74	1.05	1.84
30	1.35	1.49	1.28	1.57	1.21	1.65	1.14	1.74	1.07	1.83
31	1.36	1.50	1.30	1.57	1.23	1.65	1.16	1.74	1.09	1.83
32	1.37	1.50	1.31	1.57	1.24	1.65	1.18	1.73	1.11	1.82
33	1.38	1.51	1.32	1.58	1.26	1.65	1.19	1.73	1.13	1.81
34	1.39	1.51	1.33	1.58	1.27	1.65	1.21	1.73	1.15	1.81
35	1.40	1.52	1.34	1.58	1.28	1.65	1.22	1.73	1.16	1.80
36	1.41	1.52	1.35	1.59	1.29	1.65	1.24	1.73	1.18	1.80
37	1.42	1.53	1.36	1.59	1.31	1.66	1.25	1.72	1.19	1.80
38	1.43	1.54	1.37	1.59	1.32	1.66	1.26	1.72	1.21	1.79
39	1.43	1.54	1.38	1.60	1.33	1.66	1.27	1.72	1.22	1.79
40	1.44	1.54	1.39	1.60	1.34	1.66	1.29	1.72	1.23	1.79
45	1.48	1.57	1.43	1.62	1.38	1.67	1.34	1.72	1.29	1.78
50	1.50	1.59	1.46	1.63	1.42	1.67	1.38	1.72	1.34	1.77
55	1.53	1.60	1.49	1.64	1.45	1.68	1.41	1.72	1.38	1.77
60	1.55	1.62	1.51	1.65	1.48	1.69	1.44	1.73	1.41	1.77
65	1.57	1.63	1.54	1.66	1.50	1.70	1.47	1.73	1.44	1.77
70	1.58	1.64	1.55	1.67	1.52	1.70	1.49	1.74	1.46	1.77
75	1.60	1.65	1.57	1.68	1.54	1.71	1.51	1.74	1.49	1.77
80	1.61	1.66	1.59	1.69	1.56	1.72	1.53	1.74	1.51	1.77
85	1.62	1.67	1.60	1.70	1.57	1.72	1.55	1.75	1.52	1.77
90	1.63	1.68	1.61	1.70	1.59	1.73	1.57	1.75	1.54	1.78
95	1.64	1.69	1.62	1.71	1.60	1.73	1.58	1.75	1.56	1.78
100	1.65	1.69	1.63	1.72	1.61	1.74	1.59	1.76	1.57	1.78

Source: From J. Durbin, and G. S. Watson. "Testing for Serial Correlation in Least Squares Regression, II." *Biometrika,* 1951, 30, 159–178. Reproduced by permission of the *Biometrika* Trustees.

TABLE XIII   Critical Values for the Durbin-Watson d Statistic, $\alpha = .01$

	k = 1		k = 2		k = 3		k = 4		k = 5	
n	d_L	d_U	d_L	d_U	d_L	d_U	d_L	d_U	d_L	d_U
15	.81	1.07	.70	1.25	.59	1.46	.49	1.70	.39	1.96
16	.84	1.09	.74	1.25	.63	1.44	.53	1.66	.44	1.90
17	.87	1.10	.77	1.25	.67	1.43	.57	1.3	.48	1.85
18	.90	1.12	.80	1.26	.71	1.42	.61	1.60	.52	1.80
19	.93	1.13	.83	1.26	.74	1.41	.65	1.58	.56	1.77
20	.95	1.15	.86	1.27	.77	1.41	.68	1.57	.60	1.74
21	.97	1.16	.89	1.27	.80	1.41	.72	1.55	.63	1.71
22	1.00	1.17	.91	1.28	.83	1.40	.75	1.54	.66	1.69
23	1.02	1.19	.94	1.29	.86	1.40	.77	1.53	.70	1.67
24	1.04	1.20	.96	1.30	.88	1.41	.80	1.53	.72	1.66
25	1.05	1.21	.98	1.30	.90	1.41	.83	1.52	.75	1.65
26	1.07	1.22	1.00	1.31	.93	1.41	.85	1.52	.78	1.64
27	1.09	1.23	1.02	1.32	.95	1.41	.88	1.51	.81	1.63
28	1.10	1.24	1.04	1.32	.97	1.41	.90	1.51	.83	1.62
29	1.12	1.25	1.05	1.33	.99	1.42	.92	1.51	.85	1.61
30	1.13	1.26	1.07	1.34	1.01	1.42	.94	1.51	.88	1.61
31	1.15	1.27	1.08	1.34	1.02	1.42	.96	1.51	.90	1.60
32	1.16	1.28	1.10	1.35	1.04	1.43	.98	1.51	.92	1.60
33	1.17	1.29	1.11	1.36	1.05	1.43	1.00	1.51	.94	1.59
34	1.18	1.30	1.13	1.36	1.07	1.43	1.01	1.51	.95	1.59
35	1.19	1.31	1.14	1.27	1.08	1.44	1.03	1.51	.97	1.59
36	1.21	1.32	1.15	1.38	1.10	1.44	1.04	1.51	.99	1.59
37	1.22	1.32	1.16	1.38	1.11	1.45	1.06	1.51	1.00	1.59
38	1.23	1.33	1.18	1.39	1.12	1.45	1.07	1.52	1.02	1.58
39	1.24	1.34	1.19	1.39	1.14	1.45	1.09	1.52	1.03	1.58
40	1.25	1.34	1.20	1.40	1.15	1.46	1.10	1.52	1.05	1.58
45	1.29	1.38	1.24	1.42	1.20	1.48	1.16	1.53	1.11	1.58
50	1.32	1.40	1.28	1.45	1.24	1.49	1.20	1.54	1.16	1.59
55	1.36	1.43	1.32	1.47	1.28	1.51	1.25	1.55	1.21	1.59
60	1.38	1.45	1.35	1.48	1.32	1.52	1.28	1.56	1.25	1.60
65	1.41	1.47	1.38	1.50	1.35	1.53	1.31	1.57	1.28	1.61
70	1.43	1.49	1.40	1.52	1.37	1.55	1.34	1.58	1.31	1.61
75	1.45	1.50	1.42	1.53	1.39	1.56	1.37	1.59	1.34	1.62
80	1.47	1.52	1.44	1.54	1.42	1.57	1.39	1.60	1.36	1.62
85	1.48	1.53	1.46	1.55	1.43	1.58	1.41	1.60	1.39	1.63
90	1.50	1.54	1.47	1.56	1.45	1.59	1.43	1.61	1.41	1.64
95	1.51	1.55	1.49	1.57	1.47	1.60	1.45	1.62	1.42	1.64
100	1.52	1.56	1.50	1.58	1.48	1.60	1.46	1.63	1.44	1.65

Source: From J. Durbin, and G. S. Watson. "Testing for Serial Correlation in Least Squares Regression, II." *Biometrika,* 1951, 30, 159–178. Reproduced by permission of the *Biometrika* Trustees.

TABLE XIV   Critical Values of T_L and T_U for the Wilcoxon Rank Sum Test: Independent Samples

Test statistic is the rank sum associated with the smaller sample (if equal sample sizes, either rank sum can be used).

a. $\alpha = .025$ one-tailed; $\alpha = .05$ two-tailed

n_2 \ n_1	3		4		5		6		7		8		9		10	
	T_L	T_U	T_L	T_U	T_L	T_U	T_L	T_U	T_L	T_U	T_L	T_U	T_L	T_U	T_L	T_U
3	5	16	6	18	6	21	7	23	7	26	8	28	8	31	9	33
4	6	18	11	25	12	28	12	32	13	35	14	38	15	41	16	44
5	6	21	12	28	18	37	19	41	20	45	21	49	22	53	24	56
6	7	23	12	32	19	41	26	52	28	56	29	61	31	65	32	70
7	7	26	13	35	20	45	28	56	37	68	39	73	41	78	43	83
8	8	28	14	38	21	49	29	61	39	73	49	87	51	93	54	98
9	8	31	15	41	22	53	31	65	41	78	51	93	63	108	66	114
10	9	33	16	44	24	56	32	70	43	83	54	98	66	114	79	131

b. $\alpha = .05$ one-tailed; $\alpha = .10$ two-tailed

n_2 \ n_1	3		4		5		6		7		8		9		10	
	T_L	T_U	T_L	T_U	T_L	T_U	T_L	T_U	T_L	T_U	T_L	T_U	T_L	T_U	T_L	T_U
3	6	15	7	17	7	20	8	22	9	24	9	27	10	29	11	31
4	7	17	12	24	13	27	14	30	15	33	16	36	17	39	18	42
5	7	20	13	27	19	36	20	40	22	43	24	46	25	50	26	54
6	8	22	14	30	20	40	28	50	30	54	32	58	33	63	35	67
7	9	24	15	33	22	43	30	54	39	66	41	71	43	76	46	80
8	9	27	16	36	24	46	32	58	41	71	52	84	54	90	57	95
9	10	29	17	39	25	50	33	63	43	76	54	90	66	105	69	111
10	11	31	18	42	26	54	35	67	46	80	57	95	69	111	83	127

Source: From F. Wilcoxon, and R. A. Wilcox. "Some Rapid Approximate Statistical Procedures," 1964, 20–23. Courtesy of Lederle Laboratories Division of American Cyanamid Company, Madison, NJ.

TABLE XV   Critical Values of T_0 in the Wilcoxon Paired Difference Signed Rank Test

One-Tailed	Two-Tailed	$n = 5$	$n = 6$	$n = 7$	$n = 8$	$n = 9$	$n = 10$
$\alpha = .05$	$\alpha = .10$	1	2	4	6	8	11
$\alpha = .025$	$\alpha = .05$		1	2	4	6	8
$\alpha = .01$	$\alpha = .02$			0	2	3	5
$\alpha = .005$	$\alpha = .01$				0	2	3
		$n = 11$	$n = 12$	$n = 13$	$n = 14$	$n = 15$	$n = 16$
$\alpha = .05$	$\alpha = .10$	14	17	21	26	30	36
$\alpha = .025$	$\alpha = .05$	11	14	17	21	25	30
$\alpha = .01$	$\alpha = .02$	7	10	13	16	20	24
$\alpha = .005$	$\alpha = .01$	5	7	10	13	16	19
		$n = 17$	$n = 18$	$n = 19$	$n = 20$	$n = 21$	$n = 22$
$\alpha = .05$	$\alpha = .10$	41	47	54	60	68	75
$\alpha = .025$	$\alpha = .05$	35	40	46	52	59	66
$\alpha = .01$	$\alpha = .02$	28	33	38	43	49	56
$\alpha = .005$	$\alpha = .01$	23	28	32	37	43	49
		$n = 23$	$n = 24$	$n = 25$	$n = 26$	$n = 27$	$n = 28$
$\alpha = .05$	$\alpha = .10$	83	92	101	110	120	130
$\alpha = .025$	$\alpha = .05$	73	81	90	98	107	117
$\alpha = .01$	$\alpha = .02$	62	69	77	85	93	102
$\alpha = .005$	$\alpha = .01$	55	61	68	76	84	92
		$n = 29$	$n = 30$	$n = 31$	$n = 32$	$n = 33$	$n = 34$
$\alpha = .05$	$\alpha = .10$	141	152	163	175	188	201
$\alpha = .025$	$\alpha = .05$	127	137	148	159	171	183
$\alpha = .01$	$\alpha = .02$	111	120	130	141	151	162
$\alpha = .005$	$\alpha = .01$	100	109	118	128	138	149
		$n = 35$	$n = 36$	$n = 37$	$n = 38$	$n = 39$	
$\alpha = .05$	$\alpha = .10$	214	228	242	256	271	
$\alpha = .025$	$\alpha = .05$	195	208	222	235	250	
$\alpha = .01$	$\alpha = .02$	174	186	198	211	224	
$\alpha = .005$	$\alpha = .01$	160	171	183	195	208	
		$n = 40$	$n = 41$	$n = 42$	$n = 43$	$n = 44$	$n = 45$
$\alpha = .05$	$\alpha = .10$	287	303	319	336	353	371
$\alpha = .025$	$\alpha = .05$	264	279	295	311	327	344
$\alpha = .01$	$\alpha = .02$	238	252	267	281	297	313
$\alpha = .005$	$\alpha = .01$	221	234	248	262	277	292
		$n = 46$	$n = 47$	$n = 48$	$n = 49$	$n = 50$	
$\alpha = .05$	$\alpha = .10$	389	408	427	446	466	
$\alpha = .025$	$\alpha = .05$	361	379	397	415	434	
$\alpha = .01$	$\alpha = .02$	329	345	362	380	398	
$\alpha = .005$	$\alpha = .01$	307	323	339	356	373	

Source: From F. Wilcoxon, and R. A. Wilcox. "Some Rapid Approximate Statistical Procedures," 1964, p. 28. Courtesy of Lederle Laboratories Division of American Cyanamid Company, Madison, NJ.

TABLE XVI   Critical Values of Spearman's Rank Correlation Coefficient

The values correspond to a one-tailed test of $H_0: \rho = 0$. The value should be doubled for two-tailed tests.

n	$\alpha = .05$	$\alpha = .025$	$\alpha = .01$	$\alpha = .005$	n	$\alpha = .05$	$\alpha = .025$	$\alpha = .01$	$\alpha = .005$
5	.900	—	—	—	18	.399	.476	.564	.625
6	.829	.886	.943	—	19	.388	.462	.549	.608
7	.714	.786	.893	—	20	.377	.450	.534	.591
8	.643	.738	.833	.881	21	.368	.438	.521	.576
9	.600	.683	.783	.833	22	.359	.428	.508	.562
10	.564	.648	.745	.794	23	.351	.418	.496	.549
11	.523	.623	.736	.818	24	.343	.409	.485	.537
12	.497	.591	.703	.780	25	.336	.400	.475	.526
13	.475	.566	.673	.745	26	.329	.392	.465	.515
14	.457	.545	.646	.716	27	.323	.385	.456	.505
15	.441	.525	.623	.689	28	.317	.377	.448	.496
16	.425	.507	.601	.666	29	.311	.370	.440	.487
17	.412	.490	.582	.645	30	.305	.364	.432	.478

Source: From E. G. Olds. "Distribution of Sums of Squares of Rank Differences for Small Samples," *Annals of Mathematical Statistics,* 1938, 9. Reproduced with the permission of the Editor, *Annals of Mathematical Statistics.*

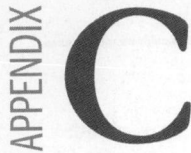

Calculation Formulas for Analysis of Variance

C.1 Formulas for the Calculations in the Completely Randomized Design

C.2 Formulas for the Calculations in the Randomized Block Design

C.3 Formulas for the Calculations for a Two-Factor Factorial Experiment

C.1 FORMULAS FOR THE CALCULATIONS IN THE COMPLETELY RANDOMIZED DESIGN

$$CM = \text{Correction for mean}$$

$$= \frac{(\text{Total of all observations})^2}{\text{Total number of observations}} = \frac{\left(\sum\limits_{i=1}^{n} y_i\right)^2}{n}$$

$$SS(\text{Total}) = \text{Total sum of squares}$$

$$= (\text{Sum of squares of all observations}) - CM = \sum_{i=1}^{n} y_i^2 - CM$$

$$SST = \text{Sum of squares for treatments}$$

$$= \left(\begin{array}{c}\text{Sum of squares of treatment totals with}\\ \text{each square divided by the number of}\\ \text{observations for that treatment}\end{array}\right) - CM$$

$$= \frac{T_1^2}{n_1} + \frac{T_2^2}{n_2} + \cdots + \frac{T_k^2}{n_k} - CM$$

$$SSE = \text{Sum of squares for error} = SS(\text{Total}) - SST$$

$$MST = \text{Mean square for treatments} = \frac{SST}{k-1}$$

$$MSE = \text{Mean square for error} = \frac{SSE}{n-k}$$

$$F = \text{Test statistic} = \frac{MST}{MSE}$$

where

$$n = \text{Total number of observations}$$

$$k = \text{Number of treatments}$$

$$T_i = \text{Total for treatment } i \ (i = 1, 2, \dots, k)$$

APPENDIX C

C.2   FORMULAS FOR THE CALCULATIONS IN
THE RANDOMIZED BLOCK DESIGN

CM = Correction for mean

$$= \frac{(\text{Total of all observations})^2}{\text{Total number of observations}} = \frac{\left(\sum y_i\right)^2}{n}$$

SS(Total) = Total sum of squares

$$= (\text{Sum of squares of all observations}) - \text{CM} = \sum y_i^2 - \text{CM}$$

SST = Sum of squares for treatments

$$= \left(\begin{array}{c}\text{Sum of squares of treatment totals with}\\ \text{each square divided by } b, \text{ the number of}\\ \text{observations for that treatment}\end{array}\right) - \text{CM}$$

$$= \frac{T_1^2}{b} + \frac{T_2^2}{b} + \cdots + \frac{T_p^2}{b} - \text{CM}$$

SST = Sum of squares for blocks

$$= \left(\begin{array}{c}\text{Sum of squares of block totals with}\\ \text{each square divided by } k, \text{ the number}\\ \text{of observations in that block}\end{array}\right) - \text{CM}$$

$$= \frac{B_1^2}{k} + \frac{B_2^2}{k} + \cdots + \frac{B_b^2}{k} - \text{CM}$$

SSE = Sum of squares for error = SS(Total) − SST − SSB

$$\text{MST} = \text{Mean square for treatments} = \frac{\text{SST}}{k-1}$$

$$\text{MSB} = \text{Mean square for blocks} = \frac{\text{SSB}}{b-1}$$

$$\text{MSE} = \text{Mean square for error} = \frac{\text{SSE}}{n-k-b+1}$$

$$F = \text{Test statistic} = \frac{\text{MST}}{\text{MSE}}$$

where

n = Total number of observations

b = Number of blocks

k = Number of treatments

T_i = Total for treatment i $(i = 1, 2, \ldots, k)$

B_l = Total for block i $(i = 1, 2, \ldots, b)$

C.3

FORMULAS FOR THE CALCULATIONS FOR A TWO-FACTOR FACTORIAL EXPERIMENT

$$CM = \text{Correction for mean}$$

$$= \frac{(\text{Total of all } n \text{ measurements})^2}{n} = \frac{\left(\sum_{i=1}^{n} y_i\right)^2}{n}$$

$$SS(\text{Total}) = \text{Total sum of squares}$$

$$= (\text{Sum of squares of all } n \text{ measurements}) - CM = \sum_{i=1}^{n} y_i^2 - CM$$

$$SS(A) = \text{Sum of squares for main effects, factor } A$$

$$= \left(\begin{array}{c} \text{Sum of squares of the totals } A_1, A_2, \ldots, A_a \\ \text{divided by the number of measurements} \\ \text{in a single total, namely } br \end{array} \right) - CM$$

$$= \frac{\sum_{i=1}^{a} A_i^2}{br} - CM$$

$$SS(B) = \text{Sum of squares for main effects, factor } B$$

$$= \left(\begin{array}{c} \text{Sum of squares of the totals } B_1, B_2, \ldots, B_b \\ \text{divided by the number of measurements} \\ \text{in a single total, namely } ar \end{array} \right) - CM$$

$$= \frac{\sum_{i=1}^{b} B_i^2}{ar} - CM$$

$$SS(AB) = \text{Sum of squares for } AB \text{ interaction}$$

$$= \left(\begin{array}{c} \text{Sum of squares of the cell totals} \\ AB_{11}, AB_{12}, \ldots, AB_{ab} \text{ divided by} \\ \text{the number of measurements} \\ \text{in a single total, namely } r \end{array} \right) - SS(A) - SS(B) - CM$$

$$= \frac{\sum_{j=1}^{b} \sum_{i=1}^{a} AB_{ij}^2}{r} - SS(A) - SS(B) - CM$$

where

$a = $ Number of level of factor A

$b = $ Number of levels of factor B

$r = $ Number of replicates (observations per treatment)

$A_i = $ Total for level i of factor A $(i = 1, 2, \ldots, a)$

$B_j = $ Total for level j of factor B $(j = 1, 2, \ldots, b)$

$AB_{ij} = $ Total for treatment (i, j), i.e., for ith level of factor A and jth level of factor B

Answers to Selected Exercises

Chapter 1

1.3 population; variables; summary tools; conclusions **1.5** published source; designed experiment; survey; observationally
1.13 qualitative; qualitative **1.15 a.** all U.S. citizens **b.** president's job performance; qualitative **c.** 2000 polled individuals **d.** estimate the proportion of all citizens who believe the president is doing a good job. **e.** survey **f.** not very likely **1.17** I. qualitative II. quantitative III. qualitative IV. qualitative V. qualitative VI. quantitative **1.19 a.** sample, if interested in CEOs of all U.S. companies; population, if interested in only the 500 CEOs in the 2005 scoreboard **b.** (1) qualitative; (2) quantitative; (3) quantitative; (4) quantitative; (5) quantitative; (6) quantitative **1.21 a.** all U.S. employees **b.** employee's job status **c.** qualitative **d.** 1000 employees surveyed **e.** majority of all workers would remain in their jobs **1.23 a.** quantitative **b.** quantitative **c.** qualitative **d.** quantitative **e.** qualitative **f.** quantitative **g.** qualitative **1.25 b.** speed of the deliveries; accuracy of the invoices; quality of the packaging **c.** total number of questionnaires received **1.27 a.** all department store executives **b.** job satisfaction; Machiavellian rating **c.** 218 department store executives **d.** survey **e.** Executives with higher job-satisfaction scores are likely to have a lower "Mach" rating. **1.31 a.** all persons over 14 in U.S. **b.** unemployment status; qualitative **c.** inferential

Chapter 2

2.1 16; .18; .45; .15; .14 **2.3 a.** pie chart **b.** task category **c.** material handling (34%) **d.** 46,080 **e.** 52% **2.5 a.** body defect **b.** paint or dents **2.7 b.** yes **c.** banks: yes; department stores: no **2.9** Channel catfish: 67.7%; large-mouth bass: 8.3%; small-mouth buffalo: 25% **2.11** Most often: F color (26.6%), clarity VS1 (26.3%); least often: D color (5.2%), IF clarity (14.3%) **2.13 a.** response time **c.** 3,570 **2.15 b.** inflation rate (58%) **c.** yes, inflation rate and real estate prices represent 78% of investors **2.17** 50, 75, 125, 100, 25, 50, 50, 25 **2.19 a.** frequency histogram **b.** 14 **c.** 49 **2.21 a.** 28.5% **b.** 82% **2.23 b.** Cardinals tend to score more runs when McGuire hit multiple home runs **2.25 d.** HRD group **2.27 c.** penalties for CAA tend to be smaller **2.29 a.** 2005 SAT scores are shifted to the right of the scores from 1990 **c.** similar conclusion **d.** Illinois (111) **2.31 a.** 44.75% **b.** .325 **2.33 a.** 12 **b.** 40 **c.** 7 **d.** 21 **e.** 144 **2.35 a.** 11.2 **b.** 12 **c.** 30 **2.37 a.** $\bar{x} = 2.717$, $m = 2.65$ **2.41** mode = 15; $\bar{x} = 14.545$; $m = 15$ **2.43 a.** mean less than median **b.** mean greater than median **c.** equal **2.45 a.** $\bar{x} = 49.88$, $m = 49.5$, mode = 51 **b.** slightly skewed right **c.** 48.75 to 51.25 **2.47 a.** $\bar{x} = .63$; average number of carats of 308 diamonds is .63 **b.** $m = .62$; 50% of the diamonds weigh less than .62 carat **c.** mode = 1.0; carat value of 1.0 occurred the most often **d.** mean or median **2.49** data are probably not skewed, but close to symmetric **2.53 a.** joint: $\bar{x} = 2.6545$, $m = 1.5$; no prefiling: $\bar{x} = 4.2364$, $m = 3.2$; prepack: $\bar{x} = 1.8185$, $m = 1.4$ **b.** three centers **2.55 c.** no; yes (if the data are between 0 and 1) **2.57 a.** R = 4, $s^2 = 2.3$, s = 1.52 **b.** R = 6, $s^2 = 3.619$, s = 1.90 **c.** R = 10, $s^2 = 7.111$, s = 2.67 **d.** R = 5, $s^2 = 1.624$, s = 1.274 **2.59 a.** $\bar{x} = 5.6$, $s^2 = 17.3$, s = 4.1593 **b.** $\bar{x} = 13.75$ feet, $s^2 = 152.25$ square feet, s = 12.339 feet **c.** $\bar{x} = -2.5$, $s^2 = 4.3$, s = 2.0736 **d.** $\bar{x} = .33$ ounce, $s^2 = .0587$ square ounce, s = .2422 ounce **2.61** Data set 1: 0,1,2,3,4,5,6,7,8,9, Data set 2: 0,0,1,1,2,2,3,3,9,9 **2.63 a.** 355 − 63 = 292 **b.** 301 − 64 = 237 **c.** no **2.65 a.** R = 34.5 cm, $s^2 = 47.36$ square cm, s = 6.88 cm **b.** R = 2,129 g, $s^2 = 141,787$ square g, s = 376.6 g **c.** R = 1,099.89 ppm, $s^2 = 9,678$ square ppm, s = 98.4 g **2.67 a.** R = 12, $s^2 = 9.37$, s = 3.06 **b.** R = 8, $s^2 = 5.15$, s = 2.27 **c.** R = 8, $s^2 = 5.06$, s = 2.25 **2.69 a.** dollars; quantitative **b.** at least $^3/_4$; at least 8/9; nothing; nothing **2.71** approx. 68%; approx. 95%; essentially all **2.73** between R/6 = 104.17 and R/4 = 156.25 **2.75 a.** (103.77, 176.85) **b.** at least $^3/_4$ **c.** nothing **2.77 a.** $\bar{x} = 94.91$, s = 4.83 **b.** (90.08, 99.74); (85.25, 104.57); (80.42, 109.40) **c.** 81.1%; 97.6%; 98.2% **2.79** $\bar{x} = 234.74$, s = 9.91; (205.0, 264.5) **2.81 a.** at least 8/9 of the velocities fall within (906, 966) **b.** no **2.83** do not buy **2.85** 11:30 **2.87 a.** 25%, 75% **b.** 50%, 50% **c.** 80%, 20% **d.** 16%, 84% **2.89 a.** z = 2 **b.** z = −3 **c.** z = −2 **d.** z = 1.67 **2.91** average score is 279; 10% of 8th-graders score below 231; 25% score below 255; 75% score below 304; 90% score below 324 **2.93 a.** $\bar{x} = 10.93$, s = 20.75 **b.** z = 3.10 **c.** z = −.47 **2.95** no **2.97 a.** 0 **b.** 21 **c.** $\bar{x} = 5.24$, s = 7.24; z = 5.90 **d.** yes **2.99 a.** z = .727, no **b.** z = −3.273, yes **c.** z = 1.364, no **d.** z = 3.727, yes **2.103 a.** z = 1.05, no **b.** greater than 194.6 or less than 88 **2.105 b.** Joint: 1.5; None firms: 3.2; Prepack: 1.4 **d.** no **e.** yes **2.107 a.** 4 outliers: 62, 72, 78, and 84 **b.** 3 outliers: 62, 72, and 78 **c.** no **2.109 b.** customers 268, 269, and 264 **c.** 2.06, 2.13, and 3.14 **2.113** increasing **2.115** increasing **2.117** length vs. weight: increasing; length vs. DDT: slightly increasing; weight vs. DDT: no trend **2.121 a.** −1, 1, 2 **b.** 0, 4, 6 **c.** 1, 3, 4 **d.** .1, .3, .4 **2.123 a.** 6, 27, 5.20 **b.** 6.25, 28.25, 5.32 **c.** 7, 37.67, 6.14 **d.** 3, 0, 0 **2.129** 60% of cars with 4-star rating **2.131** $\bar{x} = 52.04$; $m = 56.7$; mode = 56.70 **2.133 a.** frequency bar chart **c.** 70% of imprints successful **2.135 a.** grounding or fire **b.** $\bar{x} = 66.19$, s = 56.05; (0, 234.34) **2.137 b.** marketing: 6.5 days, engineering: 7.0 days; accounting: 8.5 days **2.139 a.** no scale on vertical axis **b.** add vertical axis scale **2.141 a.** skewed right **c.** ≈.38 **d.** no, z = 3.333 **2.143 b.** yes, skewed to the right **c.** 813 **d.** .007; .31 **f.** Philadelphia, Carolina, Miami, Seattle **g.** Washington **h.** operating income increases as current value increases **2.145** 7 of 25 values are less than 12; claim probably not true **2.147** Laid off: $m = 40.5$; not laid off: $m = 40$; company probably not vulnerable **2.149** yes; no observations recorded in interval just below interval centered at 1.000 cm

Chapter 3

3.1 a. .5 **b.** .3 **c.** .6 **3.3** $P(A) = .55$, $P(B) = .50$, $P(C) = .70$ **3.5 a.** 10 **b.** 20 **c.** 15,504 **3.7 a.** (B_1, B_2), (B_1, R_1), (B_1, R_2), (B_1, R_3), (B_2, R_1), (B_2, R_2), (B_2, R_3), (R_1, R_2), (R_1, R_3), (R_2, R_3) **b.** $P(E_i) = 1/10$ **c.** $P(A) = 1/10$, $P(B) = 3/5$, $P(C) = 3/10$ **3.9 a.** J, C, and U **b.** $P(J) = .35$, $P(C) = .50$, $P(U) = .15$ **c.** .85 **3.11 a.** 1/100 = .01 **b.** .0095; yes **3.13 a.** .325 **b.** .711 **3.15** 455 **3.17 a.** 6; $(G_1G_2G_3)$, $(G_1G_2G_4)$, $(G_1G_2G_5)$, $(G_2G_3G_4)$, $(G_2G_3G_5)$, $(G_2G_4G_5)$ **b.** .282, .065, .339, .032, .008, .274 **c.** .686 **3.19 a.** 1 to 2 **b.** 1/2 **c.** 2/5

3.21 a. LLLL, LLLU, LLUL, LULL, ULLL, LLUU, LULU, LUUL, ULLU, ULUL, UULL, LUUU,ULUU, UULU, UUUL, UUUU
b. 1/16 **c.** 5/16   **3.23 b.** P(A) = 7/8, P(B) = 1/2, P(A ∪ B) = 7/8, P(A^C) = 1/8, P(A ∩ B) = 1/2   **3.25 a.** 3/4 **b.** 13/20 **c.** 1 **d.** 2/5 **e.** 1/4
f. 7/20 **g.** 1 **h.** 1/4   **3.27 a.** .65 **b.** .72 **c.** .25 **d.** .08 **e.** .35 **f.** .72 **g.** 0 **h.** A and C, B and C, C and D   **3.29** .73   **3.31 a.** .43 **b.** .84   **3.33 a.** AC,
AW, AF, IC, IW, and IF **b.** .148, .066, .426, .176, .052, .132 **c.** .640 **d.** .118 **e.** .176 **f.** .786 **g.** .676   **3.35 a.** .684 **b.** .124 **c.** no **d.** .316 **e.** .717
f. .091   **3.37 a.** P(A) = .281, P(B) = .276, P(C) = .044, P(D) = .079, P(E) = .044 **b.** 0 **c.** .557 **d.** 0 **e.** .325 **f.** A and B, A and C, A and
D, A and E   **3.39 a.** .09 **b.** .09 **c.** .84 **d.** no **e.** column events not mutually exclusive   **3.41 a.** .5 **b.** .25 **c.** no   **3.43 a.** .08 **b.** .4 **c.** .52
3.45 a. .8, .7, .6 **b.** .25, .375, .375 **d.** no   **3.47 a.** .37 **b.** .68 **c.** .15 **d.** .2206 **e.** 0 **f.** 0 **g.** no   **3.49 a.** A and C, B and C **b.** none **c.** .65, .90
3.51 .545   **3.53 a.** .1875 **b.** .60   **3.55 a.** P(P) = .68, P(R | P) = .07 **b.** P(R ∩ P) = .048   **3.57 a.** .222 **b.** .183   **3.59 a.**
P(A | I) = .9, P(B | I) = .95, P(A | I^c) = .2, P(B | I^c) = .1 **b.** .855 **c.** .02 **d.** .995   **3.61 a.** (a + d)/(a + b + c + d) **b.** d/(b + d)
c. c/(a + c) **d.** d/(c + d) **e.** accuracy: .843; detection rate: .408; false alarm rate: .109; precision: .290   **3.63 a.** .3, .6 **b.** dependent **c.** independent   **3.65** .60   **3.67 a.** (.5)^{10} = .000977 **b.** .00195 **c.** .99805   **3.69 a.** 35,820,200 **b.** 1/35,820,200   **3.73 a.** .000186 **c.** no   **3.77 a.** .158
b. .074 **c.** .768   **3.79 a.** .52, .39, .09 **b.** .516   **3.81 a.** .5 **b.** .99 **c.** .847   **3.83** .6982   **3.85 a.** Supplier 4; P(S$_4$ | D) = .7147 **b.** Suppliers 4 or 6
3.87 a. 0 **b.** no   **3.89** .5   **3.91 a.** 0, .2, .9, 1, .7, .3, .4, 0   **3.93 a.** 720 **b.** 10 **c.** 10 **d.** 20 **e.** 1   **3.95** 3/650 = .0046   **3.97 a.** false **b.** true **c.** true
d. false   **3.99 a.** B ∩ C **b.** A^c **c.** C ∪ B **d.** A ∩ C^c **3.101 b.** .95 **c.** .25 **d.** .5   **3.103 a.** .5 **b.** .034 **c.** .058   **3.105 a.** .00000625 **b.** .0135
c. doubt validity of the manufacturer's claim **d.** no   **3.107** .801   **3.109 a.** .006 **b.** .012 **c.** .018   **3.111 a.** .006 **b.** .0022 **c.** .4133 **d.** .3601
e. no   **3.113** .79   **3.115 a.** .7127 **b.** .2873   **3.117 a.** 10/35 **b.** 20/35 **c.** 5/35   **3.119** .526   **3.121 a.** .0362 **b.** .0352   **3.123** Marilyn

Chapter 4
4.1 a. discrete **b.** continuous **c.** continuous **d.** discrete **e.** discrete   **4.3** discrete   **4.5** discrete   **4.11 a.** p(x) = 1/6 for all x values
4.13 a. .25 **b.** .40 **c.** .75   **4.15 b.** 1/8 **d.** 1/2   **4.17 a.** μ = 0, σ^2 = 2.94, σ = 1.72 **c.** .96   **4.19 a.** p(1) = 0, p(2) = .0408,
p(3) = .1735, p(4) = .6020, p(5) = .1837 **b.** .1837 **c.** .0408 **d.** 3.93   **4.21 a.** yes **b.** .06 **c.** .28 **d.** .82   **4.23 a.** .508 **b.** .391 **c.** .094 **d.** .007
4.25 a. .23 **b.** .0809 **c.** .77   **4.27 b.** .85 **c.** .6, 0, 0, 0, .7 **d.** a$_1$: 2.4; a$_2$: 1.5; a$_3$ − a$_5$: .90; a$_6$: 1.65 **e.** a$_1$: .86, (.68, 4.12); a$_2$: .67, (.16, 2.84) ;
a$_3$ − a$_5$: .3, (.3, 1.5); a$_6$: .57, (.51, 2.79)   **4.29 a.** p($300,000) = .3, p($0) = .7 **b.** $90,000   **4.31 a.** p(x) = .05 for all x-values **b.** 52.5
c. (−5.16, 110.16) **f.** 33.25, 33.36 **g.** .525 **i.** .20 **j.** .65   **4.33** $.25   **4.35 a.** 15 **b.** 10 **c.** 1 **d.** 1 **e.** 4   **4.37 a.** .4096 **b.** .3456 **c.** .027 **d.** .0081
e. .3456 **f.** .027   **4.39 a.** 12.5, 6.25, 2.5 **b.** 16, 12.8, 3.578 **c.** 60, 24, 4.899 **d.** 63, 6.3, 2.510 **e.** 48, 9.6, 3.098 **f.** 40, 38.4, 6.197   **4.41 a.** .5 **b.** .1
c. .9   **4.43 a.** 54 **b.** .0806, .1056   **4.45 b.** n = 20, p = .8. **c.** .175 **d.** .804 **e.** 16   **4.47 a.** .054 **b.** in 2020, more than 9% of Denver bridges
will have a rating of 4 or below   **4.49 a.** .015, .030 **b.** .0706, .0022 **c.** .1328, .0085 **d.** .9129   **4.51 a.** μ = 480, σ = 13.86 **b.** no, z = −5.77
4.53 b. μ = 2.4, σ = 1.47 **c.** p = .90, q = .10, n = 24, μ = 21.60, σ = 1.47   **4.55 a.** discrete **b.** Poisson **d.** μ = 3, σ = 1.73
4.57 a. .920 **b.** .677 **c.** .423 **d.** decreases   **4.59 a.** .125 **b.** 5   **4.61 a.** .301 **b.** .361 **c.** μ = 1.2, σ = 1.095   **4.63 a.** 2 **b.** no, P(x > 10) = .003
4.65 a. .6083 **c.** no, P(x > 2) = .0064; yes, P(x < 1) = .6907   **4.67** ≈.0498   **4.69 a.** f(x) = .04 (20 ≤ x ≤ 45), 0 otherwise **b.** 32.5,
7.22   **4.71 a.** f(x) = 1/4 (3 ≤ x ≤ 7), 0 otherwise **b.** 5, 1.155   **4.73 a.** 0 **b.** 1 **c.** 1   **4.75 a.** .133; .571 **b.** .267; 0   **4.77** yes   **4.79 a.** continuous **c.** 7, .2887 (6.422, 7.577) **d.** .5 **e.** 0 **f.** .75 **g.** .0002   **4.81 a.** 10 **b.** .05 **c.** likely not true   **4.83** .4444   **4.85 a.** .0721 **b.** .0594 **c.** .2434
d. .3457 **e.** .5 **f.** .9233   **4.87 a.** .6826 **b.** .9500 **c.** .90 **d.** .9544   **4.89 a.** −.81 **b.** .55 **c.** 1.43 **d.** .21 **e.** −2.05 **f.** .50   **4.91 a.** −2.5 **b.** 0 **c.** −.625
d. −3.75 **e.** 1.25 **f.** −1.25   **4.93 a.** .3830 **b.** .3023 **c.** .1525 **d.** .7333 **e.** .1314 **f.** .9545   **4.95 a.** .9544 **b.** .0918 **c.** .0228 **d.** .8607 **e.** .0927 **f.** .7049
4.97 a. .1442 **b.** .2960 **c.** .0023 **d.** .9706   **4.99 a.** .3755 **b.** .1969 **c.** .9693 **d.** .9292   **4.101 a.** .8413 **b.** .7528   **4.103 a.** .3050, .1020 **b.** .6879,
.8925 **c.** .003   **4.105 a.** 25.14% **b.** 90.375   **4.107 a.** Stock XYZ **b.** ABC: $105; XYZ: $107 **c.** ABC: .0475; XYZ: .0808; ABC   **4.109** 5.068
4.111 a. .68 **b.** .95 **c.** 1.00   **4.113** Plot c   **4.115 a.** 6 **b.** 5.275 **c.** IQR/s = 1.14   **4.117** no   **4.119** IQR/s = 1.3   **4.121** z = −.75 for minimum value of 128   **4.123 a.** no **b.** yes **c.** no **d.** yes **e.** yes **f.** yes   **4.125 a.** .1788 **b.** .5236 **c.** .6950   **4.127 a.** 40 **b.** 5.67 **c.** 1.86 **d.** .9686
4.129 .0537   **4.131** .1762   **4.133** .2676; no   **4.135 b.** Public: .1841, 0; Private: .6915, 0   **4.137 c.** 1/16   **4.139 c.** .05 **d.** no   **4.145 a.** 100, 5
b. 100, 2 **c.** 100, 1 **d.** 100, 1.414 **e.** 100, .447 **f.** 100, .316   **4.147 a.** 2.9, 3.29, 1.814   **4.149 a.** .0228 **b.** .0668 **c.** .0062 **d.** .8185 **e.** .0013   **4.151**
a. .8944 **b.** .0228 **c.** .1292 **d.** .9699   **4.153 a.** 141 **b.** 1.8 **c.** approx. normal **d.** 0.56 **e.** .2877   **4.155** .0838   **4.157 a.** approximately normal
with μ$_{\bar{x}}$ = .53 and σ$_{\bar{x}}$ = .0273 **b.** .0336 **c.** before: P($\bar{x}$ ≥ .59) = .0139; after: P($\bar{x}$ ≥ .59) = .3557; after tensioning   **4.159 a.** approximately normal **b.** .0322 **c.** .8925 **d.** 19.1 **e.** less than 19.1   **4.161 a.** approximately normal **b.** .0091 **c.** .9544   **4.163** Handrubbing:
P($\bar{x}$ < 30 | μ = 35) = .2743; Handwashing: P($\bar{x}$ < 30 | μ = 69) = .0047; handrubbing   **4.165 a.** .2734 **b.** .4096 **c.** .3432   **4.167 a.** .192
b. .228 **c.** .772 **d.** .987 **e.** .960 **f.** 14, 4.2, 2.049 **g.** .975   **4.169 a.** discrete **b.** continuous **c.** continuous **d.** continuous   **4.171 a.** .9821 **b.** .0179
c. .9505 **d.** .3243 **e.** .9107 **f.** .0764   **4.173 a.** .6915 **b.** .1587 **c.** .1915 **d.** .3085 **e.** 0 **f.** 1   **4.175 a.** 47.68 **b.** 47.68 **c.** 30.13 **d.** 41.5 **e.** 30.13
4.177 a. .5 **b.** .0606 **c.** .0985 **d.** .8436   **4.181 a.** .2592 **c.** .0870 **d.** .6826 **e.** 3.00   **4.183 a.** $12,500 **b.** .6 **c.** $14,000   **4.185 a.** nothing about
shape **b.** approximately normal **c.** .2843 **d.** .1292   **4.187** z = −1.71 for minimum value of 0   **4.189 b.** 20, 4.47 **c.** no, z = −3.55 **d.** 0
4.191 no   **4.193 a.** .8264 **b.** 17 times **c.** .6217 **d.** 0, −157   **4.195 a.** 1.25, 1.09; no **b.** .007 **c.** not applicable   **4.197** 292   **4.199** .9332
4.201 $\bar{x}$ = 5.935 minutes; P($\bar{x}$ < 6 | μ = 15) ≈ 0, therefore, appears drug is effective

Chapter 5
5.1 a. 1.645 **b.** 2.58 **c.** 1.96 **d.** 1.28   **5.3 a.** 28 ± .784 **b.** 102 ± .65 **c.** 15 ± .0588 **d.** 4.05 ± .163 **e.** no   **5.5 a.** 26.2 ± .96 **b.** In repeated
sampling, 95% of all confidence intervals constructed will include μ. **c.** 26.2 ± 1.26 **d.** increases **e.** yes   **5.9** yes   **5.11 a.** μ = mean
salary of all 500 CEOs **c.** $\bar{x}$ = 15.29, s = 16.22 **d.** 15.29 ± 5.92 **e.** μ = 10.93   **5.13 a.** (141.2, 141.5) **c.** random sample   **5.15 a.** (12.43,
25.57) **b.** (2.05, 11.95) **c.** SAT–Math   **5.17 a.** 66.83 ± 6.17 **c.** 45.31 ± 4.15   **5.19 a.** μ$_Y$: 4.17 ± .095; μ$_{MA}$: 4.04 ± .057; μ$_O$: 4.31 ± .062
b. more likely   **5.21 a.** z$_{.10}$ = 1.28, t$_{.10}$ = 1.533 **b.** z$_{.05}$ = 1.645, t$_{.05}$ = 2.132 **c.** z$_{.025}$ = 1.96, t$_{.025}$ = 2.776 **d.** z$_{.01}$ = 2.33, t$_{.01}$ = 3.747
e. z$_{.005}$ = 2.575, t$_{.005}$ = 4.604   **5.23 a.** 2.228 **b.** 2.228 **c.** −1.812 **d.** 1.725 **e.** 4.032   **5.25 a.** 5 ± 1.88 **b.** 5 ± 2.39 **c.** 5 ± 3.75
d. 5 ± .78, 5 ± .94, 5 ± 1.28; decreased width   **5.27** (71.67, 79.13)   **5.29 a.** 2.886 ± 4.034 **b.** .408 ± .256   **5.31 a.** (−2,237.61,

12,108.44) **b.** normally distributed   **5.33 a.** (303.3, 413.6) **c.** approximately normal **d.** no   **5.35 a.** all 339 firms in *Forbes* Largest Private Companies list **b.** (1.26, 4.32) **d.** approx. normal **e.** yes   **5.37 a.** yes **b.** no **c.** no **d.** no   **5.39 a.** yes **b.** .46 ± .065   **5.41 a.** .46 **b.** (.433, .487) **c.** 90% confident that true proportion of contractors who have a company Web site falls between .433 and .487 **d.** 90% of all similarly constructed intervals will contain the true proportion   **5.43 a.** .03 **b.** .03 ± .01   **5.45 a.** all consumers in Muncie, Indiana **b.** belief in whether "Made in the USA" means 100% **c.** .604 ± .078   **5.47 b.** .29 ± .028   **5.49 a.** .867 **b.** (.781, .953) **d.** not believable   **5.51** .85 ± .0012   **5.53 a.** 68 **b.** 31   **5.55** 34   **5.57 a.** 0.98, 0.784, 0.56, 0.392, 0.196   **5.59** 21   **5.61** 1,692   **5.63** 14,735   **5.65** 43; 171; 385   **5.67** no   **5.69 a.** .7746 **b.** .8944 **c.** .9487 **d.** .995   **5.71 a.** 1.00 **b.** .6124 **c.** 0 **d.** as n increases, standard error decreases   **5.73** .42 ± .021   **5.75 a.** 36.03 ± 3.40 **b.** .7 ± .16   **5.77** .694 ± .092   **5.79 a.** 156.46 **b.** 18.70 **c.** 156.46 ± 37.405 **d.** not reasonable   **5.81** No; .086 ± .041   **5.83 a.** −1.725 **b.** 3.250 **c.** 1.860 **d.** 2.898   **5.85 a.** 32.5 ± 5.15 **b.** 23,871   **5.87** (1) p = proportion with excellent health; (2), (3), and (4) μ = mean number of days health not good   **5.89 a.** .24 **b.** .24 ± .118   **5.91 a.** 329 **b.** 61 **c.** 61   **5.93** 184.99 ± 133.93   **5.95** .667 ± .065   **5.97 a.** 49.3 ± 8.6 **b.** 99% confident that the mean amount removed from all soil specimens using the poison is between 40.70% and 57.90% **c.** normal distribution **d.** possible   **5.99 a.** men: 7.4 ± .979; women: 4.5 ± .755 **b.** men: 9.3 ± 1.185; women: 6.6 ± 1.138   **5.101a.** .833 ± .149 **b.** no **c.** 1,337   **5.105** 154   **5.107** 818

Chapter 6

6.1 null; alternative   **6.3** α **6.5** Reject H_0 when H_0 is true; accept H_0 when H_0 is true; Reject H_0 when H_0 is false; accept H_0 when H_0 is false   **6.7** no   **6.9** H_0: p = .045, H_a: p < .045   **6.11** H_0: μ = 863, H_a: μ < 863   **6.13 a.** unsafe; safe **c.** α **6.15 c.** α **e.** decrease **f.** increase   **6.17 g.** .025, .05, .005, .10, .10, .01   **6.19 a.** z = 1.67, reject H_0 **b.** z = 1.67, do not reject H_0 **6.21 a.** z < −2.33 **b.** z = −.40 **c.** do not reject H_0 **6.23 a.** z > 2.33 **b.** z = 23.31 **c.** reject H_0 **6.25 a.** H_0: μ = .250, H_a: $\mu \neq$ .250 **b.** yes, z = 7.02   **6.27** z = −1.86, do not reject H_0 **6.29 a.** no **b.** z = .61, do not reject H_0 **d.** no **e.** z = −.83, do not reject H_0 **6.31 a.** z = 2.73, reject H_0 **c.** no   **6.33 a.** do not reject H_0 **b.** reject H_0 **c.** reject H_0 **d.** do not reject H_0 **e.** do not reject H_0 **6.35** .0150   **6.37** .03   **6.39** .06   **6.41 a.** .057 **b.** do not reject H_0 **6.43 a.** .0693 **b.** do not reject H_0 **6.45 a.** H_0: μ = 16.5, H_a: μ > 16.5 **b.** .0681   **6.47 a.** small n, data normal **b.** mound-shaped and symmetric; t is flatter than z **6.49 a.** $|t|$ > 2.160 **b.** t > 2.500 **c.** t > 1.397 **d.** t < −2.718 **e.** $|t|$ > 1.729 **f.** t < −2.353   **6.51 a.** population is normally distributed **b.** reject H_0 at α = .05 **c.** .076   **6.53 a.** H_0: μ = 2, H_a: $\mu \neq$ 2 **b.** t = −1.02 **c.** $|t|$ > 2.093 **d.** do not reject H_0 **e.** .322   **6.55** p-value = .257, do not reject H_0 **6.57** yes, t = −2.53   **6.59** no, t = 2.97   **6.61 a.** yes **b.** no **c.** no **d.** no **e.** no   **6.63 a.** −2.33 **c.** reject H_0 **d.** .0099   **6.65 a.** z = 1.13, reject H_0 **b.** .1292   **6.67 a.** .52 **b.** H_0: p = .62, H_a: $p \neq$ .62 **c.** z = −5.16 **d.** $|z|$ > 1.96 **e.** reject H_0 **f.** $\approx$0   **6.69 a.** H_0: p = .5, H_a: p < .5 **b.** .231 **c.** do not reject H_0 **6.71 a.** no, z = 1.49 **b.** .0681   **6.73** z = 4.12, reject H_0: p = .5   **6.75** z = 1.20, do not reject H_0 **6.77 b.** 532.9 **d.** .1949 **e.** .8051   **6.79 c.** .1469 **d.** .8531   **6.81 c.** .5359 **d.** .0409   **6.83 a.** .1949, Type II error **b.** .05, Type I error **c.** .8051   **6.85** .1075   **6.87 a.** χ^2 < 6.26214 or χ^2 > 27.4884 **b.** χ^2 > 40.2894 **c.** χ^2 > 21.0642 **d.** χ^2 < 3.57056 **e.** χ^2 < 1.63539 or χ^2 > 12.5916 **f.** χ^2 < 13.8484   **6.89 a.** χ^2 = 479.16, reject H_0 **6.91 a.** χ^2 < 24.3 or χ^2 > 73.1 **b.** χ^2 = 63.72 **c.** do not reject H_0 **6.93 a.** H_0: σ^2 = .000004, H_a: $\sigma^2 \neq$ .000004 **b.** χ^2 = 48.49, do not reject H_0 **c.** tee weights approx. normal   **6.95** at α = .05, yes; χ^2 = 133.90   **6.97 b.** 1.76 **c.** yes; χ^2 = 99   **6.99** alternative   **6.101** large   **6.103 a.** t = −7.51, reject H_0 **b.** t = −7.51, reject H_0 **6.105 a.** z = −1.78, reject H_0 **b.** z = −1.78, do not reject H_0 **6.107 a.** χ^2 = 63.48, reject H_0 **b.** χ^2 = 63.48, reject H_0 **6.109 a.** z = −2.22, do not reject H_0 **b.** .0132   **6.111 a.** H_0: μ = 1, H_a: μ > 1 **b.** reject H_0 if t > 1.345 **d.** t = 2.41 **e.** .01 < p-value < .025, reject H_0 **f.** χ^2 = 12.78, do not reject H_0 **6.113 a.** t = .41, do not reject H_0 **b.** yes   **6.115 a.** H_0: No disease, H_a: Disease   **6.117 a.** H_0: μ = 16, H_a: μ < 16 **b.** z = −4.31, reject H_0 **6.119 a.** z = 12.97, reject H_0: p = .5 **b.** 0 **c.** .6844   **6.121 a.** concluding percentage of shoplifters turned over to police is 50% when in fact, the percentage is higher than 50% **b.** .8461 **c.** decreases   **6.123 a.** no, z = 1.41 **b.** small **c.** .0793   **6.125 a.** no **b.** β = .5910, power = .4090 **c.** increases   **6.127 a.** z = −1.29, do not reject H_0 **b.** .0985   **6.129 a.** z = 2.73, reject H_0

Chapter 7

7.1 a. 150 ± 6 **b.** 150 ± 8 **c.** 0; 5 **d.** 0 ± 10 **e.** variability of the difference is greater   **7.3 a.** 35 ± 24.5 **b.** z = 2.8, p-value = .0052, reject H_0 **c.** p-value = .0026 **d.** z = .8, p-value = .4238, do not reject H_0 **e.** independent random samples   **7.5 a.** no **b.** no **c.** no **d.** yes **e.** no   **7.7 a.** .5989 **b.** yes, t = −2.39 **c.** −1.24 ± .98 **d.** confidence interval   **7.9 a.** do not reject H_0 **b.** .0575   **7.11 a.** t = −1.646, do not reject H_0 **b.** −2.50 ± 3.12   **7.13 a.** H_0: $\mu_1 - \mu_2$ = 0, H_a: $\mu_1 - \mu_2 \neq$ 0 **b.** t = .62 **c.** $|t|$ > 1.684 **d.** do not reject H_0 **e.** do not reject H_0 **f.** independent random samples, both populations normal, $\sigma_1^2 = \sigma_2^2$ **7.15 a.** yes **b.** z = 4.58, reject H_0 **7.17 a.** t = 1.56, do not reject H_0: $\mu_T = \mu_I$ **b.** t = −.5, do not reject H_0: $\mu_W = \mu_I$ **c.** no differences   **7.19 a.** H_0: $\mu_1 = \mu_2$, H_a: $\mu_1 \neq \mu_2$ **b.** z = 7.17, reject H_0 **c.** .51 ± .14   **7.21 a.** yes, t = 1.9557 **c.** .0579 **d.** −7.4 ± 6.38   **7.23 a.** no, t = −1.22 **b.** yes, t = −4.20   **7.25 a.** t > 1.796 **b.** t > 1.319 **c.** t > 3.182 **d.** t > 2.375   **7.27 a.** H_0: μ_d = 0, H_a: μ_d < 0 **b.** t = −5.29, p-value = .0002, reject H_0 **c.** (−4.98, −2.42) **d.** population of differences is normal   **7.29 a.** z = 1.79, do not reject H_0 **b.** .0734 **c.** no   **7.31 b.** H_0: μ_d = 0, H_a: $\mu_d \neq$ 0 **c.** do not reject H_0 **7.33** (.036, .224); Huffman-coding   **7.35 a.** yes, t = 2.864   **7.37 a.** H_0: μ_d = 0, H_a: $\mu_d \neq$ 0 **b.** t = 5.76, reject H_0 **c.** yes   **7.39** t = .46, p-value = 0.65, do not reject H_0 **7.41 a.** binomial distributions **b.** distribution is approx. normal for large n's   **7.43 a.** no **b.** no **c.** no **d.** no **e.** no   **7.45 a.** z = −4.02, reject H_0 **b.** z = −4.02, reject H_0 **c.** z = −4.02, reject H_0 **7.47 a.** .153 **b.** .215 **c.** (−.132, .008) **d.** no evidence of a difference   **7.49 a.** $p_1 - p_2$ **b.** H_0: $p_1 - p_2$ = 0, H_a: $p_1 - p_2 \neq$ 0 **c.** z = 5.16 **d.** $|z|$ > 2.58 **e.** yes **f.** reject H_0 **7.51 a.** z = 94.35, reject H_0 **b.** (−.155, −.123)   **7.53 a.** yes, z = −2.79 **b.** yes; −.011 ± .010   **7.55** yes, z = −2.25   **7.57 a.** 500, 46 **b.** sample may not be representative   **7.59** 34   **7.61 a.** 29,954 **b.** 2,165 **c.** 1,113   **7.63** 13,531 for each survey   **7.65** 1,729   **7.67** 542   **7.69 a.** 4.10 **b.** 3.57 **c.** 8.81 **d.** 3.21   **7.71 a.** F > 1.74 **b.** F > 2.04 **c.** F > 2.35 **d.** F > 2.78   **7.73 a.** F > 2.11 **b.** F > 3.01 **c.** F > 2.04 **d.** F > 2.30 **e.** F > 3.94   **7.75 a.** F = 4.29, do not reject H_0 **b.** .05 < p-value < .10   **7.77 a.** H_0: $\sigma_M^2 = \sigma_F^2$, H_a: $\sigma_M^2 < \sigma_F^2$ **b.** 1.06 **c.** F > 1.26 **d.** p-value > .10 **e.** do not reject H_0 **7.79 a.** no, F = 2.27 **b.** .05 < p-value < .10   **7.81 a.** yes, F = 8.29 **b.** no

10.27 10.10: SSE $= 1.22$, $s^2 = .244$, $s = .494$; 10.13: SSE $= 5.713$, $s^2 = 1.143$, $s = 1.069$ **10.29 a.** SSE $= 26,877.46$, $s^2 = 548.52$, $s = 23.42$ **b.** about 95% of the observed SAT scores fall within 46.84 points of their least squares predicted values **10.31 a.** SSE $= 1.017$, $s^2 = .0462$, $s = .215$ **c.** about 95% of the observed sweetness index values fall within .43 units of their least squares predicted values   **10.33 a.** $s = 5.37$; about 95% of the observed FCAT-Math scores fall within 10.74 points of their least squares predicted values **b.** $s = 3.42$; about 95% of the observed FCAT-Reading scores fall within 6.84 points of their least squares predicted values **c.** reading score   **10.35 a.** 95% CI: 31 ± 1.17; 90% CI: $31 \pm .94$ **b.** 95% CI: 64 ± 5.08; 90% CI: 64 ± 4.15 **c.** 95% CI: $-8.4 \pm .75$; 90% CI: $-8.4 \pm .62$ **10.37** 80% CI: $.82 \pm .33$; 98% CI: $.82 \pm .76$ **10.39 a.** $H_0: \beta_1 = 0$, $H_a: \beta_1 > 0$ **b.** p-value $= .0000$ **c.** $(11,005.24, 12,192.56)$ **10.41** $(30.17, 41.67)$; 90% confident that for each additional unit increase in surface area to volume, the increase in the drug release rate is between 30.17 and 41.67   **10.43** no, $t = .66$ **10.45 a.** support **b.** $\hat{y} = 15.878 + .927x$ **c.** yes, $t = 2.45$ **d.** 0 and 1   **10.47 a.** yes **c.** $1.39 \pm .10$ **d.** 90% confident that for each 1 mm increase in Winter runoff, rainfall erosivity index increases between 1.29 and 1.49   **10.49** yes, $t = -.82$ **10.51 a.** positive **b.** negative **c.** 0 slope **d.** positive or negative   **10.53 a** .9438 **b.** .8020 **10.55 a.** moderately strong positive linear relationship between skill level and goal-setting ability **b.** reject H_0 at $\alpha = .01$ **c.** .49 **10.57** $r^2 = .2286$, $r = -.478$ **10.59 a.** weak/moderate positive linear relationship between height and average earnings **b.** $r^2 = .168$; 16.8% of the total sample variation in average earnings is explained by the linear relationship with height **c.** $H_0: \rho = 0$, $H_a: \rho > 0$ **d.** t $= 4.82$ **e.** reject H_0 **10.61** $r = .243$, $r^2 = .059$ **10.63** moderate positive linear relationship between rates of returns for the two countries   **10.65 a.** .57 **c.** no   **10.67 c.** 4.64 ± 1.12 **d.** $2.28 \pm .63$; $-.41 \pm 1.17$ **10.69 a.** $\hat{y} = 1.375 + .875x$ **c.** 1.5 **d.** .1875 **e.** $(3.23, 3.89)$ **f.** $(3.81, 5.94)$ **10.71** $(19.97, 30.36)$; 90% confident that the actual value of the drug release rate is between 19.97 and 30.36 when the surface area to volume ratio is .50   **10.73 a.** $(2.955, 4.066)$; 99% confident that the mean mass of all spills with elapsed time is 15 minutes is between 2.995 and 4.066 **b.** $(1.02, 6.00)$; 99% confident that the actual mass of a single spill with elapsed time of 15 minutes is between 1.02 and 6.0 **c.** prediction interval for y; yes   **10.75 a.** yes, $t = -5.91$; negative **b.** $(.656, 2.829)$ **c.** $(1.467, 2.018)$ **10.77 a.** $\hat{y} = 37.08 - 1.6x$ **c.** 57.2 **d.** 4.4 **e.** $-1.6 \pm .5$ **f.** 13.08 ± 6.93 **g.** 13.08 ± 7.86 **10.79 b.** $r = -.1245$, $r^2 = .0155$ **c.** no, $t = -.35$ **10.81 a.** yes **b.** $\hat{y} = 1.281 + 1.372x$ **e.** $\hat{y} = 4.302 + 0.0709x$ **f.** yes, $t = 52.43$ **g.** yes, $t = 1.18$ **h.** $(46.64, 51.96)$ **j.** prediction for an x outside the range of the sample data   **10.83 a.** yes, $t = 4.98$, p-value $= .001$ **b.** .607 **d.** .461   **10.85 a.** 57.14 ± 34.82 **b.** 110 is outside range of x **c.** $\bar{x} = 44$ **10.87** $\hat{y} = -92.46 + 8.347x$, $t = 3.25$, reject H_0 **10.89 c.** $r_1 = .965$, $r_2 = .996$ **d.** yes **10.91 a.** $\hat{y} = 2.7803 + 0.01696x$ **b.** $t = 4.02$, reject H_0; $r^2 = .402$ **c.** 8   **10.93** machine hours: $t = 3.30$, $p = .008$, reject H_0, $r^2 = .521$; labor hours: $t = 1.43$, $p = .183$, do not reject H_0, $r^2 = .170$

Chapter 11

11.1 a. $E(y) = \beta_0 + \beta_1 x_1 + \beta_2 x_2$ **b.** $E(y) = \beta_0 + \beta_1 x_1 + \beta_2 x_2 + \beta_3 x_3 + \beta_4 x_4$ **c.** $E(y) = \beta_0 + \beta_1 x_1 + \beta_2 x_2 + \beta_3 x_3 + \beta_4 x_4 + \beta_5 x_5$ **11.3 a.** $t = 1.45$, do not reject H_0 **b.** $t = 3.21$, reject H_0 **11.5** $n - (k + 1)$ **11.7 a.** Yes, $s = .117$ **b.** Yes, $F = 55.2$ **11.9 a.** $\hat{y} = 1.81231 + 0.10875x_1 + 0.00017x_2$ **c.** $(.027, .190)$ **d.** $(.00009, .00025)$ **e.** $\hat{y} = 1.20785 + 0.06343x_1 + 0.00056x_2$; $(.016, .111)$; $(.00024, .00088)$ **11.11 a.** $E(y) = \beta_0 + \beta_1 x_1 + \beta_2 x_2 + \beta_3 x_3 + \beta_4 x_4$ **b.** reject H_0 **c.** yes **d.** $H_0: \beta_1 = \beta_2 = \beta_3 = \beta_4 = 0$ **e.** F < 3.37 **f.** Thrill: reject H_0; Change: do not reject H_0; Surprise: do not reject H_0 **11.13 b.** $H_0: \beta_1 = \beta_2 = \beta_3 = \beta_4 = \beta_5 = \beta_6 = 0$ **c.** $F = 32.47$, $p < .001$, reject H_0 **e.** $H_0: \beta_4 = 0$ **f.** $p = .860$, do not reject H_0 **11.15 a.** $E(y) = \beta_0 + \beta_1 x_1 + \beta_2 x_2$ **b.** $\hat{y} = -20.4 + 13.350x_1 + 243.71x_2$ **d.** no, $t = 1.74$ **e.** $(105.32, 382.10)$ **f.** .582 **g.** .513 **h.** $F = 8.36$, $p = .005$, reject H_0 **11.17 a.** $E(y) = \beta_0 + \beta_1 x_1 + \beta_2 x_2 + \beta_3 x_3 + \beta_4 x_4 + \beta_5 x_5$ **b.** $\hat{y} = 13,614.5 + 0.0888x_1 - 9.201x_2 + 14.394x_3 + 0.35x_4 - 0.848x_5$ **d.** 458.83 **e.** $F = 147.3$, $p < .001$, reject H_0 **f.** .917 **g.** yes, $t = -6.14$ **11.19 a.** $E(y) = \beta_0 + \beta_1 x_1 + \beta_2 x_2 + \beta_3 x_3 + \beta_4 x_4 + \beta_5 x_5 + \beta_6 x_6 + \beta_7 x_7$ **b.** $\hat{y} = .9981 - .0224x_1 + .1557x_2 - .0172x_3 - .0095x_4 + .4214x_5 + .4171x_6 - .1552x_7$ **d.** $F = 5.29$, $p = .007$, reject H_0 **11.21 b.** $F = 5.11$, reject H_0 **11.23 a.** Model 1: $t = 2.58$, reject $H_0: \beta_1 = 0$; Model 2: $t = 3.32$, reject $H_0: \beta_1 = 0$, $t = 6.47$, reject $H_0: \beta_2 = 0$, $t = -4.77$, reject $H_0: \beta_3 = 0$, $t = 0.24$, do not reject $H_0: \beta_4 = 0$; Model 3: $t = 3.21$, reject $H_0: \beta_1 = 0$, $t = 5.24$, reject $H_0: \beta_2 = 0$, $t = -4.00$, reject $H_0: \beta_3 = 0$, $t = 2.28$, reject $H_0: \beta_4 = 0$, $t = .014$, do not reject $H_0: \beta_5 = 0$ **c.** Model 2   **11.25 a.** $(1759.75, 4275.38)$ **b.** $(2620.25, 3414.87)$ **c.** yes   **11.27 a.** $(11,599.6, 13,665.5)$ **b.** $(12,157.9, 13,107.1)$ **c.** yes   **11.29** $(-3.44, .065)$ **11.31 a.** $\hat{y} = -3783 + .00875x_1 + 1.93x_2 + 3444x_3 + 2093x_4$ **b.** $F = 72.11$, reject H_0 **c.** $(1,449, 2,424)$ **11.33 c.** interaction is present   **11.35 a.** $\hat{y} = -2.55 + 3.82x_1 + 2.63x_2 - 1.29x_1 x_2$ **b.** twisted plane **c.** $x_2 = 1$: $\hat{y} = -.08 + 2.53x_1$; $x_2 = 3$: $\hat{y} = 5.34 - .05x_1$; $x_2 = 5$: $\hat{y} = 10.6 - 2.63x_1$ **e.** $H_0: \beta_3 = 0$ vs. $H_a: \beta_3 \neq 0$ **f.** $t = -8.06$, reject H_0 **11.37 a.** $E(y) = \beta_0 + \beta_1 x_1 + \beta_2 x_2 + \beta_3 x_1 x_2$ **b.** $\beta_3 < 0$ **11.39 a.** $\hat{y} = 1042 - 13.24x_1 + 103.3x_2 + 3.621x_1 x_2$ **b.** 22.97 **c.** 284.14 **d.** $H_0: \beta_3 = 0$ **e.** .366 **f.** do not reject H_0 **11.41 a.** $E(y) = \beta_0 + \beta_1 x_2 + \beta_2 x_3 + \beta_3 x_5 + \beta_4 x_2 x_5 + \beta_5 x_3 x_5$ **b.** $\hat{y} = 13,945 - 15.1379x_2 + 28.843x_3 - 0.689x_5 + 0.02277x_2 x_5 - 0.0543x_3 x_5$ **c.** $t = 7.59$, reject $H_0: \beta_4 = 0$ **d.** $t = -5.16$, reject $H_0: \beta_5 = 0$ **11.43 b.** yes, higher R^2 and smaller s **11.45 a.** $E(y) = \beta_0 + \beta_1 x + \beta_2 x^2$ **b.** $E(y) = \beta_0 + \beta_1 x_1 + \beta_2 x_2 + \beta_3 x_1 x_2 + \beta_4 x_1^2 + \beta_5 x_2^2$ **c.** $E(y) = \beta_0 + \beta_1 x_1 + \beta_2 x_2 + \beta_3 x_3 + \beta_4 x_1 x_2 + \beta_5 x_1 x_3 + \beta_6 x_2 x_3 + \beta_7 x_1^2 + \beta_8 x_2^2 + \beta_9 x_3^2$ **11.47 a.** yes, $F = 85.94$ **b.** $H_0: \beta_2 = 0$ vs. $H_a: \beta_2 > 0$ **c.** $H_0: \beta_2 = 0$ vs. $H_a: \beta_2 < 0$ **11.49 a.** yes, $F = 25.93$ **b.** $t = -10.74$, reject H_0 **c.** $t = .60$, do not reject H_0 **11.51 b.** first-order model; first-order model; second-order model   **11.53 a.** $E(y) = \beta_0 + \beta_1 x_1 + \beta_2 x_2 + \beta_3 x_1 x_2 + \beta_4 x_1^2 + \beta_5 x_2^2$ **b.** $\beta_4 x_1^2$ and $\beta_5 x_2^2$ **11.55 a.** $\hat{y} = 20.09 - 0.67x + .0095x^2$ **b.** yes **c.** no, $t = 1.51$ **d.** $\hat{y} = 19.28 - 0.445x$ **e.** $(-.52, -.37)$ **11.57** $E(y) = \beta_0 + \beta_1 x + \beta_2 x^2$ **11.59** $E(y) = \beta_0 + \beta_1 x$, $x = \{1$ if level 2, 0 if level 1$\}$ **11.61 a.** 10.2, 6.2, 22.2, 12.2 **b.** $H_0: \beta_1 = \beta_2 = \beta_3 = 0$ **11.63 a.** $E(y) = \beta_0 + \beta_1 x$, $x = \{1$ if developer, 0 if not$\}$ **b.** $E(y) = \beta_0 + \beta_1 x_1 + \beta_2 x_2$, $x_1 = \{1$ if low, 0 if not$\}$, $x_2 = \{1$ if medium, 0 if not$\}$ **c.** $E(y) = \beta_0 + \beta_1 x$, $x = \{1$ if fixed price, 0 if not$\}$ **d.** $E(y) = \beta_0 + \beta_1 x_1 + \beta_2 x_2$, $x_1 = \{1$ if time-of-delivery, 0 if not$\}$, $x_2 = \{1$ if cost, 0 if not$\}$ **11.65 b.** $(13.12, 24.88)$ **c.** coaching is effective   **11.67 a.** $E(y) = \beta_0 + \beta_1 x_1 + \beta_2 x_2$, $x_1 = \{1$ if group V, 0 if not$\}$, $x_2 = \{1$ if group S, 0 if not$\}$ **b.** $\hat{y} = 3.1667 - 1.0833x_1 - 1.4537x_2$ **c.** $F = 20.45$, reject H_0 **11.69 a.** $E(y) = \beta_0 + \beta_1 x$, where $x = \{1$ if Lotion/Cream, 0 if not$\}$ **b.** $\hat{y} = .7775 + .1092x$ **c.** $H_0: \beta_1 = 0$ **d.** $t = .24$, do not reject H_0 **e.** $\hat{y} = 7.56 - 1.65x$; $t = -.46$, do not reject H_0

11.71 a. $E(y) = \beta_0 + \beta_1 x_1 + \beta_2 x_2 + \beta_3 x_3$, where $x_1 = \{1$ if food, 0 if not$\}$, $x_2 = \{1$ if cleaning, 0 if not$\}$, $x_3 = \{1$ if acc/consulting, 0 if not$\}$ **b.** $\hat{y} = 141.3 + 76.4x_1 + 153.3x_2 - 84.3x_3$ **c.** no, $F = 1.26$ **11.73 a.** $E(y) = \beta_0 + \beta_1 x_1 + \beta_2 x_1^2$ **b.** $E(y) = \beta_0 + \beta_1 x_1 + \beta_2 x_1^2 + \beta_3 x_2 + \beta_4 x_3$, where x_2 and x_3 are dummy variables **c.** add terms: $\beta_5 x_1 x_2 + \beta_6 x_1 x_3 + \beta_7 x_1^2 x_2 + \beta_8 x_1^2 x_3$ **d.** $\beta_5 = \beta_6 = \beta_7 = \beta_8 = 0$ **e.** $\beta_2 = \beta_5 = \beta_6 = \beta_7 = \beta_8 = 0$ **f.** $\beta_3 = \beta_4 = \beta_5 = \beta_6 = \beta_7 = \beta_8 = 0$
11.75 b. $\hat{y} = 48.8 - 3.4x_1 + .07x_1^2$; $\hat{y} = 46.4 + .3x_1 + .05x_1^2$; $\hat{y} = 41.3 - .7x_1 + .03x_1^2$ **11.77 a.** $x_1 = \{1$ if channel catfish, 0 if not$\}$, $x_2 = \{1$ if largemouth bass, 0 if not$\}$ **b.** $E(y) = \beta_0 + \beta_1 x_1 + \beta_2 x_2 + \beta_3 x_3$, where x_3 = weight **c.** $E(y) = \beta_0 + \beta_1 x_1 + \beta_2 x_2 + \beta_3 x_3 + \beta_4 x_1 x_3 + \beta_5 x_2 x_3$ **d.** $\hat{y} = 3.1 + 25.6x_1 - 4.1x_2 + 0.0037x_3$ **f.** $\hat{y} = 3.5 + 25.6x_1 - 3.5x_2 + 0.0034x_3 + .0008x_1 x_3 - .0013x_2 x_3$ **g.** .0042 **11.79 a.** $E(y) = \beta_0 + \beta_1 x_1$; β_1 **b.** $E(y) = (\beta_0 + \beta_2) + (\beta_1 + \beta_3)x_1$; $\beta_1 + \beta_3$ **c.** no evidence of interaction at $\alpha = .01$
11.81 a. $E(y) = \beta_0 + \beta_1 x_1 + \beta_2 x_1^2 + \beta_3 x_2 + \beta_4 x_3 + \beta_5 x_4 + \beta_6 x_1 x_2 + \beta_7 x_1 x_3 + \beta_8 x_1 x_4 + \beta_9 x_1^2 x_2 + \beta_{10} x_1^2 x_3 + \beta_{11} x_1^2 x_4$, where x_1 = sales volume and $x_2 - x_4$ are dummy variables for region **b.** $E(y) = (\beta_0 + \beta_5) + (\beta_1 + \beta_8)x_1 + (\beta_2 + \beta_{11})x_1^2$ **c.** $E(y) = (\beta_0 + \beta_3) + (\beta_1 + \beta_6)x_1 + (\beta_2 + \beta_9)x_1^2$ **d.** β_3 through β_{11} **e.** yes, $F = 8.21$, $p = .000$ **11.83 a.** $E(y) = \beta_0 + \beta_1 x_1 + \beta_2 x_2 + \beta_3 x_1 x_2$, where $x_2 = \{1$ if developing, 0 otherwise$\}$ **c.** $\hat{y} = 58.786 - .557x_1 - 18.718x_2 + .354x_1 x_2$; emerging: $\hat{y} = 58.786 - .557x_1$; developed: $\hat{y} = 40.068 - .203x_1$ **e.** yes, $t = 4.64$ **11.85** a and b, a and d, a and e, b and c, b and d, b and e, c and e, d and e **11.87 a.** 5; 3 **b.** $H_0: \beta_3 = \beta_4 = 0$ **c.** $F = .38$, do not reject H_0 **11.89 a.** $E(y) = \beta_0 + \beta_1 x_1 + \beta_2 x_2 + \beta_3 x_1^2 + \beta_4 x_2^2 + \beta_5 x_1 x_2$ **b.** $H_0: \beta_3 = \beta_4 = \beta_5 = 0$ **c.** complete model: $E(y) = \beta_0 + \beta_1 x_1 + \beta_2 x_2 + \beta_3 x_1^2 + \beta_4 x_2^2 + \beta_5 x_1 x_2$; reduced model: $E(y) = \beta_0 + \beta_1 x_1 + \beta_2 x_2$ **d.** $SSE_R = 25,310,639$, $SSE_C = 19,370,350$, $MSE_C = 317,547$ **e.** $F = 6.24$ **f.** $F > 2.18$ **g.** reject H_0
11.91 a. $E(y) = \beta_0 + \beta_1 x_1 + \beta_2 x_2 + \beta_3 x_3 + \beta_4 x_4 + \beta_5 x_5 + \beta_6 x_6 + \beta_7 x_7 + \beta_8 x_8 + \beta_9 x_9 + \beta_{10} x_{10}$ **b.** $H_0: \beta_3 = \beta_4 = \cdots = \beta_{10} = 0$ **c.** reject H_0 **e.** (8.12, 19.88) **f.** yes **g.** $E(y) = \beta_0 + \beta_1 x_1 + \beta_2 x_2 + \beta_3 x_3 + \beta_4 x_4 + \beta_5 x_5 + \beta_6 x_6 + \beta_7 x_7 + \beta_8 x_8 + \beta_9 x_9 + \beta_{10} x_{10} + \beta_{11} x_1 x_2 + \beta_{12} x_3 x_2 + \beta_{13} x_4 x_2 + \beta_{14} x_5 x_2 + \beta_{15} x_6 x_2 + \beta_{16} x_7 x_2 + \beta_{17} x_8 x_2 + \beta_{18} x_9 x_2 + \beta_{19} x_{10} x_2$ **h.** Test $H_0: \beta_{11} = \beta_{12} = \cdots = \beta_{19} = 0$ using a nested model F test **11.93 a.** $E(y) = \beta_0 + \beta_1 x_1 + \beta_2 x_2 + \beta_3 x_3$ **b.** add terms: $\beta_4 x_1 x_2 + \beta_5 x_1 x_3$ **c.** AL: β_1; TDS-3A: $\beta_1 + \beta_4$; FE: $\beta_1 + \beta_5$ **d.** Test $H_0: \beta_4 = \beta_5 = 0$ using a nested model F test **11.95 b.** $F = 38.24$, reject H_0 **c.** no **11.97 a.** 7; $E(y) = \beta_0 + \beta_1 x_i$ **b.** 6; $E(y) = \beta_0 + \beta_1 x_1 + \beta_2 x_i$ **c.** 5; $E(y) = \beta_0 + \beta_1 x_1 + \beta_2 x_2 + \beta_3 x_i$
11.99 a. x_4 = ST-DEPTH, x_5 = TGRSWT, x_6 = TI **b.** no **c.** $E(y) = \beta_0 + \beta_1 x_4 + \beta_2 x_5 + \beta_3 x_6 + \beta_4 x_4 x_5 + \beta_5 x_4 x_6 + \beta_6 x_5 x_6$ **d.** Test $H_0: \beta_4 = \beta_5 = \beta_6 = 0$ **11.101** yes **11.103** x_4 and x_5 **11.105 a.** normal probability plot; yes **b.** plot of residuals versus predicted values; yes **11.107** assumptions appear to be satisfied **11.109** possibly delete outliers **11.111** confidence interval
11.113 a. $\hat{y} = 90.1 - 1.836x_1 + .285x_2$ **b.** .916 **c.** yes, $F = 64.91$ **d.** $t = -5.01$, reject H_0 **e.** 10.68 **11.117** $E(y) = \beta_0 + \beta_1 x_1 + \beta_2 x_2 + \beta_3 x_3$, where $x_1 = \{1$ if level 2, 0 otherwise$\}$, $x_2 = \{1$ if level 3, 0 otherwise$\}$, $x_3 = \{1$ if level 4, 0 otherwise$\}$ **11.121** no degrees of freedom for error **11.123 a.** type of extractor is qualitative; size is quantitative **b.** $E(y) = \beta_0 + \beta_1 x_1 + \beta_2 x_2$, where x_1 = diameter of orange, $x_2 = \{1$ if Brand B, 0 if not$\}$ **c.** $E(y) = \beta_0 + \beta_1 x_1 + \beta_2 x_2 + \beta_3 x_1 x_2$ **e.** $H_0: \beta_3 = 0$ **11.125 a.** $t = 3.88$, p-value $= .005$, reject H_0 **b.** no **c.** $F = 11.40$, reject H_0 **11.127 a.** $E(y) = \beta_0 + \beta_1 x_1 + \beta_2 x_2 + \beta_3 x_3 + \beta_4 x_4 + \beta_5 x_5$ **b.** reject $H_0: \beta_1 = \beta_2 = \beta_3 = \beta_4 = \beta_5 = 0$ **c.** $E(y) = \beta_0 + \beta_1 x_1 + \beta_2 x_2 + \beta_3 x_3 + \beta_4 x_4 + \beta_5 x_5 + \beta_6 x_6 + \beta_7 x_7$ **d.** 60.3% of the variability in GSI scores is explained by the model **e.** both variables contribute to the prediction of GSI **11.129** Importance and Support are correlated at .6991; no **11.131 b.** 51% of the variability in operating margins can be explained by the model **c.** $F = 13.53$, reject H_0
11.133 a. possibly **b.** yes **c.** no **11.135 b.** $E(y) = \beta_0 + \beta_1 x_1 + \beta_2 x_1^2 + \beta_3 x_2 + \beta_4 x_1 x_2 + \beta_5 x_1^2 x_2$, where $x_2 = \{1$ if 1-35W, 0 if not$\}$ **c.** yes, $F = 457.73$ **d.** assumptions satisfied **11.137 a.** $E(y) = \beta_0 + \beta_1 x_1 + \beta_2 x_2 + \beta_3 x_3$, where $x_1 = \{1$ if VH, 0 otherwise$\}$, $x_2 = \{1$ if H, 0 otherwise$\}$, $x_3 = \{1$ if M, 0 otherwise$\}$ **b.** no **c.** $\hat{y} = 10.2 + .5x_1 + 2.02x_2 + .683x_3$ **d.** yes, $F = 63.09$ **11.139 b.** yes, $F = 16.10$ **c.** yes, $t = 2.5$ **d.** .945 **11.141 a.** $E(y) = \beta_0 + \beta_1 x_1 + \beta_2 x_6 + \beta_3 x_7$, where $x_6 = \{1$ if good, 0 otherwise$\}$, $x_7 = \{1$ if fair, 0 otherwise$\}$ **c.** excellent: $\hat{y} = 188,875 + 15,617x_1$; good: $\hat{y} = 85,829 + 15,617x_1$; fair: $\hat{y} = 36,388 + 15,617x_1$ **e.** yes, $F = 8.43$ **f.** $(x_1$ and $x_3)$, $(x_1$ and $x_5)$, $(x_3$ and $x_5)$ are highly correlated **g.** assumptions are satisfied
11.143 a. $H_0: \beta_1 = \beta_2 = \beta_3 = \beta_4 = \beta_5 = 0$ **b.** $F = 18.24$, reject H_0 **c.** $H_0: \beta_3 = \beta_4 = \beta_5 = 0$ **d.** $F = 8.46$, reject H_0 **e.** second-order model **11.145** $\hat{y} = -11.5 + 0.189x_1 + 0.159x_2 - 0.00114x_1^2 - 0.000871x_2^2$

Chapter 12

12.7 out of control **12.9 a.** 1.023 **b.** 0.308 **c.** 0.167 **12.11 b.** $\bar{\bar{x}} = 20.11625$, $\bar{R} = 3.31$ **c.** UCL = 22.529, LCL = 17.703 **d.** Upper A–B: 21.725, Lower A–B: 18.507, Upper B–C: 20.920, Lower B–C: 19.312 **e.** yes **12.13 a.** $\bar{\bar{x}} = 23.9971$, $\bar{R} = .1815$, UCL = 24.102, LCL = 23.892, Upper A–B: 24.067, Lower A–B: 23.927, Upper B–C: 24.032, Lower B–C: 23.962 **b.** in control **c.** yes
12.15 a. $\bar{\bar{x}} = 49.129$, $\bar{R} = 3.733$, UCL = 50.932, LCL = 47.326, Upper A–B: 50.331, Lower A–B: 47.927, Upper B–C: 49.730, Lower B–C: 48.528 **b.** no **c.** no **12.17 a.** $\bar{\bar{x}} = 52.6467$, $\bar{R} = .755$, UCL = 53.419, LCL = 51.874, Upper A–B: 53.162, Lower A–B: 52.132, Upper B–C: 52.904, Lower B–C: 52.389 **b.** out of control **d.** no **12.21 a.** UCL = 16.802 **b.** Upper A–B: 13.853, Lower A–B: 2.043, Upper B–C: 10.900, Lower B–C: 4.996 **c.** in control **12.23** R-chart: $\bar{R} = 4.03$, UCL = 7.754, LCL = 0.306, Upper A–B: 6.513, Lower A–B: 1.547, Upper B–C: 5.271, Lower B–C: 2.789, in control; $\bar{x}$-chart: $\bar{\bar{x}} = 21.728$, UCL = 23.417, LCL = 20.039, Upper A–B: 22.854, Lower A–B: 20.602, Upper B–C: 22.291, Lower B–C: 21.165, out of control **12.25 a.** yes **b.** $\bar{R} = .0796$, UCL = .168, Upper A–B: .139, Lower A–B: .020, Upper B–C: .109, Lower B–C: .050 **c.** in control **d.** yes **e.** yes **12.27 a.** $\bar{R} = 3.733$, UCL = 7.481, Upper A–B: 6.231, Lower A–B: 1.235, Upper B–C: 4.982, Lower B–C: 2.484 **b.** no, Rule 1 violated **c.** yes **12.29 a.** $\bar{R} = 2.08$, UCL = 4.397, Upper A–B: 3.625, Lower A–B: .535, Upper B–C: 2.853, Lower B–C: 1.307; in control **b.** yes **c.** $\bar{R} = 1.7$, UCL = 3.594, Upper A–B: 2.963, Lower A–B: .437, Upper B–C: 2.331, Lower B–C: 1.069; out of control **12.31** 104 **12.33 a.** $\bar{p} = .0575$, UCL = .1145, LCL = .0005, Upper A–B: .0955, Lower A–B: .0195, Upper B–C: .0765, Lower B–C: .0385 **d.** no **e.** no **12.35 a.** yes **b.** UCL = .0202, LCL = .0008 **c.** Upper A–B: .0169, Lower A–B: .0041, Upper B–C: .0137, Lower B–C: .0073; in control **12.37 a.** $\bar{p} = .04$, UCL = .099, LCL = −.019, Upper A–B: .079, Lower A–B: .001, Upper B–C: .060, Lower B–C: .020 **b.** no **c.** no **12.45 a.** 126 **b.** 31.2 **c.** 660.36 **d.** .0144 **12.47** 6σ **12.49 b.** $C_p = .866$; no **12.51 a.** LSL = 3.12, USL = 3.72 **b.** .152 **c.** $C_p = .505$ **12.67 a.** $\bar{x} = 6.4$ **b.** increasing variance **12.69** out of

control   **12.71 a.** $\overline{R}$ = 7.4, UCL = 24.1758, Upper A–B: 18.5918, Lower A–B: −3.7918, Upper B–C: 12.9959, Lower B–C: 1.8041; out of control **b.** $\overline{\overline{x}}$ = 344.15, UCL = 358.062, LCL = 330.238, Upper A–B: 353.425, Lower A–B: 334.875, Upper B–C: 348.787, Lower B–C: 339.513; out of control **c.** no **d.** .25   **12.73 a.** $\overline{R}$ = 5.455, UCL = 11.532, Upper A–B: 9.508, Lower A–B: 1.402, Upper B–C: 7.481, Lower B–C: 3.429 **b.** in control **d.** $\overline{\overline{x}}$ = 3.867, UCL = 7.013, LCL = .721, Upper A–B: 5.965, Lower A–B: 1.769, Upper B–C: 4.916, Lower B–C: 2.818 **e.** in control **f.** yes   **12.75 a.** n > 141 **b.** $\overline{p}$ = .063, UCL = .123, LCL = .003, Upper A–B: .103, Lower A–B: .023, Upper B–C: .083, Lower B–C: .043 **c.** out of control **e.** no

Index

[Chapters 13 and 14 are included in this Index and appear on the CD.]

Photo Credits

Using Technology box image: Spohn Matthieu
Calculator box image: Courtesy of Texas Instruments

Title Page   James Woodson/Getty Images/Digital Vision

Table of Contents   Getty Images/Digital Vision; Photodisc/Getty Images; James Woodson/Getty Images/Digital Vision; Jack Hollingsworth/Photodisc/Getty Images; Todd Pearson/Image Bank/Getty Images; Nick Daly/Getty Images—Photonica Amana America, Inc.; Ed Horowitz/Taxi/Getty Images; Andrew Errington/Photographer's Choice/Getty Images; Nick Daly/Getty Images—Photonica Amana America, Inc.; ML Harris/Getty Images—Iconica; Getty Images/Digital Vision; Bruce Laurance/Image Bank/Getty Images; Getty Images—Stockbyte; Eric Audras/Getty Images—PhotoAlto Royalty Free

Chapter 1

p. 2 Getty Images/Digital Vision; **p. 3** David R. Frazier/Frazier Photolibrary, Inc.; **p. 10** Steve Gorton © Dorling Kindersley; **pp. 12, 19, 22** © Dorling Kindersley; **p. 14** © James Leynse/CORBIS SABA

Chapter 2

p. 38 Photodisc/Getty Images; **pp. 39, 44, 45, 56, 84, 98, 103, 128** Courtesy of http://www.istockphoto.com; **p. 68** Paul Bricknell © Dorling Kindersley; **p. 96** Photos.com

Chapter 3

p. 130 James Woodson/Getty Images/Digital Vision; **pp. 131, 142, 151, 165** Simon Ashkam/Courtesy of http://www.istockphoto.com; **p. 133** Clive Streeter © Dorling Kindersley; **p. 136** Tim Ridley/Dorling Kindersley Media Library; **p. 146** Pekka Jaakkola/Courtesy of http://www.istockphoto.com; **p. 156** Tracy Hebden/Courtesy of http://www.istockphoto.com

Chapter 4

p. 188 Jack Hollingsworth/Photodisc/Getty Images; **pp. 189, 239, 246, 269** Library of Congress; **p. 190** Dave King © Dorling Kindersley; **p. 207** John Greenleigh/Apple Computer, Inc.; **p. 212** Steve Gorton © Dorling Kindersley; **p. 234** © Judith Miller/Dorling Kindersley/Graham Cooley; **p. 238** Matthew Ward © Dorling Kindersley; **p. 258** © Dorling Kindersley; **p. 289** Bryce Flynn/Index Stock Imagery, Inc.

Chapter 5

p. 290 Todd Pearson/Image Bank/Getty Images; **pp. 291, 307, 317, 325** Pearson Education/Prentice Hall College; **p. 295** Steve Gorton © Dorling Kindersley; **p. 313** Gretchen Halverson/Courtesy of http://www.istockphoto.com; **p. 316** © Dorling Kindersley, Courtesy of the H. Keith Melton Collection; **p. 322** Dusty Cline/Courtesy of http://www.istockphoto.com

Chapter 6

p. 344 Nick Daly/Getty Images—Photonica Amana America, Inc.; **pp. 345, 351, 363, 376** Andy Crawford © Dorling Kindersley; **p. 354** © Dorling Kindersley; **p. 375** Courtesy of http://www.istockphoto.com

Chapter 7

p. 402 Ed Horowitz/Taxi/Getty Images; **pp. 403, 417, 440** AP Wide World Photos; **p. 405** Peter Wilson © Dorling Kindersley; **pp. 427, 446, 451** Courtesy of http://www.istockphoto.com; **p. 473** Diane Diederich/Courtesy of http://www.istockphoto.com

Chapter 8

p. 474 Andrew Errington/Photographer's Choice/Getty Images; **pp. 475, 494, 504** Peter Finnie/Courtesy of http://www.istockphoto.com; **pp. 479, 488** Matthew Ward © Dorling Kindersley; **p. 483** Susanna Price © Dorling Kindersley; **p. 514** Alex Balako/Courtesy of http://www.istockphoto.com

Chapter 9

p. 552 Nick Daly/Getty Images—Photonica Amana America, Inc.; **pp. 553, 559, 572** Tony Freeman/PhotoEdit Inc.; **p. 554** Jo Foord © Dorling Kindersley; **p. 558** Chas Howson © The British Museum; **p. 594** © Cathleen A. Clapper/Courtesy of http://www.istockphoto.com

Chapter 10

p. 596 ML Harris/Getty Images—Iconica; **pp. 597, 607, 624, 634, 643** Lise Gagne/Courtesy of http://www.istockphoto.com; **pp. 604, 633** Clayton Hansen/Courtesy of http://www.istockphoto.com

Chapter 11

p. 664 Getty Images/Digital Vision; **pp. 665, 690, 740, 759** Stephen Whitehorn © Dorling Kindersley; **p. 668** Frances Twitty/Courtesy of http://www.istockphoto.com; **p. 674** David Stockman/Courtesy of http://www.istockphoto.com; **p. 702** Sascha Burkard/Courtesy of http://www.istockphoto.com; **p. 713** Marilyn Nieves/Courtesy of http://www.istockphoto.com; **p. 729** Pamela Moore/Courtesy of http://www.istockphoto.com; **p. 738** Judy Foldetta/Courtesy of http://www.istockphoto.com; **p. 763** Nicky Blade/Courtesy of http://www.istockphoto.com; **p. 786** © Sean Locke/Courtesy of http://www.istockphoto.com

Chapter 12

p. 788 Bruce Laurance/Image Bank/Getty Images; **pp. 789, 818, 830** Lowell Sannes/Courtesy of http://www.istockphoto.com; **p. 815** Courtesy of http://www.istockphoto.com; **p. 837** Jim Lopes/Courtesy of http://www.istockphoto.com; **p. 864** © Nancy Louie/Courtesy of http://www.istockphoto.com

Chapter 13   (on CD only)

p. 13-2 Getty Images—Stockbyte; **pp. 13-3, 13-33, 13-37, 13-42** Gabriela Trojanowska/Courtesy of http://www.istockphoto.com; **p. 13-4** © The Granger Collection, New York; **p. 13-60** © Nancy Louie/Courtesy of http://www.istockphoto.com

Chapter 14   (on CD only)

p. 14-2 Eric Audras/Getty Images—PhotoAlto Royalty Free; **pp. 14-3, 14-8, 14-25, 14-43** Courtesy of http://www.istockphoto.com; **p. 14-7** Nathan Fultz/Courtesy of http://www.istockphoto.com; **p. 14-11** Courtesy of the Department of Statistics, Florida State University; **p. 14-21** Chen Ping-Hung/Courtesy of http://www.istockphoto.com; **p. 14-39** University College London, Department of Psychology

Critical Values of t

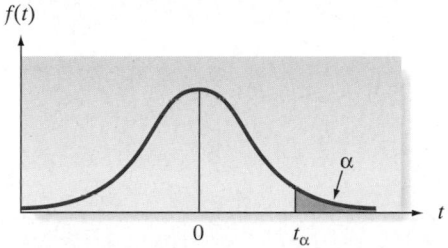

v	$t_{.100}$	$t_{.05}$	$t_{.025}$	$t_{.010}$	$t_{.005}$	$t_{.001}$	$t_{.0005}$
1	3.078	6.314	12.706	31.821	63.657	318.31	636.62
2	1.886	2.920	4.303	6.965	9.925	22.326	31.598
3	1.638	2.353	3.182	4.541	5.841	10.213	12.924
4	1.533	2.132	2.776	3.747	4.604	7.173	8.610
5	1.476	2.015	2.571	3.365	4.032	5.893	6.869
6	1.440	1.943	2.447	3.143	3.707	5.208	5.959
7	1.415	1.895	2.365	2.998	3.499	4.785	5.408
8	1.397	1.860	2.306	2.896	3.355	4.501	5.041
9	1.383	1.833	2.262	2.821	3.250	4.297	4.781
10	1.372	1.812	2.228	2.764	3.169	4.144	4.587
11	1.363	1.796	2.201	2.718	3.106	4.025	4.437
12	1.356	1.782	2.179	2.681	3.055	3.930	4.318
13	1.350	1.771	2.160	2.650	3.012	3.852	4.221
14	1.345	1.761	2.145	2.624	2.977	3.787	4.140
15	1.341	1.753	2.131	2.602	2.947	3.733	4.073
16	1.337	1.746	2.120	2.583	2.921	3.686	4.015
17	1.333	1.740	2.110	2.567	2.898	3.646	3.965
18	1.330	1.734	2.101	2.552	2.878	3.610	3.922
19	1.328	1.729	2.093	2.539	2.861	3.579	3.883
20	1.325	1.725	2.086	2.528	2.845	3.552	3.850
21	1.323	1.721	2.080	2.518	2.831	3.527	3.819
22	1.321	1.717	2.074	2.508	2.819	3.505	3.792
23	1.319	1.714	2.069	2.500	2.807	3.485	3.767
24	1.318	1.711	2.064	2.492	2.797	3.467	3.745
25	1.316	1.708	2.060	2.485	2.787	3.450	3.725
26	1.315	1.706	2.056	2.479	2.779	3.435	3.707
27	1.314	1.703	2.052	2.473	2.771	3.421	3.690
28	1.313	1.701	2.048	2.467	2.763	3.408	3.674
29	1.311	1.699	2.045	2.462	2.756	3.396	3.659
30	1.310	1.697	2.042	2.457	2.750	3.385	3.646
40	1.303	1.684	2.021	2.423	2.704	3.307	3.551
60	1.296	1.671	2.000	2.390	2.660	3.232	3.460
120	1.289	1.658	1.980	2.358	2.617	3.160	3.373
∞	1.282	1.645	1.960	2.326	2.576	3.090	3.291

Source: This table is reproduced with the kind permission of the Trustees of Biometrika from E. S. Pearson and H. O. Hartley (eds.), *The Biometrika Tables for Statisticians,* Vol. 1, 3d ed., Biometrika, 1966.

Normal Curve Areas

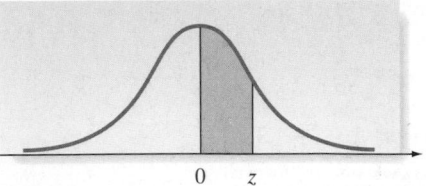

z	.00	.01	.02	.03	.04	.05	.06	.07	.08	.09
.0	.0000	.0040	.0080	.0120	.0160	.0199	.0239	.0279	.0319	.0359
.1	.0398	.0438	.0478	.0517	.0557	.0596	.0636	.0675	.0714	.0753
.2	.0793	.0832	.0871	.0910	.0948	.0987	.1026	.1064	.1103	.1141
.3	.1179	.1217	.1255	.1293	.1331	.1368	.1406	.1443	.1480	.1517
.4	.1554	.1591	.1628	.1664	.1700	.1736	.1772	.1808	.1844	.1879
.5	.1915	.1950	.1985	.2019	.2054	.2088	.2123	.2157	.2190	.2224
.6	.2257	.2291	.2324	.2357	.2389	.2422	.2454	.2486	.2517	.2549
.7	.2580	.2611	.2642	.2673	.2704	.2734	.2764	.2794	.2823	.2852
.8	.2881	.2910	.2939	.2967	.2995	.3023	.3051	.3078	.3106	.3133
.9	.3159	.3186	.3212	.3238	.3264	.3289	.3315	.3340	.3365	.3389
1.0	.3413	.3438	.3461	.3485	.3508	.3531	.3554	.3577	.3599	.3621
1.1	.3643	.3665	.3686	.3708	.3729	.3749	.3770	.3790	.3810	.3830
1.2	.3849	.3869	.3888	.3907	.3925	.3944	.3962	.3980	.3997	.4015
1.3	.4032	.4049	.4066	.4082	.4099	.4115	.4131	.4147	.4162	.4177
1.4	.4192	.4207	.4222	.4236	.4251	.4265	.4279	.4292	.4306	.4319
1.5	.4332	.4345	.4357	.4370	.4382	.4394	.4406	.4418	.4429	.4441
1.6	.4452	.4463	.4474	.4484	.4495	.4505	.4515	.4525	.4535	.4545
1.7	.4554	.4564	.4573	.4582	.4591	.4599	.4608	.4616	.4625	.4633
1.8	.4641	.4649	.4656	.4664	.4671	.4678	.4686	.4693	.4699	.4706
1.9	.4713	.4719	.4726	.4732	.4738	.4744	.4750	.4756	.4761	.4767
2.0	.4772	.4778	.4783	.4788	.4793	.4798	.4803	.4808	.4812	.4817
2.1	.4821	.4826	.4830	.4834	.4838	.4842	.4846	.4850	.4854	.4857
2.2	.4861	.4864	.4868	.4871	.4875	.4878	.4881	.4884	.4887	.4890
2.3	.4893	.4896	.4898	.4901	.4904	.4906	.4909	.4911	.4913	.4916
2.4	.4918	.4920	.4922	.4925	.4927	.4929	.4931	.4932	.4934	.4936
2.5	.4938	.4940	.4941	.4943	.4945	.4946	.4948	.4949	.4951	.4952
2.6	.4953	.4955	.4956	.4957	.4959	.4960	.4961	.4962	.4963	.4964
2.7	.4965	.4966	.4967	.4968	.4969	.4970	.4971	.4972	.4973	.4974
2.8	.4974	.4975	.4976	.4977	.4977	.4978	.4979	.4979	.4980	.4981
2.9	.4981	.4982	.4982	.4983	.4984	.4984	.4985	.4985	.4986	.4986
3.0	.4987	.4987	.4987	.4988	.4988	.4989	.4989	.4989	.4990	.4990

Source: Abridged from Table I of A. Hald, *Statistical Tables and Formulas* (New York: Wiley), 1952. Reproduced by permission of A. Hald.

CHAPTER 10 (cont'd)

$$s^2 = \frac{\text{SSE}}{n-2}$$

$$s = \sqrt{s^2}$$

$$r^2 = \frac{\text{SS}_{yy} - \text{SSE}}{\text{SS}_{yy}}$$

CI for β_1: $\hat{\beta}_1 \pm (t_{\alpha/2})s/\sqrt{\text{SS}_{xx}}$

Test for β_1: $t = \dfrac{\hat{\beta}_1 - 0}{s/\sqrt{\text{SS}_{xx}}}$

CI for $E(y)$ when $x = x_{\hat{p}}$: $\hat{y} \pm t_{\alpha/2}s\sqrt{\dfrac{1}{n} + \dfrac{(x_p - \bar{x})^2}{\text{SS}_{xx}}}$

CI for y when $x = x_{\hat{p}}$: $\hat{y} \pm t_{\alpha/2}s\sqrt{1 + \dfrac{1}{n} + \dfrac{(x_p - \bar{x})^2}{\text{SS}_{xx}}}$

CHAPTER 11

First-Order Model (QN x's):

$$E(y) = \beta_0 + \beta_1 x_1 + \beta_2 x_2 + \cdots + \beta_k x_k$$

Interaction Model (QN x's):

$$E(y) = \beta_0 + \beta_1 x_1 + \beta_2 x_2 + \beta_3 x_1 x_2$$

Quadratic Model (QN x):

$$E(y) = \beta_0 + \beta_1 x + \beta_2 x^2$$

Complete 2nd-Order Model (QN x's):

$$E(y) = \beta_0 + \beta_1 x_1 + \beta_2 x_2 + \beta_3 x_1 x_2 + \beta_4 x_1^2 + \beta_5 x_2^2$$

Dummy Variable Model (QL x):

$$E(y) = \beta_0 + \beta_1 x_1 + \beta_2 x_2$$

where $x_1 = \{1$ if A, 0 if not$\}$, $x_2 = \{1$ if B, 0 if not$\}$

$$\text{MSE} = s^2 = \frac{\text{SSE}}{n - (k+1)}$$

$$R^2 = \frac{\text{SS}_{yy} - \text{SSE}}{\text{SS}_{yy}}$$

$$R_a^2 = 1 - \left[\frac{(n-1)}{n-(k+1)}\right](1 - R^2)$$

Test for overall model: $F = \dfrac{\text{MS(Model)}}{\text{MSE}}$

Test for individual β: $t = \dfrac{\hat{\beta}_i - 0}{s_{\hat{\beta}_i}}$

CI for β_i: $\hat{\beta}_i \pm (t_{\alpha/2})s_{\hat{\beta}_i}$

Nested model F test: $F = \dfrac{(\text{SSE}_R - \text{SSE}_C)/\# \ \beta\text{'s tested}}{\text{MSE}_C}$

CHAPTER 12

Key Formulas

Control Chart	Centerline	Control Limits	A–B Boundary	B–C Boundary
$\bar{x}$-chart	$\bar{\bar{x}} = \dfrac{\sum_{i=1}^{k} \bar{x}_i}{k}$	$\bar{\bar{x}} \pm A_2\bar{R}$ or $\bar{\bar{x}} \pm 2\dfrac{(\bar{R}/d_2)}{\sqrt{n}}$	$\bar{\bar{x}} \pm \dfrac{2}{3}(A_2\bar{R})$ or $\bar{\bar{x}} \pm \dfrac{(\bar{R}/d_2)}{\sqrt{n}}$	$\bar{\bar{x}} \pm \dfrac{1}{3}(A_2\bar{R})$
R-chart	$\bar{R} = \dfrac{\sum_{i=1}^{k} R_i}{k}$	$(\bar{R}D_3, \bar{R}D_4)$	$\bar{R} \pm 2d_3\left(\dfrac{\bar{R}}{d_2}\right)$	$\bar{R} \pm d_3\left(\dfrac{\bar{R}}{d_2}\right)$
p-chart	$\bar{p} = \dfrac{\text{Total number defectives}}{\text{Total number units sampled}}$	$\bar{p} \pm 3\sqrt{\dfrac{\bar{p}(1-\bar{p})}{n}}$	$\bar{p} \pm 2\sqrt{\dfrac{\bar{p}(1-\bar{p})}{n}}$	$\bar{p} \pm \sqrt{\dfrac{\bar{p}(1-\bar{p})}{n}}$

Capability index: $C_p = (\text{USL} - \text{LSL})/6\sigma$

Selected Formulas

CHAPTER 2

Relative Frequency = (frequency)/n

$$\bar{x} = \frac{\Sigma x}{n}$$

$$s^2 = \frac{\Sigma(x - \bar{x})^2}{n - 1} = \frac{\Sigma x^2 - \dfrac{(\Sigma x)^2}{n}}{n - 1}$$

$$s = \sqrt{s^2}$$

$$z = \frac{x - \mu}{\sigma} = \frac{x - \bar{x}}{s}$$

Chebyshev = At least $\left(1 - \dfrac{1}{k^2}\right)100\%$

$$IQR = Q_U - Q_L$$

CHAPTER 3

$$P(A^c) = 1 - P(A)$$

$$P(A \cup B) = P(A) + P(B) - P(A \cap B)$$
$$= P(A) + P(B) \text{ if } A \text{ and } B \text{ mutually exclusive}$$

$$P(A \cap B) = P(A|B) \cdot P(B) = P(B|A) \cdot P(A)$$
$$= P(A) \cdot P(B) \text{ if } A \text{ and } B \text{ independent}$$

$$P(A|B) = \frac{P(A \cap B)}{P(B)}$$

$$\binom{N}{n} = \frac{N!}{n!(N - n)!}$$

Bayes's: $P(S_i|A) =$

$$\frac{P(S_i)P(A|S_i)}{P(S_1)P(A|S_1) + P(S_2)P(A|S_2) + \cdots + P(S_k)P(A|S_k)}$$

CHAPTER 5

CI for μ: $\bar{x} \pm (z_{\alpha/2})\sigma/\sqrt{n}$ (large n)

$\bar{x} \pm (t_{\alpha/2})s/\sqrt{n}$ (small n, σ unknown)

CI for p: $\hat{p} \pm z_{\alpha/2}\sqrt{\dfrac{\hat{p}\hat{q}}{n}}$

Estimating μ: $n = (z_{\alpha/2})^2(\sigma^2)/(\text{SE})^2$

Estimating p: $n = (z_{\alpha/2})^2(pq)/(\text{SE})^2$

CHAPTER 4

KEY FORMULAS

Random Variable	Prob. Dist'n	Mean	Variance
General Discrete:	Table, formula, or graph for $p(x)$	$\sum_{\text{all } x} x \cdot p(x)$	$\sum_{\text{all } x} (x - \mu)^2 \cdot p(x)$
Binomial:	$p(x) = \binom{n}{x} p^x q^{n-x}$ $x = 0, 1, 2, \ldots, n$	np	npq
Poisson:	$p(x) = \dfrac{\lambda^x e^{-\lambda}}{x!}$ $x = 0, 1, 2, \ldots$	λ	λ
Uniform:	$f(x) = 1/(d - c)$ $(c \leq x \leq d)$	$(c + d)/2$	$(d - c)^2/12$
Normal:	$f(x) = \dfrac{1}{\sigma\sqrt{2\pi}} e^{-\frac{1}{2}[(x-\mu)/\sigma]^2}$	μ	σ^2
Standard Normal:	$f(z) = \dfrac{1}{\sqrt{2\pi}} e^{-\frac{1}{2}(z)^2}$ $z = (x - \mu)/\sigma$	$\mu = 0$	$\sigma^2 = 1$
Sample Mean: (large n)	$f(\bar{x}) = \dfrac{1}{\sigma_{\bar{x}}\sqrt{2\pi}} e^{-\frac{1}{2}[(\bar{x}-\mu)/\sigma_{\bar{x}}]^2}$	$\mu_{\bar{x}} = \mu$	$\sigma_{\bar{x}}^2 = \sigma^2/n$